The Blackwell Companion
to Science and Christianity

THE BLACKWELL COMPANION TO SCIENCE AND CHRISTIANITY

Edited by

J. B. Stump and
Alan G. Padgett

WILEY-BLACKWELL

A John Wiley & Sons, Ltd., Publication

This edition first published 2012
© 2012 Blackwell Publishing

Blackwell Publishing was acquired by John Wiley & Sons in February 2007. Blackwell's publishing program has been merged with Wiley's global Scientific, Technical, and Medical business to form Wiley-Blackwell.

Registered Office
John Wiley & Sons Ltd, The Atrium, Southern Gate, Chichester, West Sussex, PO19 8SQ, UK

Editorial Offices
350 Main Street, Malden, MA 02148-5020, USA
9600 Garsington Road, Oxford, OX4 2DQ, UK
The Atrium, Southern Gate, Chichester, West Sussex, PO19 8SQ, UK

For details of our global editorial offices, for customer services, and for information about how to apply for permission to reuse the copyright material in this book please see our website at www.wiley.com/wiley-blackwell.

The right of J. B. Stump and Alan G. Padgett to be identified as the authors of the editorial material in this work has been asserted in accordance with the UK Copyright, Designs and Patents Act 1988.

Wiley also publishes its books in a variety of electronic formats. Some content that appears in print may not be available in electronic books.

Designations used by companies to distinguish their products are often claimed as trademarks. All brand names and product names used in this book are trade names, service marks, trademarks or registered trademarks of their respective owners. The publisher is not associated with any product or vendor mentioned in this book. This publication is designed to provide accurate and authoritative information in regard to the subject matter covered. It is sold on the understanding that the publisher is not engaged in rendering professional services. If professional advice or other expert assistance is required, the services of a competent professional should be sought.

Library of Congress Cataloging-in-Publication Data
The Blackwell companion to science and Christianity / edited by J.B. Stump and Alan G. Padgett.
    p. cm.
  Includes bibliographical references and index.
  ISBN 978-1-4443-3571-2 (hardcover : alk. paper)
  1. Religion and science. I. Stump, J. B. II. Padgett, Alan G., 1955– III. Title: Companion to science and Christianity.
  BL240.3.B62 2012
  261.5'5--dc23
                                        2011050474

A catalogue record for this book is available from the British Library.

Set in 10 on 12 pt Dante by Toppan Best-set Premedia Limited
Printed and bound in Singapore by Markono Print Media Pte Ltd

1   2012

Contents

CONTENTS

Acknowledgments

Any volume of this size depends on the efforts of many people. Ours is no exception. Early conversations with Ernan McMullin and Karl Giberson helped to give shape to the overall contents. Even before this project was conceived, both of us were privileged to spend three summers in Oxford as Templeton-Oxford Fellows, digging deeper into the field of science and religion. We're grateful to Jeff Dean at Wiley-Blackwell for his editorial guidance, as well as the help of his editorial assistants, Tiffany Mok and Nicole Benevenia. Kristin Joy Swartz spent many hours carefully formatting bibliographic entries. Chad Meister is a veteran of editing projects like this one; he gave sage advice at several points in the process and friendship throughout. Jim thanks Bethel College (Indiana) for graciously granting a sabbatical and lots of printer toner. Alan would like to thank the Christian community that is Luther Seminary for continued support of serious theological research. And of course our families provided seemingly endless support and encouragement.

Notes on Contributors

Denis R. Alexander is Director of the Faraday Institute for Science and Religion at St Edmund's College, Cambridge, where he is a Fellow. He was previously at the Babraham Institute, where he was Chair of the Molecular Immunology Programme and Head of the Laboratory of Lymphocyte Signaling and Development. He is editor of the journal *Science and Christian Belief*. His latest book is *The Language of Genetics: An Introduction* (Templeton Foundation Press, 2011).

Francisco J. Ayala is University Professor and Donald Bren Professor of Biological Sciences at the University of California, Irvine. He has published more than a thousand articles and is author or editor of more than 30 books. He is a member of the US National Academy of Sciences and the American Philosophical Society. He received the 2001 US National Medal of Science and the 2010 Templeton Prize. *The New York Times* named Ayala the "Renaissance Man of Evolutionary Biology."

Julian Baggini is the author of several books, including *Welcome to Everytown: A Journey into the English Mind* (Granta, 2007); *Complaint* (Profile, 2008); and, most recently, *The Ego Trick* (Granta, 2011). He has written for numerous newspapers and magazines, including the *Guardian*, the *Financial Times*, *Prospect* and the *New Statesman*, as well as for the think tanks the Institute of Public Policy Research and Demos. He is editor-in-chief and co-founder of the *Philosophers' Magazine*.

Lynne Rudder Baker is Distinguished Professor of Philosophy at the University of Massachusetts Amherst and author of *The Metaphysics of Everyday Life* (Cambridge University Press, 2007); *Persons and Bodies* (Cambridge University Press, 2000); *Explaining Attitudes* (Cambridge University Press, 1995); and *Saving Belief* (Princeton University Press, 1987), as well as numerous articles in the philosophy of mind, metaphysics, and philosophical theology.

Stephen M. Barr is Professor of Physics at the University of Delaware. He received his PhD from Princeton University in 1978. His research is in the area of theoretical particle physics, with emphasis on "grand unified theories" and the cosmology of the early universe. He writes for *First Things*, on whose editorial board he serves, and is author of *Modern Physics and Ancient Faith* (University of Notre Dame Press, 2003).

Justin L. Barrett is the Thrive Chair of Applied Developmental Science and Professor of Psychology at Fuller Theological Seminary, California and a research associate of the University of Oxford's School of Anthropology. He specializes in the cognitive science of religion, psychology of religion, and cognitive study of culture. He has authored *Why Would Anyone Believe in God?* (AltaMira Press, 2004); *Cognitive Science, Religion, and Theology* (Templeton Foundation Press, 2011); *Born Believers* (The Free Press, 2012); and scores of other scholarly and popular publications.

Peter J. Bowler is Professor Emeritus of the History of Science at Queen's University, Belfast. He is a Fellow of the British Academy, a Member of the Royal Irish Academy, and a Fellow of the American Association for the Advancement of Science. He was President of the British Society for the History of Science, 2003–2005. He has published a number of books, including *Evolution: The History of an Idea* (25th anniversary edn, University of California Press, 2009).

Jacqueline Broad is an Australian Research Council Future Fellow in the School of Philosophical, Historical, and International Studies at Monash University, Melbourne. She is the author of *Women Philosophers of the Seventeenth Century* (Cambridge University Press, 2002) and co-author (with Karen Green) of *A History of Women's Political Thought in Europe, 1400–1700* (Cambridge University Press, 2009).

Sean Carroll is a theoretical physicist at the California Institute of Technology. He received his PhD from Harvard University in 1993. His research focuses on field theory, cosmology, and gravitation. He is the author of *From Eternity to Here: The Quest for the Ultimate Theory of Time* (Dutton, 2010) and *Spacetime and Geometry: An Introduction to General Relativity* (Addison Wesley, 2004). He blogs at *Cosmic Variance* and writes for *Discover* magazine.

Robin Collins is Professor and Chair of the Department of Philosophy at Messiah College in Pennsylvania. He has graduate-level training in theoretical physics and has written over 30 articles and book chapters on a wide range of topics in philosophy of physics, philosophy of religion, and philosophy of mind. He is currently finishing two books on the fine-tuning of the cosmos for life.

Simon Conway Morris holds a chair of Evolutionary Paleobiology in the University of Cambridge, and is a Fellow of St John's College. He has published extensively, including *The Crucible of Creation* (Oxford University Press, 1998) and *Life's Solution* (Cambridge University Press, 2003). He appears frequently on radio and television, contributing to the public understanding of science. He was elected to the Royal Society in 1990, and amongst other honors has received the Walcott Medal from the National Academy of Sciences.

William Lane Craig is Research Professor of Philosophy at Talbot School of Theology in La Mirada, California. Research interests include the interface of philosophy of religion, metaphysics, philosophy of space and time, and philosophy of mathematics. He has authored or edited over 30 books, including *The Kalam Cosmological Argument* (Wipf and Stock, 2000); *Theism, Atheism, and Big Bang Cosmology* (with Quentin Smith, Clarendon Press, 1995); *Time and the Metaphysics of Relativity* (Kluwer, 2001); and *Einstein, Relativity, and Absolute Simultaneity* (edited with Quentin Smith, Routledge, 2008).

Edward B. Davis is Professor of the History of Science at Messiah College in Pennsylvania. Best known as editor (with Michael Hunter) of *The Works of Robert Boyle*, 14 vols (Pickering

& Chatto, 1999–2000), he has also written dozens of articles on historical and contemporary aspects of Christianity and science. With support from the John Templeton Foundation and the National Science Foundation, he is presently studying the religious lives and beliefs of prominent American scientists from the 1920s.

Paul Draper is Professor of Philosophy at Purdue University, Indiana. His primary area of specialization is philosophy of religion. He is the author of "Pain and Pleasure: An Evidential Problem for Theists" (*Noûs*, 1989) and the co-editor of *A Companion to Philosophy of Religion* (Wiley-Blackwell, 2010). He also edits the journal *Philo* and serves on the editorial boards of *Faith and Philosophy*, *International Journal for Philosophy of Religion*, and *Religious Studies*.

Dylan Evans is the author of several popular science books, including *Placebo: The Belief Effect* (HarperCollins, 2003). He holds a PhD in philosophy from the London School of Economics, and has lectured in robotics at the University of the West of England (UWE). In September 2008 he moved to the School of Medicine at University College Cork, where he is now Lecturer in Behavioral Science.

John H. Evans is Professor of Sociology at the University of California, San Diego. His research focuses on the sociology of religion, culture, knowledge, science, and, in particular, bioethics. He is the author of *Playing God? Human Genetic Engineering and the Rationalization of Public Bioethical Debate* (University of Chicago Press, 2002). His most recent book is *Contested Reproduction: Genetic Technologies, Religion, and Public Debate* (University of Chicago Press, 2010).

Michael S. Evans is a PhD candidate in sociology and science studies at the University of California, San Diego. His interdisciplinary research interests include science, religion, politics, and culture. He is author or co-author of several articles and chapters on these topics. His dissertation examines American public debates about religion and science in terms of representation, democracy, and morality.

Maurice A. Finocchiaro is Distinguished Professor of Philosophy (Emeritus), University of Nevada, Las Vegas; recipient of fellowships and grants from NSF, NEH, Guggenheim Foundation, and American Council of Learned Societies; and author of numerous publications in logical theory and the history and philosophy of science. Among his books are *Arguments about Arguments* (Cambridge University Press, 2005) and *Defending Copernicus and Galileo* (Springer, 2010).

Philippe Gagnon currently teaches philosophy as well as science and theology at the University of St Thomas in Minnesota. He is author of *Christianisme et théorie de l'information* (Guibert, 1998); *L'expérience de Dieu avec Pierre Teilhard de Chardin* (Fides, 2001); *La théologie de la nature et la science à l'ère de l'information* (Éditions du Cerf/Fides, 2002); and *Teilhard de Chardin: Les terres inconnues de la vie spirituelle* (Fides, 2002). He has published many articles in philosophical theology and philosophy of science.

Richard M. Gale is Professor Emeritus of Philosophy at the University of Pittsburgh, Pennsylvania. His areas of specialization include philosophy of time, negation and non-being, William James, John Dewey, and philosophy of religion. Among his major publications are

The Language of Time (Routledge & Kegan Paul, 1968); *Problems of Negation and Non-being* (AMQ monograph, 1976); *On the Nature and Existence of God* (Cambridge University Press, 1991); *The Divided Self of William James* (Cambridge University Press, 1999); and *John Dewey's Quest for Unity: The Journey of a Promethean Mystic* (Prometheus Press, 2010).

Gregory E. Ganssle is Senior Fellow at the Rivendell Institute and part-time lecturer in the philosophy department at Yale University. He has published *Thinking about God: First Steps in Philosophy* (InterVarsity Press, 2004) and *A Reasonable God: Engaging the New Face of Atheism* (Baylor University Press, 2009).

Nathan J. Hallanger currently serves as Special Assistant to the Vice-President of Academic Affairs and Dean of the College at Augsburg College in Minneapolis, Minnesota. He received his PhD in systematic theology from The Graduate Theological Union, Berkeley, and is co-editor (with Ted Peters) of *God's Action in Nature's World: Essays in Honour of Robert John Russell* (Ashgate, 2006).

William Hasker is Professor Emeritus of Philosophy at Huntington University, Indiana. He is the author of *Metaphysics* (InterVarsity Press, 1983); *God, Time, and Knowledge* (Cornell University Press, 1989); *The Emergent Self* (Cornell University Press, 1999); *Providence, Evil, and the Openness of God* (Routledge, 2004); and *The Triumph of God over Evil* (InterVarsity Press, 2008), and has authored numerous articles in journals and reference works. He was the editor of *Faith and Philosophy* from 2000 until 2007.

John F. Haught is Senior Fellow, Science and Religion, Woodstock Theological Center, Georgetown University, Washington, DC. His area of specialization is systematic theology, with a particular interest in issues pertaining to science, cosmology, evolution, ecology, and religion. He is the author of *Making Sense of Evolution* (Westminster John Knox Press, 2010) and *Is Nature Enough? Meaning and Truth in the Age of Science* (Cambridge University Press, 2006).

Noreen Herzfeld is the Nicholas and Bernice Reuter Professor of Science and Religion at St John's University, Collegeville, Minnesota. She holds degrees in computer science and mathematics from The Pennsylvania State University and a PhD in theology from The Graduate Theological Union, Berkeley. Herzfeld is author of *In Our Image: Artificial Intelligence and the Human Spirit* (Fortress Press, 2002); *Technology and Religion: Remaining Human in a Co-created World* (Templeton Foundation Press, 2009); and *The Limits of Perfection in Technology, Religion, and Science* (Pandora Press, 2010).

Rodney D. Holder is Course Director of the Faraday Institute for Science and Religion, St Edmund's College, Cambridge, and was formerly priest in charge of the parish of the Claydons, Diocese of Oxford. He carried out postdoctoral research in astrophysics at Oxford, and for 14 years worked as an operational research consultant. Dr Holder is the author of *Nothing but Atoms and Molecules?* (Monarch, 1993) and *God, the Multiverse, and Everything* (Ashgate, 2004).

Lydia Jaeger is Professor and Academic Dean at the Institut Biblique de Nogent-sur-Marne, France, and an associate member of St Edmund's College, Cambridge. She holds postgraduate degrees in physics and in theology and a PhD in philosophy. She is author of *Einstein, Polanyi and the Laws of Nature* (Templeton Foundation Press, 2010) and *Lois de la nature* *et raisons du cœur: les convictions religieuses dans le débat épistémologique contemporain* (Peter Lang, 2007).

Christopher B. Kaiser began his professional life as an astrophysicist and is now Professor of Historical and Systematic Theology at Western Theological Seminary in Michigan. His publications include *The Doctrine of God* (Wipf and Stock, 1982, 2001); *Creational Theology and the History of Physical Science* (Brill, 1992, 1997); and *Toward a Theology of Scientific Endeavour* (Ashgate, 2007).

John F. Kilner is Professor of Bioethics and Contemporary Culture, and director of Bioethics Programs at Trinity International University, Illinois. He also holds the Franklin and Dorothy Forman Chair of Christian Ethics and Theology at Trinity Evangelical Divinity School. He has authored or edited 16 books, including *Who Lives? Who Dies? Ethical Criteria in Patient Selection* (Yale University Press, 1992); *Genetic Ethics* (Eerdmans, 1997); and *Does God Need Our Help? Cloning, Assisted Suicide, and Other Challenges in Bioethics* (Tyndale, 2003).

Robin J. Klay is Professor Emerita of Economics at Hope College, Holland, Michigan. Klay's principal area of research and publication is the connections between Christian faith and practice and economic theory and policy. She is co-author of *Economics in Christian Perspective: Theory, Policy and Life Choices* (InterVarsity Press, 2007). Her articles have been published in *Christian Century, Perspectives, Faith and Economics,* and *Markets and Morality.*

Christopher C. Knight obtained a doctorate in astrophysics before studying theology. He began his serious study of the relationship between science and theology while Chaplain, Fellow, and Director of Studies in Theology at Sidney Sussex College, Cambridge. Now, while still teaching for a number of colleges within the University of Cambridge in the science–religion dialogue, he works primarily as the Executive Secretary of the International Society for Science and Religion.

E. J. Lowe is Professor of Philosophy at Durham University, UK, specializing in metaphysics, the philosophy of mind and action, the philosophy of logic and language, and the philosophy of John Locke. His recent books include *The Possibility of Metaphysics* (Oxford University Press, 1998); *The Four-Category Ontology* (Oxford University Press, 2006); *Personal Agency* (Oxford University Press, 2008); and *More Kinds of Being* (Wiley-Blackwell, 2009).

Tapio Luoma is Bishop of the Diocese of Espoo in the Evangelical Lutheran Church of Finland and has been a Research Fellow in the Project for Theology and Science in the Faculty of Theology of the University of Helsinki. He has written articles and given lectures on the relationship between theology and natural sciences. His book *Incarnation and Physics* was published by Oxford University Press in 2002.

Stephen C. Meyer, formerly a geophysicist and college professor, now directs Discovery Institute's Center for Science and Culture. He has authored, edited, or co-authored several books including *Darwinism, Design and Public Education* (Michigan State University Press, 2004); *Explore Evolution: The Arguments for and against Neo-Darwinism* (Hill House Publishers, 2007); and, most recently, *Signature in the Cell: DNA and the Evidence for Intelligent Design* (HarperOne, 2009).

J. P. Moreland is Distinguished Professor of Philosophy at Talbot School of Theology, Biola University, California. He has authored, edited, or contributed papers to over 30 books, including *Does God Exist?* (Prometheus, 1993); *Universals* (McGill-Queen's University Press, 2001); *Consciousness and the Existence of God* (Routledge, 2008); and *The Blackwell Companion to Natural Theology* (edited with William Lane Craig, Wiley-Blackwell, 2009). He has also published over 75 articles in journals such as *Philosophy and Phenomenological Research, American Philosophical Quarterly, Australasian Journal of Philosophy, MetaPhilosophy, Philosophia Christi, Religious Studies,* and *Faith and Philosophy*.

Paul K. Moser is Professor and Chair of Philosophy at Loyola University, Chicago. He is the author of *The Evidence for God: Religious Knowledge Reexamined* (Cambridge University Press, 2010); *The Elusive God: Reorienting Religious Epistemology* (Cambridge University Press, 2008); *Philosophy after Objectivity* (Oxford University Press, 1993); and *Knowledge and Evidence* (Cambridge University Press, 1991). He is co-editor of *Divine Hiddenness* (with Daniel Howard-Snyder, Cambridge University Press, 2002) and *The Wisdom of the Christian Faith* (with Michael McFall, Cambridge University Press, forthcoming). He is also editor of *Jesus and Philosophy* (Cambridge University Press, 2008) and *Rationality in Action* (Cambridge University Press, 1990), and editor of *American Philosophical Quarterly*.

Alexei V. Nesteruk is Senior Lecturer in Mathematics at the University of Portsmouth, UK, where his research is concerned with problems in the foundations of cosmology and quantum physics. His writing has increasingly focused on science from the perspective of the Eastern Orthodox tradition. He is the author of *Theology, Science and the Eastern Orthodox Tradition* (Fortress, 2003) and *The Universe as Communion: Towards a Neo-Patristic Synthesis of Theology and Science* (T&T Clark, 2008).

Graham Oppy is Professor and Head of the School of Philosophical, Historical and International Studies at Monash University, and Chair of Council of the Australasian Association of Philosophy. He is the author of *Ontological Arguments and Belief in God* (Cambridge University Press, 1995); *Arguing about Gods* (Cambridge University Press, 2006); and *Philosophical Perspectives on Infinity* (Cambridge University Press, 2006); and co-editor (with Nick Trakakis) of *The History of Western Philosophy of Religion* (Oxford University Press, 2009).

Alan G. Padgett is Professor of Systematic Theology at Luther Seminary in Saint Paul, Minnesota. He is the author of many books and articles in biblical studies, theology, and philosophy, including several works in religion and science. He advocates a mutuality model for the relationship between Christian theology and science in *Science and the Study of God* (Eerdmans, 2003).

Don N. Page is a theoretical physicist who taught physics at Penn State University and now is professor at the University of Alberta, Canada. His research focuses on quantum cosmology and black holes. He studied at the University of Cambridge and has published several articles with Stephen Hawking.

James C. Peterson is the Charles Schumann Professor of Christian Ethics and Director of the Center for Religion and Society at Roanoke College in Salem, Virginia. He is an editor of the journal *Perspectives in Science and Christian Faith* and the author of several books, including *Genetic Turning Points* (Eerdmans, 2001) and *Changing Human Nature: Ecology, Ethics, Genes, and God* (Eerdmans, 2010).

Alvin Plantinga is the John A. O'Brien Professor of Philosophy, Emeritus, at the University of Notre Dame, Indiana. His work in philosophy lies primarily in philosophy of religion, epistemology, and metaphysics. Several published volumes and dissertations discuss his work. He has twice been invited to give the Gifford lectures in Scotland, the first being published as *Warranted Christian Belief* (Oxford University Press, 2000), with the more recent course on the topic of science and religion (St Andrews, 2005).

John Polkinghorne, KBE, FRS, began his academic career in theoretical physics, and was Professor of Mathematical Physics at the University of Cambridge until 1979. He then began his studies for the Anglican priesthood, and discovered a second vocation in theology and science. Author of some 30 books on science and religion, including the published version of his Gifford lectures (*Science and Christian Belief*, SPCK, 1994), he received the Templeton Prize in 2002 for his contribution to religion and science.

Alexander R. Pruss is Associate Professor of Philosophy at Baylor University, Texas and has PhDs in mathematics (University of British Columbia) and philosophy (University of Pittsburgh). He is the author of *The Principle of Sufficient Reason: A Reassessment* (Cambridge University Press, 2006) and *Actuality, Possibility and Worlds* (Continuum, 2011).

Nicholas Rescher is Distinguished University Professor of Philosophy at the University of Pittsburgh, Pennsylvania and is Chairman of the Center for Philosophy of Science. He has served as President of the American Philosophical Association and of the American Catholic Philosophy Association. He was the founding editor of the *American Philosophical Quarterly*. He has been elected to membership in the American Academy of Arts and Sciences and received the Order of Merit (First Class) of the Federal Republic of Germany in 2011.

Michael Ruse is the Lucyle T. Werkmeister Professor of Philosophy at Florida State University. He is the author of many books, including *Can a Darwinian Be a Christian? The Relationship between Science and Religion* (Cambridge University Press, 2001) and *Science and Spirituality: Making Room for Faith in the Age of Science* (Cambridge University Press, 2010).

Robert John Russell is the Ian G. Barbour Professor of Theology and Science in Residence, at the Graduate Theological Union, Berkeley, California. He is also Founder and Director of the Center for Theology and the Natural Sciences, Berkeley, and co-editor of the journal *Theology and Science*. He is the author of *Cosmology, Evolution, and Resurrection Hope: Theology and Science in Creative Mutual Interaction* (Pandora Press, 2006). Fifteen writers engaged Russell's thought in *God's Action in Nature's World: Essays in Honour of Robert John Russell*.

James F. Salmon, SJ is a professor in the chemistry and theology departments at Loyola University Maryland and Senior Fellow at the Woodstock Theological Center at Georgetown University, Washington, DC. He founded the Annual Cosmos and Creation conference that was inspired by the writings of Teilhard de Chardin. He has authored books in both chemistry and theology, and is co-editor of *The Legacy of Pierre Teilhard de Chardin* (Paulist Press, 2011).

Hans Schwarz has been Professor of Systematic Theology and Contemporary Theological Issues at the University of Regensburg, Germany, since 1981. Before that he taught at Trinity Lutheran Seminary in Columbus, Ohio (1967–1981). He has authored more than 30 books, the most recent in English being *Theology in a Global Context* (Eerdmans, 2005), and has been the principal advisor for 40 doctoral students who teach on five continents.

Lisa H. Sideris is Associate Professor of Religious Studies at Indiana University, with research interests in environmental ethics, religion and nature, and the science-religion interface. She is author of *Environmental Ethics, Ecological Theology, and Natural Selection* (Columbia University Press, 2003) and editor with Kathleen Dean Moore of an interdisciplinary collection of essays on Rachel Carson titled *Rachel Carson: Legacy and Challenge* (SUNY Press, 2008).

Taede A. Smedes is Postdoctoral Research Fellow at the Heyendaal Program on Theology and Science of the Faculties of Theology and Religious Studies of the Radboud University Nijmegen, the Netherlands. He is the author of *Chaos, Complexity, and God: Divine Action and Scientism* (Peeters, 2004).

Lisa L. Stenmark teaches in the comparative religious studies program at San Jose State University, California. She founded and was Director of Women in Religion, Ethics and the Sciences (WiRES). Her scholarly interests include religion and culture, especially in relation to politics and science. Her current project is "A Disputational Friendship: Religion, Science and Democracy," on scientific and religious authority in public life.

Mikael Stenmark is Professor of Philosophy of Religion and Dean of the Faculty of Theology at Uppsala University, Sweden. His books include *How to Relate Science and Religion: A Multidimensional Model* (Eerdmans, 2004); *Environmental Ethics and Environmental Policy Making* (Ashgate, 2002); *Scientism: Science, Ethics and Religion* (Ashgate 2001); and *Rationality in Science, Religion, and Everyday Life* (University of Notre Dame Press, 1995).

J. B. Stump is Professor of Philosophy and directs the philosophy program at Bethel College, Indiana. He is the philosophy editor of *Christian Scholars Review*, and has published articles there as well as in *Studies in History and Philosophy of Science* and *Philosophia Christi*. He has co-authored (with Chad Meister) *Christian Thought: A Historical Introduction* (Routledge, 2010).

Richard Swinburne was Nolloth Professor of the Philosophy of the Christian Religion at the University of Oxford, 1985–2002. He is the author of many books on the meaning and justification of theism and of Christian doctrines, including his trilogy on theism, *The Coherence of Theism* (Clarendon Press, 1993); *The Existence of God* (2nd edn, Oxford University Press, 2004); and *Faith and Reason* (2nd edn, Oxford University Press, 2005). He has also written books on epistemology and on mind and body. He lectures regularly at universities around the world.

Introduction

J. B. STUMP AND ALAN G. PADGETT

The last few decades have seen an enormous increase in the scholarly attention paid to issues at the intersection of science and religion. Books and articles have been written, conferences have been organized, and even professorial chairs and programs of study have been formed to further explore this fascinating area of inquiry. The present volume is an attempt to contribute to this ongoing conversation. The original pieces collected here provide a snapshot of the current scholarly research in the area; they are written for a broad academic audience and introduce many of the important themes in the dialogue between science and Christianity.

The academic field is now maturing as the second generation of scholars in this field reflects on the seminal work of the founding generation. One of the implications of the maturing of the field is the need for a more fine-grained analysis of the issues – hence our focus on Christianity in particular rather than religion in general. There are some fine handbooks that look at world religions and science, and we commend them. In this work, we narrow the conversation to science and Christianity to allow for greater specificity and depth on the topics. Of course there are some commonalities among religions with respect to their interactions with science, but as we get into specific doctrines, it is the differences in both the sciences and in the various world religions that become important after a certain basic introduction to this fascinating interdisciplinary field. For example, the nature of God in Christian theism is very different from the understanding of God or gods in Hinduism or of ultimate (non)reality in some forms of Buddhism. And even within the traditional monotheistic religions which affirm the same Creator God, there are significant discrepancies in understanding how God relates to the natural world and how God has revealed the divine nature to humans.

Focusing more narrowly on Christianity is not at all to suggest that it is the only relevant religion in dialogue with science. Other volumes have been, and should in the future be, devoted to Buddhism, Islam, or Judaism and science, and so for all the great world faiths. These religions have their own histories and methodologies and should be accorded the respect that is due them, rather than trying to subsume them under a generic heading or by giving them a paragraph or two of attention in a work that is in reality discussing Christianity. As a matter of historical fact, it is Christianity that has been the dominant religious system interacting with modern science, because of the dominance of the Christian faith when early modern science got going in Europe. Thus, we hope it will be very helpful to the larger conversation and debate in religion and science to devote this work entirely to the mutual interaction of modern science with Christianity.

While the authors all write with Christianity in mind, they are not all themselves Christians. This is not a work defending or promoting Christian faith, apart from the normal academic sense in which better understanding should promote greater appreciation and overcome misunderstanding. Many of the authors here do have Christian commitments of various sorts, but others represent different religions or none at all. We've not attempted to give equal space to each perspective on a particular issue, but we do hope that taken as a whole the chapters give a fair representation of the kinds of perspectives found at, say, an academic conference on science and Christianity.

On the whole, the volume aims for a philosophical and historical approach to the topic. We have found that both of these disciplines – philosophy and history – provide a very helpful and insightful space in which religion and science can get down to serious talk. Many of the authors are trained as scientists, but their work here is not of the kind you'd expect to find in *Nature* or *Science*. We do not aim to "do" science in these pages, any more than we seek to "do" religion. We are seeking to introduce and advance serious thinking and talking about science and Christianity, particularly as they interconnect. We are reflecting on the work of scientists and theologians, trying to find points of contact and points of tension which help to illuminate these practices and doctrines in clear, scholarly light.

Many of the authors will be recognizable to those familiar with the literature in science and religion. We're pleased that some of the world's leading scholars have contributed to this volume in their areas of expertise. But we've also invited younger scholars who will be voices for the discipline in the next generation. We've also aimed for as much diversity as is practical among the contributors in what is admittedly a field dominated by males from America and Britain.

The articles here are not meant to be condensed overviews which cover every aspect of a topic, as one might expect from encyclopedia articles. We've asked for fair presentation of the topics, but have also encouraged authors to defend their own views and pick out salient points for discussion. This has allowed us to devote several chapters to similar topics that are treated differently by their authors. We believe this has resulted in a lively collection that encourages deeper engagement.

Books like this one can be organized variously; we have opted for a somewhat traditional ordering. The 54 chapters are grouped into 11 parts. Of course subjects like natural theology, cosmology, and evolution have substantial sections devoted to them (Parts Three, Four, and Five). And preceding these are sections on historical episodes (Part One) and methodology (Part Two). But then we aimed to broaden the typical discussion to include Christianity's interaction with some human sciences (Part Six). The interaction of Christian theology and science is seen perhaps most transparently in the discussion of various technologies; Part Seven is accordingly devoted to Christian bioethics. Part Eight collects several topics in metaphysics, and Part Nine gives significant attention to various perspectives on the mind. Part Ten looks at several points of theology that have been reconsidered in light of modern science. Finally, Part Eleven introduces some of the leading voices in the contemporary dialogue surrounding religion and science. Overall we as editors have been guided by a common vision: to provide an up-to-date and helpful resource to readers looking to become acquainted with the various scholarly discussions at the interface of science and Christianity.

Part I
Historical Episodes

Part I

Historical Episodes

Early Christian Belief in Creation and the Beliefs Sustaining the Modern Scientific Endeavor

CHRISTOPHER B. KAISER

It is widely recognized that many of the founders of modern Western science were Christians not merely incidentally, but were inspired in creative ways by their Christian faith. Johannes Kepler, Robert Boyle, Isaac Newton, and James Clerk Maxwell are some of the best-known examples. More specifically, the case has often before been made for a connection between biblical thought – particularly the biblical idea of creation – and the rise of modern science. Alfred North Whitehead and R. G. Collingwood were among the pioneers of the argument (see Whitehead 1925; Collingwood 1940). Its more recent exponents include Reijer Hooykaas and Stanley Jaki (see Hooykaas 1972; Jaki 1974). I would like to restate the case for a connection between creation and science with three major alterations to these traditional accounts.

First, I would like to avoid the procedure often used by philosophers and systematic theologians which treats creation as a timeless idea from which implications can be drawn by logical (or theo-logical) inference.[1] Instead I propose to examine the historical implications of belief in creation as that belief has actually been held and acted upon by Christians, and I shall refer here primarily to the writings of the early Church when the fundamental structures of Christian thought – common to all major branches of Christendom – were established. I hope to show, as a result, that the implications of belief in creation are much richer and much more flexible than has usually been supposed.

Second, I would like to avoid any suggestion that science and technology could not have developed, perhaps along very different lines, in non-Western cultures. For one thing, we know that significant advances in science and technology were made by the Chinese, the Hindus, and the Arabs at a time northwestern Europe was still a cultural backwater. The growth of modern Western science would not have been possible without extensive borrowing from all three of these cultures. And what of the future? Is it not possible that Western endeavors in science and technology might fail and that further progress might require the input of alternative world-and-life views from non-Western cultures?

The third alteration I would like to make in the argument is to make explicit the fact that the demonstration of a genetic relationship between theology and science has implications for both disciplines. An affiliation with theology could be intended as a kind of legitimation

The Blackwell Companion to Science and Christianity, First Edition. Edited by J. B. Stump and Alan G. Padgett.
© 2012 Blackwell Publishing Ltd. Published 2012 by Blackwell Publishing Ltd.

for modern science – and it was so understood by many apologists for the new science of the seventeenth century. But a theological affiliation also entails a set of values which would imply a standard and a direction for modern science if they were suitably updated and articulated. In other words, the separation of fact and value so commonly assumed in modern thought must be challenged by any program that roots modern science in traditional theology.

On the other hand, the claim to be the historic matrix of modern science might suggest a legitimation for Christian theology in the minds of some. In fact, much of the historical research on this topic would seem to have been motivated, at least in part, by an apologetic interest in the context of a culture where science and theology have often been regarded as antagonistic.

But parents always bear some responsibility for their children, even after they have grown up. For better or worse, modern science and technology reflect back on the credibility of the first article of the Christian faith, and there are many in our day for whom the suggestion of any genetic relationship between theology and science would be highly detrimental to the case of theology. In other words Christian laity and clergy bear a certain responsibility – responsibility to recall the creation faith and restate it in such a way that the biblical vision for science and technology will be known and possibly heeded.

Here I shall treat the implications of belief in creation as it relates to the relative autonomy and comprehensibility of the world created by God.[2] I shall briefly review the biblical background for these ideas, give examples of their usage in patristic, medieval, and early modern thought, and discuss their influence and implications for modern science.

The basic idea of creation in Scripture is that the entire universe is subject to a code of law which was established at the beginning of time. This idea has two major implications for our view of the world: (1) nature functions with a high degree of autonomy (meaning literally, "having its own laws"); and (2) the natural world is comprehended by God and therefore comprehensible to human beings created in the divine image.

Frequently we think of creation as having to do with the *origin* of the universe, but more often it is a statement about the *nature and operation* of the cosmos. The origin of the universe (or perhaps the multiverse) depends solely on the wisdom and will of God and hence may lie beyond human understanding, but its subsequent operation is autonomous by virtue of the laws God has given it. It can be understood by humans because of the fact that human reason is itself an image of the same divine reason that governs the world.

By using the phrase "relative autonomy" of nature, I mean the self-sufficiency nature possesses by virtue of the fact that God has granted it laws of operation. Like all laws, the laws of nature may come to be viewed as enslaving and inflexible, but, in their biblical sense, at least, they were viewed as liberating (from chaos) and life-giving. The autonomy of nature was therefore "relative" in the sense of being relational (to God), as well as in the sense of not being self-originate as God is.

The Old Testament and Second-Temple Judaism

As far as we know, the roots of this idea go back before the Old Testament (or Hebrew Bible) to the early stages of Mesopotamian civilization in the fourth and third millennia BCE. The Mesopotamians viewed the universe as a cosmic nation-state in which the wills of the various gods, like the wills of humans, were bound by common law. In a second-millennium revival of these ideas (the *Enuma Elish* or "Babylonian Genesis"), the Babylonian god Marduk was credited with having ordained laws for the stars (which were identified with the lesser gods). The writers of the Old Testament, particularly those associated with the Israelite monarchy, developed this tradition while stressing the unique sovereignty of Yahweh (Adonai), the God of Israel, and the complete subservience of all nature, both in heaven and on earth, to his command.[3]

Among the texts of the Old Testament contributing to the idea, Genesis 1 and Psalms 19 and 104 are particularly noteworthy. Day and night follow each other automatically once their alternation has been established by God (Gen. 1:5, 8b; Ps. 19:2); the sun rises and sets according to schedule (Gen. 1:16–19; Ps. 19:5–6; 104:19b); and new generations of plants and animals succeed each other without interference through the normal processes of reproduction (Gen. 1:11–12, 21–22, 24–25). Elsewhere in the Old Testament, lawfulness is attributed to the courses of the sun, moon, and stars (Jer. 31:35–36), the ebb and flow of the tides (Job 38:8–11), the alternation of seasons (Gen. 8:22), and even to meteorological phenomena like the wind, rain, and lightning (Job 18:25–27).

In a sense, the work of creation was complete after the work of the "six days."[4] Within the Old Testament understanding of time, however, wherever and whenever the beneficent effects of God's mighty deeds were seen to continue, God's foundational work was also viewed as continuing. Creating once and for all was also continual creation (*creatio continua* or *creatio continuata*; see Hermisson 1978, 50–51). In other words, the order of nature is a dependent or contingent order (Torrance 1981), and, like an executive decree, is subject to regular ratification or amendment by God. God can alter it when doing so would bring greater fulfillment of its ultimate ends. Such alteration would be contingent on the divine will, but would not be arbitrary.

The natural order is therefore not indifferent to human history and its final outcome. It is neither impersonal nor amoral; hence it is not to be set over against the freedom and responsibility humans experience in everyday life (Ps. 19; 93; 104). Any supposed order that might ultimately lead to chaos, anarchy, or injustice would not, in the biblical view, be true order. Hence, the upholding of natural order not only allows, but *requires* its emendation at points where irreversible damage may occur.

During the Second-Temple period (fifth century BCE to the first century CE), the Jews developed the idea of the relative autonomy of nature considerably, partly as the result of their dialogue with Greek natural philosophy. One of the earliest and best-known examples is Yeshua ben Sirah, who wrote the deuterocanonical book known as ben Sirach (or Ecclesiasticus) in the early second century BCE. Ben Sirah gives us a stunning description of the ceaseless regularity of natural rhythms:

> When the Lord created his works from the beginning, and in making them, determined their boundaries, he arranged his works in an eternal order, and their dominion for all generations. They neither hunger nor grow weary, and they do not abandon their tasks. They do not crowd one another, and they never disobey his word. (Sir. 16:26–28)

The stress here on nature's obedience to God's word was intended as a contrast to the foolishness of humans who disregard God's (moral) laws, as the context makes abundantly clear (Sir. 16; 17). The contrast between the obedience of the luminaries and the rebelliousness of humans was made even more explicit in an early segment of 1 Enoch, and it reappeared in the Testament of Naphtali, the Psalms of Solomon, and the Dead Sea Scrolls.[5]

The important point here is that the Hebrew view of nature was neither impersonal nor amoral. As God's creature, nature had laws of its own, hence a degree of autonomy and comprehensibility. And, unlike humans, nature had not violated the laws God set for it; hence it had not taken on the kind of irrationality we often associate with human behavior. Even those aspects of nature that threatened human safety were not lawless in themselves. They served God's purposes and had laws of their own, even if unknown to humans (Job 28:25–27). Hence they were open to human comprehension, at least in principle.

The idea of the comprehensibility of the natural world was reaffirmed in the New Testament, particularly in passages that portrayed Christ as the foundation of the cosmos who united all things in heaven and earth (Matt. 28:18; 1 Cor. 8:6; 15:24–28; Eph. 1:10, 20–23; 4:8–10; Phil. 2:9–11; Col. 1:15–20; Heb. 1:2–3). Christ's work was viewed in this respect as a renewal and perfection of the order in the original creation.

The Autonomy of Nature: Basil of Caesarea to John Buridan

In order to illustrate the idea of the relative autonomy and comprehensibility of the natural world in patristic thought, I turn now to Basil's sermons on the *hexaemeron*, or "work of the six days," as described in Genesis 1. Like most early Christian authors, Basil assumed that the "six days" in question were figures of speech. He followed Philo and Origen in regarding all things as having been created at the first instant of time and remaining in a steady state thereafter.[6]

While Basil is only one of many early Church figures we could examine, he is perhaps the most representative and certainly the most influential. His formal training included the classical Greek arts and sciences as well as monastic spiritual discipline. Consequently, he was well suited to provide a paradigmatic synthesis of Christian and classical learning. Moreover, Basil was a pivotal figure in all of the major areas of early Christian thought and practice. He was a devoted servant of the Church, the leading bishop of the Eastern Church after Athanasius. He was one of the founders of cenobite monasticism, the movement which was to transmit classical and patristic learning to the medieval West. He was the chief architect of post-Nicene (or neo-Nicene) orthodoxy concerning the doctrine of the Trinity. Finally, Basil's hexaemeral sermons were the principal textbook on science and Scripture through the early middle ages and were still one of the two sources recommended by John Calvin, the other being Ambrose, who was himself dependent on Basil (*Institutes of the Christian Religion* I.14.20).

Basil delivered his sermons on the *hexaemeron* on five successive weekdays to a congregation of artisans on their way to and from work. At the time (during the 360s), he was still a presbyter at Caesarea, and his responsibilities included what we would call "Christian education." He was keenly interested in the meaning of Christian faith for secular life in this context.

Perhaps the best example of Basil's views is his comment in the fifth sermon on Genesis 1:11, the text of which reads as follows: "Then God said, 'Let the earth put forth vegetation, plants yielding seed, and fruit trees of every kind on the earth that bear fruit with the seed in it.'" Basil first noted the wisdom of the basic order of the text: first pasture-land vegetation; then fruit trees. In other words, each spring the grass turns green before the trees bear fruit. This order, once given, he notes, is followed by the earth to this day, and will continue for all time:

For the voice that was then heard and this command were as a natural and permanent law [*nomos physeōs*] for it; it gave fertility and the power to produce fruit for all ages to come. (*Hexaemeron* V.1; Schaff and Wace 1890–1900, VIII:76a)

Ambrose of Milan wrote a Latin paraphrase of Basil's *Hexaemeron* which used the phrase *lex naturae* ("law of nature") at this point (*Hexaemeron* V.6.16), and this concept became commonplace in Western discourse long before its more specialized use in modern science.

In order to appreciate the force of Basil's argument about the continuing effect of God's command, recall that Aristotle restricted all natural terrestrial processes to linear motion. Fire rose up to the sky, while earth fell down, but both naturally moved in straight (vertical) lines. The cyclical phenomena of nature, on the other hand – Aristotle called them cycles of "generation and corruption" – were not natural: they were forced by the circular motion of the heavens, particularly by the sun.[7] For Basil, however, the cycles of nature were imposed on the earth by the command of God, not by the motion of the sun along the ecliptic. Basil thus eliminated the hierarchical subordination of earth to the heavens and established each process as being "natural" in that it manifested its own God-given law.

In concluding his homily on Genesis 1:11, Basil returned to the theme of the relative autonomy God had granted to nature by his command and, in so doing, gave a classic example of what later became known as the concept of impetus or momentum:

It is this command which, still at this day, is imposed on the earth. . . . Like [spinning] tops, which after the first impulse, continue their revolutions, turning upon themselves when once fixed in their centre; thus nature, receiving the impulse of this first command, follows without interruption the course of ages, until the consummation of all things. (*Hexaemeron* V.10; Schaff and Wace, 1890–1900, VIII:81b)[8]

Spinning tops were a phenomenon that strained the basic principles of Aristotelian physics and yet were known to every playful child. Belonging to the terrestrial world, they moved in circular fashion like the celestial spheres yet without dependence on the heavens.

The state of spinning was regarded as "unnatural" by Aristotle and required the ad hoc supposition of a thin layer of air whirling around the top to keep it going. For Basil, however, the motion of the spinning top was perfectly "natural," as was the regular cycle of seedtime and harvest (Gen. 8:22) to which he compared it. In either case there was an initial impulse (the twist of fingers or the pull of a string, in one case, the command of God, in the other), the effect of which continued even after the original action had ceased. In modern science, the principle exhibited in the case of the spinning top is called the law of the conservation of momentum (in this case, angular momentum). For Basil, it was not only tops but all of nature, organic as well as inorganic, that moved in regular intervals in accordance with the command of God.

The idea that motion is conserved and that its magnitude depends only on the initial impulse was developed in the sixth century by the Alexandrian John Philoponus as part of his programmatic attack on the physics of Aristotle (Sambursky 1962, 74–76). Through the writings of Philoponus, and also through the Syriac hexaemeral tradition,[9] it was passed on to Arab philosophers of the eleventh and twelfth centuries like Ibn Sina (Avicenna), Ibn Bajjah (Avempace), al-Baghdadi, and al-Bitruji (Alpetragius). The idea was taken up, with significant alterations, by Western scholastics of the thirteenth and fourteenth centuries like Thomas Aquinas, Peter John Olivi, and Francis of Marchia (Nasr 1968–1973).

Partly as a result of the influence of Neoplatonism, Ibn Sina and Ibn Bajjah had reinterpreted the impartation of momentum as a continuously impressed force, thus weakening the basic idea of the autonomy of nature and ruling out the possibility of conservation of momentum in the absence of a continuous force. In this altered form, the idea of an impressed force continued down to the mid-fourteenth century, when John Buridan revived the idea of a conserved impetus by appealing to the efficacy of God's original act of creation and citing the example of a spinning millwheel (*Questions on the Heavens and the Earth* II.12), just as Basil had done almost a thousand years earlier. Buridan's work was foundational to late medieval and early modern studies that led to the modern concept of momentum (Dales 1973, 111, 116–117).

It was another three centuries before Galileo, Descartes, and Newton were able to formulate the principle of the conservation of momentum in mathematical terms in such a way that it could be used in calculations. The ideas of laws of nature and relative autonomy that lay behind the principle were readily available by the time of Basil, however. Indeed it was deeply embedded in the Jewish–Christian tradition that Basil inherited, as we have seen. Basil merely gave practical examples from everyday experience to illustrate the principle of the relative autonomy of nature as it had been understood at least since the time of Yeshua ben Sirah.

The Comprehensibility of Nature: Gregory of Nazianzus to Johannes Kepler

The lawfulness of nature did not by itself provide any hope that humans could comprehend God's design. For early Christians, however, belief in divine creation also implied that mathematical characteristics like weight, number, and measure were imprinted on the human mind as well as on creation (based on Wis. 11:20). This idea was extremely important, because it implied that the mathematical nature of creation should be visible to anyone with the proper training to see it. One of the clearest expressions of this idea in patristic literature occurs in the orations of Basil's associate, Gregory of Nazianzus (379–380 CE):

> Is it not the Artificer of [all moving things] who implanted reason [*lógon*] in them all, in accordance with which the universe is moved and controlled? . . . Thus reason that is from God that is implanted in all from the beginning, and is the first law in us, and is bound up in all leads us up to God through visible things. (*Orations* 28.16; Schaff and Wace 1890–1900, VII:294b, modified)

According to Gregory, human intelligence is not merely a random product of chance, but deeply tuned to the same logic (*lógos*) that God has implanted in the cosmos.

Gregory did not bring out the implications of this double imprint for scientific endeavor – his main concerns were with churchmanship and theology. However, medieval heirs of the patristic tradition did apply these ideas to their efforts in their crafts (e.g., Theophilus the Presbyter, *c.* 1100) and astronomical studies (Lefèvre d'Étaples, 1503). I shall focus on one particular astronomer, Johannes Kepler (1571–1630), whose work, like that of John Buridan, lies at the basis of modern science.

Like Gregory long before him, Kepler thought of the divine ideas such as those of mathematical geometry as being imprinted on the natural world and also impressed on the human mind as part of the image of God. As he stated in the fourth book of his treatise "On the Harmony of the Universe" (*Harmonices mundi*, 1619):

Geometry, which before the origin of things was coeternal with the divine mind . . . supplied God with patterns for the creation of the world and passed over to human nature along with the image of God. (Kepler 1997, 304, modified)

As a result of this dual imprinting of mathematical truth, humans could indeed have confidence in their ability – provided they undergo suitable training – to discern the geometries and laws that God had implanted in the natural world.

Kepler was sustained by his deep faith in the providence of God in creating the world and equipping humans with the intelligence to understand it. When questioned about the possibility of solving the mystery of the planetary orbits, he wrote to one of his patrons, Johannes Georg Herwart von Hohenburg (9/10 April 1599):

Those [laws which govern the material world] are within the grasp of the human mind. God wanted us to recognize them by creating us after his own image so that we could share in his own thoughts . . . and, if piety allows us to say so, our understanding is in this respect of the same kind as the divine, at least as far as we are able to grasp something of it in our mortal life. (Baumgardt 1951, 50)[10]

Kepler's faith in the comprehensibility of the natural world continued to be an influential model for physicists right into in the early twentieth century. In fact, Albert Einstein, in his 1930 lecture on "Religion and Science," cited Kepler as the inspiration for his own efforts in mathematical physics in the early twentieth century:

What a deep conviction of the rationality of the universe and what a yearning to understand, were it but a feeble reflection of the Mind revealed in this world, Kepler and Newton must have had to enable them to spend years of solitary labour in disentangling the principles of celestial mechanics! . . . Only one who has devoted his life to similar ends can have a vivid realisation of what has inspired these men and given them the strength to remain true to their purpose in spite of countless failures. (Einstein 1954, 39–40)

Even from this brief historical sketch, it can be seen that biblical, theological ideas lay at the heart of the Western scientific enterprise. Those beliefs continue to inspire and sustain scientists the world over, even though in a secularized form.

The Twelfth-Century Reinterpretation: Nature versus God

The lawfulness, relative autonomy, and comprehensibility that early Christians attributed to the processes of nature were clearly an important factor in the rise of early modern science. However, these ideas may also have been responsible for the gradual separation that took place between matters of fact and matters of value in modern Western thought, particularly as they were reinterpreted by twelfth-century natural philosophers. Significant changes took place in the understanding of the relation between God, humanity, and nature in the twelfth century which led to a dichotomy between the sovereignty of God and the autonomy of nature (Stiefel 1977; Dales 1980; Bartlett 2008, 16–17).

There were two sides to the twelfth-century debate. On the one side, naturalists who rightly desired to comprehend the world in its own terms stressed the autonomy of nature and the power of human reason to the point where they lost sight of the dependence of all natural law on God. On the other side, conservatives who desired to defend the importance of God's role in history attacked the naturalists and stressed the absolute power of God (*potentia Dei absoluta*) and the authority of the Church. The result was a split between natural-ists and conservatives within the Church reflected in the emergence of a bifurcation between the autonomy of nature and the power of God in Christian thought.

To illustrate this dichotomy, let us look briefly at the work of Adelard of Bath (early twelfth century). Adelard (not to be confused with Peter Abelard) is often regarded as the first major contributor to Western science (Dales 1973, 37–51).

In order to defend his interest in Arabic natural philosophy against conservatives in his native England, Adelard argued that the present-day work of God was restricted to miracles and contrasted it with the work of nature. In a dialogue with his nephew, he stated:

> I am not slighting God's role. For whatever exists is from him and through him. Nevertheless, that [dependence on God] is not [to be taken] in blanket fashion, without distinction. One should attend to this [distinction] as far as human knowledge can go, but in the case *where human knowl-edge completely fails*, the matter should be referred to God. (*Natural Questions* 4; Adelard 1998, 97–99, italics added; cf. Dales 1973, 40 for a different translation)

The underlying ideas cited in this passage – the creation of all things by God, the consequent order and rationality of the cosmos, and the ability of human reason to comprehend this order – all stem from the Judeo-Christian belief in creation, dating back at least to the second century BCE. What was new was that Adelard set the natural order and the work of God, rational investigation and Christian faith, over against each other as alternatives: "where human knowledge completely fails, the matter should be referred to God."

The consequence of this polarization was that, for Adelard, God was removed from the natural order in such a way that natural law became inflexible and impersonal:

> But whoever takes away the order of things is a fool. . . . But the Disposer of things is supremely wise. He, therefore, neither wishes to, *nor is able to*, take away the order of things. . . . For this, then to occur to the mind of a philosopher is not at all appropriate. (Adelard 1998, 219, italics added; cf. Stiefel 1977, 351)

The belief that God does not normally alter his established order (*potentia Dei ordinata*) had been an essential part of the historical "creationist tradition" since the Book of Genesis, but for earlier theologians like ben Sirah and Basil, the natural order itself was upheld by God (through his word, will, power).[11] For Adelard, on the other hand, the only properly divine action was his abolition or upsetting of that order (*potentia Dei absoluta*). In this he agreed with conservatives like Peter Damian and William of St. Thierry, who stressed God's absolute power over nature. The difference was that for Adelard any alteration of the natural order was regarded as highly unlikely. The order of nature was so fixed that God was neither willing nor even able, to alter it!

Already in the Middle Ages, therefore, there were problems emerging in Western thought that have plagued us ever since. In order to see how radical the change in outlook was, con-sider whether, in our own minds today, miracles and natural processes are not two entirely different things – different in reality as well as in words. What I wish to argue is that this division of both words and reality is a social construct that does not occur in other traditional cultures and that, even in Europe, probably does not occur before the eleventh or twelfth century. Our differentiation between the natural and the supernatural allows scientists like Adelard to pursue secular goals independently of theological criteria, but at a considerable cost. Not only do problems arise for economics and ecology as a result of their isolation from theological grounding, but theology appears rather remote and unrelated to life when its implications for secular practice are ruled out by a definition of terms.

In this chapter, I have argued two theses: (1) that Christian belief in creation has historically had implications that have a bearing on the meaning of modern science and technology; and (2) that these implications have historically had an influence in the development of modern science and technology. It does not follow that people have to be theologically literate in order to be good scientists. However, intellectual honesty requires us to recognize our historical roots and their continuing influence today as much as to recognize our origins in nature with all of the strengths and weaknesses that they bring.

Notes

1   The classic example is M. B. Foster's argument (originally published in 1934) that the idea of creation implies a constitutive role for the divine will and hence a degree of contingency in the structures of creation and an empirical, rather than rationalistic, methodology in science (Foster 1969, 46–49).

2   In a full-length study (Kaiser 1997, 21–83, summarized in Kaiser 1993), I treat four beliefs implicated in the doctrine of creation: the comprehensibility of the world, the unity of nature, its relative autonomy, and the ministry of healing and restoration.

3   For example, Gen. 1:1–25; Job 28:25–26; 38:4–11; Ps. 19:4–6; 104:9; Prov. 8:29; Jer. 5:22; 31:35–36. See Schmid (1984) on the ancient Near Eastern view of the order of creation as the horizon for Old Testament theology.

4   The Greek Septuagint of Gen. 2:2 specifies that God finished his work on the sixth day, but the Hebrew text is ambiguous.

5   1 Enoch 2:1–5:5; Testament of Naphtali 3:2–4; Psalms of Solomon 18:12–14; 1QS 3:15–17 (stressing predestination); 1Q34 (Festival Prayer) frag. 3 2:1–3 (see Gowan 1985, 89, 99–100). Aramaic fragments of 1 Enoch 1–36 (The Book of the Watchers) dating from the late third or early second century BCE have been found at Qumran.

6   For example, Philo, *On the Creation of the World* 13–16, 25, 28, 43, 67–68; *Allegorical Interpretation of Genesis* 1.19–21; *Questions on Exodus* 1.1; Origen, *On First Principles* I.2.2; idem, *Against Celsus* VI.60; Basil, *Hexaemeron* 1.6; Gregory of Nyssa, *Hexaemeron* 72b–77d; Augustine, *Confessions* XII.12.15; *On Genesis Word for Word* IV.18.33; V.3.5–6, 5.12–13; VI.6.11; *City of God* XI.33.

7   See Aristotle, *On Generation and Corruption* 11.10.337a–11.338b; *Meteorology* 11.2.354b.26–28.

8   The concept of continuous spin has Stoic roots; cf. the fragment of Chrysippus in Cicero, *On Fate* XVIII.42–XIX.43, and Virgil's *Aeneid* VII.373.

9   Basil's *Hexaemeron* was translated into Syriac in the fifth century and into Arabic probably by the eighth or ninth century. Syriac *hexaemera* were written by James of Edessa (d. 708) and Moses bar Kepha (d. 903) (see Peters 1968, 116, 132–133). The illustration of a spinning wheel was used by Job of Edessa (d. *c.* 835) in his *Book of Treasures* V.12.

10 As Chancellor of Bavaria, von Hohenburg was able to help Kepler establish connections at the imperial court in Prague. He was also a mathematician and, though a Catholic, had studied under the Lutheran astronomer Michael Mästlin (Baumgardt 1951, 57–59). Kepler shares his ideas about God and creation with Herwart as if the two of them remembered them from their teacher.

11 I borrow the term "creationist tradition" from the seminal article by Richard Dales (1980, 533).

References

Adelard of Bath. 1998. *Conversations with His Nephew: On the Same and the Different; Questions on Natural Science; and On Birds*. Translated by Charles S. F. Burnett. Cambridge: Cambridge University Press.

Bartlett, Robert. 2008. *The Natural and the Supernatural in the Middle Ages*. New York: Cambridge University Press.

Baumgardt, Carola. 1951. *Johannes Kepler: Life and Letters*. New York: Philosophical Library.

Collingwood, R. G. 1940. *An Essay on Metaphysics*. Oxford: Oxford University Press.

Dales, Richard C. 1980. The De-Animation of the Heavens in the Middle Ages. *Journal of the History of Ideas*, 41, pp. 531–550.

Einstein, Albert. 1954. *Ideas and Opinions*. London: Alvin Redman.

Foster, M. B. 1969. The Christian Doctrine of Creation and the Rise of Modern Natural Science. In Daniel O'Connor and Francis Oakley, eds. *Creation: The Impact of an Idea*. New York: Charles Scribner's Sons, pp. 29–53.

Gowan, Donald E. 1985. The Fall and Redemption of the Material World in Apocalyptic Literature. *Horizons in Biblical Theology*, 7(2), pp. 83–103.

Hermisson, Hans-Jürgen. 1978. Observations on the Creation Theology in Wisdom. In John G. Gammie, Walter A. Brueggemann, W. Lee Humphreys, and James M. Ward, eds. *Israelite Wisdom: Theological and Literary Essays in Honor of Samuel Terrien*. Missoula, MT: Scholars Press, pp. 43–57.

Hooykaas, R. 1972. *Religion and the Rise of Modern Science*. Edinburgh: Scottish Academic Press; Grand Rapids, MI: Eerdmans.

Jaki, Stanley L. 1974. *Science and Creation: From Eternal Cycles to an Oscillating Universe*. Edinburgh: Scottish Academic Press.

Kaiser, Christopher B. 1993. The Creationist Tradition in the History of Science. *Perspectives on Science and Christian Faith*, 45(2), pp. 80–89.

Kepler, Johannes. 1997. *The Harmony of the World*. Translated by E. J. Aiton, A. M. Duncan, and J. V. Field. Philadelphia: American Philosophical Society.

Nasr, Seyyed Hossein. 1968–1973. Islamic Conception of Intellectual Life. In Philip P. Wiener, ed. *Dictionary of the History of Ideas*, vol. 2. New York: Scribner's, pp. 645–649.

Peters, F. E. 1968. *Aristotle and the Arabs: The Aristotelian Tradition in Islam*. New York: New York University Press.

Sambursky, Shmeul. 1962. *The Physical World of Late Antiquity*. London: Routledge.

Schaff, Philip and Wace, Henry. 1890–1900. *Nicene and Post-Nicene Fathers, Second Series*, 14 vols. Buffalo: Christian Literature Company.

Schmid, H. H. 1984. Creation, Righteousness, and Salvation: "Creation Theology" as the Broad Horizon of Biblical Theology. In Bernhard W. Anderson, ed. *Creation in the Old Testament*. Philadelphia: Fortress Press, pp. 102–117.

Stiefel, Tina. 1977. The Heresy of Science: A Twelfth-Century Conceptual Revolution. *Isis*, 68, pp. 347–362.

Torrance, Thomas F. 1981. *Divine and Contingent Order*. New York: Oxford University Press.

Whitehead, Alfred North. 1925. *Science and the Modern World*. New York: Macmillan.

Further Reading

Dales, Richard C. 1973. *The Scientific Achievement of the Middle Ages*. Philadelphia: University of Pennsylvania Press. A selection of primary sources about medieval scientific endeavor beginning with Adelard of Bath's famous dialogue on *Natural Questions* and prefaced by an introductory essay by Edward Peters.

Grant, Edward. 1996. *The Foundations of Modern Science in the Middle Ages: Their Religious, Institutional, and Intellectual Contexts*. Cambridge: Cambridge University Press. Clearly demonstrates the role of theological beliefs in the revision of Aristotelian science in the late Middle Ages.

Kaiser, Christopher B. 1997. *Creational Theology and the History of Physical Science: The Creationist Tradition from Basil to Bohr*. Leiden: Brill. Surveys the development of creational beliefs and their implications in the development of Western physical science and medicine.

Murray, Robert. 1992. *The Cosmic Covenant: Biblical Themes of Justice, Peace and the Integrity of Creation*. London: Sheed & Ward. Shows how the Old Testament and early Christian idea of covenant included the natural order.

2

The Copernican Revolution and the Galileo Affair

MAURICE A. FINOCCHIARO

The condemnation of Galileo Galilei (1564–1642) by the Inquisition in 1633 is perhaps the most significant episode in the long history of the interaction between science and Christianity. One reason is that the trial's key intellectual issue (whether the earth is a planet revolving around the sun) was identical to the key issue of what is clearly the most important episode in the history of science – the Copernican Revolution. Another reason is that the victim happened to make numerous and epoch-making contributions to physics and astronomy, so much so that he is often called the father of modern science. A third reason is that the 1633 condemnation was a *cause célèbre* that continues to be a defining moment of modern Western culture. Thus, to understand this significance we need to delve into the Copernican Revolution, the Inquisition trial proceedings, and the key points of the subsequent affair.

The Copernican Controversy

In 1543, Nicolaus Copernicus (1473–1543) published his epoch-making *On the Revolutions of the Heavenly Spheres* (Copernicus 1992). In it, he updated an idea originally advanced by the Pythagoreans and Aristarchus in ancient Greece, but almost universally rejected: the earth moves by rotating on its own axis daily and revolving around the sun once a year. This contradicted the traditional belief that the earth was standing still at the center of the universe, with all heavenly bodies revolving around it. In its essentials, this geokinetic idea turned out to be true, as we know today beyond any reasonable doubt, after five centuries of accumulating evidence. At the time, however, the situation was different (Kuhn 1957; Finocchiaro 2010, 21–36).

Copernicus's accomplishment was a *new argument* supporting an old idea: he demonstrated in quantitative detail that the known facts about the motions of the heavenly bodies could be explained more simply and coherently if the sun rather than the earth is assumed to be motionless at the center, and the earth is taken to be the third planet circling the sun. For example, from the viewpoint of simplicity, there are thousands fewer moving parts in the

The Blackwell Companion to Science and Christianity, First Edition. Edited by J. B. Stump and Alan G. Padgett.
© 2012 Blackwell Publishing Ltd. Published 2012 by Blackwell Publishing Ltd.

Copernican system than in the geostatic system, since the apparent daily westward motion of all heavenly bodies around the earth is explained by the earth's daily eastward axial rotation, and thus there is only one body rotating daily, not thousands. Regarding explanatory coherence, this concept means the ability to explain many details of the observed phenomena by means of one's basic principles, without adding ad hoc assumptions. Copernicus could thus coherently explain the periodic changes in the brightness and direction of motion of the planets, whereas the geostatic explanations of these details were improvised piecemeal.

However, Copernicus's argument was a *hypothetical* one. That is, it was based on the claim that if the earth were in motion then the observed phenomena would result; but from this it does not follow necessarily that the earth is in motion. This claim does provide a reason for preferring the geokinetic idea, but it is not a decisive reason. It would be decisive only in the absence of contrary reasons. In short, one has to look at counterarguments, and there were many.

Some of them were mechanical, namely based on physics – the science of motion. For example, according to traditional Aristotelian physics, if the earth moved then terrestrial bodies would have to move in ways that do not correspond to how they are known (and easily observed) to move: freely falling bodies could not fall vertically, but would be left behind slanting westward; westward gunshots would range farther than eastward ones, instead of ranging equally; and loose bodies not firmly attached to the ground would fly off toward the sky. There is no way of escaping these mechanical consequences unless one rejects Aristotelian physics. To reject it effectively one must put something else in its place. This in turn involves building a new physics – something easier said than done. To put it briefly, Copernicus's astronomy contradicted the physics of the time; the motion of the earth seemed to be a physical impossibility.

The idea was also considered to be a philosophical absurdity. For Copernicus did not claim that he could feel, see, or otherwise perceive the earth's motion. Like everyone else, his senses (eyes and kinesthetic awareness) told him that the earth is at rest. Thus, some people objected that if his theory were true, then the human senses would be lying to us, and it was regarded as absurd that the senses should deceive us about such a basic phenomenon as the state of the terrestrial globe on which we live. That is, the geokinetic theory seemed to be in flat contradiction with direct sense experience, and so to violate the fundamental epistemological principle claiming that under normal conditions the senses provide us with an access to reality.

The Copernican theory also faced empirical difficulties in astronomy. That is, it had observational consequences regarding the heavenly bodies that were not in fact observed. For example, it implied that the earth (being a planet) should share various physical properties with the other planets; that the planet Venus should show periodic phases similar to those of the moon; that the planet Mars should show periodic changes in apparent size and brightness of a factor of about 60; and that the fixed stars should exhibit an annual shift in apparent position.

Finally, the geokinetic theory faced religious or theological difficulties. One objection was that the earth's motion contradicted many biblical passages, which state or imply that the earth stands still. For example, Joshua 10:12–13 speaks of the miracle of stopping the sun: "On the day when the Lord gave the Amorites over to the Israelites, Joshua spoke to the Lord; and he said in the sight of Israel, 'Sun stand still at Gibeon, and Moon, in the valley of Aijalon.' And the sun stood still, and the moon stopped, until the nation took vengeance on their enemies." Other anti-Copernican passages were Ecclesiastes 1:5 and Psalm 104:5.

In Catholic circles, this biblical objection was supplemented by one appealing to the consensus of Church Fathers – the saints, theologians, and churchmen who had played a formative role in the establishment of Christianity. The argument claimed that all Church Fathers were unanimous in interpreting relevant biblical passages in accordance with the geostatic view; therefore, the geostatic system is binding on all believers, and to claim otherwise is erroneous or heretical.

A third religious objection was more theological-sounding, based on the belief in the omnipotence of God: since God is all-powerful, he could have created any one of a number of worlds, for example one in which the earth is motionless; therefore, regardless of how much evidence there is supporting the earth's motion, we can never assert that this must be so, for that would be to limit God's power to do otherwise.

Regarding the religious objections, it is important to note two things. On the one hand, they were only part of the opposition to Copernicanism, since there were also the mechanical objections, the astronomical counterevidence, and the epistemological argument. On the other hand, religious criticism of Copernicanism was immediate, indeed it even antedated the publication of the *Revolutions*; it did not have to wait for Galileo, as often alleged.[1]

Copernicus (1992, 3–50) knew that his hypothesis faced such difficulties. He realized that his novel argument did not conclusively prove the earth's motion, and that there were many counterarguments of apparently greater strength. He was also aware of the religious objections. I believe these were the reasons why he delayed publication of his book until he was near death, although his motivation was complex and is not yet completely understood and continues to be the subject of serious research.

However, Copernicus's argument was so important that it could not be ignored, and various attempts were made to come to terms with it, to assimilate it, to amplify it, or to defend it. Some thinkers (especially a group centered on the German University of Wittenberg) tried to exploit the mathematical advantages of Copernicanism without committing themselves to its cosmological claims, by adopting an instrumentalist interpretation according to which the earth's motion was just a convenient instrument for making mathematical calculations and astronomical predictions, and not a description of physical reality (Westman 1975). Tycho Brahe (1546–1601) undertook an unprecedented effort to systematically collect new observational data, and he also devised another compromise, a theory that was partly heliocentric and partly geocentric, although fully geostatic: the planets revolved around the sun, but the sun moved daily and annually around the motionless central earth (Mosley 2007). Giordano Bruno (1548–1600), an Italian Dominican friar turned apostate, undertook a multifaceted defense of Copernicanism that addressed epistemological, metaphysical, theological, and empirical issues; but Bruno's defense remained largely unknown, disregarded, or unappreciated (Bruno 1995). Johannes Kepler (1571–1630) accepted Copernicanism for metaphysical reasons and then undertook a research program to prove its empirical adequacy, by meticulously analyzing Tycho's data; the result was an improvement such that the planets revolved around the sun in elliptical, rather than circular, orbits (Kepler 1992).

The Trial of Galileo

The most significant response to the Copernican controversy was Galileo's. He was born in Pisa in 1564, became professor of mathematics at the university there in 1589, and then taught at the University of Padua from 1592 to 1610.

During this period, Galileo researched primarily the nature of motion. He was critical of Aristotelian physics; favorably inclined toward Archimedean statics and mathematics; and innovatively experimental, insofar as he pioneered the procedure of actively intervening into and manipulating natural phenomena, combining empirical observation with quantitative mathematization and conceptual theorizing. Following this approach he formulated, justified, and systematized various mechanical principles: an approximation to the law of inertia; the composition of motion; the laws that in free fall the distance fallen increases as the square of the time elapsed and the velocity acquired is directly proportional to the time; and the parabolic path of projectiles. However, he did not publish these results during that period; indeed he did not publish a systematic account of them until 1638, in *Two New Sciences* (Galilei 1974; 2008, 295–367).

A key reason for this delay was that in 1609 Galileo became actively involved in astronomy. He was already acquainted with Copernicanism and appreciative of the fact that Copernicus had advanced a novel argument. Galileo also had intuited that the geokinetic theory was generally more consistent with his new physics than was the geostatic theory; in particular, he had been attracted to Copernicanism because he felt the earth's motion could best explain why the tides occur. But he had not published or articulated this general intuition and this particular feeling. Moreover, he was acutely aware of the strength of the observational astronomical evidence against Copernicanism. Thus, until 1609 Galileo judged that the anti-Copernican arguments outweighed the pro-Copernican ones.

However, his telescopic discoveries led Galileo to a major reassessment. In 1609, he perfected the telescope to such an extent as to make it an astronomically useful instrument that could not be duplicated by others for some time. By its means he made several startling discoveries, which he published the following year in *The Sidereal Messenger* (Galilei 2008, 45–84): the moon's surface is full of mountains and valleys; innumerable other stars exist besides those visible with the naked eye; the Milky Way and the nebulas are dense collections of large numbers of individual stars; and the planet Jupiter has four moons revolving around it at different distances and with different periods. As a result, Galileo became a celebrity, resigned his professorship at Padua, was appointed philosopher and chief mathematician to the grand duke of Tuscany, and moved to Florence the same year. Soon afterwards, he also discovered the phases of Venus and sunspots; on the latter, in 1613 he published the *History and Demonstrations Concerning Sunspots* (Galilei and Scheiner 2010; Galilei 2008, 97–102).

Although most of these discoveries were made independently by others, no one understood their significance like Galileo. The reason for this was threefold. Methodologically, the telescope implied a revolution in astronomy insofar at it was a new instrument for the gathering of a new kind of data transcending the previous reliance on naked-eye observation. Substantively, those discoveries strengthened the case for Copernicanism by refuting almost all empirical astronomical objections and providing new supporting observational evidence. Finally, this reinforcement was not equivalent to settling the issue because there was still some astronomical counterevidence (mainly, the lack of annual stellar parallax); because the mechanical objections had not yet been answered and the physics of a moving earth had not yet been explicitly articulated, although it was implicit in the research he had already accomplished; and because the theological objections had not yet been refuted. Thus, Galileo conceived a work that would discuss all aspects of the question. But this synthesis of Galileo's astronomy, physics, and methodology was not published until 1632, in *Dialogue on the Two Chief World Systems, Ptolemaic and Copernican* (Galilei 2001; 2008, 190–271).

This particular delay was due to the fact that the theological aspect of the question got Galileo into trouble with the Inquisition, acquiring a life of its own that drastically changed his existence (Fantoli 2003; Finocchiaro 1989). For as it became known that he was convinced that the new telescopic evidence rendered the geokinetic theory a serious contender for real physical truth, he came increasingly under attack from conservative philosophers and clergy. They argued that Galileo was a heretic because he believed in the earth's motion, which contradicted Scripture. Although he was aware of the potentially explosive nature of this issue, he felt he could not remain silent, but decided to refute the biblical argument. To avoid scandalous publicity, he wrote his criticism in the form of long private letters, in December 1613 to his disciple Benedetto Castelli, and in spring 1615 to the Dowager Grand Duchess Christina.

Galileo's letters circulated widely and the conservatives got even more upset. Thus in early 1615, a Dominican friar filed a written complaint against Galileo with the Inquisition in Rome, and another Dominican made a formal deposition in person against him. An investigation was launched lasting about a year. As part of this inquiry, a committee of Inquisition consultants reported that the key Copernican theses were absurd or false in natural philosophy and heretical or erroneous in theology. The Inquisition also interrogated other witnesses. Galileo himself was not summoned or interrogated partly because the key witnesses exonerated him; partly because his letters had not been published, whereas his published writings contained neither a categorical assertion of Copernicanism nor a denial of the scientific authority of Scripture; and partly because he enjoyed the respect, trust, and protection of many high Church officials and powerful laymen.

However, in December 1615 Galileo went to Rome of his own accord to defend Copernicanism. He was able to talk to many influential officials and was received in a friendly manner; and he may be credited with having prevented the worst, insofar as the Inquisition did not issue a formal condemnation of Copernicanism as a heresy. However, he was otherwise unsuccessful. For in February 1616, he was privately given a personal warning by Cardinal Robert Bellarmine (in the name of the Inquisition), forbidding him to hold or defend the truth of the earth's motion; Galileo agreed to comply. And in March, the Congregation of the Index (the department in charge of book censorship) published a decree which, without mentioning Galileo, did three things: it declared that the earth's motion was physically false and contradicted Scripture; it condemned and permanently banned a book published by a clergyman in 1615 defending the earth's motion from the scriptural objection; and it temporarily and partially banned Copernicus's *Revolutions*, until and unless appropriately revised. Published in 1620, these revisions amounted to rewording or deleting a dozen passages suggesting that the earth's motion was or could be physically true, so that the revised work would clearly convey the impression that geokineticism was merely a convenient hypothesis to make mathematical calculations and observational predictions.

For the next several years, Galileo kept quiet regarding the earth's motion, until 1623, when Cardinal Maffeo Barberini became Pope Urban VIII. Since Barberini was an old admirer, Galileo felt freer and decided to write the book on the system of the world conceived earlier, adapting it to the new restrictions. He wrote the book in the form of a dialogue for three characters engaged in a critical discussion of all the arguments, except for the theological ones. This *Dialogue* was published in 1632 and its key thesis is that the arguments favoring the geokinetic theory are stronger that those favoring the geostatic view, and in that sense Copernicanism is more probable than geostaticism. When so formulated, the thesis is successfully established in the book. In the process, Galileo incorporated into the discussion the new telescopic discoveries, his conclusions about the physics of moving bodies, a geokinetic explanation of the tides, and various methodological reflections. From the viewpoint of the ecclesiastical restrictions, he must have felt that the book did not "hold" the theory of the earth's motion because it was not claiming that the geokinetic arguments were conclusive; that it was not "defending" geokineticism because it was merely a critical examination of the arguments on both sides; and that it was a hypothetical discussion because the earth's motion was being presented as a conjecture postulated to explain observed phenomena.

However, Galileo's enemies complained that the book did not treat the earth's motion as a hypothesis (in the instrumentalist sense) but as a real possibility, and that it defended the earth's motion. These features allegedly amounted to transgressions of Bellarmine's warning and the Index's decree. And there was a third charge: the book violated a special injunction issued personally to Galileo in 1616 prohibiting him from discussing the earth's motion in any way whatever; a document describing this injunction had been found in the file of the earlier Inquisition proceedings. Thus he was summoned to Rome to stand trial, which after various delays began in April 1633.

At the first hearing, Galileo was asked about the events of 1616. He admitted receiving from Bellarmine the warning that the earth's motion could not be held or defended as true, but only discussed hypothetically. He denied receiving a special injunction not to discuss the topic in any way whatever, and in his defense he introduced a certificate he had obtained from Bellarmine in 1616, which mentioned only the prohibition against holding or defending. Here it should be mentioned that the Inquisition files did not contain a signed document recording the special injunction, but merely a clerk's annotation to that effect. In the deposition, Galileo also claimed that the book did not really defend the earth's motion, but rather suggested that the favorable arguments were inconclusive, and so did not violate even Bellarmine's warning.

The special injunction must have surprised Galileo as much as Bellarmine's certificate must have surprised the Inquisitors. Thus it took three weeks before they decided on the next step. The Inquisitors opted for out-of-court plea-bargaining: they would not press the most serious charge (violation of the special injunction), but Galileo would have to plead guilty to a lesser charge (unintentional transgression of the warning not to defend Copernicanism). He requested a few days to devise a dignified way of pleading guilty to the lesser charge. Thus, at later hearings, he stated that he had reread his book and was surprised to find that it gave readers the impression that the author was defending the earth's motion, even though this had not been his intention. He attributed his error to wanting to appear clever by making the weaker side look stronger. He was sorry and ready to make amends.

The trial ended on 22 June, 1633 with a harsher sentence than Galileo had been led to believe. The verdict found him guilty of a category of heresy intermediate between the most and the least serious, called "vehement suspicion of heresy"; the objectionable beliefs were the cosmological thesis that the earth moves and the methodological principle that the Bible is not a scientific authority. He was forced to recite a humiliating "abjuration." The *Dialogue* was banned. And he was condemned to house arrest indefinitely. In such a state, he died in 1642.

The Subsequent Galileo Affair

Although the 1633 condemnation ended the original affair, it also started a new controversy – continuing to our own day – about the facts, causes, issues, and implications of the trial. This subsequent controversy partly reflects the original issues, but it has also acquired a life of its own, with debates over whether Galileo's condemnation was right; why he was condemned; whether science and religion are incompatible; and so forth. The original affair is co-extensive with Galileo's trials from 1615 to 1633; that is, it is the aspect of the Copernican Revolution consisting of Galileo's contributions to it. The subsequent affair is much more complex because of the longer historical span, the broader interdisciplinary relevance, the greater international and multi-linguistic involvement, and the ongoing cultural import. Simplifying, its highlights are as follows (Finocchiaro 2005).

One strand of this story involved the key scientific claim for which he was condemned, namely the proposition that the earth moves. The condemnation ignited a scientific controversy, which had existed since Copernicus, but which now took a more definite and intense form – more definite because it now focused on whether the earth really moves and whether this motion can be proved experimentally by terrestrial or astronomical evidence, and more intense because scores of books were published, new experiments devised, new arguments invented, and old arguments rehashed.

In 1687, Isaac Newton (1642–1727) brought the Copernican Revolution to a climax with a synthesis and extension of the work of Copernicus, Kepler, Galileo, and others, in a book entitled *Mathematical Principles of Natural Philosophy* (Newton 1999). The Newtonian system has two important geokinetic consequences. First, the relative motion between the earth and the sun corresponds to the actual motion of both bodies around their common center of mass; but the relative masses of the sun and the earth are such that the center of mass of this two-body system is a point inside the sun; so, although both bodies are moving around that point, the earth is circling the body of the sun. Second, the daily axial rotation of the earth has the centrifugal effect that terrestrial bodies weigh less at lower latitudes and least at the Equator, and the whole earth is bulged at the equator and flattened at the poles; these consequences were verified by observation.

However, the controversy over the earth's motion did not end then, because the Newtonian proofs were indirect. The search for direct evidence of the earth's motion continued. This led to the discovery of the aberration of starlight by James Bradley in 1729, showing that the earth has translational motion in space; the discovery by Giambattista Guglielmini in 1789–1792 that freely falling bodies are deflected eastward away from the vertical by a small amount, confirming terrestrial axial rotation; the discovery of annual stellar parallax by Friedrich Bessel in 1838, proving the earth's revolution in a closed orbit; and the invention of Foucault's pendulum in 1851, providing a spectacular demonstration of terrestrial rotation.

Another strand of the subsequent affair involves actions by the Catholic Church to repeal the censures against the Copernican doctrine and books. In 1744, Galileo's *Dialogue* was republished for the first time with the Church's approval, as the fourth volume of his collected works; the text was preceded by the Inquisition's sentence and Galileo's abjuration of 1633 and by an introduction written by a contemporary biblical scholar. In 1757, at the request of Pope Benedict XIV, the Congregation of the Index dropped from the forthcoming edition of the *Index of Prohibited Books* the clause "all books teaching the earth's motion and the sun's immobility"; thus, the 1758 edition of the *Index* no longer listed as an entry this general prohibition, but it continued to include several previously prohibited books, including Copernicus's *Revolutions* and Galileo's *Dialogue*. In 1820, the Inquisition gave the imprimatur to an astronomy textbook by a professor at the University of Rome that presented the earth's motion as a fact; in so doing, the Inquisition overruled the objections of the chief censor in Rome. In 1822, the Inquisition ruled that in the future this official must not refuse the imprimatur to publications teaching the earth's motion in accordance with modern astronomy; but a decision about removing from the *Index* Copernicus's and Galileo's books was postponed. In 1833, while deliberating on a new edition of the *Index*, Pope Gregory XVI decided that it would omit those books, but that this omission would be accomplished without explicit comment; thus, the 1835 edition of the *Index* for the first time omitted them from the list. This was the final and complete retraction of the book censorship begun in 1616.

However, besides the scientific issue of the earth's motion, Galileo's trial also embodied a question of principle, namely whether Scripture is a scientific authority (besides being one for matters of faith and morals). This question is partly methodological or philosophical, and partly theological or hermeneutical. It too culminated in 1633, when the Inquisition's sentence blamed Galileo in part for denying the scientific authority of Scripture. Thus, one strand of the subsequent affair involves this principle.

One crucial episode in this strand is that eventually the Church ended up agreeing with Galileo. In 1893, in the encyclical *Providentissimus Deus*, Pope Leo XIII advanced a view of the relationship between biblical interpretation and scientific investigation that corresponds to the one elaborated in Galileo's *Letter to the Grand Duchess Christina*. Although Galileo was not even mentioned in the encyclical, the correspondence was easy to detect for anyone acquainted with both documents; so the encyclical has been widely interpreted as an *implicit* vindication of Galileo's meta-hermeneutical principle.

A century later, the vindication was made *explicit* in Pope John Paul II's rehabilitation of Galileo in 1979–1992. Although this rehabilitation was incomplete, informal, and problematic in several ways, on the hermeneutical issue John Paul was clear and emphatic. In a speech given in 1979, he declared that "Galileo formulated important norms of an epistemological character, which are indispensable to reconcile Holy Scripture and science" (John Paul II 1979, 10). And in a 1992 speech, the pope specified:

> The new science, with its methods and the freedom of research that they implied, obliged theologians to examine their own criteria of scriptural interpretation. Most of them did not know how to do so. Paradoxically, Galileo, a sincere believer, showed himself to be more perceptive in this regard than the theologians who opposed him. (John Paul II 1992, 2)

This brings us to one final strand of the subsequent affair. It involves the condemnation of Galileo-the-person, and consists of various ecclesiastical attempts to revise the trial or rehabilitate him. It is the most elusive, complex, and controversial aspect of the story.

This strand began immediately after Galileo's death, when questions were raised about whether a convicted heretic like him had the canonical right to have his will executed, and whether he could be buried on consecrated ground. These issues were decided in his favor. But another question was not, namely whether it was proper to build an honorific mausoleum for him in the church of Santa Croce in Florence, which the Tuscan government was considering. This was vetoed by the Church when Galileo died in 1642. However, it finally happened in 1737.

In 1942, the tricentennial of Galileo's death occasioned a first partial and informal rehabilitation. In the period 1941–1946, this was accomplished by several clergymen who held the top positions at the Pontifical Academy of Sciences, the Catholic University of Milan, the Pontifical Lateran University in Rome, and Vatican Radio. They published accounts of Galileo as a Catholic hero who upheld the harmony between science and religion; who had the courage to advocate the truth in astronomy even against the religious authorities of his time; and who had the religious piety to retract his views outwardly when the 1633 trial proceedings made his obedience necessary.

In 1979, Pope John Paul II began a further informal rehabilitation of Galileo that was not concluded until 1992. In two speeches to the Pontifical Academy of Sciences, and other statements and actions, the pope admitted that Galileo's trial was not merely an error but also an

injustice; that, as already mentioned, Galileo was theologically right about scriptural interpretation, as against his ecclesiastical opponents; that pastorally speaking, his desire to
disseminate novelties was as reasonable as his opponents' inclination to resist them; and that
he provides an instructive example of the harmony between science and religion. This rehabilitation was informal because the pope was merely expressing his personal opinions and
not speaking *ex cathedra*. Moreover, it was partial because he deliberately avoided talk or
action regarding a formal judicial retraction or revision of the 1633 sentence. Finally, the
rehabilitation was opposed by various elements of the Church, including some in the Vatican
Commission on Galileo, which he had appointed in 1981, and which attempted to repeat
many traditional apologias.

Lessons, Problems, Conjectures

It is beyond the scope of this chapter to elaborate the issues and lessons of the preceding
fact-oriented account. However, a few pointers are in order.

First, it is important to distinguish the Copernican Revolution, the original Galileo affair,
and the subsequent Galileo affair. This distinction is important because the lessons and issues
of one of these episodes do not necessarily coincide with those of the others, and we need
to be clear where the relevant evidence comes from. On the other hand, this distinction is
not meant to preclude the possibility of formulating lessons that might involve all three
episodes, appropriately combined. For example, I have recently defended the following overarching thesis (Finocchiaro 2010): Galileo's defense of the geokinetic hypothesis is conducted
following an approach characterized by rational-mindedness, open-mindedness, and fair-
mindedness; further, it is his crucial contribution to the Copernican Revolution, his chief
crime at the trial, and a viable model for an effective defense of Galileo himself from the
many criticisms of him in the past four centuries.

Second, the most widely drawn lesson from the Copernican Revolution is the realization
that mankind is not the physical center of creation, but rather inhabits an ordinary planet
circling an ordinary star in an ordinary galaxy. This thesis was formulated with classic incisive-
ness by Sigmund Freud, who paired it with Charles Darwin's evolutionary theory demoting
the human species from the special place it had been regarded as having in the phenomenon
of organic life. Freud also speculated that his own discovery of the unconscious amounted
to a comparable revolution in the domain of the mind. This thesis has recently been criticized,
being called a myth, in part for being anachronistic (Danielson 2009). However, this criticism
is not convincing, since it is based on a one-sided analysis of the historical situation, which
contained a mixture of attitudes, one of which did indeed correspond to the Freudian interpretation. Hence, this lesson remains an open question deserving further reflection, especially
with regard to the religious implications.

Third, and more to the point, there is the problem of what, if anything, the Galileo affair
proves regarding the relationship between science and religion. As traditionally interpreted,
Galileo's trial epitomizes the conflict between science and religion. This is well known, but
it is important to stress here that this interpretation has been advanced not only by relatively
injudicious writers who have recently been widely discredited (John William Draper and
Andrew Dickson White), but also by such scientific, philosophical, and cultural icons as Bertrand Russell, Albert Einstein, and Karl Popper. At the opposite extreme, there is the revision-
ist thesis that the trial really shows the *harmony* between science and religion. Here it should

be understood that this interpretation does not merely deny the traditional thesis but *reverses* it. Its most significant advocate is Pope John Paul II, for whom this was the key point he wanted to make in his rehabilitation of Galileo in 1979–1992.

The harmony interpretation begins by distinguishing between the Catholic religion as such and men and institutions of the Church. It then goes on to say that the injustices and errors were committed by men and institutions for which they and not the Church are responsible; so the conflict was between a scientist and some churchmen. In relation to the relationship between science and religion, the correct view is the one elaborated by Galileo himself, which the Church later adopted as its own. That view says that God revealed himself to humanity in two ways, through his work and through his word. His word, namely Holy Scripture, aims to give us information which we cannot discover by examining his work. But to find out what his work is like, we need to observe it by using our bodily senses and by reasoning about it with that other aspect of the divine work which is our mind. In short, Scripture is an authority only on questions of faith and morals, not on scientific factual questions about physical reality. In Galileo's trial, a key difficulty was the misunderstanding of these principles by the churchmen in power. Once these principles are clarified, as Galileo himself ironically contributed to doing, the conflict between science and religion evaporates and continues to subsist only in the imagination of people who do not know better.

In contrast to both the conflict and harmony theses, I claim that the trial did have *both* conflictual and harmonious aspects when viewed in terms of science and religion, but that these are elements of its *surface structure* and that its most profound *deep structure* lies rather in the clash between *cultural conservation and innovation*. My argument is as follows.

First, as already mentioned, the 1633 Inquisition sentence condemned Galileo for two beliefs: that the earth moves and that Scripture is not a scientific authority. The second issue involved a disagreement between those (like Galileo) who held and those (like the Inquisitors) who denied that it is proper to defend the truth of a physical theory contrary to the Bible. That is, if in this controversy we take the Copernican theory of the earth's motion to represent science and Scripture to represent religion, then Galileo was the one claiming that there is no real incompatibility between the two, whereas the Inquisition was the one claiming that the apparent conflict between Copernicanism and Scripture was real. It follows that there is an *irreducible* conflictual element in Galileo's trial, between those who believed and those who denied that there is a conflict between Scripture and science. The irony of the situation is that it was the victim who held the more fundamentally correct view. However, insofar as that Galilean non-conflictual view is the more nearly correct one, then the content of that view suggests an important harmonious element in the trial.

Furthermore, both conflict and harmony exist at the level of the surface structure of the situation. If we move to a deeper cultural aspect, then we must say that Galileo was not the only one who held that there was no conflict: many of those who agreed with him on this question of principle were themselves churchmen. For example, the author of the first published (1622) defense of Galileo was the Dominican friar Tommaso Campanella; and the author explicitly condemned in the Index decree of 1616 was the Carmelite friar Paolo Foscarini, whose book argued that the earth's motion is compatible with Scripture. That is, in Galileo's time, there was a division within Catholicism between those who did and those who did not accept the scientific authority of Scripture. A similar split existed in scientific circles. A further division existed in both domains with regard to the other main issue of Galileo's trial, namely the proposition of the earth's motion. Thus, rather than having an ecclesiastical monolith on one side clashing with a scientific monolith on the other, the real conflict was between two attitudes crisscrossing both. The most fruitful way of conceiving the two factions is to describe them as conservatives or traditionalists on one side and pro-gressives or innovators on the other. The real conflict was between these two groups. In this sense, Galileo's trial illustrates the clash between cultural conservation and innovation, and is an episode where the conservatives happened to win. This conflict is one that operates in such other domains of human society as politics, art, economy, and technology. It cannot be eliminated without stopping social development; it is a moving force of human history.

Finally, after Galileo's condemnation, as mentioned earlier, the interpretation and evalua-tion of the trial became a *cause célèbre* in its own right. Even those who nowadays advocate the harmonious account of the trial, do not deny that the key feature of the *subsequent* affair was indeed a conflict between science and religion. For example, Pope John Paul II, believing that the lesson from Galileo's trial is the harmony between science and religion, wanted to stress this lesson in order to put an end to the subsequent, very real, but presumably unjusti-fied, science-versus-religion conflict. Regarding this subsequent controversy, the science-versus-religion conflict is indeed an essential feature of it, much more an integral part of it than of the original trial. However, underlying such surface structure there may be a cultural deep structure; but in this case the deep structure is probably the phenomenon of the birth and evolution of cultural myths and their interaction with documented facts.

Note

1   Mayaud (2005) documents several of these objections to Copernicanism by Martin Luther, Achilles Pirmin Gasser, Bartolomeo Spina, and Giovanni Maria Tolosani (3:76, 84–87; 6:134–138).

References

Bruno, Giordano. 1995. *The Ash Wednesday Supper*, 2nd edn. Translated by E. A. Gosselin and L. S. Lerner. Toronto: University of Toronto Press.

Copernicus, Nicolaus. 1992. *On the Revolutions*. Translated by E. Rosen. Baltimore: Johns Hopkins University Press.

Danielson, Dennis R. 2009. Myth 6: That Copernicanism Demoted Humans from the Center of the Cosmos. In Ronald L. Numbers, ed. *Galileo Goes to Jail and Other Myths about Science and Religion*. Cambridge, MA: Harvard University Press, pp. 50–58.

Fantoli, Annibale. 2003. *Galileo: For Copernicanism and for the Church*, 3rd edn. Translated by G. V. Coyne. Vatican City: Vatican Observatory Publications.

Finocchiaro, Maurice A., ed. 1989. *The Galileo Affair: A Documentary History*. Translated by Maurice A. Finacchiaro. Berkeley: University of California Press.

Finocchiaro, Maurice A. 2005. *Retrying Galileo, 1633–1992*. Berkeley: University of California Press.

Finocchiaro, Maurice A. 2010. *Defending Copernicus and Galileo: Critical Reasoning in the Two Affairs*. Dordrecht: Springer.

Galilei, Galileo. 1974. *Two New Sciences*. Translated by S. Drake. Madison, WI: University of Wisconsin Press.

Galilei, Galileo. 2001. *Dialogue Concerning the Two Chief World Systems, Ptolemaic and Copernican*. Translated by S. Drake. J. L. Heilbron, ed. New York: Modern Library.

Galilei, Galileo. 2008. *The Essential Galileo*. Translated by M. A. Finocchiaro. Indianapolis, IN: Hackett.

Galilei, Galileo, and Scheiner, Christoph. 2010. *On Sunspots*. Translated by E. Reeves and A. Van Helden, eds. Chicago: University of Chicago Press.

John Paul II. 1979. Deep Harmony which Unites the Truths of Science with the Truths of Faith. *L'Osservatore Romano*, 26(November), pp. 9–10.

John Paul II. 1992. Faith Can Never Conflict with Reason. *L'Osservatore Romano*, 49(November), pp. 1–2.

Kepler, Johannes. 1992. *New Astronomy*. Translated by W. H. Donahue. Cambridge: Cambridge University Press.

Kuhn, Thomas S. 1957. *The Copernican Revolution*. Cambridge, MA: Harvard University Press.

Mayaud, Pierre-Noël, ed. 2005. *Le conflit entre l'astronomie nouvelle et l'Écriture Sainte aux XVIe et XVIIe siècles [The Conflict between the New Astronomy and Holy Scripture in the Sixteenth and Seventeenth Centuries]*, 6 vols. Paris: Honoré Champion.

Mosley, Adam. 2007. *Bearing the Heavens*. Cambridge: Cambridge University Press.

Newton, Isaac. 1999. *The Principia: Mathematical Principles of Natural Philosophy*. Translated by I. B. Cohen and A. Whitman. Berkeley, CA: University of California Press.

Westman, Robert S. 1975. The Melanchthon Circle, Rheticus, and the Wittenberg Interpretation of the Copernican Theory. *Isis*, 66, pp. 165–193.

Further Reading

Fantoli, Annibale. 2003. *Galileo: For Copernicanism and for the Church*, 3rd edn. Translated by G. V. Coyne. Vatican City: Vatican Observatory Publications. An accurate, balanced, and comprehensive historical account of Galileo's trial.

Finocchiaro, Maurice A., ed. 1989. *The Galileo Affair: A Documentary History*. Translated by Maurice A. Finacchiaro. Berkeley: University of California Press. A collection of the essential documents of Galileo's trial (1613–1633), with introduction, notes, chronology, glossary, and selected bibliography.

Finocchiaro, Maurice A. 2005. *Retrying Galileo, 1633–1992*. Berkeley: University of California Press. A comprehensive but introductory survey of the subsequent Galileo affair, including sources, facts, and issues.

Finocchiaro, Maurice A. 2010. *Defending Copernicus and Galileo: Critical Reasoning in the Two Affairs*. Dordrecht: Springer. A synthesis of historical interpretation and philosophical criticism of both the original and subsequent controversy.

Kuhn, Thomas S. 1957. *The Copernican Revolution*. Cambridge, MA: Harvard University Press. A classic, still unsurpassed account of admirably clear and self-contained exposition, and historical and philosophical sophistication.

3

Women, Mechanical Science, and God in the Early Modern Period

JACQUELINE BROAD

In 1748, an anonymous work called *Adollizing* appeared on the clandestine literary scene in London. It tells the tale of a depraved young man who designs a life-size mechanical doll to console himself in the midst of bitter disappointment. For the young man, this anatomically correct doll – created "by new mechanic aid" – represents his perfect woman: mute and inanimate, she is incapable of expressing disapproval, she is "unresisting and complacent still," and (more importantly, for his purposes) "all obsequious to my wanton will" (Anonymous 2004, 328). With feminist hindsight, we might think that this story – published in the same year as La Mettrie's *L'homme machine* (*Man Machine*) – provides an apt allegory for thinking about women and the origins of mechanical science. Carolyn Merchant (1980) has highlighted the fact that, in the course of the scientific revolution (from 1500 to 1700), the Renaissance notion of a living, organic nature was reconceptualized as a dead, inanimate machine. Alongside this new mechanical model, according to Merchant, a new worldview emerged that sanctioned the mastery and domination of both nature and women. In some texts of the period, nature was personified as a passive female, completely devoid of mind and volition; in other works, it was depicted as an indocile woman, or an unruly force to be cowed and subdued. In either case, the symbolic connection between women and nature was obvious: new scientific man was urged to exploit or conquer nature, and women were figuratively associated with what must be exploited or conquered. At its very inception, Merchant claims, modern science was defined as a project to gain mastery over the stereotypically "feminine" categories of nature, matter, and the material body.

Several scholars have examined connections between the Protestant Reformation and this new mechanical science. Building on the work of Robert Merton and Charles Webster (among others), Gary Deason (1986) has highlighted thematic continuities between the Reformers' idea of God's sovereignty in nature and the mechanists' idea of nature as dead, inchoate matter governed by a divine legislator. For Reformers such as Calvin and Luther, according to Deason, God's radical sovereignty entails that God is the only independent agent or active principle in the natural world.[1] To uphold his glory, they insist that God does not require the cooperation of lesser beings to bring about his work. During the course of the scientific revolution, this concept of God's sovereignty was incorporated into the new natural philosophy of the period. The Reformers' "understanding of natural things as passive recipi-

---

The Blackwell Companion to Science and Christianity, First Edition. Edited by J. B. Stump and Alan G. Padgett.
© 2012 Blackwell Publishing Ltd. Published 2012 by Blackwell Publishing Ltd.

ents of divine power," Deason notes, "was entirely consistent with the mechanical philosophy" (Deason 1986, 175). According to mechanists, such as Pierre Gassendi, Walter Charlton,
Robert Boyle, and Isaac Newton, matter is essentially inert; it does not have an internal power
of motion. Every motion in the natural world, they argue, must be attributed to God alone,
acting externally on matter according to certain laws. Evelyn Fox Keller (1992) builds on
Deason's analysis by introducing a third term into the vocabulary of God and Nature –
Woman. She points out that, in the sixteenth and seventeenth centuries, there was a metaphorical shift in "the locus of essential secrets" from God to Nature, and this shift signaled
the rise of a negative, exploitative attitude toward nature. Because the "secrets of Nature"
did not have the privileged, sacrosanct status of the "secrets of God," Keller argues, scientists
were thereby granted permission to gain knowledge of nature's hidden recesses. The personification of nature as a woman played an important role in this discursive transformation:
in the demarcation between Nature and God, inanimate and animate, Woman was placed
decisively on the side of deanimated nature, in order to denote those secrets that *did not
belong to God*" (Keller 1992, 59). Keller sees this metaphorical use of Woman and femininity
as further evidence of misogyny in the Western scientific tradition.

More recently, however, feminist critiques such as those of Merchant and Keller have been
called into question. Some scholars suggest that their arguments are based on an outmoded
understanding of the so-called scientific revolution. Far from constituting a "clean break with
the past," the early modern period is now thought to represent the point at which the old
and new natural philosophies existed side by side (Hutton 1997, 11; Osler 2005, 77). In the
new mechanical theories of the period, one can still find traces of the ancient "organic"
approaches to nature, and the demarcation between science and religion, the rational and
the mystical, is far from clear-cut. This new historiographical framework complicates those
feminist readings in which a woman-friendly worldview was supposedly replaced (wholesale)
by a misogynistic approach to a feminized nature; as a consequence, scholars now call for a
revised understanding of the relationship between women and science in the period.

In this chapter, I take a step toward that process of revision by examining the natural
philosophy of women themselves in the early modern period.[2] Despite the fact that they were
debarred from universities and formal scientific societies, women did not remain silent at the
first inception of modern science: they commented on the theories of their famous male
contemporaries, and they developed their own opinions about nature, mechanical science,
and God in published works. Their writings provide a small snapshot of the historical complexity of the period, a period in which the mechanical theory of matter in motion was by
no means universally accepted, and science and theology were still closely intertwined. In
what follows, I focus especially on English women's responses to Descartes's work of physics,
Principia philosophiae (*The Principles of Philosophy*) of 1644, a classic statement of the mechanical philosophy of the period. In the Preface to the French edition of his book, Descartes
assures his readers that "those who have learnt the least are the most capable of learning true
philosophy," and that "there is nothing in my writings which they are not capable of completely understanding provided they take the trouble to examine them" (Descartes 1985, 183,
185) – two assurances that were highly appealing to women. Despite the fact that this work
was in Latin, a number of early modern women were familiar with Descartes's "textbook"
account of his philosophy. In 1685, one English woman, Damaris Masham (1659–1708), wrote
to her friend John Locke:

> I can but Think how you would smile to see Cowley and my Surfeit Waters Jumbled together;
> with Dr More and my Gally Potts of Mithridate and Dioscordium; My Receits and Account

Books with Antoninus's his Meditations, and Des Cartes Principles; with my Globes and my
Spining Wheel; for just in this order They at present ly. (Locke 1976–1982, 759)

Masham's juxtaposition of the *Principles* with globes and spinning-wheels is no accident: this
book represents the most mature account of Descartes's cosmology, or his theory that all the
planets (including the earth) move in giant material vortices around the sun.[3] According to
Descartes, all natural phenomena, including those of the celestial sphere, can be explained
by the movements of tiny invisible particles or "corpuscles." These material particles consist
entirely of geometrical properties (they are extended in length, breadth, and depth); they do
not have life, intelligence, or an inherent ability to move themselves. Following one initial
divine impulse, these particles generate large, circular whirlpools of matter (the vortices)
within a plenum; and the laws of motion governing these whirlpools are responsible for
everything from the circling of planets around central suns, to rainbows and comets.

In the 1630s, Descartes first formulated this heliocentric (sun-centered) theory of planetary
motion in a treatise called *Le monde* (*The World*); but he suppressed the publication following
the Church's condemnation of Galileo's defense of Copernicanism in 1633. In the *Principles*,
Descartes defends a version of Copernicanism that does not openly challenge the religious
orthodoxy that the earth does not move; according to Descartes's strict definition of motion,
the earth is in fact at rest in relation to the neighboring particles within its vortex band.
In the late seventeenth century, this theory was still one of the most popular and influential
astronomical theories, until its replacement by Newtonian physics in the eighteenth century.

The four Christian women in my study – Margaret Cavendish, Anne Conway, Aphra Behn,
and Mary Astell – all address Descartes's *Principles* in various ways in their works. I show that
their writings reveal a more positive relationship between science, Christianity, and women
in the early modern period than some recent analyses have suggested.

Margaret Cavendish (1623–1673)

In 1664, Margaret Cavendish, the Duchess of Newcastle, developed her own materialist philosophy in a work titled *Philosophical Letters: Or, Modest Reflections upon some Opinions in Natural
Philosophy*. In the first section of this work, Cavendish constructs a brief but forceful critique
of Descartes's *Principles*. Relying on an incomplete private translation of the text, she begins
by challenging the most crucial (and controversial) feature of Descartes's physics: his concept
of motion. In the *Principles*, Descartes defines motion as *"the transfer of one piece of matter, or
one body, from the vicinity of the other bodies which are in immediate contact with it, and which are
regarded as being at rest, to the vicinity of other bodies"* (Descartes 1985, II.25, 233). Using this
definition, he formulates three laws of motion (or "laws of nature"), which are founded on
the immutability of God's operations "by means of which the world is continually preserved
through an action identical with its original act of creation" (II.42, 243). The first law states
that a particular body in motion always continues to move (and likewise, a body at rest always
remains at rest), unless some external cause intervenes; the second stipulates that bodies
always move in a straight line; and according to the third, when one body *"collides with a
weaker body, it loses a quantity of motion equal to that which it imparts to the other body"* (II.40,
242). In response to the third law, Cavendish points out that if motion cannot subsist by itself
(apart from a body), and yet it can be transferred or imparted to another body, then surely
this amounts to saying that motion is both something and nothing at the same time? To dispel

the contradiction, she says, we must allow that motion is either a substance or a mode. If it is a substance, then it must transmit part of itself (i.e., some quantity of matter) to the thing with which it collides. In the case of a stick touching or poking at sand, the stick must grow bigger and the sand less. Yet experience tells us that this does not happen. If motion is nothing but a mode, however, then it cannot travel outside of body; motion cannot be separated from body (Cavendish 1664, 117).

To explain the phenomenon of collision, Cavendish maintains that every particle of matter must contain its own internal principle of self-motion. In her view, all material substance is a blend of animate ("sensitive" and "rational") matter and inanimate matter; there is no real distinction between material and thinking substances; and "there is no part of Nature that hath not life and knowledg" (Cavendish 1664, 99). When one body, a, collides with another body, b, a is merely the "occasion" for the internal self-motions of b to set itself in motion. There is no transference or translation of motion from one body to another; b simply "patterns out" or imitates a's motion for itself. In the case of a seal printing upon wax, "the seal doth not give the wax the print of its own figure, but it is the wax that takes the print or pattern from the seal, and patterns or copies out its own substance" (Cavendish 1664, 105).

Not surprisingly, Cavendish rejects the account of planetary motion that arises from the Cartesian theory of matter in motion. She dismisses the Cartesian theory of divine impulse:

> For how can we imagine that the Universe was set a moving as a Top by a Whip, or a Wheele by the hand of a Spinster, and that the vacuities were fill'd up with shavings? For these violent motions would rather have disturbed and disordered Nature. (Cavendish 1664, 108)

Because there is already inherent self-motion in every particle of matter, one almighty "shove" from God would in fact bring about chaos rather than order. Instead of three laws of nature, "Nature hath but One Law, which is . . . to keep Infinite matter in order, and to keep so much Peace, as not to disturb the Foundation of her Government" (Cavendish 1664, 146). "The Earth turns about rather than the Sun" because Nature "has ordered [the world] with great wisdom and Prudence" (Cavendish 1664, 135).

Contrary to her explicit statements on the subject, Cavendish does not develop this theory of nature in isolation from her Christian beliefs. She begins the *Philosophical Letters* by declaring that she will not mix theology with natural philosophy: "for I think it not onely an absurdity, but an injury to the holy Profession of Divinity to draw her to the Proofs in *Natural Philosophy*" (Cavendish 1664, 3). In keeping with this approach, she dismisses Descartes's theory of creation on the grounds that "it is but in vain to indeavour to know how, and by what motions God did make the World, since Creation is an action of GOD, and Gods actions are incomprehensible" (Cavendish 1664, 108). But in this same work, she herself explains the orderliness of nature with reference to God's first decree (see Detlefsen 2009, 431). While nature is co-eternal with God and without beginning, she says, it was nevertheless "a rude and indigested Heap, or chaos, without form, void and dark" (Cavendish 1664, 15) until "the material Servant of God, Nature . . . ordered her self-moving matter into such several Figures as God commanded, and God approved of them" (Cavendish 1664, 16). While nature acts independently of God, her orderliness and tendency toward peace and harmony originate with God's command.

Cavendish puts forward a positive conception of woman-as-nature to illustrate this theory of orderly, self-moving matter. Nature is personified as "a grave, wise, methodical Matron, ordering her Infinite family, which are her several parts, with ease and facility, without needless troubles and difficulties" (Cavendish 1664, 302–303). Nature does not require the direct assistance of immaterial substance in order to move: "For Nature is not a Babe, or Child, to need such a Spiritual Nurse, to teach her to go, or to move; neither is she so young a Lady as to have need of a Governess" (Cavendish 1664, 149–150). In Cavendish's philosophy, nature is composed of a thorough intermixture of animate and inanimate matter; and God's original decree has ensured that this matter has an inherent tendency to bring about order in the natural world. It is therefore appropriate that nature should be personified as a mature woman who is perfectly capable of organizing and governing her own affairs. In Cavendish's works, women and "the feminine" are not called upon to symbolize passive, inanimate bodies; nor are they symbolically aligned with that which "does not belong to God."

Anne Conway (1631–1679)

In an early correspondence with Henry More, dating from 1650, Viscountess Anne Conway (née Finch) received some tutoring in Cartesian philosophy with the assistance of More's own personal translation of Descartes's *Principles*.[4] There are only four letters extant from this "seventeenth-century correspondence course" in Cartesianism (Hutton 2004, 36) – three from More and one from Conway – but they give us a good indication of Conway's early philosophical response to parts I and II of the *Principles*.[5] In particular, Conway appears to endorse Descartes's claims that there is no vacuum in nature (Descartes 1985, II.16–18, 229–231), that the material world is infinitely (or "indefinitely") extended (II.21, 232), and that there are no indivisible atoms in nature (II.20, 231). These same views are incorporated into Conway's own *Principia philosophiae*, the *Principia philosophiae antiquissimae et recentissimae* (*The Principles of the Most Ancient and Modern Philosophy*), first published posthumously in Latin in 1690. In his Preface to the work, More praises Conway as someone who "understood perfectly, not only the true System of the World, call it Copernican or Pythagorick as you will . . . but all Descartes his Philosophy" (Conway 1996, 4). In the text itself, Conway affirms that "Descartes taught many remarkable and ingenious things" (Conway 1996, 64), but she explicitly rejects the Cartesian physics of matter in motion. Like Cavendish, Conway points to the difficulty of explaining "how motion can be transmitted from one body to another since it is certainly neither a substance nor a body" (Conway 1996, 69). If motion is only a mode, she points out, then it cannot conceivably pass out of the body in which it inheres and into another body. Motion is instead created through "real production or creation," "not from itself, but only in subordination to God as his instrument" (Conway 1996, 70). She agrees with Descartes that God gives motion to bodies, but it proceeds from his will at the moment of creation and not from external impulsion.

Conway deduces her own theory of substance from "a serious and due consideration of the divine attributes" (Conway 1996, 44). She considers what God's attributes imply for his creation – not just the attribute of divine immutability (so fundamental to Descartes's physics), but also the moral attributes of supreme justice and benevolence. We must see that "since the goodness of God is a living goodness, which possesses life, knowledge, love, and power, which he communicates to his creatures," then it is not possible for any dead thing to "proceed from him or be created by him, such as mere body or matter" (Conway 1996, 44–45). If the parts of nature did not have life and self-motion, then they would not have the capacity to perfect themselves or to achieve a greater spirituality. But this would be contrary to God's justice and goodness. Conway therefore rejects the Cartesian concept of body or matter as "merely dead mass, which not only lacks life and perception of any kind but is also utterly

incapable of either for all eternity" (Conway 1996, 63–64). There is in fact no essential difference between spirit and body: "body is nothing but fixed and condensed spirit; and spirit is
nothing but volatile body or body made subtle" (Conway 1996, 61).

Conway's vitalist theory of substance enables her to envisage a positive conception of
"mother" nature, working cooperatively with God to achieve the perfection of her
creatures:

> Thus God has implanted a certain universal sympathy and mutual love into his creatures so that
> they are all members of one body and all, so to speak, brothers, for whom there is one common
> Father, namely, God in Christ or the word incarnate. There is also one mother, that unique
> substance or entity from which all things have come forth, and of which they are the real parts
> and members. (Conway 1996, 31)

While this mother is subordinate to God, she nevertheless has her own power to bring about
change. Conway's woman-as-nature "is a living body which has life and perception, which
are much more exalted than a mere mechanism or a mechanical motion" (Conway 1996, 64).

Aphra Behn (1640–1689)

In 1688, the playwright and poet Aphra Behn published an English-language version of
Bernard le Bovier de Fontenelle's *Entretiens sur la pluralité des mondes* (1686). Behn's translation,
A Discovery of New Worlds, introduced English readers to Fontenelle's "popular science"
version of Copernican theory. Presented as a dialogue between a gentleman philosopher and
a "*Marquiese*" (a marchioness), this conversational account of seventeenth-century physics was
particularly appealing to female readers with no formal academic training in cosmology. In
the fourth discourse of this work, the male protagonist spells out the main principles of
Descartes's vortex theory in non-specialist terms. "Imagine to your self," he says,

> that the Celestial Substance which fills the vast *Tourbillion* [i.e., vortex], or Whirling of the Sun,
> is compos'd of different Coats, wrapp'd within one another, like an Onion . . . every one of the
> Planets must stop upon that Coat proportionable to its weight, and which has necessary strength
> for supporting it, and keeping it in an equal Balance. (Behn 1993, 145)

In this way, the male speaker wins the marchioness over from Ptolemaic theory to Copernicanism, and to "the Whistlings of Monsieur *Des Cartes*, whose Name is so terrible, and *Idea's*
so agreeable" (Behn 1993, 143). With her translation, Behn actively supports Fontenelle's
project to make the new natural philosophy accessible to lay philosophers: she clarifies Fontenelle's account of Cartesian physics by defining a vortex as a "*Tourbillion* of Air, call'd a
Whirl-wind, or a Hurricane" (Behn 1993, 143), and she introduces the comparison between
the vortex bands and onion layers mentioned above; neither comment appears in the original
French text (see Cottegnies 2003, 30). She also refers to Descartes's measurement of the
height "of our Air or Sphere of Activity of the Earth" in the *Principles*, in order to justify a
correction she has made to Fontenelle's text (Behn 1993, 86).

But Behn's original contributions to the subject do not end there. In a lengthy Translator's
Preface, she argues in favor of the compatibility of Copernican theory with Scripture, against
the claims of the French Jesuit Andreas Tacquet. In the King James Bible, Psalm 19:4–5, it is

said that in the heavens, God has "set a tabernacle for the sun, Which is as a bridegroom coming out of his chamber, and rejoiceth as a strong man to run a race." Behn claims that this allegorical passage is open to different interpretations: on the one hand, it might appear to suggest that the sun moves in the heavens, in accordance with Ptolemaic theory; but on the other hand, the words "set in a tabernacle" are highly suggestive of rest and stability, in keeping with Copernicanism. In Joshua 10:12–13, God commands: "Sun, stand thou still upon Gibeon; and thou, Moon, in the valley of Ajalon. And the sun stood still, and the moon stayed." Again, Behn suggests that this passage can be read metaphorically. To say that "the sun stood still" might mean only that God miraculously brought about a "wonderful stop of Time." "Time and Nature are always in motion, and this Day was a stop of that Course" (Behn 1993, 84). Behn concludes that the biblical texts are "at least, as much for *Copernicus* as *Ptolemy*," and on the whole she favors the view that "the design of the Bible was not to instruct Mankind in Astronomy, Geometry, or Chronology, but in the Law of God, to lead us to Eternal Life" (Behn 1993, 79).

This view notwithstanding, Behn does not advocate a strict separation between science and religion; while the Bible cannot have any bearing on science, science can have bearing on matters of faith. She criticizes Fontenelle because "He ascribes all to Nature, and says not a Word of God Almighty, from the Beginning to the End; so that one would almost take him to be a *Pagan*" (Behn 1993, 77). By contrast, in her preface, she highlights the fact that Fontenelle's theory of multiple inhabitable worlds gives "a magnificent *Idea* of the vastness of the Universe, and of the almighty and infinite Power of the Creator" (Behn 1993, 77). She herself says what Fontenelle fails to say: the new scientific theory provides evidence of God's omnipotence at work.

Behn also supports the inclusion of women in scientific discourse. On the one hand, she does not attempt a philosophical defense of mechanistic physics herself: as a woman, she emphasizes in "The Epistle Dedicatory," she is not "supposed to be well versed in the Terms of Philosophy" (Behn 1993, 72). On the other hand, in her translation, Behn subtly introduces a feminist agenda of her own. Line Cottegnies observes that Behn pointedly alters references to "men" in Fontenelle's text to "men and women" in her own translation (Cottegnies 2003, 26; Behn 1993, 121, 137). In the preface, Behn also complains about inconsistencies in Fontenelle's characterization of the marchioness: sometimes she displays a profound learning, and at other times she is ridiculously naive. Behn's translation corrects Fontenelle's unrealistic portrayal of a thinking woman by omitting words that suggest an unreasonable naiveté on the marchioness's part (Cottegnies 2003, 26).

Mary Astell (1666–1731)

Like Behn, Mary Astell also believes that Scripture determines nothing "between the *Copernican* and *Ptolomean* [sic] Systems" (Astell 1996, 13). Though Astell is not known for her scientific concerns (she is better known as a feminist and political thinker), a manuscript biography reveals that she planned to compile "a Book of Natural Philosophy" with the assistance of female friends (Ballard 1985, 426), and the astronomer John Flamsteed's journals report that a "Mad[ame]: Astell" was a pupil at the Royal Observatory from 1697 to 1698 (Iliffe and Willmoth 1997, 248, 264).[6] In keeping with these interests, Astell shows a strong familiarity with the central tenets of part I of Descartes's *Principles of Philosophy*. In her *Serious Proposal to the Ladies, Part II* (1697), she explicitly cites the definition of clear and distinct ideas

given in the *Principles*: "I call a perception 'clear' when it is present and accessible to the attentive mind. . . . I call a perception 'distinct' if, as well as being clear, it is so sharply separated
from all other perceptions that it contains within itself only what is clear" (Descartes 1985,
I.45, 207–208; Astell 1997, 123). These criteria of knowledge constitute the epistemological
foundations from which Descartes builds his theory of physics. In her *Christian Religion* (1705),
Astell implicitly relies on these criteria to affirm the Cartesian view that the essence of material substance is extension alone. Descartes claims that we can have a complete (clear and
distinct) idea of the mind apart from the body, if each idea can be considered without any
reference to, or abstraction from, the other. Astell likewise asserts that if I can have a complete
idea of *x* (a thing with certain "Properties and Affections") "without any Relation to, or
Dependence on" my complete idea of *y* (a thing with different "Properties and Affections"),
then *x* and *y* are "truly Distinct and of Different Natures." But I can have a complete idea of
mind as thinking being without "any Relation to, or Dependence on" my complete idea
of body as extended being; therefore mind and body are "truly Distinct and of Different
Natures" (Astell 1705, 250–251).

Astell uses the Cartesian conception of matter as extension to argue against the view that
the world was created by material substance alone. In her last work, *Bart'lemy Fair: An Enquiry
after Wit* (1709), she insists that whatever created the world must have the attribute of "self-
existence" or necessary existence. This is the case because if there were no self-existent being,
then something would have been created from nothing (an impossibility); therefore "Something must necessarily Exist, or else not any thing cou'd be" (Astell 1709, 116). Yet we cannot
attribute self-existence to any material being; we can attribute self-existence only to "One
Eternal Mind, who is Infinite in all Perfection." On this topic, Astell recalls Samuel Clarke's
cosmological argument for the existence of God in his *Demonstration of the Being and Attributes
of God* (1705) and *Discourse concerning the Unchangeable Obligations of Natural Religion* (1706).
Like Clarke, Astell draws on the new Newtonian physics to illustrate her point: if nature
consists entirely of material particles in motion, she asks, then how do we explain the phenomenon of gravitation? "Mutual Attraction or Gravitation, is one of the most Universal and
Uniform Affections of Bodies; but it is not essential to Matter" (Astell 1709, 117). This force
or power in essentially inert bodies,

> can't be a Material One, for that wou'd imply a Contradiction, as supposing a Matter Superior
> to Matter in general, and such as can give that to another which it has not in it self, nor any
> sufficient Power to produce. And yet this Mutual Attraction, tho' not essential to Matter, but
> foreign and superinduc'd by a Superior Being, is so necessary to the very Being of the Universe,
> in that Form in which we now behold it, or at least to our Solar System. (Astell 1709, 117–118)

If there were no gravity, then there would be no individuation between material things, all
"wou'd crumble into Dust," and every particle would "either remain at rest, or else proceed
in straight Lines" (Astell 1709, 118). We must then allow that the universe could neither exist
nor continue to subsist "without the Omnipotent Power and Efficacy of its Divine Cause"
(Astell 1709, 118).

Despite supporting the Cartesian concept of matter as pure extension, Astell articulates a
positive female conception of nature – one that does not sanction the exploitation of natural
resources. Astell says that:

> We may assure ourselves that Nature has no Malice. Nothing but Ill-Humour either Natural or
> Forc'd, can bring a Man to think amiss of her. The more we search into and familiarly examine

her, we shall be the more convinc'd, that she is the most inoffensive, harmless, sweetest, compassionate, good-natur'd, best sort of a Gentlewoman, that any one can settle with himself a Notion
of. (Astell 1709, 102)

Though Astell allows that we might "*search into and familiarly examine* her," there are constraints on how far we might penetrate nature's hidden recesses. On gold and other jewels,
she says that "were they really Good, they wou'd not be such Rarities, our Indulgent Mother
Nature, wou'd have bestow'd them on all her Children . . . She seems indeed rather to think
them hurtful to us, by the Care she takes to hide them in the Earth" (Astell 1709, 103). This
moral interpretation of "mother" nature's actions is consistent with Astell's view that God
himself constitutes the active principle in matter that ensures nature's order and regularity.

Conclusion

In a 1713 issue of *The Guardian* (September 8), there is a report on a group of women preserving fruit while one of them reads aloud from Fontenelle's *Plurality of Worlds*. The women
divide their thoughts between jellies and stars, apricots and suns, and Copernican theory and
cheesecake. This report illustrates the fact that Fontenelle's cosmology – and the Cartesian
theory on which it was based – was highly accessible to, and tremendously popular with,
women. Only a generation earlier, a handful of women came out of the kitchen and published
their critical responses to the new mechanical science. Despite their formal exclusion from
universities and scientific societies, these women engaged with Descartes's concept of matter
in motion, his Copernican theory of vortices, and his notion of God's causal role in the
universe. Conway and Cavendish argued against the Cartesian mechanization of nature, and
challenged the view that matter is essentially inert and passive; they both called upon God
to explain nature's orderly and regular motion. Behn argued in favor of the compatibility of
Copernicanism with the Bible, and admired the new theory for providing evidence of God's
supreme power at work in creation. Astell upheld the Cartesian conception of material substance as inert extension, while calling upon God's creative activity to explain the phenomenon
of gravity. In the process of articulating these views, all four women put forward positive
depictions of women, as matrons, mothers, gentlewomen, and thinking beings more generally. The historical union of science and Christianity is thought to have had negative implications for women and to bear some responsibility for the male-biased, anti-feminine nature of
the modern scientific enterprise. But the writings of these early modern women complicate
that view: they show that the dialogue between science and Christianity did not necessarily
lend itself to the demeaning of women and "femininity" in the literature of the period.[7]

Notes

1   Recent scholars, such as Charles Partee and Gerhard Forde, emphasize that the Reformers' views
    are somewhat more complicated than Deason suggests here. It is by no means clear, for example,
    that John Calvin maintains that God is the only independent agent in the world from a natural or
    scientific point of view. I am indebted to Alan Padgett for bringing this point to my attention.
2   To be fair, Merchant does examine the views of early modern women (Merchant 1980, 253–274),
    though she does not reach the same conclusions that I do here.

3 On Cartesian physics, see Garber 1992 and Gaukroger 2002.
4 See Hutton 2004, chapter 2.
5 For these letters, see Appendix B to Nicolson 1992, 484–494.
6 It is not possible to confirm that this student of astronomy was Mary Astell herself.
7 For their assistance in the writing of this chapter, I am extremely grateful to Patrick Spedding, Deborah Boyle, Jeremy Aarons, and participants in the 2006 mini-conference, "Women, Metaphysics and Enlightenment, 1669–1789," at the Institute of Philosophy, University of London (especially the organizers, Sarah Hutton and Susan James). A much earlier version of this paper was given at that conference. I would also like to express my gratitude to the Australian Research Council, who generously awarded me a Future Fellowship in 2010 for the purposes of studying the philosophy of Astell and her contemporaries.

References

Anonymous. 2004. *Adollizing: Or, a Lively Picture of Adoll-Worship*, vol. 2. In Deborah Needleman Armintor, ed. *Eighteenth-Century British Erotica II*. London: Pickering & Chatto.

Astell, Mary. 1705. *The Christian Religion, As Profess'd by a Daughter of the Church of England*. London: R. Wilkin.

Astell, Mary. 1709. *Bart'lemy Fair: Or, an Enquiry after Wit*. London: R. Wilkin.

Astell, Mary. 1996. *Reflections upon Marriage*. In Patricia Springborg, ed. *Astell: Political Writings*. Cambridge: Cambridge University Press.

Astell, Mary. 1997. *A Serious Proposal to the Ladies, Parts I and II*. Patricia Springborg, ed. London: Pickering & Chatto.

Ballard, George. 1985. *Memoirs of Several Ladies of Great Britain*. Ruth Perry, ed. Detroit: Wayne State University Press.

Behn, Aphra. 1993. *A Discovery of New Worlds*. In Janet Todd, ed. *The Works of Aphra Behn*, vol. 4. London: William Pickering.

Cavendish, Margaret. 1664. *Philosophical Letters: Or, Modest Reflections upon some Opinions in Natural Philosophy*. London: Privately published.

Conway, Anne. 1996. *The Principles of the Most Ancient and Modern Philosophy*. Translated by Allison P. Coudert and Taylor Corse. Cambridge: Cambridge University Press.

Cottegnies, Line. 2003. The Translator as Critic: Aphra Behn's Translation of Fontenelle's *Discovery of New Worlds* (1688). *Restoration: Studies in English Literary Culture, 1660–1700*, 27(1), pp. 23–38.

Deason, Gary B. 1986. Reformation Theology and the Mechanistic Conception of Nature. In David C. Lindberg and Ronald L. Numbers, eds. *God and Nature: Historical Essays on the Encounter between Christianity and Science*. Berkeley: University of California Press, pp. 167–191.

Descartes, René. 1985. The Principles of Philosophy. Translated by John Cottingham, Robert Stoothoff, and Dugald Murdoch. *The Philosophical Writings of Descartes*, vol. 2. Cambridge: Cambridge University Press.

Detlefsen, Karen. 2009. Margaret Cavendish on the Relation between God and World. *Philosophy Compass*, 4(3), pp. 421–438.

Garber, Daniel. 1992. *Descartes' Metaphysical Physics*. Chicago: University of Chicago Press.

Gaukroger, Stephen. 2002. *Descartes' System of Natural Philosophy*. Cambridge: Cambridge University Press.

Hutton, Sarah. 1997. The Riddle of the Sphinx: Francis Bacon and the Emblems of Science. In Lynette Hunter and Sarah Hutton, eds. *Women, Science and Medicine 1500–1700: Mothers and Sisters of the Royal Society*. Stroud: Sutton, pp. 7–28.

Hutton, Sarah. 2004. *Anne Conway: A Woman Philosopher*. Cambridge: Cambridge University Press.

Iliffe, Rob, and Willmoth, Frances. 1997. Astronomy and the Domestic Sphere: Margaret Flamsteed and Caroline Herschel as Assistant-Astronomers. In Lynette Hunter and Sarah Hutton, eds. *Women,*

Science and Medicine 1500–1700: Mothers and Sisters of the Royal Society. Stroud: Sutton, pp. 235–265.

Keller, Evelyn Fox. 1992. *Secrets of Life, Secrets of Death: Essays on Language, Gender and Science*. New York: Routledge.

Locke, John. 1976–1982. *The Correspondence of John Locke*, vol. 2. E. S. de Beer, ed. Oxford: Clarendon Press.

Merchant, Carolyn. 1980. *The Death of Nature: Women, Ecology and the Scientific Revolution*. San Francisco: Harper & Row.

Nicolson, Marjorie Hope. 1992. *The Conway Letters: The Correspondence of Anne, Viscountess Conway, Henry More and Their Friends, 1642–1684*, revised edn. Sarah Hutton, ed. Oxford: Clarendon Press.

Osler, Margaret J. 2005. The Gender of Nature and the Nature of Gender in Early Modern Natural Philosophy. In Judith P. Zinsser, ed. *Men, Women, and the Birthing of Modern Science*. DeKalb, IL: Northern Illinois University Press, pp. 71–85.

Further Reading

Broad, Jacqueline. 2002. *Women Philosophers of the Seventeenth Century*. Cambridge: Cambridge University Press. Provides an introduction to the metaphysical views of early modern women philosophers.

Keller, Evelyn Fox. 1985. *Reflections on Gender and Science*. New Haven, CT: Yale University Press. One of the first and most influential feminist critiques of science.

Schiebinger, Londa. 1989. *The Mind Has No Sex? Women in the Origins of Modern Science*. Cambridge, MA: Harvard University Press. A detailed examination of the place of women and "femininity" in the Western scientific tradition.

4

Christian Responses to Darwinism in the Late Nineteenth Century

PETER J. BOWLER

When assessing the impact of Darwin's theory in the decades immediately following the publication of the *Origin of Species* in 1859 there is a temptation to assume that there must have been a continuous tradition of opposition from religious thinkers from that time to the present. We have all heard of the confrontation between Thomas Henry Huxley (known as "Darwin's bulldog") and Bishop Samuel Wilberforce at the Oxford meeting of the British Association in 1860. We have also heard of the "Monkey Trial" of John Thomas Scopes in 1925, widely perceived as the first battle in the conflict between a resurgent Christian fundamentalism and Darwinism. In the modern world, that conflict continues, with Darwinians such as Richard Dawkins insisting that their theory makes it difficult if not impossible to believe in a wise and benevolent Creator.

It would be only natural to assume that this image of conflict should also apply to the late nineteenth century, but in fact the situation at that time was far more complex and less confrontational (Bowler 2007; Livingstone 1987; Moore 1979). Liberal Christianity was a much more powerful force then and it was able to make an accommodation with the theory of evolution, if not with the most radical form of Darwinism. Our vision of the Huxley–Wilberforce clash is itself a myth created by the exponents of "scientific naturalism" who wished to discredit the Church (James 2005). In fact, the vast majority of liberal Christians soon welcomed the idea of evolution and incorporated it into a worldview in which human spiritual progress was seen as a continuation of the Creator's great plan of universal development. Many scientists were themselves Christians, and were only too happy to look for ways of softening the impact of the most materialistic implications of Darwinism. Another factor that must be borne in mind is that Darwin's theory of natural selection was not the only game in town – there were other mechanisms of evolution that had credibility at the time (and which bear some resemblance to advances in evolutionary developmental biology which are modifying Darwinianism in the modern world). These non-Darwinian theories were much easier to fit into a worldview based on the belief that development must be predetermined to advance in a meaningful direction. The rise of what

The Blackwell Companion to Science and Christianity, First Edition. Edited by J. B. Stump and Alan G. Padgett.
© 2012 Blackwell Publishing Ltd. Published 2012 by Blackwell Publishing Ltd.

we now call "Creationism" was very much a product of the twentieth century, not of the late nineteenth.

There were several issues over which Christians and scientists had to negotiate if they were to reach an agreement over evolutionism. What was one to make of the Genesis story of creation? If this was interpreted allegorically so as to allow for some kind of extended process of historical development, did that process work in such a way as to allow the tradition of a God who designs the universe to be retained? And what about the traditional view that the human soul lifted us above the "brutes that perish" – could one really believe that our spiritual capacities had evolved from some kind of animal mentality? Attitudes on all three of these issues have changed over time, most obviously through the decline and resurgence of the literalist approach to the sacred text represented by fundamentalism. Reactions were also susceptible to geographical variation – issues that are crucial in one country or even one city, thanks to local circumstances, could be sidelined elsewhere. Thus in Belfast, John Tyndall's celebrated materialist address to the British Association in 1874 ensured that the local Presbyterians were alienated from the theory of evolution, while in Princeton the Belfast émigré James McCosh encouraged members of the same denomination to accept the idea that creative design could be seen in the workings of evolution (Livingstone 1987).

By the time Darwin published his theory it had become widely accepted that a literal interpretation of the Genesis creation story could not be maintained. The discoveries of the geologists had been widely disseminated and everyone accepted that the earth was very old, and that there had been a sequence of different populations as revealed by the fossil record (Bowler 2009). The Darwinists did not have to fight against the position which has subsequently re-emerged as Young-Earth Creationism. It should also be noted that the whole issue of a more liberal interpretation of the sacred text had become a major area of debate, as witnessed by the reaction to the collection of papers supportive of the "higher criticism" under the title *Essays and Reviews* in 1860.

For those interested in science the main question now was how to explain the progressive introduction of higher forms of life revealed by the fossil record. Paleontologists in the early nineteenth century seem to have thought in terms of a sequence of supernatural creations in the course of the earth's history. But by the 1850s there was already growing support for the idea that the appearance of new life forms might be accounted for as the consequence of some kind of divinely programmed "law of creation" probably operating through the transmutation of pre-existing species. Robert Chambers's anonymously published *Vestiges of the Natural History of Creation* had promoted this idea as early as 1844. The initial response of the scientific community had been hostile, but by the mid-1850s we know that a more positive attitude toward transmutation had begun to emerge both among scientists and the general public (Secord 2000). Chambers implied that the Creator's design could be seen in the purposeful nature of the law of development, rather than in individual acts of miraculous creation. In the 1850s the respected Anglican scientist Baden Powell also took a more positive approach to creation by law (Corsi 1988). As we shall see below, this was the position that many Christian thinkers moved toward, speeded on by the debate sparked by the *Origin of Species*. There was still concern over the status of the human soul, but all the evidence suggests that liberal Christians became willing to accept the evolution of the human spirit from an animal ancestry provided the process of evolution itself could be understood as purposeful and hence divinely preordained. More radical thinkers were already thinking in terms of natural processes shaping the evolution of the human mind, as in Herbert Spencer's *Principles of Psychology* of 1855 (Francis 2007).

Darwin's Impact

Darwin's theory of evolution by natural selection had been conceived in the late 1830s and matured over the two decades leading toward the publication of the *Origin*. Far from being a "natural" product of nineteenth-century science and culture, the selection theory was a radical idea that (when published) faced widespread misunderstanding and incomprehension. The only other naturalist to suggest the idea, Alfred Russel Wallace, had significantly different views on how the process operated and on its wider implications. Wallace was also 20 years behind Darwin in preparing a case for evolution, and it is doubtful that he could have written anything as substantial as the *Origin* in the 1860s. It is possible to argue that without Darwin, the theory of natural selection would not have come to the fore in the late nineteenth century, and an evolutionary paradigm based on the idea of progressive development would have emerged, perhaps more slowly, but certainly without the level of traumatic debate which was precipitated by the *Origin*.

Darwin's theory certainly rocked the boat, and it did so in a way that had both positive and negative consequences for the public acceptance of evolutionism (Greene 1959; Ruse 1999). The *Origin* offered new lines of evidence and new comparisons with familiar processes such as the artificial selection practiced by animal breeders. It thus speeded up the process – already underway – of converting both the scientific community and the general public to acceptance of the general idea of evolution. But Darwin's particular explanation of how evolution worked, natural selection, was profoundly disturbing because it was very hard to see how such a process could be an expression of divine providence. In the end, most scientists and laypeople accepted evolution but remained unconvinced about natural selection. The story of the late nineteenth-century response to Darwinian is thus one of a search for alternative explanations of evolution which would satisfy the expectation that the process was purposeful and progressive (Bowler 1983, 1988).

Why was the theory of natural selection so disturbing? First it must be noted that many religious thinkers (including scientists) seem to have thought that the laws governing evolution would have to somehow embody creative design in a way that would be obvious from the results they produced. Design was embodied in the laws, not in the structure of individual species, as it had been in the original version of the argument from design presented, for instance, in William Paley's *Natural Theology* of 1802. But, as Thomas Henry Huxley had complained in a review of Chambers's *Vestiges*, the vague idea that nature unfolded in a purposeful direction was not much use to the biologist who wanted to know exactly how new structures were produced. To satisfy the demands of scientific naturalism, the laws governing evolution would have to be laws of nature like any other, operating in a mechanistic manner at least as far as their immediate actions were concerned. If there was design in the system, it would have to be in the long-range consequences of those day-to-day activities. Darwin's theory certainly depended on laws that could be observed operating in the everyday world – but were its ultimate consequences those one might expect from a divinely created system? As far as most Christians were concerned, they were not.

Natural selection was a highly materialistic theory, very difficult to reconcile with design. The raw material on which selection acted was the individual differences which exist within any population. Those differences are "random" in the sense that they are multifarious and appear to have no relationship to the needs of the organism or any future goal. Most are pointless, some are harmful, and only a few will – just by chance – turn out to have some value for the organism in its daily "struggle for existence." By appealing to Thomas Malthus's principle of population expansion, Darwin portrayed nature as a scene of relentless struggle in which many must die because of the limitation of resources. Natural selection works because those few individuals which have a useful variation will succeed in the struggle and will reproduce, passing their adaptive characters on to future generations. The unfit will be rigorously eliminated. This process of what Herbert Spencer called the "survival of the fittest" did not seem like the kind of mechanism a wise and benevolent Creator would use to allow species to adapt to changes in their environment. Nor was there any way for the system to evolve toward a long-term goal – the only criterion for success was short-term advantage in the local environment.

For anyone wishing to undermine the argument from design, natural selection was the ideal theory of evolution. Indeed it is probable that T. H. Huxley welcomed the theory precisely because it had that consequence, although even he did not believe selection could be the main mechanism of change. Religious thinkers reacted with horror, seeing the theory as a recipe for undermining all faith in a God who cares about his creation. Yet they were not unsympathetic to the general idea of evolution, and there were alternative mechanisms available which might better serve their overall objective. The most popular was the so-called Lamarckian theory of the inheritance of acquired characteristic, named after the French naturalist J. B. Lamarck, who had suggested it as an explanation of adaptive evolution as early as 1809. In Lamarckism variation is not random, because it is shaped by the purposeful activities of the organisms themselves. In a changed environment animals will develop new habits and exercise their bodies in new ways, thus augmenting or diminishing their structures and faculties. If these acquired characters are inherited, they will accumulate over many generations and produce major changes. In the most popular illustration, the giraffe got its long neck thanks to generations of its ancestors stretching up to reach the leaves of trees (not, as in Darwin's theory, from generations of short-necked variants being eliminated). Here evolution seems more purposeful and does not require nature to be seen as an arena of death and suffering. Modern genetics shows that acquired characteristics cannot be inherited, of course, but at the time no one (and certainly not Darwin himself) was aware of the true mechanism of variation and heredity.

At the same time, however, we must be careful not to be too prescriptive in how we evaluate the rival theories. In the later decades of the century writers such as Samuel Butler, deeply concerned about the moral implications of the selection theory, hailed Lamarckism as an alternative that would free evolutionism from the specter of Darwinian materialism. But in the 1860s and 1870s, Herbert Spencer was popularizing an evolutionary philosophy which used both natural selection and Lamarckism, and he saw both as being driven by individual competition within the population. Struggle could eliminate the unfit, but it would also encourage all individuals to exert themselves and thus acquire useful new characters. The distinction between Darwinian selection and this model of Lamarckism was unclear to many readers, with the result that the term "Darwinism" was applied to a broadly based evolutionism, not just to the selection theory (which is the modern, more restrictive meaning of the term). Darwin became the figurehead for this broad evolutionism, even though many who counted themselves as his followers did not think his particular explanation of the process was the whole story. Much of what was later called "social Darwinism" thus did not depend on applications of the selection theory to society. Spencer's enthusiasm for free-enterprise capitalism was based more on his Lamarckian version of self-improvement than on any suggestion that vast numbers of unfit individuals needed to be eliminated from the human population.

The Initial Response

Darwin certainly feared that his book would create a public outcry, and in the short term that fear was well founded. The clash between Huxley and Wilberforce is remembered as emblematic of the opposition by churchmen to both evolutionism and the selection theory. But historians have shown that the popular image of Huxley defeating the hapless Wilberforce is a myth created by those who wanted to celebrate the new theory as a weapon in their battle against organized religion (James 2005). In fact Wilberforce had some telling points against the theory, both moral and scientific, and Huxley's response was far less effective than the popular legend implies. As one of the newly professionalized "men of science" Huxley was opposed to the influence of the Church on the nation's affairs, although he coined the term "agnostic" to indicate that he was not an outright atheist (Lightman 1987). Natural selection was a plausible explanation of adaptive evolution, but he thought it still needed to be verified by breeding experiments and seems to have thought that much evolution was not driven by adaptation in any case. But for those who shared Huxley's commitment to scientific naturalism, natural selection was useful ammunition in their fight against the claim that simple observation of nature revealed that it was a system permeated with design. Some years later Tyndall's Belfast address was widely perceived as a call for Darwinism to be seen as a key plank in what most critics saw as a campaign to establish a materialistic worldview.

Wilberforce rejected the whole idea of evolution, as well as the selection theory, but studies of the debate over the next decade or so suggest that there was a steady decline in support for what we would call the creationist alternative (Ellegard 1990; Hull 1973). In America the naturalist Louis Agassiz remained committed to a position in which every species, however little distinct from its nearest relatives, had to be seen as a product of supernatural creation. Most of Agassiz's students, however, converted to evolutionism over the next two decades (although several became prominent members of what became known as the American school of neo-Lamarckism). By the end of the 1870s Sir J. W. Dawson of Montreal was one of the very few prominent naturalists still holding out against any form of evolutionism.

Many of the converts accepted "Darwinism" only in the most general sense of the term – they did not throw their weight behind the theory of natural selection (Bowler 2007). Some retained an explicit link between evolution and design, the idea of "theistic evolution" in which the changes are divinely programmed to unfold in a particular direction. The anatomist Richard Owen has been caricatured as an anti-evolutionist because he wrote a critical review of the *Origin*, but he later proposed his own theory of "derivation" in which species were transformed in accordance with a pre-programmed law of development. The astronomer and geographer Sir J. F. W. Herschel was reported to have dismissed natural selection as the "law of higgledy-piggledy," but he too endorsed the idea of divinely planned evolution. In America, one of Darwin's leading defenders was the botanist Asa Gray, a devout Presbyterian. Gray tried hard to argue that natural selection was compatible with belief in divine providence, but in the end he conceded that variation must somehow be led along "beneficial lines" so there would be no harmful variants (the "scum of creation") needing to be removed.

The problem with theistic evolutionism was that it quite explicitly preserved a role for design. In later decades, scientists became increasingly unwilling to make explicit references to the Creator in their theories, and the Lamarckian theory of the inheritance of acquired characteristics emerged as a powerful alternative to natural selection. In effect, Lamarckism provided a natural explanation of how variation could be led along "beneficial lines" by changes in the animals' own habits. The Anglican clergyman Charles Kingsley was an early supporter of Darwinism, and his popular book *The Water Babies* is sometimes portrayed as offering support for natural selection. But Kingsley's emphasis on the importance of hard work and initiative to ensure self-development is pure Lamarckism – in effect it was the muscular Christian equivalent of the self-help form of social Darwinism being promoted along more secular lines by Herbert Spencer. As James Moore (1985) has argued, many American clergymen became, in effect, "Herbert Spencer's henchmen," including the influential Congregationalist minister Henry Ward Beecher. John Fiske modified Spencer's philosophy into a more teleological worldview in his *Outlines of Cosmic Philosophy* of 1874. Temporarily, at least, the liberal movement played a dominant role in American religion, with Beecher openly arguing that the Bible story had to be reinterpreted to allow God's plan of creation to be seen as a preordained progress in which human effort and ingenuity played a creative role. The role of original sin and the Fall had to be reinterpreted to create a worldview based on progress – now humankind's base instincts had to be seen as relics of our animal ancestry, soon to be swept aside in the course of future moral and spiritual development.

Human Origins

The reinterpretation of humanity's links with the animal kingdom was perhaps the most difficult area of negotiation between liberal Christianity and evolutionism. Following the publication of Chambers's *Vestiges*, the Scots paleontologist and religious commentator Hugh Miller had declared that, as a Christian, he could accept the idea that God's design was worked out through law rather than miracle, but he could not accept that the human spirit could have emerged from an animal origin. Although Darwin avoided discussion of the issue in the *Origin*, everyone knew that this was a crucial area of debate, and arguments immediately began over the closeness of the relationship between humans and apes. In the end, liberal Christians were prepared to bite the bullet and accept the necessary reinterpretation of humanity's status, although it became obvious by the end of the century that there were cracks in the liberal model of progress that had merely been papered over.

If humans were to be included in the Darwinian paradigm, our distant ancestors would have to be regarded not as divinely created beings immediately capable of establishing civilizations, but as primitive creatures scarcely advanced beyond the apes from which they had recently evolved. But the emergence of a model of human prehistory based on progress rather than degeneration was facilitated by a parallel revolution within archaeology which took place at the same time as that in biology, yet apparently with independent origins. As paleontology developed through the early nineteenth century, it had remained an article of faith that – however old the earth might be – humanity had appeared only a few thousand years ago. There was no sense of prehistory, of a long period of savagery predating the first written accounts of the ancient world. Occasional reports of stone artifacts turning up alongside the remains of extinct animals were dismissed as fraudulent. In the 1860s, however, the evidence for a "stone age" stretching into the distant past became inescapable, and there was a sudden revolution in which the modern science of prehistoric archaeology emerged. Charles Lyell, Darwin's geological mentor, summed up the evidence in his *Antiquity of Man* of 1863 (Van Riper 1993).

Lyell himself was reluctant to accept that the earliest humans had emerged gradually from an ape ancestry (Bartholomew 1973). But the popular image of evolutionism, displayed in a host of cartoons, was of a theory which blurred the distinction between ape and human. T. H. Huxley clashed with Richard Owen over the closeness of the physical relationship between humans and apes. Modern-day "savages" were frequently portrayed as relics of the intermediate stages in the evolution of civilized humans from apes. Archaeology thus combined with anthropology to create an almost linear model of human progress from the apes. If the "missing links" could not be found in the fossil record, their modern-day equivalents could be studied for clues about our distant ancestors' thought processes and social life. Sir John Lubbock led the campaign to establish a progressionist model of human prehistory, using derogatory models of "savage" behavior to illustrate the depths from which we have risen. The archbishop of Dublin, Richard Whately, and the Duke of Argyll tried to defend the older view that humanity had degenerated, but the evolutionary model soon became the dominant way of understanding both human origins and human diversity.

The new model required a reinterpretation of the doctrine of original sin, as liberal preachers such as Beecher were soon openly admitting. But there was already widespread dissatisfaction in the educated classes with a religion which dismissed all who had not accepted Christ to eternal damnation. It proved surprisingly easy to sidestep this issue, as long as the purposeful and progressive nature of humanity's ascent from the apes could be affirmed.

Huxley and Owen clashed over the degree of physical resemblance between apes and humans, but Owen's efforts to establish the existence of unique structures in the human brain did not really deal with the crucial issues. As Darwin had realized as soon as he became an evolutionist, the real problem was to explain the origin of the higher human mental and moral faculties by a natural process of evolution from animal origins (Desmond and Moore 1991). Spencer had made efforts in this direction, but the Darwinists added little of real value to the debate until Darwin himself published his views in his *Descent of Man* in 1871. It seemed relatively easy to explain how the level of intelligence had risen, because this characteristic was surely of benefit in the struggle for life. Indeed, one problem with the evolutionary synthesis was that it tended to assume that intellectual progress was inevitable unless delayed by environmental constraints. Darwin was one of the few to recognize that to explain why humans had progressed, but apes had not, it was necessary to imagine that their ancestors had begun adapting to different ways of life. But the origins of the moral and spiritual faculties were an obvious problem, because if survival value was the key to evolution, it would seem that characteristics such as self-sacrifice and altruism were detrimental to the individual's self-interest and hence should be eliminated by natural selection.

Darwin tackled the problem by seeing our sense of morality as the rationalization of instincts implanted in us because evolution had adapted us to a social way of life. In part he followed Spencer in assuming a Lamarckian effect in which our ancestors learned the benefits of living in a group. He also invoked what is nowadays called "group selection," noting that those groups which did not cooperate very well would be conquered by those with better-developed social instincts. Similar ideas flourished among the evolutionary psychologists and anthropologists of the late nineteenth century. Many religious thinkers seem to have gone along with the trend, yet there were some who remained unconvinced. We have already noted Charles Lyell's doubts on this score, and another prominent critic was Alfred Russel Wallace, the co-discoverer of natural selection. By the late 1860s, Wallace – who had become a convert to spiritualism – was writing openly of natural selection's inability to explain the higher mental and moral functions and invoking some form of supernatural involvement in the later stages of human evolution (Kottler 1974). Roman Catholic writers, including the anatomist St George Jackson Mivart, also criticized the adequacy of the Darwinians' explanations (Gruber 1960). Nevertheless, the liberal Christian vision of progress remained active into the early twentieth century, for instance in the Congregationalist minister R. J. Campbell's *New Theology* of 1907. By this time, however, a more widespread opposition was emerging within the Protestant churches in the form of the movement that became known as fundamentalism – although it should be noted that not all of the early fundamentalists rejected evolution (Livingstone 1987).

The Eclipse of Darwinism

Although there was some continuity within the liberal Christian tradition that found common cause with evolutionism, there were also significant developments that were in tune with a rising tide of suspicion directed against materialism. These developments also had a major impact on scientific evolutionism. The Darwinians and Spencerians of the 1860s and 1870s had accepted that Lamarckism and natural selection both had a role to play, even if they disagreed over their relative contributions. Progress worked through success in the struggle for existence, and was hence conceived in purely materialistic terms. In the later decades of the century, however, an increasingly hostile attitude toward the selection theory emerged. T. H. Huxley's grandson, the biologist and humanist Julian Huxley, later referred to the rise of explicitly anti-selectionist views in the late nineteenth century as the "eclipse of Darwinism" (Bowler 1983). Natural selection was once again hailed as an agent of materialism, and the Lamarckian mechanism was seen not as a supplement, but as an alternative. There was a temporary revival of anti-materialist thinking, even in scientific biology. At the same time, however, new developments in the study of heredity led toward the emergence of Mendelian genetics, originally seen as still another alternative to the selection theory, yet soon to be synthesized with it to give the dominant evolutionary paradigm of the mid-twentieth century.

Spencer had included a major element of Lamarckism in his thinking, but he was associated with the Darwinian view that nature is a scene of constant struggle, and he saw the organism's efforts to adapt to its environment in materialistic terms. There was thus little to distinguish Spencerianism from Darwinism, although Spencer thought that eventually humans would evolve mental functions that would render struggle superfluous – a point ignored by some of his followers (Francis 2007). In the later decades of the century, however, the Lamarckian effect was seized upon by thinkers who wanted to challenge the materialist tradition associated with the names of Darwin, Huxley, and Tyndall. The emphasis was now on the creativity of the individual organism, which was seen as something lifting the living organism above the level of a mere machine. Writers such as Samuel Butler and later Bernard Shaw depicted natural selection as a soulless and cruel mechanism which reduced animals and humans to the level of machines. For them, Lamarckism became the vehicle for promoting a vitalist philosophy in which the life force played an active and creative role by promoting behavioral innovation. The fact that Spencer's philosophy (also dismissed as materialism) had contained a significant element of Lamarckism was forgotten.

Scientists too became temporarily more open to vitalist thinking. The American paleontologist Edward Drinker Cope, a Presbyterian, became a leading figure in the American school of neo-Lamarckism. His *Theology of Evolution* of 1887 openly depicted evolution as a process that was given a purposeful direction by innovative behavior. He also attributed the active power underlying the activity of the animal body to a non-physical "growth force." Joseph LeConte also developed a form of neo-Lamarckism that presented evolution as a purposeful and harmonious process. At the start of the twentieth century, the vitalist model of an active life force struggling to impose its will on material nature was widely disseminated through the French writer Henri Bergson's philosophy of "creative evolution."

It should be noted that not all of the opposition focused on an alternative explanation of adaptive evolution. In his first paper on evolution in 1867 Cope had visualized multiple paral-lel lines of evolution within each group being propelled in the same direction by a divinely programmed internal trend. Cope and other American neo-Lamarckians later included an element of orthogenesis or predetermined nonadaptive evolution in their theory. The inten-tion of this way of thinking was to stress the orderly and predictable nature of evolution (adaptive evolution is always at the mercy of fluctuations in the environment, and is hence unpredictable and open-ended). The religious implications of this position were not always obvious, but at the philosophical level they were certainly anti-materialistic. In the case of the Roman Catholic anatomist St George Jackson Mivart the religious motivation became more apparent. Mivart began as a supporter of Darwin and Huxley but soon turned to an anti-Darwinian form of evolutionism which stressed the law-bound and predictable nature of developmental trends (Gruber 1960). His book The Genesis of Species of 1871 was a cornu-copia of anti-Darwinian arguments much exploited by later opponents of the theory. As noted above, Mivart also excluded human mental and moral functions from any form of evolution-ary explanation. Mivart tried to convince the Catholic hierarchy that in this form evolutionism should be acceptable to the Church, but he was unsuccessful and was eventually excommu-nicated (Brundell 2001; O'Leary 2006).

Much of the Christian thinking about evolutionism around the turn of the century was influenced by the nonmaterialist approach characteristic of the eclipse of Darwinism (Bowler 2007). Campbell's new theology, for instance, was inspired by idealist philosophy and stressed an immanentist viewpoint in which God's power was active within nature. A striking char-acteristic of this approach was its tendency to continue deflecting attention away from the traditional view that humans were raised above the animal kingdom by their possession of spiritual faculties. By seeing God's creative power as a nonmaterial force operating within and upon the material world, the higher faculties were, in effect, transferred into nature itself. The higher mental and moral functions expanded automatically in the course of evolution – thus denying the whole logic of the Darwinian/Spencerian emphasis on competition as the driving force of evolution. This rejection of "social Darwinism" was a key plank in the phi-losophy of writers such as Henry Drummond, whose Ascent of Man of 1894 saw altruism and cooperation as the driving forces of evolution.

Theological writers such as Drummond and Campbell were capable of arousing great enthusiasm among ordinary people dissatisfied with both traditional Christianity and mate-rialism. But in America a newly resurgent fundamentalism was creating problems for liberals such as Harry Emerson Fosdick. In the end, the liberal tradition did not have the emotional power that was necessary to engage ordinary people, who were dissatisfied with the moral effects of modernism. At the same time, however, the scientists were turning against vitalism and Lamarckism. There was a renewed interest in the role played by heredity in determining character, and in 1900 the "rediscovery" of Gregor Mendel's work led to the emergence of a new science of heredity with immense implications for evolutionism. Mendelian genetics, although at first seen as yet another alternative to natural selection, was in the end more effective in destroying the credibility of Lamarckism and the poorly defined non-Darwinian evolutionism on which many liberal Christians relied. The way was being paved for Darwin's theory to emerge as a powerful force in science, and to be identified as a major threat by increasingly influential conservative religious thinkers.

References

Bartholomew, Michael. 1973. Lyell and Evolution: An Account of Lyell's Response to the Prospect of an Evolutionary Ancestry for Man. *British Journal for the History of Science*, 6, pp. 261–303.

Bowler, Peter J. 1983. *The Eclipse of Darwinism: Anti-Darwinian Evolution Theories in the Decades around 1900*. Baltimore, MD: Johns Hopkins University Press.

Bowler, Peter J. 1988. *The Non-Darwinian Revolution: Reinterpreting a Historical Myth*. Baltimore, MD: Johns Hopkins University Press.

Bowler, Peter J. 2007. *Monkey Trials and Gorilla Sermons: Evolution and Christianity from Darwin to Intelligent Design*. Cambridge, MA: Harvard University Press.

Bowler, Peter J. 2009. *Evolution: The History of an Idea*, 25th edn. Berkeley, CA: University of California Press.

Brundell, Barry. 2001. Catholic Church Politics and Evolution Theory, 1894–1902. *British Journal for the History of Science*, 34, pp. 81–96.

Corsi, Pietro. 1988. *Science and Religion: Baden Powell and the Anglican Debate, 1800–1860*. Cambridge: Cambridge University Press.

Desmond, Adrian and Moore, James R. 1991. *Darwin*. London: Michael Joseph.

Ellegård, Alvar. 1990. *Darwin and the General Reader: The Reception of Darwin's Theory of Evolution in the British Periodical Press, 1859–1872*. Chicago: University of Chicago Press.

Francis, Mark. 2007. *Herbert Spencer and the Invention of Modern Life*. Stocksfield, UK: Acumen.

Greene, John C. 1959. *The Death of Adam: Evolution and Its Impact on Western Thought*. Ames, IA: Iowa State University Press.

Gruber, Jacob W. 1960. *A Conscience in Conflict: The Life of St. George Jackson Mivart*. New York: Columbia University Press.

Hull, David W., ed. 1973. *Darwin and His Critics: The Reception of Darwin's Theory of Evolution by the Scientific Community*. Cambridge, MA: Harvard University Press

James, Frank A. J. L. 2005. An "Open Clash between Science and the Church"? Wilberforce, Huxley and Hooker on Darwinism at the British Association. In D. Knight and M. Eddy, eds. *Science and Beliefs: From Natural Philosophy to Natural Science*. Aldershot: Ashgate, pp. 171–194.

Kottler, Malcolm Jay. 1974. Alfred Russel Wallace, the Origin of Man, and Spiritualism. *Isis*, 65, pp. 145–192.

Lightman, Bernard. 1987. *The Origins of Agnosticism: Victorian Unbelief and the Limits of Knowledge*. Baltimore MD: Johns Hopkins University Press.

Livingstone, David. 1987. *Darwin's Forgotten Defenders: The Encounter between Evangelical Theology and Evolutionary Thought*. Grand Rapids, MI: Eerdmans.

Moore, James R. 1979. *The Post-Darwinian Controversies: A Study of the Protestant Struggle to Come to Terms with Darwin in Great Britain and America*. New York: Cambridge University Press.

Moore, James R. 1985. Herbert Spencer's Henchmen: The Evolution of Protestant Liberals in Late Nineteenth-Century America. In J. R. Durant, ed. *Darwinism and Divinity: Essays on Evolution and Religious Belief*. Oxford: Blackwell, pp. 76–100.

O'Leary, Don. 2006. *Roman Catholicism and Science: A History*. New York: Continuum.

Ruse, Michael. 1999. *The Darwinian Revolution: Science Red in Tooth and Claw*, 2nd edn. Chicago: University of Chicago Press.

Secord, James A. 2000. *Victorian Sensation: The Extraordinary Publication, Reception and Secret Authorship of Vestiges of the Natural History of Creation*. Chicago: University of Chicago Press.

Van Riper, A. Bowdoin. 1993. *Men among the Mammoths: Victorian Science and the Discovery of Prehistory.* Chicago: University of Chicago Press.

Further Reading

Bowler, Peter J. 2007. *Monkey Trials and Gorilla Sermons: Evolution and Christianity from Darwin to Intelligent Design.* Cambridge, MA: Harvard University Press. Concise overview of the debates which stresses the role of liberal Christianity.

Ellegård, Alvar. 1990. *Darwin and the General Reader: The Reception of Darwin's Theory of Evolution in the British Periodical Press, 1859–1872.* Chicago: University of Chicago Press. Standard account of the public reception of Darwinism.

Greene, John C. 1959. *The Death of Adam: Evolution and Its Impact on Western Thought.* Ames, IA: Iowa State University Press. Classic survey of the development of evolutionism up to and including Darwin's theory.

Moore, James R. 1979. *The Post-Darwinian Controversies: A Study of the Protestant Struggle to Come to Terms with Darwin in Great Britain and America.* New York: Cambridge University Press. Standard work on the reception of Darwinism by religious thinkers.

5

Science Falsely So Called
Fundamentalism and Science

EDWARD B. DAVIS

The trial of John Scopes for teaching evolution in a Dayton, Tennessee high school in 1925 is undoubtedly the most famous episode in the history of fundamentalism and science. Although it was technically a criminal prosecution, everyone in the courtroom wanted and expected a conviction – including the defendant, an inexperienced teacher who was unsure that he had actually taught evolution but had agreed to stand trial at the insistence of his employers. The ultimate goal was to test the constitutionality of a new law that forbade public school teachers "to teach any theory that denies the story of the Divine Creation of man as taught in the Bible, and to teach instead that man had descended from a lower order of animal" (Larson 1997, 50). The proceedings were carefully orchestrated, resulting in an almost theatrical trial. In the penultimate scene, the noted agnostic Clarence Darrow, the greatest trial lawyer of his generation, aggressively cross-examined William Jennings Bryan, who had run three times unsuccessfully as the Democratic candidate for President decades earlier and had spearheaded the effort to pass laws against evolution in many states.

The topic of that inquisition was the Bible. For some time, Bryan had been writing regular columns about biblical stories for newspapers, and he regarded himself as something of an authority on the holy book. Bryan had gone to Dayton at the behest of William Bell Riley, pastor of the enormous First Baptist Church of Minneapolis and a bitter opponent of evolution. Riley was the founding president of the World's Christian Fundamentals Association, a confederation of conservative Protestants who vigorously opposed what they considered to be the profoundly unbiblical views of those liberal Protestants who were calling themselves "modernists." Shortly before World War One, California oil magnates Lyman and Milton Stewart had financed a transatlantic collection of 90 articles in 12 paperbound volumes, *The Fundamentals* (1910–1915), which were printed by the million and mailed free of charge to Protestant pastors, Sunday school superintendents, and other religious workers across the nation. It was in reference to the title of this collection that the word "fundamentalist" was first used in print in July 1920 by Curtis Lee Laws, editor of a leading Baptist periodical, the *Watchman-Examiner*. Laws suggested "that those who still cling to the great fundamentals and who mean to do battle royal for the fundamentals shall be called 'Fundamentalists',," adding that "when he uses the word it will be in compliment and not in disparagement" (Moore 1981, 32). Although now the term is applied far more broadly and usually with a decidedly uncomplimentary intent, the specifically Protestant and American context in which it arose must be kept in mind.

The Blackwell Companion to Science and Christianity, First Edition. Edited by J. B. Stump and Alan G. Padgett.
© 2012 Blackwell Publishing Ltd. Published 2012 by Blackwell Publishing Ltd.

Surprisingly, evolution had not been a principal target of *The Fundamentals*; the authors as a group were far more concerned about heterodox theology and the "German fancies" of higher biblical criticism. Only two of the articles can be described as mainly anti-evolutionary, and a few contributors actually favored theistic evolution – especially the Scottish theologian James Orr, who wrote that "'Evolution,' in short, is coming to be recognized as but a new name for 'creation,' only that the creative power now works from *within*, instead of, as in the old conception, in an *external*, plastic fashion" (Numbers 2006, 49). James Moore (1979) and David Livingstone (1984) have shown that some important evangelicals substantially accepted evolution among the lower animals (though always with an obvious element of divine design) for several decades prior to World War One: Harvard botanist Asa Gray (the first Darwinian in America), geologists George Frederick Wright (who later changed his mind and wrote against evolution in *The Fundamentals*) and James Dwight Dana, theologians James McCosh and Augustus Hopkins Strong, and even an author of the Princeton doctrine of inerrancy, theologian Benjamin B. Warfield. Human evolution, especially the evolution of our higher faculties, remained highly problematic for most of these thinkers – and the one exception, Gray, probably did not accept it until the final decade of his life – but none believed that evolution among the lower animals contradicted core Christian doctrines such as creation, Incarnation, and Resurrection.

Nevertheless, as George Marsden (1988, n.p.) has pointed out, most of the articles in *The Fundamentals* share the view "that true science and rationality supports traditional Christianity grounded in the supernatural and the miraculous," such that subsequent heated opposition to evolution is not too hard to understand. The concerns fundamentalists expressed about scientific naturalism, relative to the Bible, were captured brilliantly in a cartoon (Figure 5.1)

Figure 5.1 "True Science Never Wears Blinders," Ernest James Pace. From colored slide in the set "Up to Date but Deadly," no. 22, Billy Graham Center Museum, Wheaton, IL, accession no. 81.1070. Courtesy of Museum of the Billy Graham Center, Wheaton, IL.

drawn by Ernest James Pace for the *Sunday School Times*, a weekly magazine with a large circulation in the United States and more than a hundred other nations. Pace's cartoons appeared regularly in the *Sunday School Times* and other periodicals for almost 30 years, spreading fundamentalist views of science and the Bible pictorially to a very wide audience.

Bryan had personally opposed evolution for many years, but he did not seek publicly to ban its teaching until the early 1920s. He was motivated to act by what he read about links between Darwinian ideas and militarism in Germany prior to and during World War One, particularly in a book by Stanford biologist Vernon Kellogg called *Headquarters Nights* (1917). Kellogg, a pacifist who had earned his doctorate at Leipzig, volunteered to help Herbert Hoover with relief efforts in Belgium before the United States declared war on Germany. Billeted in a house that was also shared by German officers, he wrote about their conversations. Reflecting on his experiences, Kellogg said that "The creed of the *Allmacht* of a natural selection based on violent and fatal competitive struggle is the gospel of the German intellectuals," on which basis they justified "why, for the good of the world, there should be this war" (Kellogg 1917, 28 and 22). These revelations shocked Bryan, who was already convinced that belief in evolution justified monopolistic practices, enhanced class pride, and undermined the moral basis for democracy in America.

Evolution as False Science and Bad Theology

Both Bryan and Riley blamed Germany for cradling biblical criticism and Darwinian philosophy, and they both saw evolution as underlying the false theology of the modernists. It can be no accident that the anti-evolutionary screed written by Bryan in 1922, *The Menace of Darwinism*, bore a title very similar to that a book by Riley of five years earlier, *The Menace of Modernism*. As Bryan told Charles G. Trumbull, editor of the *Sunday School Times*, evolution was "the cause of modernism and the progressive elimination of the vital truths of the Bible." The Christian who accepted evolution would almost inevitably descend a staircase of increasing unbelief, on which "there is no stopping place" short of atheism – a vivid image that Pace converted into one of his most powerful cartoons (Figure 5.2). According to Bryan, "the three persons who are most affected by modernism are the student, the preacher who substitutes education for religion, and the scientist who prefers guesses to the word of God" (Moore 1981, 40). Thus, Bryan had a special revulsion for "theistic evolution," a term that had been used (not always sympathetically) by Dawson, Gray, and others since the 1870s to denote the idea that God used the process of evolution to create living things. "Theistic evolution may be described as an anesthetic which deadens the pain while the patient's religion is being gradually removed," Bryan proclaimed, making it just "a way-station on the highway that leads from Christian faith to No-God-Land" (Bryan 1922, 5).

Bryan's fears about the deleterious effects of evolution on traditional Christian beliefs were not unwarranted. Most Protestant scientists and clergy who accepted evolution at that time coupled their high view of science with a low view of orthodox Christian theology, rejecting the Incarnation, the virgin birth, the bodily Resurrection of Jesus, and even in some cases the idea of a transcendent God. American Protestants of the Scopes era were presented with a stark choice: to affirm traditional Christian beliefs while denying evolution, or to accept evolution while discarding orthodox beliefs. Thus, when Scopes's attorneys invited more than a dozen eminent scientists and theologians to testify on behalf of evolution at the trial (many of them declined), most were modernist Christians and possibly just one really believed in

Figure 5.2 "The Descent of the Modernists," Ernest James Pace. William Jennings Bryan, *Seven Questions in Dispute* (New York: Revell, 1924), frontispiece. Courtesy of Edward B. Davis.

the Incarnation – the president of the American Association for the Advancement of Science, Columbia physicist Michael Pupin, a devout Serbian Orthodox believer whose religious tradition was not involved with the fundamentalist–modernist controversy. The list included theologian Shailer Mathews, dean of the Divinity School at the University of Chicago, the most influential seminary in America. When Mathews penned his autobiography in the mid-1930s, he spoke of how the addition of laboratory science into the educational process resulted in the attitude "that orthodox theology was felt to be incompatible with intellectual integrity" (Mathews 1936, 221). Another invitee, Princeton biologist Edwin Grant Conklin, almost took the words out of Bryan's mouth, describing his own spiritual journey as one that "orthodox friends" might interpret as "descending steps," leading him further from the traditional Methodist faith of his youth. "[M]y gradual loss of faith in many orthodox beliefs," he recalled, "came inevitably with increasing knowledge of nature and growth of a critical sense" (Conklin 1953, 57–58).

In arguing against evolution, Bryan, Riley, and other fundamentalists typically distinguished "true science" of solidly proven "facts" from "false science" of speculative "theories" such as evolution. "The word hypothesis is a synonym used by scientists for the word guess," as Bryan liked to say. "If Darwin had described his doctrine as a guess instead of calling it an hypothesis, it would not have lived a year" (Bryan 1922, 21). In his closing statement from the Scopes trial (which the judge did not actually allow him to deliver in the courtroom), Bryan took this attitude even further: "Evolution is not truth, it is merely an hypothesis – it is millions of guesses strung together" (Larson 1997, 7). Following Bryan's death a few days after the trial, his role was filled by Harry Rimmer, a self-educated itinerant evangelist who became the most influential anti-evolutionist of the period between the world wars. In 1921, Rimmer had formed a one-man think tank called the Research Science Bureau to prove that science was compatible with biblical literalism and to advance "the harmony of true Science and the Word of God" (Numbers 2006, 78). Four years later, in the first of his more than two dozen pamphlets about science, Rimmer distinguished between "true science (which is knowledge gained and verified) and 'modern' science, which is so largely speculation and theory" (Davis 1995, 462). Common-sense realism of this sort, ultimately derived from Francis Bacon or Thomas Reid, was deeply embedded in nineteenth-century American thought (Marsden 1983). Even in the early twentieth century, the fundamentalists were hardly outliers in this respect, and they pushed the point at every opportunity. Another cartoon by Pace delivered this message quite effectively (Figure 5.3).

As Pace's images (Figures 5.1 and 5.3) also show, the fundamentalists often labeled evolution "science falsely so called," a reference to 1 Timothy 6:20 (Numbers and Thurs 2011). The same terminology had been used for centuries by numerous Christian authors in reference to diverse philosophical views, including Gnosticism, but since the early nineteenth century it has especially been applied to natural history. Samuel Miller, a Presbyterian minister from

Figure 5.3   "Leaking Badly and Headed for the Earth," Ernest James Pace. *Sunday School Times*, June 3, 1922, 334. Courtesy of Special Collections, Princeton Theological Seminary.

New York and a member of the American Philosophical Society, set the tone for many American Christians in 1803, when he described the previous century as "the age of infidel philosophy." One finds "in every age 'profane and vain babblings, and oppositions of science falsely so called.'" Never before have there been "so many deliberate and systematic attacks . . . on Revealed Religion, through the medium of pretended science," which was "pushed to an atheistical length by some who assumed the name, and gloried in the character of philosophers." Miller was especially concerned about natural history, which "has been pursued with unwearied diligence, to find evidence which should militate against the information conveyed in the Scriptures." By contrast, "every sober and well-directed inquiry into the natural history of man, and of the globe we inhabit, has been found to corroborate the Mosaic account of the Creation, the Fall, the Deluge, the Dispersion, and other important events recorded in the sacred volume" (Miller 1803, 431 and 434).

In short, false science contradicted a literal interpretation of Genesis while true science did not. The Anglican rector George Bugg expressed this perfectly in the title of a book that was published anonymously in 1826/27, *Scriptural Geology; or, Geological Phenomena Consistent Only with the Literal Interpretation of the Sacred Scriptures, Upon the Subjects of the Creation and Deluge*. Thus, for Bugg, the conclusion that the sun and stars "existed thousands of ages before the Mosaic creation" was nothing other than "*philosophy* [i.e., science] 'falsely *so called*'." Genuine philosophers, on the other hand, "know nothing about creation but what the Scriptures tell them" (1826/27, I, 136, emphasis in original). Strict literalism of this sort, in which a long prehuman natural history is flatly rejected on biblical grounds, mostly disappeared in America before the Civil War, surviving mainly among the Seventh-day Adventists and a few other groups on the fringes of Protestantism, only to be revived a century later with the rapid rise of scientific creationism.

Fundamentalists and the Age of the Earth

The fundamentalists of the 1920s fully accepted the geological ages, to such an extent that Riley could not identify a single "intelligent fundamentalist who claims that the earth was made six thousand years ago; and the Bible never taught any such thing" (Numbers 2006, 60). Geology and the Bible were usually reconciled in one of two ways. Bryan, Riley, and many others adopted the approach described as "progressive creation" by Benjamin Silliman (1829, 121), the first professor of natural history at Yale and the single most influential science educator in antebellum America. Silliman had pointed out that the fossil record harmonized pretty well with the order of events in Genesis, provided that one interpreted the six "days" of creation figuratively as references to the geological ages, culminating in the separate creation of humans on the final "day." Silliman's eminent successor at Yale, Dana, taught a similar position in the 1850s and continued to maintain a semi-creationist position on human origins even in the final edition (1894) of his *Manual of Geology*, the definitive text at the time. Dana's contemporaries Arnold Guyot, a Swiss-born glacial geologist who taught at Princeton, and John William Dawson, the leading Canadian geologist of his generation and a great admirer of Dana and Guyot, both made their scientific reputations while holding progressive creationist views. Both also influenced the fundamentalists long after their deaths – especially Dawson, whose many writings on biblical topics led him to be regarded as a champion for the scientific credibility of the Bible; his name was invoked at least 10 times in *The Fundamentals*. With regard to evolution, Dawson cautioned readers "to keep speculation in its proper place as distinct from science" and to bring "common-sense to bear on any hypothesis which may be suggested. Speculations as to origins may have some utility if they are held merely as provisional," but "they become mischievous when they are introduced into text-books and popular discourses, and are thus palmed off on the ignorant and unsuspecting for what they are not." Anyone who presents the common descent of species to a popular audience "as a proved result of science," he added, "is leaving the firm ground of nature and taking up a position which exposes him to the suspicion of being a dupe or a charlatan" (Dawson 1890, 54–55). This was music to fundamentalist ears.

An alternative approach to Genesis, known as the "gap theory," posited a long period of indeterminate duration after the original creation of the heavens and the earth "in the beginning," prior to the six days of creation, in which the fossil-bearing rocks (consisting of mainly extinct animals and plants) had been formed. All of the animals in our world today, however, were separately created in six literal days a few thousand years ago. That view had been endorsed early in the nineteenth century by the great evangelical preacher Thomas Chalmers, the first moderator of the Free Church of Scotland, and then by William Buckland, the first professor of geology at Oxford. Its leading American proponent, Edward Hitchcock of Amherst College, wrote the first textbook by an American geologist – a work that had more than 30 editions between 1840 and 1879 and included a detailed analysis of the relationship between the Bible, geology, and natural theology. English theologian G. H. Pember further popularized the gap theory in *Earth's Earliest Ages* (1876), a work that was frequently cited by fundamentalists in the twentieth century and remained in print until the 1980s.

By the early twentieth century, neither of these harmonizing schemes was still being endorsed by a scientist of the stature of Hitchcock, Dana, or Dawson, but both were mentioned favorably in the heavily annotated Bible edited by Charles I. Scofield (1909), a staunch dispensationalist. A footnote to the first verse of the Bible seemed to encourage a minimalist creationist approach: "But [only] three *creative* acts of God are recorded in this chapter: (1) the heavens and the earth, v[erse]. 1; (2) animal life, v. 21; and (3) human life, vs. 26, 27." These correspond to the three places in the creation story where the Hebrew verb *bara* ("created") is used. An identical interpretation had been suggested by Guyot in the late nineteenth century (Livingstone 1984, 78–79). The next sentence in the same note, however, all but endorses the gap theory, which postulated an enormous number of separate creations to produce the modern animals: "The first creative act refers to the dateless past, and gives scope for all the geologic ages." Further notes and subheadings added within the biblical text make it clear that Scofield preferred the gap theory, yet just as clearly he hedged his bets. A note attached to "the evening and the morning were the first day," for example, instructs readers that "The use of 'evening' and 'morning' may be held to limit 'day' to the solar day; but the frequent parabolic use of natural phenomena may warrant the conclusion that each creative 'day' was a period of time marked off by a beginning and ending."

Prior to the 1960s, fundamentalists generally reflected the ambivalence evidenced here: either view was acceptable, but the gap theory, with its literal creation "days," recent separate creation of humans, and complete rejection of biological evolution, was more popular than any other interpretation – despite the fact that Dawson had decisively rejected it on both scientific and biblical grounds. Scofield himself founded the Philadelphia School of the Bible (now Philadelphia Biblical University), and his Bible was also adopted at Moody Bible Institute (Chicago), the Bible Institute of Los Angeles (now Biola University), and several other Bible schools, soon becoming the most widely used version among fundamentalists and Pentecostals. The first academic dean of Biola and the last editor of *The Fundamentals*, the evangelist and biblical scholar Reuben A. Torrey, took Dana's course at Yale and embraced his overall attitude of harmonizing nature and scripture, but he adopted the gap theory as the best means to do so – and, like many other proponents of that view, he endorsed the old idea of pre-Adamite humans in order to accommodate fossil hominids to Genesis. However, like Scofield, he tried to have it both ways, combining elements of both views in his famous book, *Difficulties of the Bible* (1907). Rimmer, who revered his Scofield Bible, enthusiastically defended the gap view in his many publications and in a famous debate with Riley (who upheld the day-age view) from the late 1920s. Yet he, too, sometimes combined both views in flatly inconsistent ways. Despite the incoherence of their positions, Scofield, Torrey, and Rimmer were very persuasive, such that Baptist theologian Bernard Ramm observed with considerable frustration at mid-century, "the gap theory has become the standard interpretation throughout Fundamentalism, appearing in an endless stream of books, booklets, Bible studies, and periodical articles. In fact, it has become so sacrosanct with some that to question it is equivalent to tampering with Sacred Scripture or to manifest modernistic leanings" (1954, 197).

Fundamentalists, Progressive Creation, and the Rise of Young-Earth Creationism

The book in which Ramm made this point, *The Christian View of Science and Scripture* (1954), was based on lectures he had given shortly after the war at Biola, where the gap view still dominated; it is worth noting that he wrote his book right after leaving Biola for Bethel College and Seminary in St Paul, Minnesota. For many years Biola had offered a required course on "Bible and Science" based heavily on Rimmer's ideas; Rimmer had actually taught the course at least once himself, and one of his books was still being used as a text. Ramm was assigned to teach it while he was doing graduate study in the philosophy of science at the University of Southern California. Finding himself increasingly dissatisfied with the tone and content of Rimmer's book (Davis 1995, xxi–xxii), he soon stopped using it. The lectures he developed urged Christians to abandon the gap view in favor of "progressive creation" – the same term Silliman had used, although Silliman is not mentioned anywhere in the book. "*We believe that the fundamental pattern of creation is progressive creation*," he wrote (Ramm 1954, 113, emphasis in original). While researching his book, Ramm encountered "two traditions in Bible and science both stemming from the developments of the nineteenth century." On the one hand, there was "the ignoble tradition which has taken a most unwholesome attitude toward science" and relies on poor scholarship (Ramm 1954, preface). Although he offered no specific examples, Ramm must have put Rimmer and several other advocates of the gap theory in this camp, despite the fact that he had once held that view himself, having learned it from the Scofield Bible and Rimmer's works as a young Christian (Numbers 2006, 209). On the other hand, there was also "a noble tradition in Bible and science, and this is the tradition of the great evangelical Christians . . . who have taken great care to learn the facts of science and Scripture. No better example can be found than that of J. W. Dawson" and others, including Dana, Gray, and Orr. Unfortunately, Ramm noted, "the noble tradition . . . has not been the major tradition in evangelicalism in the twentieth century. Both a narrow evangelical Biblicism, and its narrow theology, buried the noble tradition" (Ramm 1954, preface).

Ramm clearly hoped to persuade conservative Protestants to abandon the gap theory, which no longer had any hope of matching the geological data, and to embrace what he called "*concordism* because it seeks a harmony of the geologic record and the days of Genesis interpreted as long periods of time." Two varieties are identified: the standard "age-day" view (as Ramm referred to it) and a "moderate concordism" in which "geology and Genesis tell in broad outline the same story," but there is no attempt to assign specific geological events to a given "day." Ramm favored the latter, while stressing that progressive creation "is not theistic evolution, which calls for creation from within with no acts *de novo*," yet he also found "a sure but slender thread of theistic evolutionists" among the evangelicals and spoke warmly of them (Ramm 1954, 211, 226, 228, and 284).

His message did not fall on deaf ears, creating quite a stir among the fundamentalists, from whom Ramm was obviously distancing himself, while eliciting praise from a 35-year-old Billy Graham. Graham was already drawing criticism from some fundamentalists for being too cozy with the emerging group of "neo-evangelicals" who were in the process of creating the magazine *Christianity Today* and launching a more open-minded type of conservative Protestantism. In that somewhat charged atmosphere, *The Christian View of Science and Scripture* helped split conservative Protestant scientists and scholars into two groups, one cautiously progressive and the other reactionary. Some of the progressives were members of the American Scientific Affiliation, an organization of Christians in the sciences that had been founded at Moody Bible Institute in 1941, with which Ramm became involved in the late 1940s. Although none of the five founding members was a theistic evolutionist and for at least two decades most members did not accept evolution, by the time Ramm found out about the ASA some influential members had begun to speak favorably about evolution or strongly against various forms of creationism at their meetings and in their journal – to the consternation of some other members.

One disgruntled ASA member, a youthful Southern Baptist engineer named Henry M. Morris who taught at Rice Institute (now Rice University) and who greatly admired Rimmer, had recently written a Rimmer-like book, *That You Might Believe* (1946), that was classified in Ramm's bibliography as a work "of limited worth due to improper spirit or lack of scientific or philosophic or biblical orientation." Morris presented the gap theory as a reasonable option, but then he immediately argued against various scientific methods for estimating the age of the earth and endorsed the traditional biblical chronology of a few thousand years; in the second edition he simply deleted the material about the gap view (Numbers 2006, 220). He also defended "flood geology," the view that the fossil-bearing rocks had been laid down not over millions of years, but all at once in the biblical flood. Morris got this idea from George McCready Price, a self-proclaimed geologist and Seventh-day Adventist who took it in turn from Ellen G. White, the nineteenth-century prophetess whose teachings lay at the core of the Adventist faith. Price had been attacking evolution and modern geology for decades, and fundamentalists regarded him as an authority on those topics – Bryan had tried unsuccessfully to bring him to Dayton as an expert witness – despite the fact that he belonged to a "sect" and lacked scientific credentials. Price's articles appeared frequently in the *Sunday School Times* and other fundamentalist periodicals, but even the *Catholic Weekly* and the prestigious *Princeton Theological Review* published pieces of his. Although the fundamentalists did not adopt Price's young earth, and did not usually adopt flood geology either, they shared his commitment to the recent creation of humans and appreciated how he had defended the historicity of the flood and undermined evolution – especially in his monumental work, *The New Geology* (1923), which Rimmer called "a masterpiece of REAL Science [that] explodes in a convincing manner some of the ancient fallacies of science falsely so called" (Davis 1995, 369). Ramm attributed Price's popularity among fundamentalists to "one reason alone – that he has stridden forth like David to meet the Goliath of modern uniformitarian geology and that even though the giant has not fallen Price has been slinging his smooth stones for more than forty years" (Ramm 1954, 182).

The popularity of Price notwithstanding, Morris's acceptance of both a young earth and flood geology was unusual for a fundamentalist in the late 1940s. Over the next quarter century, however, both views would become very widely held among fundamentalists, owing to a work he wrote collaboratively with another fundamentalist who did not appreciate Ramm's book – theologian John C. Whitcomb, Jr., of Grace Theological Seminary in Winona Lake, Indiana. Whitcomb took particular exception to Ramm's view that the flood had been local to Mesopotamia rather than geologically universal. He met Morris at an ASA meeting held on the Grace campus in 1953, when Morris gave a paper on "Biblical Evidence for a Recent Creation and Universal Deluge." Previously a defender of the gap view, Whitcomb was persuaded to change his mind. He proceeded to write a doctoral dissertation on the flood, in which he drew heavily on Price. When it was finished in 1957, Whitcomb invited Morris to co-author a book, *The Genesis Flood* (1961), which effectively launched the modern creationist movement. *The Genesis Flood* has all of the elements of what would later be called "scientific creationism" (a term that Morris liked but Whitcomb did not): the recent special creation of the universe, the earth, and living things – with apparent age in some cases; the production of the geological strata, including the fossils, in a single, worldwide flood in Noah's day; and the Fall of Adam and Eve, resulting in disease, suffering, and death through-out the animal kingdom. Still in print 50 years later, *The Genesis Flood* has sold more 300,000 copies in five languages.

When the book was received poorly by many ASA members, Morris and several of his friends broke with the ASA in 1963 and formed the Creation Research Society – an organiza-tion that requires members to accept the tenets of scientific creationism. Since then several other creationist organizations have appeared. Morris himself founded the Institute for Cre-ation Research in San Diego in 1970; it is now based in Dallas and directed by his son, John D. Morris, who has a doctorate in geological engineering. Although the ICR remains very influential, another creationist organization is probably now even more influential: Answers in Genesis (originally called Creation Science Ministries), founded in 1993 by Ken Ham, a former public-school science teacher from Queensland, Australia, for the stated purpose of "upholding the authority of the Bible from the very first verse." Based in northern Kentucky, AIG operates a large and technically impressive Creation Museum, completed in May 2007 at a cost reported to be about $27 million, that has drawn more than a million visitors in less than three years. Ham's daily radio feature is broadcast on more than 900 stations and he has appeared on major television networks, including Fox, ABC, CNN, and the BBC. The web sites owned by ICR and AIG are very large, and both organizations market printed materials and DVDs aggressively.

Fundamentalist Views Today

Fundamentalists today are heavily invested in scientific creationism. The gap view is almost extinct, the day-age view is seen as a dangerous "compromise" with biblical truth, and even "intelligent design" theory is often seen as too theologically minimalist to be acceptable. Several of the larger Christian colleges require science faculty to adhere to "young-earth" creationism, including Cedarville University (Ohio), Bob Jones University (South Carolina), and Liberty University (Virginia), whose founding president, the late Southern Baptist evan-gelist Jerry Falwell, also founded the Moral Majority. Many Christian day schools teach that creationism is the best, or even the only appropriate, option for students to consider, and the larger publishers catering to homeschoolers have the same basic approach. Although most Protestant denominations do not officially require pastors to accept creationism, in 1998 the General Assembly of the Presbyterian Church in America, a denomination formed in the 1970s by conservatives who left mainline churches in disputes over biblical inerrancy and the role of women in the church, appointed a committee to study the possibility of making a literal interpretation of the Genesis "days" an article of faith. Although the committee did not make such a recommendation, some important PCA clergy have been creationists, including the late D. James Kennedy, whose radio program had 3.5 million listeners. Theologian R. Albert Mohler, Jr., who helped orchestrate a conservative resurgence in the Southern Baptist Convention, the largest Protestant body in the United States, is strongly committed to creationism. Independent fundamentalist churches usually endorse creationism and often host conferences featuring creationist speakers or showing films produced by ICR or AIG. Many fundamentalists, seeking support for traditional morality in the midst of ongoing "culture wars," have connected evolution closely with diverse social ills. Morris went so far as to suggest that "Satan himself is the originator of the concept of evolution" (Morris 1974, 75), and Ham blames evolution for racism, pornography, abortion, euthanasia, divorce, and homosexuality – even though all of those things predate Charles Darwin by several millennia.

Ironically, many of the most influential and outspoken anti-evolutionists of the last century – people such as Bryan, Riley, Scofield, Rimmer, and Torrey – would not be allowed to teach at those colleges, prepare curricular materials for those publishers, or preach from those pulpits. Fundamentalist views about science have evolved since the 1920s. The biggest change involves the explicit rejection of the overall attitude displayed by Silliman, Dana, and Dawson. Like Augustine, John Calvin, Johannes Kepler, Francis Bacon, Galileo Galilei, and many other Christian thinkers from earlier ages, they viewed the Bible and nature as two "books" by the same author that had to agree when both were rightly interpreted. Whitcomb has called this idea the "double-revelation theory," and in a pamphlet written shortly after *The Genesis Flood* he spelled out its shortcomings. First, it "fails to give due recognition to the tremendous limitations which inhibit the scientific method when applied to the study of origins." Next, it "overlooks the insuperable scientific problems which continue to plague all naturalistic and evolutionary theories concerning the *origin* of the material universe and of living things." Finally, it "underestimates God's special revelation in Scripture" (1964, 9 and 25). Other creationists have pushed this idea much further, arguing for a sharp distinction between "operation science" (or experimental science) and "historical science." In their view, the historical sciences (such as geology, paleontology, and cosmology) are not really sciences at all, because we cannot put the development of the earth and the universe into a laboratory and repeat the process. Therefore, whenever the conclusions of the historical sciences conflict with the words of God, the only eyewitness of the creation events, we must reject the former in favor of the latter. Even the "big bang" theory, which many conservative Christian writers have seen as highly consistent with a belief in *creation ex nihilo*, is rejected by creationists as yet one more example of science falsely so called.

References

Bryan, William Jennings. 1922. *The Menace of Darwinism*. New York: Fleming H. Revell Co.
Bugg, George. 1826/27. *Scriptural Geology*. London: Hatchard & Son.

Conklin, Edwin Grant. 1953. Edwin Grant Conklin. In L. Finkelstein, ed. *Thirteen Americans: Their Spiritual Autobiographies*. New York: Institute for Religious and Social Studies, Jewish Theological Seminary of America, pp. 47–76.

Davis, Edward B. 1995. *The Antievolution Pamphlets of Harry Rimmer*. New York: Garland Publishing.

Dawson, J. William. 1890. *Modern Ideas of Evolution as Related to Revelation and Science*. London: The Religious Tract Society.

Kellogg, Vernon. 1917. *Headquarters Nights: A Record of Conversations and Experiences at the Headquarters of the German Army in France and Belgium*. Boston: The Atlantic Monthly Press.

Larson, Edward J. 1997. *Summer for the Gods: The Scopes Trial and America's Continuing Debate over Science and Religion*. New York: Basic Books.

Livingstone, David N. 1984. *Darwin's Forgotten Defenders: The Encounter between Evangelical Theology and Evolutionary Thought*. Edinburgh: Scottish Academic Press.

Marsden, George M. 1983. Creation versus Evolution: No Middle Way. *Nature*, 305(5935), pp. 571–574.

Marsden, George M. 1988. Introduction. In George M. Marsden, ed. *The Fundamentals: A Testimony to Truth*, vol. 1. New York: Garland Publishing.

Mathews, Shailer. 1936. *New Faith for Old: An Autobiography*. New York: Macmillan.

Miller, Samuel. 1803. *A Brief Retrospect of the Eighteenth Century*. New York: T. & J. Swords.

Moore, James R. 1979. *The Post-Darwinian Controversies: A Study of the Protestant Struggle to Come to Terms with Darwin in Great Britain and America, 1870–1900*. Cambridge: Cambridge University Press.

Moore, James R. 1981. *The Future of Science and Belief: Theological Views in the Twentieth Century*. Milton Keynes: Open University Press.

Morris, Henry M. 1974. *The Troubled Waters of Evolution*. San Diego: Creation-Life Publishers.

Numbers, Ronald L. 2006. *The Creationists: From Scientific Creationism to Intelligent Design*, expanded edn. Cambridge, MA: Harvard University Press.

Numbers, Ronald L. and Thurs, Daniel P. 2011. Science, Pseudoscience, and Science Falsely So-Called. In Peter Harrison, Ronald L. Numbers, and Michael H. Shank, eds. *Wrestling with Nature: From Omens to Science*. Chicago: University of Chicago Press, pp. 281–306.

Ramm, Bernard. 1954. *The Christian View of Science and Scripture*. Grand Rapids, MI: Eerdmans.

Silliman, Benjamin. 1829. *Outline of the Course of Geological Lectures Given in Yale College*. New Haven, CT: Hezekiah Howe.

Whitcomb, John C., Jr. 1964. *The Origin of the Solar System: Biblical Inerrancy and the Double-Revelation Theory*. Phillipsburg, NJ: Presbyterian and Reformed Publishing Co.

Further Reading

Davis, Edward B. 2008. Fundamentalist Cartoons, Modernist Pamphlets, and the Religious Image of Science in the Scopes Era. In C. L. Cohen and P. S. Boyer, eds. *Religion and the Culture of Print in Modern America*. Madison, WI: University of Wisconsin Press, pp. 175–198. Analyzes how fundamentalists and modernists used print media to reach wide audiences with competing religious interpretations of science during the 1920s.

Larson, Edward J. 1997. *Summer for the Gods: The Scopes Trial and America's Continuing Debate over Science and Religion*. New York: Basic Books. Awarded the Pulitzer Prize in history, this book revolutionized our understanding of this famous event.

Marsden, George M. 1980. *Fundamentalism and American Culture: The Shaping of Twentieth-Century Evangelicalism, 1870–1925*. New York: Oxford University Press. A comprehensive, insightful history of fundamentalism.

Numbers, Ronald L. 1998. *Darwinism Comes to America*. Cambridge, MA: Harvard University Press. Studies the reception of evolution by diverse groups of Americans.

Numbers, Ronald L. 2006. *The Creationists: From Scientific Creationism to Intelligent Design*, expanded edn. Cambridge, MA: Harvard University Press. The definitive history of creationism.

Porterfield, Amanda. 2006. *The Protestant Experience in America*. Westport, CT: Greenwood Press. Places scientific creationism and the Scopes trial in the context of fundamentalism, while linking fundamentalism with defenders of biblical authority in earlier years.

Whitcomb, John. C., Jr. and Morris, Henry M. 1961. *The Genesis Flood: The Biblical Record and Its Scientific Implications*. Philadelphia, PA: Presbyterian and Reformed Publishing Co. The most influential creationist book ever published.

Part II
Methodology

6

How to Relate Christian Faith and Science

MIKAEL STENMARK

Mary Midgley writes:

> It is, of course, quite widely believed that science and religion are in conflict. Many people, indeed, suppose that this battle has already been won – that science has in some sense "disproved" religion, and reigns instead of it. This is an extremely odd idea, since it has to mean that they have somewhere been competing for the same job, and it is not obvious what that job might be. (Midgley 1992, 51)

Midgley is on the right track here, because if we want to compare and understand the relationship between science and religion, or more specifically between science and Christian faith, it seems to be a very reasonable strategy to take into account *what kind of job* these highly influential enterprises of human life might do. So what kind of job is it that science and Christian faith do for people who participate in these activities?

I suggest that we analyze the kind of job that science and Christian faith (or religion more generally speaking) do in terms of the purpose or the goals of these two practices and the means that their practitioners have developed to achieve these goals. Once we have a good grip on this we are in a position to assess whether the two compete for the same job (the *competition view*), or do completely different jobs (the *independent view*), or do jobs that overlap to some extent (the *contact view*).

The Goals of Science and Christianity

Let us first back off a bit and think more generally about the human predicament. What problems do we have to deal with in life? Recall our situation. Human beings are contingent beings; we depend on other things for our existence and flourishing. We value practices that, very broadly speaking, do certain jobs for us such as the ones that keep us alive and healthy. Therefore, activities like religion and science do not exist in a vacuum. Instead, they are

The Blackwell Companion to Science and Christianity, First Edition. Edited by J. B. Stump and Alan G. Padgett.
© 2012 Blackwell Publishing Ltd. Published 2012 by Blackwell Publishing Ltd.

practiced and valued by finite beings with limited resources who, because of their constitution and environment, have certain needs.

For instance, things happen to us that we do not anticipate and that sometimes threaten our lives and wellbeing. We also need things that are not always easy to obtain, such as nutritious food, medicine, houses, bridges, and vehicles. In dealing with these things science has proved to be of great value. It enables us to control nature, and when we cannot control it, at least to predict it, or to adjust our behavior to an uncooperative world. We can say that science has a *technological goal* and we value science because it is useful and because it helps us control, predict, and alter the world. However, many scientists themselves think that science also has another goal, namely to theoretically understand the natural and social world or to obtain knowledge or at least justified belief about these states of affairs. Science not only has a technological goal but also an *epistemic goal*.

But we do not have to satisfy merely material needs to be alive and well. We also have to give attention to spiritual or existential needs. Our wellbeing thus also depends upon our ability to deal with our experiences of suffering, death, guilt, or meaninglessness (existential concerns) and we also need to know what is good for us, what we ought to strive towards and how we should treat others (moral concerns). In dealing with these phenomena, religion has proved to be of great value. It enables us to make sense out of these existential experiences, to diagnose them, and find a way through the barriers to our wellbeing, as well as telling us what our wellbeing consists in. We can say that religion has a *soteriological goal* and also a *moral goal*.

Christianity wants to help people realize that we are sinners in need of God's forgiveness and renewal and give guidance to how we should live a good life in relationship to other humans and to God. The job Christians have taken on themselves is to help people understand that God loves us and therefore wants to have something to do with us, but also that God expects certain things from us in return.

Christianity (and perhaps all other religions) thus contains at least: (a) a *diagnosis* of what the basic existential problem of human life is, (b) an understanding of what *ideal human flourishing* or "spiritual health" amounts to, and (c) a *remedy* for how this basic problem could be solved, how salvation could be obtained, or what constitutes a cure for our "spiritual illness." Religions differ insofar as their diagnoses, ideals of human flourishing, and remedies differ.

This analysis seems to suggest that there is good reason to embrace the independent view. Science and Christianity do different jobs, and therefore there is no overlap between the two practices or any competition between them. But we need them both to be able to satisfy our needs. Holmes Rolston maintains that "science is never the end of the story, because science cannot teach humans what they most need to know: the meaning of life and how to value it" (Rolston 1999, 161–162). Stephen Jay Gould thinks that we should use this model to understand science's relationship to all religions. He writes that "the net, or magisterium, of science covers the empirical realm: what is the universe made of (fact) and why does it work this way (theory). The magisterium of religion extends over questions of ultimate meaning and moral value. These two magisteria do not overlap, nor do they encompass all inquiry" (Gould 1999, 6). There are two jurisdictions and each party should keep off the other's turf.

There are at least two ways to respond to the claim that the independent view is the best way to understand the relationship between science and religion (including Christianity). One could like Edward O. Wilson maintain that science must take on also the soteriological mission. Science could and should today or in the near future replace religion, that is, the domain of science can be expanded in such a way that science might become our new religion. Traditional religions, the argument goes, have to go, but the mental processes of religious belief represent programmed predispositions whose components were incorporated into the neural apparatus of the brain through thousands of generations of genetic evolution (Wilson 1978). As such they are powerful, ineradicable, and at the center of human social life. Therefore we have to find a substitute for religion, and what could better take on this job than science?

Another response is to point out that these elements (a), (b), and (c) of religion we have identified entail assumptions about what exists. A religion therefore contains also (d) *beliefs about the constitution of reality*, that is, at least those beliefs that must be true for the diagnosis to be correct and for the ordinances to work and for a realization of ideal human flourishing to be possible. According to Christian faith, our problem is that although we have been created in the image of God we have sinned against God and the cure is that God, through Jesus Christ, provides forgiveness and restoration. But for this cure to work it appears that at least it must be true that God exists, that Jesus Christ is the son of God, that we are created in the image of God, that God is a creator, that God wants to forgive us, and that God loves us. Hence it seems as if Christianity, and not only science, has an *epistemic goal*, that is, it attempts to say something true about reality. If so, a religious practice like Christianity is meant to tell us something true about who God is, what God's intentions are, what God has done, what God values, and how we fit in when it comes to these intentions, actions, and values.

But I would like to stress that this epistemic goal is *subordinated* to the soteriological goal. The soteriological goal shapes the epistemic goal of Christianity. This is true, at least, in the sense that many Christians do not merely affirm the truth of beliefs such as that there is a God, that God is love, or that God created the world. Instead their primary aim is to have an appropriate relation to God so that they can implement the divine dimension of reality in their lives. Many Christians believe that God's revelation, although it is incomplete, gives knowledge that is adequate for believers' needs. For them it is sufficient to know what is necessary for them to live the life they must in relation to God. These believers aim at significant or important truths, truths that are useful for them in their relation to God.

Scientists have the epistemic goal of contributing to the long-term community project of understanding the natural and social world. In a similar fashion Christians may have the aim of contributing to the religious community's long-term goal of understanding God, to the extent that this is understood to be possible for beings in our predicament. Note that even though this formulation parallels that of science, it is, I think, a more controversial and slightly misleading characterization in the religious case. I suggest that this is because in Christianity, the emphasis is so much on *being* Christian, on *living* a life in the presence of God. The epistemic goal of Christian faith is shaped by the soteriological agenda. Therefore, it is perhaps more adequate to say that the epistemic goal of Christianity is to promote as much knowledge of God as is necessary for people to live a religious life successfully (knowing that God is love, that God wants to redeem us and how God redeems us, etc.).

A crucial difference, then, between the epistemic goal of Christianity and science is that in science the aim is to increase the general body of knowledge about the social and natural world, whereas in Christianity it is to increase the knowledge of each of its practitioners to such an extent that they can live a religious life successfully. To contribute to the epistemic goal of Christianity is first of all to increase, up to a certain level, the religious knowledge (say, at least to the level necessary for salvation) of as many people as possible. It is not, as in science, to move the frontiers of knowledge of nature and society forward as much as possible.

To achieve their epistemic goal, scientists work on different problems. They specialize and there is thus a division of labor. Moreover, scientists try to provide individuals belonging to different research groups with access to the data they discover and to the theories they develop. An integral part of this process is not only cooperation, but also competition among scientists, allowing and encouraging the critical scrutiny of other people's work, thus being aware that one's own work will probably receive the same treatment. Therefore scientists try to make certain that it will stand up to such an evaluation.

In religion, on the other hand, the process of critical evaluation is done in quite a different and less systematic way. The key question in this practice is whether the means (or in scientific terminology, the methods) that have been developed by the previous generations of practitioners of Christianity are still appropriate to allow contact with God, to enable its practitioners to live a Christian life successfully and to help other people become Christians. If not, these means need to be improved or even radically changed in some way.

The difference in the teleology of scientific and Christian practices also helps us understand why Christian journals look so different from those of science. But academic theological journals do not seem to differ radically from scientific ones, at least if we compare them with journals within the social sciences and the humanities. What does this mean? It means that we ought not automatically place religion on an equal footing with theology. The aim of academic theology is closer to that of science (these days perhaps a bit more modestly expressed) than that of religion, namely to increase our general body of knowledge or justified belief about religious matters.

Hence it seems to matter what activity within a religious practice we compare science with. This is because even though both religion and science are social activities performed by human beings, science is something more; it is a set of disciplines. A special training and a much higher degree of cognitive competence than that needed for taking part in religion is required to be able to take part in an enterprise like biology, physics, or psychology. In fact, many Christians claim that to be a part of their religious practice requires no special cognitive competence at all. To become a Christian is taken to be an act of faith alone. So science is a highly theoretical or intellectual enterprise for the cognitively well trained, whereas Christianity, on the other hand, is an activity in which anyone, if they like, can participate. In science, therefore, we have nothing similar to ordinary Christian believers. For this reason, it is sometimes better to compare religious practice with the practice of everyday life than with scientific practice.

Some Christians could perhaps be considered equals in this respect to the scientific practitioners, namely the theologians. Hence Christianity is an intellectual enterprise like science only in the form of theology. In this sense there is a crucial disanalogy between science and Christian faith. This means that we have to be careful when we analyze the relationship between science and Christianity and when we discuss the relationship between science and Christian theology. Or more generally speaking, religion and theology are not interchangeable activities.

Let us, with this in mind, go back to the evaluation of the independent view. Its proponents could still respond by saying that even if both science and Christianity have epistemic goals, they intend to tell us the truth about different things or about different aspects of reality, and therefore no contact or overlap is possible between these truth claims.

The problem with this response is that we cannot *a priori* know that no contact is possible but have to investigate it. Furthermore, we seem to be able identify cases where such contact actually takes place. For instance, on the one hand, the traditional Judeo-Christian view held that the first human beings, Adam and Eve, were created in the Garden of Eden. But evolutionary theory undermines the idea that there was a paradise without conflict, death, and suffering, and says that we are the descendants of earlier, prehuman beings. So the traditional doctrine of the Fall needs to be reinterpreted. On the other hand, Robert Wright says that "the idea that John Stuart Mill [and many modern social scientists after him] ridiculed – of a corrupt human nature, of 'original sin' – doesn't deserve such summary dismissal" (Wright 1996, 13). A tendency to sin, or to do evil, or to be selfish might be a fatal flaw in our nature that we cannot overcome by social engineering. Wright thinks that this is something that evolutionary psychology can confirm. Is this Christian idea then something that theories in evolutionary psychology can, at least to a limited extent, support? John T. Mullen thinks so. He argues that all but one of the versions of the doctrine of original sin that he identifies can "be rendered more epistemically probable upon the addition of evolutionary psychology to one's belief structure" (Mullen 2007, 269).

On the one hand, some scientists, such as George Gaylord Simpson and Stephen Jay Gould, seem to think that evolutionary theory implies both a meaningless universe and humanity's being the result of a purposeless and natural process that did not have us in mind. Gould writes, "*Homo sapiens* . . . ranks as a 'thing so small' in a vast universe, a wildly improbable evolutionary event, and [therefore] not the nub of universal purpose" (Gould 1999, 206). If we were to rewind the tape of life and play it again, presumably we would have animals of a sort, but nothing remotely like a human being. This idea undermines the Christian's belief that there is a purpose or meaning to the existence of the universe and to human life in particular. How could we be planned by God, if we are a wildly improbable and random evolutionary event? On the other hand, other scientists like Christian de Duve and Simon Conway Morris argue that far from being a contingent muddle, life is pervaded with directionality. Intelligent life is inevitable. Conway Morris maintains that "however many times we re-run the tape, we will still end up with much the same result" (Conway Morris 2010, 150).

Hence there seem to be good reasons to embrace the contact view – whether or not one thinks that these claims or ideas can be reconsolidated – rather than the independent view. But how much contact there is between the two depends on the concrete content of Christians' beliefs.

But what about the competition view, the idea that science and religion compete for the same job? Is there a way its advocates can respond to my argument so far? A fairly common reply would be to embrace *scientism* and maintain that only science can give us genuine (in contrast to apparent) knowledge about reality. For instance, Peter Atkins, in his argument for the limitless power of science, claims that:

> There is no reason to suppose that science cannot deal with every aspect of existence. Only the religious – among whom I include not merely the prejudiced but also the underinformed – hope that there is a dark corner of the physical Universe, or of the universe of experience, that science can never hope to illuminate. (Atkins 1995, 125)

Since the only epistemic job available is occupied by science, Christianity (or any other religion) cannot have such a job to fulfill. Science could perhaps not take over all the jobs that religion does, but in the cognitive realm there has been a competition and science is the winner. There is perhaps salvation, but no knowledge, to be found outside of science.

However, there are many problems with scientism (Stenmark 2001, 18–33). One problem that scientism faces is that science did not develop until around the seventeenth century. It is hard to say when exactly it began to emerge in its modern form, but science is certainly a newcomer in human history. So what about the people who lived before the development of the scientific method and the knowledge that this method (or rather cluster of methods) has generated since the seventeenth century? Did they not know anything at all? Scientism seems to entail that there would not have been any knowledge available before the dawn of science. Not until the discovery of the scientific method can human beings have known anything about themselves or the world around them. But is this standpoint a reasonable one? I would maintain, to the contrary, that people living say 10 000 years ago did know quite a lot about many things. Imagine a group of people sitting around the fire all those years ago in what we today call Africa. They knew that they had to eat to survive, that John (or whatever his name was) was in love with Maria, that John's parents were dead, and that there were, in the bushes nearby, dangerous animals that they should be careful to avoid. John knew that he was thinking about Bill, his brother, who was out hunting. They knew that you could trust some people but not others. They surely knew a lot of other things as well. It is true that, since the development of science, we know *more* than these earlier people did about the physical world, but my point is this: before the development of science human knowledge was available, and therefore there is no good reason to believe that only science can give us knowledge. It also follows that, even if the scientific project had never gotten underway, we would still know many things.

Moreover, there are many things which we must know before we are able to conduct any science or are able to derive any scientific knowledge. This is because scientific knowledge depends upon other sources of knowledge. One example will have to suffice: memorial knowledge. I remember that I am married to Anna and fell in love with her in 1986, and that I have been writing about scientism today. Furthermore, I do not merely believe these things, I also reckon that I *know* these things. In fact I am more certain that these things are true than that the theory of evolution or the big bang theory is true. But I do not think that the beliefs of memory can be scientifically established. Rather, to be able to develop and test a scientific hypothesis against a certain range of data, scientists have to be able to remember, for instance, the content of the hypothesis, the previous test results and, more fundamentally, that they are scientists and where their laboratories are located.

The biggest problem with scientism, though, is that it undermines itself. What methods in, for instance, biology, chemistry, or physics are suitable to show that the proposition "the only genuine kind of knowledge we can have is scientific knowledge" is true? Well, hardly those methods that make it possible for scientists to discover and explain electrons, protons, genes, survival mechanisms, and natural selection. The reason is not that the content of this belief is too small, too distant, or too far in the past for science to determine its truth value (or probability); rather, it is that beliefs of this sort are not subject to scientific investigation. The belief that only science can give us knowledge about reality is a view in the theory of knowledge and is, therefore, an issue for philosophy and not a matter for science. But if it is an issue for philosophy, we cannot know that the proposition "the only genuine kind of knowledge we can have is scientific knowledge" is true, because we would then have non-scientific knowledge. Hence scientism is self-referentially incoherent.

The contact view then seems to be the best option when it comes to understanding how science and Christian faith are related.

The Epistemologies of Science and Christianity

To what extent should the differences in goals shape the epistemologies of science and Christianity? The epistemology of religion and the epistemology of science can be defined in a similar way. I suggest that we define them, roughly, as the attempts to:

- understand and explain how belief (in science, typically, theory) formation and regulation is conducted within religion or science;
- assess whether these belief formations and regulations are acceptable and successful ways of carrying out one's cognitive affairs in these realms of human life; and, if it is not acceptable,
- propose alternative ways of conducting religious or scientific belief formation and regulation.

This could be done, for instance, in the case of Christianity by articulating the norms or standards implicit in the process by which people form, revise, and reject Christian beliefs and by critically comparing them with norms used in other human practices such as the sciences, everyday life, or politics.

Should the epistemology of religion be informed by the epistemology of science? Could there or should there in particular be contact between science and Christian faith at the epistemic level? Let me here briefly address two issues that arise when questions such as these are asked.

A number of scholars have recently argued that there is a methodological continuity between science and Christianity and it could be understood in terms of a similar explanatory model, namely *inference to the best explanation* (or what is sometimes called "abduction"). The idea is roughly that we infer what would, if true, provide the best of competing explanations of the data or evidence that is available at the time.

Philip Clayton and Steven Knapp write:

> On this view, many Christian beliefs are potential explanations: they tell why certain data that need to be explained are the way they are; they account for certain facts about human existence. When I believe them, I believe they do a better job of explaining the data than the other explanatory hypotheses of which I am aware. (Clayton and Knapp 1996, 134)

Arthur Peacocke quotes and agrees with Clayton and Knapp that the most appropriate theory of rationality for evaluating both scientific and religious beliefs is the inference to the best explanation model adapted from the philosophy of science (Peacocke 2001, 29).

The inference to the best explanation model as a theory of rationality may have its merits in a scientific context, but hardly in a religious context. This follows if I am right that the epistemic goal of religion is shaped by the soteriological one. If Christians primarily aim to have an appropriate relationship with God, then this practice is not about explaining and predicting events, but about transforming people's lives as a response to an encounter with God. The importance of belief in God for Christians lies in it being essential for salvation and to the practice of worship and prayer, and not in explaining facts about the universe and life. Since, according to my account, the key question in Christian religious practice is "How could we improve our relationship to God and make the path to salvation understandable and compelling to people who are not yet practitioners?" and not, as in scientific practice, "How could we improve our understanding of and control over events in the natural and social world?", the inference to the best explanation model is far from being an appropriate theory of religious rationality.

This does not mean, however, that the inference to the best explanation model cannot be used in theology, or be part of a strategy to convince people who do not participate that it would be reasonable for them to participate in a religious practice like Christianity. In theology, just as in any other academic discipline, the inference to the best explanation model could be used. Perhaps it also characterizes the methodology that theology, the humanities, the social sciences, and the natural sciences should have in common. In apologetics, it could be used as part of the framework within which evidence of different kind could be shown to support Christianity better than atheism or naturalism. The second option is possible if, as I have maintained, a life of worship and faith in God entails that some things must be taken to be true.

In fact it seems as if religious rationality is a different species of rationality from both scientific and theological rationality. It appears to be a kind of "agent-rationality," whereas rationality in science and theology looks more like a kind of "spectator-rationality" (these forms of rationality are defined below).

A temptation for scientists and philosophers is to treat the issue of religious rationality as a purely theoretical matter. The risk is that they will discuss the matter as if taking a stand on religious issues is not much different from making up one's mind about scientific issues. Thus Richard Dawkins tells us, "I pay religions the compliment of regarding them as scientific theories and . . . I see God as a competing explanation for facts about the universe and life" (Dawkins 1995, 46–47). On the basis of these assumptions he discusses the rationality of religion. Atkins talks about the different "styles for theistic and scientific explanations," about what science can explain and what religion cannot explain and even about the "omnicompetence of science". He comes to the conclusion that contemporary religious believers are irrational, uninformed, and weak-minded (Atkins 1995, 124, and 132).

At least two problematic assumptions are often made in this kind of reasoning about religion and rationality. First, it is presupposed that a rationally acceptable religious belief is, essentially, a belief that is justified with respect to its truth-promoting function and explanatory scope. However, since the relevant goal of religious practice is then taken to be merely epistemic, the "religious believer" whose beliefs are examined in fact turns out to be a purely epistemic being (a being whose sole concern is believing as many truths and as few falsehoods as possible). But the problem is that actual religious believers – whether Christian or not – are not purely epistemic beings, and if they were trying to be, it would be irrational for them to do so. This is because they (and all of us) are beings who live in the world. In that kind of situation they need, and therefore value, beliefs and activities that do certain jobs for them.

Second, this means also that what is at stake in religious matters is not only whether some beliefs are true or explanatory, or what conclusions we should draw regarding certain arguments, but how we actually should live our lives. It is not just a matter of making up one's mind: it is also a matter of choosing or denying a *way of living*. This choice cannot be postponed for real human beings. We must live right now, one way or another. Hence, real people are rationally justified, because of their predicament, in taking risks that the "religious believer" in much scientific and philosophical literature would not be justified in taking. So what it is rational for such a being to believe about religious matters cannot help us, since we are in a radically different situation.

But the choice of whether or not to accept a religious faith, in the kind of reasoning that Atkins and Dawkins exemplify, is essentially, if not completely, perceived as a *theoretical* choice: what conclusions should we draw, when it comes to certain arguments for or against the existence of God or something else religious practitioners believe? Are these arguments valid and sound? The paradigm for rationality is taken to be science. If we simplify somewhat, the scientific choice situation could be characterized as follows. A scientist or group of scientists tries to explain a particular phenomenon, for instance the speed of light or some fossils. They develop different hypotheses to explain this phenomenon. They carefully investigate the evidence supporting the different hypotheses. Should they accept hypothesis x or hypothesis y, or should they try to develop a third hypothesis z? The evidence is perhaps not unequivocal so they decide to postpone their decision. Instead they go home for the day or even take a vacation with the intention of deciding later about which hypothesis should be accepted.

Do these scientists behave in a rational way? Well, there are many things that point in that direction. It seems foolish to take any unnecessary risk if one has time to wait and acquire better grounds for the decision before one makes up one's mind. Scientific rationality is thus to a great extent a species of *spectator-rationality*, that is, an issue about how one as a human being should use one's cognitive resources in an intelligent way in a situation in which one is not required to make a decision immediately about what to believe or do. Instead, spectator-rationality allows one to postpone the decision to some point in the future or even withhold judgment altogether.

Could then the religious and the scientific context of choice be equated in this way? There are strong reasons to doubt that. Is not the situation such that religious practitioners must do something, choose a way of living, try to handle existentially important experiences, and deal – one way or another – with death, guilt, and alienation, and create opportunities for forgiveness, friendship, and meaning? Is it not the case that the religious quest is an *unavoidable existential matter* and not a theoretical decision that could be postponed? A question like "Should I continue or stop believing in God?" is asked by somebody who is in a situation in which he or she must act and must come to a decision. People could not postpone this kind of choice. We must live right now, one way or another. If we do not choose with our head then we choose with our feet. The choice can neither be avoided nor in reality postponed. Hence an adequate evaluation of religious rationality must take into account the fact that the people in question must do something, choose a way of living. Religious rationality is in other words essentially an example of *agent-rationality*, that is, an issue about how one as a human being should use one's cognitive resources in an intelligent way in a situation in which one must come to a decision about what to believe or what to do, and where it is impossible to postpone the decision to some point in the future or withhold judgment altogether.

What is the relevance of this difference between rationality in religious practice (theology excluded) and scientific practice? Let me take an example from a different area of life to clarify this. Suppose that one late winter day I am out fishing on the ice of the river at Vindeln. For some reason the ice cracks and I suddenly find myself on an ice floe, which is slowly dissolving. I pass by an area where the ice looks good and solid, but realize that it is doubtful whether I can jump that far without ending up in the cold water. I am forced to make a decision, and fast. Should I jump or wait for a better opportunity? The point is that we cannot give an adequate answer to this question unless we take into account that I am forced to make a decision about what to do and believe. The answer would probably be a different one if I did not have to make up my mind immediately. In such a situation the rational way to proceed would very likely be to refrain from jumping if even the smallest element of doubt existed that I would succeed and instead take my time and consider the different options I have.

In other words, it is rational in a situation in which we must come to a decision about what to believe and do, to take *risks* that we in a situation without time pressure and constraints on our freedom of action would not be entitled to. If you wait too long to make up your mind about what to do and believe, the drowning man would be dead, your marriage broken, and the job offered to somebody else. Therefore we cannot equate agent-rationality with spectator-rationality: the conditions when it is rational for someone to believe or do something are different in the two cases. Hence an adequate evaluation of religious rationality must take into account that the religious quest concerns an issue that people cannot avoid and which is urgent. As a result, an examination of religious rationality is inadequate if it does not take into account that religious practitioners must *do* something, choose a way of living. Religious rationality should not be treated as a purely theoretical matter (as if a response or resolution need not be more or less immediately practically implemented within people's lifetimes) because religious practitioners have other aims with their religious activities than epistemic ones.

In conclusion, the danger, constantly present in the science–religion exchange, is to forget that the aims of science and religion are quite different and that this has a great impact on how one should, in our particular case, understand how science and Christianity are related.

Note

I gratefully acknowledge financial support from the Swedish Research Council that made the writing of this chapter possible.

References

Atkins, Peter. 1995. The Limitless Power of Science. In John Cornwell, ed. *Nature's Imagination*. Oxford: Oxford University Press, pp. 122–132.

Clayton, Philip and Knapp, Steven. 1996. Rationality and Christian Self-Conceptions. In W. Mark Richardson and Wesley J. Wildman, eds. *Religion and Science: History, Method and Dialogue*. London: Routledge, pp. 131–142.

Conway Morris, Simon. 2010. Evolution and the Inevitability of Intelligent Life. In Peter Harrison, ed. *The Cambridge Companion to Science and Religion*. Cambridge: Cambridge University Press, pp. 148–172.

Dawkins, Richard. 1995. A Reply to Poole. *Science and Christian Belief*, 7, pp. 45–50.

Gould, Stephen Jay. 1999. *Rocks of Ages: Science and Religion in the Fullness of Life*. New York: Ballantine Books.

Midgley, Mary. 1992. *Science as Salvation: A Modern Myth and Its Meaning*. London: Routledge.

Mullen, John T. 2007. Can Evolutionary Psychology Confirm Original Sin? *Faith and Philosophy*, 24, pp. 268–283.

Peacocke, Arthur. 2001. *Paths from Science towards God*. Oxford: Oneworld.

Rolston, Holmes. 1999. *Genes, Genesis and God*. Cambridge: Cambridge University Press.

Stenmark, Mikael. 2001. *Scientism: Science, Ethics and Religion*. Aldershot: Ashgate.

Wilson, Edward O. 1978. *On Human Nature*. Cambridge, MA: Harvard University Press.

Wright, Robert. 1996. *The Moral Animal*. London: Abacus.

Further Reading

Barbour, Ian. 1997. *Religion and Science*. San Francisco, CA: HarperSanFrancisco. Of contemporary books written on science and religion, this is probably the best-known by academics in the field.

Huyssteen van, Wentzel, ed. 2003. *Encyclopedia of Science and Religion*, vols 1–2. New York: Thomson Gale. This is the first and the best encyclopedia of science and religion available.

Padgett, Alan G. 2003. *Science and the Study of God*. Grand Rapids, MI: Eerdmans. The author argues convincingly for a version of the contact view.

Stenmark, Mikael. 2004. *How to Relate Science and Religion*. Grand Rapids, MI: Eerdmans. In this book the author analyzes in depth different models of how to relate science and religion.

7

Authority

NICHOLAS RESCHER

Introduction

Alexis de Tocqueville sagely observed that:

> A principle of authority must . . . always occur, under all circumstances, in some part or other of the moral and intellectual world. . . . Thus the question is not to know whether any intellectual authority exists in an age of democracy, but simply by what standard it is to be measured. (1982, 229)

To be sure, authority is usually considered only in its socio-political dimension of communal authority, and it is generally viewed in its coercive aspect with a view to the power of some to control others. But this sort of thing is not the main subject of present concern. Rather, the sort of authority that will be at the forefront here is that which is at issue when we speak of someone as being a recognized authority in some field of endeavor – the kind of authority that is at work when we acknowledge someone as an expert with regard to some sector of thought and action.

It occasions surprise that this sort of authority is an unduly underdeveloped topic. Important though it is, alike in ordinary life, in the theory of knowledge, and in ecclesiastical affairs, there is a dearth of serious study of the topic. For example, philosophical handbooks and encyclopedias – even those that are themselves deemed authoritative – are generally silent on the subject.[1] Authority is a complex and many-sided significant issue which deserves closer examination.

Epistemic versus Practical Authority

We acknowledge someone as an authority insofar as we are prepared to accept what they say. Epistemic or cognitive authority is a matter of credibility in regard to matters of fact. By

---

The Blackwell Companion to Science and Christianity, First Edition. Edited by J. B. Stump and Alan G. Padgett.
© 2012 Blackwell Publishing Ltd. Published 2012 by Blackwell Publishing Ltd.

contrast, practical or pragmatic authority is at issue in regard to action. It is a matter of guidance not in relation to what we are *to accept or believe*, but in relation to what we are *to do*. There are, accordingly, two prime forms of authority, the cognitive and the practical, the former relating to information and the latter to action. Moreover practical authority can be either controlling or advising.

Practical authority can be exercised either persuasively or coercively. It can arise both with the question "What must I do?" and the question "What should I do?" Accordingly, practical authority can be either mandatory or advisory. But only mandatory authority can be delegated (e.g., by the captain of a ship to his first mate). With advisory authority, authoritativeness must be acknowledged by the recipient; it cannot simply be transferred by someone else's delegation.

As regards epistemic authoritativeness there are not only persons but also certain faculties which – like sight and memory – we must learn to trust (in contrast, say, to dreaming). With practical trust there is no analogy to this; self-reliance in this context is not a matter of learning to place trust in an internal *faculté directrice*. We may possibly learn to trust (or not trust) ourselves in certain matters of decision and action, but this is not a matter of coming to terms with a certain characteristic capacity of ours.

We thus acknowledge some person or source as a cognitive authority when we acknowledge their informative claims as true. Now there are basically two sorts of epistemic issues: issues of fact and issues of interpretation. "What did George Washington's Farewell Address say and where did he deliver it?" is a purely factual issue. "What was the objective of Washington's Farewell Address and what effect did it have on American policy?" involves a good deal of interpretation. Occurrence issues are in general purely factual; significance issues generally interpretational. (History usually involves an inextricable mixture of the two.) Being authoritative with respect to facts is a relatively straightforward and objective issue. Being authoritative on matters of interpretation is something more complex that turns on factors not just of information but of wisdom.

The trustworthiness of science – and of course information sources at large – generally requires a track record. But not always. For in the end, one must give trust not by evidentiation but by presumption: by treating the data of some source as acceptable provisionally until something conflicting comes to light. In epistemic matters one must at some point give unevidentiated trust – at least provisionally and presumptively – because otherwise one would be unable to evidentiate anything.

The scientific community is itself the prime arbiter of cognitive authority. Peer acknowledgment is the crux here. But practical authority is more democratic. It is evidentiated through public recognition at large.

However, authority is not something that operates across the board. It is logically and theoretically limited in scope.

Scientific Authority and Its Limits

Scientific authority has two prime aspects. First there is the issue of authority *in* science. This pivots on the expertise of individuals. But there is the issue of the authority *of* science as an enterprise. This is a matter of its capacity to resolve adequately the questions that intrigue us and the problems that confront us.

The authority of science is immense. It is grounded in the splendid success of the enterprise in matters of explanation, prediction, and the technological application. There is no (reasonable) way to deny the epistemic authoritativeness of science *in its own sphere*. But nevertheless, it is a decidedly limited authority – ardent enthusiasts to the contrary notwithstanding. For science as a human enterprise addresses issues of what is and can be in nature – of actual and potential fact. However, issues of value – not of what the facts are, but what they ideally should be – lie outside its scope and province. Accordingly science is effectively authoritative in issues of means – of how to go about getting ourselves from here to there. But matters of ends and goals – of where it is that we should endeavor to go with our efforts in this world – are issues on which the scientist speaks with no more authority than anyone else.

The Validation for Acknowledging Authority

The acknowledgment of cognitive authority must be earned. And the rationale for acknowledging authority in a given domain is at bottom uniform – it is a matter of the beneficiary's demonstrated competence in facilitating realizing the ends of the particular domain at issue. With cognitive authority there must be a demonstrated evidence of a capacity to provide credible answers to our questions. With practical authority there must analogously be a capacity to afford effective guidance.

Unfortunately, in matters of credibility authorities are all too often pitted against authorities. (Think here of Raphael's famous painting of *The School of Athens*.) How, then, is one to proceed?

Control authority can come to an individual simply by commission – by being "put in charge." But advisory authority must be earned via. And authority in cognitive matters has to be earned. Acknowledging someone's epistemic authority is a matter of trust. And with trust one risks error, misinformation, deceit. And in conceding (epistemic) authority to someone, I risk that they may be "talking through their hat." But in conceding practical authority to someone, I risk not just being wrong but actual damage, injury, misfortune to myself and others. I trust someone with respect to a practical issue. I *entrust* to them some aspect of my (or somebody's) interests and involve not just error but injury.

So why do people ever accept the authority of some person or source – why do they decide to concede it to some other person or agency?

The reality of it is that we cannot develop competence in all areas, nor can we make ourselves wise in all spheres of activity. Division of labor is inevitable here and means that we must, much of the time, entrust our own proceedings at least partially to others.

However, the acknowledgement of authority is not an end in itself – it has a functional rationale. It is rationally warranted only when it conduces to some significant good – when it serves a positive role in facilitating the realization of a better quality of life, enabling its adherents to conduct their affairs more productively and have them live as wiser, happier, and better people.

The key here is the inescapable fact of the limitedness of our personal capabilities. We simply cannot manage in this world all by ourselves. Neither in matters of cognitive know-that nor in those of practical know-how are we humans sufficiently competent as individuals. In both cases alike we concede authority to the experts because we acknowledge them to be more competent than ourselves. We resort to them because we believe them to afford a more promising path to issue-resolution than one we would contrive on our own. All this is simply a matter of common sense.

But is relying on the authority of others not simply taking "the easy way out"? Does the individual who concedes the authoritativeness of another person or agency not shirk his responsibility? By no means! In these matters of decision, responsibility cannot be offloaded. It stands to the individual like his own shadow. The individual himself is always the responsible decider. It is he who acknowledges that authority, seeks its counsel, and adopts it on this occasion. The "just following advice" excuse is even less exculpatory of responsibility than is its cognition of "just following orders."

In conceding authoritativeness to some individual or source we never leave responsibility behind. We are justified in acknowledging authority only where we ourselves have good ground for imputing authoritativeness.

But what can be the rationale of such a step? In the final analysis it is self-interest. For there is no point in ceding authority to someone for the guidance of one's own actions unless one has good reason to believe that this source has one's own best interest at heart. Conceding practical authority makes good sense only in the presence of substantial indications that acting on this source's counsel will actually conduce to our best interests.

As best one can tell, the ultimate aim of human endeavor and aspiration here on earth is to make us – individually and collectively – into wiser, better, happier people. These correspond to three fundamental sectors of our condition: the cognitive, moral, and affective. And these in turn are correlative with knowledge, action, and value, the concerns of the three prime branches of traditional philosophizing, namely epistemology ("logic" as usually conceived), ethics, and value theory (axiology). Man's overall wellbeing – *eudaimonia*, as Aristotle called it – is spanned by the factors of this range. As philosophers have stressed from antiquity onward, how we fare in regard to this trio of prime desideration – that is, in terms of wisdom, goodness, and happiness – provides the basis for rational self-contentment.

Ecclesiastical Authority

Let us now turn to the issue of specifically ecclesiastical authority and begin at the beginning here. Where does ecclesiastical authority come from? Any why is it needed?

Ecclesiastical authority roots in "the consent of the governed." Here to be authoritative is to be accepted as such. The endorsement of a faith community is the ultimate basis for ecclesiastical authority.

But why is such authority needed? If a church is to be more than a fellowship of kindred spirits (and there is, to be sure, no absolute necessity for this) it requires a coordinating manifold of doctrinal and behavioral principles. This stabilizing magisterium of principles is required to resolve disagreements, and a coordinative agent must be provided for in prioritizing to elucidate gentle suasion over firm discipline. And just here lies the locus of authority.

But just why is it that individuals should acknowledge the teaching authority ("magisterium") of his or her particular religion – at any rate in those religions that lay a claim thereto? The answer here lies in the fact that such acceptance is simply part and parcel of being a member of that particular religion. This is not the place to pursue this issue itself. (Why should one be a religious person – and indeed one of this or that particular faith?) The crucial point for present purposes is that the issue of relevant authoritativeness is automatically encompassed and resolved within this larger issue.

To be sure, if I am to put my trust in a bank or in an encyclopedia – or in a church – I must have good reason to think that they have at heart the best interests of people like me. And so if I am to be rational about conceding to a religious community in matters of faith and morals, there will have to be good grounds for thinking that its exponents and expositors have given hard and cogent thought to how matters can and should be taken to stand in the relevant range of issues.

But seeing that adopting a religion involves commitment taken "on faith" that goes beyond what rational inquiry (in its standard "scientific" form) can manage to validate, how can a rational person appropriately adhere to a religion? How can there be a cogent rationale for a faith whose doctrines encompass reason-transcending commitments?

The answer lies in the consideration that factual claims are not the crux here. For religious commitment is not a matter of historically factual correctness so much as one of life-orienting efficacy, since the sort of "belief" at issue in religion is at bottom a matter of life-orientation rather than historical information.

After all, religious narratives are by and large not historical reports but parables. The story of the Good Samaritan is paradigmatic here. From the angle of its role in Christian belief, its historical faithfulness is simply irrelevant. What it conveys is not historical reportage but an object-lesson for the conduct of life. And much of religious teaching is always just like that: a resource of life-guidance rather than one of information. Just this is the crux of the authority in relation to the "faith and morals" at issue with the putative authoritativeness of a church. What is at issue looks not to historical factuality but to parabolic cogency – the ability to provide appropriate life-orientation for us – putting people on the right track. It is a matter of achieving appropriate life-goals, realizing rational contentment (Aristotelian *eudemonia*), getting guidance in shaping a life one can look back on with rational contentment.

What, after all, is it that conscientious parents want for their children? That they be *happy* and *good*! (Some will say *rich*, but that clearly is a desideratum only insofar as it will conduce to happiness!) And so effectively when one asks for expert guidance the issue of effectiveness will have to be addressed in these terms. Thus, ultimately, the rationale for conceding authority will inhere in the consideration that in so doing we facilitate and foster the realization of those prime human desiderata. Two considerations will clearly be paramount here:

- leading satisfying lives
- becoming good people.

And on this basis what religious authority properly seeks to provide is not historical information but direction for the conduct of life.

Religion can thus be viewed in the light of a purposive venture. Insofar as it is based rationally (rather than just emotionally or simply on traditionary grounds), it is something we do for the sake of ends – making peace with our maker, our world, our fellows, and ourselves. And ample experience indicates that motivation to think and act toward the good flourishes in a community of shared values. In this context it makes sense to see as authoritative those who – as best we can tell – are in a good position to offer us effective guidance towards such life-enhancing affiliations.

So why would a rational person subscribe to the authority of a church (an "organized religion") in matters of faith and morals? Why would such an individual concede authority to those who speak or write on its behalf? Effectively for the same reason that one would concede authority in other practical matters that one deems it important to resolve, namely when (1) one recognizes one's own limitations in forming a cogent resolution; (2) one has grounds for acknowledging the potential authority as thoughtful and well informed with respect to the issues; and finally (3) one has good reason to see this authority as well intentioned. And it is clear that ecclesiastic authoritativeness can and should be appraised on this same basis.

On Christian principles, the doctrinal and remissive authority of the Church is based on biblical, revelatory, and rational considerations. The first two of these are evident. And the last is rooted in the fact that for the sake of communal unity and integrity there must be some agency.

And so, the ceding of authority is rationally appropriate where it serves effectively in the correlative range of humans ends, and it is life-enhancing in serving to make us wiser, better, happier people. And this is so with ecclesiastical authority in matters of faith and morals as much as authority of any other kind.

But is ceding authority not a gateway to disaster? What of the imams who turn faithful devotees into suicide bombers. What of cults and their deluded and abused adherents?

The point here is simply that like pretty much anything else, authority can be used and misused. The knife that cuts the bread can wound the innocent. The brick that forms the wall can smash the window. Authority too can be ceded reasonably and inappropriately. Here, as elsewhere, the possibility of abuse calls for sensible care with regard to such prospects, not for their abandonment.

Which One?

But just which religion are individuals to deem authoritative for themselves? Granted, there are always alternatives, and it seems plausible to think of them as being spread out before us as a matter of choice. But this is quite wrong. The fact of it is that in matters of religion, the issue of reasonable choice is in general not something people face prospectively by overtly deciding upon a religious affiliation. On the contrary, it is something they can and generally will do only retrospectively, in the wake of an already established commitment. And, perhaps ironically, the very fact that a commitment is already in place as a *fait accompli* itself forms a significant part of what constitutes a reason for continuing it.

At this point William James's classic distinction between live and dead options comes into play. Never – or virtually never – do people confront an open choice among alternative religions. For one thing, the realities of place and time provide limits. Homer could not have chosen to be a Buddhist. And cultural accessibility also comes into it. The Parisians of Napoleon's day could hardly become Muslims. Once one has "seen the light" and adopted a religion, one cannot but take the view that there is "one true religion." To do otherwise would be being unserious. Yet to say this is not to say that there are not alternatives. But in such matters, they are blocked by personal background and disposition. Benjamin Disraeli could hardly have become a Mormon. Authoritativeness must be something underpinned by a basis of personal experience.

How will these present deliberations about authority apply to the Church of Choice?

To exert ecclesiastical authority, an agency must secure from its catchment of co-religionists a fairly earned recognition as a reliable guide in matters of religious faith and practice. Appropriate acknowledgment in matters of ecclesiastical authority is – and must be – a matter of *free* acceptance, just as in the case with cognitive authority. And if such acceptance is to be rationally warranted, then it has to be rooted in cogent rationale.

First there has to be a determination of thematic range. The Church makes no claims to authority in matters of chemistry, numismatics, or Chinese literature, and there is no reason to attribute to it any authoritativeness in those matters.

But things stand rather differently in matters of doctrine and works. These are issues to which the doctors and theologians of the Church have given careful, devoted, and serious attention for generations, and insofar as the teaching institutions of the Church have reached a significant consensus in these matters it is only reasonable to acknowledge its teachings as reasonably based.

The Catholic Church teaches that the pope is the ultimate authority in matters of faith and morals, and holds every Catholic obliged through his faith to accept this fact. It bases this position partly on grounds of revelation and tradition and partly on ground of reason in that coherent doctrine requires an ultimate arbiter. And it teaches that the doctrinal claims of the papacy are maximal in this regard. It is thus the Church's position that in the existing circumstance the reasonable person is bound, by virtue of this very reasonableness, to see the matter in the Church's way, not because the Church is the Church, but because the Church is seriously committed to being as rational about these issues as the nature of the case permits.

At bottom, then, there is a uniform basis for the acknowledgment of authority, to wit the beneficial result of such a step in facilitating a realization of the particular enterprise at issue. With cognitive authority this relates to the accession of information; with positive authority this relates to effective action; and with ecclesiastical authority to a matter of achieving a life of spiritual content. In every dimension the crux is the realization of a significant benefit. But this rational aspect of the matter is not the whole of it.

Man does not live by reason alone. And there is no ineluctable necessity for religious commitment to require reason's seal of approval. True, from the strictly rational point of view religion exists to serve the interests of life. But other factors are at work in the good life apart from reason, factors that can lead a person to undertake commitment to a particular mode of religiosity: family tradition, social pressure, personal inclination, the impetus of one's experience, and so on. Nevertheless, religious commitment, and with it the acknowledgement of ecclesiastical authority, is rational insofar as there can be brought to bear the goal-oriented perspective of life-enhancement in the largest and most comprehensive sense of the idea.

Note

1   The only philosophical treatise on authority I know of is Bochenski 1974. Curiously, seeing that its author is a priest, the book treats ecclesiastical authority in only a single, rather perfunctory paragraph.

References

Tocqueville, Alexis de. 1982. *Democracy in America*, Modern Library College edn. New York: Random House.

Further Reading

Adorno, Theodor W., Else Frenkel-Brunswik, Daniel J. Levinson, and R. Nevitt Sanford. 1950. *The Authoritarian Personality*. New York: Harper. A psychological/sociological view of the subject.

Arendt, Hannah. 1956. Authority in the Twentieth Century. *Review of Politics*, 18, pp. 403–417. A politically oriented approach to the issues.

Bochenski, Joseph M. 1974. *Was ist Authorität?* Freiburg in Breisgau and Basel: Henden. The sole full-length study of the subject, but with only perfunctory treatment of ecclesiastical authority.

Bossuet, Jacques Bénigne. 1967. *Politique tirée des propres paroles de l'Écriture sainte*. Geneva: Droz. Classic statement of the indissoluble unity of ecclesiastical and political authority.

Macdonald, A. J. 1933. *Authority and Reason in the Early Middle Ages*. London: Oxford University Press. An informative historical study.

Peters, R. S. 1959. *Authority, Responsibility, and Education*. London: George Allen & Unwin. Surveys the history of the theory and practice of political authority.

8

Feminist Philosophies of Science
Towards a Prophetic Epistemology

LISA L. STENMARK

In *Resident Aliens*, Stanley Hauerwas (1989, 17) calls the Christian Church to task for adapting itself to the framework of a secular state. Christian theology has become largely apologetic, trying to make the Gospel credible to the modern world because the Church believed that with "an adapted and domesticated gospel," it could remain "culturally relevant." But, in making it possible for the Church to share power, it lost the ability to challenge that power. A theology of translation turns Christianity into something it is not: a set of ideas, rather than the struggle of a people to be faithful to the Gospel. This strategy of engagement has deprived the Church of its prophetic voice and it can no longer be God's presence in the world, challenge the powerful, or speak for the poor and disenfranchised.

Many of the criticisms Hauerwas raises in regard to the Church's relationship to the state are just as relevant to science. This is because the accommodationism he describes is in part attributable to the belief that the "poor old church" is stuck with a pre-scientific worldview. As a result, "when we took our first religion course in college, it was a course in how to fit the Bible into the scientific world view. We compared the archaic cosmology of Genesis to that of the true cosmology revealed by science" (Hauerwas 1989, 19). The question for Christians as we engage science should not be how to explain (or explain away) the doctrine of creation in a way that makes sense in light of current theories about the big bang, but whether and how we can engage science prophetically, as an expression of our Christian commitment to witness to the Gospel and live out a commitment to peace and justice. Unfortunately, the dominant framework for engagement between Christianity and science precludes this kind of engagement and undermines the development of a prophetic voice.

In this chapter, I will use feminist philosophies of science to explore some of the ways that the current framework for engagement between religion and science precludes constructive engagement, and suggest some of the ways that feminist philosophies of science lay the groundwork for an approach to science that allows Christians to be true to their commitments, a kind of Prophetic Epistemology. I will begin by providing some background on feminist philosophies of science, and outlining some current themes.

The Blackwell Companion to Science and Christianity, First Edition. Edited by J. B. Stump and Alan G. Padgett.
© 2012 Blackwell Publishing Ltd. Published 2012 by Blackwell Publishing Ltd.

Background

Early feminists focused on documenting women's exclusion from science and the ways that exclusion had created bias.[1] These arguments did not directly challenge the basic understanding of science as objective and value-free, claiming that the exclusion of women had undermined the ideal of scientific objectivity. But these revelations did pose a subtle challenge, because the epistemological foundation of science is the claim that something about its method did eliminate bias. Yet science had not only produced biased results, it had failed to detect and correct its own error. Building on sociologies of science, which revealed the ways that scientific theories and practices are "social" – influenced by and influencing society and culture – feminists began to likewise explore the ways the sciences "bear the mark of their collective and individual creators" who "in turn have been distinctively marked as to gender, class, race, and culture" (Harding 1986, 15). Feminists began to suspect that problems with science might go beyond mere exclusion of women and be woven into the fabric of science itself. Getting more women into science would not be enough, since the structure of science was itself an obstacle to making objective observations about the world.

Thus began a shift towards epistemology, and a rejection of dominant epistemologies which focused on propositional statements and the conditions under which it is reasonable to assume those statements accurately reflect an actual state of affairs (that is, how can I know that what I know is true?). Because ideal knowledge was free from contextual or individual bias, "S-knows-that-p" epistemologies render the particulars of "S" irrelevant; the ideal knower is an abstract, autonomous "any man" taking a "view from nowhere" and able to express a "universal, homogenous, and essential human nature that allows knowers to be substitutable for one another" (Code 1993, 16). But, as feminists painstakingly demonstrated, far from being a "view from nowhere," this ideal was a generalization from the *subjectivity* of "a small, privileged group of educated, usually prosperous, white men" who were privileged *enough* that they could generalize their experience "across the social order" (Code 1993, 21, 22). Despite being "an artifact" of a particular point of view, science was "upheld as a source of 'absolute truth' about how the world should be known and reported" (Code 1991, ix). Feminists claimed that "who knew" mattered, and that there were other valid ways of knowing.

Attempts to articulate these ways of knowing included *Women's Ways of Knowing*, an in-depth study of 135 women (Belenky *et al.* 1986), and psychologist Carol Gilligan's *In a Different Voice* (1982). Both of these described women's knowledge as rooted in relationships – to other knowers and to what was known – and utilizing an ongoing process of sharing and evaluating ideas. In determining what to believe, women relied not only on rational thought, but also on empathy, personal experience, and intuition. Within philosophies of science, Evelyn Fox Keller's work mirrored these findings. Drawing on her biography of Barbara McClintock, object relations theory, and her own experience as a physicist, Keller described women's knowledge as involving a relationship in which the knower understands herself as both related to and different from the world, granting it an independent integrity. This "dynamic objectivity" sees the difference between the self and the other as an opportunity for deeper kinship, in which "the scientist employs a form of attention to the natural world that is like one's ideal attention to the human world: it is a form of love" (Keller 1985, 117).

Concern that attempts to describe "women's knowledge" essentialized "women" led to standpoint theory, which grew out of Hegel's master/slave dialectic and Marxist thought. According to standpoint theory, persons with different social locations develop different assumptions and understandings of the world. Those on the margins have a less distorted and less partial view than the dominant position – that of "the master" – because the slave has to adopt the viewpoint of the master along with her own. To the extent that science is constructed by elites, it is necessarily distorted. Nancy Hartsock (1983) developed a feminist standpoint theory, arguing that women are marginalized in most cultures – incorporating men's perspectives along with their own – and often occupy a social location that is character-ized by greater interaction with material substances, constant change, and emotional invest-ment expressed as "caring." "Women's science" thus represents a more accurate, more objective, set of beliefs about the world.

Although standpoint theories have had a continuing impact on feminist philosophies of science, concerns that women were being essentialized remained. It became increasingly obvious that claiming *a* perspective or location for women was untenable. The category of "woman" itself reflected a particular perspective: no longer male, but still European and privileged. The emphasis shifted again, to describing not just how women are different, but to difference itself and its implications for science. This shift towards multiple differences – plurality – combined with ongoing theories about the social construction of knowledge generated multiple responses among feminists, and the present state of feminist thought is quite diverse. One might even question the term "feminist," at least to the extent that the term suggests that the main focus is a critique of gender, since gender is not the only – or often primary – locus of concern. Retaining the label "feminist" may be most valuable because it identifies the history of this line of thought (see Alcoff and Potter 1993, Introduction).

Themes in Feminist Philosophies of Science

Despite the diversity of feminist perspectives, it is still possible to speak of certain character-istic themes. This includes ongoing criticism of traditional epistemologies, and an attempt to develop alternative understandings of science as a socially embedded practice while maintain-ing its unique contribution to understanding the natural world. Women continue to critique "S-knows-that-p" epistemologies as inadequate for understanding actual knowledge practices, because their scope of justification is very narrow, applying only to "object oriented simples" which can be presented in propositions and verified by appeals to observational data, for example, "Susan knows the door is open" (Code 1993, 26). Unfortunately, underlying positiv-ist and empiricist assumptions of "S-knows-that-p" contribute to the perception that this model can be paradigmatic for all kinds of knowing. Because this model privileges science as "ideal, controlled, objective knowing at its best" science has come to be seen as "the best available route to reliable, objective knowledge . . . for everything one could want to know" (Code 1993, 17). Propositional statements and scientific approaches are thus applied to knowl-edge that differs in complexity and in kind from observational simples.

"S-knows-that-p" epistemologies are inadequate for describing the complexity of most knowledge practices because they ignore "S" and the context in which knowledge is sought. They leave "no place for analyses of the availability of knowledge, of knowledge-acquisition processes, or – above all – of the political considerations that are implicit in knowing anything more interesting than that the cup is on the table, now" (Code 1991, 266). A poor woman could, of course, know that a cup is on the table and could make that claim through her own resources. But real knowledge is far more complex, and S-knows-that-p epistemologies cannot register practical difficulties posed by such things as race, class, and gender. The problem is that "object oriented simples" are so simple and so shallow that they are hardly worth knowing.

As an alternative to models that approach scientists as isolated, value-free individuals, feminists argue that "the logical and cognitive structure of scientific inquiry" makes science a social practice. Science *depends* on a community; it is "a group endeavor in which models and theories are adopted/legitimated through critical processes involving the dynamic interplay of observational and experimental data and background assumptions" (Longino 1990, 13). "*S*" is not "nowhere," "*S*" is situated in a particular place and within a particular community. For this reason, all knowledge – scientific or otherwise – is value-laden, and attempts to be value-free are futile. More than futile, they are misguided; values are a cognitive resource, they allow us to see the world, and to organize what we see in new and creative ways.

Attempts to make science value-free are also misguided because they actually increase bias. Harding points out that science can only identify and exclude values external to science, while paradigmatic biases (held by virtually all scientists) cannot be questioned – or even seen. Those biases are entrenched, part of "how things just are" and are merely reinforced by false notions of objectivity that reject criticism as a result of ignorance or, ironically, lack of objectivity. To the extent that virtually all scientists share the same social location (i.e., privileged and male) science will share the paradigmatic assumptions of that social location; to the extent that social location is a dominant one in society, that paradigm will further marginalize those who are already marginalized, excluding their perspective, their knowledge, and their interests.

Rather than eliminating values, feminists try to incorporate them in a way that increases our knowledge of the world. Longino (1990, 216) achieves this by understanding objectivity "as a function of community practices rather than as an attitude of individual researchers towards their material or as a relation between representation and represented." Objectivity is a consequence of inquiry being a social activity that occurs in certain kinds of communities, one that incorporates certain values that Longino associates with objectivity. Successful knowledge-seeking takes place in communities where the assertions, assumptions, and hypotheses are available and understandable "to anyone with the appropriate background, education and interests" (Longino 1990, 70). There must be recognized avenues for criticism and shared standards that can be invoked by critics. The community must not merely tolerate criticism, there must be "uptake," meaning that beliefs and theories must (at least sometimes) change in response to them. Finally, objective communities exhibit an equality of intellectual authority, so that consensus is not the result of the exercise of political or economic power, but "of critical dialogue in which all relevant perspectives are represented" (Longino 1990, 76).

Instead of choosing particular values, as Longino advocates, Harding advocates seeking out diverse values. A standpoint theorist, she argues that social location impacts how we see the world, but rather than privileging any one perspective, she advocates thinking from multiple standpoints at once. Different cultures are exposed to different parts of nature and consequently develop "different patterns of knowledge and ignorance" (Harding 1998, 107). Therefore, "different local knowledge systems each have their own distinctive resources for and limitations on understanding ourselves and the natural and social worlds around us" (163). These resources – including metaphors, models, myths, and narratives – enable each culture to see their parts of the world in particular ways. Cultures are "tool boxes," each containing different "tools" for understanding nature. These "tools" generate both systematic knowledge and systematic ignorance about nature, and a single science – a single set of tools – produces less knowledge and is less accurate. Using the diverse resources of different cultures enables us to see more, revealing aspects of nature that may be difficult or even impossible to detect from within the dominant culture and perspective.

Lorraine Code suggests a third approach, claiming that knowers have an epistemic responsibility that resembles ethical responsibility. "Knowing well" means more than reliability in terms of the content of knowledge, it implies an obligation to be responsible knowers. There is "an accountability . . . of knowing subjects to the community, not just to the evidence" (Code 1993, 20). Knowing well means seeking knowledge that "fits the world of experience, is coherent with rationally established truths, and enables one to live well, both epistemically and morally" (Code 2006, 161). Epistemic responsibility implies certain values, including the willingness to seek out knowledge, the ability to be self-critical, and the ability to think beyond oneself and consider the impact that knowledge can have on a broader community and on the natural world. Because a community depends on knowers, all of whom also depend on one another, epistemic virtues also include trustworthiness and a willingness to deliberate in good faith.

There are several important implications of the feminist's emphasis on context, values, and social location. First, contrary to standard epistemologies, we are not passive onlookers (S) who merely "discover" facts and have "no choice but to believe that p, however unpalatable the findings may be," a view makes it possible to evade "the accountability that socially concerned communities have to demand of their producers of knowledge" (Code 1993, 28, 30). Knowers are actors, choosing what research to pursue, what viewpoints to seek out, and whether or not to be attentive to the needs of a community and to nature. Because human beings are not passive with respect to data, we can

> acknowledge our ability to affect the course of knowledge and fashion or favor research programs that are consistent with the values and commitments we express in the rest of our lives. From this perspective the idea of a value-free science is not just empty but pernicious. (Longino 1990, 191)

These approaches also reject universalized and standardized knowledge systems, which Code (2006, 8) likens to an "epistemological monoculture" that suppresses and chokes out "ways of knowing that depart from the stringent dictates of an exaggerated ideal of scientific knowledge making." As an alternative, feminist models are open-ended and dialogical, incorporating multiple perspectives, knowledge systems, and theories. Thus, Harding rejects the urge to integrate distinctive cultural understandings into an ideal knowledge system, as that sacrifices the advantages of simultaneously using differing conceptual schemes. Ideally, we would learn what to value in various knowledge systems, including modern sciences, learning which approaches provide the best set of maps for each particular journey. Difference and disagreement are not a challenge to certainty of knowledge, they are an invitation to further dialogue and exploration. This is not a different science, it is a science of difference, and once we give up the goal of telling "one true story" it becomes possible to embrace the permanent partiality of feminist inquiry.

This permanent partiality undercuts the temptation to stake out territory on the false stability of universals. Instead, knowledge-seeking involves creating "a clearing, an open middle ground where an inquirer can take up a position, a standpoint, within a forest of absolutes: the exigencies of objectivism, the fervor of ideology, the quietism of extreme relativism, and the legacy of universal truth – to mention only a few" (Code 1991, 317). It is a process which involves numerous fluid conversations and statements which are provisional and revisable. This may look like chaos – and it is – but only "thinkers wedded to a rigid conception of order and orthodoxy" could interpret this multiplicity "as chaotic in a derogatory sense" (318–319).

S-knows-that-*p* hides this messiness, and Code suggests that knowing people is therefore a better model, displacing the goal of knowledge as static with one that is a "more complex analysis in which knowledge claims are provisional and approximate" (Code 1991, 37). Knowing others is never fixed or complete, in part because the "who" we know is never fixed or complete. This doesn't mean that we abandon the desire to know another person, in part because while the "who" is in flux, human beings are nonetheless fixed enough "to permit references to and ongoing relationships with 'this person'" (34). Our relationships with other people do (or should) challenge our temptation to think "now I know all there is to know about her," and we can be surprised when what we thought we did know turns out to be wrong. While this analogy is not perfect, Code suggests "it is certainly no more preposterous to argue that people should know physical objects in the nuanced way that they know their friends than it is to argue that they should try to know people in the unsubtle way that they often claim to know physical objects" (37).

Later Code advocates "ecological thinking" as a way to combine notions of epistemic responsibility – the "locatedness" of knowing – and the open-endedness of knowledge. Ecological thinking takes note of epistemic complexity and is "animated by an informed attentiveness to local and more wide-ranging diversity and by a commitment to responsible ideals of citizenship and preservation of the public trust, all of which concerns are notably absent from putatively universal, a priori theories of knowledge and action" (2006, 4). Ecological models balance independence with mutual reliance, and emphasize diversity, community, relationships, and concern for the broader environment.

This open-endedness does not mean that feminists reject notions of science or objectivity or that they are (horrors!) relativists. These charges stem from a narrow view of "objectivity." The view that objectivity is independent of context, static, and unchanging leads feminists to be called relativists, because their epistemologies are contextual, open-ended, and dialogical. Far from being relativists, most feminists argue the opposite: women's perceptions of reality are not matters of opinion, they are real. Feminists are not relativists, because the facts are on our side and we must know the world to create a more just society. The second reason for the confusion is that standard objectivities require a value-free view from nowhere. When feminists observe that it is not possible to *be* nowhere, they are accused of rejecting objectivity. I would characterize the feminist position as "given that it is impossible to be nowhere, and given that it is impossible to be value-free, how is objectivity possible?" Feminists do not reject objectivity, they argue that by understanding scientific inquiry as what it *is* – value-laden and communal – instead of what we wish it to be, we can be *more* objective.

Further, feminists do accept that there are constraints on truth claims. Longino suggests that these constraints include the rest of the community, along with nature and logic (Longino 1990, 215). Code also acknowledges the world's intractability to wishful thinking: "Earthquakes, trees, disease, attitudes, and social arrangements are *there*, requiring different kinds of reaction and (sometimes) intervention" (Code 1993, 21). Rather than describing knowledge as either subjective or objective, feminists depict it as an interaction between subjectivity and objectivity. We do construct reality, but "the construction process is constrained by a reality that is recalcitrant to inattentive or whimsical structuring" (Code 1991, 255). More to the point, feminists tend to avoid abstract arguments about "how do we know that we know what we know" in favor of practical concerns about how that knowledge fits into broader commitments to justice and care for the earth.

Christianity and Feminist Philosophies of Science

The first contribution that feminist philosophies of science make is to remind us that Christians cannot develop a prophetic voice as long as we operate out of the same paradigm as the science we need to critique. Whether considering biology or describing sin, when virtually everyone involved in the conversation has the same social location – whatever that location is – there will be blind spots. To the extent that the conversation between Christianity and science, particularly in academia, is dominated by men from a privileged socio-economic location, our vision will be distorted. But there is a more subtle caution contained in the feminist assertion that social location and paradigmatic values distort perception, and one that resonates with Stanley Hauerwas's concerns about the Church's involvement with the state, because social location encompasses more than race, more than gender, and more than class. Western science and contemporary Western Christianity share a social location that is rooted in the European Enlightenment – even the assumed boundary between religion and science reflects this. We must be attentive to the ways that we have internalized the scientific bias of modern culture, and thus be attentive to the temptation to conform our faith to science. We should not universalize points of agreement between Christianity and science, and acknowledge that rather than being cause for confidence, these areas of agreement should be a cause for suspicion, as they may merely reflect the particular perspective of our shared culture.

These shared paradigmatic values restrict our vision with regard to science, hindering the development of a prophetic voice. As an example, several years ago at a science and religion conference a prominent presenter said to me that aging and death represented the greatest tragedy of human existence, a challenge that Christian thought had to address. This struck me as odd, since I suspect that for much of the world's population (and for much of human history), growing old and then dying would be a blessing. At a different conference, a presenter kept referring to aging genes as "abnormal," which again seemed odd since there is nothing more normal than aging. His response to my observation was that, from the perspective of genetics, aging was abnormal (as though that made it OK) and that the term reflected no value judgment (as though language had no impact on our perception).

I am not saying either position is "wrong," merely that they are a *particular* right, reflecting a *particular* perspective and that universalizing them blinds us to their implications and makes it difficult to challenge their assumptions. From the perspective of, for example, a poor Salvadoran woman, the destruction and patenting of indigenous crops and the conversion of fields from food crops to commodities with the resulting deforestation and poverty might represent a greater tragedy, and one which Christian thought had to address. Her perspective might cause us to reflect on the history of the way scientific theories and "neutral" language have contributed to racism, sexism, and classism and what it might mean that poor, largely non-Western people who could not afford expensive gene therapies would thus age "abnormally."

Developing a prophetic voice means more than simply getting more "marginalized" people into the room. It means actively seeking out alternate perspectives – whatever those perspectives might be – and giving voice to and speaking for the voiceless. It means constantly challenging dominant perspectives about the world. It means more than merely acknowledging these other perspectives, more than an occasional paper or panel from the perspective of "others." An objective community does not merely tolerate and provide avenues for criticism, there must be "uptake" of criticism: things must, at least sometimes, change in response. The challenge is analogous to the challenge of creating more diversity among Christian churches (still the most segregated hour in America). In seminary, I asked J. Alfred Smith, the Pastor of Allan Temple Baptist Church in Oakland, what he thought Lutherans could do to involve more African Americans. His response – only somewhat facetiously – was, "Are you willing to change your liturgy?" If Christians really want to engage science in a way that allows us to be Christian, we have to do more than want more diversity in the conversation. We have to be ready to change our liturgy.

Changing the Liturgy

Hauerwas (1989, 21) argues that Christianity is "not a presentation of basic ideas about God, world and humanity, but an invitation to join up, to become part of a movement, a people." And yet, the relationship between Christianity and the sciences tends to focus on propositional statements, comparing theological doctrine with scientific theories and discoveries (a "doctrines and discoveries" approach). Hauerwas argues that reducing Christianity to propositional statements distorts Christianity, can lead to an idolatrous affirmation of finitude, and undermines our ability to be prophetic. Feminist philosophies reveal the ways that an emphasis on doctrines and discoveries has a similar effect. First, this approach makes it tempting to use scientific "facts" to bolster Christian beliefs. Even when we acknowledge that science is provisional, that paradigms change, or that science is not "true" but merely "not yet falsified," S-knows-that-p is connected to a paradigm in which "Science has proved" carries "an immediate presumption of truth" (Code 1993, 18). The underlying positivism of S-knows-that-p creates the perception that scientific statements can provide a universal or absolute foundation for faith, and it is tempting to piggyback on this certainty, to claim it is possible for our faith to be unambiguous. This is, of course, idolatry. Christian thought is by nature frustratingly partial and ambiguous, but the very framework of a "doctrines and discoveries" comparison tempts us to be more certain than we have a right to be. Ultimately, a triumphalist faith in science is at odds with the Christian assertions that human life and human perspectives are always partial and provisional.

In addition to this theological concern about the positivist and empiricist underpinnings of S-knows-that-p – and thus of doctrines and discoveries – this framework inherently favors scientific pronouncements, putting Christian commitments in the position of merely responding to science (as long as that response is not a real challenge). S-knows-that-p assumes a detached objectivity that requires an independent (although often not acknowledged) ground of justification. When Christianity and science conflict, Christianity grounds its claims in Scripture and, perhaps, some form of revelation, which are "particular." Of course, scientific perspectives are also particular, but that particularity is obscured by the fiction of the neutral observer. Because S-knows-that-p disguises the particularity of science, it makes science seem neutral and objective. In this framework, scientific discoveries will always challenge and change religious doctrines, while scientific theories will rarely, if ever, be likewise challenged or even problematized by religious doctrines. If you doubt this, try to imagine saying to a scientist, "I'm sorry, I can't agree with you because that violates my religious beliefs" without being accused of being ignorant or narrow-minded.

Ultimately, an emphasis on truth claims leaves only two avenues for Christian thought: natural theology, in which the objective truths of science become the source of reflection, or ethics, in which Christians suggest what we can or can't do with scientific discoveries. While there is nothing inherently wrong with either position, both are problematic in that they preclude real dialogue by subordinating Christian faith to scientific theory. With Hauerwas, feminist epistemologies point out that in our quest to share "power" with science, we have lost our ability to threaten or even challenge the powerful.

Feminist epistemologies suggest a way to change the liturgy. Unlike S-knows-that-p, feminist epistemologies are provisional and open-ended, making them more affirming of the partial and ambiguous nature of Christian knowledge, in which we can never say "now we know all there is to know." This is a provisional approach to knowledge in which knowing is part of the human project, and thus real knowledge is possible, but difficult and never complete. Further, the feminist assertion that values matter and are an integral aspect of how we come to know creates a place at the table for Christian convictions. This is in part because Christianity contains within it long, historical conversations spanning widely divergent cultures and their speculations about nature and our relationship to it; Christians can provide valuable resources for knowledge-seeking. As long as the Christians at the table represent the diversity of Christianity, we can think from the standpoint of many different lives, contributing to a coherent, but constantly changing view.

Ultimately, feminists like Code suggest that the most important contribution Christians can make is to model what it means to be an epistemically responsible community, one that is not just attentive to the "facts" but that enables us to live well. In Hauerwas's terms, this does not mean being an activist Church (trying to change the world) or a conversionist Church (trying to change individuals), it means being a confessing Church: living in a community that conforms to the Gospel in all things. Christians are *supposed* to know a lot about what it means to live well, and this is what we need to model in our conversation with science. This is not a one-sided conversation, it is more in line with the territory mapped by feminists, the "middle ground," surrounded by those who cling to and seek certainty and absolutes, but never succumbing and, instead, living our life in a community that can live in uncertainty because of our faith.

Towards a Prophetic Epistemology

In conclusion, I would like to briefly suggest several trajectories within contemporary Christian theology that would be helpful for incorporating the insights of feminist philosophies into a more prophetic epistemology. One trajectory is process thought, and feminist theologians have been exploring this connection for over 30 years (see, e.g., Davaney 1981; Howell 2000). Narrative theologies are also helpful, in part because of resonances with process thought (Stenmark 2006b) and in part because narrative approaches encompass the open-ended and praxis-oriented middle ground of feminist thought (Stenmark 2006a). The connection to the post-liberal narrative thought of, for example, Stanley Hauerwas should be clear, and to that I would add the new crop of public theologies, including Jeffrey Stout. These trajectories do more than make metaphysical and doctrinal contributions – more doctrines and discoveries! – and each can help develop epistemological, ethical, and methodological alternatives for Christians in the engagement with science.

One additional resonance is suggested by a feminist emphasis on knowledge of persons as central for understanding knowledge, which makes knowledge of God paradigmatic for all knowledge. Charles Mathewes offers a clue as to how this might look in his comments on Augustinian epistemology. For Augustine, of course, we know the created world through our relationship to the God who creates the world. This approach begins with the assertion that we are created as fully part of creation, so that our knowledge is genuine, if muddled. There is a facticity that is beyond human control, but the mind also creates ideas beyond external influence. The mind is not a Cartesian "nowhere," it is connected to an external reality, but we also influence the conditions that produce belief, and are responsible for those conditions. It is God who connects these two poles of knowledge suggested by the feminist middle path: we know the world (objectivity) because we know God (subjectivity) (Mathewes 2007, 50). Not incidentally, Mathewes develops this epistemology in the context of an Augustinian public theology, in which knowledge is an expression of our faithfulness to God and a reflection of the ways in which knowledge is part of our responsibility to the community and the world. Mathewes suggests that an Augustinian epistemology would be relational, situated, responsible, and communal. Sounds a lot like feminism.

Note

1   While this chapter focuses largely on philosophies of science, feminist perspectives on science come from a number of disciplines, including the natural and social sciences, sociology, history, and anthropology.

References

Alcoff, Linda and Potter, Elizabeth, eds. 1993. *Feminist Epistemologies*. New York: Routledge.

Belenky, Mary Field, Clinchy, Blythe McVicker, Goldberger, Nancy Rule, and Tarrule, Jill Mattuck. 1986. *Women's Ways of Knowing: The Development of Self, Voice, and Mind*. New York: Basic Books.

Code, Lorraine. 1991. *What Can She Know? Feminist Theory and Construction of Knowledge*. Ithaca, NY: Cornell University Press.

Code, Lorraine. 1993. Taking Subjectivity into Account. In Linda Alcoff and Elizabeth Potter, eds. *Feminist Epistemologies*. London: Routledge, pp. 15–47.

Code, Lorraine. 2006. *Ecological Thinking: The Politics of Epistemic Location*. New York: Oxford University Press.

Davaney, Sheila Greeve, ed. 1981. *Feminism and Process Thought*. New York: Edwin Mellen Press.

Gilligan, Carol. 1982. *In a Different Voice: Psychological Theory and Women's Development*. Cambridge, MA: Harvard University Press.

Harding, Sandra. 1986. *The Science Question in Feminism*. Ithaca, NY: Cornell University Press.

Harding, Sandra. 1998. *Is Science Multi-Cultural? Postcolonialisms, Feminisms, and Epistemologies*. Bloomington, IN: Indiana University Press.

Hartsock, Nancy. 1983. The Feminist Standpoint: Developing the Ground for a Specifically Feminist Historical Materialism. In Sandra Harding and Merril B. Hintikka, eds. *Discovering Reality, Feminist Perspectives on Epistemology, Metaphysics, Method and Philosophy of Science*. Dordrecht: Kluwer Academic Publishers, pp. 283–310.

Hauerwas, Stanley. 1989. *Resident Aliens*. Nashville: Abingdon Press.

Howell, Nancy R. 2000. *A Feminist Cosmology: Ecology, Solidarity, and Metaphysics*. Amherst, NY: Humanity Books.

Keller, Evelyn Fox. 1985. *Reflections on Gender and Science*. New Haven, NJ: Yale University Press.

Longino, Helen. 1990. *Science as Social Knowledge*. Princeton, NJ: Princeton University Press.

Mathewes, Charles. 2007. *A Theology of Public Life*. New York: Cambridge University Press.

Stenmark, Lisa L. 2006a. Going Public: Feminist Epistemologies, Hannah Arendt, and the Science and Religion Discourse. In Philip Clayton and Zachary Simpson, eds. *The Oxford Handbook of Religion and Science*. New York: Oxford University Press, pp. 821–835.

Stenmark, Lisa L. 2006b. Story, Forgiveness, and Promise: Narrative Contributions to a Feminist Cosmology. In Paul O. Ingram, ed. *Constructing A Feminist Cosmology*. Eugene, OR: Pickwick Publications, pp. 37–55.

Further Reading

Alcoff, Linda and Potter, Elizabeth, eds. 1993. *Feminist Epistemologies*. New York: Routledge. A good collection of essays from a variety of feminist perspectives, including excellent pieces by Code, Harding, and Longino.

Bleier, Ruth. 1984. *Science and Gender: A Critique of Biology and Its Theories on Women*. Elmsford, NY: Pergamon. Bleier focuses on the ways scientific theory defends the status quo, and how biology was used to support claims of women's inferiority, such as that they are naturally subordinate.

Kahle, Jane Butler, ed. 1985. *Women in Science*. Philadelphia, PA: Falmer Press. Discusses the history and current situation of women in science, describing obstacles women face in a variety of fields.

Keller, Evelyn Fox. 1992. *Secrets of Life, Secrets of Death: Essays in Language, Gender and Science*. New York: Routledge. A collection of essays that explores the masculine psychodynamics of science.

Nelson, Lynn Hankinson. 1990. *Who Knows: From Quine to a Feminist Empiricism*. Philadelphia, PA: Temple University Press. Uses W. V. O. Quine's non-foundationalist approach to develop a feminist empiricism to give an account of the nature of science.

Tuana, Nancy, ed. 1989. *Feminism and Science*. Bloomington, IN: Indiana University Press. An important volume for early work in feminist theory on science.

Tuana, Nancy and Morgan, Sandra, ed. 2001. *Engendering Rationalities*. Albany, NY: State University of New York Press. More than an update of the earlier volume, includes several important works and suggests how quickly the depth and range of feminist theorizing on science expanded.

9

Practical Objectivity
Keeping Natural Science Natural

ALAN G. PADGETT

Should natural science go natural (so to speak) or is there room in a properly natural science for kinds of explanation other than natural ones? Is there room in a properly natural science for appeal to intelligent agency, for example?[1] This is the key question of our chapter, and it will take us some way into the philosophy of science and the relationship between science and Christian faith. I will argue that the natural sciences should stay natural, but this is a contingent and practical conclusion. We are neither putting forward some kind of essential and necessary definition, nor creating a clear and distinct "line of demarcation" that separates science from all other kinds of human knowing. Rather, I will argue that like all academic disciplines, the natural sciences embody a human, traditional, and communal form of inquiry. Because of the importance of their traditional values, practices, methods, and explanatory focus – which have pushed back the darkness for centuries and illuminated powerfully the nature of nature – the natural sciences should keep to their proven methods unless and until a very significant and powerful combination of evidence and reason forces a major change. We might say that by long practice and tradition, the natural sciences have a "nature-bias" which has proved highly successful in yielding objective knowledge about natural things. In this chapter I will introduce the notion of "practical objectivity" and a natural explanatory focus, setting these practical, traditional, and contingent concerns between advocates of methodological naturalism in natural science, and those who press for microdesign theory in biology ("intelligent design").

As we examine this intersection of ideas, other topics will have to be briefly introduced, but the focus of our chapter will remain upon the question we opened with: should natural science stay natural?

Science and Rationality as Human Practices

Philosophy of science in the twenty-first century has been deeply influenced by moves in the mid-twentieth century which connected the logic of science more closely to the actual

The Blackwell Companion to Science and Christianity, First Edition. Edited by J. B. Stump and Alan G. Padgett.
© 2012 Blackwell Publishing Ltd. Published 2012 by Blackwell Publishing Ltd.

practices of science: to its history, community, and humanity. Pierre Duhem (1954 [1906]) and the later Wittgenstein (1955) were particularly influential in this move, especially as Wittgenstein's insights were adapted and developed by N. R. Hanson (1958), and most famously by Thomas Kuhn (1962). A key element of this perspective in the history and philosophy of science is that sciences are seen as practical, human activities with an associated rationality or methodology which is grounded in a particular research program (Lakatos) or paradigm (Kuhn). Such a philosophy of science moves beyond a purely logical analysis of language, à la Wittgenstein in the *Tractatus* (Wittgenstein 1922), to seeing science and its rationality as embedded in a human community with a specific, traditional methodology and set of epistemic values which guide its quest for objective knowledge (i.e., knowledge of the object it studies). For example, in developing his own form of "post-critical philosophy" the scientist-philosopher Michael Polanyi argued that scientific knowledge is "personal knowledge" but with a universal, objective intent (Polanyi 1958, 396).

But since a science is a human practice, with its own epistemological values and methods which are contingently constructed, what about objectivity? Given this view of science as a fully human activity, can science be truly objective? There has been a massive debate on this topic by many important philosophers in the last century. Any attempt to summarize this debate would take us far off our current course and purpose. While no consensus has emerged in the history and philosophy of science concerning these important questions, a few broadly received principles will be all we need for our purposes here (see further Padgett 2003).

The notion of a value-free science has largely been replaced by a greater appreciation for the fact that all the academic disciplines or sciences are in fact *human practices* which take place within *established traditions of inquiry* (Lakatos and Musgrave 1978; MacIntyre 2006, I.3–23). To learn a natural or human science is not simply to be trained in pure *a priori* logical reasoning or in universal axiomatic systems of deductive truth, but is closer to being apprenticed into a valuable skill which requires mentoring into a community of experts, a way of thinking, an angle of vision, and a specific labor. A student of any specialized science is thus inducted into a community of truth-seeking fellow scientists, whose reasoning is shaped by that tradition of inquiry. No science is without presuppositions and important values that shape its methodology, or if you like, its rationality (McMullin 1982). The epistemological values which are embedded in the contingent, historical, and humanly constructed sciences (academic disciplines) are not pure noetic truths – at least, most of them are not – yet with successful and fruitful sciences they should be given *prima facie* epistemic warrant unless there is some reason to doubt them. So the specific sciences are best understood as using both formal and informal logics.

It was in proposing a solution to Hume's famous skeptical argument against induction that the following principles came to be important in thinking about the rationality of science, and especially informal reasoning. Following Thomas Reid's response to Hume, I conclude that the principles of informal logic are fallible and open to revision; based upon a tradition of reasoning; multiform and diverse, and applied somewhat differently in different sciences and other academic disciplines (Padgett 2003, 167–194). What counts as a beautiful solution in mathematics is one guide to a good answer to a problem, yet what counts as a beautiful solution in chemistry is quite different. In both a kind of rational elegance is seen as a kind of guide to a good answer, but what counts as elegant in these disciplines is distinct. The importance of these broad conclusions about informal reasoning will soon become apparent as we continue our discussion of natural science.

It turns out, therefore, that the nineteenth-century dream of a pure logical rationality, a scientific thinking that was value-free and based upon reason and evidence alone, has been overturned. There is no "view from nowhere" for a genuinely human epistemology (Nagel 1986). While there is thus no perfectly neutral and value-free rationality, the alternative is not the oft-feared relativism of "anything goes." Rather, a modest objectivity which sees objective truth of a certain kind as a communal goal and a practice within a tradition of inquiry, and thus engages in careful and rigorous attention *to the object of study*, is a reasonable and appropriate expectation in the natural sciences. Let us call this a "practical objectivity." As opposed to the dream of a value-free and purely logical science, this kind of objectivity is a normal part of the sciences, and does not fall into the troubles that the earlier Enlightenment exaggeration of rationality in science did (and still does). Even though the sciences represent value-laden methodologies, because of the long history of success in gaining truth about their objects of study, the values, methods, and practices embedded in scientific communities nevertheless warrant our epistemological respect.

Epistemological respect is a form of rational trust. While the principles of reason used in a particular and mature science are not absolute, *a priori* truths, we make a mistake in doubting them unless there are good reasons to do so. What is more, the smart thing to do is adopt them when investigating their area of expertise, unless significant reasons cause us to doubt one specific principle or its proper application. This general principle applies to the case at hand: should we doubt the nature-bias of the natural sciences today?

Practical Objectivity and Explanatory Focus

So what is practical about objectivity, and what does that have to do with scientific reasoning? What I am calling practical objectivity is one of those contingent values found in the tradition of any robust natural science. The sciences arose historically as ways of seeking knowledge about the world, and specialized as their range of interest grew more focused (among many sources, see Lindberg 1992; Butterfield 1953). Objectivity in science is "practical" in that it seeks objective knowledge of the things being studied. One of the goals of a science is to discover truth about some object, some element of the world. For example, economics studies monetary systems, while chemistry studies molecules (among other things). The practical objectivity of chemistry, therefore, just is the set of values, practices, and beliefs which the scientists learn in order to be good chemists, and thus to discover new things or criticize received theories about the structure and makeup of physical elements and their reactions.

In his *In Defense of Objectivity*, the philosopher Andrew Collier sets forth three definitions of objectivity. The first sense is "what is true independently of any subject judging it to be true" (Collier 2003, 134). The second sense is that in which human judgments are said to be objective, that is, the knowing subject is causally open to the influence of the object in making a truth claim or judgment (135). But the third sense is that of a "human attitude," in which one is trying to make one's beliefs and values objectively true in the second sense of the word. It is this third sense, objectivity as a human attitude or goal, which we can expand into the idea of a practical objectivity (137). And for the sciences, what we need to notice is that we are not talking about the practical objectivity of a single knower, but of a truth-seeking community and tradition.

The first aspect of keeping natural sciences natural, then, is not very controversial. In its practices and values, a natural science seeks objective knowledge about natural objects, their structure, powers, and interactions. While economics is a science, therefore, it is not a *natural* science, because financial systems are human creations and involve the study of human socie-ties – thus economics is a social or human science. Geology, on the other hand, is a natural science which studies the earth.

Somewhat more controversial is the claim that a natural science should explain things and events using *natural explanations*. Let us call the type of explanations used in any academic discipline its "explanatory focus." Mature and successful sciences (and similar academic, explanatory disciplines) explain things and events using standard, accepted models and pat-terns of explanation which have proved successful in the past. In mathematics, for example, the truth of a formula can be proved using the explanatory focus of that discipline, namely, mathematical proof. If I want to know not only if but *why* a right triangle can never be equi-lateral, a geometrical proof of this can be given. This truth about the right triangle can be explained using the explanatory focus of geometry, as this has developed in the history of mathematics. When we turn to natural sciences, there exists a long tradition in which the explanatory focus of a natural science like astronomy limits itself to natural explanations. In other words, the explanatory focus of the natural sciences upon natural explanations is also part of their practical objectivity. Human purposeful activity, of course, can and does affect the outcome of an experiment in astronomy or any natural science – but this invalidates the results. The data are then considered "corrupt." The idea in the natural sciences seems to be to understand how things work in the natural world by themselves, so to speak, without human interference. This second part of keeping natural science natural is a bit more con-troversial. To see why we need to briefly discuss "methodological naturalism" and "intelligent design."

Methodological Naturalism and Informal Reasoning

What we have been calling the nature-bias and practical objectivity of the natural sciences is generally called today "methodological naturalism." The ideas are somewhat similar, but the terminology is quite different. I find that both defenders and critics of so-called "methodologi-cal naturalism" are often led astray by their terminology. The debate all too easily switches from philosophy of science to full-blown philosophical naturalism. The term itself is objec-tionable. The nature-bias of the natural sciences is best left completely separate from any notion of "naturalism." It seems that the first published use of this phrase in the sense we are discussing was by the philosopher Paul deVries, in an article entitled "Naturalism in the Natural Sciences" (deVries 1986). Even though deVries does distinguish between two types of naturalism (methodological and full-blown philosophical), the main problem is with calling the nature-bias of natural science an "ism" as if it were some version of naturalism – which it is not. The practical nature-bias of the natural sciences which we have been discuss-ing in this chapter has nothing in fact to do with a full-blown ontology as a philosophical worldview. The discussion of this term since then shows that it is all too easy to turn "meth-odological naturalism" into some kind of worldview, or to think that it is a strict and delimit-ing methodology of some kind (Plantinga 1996). Both of these misunderstand what is no more than a contingent tradition and rational bias, rather than a "methodology" in any proper sense of the word. It is just too easy to think of methodological naturalism as simply acting in the practice of science *as if* naturalism (full-blown) were true: a highly dubious way of describing the practical objectivity of the natural sciences. Because of the serious confusions and problems with this proposed terminology from deVries in 1986, I suggest we eliminate the term, while keeping the practical observation of how natural sciences are in fact practiced, including the tradition of nature-bias. Like any tradition, it is in fact open to revision in the light of new evidence. And this point leads to a consideration of the so-called "intelligent design" proposal.

What we have called an explanatory focus and a practical objectivity are key elements in the traditions of inquiry that we call "scientific," or indeed in any of the academic disciplines. What is more, as we argued previously the natural sciences use a great deal of *informal logic* in going about the testing of theories and models, and in coming up with new ones. Both of these points will be important in considering the recent debate about intelligent design.

Despite the attempt of Karl Popper to develop a logic of scientific discovery that avoided informal reasoning (he accepted Hume's skepticism regarding the problem of induction), I find the best way forward is simply to reject Hume's rejection. Popper's philosophy of science, based upon deductive logic, is not so much false as it is limited or incomplete, just because informal thinking is so much a part of scientific reasoning from the evidence. As noted above, in defending the rationality of informal reasoning, I concluded that the principles of informal logic are fallible and open to revision, based upon a tradition of reasoning, multiform and diverse, and applied differently in different sciences and other academic disciplines. Thus this set of diverse principles must be rigorously distinguished from the system of formal and symbolic logic which has been so brilliantly developed since the nineteenth century. Once we make clear such a distinction, the so-called "problem" of induction dissipates, since the conclusion of an informal argument simply cannot be logically certain or necessary (and this conclusion *is* logically necessary!). Informal reasoning is more open than formal logic, and involves personal judgment, as well as commonly accepted principles, procedures, and evidence. Thus room exists for the deepest values and commitments of an individual researcher to shape and be shaped by the more focused and narrow discoveries and values of her particular expertise. This final point cannot be emphasized enough in the context of our present question, where issues of faith, reason, values, and rationality loom large. Sure, no discipline as a whole will share all the values of a particular scholar, but there is room for the larger worldview of a particular scholar to influence the *way* those methods and rationalities are used in the service of science. There is room in the open practice of scientific reasoning for our personal perspectives and presuppositions to rationally influence informal scientific thinking *for the individual scientist*. This is what Robert J. Russell and I mean, in part, by the "mutuality" of theology and science (Padgett 2003; Russell 2008). Larger commitments and accepted truths are bound to influence the rational investigator at the boundaries and edges of their scientific pursuits, just because a rational person will allow other truths to influence things like theory choice among otherwise equally good theories (equally good on the evidence at hand, that is).

This does not mean that our worldviews should overwhelm the evidence. Of course more basic and central epistemological values (like fit with data or coherence) can and should overrule such background commitments when there is a clearly demonstrable truth or best theory to be had – but at the growing edges of a science (among other places) such demonstrable truth is usually not available. Indeed, the very fact that the scientific discipline is "growing" in that area just means that new theories are open for consideration. The scientist is, in such situations, perfectly rational in allowing her worldview to influence areas where one looks for new discoveries, or one's best hunch as to which theory among currently disputed ones may win out over the long run.

To see this clearly it is important to make two distinctions. First we have to distinguish between the rational commitments and methods *of a whole tradition and community*, and the necessarily larger set of beliefs, values, and knowledge *of individual experts in that science*. This is simply the difference between a science and a scientist. In other words, we have to distinguish between the individual scientist and the larger community of scholars, classic texts, accepted paradigms, and practices which make up the specific science as a whole. Second, we have to distinguish between two ways in which larger truths and values from the individual's worldview may influence their scientific activity: implicitly as a background to the informal logic of their specific science; or explicitly, when researchers add their own personal commitments to the content of their scientific arguments, explanations, and publications. The importance of keeping these distinctions clear will soon become apparent in our discussion of intelligent design.

Microdesign and Macrodesign in Science

In the light of the perspective on natural scientific reasoning we have been tracing in brief compass, we are now ready to consider the case of the intelligent design debates. Since the early 1990s a small band of scholars has been seeking to insert the hypothesis of "intelligent design" into the natural sciences, especially biology (Forrest and Gross 2004). Now there is nothing unscientific in principle about appeal to the action of intelligent agents as an explanation of phenomena. Perfectly scientific disciplines like economics and linguistics do so all the time, and what counts as good evidence for design or purpose can be rationally delineated within specific sciences (Dembski 1998). Yet these are *human or social sciences* where appeal to intelligent agency is at the center of their tradition of inquiry and practical objectivity. The same could be said for the search for extra-terrestrial intelligence like the SETI project: the activities of intelligent beings are a core part of the explanatory focus and tradition of inquiry. What has been controversial is the insertion of intelligent design explanations in the *natural* sciences, and especially biology. Here proponents of intelligent design have run up against the tradition of nature-bias in what we label natural science, a tradition with a long history of success.

It is important at this point to distinguish between two notions of "design" when it comes to the universe. I have called these "macrodesign" and "microdesign" (Padgett 2008). For millennia in Western culture, going back to Plato and Aristotle, natural philosophers and scientists have simply assumed as obvious the notion that the whole universe was designed by an intelligent God. The scientific assumption that nature has an order or structure which is rational, mathematical, and can be discovered by empirical inquiry was a key element in the development of natural philosophy and early modern science. I call this scientific presupposition "macrodesign." Yet the natural philosophers did not appeal to God's action in explaining events and things within the created world – such an appeal would have been in effect to move from natural philosophy to theology. Instead, natural philosophers like Roger Bacon studied what was called "secondary causes" within the created world, while accepting all the time the *theological* presupposition that God created and sustained all things, and acts in the world. Thus macrodesign was an assumption which stimulated scientific research without prejudice as to which events were caused by God: all things and events owed their ultimate existence and powers to God, yet this theological fact was *not* accepted as a natural philosophical explanation of specific things and events within creation. The point here is not whether God does in fact act in new and surprising ways in history and nature: God's action was accepted. The point was whether appeal to God's intelligent agency was proper in *natural philosophy*.

The new innovation of intelligent design arose in the late 1980s and 1990s as a response to what its proposers thought was the inherent philosophical naturalism of Darwinian explanations. In effect, they were calling into question the late medieval division of labor in universities between natural philosophy and theology. They wanted to appeal to an unnamed "intelligent designer" to explain *within the natural sciences* the design-like character of biological phenomena, especially cellular biology. This move I label "microdesign" to distinguish it from the traditional macrodesign assumption in the history of natural science in the West. Could an explanation be natural-scientific if it appealed to the actions of an intelligent being? The being in question would not have to be God (but it is hard to imagine just who else would fit the bill here), the question was simply one of what "counts" as genuine natural scientific explanation.

In answering this question, we should first recall the difference between an assumption acting upon the individual scientist, and an assumption, method, or epistemic values being common to a community of inquiry that makes up a specific scientific tradition. Second, recall the difference between an idea being part of the implicit background of the thinking of an individual and that idea being cited explicitly in the proposed scientific explanation itself. On the basis of scientific practice and reasoning, there should be no objection to the individual scientist making use of her larger worldview (Christian or otherwise) in thinking hard about scientific issues, or in explaining the meaning of scientific discoveries to a larger audience. Of course in the end new theories and discoveries will have to be justified according to the accepted standards of the mature science concerned, but the point remains that worldviews influence questions, hunches, areas of research, scientific practice, *and* informal reasoning in science. To take one of many examples from the history of science, Geoffrey Cantor has shown that not only were Quakers, because of their distinctive theology and spirituality, more likely to be involved in science than other religious groups, they were attracted particularly to the empirical, observational sciences (Cantor 2005). Turning to matters of interpretation of scientific discoveries, it is quite obvious that larger values, assumptions, and insights well beyond science are used to illustrate and explain science to a larger intellectual audience. So in both the rational assumptions used by the sciences and in the principles of meaning and interpretation used in hermeneutics, reason must go beyond the natural sciences themselves. Put another way, this is the simple point that thinking about science requires us to go beyond science. Informal reasoning draws upon more than rational principles and evidence alone, as does the process of interpretation. There is nothing wrong with a religiously serious scientist thinking hard about her science in ways that draw upon her religious faith. The community of scientists is another thing. The principles, texts, discoveries, evidence, and procedures of any specific science (say, geology) do not draw upon any particular religious perspective. Individuals may, and groups within geology may – but not the whole community. So now we have to say two things that are in tension with each other, and both sides of this tension are equally important. First, from the perspective of the individual person of faith, no human activity or set of ideas is religiously neutral. This includes the practice and discoveries of science. The serious spiritual intellectual will want to see all of life, all human and created things (including science!), from the point of view of faith. This is of course as it should be. Second, the whole community of geologists (for example) is *not* committed to any one religious or non-religious worldview. The practical objectivity and explanatory focus of geology can proceed with quality scientific reasoning and results without necessarily embracing any larger religious or non-religious perspective. One way of making this second point would be to say that the assumptions, evidence, procedures, and epistemological values of geology (or any specific science) are *too small* to count as "religious." Of course the rational person will want to "follow the evidence wherever it leads" and this raises an important question: can the discoveries of science raise questions which science cannot answer? On the face of it, the answer would seem to be "yes." Much larger questions of truth, beauty, meaning, logic, and language can be raise by scientific discoveries without any science being able to find the answer. The question of why the universe or even the multiverse (if there be such) exists at all is one such question. But if this is so, could the evidence of geology itself not point to a designer of some type? Certainly that is possible, but *the argument would no longer be strictly geological* – it would move into an interdisciplinary conversation, where theology and philosophy would have an important place at the table. Thus questions of intelligent design go beyond geology, even if the evidence is discovered by geology. We might discover a particularly interesting layer of black rock on a geological dig, only to later discover that it is the ancient remains of a burned city, not a naturally occurring geological feature. Questions about this city and its inhabitants would necessarily take us outside geology, but not completely – geological evidence is an important part of archeology. The discussion would go interdisciplinary in a quite natural way.

But why would such an argument no longer be natural science itself? Could not a natural science like biology eventually come to embrace microdesign arguments as a normal part of the paradigm of biological science? What is wrong with making appeal to an intelligent designer as an explicit part of a scientific explanation? The philosophy of science we have been tracing in this chapter would suggest that no strict, logically necessary reason can be given to exclude microdesign arguments from natural-scientific explanations. This is just because the nature-bias of the natural sciences is a *tradition* rather than an essence, and as such is open to revision. At the same time, a very powerful burden of proof lies on those who would buck the strong currents of scientific practice and history. The practical objectivity and natural explanatory focus of biology would demand solid and convincing evidence before we set them aside, and a careful exploration of alternative natural explanations would first be called for. So far the intelligent design proponents have failed this test (see among many sources Miller 1999; Johnson, Lamoureux *et al.* 1999). In the world of scholarship and science, in the groves of academe, intelligent design has failed to be a fruitful paradigm. The promissory notes made in the 1990s of new breakthroughs in biology have simply not been paid. It would seem that microdesign is not a fruitful mode of explanation in biology.

Does such a conclusion undermine the rationality of Christian faith, or any religious faith? Of course not. The sciences as they developed over time have a specific domain of study and a narrow focus on the particular objects they seek to know, and a standard explanatory focus that excludes many things which would otherwise be important. Chemistry does not explain molecular attraction on the basis of love – does that mean love is unimportant or does not exist? Arguments for or against the existence of God are part of philosophy and theology. Such arguments can be rigorous, rational, and logical; they may draw upon the discoveries of science and history; but that does not make the arguments themselves scientific or historical. Such arguments are about the findings of history, or science, or religious studies – they do not take place *within* those disciplines. The natural sciences should stay natural not because they have to, but because it is wise given their purpose and the lessons to be learned from the history of science. Only someone naive enough to believe that natural science can answer all our questions would assume that the nature-bias of natural science undermines religion. Such an assumption is not science, but *scientism*.

Notes

My thanks to Alan Love, Philip Rolnick, and of course my excellent co-editor, Jim Stump, for comments and suggestions on earlier versions on this chapter.

1   The term "natural" has many meanings. In this chapter it will be contrasted with the human and social.

References

Butterfield, Herbert. 1953. *The Origins of Modern Science, 1300–1800*. New York: Macmillan.

Cantor, Geoffrey. 2005. *Quakers, Jews and Science*. Oxford: Oxford University Press.

Collier, Andrew. 2003. *In Defence of Objectivity and Other Essays: On Realism, Existentialism and Politics*. London: Routledge.

Dembski, William A. 1998. *The Design Inference: Eliminating Chance through Small Probabilities*. Cambridge: Cambridge University Press.

deVries, Paul. 1986. Naturalism in the Natural Sciences. *Christian Scholar's Review*, 15, pp. 388–396.

Duhem, Pierre Maurice Marie. 1954 [1906]. *The Aim and Structure of Physical Theory*. Princeton: Princeton University Press.

Forrest, Barbara and Gross, Paul R. 2004. *Creationism's Trojan Horse: The Wedge of Intelligent Design*. Oxford: Oxford University Press.

Hanson, Norwood Russell. 1958. *Patterns of Discovery: An Inquiry into the Conceptual Foundations of Science*. Cambridge: Cambridge University Press.

Johnson, Phillip E., Lamoureux, Denis O. et al. 1999. *Darwinism Defeated? The Johnson–Lamoureux Debate on Biological Origins*. Vancouver: Regent College Publishing.

Kuhn, Thomas S. 1962. *The Structure of Scientific Revolutions*. Chicago: University of Chicago Press.

Lakatos, Imre and Musgrave, Alan, eds. 1978. *Criticism and the Growth of Knowledge*. Cambridge: Cambridge University Press.

Lindberg, David C. 1992. *The Beginnings of Western Science: The European Scientific Tradition in Philosophical, Religious, and Institutional Context, 600 B.C. to A.D. 1450*. Chicago: University of Chicago Press.

MacIntyre, Alasdair C. 2006. *Selected Essays*, 2 vols. Cambridge: Cambridge University Press.

McMullin, Ernan. 1982. Values in Science. *PSA: Proceedings of the Biennial Meeting of the Philosophy of Science Association*, 2, pp. 3–28.

Miller, Kenneth R. 1999. *Finding Darwin's God: A Scientist's Search for Common Ground between God and Evolution*. New York: Cliff Street Books.

Nagel, Thomas. 1986. *The View from Nowhere*. Oxford: Oxford University Press.

Padgett, Alan G. 2003. *Science and the Study of God: A Mutuality Model for Theology and Science*. Grand Rapids, MI: Eerdmans.

Padgett, Alan G. 2008. Religion and the Physical Sciences. In D. Borchert, ed. *The Encyclopedia of Philosophy*, vol. 8. New York: Macmillan-Gale, pp. 397–401.

Plantinga, Alvin. 1996. Methodological Naturalism. In J. M. Van der Meer, ed. *Facets of Faith and Science, vol. 1, Historiography and Modes of Interaction*. Lanham: University Press of America, pp. 177–221.

Polanyi, Michael. 1958. *Personal Knowledge: Towards a Post-Critical Philosophy*. Chicago: University of Chicago Press.

Russell, Robert J. 2008. *Cosmology from Alpha to Omega: The Creative Mutual Interaction of Theology and Science*. Minneapolis: Fortress Press.

Wittgenstein, Ludwig. 1922. *Tractatus Logico-Philosophicus*. London: Kegan Paul.

Wittgenstein, Ludwig. 1955. *Philosophical Investigations*. Oxford: Blackwell.

Further Reading

Dembski, William and Ruse, Michael, eds. 2000. *Debating Design*. Cambridge: Cambridge University Press. A fine introduction to and anthology of various views on the intelligent design debate.

Marsden, George. 2001. *The Outrageous Idea of Christian Scholarship*. Oxford: Oxford University Press. A top historian introduces the perspective of faith-based rationality in academic study in general, including sciences.

Padgett, Alan G. 2003. *Science and the Study of God: A Mutuality Model for Theology and Science*. Grand Rapids, MI: Eerdmans. Develops some of the points made in this chapter more fully.

10

The Evolutionary Argument against Naturalism

ALVIN PLANTINGA

For 20 years now I have been developing what I call the "Evolutionary Argument against Naturalism." Among the ancestors of my argument are C. S. Lewis's argument in his *Miracles* and Richard Taylor in *Metaphysics*. I first proposed the argument in print in Plantinga (1991), and versions of it have since appeared in many other places.[1] I have learned much about the argument (from critics and supporters alike), and have repeatedly revised it. The version presented here is a savagely truncated condensation of the final (I hope) version, which is to be found in chapter 10 of my *Where the Conflict Really Lies: Science, Religion, and Naturalism* (Plantinga 2011b).

Take *naturalism* to be the idea that there is no such person as God or anything like God. Then the overall structure of the argument is as follows:

(1) The probability of our cognitive faculties being reliable, given naturalism and evolution, is low.
(2) If I believe both naturalism and evolution, and see that (1) is true, I have a defeater for my intuitive assumption that my cognitive faculties are reliable.
(3) If I have a defeater for *that* belief, however, then I have a defeater for *any* belief I take to be produced by my cognitive faculties, including my belief that naturalism and evolution are both true.
(4) Therefore, I have a defeater for my belief that naturalism and evolution are true.

Hence that belief defeats itself and is therefore self-referentially inconsistent; it can't be rationally accepted. Because of space constraints, I'll defend only the first premise here. The others are relatively straightforward and their details can be found in Plantinga 2011b (chapter 10).

Evolution and Naturalism

The first bit of business in defending premise (1) is to show that evolution need not go hand in hand with naturalism, as we're often led to believe. The scientific theory of evolution just

---

The Blackwell Companion to Science and Christianity, First Edition. Edited by J. B. Stump and Alan G. Padgett.
© 2012 Blackwell Publishing Ltd. Published 2012 by Blackwell Publishing Ltd.

as such is entirely compatible with the thought that God has guided and orchestrated the course of evolution, planned and directed it, in such a way as to achieve the ends he intends. Perhaps he causes the right mutations to arise at the right time; perhaps he preserves certain populations from extinction; perhaps he is active in many other ways. On the one hand, therefore, we have the scientific theory, and on the other, there is the claim that the course of evolution is not directed or guided or orchestrated by anyone; it displays no teleology; it is blind, and unforeseeing; as Dawkins says, it has no aim or goal.

This claim, however, despite its strident proclamation, is no part of the scientific theory as such; it is instead a metaphysical or theological add-on. To be fair it is not clear that naturalism, as it stands, is a religion; there is enough vagueness around the edges of the concept of religion for it to be unclear whether naturalism does or doesn't belong there. But naturalism does serve one of the main functions of a religion: it offers a master narrative, it answers deep and important human questions. Immanuel Kant identified three great human questions: Is there such a person as God? Do we human beings have significant freedom? And can we human beings expect life after death? Naturalism gives answers to these questions: there is no God, there is no immortality, and the case for genuine freedom is at best dicey. Naturalism tells us what reality is ultimately like, where we fit into the universe, how we are related to other creatures, and how it happens that we came to be. Naturalism is therefore in competition with the great theistic religions: even if it is not itself a religion, it plays one of the main roles of a religion. The question, then, is whether conjoining the scientific theory of evolution with the metaphysical or quasi-religious position of naturalism sheds any light on our natural assumption that our cognitive faculties are reliable. I shall claim that belief in evolution and naturalism taken together defeats this natural assumption. Hence if someone accepts the conjunction of naturalism and evolution, she has a defeater for the assumption that her cognitive faculties are reliable, and hence has a defeater for any belief she might have, including belief in the conjunction of naturalism and evolution itself. Hence we cannot rationally accept both evolution and naturalism.

Reliability of Our Cognitive Faculties

Our cognitive faculties are those powers or processes that produce beliefs or knowledge in us. Among these faculties is *memory*, whereby we know something of our past. There is also *perception*, whereby we know something about our physical environment – for the most part our immediate environment, but also something about distant objects such as the sun, the moon, and stars. Another is what is often called '*a priori* intuition', by virtue of which we know truths of elementary arithmetic and logic. And there is *testimony*, whereby we can learn from others, and *induction*, whereby we can learn from experience. We might also add what Thomas Reid called *sympathy*, which enables us to know the thoughts and feelings of other people, and believers in God may wish to add what John Calvin called the *sensus divinitatis*, whereby we know something of God. These faculties or powers work together in complex and variegated ways to produce a vast battery of beliefs and knowledge, ranging from the simplest everyday beliefs – it's hot in here, I have a pain in my right knee – to less quotidian beliefs such as those to be found in philosophy, theology, history, and the far reaches of science. In science, clearly enough, many of these faculties work together – perception, memory, testimony, sympathy, induction, *a priori* intuition are all typically involved. There is also the whole process of theory-building, which may or may not be reducible to the previous items.

We can speak of the reliability of a particular faculty – memory, for example. A faculty is reliable only if it produces an appropriate preponderance of true belief over false. We can also speak of the reliability of the whole battery of our cognitive faculties. And indeed we ordinarily think our faculties *are* reliable, at any rate when they are functioning properly, when there is no cognitive malfunction or disorder or dysfunction. And it is the natural thing to think, from the perspective of theistic belief, that our faculties are indeed for the most part reliable, at least over a large part of their range of operations. According to theistic religion God has created us in his image; an important part of this image consists in our resembling God in that like him, we can have knowledge. But suppose you are a naturalist: you think that there is no such person as God, and that we and our cognitive faculties have been cobbled together by natural selection. Can you then sensibly think that our cognitive faculties are for the most part reliable? I say you can't.

My position has some eminent advocates. For example, there is Friedrich Nietzsche. Ordinarily what Nietzsche (2003, 26) says inspires little confidence, but in the following he may be on to something:

> It is unfair to Descartes to call his appeal to God's credibility frivolous. Indeed, only if we assume a God who is morally our like can "truth" and the search for truth be at all something meaningful and promising of success. This God left aside, the question is permitted whether being deceived is not one of the conditions of life.

To leap to the present, there is the philosopher Thomas Nagel, himself no friend of theism: "If we came to believe that our capacity for objective theory were the product of natural selection, that would warrant serious skepticism about its results" (Nagel 1989, 79). As Patricia Churchland, an eminent naturalistic philosopher, puts it in a justly famous passage:

> Boiled down to essentials, a nervous system enables the organism to succeed in the four F's: feeding, fleeing, fighting and reproducing. The principle chore of nervous systems is to get the body parts where they should be in order that the organism may survive. . . . Improvements in sensorimotor control confer an evolutionary advantage: a fancier style of representing is advantageous *so long as it is geared to the organism's way of life and enhances the organism's chances of survival.* Truth, whatever that is, definitely takes the hindmost. (Churchland 1987, 548–549, emphasis in original)

Churchland's point, clearly, is that (from a naturalistic perspective) what evolution guarantees is (at most) that we *behave* in certain ways – in such ways as to promote survival, or more exactly reproductive success. The principal function or purpose, then (the "chore" says Churchland), of our cognitive faculties is not that of producing true or verisimilitudinous (nearly true) beliefs, but instead that of contributing to survival by getting the body parts in the right place. What evolution underwrites is only (at most) that our *behavior* is reasonably adaptive to the circumstances in which our ancestors found themselves; hence (so far forth) it does not guarantee mostly true or verisimilitudinous beliefs. Our beliefs *might* be mostly true or verisimilitudinous (hereafter I'll omit the "verisimilitudinous"); but there is no particular reason to think they *would* be: natural selection is interested, not in truth, but in appropriate behavior. What Churchland therefore suggests is that naturalistic evolution – that is, the conjunction of metaphysical naturalism with the view that we and our cognitive faculties have arisen by way of the mechanisms and processes proposed by contemporary evolutionary theory – gives us reason to doubt two things: (a) that a *purpose* of our cognitive systems is that of serving us with true beliefs, and (b) that they *do*, in fact, furnish us with mostly true beliefs.

Indeed, Darwin himself (1887, 315–316) expresses serious doubts along these lines:

> With me the horrid doubt always arises whether the convictions of man's mind, which has been developed from the mind of the lower animals, are of any value or at all trustworthy. Would any one trust in the convictions of a monkey's mind, if there are any convictions in such a mind?

Nietzsche, Nagel, Churchland, and Darwin, nontheists all, seem to concur: (naturalistic) evolution gives one a reason to doubt that human cognitive faculties produce for the most part true beliefs. Since Darwin is the standout among this group, call this thought "Darwin's Doubt." In what follows I'll explain why Darwin's Doubt seems eminently sensible and indeed correct.

Naturalists Are Committed to Materialism

The next step in defending premise (1) above is to note that nearly all naturalists are also *materialists* with respect to human beings; they hold that human beings are material objects. From this perspective a human person is not (contrary to Descartes and Augustine) an immaterial substance or self that is connected with or joined to (has?) a material body. Nor is it the case that a human being is a composite that has an immaterial component; human beings do not have an immaterial soul or mind or ego. Instead, so the materialist thinks, a person *just is* her body, or perhaps some part of her body (so that talk about "my body" is misleading). I *am* my body (or maybe my brain, or its left hemisphere, or some other part of it, or some other part of my body). Nearly all naturalists would agree. They give at least three sorts of reasons for materialism. First, naturalists often argue that dualism (the thought that a human being is an immaterial self or substance intimately related to a human body) is incoherent or subject to crushing philosophical difficulties; hence, so they say, we are rationally compelled to be materialists. You can find a typical set of such objections to dualism in Daniel Dennett's book *Consciousness Explained*. Most of these objections (including Dennett's) are astonishingly weak; no one not already convinced of materialism would (or at any rate should) find them at all persuasive. Still, they are often trotted out as showing that we are all obliged, these enlightened days, to be materialists.

A second and somewhat better reason is this: many naturalists think it is just part of naturalism as such to have no truck with immaterial souls or selves or minds. It may not be completely easy to see or say precisely what naturalism is, but, so goes the thought, at any rate it excludes things like immaterial selves or souls. Naturalism is the idea that there is no such person as God or anything like him; immaterial selves would be too much like God, who, after all, is himself an immaterial self. This reason is really quite persuasive (for naturalists), but not wholly conclusive. That is because of the vagueness of the concept of naturalism. According to naturalism, there isn't anything *like* God; but just how much similarity to God is tolerable, from a naturalistic perspective? After all, everything resembles God in *some* respect; how much similarity to God can a decently sensitive naturalist manage to accept? Plato's idea of the good and Aristotle's unmoved mover (who is also immaterial) clearly won't pass muster, but what about immaterial soul substances? Can a proper naturalist allow such a thing? That's not entirely easy to say. Far be it from me as an outsider, however, to intrude upon a delicate family dispute among naturalists; I hereby leave naturalists to decide this issue for themselves.

A third reason is as follows. Naturalists will ordinarily endorse Darwinian evolution; but how, they ask, could an immaterial soul or self have come to exist by way of the processes that evolutionary science posits? Thus Richard Dawkins (1998, n.p.):

> Catholic Morality demands the presence of a great gulf between *Homo Sapiens* and the rest of the animal kingdom. Such a gulf is fundamentally anti-evolutionary. The sudden injection of an immortal soul in the timeline is an anti-evolutionary intrusion into the domain of science.

According to contemporary evolutionary theory, new forms of life arise (for the most part) by way of natural selection working on some form of genetic variation – the usual candidate is random genetic mutation. Most mutations of this sort are lethal; but a few are advantageous in the struggle for survival. Those lucky organisms that sport them have a reproductive advantage over those that do not, and eventually the new feature comes to dominate the population; then the process can start over. But how could an *immaterial self or soul* evolve this way? What sort of genetic mutation would result in an immaterial soul? Could there be a section of DNA that codes, not for the production of proteins, but for an immaterial self? That seems doubtful.

These reasons clearly aren't conclusive, but most naturalists find them (or perhaps other arguments for materialism) at least reasonably compelling. For these reasons and perhaps others, most naturalists are materialists about human beings. For present purposes, therefore, I propose to assimilate materialism to naturalism; henceforth I'll think of naturalism as including materialism, and what I'll be arguing against is the conjunction of current evolutionary theory and naturalism, the latter including materialism.

Materialist Construal of Beliefs

Now what sort of thing will a belief *be*, from this materialist perspective? Suppose you are a materialist, and also think, as we ordinarily do, that there are such things as beliefs. For example, you hold the belief that Proust is more subtle than Louis L'Amour. What kind of a thing is this belief? Well, from a materialist perspective, it looks as if it would have to be something like a long-standing event or structure in your brain or nervous system. Presumably this event will involve many neurons connected to each other in various ways. There are plenty of neurons to go around: a normal human brain contains some 100–200 billion neurons. These neurons, furthermore, are connected with other neurons via synapses; a single neuron, on the average, is connected with a thousand of other neurons. The total number of possible brain states, then, is absolutely enormous, much greater than the number of electrons in the universe. Under certain conditions, a neuron fires, that is, produces an electrical impulse; by virtue of its connection with other neurons, this impulse can be transmitted (with appropriate modification from other neurons) down the cables of neurons that constitute effector nerves to muscles or glands, causing, for example, muscular contraction and thus behavior.

So (from the materialist's point of view) a belief will be a neuronal event or structure of this sort, with input from other parts of the nervous system and output to still other parts as well as to muscles and glands. But if this is the sort of thing beliefs are, if they are neuronal events or structures, they will have two quite different sorts of properties. On the one hand they will have *electro-chemical* or *neurophysiological* properties (NP properties, for short). Among these would be such properties as that of involving n neurons and n^* connections between neurons, properties that specify which neurons are connected with which others, what the rates of fire in the various parts of the event are, how these rates of fire change in response to changes in input, and so on.

But if the event in question is really a *belief*, then in addition to those NP properties it will have another property as well: it will have a *content*.[2] It will be the belief that p, for some proposition p. If it's the belief that Proust is a more subtle writer than Louis L'Amour, then its content is the proposition *Proust is more subtle than Louis L'Amour*. My belief that naturalism is vastly overrated has as content the proposition *Naturalism is vastly overrated*. (That same proposition is the content of the Chinese speaker's belief that naturalism is vastly overrated, even though he expresses this belief by uttering a very different sentence; beliefs, unlike sentences, do not come in different languages.) It is in virtue of having a content that a belief is true or false: it is true if the proposition which is its content is true, and false otherwise. My belief that all men are mortal is true because the proposition which constitutes its content is true; Hitler's belief that the Third Reich would last a thousand years was false, because the proposition that constituted its content is (was) false.

Given materialism, therefore, beliefs are long-standing neural events. As such, they have NP properties, but also content properties: each belief will have the property of having such and such a proposition as its content. NP properties are *physical* properties; on the other hand content properties – for example the property of having as content the proposition *all men are mortal* – are *mental* properties. Now how, according to materialism, are mental and physical properties related? In particular, how are content properties related to NP properties – how is the content property of a particular belief related to the NP properties of that belief?

Reductive and Non-reductive Materialism

Materialists offer fundamentally two theories about the relation between physical and mental properties (and hence two theories about the relation between NP properties and content properties): reductive materialism and non-reductive materialism. According to reductive materialists, mental properties are really just a special kind of physical properties. Sir Francis Crick (1995, 3) gives a good statement of reductive materialism: "your joys and your sorrows, your memories and your ambitions, your sense of personal identity and free will, are in fact no more than the behaviour of a vast assembly of nerve cells and their associ- ated molecules." The content of a belief *just is* a certain combination of NP properties.

For non-reductive materialists, there really are two kinds of properties, but the mental properties supervene on the physical properties. That is to say, mental properties are not identical with physical properties, but they are completely determined by physical properties. The basic idea is this: for any particular mental property M that you pick, there is a physical property P such that necessarily, if a thing has M, then it has P, and if a thing has P, then it has M. So take any mental property, for example the property of being in pain: there will be some physical property P (presumably an NP property), such that it's true in every possible world that whatever has P is in pain, and, conversely, whatever is in pain has P.[3] Specified to content and NP properties, the idea is that for any content property C that a neural structure can have, there is an NP property P such that if a neural structure has that content property C, it has P, and conversely, any neural structure that has P also has that content property C.

According to both reductive and non-reductive materialism, mental properties are determined by physical properties. As we go up the evolutionary scale, we find neural structures with greater and greater complexity. Near one end of the scale, for example, we find bacteria, which presumably don't have beliefs at all. At the other end of the scale there are human beings, who have a rich and varied store of beliefs. And the idea is that as you rise in the evolutionary scale, as you go through more and more complex neural structures, at a certain point belief content starts to show up, something we can properly call a belief, something that is true or false. At a certain level of complexity, these neural structures start to display belief content. Perhaps this starts gradually and early on – perhaps it is with *C. elegans*, a small but charismatic beast that enjoys the distinction of having its nervous system completely mapped. Possibly *C. elegans* displays just the merest glimmer of consciousness and just the merest glimmer of actual belief content; or perhaps belief content shows up further up the scale; that doesn't matter. What does matter is that at a certain level of complexity, neural structures begin to display content and the creatures that harbor those structures have beliefs. This is true whether content properties are reducible to NP properties or supervene on them.

So (given materialism) some neural structures at a given level of complexity of NP properties acquire content; at that level of complexity, NP properties determine belief content, and the structures in question are beliefs. And the question I want to ask is this: what is the likelihood, *given evolution and naturalism* (construed as including materialism about human beings), that the content thus arising is in fact *true*? In particular, what is the likelihood, given naturalism and evolution, that the content associated with *our* neural structures is true? What is the likelihood, on this account, that our cognitive faculties are reliable, thereby producing mostly true beliefs?

The natural thing to assume, and what we all do assume (at least before we are corrupted by philosophy (or neuroscience)), is that when our cognitive faculties aren't subject to malfunction, then, for the most part, and over a wide area of everyday life, the beliefs they produce in us are true. We assume that our cognitive faculties are reliable. But what I want to argue is that the naturalist has a powerful reason *against* this initial assumption, and should give it up. I don't mean to argue that this natural assumption is false; like everyone else, I believe that our cognitive faculties *are*, in fact, mostly reliable. What I do mean to argue is that the *naturalist* – at any rate a naturalist who accepts evolution – is rationally obliged to give up this assumption.

The Argument against Non-reductive Materialism

Let's first think about the question from the point of view of non-reductive materialism. And let's begin by returning to the evolutionary scale and *C. elegans*, that celebrated little worm. Let's suppose that it is in *C. elegans* that we first get belief. No doubt such belief will be primitive *in excelsis* (and if you don't think *C. elegans* has beliefs, you can simply go up the scale until you encounter creatures you think do have beliefs), but let's suppose members of this species have beliefs. Now given that *C. elegans* has survived for millions of years, we may assume that its behavior is adaptive. This behavior is produced or caused by the neurological structures in the *C. elegans* nervous system; we may further assume, therefore, that this neurology is adaptive. This underlying neurology causes adaptive behavior; as Churchland says, it gets the body parts where they must be in order to survive. But (in line with non-reductive materialism) the underlying neurology also determines belief content. As a result, these creatures have beliefs, which of course have a certain content.

And here's the question: what reason is there for supposing that this belief content is *true*? There isn't any. The neurology causes adaptive behavior and also causes or determines belief content: but there is no reason to suppose that the belief content thus determined is true. All that's required for survival and fitness is that the neurology cause adaptive behavior; this neurology also determines belief content, but whether or not that content is *true* makes no difference to fitness. Certain NP properties are selected for, because they contribute to fitness. These NP properties also cause or determine belief content; they associate a content or proposition with each belief. The NP properties are selected, however, not because they cause the content they do, but because they cause adaptive behavior. If the content, the proposition determined by the neurology (the NP properties of the belief), is true, fine. But if false, that's no problem as far as fitness goes.

Objection: consider a frog on a lily pad. A fly buzzes by; the frog's tongue flicks out and captures the fly. If this frog is to behave successfully, adaptively, there must be mechanisms in it that register the distance to the fly at each moment, its size, speed, direction, and so on. Aren't these mechanisms part of the frog's cognitive faculties? And don't they have to be accurate in order for the frog to behave adaptively? And isn't it therefore the case that the frog's cognitive mechanisms must be accurate, reliable, if the frog is to survive and reproduce? Or consider an animal, maybe a zebra, grazing on the veldt; a lion approaches. The zebra notices the predator; this noticing consists in part of some neural structure arising in its brain, perhaps a certain pattern of firing of neurons in the optical portion of its brain, and perhaps this pattern ordinarily arises in response to the appearance of a predator in the middle distance. If this structure isn't properly correlated with the presence of predators, the zebra won't be long for this world. And wouldn't this structure, furthermore, be part of the creatures' cognitive mechanisms? And don't those mechanisms have to be accurate, reliable, if the zebra is to survive?

Reply: that frog clearly does have 'indicators', neural structures that receive input from the frog's sense organs, are correlated with the path of the insect as it flies past, and are connected with the frog's muscles in such a way that it flicks out its tongue and captures that unfortunate fly. The same goes for the zebra: if it is to behave adaptively (evade predators, for example) it too will have to have indicators, neural structures that monitor the environment, are correlated (for example) with the presence of predators, and are connected with its muscles in such a way as to cause it to flee when a predator threatens.

Now if we like, we can include these indicators under the rubric 'cognitive faculties'. The important point to see here, however, is that indication of this sort does not require *belief*. In particular, it does not require belief having to do with the state of affairs indicated; indeed it is entirely compatible with belief *inconsistent* with that state of affairs. Fleeing predators, finding food and mates – these things require cognitive devices that in some way track crucial features of the environment, and are appropriately connected with muscles; but they do not require true belief, or even belief at all. The long-term survival of organisms of a certain species certainly makes it likely that its members enjoy cognitive devices that are successful in tracking those features of the environment – indicators, as I've been calling them. Indicators, however, need not be or involve beliefs. In the human body there are indicators for blood pressure, temperature, saline content, insulin level, and much else; in these cases neither the blood, nor its owner, nor anything else in the neighborhood ordinarily holds beliefs on

the topic. The objector is therefore right in pointing out that fitness requires accurate indication; but nothing follows about reliability of belief.

Returning to the main line of argument, we are considering the likelihood that our faculties are reliable, given naturalism, evolution, and non-reductive materialism. In order to avoid
automatically introducing into the argument our ordinary assumptions about our own mental
life, suppose we conduct a thought experiment. Consider a hypothetical species that is cognitively a lot like us: members of this species hold beliefs, make inferences, change beliefs,
and the like. And let us suppose naturalism holds for them; they exist in a world in which
there is no such person as God or anything like God. Our question, then, is this: what is the
probability that their cognitive faculties are reliable? Consider any particular belief on the part
of one of these hypothetical creatures. That belief is a neural structure of a given sort, and
one sufficiently complex to generate content. We may add, if we like, that this structure
occurs or takes place in response to something in the environment; perhaps it is a certain
pattern of firing of neurons in the optical portion of the brain, and perhaps this pattern arises
in response to the appearance of a predator. Suppose further that a certain content, a certain
proposition, is determined by the NP properties of this structure. This structure, therefore,
will be a belief, and will have a certain proposition p as its content.

But now for the crucial question: what is the probability (given naturalism, evolution, and
non-reductive materialism) that this proposition, the content of the belief in question, is true?
Well, what we know about the belief is that it is a neurological structure that has certain NP
properties, properties the possession of which is sufficient for the possession of that particular
content. We are assuming also that this structure arises in response to the presence of that
predator, and we can assume still further, if we like, that this structure is a reliable indicator
of that kind of predator: it arises when and only when there is such a predator in the middle
distance. But why think it is a *true* proposition, *true* content, that is determined by those NP
properties? Natural selection selects for adaptive NP properties; those NP properties determine content; but natural selection just has to take potluck with respect to the propositions
or content determined by those adaptive NP properties. It does not get to influence or modify
the function from NP properties to content properties: that's just a matter either of metaphysical necessity or of causal law, and natural selection can't modify either. Indeed, the
content generated by the NP properties of this structure, on this occasion, need have nothing
to do with that predator, or with anything else in the environment. True: the structure is
correlated with the presence of a predator; it indicates that presence; but indication is not
belief. Indication is one thing; belief content is something else altogether, and we know of
no reason (given materialism) why the one should follow the other; we know of no reason
why the content of a belief should match what that belief (together, perhaps, with other
structures) indicates. Content simply arises upon the appearance of neural structures of sufficient complexity; there is no reason why that content need be related to what the structures
indicate, if anything. The proposition constituting that content need not be so much as *about*
that predator; it certainly need not be true.

What, then, is the likelihood that this proposition, this content, is true? Given just this
much, shouldn't we suppose that the proposition in question is as likely to be false as true?
Here's the picture: the NP properties of a belief are adaptive in that they cause adaptive
behavior. Those NP properties also determine a content property. But as long as the NP
properties are adaptive, it doesn't matter, for survival and reproduction, what content is
determined by those NP properties. It could be true content; it could be false content; it
doesn't matter. The fact that these creatures have survived and evolved, that their cognitive
equipment was good enough to enable their ancestors to survive and reproduce – that fact

would tell us nothing at all about the *truth* of their beliefs or the reliability of their cognitive faculties. It would tell something about the *neurophysiological* properties of a given belief; it would tell us that by virtue of these properties, that belief has played a role in the production of adaptive behavior. But it would tell us nothing about the truth of the *content* of that belief: its content might be true, but might with equal probability be false. The probability that it is true, therefore, would have to be pegged at about 0.5. But then the probability that this creature's cognitive faculties are reliable is very low. If I have 100 independent beliefs, and the probability of truth with respect to each is 0.5, then the probability that three-fourths of my beliefs are true (surely a modest requirement for reliability) is about one in a million.

Reductive Materialism

That's how things stand for non-reductive materialism. We can deal more briefly with reductive materialism. On reductive materialism, mental properties are complex combinations of physical properties; more briefly, taking complex combinations of physical properties to be themselves physical properties, mental properties just are physical properties. What is the likelihood that our cognitive faculties are reliable, given naturalism, evolution, and reductive materialism?

Here we get the very same results as with non-reductive materialism. To see why, consider, again, any given belief on the part of a member of that hypothetical group of creatures – say the belief *naturalism is vastly overrated*. That belief is a neuronal event, a congeries of neurons connected in complex ways and firing away in the fashion neurons are wont to do. This neuronal event displays a lot of NP properties. Again, we may suppose that it is adaptively useful for a creature of the kind in question to harbor neuronal structures of the sort in question in the circumstances in question. The event's having the NP properties it does have is fitness-enhancing in that by virtue of having these properties, the organism is caused to perform adaptively useful action – fleeing, for example. Since the event is a belief, some subset of these NP properties together constitute its having the content it does in fact display. That is, there will be some proposition that is the content of the belief; the belief will therefore have the property of having that proposition as its content; and that property, the property of having such and such a proposition as its content, will be a (no doubt complex) NP property of the belief.

Now what is the probability that this content is *true*? What is the probability that this proposition, whatever it is, is true? The answer is the same as in the case we've already considered. The content doesn't have to be true, of course, for the neuronal structure to cause the appropriate kind of behavior. It just happens that this particular adaptive arrangement of NP properties also constitutes having that particular content. But again: it would be a piece of serendipity if this content, this proposition, were *true*; it could just as well be false. These NP properties, including those that constitute its having that content, are adaptive just as long as they cause adaptive behavior. They also constitute the property of having that particular content; but it doesn't matter at all, so far as adaptivity goes, whether that content is true. So take any particular belief on the part of one of those creatures. We may suppose (given that these creatures have come to be by way of evolution) that having this belief is adaptive; its NP properties cause adaptive behavior. These NP properties also constitute the property of having such and such content; but, clearly enough, it doesn't matter (with respect to the adaptivity of these properties) whether the content they constitute is true. It could be true: fair enough; but it could equally well be false. If these properties had constituted different content, they still would have had the same causal effect with respect to behavior. So if each of the beliefs of these creatures is just as likely false as true, we would have to rate the reliability of their cognitive faculties as very low.

Objection

Isn't it just obvious that true beliefs will facilitate adaptive action? A gazelle who mistakenly believes that lions are friendly, overgrown house cats won't be long for this world. The same goes for a rock climber who believes that jumping from a 200-foot cliff will result in a pleasant and leisurely trip down with a soft landing. Isn't it obvious both that true beliefs are much more likely to be adaptive than false beliefs? Isn't it obvious, more generally, that true beliefs are more likely to be successful than false beliefs? I want to go from New York to Boston: won't I be more likely to get there if I believe it's north of New York than if I believe it's to the south?

Yes, certainly. This is indeed true. But it is also irrelevant. We are not asking about how things *are*, but about *what things would be like if both evolution and naturalism (construed as including materialism) were true*. Like everyone else, I believe that our cognitive faculties are for the most part reliable, and that true beliefs are more likely to issue in successful action than false. But that's not the question. The question is what things would be like if naturalism and evolution were true; and in this context we can't just assume, of course, that if they (including materialism) were true, then things would still be the way they are. That is, we can't assume that if materialism were true, it would still be the case that true beliefs are more likely to cause successful action than false beliefs. And in fact, if materialism were true, it would be unlikely that true beliefs mostly cause successful action and false belief unsuccessful action.

Here you may ask, "Why think a thing like that? What has materialism to do with this question?" Here's what. We ordinarily think true belief leads to successful action because we also think that beliefs cause (part-cause) actions, and do so *by virtue of their content*. I want a beer; I believe there is one in the fridge, and this belief is a (part) cause of my going over to the fridge. We think it is by virtue of the *content* of that belief that it causes me to go over to the fridge; it is because this belief has as content that there is a beer in the fridge that it causes me to go to the fridge rather than, say, the washing machine. More generally, we think it is by virtue of the content of a belief *B* that *B* part-causes the behavior that it does cause.

But now suppose materialism were true: then, as we've seen, my belief will be a neural structure that has both NP properties and also a propositional content. It is by virtue of the NP properties, however, not the content, that the belief causes what it does cause. It is by virtue of *those* properties that the belief causes neural impulses to travel down the relevant efferent nerves to the relevant muscles, causing them to contract, and thus causing behavior. It isn't by virtue of the content of this belief; the content of the belief is irrelevant to the causal power of the belief with respect to behavior.

Consider an analogy. I am playing catch with my granddaughter, and in a vainglorious attempt to show off, I throw the ball too hard; it whistles over her head and shatters a neighbor's window. It is clear that the ball breaks the window *by virtue of* its mass, velocity, hardness, size, and the like. If it had been much less massive, been traveling at a lower rate of speed, had been as soft as a bunch of feathers, and so on, it would not have broken the window. If you ask "Why did the window shatter upon being hit by the ball?" the correct answer will involve the ball's having those properties (and of course also involve the window's having a certain degree of brittleness, tensile strength, and the like). As it happens, the ball was a birthday present; but it does not break the window by virtue of being a birthday present, or being purchased at Sears and Roebuck, or costing $5.00. Examples of this sort, clearly enough, can be multiplied endlessly; but examples of other kinds also abound. Sam has the right to fire the city manager by virtue of his being mayor, not by virtue of his being nice to his wife. Aquinas was a great philosopher by virtue of his acumen and insight and prodigious industry, not by virtue of his being called "the Dumb Ox."

   Going back to materialism and the content of belief, then, it is by virtue of the NP properties of a belief B's, not by virtue of its content, that the belief causes the behavior it does cause. Among B's NP properties are such properties as that of involving many neurons working in concert: as we learn from current science, these neurons send a signal through effector nerves to the relevant muscles, causing those muscles to contract and thereby causing behavior. It is by virtue of these NP properties that it causes those muscles to contract. If the belief had had the same NP properties but different content, it would have had the same effect on behavior.

Conclusion

So I claim that we have no reason to believe and good reason not to believe the proposition that if evolution and naturalism were true, then our cognitive faculties would be reliable. Given the other (relatively straightforward) premises I could not address in this chapter (but see the discussion in Plantinga 2011b, chapter 10), the conclusion to be drawn is that one can't rationally accept both naturalism and current evolutionary theory; that combination of beliefs is self-defeating. Thus there is deep conflict between naturalism and one of the most important claims of current science. Given that naturalism is at least a quasi-religion, there is indeed a science–religion conflict all right, but it is not between science and theistic religion: it is between science and naturalism. That's where the conflict really lies.

Notes

1   These include: Plantinga 1993, chapter 12; Plantinga 2000, 227 ff.; Beilby 2002, 1ff., 204ff; Plantinga and Tooley 2008, 30ff.; Plantinga and Dennett 2010, 16ff., 66 ff.; and Plantinga 2011a.
2   It is of course extremely difficult to see how a material structure or event could have content in the way a belief does; on the face of it, this appears to be impossible. That is one of the main problems for materialism. For development of this thought, see Plantinga 2006.
3   This is what philosophers call 'strong supervenience'. For a good account of the various kinds of supervenience, see the online *Stanford Encyclopedia of Philosophy* entry on supervenience.

References

Beilby, James, ed. 2002. *Naturalism Defeated? Essays on Plantinga's Evolutionary Argument against Naturalism.* New York: Cornell University Press.

Churchland, Patricia. 1987. Epistemology in the Age of Neuroscience. *Journal of Philosophy*, 84(10), pp. 544–553.

Crick, Francis. 1995. *The Astonishing Hypothesis: The Scientific Search for the Soul*. New York: Simon & Schuster.

Darwin, Charles. 1887. In Francis Darwin, ed. *The Life and Letters of Charles Darwin Including an Autobiographical Chapter*, vol. 1. London: John Murray.

Dawkins, Richard. 1998. When Religion Steps on Science's Turf. *Free Inquiry*, 18(2), online at www.secularhumanism.org (accessed February 14, 2011).

Nagel, Thomas. 1989. *The View from Nowhere*. Oxford: Oxford University Press.

Nietzsche, Friedrich. 2003. Notebook 36, June–July 1885. In Rüdiger Bittner, ed. *Nietzsche: Writings from the Late Notebooks*. Translated by Kate Sturge. Cambridge: Cambridge University Press, pp. 22–28.

Plantinga, Alvin. 1991. An Evolutionary Argument against Naturalism. *Logos*, 12, pp. 27–49.

Plantinga, Alvin. 1993. *Warrant and Proper Function*. New York: Oxford University Press.

Plantinga, Alvin. 2000. *Warranted Christian Belief*. New York: Oxford University Press.

Plantinga, Alvin. 2006. Against Materialism. *Faith and Philosophy*, 23(1), pp. 3–32.

Plantinga, Alvin. 2011a. Content and Natural Selection. *Philosophy and Phenomenological Research* 83(2), pp. 435–458.

Plantinga, Alvin. 2011b. *Where the Conflict Really Lies: Science, Religion, and Naturalism*. New York: Oxford University Press.

Plantinga, Alvin and Dennett, Daniel. 2010. *Science and Religion: Are They Compatible?* New York: Oxford University Press.

Plantinga, Alvin and Tooley, Michael. 2008. *Knowledge of God*. Oxford: Wiley-Blackwell.

Further Reading

Beilby, James, ed. 2002. *Naturalism Defeated? Essays on Plantinga's Evolutionary Argument against Naturalism*. New York: Cornell University Press. A collection of essays by critics and friends of the evolutionary argument against naturalism with replies by Plantinga.

Plantinga, Alvin. 2011. *Where the Conflict Really Lies: Science, Religion, and Naturalism*. New York: Oxford University Press. A monograph on the compatibility of science and religion, with a substantial treatment of the topic of this chapter.

Part III

Natural Theology

11

Arguments to God from the Observable Universe

RICHARD SWINBURNE

The Relevance of Arguments

Why believe that there is a God at all? My answer is that to suppose that there is a God explains why there is a physical universe at all; why there are the scientific laws there are; why animals and then human beings have evolved; why humans have the opportunity to mold their characters and those of our fellow humans for good or ill and to change the environment in which we live; why we have the well-authenticated account of Christ's life, death, and resurrection; why throughout the centuries millions of people (other than ourselves) have had the apparent experience of being in touch with and guided by God, and so much else. In fact, the hypothesis of the existence of God makes sense of the whole of our experience, and it does so better than any other explanation that can be put forward, and that is the grounds for believing it to be true. In this chapter I shall try to show how it makes sense of the first three of these phenomena. It has been a general Christian, Jewish, and Islamic conviction that phenomena which are evident to all – and in particular the universe and its order – provide good grounds for believing that God exists. The production of arguments to show this is called "natural theology," and it might be useful to start with a few remarks about the place of natural theology in Christian tradition.

The prophet Jeremiah wrote of the "covenant of night and day" (Jer. 33:25–26), indicating that the regularity by which day succeeded night showed that the god in charge of the universe was powerful and reliable, that is to say, that that god was God. The Wisdom literature of the Old Testament developed the idea that the details of creation showed much about the Creator. St Paul wrote that "the invisible things" of God "are clearly seen, being perceived through the things that are made" (Rom. 1:20), and pagans could see that for themselves. This biblical tradition merged in the later Greek world with the arguments of Plato and Aristotle to the existence of a supreme source of being. And so various Christian theologians, East and West, of the first millennium had their paragraph or two summarizing an argument to God from the existence or orderliness of the universe – among them Irenaeus, Gregory of Nyssa, Augustine, Maximus the Confessor, and John of Damascus. But it is normally only

The Blackwell Companion to Science and Christianity, First Edition. Edited by J. B. Stump and Alan G. Padgett.
© 2012 Blackwell Publishing Ltd. Published 2012 by Blackwell Publishing Ltd.

a paragraph or two, and the reasoning is quick. My explanation of why they directed so little energy to this issue is that they felt no need to do more. Most of their contemporaries accepted that there was a God or gods. What the theologians needed to argue was that there was only one such God, that he had certain specific characteristics and had acted in history in certain particular ways.

With the coming of the second millennium, however, the theologians of the medieval West, above all Thomas Aquinas and Duns Scotus, began to produce arguments for the existence of God of considerable length and rigor; and this enterprise of natural theology continued uninterrupted in the Catholic tradition until the nineteenth century. Classical Protestants, however, although believing that the natural world showed abundant evidence of its creator, thought that human sinfulness obscured our ability to recognize this evidence and that in any case there were better ways of getting to know God (see Calvin 1960, book 1, chapter 5). By contrast liberal Protestants (in particular those of eighteenth-century Britain) argued at some length "from nature up to nature's God." So many of them saw the wonders of nature, especially the new ones recorded by microscope and telescope, as new and positive evidence of the existence of God, and they wanted to stir their religiously sluggish contemporaries to wonder. But finally in the mid-nineteenth century a combination of what I regard as very bad reasons deriving from Hume, Kant, and Darwin led to the abandonment of the ancient project of natural theology by so many parts of the Christian tradition. That was unfortunate – for Christianity (and every other theistic religion) needs natural theology.

For the practices of the Christian religion (and of any other theistic religion) only have a point if there is a God – there is no point in worshipping a non-existent creator or asking him to do something on earth or take us to heaven if he does not exist; or trying to live our lives in accord with his will, if he has no will. If someone is trying to be rational in practicing the Christian (or Islamic or Jewish) religion, she needs to believe (to some degree) the credal claims that underlie the practice. These claims include as their central claim, one presupposed by all the other claims, the claim that there is a God. None of those thinkers of the first 1850 years of Christianity who thought that there were good arguments for the existence of God thought that all, or even most, believers ought to believe on the basis of those arguments, or that conversion always required accepting those arguments as cogent. Most Christians may well have taken God's existence for granted. Most converts may have believed beforehand that there was a God; their conversion involved accepting more detailed claims about him. And if they did not initially believe that there is a God, they may have come to believe on the basis of religious experience in some sense rather than on the basis of natural theology. But nevertheless, most Christian thinkers before 1850 held that these strong arguments are available, and that those who did not initially believe that there is a God and were rational could be brought to see that there is a God by means of them.[1]

Many post-Kantian religious thinkers have drawn our attention to the roles of our personal religious experience and religious tradition in sustaining religious belief. It is indeed a basic principle of rational belief – which I call the Principle of Credulity – that in the absence of counter-evidence, what seems to you to be so on the basis of experience probably is so. If it seems to you that you see me lean on the lectern or hear my voice, then probably you do – unless you wake up and find that it was all a dream, or someone shows you that really there is no lectern there; what seems to be a lectern is really a hologram. And it is also a basic principle of rational belief – which I call the Principle of Testimony – that in the absence of counter-evidence, what people tell you is probably true. And so if your teachers tell you that the earth is many millions of years old, or you read in a newspaper that there has been an earthquake in Turkey, these things are probably so – unless you learn something else which casts doubt on them. When doubt is cast, we need positive arguments to show that there is a lectern there, or that the earth is many millions of years old. There can be no justification for not extending these general principles of rationality to the case of religious belief. If you have had an experience apparently of God, you probably have; and if your teachers tell you that there is a God, it is rational to believe them – in the absence of counter-evidence. Counter-evidence may take various forms – the fact of pain and suffering may seem incompatible with the existence of God or render it improbable – and rival teachers may tell you that there is no God. Counter-evidence may be strong or weak; and even if fairly strong may (rationally) not disturb the belief of someone who has had an overwhelmingly strong religious experience or believes on the authority of innumerable teachers of diverse backgrounds. But in general the presence of counter-evidence opens up the question of the existence of God, which then needs to be backed up by positive arguments (or to have negative arguments rebutted) if belief that there is a God is to be rational. But since there is so much more doubt about the existence of God in the skeptical West of today than in most previous cultures and centuries, the need for natural theology is far greater than it ever has been before – both to deepen the faith of the believer, and to convert the unbeliever.

The Nature of Inductive Arguments

The medievals, paradigmatically Aquinas, tried to cast reasoning from the world to God into the form of a deductive argument. But all that a deductive argument can do is to draw out in its conclusion what you are committed to by its premises. A valid deductive argument is one in which, if you affirm the premises but deny the conclusion, you contradict yourself. Yet it is most implausible to suppose that such a statement as "there is a physical universe but no God" (irrational though it may be to believe it) contains any internal contradiction. It's not like "there exists a round square." "There is a God" goes beyond premises affirming the existence or orderliness of the universe to something far bigger. But an argument that purports to be a valid deductive argument and is not valid, is invalid. And in the centuries subsequent to Aquinas many have pointed out the fallacies in the details of Aquinas's arguments.

However, an argument from the existence and orderliness of the universe to the existence of God is best represented not as a deductive, but as an inductive argument – one in which the premises make the conclusion to some extent probable, perhaps very probable, but not certain. All arguments in science and history from evidence to theory are inductive; but Aristotle and his successors, who tried (with moderate success) to codify deductive arguments by the forms of the syllogism, had very little understanding of the distinction between deduction and induction, let alone of the criteria of a good inductive argument. Only today are we beginning to have some understanding of induction. One feature of inductive arguments is that they are cumulative. One piece of evidence stated in the premises may give a certain amount of probability to the conclusion, and another piece of evidence may increase that probability. And if arguments from the universe and its order yield only a probable conclusion, not a certain one, there is room for religious experience and tradition. I wish now to argue that three arguments – from the existence of the universe, from there being simple scientific laws, and from those laws leading to the evolution of human beings – to the existence of God are strong inductive arguments. There will not be space to discuss other arguments, or to discuss arguments against the existence of God.[2]

Each of the phenomena cited in my opening paragraph has formed the starting point of an argument for the existence of God. These arguments seem to me to have a common pattern. Some phenomenon E, which we can all observe, is considered. It is claimed that E is puzzling, strange, not to be expected in the ordinary course of things; but that E is to be expected if there is a God; for God has the power to bring about E and he might well choose to do so. Hence the occurrence of E is a reason for supposing that there is a God.

This pattern of argument is one much used in science, history, and all other fields of human inquiry. A detective, for example, finds various clues – John's fingerprints on a burgled safe, John having a lot of money hidden in his house, John being seen near the scene of the burglary at the time when it was committed. He then suggests that these various clues, although they just *might* have other explanations, are not in general to be expected unless John had robbed the safe. Each clue is some evidence that he did rob the safe, and "confirms" (that is, strengthens) the hypothesis that John robbed the safe; the evidence is cumulative – when put together it makes the hypothesis probable.

Arguments of this kind are inductive arguments to the cause of the phenomena cited as evidence in the premises. Scientists use this pattern of argument to argue to the existence of unobservable entities as causes of the phenomena they observe. For example, at the beginning of the nineteenth century, scientists observed many varied phenomena of chemical interaction, such as that substances combine in fixed ratios by weight to form new substances (e.g., hydrogen and oxygen always form water in a ratio by weight of $1:8$). They then claimed that these phenomena would be expected if there existed a hundred or so different kinds of atoms, particles far too small to be seen, which combined and recombined in certain simple ways. In their turn physicists postulated electrons, protons, neutrons, and other particles in order to account for the behavior of the atoms, as well as for larger-scale observable phenomena; now they postulate quarks in order to explain the behavior of protons, neutrons, and other particles.

To be good arguments (that is, to provide evidence for their hypothesis), arguments of this kind must satisfy four criteria. First, the phenomena they cite as evidence must be the sort of phenomena you would expect to occur if the hypothesis is true. If John did rob the safe it is quite likely that his fingerprints would be found on it. Second, the phenomena must be much less likely to occur in the normal course of things, that is if the hypothesis is false. We saw in the burglary example how the various clues, such as John's fingerprints on the safe, were not much to be expected in the normal course of things. Third, the hypothesis must be simple. That is, it must postulate the existence and operation of few entities, few kinds of entities, with few easily describable properties behaving in mathematically simple kinds of ways. We could always postulate many new entities with complicated properties to explain anything which we find. But our hypothesis will be supported by the evidence only if it postulates few entities that lead us to expect the diverse phenomena that form the evidence. Thus in the detective story example we could suggest that Brown planted John's fingerprints on the safe, Smith dressed up to look like John at the scene of the crime, and without any collusion with the others Robinson hid the money in John's flat. This new hypothesis would lead us to expect the phenomena we find just as well as does the hypothesis that John robbed the safe. But the latter hypothesis is confirmed by the evidence whereas the former is not. And this is because the hypothesis that John robbed the safe postulates one object (John) doing one deed (robbing the safe) which leads us to expect the several phenomena we find. Scientists always postulate the fewest new entities (e.g., subatomic particles) that are needed to lead us to expect to find the phenomena we observe. They also postulate that those entities do not behave erratically (behave in one way one day, and a different way the next day), but that they behave in accordance with as simple and smooth a mathematical law as is compatible with what is observed. And fourth, the hypothesis must fit in with our knowledge of how the world works in wider fields – what I shall call our background knowledge. The hypothesis that John robbed the safe must fit with what we know from other occasions about whether John often robs safes. But the more we are dealing with a hypothesis which purports to explain a vast range of phenomena, the more this criterion tends to drop out, since there will be no wider fields of inquiry. There are no wider scientific fields relevant to assessing a very general theory of physics, such as Einstein's general theory of relativity purporting to explain all physical phenomena. And this criterion will not be relevant in assessing the hypothesis of theism – that there is a God – which is put forward as a hypothesis to explain everything we know (a hypothesis more general than the widest-ranging hypothesis of physics). An inductive argument from phenomena to a cause will be stronger the better the four criteria are satisfied, that is, the more probable it is that the phenomena will occur if the postulated cause occurred, the less probable it is that the phenomena will occur if the postulated cause did not occur, the simpler is the postulated cause, and the better the explanation fits with background knowledge. The better the criteria are satisfied, the more probable it is that the purported explanation is true.

Arguments from the Existence of the
Universe and Laws of Nature

The most general phenomenon that provides evidence for the existence of God is the existence of the physical universe for as long as it has existed (whether a finite time or, if it has no beginning, an infinite time). This is something evidently inexplicable by science. For a scientific explanation as such explains the occurrence of one state of affairs $S1$ in terms of a previous state of affairs $S2$ and some law of nature which makes states like $S2$ bring about states like $S1$. Thus it may explain the planets being in their present positions by a previous state of the system (the sun and planets being where they were last year) and the operation of Kepler's laws, which claim that states like the latter are followed a year later by states like the former. But what science by its very nature cannot explain is why there are any states of affairs at all.

My next phenomenon is the operation of the most general laws of nature, that is, the orderliness of nature in conforming to very general laws of physics, from which the regularities of chemistry and biology follow. What exactly the most general laws are, science may not yet have discovered – perhaps they are the field equations of Einstein's general theory of relativity, or more likely there are some yet more fundamental laws, perhaps the laws of a "Theory of Everything." Now science can explain why one law operates in some narrow area, in terms of the operation of a wider law in the particular conditions of that narrow area. Thus it can explain why Galileo's law of fall holds – that small objects near the surface of the earth fall with a constant acceleration towards the earth. Galileo's law follows from Newton's laws, given that the earth is a massive body far from other massive bodies and the objects on its surface are close to it and small in mass in comparison. But what science by its very nature cannot explain is why there are the most general laws of nature that there are; for *ex hypothesi*, no wider laws can explain their operation.

That there is a universe and that there are laws of nature are phenomena so general and pervasive that we tend to ignore them. But there might so easily not have been a universe at all, ever. Or the universe might so easily have been a chaotic mess. That there is an *orderly* universe is something very striking, yet beyond the capacity of science ever to explain. Science's inability to explain these things is not a temporary phenomenon, caused by the back-wardness of twenty-first-century science. Rather, because of what a *scientific* explanation is, these things will ever be beyond its capacity to explain. For scientific explanations by their very nature terminate with some ultimate natural law and ultimate arrangement of physical things, and the questions I am raising are why there are natural laws and physical things at all.

Personal Explanation

However, there is another kind of explanation of phenomena which we use all the time and which we see as a proper way of explaining phenomena. This is what I shall call personal explanation. We often explain some phenomenon E as brought about by a person P in order to achieve some purpose or goal G. The present motion of my fingers is explained as brought about by me for the purpose of writing an article. The cup being on the table is explained by a person having put it there for the purpose of drinking out of it. Yet this is a different way of explaining things from the scientific. Scientific explanation involves laws of nature and previous states of affairs. Personal explanation involves persons and purposes. If we cannot give a scientific explanation of the existence and orderliness of the universe, perhaps we can give a personal explanation.

But why should we think that the existence and orderliness of the universe has an explana-tion at all? We seek for an explanation of all things; but we have seen that we only have reason for supposing that we have found one if the purported explanation is simple, and leads us to expect what we find when that is otherwise not to be expected. The history of science shows that we judge that phenomena that are many and complex need explaining, and that they are to be explained in terms of something simpler. The motions of the planets (subject to Kepler's laws), the mechanical interactions of bodies on earth, the behavior of pendula, the motions of tides, the behavior of comets, and so forth formed a pretty miscellaneous set of phenom-ena. Newton's laws of motion constituted a simple theory that led us to expect these phenomena, and it was judged to be a true explanation of them. The existence of thousands of different chemical substances combining in different ratios to make other substances was complex. The hypothesis that there were only a hundred or so chemical elements of which the thousands of substances were made was a simple hypothesis that led us to expect the complex phenomenon.

Our universe is a complex thing. There are lots and lots of separate chunks of matter in the universe. The chunks have each a different finite and not very natural volume, shape, mass, and so on – consider the vast diversity of the galaxies, stars and planets, and pebbles on the sea-shore. Matter is inert and has no powers that it can choose to exert; it does what it has to do. There is a limited amount of it in any region and it has a limited amount of energy and velocity. The universe is a large and complex thing.

The conformity of objects throughout endless time and space to simple laws is likewise something which cries out for explanation in yet simpler terms. For let us consider what this amounts to. Laws are not things, independent of material objects. To say that all objects conform to laws is simply to say that they all behave in exactly the same way, that they have certain powers which they exert on other objects, and liabilities to exert those powers in certain circumstances. To say, for example, that the planets obey Kepler's laws is just to say that each planet at each moment of time has the power of moving in the way that Kepler's laws state, and the liability to do so while the sun and other planets are there. There is there-fore this vast coincidence in the powers and liabilities of objects at all times and in all places. If all the coins of some region have the same markings, or all the papers in a room are written in the same handwriting, we seek an explanation in terms of a common source of these coincidences. We should seek a similar explanation for that vast coincidence we describe as the conformity of objects to laws of nature, for example the fact that all electrons are pro-duced, attract and repel other particles, and combine with them in exactly the same way at each point of endless time and space.

The hypothesis of theism is that the universe exists because there is a divine person who keeps it in existence and that laws of nature operate because there is a divine person who brings it about that they do.[3] He brings it about that the laws of nature operate by sustaining in every object in the universe its liability to behave in accord with those laws. He brings it about that the universe exists by sustaining at each moment (of finite or infinite time) objects with the powers and liabilities codified by laws of nature including the laws of the conserva-tion of matter energy, that is by making it the case at each moment that what there was before continues to exist. The hypothesis is a hypothesis that a person brings about these things for some purpose. He acts directly on the universe, as we act directly on our brains, guiding them to move our limbs (but the universe is not his body – for he could at any moment destroy it, and act on another universe, or do without a universe).

As we have seen, personal explanation and scientific explanation are the two ways we have of explaining the occurrence of phenomena. Since there cannot be a scientific explanation of the existence of the universe, either there is a personal explanation or there is no explana-tion at all. The hypothesis that there is a divine person is the hypothesis of the existence of the simplest kind of person there could be. A person is a being who exists for some time with *power* to bring about effects, *knowledge* of how to do so, and *freedom* to make choices of which effects to bring about. A divine person is by definition an everlasting omnipotent (that is, infinitely powerful), omniscient (that is, all-knowing), and perfectly free person; he is an everlasting person of infinite power, knowledge, and freedom; a person to whose existence, power, knowledge, and freedom there are no limits except those of logic. The hypothesis that there exists a being with infinite degrees of the qualities essential to a being of that kind is the postulation of a very simple being. And it is simpler to suppose that these properties are not accidentally correlated with each other but follow necessarily from the essence of the divine person. The hypothesis that there is such a divine person is a much simpler hypothesis than the hypothesis that there is a God who has such and such a limited power. It is simpler in just the same way that the hypothesis that some particle has zero mass or infinite velocity is simpler than the hypothesis that it has 0.32147 of some unit of mass or a velocity of 221.000 km/sec. A finite limitation cries out for an explanation of why there is just that par-ticular limit, in a way that limitlessness does not. It follows from God's perfect freedom that he will be subject to no influences deterring him from doing what he sees reason to do. That is what he believes good to do; and since being omniscient, he will always know what is good, he will always do what is good. He will be perfectly good.

That there should exist anything at all, let alone a universe as complex and as orderly as ours, is exceedingly strange. But if there is a God, it is not vastly unlikely that he should create such a universe. A universe such as ours is a thing of beauty, and a theatre in which humans and other creatures can grow and work out their destiny. The orderliness of the universe makes it a beautiful universe, but, even more importantly, it makes it a universe which humans can learn to control and change. A good God will want to create creatures such as humans, having a free choice between good and evil, a deep responsibility for themselves and each other, and an ability to form their own character in such a way as to love God; and for that we need bodies, places where we can take hold of each other and so hurt or benefit each other. But we can only look after ourselves and each other (or choose not to do so) if there are simple laws governing a universe in which humans are embodied. If we have bodies, then there are ways in which we can hurt or benefit each other. But only if there are simple laws of nature which we can come to know will there be ways in which my doing this or that will make a predictable difference to me or you. Only if humans know that by sowing certain seeds and weeding and watering them, they will get corn, can they develop an agriculture. And only if they know that by rubbing sticks together they can make fire will they be able (if that is what they choose) to burn the food supplies of others. Graspable laws of nature allow agents a choice of how to treat each other. So God has good reason to make an orderly universe and, *ex hypothesi*, being omnipotent, he has the power to do so. So the hypothesis that there is a God makes the existence of the universe much more to be expected than it would otherwise be, and it is a very simple hypothesis. Hence the arguments from the existence of the universe and its conformity to simple natural laws are good arguments to an explanation of the phenomena, and provide substantial evidence for the existence of God.

The Argument from Fine-Tuning

The last phenomenon I shall consider is the evolution of animals and humans. In the middle of the nineteenth century Darwin set out his impressive theory of evolution by natural selection to account for the existence of animals and humans. Once upon a time there were primitive organisms. These animals varied in various ways from their parents (some were taller, some shorter, some fatter, some thinner, some had the beginnings of a wing, others did not; and so on). Those animals with characteristics that made them best fitted to survive, survived and handed on their characteristics to the next generation. But, although in general resembling their parents, their offspring varied from them, and those variations that best fitted the animal to survive were again the ones most likely to be handed on to another generation. This process went on for millions of years producing the whole range of animals we have today, each adapted to survive in a different environment. Among the characteristics giving advantage in the struggle for survival was intelligence, and the selections for this characteristic eventually led to the evolution of man. Such is Darwin's account of why we have today animals and humans.

As far as it goes, his account is surely right. But there are crucial matters beyond its scope. The evolutionary mechanism Darwin describes works only because there are certain laws of biochemistry (animals produce many offspring, these vary in various ways from the parents, etc.). But why are there these laws rather than other laws? No doubt because these laws follow from the basic laws of physics. But then why do the basic laws of physics have such a form as to give rise to laws of evolution? And why were there the primitive organisms in the first place? A plausible story can be told of how the primeval "soup" of matter-energy at the time of the "big bang" (a moment some 13 500 million years ago at which, scientists now tell us, the universe, or at least the present stage of the universe, began) gave rise over many millennia, in accordance with physical laws, to those primitive organisms. But then why was there matter suitable for such evolutionary development in the first place? With respect to the laws and with respect to the primeval matter, we have again the same choice: of saying that these things cannot be further explained, or of postulating a further explanation. The issue here is not why there are laws at all or why there is matter at all, but why the laws and the matter have this peculiar character, that they are ready wound-up to produce plants, animals, and humans. Since it is the most general laws of nature that have this special character, there can be no scientific explanation of why they are as they are. And although there might be a scientific explanation of why the matter at the time of the big bang had the special character it did, in terms of its character at some earlier time, clearly if there was a first state of the universe, it must have been of a certain kind; or if the universe has lasted forever (in addition to having the right kind of laws), its matter needed to have had at all times certain general features (e.g., in respect of the quantity of its matter-energy) if at any time there was to be a state of the universe suited to produce plants, animals, and humans. Scientific explanation comes to a stop. The question remains whether we should accept these particular features of the laws and matter of the universe as ultimate brute facts or whether we should move beyond them to a personal explanation in terms of the agency of God.

What the choice turns on is how likely it is that the laws and initial conditions should by chance have just this character. Recent scientific work has drawn attention to the fact that the universe is fine-tuned. Given laws of the present type (the four forces, constrained by the requirements of quantum theory), the matter-energy at the time of the big bang had to have a certain density and a certain velocity of recession; increase or decrease in these respects by one part in a million would have had the effect that the universe was not life-evolving. For example, if the big bang had caused the quanta of matter-energy to recede from each other a little more quickly, no galaxies, stars, or planets, and no environment suitable for life, would have been formed. If the recession had been marginally slower, the universe would have collapsed in on itself before life could be formed. Similarly, the constants in laws of nature needed to lie within very narrow limits if life was to be formed.[4]

Some contemporary physicists will tell you that we live in a multiverse such that many different universes with different laws and initial conditions will eventually be caused to occur, and so – they claim – it is not surprising that there is one with laws and initial conditions like ours. But, even if that were so, it is then immensely improbable that we should live in a multiverse that has the characteristic of producing at some stage a universe with laws and initial conditions like ours, when almost all possible multiverses would not produce such a universe. So, whether or not there is a multiverse, it is most unlikely that the laws and initial conditions of any universe should have by chance a life-producing character. God is able to give matter and laws this character either directly or by making a multiverse which produces a universe of our kind. If we can show that he would have reason to do so, then that gives support to the hypothesis that he has done so. There is available again the reason which (additional to the reason of its beauty) was a reason why God would choose to bring about an orderly universe at all – the worthwhileness of the sentient embodied beings that the evolutionary process would bring about, and above all of humans, who can themselves make informed choices as to what sort of a world there should be.

Conclusion

So the three arguments I have considered – from the existence of the universe, from its conformity to natural laws, and from the existence of humans and animals – to the hypothesis of the existence of God are all arguments that satisfy well the three criteria given earlier for inductive arguments to an explanation. The phenomena cited by the premises are not ordinarily to be expected, they are to be expected if the cause postulated in the conclusion exists, and the hypothesis of the existence of that cause is simple. Indeed, I suggest that not merely are these good arguments for the existence of God, but they are very strong ones. The postulated divine person is a very simple one, and it is vastly improbable that the phenomena cited should occur by chance, for instance that there should exist such an enormous number of atoms in the universe, all of which behave in exactly the same human-life-producing way.

Of course, the God to whom these arguments point is a person (or persons) about whom we can know only those properties responsible for the phenomena I have been discussing – his omnipotence, omniscience, and perfect freedom (and other properties which, I believe, are consequences of these, e.g. omnipresence and perfect goodness). Of what underlies these properties, of that in which the properties inhere, we cannot have any full understanding. But for the human pilgrim in this life, the former is quite enough; and some human pilgrims in the modern world need the strong inductive arguments that are available to show the existence of a God having these properties.

Notes

1 The great fourth-century theologian Gregory of Nyssa put the point like this: "Not that the same method of instruction will be suitable in the case of all who approach the word. . . . the method of recovery must be adapted to the form of the disease. . . . [It] is necessary to regard the opinions which the persons have taken up, and so frame your argument in the accordance with the error into which each have fallen, by advancing in each discussion certain principles and reasonable propositions, that thus, through what is agreed on both sides, the truth may be conclusively brought to light. Should [your opponent] say there is no God, then, from the consideration of the skilful and wise economy of the Universe he will be brought to acknowledge that there is a certain over-mastering power manifested through these channels" (1893, Prologue).

2 Positive arguments for the existence of God need to be weighed against arguments against the existence of God, by far the strongest of which is the argument from the existence of evil. On this see the article by Gale in part 6 of Meister and Copan (2007), chapter 9 of Mackie (1982), and chapter 6 of Swinburne (2010).

3 While Christians have always maintained that God is a personal being in the sense of being someone who has powers, knowledge, and freedom, they have also maintained that in a certain sense God is "three persons of one substance," Father, Son, and Holy Spirit. This is the doctrine of the Trinity. The arguments which I give are arguments to the existence of one divine person, on whom everything else depends. In terms of other monotheistic religions, such as Judaism and Islam, they are arguments to the existence of the one and only divine person. But given the Christian doctrine of the Trinity these arguments are to be construed as arguments to the existence of God the Father. That God the Father would inevitably cause the Son and Spirit requires further argument. For such an argument see Swinburne (2008, chapter 2).

4 For a fuller description of the evidence for fine-tuning see, for example, Collins (2003).

References

Calvin, John. 1960. *Institutes of the Christian Religion*. Translated by F. L. Battles. Philadelphia, PA: West-
    minster Press.
Collins, Robin. 2003. The Evidence for Fine-Tuning. In Neil A. Manson, ed. *God and Design: The Teleologi-
    cal Argument and Modern Science*. London: Routledge, pp. 178–199.
Gregory of Nyssa. 1893. The Great Catechism: Prologue. Translated by W. Moore and H. A. Wilson.
    In *Selected Writings of Gregory of Nyssa*. Oxford: Parker and Co.
Mackie, J. L. 1982. *The Miracle of Theism*. Oxford: Clarendon Press.
Swinburne, Richard. 2008. *Was Jesus God?* Oxford: Oxford University Press.
Swinburne, Richard. 2010. *Is There a God?*, revised edn. Oxford: Oxford University Press.

Further Reading

Craig, William Lane and Moreland, J. P., eds. 2009. *The Blackwell Companion to Natural Theology*. Oxford:
    Wiley-Blackwell. A large volume containing very full, high-level discussion of arguments, ancient
    and modern, for the existence of God.
Mackie, J. L. 1982. *The Miracle of Theism*. Oxford: Clarendon Press. Seeks to show that arguments for
    the existence of God are not cogent.
Meister, Chad and Copan, Paul. 2007. *The Routledge Companion to the Philosophy of Religion*. London:
    Routledge. Contains various arguments for the existence and non-existence of God, including
    those discussed in this chapter.
Swinburne, Richard. 2010. *Is There a God?*, revised edn. Oxford: Oxford University Press. A fuller pres-
    entation of the arguments discussed in this chapter as well as a response to the argument from
    evil to the non-existence of God.

12

"God of the Gaps" Arguments

GREGORY E. GANSSLE

Introduction

It is often the case that certain arguments for the existence of God, or for the claim that God has acted in the world, are branded with the label "God of the gaps argument." Such arguments are taken to be fallacious in a particularly ignorant sort of way. The label "God of the gap argument" ("gap argument" for short) is always pejorative, and it is thrown around readily. The label began to be used in discussions of the old-fashioned design arguments. The earliest reference to the phrase cited in the *OED* (online edition) is from 1894. Henry Drummond wrote, "There are reverent minds who ceaselessly scan the fields of Nature and the books of Science in search of gaps – gaps which they will fill up with God. As if God lived in gaps?" (Drummond 1894, 333). Today, the accusation of endorsing gap arguments is especially prevalent in disputes about intelligent design. For example, Dawkins has written, "Creationists eagerly seek a gap in present-day knowledge or understanding. If an apparent gap is found, it is *assumed* that God, by default must fill it" (Dawkins 2006, 125). Given the fairly common accusation that theists trade in gap arguments, it might pay to get clear on what sort of inferences gap arguments are supposed to be. Consider the following argument about some event in the world.[1]

(1)   Natural means cannot explain event *E*.
(2)   Therefore there is a supernatural explanation of event *E*.

Is this a bad argument? It can be shown to be valid, provided we add two premises:

(3)   There is an explanation of event *E*.
(4)   Every explanation is either natural or supernatural.[2]

The accusation of failure that goes with labeling this argument a gap argument cannot land on the *form* of this argument. The conclusion (2) follows clearly from premises (1), (3), and (4). If the argument is to be judged wanting, the problem must be somewhere else. The

---

The Blackwell Companion to Science and Christianity, First Edition. Edited by J. B. Stump and Alan G. Padgett.

charge of fallacy, it turns out, lands on the *justification* for the first premise. The first premise, after all, is the claim that does most of the work in the argument. Such a premise might be justified as follows:

(1a) No natural means we know of can explain event E.
(1b) Therefore probably no natural means can explain event E.

Notice that we cannot get more than probability in (1b). We cannot conclude that there is *definitely* no natural means of explaining the event. It is always possible that there is a natural explanation that is outside of our grasp. Therefore, we need to revise the original argument to accommodate the introduction of probability. The revised form can be expressed as follows (I shall call this the *central argument*):

(1) It is probably the case that natural means cannot explain event E.
(2) Therefore, it is probably the case that there is a supernatural explanation of event E.

If premise (1) of this argument is justified by the kind of reasoning we discussed, then it looks as if the argument *is* about a gap. The argument moves from a gap in our knowledge of possible natural explanations to a gap in reality. The question is why this kind of argument should be considered fallacious. More specifically, the question is why it should warrant the naming of an entirely new kind of fallacy. The "gaps argument" label is unique, but the argument form is not. The argument that the key premise is true turns out to be an instance of a more general kind of argument:

(a) No X we know of can do Y.
(b) Therefore probably no X can do Y.

We do not employ the "gap argument" label for *all* arguments of this basic kind. It is only when the argument is about natural and supernatural explanations that it is labeled a gap argument. Some might be tempted to think that there is something special about arguments that are about *God* such that they get labeled gap arguments while other arguments of the same structure will not earn the label. But what is special about the arguments that earn the "gap argument" label is not something about God, as we all know, but something about *science*. The gap in our knowledge appealed to is a gap in our scientific knowledge. From a gap in the current state of our scientific knowledge, we infer a gap in reality. We argue for a gap in what naturalistic items can explain.

The problem with this kind of reasoning, many argue, is that gaps in our scientific knowledge are shrinking. What we know today will be supplemented by more accurate, more detailed, and wider-reaching knowledge tomorrow. Locating our argument for a supernatural explanation in this kind of gap, then, is locating it on shrinking ground. As Dawkins suggests, "What worries thoughtful theologians such as Bonhoeffer is that gaps shrink as science advances, and God is threatened with eventually having nothing to do and nowhere to hide" (Dawkins 2006, 125). So the problem with the sort of gaps at work in these arguments is that they are shrinking.

Robert Larmer offers an analysis of gap arguments that will help us sort through the "shrinking gap" objection (Larmer 2002). Larmer thinks that people who apply the "gaps" label see these arguments as *arguments from ignorance*. They amount to an argument from "There is no proof (or you have not proved) that E is a natural event" to the conclusion

"Therefore E is not a natural event." You can see this connection in the comment of Dawkins. Creationists eagerly seek those places where they can say that there is no proof that some event is natural. Arguments from ignorance, of course, are fallacious.

Larmer mentions the fact that it is rare to encounter anyone defending any claim or position solely based on an argument from ignorance. What appears to be an argument from ignorance is usually an argument of a different form. Larmer provides a story to make this point clear:

> If my son tells me that there is a Great Dane in the bathroom and I go look and find no evidence of a Great Dane, I conclude that it is false there is a Great Dane in our bathroom. My lack of evidence of it being the case that there is a Great Dane in our bathroom is good evidence that there is not a Great Dane in our bathroom because I have knowledge that if a Great Dane were there, there should be positive evidence to confirm its presence. (Larmer 2002, 131)

Rather than being a straightforward example of an argument from ignorance, what Larmer employs in his reasoning is a principle that can be articulated as "If there were a Great Dane in the bathroom, it would be fairly obvious." His argument, then, is not the following:

(1)   There is no evidence that there is a Great Dane in the bathroom.
(2)   Therefore, there is no Great Dane in the bathroom.

Larmer's actual argument is:

(3)   If there were a Great Dane in the bathroom, there would be clear evidence of it.
(4)   There is no clear evidence that there is a Great Dane in the bathroom.
(5)   Therefore, there is no Great Dane in the bathroom.

Larmer has transformed the argument from ignorance into a positive argument of the form *modus tollens*.[3] The main philosophical premise is the conditional. As a result, we can see that what is at stake is not the *structure* of the argument but the truth of the conditional. What makes the conditional true (or false) is a series of facts about Great Danes and bathrooms. To know or to believe reasonably that the conditional is true requires that we know or believe reasonably the relevant facts.

Larmer's conditional analysis of gap arguments can be brought into my analysis above. Consider again the central argument:

(1)   It is probably the case that natural means cannot explain event E.
(2)   Therefore, it is probably the case that there is a supernatural explanation of event E.

The premise that does the work is (1): "It is probably the case that natural means cannot explain event E." This premise, as we saw, is justified as follows:

(1a) No natural means we know of can explain event E.
(1b) Therefore probably no natural means can explain event E.

As we noted, this argument is an instance of the following:

(a)   No X we know of can do Y.
(b)   Therefore probably no X can do Y.

This kind of inference is sometimes strong and sometimes weak. It all depends upon what we fill in for X and Y. We can go a long way towards specifying a *criterion* for determining the strength of the argument by appealing to the relevant conditional:

(c)   If there were an X that could do Y, we would probably know that this is the case.

If conditional (c) is true, then the inference from (a) to (b) is a strong inference. If the conditional (c) is false, then the inference is weak. Let us turn back to our justification for the main premise of the central argument. The relevant conditional is:

(1c) If there were a natural means to explain event E, we would probably know that this is the case.

Note that the conditional does not require that we know what the natural means to explain E is. We only need to know that it is probably the case that there is a natural explanation. If this conditional (1c) is true, then the inference from (1a) to (1b) is a strong inference. If it is a strong inference, then premise (1) of the central argument is justified. As a result, we have a strong argument. We have shown that it is probably the case that there is a supernatural explanation of event E. A successful argument like this one does not deserve a pejorative label or adverse judgment. If the conditional is false, however, the inference is weak. If it is weak, premise (1) is not justified and the central argument is not strong.

Larmer applies the conditional analysis to arguments that are likely to be branded as "God of the gaps arguments":

> Applying this analysis to the "God of the gaps" objection, we can ask whether those who appeal to gaps in our scientific understanding of nature as evidence of supernatural intervention in the course of nature do so solely or simply on the basis of ignorance of how natural causes operate or rather on the basis of presumed positive knowledge of how natural causes operate. (Larmer 2002, 131)

It seems clear that one who argues in the way we have analyzed is not appealing to what he does *not* know about natural causes and explanations. Rather, he is appealing (rightly or wrongly) to what he *does* know about them. It turns out, then, that an argument of this kind is not about gaps in our knowledge after all. It is not our ignorance of natural explanations that motivates the inference. It is our knowledge of natural explanations. Unless we have sufficient knowledge of natural explanations, we cannot make the inferences in question.

Shrinking Gaps?

How should the proponent of an argument that some event requires a supernatural explanation (call this a *supernatural argument*) respond to developing scientific advances? Suppose that when someone puts forward such an argument, the relevant conditional seems highly likely to be true. Everything we seem to know about the event and the facts relevant to it leads us to hold that, if a natural means to explain the event were available, we would probably know that this is the case. This fact grounds the inference to the supernatural explanation, at least for the time being. Now, there are two ways that advances in particular sciences might affect this argument adversely. First, these advances may result in the availability of a brand-new naturalistic explanation for the event. In this case, we would have to change our assessment of the original argument. The key premise, *it is probably the case that natural means cannot explain event* E, would be revealed to be false. As a result of the scientific advance, it is likely that there is a natural means to explain E.

Second, it is possible that advances in particular sciences will introduce other facts that are relevant to the event in question. These facts might not consist of new natural means of explanation, but they still might be facts that affect our assessment of the truth value of the relevant conditional. Suppose an argument for a supernatural explanation for event E turns on the fact that events and states relevant to E cannot be generated biochemically. (I have no particular argument in mind, here. This is just an example.) Because these events and states cannot be generated biochemically, E is the sort of event to which various possible natural explanations do not apply. The advances in scientific learning might reveal that those events and states relevant to E can be generated biochemically after all. In this case, what we took to be the relevant facts on the basis of which we judged the conditional to be true turned out not to be facts at all. We will need to reassess the truth of the conditional. This reassessment is necessary not because science has discovered new natural explanations that apply but because it has discovered new facts that reveal that old natural explanations might turn out to apply to the event in question.

In each of these cases a supernatural argument is overturned. The argument *was* a good argument, given the empirical knowledge we had at the time. What should we make of the fact that advances in science can overturn supernatural arguments? Advances in the sciences do not show that these arguments are simply attempts to find room for God in a shrinking gap. What we learn from the possibility of having these arguments overturned is that they are similar to any other argument that depends crucially on empirical premises. Our justification for any empirical premise may change with scientific and other empirical advances. This fact is not unique to arguments for supernatural explanations. Every argument that has empirical premises is subject to revision in these ways. The possibility that one will need to revise an argument on the basis of new knowledge, then, does not indicate that the argument was fallacious in any way.

The accusation that an argument aims at shrinking gaps, though, often comes from a conviction that *all* such arguments will be overturned eventually. One who shares this conviction will see the project of putting forward a supernatural argument as a task that can have only temporary success. It might look as though we need a supernatural explanation for an event, but it looks this way because we have yet to discover the grounds for the possibility of a natural explanation.

It might be possible to support the conviction that all such arguments will be overturned with an inductive argument. The term "shrinking gaps" suggests that there is a steady progress in the direction of there being less and less ground for these arguments. How strong could such an inductive argument be? There are some famous historical cases where scientists have posited the activity of God, only to have naturalistic explanations discovered by later theorists. We can think of Laplace's advances on Newton's theories of planetary motion as well as the impact of Darwin's theories on the design argument put forward by Paley and others. Clearly there have been supernatural arguments that were overthrown by advances in the sciences.

It is uncertain, however, if the historical record reveals enough cases to make a strong enumerative inductive generalization. There are two worries here. First, advances in the sciences might go in either direction. We may discover new facts that generate new arguments in favor of supernatural explanations. Surely advances in cosmology have done so in recent years. Second, what looks like an appeal to an inductive generalization might serve to conceal an *a priori* commitment to naturalism. The objector's conviction that the gaps are shrinking might be as much the result of a conviction that they *must* shrink as they are the outcome of inductive reasoning. There is nothing wrong, in this context, with a commitment to naturalism on the part of the objector. We might want to insist, however, that the objector recognize when his conviction about shrinking gaps is a result of this commitment, and not a result of an inductive argument that science advances steadily towards the elimination of the need for supernatural explanations.

The conviction that supernatural arguments will be overturned might be grounded in another way as well. The objector might think that we can never be in a position to assent to the relevant conditional. Perhaps the claim that *if there were a natural means to explain event E, we would probably know that this is the case* is not one we can be justified in holding. This posture does not require a commitment to naturalism or to an inductive argument that all gaps will be filled. Even if he is impressed with a particular argument for the supernatural, the objector might still refrain from affirming the truth of the conditional. Scientific discovery often proceeds along unpredictable paths. There might be little ground to think that the facts we grasp now are representative enough of what will be discovered to ground any degree of confidence in the truth or falsity of the conditional. The unpredictability of scientific progress might reasonably undermine such confidence. The best we might be able to do is to withhold judgment. There may be no way of justifying the claim that there is no natural explanation on the horizon.

The motivation for this criticism is similar to that of those who support the inductive argument that natural explanations will be found for every event. In each case, there is a concern that the variety of possible directions in the future of scientific discovery is not being taken seriously enough. As we have seen, supernatural arguments that employ a conditional of the form discussed thus far are not really arguments about *gaps*. Yet the deeper concern of the one who accuses theists of gap arguments and the one who withholds judgment about the conditional is the same. The one who withholds judgment is putting forward a more significant criticism insofar as it is not based either on a dubious inductive argument or on an *a priori* commitment to naturalism.

Strengthening Supernatural Arguments

If we are justified in our appeal to the relevant conditionals in these arguments, it is in virtue of our knowledge of the facts about the events in question and about kinds of natural explanations available to us. Many of these factual claims are empirical and, as we have seen, are subject to revision by advances in science. In spite of the possible need for revision, we can strengthen some of our supernatural arguments by appealing to relevant facts of another kind. These are facts about divine agency.

Michael Murray (2003) has argued against some proponents of intelligent design that we ought not to think of God's action in the world in interventionist ways. Murray is confident that we do distinguish validly between designed and non-designed systems, but he is unsure how we make this inference. It is in this context that he makes a passing suggestion about the role of divine agency:

Perhaps, we should take a cue from the old fashioned design arguments which said that "specified outcomes" are ones that exhibit patterns that intelligent beings often purpose to bring about in the world. So, when events exemplify patterns which are useful or aesthetically pleasing, we can regard them as likely to have resulted from design rather than chance. (Murray 2003, 312)

Murray's suggestion is that understanding personal agency may help us sort out cases in which a design inference is strong from those in which it would be weak. We can (and do) make judgments ahead of time as to what sort of outcomes we would expect from intelligent agents, human or otherwise.

J. P. Moreland has also appealed to divine agency to understand supernatural arguments. Contrary to Murray, he argues that thinking of divine agency in a libertarian manner should lead us to expect gaps in the natural world. He writes, "[B]elief in gaps should not be based on ignorance of a natural causal mechanism, but on positive theological, philosophical or scientific arguments that would lead one to expect such a gap" (Moreland 1997, 136). Both Murray and Moreland indicate that our understanding of intelligent agency can lead us to expect divine action in particular places. This in turn will direct our search for evidence of the supernatural in new ways. These new directions will strengthen arguments for supernatural explanations. Rather than relying only on one relevant conditional, we can employ an additional conditional in our argument:

(1d) If there were a supernatural agent at work in this context, we would expect an event like event E.

This new conditional allows for a stronger sort of argument for a supernatural explanation. We can compare two supernatural argument forms, each of which is immune from the shrinking-gap objection. The first adds the relevant conditional to the central argument (and fills in the premises needed to show the argument to be valid).

(1) No natural means we know of can explain event E.
(2) There is an explanation of event E.
(3) Every explanation is either natural or supernatural.
(4) If there were a natural means to explain event E, we would probably know that this is the case.
(5) Therefore probably no natural means can explain event E.
(6) Therefore, it is probably the case that there is a supernatural explanation of event E.

If we also include a premise about divine agency, we arrive at the *final argument form*:

(7)   No natural means we know of can explain event E.
(8)   There is an explanation of event E.
(9)   Every explanation is either natural or supernatural.
(10) If there were a natural means to explain event E, we would probably know that this is the case.
(11) Therefore probably no natural means can explain event E.
(12) If there were a supernatural agent at work in this context, we would expect something like event E.
(13) Therefore, it is probably the case that there is a supernatural explanation of event E.

Note that the first of these two arguments supports the need for a supernatural explanation simply on the basis of a low probability of an adequate natural explanation. If we *can* judge that the conditional (4) is true, then the likelihood of a natural explanation is low enough to support the conclusion. In contrast, the final argument also raises the likelihood that a supernatural agent is at work *independent* of the likelihood of a natural explanation. It does not rely solely on the task of lowering the likelihood of a natural explanation. Nor does it rely solely on our confidence in the truth of (4). As a result, this is a stronger argument form.

It may be fruitful to think about what grounds we could have to affirm the claim that *if there were a supernatural agent at work in this context, we would expect something like event* E (premise 12). It is at this point that the details of various concepts of God are relevant. Most philosophical discussions of religious belief begin with a concept of God something like the following: God is a being of unlimited power and knowledge who created the universe and who is wholly good. We will call this position *minimalistic monotheism*. Minimalistic monotheism is the bare minimum necessary for a position to count as theism. Using minimalistic monotheism as a starting point is appropriate in many philosophical discussions. Few philosophers who are theists, however, embrace minimalistic monotheism. Rather most hold to some form of *particularistic monotheism* (Ganssle 2003). Particularistic monotheism entails minimal monotheism, but it includes a lot more. For example, many of the theistic philosophers writing today are Christian theists. Other theists hold to other kinds of particularistic monotheism, such as Islamic theism or Jewish theism.[4] Each kind of particularistic monotheism brings different resources to bear on various philosophical problems. In trying to solve these problems, philosophers who are theists of a particular sort ought to draw on the resources provided by the particularities of their system of beliefs.

Christian theists hold to a significantly developed understanding of the nature and purposes of God. Some of the more detailed understanding held to by Christian theists is shared by other kinds of particularistic monotheism, although other aspects are distinct to Christianity. Christian theists, along with others, hold that God created the universe and human beings for reasons of his own. Furthermore, human beings are seen to be made in the image of God. These two features of creation help expand our understanding of the purposes of God. The fact that God made us the kinds of beings that seek knowledge reflects his character as omniscient. In addition, it helps explain his purposes in creating a world with stable physical laws. He made us as knowers and placed us in a specially designed knowable world. In addition, our moral sense, on a Christian view, reveals that the purposes of God include our engaging in interpersonal relationships through embodying certain virtues and practices.

Christian theists also believe that God's purposes include communicating knowledge about his own nature, human nature, and how we are to be related to him. God communicates through special events in history such as his acts of bringing his people out of Egypt, the sending of the prophets, and most decisively in the person of Jesus. In addition, Christians hold that God's revelation is captured in an authoritative form in the Scriptures. As a result, we are given much greater insight into the plans and purposes of God than we could discover through philosophical reflection alone.

God's action on our behalf in redemption also expands our notion of divine purpose and agency. Jesus is thought to be fully God and fully human. Whatever it means to be a human being is captured by the person of Jesus. This fact shapes the way Christians think of human flourishing as well as the metaphysics of the human person. God's action in our redemption also indicates that his purposes for us are not only moral, they are spiritual as well. We are made to know him.

In these ways, the Christian theist is in the position of having a more precise understanding of the aims of the divine agent than the minimal theist can have. Given a Christian understanding of the overall plan of God in creation and redemption, we have grounds to expect that God would be especially interested in the creation of beings that have specific capabilities. There is good reason to think that he would create conscious beings that are able to understand moral reality, use language, and act in the world for reasons. Furthermore, his purposes seem to include the sorts of beings who have sufficient freedom to engage in morally significant behavior.

One application of this analysis is that it might be more fruitful to look for the presence of supernatural agency at those points where we would expect such an agent to act. If there are two spots in the natural world where it seems that a natural explanation has equally low chances of being available, one might be a better candidate for a supernatural argument because it better fits our expectations of the activity of a supernatural agent.

For example, it may be that arguments that the flagellum involves a system that cannot be explained naturalistically will not be as strong as similar arguments pertaining to the origin of life, the emergence of consciousness, and the development of language. Each of these latter steps in the development of complex life looks a great deal more like the kind of step a supernatural agent would especially want to bring about. The transition from pre-bacteria to bacteria is less likely to be the sort of thing that is recognizably what we would expect an intelligent supernatural agent to accomplish.

Although theists are often accused of putting forward God of the gaps arguments that are obviously fallacious, we have seen that these arguments actually are not about gaps at all. Furthermore, they can be strong arguments, provided the truth of the relevant conditional can be affirmed. There remains a legitimate objection that we may not be in a position to assent to this conditional. In the face of this objection, I suggest that these arguments can be strengthened by the appeal to the nature of divine agency.

Notes

1   These are argument forms rather than arguments because they involve variables. Filling in the variables with appropriate values will turn the argument form into an argument proper.
2   For clarity of exposition, I will take the category of natural explanation to cover all explanations not involving supernatural persons. As a result, what Richard Swinburne calls a personal explanation, if it is taken to involve non-supernatural persons, counts as a natural explanation. I also assume, for simplicity, that all supernatural explanations involve supernatural agents. See Swinburne (2004, chapter 2).
3   Larmer here cites Walton (1996).
4   There may be other possibilities as well. Some theists will deny some of the positions that count as minimal theism but hold to a more robust overall view. An example is process theism, which denies that God is the creator of the universe.

References

Dawkins, Richard. 2006. *The God Delusion*. Boston: Houghton Mifflin Co.
Drummond, H. 1894. *The Ascent of Man*, 3rd edn. New York: James Pott & Co.
Ganssle, Gregory E. 2003. God and Evil. In Paul Copan and Paul K. Moser, eds. *The Rationality of Theism*. London: Routledge, pp. 259–277.

Larmer, Robert. 2002. Is There Anything Wrong with "God of the Gaps" Reasoning? *International Journal for Philosophy of Religion*, 52, pp. 129–142.

Moreland, J. P. 1997. Science, Miracles, Agency Theory and the God-of-the-Gaps. In R. Douglas Geivett and Gary R. Habermas, eds. *In Defense of Miracles: A Comprehensive Case for God's Action in History*. Downers Grove, IL: InterVarsity Press, pp. 132–148.

Murray, Michael. 2003. Natural Providence (or Design Trouble). *Faith and Philosophy*, 20, pp. 307–327.

Swinburne, Richard. 2004. *The Existence of God*, 2nd edn. Oxford: Oxford University Press.

Walton, Douglas. *Arguments from Ignorance*. Philadelphia: Pennsylvania State University Press, 1996.

Further Reading

Dawkins, Richard. 2006. *The God Delusion*. Boston: Houghton Mifflin Co. Presses the case that the question of God's existence is a scientific question and can be evaluated in terms of scientific evidence.

Ganssle, Gregory E. 2009. *A Reasonable God: Engaging the New Face of Atheism*. Waco: Baylor University Press. My response to the case for atheism as it is found in Dawkins, Dennett, Harris, and Hitchens.

Larmer, Robert. 2002. Is There Anything Wrong with "God of the Gaps" Reasoning? *International Journal for Philosophy of Religion*, 52, pp. 129–142. The most thorough investigation of the nature of God of the gaps arguments to date.

Moreland, J. P. 1997. Science, Miracles, Agency Theory and the God-of-the-Gaps. In R. Douglas Geivett and Gary R. Habermas, eds. *In Defense of Miracles: A Comprehensive Case for God's Action in History*. Downers Grove, IL: InterVarsity Press, pp. 132–148. Argues that we ought to expect gaps in nature as a result of divine intervention.

Murray, Michael. 2003. Natural Providence (or Design Trouble). *Faith and Philosophy*, 20, pp. 307–327. Defends a non-interventionist account of God's action in the world and criticizes some prominent proponents of intelligent design theory.

13

Natural Theology
after Modernism

J. B. STUMP

Natural theology is generally understood to be systematic inquiry into what can be known about God apart from what God has specially revealed. Because of the influence of the scientific revolution, natural theology gained popularity during the modern period (roughly the seventeenth through the nineteenth centuries) as a method of using scientific data to demonstrate the existence and attributes of God. But this version of natural theology depends on certain understandings of nature and science which were part of the modern worldview. Now that much of this worldview has changed, what are the prospects and challenges for natural theology? I'll trace some of the history of this problem and suggest that natural theology can no longer be properly understood as theological conclusions drawn from neutral, natural premises. Instead, natural theologians bring to their study of nature religious commitments which are corroborated when they find that nature behaves the way their religious commitments lead them to expect it to behave. Their articulation of a consistent explanation of the natural world is incorporated into Christians' proclamation of the Gospel message.

Natural Theology and Its Dissolution in the Modern Period

The nineteenth-century British mathematician and philosopher Augustus de Morgan included this now famous story in his *A Budget of Paradoxes*:

> Laplace once went in form to present some edition of his "Systeme du Monde" to the First Consul, or Emperor. Napoleon, whom some wags had told that this book contained no mention of the name of God, and who was fond of putting embarrassing questions, received it with – "M. Laplace, they tell me you have written this large book on the system of the universe, and have never even mentioned its Creator." Laplace, who, though the most supple of politicians, was as stiff as a martyr on every point of his philosophy or religion . . . drew himself up, and answered bluntly, "Je n'avais pas besoin de cette hypothèse-là." (1872, 249–250)[1]

The Blackwell Companion to Science and Christianity, First Edition. Edited by J. B. Stump and Alan G. Padgett.
© 2012 Blackwell Publishing Ltd. Published 2012 by Blackwell Publishing Ltd.

"I had no need of that hypothesis." Laplace's religious beliefs are debated, and his remark here is no help. He was not professing atheism to Napoleon, as his comments are sometimes construed. Rather, the point is one of disciplinary autonomy or completeness. In the seventeenth century, Newton's laws had elegantly shown how the mechanical laws of the celestial bodies were the same as those of terrestrial bodies. But like any scientific theory, there were some anomalies among the increasingly accurate observations of the heavens – phenomena for which Newton's science had no explanations. Why doesn't the gravitational force between the fixed stars cause them to collapse together? And why don't the gravitational effects of the planets on each other undermine the observed stability of the solar system? Newton could only call on God to intervene and tinker with creation in order to preserve it. To some, this spoke to God's continued role of sustaining the universe beyond merely creating it; to others, it stained God with incompetence for not being able to get creation right in the first place. Newton's great rival Leibniz charged him with a "very mean notion of the wisdom and power of God" since his God has to wind up, clean out, and even mend the "watch" of creation from time to time in order to set it right (Alexander 1998, 11–12). Laplace was on the side of Leibniz. His 1796 *System of the World* recast Newton's work in the more powerful differential calculus to show how the solar system did indeed obey the laws of motion without exception and so needed no tinkering to keep it going. Physics did not need to assume the existence of the Creator in order to explain the observed phenomena in physical terms. Physics could do just fine on its own.

This creates a problem for a certain kind of natural theology. In this original Newtonian variety of natural theology, God is a kind of corollary to scientific theories. These natural theologians begin by looking at natural phenomena and conclude that the natural order could not work that way on its own; supernatural intervention is required. This God of the modern period had taken up residence in the gaps that were unable to be explained by natural means. But throughout the period, the science got better at closing those gaps. So this version of natural theology became less and less plausible in both the physical sciences and in biology.

But natural theology came in another variety during the modern period. Instead of a corollary, God was more like a presupposition for the scientific theories of Descartes and those in his wake.[2] They didn't see God's existence as a consequence of their scientific theories; they began with God as the necessary supposition for the rationality of those theories in the first place. Descartes was concerned to answer the skepticism regarding claims to religious knowledge which had arisen through Michel de Montaigne's influential reading of the natural theology of a fifteenth-century writer, Raymond Sebond. Montaigne translated Sebond's work into French in 1569 and believed that it led to skepticism; Descartes's aim was to reverse that movement from natural theology to skepticism and show instead that skepticism could lead to natural theology.

He famously began by turning skeptical doubt on its head. In the very act of doubting Descartes found an absolutely certain foundation in the immediate consciousness of himself as the thing which doubts and thinks, and therefore exists. From there he would demonstrate the reliability of our ordinary empirical and rational beliefs from which science is derived. But in order to do that, he needed God to guarantee the non-existence of the evil genius who was invoked in the stage of radical doubt and who might be systematically deceiving us even in matters of mathematics and logic. Descartes needed God to ensure that mathematics works as we think it does. Once he had this, the rest of his scientific system was given in purely natural terms.[3] In this way he claimed to defeat skepticism and bring back natural theology on more secure, non-theological ground: God is the foundation without which natural science would not be reliable.

So far in this brief survey we have found belief in God as the fruit of natural science in Newton's view, or belief in God as the root of natural science in Descartes's view. In the climax of the modern period, Immanuel Kant showed to the satisfaction of most in his day that both of these approaches to natural theology are illegitimate. In his *Critique of Pure Reason* Kant argued that the application of pure concepts beyond the manifold of experience leads to the paralogisms and the antinomies of pure reason. The former undermine the Cartesian attempt to ground belief in God on the supposed certainty of self-knowledge; the latter undermine the Newtonian attempt to ground belief in God on our knowledge of nature. But according to Kant, proofs of atheism which are based on modern science are just as spurious. Proof or disproof for God's existence is not to be found in reason's theoretical realm. This was not his last word on the subject, however, for he went on to conduct a critique of practical reason as well. In Kant's *Critique of Practical Reason*, God became a presupposition or ground, not for science and theoretical reason, but for the moral life. As such, theology found itself less in conversation with metaphysics than with ethics; it was transferred from reason to practice, and from fact to value.

A stark separation between the external world of facts and the internal world of values was effected in the modern period and is crucial for understanding our topic.[4] It began with Descartes's bifurcation of reality into the outer world of extension and the inner world of thinking. Hume furthered the distinction by maintaining that facts are anything that could give us a sense impression. Kant sealed the separation with his critiques on pure reason and practical reason. Facts were objective, publicly accessible, and treated by science; values were subjectively chosen matters of conscience. God still had relevance for the ethical life, but in and amongst the hard facts of science, there were no theological facts to be found. Theological facts became religious convictions, and religious convictions were a species of valuing. And since we can't get "ought" (value) from "is" (fact), as Hume famously taught, natural theology in its modern guise was rendered impotent.

But we are not living in the modern period today. These are postmodern times. And while many still blindly assume the legitimacy of the fact–value distinction, the story of its dissolution is well known in philosophy of science circles. In brief, Hume's definition of a fact as something that can give us a sense impression became deeply problematic with the continuing development of the physical sciences in which unobservables like electrons came to play significant roles. The logical empiricists of the first half of the twentieth century tried various solutions to keep the realm of fact pure and untainted, but ultimately Quine (1980) showed to the satisfaction of most philosophers that we experience the world through complex webs of beliefs in which there is deep entanglement of facts and values. And more specifically to the realm of science, Kuhn (1970) contended that scientific theories are more like paradigms through which we view the world, so that even the observation of "facts" is influenced by and laden with our complex systems of belief. Theory choice, then, will depend on more than just the data or hard facts. Facts and values are difficult to sort out from each other, and values are part and parcel of the scientific process.

Is there hope for natural theology with this unraveling of the modern worldview? Since there is no stark separation of fact and value, and since there are values entangled with any interpretation of science, perhaps we really can begin with science and end with God after all? I do think there is hope for natural theology, but it is not simply reclaiming the kind of natural theology inspired by Newton or Descartes. For the lesson we should have learned during the twentieth century is that there are no neutral premises from which to begin and that that everyone will agree to. Instead, there is a different kind of natural theology that is more appropriate to our time and place; one which sees the natural sciences not as providing evidences for the existence of God from some supposed natural realm of objective facts, but as domains of knowledge in which faith commitments can be worked out in the language of science. To see this, we need to first examine more closely what kinds of values science depends on.

The Valueladenness of Science and the Example of Intelligent Design

There is an obvious influence that values can have on the development of science when we talk about the funding of scientific research. If funds are given by organizations with clearly articulated funding priorities, then these "values" cannot help but have an effect on the development of science. This is not the kind of value-influence on science that concerns us here. Rather, we're interested first in what Gerald Doppelt calls the influence of epistemic values on scientific knowledge. He has provided a careful and insightful analysis of this kind of valueladenness, and he sees three ways in which such epistemic values are operative in the production of scientific knowledge:

(1) normative commitments to *the value* of certain kinds or patterns of phenomena and *not others*, as what the theories of a science must or should explain, predict, and so on to constitute knowledge of the domain of that science (e.g., a physics of motions);

(2) normative commitments to (or interests in) *the value* of certain kinds of types of theory *and not others*, such [as] deterministic or indeterministic, possessing this or that mathematical structure, explanatory and/or predictive, as what theories must or should be like to constitute scientific knowledge of the domain (or in the discipline); and

(3) normative commitments to the *value* of *certain* kinds of inference, reasoning, or proof and *not others* (deduction, empiricist induction, the method of hypothesis, the consilience of induction) as how scientific theories must or should be established to constitute a knowledge of phenomena. (Doppelt 2007, 190)

Doppelt's careful analysis demonstrates that these values are not merely the product of scientific knowledge, as though all successful scientific theories have espoused the same epistemic values or we can use the methods of science to show that the epistemic values we use in our scientific theories are in fact the most reliable. Critics might try to show that, for example, the kinds of phenomena we look at, the kinds of theories we use to explain the phenomena, and the methods we use for arriving at those theories are in fact the most reliable in attaining true theories about the world. But this only pushes the problem back another level: what count as true theories about the world? Predictive success or explanatory power? The simplest theory or the one that unifies the most disparate phenomena? And so on. This supposedly naturalistic reliabilism is as value-laden as the bodies of scientific knowledge it hopes to evaluate (Doppelt 2007, 206).

The upshot of this is that the aims, problems, and methods of science change from time to time, varying with local evaluations of what counts as a legitimate scientific theory. For example, currently there is strong support from the scientific community for what is usually called methodological naturalism. On Doppelt's typology, this is a normative commitment to certain types of theories and not others. Specifically, theories which appeal to any sort of *super*natural agency are ruled out as unscientific. On this account, if at any point in an explanation we have to say, "and then a miracle happens," we are not giving a *scientific* explanation. Notice that methodological naturalists need not claim that no miracles happen or that there is no such thing as supernatural agency in the world; they just claim (qua methodological naturalists) that explanations appealing to the supernatural are not scientific explanations. One of the fundamental claims of the prosecution in Pennsylvania's *Kitzmiller vs. Dover Public Schools* case was that it is the intention of the intelligent design community to change what is accepted as science to include the supernatural. Judge Jones concluded, "It is therefore readily apparent to the Court that ID fails to meet the essential ground rules that limit science to testable, natural explanations" (Jones 2005, 70).

But if methodological naturalism is a normative commitment, it is hubris on the part of its proponents to declare that they have discovered the heretofore elusive criterion of demarcation that separates all legitimate natural science from the illegitimate. The supposed universality of methodological naturalism in the sciences just doesn't hold historically – science changes, and not just the conclusions of science, but the methods and aims of science. Even one with impeccable naturalist credentials like Quine recognized this, saying "If I saw indirect explanatory benefit in positing sensibilia, possibilia, spirits, a Creator, I would joyfully accord them scientific status too, on a par with such avowedly scientific posits as quarks and black holes" (Quine 1995, 252). Jeffrey Koperski (2008, 440) sums up the situation:

> The bottom line is this: The future use or suspension of [methodological naturalism] depends on what is discovered. If the best explanation for some new phenomenon is design, even supernatural design, it would still count as a scientific explanation. It borders on academic incompetence to pretend that science has strict boundaries and then gerrymander those boundaries to keep out the riffraff. Philosophers of science in particular should know better.

It is true, however, that the mainstream of the specific natural sciences right now purports to operate according to methodological naturalism. The proponents of intelligent design are perfectly free to adopt local values different from the mainstream regarding what counts as legitimate scientific explanation. It is even possible that they could ultimately win the day and persuade the mainstream that their view of science is "better." But even if they do, it would not be on the basis of objective, neutral criteria. However Quine's "explanatory benefit" is described, it will have normative commitment – values – as part of it.

A Religiously Neutral Concept of Nature?

It might be argued that even though there are no neutral premises that are free from these epistemic values, we might still use premises that are *religiously* neutral. We could appeal to nature as a non-religious realm which provides us with data from which we can draw conclusions with some import for theism. For example, the cosmological argument shows the necessity of a first cause or mover that is outside the realm of contingent causation; and the teleological argument provides compelling evidence that our universe was designed so that beings like us could flourish. These may not generate all of what Christian theists want to see in their concept of God, but they do provide an opening for the supernatural based only on neutral, natural premises. Or so the argument goes.

Our question here continues to be whether these really are neutral premises – religiously neutral in this instance. Consider the case of Aquinas, the natural theologian *par excellence*: his premises were certainly not religiously neutral. They couldn't be. His natural theology was an appeal to nature and drew from Greek and Arabic sources, but nature was a concept infused with theology in the Middle Ages. Nature was seen as God's creation (see Murray 1992). Even when it seemed that Aquinas employed his natural theology as apologetics directed at those outside the Christian faith, the overwhelming intellectual climate was mono-theistic (whether Christian, Jewish, or Islamic), and therefore the generic monotheism of Aquinas's arguments resonated within this common mindset. It might be argued that Aquinas upheld a distinction between nature and grace, and therefore there are two distinct realms, one of which makes no appeal to religious notions.[5] But for Aquinas (unlike some interpreta-tions of Augustine) the grace of God has already touched nature, and as such the two can never really be separated – hence the "synthesis" for which Aquinas is famous.

But then nominalist theology of the later Middle Ages dis-integrated the synthesis and allowed the theologians of the sixteenth century to adopt a concept of nature that seemed free from theological entanglement. What seemed autonomous, though, actually drew heavily from ancient Stoic authors for whom the cosmos had religious significance of a very different type from that of the Christian conception (Dupré 1999, 68–71). This is why the Reformers had serious misgivings about that supposedly "neutral" realm of nature. It is essentially their objection that lived on in Barth's rejection of natural philosophy (see Brunner and Barth 2002).

Still, couldn't it be argued that despite its origins the concept of the natural world used by scientists today is free from religious significance? This is a difficult argument to make, because just as the demarcation of science from non-science is notoriously difficult, here too the identification of what counts as religious will not be agreed upon by all. The case can be made that the naturalistic lens through which most scientists view nature does in fact func-tion as a religion in at least the cognitive sense. That is to say, a commitment to naturalism may not always involve the sorts of ritualistic worship generally associated with religions – though even on this count we might interpret the awe and reverence of some naturalists toward nature as instances of this – but naturalism fulfills the cognitive dimension of religion by supplying answers to ultimate questions: What is the ultimate nature of reality? Is there a God? Why are we here? What happens to us after death? In this sense, naturalism is a world-view and contributes to one's noetic structure in the same way that religious commitment does.[6] And it does no good in this regard to distinguish between methodological naturalism and metaphysical naturalism. Those who treat nature "as if" naturalism is true are still working qua scientists within a tradition of thinking which supplies (often unspoken) value commitments that color our understanding of nature. Mine is not an argument that scientists should not seek answers that are thoroughly naturalistic; again, that value has prevailed in the current climate of natural science. My argument is that we should not mistake the concept of nature from which they work as neutral – perhaps not even in the religious sense.

Nature has been understood in significantly different ways throughout the centuries. From Aristotle, Augustine, and Aquinas; to Descartes, Newton, and Paley; to present-day environ-mentalists, pantheists, and naturalists. In all of these instances, the preferred image of nature corresponds to the prejudices of a particular community which are read onto their subject. Nature is not an uninterpreted concept (cf. McGrath 2006, 81–135).

Such considerations make it very difficult to maintain that natural theology is argumenta-tion from neutral premises about the natural world to theistic conclusions. How might we re-envision natural theology in this context?

Natural Theology and *credo ut intelligam*

In the eleventh century Anselm, drawing explicit inspiration from Augustine's words (700 years earlier), wrote *credo ut intelligam* – I believe in order to understand.[7] It's not plausible to understand this *credo* as some sort of fideism for Augustine and Anselm – at least in the sense of fideism which finds its meaning in the context of modernism: religious belief ungrounded on (and even in spite of) reason. A huge component of Augustine's path to Christian faith was his use of reason against the spurious arguments of the Manichees, and Anselm claimed to prove that the existence of God and the Incarnation were necessary truths of logic. These were not stick-your-head-in-the-sand-and-just-believe simpletons. Furthermore, it doesn't appear that either of them had in mind the process of converting to Christianity when they claimed that they believed in order to understand.

The point of *credo ut intelligam* for them was that faith is the starting point for working out Christian understanding. That is, faith provides a stock of beliefs through revelation, for example God exists as a Trinity, the Incarnate Christ is fully God and fully human, the dead in Christ will be resurrected, and so on. But these are only the "data points" that need to be explained – much the way experiments provide data that must be explained via theories in the sciences.[8] Saying that faith is the starting point for understanding is not commentary on how any person came to faith; there are all sorts of ways and reasons people come to align themselves with Christianity and accept the truths of revelation – including reason. But it is an acknowledgement that there is much intellectual work to be done once we've accepted the faith; there is still the business of working out our faith (in fear and trembling, says the Apostle Paul), and if this is what they meant by understanding, then of course it would have to come after faith rather than before it.

Furthermore, the understanding, or what we might call an explanation or a theory, provides some justification for the "data." Again by analogy with the sciences, a theory explains the empirical data by providing a coherent story for why the data are the way they are. We understand the data, then, when we see through our theories why we should expect the world to generate such data. If the analogy works, faith generates the data of revelation; we understand these data more and more as we develop explanations for why we should expect those articles of faith to be what they are.

What are the implications for natural theology? Certainly arguments are offered which purportedly start from nature and argue to the existence of God. These have been powerful and useful tools that have contributed to the conversions of many to Christianity. That much is not in dispute. The relevant question here, though, is whether this is really natural theology in the modern sense of beginning with neutral scientific premises and arguing to conclusions with theological content. And if the foregoing is close to correct, then the answer must be that it is not. Science is never completely value-neutral and objective in the modern sense.

So even scientists work from a concept of nature that is not merely "the given." We see things "as" something according to theoretical presuppositions – especially as we move away from individual observances of a tree or an elephant or a waterfall and talk about a giant collective entity we call nature. But rather than despairing of this situation or pretending it isn't so, Alister McGrath (2009) sees it as an opportunity to reclaim the Christian notion of nature as creation. Nature is not uninterpreted, but that doesn't mean in some postmodern sense that every interpretation is just as good as the others. Seeing nature as God's creation may be an interpretation, but if Christians are right, it is the *correct* interpretation of what nature is. Furthermore, it has been argued many times that the Christian understanding of nature as God's creation was immensely important in the rise and development of modern science. Christians no less than others bring their values to the explanation of scientific data.

By analogy (and it's just an analogy), we might consider the perplexing nature of light and how if we put a wave-like question to it, like double-slit experiments, we get a wave-like answer; and if we put a particle-like question to it, like the photoelectric effect experiments, we get a particle-like answer. Similarly, the kind of answers that nature yields will depend on the kinds of questions put to it. And in this regard, the "questions" involve all sorts of assumptions – or value commitments along the lines detailed by Doppelt – about nature and about the methodology used to investigate nature. It is not surprising, then, that when some look at nature through the lens of their commitment to naturalism, they see only natural entities and natural laws.

Here we are back at *credo ut intelligam*. The data of revelation are being worked out in a scientific understanding of nature. Nature is rendered intelligible to us as explanatory theories are offered which are consistent with what we believe by revelation, and revelation is further understood as we see nature testifying to its creator. There is no escaping some circularity here, but that too is part of the dissolution of some elements of modernism. We need not embrace all the silliness of postmodernism, but when we realize that there will be no incorrigible or indubitable foundations from which we can deduce all truths to the satisfaction of all people, we're driven to accept some sort of hermeneutical circle. We do not have access to a standpoint from which there is perfect objectivity. Not only do we see the world through our values, we also judge the appropriateness of our values and the worldview they produce through our values. Hilary Putnam (2002, 32–33) said in this regard:

> If these epistemic values do enable us to correctly describe the world (or to describe it *more correctly* than any alternative set of epistemic values would lead us to do), that is something we see *through the lenses of those very values.*

It is my claim, then, that natural theology cannot be rational argumentation to theistic conclusions from value-neutral data provided by natural science. We'll not argue people to Christian theism from value-neutral premises, for there are no value-neutral premises. But what Christian natural theologians can do is to consistently proclaim the truth about the natural world as it is seen from the perspective of Christian theism. Perhaps this witness will be persuasive to others to accept Christianity when we show how our understanding makes a "better" explanation for why the world is the way it is, when we show that the world is the way we would expect it to be if it is the creation of the Christian God. In this sense, we are taking the approach promulgated by the pre-moderns. We are rendering revelation intelligible in the language of the day and showing Christian theism to be credible on the evidence we have, whether from science or elsewhere. This is what Augustine attempted to do in the language of Platonism; this is what Anselm attempted in the language of medieval logic; it's what Aquinas attempted in the language of Aristotelianism; and what Descartes and Newton attempted in the language of modernism. In each of these cases, there are facets of the schema language which stand in tension with Christianity, and so we see that any particular understanding that has been worked out doesn't last for all times, because those explanations are culture-bound to some degree. But the data of revelation persist and are there to be worked out again in a new cultural context.

The cultural context of contemporary science is methodological naturalism, which presupposes some kind of disciplinary autonomy. As in Laplace's remark with which we began this investigation, physics (or any other scientific discipline) strives to be able to answer questions in the domain of physics using just the resources of physics. We've seen that there will necessarily be some elements which come from outside of physics because of the role of epistemic values. But given the epistemic values of the current climate, supernatural elements have no purchase in these scientific explanations. Can the data of Christian revelation be worked out in such a climate that seems so inimical to the supernatural? Yes, they can.

To assume that biology (again to take just one scientific discipline) cannot give a coherent and reasonably complete explanation of living things from the perspective of biology is to claim there are gaps in the laws of biology – not just in our understanding of them, which may always be incomplete – but in the integrity of the biological order itself. It is these ontological gaps that intelligent design counts on for the success of its theories: irreducibly complex structures could not have come about according to the mechanisms of evolution, or information could not have been generated through natural processes to code for life. Such a perspective suggests that the Creator did not endow creation with its own fruitful, creative capacities to grow and develop without some kind of divine intervention or tinkering (remember Leibniz's comment about Newton's God).

But we can instead assume a different stance, one that takes the natural order as complete in itself. Then it is the laws themselves – rather than the gaps in the laws – that point to the God who creates and sustains the natural order. Scientists (whether Christians or not) are free to investigate this natural order without considering why it is ordered in the way it is, taking the laws as brute facts. But Christian natural theologians will see the natural order as imbued with purpose, and the more scientists reveal the ordered and lawful behavior of the natural realm, the more natural theologians will revel in God's provision for creation. Scientists discover "facts" about the natural order that are surprising and incredible (in the literal sense of not easily believed) – perhaps the cosmological constants that seem to have been selected to allow for life; perhaps the evolutionary convergences that seem to be conspiring to bring about life forms like us. These are not so incredible, though, when viewed through the lens of Christian theism. In fact, they're just what we would expect from the God revealed to us in the Christian tradition. The data of faith are corroborated by this view of science. We are working out an understanding of our beliefs which supports the coherence and rationality of a deeply Christian worldview. That is natural theology for our era.

Notes

My thanks to Chad Meister and Alan Padgett for helpful comments on earlier drafts of this chapter.

1   De Morgan's account is not very accurate in its detail, but there is probably some truth to this supposed encounter between Napoleon and Laplace. William Herschel preserved a record of a visit by Napoleon to Malmaison (Josephine's estate) on August 8, 1802, where Hershel and Laplace were visiting. After a discussion with Herschel, Napoleon also addressed himself to Laplace and had a considerable disagreement with him: "The difference was occasioned by an exclamation of the First Consul's, who asked in a tone of exclamation or admiration (when we were speaking of the extent of the sidereal heavens), 'and who is the author of all this?' M. de LaPlace wished to shew that a chain of natural causes would account for the construction and preservation of the wonderful system; this the First Consul rather opposed" (Lubbock 1933, 310).

2   These characterizations of Newtonian and Cartesian approaches to natural theology are admittedly superficial. In reality, both are more complex. For my purposes here, they serve to highlight or illustrate types or tendencies within the natural theology of the seventeenth and eighteenth

centuries. See Buckley 1987 for a more elaborate discussion of these approaches to natural theology.

3 Of course this move generates the infamous problem of the Cartesian Circle: Descartes needs God to prove that reason is not systematically deceived, but he can only prove the existence of God using reason. This is a serious interpretive difficulty for understanding Descartes, but that lies outside the scope of this chapter.

4 For a more complete account than can be given here, see Putnam 2002.

5 Here "nature" takes on a different connotation to our ears today, more like "human nature" than "the natural world." But both these "internal" and "external" senses spring from the same source and were much more closely linked in the Middle Ages. See Murray 1992, 26–27.

6 See Plantinga 2011, chapter 10, and his contribution to the current volume, THE EVOLUTIONARY ARGUMENT AGAINST NATURALISM.

7 Augustine wrote, "For understanding is the reward of faith. Therefore do not seek to understand in order to believe, but believe that thou mayest understand" (Lectures or Tractates on the Gospel According to St. John, tractate XXIX, 6). Anselm wrote, "For I do not seek to understand that I may believe, but I believe in order to understand. For this also I believe, that unless I believed, I should not understand" (Proslogion, chapter 1).

8 This insight is taken from Gilson (1938, 32). He does not push the analogy with science any further, though, as I'm attempting to do.

References

Alexander, H. G., ed. 1998. The Leibniz–Clarke Correspondence. Manchester: Manchester University Press.

Brunner, Emil and Barth, Karl. 2002. Natural Theology: Comprising "Nature and Grace" by Professor Dr. Emil Brunner and the Reply "No!" by Dr. Karl Barth. Eugene, OR: Wipf and Stock Publishers.

Buckley, Michael J. 1987. At the Origins of Modern Atheism. New Haven: Yale University Press.

De Morgan, Augustus. 1872. A Budget of Paradoxes. London: Longmans, Green, and Co.

Doppelt, Gerald. 2007. The Valueladenness of Scientific Knowledge. In Harold Kincaid, John Dupré, and Alison Wylie, eds. Value-Free Science? Ideals and Illusions. Oxford: Oxford University Press, pp. 188–217.

Dupré, Louis. 1999. Secular Philosophy and Its Origins at the Dawn of the Modern Age. In Francis J. Ambrosio, ed. The Question of Christian Philosophy Today. New York: Fordham University Press, pp. 61–79.

Gilson, Etienne. 1938. Reason and Revelation in the Middle Ages. New York: Charles Scribner's Sons.

Jones, John E. 2005. In the United States District Court for the Middle District of Pennsylvania. Case no. 04cv2688. Memorandum Opinion, December 20, 2005, online at www.pamd.uscourts.gov/kitzmiller/kitzmiller_342.pdf (accessed March 15, 2011).

Koperski, Jeffrey. 2008. Two Bad Ways to Attack Intelligent Design and Two Good Ones. Zygon, 43(2), pp. 433–449.

Kuhn, Thomas. 1970. The Structure of Scientific Revolutions, 2nd edn. Chicago: University of Chicago Press.

Lubbock, Constance Ann. 1933. The Herschel Chronicle: The Life-Story of William Herschel and His Sister, Caroline Herschel. New York: The Macmillan Company.

McGrath, Alister E. 2006. A Scientific Theology: Nature. London: T&T Clark.

McGrath, Alister E. 2009. A Fine-Tuned Universe: The Quest for God in Science and Theology. Louisville: Westminster John Knox Press.

Murray, Alexander. 1992. Nature and Man in the Middle Ages. In John Torrance, ed. The Concept of Nature. Oxford: Oxford University Press, pp. 25–62.

Quine, W. V. O. 1980. Two Dogmas of Empiricism. In *From a Logical Point of View*, 2nd edn. Cambridge, MA: Harvard University Press, pp. 20–46.

Quine, W. V. O. 1995. Naturalism; or Living within One's Means. *Dialectica*, 49, pp. 251–261.

Plantinga, Alvin. 2011. *Where the Conflict Really Lies: Science, Religion, and Naturalism*. Oxford: Oxford University Press.

Putnam, Hilary. 2002. *The Collapse of the Fact/Value Dichotomy*. Cambridge, MA: Harvard University Press.

Further Reading

Buckley, Michael J. 1987. *At the Origins of Modern Atheism*. New Haven: Yale University Press. An important book on the origins of atheism during the modern period, with significant implications for the topic of this chapter.

Gilson, Etienne. 1938. *Reason and Revelation in the Middle Ages*. New York: Charles Scribner's Sons. A short study that sets the "natural theology" of the Middle Ages in its proper intellectual context, which is very different from the context of natural theology in the modern period.

McGrath, Alister E. 2009. *A Fine-Tuned Universe: The Quest for God in Science and Theology*. Louisville: Westminster John Knox Press. McGrath's 2009 Gifford lectures, which argue for an understanding of natural theology along the lines of this chapter.

Torrance, John, ed. 1992. *The Concept of Nature*. Oxford: Oxford University Press. A collection of articles documenting how the concept of nature has changed since antiquity.

14

Religious Epistemology Personified
God without Natural Theology

PAUL K. MOSER

> Jesus answered . . . "Truly, truly, you seek me, not because you saw signs, but because you ate your fill of the loaves. Do not labor for the food which perishes, but for the food which endures to eternal life, which the Son of man will give to you; for on him has God the Father set his seal." (John 6:26–27, RSV)

According to John's Gospel, God cares about human motives in seeking and believing regarding God. More generally, John's Gospel suggests that God cares about how we fill in the blank in this locution: "I inquire or believe regarding God's existence because I want –." As a result, we should begin by asking what human motive(s) God would want to underlie human inquiry and belief regarding God. This strategic lesson is widely neglected among philosophers and others, but its answer can illuminate religious epistemology. In particular, as we shall see, this lesson can highlight the shortcomings of the arguments of traditional natural theology.

What has traditional natural theology to do with Christian belief, particularly with belief regarding the Jewish–Christian God? Such natural theology offers arguments, in *a priori* and *a posteriori* forms, for the conclusion that God exists, and some of these arguments have been highly influential in many movements and eras. They include various ontological, contingency, cosmological, teleological, moral, and psychological arguments, among others, and the pertinent details can be remarkably elaborate. We shall see that such arguments fail to accommodate the motive(s) that God, as worthy of worship, would want in human inquiry and belief regarding God. The Jewish–Christian God, according to this chapter, does not need the arguments of natural theology and is not the god represented by such arguments. The Jewish–Christian God, in other words, is not the god of the philosophers' traditional theological arguments.

Natural Theology and God

Philosophers and theologians do not all mean the same thing by "natural theology." Some have in mind any theological information or beliefs independent of Scripture, whereas some

The Blackwell Companion to Science and Christianity, First Edition. Edited by J. B. Stump and Alan G. Padgett.
© 2012 Blackwell Publishing Ltd. Published 2012 by Blackwell Publishing Ltd.

others have in mind theological arguments of a certain sort that are independent of Scripture. James Barr offers the following characterization:

> Traditionally "natural theology" has commonly meant something like this: that 'by nature', that is, just by being human beings, men and women have a certain degree of knowledge of God and awareness of him, or at least a capacity for such an awareness; and this knowledge exists anterior to the special revelation of God made through Jesus Christ, through the Church, through the Bible. (Barr 1993, 1)

This characterization is very broad in that it does not require of natural theology any arguments for God's existence, certainly not the traditional arguments for God's existence. In focusing on these traditional arguments, this chapter will work with a narrower conception of natural theology. It will understand "natural theology" to require reliance on (a variation of) at least one of the aforementioned traditional arguments for God's existence.

Barr's characterization mentions "a certain degree of knowledge of God and awareness of him, or at least a capacity for such an awareness" independent of special revelation from God through Jesus, the Christian church, and the Bible. This is vague talk, because it does not indicate whether the relevant knowledge of God has certain propositional content, such as the content that God exists. Initially, one might think that the relevant knowledge requires a direct awareness of God, regardless of the propositional content one accepts. This would be mistaken, however, because the characterization allows for just "a capacity" for awareness of God, and such a capacity does not require actual awareness of God. Accordingly, Barr's characterization is unacceptably vague. We can remove the vagueness by requiring of natural theology reliance on (a variation of) at least one of the aforementioned traditional arguments for God's existence.

The arguments of natural theology seek to establish, or at least to confirm, God's existence on the basis of *natural* sources of human knowledge, without an appeal to a special revelation from God. If an argument appeals to a special revelation from God, it arguably qualifies as an argument of *supernatural* theology rather than of natural theology. The distinction between what is natural and what is supernatural may not be altogether clear, but we can exclude from what is natural at least a direct word from God or a word from God through God's prophets. Traditional natural theology proceeds with this exclusion.

Philosophers rarely note that we have no distinctively *Jewish–Christian* natural theology that concludes with the claim that the Jewish–Christian God exists. The lack of a distinctively Jewish–Christian natural theology suggests that the distinctive features of the Jewish–Christian God demand more than what we humans can confirm by our natural sources of information. I take this suggestion seriously, and will contend that traditional natural theology is inadequate and dispensable relative to the standard of the Jewish–Christian God.

If an argument is to establish the existence of the Jewish–Christian God, it must establish the existence of a *personal agent worthy of worship*. Worthiness of worship is, of course, no small matter. It requires worthiness of full, unqualified commitment, because worship requires full, unqualified commitment. In addition, one will be worthy of full, unqualified commitment only if one is morally perfect, that is, morally without defect. Moral defectiveness, such as selfishness, undermines worthiness of full commitment and therefore precludes worthiness of worship. As a result, given the title "God" as used in central parts of Jewish–Christian monotheism, God's character must be free of selfishness and characterized by unselfish love, or *agape*, toward all persons, even toward enemies of God. The title "God," accordingly, is a maximally exalted title regarding moral character.

Advocates of natural theology have the burden of establishing via an argument limited to natural sources of evidence that a personal agent worthy of worship exists. None of the arguments of natural theology, however, enjoys widespread support as having actually discharged this burden. We can characterize the history of natural theology as the history of attempting to secure knowledge of God's reality solely via natural sources of evidence, without acknowledging evidence of God's authoritative call to humans. We should consider some reasons why this widely influential attempt fails.

Inadequate Arguments

One big problem for natural theology is this: the traditional *a posteriori* arguments for God's existence confirm *at most* the existence of causes *just adequate*, and not beyond just adequate, to yield their selected features. These features include observed causal chains of contingent events, perceived order or fine-tuning in nature, moral duties binding on humans, human self-reflective consciousness, and so on. The relevant just-adequate causes of these features fail to establish or confirm the existing moral character of a personal agent worthy of worship, who is perfectly loving toward all agents. Some friends of natural theology have conceded this inadequacy, but they then have retreated to arguments for something inferior to God as a personal agent worthy of worship. If, however, the desired conclusion is to yield a personal God worthy of worship, such as the Jewish–Christian God, who seeks fellowship with humans on divine terms, then the familiar *a posteriori* arguments fail to yield the desired conclusion. We shall use a few familiar examples to illustrate the problems for the arguments of natural theology.

Cosmological arguments

Consider Thomas Aquinas's cosmological argument, in the *Summa Theologica*, I, q.2, a.3, that begins by acknowledging a case of efficient causation in the empirical world. The argument then claims that nothing is either the efficient cause of itself or part of an infinite causal chain, and it concludes that it is necessary to acknowledge "a first efficient cause, *which everyone gives the name of God.*" Let's grant, for the sake of argument, Aquinas's inference that there is a *first* efficient cause, although there is serious philosophical controversy over this inference. The big problem is that the inference to a first cause gives us, at most, a first cause *just adequate*, and not beyond just adequate, for the observed causal chains in the empirical world. Clearly, however, *this* first cause falls far short of a living personal God who is worthy of worship and who therefore, out of *agape*, seeks fellowship with humans. In particular, we have no good reason to ascribe *moral perfection* to the inferred first cause in question. It is also doubtful that we have good grounds to assign fellowship-seeking *personal agency* to this first cause. Minimally, it is not obvious that such personal agency is needed to accommodate the relevant empirical data regarding causal chains. Those data offer no definite indication, *de re* or otherwise, of the reality of a personal agent, let alone a personal agent who is worthy of worship and seeks fellowship with humans.

It is dubious at best for Aquinas to refer to "a first efficient cause, *which everyone gives the name of God*," and a similar dubious reference to God occurs in the corresponding argument in his *Summa contra Gentiles*. We should be suspicious of this reference to God, given the exalted demand of morally perfect personal agency in one's satisfying the title "God," particularly in the case of the Jewish–Christian God. If Aquinas's argument does not establish or confirm the existence of a morally perfect intentional agent, then that argument does not establish or confirm that *God* exists, whatever else it establishes or confirms. Proponents of natural theology often overlook this kind of consideration, and their natural theology suffers accordingly.

A related problem for natural theology stems from the elusiveness of the Jewish–Christian God, as indicated in Isaiah 45:15: "Truly, you are a God who hides yourself" (cf. Matt. 11:25–26; Luke 10:21). Consider Aquinas's evidence consisting of efficient causation in the empirical world. That empirical evidence is static in a way that occurrent evidence of the presence and the reality of the Jewish–Christian God is not, given God's elusiveness. Aquinas's evidence involving efficient causation is not variable relative to the volitional tendencies of human agents toward God and God's will. Accordingly, Aquinas's empirical evidence fails to accommodate the personally interactive character of God's self-revelation, which includes God's intermittent hiding and seeking relative to humans and their volitional tendencies. The self-revelation of the Jewish–Christian God would include a redemptive aim to transform humans, and this revelation therefore should be expected to be personally interactive, variable, and intermittent in ways not found in mere efficient causation in the empirical world. Aquinas's proposed evidence in the cosmological argument, accordingly, is not suited to the cognitively and personally dynamic Jewish–Christian God. The same problem bears on the other cosmological arguments offered by proponents of natural theology.

Teleological arguments

The two aforementioned problems bear on other influential arguments of natural theology that rely on empirical observation, including Aquinas's teleological arguments in the *Summa Theologica* (I, q.2, a.3) and the *Summa contra Gentiles* (I, chapter 13, section 35). First, the just-adequate cause of Aquinas's observed complex structures in nature does not yield the morally perfect Jewish–Christian God who is a personal agent worthy of worship, even *if* it involves some lesser designer. Aquinas therefore had no adequate ground in his *natural* theology for ascribing the title "God" to his alleged designer. Likewise, more recent variations on Aquinas's teleological argument cannot escape this problem while remaining within *natural* theology based on natural sources of belief. Warranted application of the exalted title "God" to an agent requires evidence of a morally perfect personal agent who calls receptive humans to fellowship with himself on divine terms. A response that would attempt to extend natural theology to include a humanly experienced divine call to humans will not serve natural theology, because it will move beyond natural theology proper to *supernatural* theology.

Second, teleological arguments cannot avoid the aforementioned problem of divine elusiveness. Aquinas's evidence, consisting of certain complex structures in nature, is static in a way that occurrent evidence of the reality of the Jewish–Christian God is not. Aquinas's evidence from complex structures in nature does not vary relative to the wills of human agents toward God's will. Accordingly, this evidence does not fit with God's personally interactive hiding and seeking relative to humans for the sake of their character transformation. As suggested, God's self-revelation would aim at transforming humans morally and therefore would be personally variable and interactive in ways that mere complex structures in nature are not. As a result, the evidence offered in Aquinas's teleological argument does not conform to the personally and cognitively dynamic Jewish–Christian God who seeks human transformation toward God's moral character. The same is true of the various other teleological arguments in circulation.

Ontological arguments

Ontological arguments might seem more promising than cosmological and teleological arguments. Characteristically, they proceed *a priori* from a *concept* of a perfect being to the *actual existence* of such a being, on the assumption that such a concept without the actual existence of its represented object would not genuinely be that of a truly perfect being. The lack of existence in the represented object, according to this assumption, precludes the concept from being a genuine concept of a perfect object. As a result, an ontological argument might seem to sustain natural theology in the face of the aforementioned problems. In particular, an ontological argument might seem to guarantee the existence of a being worthy of worship rather than a being just adequate to yield some empirical, moral, or psychological feature of the world. Let's briefly explore this prospect.

We can distinguish between an *existence-affirming* concept of a perfect being and an *existence-guaranteeing* concept of a perfect being. An existence-affirming concept of a perfect being includes, if only implicitly, either *correct or incorrect* affirmation of the existence of that being. Such a concept does not guarantee, by itself, the existence of a perfect being. One could have the existence-affirming concept even though the conceptualized perfect being does not exist. By analogy, one could have the concept of a perfect unicorn while such a unicorn does not actually exist. In contrast, an existence-guaranteeing concept of a perfect being would logically preclude *incorrect* affirmation of the existence of that being, at least in any world where the concept exists, in virtue of guaranteeing the existence of that being. A concept of a perfect being typically affirms, if only implicitly, the existence of that being, but this affirmation may be mistaken.

As suggested, an ontological argument characteristically includes an existence-affirming concept of a perfect being. This should prompt us to ask whether its (possibly implicit) affirmation of the existence of the perfect being is correct rather than incorrect. In other words, we should ask whether reality actually includes the perfect being in question. Perhaps reality does not actually include a perfect being, despite the concept's (possibly implicit) affirmation to the contrary. Accordingly, an existence-affirming concept of a perfect being will not settle by itself the issue of whether God actually exists. As a result, ontological arguments fail to supply a logically conclusive move from a concept of a perfect being to the existence of a perfect being, even if the existence of a perfect being is thereby affirmed.

We can put the concern in somewhat different terms. A simple question arises when an ontological argument offers an alleged existence-guaranteeing concept of a perfect being, on the ground that if the concept's represented object fails to exist, then the concept is not genuinely that of a *perfect* object. We then need to ask whether we actually have a genuine concept of a perfect being that guarantees the existence of a perfect being. In other words, we must ask whether, necessarily, given the concept, reality includes a perfect being. Likewise, we must ask whether the concept in question is actually existence-*affirming* but *not* existence-*guaranteeing* regarding a perfect being. We can grant that the concept is existence-affirming, but this leaves open the question of whether a perfect being actually exists.

It would be fatally question-begging to assume that the concept's affirmation of the existence of a perfect being is correct just by virtue of the affirmation. We can have a concept that is *incorrect* in its affirmation of the existence of a perfect being, even if that affirmation is integral to the concept. In that case, we can have a concept of a perfect being without a corresponding real object, or real perfect being. Such a concept–object disconnect threatens any alleged existence-guaranteeing concept of a perfect being by raising the question of whether we have a genuine existence-guaranteeing concept after all. It is not automatic that we actually have a *concept* of a perfect divine being that guarantees, beyond merely affirming, the existence of that being.

It would be pointlessly question-begging to construe the use of the word "of" in the phrase "concept of a perfect being" as *de re* or denoting, as though it actually refers to a perfect being. Anselm may have made such a serious mistake, given a certain Platonic view of meaning as naming (for discussion, see McGill 1967). Whatever the role of semantic Platonism in Anselm's argument, an alleged existence-guaranteeing concept of a perfect being will not settle by itself the issue of whether God exists. The reality of a perfect divine being is not guaranteed by a concept in the manner supposed.

Ontological arguments must also face the aforementioned problem of divine elusiveness that challenges cosmological and teleological arguments. The evidence based just on a concept of God offered in ontological arguments is static in a way that the personally interactive occurrent evidence of the reality of the Jewish–Christian God is not. More specifically, the evidence based just on a concept of God is not personally variable relative to the wills of humans toward God's will. As a result, the evidence offered in ontological arguments does not accommodate the personally interactive divine self-revelation that would involve God's intermittent hiding and seeking relative to humans. As suggested, God's self-revelation would aim at the transformation of humans toward God's moral character, and it therefore would be personally variable and interactive in ways that a concept of God is not. As a result, the evidence offered in ontological arguments is at odds with the personally and cognitively dynamic God of Jewish–Christian theism. Natural theology, then, is not resuscitated by ontological arguments.

Natural Theology Undone

The standard arguments of natural theology fail to supply evidence of a divine call to humans that includes human confrontation *de re*, via noncoercive volitional pressure, with a living perfect will, and therefore they offer no human confrontation *de re* with a living personal God who is worthy of worship and seeks fellowship with humans. The neglected divine–human volitional confrontation involves an authoritative divine call for a human to undergo moral transformation by way of response to a divine offer of fellowship. The arguments of natural theology omit and neglect evidence of an authoritative divine call for a human to commit to undergo such a transformation toward God's perfect will. Accordingly, whatever the arguments of natural theology actually confirm, they do not yield conclusive evidence of a volitionally interactive personal God who is worthy of worship and seeks fellowship with humans. The god of the philosophers' arguments does not match or deliver the redemptive Jewish–Christian God.

The arguments of natural theology offer volitionally static evidence that is independent, in terms of its content, of authoritative evidence of a divine personal call to a human. These arguments offer, at best, evidence for mere spectators, in contrast with people called by God to repentance and transformation. A key deficiency is that the volitionally static evidence of natural theology is insensitive to the direction of a human will relative to God and God's will. Such static evidence does not increase or decrease relative to the orientation of a human will toward God's perfect will. As a result, the evidence of natural theology does not provide for the personally dynamic evidential variability that is central to divine elusiveness toward humans. It neglects the personally variable but characteristic divine activity in which God intentionally hides and seeks in interaction with humans for the sake of divine redemptive purposes. Such divine hiding and seeking intends to challenge and transform humans toward God's perfect will and thereby to lead humans in fellowship and new life with God as their living Lord. In contrast, the evidence offered by natural theology is volitionally casual and ineffectual relative to God's morally perfect authoritative will.

We should acknowledge the distinctiveness of conclusive evidence of a personal God who, in virtue of being worthy of worship and thus perfectly loving, calls and hides from people at different times for redemptive purposes. Such evidence will include an evident divine redemptive call in its content. An undermining defeater would emerge from the absence of such a call, given this true and justifiable conditional: if there is a perfectly loving God, then this God would call receptive people at opportune times into divine–human fellowship and new life with God for their own redemption. Natural theology is devoid of evidence of such a divine call, and therefore fails to supply conclusive evidence of God's existence.

If we have conclusive evidence of a divine call to humans, then we will not need the arguments of natural theology for purposes of our knowing God and God's reality. Of course, some people might find those arguments to be helpful in various noncognitive ways, such as in psychological or aesthetic ways. Even so, the kind of philosophy-to-theology sequence familiar from many natural theologians ultimately fails for lack of adequate natural theological evidence for God. A perfectly loving God would not need to use this sequence, because such a God would seek to be, himself, the objective cognitive ground of human belief in God's reality, thus unifying the object and the objective cognitive ground of human faith in God.

We can capture the main point in terms of our previous talk of a divine concern about human motives in inquiry and belief regarding God. The arguments of natural theology do not accommodate the concern of the Jewish–Christian God regarding human motives in inquiry and belief regarding God. Being inherently loving and redemptive, this God would self-reveal in ways that noncoercively challenge humans to undergo transformation toward God's character of *agape*, or unselfish love, and away from human selfishness. As a result, the Jewish–Christian God would seek human motives in inquiry and belief regarding God that line up with or aid this kind of transformation. The arguments of natural theology do nothing to encourage such motives; in fact, they offer no challenge at all to human indifference toward such motives, and they thereby omit the distinctive character of the Jewish–Christian God.

The elusive call of the Jewish–Christian God to us to become, ourselves, personifying evidence of God is morally demanding and thus challenging toward any selfish human motives. In sharp contrast, the arguments of natural theology are not morally demanding at all in this respect. As a result, they fail to point to a redemptive personal God worthy of worship; accordingly, they fail to point to the Jewish–Christian God. The empirical versions of these arguments apparently confuse the *effects* of a Creator (for example, in contingent observable causation and perceived order in nature) with *evidence* for the existence of God. In doing so, they omit (evidence of) the inherent moral character of the God worthy of worship, and therefore neglect what is required for being God. It is no surprise, then, that these arguments do not deliver (evidence of) the Jewish–Christian God. They end up as a distraction from crucial matters regarding the God worthy of worship.

Can the arguments of natural theology benefit people who are altogether unreceptive to God's call to redemption? The answer depends on what it is to *benefit* such people. We have seen good reasons to doubt that the arguments of natural theology deliver adequate evidence of a personal God worthy of worship. Conclusive evidence of a personal God worthy of worship would include evidence of a divine call to receptive persons, and it would be sensitive, in terms of its depth and salience, to one's willingness to obey God's call to human transformation toward God's moral character. The arguments of natural theology fail in this connection.

Some advocates of natural theology will seek refuge in the claim that some arguments of natural theology are at least "confirmatory" of theism even if they fail to supply conclusive evidence of God's existence. The suggested idea is that some of the arguments in question raise the probability of theism to some extent, even if they do not settle the question of whether theism is true. Two obstacles arise. First, the arguments of natural theology will not be confirmatory of theism if they do not confirm to some extent that a personal agent worthy of worship exists. We have seen definite reasons to doubt that the relevant confirmation concerns a personal agent worthy of worship, even if there is some confirmation that a lesser being exists. Second, the proposed standard for evidence being "confirmatory" must avoid being question-begging regarding the significant role of a personal agent worthy of worship, but this, as suggested, is no small task. (For related doubts in connection with fine-tuning arguments, see Colyvan *et al.* 2005.)

God, *Agape*, and Personifying Evidence

Given the previous line of argument, we can conclude that natural theology is, at best, beside the point regarding the Jewish–Christian God. Jesus and Paul, among other biblical figures, could have used arguments from natural theology to make their case on behalf of the Jewish–Christian God, but they did not take that option. Paul, in particular, presented his case for the Jewish–Christian God before Epicurean and Stoic philosophers in Athens, but he did not resort to any argument of natural theology (see Acts 17:18–34). If the arguments of natural theology were important to the case for the Jewish–Christian God, they would emerge at least in outline somewhere in the Jewish–Christian scriptures, but they do not. This is telling indeed, and often neglected by advocates of natural theology.

According to the Christian message of various New Testament writers, God's distinctive moral character is imaged perfectly in the evidence representing who Jesus Christ is as an intentional agent with definite gifts, demands, and goals from God himself. As this message shows, God did not send humans just additional information or more laws or arguments. Instead, God sent revelatory personifying evidence in Jesus and thereby in the followers of Jesus who are being conformed to his *agape*-oriented moral image. John's Gospel therefore portrays Jesus as saying that people will know his disciples by the intentional *agape* they manifest in themselves for one another, after the pattern of Jesus' *agape* (see John 13:35). A cognitive role for *agape* also emerges in the following striking remark in 1 John 4:7–16: "let us love one another; for love [*agape*] is of God, and he who loves is born of God and knows God. He who does not love does not know God; for God is love." Similarly, a cognitive role for *agape* is found in the following remark by Paul: "hope [in God] does not disappoint us, because God's love [agape] has been poured into our hearts through the Holy Spirit . . . given to us" (Rom. 5:5). (For relevant discussion, see Gorman 2001, chapter 8; Gorman 2009, chapter 2; Moser 2008, chapter 2; Moser 2010, chapter 4.)

Some philosophers and theologians try to portray the Apostle Paul as an advocate of natural theology, given his remarks in Romans 1:19–20. This is a serious mistake. Paul does not claim that nature *alone* reveals, establishes, or otherwise confirms divine reality; nor does he argue for God's existence on the basis of certain features of nature. In particular, he does not offer a cosmological or a teleological argument for God's existence. Instead, Paul explicitly claims that "*God* has shown" divine reality to people (Rom. 1:19), even if through nature, which is not equivalent to a claim about divine revelation "through nature *alone*." If he were inclined to natural theology, Paul easily could have claimed that nature *by itself* manifests God's reality, but he definitely does not suggest this.

We should observe a simple distinction between God's being revealed "through nature" and God's being revealed "in nature by itself." As Hendrikus Berkhof remarks, "Nature in itself does not reveal God. [God] reveals Himself in history through his words and deeds" (1968, 52). An analogy can help. When I call my friend on the phone, the phone is not evidence of my existence for my friend; my voice, however, could supply such evidence for my friend. In other words, my existence is not revealed in the phone by itself, but it can be revealed *through* the phone as I speak to my friend, say, as I call out my friend's name. In Romans 1, Paul assumes that *God's showing* what can be known of God to humans includes God's showing his being worthy of honor, thanksgiving, and even worship (see Rom. 1:21, 25). On this ground, rather than on the basis of natural theology, Paul infers that people who resist worship of God are "without excuse" (Rom. 1:20).

Seeking to redeem humans, the Jewish–Christian God has a specific purpose different from our casually knowing, via morally neutral spectator-evidence, that God exists. (Spectator-evidence, unlike divine authoritative evidence, does not challenge one to conform to God's morally perfect will.) The divine purpose is to bring humans into lasting reconciliation with God, in loving and obedient fellowship with God. Accordingly, we should expect God to offer purposively available evidence of God's reality that promotes this redemptive purpose. It is doubtful that the alleged spectator-evidence of natural theology serves such a purpose, because such evidence does not engage us with a challenge to our tendencies that need redemption. In particular, such alleged evidence does not challenge us to undergo transformation toward God's loving character and away from our selfishness. In other words, it does not encourage us, ourselves, to become personifying evidence of God.

The role of divine concern about human motives in inquiry and belief regarding God admits of straightforward elaboration by way of contrast with natural theology. The transformative motives sought by God in human inquiry and belief regarding God include primarily human love for God and human trust, or faith, in God, for the sake of lasting fellowship with God and other receptive humans. As a result, the divine aim would be to exclude such motives as human selfish fear, self-righteous pride, and *purely* alethic or cognitive interest in human inquiry and belief regarding God. Natural theology is no help here. In the best interest of humans, God would seek a morally profound motive and therefore would not settle for pure, morally indifferent truth-seeking or knowledge-seeking. Truth-seeking and knowledge-seeking have an important role in God's redemptive plan, but they do not capture the kind of redemptive transformation of humans sought by the Jewish–Christian God. That transformation includes humans, themselves, becoming personifying evidence of God's moral character and reality, for the sake of realizing God's noncoercive kingdom of *agape* toward all agents.

My case against natural theology relies on an understanding of the title "God" in terms of a personal agent worthy of worship, in accordance with the Jewish–Christian God. Someone might wonder whether this case itself is a variation on natural theology. It is not, because it does not offer, on the basis of natural sources of knowledge, an inference to the existence of a supernatural being. My case relies on a notion of God, as a personal agent worthy of worship, but this notion does not figure in an argument for God's existence from natural sources of information. As a result, we do not need to rely on natural theology to challenge natural theology.

The details of a robust epistemological alternative to natural theology are available else-where (see Moser 2008, 2010), but we should acknowledge that without divine self-revelation the Jewish–Christian God will not be an object of knowledge for humans. We have no reason to suppose that by means of their own natural sources of evidence humans can acquire knowledge of the Jewish–Christian God. The more plausible view is that through self-revelation this God must supply for humans the needed evidence of divine reality. This view explains the absence of the arguments of natural theology in the Jewish–Christian scriptures.

We are not left now with fideism, the troubled view that belief in the Jewish–Christian God needs or has no supporting evidence (on which see Moser 2010, chapter 3; Moser and McCreary 2010). In providing self-revelation to humans at the opportune times, which are not always times preferred by humans, God proves himself as living and faithful, on his morally profound and challenging terms. Alan Richardson explains:

> The answer . . . to the question why God does not offer proofs of his existence as the sovereign Lord of all things is that he has in fact done so, but only to those who have understood the true nature of kingship. Divine kingship consists not in coercive power but in patient love. God, because he is God, chooses to win man's love where he could have coerced his assent. . . . God does not want us to believe in him because we have been overawed by his power or impressed by his wonder; he does not want us to give him our allegiance as a result of our misunderstanding of his true nature, so that we should seek him because we desire the material prosperity that might be assured to us by being on the winning side (cf. John 6:26). He wants us to respond to what he is, not to what he is not, and he is the one who loves without asking for reward and who expects us to serve him by loving other people in the same way. . . . [N]o cosmic demonstration, no metaphysical proof, could elicit the kind of faith which God desires. . . . To seek any other sign [than divine *agape*] . . . is a seeking after a false image of God, which is idolatry (cf. Matthew 16:4). (Richardson 1966, 107–108)

Accordingly, the Jewish–Christian God proves himself with the rare but sacred evidence of self-giving *agape*, as seen paradigmatically (but not exclusively) in the self-giving life and death of Jesus as God's unique emissary and beloved Son. Humans are called to become personifying evidence of this God of self-giving *agape* as they learn to (struggle to) receive and reflect God's distinctive moral character.

We can give sound arguments for God's reality, but they cannot be reduced to natural theology limited to natural sources of evidence. They need to allow for *supernatural* evidence that comes from the power of a God of self-giving love, and they can recruit abductive, explanatory inference to avoid pointless question-begging (see, for example, Moser 2008, chapter 2; Moser 2010, chapter 4). Even so, any arguments offered will not be themselves the ultimate source of the evidence for God. God's self-revelation will be the needed ultimate source, and given that God is worthy of worship, God's self-revelation will manifest God's character of self-giving love, in keeping with the insight that "God is love" (1 John 4:8).

Humans can ignore or reject this self-revelation, but a receptive motive in inquiry about God will open a door to evidence beyond ordinary imagination and belief. The outstanding question is whether humans are willing to open the door to a God of self-giving *agape*. This God, unlike the god of the philosophers, promises to renew everything under the power of *agape*.

References

Barr, James. 1993. *Biblical Faith and Natural Theology: The Gifford Lectures for 1991 Delivered in the University of Edinburgh*. Oxford: Clarendon Press.

Berkhof, Hendrikus. 1968. Science and the Biblical World-View. In Ian G. Barbour, ed. *Religion and Science: New Perspectives on the Dialogue*. New York: Harper & Row, pp. 43–53.

Colyvan, Mark, Garfield, Jay L., and Priest, Graham. 2005. Problems with the Argument from Fine-Tuning. *Synthese*, 145(3), pp. 325–338.

Gorman, Michael J. 2001. *Cruciformity: Paul's Narrative Spirituality of the Cross*. Grand Rapids, MI: Eerdmans.

Gorman, Michael J. 2009. *Inhabiting the Cruciform God: Kenosis, Justification, and Theosis in Paul's Narrative Soteriology*. Grand Rapids, MI: Eerdmans.

McGill, Arthur C. 1967. Recent Discussions of Anselm's Argument. In John Hick and Arthur C. McGill, eds. *The Many-Faced Argument: Recent Studies on the Ontological Argument for the Existence of God*. New York: Macmillan, pp. 33–110.

Moser, Paul K. 2008. *The Elusive God: Reorienting Religious Epistemology*. Cambridge: Cambridge University Press.

Moser, Paul K. 2010. *The Evidence for God: Religious Knowledge Reexamined*. Cambridge: Cambridge University Press.

Moser, Paul K. and McCreary, Mark L. 2010. Kierkegaard's Conception of God. *Philosophy Compass*, 5(2), pp. 127–135.

Richardson, Alan. 1966. *Religion in Contemporary Debate*. Philadelphia: The Westminster Press.

Further Reading

Farmer, Herbert H. 1936. *The World and God: A Study of Prayer, Providence, and Miracle in Christian Experience*. London: Nisbet. A comprehensive statement and defense of a personalist approach to Christian theism, without reliance on the arguments of natural theology.

Farmer, Herbert H. 1954. *Revelation and Religion: Studies in the Theological Interpretation of Religious Types*. London: Nisbet. A defense of a Christian personalist approach to religions, accompanied by a discussion of natural theology.

Moser, Paul K. 2010. *The Evidence for God: Religious Knowledge Reexamined*. Cambridge: Cambridge University Press. A case for evidential personalism regarding God's existence, according to which the ultimate evidence is irreducibly personal.

Oman, John. 1931. *Grace and Personality*. Cambridge: Cambridge University Press. An examination of the main implications of the Christian view that God is personal.

15

Problems for Christian Natural Theology

ALEXANDER R. PRUSS AND RICHARD M. GALE

Christian natural theology presents arguments for the existence of God that are based solely on reason and experience without any appeal to revelation. Many different types of objections have been made to this effort. The most radical ones charge these arguments with making use of an incoherent concept of God. Another type of objection charges them, whether taken individually or collectively, with failing to establish the existence of God. And there are, of course, arguments against the existence of God, some of which appeal to what is scientifically vouchsafed or find some support in science. Each of these different types of objection will be considered in turn.

Incoherency Objections

Christian natural theology conceives of God as essentially having every perfection to an unlimited degree, among which are omnipotence, omniscience, benevolence, sovereignty, and freedom. Each is essential to God in that he could not exist and lack that property. Each of these perfections, taken either in isolation or in conjunction with other ones, is the target of an "atheological argument" that attempts to deduce from the proposition that God has the perfection(s) in question an explicit contradiction, making use only of additional premises that are either necessarily true or accepted by the theist.

With respect to God's omnipotence there is the famous paradox of the stone that asks whether God can create a stone so heavy that he cannot lift it. If God cannot create the stone, he is not omnipotent since there is something that he can't do; and, if he can create it but can't lift it, there is again something that he cannot do. To escape this atheological argument some restriction must be placed upon God's omnipotence. Traditionally this has been done by restricting his omnipotence to being able to bring about anything that is possible. Since it is not possible that there be a stone so heavy that God cannot lift it, he is excused from having to be able to bring this about. There is, however, a need for a more stringent restriction since there are possible states of affairs that it is not possible for God to bring

The Blackwell Companion to Science and Christianity, First Edition. Edited by J. B. Stump and Alan G. Padgett.
© 2012 Blackwell Publishing Ltd. Published 2012 by Blackwell Publishing Ltd.

about: God cannot bring it about that God exists. To meet this difficulty it is necessary to restrict God's omnipotence to being able to bring about anything that it is consistent for God to bring about.

There is an atheological argument that is directed against the conjunction of God's freedom and essential benevolence: Because God is essentially benevolent he cannot do what is morally wrong; but, because he is free, he can do what is morally wrong. We say of a person of sterling character that she is unable or can't bring herself to do what is morally wrong, although in some possible world she does. God's inability is stronger than this since in no possible world in which he exists does he do what is morally wrong. Maybe we are being overly anthropomorphic in modeling God's goodness on human goodness. Maybe we can't afford to have a God who is less than essentially benevolent. Similar considerations apply to whether God is free to commit suicide.

There is another atheological argument that targets freedom, only this time it is human rather than divine freedom that is the target: God is essentially sovereign, meaning that he determines everything. Theism holds that human beings perform free actions. But most theists, with the exception of Augustine, Aquinas, Leibniz, and Calvin, believe that if God determines everything, he determines these actions and therefore they are not done freely. There have been in contemporary times three different ways of reconciling God's sovereignty with human freedom, all of which involve a restriction on his sovereignty.

All three make use of a libertarian theory of freedom according to which a free action is not wholly determined by anything that is external to the performer of the action. In one version God foreknows what actions will result from his creating persons who are free with respect to certain acts, but he does not determine that it is true that these persons will so act if made free with respect to these acts, and thereby he does not completely determine them. According to the other two versions, God does not know what will result from his creating free persons. In one version there is no fact of the matter as to what will result from God's creating persons who are free with respect to certain actions and thus there was nothing for God to know prior to his creative decision. For the other version there is a fact of the matter but God cannot access it. The reason is that God's omniscience does not require him to know those true propositions that it is not possible for him to know, and on this theory it is not possible for God to create free persons whose actions he knows in advance.

God's essential omniscience has also been a breeding ground for atheological arguments. God is not only omniscient, that is, believes and knows all and only true propositions, but is *essentially* omniscient. Boethius presented but did not endorse an argument to show that God's essential omniscience negates human freedom. Because it is impossible for God to believe falsely or fail to believe some true proposition, it follows that:

(1)   If God believes a proposition, then it is necessary that this proposition is true.

For any human action there is a true proposition that reports this action. And because God is omniscient he will believe this proposition. So, given (1)'s rendering of God's essential omniscience, it follows, by *modus ponens*, that this proposition is not only true but necessarily true, which, in turn, entails that the human being who performed this action could not have done otherwise. And since a necessary condition for acting freely is being able to act otherwise, it follows that the action is not a free one. Notice that this argument works equally well for a timelessly eternal God – one not subject to any temporal determinations or distinctions – as it does for an omnitemporally eternal God – one who endures throughout a beginningless and endless time.

This argument wears its refutation on its sleeve, for it is clear that the rendering of God's essential omniscience in terms of (1) is unacceptable. The "it is necessary" operator is placed incorrectly before the consequent proposition of the conditional proposition, the one that follows the "then," when it should be applied to the entire conditional, resulting in:

(1′)   It is necessary that (if God believes a proposition, then it is true).

The parentheses indicate that the necessity operator has the entire if–then proposition within its scope. What is necessary is the connection between the antecedent and consequent. When (1′) is conjoined with the proposition that God believes some proposition, it follows by *modus ponens* only that this proposition is true, not that it is necessarily true.

In the last century attempts have been made to improve on this ill-fated argument, most notably by Nelson Pike (1965). The most vulnerable of the lot is the one that argues that if persons can act otherwise than God truly believes – either in advance or timelessly – that they do, they can bring it about that God's belief is false, which violates his essential omniscience. The response to this argument is that in the counterfactual circumstance in which persons refrain from acting as they do in the actual world God believes differently than he does in the actual world. Caution must be exercised when we move from the actual world to some counterfactual situation as to what features of the actual world we carry over into this situation, which is the point of Clarence Darrow's quip that he is glad that he hates spinach for if he were to have liked it that would have been awful. Just as we are not to carry over into the counterfactual situation in which Darrow likes spinach that Darrow hates spinach, we must not carry over into the counterfactual world (in which persons refrain from performing the actions that God actually believes they perform) that God believes that they perform these actions. That God's beliefs will vary across possible worlds does not violate his immutability, since within each world in which he exists he is immutable.

There is a more promising argument that is directed only at an omnitemporal God who exists at every moment of time. The argument assumes the law of bivalence – that every proposition is true or false. In advance of every free human action God truly believes that it will occur. Because the action is a free one, the human who performs it can do otherwise. But this gives this person the power to bring it about that God believed differently than he actually did. Assuming that it is a necessary truth that causation cannot go backwards, this is a conceptual absurdity since it gives this person the power to causally affect the past.

There are, however, numerous cases in which a person can now act so as to bring it about that a proposition about the past is false. For example by acting as I do now (e.g., selling state secrets to a foreign power) I bring it about that the patriots labored in vain, by pumping out Smith's stomach that he did not take a fatal overdose, by engaging in a great buffalo hunt that yesterday Jones had not engaged in the last great buffalo hunt. What these past-tensed propositions have in common is that they report what obtains during some time interval in a way that makes demands on what happens or fails to happen at later or earlier times. They could be called "temporally impure propositions." Consider a proposition of the form "S is F." It reports what its participial nominalization, "S's being F", refers to (e.g., the proposition that Socrates is seated reports Socrates' being seated). The proposition that "S is F" is temporally impure just in case the proposition that S's being F obtains during an interval of time t either entails that there is a time earlier or later than t or is not consistent with any number of occurrence of S's being F earlier or later than t. Thus, any proposition that reports a first or last occurrence of S's being F will count as temporally impure as well any proposition that reports what obtains at some interval of time that entails that something happens or fails to happen at some earlier or later time, which entails that there is some time earlier or later than that time.

There are yet other atheological arguments directed at God's omniscience. There are true tensed propositions that report what is happening now, as well as what did and will happen. Being omniscient, God will have to know these propositions, but because time passes he will have to continually change how he expresses tensed propositions so as to literally remain up to date. First, he says that event E is happening now and at a later time says that E happened. And this violates his immutability. This raises the question of how strictly his immutability is to be taken. Such changes seem quite harmless, which would not be the case were God to vary with respect to his character and purposes or believe at one time what he disbelieves at another. This way of meeting the atheological argument avoids the problem of whether God is able to know any tensed proposition that faces any account on which God is outside of time. The problem is that to know a proposition requires being able to express it, but only a being in time could express the proposition that an event E is happening now. This problem could be avoided if one of the following three theses were true. First, tensed propositions are reducible to tenseless propositions that describe a temporal relation between two events or times. Second, there are no tenseless de dicto propositions, only de re tenseless propositions, as was argued by Bertrand Russell, David Kaplan, and John Perry. Third, as Hector Casteñeda argued, God can tenselessly know a tensed proposition by the use of a "quasi-indicator," knowing, for example, that it is tenselessly true that at a time t, event E is then occurring.

There is another problem with placing God outside of time and having him timelessly know and cause things. The worry is that such a God is not religiously available to working theists who want a personal God with whom they can interact, have an interactive dialogue with. Herein God timelessly knows what they say to him and timelessly wills his response. Again, the problem arises of just how anthropomorphic we want our concept of God to be.

There is another atheological argument that seems to require placing God outside of time, not subject to any temporal distinctions or determinations. This argument plays God's immutability off against the theist's claim that that world came into being a finite number of years ago through God's creative activity. But this involves a change in God, since prior to the world's coming into being God was not exercising his creative power but subsequently did. St Augustine's way out was to say that God is timeless and that he timelessly wills in his eternal now that the world comes into being just when it did. How satisfactory this is depends on whether the difficulties the preceding two paragraphs raise for a timeless God can be met.

There have been atheological arguments directed against the doctrine of the Trinity and God's simplicity. But since these matters are knowable only by faith, they fall outside the purview of Christian natural theology and will not be considered in this chapter.

Objections to Theistic Arguments

The major theistic arguments are the ontological, cosmological, teleological, moral, and religious experience arguments. Historically, the opponents of theistic arguments have adopted a divide-and-conquer strategy in which each theistic argument is considered in isolation and found to be wanting. But this fails to deal with what results if all of these arguments are agglomerated. Initially, the divide-and-conquer strategy will be pursed and then the latter issue will be addressed.

Ontological argument

This argument invented by St Anselm attempts to deduce the existence of God from a mere analysis of the concept of God as a greatest conceivable being. If God were to lack existence, he would be seriously defective and thus not qualify as a greatest conceivable being. From Kant to the logical positivists it has been argued that existence cannot be deduced from a mere analysis of concepts. This ontological argument does not show that God exists, only that we must conceive of God as existent.

There are modern modal versions of the ontological argument by Charles Hartshorne (1965), Norman Malcolm (1960), and Alvin Plantinga (1974) that escape this objection. They hold that God must be conceived of not just as having existence but as having necessary existence. A necessarily existent being exists in every possible world. They ask the biblical fool who said in his heart that God does not exist to at least grant the possibility that he does, which means that it is possible that there exists a necessarily existent being who has all of God's omni-perfections. But this is equivalent to saying that it is possible that it is necessary that there exists a being who has all of God's omni-perfections. A proposition that is possible is true in some possible world. Therefore, in some possible world it is true that it is necessary that there exists a being who has all of God's omni-perfections. But if a proposition is necessarily true in any possible world it is true in every possible world, including the actual one. And thus God exists in the actual world.

Opponents of this argument charge its possibility premise with begging the question, since in granting that it is possible that there exists a necessarily existent being who has all of God's omni-perfections they are in effect granting that it is possible that it is necessary that there exists a being who has all of God's omni-perfections, from which it follows by the S-4 rule of modal logic that it is necessary that there exists a being who has all of God's omni-perfections. Furthermore, it has been contended that the possibility premise is inconsistent with the possibility that there exist an unjustified evil, that is, an evil that could not coexist with God. And if, as many contend, it is more likely that there could exist such an evil than that it is possible that there exist a necessarily existent being who has all of God's omni-perfections, the latter proposition should not be accepted.

Cosmological argument

The basic idea behind the cosmological argument is to start with some very general and uncontroversially real feature of our world, such as that there is motion or that there is something rather than nothing, and then to claim that the only or best explanation of that feature involves a being like God.

One traditional response to the cosmological argument is to ask for the explanation of the existence of God. There, the theist has a simple response: God is a *necessary* being, namely one that could not fail to exist, and hence his existence does not call out for an explanation in the same way that contingent states of affairs – ones that could have failed to obtain – do.

A classic challenge to the cosmological argument is to offer to explain the feature by an infinite causal chain: feature F_1 is causally explained by F_2, F_2 is causally explained by F_3, and so on, with no first cause. Cosmological arguments divide into three types depending on how they handle this regress objection.

The Kalām cosmological argument, in our day defended by William Lane Craig (1979), responds to the regress objection via philosophical and empirical arguments against the possibility of an infinite past. The philosophical arguments purport to find absurdities in actual infinities, such as that when one subtracts one item from an infinite set, one has a set of the same size: the sets {1, 2, 3, . . .} and {2, 3, 4, . . .} have the same size, as can be checked by pairing 1 with 2, 2 with 3, 3 with 4, and so on. The difficulty with such arguments is that many, if not all, of the consequences may simply appear absurd as a result of our being used to working with finite collections. The empirical side is more solid. Here, one might cite the evidence for a big bang, and the more recent work of Borde et al. (2003) that proves that under weak assumptions an inflationary cosmological model (and we have good evidence for our universe being an inflationary one) cannot have an infinite past.

Thomistic cosmological arguments proceed by making an intrinsic distinction between intermediate and first causes. Only first causes produce causal influence. Intermediate causes are mere transmitters of causal influence. St Thomas Aquinas concludes that one cannot have an infinite chain of intermediate causes with no first cause, since explanation by mere transmitters of causal influence depends on first causes. Evaluation of this argument would require subtle and difficult analysis of the nature of causation, and would take us too far afield.

Leibniz and Clarke, on the other hand, removed the worries about infinite regresses by basing their arguments on the demand for the explanation of a feature F_1 which is so all-encompassing that there is no room for a regress. For instance, one might take F_1 to be an enormous proposition reporting all of the world's contingent states of affairs. If the explanation F_2 of F_1 involves the causal activity of merely contingent beings, then the explanation is viciously circular, since the existence of these beings is itself a part of F_1. Thus, the Leibnizian argues, the explanation F_2 must involve the activity of one or more necessary beings.

A different kind of response to the cosmological argument is to provide a scientific explanation of the feature of the universe that is being explained. For instance, Stephen Hawking has recently contended that our universe's existence can simply be explained by means of gravity (Hawking and Mlodinow 2010). A difficulty with offering an ultimate explanation that is scientific is that the laws of nature involved in such an explanation appear to be contingent – they might have been otherwise, and an explanation is called for why they are as they are.

A second response is to block the inference from the existence of a first cause, which is what the cosmological argument argues towards, to the existence of God. A recent theistic move by Robert Koons (1997) has been to combine the cosmological argument with the teleological argument to argue that the first cause was most likely a highly intelligent and at least somewhat benevolent being.

A final response is to insist that the feature F for which the theist demands an explanation might simply not have one. There is something rather than nothing, but there is no explanation as to why. The theist can insist that F calls out for an explanation, and the atheist can respond that one cannot conclude from the fact that something calls out for an explanation that, in fact, it *has* an explanation.

Here, the cosmological arguer can attempt to argue for the principle of sufficient reason (PSR), which says that every contingent fact has an explanation. But there is another strategy available: instead of basing the argument on the PSR, one can base it on a less controversial principle. For instance, Gale and Pruss (1999) have shown that one can run a cosmological argument based on the weak PSR that says that each contingent fact *possibly* has an explanation, and Pruss (2004) has shown it can be done on the basis of a restricted PSR that says that each contingent fact that it is logically possible to explain does in fact have an explanation.

Teleological argument

The teleological argument typically proceeds by asking for an explanation of complex biologi-cal phenomena. Darwin struck a serious blow against this sort of argument by showing how various complex biological phenomena could be explained by a process of random mutation and natural selection that does not need to involve any intelligent agent.

The most common contemporary versions of the teleological argument exist in two ver-sions. The intelligent design (ID) version claims that the Darwinian explanations are not in fact satisfactory, because the probabilities of the right sequences of mutations needed to produce some complex biological phenomena are simply too small. However, it does not appear that current science is capable of giving us sufficiently good estimates of the probabili-ties to support or refute such a claim.

The fine-tuning version of the teleological argument observes that the constants in the laws of nature, such as the cosmological constant or the mass of the proton, appear to be fine-tuned for the possibility of complex life. If the constants were a bit different, galaxies and stars would not be able to form, and complex life as we know it would be impossible.

An initial worry is that this only shows that life *as we know it* would be impossible. Could there not, for instance, be complex living organisms constituted out of complex large-scale gravitational interactions in a universe with no stars (they would be very slow, of course), or some other equally or more exotic form of life? It does not seem, however, to be a fatal objection to the fine-tuning argument that it is based on the only sort of organic life we know of. One might also hold out hope that a future physics will find a simple, elegant law of nature, all constants in which will be "very natural" numbers like 1, 2, e, and π, which would damage the fine-tuning argument.

But perhaps the most powerful contemporary objection to the fine-tuning argument is the multiverse. On this view, our universe is a single island universe in a multiverse that consists of either an infinite or a very large finite number (say, of the order of 10^{500}) of universes. While in the past multiverses have been fodder for speculative metaphysics and imaginative fiction, they are now a part of a number of mainstream scientific theories. For instance, it is widely accepted that our universe's cosmology is driven by cosmic inflation, and a number of models of inflation predict a process in which new universes bud off old ones. Likewise, string theory is quite likely to generate a large multiverse.

Now, if there is a sufficiently large multiverse, and the constants in the laws of nature vary between island universes, it is likely that in some island universes the constants will be appro-priate for complex life, and in some of these intelligent life will likely evolve. Moreover, observers like us are only going to be found in those universes in which the constants are life-permitting, and so we should not be surprised that we observe such constants. Somebody will probably observe life-permitting constants, and nobody (at least nobody like us) will observe non-life-permitting constants.

Unfortunately, as Robin Collins (2009) has argued, many multiverse hypotheses face the Boltzmann brain problem. Given enough random variation in the universes, it is likely that in many places in the multiverse matter will locally and temporarily find itself arranged in configurations just like the present arrangement of the matter in your brain, in isolation from any larger ecosystem or even body. If we are purely physical, as most atheists think, these "Boltzmann brains" will have the same subjective states as you do. Furthermore, it has been argued that there is reason to think on thermodynamic grounds that cases where the chaos temporarily and locally lifts to produce a Boltzmann brain are going to be more common than cases where the entropy is low in a large spatiotemporal region, like that of a body, planet, or galaxy. Thus, brains like yours that are found within an enduring body are going to be more rare than brains like yours that arise randomly and temporarily in isolation from a larger system. Therefore, on such more modest multiverse hypotheses, you should think that you are a temporarily existing Boltzmann brain, since most people who think as you do are Boltzmann brains! But of course that supposition undercuts science, because the Boltzmann brain has almost no scientific knowledge, as it has never received information from any other scientists and it itself probably did not exist long enough to make significant scientific observations (maybe it only exists for a few seconds).

Multiverse hypotheses with a large amount of random variation and an infinite number of universes face a different problem of undercutting science: it is not clear that it is possible to make any interesting probabilistic claims in such a world, and yet probabilistic claims are central to modern science. For instance, suppose you toss a coin and roll a die, and prior to observing the outcome you want to say that it's more likely that the coin lands heads than that the die shows a six. But if you accept an infinitary multiverse hypothesis, then you will think that there are infinitely many coin-tossers and die-rollers relevantly like you, and of these, infinitely many get heads and just as infinitely many get a six. Therefore, the number of observers who will see heads is the same as the number of observers who will see a six, and it is challenging to reconcile this with the greater confidence that we should have in our seeing heads than in our seeing a six.

Moral and religious experience arguments

The standard moral argument holds that some facts involving God (such as what he commands or wills) are the best explanation of moral truths. This is countered by alternate non-realist and naturalistic accounts of morality, and space does not allow us to evaluate whether the response is successful. The most popular contemporary version of the argument from religious experience is based on an analogy between ordinary sense experience and religious experience that involves an apparent direct, nonsensory perception of God as a very powerful, loving being, and the most powerful criticisms of this argument are based on disanalogies between sensory and religious experience. Again, space does not allow us to evaluate the strength of the analogy and disanalogies.

Cumulative case

A question that must be faced by the opponent of theistic arguments is what results from the agglomeration of all of their premises. Although each of these arguments in isolation might not do the job of showing that it is more likely than not that God exists, their agglomeration might. According to Richard Swinburne (2004), each of these arguments (with the ontological argument excluded) increases the probability that God exists and when combined render this probability greater than one half. Unfortunately, there is no way to assign specific numerical probabilities of God's existence relative to the premises of these several arguments and thus no way of determining the probability of God's existence when they are combined. Furthermore, as will be seen in the next section, there are numerous arguments against God's existence, especially arguments from evil, and again there is no way to determine the numerical probability of their conclusion that God does not exist relative to their premises.

Empirical Arguments against God's Existence

These arguments pose a far greater challenge to Christian natural theology than objections to natural-theological arguments since failure to be able to establish God's existence is a far less serious problem for theism than arguments that establish God's nonexistence. By far the greatest problem for Christian natural theology is posed by the widespread existence of evil, especially evil of the most horrendous kind. Although it is generally conceded that no contradiction can be deduced from the fact that God and evil coexist, the evidential argument from evil contends that the known evils of the world significantly lower the probability that God exists, maybe even making this probability less than one half.

Some credible free-will theodicies, such as those implicit in the three reconciliations of free will and sovereignty, have attempted to neutralize the challenge of moral evil – evil that results from the improper use of free will by finite beings – by making the buck of moral blame stop with these finite middlemen and thus not reaching through to God. For natural evils there are a battery of theodicies, the most important of which is the soul-building one according to which such evils serve the outweighing good of giving humans the opportunity to freely develop the good character traits of courage, compassion, charity, and the like, which require the occurrence of evil for their development. And then there is the cover-all theodicy of a heavenly post-mortem compensation. Assuming that the Christian does not have an independent argument for survival in a Christian-type heaven, if the other theodicies fail, then what the atheist has shown is that (a) God doesn't exist or (b) there is post-mortem compensation. Which of (a) and (b) is more probable will then depend on the relative strengths of the arguments for the existence of God and the (typically neuroscience-based) arguments against an afterlife.

Many contemporary theists eschew giving theodicies and go instead with skeptical theism, according to which our radically limited understanding and knowledge preclude us from being able either to know God's morally exonerating excuse for allowing evils or whether there will be future outweighing goods for these evils. It is plausible for people to believe skeptical theism only if they experience a favorable balance of good over evil. It would not be plausible for people to believe skeptical theism if their experience was limited to their being stretched on a rack.

The danger of skeptical theism is that it makes theism susceptible to the argument against the existence of God based on his hiddenness. This argument marshals many quotations from the Bible that indicate that God's purpose in creating humans was to have people who could come to know, love, obey, and worship him. But if he remains as hidden as skeptical theism holds, he undermines the realization of this purpose and thus gives humans a good reason not to believe he exists.

There are and have been numerous arguments against the existence of God that appeal in some way to science. Herein it is crucial to distinguish between scientific and scientistic argument for God's nonexistence. A scientific argument contains a premise that appeals to what is scientifically vouchsafed, such as a law, theory, or evolutionary process. A scientistic argument contains in addition a premise that imputes to science a privileged authority to legislate everything that is (and isn't) the case and the proper way to explain everything.

Among the scientific arguments are those that appeal to the account that psychologists and social scientists give of the causes of theistic beliefs. It is argued that the manner in which theistic beliefs are caused makes them unlikely to be true. According to Freud, theistic beliefs result from an illusion, by which he means that they result from wish fulfillment – a desire for them to be true. This alone does not indict theistic belief since there are many perfectly respectable beliefs that we desire to be true that are not rendered suspect on that count alone, such as the belief that bread will nourish us or that our cognitive faculties are generally in tune with reality. But, for Freud, theistic belief is more than illusory. It is delusory as well since there is no evidence for its truth. And we know that delusory beliefs usually are false.

In addition to begging the question against the claim of Christian natural theology to have made out a good epistemic case for theistic belief based on the preceding arguments, this principle faces numerous counter-examples. We certainly are justified in believing that that our apparent memories are generally reliable, but this is a delusion according to Freud. Not only do we desire that our apparent memories are generally reliable, any attempt to show that they are by appeal to the fact that they have usually been so in the past falls prey to vicious epistemic circularity in that the evidence that is marshaled assumes that they are generally reliable – the very thing that we are trying to establish.

Probably the most powerful scientifically based atheistic argument is the one based on the increasing success of neuro-physiology (and perhaps artificial intelligence as well, though progress in artificial intelligence has been slower than expected) in giving a materialistic account of the mind. This gives us inductive reasons for believing that our consciousness supervenes on the brain. This would undermine traditional Christianity's dualism between the physical and the mental, and endanger the possibility of post-mortem survival.

Scientistic arguments, on the other hand, get impaled on their own sword. Their premise that accords a privileged status to science to determine, as Wilfrid Sellars said, of what is that it is and of what is not that it is not, is not something that is itself scientifically vouchsafed, and thus, by their own scientistic standard, is not to be accepted. Another type of scientistic argument upholds the scientific modes of explanation as being the only legitimate modes of explanation. On this basis the theistic mode of explaining why there is something rather than nothing in terms of God's creative will is illegitimate because, unlike scientific types of explanations, there is no covering law of either a deterministic or statistical nature that connects the cause with its effect. But, again, that scientific modes of explanation are alone legitimate is not a scientifically confirmed result.

References

Borde, Arvind, Guth, Alan H., and Vilenkin, Alexander. 2003. Inflationary Spacetimes Are Incomplete in Past Directions. *Physical Review Letters*, 90, 151301.

Collins, Robin. 2009. The Teleological Argument: An Exploration of the Fine-Tuning of the Universe. In W. L. Craig and J. P. Moreland, eds. *The Blackwell Companion to Natural Theology*. Oxford: Wiley-Blackwell, pp. 202–281.

Craig, William Lane. 1979. *The Kalam Cosmological Argument*. London: Macmillan.

Gale, Richard M. and Pruss, Alexander R. 1999. A New Cosmological Argument. *Religious Studies*, 35, pp. 461–476.

Hartshorne, Charles. 1965. *Anselm's Discovery: A Re-examination of the Ontological Proof for God's Existence*. La Salle, IL: Open Court.

Hawking, Stephen and Mlodinow, Leonard. 2010. *The Grand Design*. New York: Bantam.

Koons, Robert C. 1997. A New Look at the Cosmological Argument. *Philosophical Quarterly*, 34, pp. 171–192.

Malcolm, Norman. 1960. Anselm's Ontological Argument. *Philosophical Review*, 69, pp. 41–62.

Pike, Nelson. 1965. Divine Omniscience and Voluntary Action. *Philosophical Review*, 74, pp. 27–46.

Plantinga, Alvin. 1974. *The Nature of Necessity*. Oxford: Clarendon Press.
Pruss, Alexander R. 2004. A Restricted Principle of Sufficient Reason and the Cosmological Argument. *Religious Studies*, 40, pp. 165–179.
Swinburne, Richard. 2004. *The Existence of God*, 2nd edn. Oxford: Oxford University Press.

Further Reading

Craig, William Lane and Moreland, J. P., eds. 2009. *The Blackwell Companion to Natural Theology*. Oxford: Wiley-Blackwell. An anthology of extensive review articles on the major theistic arguments.
Gale, Richard M. 1999. *On the Nature and Existence of God*. Cambridge: Cambridge University Press. A critical analytic examination of the major arguments for and against the existence of God.
Gale, Richard M. and Pruss, Alexander R., eds. 2003. *The Existence of God*. Aldershot: Ashgate Publishing. Contains central classic analytic philosophy papers arguing for and against the existence of God.
Howard-Snyder, Daniel, ed. 1996. *The Evidential Argument from Evil*. Bloomington, IN: Indiana University Press. An anthology evaluating the argument that our inability to find justifications for evils gives good reason to deny the existence of God.
Oppy, Graham. 1995. *Ontological Arguments and Belief in God*. New York: Cambridge University Press. A magisterial survey of arguments on the existence of God.
Smart, J. J. C. and Haldane, J. J. 2003. *Atheism and Theism*, 2nd edn. Oxford: Blackwell. A lively debate book – Smart is arguing for atheism and Haldane for theism.

Part IV
Cosmology and Physics

16

Modern Cosmology and Christian Theology

STEPHEN M. BARR

The Beginning and Creation

The first words of Genesis declare that, "In the beginning, God created the heavens and the earth." This contains two distinct ideas: beginning and creation. These are often conflated, for reasons that are understandable. Anything we humans "create" does indeed begin at some time. And in human experience anything that begins to exist is found to have some cause of its origination. However, when one speaks of the "creation" of the universe in the theological sense, it is important to distinguish it from the idea of the universe having a temporal beginning. On the one hand, many atheists would concede that the universe probably had a temporal beginning but deny that it was created. On the other hand, no less a theologian than St Thomas Aquinas argued that the world's creation can be proven philosophically, whereas its having a temporal beginning cannot be (Aquinas 1975, 113).

The distinction between creation and beginning is made clearer by the old analogy of the universe as a book with God as its author. Time in the physical universe is analogous to the ordering of events in a book by page, line, and word. The "beginning" of a book refers to its first words, whereas the "creation" of the book refers to the fact that the book has an author. The author's creative activity does not extend only to the book's opening words; rather, every word of the book is equally and in exactly the same way a direct creation of the author. By analogy, we see that God is equally and in exactly the same way the creator of events that happen at any point of space and time, including those that happened in its first moments. That is why, according to medieval scholastic theology, God's act of "creating" the universe "in the beginning" and his act of "conserving" the universe in existence at later times were held to be one and the same act.

It may be wondered whether the two ideas can really be so clearly distinguished. Does not creation imply a beginning? If, hypothetically speaking, the universe has always been in existence, how could it have been created? Would not a beginning-less universe also have to be an uncreated universe, contrary to the view of Aquinas? Here another analogy may be helpful. Imagine a lamp that has been illuminating a piece of paper forever, throughout infinite past

The Blackwell Companion to Science and Christianity, First Edition. Edited by J. B. Stump and Alan G. Padgett.
© 2012 Blackwell Publishing Ltd. Published 2012 by Blackwell Publishing Ltd.

time. While the paper's illumination has no temporal beginning, it has nevertheless always had a cause, namely the lamp. In an analogous way, God may be the cause of every moment of the universe's existence, even though the universe has existed for infinite past time.

One of the things that has helped confuse these questions is a basic misunderstanding of what philosophers and theologians, such as Aquinas, meant by saying that God is the "First Cause." Many naively think that what is meant is a cause that is first in time, that is, first in a temporal chain of events. Creation then would be like the cue ball breaking a rack of balls in a game of pool: a "first event" that set in motion all subsequent events. In that case, the creation event would indeed be the same as the beginning. But that is not what St Thomas meant by "First Cause." In fact, he was quite clear that there is no compelling philosophical reason that a temporal chain of events must have a first link, rather than extending back infinitely into the past (Aquinas 1975, 114). His proof of a "First Cause" was not a proof of a temporally first event, but of an *ultimate* cause or explanation of things. He was thinking of an *explanatory* chain, not of a *temporal* chain (Gilson 1994, 67–68).

The foregoing distinctions are important if one is to think clearly about the theological implications of various ideas in modern cosmology that will be discussed in later sections of this chapter.

While one can and ought to distinguish between the ideas of the universe having a temporal beginning and having a Creator (i.e., an ultimate cause, source, or author of its being), it is in fact the traditional Christian teaching that the universe has both a Creator and a temporal beginning. That is the standard interpretation of the first words of Genesis. It is also implied by the statements of the Fourth Lateran Council and First Vatican Council, which spoke of God creating the universe *"ab initio temporis"* ("from the beginning of time") (Denziger and Schönmetzer 1976, 259 and 587).

As is well known, the Christian belief that the universe had a beginning occasioned much ridicule from ancient pagans, who believed that the universe had always existed. They asked derisively what the Christian God was doing for all the infinite time "before" he got around to creating the universe (Augustine 1960, 284–285). To this, St Augustine gave a profound answer: there was no "before." Time, he argued, is a relationship among created things. Consequently, if there were no created things, there would be no such thing as time. In fact, since time is an aspect of the created world, it is itself something created. This means that if time is passing there is already something created in existence, namely time itself. It follows that to speak of time passing when creation has not yet taken place is a contradiction in terms. It is therefore quite meaningless to speak of a "time before creation." "Why," asked St Augustine, "do they ask what God was doing 'then'? There was no 'then' where there was no time" (Augustine 1960, 287).

This was a brilliant and remarkable anticipation of an insight that modern physics did not arrive at until Einstein's theory of gravity (general relativity) was developed in the early twentieth century. Physics arrived at it by a different, but parallel path. For St Augustine, the crucial insight was that time is something *created*. For modern physics the crucial insight is that time is something *physical*. In Newtonian physics, time is just a backdrop to physical events. But in general relativity it is found that space-time is a physical fabric that stretches, flexes, and vibrates in response to the energy, momentum, pressure, and stresses of matter. Indeed, the movements of this space-time manifold themselves carry energy and momentum. In short, space and time are just as physical as rocks or trees. If the physical universe had a beginning, therefore, it was not only the beginning of matter, but the beginning of space and time as well. All of which implies that to speak about a "time before" the beginning of the physical universe is utterly meaningless.

This seems to raise a difficulty for the notion that God is the cause of the universe. In our experience, causes always precede their effects in time. But how can God precede the universe in time? There is no such thing as a time "before" the universe; and that is true whether the universe has always existed (in which case it is obvious) or had a beginning (in which case it follows from the reasoning of both St Augustine and of modern physics). The solution to this seeming difficulty lies in another deep insight of St Augustine's, which is that God is outside of time, and that the divine act of creation should be conceived of as occurring a-temporally (Augustine 1960, 303).

The point is that if time and space are created (and indeed physical) realities, then spatio-temporal relations cannot pertain to God, who is neither created nor physical. (We are speaking of the divine nature, not of the human nature "assumed" in the Incarnation.) Here again the analogy of the universe as a book is useful. The words of a book and the events in its plot form a sequence, which is the internal "time" of the book, which can be measured by page, line, and word. Moreover, there are causal relationships within the book's plot. An event on page 10 may be caused by an event on page 7. But the author of the book and his actions are not a part of this *internal* timeline or causal chain. An author generally does not appear as a character in his book (unless it is autobiographical) and his actions are not events in its plot. The author conceiving the idea for what happens on page 73, is not itself an event that happens on page 73 or any other page. And the author's causing what happens in the plot is on a quite different level from the internal cause and effect within the plot. On one level, Hamlet stabbing Polonius is the cause of Polonius dying. But on a different level, Shakespeare is the cause of both Hamlet stabbing Polonius and Polonius dying, and indeed of the fact that the former causes the latter.

Analogously, God is completely *outside* of the temporal chain – or more accurately, four-dimensional spatio-temporal web – of events in the universe and also of the web of causal relations that are "internal" to the universe. God ordains that events A and B occur – in terms of the book analogy, they are in the script he has written. He also ordains that A shall precede B in the universe's time and that B shall happen "because" of A. But God's *act of willing A* to happen does not "precede in time" his *act of willing B* to happen. The temporal "before–after" relation is one that obtains between A and B, not within God or between God and anything else. He is the cause of both A and B – and indeed of their temporal relationship *to each other*, but he himself is not *temporally* before A or B, or temporally related to A and B at all. Thus God is only "prior" to the things and events he creates in a causal sense, *not* in a temporal sense. In the traditional understanding, the fact that God is the First Cause of the universe does not entail that his act of creating the universe occurs temporally prior to the universe, and therefore the fact that it is meaningless to speak of a time "before the universe" does not constitute any difficulty for Christian theology, if conceived along traditional lines.

Attitudes about a Beginning and the Big Bang Theory

The pagan thinkers of antiquity generally believed the universe always to have existed. Though in Plato one finds the idea of a Demiurge forming matter, he assumed that the matter itself as well as space and time had always existed. Aristotle too thought the universe was without beginning or end. It was the Bible which introduced into Western thought the idea of a beginning, and as noted above, this idea was the object of pagan ridicule.

(Admittedly, the first words of Genesis do not unambiguously assert creation *ex nihilo*. However, with the unfolding of revelation, creation came to be understood as *ex nihilo*. Cf. 2 Mac. 7:28: "God did not make them out of things that existed." Also cf. Rom. 11:36; 1 Cor. 8:6; Col. 1:16. The great majority of the Church Fathers understood creation as *ex nihilo*.)

For the first two or three centuries after modern science began in the early seventeenth century, most scientists were Christian believers, and so continued to believe in a beginning. Science itself, however, gave little if any support to such a belief. Indeed, there were a number of scientific considerations that seemed to tell strongly against it. In Newtonian physics, it was natural to imagine the time coordinate, like the space coordinates, stretching unbroken from $-\infty$ to $+\infty$. And in the nineteenth century physicists discovered the law of conservation of energy, which says that energy can neither be created nor destroyed. Similarly, chemists found that the amount of mass remains unchanged in chemical processes. (In the twentieth century, the equivalence of mass and energy showed these two conservation laws to be the same.) So virtually every indication from science as of a hundred years ago was that matter, energy, space, and time had always existed and always would.

Because of this and the waning of traditional religious belief, the view began to prevail among scientists that the universe had always existed. For instance, the eminent physicist Walther Nernst declared, "To deny the infinite duration of time would be to betray the very foundations of science" (cited in Jastrow 1992, 104). There were two clear positions, the biblical teaching that there was a beginning, and the apparent verdict of modern science that there was not.

This changed soon after Einstein proposed his theory of gravity in 1916. As already noted, general relativity tells us that space-time is a four-dimensional manifold that can stretch and warp. This is governed by Einstein's equations, which relate the curvature of space-time to the density of matter. According to Einstein's equations, a universe that is filled with matter cannot be static: the curvature of space-time produced by the matter requires space to expand or contract. This can be understood as being due to the mutual gravitational attraction of all the matter in the universe. It is analogous to the fact that the gravitational attraction of a ball toward the earth does not allow it to hover motionless in midair for more than an instant: the ball must be rising or falling.

Einstein preferred the idea of a static (i.e., non-expanding, non-contracting) universe, since it comported with his philosophical preference for a universe that is eternal into both past and future. He therefore suggested the possibility that a certain term in his equations (now called the "cosmological constant term") exactly balances matter's mutual gravitation to allow a "static" solution. However, Arthur Eddington soon showed that such a balance would be unstable, making the static solution unrealistic. In 1922 a Russian mathematician named Alexander Friedmann, and independently in 1927 a Belgian physicist and Catholic priest named Georges Lemaître, found solutions of Einstein's equations that described an expanding universe filled with matter. Relating his own theoretical work to the 1929 discovery by the American astronomers Hubble and Humason that galaxies were flying away from each other, Fr Lemaître developed the idea that the universe had exploded from an initial state in which matter was highly compressed, which he called the "primeval atom" – essentially what we now call the Big Bang. On the basis of Einstein's theory of general relativity, Lemaître realized that the mutual recession of the galaxies was not the result of their moving *through* space away from each other, but actually the consequence of *space itself* expanding in accordance with Einstein's equations and carrying the galaxies with it.

In what is now called the Big Bang theory, the primeval explosion that began the expansion of the universe was also quite literally the "beginning of time" (the *initio temporis*) and of space. As profoundly anticipated by St Augustine, there is no such thing in the standard Big Bang model as a time "before the Big Bang." It is justifiable to regard this as a scientific vindication of the Jewish and Christian idea of a temporal beginning against the expectations of most modern atheists as well as most modern scientists. (Even as late as 1959, a poll showed that a majority of American physicists and astronomers believed the universe had no beginning (Brush 1992, 62–70).) Indeed, it is generally acknowledged that the scientific community was slow to take the Big Bang theory seriously in part because of a widespread philosophical prejudice against the idea of a beginning. In 1964, however, Penzias and Wilson discovered the so-called cosmic background radiation, which is the highly attenuated afterglow of the Big Bang. Since then, the confirmatory evidence has mounted to such an extent that the Big Bang theory is now regarded as solidly established.

Was the Big Bang Indeed the Beginning?

While there is no longer significant doubt that there was a Big Bang about 14 billion years ago, it has not been proved that it was the beginning of the universe and of time. In fact, over the years a number of speculative cosmological scenarios have been proposed in which the Big Bang was not the beginning. We will consider two of them: the "bouncing universe" scenario and the "eternal inflation" scenario.

The bouncing universe scenario works as follows. If there is no "cosmological constant term" to counteract it, the mutual gravitation of all the matter in the universe will slow its expansion. If the density of matter is greater than the "critical density," the expansion will eventually come to a standstill and reverse, leading the universe to contract. In this contracting phase, the effect of gravity is to accelerate the contraction. Eventually, all the matter collapses upon itself in a fiery mass of enormous density and pressure. In the standard picture, such a collapse ends in a "final singularity," called the "Big Crunch," which is the reverse of the Big Bang singularity. At the final singularity, matter reaches infinite density and the universe and time itself abruptly end. One can imagine, however, a less drastic possibility. Perhaps before a singularity is reached, the universe might rebound sharply and start expanding again, that is, "bounce." This bounce is like a new Big Bang, and the whole process starts over again. One can imagine a never-ending cycle of bounce, expansion, contraction, and bounce; and that this cycle has been going on forever.

There are several difficulties with this scenario. First, in 1998 it was discovered that the expansion of the universe has actually been accelerating for the last several billion years, rather than slowing down. This is due either to the effect of the "cosmological constant" term in Einstein's equations, or to a form of matter called "dark energy" that acts very much like the cosmological constant term. Unless this accelerated expansion eventually stops, the universe will never enter a contracting phase. Second, there is no reason to believe that a collapse of the universe would lead to a "bounce." Theoretically, it seems more likely to end in a final singularity that brings the universe and time to an end.

But even setting aside these difficulties, there is a strong argument that a bouncing universe cannot have been bouncing forever. The argument goes back to the physicist Richard Tolman, who showed that the lengths of the cycles – that is, the times between successive bounces – of a bouncing universe would grow longer and longer. Looking into the past, therefore, they get shorter and shorter the farther back one looks. Tolman showed that if one adds up the lengths of all the past cycles they must sum to a *finite* total time. Thus, even in the bouncing universe scenario, the age of the universe would be finite. In other words, even though in the bouncing universe scenario the Big Bang was not necessarily the beginning of time, there would nevertheless have been a beginning of time at *some* point, if not at the Big Bang, then at some finite time before the Big Bang (Silk 1980, 311).

The reason the cycles grow ever longer in duration in the bouncing universe scenario has to do with the increase of "entropy" from one cycle to the next. (Entropy is a measure of the amount of disorder in a system.) The Second Law of Thermodynamics states that the entropy of a closed system can increase, but never decrease, which is why many processes in real life are "thermodynamically irreversible." (For example, milk spills; it doesn't un-spill. Glass shatters; it doesn't un-shatter.) It is due to the Second Law of Thermodynamics that things in this world are subject to decay, aging, and wearing out. It is the reason why it is impossible to build a "perpetual motion machine." And it is one of the reasons that it is difficult, and perhaps impossible, to construct a realistic and self-consistent theory in which the universe has been going on forever, without a beginning – such a universe is very much like a perpetual motion machine.

A second speculative scenario in which the Big Bang is not the beginning of the universe is called "eternal inflation." If most of the energy in the universe is in the form of particles, such as atoms or photons (particles of light), then the universe expands in a gradual way. Moreover, because of the mutual gravitation of the particles, the expansion slows down and may even come to a halt and reverse, as noted above. If, however, the universe is dominated by "dark energy" or "cosmological constant" rather than particles, then the universe grows "exponentially" with time. Such an exponentially growing universe is said to be "inflating." The solution of Einstein's equations that describes such an exponentially inflating universe is called the "de Sitter solution."

There are strong reasons to believe that near the time of the Big Bang our universe underwent a very brief period of extremely rapid inflation, before it settled down to several billions years of the gradual type of expansion (which has, in the last few billion years, begun to pick up speed a little). This idea of an early inflationary epoch helps to explain several otherwise extremely puzzling features of the universe (e.g., its almost exact "spatial flatness" and "homogeneity" on large scales), and is now accepted as highly probable.

The idea of eternal inflation takes this idea a step further. It says that the part of the universe we can see is just part of a bubble or island within a much vaster (perhaps infinitely large) universe that is *perpetually* undergoing extremely rapid inflation. There would be many such bubbles, inside each of which space undergoes the kind of gradual, non-inflationary expansion that we now observe. We cannot see outside our bubble, because in this scenario our bubble is much larger than our "horizon." (This "horizon" exists because in the 14 billion years since the Big Bang, light hasn't had time to travel more than 14 billion light years. Therefore, no light can reach us from farther away than that – nor can any other information, since no information can travel faster than light.) The perpetual inflation of space that goes on in the greater universe outside the bubbles is driven by an ultra-large density of dark energy (or cosmological constant). The bubbles are regions in which this dark energy has converted into ordinary forms of energy (particles and heat), which is why the space inside the bubbles does not inflate, but expands in an ordinary, gradual way. The interior of each of these bubbles therefore starts out as extremely hot and densely filled with particles. From inside a bubble, this looks just like a Big Bang explosion. As the space inside a bubble gradually expands, the interior of the bubble cools, and the matter gets less dense, and begins to form galaxies and stars.

In this scenario, "our" Big Bang was just the beginning of our bubble, not the beginning of the whole universe. Indeed, it has been suggested by the cosmologist Andrei Linde, one of the architects of the eternal inflation scenario, that the rapidly inflating universe in which these bubbles are contained has been inflating forever, without beginning. Is this actually possible? There are several theoretical considerations that suggest that the answer is no.

One such consideration is a powerful theorem proved by the cosmologists Borde, Guth, and Vilenkin (2003). If one follows the trajectory of an object moving "freely" through an expanding universe, one finds that it appears to move ever more slowly (with respect to objects that are "comoving" with the cosmic expansion) – this effect is called "the red-shift of velocity." Consequently, if one looks back in time, such a freely moving object will appear to move faster and faster the farther back one looks. But since nothing can move faster than light, there is a limit to how far back in time one can trace the history of a freely moving object. Thus, a universe that is always expanding cannot have been expanding forever.

At first glance, this seems to contradict the fact that there is a self-consistent "de Sitter solution" to Einstein's equations that describes a universe that has always been expanding exponentially. (In fact, it is just this de Sitter solution that describes the inflating greater universe in the eternal universe scenario.) It turns out, however, that if one looks carefully at the mathematics of the de Sitter solution (Misner *et al.* 1970, 745) it does not actually describe a perpetually expanding universe. It actually describes a universe that *deflates* (contracts) exponentially from $t = -\infty$ until some point at which it reaches its minimum size, and then inflates exponentially for all subsequent time. This evades the Borde-Guth-Vilenkin (BGV) theorem, which applies only to expanding universes. Therefore, a de Sitter universe can have existed forever. However, a universe that *contracts* for infinite time from $t = -\infty$ is regarded as extremely unrealistic (or "unphysical"). Moreover, in such a universe, it would be extremely hard to account for the very low entropy that existed in our bubble at the time of our Big Bang. (This gets back to the Second Law of Thermodynamics, and the argument against perpetual motion machines.)

To summarize, in the eternal inflation scenario, one either has to say that the universe began some finite time ago, or one has to say that it contracted for infinite time before starting to inflate (which is "unphysical"). The upshot is that the eternal inflation scenario seems to require a beginning. That is the view of the great majority of cosmologists (with the notable exception of Linde himself).

Other scenarios have been proposed as ways in which the universe can have existed forever. One that is much discussed is the so-called cyclic "ekpyrotic universe" of Steinhardt and Turok (2002). This idea involves the existence of a fourth space dimension in which two universes of three spatial dimensions move relative to each other in a cyclical fashion. They repeatedly bounce off each other, each bounce being experienced in one of the three-dimensional universes as an explosive event – a Big Bang. This is, in essence, a more sophisticated version of the old bouncing universe scenario. It seems to avoid the Tolman argument. It turns out, however, that the BGV theorem applies to the ekpyrotic universe scenario, and implies that it must have a beginning, too.

No one has succeeded up to now in developing a mathematically self-consistent and realistic cosmological model that describes a universe that has existed forever. There are several strong reasons to suspect that this may be impossible, notably the Second Law of Thermodynamics and the BGV theorem. So, while one cannot say with absolute certainty that the universe had a beginning, the theoretical arguments point very strongly in that direction. The "beginning" seems to be a historical fact.

Can Science Explain the Beginning?

Can science explain the beginning of the universe? That depends on what one means. If the question is whether the events that occurred at the beginning of the universe obeyed the laws of physics and were in that sense "natural events," of which a natural account can be given, then the answer is quite likely to be yes – at least there is no solid reason to doubt it. But if one is asking whether such an "explanation" would constitute a scientific theory of "creation" that is an alternative to divine creation, then the answer is no.

To return to the book analogy, it is one thing to ask why a book starts with the particular sequence of letters it does, and something else to ask why there is a book at all. If the book is written in English, much about the beginning sequence of letters can be understood in terms of the rules of English grammar, syntax, and spelling, and in terms of the meanings of the opening words and their relation to the rest of the book. One can to a large extent explain why it begins, "It was the best of times, it was the worst of times," say, rather than beginning "Wxrh tys ystpmd akd hgtwo." But such an explanation does not explain why there is a book at all, or why it is written in English, or why it has one plot rather than another. "Scientific explanation" is about finding patterns in the Book of Nature and the fundamental grammatical rules ("laws of nature") that govern those patterns. But science cannot explain why there is a Book of Nature in the first place. It cannot tell us, in other words, about the "source of being" of the universe, which is to say its "creation" in the theological sense.

The word "creation" is also used in physics, and that probably produces or at least abets some conceptual confusion. In quantum field theory, for example, one speaks of "creation operators" and "annihilation operators" and there is also some discussion in recent decades of "quantum creation of universes," which certainly *sounds* like it is an attempt to explain the creation of the universe in purely naturalistic terms. And many scientists see it that way (Hawking and Mlodinow, 2010). But there is less here, metaphysically speaking, than the "creation" language suggests.

It will help dispel possible misunderstandings to give a brief sketch of the idea of "quantum creation of universes." The idea is inspired by a real effect in physics called the "pair creation" or "pair production" of particles, which has been observed many times and is well understood. An example of pair creation is that a charged particle and its associated anti-particle (e.g., an electron and a positron) may suddenly and spontaneously appear in a volume of space that initially had nothing in it except a non-zero electric field. The probability of this happening in a given period of time can be calculated using the rules of "quantum electrodynamics." The particle–antiparticle "pair" isn't produced from "nothing." Some of the energy in the electric field is converted into the mass and kinetic energy of the particles. This is really just a transformation of one thing into another.

In quantum theory, one considers "systems" that have a multiplicity of possible "states." A system can make a "transition" from one of its possible states to another, as long as no conservation law (such as conservation of energy, or of charge) is violated in the process. These transitions are governed by the general principles of quantum theory (which apply universally) and by the particular dynamical laws that define and characterize the system in question. In the case of systems made up of electric fields, electrons and positrons, for example, the dynamical laws are those of quantum electrodynamics. The initial situation (which consisted of space filled with an electric field) and the situation that emerged from it (which consisted of an electron, a positron, and a weaker electric field) should be regarded as two "states" of one and the same physical system. That same "system" has many other possible states – for example, states with two electrons and two positrons and an electric field. What is happening in the case of "pair creation," is not that a physical system is being created *ex nihilo*, but that a physical system is making a transition from one of its possible states to another.

In the quantum creation of universes, one applies the same ideas to "universes" instead of particles. A "universe" here does not mean the totality of all physical things. It means a "space-time manifold" that possesses some well-defined geometrical properties and that may or may not be filled with certain kinds of matter and fields. One can imagine there being in existence simultaneously any number of such "universes." One can also imagine a universe splitting into two disconnected universes. (Think of a balloon that has a part of it "pinch off" to make another balloon.) Or a new universe may appear by growing from "zero size" to finite size. By such processes, the number of universes in existence can change – increase or decrease. Now, suppose that the dynamical laws that govern these "universes" do indeed allow processes to occur in which the number of such "universes" changes. Then such processes should be thought of as transitions among various possible states *of one and the same system*. That is, the same system has some states with zero "universes," some states with one "universe," some states with two "universes," and so forth.

One sees from this that in discussing "quantum creation of universes" from a "zero-universe state" one is not starting with sheer nothingness or blank non-existence. One starts by assuming a "system" that has a number of possible states, governed by specific dynamical laws that have a precise logical and mathematical form. For example, in a certain "system" the only kinds of "universes" that the dynamical laws may allow to exist in its various "states" might be ones with exactly three space dimensions, one time dimension, certain kinds of particles (say, electrons and positrons), and certain kinds of forces (say, electromagnetic forces). But one can imagine a different system, governed by different laws, in which the only kinds of "universes" allowed to exist in its various states have exactly seven space dimensions, one time dimension, and different types of particles and forces. The "zero-universe state" of the former system would not be the same thing as the "zero-universe state" of the latter system. In each case, the "zero-universe state" is not pure nothingness, it is a quite definite something – a particular state of a particular system governed by particular rules.

An analogy may help. Your having a bank account at Wilmington Trust Bank with a balance of zero dollars in it, is not the same thing as your having no bank account at all – even if the difference is not a spendable one. A bank account, even one with a zero balance, is a particular state of a highly elaborate system. There has to be a legal entity called a bank, a system of money, a contract between you and the bank, with all of this being governed by various laws and regulated by various government entities. The situation of "not having a bank account at all" does not require any of these things.

To conclude, Jewish and Christian revelation made two fundamental assertions about the universe: it had a temporal beginning, and it owes its being to God's free creative decision. The first assertion seemed for a long time to fly in the face of scientific evidence; but the evidence now points strongly in its favor. Some have claimed that the second assertion is undermined by recent ideas about the quantum creation of universes. But this is based on a fundamental misunderstanding of what the word "creation" means in theological parlance as opposed to physics jargon.

References

Aquinas, Thomas. 1975. *Summa contra Gentiles, Book Two: Creation*. Translated by James F. Anderson. Notre Dame: University of Notre Dame Press.

Augustine. 1960. *Confessions*. Translated by John K. Ryan. Garden City, NY: Doubleday Publishing Group.

Borde, A., Guth, A. G. and Vilenkin, A. 2003. Inflationary Spacetimes Are Incomplete in Past Directions. *Physical Review Letters*, 90, 151301.

Brush, Stephen G. 1992. How Cosmology Became a Science. *Scientific American*, August, pp. 62–70.

Denziger, Heinrich and Schönmetzer, Adolf. 1976. *Enchiridion Symbolorum, Declarationem et Definitionem*. Barcelona: Herder.

Gilson, Etienne. 1994. *The Christian Philosophy of St. Thomas Aquinas*. Translated by I. K. Shook. Notre Dame: University of Notre Dame Press.

Hawking, Stephen and Mlodinow, Leonard. 2010. *The Grand Design*. New York: Bantam.

Jastrow, Robert. 1992. *God and the Astronomers*. New York: Norton.

Misner, Charles W., Thorne, Kip S. and Wheeler, John Archibald. 1970. *Gravitation*. New York: Freeman.

Silk, Joseph. 1980. *The Big Bang: The Creation and Evolution of the Universe*. New York: Freeman.

Steinhardt, Paul J. and Turok, Neil. 2002. Cosmic Evolution in a Cyclic Universe. *Physical Review*, D65(12), 126003.

Further Reading

Aquinas, Thomas. 1975. *Summa contra Gentiles, Book Two: Creation*. Translated by James F. Anderson. Notre Dame: University of Notre Dame Press. Expounds the traditional doctrine of creation.

Augustine. 1960. *Confessions*. Translated by John K. Ryan. Garden City, NY: Doubleday Publishing Group. The eleventh book contains a profound reflection on the nature of time much respected by modern cosmologists.

Barr, Stephen M. 2003. *Modern Physics and Ancient Faith*. Notre Dame: University of Notre Dame Press. Contains more extended treatment of the issues discussed in this chapter.

Gilson, Etienne. 1994. *The Christian Philosophy of St. Thomas Aquinas*. Translated by I. K. Shook. Notre Dame: University of Notre Dame Press. An accessible account of traditional metaphysics.

17

Does the Universe Need God?

SEAN CARROLL

In the beginning, God created the heavens and the earth.

In many religious traditions, one of the standard roles of the deity has been to create the universe. The first line of the Bible, Genesis 1:1, is a plain statement of this role. Much has happened, both in our scientific understanding of the universe and in the development of theology, since that line was first written. It's worth examining what those developments imply for the relationship between God and cosmology.

In some ways of thinking about God, there's no relationship at all; a conception of divinity that is sufficiently ineffable and transcendent may be completely separate from the workings of the physical world. For the purposes of this chapter, however, we will limit ourselves to versions of God that play some role in explaining the world we see. In addition to the role of creator, God may also be invoked as that which sustains the world and allows it to exist, or more practically as an explanation for some of the specific contingent properties of the universe we observe.

Each of these possibilities necessarily leads to an engagement with science. Modern cosmology attempts to come up with the most powerful and economical understanding possible of the universe that is consistent with observational data. It's certainly conceivable that the methods of science could lead us to a self-contained picture of the universe that doesn't involve God in any way. If so, would we be correct to conclude that cosmology has undermined the reasons for believing in God, or at least a certain kind of reason?

This is not an open-and-shut question. We are not faced with a matter of judging the merits of a mature and compelling scientific theory, since we don't yet have such a theory. Rather, we are trying to predict the future: will there ever be a time when a conventional scientific model provides a complete understanding of the origin of the universe? Or, alternatively, do we already know enough to conclude that God definitely helps us explain the universe we see, in ways that a non-theistic approach can never hope to match?

Most modern cosmologists are convinced that conventional scientific progress will ultimately result in a self-contained understanding of the origin and evolution of the universe,

---

The Blackwell Companion to Science and Christianity, First Edition. Edited by J. B. Stump and Alan G. Padgett.
© 2012 Blackwell Publishing Ltd. Published 2012 by Blackwell Publishing Ltd.

without the need to invoke God or any other supernatural involvement.[1] This conviction necessarily falls short of a proof, but it is backed up by good reasons. While we don't have the final answers, I will attempt to explain the rationale behind the belief that science will ultimately understand the universe without involving God in any way.

The Universe We Know

Cosmology studies the universe on the largest scales, and over large scales the most important force of nature is gravity. Our modern understanding of gravity is the theory of general relativity, proposed by Einstein in 1915. The key insight in this theory is the idea that space and time can be curved and have a dynamical life of their own, changing in response to matter and energy. As early as 1917, Einstein applied his new theory to cosmology, taking as an assumption something we still believe is true: that on the largest scales, matter in the universe (or at least our observable part of it) is uniform through space. He also assumed, consistent with the apparent implication of observations at the time, that the universe is static. To his surprise, Einstein found that general relativity implied that any uniform universe would necessarily be non-static – either expanding or contracting. In response he suggested modifying his theory by adding a new parameter called the "cosmological constant," which acted to push against the tendency of matter to contract together. With that modification, Einstein was able to find a static (but unstable) solution if the cosmological constant were chosen precisely to balance against the attraction of matter on large scales.

This discussion became somewhat academic when Edwin Hubble and Milton Humason announced in 1929 that the universe is expanding: distant galaxies are receding from us at speeds that are proportional to their distance. If the universe is expanding now, it was smaller in the past. (More properly, galaxies were closer together and the universe was more dense; it's possible that space is actually infinite in extent.) Using the rules provided by general relativity, and some assumptions about the types of matter and energy that pervade the universe, we can play the movie backwards in time to reconstruct the past history of our universe. Eventually, about 13.7 billion years ago, we reach a moment of infinite density and spacetime curvature. This singularity is known as the "Big Bang." Note that the phrase "Big Bang model" refers to the entire history of the expanding universe that began in a hot, dense state, the broad outlines of which are established beyond reasonable doubt. In contrast, the "Big Bang" itself, the initial singularity, is really just a placeholder for our lack of complete understanding.

One second after the Big Bang, we enter the realm of empirical testability. That's the era of primordial nucleosynthesis, when protons and neutrons were being converted into helium and other light elements. The theory of nucleosynthesis makes precise predictions for the relative abundance of these elements, which have passed observational muster with flying colors, providing impressive evidence in favor of the Big Bang model. Another important test comes from the cosmic microwave background (CMB), the relic radiation left over from the moment the primordial plasma cooled off and became transparent, about 380 000 years after the Big Bang. Together, these observations provide not only evidence in favor of the basic cosmological picture, but stringent constraints on the parameters describing the composition of our universe.

One implication of these data is that only about 4% of the total energy of the current universe is in the form of "ordinary matter" – the atoms and molecules consisting of protons, neutrons, and electrons, as well as photons and neutrinos and all the other known elementary particles. Another 23% of the universe is "dark matter" – a completely new kind of particle, as yet undiscovered here on earth. In addition to constraints from nucleosynthesis and the CMB, strong evidence for dark matter comes from the dynamics of galaxies, clusters of galaxies, and large-scale structure in the universe.

This leaves us with 73% of the universe in an even more mysterious form – "dark energy." Once the expansion of the universe was discovered, Einstein's original motivation for introducing the cosmological constant evaporated. But the idea didn't go away, and physicists later realized that this parameter had a very natural interpretation – the energy density of empty space, or "vacuum energy" for short. In 1998 two groups of astronomers made a surprising discovery: the universe is not only expanding, but accelerating – distant galaxies are moving away from us faster and faster over time. This is contrary to our expectation that the gravitational pull between galaxies should slow the expansion down. The most straightforward explanation for this acceleration is to posit dark energy – a smooth, persistent form of energy that isn't localized into particles, but is spread throughout space. Vacuum energy, or Einstein's cosmological constant, is the simplest candidate for dark energy; it features a density that is strictly constant, unchanging through space or time. But more complicated models are possible, and cosmologists are currently working hard to test the hypothesis that the dark energy density is truly a constant. If it is, we can predict the future of the universe – it will expand forever, gradually cooling and diluting away until nothing is left but empty space.

Concerning the first second of the universe's existence, we are necessarily speculating. Even the formulation "one second after the Big Bang" should be interpreted as "one second after what would be the moment of infinite curvature in the most straightforward extrapolation to earlier times." From one second back to about 10^{-43} seconds, we expect the *kinds* of physics we understand – general relativity and quantum field theory – to be applicable, even if the details are unclear. That is, we think we can successfully model the world in terms of fields that obey the rules of quantum mechanics, evolving within a curved spacetime obeying the laws of general relativity. The value 10^{-43} seconds is the "Planck time," before which we expect spacetime itself to be subject to quantum behavior. Currently we don't have a reliable theory that describes gravity in quantum-mechanical terms; the search for a theory of "quantum gravity" is one of the most pressing concerns of modern physics. The leading candidate for such a synthesis, string theory, has been the subject of an enormous amount of attention in recent decades. Unfortunately, despite a number of intriguing theoretical discoveries, string theory has neither made direct contact with experiments, nor provided an unambiguous answer to what happened at the Big Bang.

One sometimes hears the claim that the Big Bang was the beginning of both time and space; that to ask about spacetime "before the Big Bang" is like asking about land "north of the North Pole." This may or may not be true. The singularity at the Big Bang doesn't indicate a beginning to the universe, only an end to our theoretical comprehension. It may be that this moment does indeed correspond to a beginning, and a complete theory of quantum gravity will eventually explain how the universe started at approximately this time. But it is equally plausible that what we think of as the Big Bang is merely a phase in the history of the universe, which stretches to long before that time – perhaps infinitely far in the past. The present state of the art is simply insufficient to decide between these alternatives; to do so, we will need to formulate and test a working theory of quantum gravity.

Theories of Creation

The inability of established physics to describe the Big Bang event makes it tempting to consider the possibility that God has a crucial role to play at this unique moment in the history of the universe. If we were able to construct a complete and compelling naturalistic account, the necessity of appealing to God would be diminished. A number of avenues toward this goal are being explored. They can be divided into two types: "beginning" cosmologies, in which there is a first moment of time, and "eternal" cosmologies, where time stretches to the past without limit.

"Beginning" cosmologies typically attempt to replace the Big Bang singularity of classical general relativity with some sort of quantum-mechanical event, and often go by the name "quantum cosmology" (Hartle and Hawking 1983; Vilenkin 1984). These models imagine that spacetime is a classical approximation to some sort of quantum-mechanical structure. In particular, *time* may be just an approximate notion, useful in some regimes but not others. Near the Big Bang is an obvious candidate for an era in which time loses its conventional meaning. The important ingredient is then a "boundary condition" that describes the state of the universe at the moment when time is first an intelligible concept. The most famous example is the "no-boundary proposal" of Hartle and Hawking, which constructs the state of the universe by integrating over all possible geometries with no other boundaries.

A provocative way of characterizing these beginning cosmologies is to say that "the universe was created from nothing." Much debate has gone into deciding what this claim is supposed to mean. Unfortunately, it is a fairly misleading natural-language translation of a concept that is not completely well defined even at the technical level. Terms that are imprecisely defined include "universe," "created," "from," and "nothing."

The problem with "creation from nothing" is that it conjures an image of a pre-existing "nothingness" out of which the universe spontaneously appeared – not at all what is actually involved in this idea. As human beings embedded in a universe with an arrow of time, we reflexively attempt to explain events in terms of earlier events, even when the event we are trying to explain is explicitly stated to be the earliest one. It would be more accurate to characterize these models by saying "there was a time such that there was no earlier time."

To make sense of this, it is helpful to think of the present state of the universe and work backwards, rather than succumbing to the temptation to place our imaginations "before" the universe came into being. The beginning cosmologies posit that our mental journey backwards in time will ultimately reach a point past which the concept of "time" is no longer applicable. Alternatively, imagine a universe that collapsed into a Big Crunch, so that there would be a future end point to time. We aren't tempted to say that such a universe "transformed into nothing"; it simply has a final moment of its existence. What actually happens at such a boundary point depends, of course, on the correct quantum theory of gravity.

The important point is that we can easily imagine self-contained descriptions of the universe that have an earliest moment of time. There is no logical or metaphysical obstacle to completing the conventional temporal history of the universe by including an atemporal boundary condition at the beginning. Together with the successful post-Big-Bang cosmological model already in our possession, that would constitute a consistent and self-contained description of the history of the universe. As Hawking (1988, 156) put it in a celebrated passage:

So long as the universe had a beginning, we could suppose it had a creator. But if the universe is really self-contained, having no boundary or edge, it would have neither beginning nor end, it would simply be. What place, then, for a creator?

The issue of whether there actually is a beginning to time remains open. Even though classical general relativity predicts a singularity at the Big Bang, it's completely possible that a fully operational theory of quantum gravity will replace the singularity by a transitional stage in an eternal universe. Various approaches along these lines are being pursued by physicists: bouncing cosmologies in which a single Big Crunch evolves directly into our observed Big Bang; cyclic cosmologies in which there are an infinite number of epochs separated by Big Bangs; and baby-universe scenarios in which our Big Bang arises spontaneously out of quantum fluctuations in an otherwise quiet spacetime. There is no way to decide between beginning and eternal cosmologies on the basis of pure thought; both possibilities are being actively pursued by working cosmologists, and a definitive judgment will have to wait until one or the other approach develops into a mature scientific theory that makes contact with observations.

Why This Universe?

In recent years, a different aspect of our universe has been seized upon by natural theologians as evidence for God's handiwork – the purported fine-tuning of the physical and cosmological parameters that specify our particular universe among all possible ones. These parameters are to be found in the laws of physics (the mass of the electron, the value of the vacuum energy) as well as in the history of the universe (the amount of dark matter, the smoothness of the initial state). There's no question that the universe around us would look very different if some of these parameters were changed (Rees 1999). The controversial claims are two: that intelligent life can exist for only a very small range of parameters, in which our universe just happens to find itself; and that the best explanation for this happy circumstance is that God arranged it that way.

The clearest example of apparent fine-tuning is the vacuum energy. The value of the vacuum energy is not greater than (and is probably equal to) that of the dark energy, about 10^{-8} ergs per cubic centimeter. Using techniques from quantum field theory, we can do a rough calculation of what we would expect the vacuum energy to be, if we hadn't already measured it. The answer is quite a bit larger: about 10^{112} ergs per cubic centimeter. The fact that the actual value of the vacuum energy is at least 120 orders of magnitude smaller than its natural value is a fine-tuning by anyone's estimation.

Cosmologists don't have a compelling model for why the vacuum energy is so much smaller than it should be. But if it were anywhere near its "natural" value, we would not be here talking about it. Vacuum energy pulls objects away from each other, and a value much larger than what is observed would prohibit galaxies and stars from forming, presumably making it harder for life to exist.

Other constants of nature, such as those that govern atomic and nuclear physics, seem natural by themselves, but would give rise to very different macroscopic phenomena if they were changed even slightly. For example, if the mass of the neutron were a bit larger than its actual value, hydrogen would not fuse into deuterium and conventional stars would be impossible; if the neutron mass were a bit smaller, all the hydrogen in the early universe would fuse into helium, and helium stars in the late universe would have much shorter lifetimes (Collins 2003). On the other hand, Adams has argued that a wide range of physical parameters leads to stars sustained by nuclear fusion (Adams 2008).

In the face of these apparent fine-tunings, we have several possible options:

(1) Life is extremely robust, and would be likely to arise even if the parameters were very different, whether or not we understand what form it would take.
(2) There is only one universe, with randomly chosen parameters, and we just got lucky that they are among the rare values that allow for the existence of life.
(3) In different regions of the universe the parameters take on different values, and we are fooled by a selection effect: life will arise only in those regions compatible with the existence of life.
(4) The parameters are not chosen randomly, but designed that way by a deity.

Generally, not nearly enough credence is given to option (1) in this list. We know very little about the conditions under which complexity, and intelligent life in particular, can possibly form. If, for example, we were handed the Standard Model of particle physics but had no actual knowledge of the real world, it would be very difficult to derive the periodic table of the elements, much less the atoms and molecules on which earth-based life depends. Life may be very fragile, but for all we know it may be ubiquitous (in parameter space); we have a great deal of trouble even defining "life" or for that matter "complexity," not to mention "intelligence." The tentative nature of our current understanding should make us reluctant to draw grand conclusions about the nature of reality from the fact that our universe allows for the existence of life.

Nevertheless, let's imagine that intelligent life arises only under a very restrictive set of circumstances. Following Swinburne (1990), we can cast the remaining choices in terms of Bayesian probability. The basic idea is simple: we assign some prior probability – before we take into account what we actually know about the universe – to each of the three remaining scenarios. Then we multiply that prior probability by the probability that intelligent life would arise in that particular model. The result is proportional to the probability that the model is correct, given that intelligent life exists.[2] Thus, for our second option (2) (a single universe, no supernatural intervention), we might put the prior probability at a relatively high value by virtue of its simplicity, but the probability of life arising (we are imagining) is extremely small, so much so that this model could be considered unlikely in comparison with the other two.

We are left with option (3), a "multiverse" with different conditions in different regions (traditionally called "universes" even if they are spatially connected), and (4), a single universe with parameters chosen by God to allow for the eventual appearance of life. In either case we can make a plausible argument that the probability of life arising is considerable. All of the heavy lifting, therefore, comes down to our prior probabilities – our judgments about how a priori likely such a cosmological scenario is. Sadly, prior probabilities are notoriously contentious objects.

The Multiverse and Fine-Tuning

There are two popular mechanisms to obtain a multiverse. One is the many-worlds or Everett interpretation of quantum mechanics; I won't discuss this idea here, because the various "branches of the wave function" describing different worlds all share the same basic laws of physics. The other kind of multiverse is more prosaic, in that it simply posits regions of spacetime outside our observable horizon, in which conditions are very different – including, in principle and often in practice, the parameters specifying the laws of physics, such as the mass of the neutron or the vacuum energy.

This latter scenario has garnered a great deal of attention in recent years, in part because it seems to be a natural outcome of two powerful ideas that were originally pursued for other reasons: inflationary cosmology and superstring theory. Inflation uses the fact that dark energy makes the universe accelerate, but posits an initially small region of space filled with a temporary form of super-dark energy at an enormously high density. This causes this small region to grow to fantastic size, before the dark energy ultimately decays. In many versions of the theory, the decay isn't complete, and at least some region is always undergoing ultra-fast inflationary expansion (Guth 1998). From string theory we get the idea of a "landscape" of possible vacuum states. A "vacuum state" is simply a configuration of empty space with an associated set of physical laws. That is, what we think of as spacetime comes in a variety of phases, much as water can be in solid, liquid, or gaseous forms. In string theory there seems to be a mind-boggling number of possible phases (over 10^{500}), each characterized by different physical constants, including the set of elementary particles and the number of macroscopic dimensions of space (Greene 2011).

The multiverse comes to life by combining inflation with string theory. Once inflation starts, it produces a limitless supply of different "pocket universes," each in one of the possible phases in the landscape of vacuum states of string theory. Given the number of potential universes, it wouldn't be surprising that one (or an infinite number) were compatible with the existence of intelligent life. Once this background is in place, the "anthropic principle" is simply the statement that our observable universe has no reason to be representative of the larger whole: we will inevitably find ourselves in a region that allows for us to exist.

What prior likelihood should we assign to such a scenario? One popular objection to the multiverse is that it is highly non-parsimonious; is it really worth invoking an enormous number of universes just to account for a few physical parameters? As Swinburne (1996, 68) says, "To postulate a trillion trillion other universes, rather than one God in order to explain the orderliness of our universe, seems the height of irrationality."

That might be true, even with the hyperbole, if what one was postulating were simply "a trillion trillion other universes." But that is a mischaracterization of what is involved. What one postulates are not universes, but laws of physics. Given inflation and the string-theory landscape (or other equivalent dynamical mechanisms), a multiverse happens, whether you like it or not.

All else being equal, a simpler scientific theory is preferred over a more complicated one. But how do we judge simplicity? It certainly doesn't mean "the sets involved in the mathematical description of the theory contain the smallest possible number of elements." In the Newtonian clockwork universe, every cubic centimeter contains an infinite number of points, and space contains an infinite number of cubic centimeters, all of which persist for an infinite number of separate moments each second, over an infinite number of seconds. Nobody ever claimed that all these infinities were a strike against the theory. Indeed, in an open universe described by general relativity, space extends infinitely far, and lasts infinitely long into the future. It is only when space extends without limit and conditions change from place to place, representing separate "universes," that people grow uncomfortable.

A scientific theory consists of some formal structure, as well as an "interpretation" that matches that structure onto the world we observe. The structure is a statement about patterns that are exhibited among the various objects in the theory. The simplicity of a theory is a statement about how compactly we can describe the formal structure (the Kolmogorov complexity), not how many elements it contains. The set of real numbers consisting of "11, and 13 times the square root of 2, and pi to the twenty-eighth power, and all prime numbers between 4982 and 34950" is a more complicated set than "the integers," even though the latter set contains an infinitely larger number of elements. The physics of a universe containing 10^{88} particles that all belong to just a handful of types, each particle behaving precisely according to the characteristics of its type, is much simpler than that of a universe containing only a thousand particles, each behaving completely differently.

Likewise, a multiverse that arises as a result of the natural dynamical consequences of a relatively simple set of physical laws should not be discounted because it involves a lot of universes. The multiverse is not a theory; it is a prediction of a theory, namely the combination of inflationary cosmology and a landscape of vacuum states. Both of these ideas came about for other reasons, having nothing to do with the multiverse. If they are right, they predict the existence of a multiverse in a wide variety of circumstances. It's our job to take the predictions of our theories seriously, not to discount them because we end up with an uncomfortably large number of universes.

By itself, the multiverse doesn't successfully explain every cosmological fine-tuning problem. If a parameter needs to be smaller than a certain value for life to exist, there's no anthropic reason for it to be *much* smaller than that value. We therefore have a prediction: anthropically selected parameters should be of the same order of magnitude as the largest value compatible with the existence of life. Indeed, this prediction was successfully made by Weinberg for the vacuum energy, over a decade before it was actually discovered (Weinberg 1987).

An example of fine-tuning well beyond anthropic constraints is the initial state of the universe, often characterized in terms of its extremely low entropy (Penrose 1989). Roughly speaking, the large number of particles in the universe were arranged in an extraordinarily smooth configuration, which is highly unstable and unlikely given the enormous gravitational forces acting on such densely packed matter. While vacuum energy is tuned to 1 part in 10^{120}, the entropy of the early universe is tuned to 1 part in *10 to the power of* 10^{120}, a preposterous number. The entropy didn't need to be nearly that low in order for life to come into existence. One way of thinking about this is to note that we certainly don't need a hundred billion other galaxies in the universe in order for life to arise here on earth; our single galaxy would have been fine, or for that matter a single solar system.

That doesn't mean that we can't possibly explain the low entropy of our early universe by invoking the multiverse; it just means that the explanation must rely on detailed dynamical properties of the multiverse, rather than simply the requirement that life can exist. We would need to show that, in the context of the particular multiverse scenario under consideration, when life arises at all it typically does so in the aftermath of an extremely low-entropy event like our Big Bang. This is a challenge, but not obviously an insuperable one, and researchers are actively tackling this question (Carroll 2010).

If anything, the much-more-than-anthropic tuning that characterizes the entropy of the universe is a bigger problem for the God hypothesis than for the multiverse. If the point of arranging the universe was to set the stage for the eventual evolution of intelligent life, why all the grandiose excess represented by the needlessly low entropy at early times and the universe's hundred billion galaxies? We might wonder whether those other galaxies are spandrels – not necessary for life here on earth, but nevertheless a side effect of the general Big Bang picture, which is the most straightforward way to make the earth and its biosphere.

This turns out not to be true; quantitatively, it's easy to show that almost all possible histories of the universe that involve earth as we know it don't have any other galaxies at all.[3] It's unclear why God would do so much more fine-tuning of the state of the universe than seems to have been necessary.

Accounting for the World

So far we've been discussing roles for God that match those of a conventional scientific theory – providing a clear and compelling account of the observational facts. There is another angle often taken in explaining God's usefulness to cosmology: that whatever the facts of the world might be and whatever patterns they might follow, only a divine being can offer a "reason why" things are that way, over and above the facts and patterns themselves.

This approach takes a number of different forms. One is to give God credit for simply allowing the universe to exist:

> For Judeo-Christianity, God is not a person in the sense that Al Gore arguably is. . . . He is, rather, the condition of possibility of any entity whatsoever, including ourselves. He is the answer to why there is something rather than nothing. (Eagleton 2006, 32)

Another is to sustain the existence of the universe. In response to Hawking's question "What place, then, for a creator?", Polkinghorne (1994, 73) answers: "[I]t would be theologically naïve to give any answer other than: 'Every place – as the sustainer of the self-sustained spacetime egg and as the creator of its quantum laws.'" Along similar lines, God is sometimes credited with maintaining the regularities observed in nature, which would otherwise simply be a coincidence.

> The same laws of nature govern the most distant galaxies we can observe through our telescopes as operate on earth, and the same laws govern the earliest events in time to which we can infer as operate today. . . . If there is no cause of this, it would be a most extraordinary coincidence – too extraordinary for any rational person to believe. (Swinburne 1996, 49)

A final example comes from the traditional "cosmological" arguments for God's existence. In the "Kalam" formulation championed by William Lane Craig (1979), the first premise of the argument states "everything that has a beginning in time has a cause." Things cannot simply begin; something must begin them.

These are very different arguments, but they all arise from a conviction that, in various contexts, it is insufficient to fully understand what happens; we must also provide an explanation for *why* it happens – what might be called a "meta-explanatory" account.

It can be difficult to respond to this kind of argument. The ultimate answer to "We need to understand why the universe exists/continues to exist/exhibits regularities/came to be" is essentially "No, we don't." That is unlikely to be considered a worthwhile comeback to anyone who was persuaded by the need for a meta-explanatory understanding in the first place.

It is always nice to be able to provide reasons why something is the case. Most scientists, however, suspect that the search for ultimate explanations eventually terminates in some final theory of the world, along with the phrase "and that's just how it is." It is certainly conceivable that the ultimate explanation is to be found in God; but a compelling argument to that effect would consist of a demonstration that God provides a better explanation than a purely materialist picture, not an *a priori* insistence that a purely materialist picture is unsatisfying.

Why are some people so convinced of the need for a meta-explanatory account, while others are perfectly happy without one? I would suggest that the impetus to provide such an account comes from our experiences within the world, while the suspicion that there is no need comes from treating the entire universe as something unique, something for which a different set of standards is appropriate.

For example, we could imagine arguing that there is no puzzle associated with the value of the vacuum energy. It had to be some number, and we have (perhaps) measured what that value is, and there's nothing more to be said. The counter-argument is that the vacuum energy is really a parameter that we measure in the "effective field theory" that governs physics at low energies, regardless of the virtual high-energy processes we have not yet explored in experiments. Even though there is only one universe, there are many effective field theories, and many parameters in the theories relevant to low-energy physics. So the vacuum energy is not a unique object; we have expectations for it based on our experience with other parameters in effective field theories, and can sensibly compare its measured value to those expectations. It is in terms of that comparison that we can legitimately call the vacuum energy finely tuned.

States of affairs require an explanation only if we have some contrary expectation, some reason to be surprised that they hold. Is there any reason to be surprised that the universe exists, continues to exist, or exhibits regularities? When it comes to the universe, we don't have any broader context in which to develop expectations. As far as we know, it may simply exist and evolve according to the laws of physics. If we knew that it was one element of a large ensemble of universes, we might have reason to think otherwise, but we don't. (I'm using "universe" here to mean the totality of existence, so what would be called the "multiverse" if that's what we lived in.)

In his *Metaphysics*, Aristotle suggested the need for an "unmoved mover" to explain the motion of ordinary objects. That makes sense in the context of Aristotle's physics, which was fundamentally teleological: objects tended toward their natural place, which is where they wanted to stay. How, then, to account for all the motion we find everywhere around us? But subsequent developments in physics – conservation of momentum, Newton's laws of motion – changed the context in which such a question might be asked. Now we know that objects that are moving freely continue to move along a uniform trajectory, without anything moving them. Why? Because that's what objects do. It's often convenient, in the context of everyday life, for us to refer to this or that event as having some particular cause. But this is just short-hand for what's really going on, namely: things are obeying the laws of physics.

Likewise for the universe. We have no reason to think of the existence and persistence and regularity of the universe as things that require external explanation. Indeed, for most scientists, adding on another layer of metaphysical structure in order to purportedly explain these nomological facts is an unnecessary complication.

God as a Theory

Religion serves many purposes other than explaining the natural world. However, accounting for the universe is certainly a traditional role for God, and arguably a foundational one. How we think about other religious practices depends upon whether our understanding of the world around us gives us a reason to believe in God. And insofar as it attempts to provide an explanation for empirical phenomena, the God hypothesis should be judged by the standards of any other scientific theory.

Consider a hypothetical world in which science had developed to something like its current state of progress, but nobody had yet thought of God. It seems unlikely that an imaginative thinker in this world, upon proposing God as a solution to various cosmological puzzles, would be met with enthusiasm. All else being equal, science prefers its theories to be precise, predictive, and minimal – requiring the smallest possible amount of theoretical overhead. The God hypothesis is none of these. Indeed, in our actual world, God is essentially never invoked in scientific discussions. You can scour the tables of contents in major physics journals, or titles of seminars and colloquia in physics departments and conferences, looking in vain for any mention of possible supernatural intervention into the workings of the world.

At first glance, the God hypothesis seems simple and precise – an omnipotent, omniscient, and omnibenevolent being. (There are other definitions, but they are usually comparably terse.) The apparent simplicity is somewhat misleading, however. In comparison to a purely naturalistic model, we're not simply adding a new element to an existing ontology (like a new field or particle), or even replacing one ontology with a more effective one at a similar level of complexity (like general relativity replacing Newtonian spacetime, or quantum mechanics replacing classical mechanics). We're adding an entirely new metaphysical category, whose relation to the observable world is unclear. This doesn't automatically disqualify God from consideration as a scientific theory, but it implies that, all else being equal, a purely naturalistic model will be preferred on the grounds of simplicity.

There is an inevitable tension between any attempt to invoke God as a scientifically effective explanation of the workings of the universe, and the religious presumption that God is a kind of *person*, not just an abstract principle. God's personhood is characterized by an essential unpredictability and the freedom to make choices. These are not qualities that one looks for in a good scientific theory. On the contrary, successful theories are characterized by clear foundations and unambiguous consequences. We could imagine boiling God's role in setting up the world down to a few simple principles (e.g., "God constructs the universe in the simplest possible way consistent with the eventual appearance of human beings"). But is what remains recognizable as God?

Similarly, the apparent precision of the God hypothesis evaporates when it comes to connecting to the messy workings of reality. God is not described in equations, as are other theories of fundamental physics. Consequently, it is difficult or impossible to make predictions. Instead, one looks at what has already been discovered, and agrees that that's the way God would have done it. Theistic evolutionists argue that God uses natural selection to develop life on earth; but religious thinkers before Darwin were unable to predict that such a mechanism would be God's preferred choice.

Ambitious approaches to contemporary cosmological questions, such as quantum cosmology, the multiverse, and the anthropic principle, have not yet been developed into mature scientific theories. But the advocates of these schemes are working hard to derive testable predictions on the basis of their ideas: for the amplitude of cosmological perturbations (Hartle *et al.* 2008), signals of colliding pocket universes in the cosmic microwave background (Aguirre and Johnson 2009), and the mass of the Higgs boson and other particles (Feldstein *et al.* 2006). For the God hypothesis, it is unclear where one would start. Why does God favor three generations of elementary particles, with a wide spectrum of masses? Would God use supersymmetry or strong dynamics to stabilize the hierarchy between the weak scale and the

Planck scale, or simply set it that way by hand? What would God's favorite dark-matter particle be?

This is a venerable problem, reaching far beyond natural theology. In numerous ways, the world around us is more like what we would expect from a dysteleological set of uncaring laws of nature than from a higher power with an interest in our welfare. Imagine a hypothetical world in which there were no evil, people were invariably kind, fewer natural disasters occurred, and virtue was always rewarded. Would inhabitants of that world consider these features to be evidence *against* the existence of God? If not, why don't we consider the contrary conditions to be such evidence?

Over the past 500 years, the progress of science has worked to strip away God's roles in the world. He isn't needed to keep things moving, or to develop the complexity of living creatures, or to account for the existence of the universe. Perhaps the greatest triumph of the scientific revolution has been in the realm of methodology. Control groups, double-blind experiments, an insistence on precise and testable predictions – a suite of techniques constructed to guard against the very human tendency to see things that aren't there. There is no control group for the universe, but in our attempts to explain it we should aim for a similar level of rigor. If and when cosmologists develop a successful scientific understanding of the origin of the universe, we will be left with a picture in which there is no place for God to act – if he does (e.g., through subtle influences on quantum-mechanical transitions or the progress of evolution), it is only in ways that are unnecessary and imperceptible. We can't be sure that a fully naturalist understanding of cosmology is forthcoming, but at the same time there is no reason to doubt it. Two thousand years ago, it was perfectly reasonable to invoke God as an explanation for natural phenomena; now, we can do much better.

None of this amounts to a "proof" that God doesn't exist, of course. Such a proof is not forthcoming; science isn't in the business of proving things. Rather, science judges the merits of competing models in terms of their simplicity, clarity, comprehensiveness, and fit to the data. Unsuccessful theories are never disproven, as we can always concoct elaborate schemes to save the phenomena; they just fade away as better theories gain acceptance. Attempting to explain the natural world by appealing to God is, by scientific standards, not a very successful theory. The fact that we humans have been able to understand so much about how the natural world works, in our incredibly limited region of space over a remarkably short period of time, is a triumph of the human spirit, one of which we can all be justifiably proud.

Notes

1   See Carroll 2005, 62. For different views, see chapters in this volume by Don Page, Robin Collins, and Steve Barr.
2   It's not obvious that this line of reasoning is valid. One could imagine taking the position that our existence offers exactly zero information about the probability of any cosmological scenario, because if we didn't exist we wouldn't be here debating the alternatives.
3   Given laws of motion, the space of histories of the universe is isomorphic to the space of states at some fixed time. The entropy is the logarithm of the number of macroscopically similar states. The fact that we can imagine much higher-entropy configurations of the universe today without disturbing the earth (e.g., by putting the rest of the universe into black holes) demonstrates that histories like ours are an incredibly tiny fraction of histories that give rise to something like our current earth.

References

Adams, Fred C. 2008. Stars in Other Universes: Stellar Structure with Different Fundamental Constants. *Journal of Cosmology and Astroparticle Physics*, 2008(August), 010.

Aguirre, A. and Johnson, M. C. 2009. A Status Report on the Observability of Cosmic Bubble Collisions. ArXiv: 098.4105v2 [hep-th].

Carroll, Sean. 2005. Why (Almost All) Cosmologists Are Atheists. *Faith and Philosophy*, 22, pp. 622–635.

Carroll, Sean. 2010. *From Eternity to Here: The Quest for the Ultimate Theory of Time*. New York: Dutton.

Collins, Robin. 2003. The Evidence for Fine-Tuning. In Neil Manson, ed. *God and Design: The Teleological Argument and Modern Science*. London: Routledge, pp. 178–199.

Craig, William L. 1979. *The Kalam Cosmological Argument*. London: Macmillan.

Eagleton, Terry. 2006. Lunging, Flailing, Mispunching. *London Review of Books*, 28(October 19), pp. 32–34.

Feldstein, B., Hall. L. J., and Watari, T. 2006. Landscape Predictions for the Higgs Boson and Top Quark Masses. *Physical Review D*, 74, pp. 095011.

Greene, Brian. 2011. *The Hidden Reality: Parallel Universes and the Deep Laws of the Cosmos*. New York: Knopf.

Hartle, J. B. and Hawking, S. W. 1983. Wave Function of the Universe. *Physical Review D*, 28, pp. 2960–2975.

Hartle, J. B., Hawking, S. W., and Hertog, T. 2008. Classical Universes of the No-Boundary Quantum State. *Physical Review D*, 77, pp. 123537–123568.

Hawking, S. W. 1988. *A Brief History of Time*. New York: Bantam.

Penrose, Roger. 1989. *The Emperor's New Mind: Concerning Computers, Minds, and the Laws of Physics*. Oxford: Oxford University Press.

Polkinghorne, John. 1994. *The Faith of a Physicist: Reflections of a Bottom-Up Thinker*. Princeton, NJ: Princeton University Press.

Rees, Martin. 1999. *Just Six Numbers: The Deep Forces that Shape the Universe*. New York: Basic Books.

Swinburne, Richard. 1990. Argument from the Fine-Tuning of the Universe. In J. Leslie, ed. *Physical Cosmology and Philosophy*. New York: Macmillan, pp. 154–172.

Swinburne, Richard. 1996. *Is There a God?* Oxford: Oxford University Press.

Vilenkin, A. 1984. Quantum Creation of Universes. *Physical Review D*, 30, pp. 509–511.

Weinberg, Steven. 1987. Anthropic Bound on the Cosmological Constant. *Physical Review Letters*, 59, pp. 2607–2610.

Further Reading

Carroll, Sean. 2010. *From Eternity to Here: The Quest for the Ultimate Theory of Time*. New York: Dutton. An examination of why the early universe has a low entropy, including the possible role of the multiverse.

Greene, Brian. 2011. *The Hidden Reality: Parallel Universes and the Deep Laws of the Cosmos*. New York: Knopf. A modern survey of the multiverse.

Guth, Alan H. 1998. *The Inflationary Universe: The Quest for a New Theory of Cosmic Origins*. New York: Basic Books. An exposition of inflation and the quantum creation of universes.

Rees, Martin. 1999. *Just Six Numbers: The Deep Forces that Shape the Universe*. New York: Basic Books. A survey of the role of fine-tuning in physics and cosmology.

18

Does God Love the Multiverse?

DON N. PAGE

A central point of the Judeo-Christian tradition is that God loves everyone. One of the most famous verses in the Bible is in the Gospel of John: "For God so loved the world that he gave his only begotten Son, that whoever believes in him should not perish but have everlasting life" (John 3:16). Furthermore, according to this tradition, God not only loves all people, but he also created them in his own image. As it is written in the Book of Genesis: "So God created man in his own image; in the image of God he created him; male and female he created them" (Gen. 1:27). For us to receive both the love and the image of God, it seems that humanity is unique in some sense – different from the rest of creation.

In light of modern science, however, we have to ask how unique we really are. Some have taken the image of God for humans to imply that God created us individually and separately from other living beings. This is challenged by Darwin's theory of evolution, which suggests that we were not created separately by an individual act, independent of the creation of the remainder of the earth's biosphere. Rather, we are related to the rest of life on earth. A new challenge to the beliefs of some Christians has arisen from the idea of a multiverse, that our universe is not unique but instead is one among many.

Parallels between Evolution and Multiverse Ideas

When Darwin proposed evolution, many conservative Christians accepted it as not necessarily contrary to Christianity. One famous example was Benjamin B. Warfield (1851–1921), the conservative Christian theologian and principal of Princeton Seminary from 1887 to 1921. Warfield wrote the chapter on "The Deity of Christ" in *The Fundamentals*, the source of the term "fundamentalism." Thus one of the most famous original fundamentalists accepted the possibility of Darwinian evolution, writing:

> I am free to say, for myself, that I do not think that there is any general statement in the Bible or any part of the account of creation, either as given in Genesis 1 and 2 or elsewhere alluded to, that need be opposed to evolution. (Warfield 2000, 130)

The Blackwell Companion to Science and Christianity, First Edition. Edited by J. B. Stump and Alan G. Padgett.
© 2012 Blackwell Publishing Ltd. Published 2012 by Blackwell Publishing Ltd.

However, many Christians later came to oppose evolution, perhaps most famously some other fundamentalists. Although this has a complex history which cannot be told here, one of the central reasons for resistance to evolution by some Christians is their belief that evolution removes one particular design argument for the existence of God, the argument that all of the marvelously many different species of living things on earth had been separately designed and created by God. Nevertheless, evolution did not disprove the existence of God or even of some overall design. Indeed, there are many leading theologians and scientists today who accept both evolution and creation by God.

It seems to me that there may be a parallel development occurring today in cosmology. Before Darwin, some Christians took the marvels of humanity as evidence of separate and individual design. Now, some Christians take the marvels of the fine-tuning of the physical constants of the universe as evidence of theism and often of separate and individual design of these constants by God. Here I wish to argue that this approach to cosmology could be just as mistaken as the approach of those who held to the separate and individual design of human beings. Embracing the multiverse is not yet a popular view among theists, but a minority of theists (e.g., Leslie 1989, 64–65; Leslie 2001, 211–214; Collins 2002; Barr 2003; Swinburne 2011) have broken with tradition and argue that a multiverse could reveal an even more grand design of the universe. If our observable universe is only a part of a much more complex structure, the physical process that would generate such a "multiverse" would have to have suitable basic laws and initial conditions to produce any life at all. The laws and initial conditions would apparently have to be even more special to produce not just life, but life like ours, in view of the order we actually do see around us. Stephen Barr, Gerald Cleaver, Robin Collins, Klaas Kraay, John Leslie, Richard Swinburne, and others claim that since God is infinitely creative, it makes sense to say that he might create a physical reality much larger than the single visible part of the universe or multiverse that we can observe directly (see, e.g., Leslie 1989, 180; Leslie 2001, 18–19, 215–216; Barr 2003, 151–153; Collins 2007, 460–462; Kraay 2010, 361–366). To understand this reasoning, we need to address the apparent fine-tuning of the physical constants in our universe.

Fine-Tuning in Our Universe

Now it does seem to be true that we could not be here if many of the constants of physics were significantly different, so that in our part of the universe, the constants of physics do in fact seem to be fine-tuned for our kind of life. This is generally agreed upon both by those who attempt to use this fine-tuning to support theism (as in Swinburne 2011), and by many scientists who are usually neutral or opposed to such an attempt (e.g., Carter 1990, 125–133; Carr and Rees 1979, 605–612; Davies 1982; Barrow and Tipler 1986; Rees 2000; Barrow 2002; Bostrom 2002; Susskind 2006; Carr 2007). Of course, no one knows what other forms of life might be possible if the constants of physics were significantly different, but the general consensus seems to be that it would be very difficult to imagine the possibility of any complex life at all existing if certain combinations of the constants of physics were greatly different.

For example, one of the most remarkable fine-tunings is the value of the cosmological constant or energy density of the "dark energy" responsible for the current acceleration of distant galaxies away from each other. Measurements show that the cosmological constant is more than 120 orders of magnitude smaller than unity in certain natural units (called Planck units, obtained by setting to unity the speed of light, Planck's quantum constant of action, and Newton's gravitational constant). With the other constants kept fixed, it would be difficult to have a universe with gravitationally formed structures lasting long enough for life if the cosmological constant were even just a few orders of magnitude larger than its observed value. But even if one tuned the other constants to allow the possibility of such structures when the cosmological constant has a value many orders of magnitude larger than its observed value, one still seems to need it to be many orders smaller than unity. So it is hard to see how to avoid at least some significant amount of fine-tuning of this parameter. (Basically, if the cosmological constant were of the order of unity in the natural Planck units, the spacetime of the universe would always have large quantum mechanical fluctuations, and no one knows any plausible way to have persisting complex structures that one could call life in such a case.)

Another constant that is many orders of magnitude away from unity, in this case about 36 orders of magnitude larger than unity, is the ratio of the electrostatic repulsion to the gravitational attraction between two protons (the nuclei at the centers of hydrogen atoms). With other constants kept fixed, it seems that one could not have the types of stars that appear to be necessary for life if this constant differed by much more than even one order of magnitude from its actual value. Again one could try to imagine a universe hospitable to some other form of life when this constant is significantly different by also tuning other constants to an appropriate range, but again it seems that complex life of any form relying mainly on the electromagnetic and gravitational forces would be impossible if this constant were close to unity. (Then it seems that one could not have stars, planets, and living organisms with large numbers of atoms, since the number of atoms in such structures generally scales as a positive power of this constant and would approach some small number near unity if this constant were itself near unity.)

Martin Rees (2000) discusses in much more detail these two constants and four others in our universe that are crucial for its properties. Life as we know it would apparently be impossible if anyone of them were greatly different (with the others held fixed). So although it might not be necessary for all of them to have their observed values, there are some combinations of them that apparently could not be very much different and yet give a universe with life, at least life at all similar to present life on earth. So we need some explanation for why these values are the way they are.

Explanations for Fine-Tuning

There is a general consensus that there appears to be "fine-tuning" of some of the constants of physics in our part of the universe. That is to say, if these constants had been sufficiently different, life as we know it could not have existed. So what is the explanation for this phenomenon? Three general types of explanations are often put forward.

Some suggest that the fine-tuning was done by a separate act of God to allow life. Others say that it is accidental, a fluke. And yet others propose that it arises from a huge multiverse of very many different possible constants of physics. It is also noted in several sources (such as Leslie 1989, 22; Leslie 2001, 211; Bostrom 2002, 11; Barr 2003, 153–154; Carr 2007, 16–17, 27, 411–412, 459–480) that the three explanations are not mutually exclusive, so that virtually any combination of them is logically possible. Also it should be noted that each of these three explanations really stands for a class of explanations, so that one should actually compare specific proposals taken from these classes rather than the classes themselves. For example, theists of different theological convictions might propose different ideas of how God would choose the constants. Those saying that the fine-tuning is a fluke might say that the constants are determined by any number of different mathematical structures that just happened to give biophilic values, or they might propose that there is truly some random process determining the constants in some way not derivable from any simple mathematical structure. And of course there are a huge number of possible multiverse theories. These theories are rapidly growing in favor, though not without a lot of opposition from both theists and nontheists.

Some multiverse theories seem to me to be too general to be plausible, such as the idea of David Lewis (1990) that all logical possibilities actually exist, or the original idea of Max Tegmark (1998, 1–51) that all mathematical structures have physical reality. These seem to leave it unexplained why what we see has the order that it does, whereas a random possibility from all logical possibilities or from all mathematical structures would surely be far more chaotic (Leslie 1989, 97–98; Leslie 2001, 23–30; Barr 2003, 156; Vilenkin 2006, 203). However, there might be other multiverse theories that better explain the order we observe, perhaps arising naturally out of elegant but specific laws of nature.

One natural way to get a multiverse is to have a universe so large that highly varied conditions occur somewhere. Another is from Everett many-worlds (DeWitt and Graham 1973), that all the quantum possibilities are actually realized. However, those possibilities do not necessarily give varying constants of physics.

One scenario that seems more hopeful is to get multiverses from inflation (Linde 1990, 292–317; Guth 1997, 245–252; Vilenkin 2006, 203–205), which is a very rapid exponential expansion of the early universe that may make the universe enormously larger than what we can observe of it. If the inflationary scenario can include phase transitions, and if the constants of physics can differ across phase transitions, inflation tends to produce all such possibilities.

Recently it has been realized that string/M theory apparently leads to a huge multiverse of 10^{500} or so different vacua or sets of constants. This would be enough for the constants we see to randomly occur somewhere (maybe once per 10^{200} vacua or so). Then perhaps 10^{300} or so vacua would reasonably allow for what we see.

If only one universe in 10^M could fit our observations, but if 10^N different universes exist in the multiverse, then it might not be surprising that what we observe exists if $N > M$. So if N is around 500 as suggested by string/M theory and M is around 200, so then indeed $N > M$. However, the actual numbers are scarcely known. We really don't yet know whether $N > M$ in string/M theory, but it does seem plausible. If this is the case, then what we see could be explained without its having to be individually selected.

One might still ask whether the multiverse explanation always works, assuming that it has enough universes (e.g., $N > M$). Is it sufficient to explain what we see by a multiverse theory in which there are enough different conditions that ours necessarily occurs somewhere? I would say not. Rather, it seems to me there is the further requirement that the conditions we observe should not be too rare out of all the conditions that are observed over the entire multiverse. A theory making our observations extremely rare should not be considered a good theory.

Good theories should be both intrinsically plausible and fit observations. Intrinsic plausibility is quantified by what is called the *a priori* probability of the theory, the probability that one might assign to it from purely theoretical background knowledge, without considering any observations. The fit to observations is quantified by the conditional probability of the observation given the theory, what is called the *likelihood*. Then the probability of the theory after taking into consideration the observation, what is called the *a posteriori* probability of the theory, is given by Bayes's theorem as being proportional to the product of the *a priori* probability and the likelihood.

I take the *a priori* probabilities of theories (intrinsic plausibilities before considering the observations) to be subjective but to be generally assigned higher values for simpler theories, by the principle known as Occam's razor. However, the recognition of simplicity depends on one's background knowledge, which itself depends on the laws of physics.

The *likelihood* of a theory is itself neither the *a priori* nor the *a posteriori* probability of the theory, but rather the conditional probability, not of the theory, but of the observation given the theory. A theory that uniquely gives one's observation would have unit likelihood but might have very low *a priori* probability.

For example, consider an extreme solipsistic theory that only one's actual momentary observation exists, not anyone else's or even any of one's own in either the past or the future, and perhaps not even that an external world exists at all. This theory would predict that observation with certainty if it were correct. (If the theory were true, certainly the observation would be that single one predicted by the theory.) Therefore, for that observation the likelihood is unity. However, such an extreme solipsistic theory, giving all the details of one's observation or conscious perception without an external world giving other observations, would surely be highly complex and so would be viewed as extremely implausible, much more implausible than an alternate theory in which the observation resulted from the existence of an external world that also gives other observations. Therefore, this extreme solipsistic theory would be assigned very low *a priori* probability.

At the other extreme, consider the simple theory that predicts all possible observations equally (arguably a consequence of something like the modal realism of David Lewis (1990)). Since this theory is so simple, it might be assigned a high *a priori* probability, but then because of the enormous number of observations it predicts with equal probability (presumably infinitely many), it would give very low likelihood (presumably zero).

The Growth of Our Knowledge of the Universe

Our whole growth of knowledge about the universe has been an expansion of its scope. As one grows as an infant, one rapidly grows beyond the view that one's present observation is all that is real, as one develops memories about the past and anticipations of the future. One then goes beyond solipsism and gains an understanding that other persons or observers exist as well. In the early stage of human development, there was the focus on one's family, which was then gradually extended to one's tribe, one's nation, one's race, and, one might hope, to all humans. But then when one further considers what other conscious observations may be going on, one might well believe that consciousness extends to other creatures, such as other animals.

Of course, one's direct observation never extends beyond one's own immediate conscious perception, so one can never prove that there are past or future perceptions as well (and I know philosophers who do not believe the future exists). Similarly, one can never directly experience even the present conscious perceptions of another, which engenders the problem of other minds in philosophy. Nevertheless, most of us believe that we have fairly good indirect evidence for the existence of other conscious experiences, at least for other humans on earth with whom we can communicate, though it is logically possible that neither they nor any external world actually exists. (My belief is that it is much simpler to explain the details of my present observation or conscious perception or experience by assuming that an external world and other conscious experiences also exist, than by assuming that just my own momentary conscious perception exists.)

We may now extend the reasoning to suppose that if the universe is large enough, it will also include conscious extraterrestrials, even though we do not have even indirect evidence for them that is so nearly direct as our (inevitably still indirect) evidence for other conscious beings on earth. We can further theorize that if the universe is so large that there never will be any contact between its distant parts and our part, there still might be other conscious beings not in causal contact with us, so that we never could communicate with them to get, even in principle, the indirect evidence of the same qualitative nature that we have for other humans here on earth with us.

A next step might be to postulate conscious beings and experiences in other universes totally disconnected from ours, so that even if one could imagine traveling faster than the speed of light, there would simply be no way to get there from here; the two parts would be in totally disconnected spacetimes. A similar situation would occur for putative conscious experiences in other branches of an Everett "many-worlds" wavefunction or quantum state. From accepting the existence of such disconnected observers, it hardly seems an excessive additional step to imagine observers in universes or parts of the multiverse with different constants of physics. One might even imagine observers in entirely different universes, not related to ours in the way an entire multiverse might be related by having one single overarching set of natural laws.

So in this sense, the idea of a multiverse seems to be rather a natural extension of our usual ideas of accepting a reality beyond one's immediate conscious perception, which is all the experience for which one has direct access. All the rest of one's knowledge is purely theoretical, though one's brain (assuming it exists) is apparently constructed to bring this knowledge into one's awareness without one's needing to be consciously aware of the details of *why* one seems to be aware of the existence of other conscious beings.

Despite the naturalness of the progression of ideas that leads to multiverse theories, there are various objections to the multiverse theory. However, none of the objections seem to me to be convincing, as there are highly plausible rebuttals to the objections.

Objections to Multiverse Ideas

A scientific objection to a multiverse theory might be that the multiverse (beyond our observed part, which is within one single universe) is not observable or testable. But if one had precise theories for single universes and for multiverses that gave the distributions of different conditions, one could make statistical tests of our observations (likely or unlikely in each distribution). Unfortunately, no such realistic theory exists yet for either a single universe or a multiverse, so I would agree that at present we simply do not have any good theories for either to test.

Another objection is that a multiverse is not a clear consequence of any existing theory. Although it is beginning to appear to be a consequence of string/M theory, that is not yet certain, which is why there can be theorists like David Gross who are still holding out hope that string/M theory might turn out to be a single-universe theory after all, possibly enabling theorists (if they could perform the relevant calculations) to fulfill their wildest dreams of being able to calculate the constants of physics uniquely from some simple principles. One first needs to make string/M theory into a precise theory and calculate its consequences, whether single universe or multiverse. And if that theory gives predictions that do not give a good statistical fit to observations, one needs to find a better theory that does.

A philosophical objection to a multiverse theory is that it is extravagant to assume unfathomable numbers of unobservable universes. This is a variant upon the psychological gut reaction that surely a multiverse would be more complex than a single universe, and hence should be assigned a lower *a priori* probability. But this is not necessarily so. The whole can be simpler than its parts, as the set of all integers is quite simple, certainly simpler than nearly all the (arbitrarily large) individual integers that form its parts.

As a further rebuttal of the accusation of extravagance, a theist can say that since God can do anything that is logically possible and that fits with God's nature and purposes, then there is apparently no difficulty for God to create as many universes as he pleases. God might prefer elegance in the principles by which he creates a vast multiverse over paucity of universes, that is, economy of principles rather than economy of materials.

Another philosophical objection to multiverses is that they can be used to explain anything, and thereby explain nothing. I would strongly agree with this criticism of multiverse theories that are too vague or diffuse, which do not sufficiently restrict the measure on the set of observations to favor ordered ones such as what we observe. There is a genuine need for a multiverse theory not to spread out the probability measure for observations so thinly that it makes our observation too improbable. So this objection would be a valid objection to vast classes of possible multiverse theories, but I do not see that it is an objection in principle against a good multiverse theory. Certainly not just any multiverse theory is acceptable, and even if simple single-universe theories do not work for explaining our observations, it will no doubt be quite a challenge to find a good multiverse theory that does succeed.

Most of the objections I have raised and attempted to answer so far would apply both to theistic and nontheistic scientists. However, if one is a theist, one might imagine that there are additional objections to multiverse theories, just as some theists had additional objections to Darwin's theory of evolution beyond the scientific objections that were also raised when that theory had much less support.

For example, a theist might feel that a multiverse theory would undercut the fine-tuning argument for the existence of God. I shall not deny that it would undercut the argument at the level of the constants of physics (though I think there would still be such a design argument from the general apparently elegant structure of the full laws of nature once they are known). However, the loss of one argument does not mean that its conclusion is necessarily false.

I personally think it might be a theological mistake to look for fine-tuning as a sign of the existence of God. I am reminded of the exchange between Jesus and the religious authorities recorded in the Gospel of Matthew (12:38–41):

> Then some of the scribes and Pharisees answered, saying, "Teacher, we want to see a sign from you." But He answered and said to them, "An evil and adulterous generation seeks after a sign, and no sign will be given to it except the sign of the prophet Jonah. For as Jonah was three days and three nights in the belly of the great fish, so will the Son of Man be three days and three nights in the heart of the earth. The men of Nineveh will rise up in the judgment with this generation and condemn it, because they repented at the preaching of Jonah; and indeed a greater than Jonah is here."

In other words, I regard the death and Resurrection of Jesus as the sign given to us that he is indeed the Son of God and Savior he claimed to be, rather than needing signs from fine-tuning.

Another theistic objection might be that with a multiverse explanation of the constants of physics, there is nothing left for God to design. But God could well have designed the entire multiverse, choosing elegant laws of nature by which to create the entire thing. In any case, whatever the design is, whether a logically rigid requirement, a simple free choice God made, or a complex free choice God made, theists would ascribe to God the task of creating the entire universe or multiverse according to this design.

A third more specifically Christian objection might be that if the multiverse (or even just our single part of the universe) is large enough for other civilizations to have sinned and needed Christ to come redeem them by something similar to his death on the cross here on earth for our sins, then his death may not sound as unique as the Bible says it is in Romans 6:10: "For the death that he died, he died to sin once for all; but the life that he lives, he lives to God." The Bible, however, was written for us humans here on earth, so it seems unreasonable to require it to describe what God may or may not do with other creatures he may have created elsewhere. We could just interpret the Bible to mean that Christ's death here on earth is unique for our human civilization.

Conclusion

In conclusion, multiverses are serious ideas of present science, though certainly not yet proven. They can potentially explain fine-tuned constants of physics but are not an automatic panacea for solving all problems; only certain multiverse theories, of which we have none yet in complete form, would be successful in explaining our observations. Though multiverses should not be accepted uncritically as scientific explanations, I would argue that theists have no more reason to oppose them than they had to oppose Darwinian evolution when it was first proposed.

God might indeed love the multiverse.

References

Barr, Stephen. 2003. *Modem Physics and Ancient Faith*. Notre Dame, IN: University of Notre Dame Press.

Barrow, John D. 2002. *The Constants of Nature*. New York: Pantheon Books.

Barrow, John D. and Tipler, Frank J. 1986. *The Anthropic Cosmological Principle*. Oxford: Clarendon Press.

Bostrom, Nick. 2002. *Anthropic Bias: Observation Selection Effects in Science and Philosophy*. New York: Routledge.

Carr, Bernard, ed. 2007. *Universe or Multiverse?* Cambridge: Cambridge University Press.

Carr, Bernard J. and Rees, Martin J. 1979. The Anthropic Principle and the Structure of the Physical World. *Nature*, 278, pp. 605–612.

Carter, Brandon. 1990. Large Number Coincidences and the Anthropic Principle in Cosmology. In J. Leslie, ed. *Physical Cosmology and Philosophy*. New York: Macmillan, pp. 125–133.

Collins, Robin. 2002. Design and the Many-Worlds Hypothesis. In William Lane Craig, ed. *Philosophy of Religion: A Reader and Guide*. New Brunswick, NJ: Rutgers University Press, pp. 130–148.

Collins, Robin. 2007. The Multiverse Hypothesis: A Theistic Perspective. In Bernard Carr, ed. *Universe or Multiverse?* Cambridge: Cambridge University Press, pp. 459–480.

Davies, Paul. 1982. *The Accidental Universe.* Cambridge: Cambridge University Press.

DeWitt, Bryce and Graham, R. Neill, eds. 1973. *The Many-Worlds Interpretation of Quantum Mechanics.* Princeton, NJ: Princeton University Press.

Guth, Alan. 1997. *The Inflationary Universe: The Quest for a New Theory of Cosmic Origins.* Reading, MA: Addison-Wesley.

Kraay, Klaas J. 2010. Theism, Possible Worlds, and the Multiverse. *Philosophical Studies,* 147, pp. 355–368.

Leslie, John. 1989. *Universes.* London: Routledge.

Leslie, John. 2001. *Infinite Minds: A Philosophical Cosmology.* Oxford: Oxford University Press.

Lewis, David. 1990. *On the Plurality of Worlds.* Cambridge: Blackwell.

Linde, Andrei. 1990. *Particle Physics and Inflationary Cosmology.* Chur, Switzerland: Harwood.

Rees, Martin. 2000. *Just Six Numbers: The Deep Forces that Shape the Universe.* New York: Basic Books.

Susskind, Leonard. 2006. *The Cosmic Landscape: String Theory and the Illusion of Intelligent Design.* New York: Little, Brown & Company.

Swinburne, Richard. 2011. Bayes, God, and the Multiverse. In J. Chandler and V. Harrison, eds. *Probability in the Philosophy of Religion.* Oxford: Oxford University Press.

Tegmark, Max. 1998. Is "The Theory of Everything" Merely the Ultimate Ensemble Theory? *Annals of Physics,* 270, pp. 1–51.

Vilenkin, Alex. 2006. *Many Worlds in One: The Search for Other Universes.* New York: Hill & Wang.

Warfield, Benjamin Breckinridge. 2000. *Evolution, Science and Scripture: Selected Writings.* Mark A. Noll and David N. Livingstone, eds. Grand Rapids, MI: Baker Books.

Further Reading

Collins, Francis. 2006. *The Language of God: A Scientist Presents Evidence for Belief.* New York: Free Press. The leader of the Human Genome Project recounts his personal Christian faith and the thesis that it is not contradictory to evolution.

Page, Don N. 2010. Does God So Love the Multiverse? In Melville Y. Stewart, ed. *Science and Religion in Dialogue,* vol. 1. Oxford: Wiley-Blackwell, pp. 396–410. Also available online at http://arxiv.org/abs/0801.0246, this is the original and longer version of the present chapter.

19

The Fine-Tuning of the Cosmos
A Fresh Look at Its Implications

ROBIN COLLINS

Introduction

The fine-tuning of the cosmos for life refers to the claim that the laws of nature, the fundamental parameters of physics, and the initial conditions of the universe are set just right for life to occur. As I have argued elsewhere (Collins 2009, 254–255), the relevant kind of life is embodied conscious agents (ECAs) who can make what they take to be moral choices.

The key assumption for all cases of fine-tuning is that ECAs require the existence of relatively stable, reproducible complex material structures. With that in mind, consider the fine-tuning of the laws of nature. The existence of the aforementioned complex structures depends on having precisely the right set of laws – such as those for the forces of nature. For example: if gravity did not exist, masses would not clump together to form stars or planets; if the electromagnetic force didn't exist, there would be no chemistry; if the strong force didn't exist (which binds protons and neutrons together in a nucleus), no atoms could exist with atomic number greater than hydrogen, and thus no complex chemistry. Other laws and principles of physics also appear necessary for ECAs. For example, as Princeton physicist Freeman Dyson has pointed out (1979, 251), if the Pauli-exclusion principle did not exist – which is what keeps two electrons from occupying the same energy state in an atom – all electrons would occupy the lowest atomic energy state, and thus no complex atoms could exist.

Next, consider the fundamental parameters of physics. These are fundamental numbers that when plugged into the laws of physics determine the basic structure of the universe. Newton's gravitational constant G is an example, determining the strength of the force of gravity via Newton's law $F = Gm_1m_2/r^2$. G, and several other fundamental parameters, must fall into a narrow range in order for complex life to exist.[1]

The most discussed case of this sort of fine-tuning is that of the dark-energy density of the universe. When this density is positive, it acts as a repulsive force, causing space to expand; when negative, it acts as an attractive force, causing space to contract. If it were too large, space would expand so rapidly that galaxies and stars could not form and hence no habitats for ECAs would exist; if too small, the universe would collapse before ECAs could evolve.

The Blackwell Companion to Science and Christianity, First Edition. Edited by J. B. Stump and Alan G. Padgett.
© 2012 Blackwell Publishing Ltd. Published 2012 by Blackwell Publishing Ltd.

The fine-tuning for life of the dark energy is estimated to be around 1 part in 10^{120} – that is, 1 part in 1 followed by 120 zeros. The precision of this is comparable to that required to hit a bull's-eye on earth less than the size of a proton when throwing a dart from outer space.

Finally, according to Roger Penrose – one of Britain's leading theoretical physicists – the initial distribution of mass-energy in the universe has to be fine-tuned to 1 part in 10 raised to the power of 10^{123} in order for a universe with as low entropy as ours to exist (Penrose 1989, 343). This precision is much, much greater than that required to hit an individual proton if the entire visible universe were a dart board!

There are three major responses to the fine-tuning: the multiverse explanation, theism, and the naturalistic single-universe hypothesis. I will begin with the multiverse explanation. Although I have addressed these alternatives in much detail elsewhere, in this chapter I will present condensed versions of new and I believe powerful arguments against the two non-theistic ones.

Multiverse Explanation

The multiverse explanation of the fine-tuning begins with the multiverse hypothesis. This hypothesis claims that there are a very large, if not infinite, number of regions of space-time with different values of the fundamental parameters of physics, different initial conditions, and perhaps even different laws of nature. It then claims that in a sufficiently varied multiverse, it is no surprise that some universe is observer-structured – that is, structured so that observers will arise in it. Finally, it invokes the so-called *observer-selection principle*, which is the tautological claim that embodied observers can exist only in a region of space-time that allows for them to exist. This renders it unsurprising that as observers we find ourselves in an observer-structured region of space-time since it is impossible for us to exist in any other type of region.

The observer-selection principle is essential to the multiverse explanation because it prevents it from undercutting the need to explain other seemingly surprising events and features of the universe. For example, normally one would think that it is too coincidental for a 6-sided die to land 50 times in a row on 4 just by chance. Yet, in a large enough multiverse, someone will observe this to happen. Nonetheless, it is still improbable that a "randomly selected" observer will see such an occurrence. Hence, purportedly, the multiverse hypothesis combined with the observer-selection principle can render it unsurprising both that we exist and that we find ourselves in an observer-structured universe while at the same time not undercutting ordinary claims of improbability.

Elsewhere (Collins 2007; 2009, 262–269), I have argued that by far the most popular versions of the multiverse hypothesis – namely, those that postulate that the multiverse was generated by some physical process – push the problem of fine-tuning up one level to the laws required to generate the multiverse. For, I argued, in order to generate even one life-permitting universe, this process must be governed by precisely the right set of laws. Here, I want to briefly outline what I believe to be an even more powerful objection to the multiverse explanation, one that applies to any type of multiverse.

The objection begins by noting that the universe is *not* fine-tuned so that observers can exist; rather it is fine-tuned so that, at least within some epoch, the kind of observers who are most likely to occur are ECAs who can interact with each other for good or ill. Indeed, it appears to be additionally fine-tuned so that those observers can develop scientific technol-

ogy and discover the universe. The reason that it is not fine-tuned for observers is that sufficiently large non-fine-tuned universes will still contain observers, at least for many of the
fundamental parameters of physics. Specifically, as one moves further and further away from
the fine-tuned values that the fundamental parameters have in our universe, the resulting
universe becomes first less optimal for scientific discoverability and the concurrent development of technology; then, given the universe is large enough, it becomes overwhelmingly
dominated by "fluctuation observers" who are isolated and last for only a brief time. Thus,
sufficiently large non-fine-tuned universes will be populated by observers, but for any finite
volume in such universes, fluctuation observers will be much more likely to occur than ECAs.

What is a fluctuation observer? The idea of a fluctuation observer presupposes a view of
consciousness almost universally assumed by naturalists who advocate a multiverse: namely,
one in which the mind – and hence being an observer – is a result of the right structural
arrangement of matter. A fluctuation observer can then be defined as a localized fluctuation
in the organization of mass-energy in some region that results in a sufficiently organized
material structure to constitute an observer. In the literature, both thermal fluctuations and
quantum fluctuations have been postulated to give rise to these observers. However, because
the former type of fluctuation is conceptually clearer than the latter, I will focus on it.[2]

Thermal fluctuations refer to the constantly varying states of individual particle and field
states in a material system as a result of thermal energy contained in the system. For instance,
the molecules of a gas in the box at room temperature will have constantly changing velocities and positions as they collide with each other. Because of thermal fluctuations, there is a
finite, though very, very small probability for the mass-energy in a system to move from
a highly disorganized (high-entropy) state to a highly organized (low-entropy) state. One such
highly organized state is that needed for the existence of an observer. Originally, Ludwig
Boltzmann (1844–1906) – one of the most significant founders of the branch of physics
known as statistical mechanics – attempted to use this idea to explain why we live in a universe
with the enormously improbable arrangement of mass-energy mentioned in the introductory section. He proposed that if we were in a large enough universe, eventually some region
would undergo a random thermal fluctuation to a sufficiently low-entropy state to produce
observers, thus explaining why we find ourselves in a low-entropy universe.

In response, it was pointed out that it is vastly more likely for such a localized fluctuation
to give rise to an observer that is surrounded by a chaotic, high-entropy arrangement of
mass-energy than one surrounded by an ordered, low-entropy universe such as ours. Such
an isolated observer came to be called a "Boltzmann brain." The claim that isolated local
islands of order are vastly more probable than larger regions of order is illustrated by the
well-worn analogy of monkeys randomly typing on a typewriter. It is enormously more likely
for the monkeys to occasionally produce a meaningful word than for them to produce a
meaningful paragraph, let alone a play by Shakespeare. Similarly, if one randomly shook 100
coins laid out in a row, it would be vastly more likely for a small number of coins in a row
– say 5 coins – to come up on all heads somewhere than for the entire set of coins to all land
on heads. In the case of fluctuation observers, calculations by Roger Penrose show that using
the probability measure of statistical mechanics, it is around 10 raised to 10^{120} times more
likely for an isolated fluctuation observer to arise in a region of space surrounded by chaos
than in a large, low-entropy universe such as ours (2004, 762–765).

Since the time of Boltzmann, the existence of fluctuation observers has been considered
the outstanding problem with multiverse explanations of the low entropy of the universe;
more recently, it has also been discussed as a problem for some types of infinitely expanding
universes, since purportedly these could give rise to an unlimited number of fluctuation

observers via quantum fluctuations (Davenport and Olum 2010). What has not been recognized is that isolated fluctuation observers would exist in universes in which the fundamental parameters are not fine-tuned, and that this undercuts the ability of a multiverse to explain many other cases of fine-tuning.

The existence of such observers is especially clear for those fine-tuned parameters – such as the strength of gravity, the dark-energy density, and the strength of the primordial density fluctuations – that can be varied without affecting the properties of atoms or molecules. If these "chemistry-irrelevant" parameters were changed, any atom in the periodic table could still come into existence as a result of thermal fluctuations; further, any organized combination of such atoms could fluctuate into existence in this way. Hence material structures identical to our brains – and that last for as long as necessary to be counted as observers – would exist in sufficiently large universes that have non-fine-tuned values for the chemistry-irrelevant parameters. In particular, as if we imagine these chemistry-irrelevant parameters being moved further and further away from their current value, the universe first becomes less conducive for scientific discoverability and technology, with eventually the predominant kind of observers being fluctuation observers.

For example, consider a universe with a dark-energy density a million times the value in our universe, but otherwise having the same laws and initial conditions as ours. Even if observers could form via a standard evolutionary process, the universe would have expanded so much by the time a typical observer formed that it would find itself in the only galaxy in its visible universe. As Tegmark and Rees comment, "When the Universe had reached its current age . . . ours would be the only galaxy in the local Hubble volume – alas, a drab and dreary place for extragalactic astronomers" (Tegmark and Rees 1997, 6). Further increases in the dark-energy density would not allow ECAs to form at all. Fluctuation observers would still exist, however. For example, during the early part of such a universe's expansion, it would contain a high density of mass-energy undergoing thermal fluctuations; since one possible, though enormously improbable, configuration of this mass-energy would consist of a structure the same as that of our brains, if the universe were large enough, many such structures would form. It would be vastly more likely for a given structure to exist in isolation, however, than in a community of interacting agents; the reason is that a community of agents requires much more organized complexity than a single observer, and thus is much less likely to arise by a chance fluctuation.

As another example, consider varying the strength of gravity as given by the dimensionless gravitational constant, $\alpha_G \equiv 2\pi G(m_p)^2/hc$, where m_p is the mass of the proton, h is Planck's constant, and c is the speed of light. As I pointed out elsewhere (Collins forthcoming b), the range of values for α_G is zero to the Planck scale, which is about 10^{38} the current value of α_G. Now consider a planet of the same size and composition as earth. As α_G is moderately increased – say tenfold – any kind of technology would become more difficult, for example, building a structure to live in or perform scientific experiments would become more difficult since it would be more difficult for ECAs to lift the material. As α_G is increased further, terrestrial ECAs would become impossible since a life form with a brain large enough to qualify as an ECAs would be crushed; this would only allow for ECAs to evolve under water, which clearly would not allow them to develop scientific technology since they could not forge metals. Further increases would make even this sort of life impossible. Although decreasing the size of the planet would compensate for increasing α_G, this can only partially compensate for an increase in α_G for several reasons (Collins forthcoming b). For example, at some point one would have to decrease the size of the planet so much that it could not contain an ecosystem for ECAs to evolve; to keep enough gravitational attraction to retain an atmosphere, the size of a planet cannot be decreased fast enough to keep the force on the surface from increasing with an increase in α_G. The result is that even taking into account the possibility of ECAs evolving on smaller planets than earth, as α_G is moderately increased (say by a hundredfold), it becomes much more difficult for the ECAs that do evolve to develop scientific technology; then, at some point – for example, a billionfold increase in α_G (which is only one part in 10^{29} of its possible range of values) – it becomes impossible for ECAs to evolve at all. Yet, isolated fluctuation observers would still exist.

The existence of these fluctuation observers in non-fine-tuned universes shows that the chemistry-irrelevant parameters of physics are not fine-tuned for observers, but rather for ECAs that can significantly interact with each other, and moreover, that can develop scientific technology and discover the universe. Yet because of its reliance on the observer-selection principle, without additional postulates the multiverse hypothesis can only take away the surprise that we exist in an observer-structured universe, not in a universe structured for ECAs (see Figure 19.1).

In response, multiverse advocates could point out that non-fine-tuned universes will have a much lower density of observers than fine-tuned universes: even in a non-fine-tuned region of space as large as our visible universe (about 30 billion light years across), a fluctuation observer would be rare. They could then argue that if one considers oneself a generic observer and weights the probability of finding oneself in a given universe by its density of observers, then one should not be surprised to be in a fine-tuned universe. The problem with this response is that density seems irrelevant for such probabilistic weightings across universes. Rather, if anything, it is the relative number of observers per universe that should

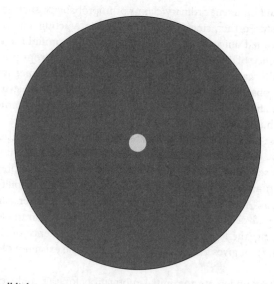

Figure 19.1 The small lighter region at the center represents the region of parameter space in which the chemistry-irrelevant constants are fine-tuned for ECAs to evolve. Since observers can exist for all the other values of these constants (as represented by the darker region), the universe is not fine-tuned for observers. Thus, since the multiverse hypothesis relies on the observer-selection principle, it can only render unsurprising that we exist in the darker region, not that we find ourselves in the lighter region. It thus fails to account for the fine-tuning.

matter. Consider, for instance, two universes – A and B – with universe A having 1/10 the density of observers as universe B but being 100 times as large. If one did not have any other information about which universe one is in, if anything one should expect to find oneself in universe A, not B, since it contains 10 times as many observers. Since there is no upper bound on the size of the universe in current multiverse theories, however, we have no basis for thinking that the number of observers in fine-tuned universes is greater than in non-fine-tuned universes.

In fact, in the typical current inflationary multiverse models, each universe is infinite (Vilenkin 2006, 96–101; Susskind 2006, 312–313); hence there are infinitely many observers in both fine-tuned and non-fine-tuned universes. Although density could suddenly become relevant in the transition from finite to infinite universes, in absence of a positive argument for this happening, our intuitions in the finite case remain the only guide we have to the infinite case. Further, even if one accepted density as relevant, of itself the multiverse would still not be able to explain the low entropy of the universe: even when restricted to a finite region of space the size of our visible universe, a random configuration of mass-energy in that region is vastly more likely to result in an isolated observer surrounded by chaos than of group of interacting agents surrounded by low-entropic conditions as in our universe. Finally, although multiverse advocates might reply that there being infinitely many observers in both fine-tuned and non-fine-tuned universes undercuts any claim of surprise or impro-bability regarding the fine-tuning, such a reply threatens to undermine all probabilistic inferences, since for almost any improbable occurrence O, in a sufficiently large and varied multiverse there will always be an infinite number of observers who observe O.

Another possibility is to build into the definition of the relevant kind of observer that it is part of a community of interacting agents. The problem here is that one can always do this for any attribute F of the universe, thus making it certain that a generic observer will observe F. This would undercut ordinary claims of improbability, such as the case of the die mentioned previously. Further, since a community of interacting agents is itself a material structure, non-fine-tuned universes will also contain such communities. However, the prob-ability of a community of ECAs forming in any finite region drops precipitously with the size of and material organization required for the community. Hence it is still vastly more likely for a generic observer to find itself in the smallest and least structured community required for it to be an observer than in a larger, highly structured community of observers, such as that of the human race.

Finally, multiverse advocates could postulate that, contrary to the usual measure used in statistical mechanics, there is a true probability measure that will make it likely that a generic observer will find itself in an ECA-structured universe. In this case, however, the work of explaining the fine-tuning is being done by the right choice of probability measure, not the multiverse hypothesis. Accordingly, it is difficult to see how multiverse advocates do better than single-universe advocates in explaining the fine-tuning. For example, in an attempt to explain the fine-tuning, the latter could also postulate the existence of the right probability measure, namely one that gives a significant probability to the existence of an ECA-structured universe.

The above analysis undercuts the initial motivation for the multiverse explanation by showing that its seeming ability to explain the fine-tuning was based on conflating the real fine-tuning for ECAs (and secondarily, technology and discoverability) with a non-existent fine-tuning for observers. This in turn was the result of conflating conscious observers that arise through a normal evolutionary process – which are likely to be interacting agents – with mere observers, which need not arise through such a process. Without this initial motivation, however, it is hard to see why we should take the multiverse explanation more seriously than other naturalistic contenders. Finally, it should be clear that the existence of these fluctuation observers also undercuts the so-called *weak anthropic principle objection*, which claims that, even if there is only one universe, it is illegitimate to claim that the fine-tuning is surprising or "improbable" since a universe that is not fine-tuned could not be observed.

Theistic Explanation

In contrast to the naturalistic multiverse explanation, theism does render it unsurprising that an ECA-structured universe exists. To begin, we would expect an all-good God to create a reality with at least a positive, if not optimal, balance of good over evil. Thus, arguably, theism should lead us to expect a universe structured toward the realization of moral and aesthetic value. Given that we can glimpse some special value that highly vulnerable embodied conscious agents like us can realize that could plausibly be thought to outweigh the evils – such as suffering –resulting from such embodiment, it follows that it is not surprising that God would create an ECA-structured universe. I propose that one such value is the ability to engage in particular kinds of virtuous actions – such as self-sacrificial love, courage, and the like – that the vulnerability that comes from embodiment allows. In a theodicy I have developed elsewhere (Collins forthcoming a), I claim that these actions allow for eternal connections of appreciation, contribution, and intimacy between conscious agents. For example, if someone significantly helps me in times of suffering, it can create a connection of appreciation in me that has the potential of lasting all eternity, and hence growing in value.

Single-Universe Naturalism

By single-universe naturalism I mean the claim that the universe is a brute, inexplicable fact with no further explanation. Elsewhere (Collins 2009) I argued that, given the fine-tuning evidence, the existence of an ECA-structured universe is very surprising (i.e., epistemically improbable) under single-universe naturalism but not under theism. Then, using a variation of the likelihood principle of confirmation theory, I concluded that the fine-tuning evidence strongly confirms theism over single-universe naturalism. Since, as we saw above, the naturalistic multiverse hypothesis does not take away the seeming improbability associated with the fine-tuning, theism is also strongly confirmed over it. Consequently, theism can be said to be strongly confirmed over naturalism.

One response naturalists can give to this argument is that the existence of evil provides a counterbalancing reason against theism. As I have argued elsewhere (Collins 2009, 255–256), a universe with agents that are highly vulnerable to their environment and to one another will almost inevitably contain the kind of evils we find in our universe. Consequently, even though the problem of evil is a serious problem, insofar as we can glimpse a reason for God's creating such a universe – such as the reasons cited in the last section – the combination of the existence of such a universe with its consequent evils is rendered unsurprising under theism. Under naturalism, however, it is still very surprising that such a universe exists, and hence theism is strongly confirmed over naturalism even when the existence of evil is taken into account.

Naturalists have another common response – that hypothesizing the existence of God merely transfers the problem posed by the order and fine-tuning of the universe up one level to that of the order in God's mind; thus no explanatory progress is made. It is crucial to recognize here that the leading theistic thinkers in all the major theistic traditions (Judaism, Christianity, Islam, and Hindu theistic traditions) have conceived of God as a being that has great, if not absolute, ontological simplicity, without anything resembling an ordering of elements of the type expressed by the laws of nature; those who raise this objection, there-fore, are assuming an anthropomorphic conception of God explicitly disavowed by these leading theistic philosophers and theologians. The real question is thus not whether theism transfers the problem up one level, but whether this traditional conception of God is logically consistent. If it is, then it removes the coincidence or improbability posed by fine-tuning without transferring it up. In my judgment, traditional theism has neither been shown to be logically consistent nor logically inconsistent. Consequently, it offers the *promise* of a logically consistent solution, even though no one has been able to show that it can fulfill that promise.

At this point, a naturalist might argue that even if naturalism involves accepting the huge coincidence of the existence of an ECA-structured universe as a brute fact, at least it does not involve an unjustified commitment in some ontological reality whose intelligibility is not even clear. In fact, naturalism is often presented as being based on an unwillingness to go beyond what the evidence warrants, and thus as not involving a *faith commitment* – by which I mean a commitment that goes beyond what can be derived from a combination of one's immediate sense experience and the standard rules of deductive and probabilistic logic.[3] This portrayal of naturalism is false: even apart from the fine-tuning evidence, naturalism involves a faith commitment regarding the structure of reality that goes as much beyond the evidence as naturalists accuse theists of doing.

To show this, I begin with what has become known as the *underdetermination of theory by data problem*. This is the problem that for any set of extant observational data, there is always an indefinite number of logically consistent hypotheses that can account for the data but which have different predictive consequences in untested domains. Consequently, in order for scientists to choose one theory over another – even merely for its potential predictive success in unobserved domains or new applications – scientists must go beyond mere logical consist-ency and fit with data. Rather, they must rely on what are called *theoretical virtues*. The most commonly cited theoretical virtue is that of simplicity, a virtue that says that everything else being equal, we should prefer simple theories over complex ones. Using this virtue commits one to a claim in the neighborhood of the idea that the relevant aspects of the world (such as the fundamental laws of nature) are more likely to be simple than complex.

The need to invoke simplicity is nicely illustrated by the case of "curve fitting," in which scientists attempt to find the right equation that both accounts for a body of data and can serve as a trustworthy basis for future predictions or extrapolations. For example, suppose that one collects data on the relation between the magnitude of force exerted on a mass and the magnitude of the mass's acceleration. The data will consist of measurements of accelera-tions that result from various forces. Graphically, this could be represented by a plot of data points (with error bars), with the amount of force on the y-axis and the amount of accelera-tion on the x-axis (see Figure 19. 2). It is a mathematical fact that for any number of data points, there always exist an infinite number of functions that will perfectly go through the data points, but radically disagree about the values of the force associated with unobserved values of acceleration. Consequently, to choose the appropriate function to use for predic-

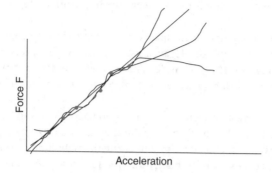

Figure 19.2   In extrapolating from the data points using the straight line instead of the other possible curves, scientists are implicitly assuming that the world is in some sense more likely to be simple than complex.

tions, scientists must consider something more than fit with data. Typically, scientists consider the simplicity, naturalness, or some other purported feature of an equation – such as how well it fits with background information (such as previous theories or similar cases). Indeed, the equation they ultimately choose might even miss one or more of the points by a greater amount than experimental error.

In the terminology I will now introduce, the use of a theoretical virtue implicitly commits one to claiming that some corresponding property is what I call an *ideal of natural order* (INO). Roughly, I define some overarching property as an INO for a person if and only if: (i) the person is explicitly or implicitly committed to the claim that the world is, or is likely to be, structured in such a way that there is a positive realization of that property; and (ii), that commitment guides their inductive practices and choice of theories. For example, the use of simplicity in scientific theory choice implicitly commits one to something in the neighbor-hood of the claim that the world is more likely to be simple than complex (at least in its basic law structure). Thus, insofar as scientists use simplicity in this way, they are committed to simplicity being an INO. Finally, I define a *primitive* INO (a PINO) as an INO for which one has no further explanation in terms of another INO.

As shown by the curve-fitting example, INOs form the basis of our inductive practices, such as extrapolating from observed data and choosing the best explanation of some set of phenomena. This means that one's primitive INOs cannot be justified by their past success, since any argument from their past success to their future reliability would be an argument from observed data (namely, their past success) to unobserved data (namely, their future success), and thus would itself require assuming the PINOs in question. Nonetheless, one should require that they be consistent with their past success.

In general, naturalists and theists share the same INOs, with some qualifications to be discussed below. Where they differ is in their PINOs. Consider simplicity. Both theists and naturalists would accept simplicity as an INO. Non-theists would likely take that INO as primitive – it is a brute fact that the universe is structured in a simple way, and it is a brute fact that simplicity should be an epistemic norm to decide between scientific theories. In contrast, theists are committed to saying that God has structured reality for a positive realiza-tion of moral and aesthetic value. Therefore, the commitment to non-contingent divine reality being structured in this way constitutes theism's PINO. A theist could then explain the success and normativity of simplicity and elegance in scientific theory choice in terms of this PINO.

In the case of simplicity, one such explanation is that simplicity contributes to elegance, at least for the classical notion of elegance as simplicity with variety, famously stated by William Hogarth (Hogarth, 1753). Thus, for this reason alone, theism renders it unsurprising that an elegant universe has a high degree of complexity while having a highly simple underlying law structure.

Theists could also argue that there are certain moral goods that can be more fully realized in a world structured for scientific technology and discoverability; they could then go on to argue, as I will below, that the universe's manifesting the right kind of simplicity greatly aids in its discoverability. For instance, with regard to the first point, technology allows for ECAs to influence each other for good or for ill on a much larger scale, thereby greatly increasing the range and extent of potential virtuous responses and positive connections between these agents. In addition, one might think scientific discovery is valuable in and of itself. So, we can glimpse a reason for God creating a discoverable world.

My analysis so far can be summarized as follows: theists must make a faith commitment in believing in God, but since God's existence can plausibly explain why we should trust our theoretical and inductive practices, *theists do not have to make an additional faith commitment in the continued reliability of these practices*. On the other hand, in order to engage in empirical enquiry, naturalists must make a faith commitment to their continued reliability. Consequently, apart from other considerations, there is a stalemate of one faith commitment versus another.

Arguably, the fine-tuning data tip the balance in favor of theism. But that is not all. I will now argue that the use of simplicity in scientific theory choice implicitly assumes that the kind of simplicity exemplified by the universe is one that makes it discoverable for the ECAs that arise in it, and this ends up building in a teleological assumption that is highly problematic for naturalism. Specifically, the kind of simplicity that has been successful in science, and is now implicitly considered normative, is simplicity in the *humanly practical limit*, not absolute simplicity or elegance. To illustrate, consider Newton's equation of gravity, $F = Gm_1m_2/r^2$. This equation is very simple when written in the Newtonian mathematical framework (namely, one based on Euclidean geometry with its three spatial dimensions and one independent time dimension). Similarly, Einstein's equation of gravity has great simplicity when expressed in the mathematical framework of general relativity (namely, a four-dimensional semi-Riemannian manifold). Yet, if one wrote Einstein's equations of motion in a Newtonian conceptual framework, one would obtain Newton's law, $F = Gm_1m_2/r^2$, plus an infinite number of small correction terms. These correction terms would only become important for large gravitational fields or relativistic velocities. Yet, they exist, and hence within the Newtonian framework the experimentally correct equation of gravity is actually enormously complex – its simplicity lies in its humanly practical limit. Furthermore, the fact that it has such a simple limiting form for *practical purposes* depends on specific contingent facts about our existence – for example, that our planet is not orbiting close to a black hole; thus it need not have been that way.

Similar things could be said about the relation of quantum mechanics to classical mechanics: if the predictions of quantum mechanics (in terms of expectation values) are written out in the classical mathematical framework with real numbers denoting quantities, one obtains simple equations (corresponding to the equations of classical mechanics), with an infinite number of correction terms that are very small except when quantum effects become important. This simplicity in the humanly practical limit – which I henceforth call *qualified simplicity*

– has allowed us to discover the classical equations while at the same time providing the experimental basis for moving to the quantum framework.

To make sense of the success and continued use of this qualified simplicity, one cannot merely assume that the underlying law structure of the world is likely to be simple or elegant. Neither of these would give us any grounds for thinking that the equations of physics would be simple in the humanly accessible limits within ultimately unsatisfactory mathematical frameworks (such as the Newtonian framework), but not simple outside those practically useable limits. Being structured for discoverability, however, does make sense of it. Given our limited cognitive capacities, natural selection would favor creatures that prefer simplicity over complexity. Thus if God wanted to make a universe optimally discoverable, it would make sense for God to structure the world so that (i), at each conceptual framework (such as the flat space-time of Newtonian mechanics), simplicity would offer a generally good guide; but (ii), it would fail at the boundaries, thereby forcing the ECAs in that universe to go to the next theoretical rung (e.g., such as to the curved space-time of Einstein) in their scientific quest.

The naturalist could respond that it is also a lucky brute fact that the universe has exhibited this anthropocentric form of simplicity. This response, however, misses an important point: scientists continue to be confident in this form of simplicity. If the success of qualified simplicity is merely considered an accidental regularity – something that just happens by chance – there are no grounds for expecting it to continue. If, for instance, one tossed a 2-sided coin 10 times in a row and if by accident it came up heads every time, one would have no basis for expecting this regularity to continue. Only if there is a deeper explanation for this occurrence – such as a natural law or something else – would there be a basis for this expectation. Yet, scientists do expect qualified simplicity to continue to work – and this is true even in the practice of predictively relying on virtually any equation of physics, since as illustrated by the curve-fitting example, there are always an indefinite number of competitors that account for the data but yield radically different predictions. Qualified simplicity is what separates out the equations actually used from these competitors. (It is not absolute simplicity, since most physicists think that current physics is a low-energy approximation to some higher-level set of theories, most likely formulated in a mathematical framework as different from the current one as the framework of general relativity is from Newtonian mechanics.)

If scientific practice really does implicitly take as more likely to be predictively accurate those theories that are simple *in the ECA-assessable limit*, but not in other limits, it is difficult to see how scientific practice can avoid implicitly assuming that the world is likely to be constructed for human discoverability. This in turn involves an implicit teleological commitment, which is at best difficult to reconcile with naturalism.[4]

Concluding Thoughts

Finally, one might worry that the two faith commitments – that of the naturalist and that of the theist – are at different levels, and so cannot really be compared. The theist's is about a transcendent ontological reality whereas the naturalist's is about the structure of this universe. To compare them, one can divide the theistic thesis into three parts:

(a)   the universe (and reality in general) is non-accidentally structured to positively realize moral and aesthetic value (the theist's PINO);

(b)   some kind of transcendent unified ontological reality grounds this structure; and
(c)   this reality is more appropriately described as personal than impersonal.

Like the naturalist's commitment, thesis (a) is about the structure of the universe. Further, it has cross-cultural intuitive appeal in itself, apart from theism: for example, many non-theists have held something in the neighborhood of this thesis, such as Plato and the some of the most important Chinese philosophers.[5] My argument in the last section above is that thesis (a) makes much more sense of the success, and actual practice, of empirical enquiry than the corresponding naturalist PINO, whatever exactly they take that to be. But it does more than that: thesis (a) renders unsurprising the existence of a universe with embodied conscious agents. Since naturalists typically reject (a), however, their view renders it enormously coincidental that we find ourselves in an ECA-structured universe – for example, a coincidence on the order of 1 part in 10 raised to 10^{123} in the case of the low entropy of the universe and 1 part in 10^{120} in the case of the dark-energy density.

Notes

I would like to thank the John Templeton Foundation for grant support for research that undergirds this paper.
1   See Collins (2003) for an examination of some of these cases. Further examples of fine-tuning are presented in Collins (forthcoming a), where I respond to the major criticisms raised by physicist Victor Stenger, the leading skeptic on fine-tuning. Also see Martin Rees (2000) and Paul Davies (1982) for evidence for fine-tuning.
2   There is a significant literature on this issue. A good place to begin is Davenport and Olum (2010). For a discussion of the history of the problem, see Davies (1974, 103f.).
3   For example, in his *Atheism: A Very Short Introduction*, Julian Baggini states that "Atheism is not a faith position because it is belief in nothing beyond which there is evidence and argument for" (2003, 32).
4   Philosopher Mark Steiner (1998) has developed this idea in some depth for the case of physics. By looking at many examples, he argues that the practice of scientists assumes that the world is more user-friendly than would make sense under naturalism. He does not use my example of simplicity, however.
5   See, for example, book VI of Plato's Republic; for an example of one major Chinese philosopher (Chu Hsi (1140–1200)) who held this view, see Fung (1948, 297–298).

References

Baggini, Julian. 2003. *Atheism: A Very Short Introduction*. Oxford: Oxford University Press.
Collins, Robin. 2003. The Evidence for Fine-Tuning. In Neil Manson, ed. *God and Design: The Teleological Argument and Modern Science*. New York: Routledge, pp. 178–199.
Collins, Robin. 2007. The Multiverse Hypothesis: A Theistic Perspective. In Bernard Carr, ed. *Universe or Multiverse?* New York: Cambridge University Press, pp. 459–480.
Collins, Robin. 2009. The Teleological Argument: An Exploration of the Fine-Tuning of the Universe. In William Lane Craig and J. P. Moreland, eds. *The Blackwell Companion to Natural Theology*. Oxford: Wiley-Blackwell, pp. 202–281.

Collins, Robin. Forthcoming a. The Connection-Building Theodicy. In Dan Howard-Snyder and Justin McBrayer, eds. *The Blackwell Companion to the Problem of Evil*. Oxford: Wiley-Blackwell.

Collins, Robin. Forthcoming b. The Fine-Tuning Evidence Is Convincing. In Chad Meister, J. P. Moreland and Khaldoun Sweis, eds. *Oxford Dialogues in Christian Theism*. Oxford: Oxford University Press.

Davenport, Matthew and Olum, Ken. 2010. Are There Boltzmann Brains in the Vacuum? ArXiv:1008.0808v1 [hep-th].

Davies, P. C. W. 1974. *The Physics of Time Asymmetry*. Berkeley, CA: University of California Press.

Davies, P. C. W. 1982. *The Accidental Universe*. Cambridge: Cambridge University Press.

Dyson, Freeman. 1979. *Disturbing the Universe*. New York: Harper and Row.

Fung, Y-Lan. 1948. *A Short History of Chinese Philosophy*. New York: The Free Press.

Hogarth, William. 1753. *The Analysis of Beauty*. London: J. Reeves.

Penrose, Roger. 1989. *The Emperor's New Mind: Concerning Computers, Minds, and the Laws of Physics*. New York: Oxford University Press.

Penrose, Roger. 2004. *The Road to Reality: A Complete Guide to the Laws of the Universe*. New York: Alfred A. Knopf.

Rees, Martin. 2000. *Just Six Numbers: The Deep Forces that Shape the Universe*. New York: Basic Books.

Steiner, Mark. 1998. *The Applicability of Mathematics as a Philosophical Problem*. Cambridge, MA: Harvard University Press.

Susskind, Leonard. 2006. *The Cosmic Landscape: String Theory and the Illusion of Intelligent Design*. New York: Little, Brown & Company.

Tegmark, Max and Rees, Martin. 1997. Why Is the CMB Fluctuation Level 10^{-5}? ArXiv:astro-ph/9709058v2.

Vilenkin, Alex. 2006. *Many Worlds in One: The Search for Other Universes*. New York: Hill & Wang.

Further Reading

Collins, Robin. 2009. The Teleological Argument: An Exploration of the Fine-Tuning of the Universe. In William Lane Craig and J. P. Moreland, eds. *The Blackwell Companion to Natural Theology*. Oxford: Wiley-Blackwell, pp. 202–281. A careful rendition of the fine-tuning argument for theism.

Leslie, John. 1989. *Universes*. New York: Routledge. A semi-popular treatment of the fine-tuning evidence and what it might tell us about ultimate reality.

Manson, Neil, ed. 2003. *God and Design: The Teleological Argument and Modern Science*. New York: Routledge. The 19 chapters in this collection address modern design arguments from a wide variety of perspectives.

Rees, Martin. 2000. *Just Six Numbers: The Deep Forces that Shape the Universe*. New York: Basic Books. A popular presentation by the thirteenth British Astronomer Royal on the way in which six fundamental numbers must be precisely set for life to exist.

Smith, Quentin, Draper, Paul, and Collins, Robin. 2008. Section Three: Science and the Cosmos. In *God or Blind Nature? Philosophers Debate the Evidence (2007–2008)*. Online at http://www.infidels.org/library/modern/debates/great-debate.html (accessed July 4. 2011). A debate as to whether the structure of the cosmos provides evidence for or against the existence of God.

20

Quantum Theory and Theology

RODNEY D. HOLDER

Anyone not shocked by quantum theory has not understood it. (Niels Bohr)

If all this damned quantum jumping were really here to stay, I should be sorry I ever got involved with quantum theory. (Erwin Schrödinger)

Quantum mechanics is certainly imposing. But an inner voice tells me that it is not the real thing. The theory says a lot, but does not bring us any closer to the secret of the old one. I, at any rate, am convinced that He [God] does not throw dice. (Albert Einstein)

I think I can safely say that nobody understands quantum mechanics. (Richard Feynman)

Introduction

The above quotations from some of the founders of quantum theory plainly demonstrate the radical revolution in our understanding of the world which the theory has wrought. In this chapter I describe some simple experiments, including thought experiments, which illustrate this revolution. I then go on to explore what implications or opportunities for theology there may be in the light of these developments.

The Two-Slit Experiment and Wave-Particle Duality

Richard Feynman thought that the whole mystery of quantum theory was encapsulated in the following experiment. Neutrons are fired at a screen with two slits in it, so as to be detected by a photographic plate on a target screen beyond. Unsurprisingly individual neutrons behave like particles in that each produces a definite mark. However, as more and more

The Blackwell Companion to Science and Christianity, First Edition. Edited by J. B. Stump and Alan G. Padgett.
© 2012 Blackwell Publishing Ltd. Published 2012 by Blackwell Publishing Ltd.

neutrons are fired, the pattern that builds up comprises not two clusters of hits, but alternating bands of high and low intensity. This is exactly like an interference pattern arising from a wave motion, whereby peaks combine with peaks to reinforce the intensity but peaks and troughs cancel out.

If one of the slits is closed, the interference pattern disappears. However, the results from the two slits considered separately do not add up to the pattern produced when both slits are open. The inference is that the neutron possesses both particle and wave properties. Neutrons arrive at the target as distinct "hits," but with an intensity pattern characteristic of a wave.

One way of thinking about this is to observe the bands of zero intensity on the screen. These are places which an individual neutron could reach when only one slit was open, but when both slits are open, even if the neutrons are fired individually, no neutron can now reach these points!

Suppose we try to resolve the wave-particle ambiguity by attempting to determine by observation which slit an individual neutron actually passed through on its way to the target. If we do this we find, amazingly, that the interference pattern disappears.

How on earth can we resolve these strange ambiguities? The only way seems to be to say that when both slits are open an individual neutron interferes with itself. In fact we are forced to say that an individual neutron passes through both slits!

Suppose we replace the neutrons by light, which had been classically thought of as a wave motion. The pattern observed is the same as that for neutrons. However, light has been shown to occur in discrete quanta of energy known as photons. Therefore light arrives at the screen as individual localized units of energy, just as the neutrons did. When the light intensity is low one can make out the individual spots. But wavelike behavior is observed when both slits are open and there is strong light intensity. Then one obtains just the same sort of interference pattern as with the neutrons. Again, if a photon detector is placed at one slit to determine which slit any photon has gone through, the interference pattern disappears.

The two-slits experiment shows that atomic particles such as neutrons or electrons have wavelike properties and that light, which propagates as a wave, also has particle properties. Which kind of property is exhibited in an experiment depends on the question being asked by the experiment itself, that is, just what is being measured. This phenomenon is known as wave-particle duality.

This experiment, and others, have led to the formulation of the rules of quantum mechanics, according to which a system remains in a combination, called a "superposition," of alternative possible states until a measurement is made. The state of a system is described by a quantity called the wave function, whose change over time is described by a differential equation, Schrödinger's equation. But this wave function only gives us the probability of finding the system in any of the possible states at any given time. When a measurement is made we say that the wave function "collapses" to a particular value.

Heisenberg's Uncertainty Principle

In the year 1814 the French mathematician the marquis de Laplace famously made the leap from Newton's laws of motion, discovered a century earlier, to universal determinism. He said:

We ought then to regard the present state of the universe as the effect of its anterior state and as the cause of the one which is to follow. Given for one instant an intelligence which could comprehend all the forces by which nature is animated and the respective situation of the beings who compose it – an intelligence sufficiently vast to submit these data to analysis – it would embrace in the same formula the movements of the greatest bodies of the universe and those of the lightest atom; for it, nothing would be uncertain and the future, as the past, would be present to its eyes. (Laplace 1902, 4)

The Laplacian universe runs by itself on mechanical principles, just like a watch that has been wound up and allowed to run. The laws of physics, as discovered by Newton, imply that the universe is a closed causal system. We can imagine God upholding or sustaining these mechanistic laws, but not of having any further interaction with his creation.

That picture of the way the world works has been completely overturned by quantum mechanics. This is made particularly clear by Heisenberg's Uncertainty Principle, which tells us that it is not possible simultaneously to measure with total precision (for example) both the position and the momentum of an electron. If we measure the one accurately, the other is infinitely imprecise.

Heisenberg conducted a thought experiment in which a γ-ray microscope was used to measure the position of the electron. This is done by bouncing photons off the electron into the microscope. The problem is that if light of long wavelength is used then the accuracy of position measurement is poor, but using short-wavelength (high-frequency) light (γ-rays) imparts energy to the electron and makes its momentum more uncertain.

Most physicists believe that this indeterminacy reflects "the way the world is," that is, it is ontological and not merely epistemological. It is not due to some fault or inaccuracy in our measuring instruments. The wave function does indeed evolve deterministically (according to Schrödinger's equation), but it only tells us the probability of a particular event occurring.

The main alternative interpretation is that of David Bohm. This maintains determinism but at the cost of introducing "hidden variables." It must also account for "non-locality," that is, the possibility that widely separated particles can form a unified quantum system, as discussed below. Most physicists consider this to be too ad hoc to be plausible, though in doing so they are making a metaphysical decision rather than adopting a position demanded by the science.

The picture that emerges is one in which successive events occur according to chance, though with a definite probability, in total contrast to the Laplacian deterministic picture, in which each successive event is totally determined by those which have gone before. However, when matter is aggregated together to the macroscopic scale, the scale of everyday objects, the quantum uncertainty tends to disappear and determinism rules again. The motion of all the atoms comprising a billiard-ball is probabilistic, but when these motions are aggregated, the motion of the ball is determined by Newton's laws. Newton's laws are a highly accurate approximation to the laws of quantum mechanics at the macroscopic scale, so accurate that all uncertainty is effectively removed. However, quantum theory has more surprises in store, as we now discuss.

Schrödinger's Cat

This unfortunate animal, in Schrödinger's vivid thought experiment, is incarcerated in a sealed box which also contains a radioactive atom with a fifty-fifty chance of decaying in the next hour, emitting a γ-ray in the process (Polkinghorne 2002, 51–52). If this emission takes place it is recorded by a Geiger counter, which triggers the breaking of a vial of poisonous gas into the box, and this quickly kills the cat. If the atom does not decay in the allowed time the cat survives. The experiment ends when we lift the lid from the box to see if the cat is alive or dead.

The paradox arises because the orthodox interpretation of quantum theory tells us that before I lift the lid from the box the cat is in a fifty-fifty superposition of the two states "alive" and "dead." The question as put by John Barrow is:

> When and where does this crazy mixed-up, half dead, half alive cat change state from being neither dead nor alive into one or the other? Who collapses the cat's wave function, the cat itself, the Geiger counter, or the physicist? Or does quantum theory not apply to "large", complicated objects, though it does to the smaller ones of which the large are composed? (Barrow 1988, 152).

This seems to be a macroscopic effect of considerable magnitude arising out a quantum mechanical substrate and posing some perplexing philosophical questions.

The Einstein-Podolsky-Rosen Experiment

Einstein was deeply skeptical about quantum theory, as indicated by the quotation at the beginning of this chapter. He and two collaborators, Boris Podolsky and Nathan Rosen, conceived a famous thought experiment which they believed undermined the theory and which has given rise to what is now known as the Einstein-Podolsky-Rosen (EPR) paradox.

In quantum theory, elementary particles possess a property called "spin" and for convenience we can think of them as tiny tops, although in reality they are unpicturable. Suppose that an electrically neutral particle with spin 0 decays into an electron and a positron, each possessing spin ½ in natural quantum mechanical units. Suppose these particles move directly outwards in opposite directions. Since spin is conserved in this process, if we measure the spin of the electron in some direction, then the spin of the positron must automatically be in the opposite direction. These particles might now be light years apart, even at opposite ends of the universe. Measurement on the one seems to communicate its effect to the other faster than the speed of light – in fact, instantaneously – in violation of Einstein's own theory of relativity.

Everything would be alright for this experiment on a classical picture, since the spin states would then be fixed at the decay time. The experiment would only bring to light an already existing state of affairs. The problem arises because in quantum theory it is the act of measurement which fixes the spin of the electron – it is indeterminate up to that point. Hence the instantaneous transmission of the opposite value to the positron and hence the paradox.

It is possible to design an experiment to test whether quantum mechanical systems have the property known as "local realism." If a system is "locally realistic" then measurement on it is independent of measurement on another system from which it is widely separated. John Bell derived a set of inequalities which would apply to the classical case but be violated in the quantum case, and experiments by French physicist Alain Aspect have confirmed the reality of the EPR paradox – these effects do in essence travel faster than light. Quantum theory thus exhibits non-local effects; there is an interrelatedness between different parts of the universe of a most fundamental kind. Isolation of the phenomena under discussion, as traditionally done in science, is intrinsically impossible, and a new holism reigns.

Physics has traditionally been thought of as the most reductionist of the sciences. Physicists have always wanted to split things up into smaller and smaller constituents with a view to treating these constituents independently and isolating systems from extraneous effects. The EPR experiment and the verification of its paradoxical predictions show that holism, and not reductionism, reigns at the most fundamental level in physics (Polkinghorne 2002, 80).

Interpretation: Quantum Reality?

Quantum theory is quite clearly saying something very strange about reality. Most physicists just get on with the job, and ignore the philosophical implications of their subject. Quantum mechanics is highly successful. It has been verified by countless experiments and keeps making predictions which are verified. But what does it all mean?

The interpretation we have been implicitly working with is the so-called "Copenhagen interpretation," associated especially with Niels Bohr, who worked in Copenhagen. This would be the working interpretation of most physicists who give any thought to such issues. It embraces the features we have described: wave-particle duality, ontological indeterminism, and collapse of the wave function when a quantum system interacts with a classical, macro-scale measuring device.

One way of understanding this interpretation is in a positivist or instrumentalist sense, as Bohr himself appeared to do. The concern then would be with only what is measurable – pointers on scales, marks on photographic plates, and so on. Reality would be understood as "created" by acts of measurement, and physics would be merely a set of calculational procedures. I agree with Polkinghorne that such an approach should be rejected, on the grounds that it denies a fundamental motivation which physicists generally have in doing science – that is, to understand the underlying reality (Polkinghorne 2002, 84–86).

One of the main problems with the Copenhagen interpretation is that it creates a divide between the classical and the quantum mechanical. The classical measuring instrument is made up of parts which are ultimately quantum-mechanical in character. How does it come about that the quantum-mechanical level is obliterated in the large-scale instrument? This is the so-called "measurement problem." One development which seems to help in solving this problem is the notion of "decoherence." This relates to the interaction of a classic object with its environment. For example Schrödinger's cat, whether alive or dead, will interact with the air molecules in the box and the "alive" and "dead" states will not interact but "decohere." The upshot would be that the cat is not in a superposition of states but definitely alive or dead.

An extreme interpretation of quantum theory is that reality is not instrument-created but "observer-created." This idealist view gives consciousness pride of place in bringing about reality through a kind of "backwards causation." The physicist John Wheeler has adopted a view like this which he calls "it from bit." It is, however, highly paradoxical to assert both that non-conscious matter pre-exists and causes my existence and that I cause its existence. And surely the result of an experiment is decided by the imprint on the photographic plate at the time the experiment happens, rather than by me three months later when I take the plate out of the cupboard and look at it! However, there is an interesting theological analog to this.

As noted by Barrow and Tipler (1986, 470–471), this line of speculation can lead to the idea that all quantum events are coordinated by an Ultimate Observer who, by making the Final Observation, brings the whole universe into existence. This being would resemble the idealist Bishop Berkeley's picture of God, albeit a resemblance which Wheeler may well not welcome (Midgley 1992, 206–211).

A realist interpretation in contrast stresses the belief that the world has an objective existence independent of any observer; it stands over against us as an entity in its own right. This world is populated by entities such as electrons and positrons. By observation we can probe what this world is like and attempt to understand its laws. In doing so we submit to the way things actually are.

This realist view is certainly the way scientists in general view their activities and their discoveries. It is supported by the success of science, and the way in which the world has a habit of surprising us (not least through quantum phenomena) speaks against it being merely constructed by our minds. But quantum theory clearly leads us to question a straightforwardly objective view of the world.

The wave function must play a pivotal role in our interpretation. It is clearly not a physical object in the way a billiard-ball is a physical object. Yet it would seem that neither is it merely a calculational device. It describes the objectively real state of the electron even if the reality of the electron itself is "veiled" from us and unpicturable. The wave function evolves in time according to Schrödinger's equation, which is a differential equation just like the differential equations of classical physics. The difference is that the wave function gives only the probability that a measurement will give a particular result. To say that the electron does not exist between measurements seems far too pessimistic: it is a real entity which has the potentiality to exhibit definite properties when measurements are made.

There is another, highly extreme and quite bizarre, version of realism. This is Hugh Everett III's many-worlds interpretation. This states that wave functions do not actually collapse, but that all possibilities are realized. Each time an experiment is done which has several possible outcomes, the world splits into different branches which have no causal contact with each other. I am being repeatedly cloned as copies of myself multiply and pursue separate lives in the many worlds into which my world is splitting.

William of Occam advocated that in any explanation entities should not be multiplied beyond necessity. This principle of "Occam's razor" has proved highly successful in sifting and selecting scientific theories. Everett's many-worlds interpretation of quantum mechanics would seem to be highly anti-Occamite.

Critical Realism in Science and Theology

One area of comparison between science and theology is the realist–positivist–idealist debate. It would seem that in both science and theology some form of critical realism is the preferred option. In the case of physics, realism states that there is a real world out there to be discovered. Genuine scientific discoveries disclose something about real things. Theology would endorse that, the doctrine of creation telling us that this world is the free creation of an omnipotent, omniscient, all-good God. Orthodox theological discourse would also speak of God as real, indeed as the ultimately real who gives reality to everything else.

In physics, quantum theory shows us that a naive, common-sense realism is inadequate, but that some form of critical realism is more appropriate. Subatomic particles exist as real entities but are totally unlike the macroscopic objects we can readily grasp. Similarly in theology, God is real and has effects, but, since he is "qualitatively other," his reality is veiled and our knowledge of him has to be mediated in a number of ways – through creation itself; through revelation in Scripture; and through religious experience, which is mediated through the senses. All of these sources of revelation need careful interpretation, of course. So again, a critical realist position is reasonable (Polkinghorne 1998, chapter 5).

The great Protestant theologian Karl Barth said that we have to know God as he has revealed himself to be, on his terms, and for Barth this is uniquely in the person of the incarnate Son and as Trinity. This is why Barth (1957) repudiated all natural theology, which he saw as the human attempt to have God on our terms, not his. Barth's disciple Thomas Torrance took a similar line (Holder 2009). While I take a more positive view of natural theology than Barth or Torrance, I agree that God's clearest disclosure of himself to humans is in Christ. The analogy here with quantum theory is that just as we have to accept the reality of the world, in all its strangeness, as it is disclosed to us by observation and experiment, and not according to any preconceived notions we might have, so also if God has revealed himself to us in Christ then that is where to look for the reality of God. Moreover, the methods and tools of theology need to be appropriate to the task of theology, just as the methods and tools of quantum theory are appropriate to that realm of enquiry and not simply adopted from elsewhere, which in this case would be classical physics.

Determinism, Human Free Will, and Divine Action

Quantum theory, at least under the interpretation favored by the overwhelming majority of physicists, shows that nature is not deterministic but probabilistic. Determinism is, I believe, damaging for a religious perspective. It means that we have no genuine free choice. How then could we be held responsible for our actions?

One answer to this question would be to affirm the compatibilist account of free will. This merely requires that I do what I want and am not constrained, say by another person, to do what I do. The determining factors of my actions are within my biological makeup (my neurons really did "make me do it" and their deterministic behavior does not negate this kind of free will).

Many philosophers, however, conceive of free will in the libertarian sense whereby I could have acted otherwise. There are genuine choices open to me and I choose which of several possible actions to take. For this kind of freedom indeterminism is a necessary but not sufficient condition. Thus the standard probabilistic, Copenhagen interpretation makes libertarian freedom possible but by no means guarantees it. Similarly with regard to divine action, God is not simply upholding deterministic laws which he has decreed from the foundation of the world but is able to act within the openness and flexibility of indeterminate, unpredictable processes.

Compatibilism therefore fits with the Bohmian interpretation of quantum theory because it does not require genuine uncertainty. The many-worlds interpretation is also deterministic, insofar as all possible outcomes of my decisions occur, but that makes both compatibilist and libertarian freedom look decidedly odd. Of course it may be preferable to speak of clones of me making these alternative choices, but then, if they are all of identical makeup, there is no sufficient reason for *me* to do what *I* do in this particular universe.

For some significant figures in the modern dialogue between science and religion, then, it is the probabilistic nature of quantum theory as standardly interpreted which makes possible both human free will and divine action in the world. A significant recent exemplar would be Robert John Russell.

Russell calls his a "bottom-up, noninterventionist, objective approach" to divine action. It is clearly "bottom-up" since it sees God as acting at the lowest level of the hierarchy of sciences rather than through higher-level influences of complex systems on their parts ("whole–part influence" or "downward causation"). However, Russell stresses his belief that other modes of divine action besides that at the quantum level will be required in an overall picture (Russell 2001, 294). His view is non-interventionist because the probabilistic laws of quantum physics are not violated. It does not, therefore, invalidate a "methodologically naturalist" approach to the scientific enterprise, nor does it invoke a "God of the gaps." It is objective because these acts are objectively special acts, bringing about objective changes in the physical world which would not occur otherwise. Russell lists many quantum events which are not simply acts of measurement, and many ways in which quantum events influence the macro level.

Does God act in every single quantum event on this kind of model? The danger here is that determinism returns, albeit in the different sense that God determines everything and there is no real role for secondary causes. This was the view of physicist-turned-theologian William Pollard (1958), who pioneered this way of thinking about divine action, and also of neuroscientist Donald MacKay (1978, 30–31). Chance events at the level of physics would then not really be chance events at the deepest level of theological truth about reality. This theological determinism would, like physical determinism, negate the possibility of libertarian free will, and in addition exacerbate the theodicy problem.

Nancey Murphy, another significant contributor to the discussion, believes that God does indeed act intentionally in all quantum events. Regarding Pollard's view as occasionalism (God alone determines every natural process), Murphy is more nuanced, seeing God's action as mediated, that is, God acts together with nature. Thus on the one hand subatomic particles possess innate powers given to them by God, such as that of electrons to repel rather than attract other electrons, and God respects the integrity of these devolved powers. On the other hand, there is no sufficient reason for the results of quantum measurements to come down one way rather than another. Murphy says that "God must not be made a competitor with processes that on other occasions are sufficient in and of themselves to bring about an effect," and there is indeed no such competition because "the efficient natural causes at this level are insufficient to determine all outcomes" (Murphy 1995, 343).

Russell is impressed by Murphy's approach (Russell 2001, 315) but disagrees with Murphy about human free will. Murphy thinks that quantum indeterminacy is not necessary for top-down causation to be effectual for this, whereas for Russell "the somatic enactment of incompatibilist human freedom requires lower-level indeterminism" (317). This leads Russell to see God acting in all quantum events in the universe until life and consciousness arise but then gradually refraining from determining outcomes (318). Both Russell and Murphy agree that God is continuously active in upholding the laws of nature with which he has endowed the universe, but see this as insufficient adequately to describe God's action in history as revealed in Scripture. They also believe that divine action in their sense is necessary for intercessory prayer to be meaningful.

A problem arises because, as noted above, quantum indeterminacies tend to disappear at the macroscopic level. Peter Clarke, for example, argues that they are irrelevant at the level of brain function (Clarke 2010), and in any case free will requires more than randomness.

For both human and divine action, quantum events would need to be agent-controlled and yet would not have to conflict with the probabilistic laws. John Polkinghorne sees the influences that do or might occur, by their "episodic nature," to be inadequate to describe the "flexible actions of agents" (Polkinghorne 2001, 189), and therefore turns to chaos theory as a more promising locus for both human and divine action in the world.

Chaotic systems are theoretically deterministic but unpredictable in practice. This is because errors in the initial measurements propagate exponentially, rather than linearly as in predictable systems. To obtain accurate predictions the initial errors will ultimately have to be reduced to infinitesimal proportions. Polkinghorne gives the example of molecules in a gas, which behave essentially like small billiard-balls:

> After less than a microsecond, fifty or more collisions have taken place for each molecule. After even so few collisions the resulting outcome is so sensitive that it would be affected by the variation in the gravitational field due to an extra electron on the other side of the universe – the weakest force due to the smallest particle the furthest distance away! (Polkinghorne 2005, 35)

Of course unpredictability and indeterminism are not the same thing. However, the requirement of infinitesimal accuracy leads us back to the quantum world with its intrinsic uncertainty. But then a further problem arises owing to the severe, and as yet unsolved, technical problems of matching the quantum and macroscopic realms.

Meanwhile Polkinghorne questions whether we are right to stipulate deterministic laws with unpredictable behavior following from them. "Which is the approximation and which is the reality?" he asks (Polkinghorne 1991, 41). Indeed, why should we take deterministic laws as anything other than useful approximations to reality, especially when we know we have free will because we experience it? Moreover, we have obtained the lower-level laws by treating systems as if they were isolated from the whole, a procedure intrinsically impossible. Polkinghorne writes:

> There is an emergent property of flexible process, even within the world of classical physics, which encourages us to see Newton's rigidly deterministic account as no more than an approximation to a more supple reality. (Polkinghorne 2005, 35–36)

Polkinghorne suggests a form of downward causation through the input of active information, whereby the simple deterministic, and approximate, laws emerge at a lower level from high-level behavior which does not possess this property (Polkinghorne 1998, 63ff.). To see God acting by downward causation would be analogous to our minds influencing matter. This happens in any act of will, for example when I intentionally raise my arm, and without violating any laws of nature. Might not the mind of God similarly, yet far more powerfully, act on the matter of his created universe?

Whether God acts in any of the ways suggested is of course highly speculative, and it would be dangerous to dogmatize, yet modern science does seem to be opening up possibilities denied to us by the viewpoint of Laplace. The world of modern physics is a world of regularities described by natural law (these laws given and faithfully sustained by God), but also a world with a genuine openness, flexibility, and freedom. Within that freedom lies man's own free will as a conscious, rational being, and also God's freedom to fulfill his special providential care for humans and the rest of creation. And rather than focusing on one route to divine action, perhaps we should humbly leave the question open as to exactly how in fact God does act.

Consonance with Christian Doctrine

Although we could not predict the kind of world shown to us by quantum theory without doing the experiments, it does seem to be a world consistent with the kind of world the Christian God would create. And we can say more about this with regard to specifically Christian doctrine as opposed to mere theism: these strange features are consonant with the kind of world one would expect the God described by the Nicene and Chalcedonian formulations to create.

According to Christian doctrine, God is fundamentally relational. God is one, yet God is also Trinity; God is three persons enfolded in a relationship of perfect love. Moreover, each of the persons is fully God. The persons are distinct yet inseparable and interrelated. According to the doctrine of perichoresis formulated in the early Church, the three persons are bound together in a kind of mutual indwelling.

Quantum holism, as demonstrated by the EPR thought experiment, is analogous to this. The electron and positron, though distinct and widely separated, yet form a unified quantum system (Polkinghorne 2004, 73ff.; 2010).

According to the Chalcedonian definition, our Lord Jesus Christ is fully God and fully man. He is one person, the Son of God, but with two natures, divine and human. This reminds us of the wave-particle duality of subatomic particles discussed above. An electron is one thing but possesses both particle and wave properties.

A further analogy might be drawn with the distinction made by the Fathers between the "immanent" Trinity and the "economic" Trinity. The idea of the immanent Trinity concerns what God is in himself, the inner relations between the persons. The economic Trinity concerns how he reveals himself for the sake of the "economy," that is, how in the divine plan the persons of the Trinity relate to the world and its salvation. Thus, while the Son and Spirit are eternally one with the Father in the being of the Godhead, they are manifested in the economy, and thus made known to us as distinct from the Father, in the Incarnation and in our sanctification. In a somewhat analogous way, the electron's reality is veiled until a measurement is made.

Of course, none of this is to claim that quantum theory proves Christian doctrine correct. However, I believe it does two things. First, it shows that theology and science are alike in using analogical language, even apparently paradoxical language. For example, the mystery of God is expressed in the phrase "one God, Father, Son and Holy Spirit." Wave-particle duality would be doing a similar job in quantum theory to express the veiled mystery of the electron.

Second, it links theology to science by saying that the world revealed by quantum theory is consonant with what would be expected on the basis of Christian doctrine, so that a relational God is likely to create a relational world. As Polkinghorne rightly says, this is indeed not to prove that God is relational, or that theology can make predictions from its doctrines about the physical world, but it is to say that theology and science fit together very comfortably and are far from contradictory.

References

Barrow, J. D. 1988. *The World within the World*. Oxford: Oxford University Press.
Barrow, J. D. and Tipler, F. J. 1986. *The Anthropic Cosmological Principle*. Oxford: Clarendon Press.

Barth, K. 1957. *Church Dogmatics*, vol. 2.1. Edinburgh: T. & T. Clark, pp. 162–178.

Clarke, P. G. H. 2010. Determinism, Brain Function and Free Will. *Science and Christian Belief*, 22(2), pp. 133–149.

Holder, R. D. 2009. Thomas Torrance: "Retreat to Commitment" or a New Place for Natural Theology? *Theology and Science*, 7(3), pp. 275–296.

Laplace, P. S. 1902. *A Philosophical Essay on Probabilities*. Translated by F. W. Truscott and F. L. Emory. New York: Wiley.

MacKay, D. M. 1978. *Science, Chance, and Providence*. Oxford: Oxford University Press.

Midgley, M. 1992. *Science as Salvation: A Modern Myth and Its Meaning*. London: Routledge.

Murphy, N. 1995. Divine Action in the Natural Order: Buridan's Ass and Schrödinger's Cat. In R. J. Russell, N. Murphy, and A. R. Peacocke, eds. *Scientific Perspectives on Divine Action*, vol. 2, *Chaos and Complexity*. Vatican City: Vatican Observatory and Center for Theology and the Natural Sciences, pp. 325–358.

Polkinghorne, J. C. 1991. *Reason and Reality: The Relationship between Science and Theology*. London: SPCK.

Polkinghorne, J. C. 1998. *Belief in God in an Age of Science*. New Haven, CT: Yale University Press.

Polkinghorne, J. C. 2001. Physical Process, Quantum Events, and Divine Agency. In R. J. Russell, P. Clayton, K. Wegter-McNelly, and J. C. Polkinghorne, eds. *Scientific Perspectives on Divine Action*, vol. 5, *Quantum Mechanics*. Vatican City: Vatican Observatory and Center for Theology and the Natural Sciences, pp. 181–190.

Polkinghorne, J. C. 2004. *Science and the Trinity: The Christian Encounter with Reality*. London: SPCK.

Polkinghorne, J. C. 2005. *Science and Providence: God's Interaction with the World*, 2nd edn. West Conshohocken, PA: Templeton Foundation Press.

Polkinghorne, J. C., ed. 2010. *The Trinity and an Entangled World: Relationality in Physical Science and Theology*. Grand Rapids, MI: Eerdmans.

Pollard, W. G. 1958. *Chance and Providence: God's Action in a World Governed by Scientific Laws*. London: Faber and Faber.

Russell, R. J. 2001. Divine Action and Quantum Mechanics: A Fresh Assessment. In R. J. Russell, P. Clayton, K. Wegter-McNelly, and J. C. Polkinghorne, eds. *Scientific Perspectives on Divine Action*, vol. 5, *Quantum Mechanics*. Vatican City: Vatican Observatory and Center for Theology and the Natural Sciences, pp. 293–328.

Further Reading

Penrose, R. 1989. *The Emperor's New Mind: Concerning Computers, Minds, and the Laws of Physics*. Oxford: Oxford University Press. A critique of strong artificial intelligence with helpful discussions of quantum theory, especially in chapter 6, Quantum Magic and Quantum Mystery.

Polkinghorne, J. C. 2002. *Quantum Theory: A Very Short Introduction*. Oxford: Oxford University Press. Excellent introductory text, including philosophical discussion.

Polkinghorne, J. C., ed. 2010. *The Trinity and an Entangled World: Relationality in Physical Science and Theology*. Grand Rapids, MI: Eerdmans. A valuable collection of essays on relationality in God and the physical world.

R. J. Russell, P. Clayton, K. Wegter-McNelly, and J. C. Polkinghorne, eds. 2001. *Scientific Perspectives on Divine Action*, vol. 5, *Quantum Mechanics*. Vatican City: Vatican Observatory and Center for Theology and the Natural Sciences. A wide-ranging and invaluable collection of essays, with much that is worthy of attention besides the chapters by Polkinghorne and Russell cited above.

Part V
Evolution

21

Creation and Evolution

DENIS R. ALEXANDER

Creation in Christian theology refers to the belief that God is the ultimate creative source, power and will of all that exists. The Christian understanding of creation relates to ontology, to the question of existence. Why does anything exist and for what purpose?

Evolution in its contemporary biological sense refers to the differential reproductive fitness of living organisms such that those better adapted to their environments leave more offspring. Evolution seeks to answer the question "How?" How has God brought into being all the living diversity that characterizes planet earth?

Traditional Christian theology has seen little problem in incorporating evolution within its understanding of the created order. At the same time, some Christians see evolution as problematic, either because they believe it contradicts the early chapters of Genesis, or because they do not think this is how God should have brought biological diversity into being. To understand such responses, a brief historical overview will be provided, followed by a discussion of the various ways in which Christian faith has engaged with evolution.

The Historical Background

Evolution as natural history began with Jean-Baptiste Lamarck (1744–1829), who became Professor of Lower Animals at the newly founded Natural History Museum in Paris in 1800. Lamarck envisaged the continuous spontaneous generation of new species which then move up the escalator of life, with all steps occupied at all moments. This is the primary process and it is then the differing circumstances on each step that lead to different adaptations and consequent variations. The idea for which Lamarck is now chiefly remembered – the inheritance of acquired characteristics – played a relatively small role in his grand evolutionary scheme. This scheme was much modified by Charles Darwin (1809–1882) in his *On the Origin of Species*. It was Darwin's inspiration to bring history into biology, so that now all living things were joined up in one single evolutionary tree of life. In the struggle for life those

The Blackwell Companion to Science and Christianity, First Edition. Edited by J. B. Stump and Alan G. Padgett.
© 2012 Blackwell Publishing Ltd. Published 2012 by Blackwell Publishing Ltd.

organisms better adapted to their environments would be more likely to pass on their adaptations to their offspring, so leaving more progeny to subsequent generations, the process of "natural selection."

Following Darwin's death in 1882 the idea of natural selection as the main mechanism for evolutionary change declined in popularity, being displaced by a range of more Lamarckian ideas. But it was eventually revived following the rediscovery of Mendel's laws of inheritance around 1900, which led to the discovery of the unit of inheritance, the gene. The fusion of genetics with the idea of natural selection which took place during the 1920s and 1930s became known as the neo-Darwinian synthesis. Indeed, it was mathematical genetics that rescued natural selection from oblivion, showing how many variant genes within a single organism could contribute to reproductive fitness (Alexander 2011).

Today Darwinian evolution is perceived as involving two key steps. In the first step variation is introduced into the genome, meaning the sum total of all the information encoded in the DNA of a single living organism, known as the "genotype." Variation in the DNA can increase by a wide range of mechanisms, including mutations, gene flow, and that arising from the exchange of DNA material that occurs between paired chromosomes during the generation of the sperm and eggs ("recombination"). Each genotype generates a "phenotype," meaning the visible characteristics of the organism. In the second step in the evolutionary process, that of natural selection, the slightly different phenotypes are tested out in the workshop of life, and those that are more successful at contributing more progeny to subsequent generations spread their particular sets of beneficial variant genes through an interbreeding population. Speciation occurs when one population no longer interbreeds with another. Speciation can occur suddenly, as often occurs in plants, and some animals, when the number of chromosomes is increased ("polyploidy"), or gradually, as in most animal populations, a process associated with reproductive isolation.

Initial Christian responses to Darwin's *On the Origin of Species* were varied. The first written response to Darwin in existence is a letter from Charles Kingsley, rector of Eversley, to whom Darwin had sent an advance copy of the *Origin of Species*. Kingsley wrote to Darwin on November 18, 1859, six days before the book's publication date, that: "All I have seen of it awes me," going on to comment that it is "just as noble a conception of Deity, to believe that He created primal forms capable of self-development . . . as to believe that He required a fresh act of intervention to supply the lacunas [gaps] which He Himself had made" (Kingsley 1859). Darwin was so impressed with this response that he quoted these lines in the second edition of the *Origin*.

Another Anglican cleric, Adam Sedgwick (1785–1873), Professor of Geology at Cambridge and Darwin's old mentor and teacher, was less enthusiastic. Sedgwick had also received an advance copy of the *Origin*, and on November 24, the official publication day, wrote to Darwin, "I have read your book with more pain than pleasure. Parts of it I admired greatly; parts I laughed at till my sides were almost sore; other parts I read with absolute sorrow; because I think them utterly false & grievously mischievous" (Sedgwick 1859). Sedgwick did not like what he saw as Darwin's departure from the sound inductive approach of true science, he wanted to maintain a role for God in creating species separately, and above all he feared that human moral dignity was being undermined by Darwin's theory.

Kingsley and Sedgwick typify two of the contrasting voices that can be heard amongst the initial responses to the *Origin*. The idea that there was a universal chorus of disapproval from the Church is a myth. What is perhaps more surprising in retrospect is how quickly Darwinian evolution was baptized into a traditional Christian understanding of creation. A future archbishop of Canterbury, Frederick Temple, extolled Darwinian ideas in his official sermon at the annual meeting of the British Association for the Advancement of Science at Oxford in 1860, and would later develop this theme more fully in his Bampton lectures of 1884 (Temple, 1903). Questions about Darwinian evolution were already beginning to appear by the mid-1860s in the science examination papers of Cambridge University, that bastion of Anglican respectability.

Some of the warmest support for Darwinian evolution came from evangelical Protestants. Henry Drummond, Scottish naturalist and professor in the Free Church College in Glasgow, thought that natural selection was "a real and beautiful acquisition to natural theology" and that the *Origin* was "perhaps the most important contribution to the literature of apologetics" to have appeared during the nineteenth century (Smith 2005, 47).

Meanwhile in the USA the *Origin* was widely promoted by Christian academics. Asa Gray, Professor of Natural History at Harvard and a committed Christian, was Darwin's long-term correspondent and confidant and helped organize the publication of the *Origin of Species* in America. The Calvinist James McCosh, president of the College of New Jersey (later to become Princeton University), held strongly to the concept of natural selection, but equally strongly believed that "the natural origin of species is not inconsistent with intelligent design in nature or with the existence of a personal Creator of the world." Upon looking back over his 20 years as president, McCosh remarked "I have been defending Evolution but, in so doing, have given the proper account of it as the method of God's procedure, and find that when so understood it is in no way inconsistent with Scripture." Even amongst the writers of *The Fundamentals*, that mass-produced series of 12 booklets published in the period 1910–1915 which later contributed to the emergence of the term "fundamentalism," we find a number of evangelical writers committed to Darwinism, such as James Orr and Benjamin Warfield.

The historian James Moore (1981, 79) writes that "with but few exceptions the leading Christian thinkers in Great Britain and America came to terms quite readily with Darwinism and evolution," and the American historian George Marsden (1984, 101) reports that "with the exception of Harvard's Louis Agassiz, virtually every American Protestant zoologist and botanist accepted some form of evolution by the early 1870s." Where there was opposition to evolution, it was not connected with the age of the earth, since by the time the *Origin* was published, everyone knew that the earth was very old, although the precise age remained a topic of ongoing investigation. More commonly, opposition arose from the concern that common descent with the rest of the animal kingdom might reduce humanity's special role and value in God's creation. There was also concern about subversion of the moral order if Man began to be perceived as "just another animal." The dynamic nature of the evolutionary process also challenged ancient ideas of Platonic essentialism, replacing the static notion of a species with that of historical process, and subverting the teleological idea of Aristotelian final cause in which humanity lies at the center of the cosmos – instead portraying Man as but one little twig in a very large evolutionary tree.

Creationism in the contemporary sense of that term is a twentieth-century phenomenon and arose in the USA partly as a reaction against the inroads made by German liberal theology into American denominations, partly in response to the supposed Darwinian threat to morality posed by the philosophy of "might is right" that was used to justify German military expansion during World War One, and partly as a reaction against the perceived centralized US government control of educational curricula (Numbers 2006). The Seventh-day Adventist writer George McCready Price published *New Geology* in 1923, an attempt to interpret the geological column based on the Mosaic flood story. In 1925 a teacher called John Scopes "confessed" to violating the recently passed law banning the teaching of human evolution in his state of Tennessee, but was acquitted on a technicality in the subsequent farcical trial (Larson 2003). The term "creationism" began to be associated with this early anti-evolutionary movement, which eventually ran out of steam in the late 1920s, particularly with the advent of the Depression. Nevertheless there is good evidence that the campaign had a long-lasting impact on the contents of the nation's biology textbooks. In 1942, a nation-wide survey of secondary school teachers in the USA indicated that less than 50% of high-school biology teachers were teaching anything about organic evolution in their science courses.

In 1957 the Russians launched *Sputnik*, the first space satellite, and US alarm at falling behind in the space race led to reforms in science teaching, including increased emphasis on the teaching of evolution. This in turn helped to boost interest in Henry Morris and John Whitcomb's new book *The Genesis Flood*, published in 1961, a reformulation of the ideas in Price's *New Geology*. Within a quarter of a century *The Genesis Flood* went through 29 print-ings and sold over 200 000 copies (Numbers 2006). The interest stimulated by this book led to the formation of the Creation Research Society (CRS) in 1963 and other creationist organi-zations since that time. Whereas the earlier creationist movement of the 1920s still main-tained that the earth was very old, the late twentieth-century movement initiated by Morris and Whitcomb promoted the idea that the earth is only about 10 000 years old, a belief not otherwise widely held since the eighteenth century. The term "creationism" began to be associated specifically with this brand of "young-earth creationism." Various forms of anti-Darwinian creationism are held by around 40–45% of the US population, whereas in European countries the level of creationist beliefs is generally much lower (Spencer and Alexander 2009).

In considering the various responses to evolution since 1859, it is worth noting that the biological theory has often been used and abused for ideological purposes, for example in support of capitalism, socialism, communism, racism, militarism, feminism, atheism, and other political and social ideas, many of them mutually exclusive (Alexander and Numbers 2010). These are parasitic upon the scientific theory and none are intrinsic to the theory itself, but the deployment of evolution in their support helps us to understand why there has been such a heterogeneous and often robust range of responses to evolution.

The Contemporary Discussion

Four main positions are held by Christians in relation to the contemporary discussion between creation and evolution, though each position can be sub-divided into many further variants.

First, young-earth creationism rejects the mainstream scientific view that the earth is 4.6 billion years old and maintains that all the main "kinds" of living things were created in six literal days of 24 hours about 10 000 years ago. Since that time very rapid evolution has occurred in which the "kinds" have diversified into all the species extant today. In this view there was no physical death of animals before the Fall, death being seen as punishment for the disobedience of Adam and Eve (Whitcomb and Morris 1960; Ham 1987).

Second, old-earth creationism accepts the date of the earth provided by science, but sees the creation of life, of the main kinds of living organisms, and especially the creation of Adam and Eve, as a series of miraculous events, that in some versions of this per-spective are identified with six literal days of creation. In some variants of this position physical death was already present before the Fall, whereas in others it came afterwards (Ross 2009).

Third, intelligent design (ID) is an anti-Darwinian movement that emerged in the USA during the early 1990s which is distinct from creationism, although some of its proponents maintain creationist beliefs. ID maintains that Darwinian evolution is intrinsically materialistic and therefore a threat to religious belief. At the same time, it is maintained, science itself can be used to detect "signs of intelligence" which point to design, and so by inference a designer. Certain entities in biology are deemed to be "irreducibly complex" and their origins supposedly inexplicable by evolution, so pointing to "design." ID proponents look not to the Bible but to science in order to support their position (Behe 1996; Dembski 2004).

Fourth, theistic evolution, sometimes known as evolutionary creationism, fully accepts the current mainstream scientific understandings of evolutionary theory. In this view, God is seen as the author of all that exists, fulfilling his intentions and purposes through the evolutionary process. The adjective "theistic" does not imply that there is anything distinctive about the scientific theory itself, but simply points out that it can be incorporated within a Christian worldview, as indeed can all other scientific descriptions, given that their goal is the understanding of God's creation. Of course some scientific theories turn out to be wrong, but all are attempts to understand the created order, even though the attempts are always open to revision and improvement (Falk 2004; Collins 2007; Alexander 2008).

Theistic evolution comes in three distinctive flavors. In the first, sometimes known as "directed evolution," God is seen as providentially orchestrating the process, for example by bringing about specific events, such as mutations, that influence the course of evolutionary history. Some of the early theological responses to the *Origin of Species* constructed schemes of this kind. The second and rather more nuanced notion of theistic evolution derives from later twentieth-century thinkers such as the biochemist Arthur Peacocke and others (Peacocke 1993), who perceive God's actions and purposes as being immanent within the evolutionary process. The properties of matters are only what they are because of God's faithfulness in willing and sustaining those properties and, as a matter of fact, evolution will happen with matter possessing these properties given the appropriate conditions. This is what God's materials do. The third very different brand of theistic evolution derives from the writings of the Catholic paleontologist and philosopher Pierre Teilhard de Chardin (1881–1955), who built a Lamarckian version of evolution into an ambitious theological scheme in which the whole universe is evolving towards the "omega point," the stage of maximum organized complexity (Teilhard de Chardin 2002). Censured by the Catholic Church during his lifetime for departing from theological orthodoxy, Teilhard de Chardin's ideas have been influential in popularizing evolution within Catholic circles, albeit of a kind barely recognized by contemporary Darwinian biology.

An assessment of these various Christian responses to evolution can best be made by considering them from the perspective of the Christian doctrine of creation.

The Christian Doctrine of Creation

Traditional Christian notions of creation are largely derived from the biblical literature, from the early Church Fathers such as Augustine of Hippo, from medieval theologians such as Thomas Aquinas, and from Reformation theologians such as John Calvin.

There are three key aspects of God's character in creation: his transcendence, his immanence, and his personal Trinitarian character. God's transcendence refers to his eternal being, to his "otherness," the fact that God's power and actions lie beyond human understanding or ultimate comprehension (Ps. 90:2; Jer. 10:10). "My thoughts are not your thoughts, neither are your ways my ways, declares the Lord. As the heavens are higher than the earth, so are my ways higher than your ways and my thoughts than your thoughts" (Isa. 55:8–9). This implies that we cannot tell God how he should be writing the book of creation. The properties of creation are contingent upon God's will and actions; we cannot derive them from first principles. Scientists can only describe what God does in the created order for there is nothing else to describe.

This presents a challenge to those who maintain that the evolutionary process is wasteful. Wasteful compared to what? We now know that the universe with its 10^{11} galaxies each containing an average 10^{11} stars has to be this large and this old in order for us to exist. It is difficult to know what "waste" means to the God who is the ground of all existence. Equally with those who wonder why evolution has taken "so long" before arriving at humans, one may question the anthropocentric assumption that the only purpose of evolution is to produce humanity, when God clearly enjoys and values all his works of creation (Gen. 1; Job 38–39; Ps. 104). Furthermore, God in his transcendence is not encompassed by space nor by time, so the question "why so long?" hardly seems relevant to such a creator.

God's immanence refers to his continuing creative activity in relation to his universe and intimate involvement in upholding and sustaining its properties. All that exists continues to do so only because of his continued say-so. The properties of matter continue to be what they are because God wills that they should continue to have such properties. It is what makes science possible. The biblical literature frequently draws attention to God's creative power in every aspect of the created order. God is the one who "gives life to everything" (Neh. 9:6) in the present tense. In the Book of Job, God is the one, in the present tense, who generates earthquakes (Job 9:5–6), brings about eclipses (9:7), wraps up water in the clouds (26:8), spreads his clouds over the moon (26:9), brings down hail and snow from his storehouses (38:22), and molds Job himself like clay (10:9). In the New Testament the emphasis shifts to Christ the Word of God, in whom and through whom the whole created order exists (John 1:3). "He is before all things, and in him all things hold together" (Col. 1:17). The Son is the one who "sustains all things by his powerful word" (Heb. 1:3).

The immanence of God in creation is an important reminder that creation in Scripture is seen as a continuous process with past, present, and future aspects. Christians are "theists," those who see God's continuing involvement in the whole created order, not "deists" who perceive a distant God who endows the universe with a suite of laws, but otherwise remains aloof. Discussion of creation and evolution too often focuses on distant origins, but this is not where Scripture chooses to place its emphasis. Furthermore, the immanence of God subverts "God-of-the-gaps" or "designer-of-the-gaps" types of argument in which attempts are made to locate special divine action within current domains of scientific ignorance. For example, our scientific understanding of the processes whereby complex biological systems arose during the origin of life is very limited, so attempts have been made to argue for a designer based on our current lack of knowledge of these processes, the approach of intelligent design advocates. But if all things hold together in Christ, then it is unclear why current human ignorance should have any particular theological relevance. And as science continues to extend its understanding, so the role for the putative designer will inevitably shrink, and the gaps will close. "Designer-of-the-gaps" arguments are disastrous when deployed in Christian apologetics, and a firm grasp of the biblical understanding of God's immanence in creation will in any case render them superfluous.

God's personal Trinitarian character in creation is rooted in the eternal relationship of love that has always existed in the Godhead between Father, Son, and Holy Spirit. The creation of other personalities is therefore what one expects in a universe which exists because of his creative activity. We live in a relational universe. Our own human existence continues to maintain its sense of value and purpose only insofar as we are enmeshed within a network of meaningful relationships. As God's intentions and purposes have been worked out through the evolutionary process, so this has involved the emergence of mind, consciousness, and free will, so rendering possible the practice of human relationships that reflect something of God's Trinitarian character. That same suite of human abilities also renders feasible a personal relationship with God. Without our brains' large frontal lobes, which have come into existence through a long evolutionary process, our minds would lack the subtle properties that make possible practices such as prayer and worship.

Once the personal Trinitarian character of God in creation is fully grasped, then it comes as no surprise to note that the main metaphor used in the Bible to describe God's creative actions is that of speaking. In Genesis 1 God speaks and calls no less than 14 times to instantiate the created order. When Jesus wanted to calm the storm he spoke to the wind and waves and said "Quiet! Be still!" (Mark 4:39). In John 1 it is through the divine Logos, the incarnate Son of God, that the whole universe has been brought into being, for "without him nothing was made that has been made" (John 1:3). It is through the Son that God has made the universe (Heb. 1:2).

What is striking in this brief overview of the character of God in creation is the realization that creation theology is thoroughly integrated into the biblical literature from its first page until its last. We look forward to a new heaven and a new earth (2 Pet. 3:13; Rev. 21:1). There is plenty more creation yet to come. This is not to downplay the importance of the early chapters of Genesis, only to place them within the context of the biblical corpus as a whole.

The Bible contains more than 20 different genre of literature, and it is important that we interpret different biblical narratives according to their own particular genre and context. Clearly the early chapters of Genesis cannot represent scientific literature for the simple reason that scientific literature, with its specialized language involving very specific meanings for words, did not exist at the time, only developing during the past few centuries. Indeed the literary genre of Genesis 1 is unique in the whole of Scripture, defying ready classification. It is not Hebrew poetry, but has poetic elements, leading to its description as "elevated prose." The first few chapters of Genesis may be read as a theological essay that embodies great truths expressed in figurative language. For example, it really is true that God, and not many gods, has created all that exists (Gen. 1). It really is true that only humankind is made in the image of God with the particular responsibilities that this entails (Gen. 1:26–27). And it really is true that human disobedience to God's commands leads to alienation from God and to bitter consequences (Gen. 2 and 3). Those coming to such ancient texts with a set of questions to do with science and chronology will find that the early chapters of Genesis are addressing a quite different set of priorities; for example, who is the one who creates and for what purpose, and how are the status and role of humankind to be understood in relation to God's intentions (Lamoureux 2008)? Commentators have emphasized the way in which Genesis 1 involves the creation of function more than form, reflecting the assumptions of the contemporary literature of that era (Walton 2009). Others have focused on the covenantal features of the texts (Godfrey 2003). Many have drawn attention to the way in which Genesis

1 is best understood by reference to its cultural and religious context (Wenham 1987; Lucas 2001; Alexander 2008).

The handling of the early chapters of Genesis by early Jewish and Christian commentators during the first few centuries AD is of particular interest given their pre-scientific context. The first-century Jewish philosopher and theologian Philo taught that God had made all things instantaneously and that the days of creation, Adam and Eve, and the garden of Eden were all "intended symbolically rather than literally," being "no mythical fictions . . . but modes of making ideas visible." The six days of creation therefore provided a way for Moses to explain God's orderly manner of creation.

The early Church Fathers likewise interpreted the Genesis narratives figuratively. Origen wrote:

> What man of intelligence, I ask, will consider that the first and second and the third day, in which there are said to be both morning and evening, existed without sun and moon and stars, while the first day was even without a heaven? And who could be found so silly as to believe that God, after the manner of a farmer "planted trees in a paradise eastward in Eden" . . . I do not think anyone will doubt that these are figurative expressions which indicate certain mysteries through a semblance of history. (Origen 1936, book IV, chapter 3)

In his commentary entitled "The Literal Interpretation of Genesis," the final version of which was published in AD 415, Augustine also adopted a distinctively figurative interpretation of the days of Genesis, seeing God's creative activity as having two different aspects: "Some works belonged to the invisible days in which he created all things simultaneously, and others belong to the days in which he daily fashions whatever evolves in the course of time from what I call the primordial wrappers" (Augustine 1982, 6.6.9, 183–184).

The "invisible days" in Augustine's exposition were the days as described in Genesis 1, which he understood not chronologically but as a kind of inventory of all God's acts of creation which were performed simultaneously. This single act of creation then brought forth, in due course, all the rest of the diversity of the created order. All the potentiality of the created order was encompassed within those original "primordial wrappers."

Later Calvin promoted the principle of accommodation whereby the biblical writers used everyday language so that essential truths could be understood by the general reader. As Calvin put it, Moses "adapted his writing to common usage." The Bible was "a book for laymen" and "he who would learn astronomy and other recondite arts, let him go elsewhere."

> The Holy Spirit had no intention to teach astronomy; and, in proposing instruction meant to be common to the simplest and most uneducated persons, he made use by Moses and the other prophets of popular language. . . . the Holy Spirit would rather speak childishly than unintelligibly to the humble and unlearned. (Calvin 1847–1850, Ps. 136:7)

Christians who today continue to interpret the language of the early chapters of Genesis figuratively stand in a long tradition which represents not a response to science, but concern for the integrity of the text. This is not to say that Christians today would accept all the interpretations of Genesis provided by the early Church Fathers; some, like Origen, went too far in their allegorical musings. The point is that it is not modern science that dictates how the text should be interpreted. By contrast the interpretative stance adopted by creationists tends to be influenced more by modernism, the idea that the only "real" truths are scientific truths, leading to the interpretation of texts as if they were making claims about science.

This modernistic tendency is widespread also amongst Muslims in their interpretation of the Qur'an.

Questions Posed by Evolution for Christian Theology

Evolution raises three main questions for theology: first, how can a God of love use a process involving so much death to bring about his intentions? Second, how do we understand Adam and Eve in light of human evolution? And, third, what about the Fall? Many books have been written on these topics. Brief summaries are provided here of some of the common responses to these questions.

Death in the evolutionary process

There is no doubt that 3.8 billion years of evolution have involved pain and death on a vast scale. More than 99% of the species that ever lived have become extinct. Carbon-based life is impossible without death. All living things are embedded in huge food-chains in which ultimately most of the energy used in living organisms is derived from the sun. We are all on the great escalator of life and the dead are constantly making space for the living. If there were no death on this planet, then it would be packed full of life forms within weeks, as crowded as a New York subway.

In fact science is of considerable help in reflecting on the challenges of death and suffering, for it demonstrates all the various ways in which carbon-based life is a "package deal." Every aspect of our genetics and biochemistry that is positive for our survival and wellbeing has by the same token a down side as well. Without genetic variation there would be no evolution and we would not exist. If we suddenly came into existence with identical genomes, then we would comprise one giant clonal population, there would be no sexual differentiation, and life would be boring. But genetic variation is also the cause of cancer and of genetic diseases, and our genomes encode our ultimate demise as well as our present ability to live (Southgate 2008).

All of these aspects of our biology reflect "nomic regularity," the lawlike behavior of the matter and energy comprising our universe that provides it with its inherent intelligibility and functioning properties. It is this internal consistency and reproducibility in the properties of the universe that renders life possible, that enables rational existence, and that makes science feasible. Christians see this as an aspect of God's faithfulness in creation, without which existence could have no coherence (Murray 2008).

All living organisms have a means of detecting and interpreting their environments, which can be experienced as "pain" as the nervous system increases in complexity. The more developed the brain, the more developed is the acute awareness of pain. The experience of pain is essential for human survival. Those rare individuals born without functioning pain responses do not live for long without clinical intervention. Since carbon appears to be ubiquitous in the universe, it is likely that there are carbon-based life forms in other parts of the universe, since of all the elements carbon seems to be uniquely suited to functioning as a key building block for life. If these life forms have likewise evolved complex nervous systems, then they also will experience pain, and in any case will certainly die and be involved in food-chains similar to those on planet earth.

Nothing in biological evolution is gratuitous. All makes perfect sense in the light of the evolutionary mechanisms that in turn reflect the chemical composition of the universe. But clearly the evolutionary process is very costly in terms of life and death. We are used to the idea of costly processes leading to outcomes that are of particular value. The Christian claim is that the cost is worth it – the generation of a planet full of fascinating life forms that have intrinsic worth in their very existence, and the generation of humans with cognitive abilities that enable them to enjoy the richness of this diversity. More than that, perhaps this is the only way in which beings can come into existence who are genuinely free, able to make moral decisions, and free to respond, or not, to God's love. Freedom is costly, gained at great price. Of course, ultimately we cannot know the mind of God to know whether this really is the only way to create beings who can freely respond to his love, but even supposing it might be the case provides us with a potentially helpful insight (Hebblethwaite 2000; Alexander 2008).

If this present life were the only one, then the potent objection would remain that the costs involved in generating conscious intelligent beings are simply not worth the benefits. But for the Christian who sees God as the creator of the new heavens and the new earth, to be enjoyed forever clothed in new resurrection bodies, the pain and suffering of the present order are but stepping-stones on the path to eternity. Our new resurrection bodies will certainly not be carbon-based, and will experience neither pain nor suffering. The present "vale of soul-making" makes far more sense viewed in the light of eternity, even if we will never ultimately know, in this life at least, the final answer as to why God has created a universe with these particular properties to bring about God's purposes.

Adam and Eve, and the Fall

It makes sense to take these two topics together because the way one interprets one will strongly influence interpretation of the other. The main question is how to relate the Adam and Eve narrative provided in the early chapters of Genesis with current anthropological accounts of human evolution. In the "Out-of-Africa" model that currently holds sway, anatomically modern humans first emerged in Africa about 200 000 years ago, before a small group emigrated out of Africa to populate the rest of the world around 60 000 years ago. Speciation in mammals involves reproductive isolation and, in the case of humans, an interbreeding population that may have numbered only a few hundred individuals. A new species does not start with a single breeding pair.

Some Christians do not think that one should seek any kind of connection between the Genesis narrative and anthropology. In this view the Genesis 2 account is about the human responsibility to obey God's commands and the Genesis 3 narrative of human disobedience is the "story of everyman." We have all sinned and fallen short of the glory of God (Rom. 3:23), and these passages present this truth in a vivid narrative style that is about theology rather than historical events (Lamoureux 2008).

Whereas these theological convictions are entirely appropriate, other Christians think that the approach of model-building can be helpful in bringing the theological and anthropological truths into conversation with each other. Our last common ancestor with our nearest living genetic relative, the chimpanzee, lived about 6 million years ago. Since our evolutionary lineages parted ways, chimpanzees have emerged from the ape lineage without religion, whereas we have religious capacities. Furthermore, there must have been a time when humans first started knowing God in a personal way such that they could engage in prayer and worship. How and when did that happen? Rejecting the concordist idea that scientific meanings can be imposed on theological texts, models can nevertheless be constructed that incorporate theological and anthropological insights into a single integrated narrative. The notion of models is common in science, referring to the way in which certain sets of data can be rendered coherent by explaining them in terms of a physical, mathematical, or even metaphorical representation.

Two general models have been proposed for the purposes of bringing the theology of Genesis into conversation with anthropology, which we will here label the "Retelling model" and the "*Homo divinus* model." The Retelling model suggests that as anatomically modern humans evolved in Africa from 200 000 years ago, or during some period of linguistic and cultural development since then, there was a gradual growing awareness of God's presence and calling upon their lives to which they responded in obedience and worship. The earliest spiritual stirrings of the human spirit meant that it was natural at the beginning for humans to turn to their Creator, in the same way that children today seem readily to believe in God almost as soon as they can speak (Barrett 2004). The Fall is then interpreted as the conscious rejection by humankind of the awareness of God's presence and calling upon their lives in favor of choosing their own way rather than God's way. In this model, the early chapters of Genesis represent a retelling of this early episode, or series of episodes, in our human history in a form that could be understood within the Middle Eastern culture of the Jewish people of that time.

A possible problem with the Retelling model is the way in which it evacuates the Genesis narrative of any Near Eastern context, detaching the account from its Jewish roots. The *Homo divinus* model addresses this question, and places emphasis on the way that the Bible treats Adam as a real historical figure, particularly in the genealogies (Gen. 5; Luke 3), and in passages such as Romans 5 and 1 Corinthians 15 (Berry and Jeeves 2008; Alexander 2008). According to this model, God chose a couple of neolithic farmers in the Near East, or maybe a community of farmers, to whom he chose to reveal himself in a special way, calling them into fellowship with himself – so that they might know him as the one true personal God. From now on there would be a community who would know that they were called to a holy enterprise, called to be stewards of God's creation, called to know God personally. It is for this reason that this first couple, or community, have been termed *Homo divinus*, the divine humans, those who know the one true God, the Adam and Eve of the Genesis account. Being an anatomically modern human was necessary but not sufficient for being spiritually alive, as remains the case today. *Homo divinus*, in this model, were the first humans who were truly spiritually alive in fellowship with God, providing the spiritual roots of the Jewish faith. In this model the Fall then becomes the disobedience of Adam and Eve to the expressed revealed will of God, bringing spiritual death in its wake, a broken relationship between humankind and God. And as with the Retelling model, the physical death of both animals and humans is seen as happening throughout evolutionary history. Both models suggest that it is spiritual death that is the consequence of sin, Genesis 3 providing a potent description of the alienation that humankind suffers as a result of sin, with a fiery barrier separating them from the Tree of Life (3:24). But under the New Covenant the way back to the tree of life is opened up through the atoning work of Christ on the cross (Rev. 22:14).

Conclusions

There is no need to see creation and evolution as rival explanations for the origins of biological diversity. Creation provides ontological explanations for why things exist, interpretations of existence, insights into its meaning. Evolution describes the mode whereby living things come into existence and have their being, its mechanisms. Mechanism and meaning provide complementary insights into reality; both are needed. The long process of evolutionary history provides some challenges for Christian theology, but also provides a great deal of help. As that great Victorian clerical enthusiast for Darwinism, Aubrey Moore, Fellow of St John's College, Oxford, once put it: "Darwinism appeared, and, under the guise of a foe, did the work of a friend."

References

Alexander, Denis. 2008. *Creation or Evolution: Do We Have to Choose?* Oxford: Monarch.

Alexander, Denis. 2011. *The Language of Genetics: An Introduction.* West Conshohocken: Templeton Foundation Press.

Alexander, Denis and Numbers, Ronald, eds. 2010. *Biology and Ideology: From Descartes to Dawkins.* Chicago: Chicago University Press.

Augustine. 1982. *The Literal Meaning of Genesis*, vol. 1. John Hammond Taylor, ed. Mahwah, NJ: Paulist Press.

Barrett, Justin. 2004. *Why Would Anyone Believe in God?* Lanham, MD: Altamira Press.

Behe, Michael J. 1996. *Darwin's Black Box.* New York: The Free Press.

Berry, R. J. and Jeeves, Malcolm. 2008. The Nature of Human Nature. *Science and Christian Belief*, 20(1), pp. 3–47.

Calvin, John. 1847–1850. *Calvin's Commentaries*, vol. 12, part V. Translated by John King. Edinburgh: Calvin Translation Society.

Collins, Francis. 2007. *The Language of God.* New York: The Free Press.

Dembski, William A. 2004. *The Design Revolution: Answering the Toughest Questions about Intelligent Design.* Downers Grove, IL: InterVarsity Press.

Falk, Darrel L. 2004. *Coming to Peace with Science.* Downers Grove, IL: InterVarsity Press.

Godfrey, W. Robert. 2003. *God's Pattern for Creation.* Phillipsburg, NJ: P&R Publishing.

Ham, Ken. 1987. *The Lie: Evolution.* Green Forest, AR: Master Books.

Hebblethwaite, Brian. 2000. *Evil, Suffering and Religion.* London: SPCK.

Kingsley, Charles. 1859. Letter to Charles Darwin, November 18. University of Cambridge: Darwin Correspondence Project, online at http://www.darwinproject.ac.uk/entry-2534 (accessed January 14, 2011).

Lamoureux, Denis O. 2008. *Evolutionary Creation.* Eugene. OR: Wipf and Stock.

Larson, Edward J. 2003. *Trial and Error: The American Controversy over Creation and Evolution.* New York: Oxford University Press.

Lucas, Ernest. 2001. *Can We Believe Genesis Today?*, 2nd edn. Leicester: InterVarsity Press.

Marsden, George M. 1984. Understanding Fundamentalist Views of Science. In Ashley Montagu, ed. *Science and Creationism.* Oxford: Oxford University Press, pp. 95–116.

Moore, James. 1981. *The Post-Darwinian Controversies: A Study of the Protestant Struggle to Come to Terms with Darwin in Great Britain and America, 1870–1900.* Cambridge: Cambridge University Press.

Murray, Michael. 2008. *Nature Red in Tooth and Claw: Theism and the Problem of Animal Suffering.* New York: Oxford University Press.

Numbers, Ronald L. 2006. *The Creationists: From Scientific Creationism to Intelligent Design.* Cambridge, MA: Harvard University Press.

Origen. 1936. *On First Principles.* Translated by G. Butterworth. London: SPCK.

Peacocke, Arthur. 1993. *Theology for a Scientific Age: Being and Becoming – Natural, Divine and Human,* enlarged edn. Minneapolis, MN: Fortress Press.

Ross, Hugh. 2009. *More Than a Theory: Revealing a Testable Model for Creation.* Ada, MI: Baker Books.

Sedgwick, Adam. 1859. Letter to Charles Darwin, November 24. University of Cambridge: Darwin Correspondence Project, online at http://www.darwinproject.ac.uk/entry-2548 (accessed January 14, 2011).

Smith, George Adam. 2005. *The Life of Henry Drummond*. Whitefish, MT: Kessinger Publishing.

Southgate, Christopher. 2008. *The Groaning of Creation*. London: Westminster John Knox Press.

Spencer, Nick and Alexander, Denis. 2009. *Rescuing Darwin: God and Evolution in Britain Today*. London: Theos.

Teilhard de Chardin, Pierre. 2002. *Christianity and Evolution*. New York: Mariner Books.

Temple, Frederick. 1903. *The Relations between Religion and Science: Eight Lectures Preached Before the University of Oxford in the Year 1884*. London: Macmillan.

Walton, John H. 2009. *The Lost World of Genesis One: Ancient Cosmology and the Origins Debate*. Downers Grove, IL: IVP Academic.

Wenham, Gordon J. 1987. *Word Biblical Commentary*, vol. 1, *Genesis 1–15*. Waco, TX: Word Books.

Whitcomb, John C. and Morris, Henry M. 1960. *Genesis Flood*. Phillipsburg, NJ: P&R Publishing.

Further Reading

Alexander, Denis. 2008. *Creation or Evolution: Do We Have to Choose?* Oxford: Monarch. Surveys the biblical understanding of the term "creation" and explains the contemporary understanding of evolution, concluding that there is no need to choose between these two narratives describing the created order.

Falk, Darrel L. 2004. *Coming to Peace with Science*. Downers Grove, IL: InterVarsity Press. Surveys the main biological evidence for evolution showing how this can readily be incorporated within a traditional Christian understanding of creation.

Lamoureux, Denis O. 2008. *Evolutionary Creation*. Eugene. OR: Wipf and Stock. A detailed examination of the hermeneutics of biblical texts showing how they can be interpreted within their context without recourse to concordism, illustrating also the ways in which Darwinian evolution can be understood from the perspective of the Christian understanding of creation.

Lucas, Ernest. 2001. *Can We Believe Genesis Today?*, 2nd edn. Leicester: InterVarsity Press. Examines the hermeneutics and cultural context of the early chapters of Genesis in the light of contemporary Near East creation accounts.

Numbers, Ronald L. 2006. *The Creationists: From Scientific Creationism to Intelligent Design*. Cambridge, MA: Harvard University Press. An extensive overview of the way in which creationism became popular in the USA during the twentieth century, providing detailed analysis of the growth of specific creationist institutes and movements.

22

Darwinism and Atheism
A Marriage Made in Heaven?

MICHAEL RUSE

My aim in this chapter is to consider the relationship between Darwinism and atheism. I take it that by Darwinism is meant today's version of the theory given in Charles Darwin's *On the Origin of Species*, evolution through natural selection (Ruse 2006, 2008). Of course no one believes that natural selection is the only cause of change, but the Darwinian is committed to the belief that natural selection is by far the greatest force. It should be noted that natural selection does not lead simply to change but change of a particular kind, namely in the direction of adaptive advantage. By atheism in this chapter is meant the denial of religious belief, and specifically in the context of this volume the denial of Christian belief. In other words, this essay could as well have been titled "Can a Christian Be a Darwinian?"

Biblical Literalism

I shall take in turn a number of points of potential conflict, starting with the most obvious potential conflict of all, namely the clash between the claims made in the Holy Bible and the claims made by Darwinians. If one reads the Bible in any sense literally then clearly there are problems. The Bible tells us that God created the earth and all of the organisms on it in six days. The Bible tells us that humans are all descended from one man and one woman who were likewise created miraculously. The Bible tells us that, at some point after the initial creation, God being displeased with what he saw, decided to destroy almost everything by means of a universal flood. All of these claims and more are denied by Darwinian evolutionary theory. The Darwinian accepts the standard cosmological picture of the universe, namely that everything began some 15 billion years ago with a so-called Big Bang. The Darwinian accepts that the earth is about 4½ billion years old. The Darwinian believes that life began just under 4 billion years ago. The Darwinian believes that organisms developed slowly and naturally (meaning without divine miraculous intervention) from common ancestors. The Darwinian believes that humans are part of the natural evolutionary process, and that we

The Blackwell Companion to Science and Christianity, First Edition. Edited by J. B. Stump and Alan G. Padgett.
© 2012 Blackwell Publishing Ltd. Published 2012 by Blackwell Publishing Ltd.

appeared some million or so years ago. The Darwinian believes that human population numbers were once much smaller than they are now, but that they never dropped below about 20 000 organisms. The Darwinian accepts plate tectonics and finds no evidence whatsoever for a universal flood.

Obviously, if religion and science are to be brought together in harmony, something must give. Most particularly something must give on the side of religion. One simply cannot interpret the Bible in the literal way just sketched in the last paragraph. However, as is well known, Christians have long had resources to tackle this problem (McMullin 1985, 1993; Ruse 2001). The greatest theologian that the church has known, St Augustine of Hippo (who lived around AD 400), stressed that although the Bible is the word of God and hence true throughout, this does not mean that the Bible must always be read in a literal fashion. Reasonably, Augustine stressed that had God expressed his views in the terms of modern science the people of the Bible simply would not have understood what he was talking about. Hence, to use the language of the great reformer John Calvin, God had to "accommodate" his speech to the common people. As it happens, Augustine did take most of the early chapters of the Bible fairly literally. But he set in place the methodology to deal with ongoing discoveries and theories of science. In other words, so long as one sees the creation story of the Bible as telling us something about God and his creative power, and also about the special relationship that humans have with God, it is open to the Christian to understand everything else in the terms of modern science. Indeed many would argue that the Christian must understand things in terms of modern science. The Bible tells us that we are made in the image of God. Whatever else that might mean, it clearly means that we have powers of sense and reason which are godlike. Hence, using them is using gifts given to us by God, and not to explore our wonderful world is itself positively unchristian.

Of course, particularly in the USA today, many Christians (particularly evangelical Protestants) find this kind of argument unconvincing. They feel strongly that a true Christian must be guided by the unaltered, uninterpreted word of God (Numbers 2006). Ultimately, I suppose, there is little reconciliation possible. However, it is worth pointing out that almost no one in fact takes every part of the Bible completely literally. For example, Revelation talks much about such individuals as the Whore of Babylon. There is a long tradition in Christianity, especially for evangelicals, of interpreting the Whore in all sorts of nonliteral ways. Hardly anyone thinks that she is an actual person. Rather it is taken to be a metaphorical way of describing evil forces, often for traditional Protestants the Catholic Church or its leader, the pope. So when people argue that Darwinism clashes with the Bible, it is worth pointing out that even the most fervent are usually cherry-picking those parts of the Bible that they insist must be read literally (Ruse 2005).

Miracles

Matters of faith, including interpretation of the Bible, fall under what is known as revealed religion. Let us turn now to the other side of the coin, natural religion or theology, that area of inquiry that deals with religion from the viewpoint of reason. Here we encounter the well-known proofs for the existence of God. I assume that Darwinian evolutionary theory has nothing to say about an argument like the ontological argument for God's existence, namely that which derives God's existence from the very nature of his being. I am not sure, to be candid, whether Darwinism has much to say either about causal arguments. However, it certainly does seem pertinent to some of the other arguments and so let us run through a number.

Start with the argument from miracles. This is the argument that says miracles, however defined, point to the existence of a deity (remember we are thinking in terms of the Christian deity). The trouble here is that if miracles are defined in the usual way, that is to say as breaks with the regular laws of nature, this goes against science in general and Darwinian science in particular. The absolutely fundamental, metaphysical presupposition is that the world is regular, governed by unbroken rules or laws.

There are two traditional approaches that one can take at this point (Mullin 2000). The first, going back to St Augustine, suggests that even miracles are governed by laws, albeit laws that we do not necessarily yet know. Hence there need be no conflict with science. Of course today we know a lot more about the laws of nature than did St Augustine. In the modern version, the argument that there need be no conflict is more likely to be phrased less in terms of unknown laws and more of known laws coming together in some significant and perhaps unexpected way. For instance, when the British Army escaped in 1940 from Dunkirk, most atypically the English Channel was very smooth, without any storms or other unpleasant weather effects. Many thought that this was miraculous, but I suspect few thought that any laws of nature were actually being broken or that indeed any unknown laws of nature were involved. It was more a question of things coming together serendipitously.

I presume therefore that pursuing this line of argument, the claim would be that such miracles as feeding the 5000 were in fact law-bound phenomena. Perhaps Jesus' influence so affected the multitude that spontaneously and atypically they shared their food. The real miracle was this outpouring of love rather than Jesus acting rather like a high-class caterer. Even something like the Resurrection could be dealt with in this way. Presumably one might say something along the lines that Jesus physically actually died and remained dead, but that on the third day the disciples suddenly felt in their hearts that they were not alone and that their savior had arisen. If one goes in this sort of direction then clearly there is no conflict with science, specifically including Darwinian science.

For many Christians, however, this is too weak or radical a solution. They opt rather to go with a line of thinking endorsed by St Thomas Aquinas. He argued that there were indeed actual breaks or violations of natural law. On the third day one would rightly expect the body of Jesus to go on rotting. However, miraculously, Jesus came back from the dead and arose to meet his followers. What can be said by the Darwinian reconciler in the face of this kind of thinking? I suspect that the best solution is that one argues that God is ever immanent and that, no matter how lawlike any situation may be, it would collapse into nothingness without his support. There is therefore no reason why God should not at any point that suits him intervene and break with natural law, which after all is something he created and sustained. Here, therefore, I think one would argue that one is not so much violating science, including Darwinian science, but going beyond the scope of science.

I suspect that many Darwinians would feel uncomfortable with this, but I'm not sure that logically they are in a position to object. I do suspect, however, that if one starts to look for actual evidence of miracles, for instance speculating about how the Virgin Mary might have become pregnant, one is going to run into all of the objections philosophers like David Hume have long detailed. Better therefore take things on faith. Also, I suspect one should be very wary about how far one is prepared to extend the notion of miracle. We shall come later to human evolution, but it is probably a mistake to start introducing miracles to get the arrival of *homo sapiens*. Better to restrict the notion of miracle strictly to situations needed for our salvation. Let God's laws do the rest.

Design

The design argument comes in various forms (Ruse 2003). One version, which goes back to Plato, sees design in the very existence of laws of nature themselves. If this argument be found convincing, then clearly Darwinian evolutionary theory adds to its strength. Darwinism extends the rule of law into the area of organic origins, something that previously had been thought miraculous. However, there is another version which goes back particularly to Aristotle, focusing on the nature of organisms. In Aristotle's terminology, organisms show evidence of ends or purposes, what he called "final causes." It was Aristotle's opinion, and this was shared by many down through the course of history, that final causes cannot just have happened randomly. There must be some kind of designing intention behind them. Christians have taken this up and argued that the designer is in fact the God of the Old and New Testaments. After the Reformation, particularly in Britain, the argument for organic design was much cherished, and naturalists like John Ray made much of it, as did theologians like Archdeacon William Paley a century later. In recent years the argument has been reinvigorated, if that is the right word, by a group of American evangelical Christians, who argue that organisms show evidence of an "intelligent design" (Dembski and Ruse 2004).

Well before Darwin appeared on the scene there were strong critics of the organic design argument. Most particularly, the eighteenth-century Scottish philosopher David Hume (1947) showed that there are many problems, particularly for the Christian. For instance, why should there not be more than one designer? And why should we think that this world of ours is the one and only attempt made by the designer? It may be that we had a series of predecessors and that there will be many successors in future years, after we are long gone and forgotten. However, it seems fair to say that even Hume did not demolish the argument entirely, and indeed he himself admitted this. Supporters of the argument invoked a version of what is today known as the "argument to the best explanation." They pointed out, reasonably, that Aristotle was indeed right. Organisms show final causes, final causes cannot have come about by chance, and that failing some other alternative one really has no choice but to suppose that a designer of some form or another. Here, obviously, Darwin's thinking did have major implications. He gave a law-bound explanation not only of the evolution of organisms but also, as pointed out earlier, their designlike or adapted nature. Natural selection speaks directly to final causes. Organisms like the eye and the hand show evidence of intention, not because there was a conscious intention but because those that were intention- or designlike succeeded in the struggle for existence and those that were not did not. In the notorious words of Britain's best-known popularizer of science, "Darwin made it possible to be an intellectually fulfilled atheist" (Dawkins 1986, 6).

Note, however, what Darwin's argument does and does not do. It does not disprove the existence of God. Rather, it shows that we do not need directly to invoke God to explain the designlike nature of organisms. In other words, at this level it makes God redundant. (In fact at the time of writing the *Origin of Species* in 1859, Darwin believed that there was a designer who worked through the medium of law. Later, he became more of an agnostic, although never an atheist. Darwin would have agreed fully with Dawkins at this point. God is redundant.) My suspicion is that many thinkers today, probably including Dawkins himself, think that Darwinism at this point actually refutes Christianity. This is simply not so. Showing that something is not necessary is not the same as showing that something is not possible. One should not underestimate the significance of Darwinism, but at the same time one should not over exaggerate the significance of Darwinism.

Morality

Many would argue that morality proves the existence of God in some sense. They would argue that without God's backing, morality degenerates into mere subjective feelings, and not only is this an undesirable state of affairs but in the light of all that we know and think it is a completely unconvincing state of affairs. Morality does not come across to us as mere subjective feeling rather like a fondness for spinach. It is more, and this more implies God.

Does Darwinism have anything to say at this point? Many evolutionists think that it does (Ruse 2009). In the past 30 or 40 years there has been much interest in the possibility of morality emerging as part of our evolved human nature. In fact, following Darwin himself in his *Descent of Man*, today's evolutionists generally claim that morality is highly adaptive. This may seem paradoxical given that evolution forges us all in a struggle for existence. But, as Darwin recognized and as today's evolutionists endorse, often in the struggle one gets far more by cooperating rather than by fighting flat out. It is argued that what really matters for social organisms like humans are sentiments of warm feeling, extending even to obligations towards our fellows.

It is true that Darwinians are not in total unity about the actual mechanism of evolution at this point. Some favor a fairly rigorous selective process, often known as the "selfish gene" perspective (Williams 1966; Dawkins 1976; Ruse 1998). Here, all benefits ultimately come down to the individual and no one does anything without some hope of personal gain. Others favor a more holistic approach, where selection can work for the good of the group (Sober and Wilson 1994, 1998). But although these differences cause much heated debate among Darwinians, the overall result is the same. Natural selection produces morality. The actual nature of the moral claims is sometimes disputed. Some (like Peter Singer) incline more to utilitarianism, the greatest happiness of the greatest number. Others (like John Rawls) are more inclined towards some kind of Kantian position, where there is a great emphasis on fairness and treating others as ends rather than as means. But ultimately again one finds a fair amount of overlap, and most would surely be inclined to endorse something along the lines of Jesus' Love Commandment, namely one ought to treat one's neighbor as oneself.

What does all of this have to say about questions of objectivity and subjectivity? I think it's fairly clear that Darwinians unite in thinking that morality is ultimately a matter of emotions. Note, however, that these are not individual emotions. Morality only works if everyone shares basically the same emotions. In other words, there is no relativity implied by the Darwinian approach to morality. But surely one might argue that morality being in some sense a matter of human emotions does not deny some kind of objective reality out there. After all, who would doubt that ultimately morality has to be a human thing? Think analogously about our perception of the external world. We have eyes and ears which enable us to recognize and track external objects. Thus, for example, if a truck is bearing down on us we can see and hear it, and clearly it is to our adaptive advantage to get out of its way. Our eyes and ears are products of evolution, as is the use that we make of them. But this does not in any sense deny the reality of the speeding truck. Surely analogously one might argue that although morality is something given to us through evolution, it is not to deny that there is an objective morality behind everything, not excluding the possibility of an objective morality put in place and endorsed by God (Kitcher 1994).

However, some Darwinians would push the argument rather more strongly and deny this can be so. They would argue that there is often more than one way of skinning the cat, or less metaphorically that there is nothing in the Darwinian picture to deny that we might have evolved other ways of interacting with our fellow species members. Rather than evolving with the belief that we ought to love each other, possibly we might have evolved with the belief that we ought to hate each other, but that knowing others feel the same way about us we see that it is in our interests to cooperate. In other words, there is no guarantee in the Darwinians' scenario that what we believe in fact corresponds to the objective moral truth. And, surely, if the objective moral truth is unknown to us it is hardly likely that such truth is something put in place by a loving God. In still other words, perhaps the Darwinian picture cuts more deeply. Completing the argument, Darwinians suggest also that even though morality may be a matter of emotion, it is a matter of emotions of a rather strange kind. Most particularly, our biology deceives us into thinking that these emotions truly do reflect objective morality. If we did not think that morality was objective then we would start to disregard it and, before long, everything would break down. In other words, for our own biological good, natural selection makes us think morality is objective even though it is really subjective (Ruse 1998).

Is this the final word on the matter? Possibly not. The above picture has been sketched deliberately without any reference to the Christian God. If it is well taken, then clearly one does not need God to explain morality. However, this is not to stop the Christian from suggesting that God might be the author of all things, including our moral sentiments. In fact, someone inclined to a natural-law theory of morality might well embrace this route. The natural-law theorist believes that the objectivity of morality comes about, not from God's arbitrary decrees, but because of the way that God has made us. It is right and proper, for instance, for man and woman to come together and have children, not because God laid down the law, as it were, but because God made us as sexual beings and having children is a natural outcome. There is therefore no reason why the Christian should not accept the Darwinian position and simply say that morality has come about because this was what God intended. Morality is as natural as sex. In other words, although one does not have a proof of the existence of God from the nature and existence of morality, one has no refutation of the existence of God from the nature and existence of morality. Therefore, it seems that Christianity and Darwinism can be quite good friends at this point (Ruse 2001, 2010).

Original Sin

The move now is to one of the biggest problems for the Christian, irrespective of any science, including Darwinism. I refer to the problem of evil. How is one to reconcile Christian claims about a creator God, who is not only all-powerful but also all-loving, and the existence of evil in the world? The point of relevance for us here is that many critics think that Darwinism exacerbates the problem (Dawkins 1995). Attention is drawn to the fact that natural selection starts with a struggle for existence, a phenomenon which is often very painful and almost inevitably ends in death and destruction. How is it that such a process could have been brought about by an all-loving, all-powerful God? Charles Darwin (1985–, 8, 224) himself drew attention to some of the terrible ways in which organisms are adapted to succeed in life's struggles. He concluded, and many have concluded with him, that it is very hard to see at a point like this how Christianity can be maintained.

To speak to these issues, let us stress, first, that the question is not whether the Christian can give an adequate answer to evil. The question rather is whether Darwinism makes the problem worse. Let us stress, second, that Christians have thought hard about these issues, and that it would be wrong to ignore the fruits of their inquiry. In particular, following this prescription, let us note that traditionally a distinction is drawn between moral evil and physical evil. The Christian argues that some evils, like the Holocaust, are the results of human actions. They therefore demand an explanation that takes account of this fact. The Christian also argues that some evils, like earthquakes and tsunamis, are the results of natural causes. Any explanation must likewise take account of this fact.

Start with moral evil. What does the Christian have to say here? The answer is that moral evil is brought about by human actions and that humans act in bad ways because they are sinful, in some sense tainted. But how does one explain human sinfulness, given that we are made in the image of a loving God? Here the answer is traditionally given in terms of the Fall. Following St Augustine, Christians argue that sin came into the world because of human disobedience and that God should not be blamed for it. (Christians also argue that Jesus' death on the cross in some way counters this disobedience, but this is not something of direct relevance to us here.) Surely we have a point of conflict with Darwinism. It was not just any disobedience that brought in sin. It was the disobedience of the actual historical figures Adam and Eve. But we have just seen that modern evolutionary theory denies the existence of such figures and so there is a point of breakdown here.

There is one fairly obvious solution to this problem, namely suggesting that original sin should not be ascribed directly to Adam and Eve. As it happens, there is an alternative theological position going back even before Augustine to Irenaeus, one which has long been favored by Eastern Christianity (Schneider 2010). Here one does not see sin coming about as the direct result of moral disobedience by fully aware and formed beings. Rather it is seen as something which was a natural consequence of our immature, evolving nature. Instead of seeing the coming of Christ and his atoning death on the cross as a rather contingent response to an unplanned fall, one sees that the death on the cross was something anticipated and planned from the first. Humans, although made in the image of God, only came slowly to intellectual and moral maturity. Expectedly, when they first appeared, they were incomplete and imperfect beings. God knew that this would be so and anticipated from the first that he would have to suffer on our behalf.

This kind of theological approach lends itself naturally to a Darwinian interpretation (Ruse 2001). Humans are bound to be selfish, because unless we are self-regarding we are not going to succeed in the struggle for existence. We are also going to be moral or, as evolutionists say, "altruistic," because altruism is a good strategy in the struggle for existence. In other words, we are an uneasy *mélange* of good and bad, and this is something which emerges naturally out of our background. Sin has not come about because of one individual act, but because this is the natural consequence of an evolutionary process that makes natural selection the central cause. In short, far from refuting the Christian position on original sin, if one goes with Irenaeus rather than Augustine, if anything, natural selection offers support for this way of thinking.

Natural Evil

What then of natural evil? What about the child burnt by the fire or the family destroyed by an earthquake? The traditional Christian position is that best articulated by the German philosopher Gottfried Leibniz (Reichenbach 1982). He argued that God's being all-powerful did not imply that God could do the impossible. God could not make $2 + 2 = 5$. But such a limitation was no reflection on his omnipotence. Leibniz argued that the laws of nature that we have maximize the good even though there are sometimes costs. It is true the burning fire is very painful, but without the pain we would never learn to avoid fire. Better the pain than major burning. It is true that while Voltaire parodied this way of thinking in his satire *Candide*, many Christians nonetheless feel that essentially Leibniz's position is the right answer to natural evil.

Does Darwinism have anything to say at this point? It may be that it does. Richard Dawkins (1983) of all people has argued that the only way in which one can get designlike attributes naturally, that is the only way in which unguided laws can bring about final causes, is through the process of natural selection. Dawkins argues that earlier thinkers were indeed right. Normally, blind law leads to randomness and things going wrong. For instance, new variations or mutations, particularly if they are large, almost invariably are deleterious to their possessors rather than helpful. The only way one can get designlike features is either through genuine design or through a lawlike, designlike producing mechanism, namely natural selection. One can see immediately how this argument can bring comfort to the Christian. It certainly does not answer or speak to all of the instances of natural evil. However, it does explain many instances, for example those cases of adaptation which bring about such cruelty that so troubled Charles Darwin himself. If Dawkins is right, since natural selection is the only way to get designlike features, it is no reflection on God's omnipotence that the process involves pain and suffering.

Of course this does all rather presuppose that God in his wisdom created through law rather than miraculously. However, there are arguments that one can use to suggest that creation through law is preferable to creation through miracle. For instance, if you are going to produce humanlike beings then necessarily we will have all sorts of features that seemingly reflect our past. If God created miraculously, then it seems we are in the kind of position that the nineteenth-century English naturalist Philip Gosse (1857) proposed, namely that God made things all in one fell swoop but then rather dishonestly put in seeming traces of evolution. One might, I suppose, argue that humans could have been made without any seeming marks of the past, but it is difficult indeed to see how this could be done without completely altering the ground plan. So one can see, at the very least, that if one rushes in and denies the importance of law-bound creation, one is probably raising as many new difficult problems as one is supposedly solving.

Contingency

I want finally to turn to an issue which many, myself included, think is the most difficult problem of all to be solved if one is trying to reconcile Darwinism and Christianity (Ruse 2010). It is surely the case in the Christian scheme of things that humans cannot be contingent. It does not at all follow that we must be the only beings that exist, but that we exist is something that in some sense must be necessary. I doubt very much that we have to be exactly as we are. Presumably we could have green skin. We might have 12 fingers rather than 10. Perhaps even we might not have sexuality, at least as we know it, although this does start to stretch the outer limits of conceivability. But, if beings made in the image of God do not exist or might not have existed, then we have a major challenge to Christian belief.

Unfortunately it is absolutely central to Darwinian evolutionary theory that the course of evolution is contingent. This does not at all mean that it is uncaused. What it does mean is that its path is not predetermined. As the late Stephen Jay Gould (1989) used to say, play the tape of life one time and you get one result. Play the tape of life another time, and you get another result. The reason for this is simple. First of all, natural selection does not insist that one form rather than another must always succeed in life's struggles. Depending on the circumstances, one kind of organism might be better or fitter than another. Depending on the circumstances, the second kind of organism might be better or fitter than the first. Second, genetics – whether it be Mendelian or the later molecular form – insists that new variations or mutations do not come about according to the needs of their possessors. We know a lot about the causes of mutation, but there is nothing in the theory to say that mutation comes to order, as it were. Indeed, usually mutations are deleterious. These two things, the working of selection and the nature of mutation, mean that there is no direction to the evolutionary process. What evolves is, in a very real sense, a matter of chance.

We have here an area of significant potential conflict. For the Christian, the existence of humans is necessary. For the Darwinian, the existence of humans is contingent. Nor should you think that humans are special and must have evolved (Ruse 2011). If anything, Darwinism suggests that in this case evolution is highly improbable. For a start, beings with brains as large as ours require huge amounts of fuel, namely protein. This is very expensive to obtain, usually involving the pursuit and killing of large mammals. There are many other evolutionary strategies which might be at least as good, if not more efficient, than the one taken by us. For instance, cows have the ability to eat and digest large amounts of very low-grade material. There is nothing in the Darwinian picture to suggest that humans are in some sense innately better or likely to be more successful than dumb brutes like cows.

A number of solutions have been offered to this dilemma. Once again, somewhat paradoxically, the greatest atheist of them all, Richard Dawkins (1986), comes to the Christian's aid. Dawkins argues that organisms engage in (what are known by biologists as) "arms races." Two lines of organisms compete and as they do their adaptations are refined and made yet stronger. Thus the antelope is pursued by the cheetah and so the antelope gets faster and in tandem the cheetah gets faster too. Dawkins argues that these arms races lead ultimately up the chain of being to intelligence. He draws attention to the fact that, in the military world, arms races have changed, from the development of heavier and heavier weaponry and armory, to the use of more sophisticated methods of attack and destruction, often if not always involving large amounts of electrical hardware like computers. It is Dawkins's belief that, in the biological world, arms races sooner or later would lead to humanlike beings.

Perhaps this is true, but even the non-expert can see a great deal is being presupposed here. First, do arms races exist and do they always have the results of that Dawkins suggests? Paleontological evidence rather implies that predators and prey fairly rapidly reached the peak of their abilities and get little or no faster after that. Likewise paleontological evidence suggests that the opportunism of evolution can lead to many different forms, not all of which involve intelligence. Without something more being added there is certainly no necessity for the emergence of beings like ourselves.

Another approach has been suggested recently by the British invertebrate paleontologist Simon Conway Morris (2003). Conway Morris suggests that convergence is a major feature of the evolutionary picture. Ecological niches exist before organisms. Organisms seek these out and evolve into them. Thus, for instance, in the jungle there is going to be an ecological niche for aerial insects at the tops of trees. Likewise, once one has herbivores one is going to have an ecological niche for carnivores. Conway Morris makes much of the fact that saber-tooth tigers evolved separately in both the placental mammalian line and the marsupial mammalian line. He suggests even that there might have been saber-tooth-tiger-like beings amongst the dinosaurs. Working from this, Conway Morris suggests also that ecological niches have a kind of hierarchy, and at the top exists a slot open to cultural beings. It is this niche that humans occupied. Conway Morris argues that in some sense it was inevitable that some evolving line would occupy the cultural niche. Had humans not found it then some other beings surely would have. This gives us all the necessity required by Christianity.

Once again, ingenious though the solution may be one can see that there are many unfounded assumptions. For a start, many deny strongly that ecological niches exist objectively waiting to be occupied. Rather it is argued they are as much a construction from what already exists as anything else. Had herbivores not evolved in the way that they did, then surely the carnivore niche as we know it would not exist. Likewise there is absolutely no necessity to suppose a cultural niche existing independently on its own. There is certainly no reason to think that it waits there asking to be occupied by some group of organisms. And even if it does, then there may well be so many barriers or impediments to reaching it that the chances of its ever being occupied are vanishingly small. As with arms races, one should probably not assume that one has a full answer, totally satisfying for the Christian.

What about a more theological kind of solution? The physicist-theologian Robert John Russell (2008) has offered one candidate. He argues that God gives direction to mutations, but not at the visible level. Rather God directs change down at the quantum level, where it is essentially undiscoverable by us humans. It is hardly a surprise to learn that many find Russell's solution problematic. One surely has here some version of the "God-of-the gaps argument." One is breaking with science in order to achieve a theologically acceptable outcome. At the very least, one is putting strain on one's understanding of Darwinism. Indeed, one has a replay of the debate between Charles Darwin and his great American supporter Asa Gray (Ruse 1999). Gray did not think that evolution could lead to design and ultimately to humans, at least not if one relied solely on natural selection. Therefore, anticipating Russell, Gray argued that some variations are directed. Darwin was horrified and responded that to make such a move as this was to take evolutionary discussion out of the realm of science. Many feel this objection still holds today.

Is there any other possible solution? Stephen Jay Gould (1996) thought that (irrespective of the workings of selection) complexity is bound to occur naturally over time, and that this could lead to intelligence. But again I am not sure that this must lead to intelligence. The solution which I favor invokes (for theological not scientific reasons) some kind of multiverse state of affairs (Ruse 2010). There are many, an infinite number, of universes. I point out that humans *have* evolved and therefore, however difficult, they *could* have evolved. In other words, run the process enough times and humans will evolve. Note that "enough times" might mean many, many billions of times – an infinite number in some sense. If God creates universes enough times then humans will evolve. The fact that it takes a great deal of time is irrelevant. It would bore us to wait, but God is outside time and space. He sees always that humans will evolve. I argue, therefore, that although evolution is unguided, the coming of humans was not unplanned.

Does this not imply an awful lot of waste on the part of God? Obviously it does from one perspective. However, note that God may not think a universe totally wasted even if we do not exist in it. Already in this universe we have many worlds which presumably are unoccupied, at least unoccupied by humanlike beings. So, if we are going to talk of waste, we are already up to our necks in that problem. (This is an old problem for those reconciling science and religion. Known as the "plurality-of-worlds" problem, it much engaged philosophers and theologians in the nineteenth century. The philosopher and historian of science William

Whewell (2001) wrote an engaging book on the subject, trying to reconcile an essentially empty universe with the purposes of a good and intelligent divine being.)

Conclusion

I doubt my proposal will convince everyone or perhaps anyone. So this is a good point on which to end this essay. One can make considerable progress on the Darwinism and Christianity problem or (if you prefer) the counter-problem of whether Darwinism implies atheism. If what I have covered in this essay is at all well taken, it is clear that those who argue that Darwinism leads inevitably to atheism are simply mistaken. There are, however, many difficult problems and perhaps not all have been tackled successfully. This surely is a challenge rather than refutation. There is work in need of completion.

References

Conway Morris, Simon. 2003. *Life's Solution: Inevitable Humans in a Lonely Universe*. Cambridge: Cambridge University Press.

Darwin, Charles. 1985–. *The Correspondence of Charles Darwin*. Cambridge: Cambridge University Press.

Dawkins, Richard. 1976. *The Selfish Gene*. Oxford: Oxford University Press.

Dawkins, Richard. 1983. Universal Darwinism. In D. S. Bendall, ed. *Evolution from Molecules to Men*. Cambridge: Cambridge University Press, pp. 403–425.

Dawkins, Richard. 1986. *The Blind Watchmaker*. New York: Norton.

Dawkins, Richard. 1995. *River Out of Eden: A Darwinian View of Life*. New York: Basic Books.

Dembski, William and Ruse, Michael, eds. 2004. *Debating Design: Darwin to DNA*. Cambridge: Cambridge University Press.

Gosse, Philip. 1857. *Omphalos: An Attempt to Untie the Geological Knot*. London: John Van Voorst.

Gould, Stephen Jay. 1989. *Wonderful Life: The Burgess Shale and the Nature of History*. New York: W. W. Norton & Co.

Gould, Stephen Jay. 1996. *Full House: The Spread of Excellence from Plato to Darwin*. New York: Paragon.

Hume, David. 1947. *Dialogues Concerning Natural Religion*. N. K. Smith, ed. Indianapolis, IN: Bobbs-Merrill Co.

Kitcher, Philip. 1994. Four Ways to "Biologicize" Ethics. In Elliott Sober, ed. *Conceptual Issues in Evolutionary Biology*. Cambridge, MA: MIT Press, pp. 439–450.

McMullin, Ernan, ed. 1985. *Evolution and Creation*. Notre Dame, IN: University of Notre Dame Press.

McMullin, Ernan. 1993. Evolution and Special Creation. *Zygon*, 28, pp. 299–335.

Mullin, R. B. 2000. Miracle. In A. Hastings, A. Mason, and H. Pyper, eds. *The Oxford Companion to Christian Thought*. Oxford: Oxford University Press, pp. 438–440.

Numbers, Ronald L. 2006. *The Creationists: From Scientific Creationism to Intelligent Design*, expanded edn. Cambridge, MA: Harvard University Press.

Reichenbach, Bruce R. 1982. *Evil and a Good God*. New York: Fordham University Press.

Ruse, Michael. 1998. *Taking Darwin Seriously: A Naturalistic Approach to Philosophy*, 2nd edn. Buffalo, NY: Prometheus.

Ruse, Michael. 1999. *The Darwinian Revolution: Science Red in Tooth and Claw*, 2nd edn. Chicago: University of Chicago Press.

Ruse, Michael. 2001. *Can a Darwinian Be a Christian? The Relationship between Science and Religion*. Cambridge: Cambridge University Press.

Ruse, Michael. 2003. *Darwin and Design: Does Evolution Have a Purpose?* Cambridge, MA: Harvard University Press.

Ruse, Michael. 2005. *The Evolution–Creation Struggle.* Cambridge, MA: Harvard University Press.

Ruse, Michael. 2006. *Darwinism and Its Discontents.* Cambridge: Cambridge University Press.

Ruse, Michael. 2008. *Charles Darwin.* Oxford: Wiley-Blackwell.

Ruse, Michael, ed. 2009. *Philosophy after Darwin: Classic and Contemporary Readings.* Princeton, NJ: Princeton University Press.

Ruse, Michael. 2010. *Science and Spirituality: Making Room for Faith in the Age of Science.* Cambridge: Cambridge University Press.

Ruse, Michael. 2011. *The Philosophy of Human Evolution.* Cambridge: Cambridge University Press.

Russell, Robert J. 2008. *Cosmology from Alpha to Omega: The Creative Mutual Interaction of Theology and Science.* Minneapolis, MN: Fortress Press.

Schneider, John. 2010. Recent Genetic Science and Christian Theology on Human Origins: An "Aesthetic Supralapsarianism." *Perspectives on Science and Christian Faith,* 62, pp. 196–212.

Sober, Elliot and Wilson, David S. 1994. A Critical Review of Philosophical Work on the Units of Selection Problem. *Philosophy of Science,* 61, pp. 534–555.

Sober, Elliot and Wilson, David S. 1998. *Unto Others: The Evolution of Altruism.* Cambridge, MA: Harvard University Press.

Whewell, William. 2001. *Of the Plurality of Worlds: A Facsimile of the First Edition of 1853; Plus Previously Unpublished Material Excised by the Author Just Before the Book Went to Press; and Whewell's Dialogue Rebutting His Critics, Reprinted from the Second Edition.* Michael Ruse, ed. Chicago: University of Chicago Press.

Williams, George C. 1966. *Adaptation and Natural Selection.* Princeton, NJ: Princeton University Press.

Further Reading

Conway Morris, Simon. 2003. *Life's Solution: Inevitable Humans in a Lonely Universe.* Cambridge: Cambridge University Press. An interesting attempt by a paleontologist who is also a practicing Christian to show how the randomness of Darwinian evolution does not necessarily preclude the evolution of human beings.

Dawkins, Richard. 2006. *The God Delusion.* New York: Houghton Mifflin Harcourt. A slash-and-burn attack on religion by today's most popular biology writer.

Numbers, Ronald L. 2006. *The Creationists: From Scientific Creationism to Intelligent Design,* expanded edn. Cambridge, MA: Harvard University Press. The definitive history of the creationist movement.

Ruse, Michael. 2001. *Can a Darwinian Be a Christian? The Relationship between Science and Religion.* Cambridge: Cambridge University Press. A systematic examination of the claims of Christianity in the light of modern evolutionary theory.

Ruse, Michael. 2010. *Science and Spirituality: Making Room for Faith in the Age of Science.* Cambridge: Cambridge University Press. What questions does science not answer and why can religion try to offer answers?

23

Creation and Evolutionary Convergence

SIMON CONWAY MORRIS

The present-day polarization – or should I say circus? – between science and religion, and more specifically evolution and Christianity, needs no introduction. Militant atheists and creationists continue to build what they suppose to be impregnable fortresses of evidence, while in all directions their sappers extend subterranean tunnels of argument convinced that with sufficient explosives the opposing side will see the light, literally. Pity those who wander into no man's land: reconciliation is a word unheard, and the slightest hint that one finds favor with either of the entrenched positions is a cause for fervent rejoicing. The reality may be more complex, more subtle, but since the publication of Darwin's *Origin* on November 24, 1859, it has been a tangled web.

Darwin's metaphysical position on the evidence of evolution as a blind process as against the curious fact that somehow at least one of its products manages to extract meaning might be politely referred to as ambiguous (sterner critics might say evasive, if not incoherent). And think of St George Mivart, naturalist, controversialist, and theologian manqué (Mivart 1871; Artigas *et al.* 2006). His criticisms of Darwinian evolution were not entirely misplaced, but in a way somewhat reminiscent of Richard Owen (see Rupke 2009) Mivart's reservations about aspects of Darwinism (but certainly not the evidence for evolutionary change) have led to him being cast by the new secular priesthood into the outer darkness. To be sure in both the case of Mivart and Owen there were aspects of the Darwinian world-picture that they failed to grasp. But at least some of this is apparent only with hindsight, even though it confirms the genius of Darwin.

A more important point, however, is in danger of being lost, even though it has an immediate bearing on the current tension between evolutionary biology and religion. In the case of both Mivart (Gruber 1960) and Owen (Rupke 2009) the positions they arrived at, and the intellectual currents that took them in particular directions, are far more subtle and complex than the usual demonization might suggest. Their principal opponent, T. H. Huxley, was beyond doubt not only intensely energetic and a skilled debater, but his capacity at times to miss the point verges on the breathtaking. The net result – then as now – has been intensely corrosive. Most obvious is the poisoning of the wells from which biologists and theologians

The Blackwell Companion to Science and Christianity, First Edition. Edited by J. B. Stump and Alan G. Padgett.
© 2012 Blackwell Publishing Ltd. Published 2012 by Blackwell Publishing Ltd.

might wish to share a common libation. But even within orthodox biology, views that in any way question the absolute primacy of the Darwinian explanation are usually given short shrift.

Yet even if we are willing to acquaint ourselves with unfamiliar philosophies, prepared to show a modicum of historical sophistication, and engage in a dialogue where the default assumption is that your opponents may be misinformed (quite possibly grievously) but that they are not idiots, the fact remains that the present-day zeitgeist has not been arrived at accidentally. If we fail to appreciate where we came from, we may be poorly equipped to see how we might choose to dig ourselves out of the present morass. Although there is much in the past with which we can find an immediate resonance, in other respects L. P. Hartley was right: they do things differently there. Scientific knowledge changes the world-picture irrevocably and permanently. All too often the advances of science lead to an irritating triumphalism, which might be tempered by the recollection that what we know may be an infinitesimally small fraction of what we don't know. Nevertheless, it is not difficult to see how in the light of scientific knowledge, not least that of evolution, many now find Christianity entirely absurd.

Darwin characteristically harrumphed, but Huxley's position was clear enough, as indeed is that of many of his intellectual descendants. Yet it is curious that generation by generation even as the hearse drawing the remains of religion (or as some prefer to regard it, a superstition) is dispatched towards the graveyard, so for each generation the funeral obsequies have to be solemnly reobserved. Indeed it is ironic that despite the manifest advances in evolutionary biology the science–religion debate is more likely to sound like an old-fashioned record, with the needle permanently stuck in the groove. Maybe religion, and from now on I will address only Christianity, is taking an unconscionably long time to expire because in the final analysis people hardly warm to the idea that they are meaningless products of a blind process. After all, aren't we repeatedly told that this is a process where indeed some get lucky and most don't, but irrespective of whether or not you are a wealthy and successful Anglo-Saxon male don't forget that ultimately the whole show is massively and stupendously pointless. Perhaps so. Possibly, however, the supposed difficulties lie in quite another direction. Could it be that there is a far more fundamental misapprehension of not only what Christianity purports to claim but what metaphysical burden scientific knowledge can be reasonably expected to bear? And linked to the second point, is it conceivable that just as we condescendingly look to the exponents of phlogiston or more topically "cold fusion," so even today there are clear signs that aspects of reality remain scientifically intractable. This is not because we lack the machinery or money, but because the phenomena they entail are simply inaccessible to the current scientific method.

Christianity and Science

Perhaps we should also consider whether science and Christianity might have more in common than is supposed by either group of partisans? Although it is not universally accepted, I remain impressed by the suggestion that science was only likely to arise in a society which believed the world to have had a beginning (and so a particular history that might in principle point to a culmination), to be organized in a way that was open to rational investigation, and where beauty was not an accident of the beholder. And where might the identities of science and Christianity begin to coincide? Both, of course, depend on fundamental tenets that are themselves not open to verification, even if one is encouraged by the continued emergence of consistencies. Christians can provide no proof of God, scientists no proof of why their understanding actually works. Both seek an increase of knowledge, and although non-theists may parody the dogma of Christianity they mistake the fundamentals with its application to new scientific insights (say, the Big Bang) or ethical problems (say, abortion as a great evil; see Beckwith 2007). This is not to say that either can avoid being reactionary: who is not familiar with the entrenched position? But far more important is that both enterprises are open-ended.

In some ways Christianity is the more remarkable because it makes such startling claims, but it is important to remember that so far as science is concerned the widespread belief (or rather faith) that we are in any way close to a totality of knowledge is surely risible. If, in addressing the phenomenon of quantum non-locality and the apparently baffling phenomenon of quantum entanglement, Nicolas Gisin (2009, 1358) can write "No story in space-time can tell us how nonlocal correlations happen; hence, nonlocal quantum correlations seem to emerge, somehow, from outside space-time," then this might suggest that we are dealing with unfinished business. Could indeed the world around us prove to be far stranger than we care to believe? Emphatically, this thought is not intended as any sort of "proof of God"; as already noted, such do not exist. But the area of science addressed by Gisin, counterparted most obviously in the enigma of consciousness (and indeed some investigators believe that quantum processes are our best avenue to explain consciousness), is a powerful reminder that the universe we perceive may be but one tiny island in an ocean of as yet ungrasped potentialities.

This view is not to imply that one day science and Christianity will somehow come to mean the same thing in some sort of Comtian bliss of positivist reconciliation. Rather the reverse. Attempts to wed the two in one or other syncretistic project usually make for embarrassing reading. Reconciliation is not the same as fusion. Christianity effectively is an account of what happens when the Creator makes an apparently surprise visit (although with the benefit of hindsight one that was very much on the cards) to his fallen creation. Science tells us not only how this creation works, and in doing so increasingly reveals its extraordinary subtlety, but also poses the still unanswered question as to why at least one of its products is so uncannily effective in understanding it.

Evolutionary Myths

From this perspective evolution might be seen in a more interesting light. What if evolution is the entirely unremarkable mechanism that ensures that the universe becomes self-aware? As ever, one can see the secular agents raising their hands in horror, although they might do well to consider how very peculiar this self-awareness is. But so too they might protest that even if one species is gifted enough to understand, however dimly, the world from which it arose, what importance can this possibly hold given the billions of other species that have evolved? And this allows us to consider one of the most tenacious of evolutionary myths, that of the "twig."Geometrically, of course, we are just that, one slender end point in the vast arborescence that forms the Tree of Life. One tiny "twig" we may be, but recall we are the only species to know this. Second, even if almost the entire Tree is ossified (that is, extinct and effectively known only from the fossil record), all the surrounding "twigs" represent the exploration of a potentially immense biological hyperspace. But the most important question to ask is as follows. As the Tree of Life grew to its current size (and although there is no space here to discuss this aspect, there is some reason to think that it is now not far off its maximum possible size), was its shape effectively accidental, that is determined by the innumerable contingencies in the history of life? At first sight it would seem difficult to avoid this point of view, perhaps most obviously because of the evolutionary mayhem that arises from a mass extinction or comparable environmental disasters. To be sure life bounces back, but, so it is argued, in a completely unpredictable direction. So a giant tsunami rolls across the edge of a continent, but by a freak of circumstance one chattering group of monkeys watches the water swirl beneath them while other species are swept to their doom. It is all a matter of luck. I suggest that this view, however deeply embedded in the neo-Darwinian zeitgeist, is fundamentally incorrect because a good argument can be made that evolution is a much more predictable process than has been thought (Conway Morris 2010b). Should this view prove correct then it is important to insist at once that in no sense is this a hostage to fortune so far as non-scientific manifestations such as "intelligent design" are concerned.

What science, including that of evolution, does reveal is the deeply interpenetrating order of the world. This, when combined with our capacity to understand it, indicates that if it is all a splendid accident then it is a very odd sort of accident. And here, I would suggest, we begin to find theological resonances. As with Christianity, although the rules of organization are evident the actual results still continue to surprise us. Woven into a deeply embedded order one senses an extraordinary creativity, so in its long history the universe demonstrates an astonishing capacity for self-fructification. From an unpromising sea of elementary particles to roughly 14 billion years later, so the component atoms form our brains by which the universe blinks into self-consciousness. In parentheses we might also observe that the view as to how the immense size and age of the universe can only reinforce our utter insignificance can be countered by the argument that in no other circumstances would we have been able to evolve. Making carbon, making animals, not to mention making brains, all take time. From the instantiation of the Big Bang (which is the closest we will ever get to observing, *per impossible, creation ex nihilo*; Conway Morris 2010c) it was inevitable that we would see the universe only at a given time. And this too echoes the claims of historical Christianity.

Predictable Evolution?

So what is the evidence for evolution being predictable? Whilst most evidence has been derived from the phenomenon of evolutionary convergence, there are several other lines of argument that reinforce this argument. Emphatically this view denies nothing Darwin (or his successors) said, neither does it claim the predictions are precise. Nor for that matter does it regard history and its contingencies as irrelevant. It does, however, insist that renewed emphasis should be given to the emergence of biological properties. In other words if biological form is constrained then the Darwinian mechanism simply provides the means to get from A to B, but it is ill equipped to say what either A or B might actually look like. Thus in evolutionary biology one could look to a Heraclitean flux of process, an Aristotelian set of causations, and the identification of Platonic forms, but all set in a creative act, freely given.

Evolutionary convergence is familiar to all biologists, and simply observes that from different starting points in the Tree of Life similar forms emerge. Often a distinction is made between parallelism and convergence, with the former identifying similar forms evolving in relatively closely related forms. Thus, one might argue that the evolution of a saber-tooth marsupial (thylacosmilid) is less surprising given that its placental cousin shares a mammalian dentition. Conversely, the evolution of a camera-eye in the octopus (and related cephalopods) is the more remarkable given that the common ancestor of this group and the vertebrates did not look remotely like any sort of octopus or fish, and this primitive form at most would have had a simple eye-spot. Yet whilst marsupial and placental mammals are patently more closely related to each other than are cephalopods to vertebrates, the parallelism of the former grades into the convergence of the latter. There is, therefore, a continuum (see Kaster and Berger 1977).

This observation extends to the more general principle that homoplasy (that is, employing the standard term in cladistic methodology, characters that have evolved independently) is ubiquitous in all parts of the Tree of Life. In other words in any clade, of any size, the diversification of taxa (which might be modest or exuberant) is accompanied by rampant homoplasy. This has two implications. The first, and more obvious, is that however spectacular the adaptive radiation may be, the various forms that evolve do not have unlimited potentiality. Certain combinations of characters are much more likely to evolve, hence the prevalence of homoplasy. This is not completely deterministic, and all biologists are familiar with particular taxa (usually of low diversity) that consist of unusual character combinations. Of course the mathematics of combinatorials ensures that even with a fairly limited number of characters the range of alternatives can be quite substantial. It remains, however, to be established just how many are viable in practice rather than in principle. A reasonable suspicion is that some, possibly many, combinations work in theory but are disastrously maladaptive in the wider world.

The second implication may be the more profound, even though it arises from the first. If any radiation (large or small) is constrained in terms of the number of outcomes (because the starting point can necessarily only be a small fraction of all biological possibilities), then one might presume that if the evolutionary processes remain the same at each and any bifurcation (in other words, there are no specifically distinct macroevolutionary processes), then presumably these restrictions on what can evolve will apply across the entire Tree of Life. In other words the areas open to biological occupation are much more highly constrained than is often imagined, and whilst indeed from our perspective the Tree of Life has occupied an immense area, it is an infinitesimally small fraction of all theoretical possibilities. This rather deterministic view of the Tree of Life, suggesting that not only is any future diversification constrained by a "memory" of its immediate antecedents but that the area available for occupation is smaller, possibly much smaller, than the theoretical maximum, might be undermined by at least three pitfalls. None, however, appears to be fatal.

Three Evolutionary Pitfalls

The first is the least important and revolves around the idea of "deep homology" (Shubin *et al.* 2009). This argues that if, for instance, animal eyes all employ a particular developmental gene (in this case *Pax-6*), then notwithstanding the diversity of eyes all are homologous, and to say they are convergent misses the point. "Deep homology," however, suffers from overliteralism (Conway Morris 2009). First, some of the genes central to eye development (such as one known as *sine oculis*) appeared before the first eye. Second, in the most primitive animals with complex eyes (a group of jellyfish known as cubozoans or box jellies) the gene involved is a *Pax* gene, but is not close to *Pax-6*. Third, eye development involves much more than just *Pax-6*, and more tellingly the complex of genes are deployed in a variety of other roles in the nervous system. Finally, in a classic case of cooption the eye genes are also known to be involved in muscle development in birds. If "deep homology" meant anything then we would be forced to equate eye and muscle. These observations also resonate with evolutionary convergence. We should not be surprised if in stickle-back fish and manatees a reduction of the pelvis (including a characteristic asymmetry) employs the same genetic mechanism (*Pitx1*), even though a considerable evolutionary gap separates them (Shapiro *et al.* 2006). If their common ancestor possessed *Pitx1*, it makes "sense" that they continue to employ it. But this is by no means always the case, and in many other instances strikingly similar morphological arrangements in even closely related groups have different genetic bases.

The second potential pitfall is the possibility that many major transitions, say the origin of the eukaryotic cell, are the result of a fortuitous concatenation of unrelated events, the probability of which is extremely small. Unfortunately these sorts of question are largely frustrated by our ignorance of precisely how the eukaryotic cell evolved. Yet two lines of evidence suggest that eukaryosis, arguably the single most important evolutionary event in the history of life given it is the necessary prerequisite for any sort of complex body, is far from improbable. First, within certain bacteria features crucial to eukaryotic organization, such as a nuclear envelope, organelle-like structures and internal membranes have evolved independently (e.g., Fuerst and Webb 1991; Lindsay *et al.* 2001; Herskovits *et al.* 2002). So too proteins that are central to eukaryotic function, such as tubulin, are present in bacteria (e.g., Graumann 2007), and in some cases even adopt eukaryote-like functions (Wang *et al.* 2010). Second, endosymbiotic events that involved the incorporation of once free-living bacteria are central to eukaryotic success as manifested by the chloroplasts (once cyanobacteria) and mitochondria (once rickettsialean-like proteobacteria), yet examples such as the ongoing endosymbiosis between an amoeba (*Paulinella*) and a cyanobacteria (e.g., Marin *et al.* 2005; Nakayama and Ishida 2009) suggest such events may be crucial but are far from fortuitous. The example of bacterial tubulin is also a reminder of what might be termed molecular inherency, that is the extraordinary capacity by which a given protein can be redeployed in a completely new context. And of this principle the crystallins of eyes are perhaps the best-known example.

These two pitfalls together indicate that not only are evolutionary transformations facile (in so much as they look to a substrate that is largely pre-existent and depends as much on a modular redeployment), but are consistent with the restriction of possibilities that is reflected in the ubiquity of evolutionary convergence.

The third pitfall, however, is non-biological and historical, and reminds the student of the history of life that it is punctuated by numerous disasters that if sufficiently traumatic might radically redirect the courses of evolution given that the extent of extinction (that amongst Permian marine species might have exceeded 90%) is so severe that the grim reaper is effectively indiscriminate. A new, if battered world emerges, but the ensuing trajectories are largely governed by chance survival. If correct, this would fundamentally undermine any likelihood that evolution has probable, let alone predictable, outcomes. But is it correct? The most-cited example of why mass extinctions are radically contingent concerns the end-Cretaceous or K/T event and the extirpation of the great reptiles (notably the terrestrial dinosaurs, marine mosasaurs, and aerial pterosaurs). Their removal led to a vacant ecology that the mammals were quick to occupy, not least those arboreal excursionists who in due course evolved into monkeys and apes. No extinction, so the argument goes, ultimately no us. But suppose for whatever reason the great reptiles survived the disaster and reclaimed their dominance? Their fate was still sealed. Some 20 Ma after their narrow shave the glaciations that culminated in the current Ice Age began, with cooling of the planet, especially in the temperate and polar zones. If the great reptiles survived, there is no reason to think that the birds and mammals would not have done so (and, of course, both groups evolved in the Mesozoic, alongside the dinosaurs), but their response to this climatic change would have been very different. Sooner rather than later, one or other species – warm-blooded, socially adept, more intelligent and independently arriving at tool-making –would regard a dinosaur not as a thing to be avoided, but a thing to be hunted (just as in fact happened with the mammalian megafaunas). Far from radically redirecting the course of evolutionary history, mass extinctions have a far more valuable role. They provide evolutionary time for free, accelerating an inevitable process, perhaps lopping off an equivalent of 50 Ma.

The Emergence of Cognition

The idea that dinosaurs would disappear under a hail of arrows and spears, rather than the choking dust, blazing forests, and towering tsunami of the actual K/T event, might seem more appropriate to science fiction, until we recall perhaps the most important aspect of evolutionary convergence, that is, the inevitable emergence of cognitive capacity and consciousness. Not only has the universe become self-aware, but it is enabled in its investigatory program with an ability not just to reveal its own origins (McNamara 2004), but a dawning realization that the world about us is not only very cannily organized but also offers the favored species the opportunities of transcendence. Recent work has very much focused on the convergence of cognitive capacities between the birds (especially corvids, and also parrots) and the great apes (e.g., Emery and Clayton 2004). Particularly telling in this context are the tool-making capacities of such birds as the New Caledonian crow (e.g., Chappell and Kacelnik 2002) that involve both combined tool use (e.g., Taylor et al. 2007) and successive modification that deserves the cognomen of a prototechnology (e.g., Hunt 2000; Hunt and Gray 2003). It might be objected that notwithstanding the disparate structure of the bird brain in comparison with that of an ape, other similarities are driven by not only a terrestrial but also primarily arboreal existence. This in turn, it might be argued, will constrain the cognitive capacity so that ultimately this particular convergence is rather trivial. Tree-dwellers will think alike. That this is unlikely is evident from the cognitive world of the dolphins, which again converges on that of the apes (e.g., Marino 1996). True, both are mammals, but again the brain structures show significant divergences, and as importantly we are dealing with a handless oceanic creature (but one which can still employ tools; Krützen et al. 2005) whose sensory modalities include a central role for echolocation. These similarities in cognitive worlds are unlikely to be accidental.

It is important also to recall that the capacity for some sort of intelligence probably goes much deeper into the Tree of Life than is sometimes realized, and it is likely that some aspects of its molecular underpinning also arose at a very early stage. Evidence, for instance, continues to accumulate as to the convergences between the intelligence of the vertebrates and the octopus, and the likelihood that the latter are also conscious (e.g., Mather 2008). So too at a much deeper phylogenetic level experiments with the protistan plasmodium involving the solving of maze experiments (e.g., Nakagaki 2001) and a capacity for memory (Saigusa et al. 2008) can be taken to represent "a primitive intelligence" (Nakagaki et al. 2000). Nor should any of this particularly surprise us. A basis of sentience and ultimately consciousness must in part be molecular, employing specific compounds (such as acetylcholine; see, e.g.,

Kawashima *et al.* 2007) and cell communication (including the employment of vesicles) that evolved long before any nervous system. So, too, in plants and fungi some 30% of the genes required in the nervous system have already evolved (Mineta *et al.* 2003).

The capacity for mind is, therefore, inherent in the evolutionary process, but it would be entirely mistaken to extrapolate such an observation to argue that this thereby explains either mind or consciousness. Rather the reverse. The very success of scientific investigation in documenting both the cellular processes within the brain and the pathways whereby a physical stimulus, say photon or molecule, impinging onto the appropriate sensory receptor (in this case eye or nose) is perceived as red or the taste of Château Petrus ("the '49, I do believe") provides no insight as to why that first sip of wine immediately propels us back decades, to holding a girl's hand, in the cool of an evening on a terrace in France, as the bats twittered overhead, and the conjunction of Venus and Jupiter hung as a jewel in the sky. In fact, the very precision of detail that is now available to neurobiologists seems to lead paradoxically to a deeper incoherence. It is not just that we have no clue as to why any of these molecular gyrations equate to a conscious sensation; we should have no trust in a particular chemical configuration being in any way trustworthy.

To know, for example, that in the part of the brain that deals with numerosity, particular neurons are coded for particular numbers (and so the basis of all mathematics) gives us no understanding as to why we should understand even $2 + 2$. This particular case is also of importance because of evidence that numerosity (and such features as magnitude differences), which we might assume entails cognitive decisions, is actually perceived in the same way as sensory processes (and follow the Weber–Fechner law of non-proportionality; see Nieder and Miller 2003). Here, too, do we simply delude ourselves that what we fondly believe to be ratiocination is simply a phantom? Such existential bleakness is difficult to square with not only the effectiveness of mathematics (why should Fermat's last theorem actually *mean* anything?), but our capacity to employ hypotheses, let alone imagination. Nevertheless the divergence of opinion regarding the nature of mind is simply startling. By the majority of evolutionary biologists it is regarded as some sort of emergent property, or at least is regarded as a problem "solved" by reference to various sorts of brain imaging, effects of drugs, or damage to brain tissue. Clearly, in this view the mind can reside nowhere else, and that is the end of the matter. "Neuromythologists," as Raymond Tallis (2008) pithily calls them. For the great majority of philosophers matters are not nearly so straightforward, and at their first approximation the questions seem intractable. There seems no *a priori* reason why mind should emerge from matter. The solution (if that is the word) is to postulate that mind is identifiably different. This need not lead to dualism. Consider this alternative, that whilst mind is certainly embodied in one sense, we serve as receptacles, or perhaps better an "antenna," for mind. From this perspective, we should be neither surprised that we have access to truths that are themselves immaterial, nor immediately dismiss "out-of-body" experiences.

The implications of this for both evolutionary biology and theology are interesting. Nothing in the biological organization of the brain appears to explain why it is conscious. Recall that although much is made of its electrical activity induced by the polarization of the membranes, for all intents and purposes the brain is a chemical machine. For this reason alone we should not be surprised if in some form sentience extends far beyond the animals (some investigators cheerfully refer to plant neurobiology) and might suggest that the metaphor of "dawning consciousness" is not inappropriate. But it is the theological implications that are even more intriguing. Talk of mind as a real property invites consideration of a wide spectrum of issues, such as the nature of free will (the emergence of which from a materiality which is oblivious to intentionality seems to be incoherent), the sense of purpose, and the likelihood that whilst our minds are necessarily embodied (although near-death experiences suggest this is not essential) in other agencies mind could still be very much part of the universe but from our mundane perspective immaterial.

As already argued evolution appears to act as a search engine for all possibilities, not only reaching the physico-chemical limits of the world (as shown in extremophiles; Conway Morris 2010a) but also evolving a recurrent configuration that allows the universe to begin to understand itself. None of this, of course, would have been possible without the initial fine-tuning of the universe at its instantiation, but neither would these constants of nature be identified in the absence of a conscious agent.

And Christianity?

What then of Christianity? It should be evident that the above arguments should do no violence to the outlook of a theist. But Christianity makes very specific claims about not only the nature of creation but God's agency in it. Not only does it diverge from its sister monotheisms, who one might say are peoples of the Book rather than peoples of Jesus Christ, but more importantly, in the context of the secular agents whose self-appointed task is to act as guardians of the flame to Darwinism, any claims of Christianity must by definition be absurd. The idea of a god may be bad enough, but to have him wandering around in an out-of-the-way nook of the Roman empire, with a raggle-taggle band of followers, then fizzling out in an all too common method of execution, and to cap it all to claim he was God incarnate seems risible. They might, however, benefit from a refresher course in theology rather than sitting at the feet of the village atheist.

What we seem to see is an interpenetration of worlds, with the unavoidable conclusion that much lies beyond our mundane expectations. Such is evident from the Transfiguration, Resurrection, and Ascension. Science in its present primitive state has very little useful to say about any of these events: just because they are inexplicable does not mean they did not happen. In this context note too that any species inhabits a specific *Umwelt* (Kováč 2010), and as this author notes:

> There is undeniably a world outside the confinements of our species-specific *Umwelt*, but if the world of humans is too complex for the neural ganglia of beetles, the world beyond Kant's barriers may similarly exceed the capacity of the human brain. (Kováč 2010, 410)

Maybe so, and quantum mechanics is a warning to the curious. But we can also enquire not only whether there are limits of rational investigation, but also transcendence. And in this context we can observe two things. First, Jesus could explain what he was about only to a species that had evolved to a necessary stage. And in this context we need to recall that attempts to extrapolate what defines our humanness from even our closest relatives seem forced. This is certainly not to invoke some "God-of-the gaps" argument, let alone attempt to circumvent our evolutionary origins. The former is unnecessary, the latter ludicrous. Yet as the Australian philosopher David Stove (2006) reminds us, attempts to extrapolate across the gulf that separates us from the animals are "Darwinian fairytales." As an atheist he has no theological axe to grind, but his insistence suggests we might need to seek yet another order of explanation if we are to account for this emergence. Jesus, so I suppose, would have talked to the crows and dolphins if they had anything to say.

But these claims of Christianity – especially the Resurrection – not only remain central to this religion, but by their very nature define a universe of which we can only see a very small part. Science could explain the Resurrection only if it knew something of what lies beyond our mundane world, but by definition it cannot. Neither, by definition, can it even know everything about our world – it is silent as to the virtues of Mozart's Mass in C minor or T. S. Eliot's *Four Quartets*. But they too are in fact pointers to other worlds, which Paul clearly understood. Let us conclude with an imaginary dialogue between Paul of Tarsus and Charles Darwin.

Paul: Before my last imprisonment I saw many animals, the dog that swam ashore with us at Malta, a cur being whipped on the road to Ephesus, but most vividly I recall what happened a week after I first arrived in Rome. A caravan of beasts, being taken to the Circus; they were miserable, but I was most struck with some monkeys, larger than I had ever seen, and evidently of immense strength. An attendant slave told me that they had come from far to the south of Carthage.

Darwin: Did they not remind you of ourselves?

Paul: Grotesquely, yes, not least with a female who continued to nurse a young, unaware that within a few days they would be brief sport to the braying mob.

Darwin: If I was to tell you that we humans evolved from just such an animal, would you not be shocked and dismayed?

Paul: Once certainly, but for many years I have pondered all that suddenly became clear on that dusty road. As I told Luke and the others, the scales fell from my eyes, and from that moment I saw not just the world, not just the cosmos, but all of Creation, joined and despite all the evil loved beyond compassion.

Darwin: I've heard the story, and similar, but they are too fantastical. Consider those monkeys. My dear friend Huxley tells me our brains are scarcely to be distinguished, and to be honest now I wonder why as a descendant of such brutes I should have faith that what I myself think is even remotely true.

Paul: You are to be pitied; all those years of investigation into God's glory and you even begin to distrust your own mind.

Darwin: Not distrust, only –

Paul: The Greeks, and, yes, I know them better than might appear, would see you as a victim of Irony, even Tragedy. Those years of thought, as your path turned ever more arid, as mine was of shipwreck, hunger, and beatings, but which far more importantly led to the dawning realization that as God made everything so the Resurrection must echo to the stars. So before Adam, a monkey? Well, are we not all one creation?

References

Artigas, Mariano, Glick, Thomas F., and Martínez, Rafael A. 2006. *Negotiating Darwin: The Vatican Confronts Evolution 1877–1902*. Baltimore: Johns Hopkins University Press.

Beckwith, Francis J. 2007. *Defending Life: A Moral and Legal Case against Abortion Choice*. Cambridge: Cambridge University Press.

Chappell, Jackie and Kacelnik, Alex. 2002. Tool Selectivity in a Non-Primate, the New Caledonian Crow (*Corvus moneduloides*). *Animal Cognition*, 5, pp. 71–78.

Conway Morris, Simon. 2009. The Predictability of Evolution: Glimpses into a Post-Darwinian World. *Naturwissenschaften*, 96, pp. 1313–1337.

Conway Morris, Simon. 2010a. Aliens at Home? *EMBO Reports*, 11(8), p. 563.

Conway Morris, Simon. 2010b. Evolution: Like Any Other Science It Is Predictable. *Philosophical Transactions of the Royal Society of London B*, 365(1537), pp. 133–145.

Conway Morris, Simon. 2010c. What Is Written into Creation? In David B. Burrell, Carlo Cogliati, Janet M. Soskice and William R. Stoeger, eds. *Creation and the God of Abraham*. Cambridge: Cambridge University Press, pp. 176–191.

Darwin, Charles. 1859. *On the Origin of Species, by Means of Natural Selection, etc.* London: John Murray.

Emery, Nathan J. and Clayton, Nicola S. 2004. The Mentality of Crows: Convergent Evolution of Intelligence in Corvids and Apes. *Science*, 306(5703), pp. 1903–1907.

Fuerst, John A. and Webb, Richard I. 1991. Membrane-Bounded Nucleoid in the Eubacterium *Gemmata obscuriglobus*. *Proceedings of the National Academy of Sciences of the USA*, 88(18), pp. 8184–8188.

Gisin, Nicolas. 2009. Quantum Nonlocality: How Does Nature Do It? *Science*, 326(5958), pp. 1357–1358.

Graumann, Peter L. 2007. Cytoskeletal Elements in Bacteria. *Annual Review of Microbiology*, 61, pp. 589–618.

Gruber, Jacob W. 1960. *A Conscience in Conflict: The Life of St. George Jackson Mivart*. New York: Columbia University Press.

Herskovits, Anat A., Shimoni Eyal, Minsky, Abraham and Bibi, Eitan. 2002. Accumulation of Endoplasmic Membranes and Novel Membrane-Bound Ribosome-Signal Recognition Particle Receptor Complexes in *Escherichia coli*. *Journal of Cell Biology*, 159(3), pp. 403–410.

Hunt, Gavin Raymond. 2000. Human-Like, Population-Level Specialization in the Manufacture of Pandanus Tools by New Caledonian Crows *Corvus moneduloides*. *Proceedings of the Royal Society of London B*, 267(1441), pp. 403–413.

Hunt, Gavin Raymond and Gray, Russell D. 2003. Diversification and Cumulative Evolution in New Caledonian Crow Tool Manufacture. *Proceedings of the Royal Society of London B*, 270(1517), pp. 867–874.

Kaster, Jerry and Berger, Joel. 1977. Convergent and Parallel Evolution: A Model Illustrating Selection, Phylogeny, and Phenetic Similarity. *Biosystems*, 9(4), pp. 195–200.

Kawashima, Koichiro, Misawa, Hidemi, Moriwaki, Yasuhiro *et al.* 2007. Ubiquitous Expression of Acetylcholine and Its Biological Functions in Life Forms without Nervous Systems. *Life Sciences*, 80(24–25), pp. 2206–2209.

Kováč, Ladislav. 2010. A "Metaphising" Dung Beetle. *EMBO Reports*, 11(6), p. 410.

Krützen, Michael, Mann, Janet, Heithaus, Michael R. *et al.* 2005. Cultural Transmission of Tool Use in Bottlenose Dolphins. *Proceedings of the National Academy of Sciences of the USA*, 102(25), pp. 8939–8943.

Lindsay, Margaret R., Webb, Richard I., Strous, Marc *et al.* 2001. Cell Compartmentalisation in Planctomycetes: Novel Types of Structural Organization for the Bacterial Cell. *Archives of Microbiology*, 175(6), pp. 413–429.

Marin, Birger, Nowack, Eva C. M., and Melkonian, Michael. 2005. A Plastid in the Making: Evidence for a Secondary Primary Endosymbiosis. *Protist*, 156(4), pp. 425–432.

Marino, Lori. 1996. What Can Dolphins Tell Us about Primate Evolution? *Evolutionary Anthropology*, 5(3), pp. 81–85.

Mather, Jennifer A. 2008. Cephalopod Consciousness: Behavioural Evidence. *Consciousness and Cognition*, 17(1), pp. 37–48.

McNamara, Ken. 2004. *It's True! We Came from Slime*. Sydney: Allen & Unwin.

Mineta, Katsuhiko, Nakazawa, Masumi, Cabrià, Francesc *et al.* 2003. Origin and Evolutionary Process of the CNS Elucidated by Comparative Genomics Analysis of Planarian ESTs. *Proceedings of the National Academy of Sciences of the USA*, 100(13), pp. 7666–7671.

Mivart, St George Jackson. 1871. *On the Genesis of Species*. New York: D. Appleton and Company.

Nakagaki, Toshiyuki. 2001. Smart Behavior of True Slime Mold in a Labyrinth. *Research in Microbiology*, 152(9), pp. 767–770.

Nakagaki, Toshiyuki, Yamada, Hiroyasu, and Tóth, Ágota. 2000. Intelligence: Maze-Solving by an Amoeboid Organism. *Nature*, 407(6803), p. 470.

Nakayama, Takuro and Ishida, Ken-ichiro. 2009. Another Acquisition of a Primary Photosynthetic Organelle Is Underway in *Paulinella chromatophora*. *Current Biology*, 19(7), pp. R284–R285.

Nieder, Andreas and Miller, Earl K. 2003. Coding of Cognitive Magnitude. *Neuron*, 37(1), pp. 149–157.

Rupke, Nicholas A. 2009. *Richard Owen: Biology without Darwin*. Chicago: University of Chicago Press.

Saigusa, Tetsu, Tero, Atsushi, Nakagaki, Toshiyuki, and Kuramoto, Yoshiki. 2008. Amoebae Anticipate Periodic Events. *Physical Review Letters*, 100(1), art. 018101.

Shapiro, Michael D., Bell, Michael A., and Kingsley, David M. 2006. Parallel Genetic Origins of Pelvic Reduction in Vertebrates. *Proceedings of the National Academy of Sciences of the USA*, 103(37), pp. 13753–13758.

Shubin, Neil, Tabin, Cliff, and Carroll, Sean. 2009. Deep Homology and the Origins of Evolutionary Novelty. *Nature*, 457(7231), pp. 818–823.

Stove, David. 2006. *Darwinian Fairytales: Selfish Genes, Errors of Heredity and Other Fables of Evolution*. New York: Encounter Books.

Tallis, Raymond. 2008. *The Kingdom of Infinite Space: A Fantastical Journey around Your Head*. London: Atlantic Books.

Taylor, Alex H., Hunt, Gavin R., Holzhaider, Jennifer C., and Gray, Russell D. 2007. Spontaneous Meta-tool Use by New Caledonian Crows. *Current Biology*, 17(17), pp. 1504–1507.

Wang, Siyuan, Arellano-Santoyo, Hugo, Combs, Peter A., and Shaevitz, Joshua W. 2010. Actin-Like Cytoskeleton Filaments Contribute to Cell Mechanics in Bacteria. *Proceedings of the National Academy of Sciences of the USA*, 107(20), pp. 9182–9185.

Further Reading

Conway Morris, Simon. 2004. *Life's Solution: Inevitable Humans in a Lonely Universe*. Cambridge: Cambridge University Press. A monograph in which examples of convergence are compiled and the thesis defended that evolution is remarkably predictable.

Conway Morris, Simon, ed. 2008. *The Deep Structure of Biology: Is Convergence Sufficiently Ubiquitous to Give a Directional Signal?* West Conshohocken, PA: Templeton Foundation Press. A collection of articles by 12 scientists, philosophers, and theologians reflecting on evolution.

24

Signature in the Cell
Intelligent Design and the DNA Enigma

STEPHEN C. MEYER

When James Watson and Francis Crick elucidated the structure of DNA in 1953, they solved one mystery but created another.

For almost a hundred years after the publication of Charles Darwin's *The Origin of Species*, biology had rested secure in the knowledge that it had explained one of humankind's most enduring enigmas. From ancient times, observers had noticed organized structures in living organisms that gave the appearance of having been designed for a purpose – the elegant form and protective covering of the coiled nautilus, the interdependent parts of the eye, the interlocking bones, muscles and feathers of a bird wing.

But with the advent of Darwinism, and later neo-Darwinism, modern science claimed to explain the appearance of design in life as the product of a purely undirected process. In the *Origin*, Darwin argued that the striking appearance of design in living organisms – in particular, the way they are so well adapted to their environments – could be explained by natural selection working on random variations, a purely undirected process that nevertheless mimicked the powers of a designing intelligence. Thus, as evolutionary biologist Francisco Ayala (2007, 8567) notes, Darwin accounted for "design without a designer." Indeed, since 1859 the appearance of design in living things has been understood by most biologists to be an illusion – a powerfully suggestive illusion but an illusion nonetheless. Or as Francis Crick put it, biologists must "constantly keep in mind that what they see was not designed, but rather evolved" (Crick 1988, 138).

But thanks in large measure to Watson and Crick's own discovery of the information-bearing properties of DNA, scientists have become increasingly, and in some quarters acutely, aware that there is at least one appearance of design in biology that has not been explained by natural selection or any other purely naturalistic mechanism. When Watson and Crick discovered the structure of DNA, they also discovered that DNA stores information in the form of a four-character alphabetic code. Strings of precisely sequenced chemicals called *nucleotide bases* store and transmit the assembly instructions – the information – for building the crucial protein molecules and protein machines the cell needs to survive.

Crick later developed this idea with his famous "sequence hypothesis," according to which the chemical parts of DNA (the nucleotide bases) function like letters in a written language

The Blackwell Companion to Science and Christianity, First Edition. Edited by J. B. Stump and Alan G. Padgett.
© 2012 Blackwell Publishing Ltd. Published 2012 by Blackwell Publishing Ltd.

or symbols in a computer code. Just as letters in an English sentence or digital characters in a computer program may convey information depending on their arrangement, so too do certain sequences of chemical bases along the spine of the DNA molecule convey precise instructions for building proteins.

Moreover, DNA sequences do not just have a mathematically measurable degree of improbability. Thus, they do not just possess "information" in the strictly mathematical sense of the theory of information developed by the famed MIT scientist Claude Shannon in the late 1940s. Instead, DNA contains information in the richer and more ordinary dictionary sense of "alternative sequences or arrangements of characters that produce a specific effect." DNA base sequences convey instructions. They perform functions and produce specific effects. Thus, they do not possess mere "Shannon information," but instead what has been called "specified" or "functional information." Indeed, like the precisely arranged 0s and 1s in a computer program, the chemical bases in DNA convey instructions in virtue of their "specificity" of arrangement. Thus, Richard Dawkins (1995, 17) notes that "the machine code of the genes is uncannily computer-like," and software developer Bill Gates (1995, 188) observes that "DNA is like a computer program." Similarly, biotechnology specialist Leroy Hood (Hood and Galas 2003) describes the information stored in DNA as "digital code."

But if this is true, how did the *functionally specified information* in DNA arise? Is this striking appearance of design the product of actual design or a natural process that can mimic the powers of a designing intelligence? This question is related to a long-standing mystery in biology – the question of the origin of the first life. Indeed, since Watson and Crick's discovery, scientists have increasingly come to understand the centrality of information to even the simplest living systems. DNA stores the assembly instructions for building the many crucial proteins and protein machines that service and maintain even the most primitive one-celled organisms. It follows that building a living cell in the first place requires assembly instructions stored in DNA or some equivalent molecule. As origin-of-life researcher Bernd-Olaf Küppers (1990, 170) has explained, "The problem of the origin-of-life is clearly basically equivalent to the problem of the origin of biological information."

Today the question of how life first originated is widely regarded as a profound and unsolved scientific problem, largely because of the mystery surrounding the origin of functionally specified biological information. This chapter will examine the various attempts that have been made to solve this mystery – what I call "the DNA enigma" – and it will argue that intelligent design, rather than an undirected mechanism that merely mimics design, best explains it.

Early Theories of the Origin of Life

Darwin's theory sought to explain the origin of new forms of life from simpler forms. It did not explain how the first life – presumably a simple one-celled organism – might have arisen to begin with. Nevertheless, in the 1860s and 1870s scientists assumed that devising a materialistic explanation for the origin of life would be fairly easy and, therefore, they did not worry that one-celled organisms might betray evidence of design.

Instead, scientists at the time assumed that life was essentially a rather simple substance called protoplasm that could be easily constructed by combining and recombining simple chemicals such as carbon dioxide, oxygen, and nitrogen. German evolutionary biologist Ernst Haeckel likened cell "autogeny," as he called it, to the process of inorganic crystallization.

Haeckel's English counterpart, T. H. Huxley, proposed a simple two-step method of chemical recombination to explain the origin of the first cell. Just as salt could be produced spontaneously by adding sodium to chloride, so they thought could a living cell be produced by adding several chemical constituents together and then allowing spontaneous chemical reactions to produce the simple protoplasmic substance that they assumed to be the essence of life (Meyer 1990, 143–161).

During the 1920s and 1930s a more sophisticated version of this "chemical evolutionary theory" was proposed by a Russian biochemist named Alexander I. Oparin. Oparin, like his nineteenth-century predecessors, suggested that life could have first evolved as the result of a series of chemical reactions. Nevertheless, he envisioned that this process of chemical evolution would involve many more chemical transformations and reactions and hundreds of millions of years. Oparin postulated these additional steps and additional time because he had a more accurate understanding of the complexity of cellular metabolism than did Haeckel and Huxley (Kamminga 1980, 222–245). Nevertheless, neither he, nor anyone else in the 1930s, fully appreciated the complexity – and information-bearing properties – of the DNA, RNA, and proteins that make life possible.

Though Oparin's theory appeared to receive experimental support in 1953 when Stanley Miller simulated the production of the amino acid "building blocks" of proteins under ostensibly pre-biotic atmospheric conditions, his textbook version of chemical evolutionary theory is riddled with difficulties. Miller's simulation experiment is now understood by origin-of-life researchers to have little, if any, relevance to explaining how amino acids – let alone their precise sequencing, which is necessary to produce proteins – could have arisen in the actual atmosphere of the early earth. Moreover, Oparin proposed no explanation for the origin of the information in DNA (or RNA) that present-day cells use to build proteins. As a result, a search for pre-biotic chemical mechanisms to explain the origin of biological information has ensued. Since the 1950s, three broad types of naturalistic explanations have been proposed by scientists in an attempt to explain the origin of the information necessary to produce the first cell.

Beyond the Reach of Chance

One naturalistic view of the origin of life is that it happened exclusively by chance (Wald 1954, 44–53). Since the late 1960s, however, few serious scientists have supported this view (Shapiro 1986, 121; Kamminga 1980, 303–304). Since molecular biologists began to understand how the digital information in DNA directs the construction of protein synthesis in the cell, many calculations have been made to determine the probability of formulating functional proteins and nucleic acids (DNA or RNA molecules) at random. Even assuming extremely favorable pre-biotic conditions (whether realistic or not) and theoretically maximal reaction rates, such calculations have invariably shown that the probability of obtaining functionally sequenced (information-rich) bio-macromolecules at random is, in the words of physicist Ilya Prigogine and his colleagues, "vanishingly small . . . even on the scale of . . . billions of years" (Prigogine et al. 1972, 23).

Even so, origin-of-life scientists recognize that the critical problem is not just generating an improbable sequence of chemical constituents – an improbable arrangement of nucleotide bases in DNA, for example. Instead, the problem is relying on a random search or shuffling of molecular building blocks to generate one of the very rare arrangements of bases in DNA (or amino acids in proteins) that also *perform a biological function*. Very improbable things do occur by chance. Any hand of cards or any series of rolled dice represents an improbable occurrence. Observers often justifiably attribute such events to chance alone. What justifies the elimination of chance is not just the occurrence of a highly improbable event but also the occurrence of an improbable event that conforms to a discernible pattern (either what statisticians call a "conditionally independent pattern" or what I call a "functionally significant pattern," i.e., one that accomplishes a discernable purpose).

If, for example, someone repeatedly rolls two dice and turns up a sequence such as 9, 4, 11, 2, 6, 8, 5, 12, 9, 6, 8, and 4, no one will suspect anything but the interplay of random forces, though this sequence does represent a very improbable event given the number of possible numeric sequences that exist corresponding to a sequence of this length. Yet rolling 12 (or 1200!) consecutive sevens in a game that rewards sevens will justifiably arouse suspicion that something more than chance is in play.

Origin-of-life researchers employ this kind of statistical reasoning to justify the elimination of the chance hypothesis. Christian de Duve (1995a, 437), for example, has made this logic explicit in order to explain why chance fails as an explanation for the origin of life: "A single, freak, highly improbable event can conceivably happen. Many highly improbable events – drawing a winning lottery number or the distribution of playing cards in a hand of bridge – happen all the time. But a string of improbable events – drawing the same lottery number twice, or the same bridge hand twice in a row – does not happen naturally."

In my book *Signature in the Cell* (2009), I perform updated calculations of the probability of the origin of even a single *functional* protein or corresponding *functional* gene (the section of a DNA molecule that directs the construction of a particular protein) by chance alone. My calculations are based upon recent experiments in molecular biology establishing the extreme rarity of functional proteins in relation to the total number of possible arrangements of amino acids corresponding to a protein of a given length. I show that the probability of producing even a single functional protein (a gene product) of modest length (150 amino acids) by chance alone stands at a "vanishingly small" 1 chance in 10^{164}.

Moreover, in *Signature*, I not only demonstrate that the probability of a single functional protein arising at any given time is absurdly small, but also that the probability is even extremely small *in relation to* all the opportunities that have existed for that event to occur since the beginning of time (what are called the "probabilistic resources" of the universe). I show that even if every event in the entire history of the universe (where an event is defined minimally as an interaction between elementary particles) were devoted to producing combinations of amino acids of a given length (an extravagantly generous assumption), the number of combinations thus produced would still represent a tiny portion – fewer than 1 out of a trillion trillion – of the total number of possible amino acid combinations corresponding to a functional protein – *any* functional protein – of that given length. In short, it is extremely unlikely that even a single protein would have arisen by chance on the early earth even taking the probabilistic resources of the entire universe into account. For this and other similar reasons, serious origin-of-life researchers now consider "chance" an inadequate causal explanation for the origin of biological information (de Duve 1996, 112; Crick 1981, 89–93).

Self-Organization Scenarios

Because of these difficulties, many origin-of-life theorists after the mid-1960s addressed the problem of the origin of biological information in a different way. Rather than invoking chance events or "frozen accidents," many theorists suggested that the laws of nature or lawlike forces of chemical attraction might have generated the information in DNA and proteins. Some have suggested that simple chemicals might possess "self-ordering properties" capable of organizing the constituent parts of proteins, DNA, and RNA into the specific arrangements they now possess. Just as electrostatic forces draw sodium (Na+) and chloride ions (Cl−) together into highly ordered patterns within a crystal of salt (NaCl), so too might amino acids with special affinities for each other arrange themselves to form proteins. Kenyon and Steinman (1969) developed this idea in a book entitled *Biochemical Predestination*.

Prigogine and Nicolis (1977, 339–353, 429–447) proposed another theory of self-organization based on their observation that open systems driven far from equilibrium often display self-ordering tendencies. For example, gravitational energy will produce highly ordered vortices in a draining bathtub; and thermal energy flowing through a heat sink will generate distinctive convection currents or "spiral wave activity."

For many current origin-of-life scientists, self-organizational models now seem to offer the most promising approach to explaining the origin of biological information. Nevertheless, critics have called into question both the plausibility and the relevance of such models. Ironically, perhaps the most prominent early advocate of self-organization, Dean Kenyon, has now explicitly repudiated his own and similar theories as both incompatible with empirical findings and theoretically incoherent.

The difficulty in using self-organizational scenarios to explain the origin of biological information can be illustrated by examining the structure of the DNA molecule. Figure 24.1 shows that the structure of DNA depends upon several chemical bonds. There are bonds, for example, between the sugar molecules (designated by the pentagons) and the phosphate molecules (designated by the circled Ps) that form the twisting backbones of the DNA helix. There are bonds fixing individual (nucleotide) bases to the sugar–phosphate backbones on each side of the molecule. Notice, however, that there are no chemical bonds (and thus forces of attraction) between the bases that run along the spine of the helix. Yet it is precisely along this axis of the molecule that the genetic instructions in DNA are encoded.

Further, just as magnetic letters can be combined and recombined in any way to form various sequences on a metal surface, so too can each of the four bases A, T, G, and C attach to any site on the DNA backbone with equal facility, making all sequences equally probable (or improbable). The same type of chemical bond (an N-glycosidic bond) occurs between the bases and the backbone regardless of which base attaches. All four bases are acceptable; none is preferred. Thus, *differences in* bonding affinity do not determine the arrangement of the bases – that is, forces of chemical attraction do not account for the information in DNA.

For those who want to explain the origin of life as the result of self-organizing properties intrinsic to the material constituents of living systems, these rather elementary facts of molecular biology have devastating implications. The most logical place to look for self-organizing properties to explain the origin of genetic information is in the constituent parts of the molecules carrying that information. But biochemistry and molecular biology make clear that the forces of attraction between the constituents in DNA (and RNA) do not explain the sequence specificity (the information) present in these large information-bearing molecules.

Significantly, information theorists insist that there is a good reason for this. If chemical affinities between the bases in the DNA instruction set determined the arrangement of the bases, such affinities would dramatically diminish the capacity of DNA to carry information. Consider what would happen if the individual nucleotide "letters" (A, T, G, C) in a DNA molecule *did* interact by *chemical* necessity with each other. Suppose every time adenine (A)

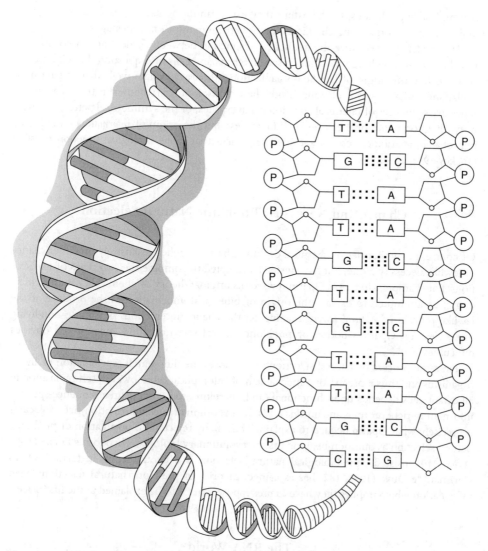

Figure 24.1   The bonding relationship between the chemical constituents of the DNA molecule. Note that no chemical bonds exist between the nucleotide bases along the message-bearing axis of the DNA helix. Courtesy of Fred Heeren.

occurred in a growing genetic sequence, it dragged guanine (G) along with it. And every time cytosine (C) appeared, thymine (T) would follow. As a result, the DNA message text would be peppered with repeating sequences of As followed by Gs and Cs followed by Ts.

Rather than having a genetic molecule capable of unlimited novelty, with all the unpredictable and aperiodic sequences that characterize informative texts, we would have a highly repetitive text awash in redundant sequences – much as happens in crystals. Indeed, in a crystal the forces of mutual chemical attraction do completely explain the sequential ordering of the constituent parts, and consequently crystals cannot convey novel information. For this reason, bonding affinities, to the extent they exist, cannot be used to explain the origin of information. Self-organizing chemical affinities create mantras, not messages.

The tendency to confuse the qualitative distinction between "order" and "information" has characterized self-organizational research efforts and calls into question the relevance of such work to the origin of life. Self-organizational theorists explain well what doesn't need explaining. What needs explaining is not the origin of order (whether in the form of the repetitive sequences of chemical constituents in crystals, or the symmetrical patterns evident in swirling tornadoes or the "eyes" of hurricanes), but the origin of *information* – the highly improbable, aperiodic, and yet specified sequences that make biological function possible (Yockey 1992, 274–281).

Chance and Necessity: Pre-biotic Natural Selection

Of course, many theories of chemical evolution have not relied exclusively on either chance or lawlike necessity alone, but have instead attempted to combine the two types of explanations. For example, after 1953 Oparin revised his original theory of chemical evolution. In so doing, he attempted to explain the origin of biological information as the product of the lawlike process of *natural selection* acting on the chance interactions of simple non-living molecules. Yet Oparin's notion of pre-biotic natural selection soon encountered obvious difficulties.

First, the process of natural selection presupposes the differential reproduction of living organisms and thus a pre-existing mechanism of self-replication. However, self-replication in all extant cells depends upon functional (and, therefore, to a high degree sequence-specific, information-rich) proteins and nucleic acids. Yet the origin of such information-rich molecules is precisely what Oparin needed to explain. Thus many rejected his postulation of pre-biotic natural selection as question-begging. As the evolutionary biologist Theodosius Dobzhansky (1965, 310) insisted, "pre-biological natural selection is a contradiction in terms." Or as Christian de Duve (1991, 187) has explained, theories of pre-biotic natural selection "need information which implies they have to presuppose what is to be explained in the first place."

The RNA World

More recently, some have claimed that another scenario – the RNA-world hypothesis, combining chance and pre-biotic natural selection – can solve the origin-of-life problem and with it, presumably, the problem of the origin of genetic information. The RNA world was proposed as an explanation for the origin of the interdependence of nucleic acids and proteins in the cell's information-processing system. In extant cells, building proteins requires genetic information from DNA, but information in DNA cannot be processed without many specific proteins and protein complexes. This poses a chicken-or-egg problem. The discovery that RNA (a nucleic acid) possesses some limited catalytic properties similar to those of proteins suggested a way to solve that problem. "RNA-first" advocates proposed an early state in which RNA performed both the enzymatic functions of modern proteins and the information-storage function of modern DNA, thus allegedly making the interdependence of DNA and proteins unnecessary in the earliest living system.

Nevertheless, many fundamental difficulties with the RNA-world scenario have emerged. First, synthesizing (and/or maintaining) many essential building blocks of RNA molecules under realistic conditions has proven either difficult or impossible (Shapiro 1999, 4396–4401). Second, naturally occurring RNA possesses very few of the specific enzymatic properties of proteins necessary to extant cells. Indeed, RNA catalysts do not function as true enzyme catalysts. Enzymes are capable of coupling energetically favorable and energetically unfavorable reactions together. RNA catalysts, so-called "ribozymes," are not. Third, RNA-world advocates offer no plausible explanation for how primitive RNA replicators might have evolved into modern cells that do rely almost exclusively on proteins to process and translate genetic information and regulate metabolism (Wolf and Koonin 2007, 14). Fourth, attempts to enhance the limited catalytic properties of RNA molecules in so-called ribozyme engineering experiments have inevitably required extensive investigator manipulation, thus simulating, if anything, the need for intelligent design, not the efficacy of an undirected chemical evolutionary process.

Most importantly for our present considerations, the RNA-world hypothesis presupposes, but does not explain, the origin of sequence specificity or information in the original functional RNA molecules. Indeed, the RNA-world scenario was proposed as an explanation for the functional interdependence problem, not the information problem. Even so, some RNA-world advocates seem to envision leapfrogging the sequence-specificity problem. They imagine sections of RNA arising by chance on the pre-biotic earth and then later acquiring an ability to make copies of themselves – that is, to self-replicate. In such a scenario, the capacity to self-replicate would favor the survival of those RNA molecules that could do so and would thus favor the specific sequences that the first self-replicating molecules happened to have.

This suggestion merely shifts the information problem out of view, however. To date scientists have been able to design RNA catalysts that will copy only about 10% of themselves (Johnston et al. 2001). For strands of RNA to perform even this limited replicase (self-replication) function, however, they must, like proteins, have very specific arrangements of constituent building blocks (nucleotides in the RNA case). Further, the strands must be long enough to fold into complex three-dimensional shapes (to form so-called tertiary structures). Thus, any RNA molecule capable of even limited function must have possessed considerable (specified) information content. Yet explaining how the building blocks of RNA arranged themselves into functionally specified sequences has proven no easier than explaining how the constituent parts of DNA might have done so, especially given the high probability of destructive cross-reactions between desirable and undesirable molecules in any realistic pre-biotic soup. As de Duve (1995b, 23) has noted in a critique of the RNA-world hypothesis, "hitching the components together in the right manner raises additional problems of such magnitude that no one has yet attempted to do so in a prebiotic context."

The Return of the Design Hypothesis

If attempts to solve the information problem only relocate it, and if neither chance nor physical–chemical necessity, nor the two acting in combination, explains the ultimate origin of specified biological information, what does? Do we know of any entity that has the causal powers to create large amounts of specified information? We do. As information scientist Henry Quastler (1964, 16) recognized, the "creation of new information is habitually associated with conscious activity."

Experience affirms that functionally specified information routinely arises from the activity of intelligent agents. A computer user who traces the information on a screen back to its source invariably comes to a mind, that of a software engineer or programmer. Similarly, the information in a book or newspaper column ultimately derives from a writer – from a mental, rather than a strictly material, cause.

But could this intuitive connection between information and the prior activity of a designing intelligence justify a rigorous scientific argument for intelligent design? I first began to consider this possibility during my PhD research at the University of Cambridge in the late 1980s. At that time, I was examining how scientists investigating origins events developed their arguments. Specifically, I examined the method of reasoning that historical scientists use to identify causes responsible for events in the remote past.

I discovered that historical scientists often make inferences with a distinctive logical form (known technically as *abductive inferences*; Peirce 1931, 372–388). Paleontologists, evolutionary biologists, and other historical scientists reason like detectives and infer *past* conditions or causes from *present* clues. As Stephen Jay Gould (1986, 61) notes, historical scientists typically "infer history from its results."

Nevertheless, as many philosophers have noted there is a problem with this kind of historical reasoning, namely, there is often more than one cause that can explain the same effect. This makes reasoning from present clues (circumstantial evidence) tricky because the evidence can point to more than one causal explanation or hypothesis. To address this problem in geology, the nineteenth-century geologist Thomas Chamberlain delineated a method of reasoning he called "the method of multiple working hypotheses" (Chamberlain 1965).

Contemporary philosophers of science such as Peter Lipton have called this the method of "inference to the best explanation." That is, when trying to explain the origin of an event or structure from the past, scientists often compare various hypotheses to see which would, if true, best explain it (Lipton 1991, 1). They then provisionally affirm the hypothesis that best explains the data as the one that is most likely to be true. But that raised an important question: exactly what makes an explanation best?

As it happens, historical scientists have developed criteria for deciding which cause, among a group of competing possible causes, provides the best explanation for some event in the remote past. The most important of these criteria is called "causal adequacy." This criterion requires that historical scientists, as a condition of a successful explanation, identify causes that are known to have the power to produce the kind of effect, feature, or event that requires explanation. In making these determinations, historical scientists evaluate hypotheses against their present knowledge of cause and effect. Causes that are known to produce the effect in question are judged to be better candidates than those that are not. For instance, a volcanic eruption provides a better explanation for an ash layer in the earth than an earthquake because eruptions have been observed to produce ash layers, whereas earthquakes have not.

One of the first scientists to develop this principle was the geologist Charles Lyell, who also influenced Charles Darwin. Darwin read Lyell's *magnum opus*, *The Principles of Geology*, on the voyage of the *Beagle* and employed its principles of reasoning in *The Origin of Species*. The subtitle of Lyell's *Principles* summarized the geologist's central methodological principle: *Being an Attempt to Explain the Former Changes of the Earth's Surface, by Reference to Causes Now in Operation* (1800–1803). Lyell argued that when scientists seek to explain events in the past, they should not invoke unknown or exotic causes, the effects of which we do not know. Instead they should cite causes that are known from our uniform experience to have the power to produce the effect in question (see Lyell 1830–1833, vol. 1, 75–91). Historical scientists should cite *"causes now in operation"* or presently acting causes. This was the idea behind his uniformitarian principle and the dictum: "The present is the key to the past." According to Lyell, our *present* experience of cause and effect should guide our reasoning about the causes of *past* events. Darwin himself adopted this methodological principle as he sought to demonstrate that natural selection qualified as a *vera causa*, that is, a true, known, or actual cause of significant biological change (Kavalovski 1974, 78–103.) He sought to show that natural selection was "causally adequate" to produce the effects he was trying to explain.

Both philosophers of science and leading historical scientists have emphasized causal adequacy as the key criterion by which competing hypotheses are adjudicated. But philosophers of science have also noted that assessments of explanatory power lead to conclusive inferences only when it can be shown that there is *only one known cause* for the effect or evidence in question (Scriven 1959, 480). When scientists can infer a *uniquely* plausible cause, they can avoid the fallacy of affirming the consequent and the error of ignoring other possible causes with the power to produce the same effect (Meyer 1990, 96–108).

Intelligent Design as the Best Explanation?

What did all this have to do with the DNA enigma? As a PhD student I wondered if a case for an intelligent cause could be formulated and justified in the same way that historical scientists would justify any other causal claim about an event in the past. My study of historical scientific reasoning and origin-of-life research suggested to me that it was possible to formulate a rigorous scientific case for intelligent design as an inference to the best explanation, specifically, as a best explanation for the origin of biological information. The action of a conscious and intelligent agent clearly represents a known (presently acting) and adequate cause for the origin of information. Uniform and repeated experience affirms that intelligent agents produce information-rich systems, whether software programs, ancient inscriptions, or Shakespearean sonnets. Minds are clearly capable of generating functionally specified information.

Further, the functionally specified information in the cell also points to intelligent design as the *best* explanation for the ultimate origin of biological information. Why? Experience shows that large amounts of such information (especially codes and languages) *invariably* originate from an intelligent source – from a mind or a personal agent. In other words, intelligent activity is *the only known cause of* the origin of functionally specified information (at least, starting from a non-living source, that is, from purely physical or chemical antecedents). Since intelligence is the only known cause of specified information in such a context, the presence of functionally specified information sequences in even the simplest living systems points definitely to the past existence and activity of a designing intelligence.

Ironically, this generalization – that intelligence is the only known cause of specified information (starting from a non-biological source) – has received support from origin-of-life research itself. During the last 50 years, every naturalistic model proposed has failed to explain the origin of the functionally specified genetic information required to build a living cell (Thaxton *et al.* 1984; Shapiro 1986; Dose 1988; Yockey 1992, 259–293; Thaxton and Bradley 1994; Meyer 2009). Thus, mind or intelligence, or what philosophers call "agent causation," now stands as the only cause known to be capable of generating large amounts of information starting from a non-living state.[1] As a result, the presence of specified information-rich sequences in even the simplest living systems would seem to imply intelligent design.

When I first noticed the subtitle of Lyell's book, referring us to *"causes now in operation,"* a light came on for me. I immediately asked myself a question: "What causes 'now in operation' produce digital code or specified information?" Is there a known cause – a *vera causa* – of the origin of such information? What does our uniform experience tell us? As I thought about this further, it occurred to me that by Lyell's and Darwin's own rule of reasoning and test of a sound scientific explanation, intelligent design must qualify as the currently best scientific explanation for the origin of biological information. Why? Because we have independent evidence – "uniform experience" – that intelligent agents are capable of producing specified information and, as origin-of-life research itself has helped to demonstrate, we know of no other cause capable of producing functional specified information starting from a purely physical or chemical state.

Scientists in many fields recognize the connection between intelligence and information and make inferences accordingly. Archaeologists assume that a scribe produced the inscriptions on the Rosetta stone. The search for extraterrestrial intelligence (SETI) presupposes that any specified information imbedded in electromagnetic signals coming from space would indicate an intelligent source (McDonough 1987). As yet, radio astronomers have not found any such information-bearing signals. But closer to home, molecular biologists have identified information-rich sequences and systems in the cell, suggesting, by the same logic, the past existence of an intelligent cause for those effects.

Indeed, our uniform experience affirms that specified information – whether inscribed in hieroglyphics, written in a book, encoded in a radio signal, or produced in an RNA-world ribozyme engineering experiment – *always* arises from an intelligent source, from a mind and not a strictly material process. So the discovery of the functionally specified digital information in the DNA molecule provides strong grounds for inferring that intelligence played a role in the origin of DNA. Indeed, whenever we find specified information and we know the causal story of how that information arose, we always find that it arose from an intelligent source. It follows that the best, most likely explanation for the origin of the specified, digitally encoded information in DNA is that it too had an intelligent source. Intelligent design best explains the DNA enigma.

Note

1 Of course, the phrase "large amounts of specified information" raises a quantitative question, namely, "How much specified information would the minimally complex cell have to have before it implied design?" In Meyer 2009, I give and justify a precise quantitative answer to this question. I show that the *de novo* emergence of 500 or more bits of specified information reliably indicates design.

References

Ayala, Francisco J. 2007. Darwin's Greatest Discovery: Design without Designer. *Proceedings of the National Academy of Sciences*, 104, pp. 8567–8573.

Chamberlain, Thomas C. 1965. The Method of Multiple Working Hypotheses. *Science*, 148, pp. 754–759.

Crick, Francis. 1981. *Life Itself*. New York: Simon & Schuster.

Crick, Francis. 1988. *What Mad Pursuit: A Personal View of Scientific Discovery*. New York: Basic Books.

Dawkins, Richard. 1995. *River Out of Eden: A Darwinian View of Life*. New York: Basic Books.

de Duve, Christian. 1991. *Blueprint for a Cell: The Nature and Origin of Life*. Burlington, NC: Neil Patterson Publishers.

de Duve, Christian. 1995a. The Beginnings of Life on Earth. *American Scientist*, 83, pp. 249–250, 428–437.

de Duve, Christian. 1995b. *Vital Dust: Life as a Cosmic Imperative*. New York: Basic Books.

de Duve, Christian. 1996. The Constraints of Chance. *Scientific American*, January, p. 112.

Dobzhansky, Theodosius. 1965. Discussion of G. Schramm's Paper. In Sidney W. Fox, ed. *The Origins of Prebiological Systems and of Their Molecular Matrices*. New York: Academic Press, pp. 309–315.

Dose, K. 1988. The Origin of Life: More Questions than Answers. *Interdisciplinary Science Review*, 13, pp. 348–356.

Gates, Bill. 1995. *The Road Ahead*. New York: Viking.

Gould, Stephen Jay. 1986. Evolution and the Triumph of Homology: Or, Why History Matters. *American Scientist*, 74, pp. 60–69.

Hood, Leroy and Galas, David. 2003. The Digital Code of DNA. *Nature*, 421, pp. 444–448.

Johnston, Wendy K., Unrau, Peter J., Lawrence, Michael S. *et al*. 2001. RNA-Catalyzed RNA Polymerization: Accurate and General RNA-Templated Primer Extension. *Science*, 292, pp. 1319–1325.

Kamminga, Harmke. 1980. Studies in the History of Ideas on the Origin of Life. PhD dissertation, University of London.

Kavalovski, V. 1974. The Vera Causa Principle: A Historico-Philosophical Study of a Meta-theoretical Concept from Newton through Darwin. PhD dissertation, University of Chicago.

Kenyon, Dean and Steinman, Gary. 1969. *Biochemical Predestination*. New York: McGraw-Hill.

Küppers, Bernd-Olaf. 1990. *Information and the Origin of Life*. Cambridge, MA: MIT Press.

Lipton, Peter. 1991. *Inference to the Best Explanation*. London: Routledge.

Lyell, Charles. 1830–1833. *Principles of Geology: Being an Attempt to Explain the Former Changes of the Earth's Surface, by Reference to Causes Now in Operation*, 2 vols. London: John Murray.

McDonough, T. R. 1987. *The Search for Extraterrestrial Intelligence: Listening for Life in the Cosmos*. New York: Wiley.

Meyer, Stephen C. 1990. Of Clues and Causes: A Methodological Interpretation of Origin of Life Studies. PhD dissertation, University of Cambridge.

Meyer, Stephen C. 2009. *Signature in the Cell: DNA and the Evidence for Intelligent Design*. San Francisco, CA: HarperOne.

Peirce, Charles S. 1931. *Collected Papers*, vol. 2. C. Hartshorne and P. Weiss, eds. Cambridge, MA: Harvard University Press.

Prigogine, Ilya and Nicolis, Grégoire. 1977. *Self Organization in Nonequilibrium Systems*. New York: John Wiley & Sons, Inc.

Prigogine, Ilya, Nicolis, Grégoire, and Babloyantz, Agnessa. 1972. Thermodynamics of Evolution. *Physics Today*, 23, pp. 23–31.

Quastler, Henry. 1964. *The Emergence of Biological Organization*. New Haven, CT: Yale University Press.

Scriven, Michael. 1959. Explanation and Prediction in Evolutionary Theory. *Science*, 130, pp. 477–482.

Shapiro, Robert. 1986. *Origins: A Skeptic's Guide to the Creation of Life on Earth*. New York: Summit Books.

Shapiro, Robert. 1999. Prebiotic Cytosine Synthesis: A Critical Analysis and Implications for the Origin of Life. *Proceedings of the National Academy of Sciences*, 96, pp. 4396–4401

Thaxton, Charles and Bradley, Walter L. 1994. Information and the Origin of Life. In J. P. Moreland, ed. *The Creation Hypothesis: Scientific Evidence for an Intelligent Designer*. Downers Grove, IL: InterVarsity Press, pp. 173–210.

Thaxton, Charles, Bradley, Walter L. and Olsen, Roger. 1984. *The Mystery of Life's Origin*. New York: Philosophical Library.

Wald, G. 1954. The Origin of Life. *Scientific American*, 191, pp. 44–53.

Wolf, Huri I. and Koonin, Eugene V. 2007. On the Origin of the Translation System and the Genetic Code in the RNA World by Means of Natural Selection, Exaptation, and Subfunctionalization. *Biology Direct*, 2, pp. 1–25.

Yockey, Hubert P. 1992. *Information Theory and Molecular Biology*. Cambridge: Cambridge University Press.

Further Reading

Meyer, Stephen C. 2009. *Signature in the Cell: DNA and the Evidence for Intelligent Design*. San Francisco, CA: HarperOne. In this book I respond in detail to various objections to the case for intelligent design sketched in this short article. I address objections such as: "intelligent design (a) is religion, (b) is not science, (c) makes no predictions, (d) is based on flawed analogical reasoning, (e) is a fallacious argument from ignorance," and many others. I direct intrigued, but still skeptical, readers to my book for a more thorough consideration of popular objections to my argument. I also provide more extensive documentation there of the scientific discussion provided in this chapter.

25

Darwin and Intelligent Design

FRANCISCO J. AYALA

Introductory Summary Statement

The steering-wheel of a car has been designed for turning; the human eye has been designed for seeing. Most of us would be willing to accept these two statements, but would probably balk if somebody claimed that a mountain has been designed for climbing. We might note that mountain slopes are there whether or not there is anybody to climb them, but steering-wheels would never have been produced if it were not for the purpose they serve. Mountain slopes and steering-wheels have in common that they are used for certain purposes, but differ because steering-wheels, but not mountain slopes, have been specially created for the purpose they serve. This is what we mean when we say that steering-wheels are "designed" for turning: the reason why steering-wheels exist at all and exhibit certain features is that they have been designed for turning the car. This is not so with mountain slopes.

But what about eyes? Human eyes share something in common with steering-wheels and something with mountain slopes. Human eyes like steering-wheels have been "designed," but only in the sense that were it not for the function of seeing they serve, eyes would have never come to be; and the features exhibited by eyes specifically came to be in order to serve for seeing. But eyes share in common with mountain slopes that both came about by natural processes, the eyes by natural selection, the mountain slopes by geological movements and erosion. Steering-wheels, on the contrary, are designed and produced by human engineers.

In *The Origin of Species* Darwin accumulated an impressive number of observations supporting the evolutionary origin of living organisms. Moreover, and most importantly, he advanced a causal explanation of evolutionary change – the theory of natural selection, which provides a natural account of the design of organisms, or as we say in biology, their adaptations. Darwin accepted that organisms are adapted to live in their environments, and that their parts are adapted to the specific functions they serve. Penguins are adapted to live in the cold, the wings of birds are made to fly, and the eye is made to see. Darwin accepted the facts of adaptation, but advanced a scientific hypothesis to account for the facts. It may count

The Blackwell Companion to Science and Christianity, First Edition. Edited by J. B. Stump and Alan G. Padgett.
© 2012 Blackwell Publishing Ltd. Published 2012 by Blackwell Publishing Ltd.

as Darwin's greatest accomplishment that he brought the design aspects of nature into the realm of science. The wonderful designs of myriad plants and animals could now be explained as the result of natural laws manifested in natural processes, without recourse to an external Designer or Creator.

Biologists need to account for the functional features of organisms, their "design," in terms of the goals or purposes they serve, which is accomplished by means of hypotheses ultimately based on natural selection. Physical scientists do not face similar demands. Inanimate objects and processes (other than those created by humans) are not directed toward specific ends, they do not exist to serve certain purposes. The configuration of sodium chloride depends on the structure of sodium and chlorine, but it makes no sense to say that that structure is made up so as to serve a certain end. Similarly, the slopes of a mountain are the result of certain geological processes and weather erosion, but did not come about so as to serve a certain end, such as skiing.

The Design Argument

The argument from design is a two-pronged argument. The first prong, as formulated for example by the English author William Paley, asserts that organisms, in their wholes, in their parts, and in their relations to one another and to the environment, appear to have been designed for serving certain functions and to fulfill certain ways of life. The second prong of the argument affirms that only God, an omnipotent and omniscient creator, could account for the diversity, perfection, and functionality of living organisms and their parts.

The argument from design has been formulated in different versions through history. The first prong comes, importantly, in at least two flavors. One version refers to the order and harmony of the universe as a whole; as for example, in St Augustine: "The world itself, by the perfect order of its changes and motions and by the great beauty of all things visible" (1998, 452–453); or in St Thomas Aquinas: "It is impossible for contrary and discordant things to fall into one harmonious order except under some guidance, assigning to each and all parts a tendency to a fixed end. But in the world we see things of different natures falling into harmonious order" (1905, 12). The second version of the first prong refers to the living world, the intricate organized complexity of organisms, as formulated, among others, by William Paley (1802) and the modern proponents of intelligent design (ID).

The second prong of the argument from design has been formulated in three important versions. One formulation of the Designer appears in classical Greece, including Plato, who postulates in his *Timaeus* the existence of a Demiurge, a creator of the universe's order, who is a universal and impersonal ordering principle, rather than the personalized Judeo-Christian God. Plato's Demiurge is an orderer of the world who accounts for the world's rationality, but not necessarily for its creation. A second version of the Designer is the familiar one of the Judeo-Christian God, as formulated by Paley and other Christian philosophers and theologians, who is a "person," the creator and steward of the universe, who creates a world from nothing and is omniscient, omnipotent, omnibenevolent, and is provident for humans.

Proponents of ID have in recent years formulated a third version of the second prong of the argument: an unidentified Designer who may account for the order and complexity of the universe, or that may simply intervene from time to time in the universe so as to design organisms and their parts, because the complexity of organisms, it is claimed, cannot be accounted for by natural processes. According to ID proponents, this intelligent designer could be, but need not be, God. The intelligent designer could be an alien from outer space or some other creature, such as a "time-traveling cell biologist," with amazing powers to account for the universe's design. Explicit reference to God is avoided, so that the "theory" of ID can be taught in the public schools as an alternative to the theory of evolution without incurring conflict with the US Constitution, which forbids the endorsement of any religious belief in public institutions.

The Design Argument in Antiquity

Anaxagoras of Clazomenae (c. 500–428 BCE) was among the early pre-Socratic Greek philosophers who formulated versions of the argument from design. Anaxagoras primarily concerned himself with astronomical and meteorological questions, but also addressed biological doctrines. He postulated a Mind that accounts for order in the world: "All things that were to be . . . those that were and those that are now and those that shall be . . . Mind arranged them all, including this rotation in which are now rotating the stars, the sun and moon" (Kirk et al. 1983, 363). Diogenes of Apollonia, a near-contemporary of Anaxagoras, asserts that "what men call air . . . seems to me to be a god and to have reached everywhere and to dispose all things and to be in everything" (Kirk et al. 1983, 442).

In the *Phaedo*, Plato (427–347 BCE) puts the argument in Socrates' mouth: "I have heard someone reading . . . from a book by Anaxagoras, and saying that it is Mind that directs and is cause of everything and placed each thing severally as it was best that it should be" (Plato 1997, 97c). In the *Timaeus*, Plato attributes creative powers to this Mind, which does not create by making something out of nothing, but accounts for rational order in the world and for the configuration of organisms.

Among the ancient Romans, it was particularly Marcus Tullius Cicero (106–43 BCE), the great statesman and orator, who argued that the purposeful complexity of the living world, such as we see in the eye, could not come about by chance, or without guidance.

Christian Authors

The argument from design was advanced in the early centuries of the Christian era on the basis of the overall harmony and perfection of the universe by St Augustine (354–430 CE), for example, and, according to St Thomas Aquinas, by St John of Damascus (675–749 CE).

Aquinas (1225–1274), in his *Summa Theologiae*, advances five ways to demonstrate, by natural reason, that God exists. The fifth way derives from the orderliness and designed purposefulness of the universe, which evince that it has been created by a Supreme Intelligence.

The most forceful and elaborate formulation of the argument from design, before William Paley's, was *The Wisdom of God Manifested in the Works of Creation* by the English clergyman and naturalist John Ray (1627–1705). Ray regarded as incontrovertible evidence of God's wisdom that all components of the universe – the stars and the planets, as well as all organisms – are wisely contrived from the beginning and perfect in their operation. The "most convincing argument of the Existence of a Deity," writes Ray, "is the admirable Art and Wisdom that discovers itself in the Make of the Constitution, the Order and Disposition, the Ends and uses of all the parts and members of this stately fabric of Heaven and Earth" (1691, 33).

The design argument was advanced, in greater or lesser detail, by a number of authors in the seventeenth and eighteenth centuries. John Ray's contemporary Henry More (1614–1687) saw evidence of God's design in the succession of day and night and of the seasons. Robert Hooke (1635–1703), a physicist who became Secretary of the Royal Society, formulated the watchmaker analogy that would become common among British natural theologians of the time: God had furnished each plant and animal "with all kinds of contrivances necessary for its own existence and propagation . . . as a Clock-maker might make a Set of Chimes to be a part of a Clock" (Hooke 1665, 124). On the Continent, Voltaire (1694–1778), like other philosophers of the Enlightenment, accepted the argument from design. Voltaire asserted that in the same way as the existence of a watch proves the existence of a watchmaker, the design and purpose evident in nature prove that the universe was created by a Supreme Intelligence (Torrey 1967, 262–270).

William Paley's *Natural Theology*

William Paley (1743–1805), one of the most influential English authors of his time, argued forcefully in his *Natural Theology* that the complex and precise design of organisms and their parts could be accounted for only as the deed of an Intelligent and Omnipotent "Designer." With *Natural Theology*, Paley sought to update Ray's *Wisdom of God*, but he could now carry the argument much further than Ray, by taking advantage of one century of additional biological knowledge. Paley's keystone claim was that there "cannot be design without a designer; contrivance, without a contriver; order, without choice . . . means suitable to an end, and executing their office in accomplishing that end, without the end ever having been contemplated" (Paley 1802, 15–16).

Natural Theology is a sustained argument for the existence of God based on the obvious design of humans and their organs, as well as the design of all sorts of organisms, considered by themselves and in their relations to one another and to their environment. Paley's first extended example is the human eye. He points out that the eye and the telescope "are made upon the same principles; both being adjusted to the laws by which the transmission and refraction of rays of light are regulated" (Paley 1802, 20). Specifically, there is a precise resemblance between the lenses of a telescope and "the humors of the eye" in their figure, their position, and the ability of converging the rays of light at a precise distance from the lens – on the retina, in the case of the eye.

Natural Theology has chapters dedicated to the human frame, which displays a precise mechanical arrangement of bones, cartilage, and joints; to the circulation of the blood and the disposition of blood vessels; to the comparative anatomy of humans and animals; to the digestive tract, kidneys, urethra, and bladder; to the wings of birds and the fins of fish; and much more. Across 352 pages, *Natural Theology* conveys Paley's expertise: extensive and accurate biological knowledge, as detailed and precise as was available in the year 1802. After detailing the precise organization and exquisite functionality of each biological entity, relationship, or process, Paley draws again and again the same conclusion: only an omniscient and omnipotent Deity could account for these marvels of mechanical perfection, purpose, and functionality, and for the enormous diversity of inventions that they entail.

In 1829, Francis Henry Egerton (1756–1829), the eighth earl of Bridgewater, bequeathed the sum of £8000 to the Royal Society with instructions that it commission eight treatises that would promote natural theology by setting forth "The Power, Wisdom and Goodness of God as manifested in the Creation." Eight treatises were published in the 1830s by distinguished British scientists, several of which artfully incorporate the best science of the time and had considerable influence on the public and among scientists. *The Hand, Its Mechanisms and Vital Endowments as Evincing Design* was written in 1833 by Sir Charles Bell, a distinguished anatomist and surgeon, famous for his neurological discoveries. William Buckland, Professor of Geology at Oxford University, wrote *Geology and Mineralogy* in 1836. In 1857, Hugh Miller, in *The Testimony of the Rocks*, would formulate what I call the *argument from beauty*, which allows that it is not only the perfection of design, but also the beauty of natural structures found in rock formations and in mountains and rivers that manifests the intervention of the Creator.

The "Theory" of Intelligent Design

Darwin's *On the Origin of Species* (1859) very much disposed of natural theology as an attempt to prove the existence of God based on the argument from design. Nevertheless, since the 1990s, several authors in the United States have revived the argument from design, notably Michael Behe, William Dembski, and Stephen C. Meyer, among others. These modern proponents, at times, claim that the Intelligent Designer need not be God, but could be a space alien or some other intelligent superpower unknown to us. The folly of this pretense is apparent to anyone who takes the time to consider the issue seriously.

Proponents of ID call for an Intelligent Designer to explain the supposed irreducible complexity in organisms. An *irreducibly complex system* is defined by Behe as an entity "composed of several well-matched, interacting parts that contribute to the basic function, wherein the removal of any one of the parts causes the system to effectively cease functioning" (Behe 1996, 39). The claim is that irreducibly complex systems cannot be the outcome of natural selection, which proceeds by small steps, slowly accumulating over thousands or millions of generations the components of complex systems. Evolutionists have pointed out, again and again, with supporting evidence, that organs and other components of living beings are not irreducibly complex – they do not come about suddenly, or "in one fell swoop" (see, for example, Miller 1999, 2004; Brauer and Brumbaugh 2001; Pennock 2002; Perakh 2004; Ayala 2007). Evolutionists have shown that organs such as the human eye are not irreducible at all; rather, less complex versions of the same systems have existed in the past, and some can be found in today's organisms as well.

Natural Selection

Natural selection was proposed by Darwin (1859) primarily to account for the adaptive organization, or design, of living beings; it is a process that preserves and promotes adaptation. Evolutionary change through time and evolutionary diversification (multiplication of species) often ensue as by-products of natural selection, fostering the adaptation of organisms to their milieu. Evolutionary change is not directly promoted by natural selection and, therefore, it is not its necessary consequence. Indeed, some species remain unchanged for long periods of time, as Darwin noted. *Nautilus, Lingula,* and other so-called "living fossils" are Darwin's examples of organisms that have remained unchanged in their appearance for millions of years. Nor does natural selection ensure that features that have evolved at a certain time and place as adaptations will be successful over long time spans. Indeed, more than 99% of all species that ever existed have become extinct.

Evolution affects all aspects of an organism's life: morphology (form and structure), physiology (function), behavior, and ecology (interaction with the environment). Underlying these changes are changes in the hereditary materials. Hence, in genetic terms, evolution consists of changes in the organisms' hereditary makeup.

As a genetic process, evolution can be seen as a two-step process. First, hereditary variation arises by mutation; second, selection occurs by which useful variations increase in frequency and those that are less useful or injurious are eliminated over the generations. As Darwin saw it, individuals having useful variations "would have the best chance of surviving and procreating their kind" (Darwin 1859, 81). As a consequence, useful variations increase in frequency over the generations, at the expense of those that are less useful or are injurious.

Natural selection is able to generate novelty and complexity by increasing the probability of otherwise extremely improbable genetic combinations. Natural selection, in combination with mutation, becomes, in this respect, a creative process. It is a process that has been occurring for many millions of years, in many different evolutionary lineages, and in a multitude of species, each consisting of a large number of individuals.

Natural selection is an incremental process, operating over time and yielding organisms better able to survive and reproduce than others, under the conditions prevailing in a given place and at a certain time. Individuals of a given species differ from one another, at any one time, only in small ways; for example, the difference between bacteria that have or lack an enzyme able to synthesize the sugar lactose, or between moths that have light or dark wings. These differences typically involve one or only a few genes (Carroll 2005), but they can make the difference between survival and death, as in the evolution of resistance to DDT in disease-transmitting mosquitoes or to antibiotics in people. Consider a different sort of example. Some pocket mice (*Chaetodipus intermedius*) live in rocky outcrops in Arizona. Light, sandy-colored mice are found in light-colored habitats, whereas dark (melanic) mice prevail in dark rocks formed from ancient flows of basaltic lava. The match between background and fur color protects the mice from avian and mammal predators that hunt guided largely by vision. Mutations in one single gene (known as *MC1R*) account for the difference between light and dark pelage (Nachman *et al.* 2003).

Adaptations that involve complex structures, functions, or behaviors involve numerous genes. Many familiar mammals, but not marsupials, have a placenta. Marsupials include the familiar kangaroo and other mammals native primarily to Australia and South America. Dogs, cats, mice, donkeys, and primates are placental. The placenta makes it possible to extend the time the developing embryo is kept inside the mother and thus make the newborn better prepared for independent survival. However, the placenta requires complex adaptations, such as the suppression of harmful immune interactions between mother and embryo, delivery of suitable nutrients and oxygen to the embryo, and the disposal of embryonic wastes. The mammalian placenta evolved more than 100 million years ago and proved a successful adaptation, contributing to the explosive diversification of placental mammals in the Old World and North America.

The placenta also has evolved in some fish groups, such as *Poeciliopsis*. Some *Poeciliopsis* species hatch eggs. The females supply the yolk in the egg, which furnishes nutrients to the developing embryo (as in chicken). Other *Poeciliopsis* species, however, have evolved a placenta through which the mother provides nutrients to the developing embryo. Molecular biology has made possible the reconstruction of the evolutionary history of *Poeciliopsis* species. A surprising result is that the placenta evolved independently three times in this fish group. The required complex adaptations accumulated in each case in less than 750 000 years (Reznick *et al.* 2002; see Avise 2006).

Natural selection produces combinations of genes that would seem highly improbable, because natural selection proceeds stepwise over long periods of time. Consider the evolution of the eye in humans and other vertebrates. Perception of light, and later vision, were important for the survival and reproductive success of their ancestors, because sunlight is a predominant feature of the environment. Accordingly, natural selection favored genes and gene combinations that increased the functional efficiency of the eye, according to the needs of different sorts of organisms. Such mutations gradually accumulated, eventually leading to the highly complex and efficient vertebrate eye.

Several hundred million generations separate modern animals from the early animals of the Cambrian geological period (542 million years ago). The number of mutations that can be tested, and those eventually selected, in millions of individual animals over millions of generations is difficult for a human mind to fathom, but we can readily understand that the accumulation of millions of small, functionally advantageous changes could yield remarkably complex and adaptive organs, such as the eye.

Natural Selection and Design

An engineer has a preconception of what a design is supposed to achieve, and will select suitable materials and arrange them in a preconceived manner so that the design fulfills the intended function. On the contrary, natural selection does not operate according to some preordained plan. It is a purely natural process resulting from the interacting properties of physicochemical and biological entities. Natural selection is simply a consequence of the differential survival and reproduction of living beings. It has some appearance of purposefulness because it is conditioned by the environment: which organisms survive and reproduce more effectively depends on which variations they happen to possess that are useful or beneficial to them, in the place and at the time where they live.

Natural selection does not have foresight; it does not anticipate the environments of the future. Drastic environmental changes may introduce obstacles that are insuperable to organisms that were previously thriving. In fact, species extinction is a common outcome of the evolutionary process. The species existing today represent the balance between the origin of new species and their eventual extinction. The available inventory of living species describes nearly 2 million species, although at least 10 million are estimated to exist. But again, we know that more than 99% of all species that have ever lived on earth have become extinct (Aitken 1998).

The arguments of ID proponents that state the incredible improbability of chance events, such as mutation, in order to account for the adaptations of organisms (e.g., Meyer 2009) are irrelevant because evolution is not governed by chance processes. Genetic mutations are random events that occur with certain probabilities. But mutations do not determine the outcomes of evolution. Rather, there is a natural process (namely, natural selection) that is not random, but oriented and able to generate order or "create." The traits that organisms acquire in their evolutionary histories are not fortuitous but, rather, determined by their functional utility to the organisms, designed, as it were, to serve their life needs. Natural selection preserves the mutations that are useful and eliminates those that are harmful. Without hereditary mutations, evolution could not happen, because there would be no variations that could be differentially conveyed from one to another generation. But without natural selection, the mutation process would yield disorganization and extinction because most mutations are disadvantageous. Mutation and selection have jointly driven the marvelous process that, starting from microscopic organisms, has yielded orchids, birds, and humans.

The theory of evolution conveys chance and necessity jointly enmeshed in the stuff of life; randomness and determinism interlocked in a natural process that has spurted the most complex, diverse, and beautiful entities that we know of in the universe: the organisms that populate the earth, including humans who think and love, endowed with free will and creative powers, and able to analyze the process of evolution itself that brought them into existence.

Unintended Consequences: ID's Denigration of Religion and God

The point I now want to make may come as a surprise to people of faith and scientists alike. I assert that scientific knowledge, the theory of evolution in particular, is consistent with a religious belief in a personal God, whereas creationism and intelligent design are not. This point depends on a particular view of God – shared by many people of faith – as omniscient, omnipotent, and benevolent. This point also depends on our knowledge of the natural world and, particularly, of the living world.

Before modern physical science came about, God (in some religious views) caused rain, drought, volcanic eruptions, and so forth to reward or punish people. This view entails that God would have caused the tsunami that killed 200 000 Indonesians a few years ago, or the earthquake that more recently killed tens of thousands of people in Haiti. Thus, it would seem incompatible with a benevolent God. However, we now know that tsunamis and other "natural" catastrophes come about by natural processes. Natural processes don't entail moral values. Some critics might say "that does not excuse God, because God created the world as it is. God could have created a different world, without catastrophes." Yes, according to some belief systems, God could have created a different world. But that would not be a creative universe, where galaxies form, stars and planetary systems come about, and continents drift causing earthquakes. The world that we have is creative and more exciting than a static world. This argument will not convince all, but is persuasive for some as an account of physical evil, and many theologians use it, whether implicitly or explicitly.

Turn now to badly designed human jaws, parasites that kill millions of children, and a poorly designed human reproductive system that accounts for millions of miscarriages every year in the world. If these dreadful happenings come about by direct design by God, God would seem responsible for the consequences. If engineers design cars that explode when you turn on the ignition key, they are accountable. But if the dreadful happenings come about by natural processes (evolution), there are no moral implications, because natural processes don't entail moral values.

Nevertheless, some would say, once again, that because the world was created by God, so God is ultimately responsible: God could have created a world without parasites or dysfunctionalities. Yes, others would answer, but a world of life with evolution is much more exciting; it is a creative world where new species arise, complex ecosystems come about, and humans have evolved. This account will not satisfy some people of faith and many unbelievers will surely find it less than cogent: a *deus ex machina*. But I am suggesting that it may provide the beginning of an explanation for many people of faith, as well as for theologians.

One difficulty with attributing the design of organisms to the Creator is that imperfections and defects pervade the living world. Consider the human eye. The visual nerve fibers in the eye converge to form the optic nerve, which crosses the retina (in order to reach the brain) and thus creates a blind spot, a minor imperfection, but an imperfection of design, nevertheless; squids and octopuses do not have this defect. Did the Designer have greater love for squids than for humans and, thus, exhibit greater care in designing their eyes than ours?

The theory of ID leads to conclusions about the nature of the Designer quite different from those of omniscience, omnipotence, and benevolence that Christian theology predicates of God. It is not only that organisms and their parts are less than perfect, but also that deficiencies and dysfunctions are pervasive, evidencing "incompetent" rather than "intelligent" design. Consider the human jaw. We have too many teeth for the jaw's size, so that wisdom teeth need to be removed and orthodontists can make a decent living straightening the others. Would we want to blame God for this blunder? A human engineer would have done better.

Evolution gives a good account of this imperfection. Brain size increased over time in our ancestors; the remodeling of the skull to fit the larger brain entailed a reduction of the jaw, so that the head of the newborn would not be too large to pass through the mother's birth canal. Evolution responds to the organisms' needs through natural selection, not by optimal design but by "tinkering," by slowly modifying existing structures. Evolution achieves "design," as a consequence of natural selection while promoting adaptation. Evolution's ID is *imperfect* design, not *intelligent* design.

Consider the birth canal of women, much too narrow for easy passage of the infant's head, so that thousands upon thousands of babies and many mothers die during delivery. Surely we don't want to blame God for this dysfunctional design or for the children's deaths. Science makes it understandable, a consequence of the evolutionary enlargement of our brain. Females of other primates do not experience this difficulty. Theologians in the past struggled with the issue of dysfunction because they thought it had to be attributed to God's design. Science, much to the relief of theologians, provides an explanation that convincingly attributes defects, deformities, and dysfunctions to natural causes.

Examples of deficiencies and dysfunctions in all sorts of organisms can be listed endlessly, reflecting the opportunistic, tinkerer-like character of natural selection, which achieves imperfect, rather than intelligent, design. The world of organisms also abounds in characteristics that might be called "oddities," as well as those that have been characterized as "cruelties," an apposite qualifier if the cruel behaviors were designed outcomes of a being holding on to human or higher standards of morality. However, the cruelties of biological nature are only metaphoric cruelties when applied to the outcomes of natural selection.

Examples of "cruelty" involve not only the familiar predators tearing apart their prey (say, a small monkey held alive by a chimpanzee biting large flesh morsels from the screaming monkey), or parasites destroying the functional organs of their hosts, but also – and very abundantly – between organisms of the same species, even between mates. A well-known example is the female praying mantis that devours the male after coitus is completed. Less familiar is that, if she gets the opportunity, the female praying mantis will eat the head of the male *before* mating, which thrashes the headless male mantis into spasms of "sexual frenzy" that allow the female to connect his genitalia with hers. In some midges (tiny flies), the female captures the male as if he were any other prey, and with the tip of her proboscis she injects into him her spittle, which starts digesting the male's innards which are then sucked by the female; partly protected from digestion are the relatively intact male organs that break off inside the female and fertilize her. Male cannibalism by their female mates is known in dozens of species, particularly spiders and scorpions. The world of life abounds in these kinds of "cruel" behaviors.

The design of organisms is often so dysfunctional, odd, and cruel that it possibly might be attributed to the gods of the ancient Greeks, Romans, and Egyptians, who fought with one another, made blunders, and were clumsy in their endeavors. For a modern biologist who knows about the world of life, the design of organisms is not compatible with special action by the omniscient and omnipotent God of Judaism, Christianity, and Islam. The God of revelation and faith is a God of love and mercy, and of wisdom. A major burden was removed from the shoulders of believers when convincing evidence was advanced that the design of organisms need not be attributed to the immediate agency of the Creator, but rather is an outcome of natural processes. If we claim that organisms and their parts have been specifically designed by God, we have to account for the incompetent design of the human jaw, the narrowness of the birth canal, and our poorly designed backbone, less than fittingly suited for walking upright.

Most disturbing for ID proponents has to be the following consideration. About 20% of all recognized human pregnancies end in spontaneous miscarriage during the first two months of pregnancy. This misfortune amounts at present to more than 20 million spontaneous abortions worldwide every year. Do we want to blame God for the deficiencies in the pregnancy process? Is God the greatest abortionist of them all? Most of us might rather attribute this monumental mishap to the clumsy ways of the evolutionary process than to the incompetence of an intelligent designer.

The "Disguised Friend"

Proponents of ID would do well to acknowledge Darwin's revolution and accept natural selection as the process that accounts for the design of organisms, as well as for the dysfunctions, oddities, cruelties, and sadism that pervade the world of life. Attributing these to specific agency by the Creator amounts to blasphemy. Proponents and followers of ID are surely well-meaning people who do not intend such blasphemy, but this is how matters appear to a biologist concerned that God not be slandered with the imputation of incompetent design.

The late theologian Sir Arthur Peacocke found it surprising "the way in which the 'disguised friend' of Darwinism, of evolutionary ideas, has been admitted (if at all) only grudgingly into Christian theology" (Peacocke, 2005, 60). Peacocke had in mind the statement of Aubrey Moore, a Protestant theologian who in 1891 wrote, "Darwinism appeared, and under the guise of a foe, did the work of a friend. It has conferred upon philosophy and religion an inestimable benefit" (Ayala 2007, 159).

Darwin's theory of evolution is one of the great scientific developments of all times. It is also, in my view, a great gift to religion.

References

Aitken, G. M. 1998. Extinction. *Biology & Philosophy*, 13, pp. 393–411.

Aquinas, Thomas. 1905. Of God and His Creatures. In Joseph J. Rickaby, ed. *Summa contra gentiles*. London: Burns & Oates.

Augustine. 1998. *The City of God against the Pagans*. Robert Dyson, ed. Cambridge: Cambridge University Press.

Avise, John C. 2006. *Evolutionary Pathways in Nature: A Phylogenetic Approach*. Cambridge: Cambridge University Press.

Ayala, Francisco J. 2007. *Darwin's Gift to Science and Religion*. Washington, DC: Joseph Henry Press.

Behe, Michael. 1996. *Darwin's Black Box: The Biochemical Challenge to Evolution*. New York: The Free Press.

Brauer, Matthew J. and Brumbaugh, Daniel R. 2001. Biology Remystified: The Scientific Claims of the New Creationist. In Robert T. Pennock, ed. *Intelligent Design Creationism and Its Critics: Philosophical, Theological, and Scientific Perspectives*. Cambridge, MA: MIT Press, pp. 289–334.

Carroll, Sean B. 2005. *Endless Forms Most Beautiful: The New Science of Evo Devo and the Making of the Animal Kingdom*. New York: W. W. Norton.

Darwin, Charles. 1859. *On the Origin of Species by Means of Natural Selection*. London: John Murray.

Hooke, Robert. 1665. *Micrographia, or, Some Physiological Descriptions of Minute Bodies Made by Magnifying Glasses with Observations and Inquiries Thereupon*. London: Martyn & Allestry.

Kirk, Geoffrey K., Raven, John E., and Schofield, Malcolm. 1983. *The Presocratic Philosophers: A Critical History with a Selection of Texts*. Cambridge: Cambridge University Press.

Meyer, Stephen C. 2009. *Signature in the Cell: DNA and the Evidence for Intelligent Design*. New York: HarperCollins.

Miller, Kenneth R. 1999. *Finding Darwin's God: A Scientist's Search for Common Ground*. New York: HarperCollins.

Miller, Kenneth R. 2004. The Flagellum Unspun: The Collapse of "Irreducible Complexity". In William Dembski and Michael Ruse, eds. *Debating Design: From Darwin to DNA*. Cambridge: Cambridge University Press, pp. 81–97.

Nachman, Michael W., Hoekstra, Hopi E., and D'Agostino, Susan L. 2003. The Genetic Basis of Adaptive Melanism in Pocket Mice. *Proceedings of the National Academy of Sciences USA*, 100, pp. 5268–5273.

Paley, William. 1802. *Natural Theology, or Evidences of the Existence and Attributes of the Deity Collected from the Appearances of Nature*. New York: American Tract Society.

Peacocke, Arthur. 2005. *The Palace of Glory: God's World and Science*. Adelaide: ATF Press.

Pennock, Robert T. 2002. *Tower of Babel: The Evidence against the New Creationism*. Cambridge, MA: MIT Press.

Perakh, Mark. 2004. *Unintelligent Design*. New York: Prometheus Books.

Plato. 1997. *Phaedo*. In John M. Cooper, ed. *Plato: Complete Works*. Indianapolis, IN: Hackett Publishing Company.

Ray, John. 1691. *The Wisdom of God Manifested in the Works of Creation*. London: Wernerian Club.

Reznick, David N., Mateos, Mariana, and Springer, Mark S. 2002. Independent Origins and Rapid Evolution of the Placenta in the Fish Genus *Poeciliopsis*. *Science*, 298, pp. 1018–1020.

Torrey, Norman L. 1967. Voltaire (François-Marie Arouet de Voltaire). In Paul Edwards, ed. *Encyclopedia of Philosophy*, vol. 8. London: Macmillan, pp. 262–270.

Further Reading

Ayala, Francisco J. 2007. *Darwin's Gift to Science and Religion*. Washington, DC: Joseph Henry Press. Offers a way to reconcile science and religion on the issue of evolution by showing the different roles each discipline plays in human understanding.

Ayala, Francisco J. 2010. *Am I a Monkey? Six Big Questions about Evolution*. Baltimore, MD: Johns Hopkins University Press. Provides succinct answers to important questions that religious believers have about evolution.

Peacocke, Arthur. 2005. *The Palace of Glory: God's World and Science*. Adelaide: ATF Press. A collection of essays on science and religion by one of the field's leading voices.

Pennock, Robert T. 2002. *Tower of Babel: The Evidence against the New Creationism*. Cambridge, MA: MIT Press. Catalogs the wide range of beliefs and weaknesses of creation science, focusing particularly on the scientific claims of intelligent design.

26

Christianity and Human Evolution

JOHN F. HAUGHT

The innumerable species, genera and families, with which this world is peopled, are all descended, each within its own class or group, from common parents, and have all been modified in the course of descent. (Charles Darwin, *The Origin of Species*)

The topic of human evolution and what it means in the context of Christian faith requires above all a consideration of how to understand the venerable teaching that human beings are created in the "image and likeness of God." If our species has descended in a continuous way from a nonhuman animal ancestry, can Christians now justify their traditional claim that human beings have a special place among created beings? Of course, other theological questions also arise in connection with the theme of human evolution – and the present contribution makes brief allusion to some of them – but our main focus here is on the question of whether and how to measure human worth after Darwin.

Human Evolution and the Image of God

By the time Charles Darwin had published *On the Origin of Species* in 1859, many naturalists in Europe and America had already concluded that all extant living beings share a common ancestry. Even Charles's own grandfather, Erasmus Darwin, had expressed the opinion that life has unfolded and diversified gradually from a single common source over a long span of time. Furthermore, according to traditional theology, God's creativity is not limited to the beginning of time. There is *original* creation, of course, but also *continuous* and *new* creation. The Creator works not only at the time of origins but also over the course of time, allowing for new beings to come into existence spontaneously during the unfolding of natural history. This creativity can take place, moreover, without disturbing the regularity of natural laws.

Augustine of Hippo (354–430) long ago proposed that new kinds of beings, including unprecedented forms of life, can come into existence quite naturally subsequent to the initial

The Blackwell Companion to Science and Christianity, First Edition. Edited by J. B. Stump and Alan G. Padgett.
© 2012 Blackwell Publishing Ltd. Published 2012 by Blackwell Publishing Ltd.

creation of the world (*De Genesi ad Litteram*). According to Augustine, the Creator originally planted "seed principles" (*semines rationales*) in nature, and these potentialities blossomed into actualities only later on. Nowadays it is standard Christian theology to acknowledge that the world is still being created with the complicity, rather than violation, of natural causes. To maintain that natural laws can proximately explain the existence of various phenomena is not to deny that God is the ultimate explanation of the existence of the heavens and the earth. In the biblical understanding of creation, God continues to create by making all things *new* (Isa. 42:9; Rev. 21:5). Such a religious understanding of nature is in principle completely consistent with an evolutionary account of human emergence.

Consequently, Christians are not contradicting their fundamental beliefs or theological tradition when they embrace the scientific idea of life's common descent. According to many Christian evolutionists, Darwin's new science now makes it possible to think of God's power to create as more impressive than ever. A creator who brings into being a world that in turn gives rise to new kinds of being from out of its original resourcefulness is certainly more impressive than a hypothesized "designer" who molds and manages everything in the world directly. As Charles Kingsley (1819–1875), Frederick Temple (1821–1902), and the Jesuit geologist Pierre Teilhard de Chardin (1881–1955) have all put it, the remarkableness of creation consists not only of the fact that God makes things but, even more, that God makes things that can make themselves.

Long before Darwin, Christian theology had already proposed that God, the primary cause of the world, characteristically creates by way of secondary or instrumental natural causes. Even in Genesis, God is portrayed as creating through natural causes: "Let the *earth* bring forth living creatures after their kind: cattle and creeping things and beasts of the earth after their kind; and it was so" (Gen. 1:24). Darwin, who was in no way the atheist that some contemporary evolutionists have made him out to be, also occasionally employed the classic theological distinction between a primary creative cause (God) and secondary, or instrumental, natural causes. The latter include the causal agency that Darwin and neo-Darwinians have referred to as "natural selection." The creation of human beings by natural causes, therefore, does not diminish the creative role of God in bringing about a world inventive enough to produce by evolutionary process not only living beings but conscious, moral, and religious beings as well.

However, what can it mean, after Darwin, to claim that human beings are created in the image and likeness of God? According to the Bible, we are special in the context of creation (Gen. 1:26), but evolutionary theory seems to challenge this status by washing out what were earlier thought of as clearly defined lines of discontinuity between ourselves and other living beings. Evolution situates humans in an unbroken line of descent involving millions of other kinds of living beings that share our metabolic, genetic, and chemical constitution. Even though traditional Christian theologies of creation possess a doctrinal latitude sufficient to accommodate Darwin's theory of life's gradual descent, many believers remain troubled that human life has emerged only recently, and apparently without any sharp breaks, from a nonhuman line of descent going back millions of years. The evolutionary proximity of human life to that of primates and other mammals has been especially hard for countless Christians to embrace enthusiastically.

According to virtually all paleontologists, human beings did not appear on earth abruptly, but only stepwise, from a long lineage of hominid and, before that, primate species going back to a latest common ancestor 6–8 million years ago. Most scientists agree that contemporary human beings have descended from anatomically modern forebears who appeared in Africa as recently as 50 000–100 000 years ago (for details see Wood 2006). Because of our own evolutionary proximity to nonhumans, the question arises as to whether we can legitimately claim to be special in any significant sense. How are we to understand such declarations as those of Jesus that we are "worth more than many sparrows" (Matt. 10:21), or of the psalmist that we were created only slightly lower than the angels (Ps. 8:5)?

This chapter proposes that there should be no theological difficulty accepting common descent, but it recognizes that for countless believers, such as Darwin's nemesis, the highly respected Anglican bishop Samuel Wilberforce (1805–1873), the idea of human evolution provokes a palpable sense of disgust. A good many Christians still agree with Wilberforce's sermon on the implications of Darwinian science:

> Man's derived supremacy over the earth; man's power of articulate speech; man's gift of reason; man's free will and responsibility; man's fall and man's redemption; the incarnation of the Eternal Son; the indwelling of the Eternal Spirit– all are equally and utterly irreconcilable with the degrading notion of the brute origin of him who was created in the image of God. (Cited by Phipps 2002, 89)

Darwin himself was reluctant to dwell on the idea of human descent in the *Origin of Species* (1993 [1859]), even though the notion is clearly implicit there, as Wilberforce rightly grasped. However, Darwin's later *Descent of Man* (1998 [1871]) made human evolution its main theme. Many if not most of Darwin's contemporaries interpreted *Descent* as a subversion of the ageless Christian teaching on the exceptional dignity of human beings. By the beginning of the early twenty-first century, as a result of impressive post-Darwinian developments in biology and other sciences such as geology, paleontology, ecology, archaeology, and especially genetics, evolutionary science appears to have erased any decisive historical demarcation between the human species and its animal past.

Consequently, if Darwin and contemporary evolutionary biologists are right, religious and theological inquiry cannot help asking such questions as whether human moral activity, even in its most noble expressions, is fully distinguishable from the instinctive and adaptive behavior of nonhuman animals. The human commitment to living a serious moral life would seem to require that people think of themselves as endowed in an exceptional way with freedom and responsibility, but doesn't evolution undermine this belief? The conviction most people have of an interior freedom suggests that human persons are qualitatively distinct from non-human forms of life, but evolutionary science challenges any such assumption. Isn't freedom an illusion, and haven't our own moral tendencies been inherited by a gradual modification of the adaptive behavioral repertoire of beasts that in previous ages were thought to lie morally far beneath us in nature's hierarchy of beings?

The human treasuring of personal freedom and a sense of moral responsibility has traditionally reinforced the assumption of human dignity. Yet, if one assumes that human beings are linked in a continuous biological chain of inheritance to the simplest forms of life, can human beings still claim to be qualitatively different from other forms of life? According to Darwin all the various orders, families, genera, and species of life, including ourselves, have descended slowly and gradually from a single common ancestor over an immensely long span of time. The mechanism for change is said to be a combination of accidental organic variations (now traced especially to genetic mutations) and natural selection. At what point in evolution's long descent does freedom or responsibility enter in? Or, as traditional religious believers would ask: at what point in the process do immortal souls take up their dwelling within the newly evolved bodies of human beings? Moreover, how can the combination of accidents and impersonal selection give rise to beings endowed with freedom, self-awareness, moral seriousness, and religious longing, qualities that at least appear to make us quite special in a world otherwise ruled by fate as the ancients named it, or by inviolable natural laws as contemporary scientists suppose?

Not only are persons tied tightly to the evolutionary continuum, their existence seems to have required no special divine creation or intervention in the evolutionary process. Long before Darwin, Carolus Linnaeus (1707–1778) classified living beings into a static system of distinct genera and species. In his binomial system of classification all species were qualitatively distinct from one another as a result of their separate creation by God. Linnaeus's crisp distinctions, however, have now given way to the idea of life as a continuously rolling stream of genetic experiments. Contemporary gene-centered biology pictures life as ultimately a matter of genes flowing aimlessly – that is without any intelligent direction – from one generation to the next.

This "gene's eye" perspective is the result of uniting Darwin's notion of natural selection with the Mendelian discovery of discrete units of inheritance now known as genes. According to this modern biological synthesis, sometimes labeled "neo-Darwinism," genetic mutations provide the raw material for most evolutionary change. The genetic changes, moreover, are said to be accidental, in the sense of not being directed by any intelligent agency. It is the function of combinations of genes (segments of DNA) to instruct proteins how to take specific organic shapes. A relatively small number of these organic experiments prove to be adaptively fit, in the sense of being able to survive and reproduce. Moreover, both genes and proteins are composed of complex molecules that in turn are resolvable into arrays of lifeless atomic units. Consequently, an even more disturbing question arises for theological reflection on human specificity: is there really any clear distinction between life and lifeless matter? Each of the following two sections, one on "information" and the other on cosmology, proposes a way for theology after Darwin to respond to what might seem at first to be a decisive Darwinian defeat of any religious or ethical attempts to justify the theologically indispensable Christian vision of human dignity.

The Significance of "Information"

The science of genetics allows theology to consider the question of human dignity and the meaning of being created "in the image and likeness of God" in a new way. Information science, especially as applied to genetics, can neutralize the claims of those evolutionists who take the historical arrival of Darwinian biology to be the final victory of materialist monism over religious claims to human specific difference. With the arrival of life there quietly emerged in natural history an "information explosion," as Holmes Rolston III has put it (Rolston 2010). When applied to living beings "information" means the encoding and transmission of messages in the letters of the genetic code. The DNA molecule in the nucleus of each cell, for example, comprises something like a patterned series of "letters" (A, T, C, G, and sometimes R) embodying various informational sequences. Chemical and biological processes translate the "messages" embedded in these sequences into corresponding arrangements of amino acids. The latter are the constituents of the proteins whose three-dimensional patterns make up the diverse body types in the realm of life.

Were it not for the informationally distinct sequences in the nucleus of living cells, however, there would be no evolution by natural selection, and hence no speciation, in the story of life on earth. By recognizing the role of information in the life process, modern science has finally bumped into a dimension of nature that is radically different, though certainly not separate, from the purely physical causes which, according to scientific materialists, provide the ultimate explanation of literally everything going on in the natural world. To materialists, those who believe that matter is ultimately "all there is," the DNA molecule may seem to be "just chemistry." However, at another level of understanding, something non-material – namely, the informational sequence of letters (A, T, C, and G) – is the most remarkable aspect of the living cell. The specific sequence of nucleotides determines whether the coded organism will turn out to be a vegetable, monkey, or human being. The specific arrangement of letters (nucleotides) in the DNA molecule does not violate the laws of chemistry, and the informational content goes unnoticed by the physical sciences. From an informational point of view, however, the specific sequence of "letters" in DNA is all-important (Polanyi 1969, 225–239).

Why so? The informational aspect of DNA creates sharp distinctions, in the form of informational discontinuity, among different species, say, radishes, alligators, chimpanzees, and human beings, even though physically, chemically, biologically, and historically they all form an unbroken continuum. Human beings, for example, share with other species a common evolutionary history, as well as the same or similar molecular and metabolic characteristics. However, even a quantitatively small difference in the specific sequence of "letters" in the human or any other species' genome makes it qualitatively distinct from other kinds of life. Even if human beings and chimpanzees have descended only gradually from a common living ancestor, and even if their respective genomes differ only fractionally from each other, even a small informational divergence is enough to make each species and each individual within a species ontologically unique. We need not deny the atomic, physical, and chemical continuity, or the biological kinship, humans have with all other forms of life, in order to claim with logical consistency that even miniscule informational differences can render each species and each member of a species distinctly different (Polanyi 1969, 225–239).

The relatively new appreciation of information by life-scientists is significant for our question of human dignity. By itself the fact of informational differences cannot provide the foundation of human dignity, but it is a necessary condition for doing so. First, it implies that no living organism is simply reducible to mindless "matter." Logically speaking, biologists can no longer plausibly claim to have gotten to the very essence of life simply by resolving living cells into lifeless chains of atoms and molecules. The informational dimension in the cell implies that life is much more than "just chemistry." After all, nothing in the science of chemistry or physics is able to specify or explain precisely the particular succession of letters in the DNA of a particular species (Polanyi 1969, 225–239). Another "reading level," one capable of detecting informational differences, is required.

Materialist biologists, including especially Francis Crick and James Watson, the co-discoverers of the double-helix formation of DNA, assumed that their discoveries meant that all of life is now reducible to physics and chemistry (Crick 1996, 10; Watson 1965, 67). Further reflection, however, demonstrates that this assumption is logically mistaken. It is not the chemistry at work in the cell but mainly the specific sequence of letters in DNA that makes the difference between whether an organism is a carrot, amoeba, monkey, or human being. DNA, as we now realize, carries a considerable amount of "junk" segments, but this in no way rules out the specificity resident in the general sequence of letters in the DNA molecule. Even though there is atomic and molecular continuity, the element of information crisply differentiates one species from another.

Scientists must not attribute this sequence to supernatural intervention or to anything miraculous. However, the fact of information does require a richer understanding of the resourcefulness of nature than has been customary in mechanistic and atomistic philosophies of biology. An informational perspective shows, at the very least, that modern humans can be qualitatively differentiated from all other species, including other primates, in spite of their physical, chemical, and biological continuity. Scientists, it is true, have produced an increasingly reliable record of the genetic similarities between primates and human beings, but genes are much more than mere chains of atoms. They are carriers of information. The genome of one species employs the same alphabet and lexicon but not the same "message" as others. Seen in terms of coded information, even a slight modification of the sequence of "letters" or "words" carried by the DNA of a chimp is enough to differentiate it sharply from anatomically modern humans.

We may clarify this point by way of a simple analogy. In writing an essay any author employs the same alphabet, lexicon, and grammatical rules that others do. As far as relying on these ingredients is concerned, there will be no important differences among writers. But at a higher reading level, that of the specific sequence of letters and words, the essays differ considerably from one another. Likewise in the domain of life, even a quantitatively slight difference in the sequence of letters and "words," say, in the respective genomes of chimps and humans, can generate a disproportionately large difference when this information is expressed at the level of the whole organism in a specific environment. Figuratively speaking, the genetic alphabet, lexicon, and syntax can be shared across species. Yet, at a different level of understanding from that of chemistry and physics, information's openness to an endless variety of arrangements allows for sharp discontinuity among species. This is why the natural sciences, including biochemistry and evolutionary biology, cannot by themselves settle the question of whether humans are created in the image and likeness of God. Even after Darwin, however, the informational dimension of life and heredity leaves ample logical space for a genuinely religious interpretation of what it means to be specifically human.

The Perspective of Cosmology

As we have just seen, an informational perspective provides new insights into the evolution of life and human evolution. It provides a framework within which human dignity can, at least in principle, be affirmed without conflicting with evolutionary science. It offers an alternative to the narrowly materialist perspective on life that has dominated biology since the time of Darwin.

In a radically different way recent discoveries in the fields of astronomy and cosmology can also open a new window onto the specificity of human life and evolution within the larger history of nature. Big Bang cosmology now implies that the emergence of life and the ongoing story of biological evolution are part of a much larger cosmic drama than our species had ever known about prior to the twentieth century. In this recent and more sweeping cosmological setting evolution may be seen to carry a meaning that accentuates human difference and dignity in a surprising new way. In a word, a contemporary cosmological perspective allows us to realize that, at least on our planet, it is through human beings that "critical consciousness," along with freedom, moral aspiration, and religious longing, has broken into the sphere of finite being.

By placing biology in the context of cosmology, science has now shown that human beings have recently come into existence from a universe that is estimated to be around

14 billion years old. Moreover, judging from all that the physical sciences have discovered recently, this universe remains unfinished. In theological terms, the cosmos is still being created. It may be instructive, therefore, to locate the question of human significance within the framework of the newly revealed cosmic drama. Christian theology may now ask what human evolution means not only in conversation with biology but also with cosmology.

It is only recently that scientists and theologians alike have been able even to raise the question of human specificity in this way. Thanks to astrophysics and cosmology, beginning in the twentieth century, scientific inquiry has come to realize that the existence of human consciousness entails a very specific kind of universe, one that possesses just the right physical characteristics that have allowed for the eventual emergence of "thought." Thus our question of human specificity now merges with the much larger question of cosmic specificity: "Why this particular universe?"

Many scientists have now concluded that the Big Bang universe has been pregnant with life and mind from its very inception 14 billion years ago. Contrary to what materialist or "physicalist" philosophies of nature have traditionally held, the stuff of the universe has never been essentially mindless. The emergence of beings endowed with the capacity to understand, reflect, and decide, therefore, really begins during the first microseconds of the universe's existence. Christianity's declaration that human beings have been specially endowed by the Creator with a unique significance and a special vocation within the total scheme of things is at least logically consistent with contemporary cosmology. We have emerged, science suggests, from a cosmos whose primordial physical makeup was such as to make the eventual appearance of mind highly probable. Even though mind has appeared relatively recently in the cosmic story, the physical prelude to this emergent wonder was already playing from the very start of the symphony. During the earliest moments of cosmic existence, mind was already beginning to stir, as it were, in the very heart of matter.

The relatively recent debut of life 3.8 billion years ago, and of conscious self-awareness only a few million years ago, points to an immense awakening, still in progress, in which the universe is now becoming conscious of itself through the medium of our own species. In our specifically human mode of existence the cosmos is finally bringing one of its deepest potentialities out into the open. Our special place in the universe is to be the agents and instruments of this precious awakening. With the appearance of human beings, the phenomenon of reflective self-consciousness has now made its entrance into the universe.

This entry onto the cosmic stage may seem unimpressive from the perspective of physics, chemistry, and even biology. No laws of nature are broken in the process. Cosmologically speaking, however, the recent emergence of conscious self-awareness – accompanied by moral, aesthetic, and religious sensitivity – is the most dramatic development ever to have occurred in the unimaginably long journey of our universe, at least until now. Looking at human evolution panoramically, as part of the impressive drama of cosmic emergence, the appearance of humans is hardly the trivial occurrence that entrenched materialists take it to be.

Critical Consciousness and Human Dignity

Along with the emergence of consciousness, of course, other human propensities associated with the *imago Dei* such as freedom, creativity, ability to form deep relationships, and the capacity to love and keep promises have also made their way into the universe (Haught 2006). In spite of the claim by Darwinian materialists that the high degree of accident and blind necessity in biological evolution renders humanity nothing more than a fluke of nature, the cosmological perspective proposed here provides a wider point of view and a necessary corrective. Indeed, after Einstein an exclusively Darwinian contextualizing of human existence turns out to be unnecessarily cramped. A cosmological perspective, of course, does not render Darwinian biology irrelevant to our understanding of human specificity. It does, however, challenge the common assumption that biology is the most comprehensive intellectual setting within which to discern the meaning of human existence in the age of science.

Biology's inability to take into account the much broader cosmological context of human emergence has led much contemporary scientific thought and philosophy to the dubious conclusion that the human phenomenon is nothing more than an absurd and unintended effluence of an essentially pointless universe. Cosmologically understood, however, the arrival in natural history of consciousness, freedom, and moral sensitivity are ways in which the universe unfolds and reveals something of its true being and potential. Of course, the universe expresses its inner depths uniquely in the emergence of every form of life, and not just in the arrival of modern humans. Nevertheless, in the recent emergence of human beings – and any other instances of consciousness that may exist in extraterrestrial zones – the universe has made a momentous leap. The universe has at last awakened into thought and freedom, and now through us it begins to reflect upon itself and on the many possible ways it may continue to unfold in the future. By producing beings that have the capacity for reflection and moral sensitivity, the universe demonstrates that it still has the reserves to become even "more" than it has become thus far. The fact that we humans can contribute in diverse ways to the process of the universe's becoming "more" implies that we have a special standing within the whole of creation. Our special dignity is already implied in the experience of ourselves as having a vocation to contribute, each in our own modest ways, to the ongoing creation of the universe (Teilhard de Chardin 1999). In our creativity, our intense capacity to form relationships, to act responsibly, and even to worship, we mirror the image of God in an exceptional way. In view of astronomy and astrophysics, members of our species may now realize that the cosmos is a still unfolding, unfinished drama, and that the very meaning of our lives consists, at least in part, of our awareness that we may now take a more deliberate role in the continuation of this drama.

Like freedom, creativity is one of the traits that grounds our sense of self-worth. While other species may be to some degree sentient and even conscious, there is no evidence that they perceive themselves as having a special cosmic vocation and responsibility. They do not appear to possess a self-conscious concern about who they are, about what they should be doing with their lives, or about what their destiny is. Nor is their specific mode of awareness developed to the point where they can ask what is really going on in the universe and whether the universe has a purpose or meaning.

For this reason it seems rather ridiculous to maintain that there is nothing special about human existence. A cosmological window onto human evolution challenges the nearsighted claim that Darwinian biology has deposed humans from some illusory perch that they may formerly have occupied, reducing them to mere accidents of nature in an ultimately absurd universe. The dangers of anthropocentrism are, of course, still present, and subject to criticism, but instead of depleting our self-confidence, the cosmological perspective has the potential to renew it (Teilhard de Chardin 1964).

Summary and Conclusion

Situating biology and anthropology within the context of a universe that is still being created renders dubious all the shortsighted assertions by contemporary evolutionary materialists that biology alone can make adequate and ultimate sense of human nature. Unfortunately, the separating of scientific disciplines from one another in an age of over-specialization has led many scientists and philosophers to exaggerate the explanatory power of their own particular areas of expertise. This has been especially the case with evolutionary biologists, who have maintained that biology provides the ultimate and adequate framework for making (adaptive) sense of human existence, of mind, morality, freedom, and the human capacity to worship (for example, Dawkins 1986; Dennett 1995).

The absence of a cosmological perspective on humanity has led to a distortion of human specificity, especially in the writings of late twentieth- and early twenty-first-century evolutionary materialists. Their arbitrary decree that biological evolution is now the ultimate explanatory context for all living beings, including humans, inevitably makes our existence seem profoundly absurd and vocationally futile. The ultra-Darwinian debunkers have assumed, on the basis of the impersonal way in which natural selection seems to work, that any universe that sponsors the Darwinian mode of creating diversity is an indifferent and even hostile setting for the story of life and humanity. Nevertheless, as suggested above, natural selection may also be interpreted from a cosmological perspective. It may be situated within the context of a universe that is held together by a whole suite of reliable and predictable habits known as natural laws. In such a context natural selection should be no more theologically troubling than are the physical and chemical laws essential for the emergence of mind. The evolutionary materialists have overlooked the possibility that the universe itself is the more fundamental drama and that quite possibly something of great significance is slowly and quietly working itself out on a much larger scale than evolutionary biology – accurate though it may be – has been able to discern.

By moving our main point of view from biology to that of cosmology the emergence of consciousness and cognate traits is seen to be the most dramatic set of events ever to have occurred in the unfolding of the whole universe (or "multiverse," if it turns out that there exists a plurality of worlds empirically cut off from our own Big Bang cosmos). Theologically speaking, therefore, it makes good sense to situate human evolution in the context of a momentous cosmic process – in a way that biology alone cannot comprehend.

Unfortunately, however, many Christians, rather than widening their scientific vision of nature, have been content to ignore both evolutionary biology and cosmology as irrelevant to their understanding of human specificity. Christian thinking traditionally affirmed human dignity by appealing to the classical dualistic notion in which the human "soul" is said to be separable from the body, just as matter seemed separate from spirit. This dualistic understanding has provided an excuse to avoid any deep reflection on human specificity within the framework of a still unfolding universe. The typical approach of Christian education has been to salvage human dignity after Darwin by first allowing that our bodies may be the products of evolution but that an immortal soul has been infused in each person directly by God. Accordingly, even if humans and chimps have emerged from a shared ancestry, and even if our existence is part of a larger cosmic adventure, it is the divinely created human soul that assures us of our special value.

To those content with this interpretation, there is little or no interest in theologically connecting human identity tightly to the story of the universe. According to dominant strains of traditional theological anthropology and eschatology, the only important future that awaits human souls lies in an extraterrestrial heaven. So why worry about our relationship to nature and its history here and now? To those whose spiritual aspirations are limited to the "next world," both evolution and cosmology seem humanly inconsequential. To many believers a cosmological interpretation of human evolution is still seldom considered important.

However, the idea of a directly infused human soul can scarcely be the last word of theology on the relationship of humans to nature and God. Is there not some way in the age of evolution and Big Bang physics to affirm human dignity without trying to outflank biology and cosmology? Perhaps a biblically based faith may learn to understand the special value of human beings in a manner that now takes fully into account both the enormous amount of paleontological evidence for human evolution and the physical evidence of a cosmological drama that sponsors life and its evolution.

The longing for an eventual divorce of humanity from the cosmos, after all, is quite unbiblical. The Apostle Paul rejected such dualism when he declared that the whole of creation longs for the redemption proclaimed by Christian faith. In Christianity's foundational phase devotees of Christ did not separate either the Redeemer's destiny or their own from that of the universe. Contemporary cosmology, therefore, provides the opportunity for a fresh theological discernment of who we are and what our lives are all about. Such reflection by theology has still just barely begun, but even now at the very least it seems reasonable to acknowledge that the natural sciences provide no justifiable reason for Christians to abandon hope for the liberation of the entire creation. On the contrary, biology and cosmology together can help re-energize the belief that the grand story of life and the universe will be swept up into the fulfillment promised by the Christian Gospel.

References

Crick, Francis H. C. 1966. *Of Molecules and Men*. Seattle: University of Washington Press.

Darwin, Charles. 1993 [1859]. *The Origin of Species*, 6th edn. New York: Random House.

Darwin, Charles. 1998 [1871]. *The Descent of Man*. Amherst, NY: Prometheus Books.

Dawkins, Richard. 1986. *The Blind Watchmaker*. New York: W. W. Norton & Co.

Dennett, Daniel C. 1995. *Darwin's Dangerous Idea: Evolution and the Meaning of Life*. New York: Simon & Schuster.

Haught, John F. 2006. *Is Nature Enough? Meaning and Truth in the Age of Evolution*. New York: Cambridge University Press.

Phipps, William P. 2002. *Darwin's Religious Odyssey*. Harrisburg, PA: Trinity Press International.

Polanyi, Michael. 1969. Life's Irreducible Structure. In Marjorie Grene, ed. *Knowing and Being: Essays by Michael Polanyi*. London: Routledge & Kegan Paul, pp. 225–239.

Rolston, Holmes, III. 2010. *Three Big Bangs: Matter-Energy, Life, Mind*. New York: Columbia University Press.

Teilhard de Chardin, Pierre. 1964. *The Future of Man*. Translated by Norman Denny. New York: Harper & Row.

Teilhard de Chardin, Pierre. 1999. *The Human Phenomenon*. Translated by Sarah Appleton-Weber. Portland, OR: Sussex Academic Press.

Watson, J. D. 1965. *The Molecular Biology of the Gene*. New York: W. A. Benjamin, Inc.

Wood, Bernard. 2006. *Human Evolution: A Very Short Introduction*. New York: Oxford University Press.

Further Reading

Darwin, Charles. 1998 [1871]. *The Descent of Man*. Amherst, NY: Prometheus Books. Darwin's lengthy and detailed study of the evolution of modern humans from a nonhuman ancestry.

Haught, John F. 2010. *Making Sense of Evolution: Darwin, God, and the Drama of Life*. Louisville: Westminster John Knox Press. Argues that Darwinian evolution makes sense not only scientifically but also theologically.

Polanyi, Michael. 1969. Life's Irreducible Structure. In Marjorie Grene, ed. *Knowing and Being: Essays by Michael Polanyi*. London: Routledge & Kegan Paul, pp. 225–239. An important philosophical critique of the materialist assumption that life can be fully explained in terms of physical and chemical processes.

Teilhard de Chardin, Pierre. 1999. *The Human Phenomenon*. Translated by Sarah Appleton-Weber. Portland, OR: Sussex Academic Press. Arguably the most important Christian attempt in the twentieth century to show the consonance of geology, paleontology, contemporary cosmology, and evolutionary biology with the fundamental tenets of Christian faith.

Wood, Bernard. 2006. *Human Evolution: A Very Short Introduction*. New York: Oxford University Press. A clear and reliable presentation of the paleontological evidence for the evolution of modern humans.

27

Christian Theism and Life on Earth

PAUL DRAPER

Introduction

Some facts about life on earth appear to support theism. Indeed, perhaps the strongest evidence we have for theism is the existence of intelligent life. The complexity, value, and fragility of intelligent life on earth make its existence extraordinary and in some sense surprising; yet it is just the sort of thing one would expect to exist if theism were true. Theism does not, however, appear to fit as well with certain other facts about life, especially facts about the history and condition of life on earth. In this chapter, I want to focus on some of these other facts, and I want to examine their impact, not on the credibility of theism in general, but instead on the credibility of specifically Christian theism.

Arguments against Christian theism can be divided into two main types. "Logical" arguments attempt to show either that Christian theism is self-contradictory or that Christian theism is inconsistent (in the broadly logical sense) with some known truth. "Evidential" arguments attempt to show that certain known facts that are (at least so far as we can tell) consistent with Christian theism nevertheless provide evidence against it. The arguments in this chapter will be evidential. I will compare Christian theism ("CT" for short) to a serious alternative "hypothesis" that I will call "indifference naturalism" ("IN" for short), arguing for the thesis that IN is much more accurate than CT with respect to certain known facts about the history and condition of life on earth. In other words, I will show that, antecedently, we have much more reason to expect those facts to obtain on the assumption that IN is true than we have on the assumption that CT is true. Thus, while those facts may for all we know be consistent with CT, they nevertheless *strongly* support IN over CT (in the sense that they raise the ratio of the probability of the former to the probability of the latter *many*-fold).

The truth of my thesis is a threat to CT partly because IN is at least as probable prior to inquiry as CT is and partly because IN and CT are alternatives – they cannot both be true. Thus, in the absence of offsetting evidence strongly favoring CT over IN, establishing my thesis suffices to show that CT is very probably false. Before arguing for my thesis, I need to

---

The Blackwell Companion to Science and Christianity, First Edition. Edited by J. B. Stump and Alan G. Padgett.
© 2012 Blackwell Publishing Ltd. Published 2012 by Blackwell Publishing Ltd.

define both "IN" and "CT" and explain why I believe that IN is at least as probable prior to inquiry as CT.

Since IN is a form of naturalism and CT is a form of supernaturalism, I will begin by defining "naturalism" and "supernaturalism." I take naturalism to be the view that physical entities causally explain why there are any mental entities. Supernaturalism is the opposite view. Supernaturalists contend that the mental has ontological priority: in other words, that physical reality depends for its existence on one or more conscious beings. Theism is a form of supernaturalism. It claims that what ultimately explains the existence of physical entities is the productive power and purposes of a single conscious being: an omnipotent, omniscient, and morally perfect person (i.e., God). CT – Christian theism – adds to theism the view that Jesus of Nazareth was God incarnate and that, after being crucified, he literally and miraculously rose from the dead. IN – indifference naturalism – is a form of naturalism. It claims that the existence of all mental entities is explained by the productive power and natural laws of a morally indifferent physical universe.

Naturalism and supernaturalism are highly symmetrical views both syntactically and semantically. Both assert that physical and mental reality exists and that one of these two parts of reality ultimately explains the existence of the other. Thus, they have symmetrical metaphysical commitments. Neither is compatible with eliminative physicalism or eliminative idealism. Naturalism is compatible with dualism and identity physicalism but not with identity idealism, while supernaturalism is compatible with dualism and identity idealism but not with identity physicalism.[1] Given this symmetry, it is difficult to see how one could successfully argue that one view is more probable than the other *prior to inquiry*. As Hume taught us, one cannot determine *a priori* that the mental is better suited to serve as an ultimate cause than the physical or vice versa. IN and theism are not as symmetrical as naturalism and supernaturalism, but they are symmetrical enough to justify the claim that theism is not *much* more probable prior to inquiry than IN. (Indeed, the great specificity of theism suggests that it is less probable prior to inquiry than IN.) CT, however, is much more specific than theism and for that reason is much less probable prior to inquiry than theism and so less probable prior to inquiry than IN. (The general principle here is that the more specific a theory is, the more it says about the world, and so the more likely it is independent of evidence to say something false and so to be false.) To be safe, however, I will assume in this chapter only that IN is *at least as* probable prior to inquiry as CT. This means that, in order for CT to be more probable all things considered than IN, it will have to be the case that, on balance, the (total) available evidence raises the ratio of the probability of CT to the probability of IN.

In this brief chapter I will be able to examine only a small portion of the available evidence – just a few known facts about the history and condition of life on earth, beginning in the next section with the fact of evolution. The issue of whether the rest of the available evidence raises the ratio of the probability of CT to IN (or vice versa) and, if so, how much – not to mention the issue of how CT and IN fare when compared to other alternative "theories" – is beyond the scope of this chapter. For example, I will not assess the evidential value of the fact that (intelligent) life exists, the fact that the only intelligent life we know to exist is merely human instead of something more impressive, the (alleged) fact that the universe had a beginning, the (alleged) fact that human beings have free will, the fact that human mental activity is dependent to a very high degree on physical processes occurring in the brain, and the (alleged) fact that non-belief in God is often blameless and reasonable. In my opinion, some of these facts support IN over CT, some support CT over IN, and some are not, contrary to widespread belief, actually known to obtain; but these opinions will not be defended here.

Evolution

Ever since the publication of Darwin's *The Origin of Species*, countless theologians, philosophers, and scientists have pointed out that evolution could be the means by which God has chosen to create human beings and the rest of the living world. This is thought to show that, while the truth of evolution does refute the biblical story of creation, interpreted literally, it in no way threatens the more general belief that the universe was created by the Christian God; for one can be a Christian, indeed even an orthodox Christian, and not interpret the account of creation in the Book of Genesis literally. Thus, evolution provides little or no reason to doubt CT. The plausibility of this argument seems to be confirmed by the fact that many scientists are both evolutionists and Christian theists. Commenting on this fact (or something close to it), Stephen Jay Gould (1987, 70) says:

> Unless at least half my colleagues are dunces, there can be – on the most raw and direct empirical grounds – no conflict between science and religion. I know hundreds of scientists who share a conviction about the fact of evolution, and teach it in the same way. Among these people I note an entire spectrum of religious attitudes – from devout daily prayer and worship to resolute atheism. Either there's no correlation between religious belief and confidence in evolution – or else half these people are fools.

What Gould neglects to mention is that many well-educated people, including many of Gould's colleagues on the irreligious end of the spectrum, reject CT precisely because they believe in evolution. For example, William B. Provine (1988), a leading historian of science, maintains that those who manage to retain their religious beliefs while accepting evolution "have to check their brains at the church-house door."

So who is correct? Is it compatibilists like Gould and the liberal preacher Henry Ward Beecher (1885, 53), who predicted in 1885 that evolution "will change theology, but only to bring out the simple temple of God in clearer and more beautiful lines and proportions"? Or is it incompatibilists like Provine and the fundamentalist preacher William Jennings Bryan, who once defined "theistic evolution" as "an anesthetic which deadens the patient's pain while atheism removes his religion" (Kennedy 1957, xiv)? My own position, as my introductory remarks suggest, lies somewhere between the view that the marriage of CT to evolution is a happy one and the view that it must end in divorce. I agree with the compatibilists that CT and evolution are logically consistent. What I disagree with is the compatibilist's inference from no inconsistency to no conflict. For while consistency implies that the truth of evolution does not conclusively disprove CT – that there is no good "logical" argument from evolution against CT just as there is no good logical argument from evil against theism – it does not imply that the truth of evolution is no evidence at all against CT. My position is that evolution is evidence strongly favoring IN over CT.

By "evolution" I mean the conjunction of two theses. The first, which I will call "the genealogical thesis," asserts that evolution did in fact occur – complex life did evolve from relatively simple life. Specifically, it is the view that all multicellular organisms and all (relatively) complex unicellular organisms on earth (both present and past) are the (more or less) gradually modified descendants of a small number of relatively simple unicellular organisms. The second thesis, which I will call "the genetic thesis," addresses the issue of how evolution occurred. It states that all evolutionary change in populations of complex organisms either is, or is the result of, trans-generational genetic change (or, to be more precise, trans-generational change in nucleic acids). It is important to distinguish this claim about the mechanisms by which evolution takes place from the much more specific claim that natural selection operating on random genetic mutation is the principal mechanism driving evolutionary change (or the principal mechanism driving the evolutionary change that results in increased complexity). Let's call this more specific claim "the theory of natural selection" and its conjunction with evolution "Darwinian evolution." The evidence for evolution, unlike the evidence for Darwinian evolution, is overwhelming – so overwhelming that evolution can without begging any questions legitimately be taken as fact rather than mere theory for the purpose of arguing against CT.

The specific claim I wish to defend in this section is the following: IN is much more accurate with respect to evolution than CT is. This means that, if we were to abstract from the observations and testimony upon which our knowledge of the history and condition of life on earth is based, but not ignore other knowledge we have, such as the knowledge that complex life of various forms, including intelligent life, exists (but did not always exist), then we would have much more reason to expect evolution to be true on the assumption that IN is true than we would have on the assumption that CT is true. Again, it is an interesting and difficult question whether any of the knowledge from which we do *not* abstract favors CT over IN or vice versa, but as I said earlier that issue is beyond the scope of this chapter.

Now consider special creationism, by which I mean the statement that some relatively complex living things did not descend from relatively simple single-celled organisms but rather were independently created by God. The use of the word "independently" here signifies, not just that the creation in question violates genealogical continuity, but also that it involves direct divine action in the world. Thus, evolution entails that special creationism is false. Accordingly, we can divide the issue of the relative accuracy of CT and IN with respect to evolution into two parts. First, how accurate are these two theories with respect to the falsity of special creationism? And second, *given the falsity of special creationism*, how accurate are they with respect to evolution? IN entails that God does not exist and so entails that special creationism is false. Thus, IN predicts the falsity of special creationism with maximal accuracy. CT, however, does not predict this. Were it not for the evidence we have for evolution, Christian theists would be justifiably uncertain about whether special creationism is true or false. So CT is clearly not as accurate as IN with respect to the falsity of special creationism. But how much less accurate is it? In the remainder of this section, I will argue for the position that it is much less accurate.

At first glance, it seems that the evidence for evolution is the only strong reason theists have for believing that God is not a special creator. After all, for all we know independent of that evidence, God might have chosen to create in a variety of different ways. For example, while he might have created life in a way consistent with genealogical continuity, he might also have created each species independently. Or he might have created certain basic types of life independently, allowing for evolutionary change, including change resulting in new species, within these types. Or he might have independently created only a few species or even only a single species, humans perhaps. Antecedently – that is, independent of the evidence for evolution – it appears we have no reason at all to think that an omnipotent, omniscient, and morally perfect creator would prefer evolution to one of these forms of special creation.

Some theists, however, are quite confident on purely *a priori* grounds that God is not a special creator. According to Diogenes Allen (1989, 59) and Howard J. Van Till (1991, 43), for example, special creationism was implausible even before the evidence for evolution was discovered, because it is an implication of God's "rationality" or God's status as creator rather than as "member of the universe" that God "creates a universe with members that are coherently connected." This coherence precludes God's acting directly in the world and hence precludes special creation. Thus, according to these theists, the only sort of explanations of natural phenomena that theistic scientists should look for are ones that are consistent with naturalism. In short, these theists are committed methodological naturalists.

I do not, however, find their arguments at all convincing. What possible justification could be given for thinking that if God were the immediate cause of a natural event then that would reduce God's status from creator to "member of the universe"? Also, what does God's rationality have to do with this? Perhaps the idea is that, just as a perfectly rational car manufacturer would produce a car that never needed its gas tank filled or its air filter replaced, a perfectly rational creator would make a universe that ran on its own. But such a car would be preferable because filling up with gas or replacing parts has a cost in terms of time, energy, and so forth. An omnipotent and omniscient creator would not have such worries. In general, what counts as a rational or perfect or defective universe depends on the creator's goals. What goal or plan of God would be better served by a universe in which God never acts directly? Of course, human freedom may place limitations on the amount and type of God's "interventions." But it does not rule out special creation. For all we know, it could be the case both that God has some goal that is furthered by creating a universe governed for the most part by natural laws and that God must on occasion directly act in this universe in order to accomplish God's goals, including the goal of actualizing the precise sort of complex life God wants. If this were the case, then God might independently create that life. Surely such intervention in the course of nature would conflict neither with God's status as creator nor with God's rationality. Nor would it imply that the universe is in some way defective or inferior to universes in which God never intervenes. Perhaps no such universes are compatible with God achieving God's goals.

Another theist who holds that we have antecedent reasons for believing that God would not perform any special creative acts is the philosopher Ernan McMullin. In response to Alvin Plantinga's (1991b) defense of special creationism, McMullin (1991, 74) says that "from the theological and philosophical standpoints, such intervention is, if anything, antecedently improbable."[2] He claims further that, "the eloquent texts of Genesis, Job, Isaiah, and Psalms" support his position, because "the Creator whose powers are gradually revealed in these texts is omnipotent and all-wise, far beyond the reach of human reckoning. His Providence extends to all His creatures; they are all part of His single plan, only a fragment of which we know, and that darkly" (1991, 75). But how this is supposed to support his position is never explained. It seems to do the opposite, since any claim to know that God would never intervene in the natural order will be difficult to justify if we are as much in the dark about God's plans as these texts suggest.[3]

Incidentally, I find it interesting that when confronted with arguments against theism based on the idea that it is antecedently unlikely that God would permit heinous evil, many theists are quick to suggest that, since God is omniscient, humans are not in a position to make such a judgment. Yet, if we are to believe Allen and Van Till (McMullin has his doubts), then humans are in a position to judge that it is antecedently unlikely that God would create any life forms independently! Personally, I find the claim that the torturing of innocent children is antecedently improbable given theism vastly more plausible than the claim that special creationism is antecedently improbable given theism.

The problem with the theistic objections to special creationism considered so far is that they all involve *a priori* theological or philosophical speculation the direction of which is influenced far too much by the conclusion desired (cf. Plantinga 1991a, 100). Indeed, these attempts to make special creation seem incompatible with theism are no more objective and no more plausible than Provine's attempt to make evolution seem incompatible with theism. While Allen, Van Till, and McMullin claim that God would never intervene in nature to create life, Provine claims that the idea of a God who "works through the laws of nature" is "worthless" and "equivalent to atheism" (McMullin 1991, 58). How convenient!

A more serious attempt to show that the truth of special creationism would actually be surprising on CT is *a posteriori* in nature. We know by past experience that God, if he exists, has at least latent "deistic tendencies." Teleology was, after all, eliminated from the physical sciences well before Darwin wrote *The Origin of Species*. And even independent of the evidence for evolution there is considerable evidence that various biological processes work quite well without direct divine action in the world. In general, even independent of the evidence upon which evolution is based, the history of science is a history of success for naturalistic explanations and failure for supernaturalistic ones. Thus, we have a good antecedent *a posteriori* reason to believe that, assuming theism is true, God does not act directly in nature.

Although the past success of methodological naturalism in the physical sciences does provide some reason for theists to believe that God is not a special creator, Christian theists should not be convinced, because Christian theism implies that Jesus was and is God incarnate and that he literally and miraculously rose from the dead. It seems unlikely, to say the least, that this could be true without direct divine action. Therefore, the success of methodological naturalism should not make anyone who believes that CT is true confident that God did not create at least some complex life independently.

In addition, theists of all stripes have reason to believe that God would specially create. This is because the division between conscious and non-conscious life is enormously significant if theism is true, at least if one assumes that idealism is false, which is an assumption that few people nowadays are inclined to challenge. By claiming that a mind existed prior to the physical world and was responsible for its existence, theism entails the falsity of physicalism and so supports metaphysical dualism. Thus, since theism entails that God's mind is not physical, it makes it antecedently likely that all minds are non-physical and hence that conscious life is fundamentally different from non-conscious life. But this in turn makes it antecedently likely that conscious living things are not just the genetically modified descendants of non-conscious living things – that conscious life was created independently. And since special creationism is defined as the position that at least some complex life was created independently, it follows that theism would lead one to expect (though granted not with certainty) that special creationism is true.

This may explain why so many theists were drawn to the idea of special creationism before (and in many cases even after) conclusive evidence for evolution was discovered. For those theists who recognized that theism supports a dualistic view of concrete reality, which in turn supports a dualistic view of human nature, the idea that conscious life is the natural effect of altering the nucleic acids of non-conscious life must have seemed rather absurd. Granted, changes in genotype can result in large changes in phenotype, but surely one would not expect genetic change to result in the crossing of fundamental metaphysical lines! Thus, even if we know by past experience that God, assuming God exists, rarely intervenes in nature, the sort of metaphysics presupposed or at least supported by theism gives theists reason to believe that God did intervene in the physical world in order to create a mental world within it. So it is hardly surprising that, prior to the discovery of overwhelming evidence for evolution, many theists were special creationists. They had good reason to be! This means, however, that CT is more than just slightly less accurate than IN with respect to the falsity of special creationism. IN entails the falsity of special creationism, while CT leads one to expect its truth.

Recall that, in order to show that IN is much more accurate than CT with respect to evolution, it is sufficient to show that IN is much more accurate than CT with respect to the falsity of special creationism and that, given the falsity of special creationism, IN is at least as accurate as CT with respect to evolution. I have completed the first of these two tasks. Turning to the second, we are now assuming that special creationism is false and asking how surprising evolution is on IN and on CT (relative to background information that includes the fact that complex life forms do exist). As previously noted, naturalism entails that special creationism is false; so the assumption that special creationism is false adds nothing to IN. I will call the denial of special creationism conjoined with CT "Augustinian CT," since St Augustine famously rejected a special creationist interpretation of Genesis. So my task is to show that, antecedently, we have at least as much reason to expect evolution to be true given IN as we have given Augustinian CT.

Given that complex life exists, the truth of evolution is unsurprising on IN primarily because of a complete lack of plausible naturalistic alternatives. As Alvin Plantinga (1991b, 18) says, "For the non-theist, evolution is the only game in town." On Augustinian CT, alternatives to evolution are somewhat more likely, partly because there is less reason to assume that the complex must arise from the simple. When one starts with omnipotence and omniscience, so much is possible (and equally easy)! Even if the Augustinian Christian theist grants that these considerations favor IN, she might counter that evolution is more likely given Augustinian CT because evolutionary processes could not produce the sort of life we find in the world without supernatural assistance. For example, without some intelligent being guiding genetic change, such magnificent ordered systems as the human body could never have evolved from single-celled organisms in a few billion years. The problem is that the arguments that have been offered in defense of these claims are rejected by the vast majority of evolutionary biologists and philosophers of science (see Kitcher 1982). All things considered, then, the modest conclusion that IN is at least as accurate as Augustinian CT with respect to evolution is justified. Therefore, since, for the reasons explained earlier, CT is much less accurate with respect to the falsity of special creationism than IN is, it follows that CT is much less accurate with respect to evolution than IN is.

Flourishing and Floundering

The next question is how accurate IN and CT are with respect to the condition of life on earth.[4] (Here we assume background information that includes the truth of evolution.) What we find when we examine our biosphere is that, for a variety of biological and ecological reasons, organisms compete for survival, with some having an advantage in the struggle for survival over others; as a result, many organisms, including many sentient beings, never flourish because they die before maturity, many others barely survive, but languish for most or all of their lives, and those that reach maturity and flourish for much of their lives usually flounder in old age; further, in the case of human beings and very probably some non-human animals as well, floundering or languishing often involves intense and prolonged suffering.

In this section, I will defend the claim that, given evolution, IN is much more accurate with respect to these facts than CT is. I will provide two supporting arguments for this claim. First, I will show that, on the assumption that CT is true, we have good reasons to be surprised by these facts, reasons that we do not have when we assume that IN is true. Second, I will show that, on the assumption that IN is true, there are good reasons to expect these facts, reasons that we do not have when we assume that CT is true.

Christian theists must at least start from the position that human beings and other sentient organisms are *supposed* to flourish (hence the motivation for the doctrine of the Fall). After all, almost all sentient organisms are *capable* of flourishing in biologically realistic circumstances. This is proven by the fact that many do flourish and by the fact that the differences between those that do flourish and those that do not are in almost all cases relatively small. Second, sentient organisms have a good – they certainly can be benefited or harmed – and no sentient organism can achieve that good without flourishing. Third, a God, being perfect in moral goodness, could not care more deeply about sentient beings achieving their good, and being perfect in power and knowledge, could not be better positioned to ensure that sentient beings achieve their good. Therefore, what we know about the condition of living things on earth, including the fact that huge numbers of human and other sentient beings never flourish at all before death and countless others flourish only briefly, is extremely surprising given CT. It is not what one would expect to find in a living world created by the Christian God.

Granted, it is *possible* that an omniscient God would have good moral reasons unknown to us to permit sentient organisms to flounder. This is why claims about what God would prefer must be prefaced with "other moral considerations held equal." But it is also possible, *and no less likely*, that such a God would have good moral reasons unknown to us to *prevent* sentient organisms from languishing – reasons in addition to the reasons that are known to us. Thus, the accuracy of CT with respect to the condition of life on earth will depend largely on the moral reasons that we know about, not on the ones we do not know about, and the reasons we know about all make the distribution of flourishing and floundering that we observe in the living world very surprising given CT. Further, no parallel reasons make this distribution surprising given IN; so other considerations held equal, it follows that IN is more accurate with respect to the condition of life on earth than CT is.

Other considerations, however, are not equal – they are actually even worse for the Christian theist. Evolution greatly increases IN's advantage over CT because, when it is combined with IN, it provides good reasons to expect what we observe about the condition of terrestrial life. This is so, because IN together with our background knowledge is not neutral with respect to the theory of natural selection, which in turn is not neutral with respect to what we know about the condition of life on earth. In other words, given IN, it is to be expected, not only that common descent is true, but also that what I earlier called the theory of natural selection is true: natural selection accounts for most of the fantastic complexity we find in the living world. And given the truth of the theory of natural selection, we should not find the various facts mentioned above about the condition of life on earth at all surprising.

Of course, when we assess the accuracy of IN with respect to the condition of life on earth, we must abstract from the observations and testimony upon which our knowledge of that condition is based, and that involves abstracting from much of the evidence we have for the operation of natural selection. But even apart from that evidence, the theory of natural selection is almost certainly true given IN because no other viable naturalistic explanation of biological complexity is available, nor is one likely to become available. Granted, evolutionary change may have many causes besides natural selection (e.g., genetic drift), but that's because not all evolutionary change involves increased complexity. The gradual development of highly complex organic systems requires something that can coordinate or give direction to a series of small evolutionary changes across many generations. And if IN is true, then what could possibly do that besides natural selection, broadly understood? (Dembski 2004, chapter 6, makes this point. See especially pp. 261–263.) Thus, when we assess the predictive power of IN with respect to the observed condition of life, we can assume that the theory of natural selection is true. And what we observe about the distribution of flourishing and floundering is far from surprising given the theory of natural selection, for natural selection (and in particular "survival selection"[5]) cannot operate unless there are winners and losers in the struggle to survive and reproduce. Thus, in the absence of supernatural assistance, a "Darwinian world" containing sentient organisms is very likely to be a world where early death, languishing, and suffering are common.

One might object that what works for the naturalistic goose will also work for the theistic gander. In other words, if the proponent of IN can use the theory of natural selection to help it "predict" the condition of life on earth, then why can't the Christian theist do the same? This objection misses the mark for two reasons. The first is that CT undercuts many of the predictions that the theory of natural selection makes about good and evil. For example, while survival selection is not at all surprising given IN and the theory of natural selection, other less brutal forms of natural selection would be more likely on CT. Thus, even assuming that the theory of natural selection is true, CT is not as accurate as IN is with respect to the observed distribution of flourishing and floundering.

The main reason, however, that this objection fails is that, given CT, we have no good reason to believe that the theory of natural selection is true. Of course, as I mentioned previously, whether IN or CT or something else is true, we have overwhelming reason to believe that evolution is true; but the theory of natural selection, though perhaps compatible with CT, is not particularly likely on CT (especially when one abstracts from the observations and testimony upon which our knowledge of the condition of life on earth is based). Keep in mind that the theory of natural selection is more than the claim that natural selection causes some evolutionary change – that has been proven experimentally and so is certain given either IN or CT. The theory of natural selection, as I have defined it, claims that natural selection accounts for most of the biological complexity in the world. Given IN, we are justly confident of this, not because we know in any historical detail exactly how natural selection led to biological complexity, but rather because natural selection provides a way of explaining such complexity without having to appeal to the purposes of a supernatural designer. If CT is true, however, then natural selection is not needed to solve the problem of apparent teleological order in the living world. It is *possible*, of course, that the Christian God would use natural selection and in particular survival selection to drive the evolution of increasingly complex organisms; but for all we know, such a God would proceed in any of a variety of other non-Darwinian ways. As long as an omnipotent God is the ultimate source of evolutionary change, natural selection is not crucial for the development of biological complexity. Further, CT implies or at least makes it very likely that God does on occasion directly act in the natural world – it's certainly hard to see how the Incarnation and Resurrection, taken literally, could result from purely natural processes! Thus, for example, on the assumption that CT is true, it must be regarded as a *real* possibility that God has guided evolution by directly causing genetic changes throughout an entire population of organisms to occur, making survival selection unnecessary. Therefore, given CT, it would not be surprising at all if natural selection did not play a major role in the development of biological complexity.

So not only do we have reasons on CT that we do not have on IN to be surprised by the condition of life on earth; we also have reasons on IN that we do not have on CT not to be surprised by the condition of life on earth. The latter reasons are parasitic on the theory of natural selection. That theory is very accurate with respect to the relevant facts about the condition of life on earth. This increases the accuracy of IN with respect to those facts but not CT because the theory of natural selection is much more likely to be true if IN is true than if CT is true. Therefore, IN is clearly much more accurate than CT is with respect to the relevant facts about the condition of life on earth.

Conclusion

I have argued that IN is much more accurate than CT with respect to evolution and also that, given evolution, IN is much more accurate than CT with respect to certain known facts about the condition of life on earth. Thus, since IN is also at least as probable as CT prior to inquiry, it follows that the history and condition of life on earth provide the resources for a powerful cumulative case against the truth of Christian theism. Unless one possesses strong offsetting evidence favoring CT over IN, the correct conclusion to draw is that CT is much less likely to be true than IN. And while this conclusion does not imply that indifference naturalism is probably true, it does imply that Christian theism is very probably false.

Notes

1 Some supernaturalists (e.g., so-called physicalist Christians) are identity physicalists about some minds (e.g., human and animal minds), but not about all minds (e.g., God's). I take this to be a form of dualism because I define terms like dualism and physicalism at the global level of reality as a whole, not at the local level of human beings. If one believes that at least one non-physical mind exists and that at least one non-mental physical object exists, then one is a dualist, even if one believes that human minds are physical objects or that tables are mental objects.

2 Plantinga (1991b, 21) refers to the sort of position that McMullin defends as "semi-deistic." McMullin (1991, 76) complains that this terminology is loaded, yet he describes his own position as believing in "the integrity of the natural order." It would seem then that Christians have a dilemma. No good Christian wants to be called a "deist," but no good Christian would want to deny that God's creation has "integrity"!

3 For additional criticisms of the positions of Van Till and McMullin, see Plantinga (1991a).

4 Some will object to this new question on the grounds that, by presupposing that there are "facts" about the "condition" of life on earth, it presupposes that there are evaluative facts when in fact there are no such facts if naturalism is true. I find it difficult to take this objection seriously. Super-naturalists and naturalists may disagree about whether the teleological organization of living organisms is reducible to non-teleological facts, but they should not disagree about whether organisms are organized teleologically, nor should they disagree on whether that organization provides a foundation for objective (and often obvious) truths about whether a particular organism is flourishing or floundering. Evaluative facts, in other words, are built into nature – they supervene on certain non-evaluative facts, and they do so whether or not a divine mind or any other mental entity is the ultimate source of the physical world.

5 I use the term "natural selection" to refer, not just to cases in which a characteristic is selected because it enables an organism to survive long enough to reproduce ("survival selection"), but also to cases in which a characteristic is selected either because it makes an organism that survives long enough to reproduce more likely to find a willing mate (sexual selection) or because it makes an organism that finds a willing mate likely to have a greater than average number of

surviving fertile offspring (fecundity selection). Other variations involving group selection are also possible.

References

Allen, Diogenes. 1989. *Christian Belief in a Postmodern World*. Louisville, KY: Westminster John Knox Press.

Beecher, Henry Ward. 1885. *Evolution and Religion*. Boston: The Pilgrim Press.

Dembski, William. 2004. *The Design Revolution: Answering the Toughest Questions about Intelligent Design*. Downers Grove, IL: InterVarsity Press.

Gould, Stephen Jay. 1987. Darwinism Defined: The Difference between Fact and Theory. *Discover* (January), pp. 64–70.

Kennedy, Gail, ed. 1957. *Evolution and Religion*. Boston: D. C. Heath & Company.

Kitcher, Philip. 1982. *Abusing Science: The Case against Creationism*. Cambridge, MA: MIT Press.

McMullin, Ernan. 1991. Plantinga's Defense of Special Creation. *Christian Scholar's Review*, 21(1), pp. 55–79.

Plantinga, Alvin. 1991a. Evolution, Neutrality, and Antecedent Probability: A Reply to Van Till and McMullin. *Christian Scholar's Review*, 21(1), pp. 80–109.

Plantinga, Alvin. 1991b. When Faith and Reason Clash: Evolution and the Bible. *Christian Scholar's Review*, 21(1), pp. 8–32.

Provine, William B. 1988. Evolution and the Foundation of Ethics. *MBL Science*, 3(1), pp. 25–29.

Van Till, Howard J. 1991. When Faith and Reason Cooperate. *Christian Scholar's Review*, 21(1), pp. 33–45.

Further Reading

Draper, Paul, ed. 2007–2008. *God or Blind Nature? Philosophers Debate the Evidence*. Online at http://www.infidels.org/library/modern/debates/great-debate.html. A set of four debates about the evidence for and against theism and naturalism.

Rachels, James. 1990. *Created from Animals: The Moral Implications of Darwinism*. Oxford: Oxford University Press. An introductory book defending the view that Darwinian evolution undermines traditional religion and morality.

Stump, Eleonore. 2010. *Wandering in Darkness: Narrative and the Problem of Suffering*. New York: Oxford University Press. Includes an attempt to show how suffering might contribute to human flourishing.

Part VI
The Human Sciences

28

Toward a Cognitive Science of Christianity

JUSTIN L. BARRETT

My task for this chapter is to prime the pump. The time is right for theologically informed scholars to build upon the accomplishments of the cognitive science of religion (CSR) to create a new, rigorous engagement between Christianity and science. It is time for a cognitive science of Christianity.

Like most sciences involved in the "science–religion dialogue," cognitive science has the potential to reveal fresh insights about the natural world, which could encourage or discourage particular theological positions. Unlike many of these sciences, cognitive science has the additional potential to reveal to us previously undiscovered insights into human nature itself, and particularly how human nature comes to embrace (or reject) and act upon (or ignore) these same theological positions. Consequently, cognitive science could be an especially valuable "dialogue partner" for theological traditions. A cognitive science of Christianity could provide a blueprint.

CSR was begun by scholars of religion principally interested in scientifically explaining patterns of cross-culturally recurrent ideas and practices. For this reason, careful examinations of particular traditions have been relatively rare. Nevertheless, a thorough treatment of one familiar religious and theological tradition would benefit CSR by forcing the area to join up various theories into a coherent and comprehensive account of not just "religion" or "religious ideas" but a particular religion. Further, philosophers have begun discussing the implications of CSR for justified religious beliefs (Schloss and Murray 2009). Do cognitive explanations of religion explain religion away? The answer will surely be yes and no. At least some religious and theological perspectives – particularly those that are empirical claims about, say, human nature – will prove to be difficult to square with findings from CSR. Others, however, will be reinforced or remain untouched. By examining the specific claims of a specific religion (in this case, Christianity) lessons will be learned faster and more clearly than from a generic treatment, and these lessons may then be applied to other religions.

My job in this chapter, then, is twofold: I must introduce CSR, but I must do so in such a way that its exciting promise for generating new perspectives on Christianity is clear. For

The Blackwell Companion to Science and Christianity, First Edition. Edited by J. B. Stump and Alan G. Padgett.
© 2012 Blackwell Publishing Ltd. Published 2012 by Blackwell Publishing Ltd.

this reason, I begin with a cursory summary of the field and then provide a sampling of applications of CSR to Christianity. Many of these applications could be made to other religions, but for the sake of brevity I will not flag such parallels in my presentation.

Cognitive Science of Religion in Brief

Primarily, CSR draws upon the cognitive sciences to explain how cross-culturally regular features of human minds inform and constrain religious thought and action, therefore accounting for recurrent patterns in their expression. For instance, how might belief in super-human intentional beings (gods) be explained in terms of underlying cognitive structures? Do cognitive regularities help explain the prevalence of afterlife beliefs?

Basic commitments

A number of basic commitments motivate the CSR approach:

(1) *Tabula rasa* and radical relativist views of minds are mistaken. Drawing upon break-throughs in the cognitive sciences over the past 60 years, CSR scholars reject full-bodied cultural relativism. Minds are not passive sponges or blank slates, equally able and willing to learn and use any type of information equally well. By virtue of our biological endowment as *homo sapiens* plus regularities of the environments in which we grow up, humans naturally acquire numerous cognitive biases and predilections – independent of cultural particulars (Pinker 1997).

(2) By extension some important and content-rich aspects of human cognition are extra-cultural. Well-supported examples include preferential processing of human faces (Melt-zoff and Moore 1983), reasoning about the properties and movement of bounded physical objects, basic numeracy, and the distinction between ordinary physical objects and those that can move themselves in a goal-directed manner, that is, agents (Spelke and Kinzler 2007). Other well-supported domains of thought that appear largely invariant across cultures in terms of their basic parameters and developmental courses include language, folk psychology (or Theory of Mind), folk biology (people's intuitions about living things), and some aspects of moral thought and social exchange reasoning (Hirschfeld and Gelman 1994). I have referred to these various extra-cultural, content-rich cognitive systems as *mental tools* (Barrett 2004).

(3) Such mental tools inform and constrain religious thought, experience, and expression. Certainly the operation of mental tools does not *determine* human cultural expression in all of its diversity. Rather, mental tools can be likened to the foundation and supports of a house. They give a basic shape and size to the house, but the particulars that make a house unique and beautiful are free to vary considerably.

(4) Following Sperber's epidemiological approach to explaining cultural expression (Sperber 1996), CSR scholars typically focus on ideas and practices that are distributed across individuals, regarding ideas that are not shared as idiosyncratic rather than "religious."

(5) It follows that the task for CSR is to account for recurrent patterns of religious expression – types of ideas, experiences, identifications, and practices – that are distributed

across a population or even across cultures. Explaining religion, then, is explaining how mental tools working in particular environments resist or encourage the spread of these ideas and practices we might call "religious."

Additional characteristic features of CSR

Typically CSR scholars have avoided trying to define *religion* as a whole, but rather generally chosen to approach "religion" in a piecemeal fashion, by identifying human thoughts and behaviors that are generally considered religious and then trying to explain why those thought or behavioral patterns are cross-culturally recurrent. If the explanations turn out to be part of a grander explanation of "religion", so be it, but there is no assumption that *religion* is a coherent natural kind.

As CSR is an interdisciplinary enterprise, it is marked by methodological pluralism. CSR scholars have turned to whichever data collection and analysis methods appear appropriate to particular questions. These methods include archeological (Whitehouse and Martin 2004); ethnographic (Malley 2004; Cohen 2007; Whitehouse and Laidlaw 2004); historiographic (Lisdorf 2001; Whitehouse and Martin 2004; Vial 2004); interview (Malley and Barrett 2003); and experimental (Barrett and Keil 1996), including cross-cultural (Knight 2008; Astuti and Harris 2008) and developmental techniques (Bering and Parker 2006; Barrett and Richert 2003).

Topics of exploration

CSR has made starts on many topics, including: children's ideas about the design and origin of the natural world (Kelemen 2004; Evans 2001); death and afterlife beliefs (Astuti and Harris 2008; Bering *et al.* 2005); magic (Sørensen 2005); prayer (Barrett 2001); the relationship among souls, minds, and bodies (Cohen and Barrett forthcoming; Bloom 2004); super-human agent concepts such as gods (Barrett 2008); religion and morality (Boyer 2001); religious development in children (Barrett 2012); religious ritual and ritualized behaviors (Liénard and Boyer 2006; McCauley and Lawson 2002; Malley and Barrett 2003); religious social morphology (Whitehouse 2004); scripturalism (Malley 2004); spirit possession (Cohen and Barrett 2008); transmission of religious ideas (Gregory and Barrett 2009; Boyer and Ramble 2001).

The Naturalness of Christianity

CSR has converged on the claim that religion is so common within and across cultures because of its "cognitive naturalness," its relative ease, and automaticity owing to strong undergirding in normally developing cognitive systems (Boyer 1994; Atran 2002; Barrett 2004; Pyysiäinen 2009; Bloom 2007; McCauley 2011). Normal human cognitive systems operating in normal human environments generate converging intuitions that find satisfaction in some core religious ideas (and subsequent practices). From early childhood people easily acquire ideas about gods, a non-physical aspect of humans, and some kind of afterlife (Barrett 2012).

And because these ideas are naturally and largely intuitive, they have a plausible feel about them, too. Rather than particular social or cultural conditions driving people to religion, religions are going to be there unless specific, unusual social and cultural conditions tamp them down. These natural intuitions, then, are the building blocks for specific religious traditions and theologies.

Natural religion

The core natural intuitions collaborate to form what I have called Natural Religion, the religious thoughts that naturally developing cognition encourages people toward (Barrett 2011, 2012; contrast with natural theology, a reflective intellectual exercise). The contours of Natural Religion are still under exploration, but evidence from cross-cultural recurrence and early appearance in children suggests the following candidate features:

(A)   Elements of the natural world such as rocks, trees, mountains, and animals are purposefully and intentionally designed by someone(s), who must therefore have superhuman power (Kelemen 2004).

(B)   Things happen in the world that unseen agents cause. These agents are not human or animal (Guthrie 1993).

(C)   Humans have internal components (such as a mind, soul, and/or spirit) that are distinguishable from the body (Bloom 2004, 2007, 2009).

(D)   Moral norms are unchangeable – even by gods (Hauser 2006; Katz 2000).

(E)   Immoral behavior leads to misfortune; moral behavior to fortune (Jose 1990; Hafer and Begue 2005).

(F)   Ritualized behaviors such as marking off special spaces or ritual cleansings can protect from unseen hazards (including those caused by gods) (Liénard and Boyer 2006; Boyer and Liénard 2006).

(G)   Some component(s) of humans that has agency (such as souls or minds) may continue to exist without earthly bodies after death (thereby becoming gods) (Cohen and Barrett forthcoming; Bloom 2004).

(H)   Gods exist with thoughts, wants, perspectives, and free will to act (Guthrie 1993; Barrett 2012).

(I)   Gods may be invisible and immortal, but they are not outside of space and time (Barrett and Keil 1996; Barrett 1999).

(J)   Gods can and do interact with the natural world and people, perhaps especially those that are ancestors of the living, and hence, have an interest in the living. This interaction with the world accounts for perceived agency and purpose in the world that cannot be accounted for by human or animal activity (Barrett 2008; Bering 2006, 2002; Boyer 2001).

(K)   Gods generally know things that humans do not (they can be super-knowing or super-perceiving or both), perhaps particularly things that are important for human relations (Boyer 2001; Barrett and Richert 2003).

(L)   Gods, because of their access to relevant information and special powers, may be responsible for instances of fortune or misfortune; they can reward or punish human actions (Bering and Johnson 2005; Johnson 2005; Boyer 2001; Bering and Parker 2006).

(M) Because of their superhuman power, when gods act, they act permanently, and so when they act in religious rituals, the religious ritual need not be repeated as in baptisms or ordinations (McCauley and Lawson 2002).

How is Christianity natural?

Because many components of Christianity consist of only small elaborations on Natural Religion, they are readily understood, believed, communicated, and used to generate inferences and explanations. Here again are features of Natural Religion, but this time with elaborations common (but not necessarily uncontroversial) in Christianity (indicated by italics):

(A_χ) Elements of the natural world are purposefully and intentionally designed by someone, who must therefore have superhuman power. *The Creator of the cosmos is God.*

(B_χ) Things happen in the world that unseen agents cause. These agents are not human or animal. *God, angels, and demons account for these happenings.*

(C_χ) Humans have internal components that are distinguishable from the body. *Humans have a soul.*

(D_χ) Moral norms are unchangeable (even by gods). *Moral norms are an expression of God's unchangeable will.*

(E_χ) Immoral behavior leads to misfortune; moral behavior to fortune. *God punishes immoral behavior and rewards moral behavior, but not necessarily in this lifetime.*

(F_χ) Ritualized behaviors such as marking off special spaces or ritual cleansings can protect from unseen hazards (including those caused by gods). *Churches are sacralized through prayer and ritual.*

(G_χ) Some component(s) of humans that has agency may continue to exist without earthly bodies after death. *Human souls are resurrected in new bodies.*

(H_χ) Gods exist with thoughts, wants, perspectives, and free will to act. *God, angels, and demons are all persons with minds.*

(I_χ) Gods may be invisible and immortal, but they are not outside of space and time. *God is invisible and immortal.*

(J_χ) Gods can and do interact with the natural world and people, perhaps especially those that are ancestors of the living and, hence, have an interest in the living. This interaction with the world accounts for perceived agency and purpose in the world that cannot be accounted for by human or animal activity. *Some happenings in the world are caused by God, angels, or demons.*

(K_χ) Gods generally know things that humans do not, perhaps particularly things that are important for human relations. *God knows everything.*

(L_χ) Gods, because of their access to relevant information and special powers, may be responsible for instances of fortune or misfortune; they can reward or punish human actions. *God punishes immoral behavior and rewards moral behavior, but not necessarily in this lifetime.*

(M_χ) Because of their superhuman power, when gods act, they act permanently, and so when they act in religious rituals, the religious ritual need not be repeated. *Marriage, baptism, and ordination rituals are performed once for life and produce permanent changes in status.*

These Christian ideas are not strange, opaque, or even arbitrary from a cognitive perspective. They build upon a firm, natural conceptual foundation.

Christian views on divinely implanted intuitions

Research from CSR provides empirical support for at least two themes in traditional Christian theology that pertain to human nature. Both can find expression in St Paul's letter to the Romans. Romans 1:18–20 speaks to all humans possessing some knowledge of God:

> For the wrath of God is revealed from heaven against all ungodliness and unrighteousness of men, who suppress the truth in unrighteousness, because that which is known about God is evident within them; for God made it evident to them. For since the creation of the world His invisible attributes, His eternal power and divine nature, have been clearly seen, being understood through what has been made, so that they are without excuse. (NASV)

CSR provides evidence that humans do have natural propensities toward believing in some kind of god, and perhaps particularly a super powerful, immortal, creator. Many subtly different theological perspectives concerning exactly what knowledge of God is a natural part of human experience (apart from special revelation) have been developed. Even considering just the Calvinist tradition, at least two versions of the *sensus divinitatis* (sense of the divine) have been prominently defended, John Calvin's and Alvin Plantinga's (Clark and Barrett 2010). In addition to providing support for the basic thrust of these related theological notions, perhaps CSR could also help decide which of the competing conceptions of this natural *sensus divinitatis* is likely to be accurate.

Similarly, it is not uncommon for Christian theologians to comment on the condition of people's natural access to moral truths. As a result of biblical passages such as Romans 2:14–15, Christians commonly regard everyone – regardless of culture – as having some access to genuine morality:

> Indeed, when Gentiles, who do not have the law, do by nature things required by the law, they are a law for themselves, even though they do not have the law. They show that the requirements of the law are written on their hearts, their consciences also bearing witness, and their thoughts sometimes accusing them and at other times even defending them. (NIV)

Here, too, cognitive scientists and evolutionary psychologists are beginning to generate supportive data, addressing questions such as what moral intuitions humans have in common (Haidt 2007; Hauser 2006; Hinde 2002). We might also wonder about the evolution and development of moral intuitions. When did they arise in our ancestry? When do they appear in children? At stake could be the species boundary and age boundary of moral culpability and, hence, need for salvation (setting aside the consequences of original sin).

These examples illustrate that some theological claims are empirically tractable, and a collaboration of Christian theology and CSR bears potential to support, challenge, or disambiguate competing theological claims.

How Christianity Deviates from Natural Religion

Of course, there is more to Christianity than these claims, and even a couple of these claims are either rejected or amplified by theologians such that they are not nearly so natural. For instance, the most natural cultural instantiation of (J) might be beliefs in ancestor spirits or ghosts that act in the world. The common official Christian rejection of such beings rebuffs a natural tendency. Perhaps this is one reason why beliefs in ghosts and saints coexist with other more uniformly sanctioned beliefs in superhuman agency. Similarly, point (G_χ) concerning souls requiring bodily resurrection also deviates somewhat from the natural anchor. Again, disembodied spirits living in a spirit world or acting in this one might be more cognitively intuitive than souls lying in wait for resurrection at the final judgment.

When religious traditions or theologies develop ideas that deviate from Natural Religion, CSR predicts two accompanying problems: *theological correctness* and *theological incorrectness*.

Theological correctness

The more complex theological ideas are – that is, the more they deviate from the ordinary cognition that undergirds Natural Religion – the more effort will be required to teach them and maintain them, a point illustrated by my research on *theological correctness*, the tendency for the religious concepts we use in ordinary tasks to be much simpler and cognitively natural than the theological propositions we affirm when in a reflective mode (Barrett 1999).

Christian theologian Gordon Spykman, in discussing the biblical view of God, explains that:

> On this view, God and the world are two uniquely distinct realities. The difference between them is not merely quantitative but qualitative. God is not simply more of what we are. There is an essential discontinuity, not just a share of difference, nor a gradual more-or-less distinction, as though God has only a "running head start" on us. God is absolutely sovereign, "the Other," not simply "Another." (Spykman 1992, 64–65)

Though someone might sincerely believe that God is the unknowable, indescribable, wholly transcendent otherness that is reality outside of time and existing in an infinite number of dimensions of reality, such a concept of God is difficult to use to solve problems, generate inferences, and make predictions, especially in the course of normal events – in *real-time* thinking.

Christians commonly say things like, "When I went through that ordeal, I felt like God was walking right beside me," or "Sometimes when I pray, I imagine myself embraced in God's arms." This sort of language suggests a conception of God far more human-like and far less abstract than what theologians produce and believers affirm. Adults – even theologically savvy ones – do not always seem to *use* these theologically sophisticated concepts all the time. To try to clarify the relationship among various conceptions of God, my collaborators and I conducted several experiments. In these experiments we contrasted what adults *said* they believed about God with how they thought about God in a less reflective, real-time situation – understanding stories (Barrett 1999; Barrett and VanOrman 1996; Barrett 1998; Barrett and Keil 1996).

Cognitive psychologists have shown that we automatically fill in the gaps in stories to the point that we actually misremember what was in the original story as being more complete than it was. That is, we use our current knowledge to complete what was presented, leading to *intrusion errors*, remembering things as being in the story that were not actually there. For instance, in one set of experiments, participants heard: "John was trying to fix the birdhouse.

He was pounding the nail when his father came out to watch him and to help him do the work." Subsequently, a large portion of the listeners confidently agreed that the following sentence was one of the sentences they heard: "John was *using the hammer* to fix the bird house when his father came out to watch him and to help him do the work." Notice that in the original sentences, no hammer was mentioned. Listeners who know that nails are typically "pounded" with hammers naturally inserted the presence of a hammer in their memory of the sentences (Johnson *et al.* 1973).

My collaborators and I took advantage of this tendency for the hearer to automatically fill in the gaps to create an indirect measure for people's ideas about God. We constructed a number of stories that included God as a character but carefully left gaps for our audience to fill. For instance, one story read:

> On a dry, dirt road in Australia was a beautiful and interesting rock. One day, God was looking at the rock. It was green with blue, red, and gold flakes. While God was looking at the rock, a stampede of brown, long-horned cattle came charging down the road over where the rock was. God watched them go. They were kicking up dust and bellowing. The noise was thunderous. God finished looking at the rock, which was then dust-covered and had hoof prints all around it.

After each story we asked: "Which of the following pieces of information were included in the story?" Listeners answered simply "Yes" if they remembered it being in the story or "No" if they didn't remember it. We assured our participants that the wording did not have to be exact. Some of the items checked for general memory of the story, for instance, "The rock was in Asia." The other items checked for intrusion errors related to hearers' ideas about God. To illustrate, one item read, "God resumed looking after the rock after the cattle went past." (Was that in the story? Yes or no?) If participants understood God as someone that can attend to any number of things at once, the answer is no. God might have been watching the cattle *and* looking at the rock. Alternatively, if we tacitly attribute to God more human-like serial attention, then the story might be misremembered as saying that God *resumed* looking at the rock after the cattle went past because God could not attend to both at once.

Using stories and questions like these, intrusion errors revealed that our participants used a very human-like or *anthropomorphic* understanding of God to make sense of the stories. There is something hard about understanding the story with an all-present, all-powerful, non-anthropomorphic God. At least when trying to *use* our ideas of God in these kinds of tasks, a more human-like concept of God seems easier, more natural. For instance, in the stories people tended to incorrectly remember God as being in one place at a time, but when asked directly they claimed God was everywhere or nowhere; they incorrectly remembered God as doing one thing at a time, but claimed God could do any number of things at once when asked directly.

These experimental results demonstrate that in a sense adults may actually have two (or more) different sets of ideas about God: one set is the complex theological set about an all-present, all-knowing, and radically different kind of being that comes up in reflective situations; and the other set is the one that looks much more like a human and is easier to use in real-time situations. The gap between these two conceptions is *theological correctness*. Like political correctness, when our intellectual guard is up, we use the ideas we know we are supposed to use; different ideas than those that come naturally. The farther religious ideas deviate from Natural Religion, the harder they are to use in reflexively in real-time situations.

Theological *incorrectness*

Because it is difficult for individuals to use relatively unnatural theological ideas in real-time, attempts to teach theological concepts that deviate too far from Natural Religion run the risk of confusion and misappropriation. Pascal Boyer refers to this tendency as the "Tragedy of the Theologian" (Boyer 2001) and Jason Slone calls it *theological incorrectness* as it is a corollary of theological correctness (Slone 2004).

Slone has described many cases of theological incorrectness caused by the restrictive influence of natural cognition on the successful up-take of theological concepts. For instance, one illustration Slone develops is how to square the status of individual free will with traditional predestination within Calvinist theology. Theologians may offer intellectual ways to bring the idea that God sovereignly determines who does and does not become a Christian together with the idea that humans freely choose whether or not to accept the Gospel of Jesus Christ. The apparent mutual incompatibility, however, and the counterintuitiveness of humans not having freedom in this regard, lead people to positions that theologians might regard as distortions.[1] This case illustrates that while general religious thought and action may have largely natural cognitive foundations, Christian theology need not have anything like the same naturalness.[2]

The counterintuitiveness of grace

To develop just one example of potentially unnatural, counterintuitive theology, consider the Christian doctrine of grace. Grace is sometimes defined as "unmerited favor" or "not getting the punishment we deserve". Grace captures the idea that salvation is not earned or deserved but is a free gift from God to those that receive it. Think of a Christmas present from parents when you were a child. You didn't earn it and there is no expectation of reciprocating; no *quid pro quo*. To get it, all you have to do is say "thank you" and unwrap it. Many Christians say God's grace is like this present: receiving it and expressing gratitude is the only reasonable response.

Through the ages Christians seem compelled to add stipulations to the "gift" of salvation: that you have to behave yourself, go to church, wear trousers if male and dresses if female (instead of traditional ethnic attire), read your Bible frequently, pray daily, and so forth. That so many preachers include sermons on grace in their regular offerings of topics, month after month, year after year, attests that the message just isn't sticking. People seem to have a deeply ingrained sense of fair-exchange practices. If you give me something, I'm obligated to give you something of comparable value. If I don't reciprocate, I am in your debt. Being in someone else's debt is uncomfortable, so we try to settle the account. Worse still is when someone else receives grace instead of justice. Theologian Donald McCullough puts the situation thus:

> Grace set to music is one thing, but what about grace itself? What about grace as an idea? Grace as an act? Grace as a force? We don't like it. . . . To be sure, we appreciate brief encounters with it, such as when we forget to pay the health insurance premium and we're told not to worry because there is a "grace period." . . . We're thankful for these minor reprieves, for Grace Lite. But if the real thing happens, if we're seized by a full-bodied, take-no-prisoners grace, we have far more ambivalent feelings. When a muscled arm of mercy lifts us by the scruff of the neck and sets us in a new place, a better place we neither earned nor deserved, we're likely to protest

that, given time, we could have gotten ourselves there, thank you very much, and without the rough treatment. Even worse, if grace happens to someone else, someone we *know* doesn't deserve it, someone we can't stand, then we don't want to hear about grace, let alone see it in operation. In such circumstances, grace seems more like a miscarriage of justice. (McCullough 2005, 4–5)

Evolutionary psychologists Leda Cosmides and John Tooby have provided evidence that people are sensitive to social exchange rules and have argued that this sensitivity is an evolved cognitive capacity (Cosmides and Tooby 1989). Even the feeling of gratitude may be tough for us. If someone pays us an enormously generous kindness, we may feel embarrassed, guilty, or indebted instead of grateful (Emmons 1999, 2008). So, no matter how many times preachers tell us that "God doesn't need anything from you," or "The price Jesus paid is too big for any mortal to reciprocate," or the like, we just can't seem to shake that nagging feeling that God wants something from us in exchange for salvation. These sorts of considerations have led me to think sometimes that grace is something counterintuitive to the way people think.[3]

Of course, grace is not the only Christian doctrine or theological teaching that seems to push away from Natural Religion. The idea of God being outside of time or being a Trinity, for instance, does not appear to be natural in the least. At the center of Christianity is the idea of the Incarnation of God in the form of Jesus of Nazareth, born of a virgin, executed, but conquered death. The points at which the Incarnation is relatively natural and those at which it is unnatural or counterintuitive is a question presenting a potentially fruitful interaction between CSR and theology.

How unnatural theology is spread

Recognizing that not all religious beliefs are terribly natural, cognitive scientists of religion have begun specifying the *cultural scaffolding* – irregularly available tools or resources – that help build theologies far removed from the foundation of Natural Religion. As a result of dynamics such as theological correctness and incorrectness, a standard rule of thumb is that the more unnatural an idea is, the more cultural scaffolding is required for the idea to spread successfully.

Successful theological traditions, such as Christianity, have developed just this cultural scaffolding to make complex ideas more accessible. Christian activities include teaching, preaching, and other instructive occasions in which religious ideas are communicated. The use of written texts, particularly the Bible, is an example of cultural scaffolding that aid in transmitting relatively unnatural theological ideas. People can believe in concepts that they have trouble articulating if they use a text as a cognitive prosthetic – indeed for this reason texts, tables, and figures are commonplace in science.

Cognitive anthropologist Harvey Whitehouse has argued that religious communities tend to gravitate toward at least one of two strategies for communicating counterintuitive ideas and practices, and the two strategies yield religious communities with very different characteristics, two clusterings of variables that Whitehouse has dubbed *modes of religiosity* (Whitehouse 2000, 2004). Christianity provides a strong example of what Whitehouse has called the *doctrinal mode*. In the doctrinal mode of religiosity, weekly or even daily practices in which religious ideas are communicated serve as a central device for helping to transmit and maintain a common body of beliefs and practices, and that can help a community identify its members. The doctrinal mode triggers the development of *semantic memory* (the meanings of ideas) for large bodies of doctrine. Complex ideas and intricate ceremonies are scaffolded by heavy repetition and socially sanctioned doctrinal specialists who help maintain orthodoxy and orthopraxy. The resulting religious communities tend to be bound together by common bodies of ideas and hierarchical power structures. Because having the right commitments to ideas (and related practices) mark out the religious community, the communities can be very large and the religions can spread rapidly.

Cognitive considerations of the various forms of cultural scaffolding that characterize Christian practice and transmission of ideas have only begun. For instance, Brian Malley has applied CSR insights and the cognitive *relevance theory* of communication (Sperber and Wilson 1995) to begin understanding how Christians use the Bible (Malley 2004). Cognitive treatments of Christian pilgrimage, prayer, rituals, and sermons are all needed.

Is Cognitive Science a Threat to Theism?

As CSR and related evolutionary explanations of religious beliefs have become more prominent, philosophers have begun exploring whether such scientific approaches to religion are a threat to justified theistic belief (Murray and Goldberg 2009; Murray 2009; Barrett 2007; van Inwagen 2009; Murray 2008; Barrett *et al.* forthcoming). A review of treatments to date falls beyond the scope of this chapter, but I offer that the consensus seems to be gravitating toward a negative answer. That CSR can offer explanations for why people tend to believe in some kind of god does not mean that there is no God, nor does it mean that belief in the existence of God is unjustified or irrational.

The collection of mental tools that encourage religious beliefs can be compared to a radio. Non-obvious and transient signals get detected and processed to reveal to some possessors of the radio that there is an unseen, intelligent, intentional being out there somewhere. Some people possess a radio but haven't formed the belief that someone is out there. Perhaps their radios aren't tuned properly or there is some environmental interference jumbling the message reception. In either case, learning how a radio works does not bear upon whether there really is an unseen someone "out there" broadcasting. Maybe there is, and maybe there isn't. Similarly, explaining the cognitive equipment relevant for forming beliefs in gods, souls, the afterlife, and other religious concepts does not importantly impact whether one is justified in holding such beliefs.

Findings from CSR would be much more troubling for Christian beliefs if the proposed factors promoting beliefs bore no connection to the outside world. Radios, like our mental tools, use inputs from the environment. They very well could be detecting real patterns from someone. Similarly, if the subsequent beliefs were 100% uniform, whether or not the cognitive systems in play received inputs from the outside, you would believe whether or not the beliefs were true. If 100% of humans believed in the existence God, for instance, and cognitive science was able to demonstrate that we have cognitive systems that unswervingly make us believe in God, then we might have reason to doubt the actual existence of God. We wouldn't be justified in saying there is no God, but only that our reason for believing in God (namely our strong intuition produced by cognitive mechanisms) would be seriously damaged. Whether or not God existed we would believe in God's existence. Ironically, then, the fact that no religious belief is completely universal and uncontroversial helps protect religious beliefs from being "explained away" by cognitive science.

Nevertheless, as mentioned above, the apparent immunity of core religious ideas from being undercut by cognitive science does not necessarily apply to all specific religious or theological claims. Christian theology often contains claims about the nature of human thought, moral sensibilities, and the like. Many of these are empirical claims that fall into the domain of cognitive science and are, hence, open to empirical challenges from cognitive science.

Conclusion

The cognitive science of religion has revealed that ordinary cognitive systems inform and constrain religious expression, thereby accounting in part for why certain ideas and practices are cross-culturally recurrent. Christianity shares many features with other religions, features that can be located in a theoretical Natural Religion generated by cognitive systems working in common human environments. Christian ideas and practices that deviate too far from Natural Religion – that are relatively counterintuitive – will be more difficult for believers to use to generate inferences, predictions, and explanations in real-time, non-reflective situations. Similarly, theological ideas will predictably suffer distortion and simplification because of cognitive dynamics. To fight these tendencies and successfully spread many aspects of Christian theology, therefore, cultural scaffolding is required.

Exactly which aspects of Christianity are more or less natural, and how cultural scaffolding works most effectively in the Christian tradition are two promising areas of study for a cognitive science of Christianity. Likewise, examining how such scientific treatments might support or challenge justified Christian belief will be required scholarly activities as such a cognitive science of Christianity develops.

Notes

1 Indeed, I am deliberately not taking care here to spell out the theologically correct positions, because they are somewhat beside the point, and any distortion I introduce underlines the point that counterintuitive theology is bound to be distorted.
2 For a more thorough discussion of these issues and an enlightening comparison among religion, theology, and modern science, see McCauley (2011).
3 I thank Nick Gibson for his perspectives on how cognitively natural or unnatural grace might be. In my book *Born Believers*, I suggest that, perhaps, grace is not as difficult for children as for adults. If I am correct there, the intuitions that adults have that work against accepting grace might be late developing and subject to cultural particularities, rather than reflecting natural cognition (Barrett 2011).

References

Astuti, Rita and Harris, Paul L. 2008. Understanding Mortality and the Life of the Ancestors in Rural Madagascar. *Cognitive Science*, 32, pp. 713–740.
Atran, Scott. 2002. *In Gods We Trust: The Evolutionary Landscape of Religion*. Oxford: Oxford University Press.

Barrett, Justin L. 1998. Cognitive Constraints on Hindu Concepts of the Divine. *Journal for the Scientific Study of Religion*, 37, pp. 608–619.

Barrett, Justin L. 1999. Theological Correctness: Cognitive Constraint and the Study of Religion. *Method and Theory in the Study of Religion*, 11, pp. 325–339.

Barrett, Justin L. 2001. How Ordinary Cognition Informs Petitionary Prayer. *Journal of Cognition and Culture*, 1(3), pp. 259–269.

Barrett, Justin L. 2004. Bringing Data to Mind: Empirical Claims of Lawson and McCauley's Theory of Religious Ritual. In B. C. Wilson and T. Light, eds. *Religion as a Human Capacity: A Festschrift in Honor of E. Thomas Lawson*. Leiden: Brill, pp. 265–288.

Barrett, Justin L. 2007. Is the Spell Really Broken? Bio-psychological Explanations of Religion and Theistic Belief. *Theology and Science*, 5(1), pp. 57–72.

Barrett, Justin L. 2008. Why Santa Claus Is Not a God. *Journal of Cognition and Culture*, 8(1–2), pp. 149–161.

Barrett, Justin L. 2011. *Cognitive Science, Religion, and Theology: From Human Minds to Divine Minds*. Conshohocken, PA: Templeton Foundation Press.

Barrett, Justin L. 2012. *Born Believers: The Science of Childhood Religion*. New York: Free Press.

Barrett, Justin L. and Keil, Frank C. 1996. Anthropomorphism and God Concepts: Conceptualizing a Non-natural Entity. *Cognitive Psychology*, 31, pp. 219–247.

Barrett, Justin L., Leech, David, and Visala, Aku. Forthcoming. Can Religious Belief Be Explained Away? Reasons and Causes of Religious Belief. In U. Frey, ed. *Evolution and Religion*. Brussels: Tectum.

Barrett, Justin L. and Richert, Rebekah A. 2003. Anthropomorphism or Preparedness? Exploring Children's God Concepts. *Review of Religious Research*, 44, pp. 300–312.

Barrett, Justin L. and VanOrman, Brant. 1996. The Effects of Image Use in Worship on God Concepts. *Journal of Psychology and Christianity*, 15(1), pp. 38–45.

Bering, Jesse M. 2002. Intuitive Conceptions of Dead Agents' Minds: The Natural Foundations of Afterlife Beliefs as Phenomenological Boundary. *Journal of Cognition and Culture*, 2, pp. 263–308.

Bering, Jesse M. 2006. The Folk Psychology of Souls. *Behavioral and Brain Sciences*, 29, pp. 453–462.

Bering, Jesse M., Hernández-Blasi, C., and Bjorkland, D. F. 2005. The Development of "Afterlife" Beliefs in Secularly and Religiously Schooled Children. *British Journal of Developmental Psychology*, 23, pp. 587–607.

Bering, Jesse M. and Johnson, Dominic D. P. 2005. "O Lord . . . You Perceive My Thoughts from Afar": Recursiveness and the Evolution of Supernatural Agency. *Journal of Cognition and Culture*, 5, pp. 118–142.

Bering, Jesse M. and Parker, B. D. 2006. Children's Attributions of Intentions to an Invisible Agent. *Developmental Psychology*, 42, pp. 253–262.

Bloom, Paul. 2004. *Descartes' Baby: How Child Development Explains What Makes Us Human*. London: William Heinemann.

Bloom, Paul. 2007. Religion Is Natural. *Developmental Science*, 10, pp. 147–151.

Bloom, Paul. 2009. Religious Belief as an Evolutionary Accident. In M. Murray and J. Schloss, eds. *The Believing Primate: Scientific, Philosophical, and Theological Reflections on the Origin of Religion*. New York: Oxford University Press, pp. 118–127.

Boyer, Pascal. 1994. *The Naturalness of Religious Ideas: A Cognitive Theory of Religion*. Berkeley: University of California Press.

Boyer, Pascal. 2001. *Religion Explained: The Evolutionary Origins of Religious Thought*. New York: Basic Books.

Boyer, Pascal and Liénard, Pierre. 2006. Why Ritualized Behavior? Precaution Systems and Action-Parsing in Developmental, Pathological, and Cultural Rituals. *Behavioral and Brain Sciences*, 29(6), pp. 595–613.

Boyer, Pascal and Ramble, Charles. 2001. Cognitive Templates for Religious Concepts: Cross-cultural Evidence for Recall of Counter-intuitive Representations. *Cognitive Science*, 25, pp. 535–564.

Clark, Kelly James and Barrett, Justin L. 2010. Reformed Epistemology and the Cognitive Science of Religion. *Faith and Philosophy*, 27(2), pp. 174–189.

Cohen, Emma. 2007. *The Mind Possessed: The Cognition of Spirit Possession in an Afro-Brazilian Religious Tradition*. New York: Oxford University Press.

Cohen, Emma and Barrett, Justin L. 2008. Conceptualising Possession Trance: Ethnographic and Experimental Evidence. *Ethos*, 36(2), pp. 246–267.

Cohen, Emma and Barrett, Justin L. Forthcoming. In Search of "Folk Anthropology": The Cognitive Anthropology of the Person. In W. van Huyssteen and E. Wiebe, eds. In *Search of Self: Interdisciplinary Perspectives on Personhood*. Grand Rapids, MI: Eerdmans, pp. 104–125.

Cosmides, Leda and Tooby, John. 1989. Evolutionary Psychology and the Generation of Culture, Part 2. Case Study: A Computational Theory of Social Exchange. *Ethology and Sociobiology*, 10, pp. 51–97.

Emmons, Robert A. 1999. *The Psychology of Ultimate Concerns: Motivation and Spirituality in Personality*. London: Guildford Press.

Emmons, Robert A. 2008. *Thanks! How Practicing Gratitude Can Make You Happier*. New York: Houghton Mifflin.

Evans, E. Margaret. 2001. Cognitive and Contextual Factors in the Emergence of Diverse Belief Systems: Creation versus Evolution. *Cognitive Psychology*, 42, pp. 217–266.

Gregory, Justin and Barrett, Justin L. 2009. Epistemology and Counterintuitiveness: Role and Relationship in Epidemiology of Cultural Representations. *Journal of Cognition and Culture*, 9, pp. 289–314.

Guthrie, Stewart E. 1993. *Faces in the Clouds: A New Theory of Religion*. New York: Oxford University Press.

Hafer, Carolyn L. and Begue, Laurent. 2005. Experimental Research on Just-World Theory: Problems, Developments, and Future Challenges. *Psychological Bulletin*, 131(1), pp. 128–167.

Haidt, Jonathan. 2007. The New Synthesis in Moral Psychology. *Science*, 316, pp. 998–1002.

Hauser, Marc D. 2006. *Moral Minds: How Nature Designed Our Universal Sense of Right and Wrong*. New York: Ecco/HarperCollins.

Hinde, Robert. 2002. *Why Good Is Good: The Sources of Morality*. London: Routledge.

Hirschfeld, Lawrence A. and Gelman, Susan A., eds. 1994. *Mapping the Mind: Domain Specificity in Cognition and Culture*. Cambridge: Cambridge University Press.

Johnson, Dominic D. P. 2005. God's Punishment and Public Goods: A Test of the Supernatural Punishment Hypothesis in 186 World Cultures. *Human Nature*, 16, pp. 410–446.

Johnson, Marcia K., Bransford, John D., and Solomon, Susan K. 1973. Memory for Tacit Implications of Sentences. *Journal of Experimental Psychology*, 98, pp. 203–205.

Jose, Paul E. 1990. Just-World Reasoning in Children's Immanent Justice Judgments. *Child Development*, 61(4), pp. 1024–1033.

Katz, Leonard D., ed. 2000. *Evolutionary Origins of Morality: Cross-Disciplinary Perspectives*. Thoverton: Imprint Academic.

Kelemen, Deborah. 2004. Are Children "Intuitive Theists"? Reasoning about Purpose and Design in Nature. *Psychological Science*, 15, pp. 295–301.

Knight, Nicola. 2008. Yukatek Maya Children's Attributions of Beliefs to Natural and Non-natural Entitites. *Journal of Cognition and Culture*, 8(3–4), pp. 235–243.

Liénard, Pierre and Boyer, Pascal. 2006. Whence Collective Ritual? A Cultural Selection Model of Ritualized Behavior. *American Anthropologist*, 108, pp. 814–827.

Lisdorf, Anders. 2001. The Spread of Non-natural Concepts. *Journal of Cognition and Culture*, 4, pp. 151–174.

Malley, Brian. 2004. *How the Bible Works: An Anthropological Study of Evangelical Biblicism*. Walnut Creek, CA: AltaMira Press.

Malley, Brian and Barrett, Justin L. 2003. Does Myth Inform Ritual? A Test of the Lawson–McCauley Hypothesis. *Journal of Ritual Studies*, 17(2), pp. 1–14.

McCauley, Robert N. 2011. *Why Religion Is Natural and Science Is Not*. New York: Oxford University Press.

McCauley, Robert N. and Lawson, E. Thomas. 2002. *Bringing Ritual to Mind: Psychological Foundations of Cultural Forms*. Cambridge: Cambridge University Press.

McCullough, Donald. 2005. *If Grace Is So Amazing, Why Don't We Like It?* San Francisco, CA: Jossey-Bass.

Meltzoff, Andrew N. and Moore, N. Keith. 1983. Newborn Infants Imitate Adult Facial Gestures. *Child Development*, 54, pp. 702–709.

Murray, Michael J. 2008. Four Arguments That the Cognitive Psychology of Religion Undermines the Justification of Religious Beliefs. In J. S. Bulbulia, Richard Sosis, and Erica Harris *et al.*, eds. *The Evolution of Religion: Studies, Theories, and Critiques*. Santa Margarita, CA: Collins Foundation Press, pp. 365–370.

Murray, Michael J. 2009. Scientific Explanations of Religion and the Justification of Religious Belief. In M. Murray and J. Schloss, eds. *The Believing Primate: Scientific, Philosophical, and Theological Reflections on the Origin of Religion*. Oxford: Oxford University Press, pp. 168–178.

Murray, Michael J. and Goldberg, Andrew. 2009. Evolutionary Accounts of Religion: Explaining and Explaining Away. In M. Murray and J. Schloss, eds. *The Believing Primate: Scientific, Philosophical, and Theological Reflections on the Origin of Religion*. New York: Oxford University Press, pp. 179–199.

Pinker, Steven. 1997. *How the Mind Works*. New York: W. W. Norton & Co.

Pyysiäinen, Ikka. 2009. *Supernatural Agents: Why We Believe in Souls, Gods, and Buddhas*. New York: Oxford University Press.

Schloss, Jeffrey P. and Murray, Michael J., eds. 2009. *The Believing Primate: Scientific, Philosophical, and Theological Reflections on the Origin of Religion*. Oxford: Oxford University Press.

Slone, D. Jason. 2004. *Theological Incorrectness: Why Religious People Believe What They Shouldn't*. New York: Oxford University Press.

Sørensen, Jesper. 2005. *A Cognitive Theory of Magic*. Lanham, MA: Rowman & Littlefield.

Spelke, Elizabeth S. and Kinzler, K. D. 2007. Core Knowledge. *Developmental Science*, 11, pp. 89–96.

Sperber, Dan. 1996. *Explaining Culture: A Naturalistic Approach*. Oxford: Blackwell.

Sperber, Dan and Wilson, Deirdre. 1995. *Relevance: Communication and Cognition*, 2nd edn. Oxford: Blackwell.

Spykman, Gordon. 1992. *Reformational Theology: A New Paradigm for Doing Dogmatics*. Grand Rapids, MI: Eerdmans.

van Inwagen, Peter. 2009. Explaining Belief in the Supernatural: Some Thoughts on Paul Bloom's "Religious Belief as an Evolutionary Accident." In M. Murray and J. Schloss, eds. *The Believing Primate: Scientific, Philosophical, and Theological Reflections on the Origin of Religion*. New York: Oxford University, pp. 128–138.

Vial, Theodore M. 2004. *Liturgy Wars: Ritual Theory and Protestant Reform in Nineteenth-Century Zurich*. New York: Routledge.

Whitehouse, Harvey. 2000. *Arguments and Icons: Divergent Modes of Religiosity*. Oxford: Oxford University Press.

Whitehouse, Harvey. 2004. *Modes of Religiosity: A Cognitive Theory of Religious Transmission*. Walnut Creek, CA: AltaMira Press.

Whitehouse, Harvey and Laidlaw, James A., eds. 2004. *Ritual and Memory: Towards a Comparative Anthropology of Religion*. Walnut Creek, CA: AltaMira Press.

Whitehouse, Harvey and Martin, Luther H., eds. 2004. *Theorizing Religions Past: Archaeology, History, and Cognition*. Walnut Creek, CA: AltaMira Press.

Further Reading

Barrett, Justin L. 2011. *Cognitive Science, Religion, and Theology: From Human Minds to Divine Minds*. Conshohocken, PA: Templeton Foundation Press. The cognitive science of religion is placed in a broader context of cognitive science generally.

Barrett, Justin L. 2012. *Born Believers: The Science of Childhood Religion*. New York: The Free Press. Develops the theme that religion is cognitively natural, with particular attention to how children are naturally disposed to acquire religious beliefs.

Bering, Jesse M. 2011. *The Belief Instinct: The Psychology of Souls, Destiny, and the Meaning of Life*. New York: W. W. Norton & Co. Religious thought is explained as the outcome of an over-active theory of mind system in humans.

Schloss, Jeffrey P. and Murray, Michael J., eds. 2009. *The Believing Primate: Scientific, Philosophical, and Theological Reflections on the Origin of Religion*. Oxford: Oxford University Press. A collection of essays by cognitive and evolutionary scientists as well as philosophers grappling with the potential implications of evolutionary approaches for rational justification of religious beliefs.

29

The Third Wound
Has Psychology Banished the Ghost from the Machine?

DYLAN EVANS

Introduction

The advance of science has challenged some of humanity's most cherished beliefs. Sigmund Freud noted three such scientific disturbances, describing them as "severe wounds" (*schwere Kränkungen*[1]). The first was the *cosmological* wound inflicted by Copernicus. Then there was the *biological* injury caused by Darwinism. The third wound was the *psychological* one which Freud modestly attributed to his own theory of psychoanalysis (Freud 1917). For Freud, the victim of these three assaults was "the universal narcissism of men," but it would be more historically accurate to identify the Christian faith as the real victim of these particular scientific revolutions. It would also be more accurate to credit psychology in general, rather than psychoanalytic theory, with inflicting the third wound, but Freud was right in thinking that this was the deepest cut.

Despite what churchmen thought in the fifteenth and sixteenth centuries, no deep theological question hinges on whether the sun orbits the earth or vice versa. Nor is there any fundamental incompatibility between belief in a Christian God and Darwin's theory of evolution by natural selection. As I will argue in this chapter, however, the various developments in scientific psychology over the past century are far more corrosive of Christian faith than the earlier revolutions in astronomy and biology. I will focus on three strands of psychological research in particular: the study of human error, research into the placebo effect, and the demonstration that psychological properties can be exhibited by purely physical systems.

Human Error

One way in which psychology tends to undermine Christian faith is by exposing the extent of human error. In particular, the "feeling of knowing" often fails to correspond with real knowledge (Koriat *et al.* 1980). The fact that people can feel utterly convinced of something

---

and yet be completely mistaken was of course well known long before the advent of scientific psychology in the mid-nineteenth century. Descartes famously illustrated the problem by imagining a malignant demon, "who has employed all his energies in deceiving me," and proceeded to ask, rhetorically: "could not an all-powerful demon make me believe those propositions are true when, as a matter of fact, they are not?" (*Meditations*, AT 22). In the past few decades, however, psychological research has gone well beyond such blanket forms of skepticism, identifying certain systematic patterns of error which cast more empirically founded doubts on Christian beliefs.

One way of categorizing types of error is to divide them into two groups: false positives (in which x is mistakenly identified as y) and false negatives (in which x is not recognized as y, even though it is). Psychologists have identified many cognitive systems in which these errors are not randomly distributed but systematically skewed in one direction (Haselton and Nettle 2006). That is, instead of making an equal number of each type of mistake, many cognitive systems make more of one kind than the other. For example, the psychological mechanisms responsible for spotting patterns are biased towards false positives; they are more likely to see a pattern in what is, in fact, a random series than to mistake order for chaos. A classic example is the so-called "clustering effect," in which people are more likely to mistake a random sequence of coin tosses for a nonrandom one than vice versa.

Experimental evidence suggests that there are similar biases in the cognitive mechanisms for spotting causal relations and intentional agents. That is, we are more likely to imagine that things are causally related when they are not, rather than vice versa, and more likely to see an intentional agent where there is none than fail to spot one that is there. Several psychologists and anthropologists have argued that these cognitive biases provide a naturalistic explanation for the origin of many religious beliefs. Skinner, for example, argued that the tendency to see causal relations where there is none, which is also evident in nonhuman animals, was at the root of many superstitions. In a famous experiment, Skinner placed hungry pigeons in cages fitted with automatic mechanisms which delivered food to the pigeons "at regular intervals with no reference whatsoever to the bird's behavior" (Skinner 1948, 168). He found that the pigeons associated the delivery of the food with whatever chance actions they had been performing as it was delivered, and that they subsequently continued to perform these same actions:

> One bird was conditioned to turn counter-clockwise about the cage, making two or three turns between reinforcements. Another repeatedly thrust its head into one of the upper corners of the cage. A third developed a "tossing" response, as if placing its head beneath an invisible bar and lifting it repeatedly. Two birds developed a pendulum motion of the head and body, in which the head was extended forward and swung from right to left with a sharp movement followed by a somewhat slower return. (Skinner 1948, 168)

Skinner suggested that the pigeons behaved as if they were influencing the automatic mechanism with their rituals and that this experiment shed light on human behavior:

> The experiment might be said to demonstrate a sort of superstition. The bird behaves as if there were a causal relation between its behavior and the presentation of food, although such a relation is lacking. There are many analogies in human behavior. Rituals for changing one's fortune at cards are good examples. A few accidental connections between a ritual and favorable consequences suffice to set up and maintain the behavior in spite of many unreinforced instances. The bowler who has released a ball down the alley but continues to behave as if she were controlling it by twisting and turning her arm and shoulder is another case in point. These behaviors have,

of course, no real effect upon one's luck or upon a ball half way down an alley, just as in the present case the food would appear as often if the pigeon did nothing – or, more strictly speaking, did something else. (Skinner 1948, 171)

Superstition might then be a natural result of a "hyperactive causation detector." In a similar way, Scott Atran and Pascal Boyer have argued that beliefs in spirits and gods may be a natural result of a parallel tendency to mistake inanimate things for intentional agents (Boyer 2001; Atran 2002). Justin Barrett attributes this tendency to what he calls a "hyperactive agent detection device," or HADD, which errs on the safe side by mistaking sticks for snakes rather than vice versa, but which also leads us to attribute agency to thunder and lightning (Barrett 2000).

It is interesting to note that in these examples of systematic error, all the cognitive biases favor religious beliefs rather than nonreligious ones. This poses a serious challenge to the Christian notion that God has left man free to disbelieve. A Christian who accepts the evidence from psychology would have to concede that the creator had endowed the human mind with a strong innate tendency to believe in him. Far from allowing his creatures the freedom to make their own minds up on matters of faith, then, it would appear that God had heavily loaded the dice in his favor.

Similar biases can also shed light on cases of pareidolia, in which people perceive religious imagery in natural phenomena. In 1978, for example, a New Mexican woman found that the burn marks on a tortilla she had made appeared similar to the traditional Western depiction of Jesus' face. Thousands of people subsequently came to see the framed tortilla. In 2009, an equally abundant number of Irish Catholics flocked to a church in Rathkeale, County Limerick, to pray at the stump of a recently cut willow tree in which many observers claimed to see the silhouette of the Virgin Mary. It would appear that the cognitive mechanisms responsible for face recognition are just as prone to false positives as the mechanisms for spotting causal relations and intentional agents.

Although these biases are found in most people, there are of course individual differences in the degree to which they influence cognition. In a particularly revealing experiment carried out by Peter Brugger, a neurologist at the University Hospital in Zurich, volunteers were asked to distinguish real faces from scrambled faces as the images were flashed up briefly on a screen, and then to distinguish real words from made-up ones (Krummenacher et al. 2010). Those who believed in the paranormal were much more likely than skeptics to see a word or face when there was not one, whereas skeptics were more likely to miss real faces and words when they appeared on the screen. The researchers then gave the volunteers a drug called L-dopa, which is usually used to relieve the symptoms of Parkinson's disease by increasing levels of dopamine in the brain. Under the influence of the drug, both groups made more mistakes, but the skeptics became more likely to interpret scrambled words or faces as the real thing. This suggests that paranormal thoughts are associated with high levels of dopamine in the brain and that L-dopa makes skeptics less skeptical. More generally, people with higher levels of dopamine are more likely to find significance in coincidences, and pick out meaning and patterns where there are none. This fits in well with the dopamine hypothesis of schizophrenia, according to which some of the symptoms of disease are caused by hyperactive dopaminergic signal transduction; paranoid delusions often involve the attribution of sinister meanings to random events such as lottery numbers or freak accidents.

Another symptom of schizophrenia which may be caused by high levels of dopamine in the brain is hallucination. Psychologists now think that hallucinations are more common than was previously suspected, and are by no means limited to schizophrenics. Indeed, there seems to be a continuum from the bizarre visions of the latter to the almost imperceptible illusions which are common features of everyday life. Reports of religious statues nodding should not be taken at face value, therefore, even if the observers are not mad. Indeed, the disciples may have hallucinated some of the more bizarre episodes recounted in the gospels, such as the ascent of Jesus into heaven, and the Book of Revelation was almost certainly written by a schizophrenic.

It is not necessary, however, to appeal to such extreme examples of human error as visual hallucinations to explain the many weird stories in the gospels. Since the pioneering work of Sir Frederic Bartlett in the 1930s, psychologists have known that remembering does not involve retrieving an exact copy of the original experience but rather a process of reconstruction (Bartlett 1932). This process is often biased by a tendency to force remembered details into the procrustean bed of pre-existing schemata. Sometimes whole chunks can be fabricated unconsciously in a process that psychologists call confabulation. Given that the earliest of the four gospels – that of Mark – was not written down until at least 40 years after the death of Jesus, there would have been more than enough scope for the Chinese whispers of human remembering and the distortions of confabulation to transform perfectly normal events into magical wonders. I do not mean to imply, of course, that the gospel was the product of a single author who attempted to recall events that he had personally witnessed four decades before; clearly it was a communal effort, and may well have drawn on earlier written sources that are no longer extant. These qualifications, do not, however, alter my point about Chinese whispers; if anything, they reinforce it.

Besides the particular conclusions that can be drawn by applying theories of various types of human error to the gospels and to the faith of ordinary believers, there is a more general lesson that emerges from subjecting religious experience to the same scientific scrutiny as any other natural phenomenon. The pioneer in this endeavor, William James, was careful to state in his lectures on *The Varieties of Religious Experience* that such research could be conducted without taking any view on whether or not religion was also a *supernatural* phenomenon (James 1997 [1902]). Nevertheless, both believers and nonbelievers have tended to feel that, by shining a harsh light on the often prosaic nature of religious experience as a natural phenomenon, psychological research could not help but cast doubt on its supposed supernatural aspects. Indeed, this may be why Christians have often resisted scientific scrutiny of their beliefs; as Dan Dennett observes, "the religious . . . often bristle at the impertinence, the lack of respect, the *sacrilege*, implied by anybody who wants to investigate their views" (Dennett 2006, 17, emphasis in original). Dennett suggests that this "taboo against a forthright, no-holds-barred scientific investigation of one natural phenomenon among many" is bound together with religion itself in a "curious embrace" (17–18). Part of the strength of religion itself may be due to the protection it receives from this taboo.

The Placebo Effect and "Faith Healing"

Another way in which psychological research tends to undermine Christian faith is by providing naturalistic explanations for cases of healing which believers had thought to be "miraculous." Many Christians have placed great store on the gospel accounts of how Jesus restored sight to blind people, cured people of leprosy, and restored movement to a paralytic man, merely by saying a few words. The Catholic Church stipulates that at least one miracle is necessary before canonizing someone as a saint, and these miracles are often putative cures.

Since the 1860s, thousands of pilgrims have left their crutches and canes at the Sanctuary of Our Lady of Lourdes in France, and hundreds of other visitors claim to have been cured of advanced cancers after visiting the shrine. During the past 50 years, television evangelists such as Oral Roberts have attracted millions of viewers worldwide with their dramatic displays of "divine healing."

Catholics and evangelicals alike agree that such cases count as miracles only if they cannot be explained in scientific terms. Indeed, for many years they could not. Since the emergence of psychoneuroimmunology in the 1970s, however, a number of biological mechanisms have been identified that could explain a variety of cures previously attributed to divine intervention. Some of these go under the general umbrella of the "placebo effect"; this is a process that begins in the brain with the formation of a particular sort of belief – the belief that one has taken, or been given, a powerful therapy of some sort or another (Evans 2003). The precise nature of the therapy is not important, provided that the person receiving it believes it can help to relieve the condition that he or she is suffering from. Pills, injections, surgery, psychotherapy, and acupuncture are just some of the many medical procedures that, depending on one's belief in their effectiveness, are capable of inducing placebo responses. When someone comes to believe that he has received some such therapy, this belief tends to activate a cascade of chemical messengers which ends in some (perhaps all) cases with the local release of endorphins, the body's natural pain killers.

A key difference between this scientific account of the placebo response and faith healing from a Christian perspective is that the former views the power of the mind to heal the body as entirely dependent on the various physical mechanisms just described. In the scientific accounts, if there is no chemical messenger to act as a go-between, the brain is powerless to alter the action of the immune system, and even when such molecules do exist, they cannot endow the immune system with supernatural powers. All they can do is tell the immune system to behave in one way rather than another. If something is beyond the power of the immune system altogether, then no amount of chemical messengers secreted by the brain will change this.

The scientific accounts therefore predict that the range of "mysterious" cures will be highly circumscribed. Far from being a universal panacea, "divine" healing will exhibit systematic patterns which coincide with underlying biological mechanisms. Indeed, this is exactly what we find. The shrine at Lourdes proudly displays hundreds of crutches cast off by pilgrims who feel able to walk without them after taking the holy water, but no wooden legs. Nor does the shrine display any glass eyes or prostheses left behind by pilgrims whose eyes and hands have grown back. Nicholas Humphrey calls this the "argument from unwarranted design" (Humphrey 1996).

Of course, before attempting to explain any cure, we should first establish that it did, in fact, occur. This means establishing that the disease was present before the alleged miracle. In his wonderful exposé of faith healing in the US, James Randi reports many instances of evangelists who have cured people of diseases they never had (Randi 1989). Even when a disease really is present before the putative cure, one must take care to verify that it is absent afterwards. More observant visitors have noticed that the crutches on display at Lourdes change with an alarming frequency. That is because many are reclaimed a few days after being cast aside by pilgrims who find that they cannot, in fact, do without them.

Even more fascinating than the scientific explanations for cures that Christians have falsely attributed to divine intervention are the psychological mechanisms that allow the fraudulent healers to act with wholehearted sincerity. Randi has also documented the process by which many faith healers start off with deliberate deception, employing methods which they know full well to be tricks. As their reputation grows and they gather followers, however, these healers gradually come to believe their own lies, and eventually become capable of breathtaking doublethink (Randi 1989).

Nicholas Humphrey has made a persuasive case that this is exactly what happened with Jesus himself (Humphrey 1996). He notes that Jesus' miracles were entirely typical of the conjuring tricks that were popular around the Mediterranean at the time. Hippolytus, for example, describes a certain Marcus who had mastered the art of turning the water in a cup red by mixing liquid from another cup while the onlookers' attention was distracted. Humphrey then asks, rhetorically:

> Is it possible that, even though Jesus was regularly using deception and trickery in his public performances like any common conjuror, he actually believed that he was more than a conjuror: believed that sometimes he could *genuinely* exert the powers he claimed? (Humphrey 1996, 99)

If this is indeed what happened, it would reveal a different kind of pathos in those famous words spoken from the cross, echoing the twenty-second psalm: "My God, my God, why hast thou forsaken me?" If Jesus really did say something like this as he was dying, then might these words express genuine bewilderment on Jesus' part about why he could not summon up any supernatural help when he most needed it.

Humphrey's speculations on the psychology of Jesus are just that – speculations. Nevertheless, they do point to another way in which psychology can undermine Christian faith – namely, by providing plausible accounts of how a normal, fallible human being could behave like Jesus, and thus disposing of the false dilemma posed by C. S. Lewis, according to which Jesus must be either mad or divine (Lewis 1952). Instead, he was just mistaken in believing himself to be the messiah and Son of God.

The Mechanical Mind

The third way in which psychology tends to undermine Christian faith is by demonstrating that psychological properties can be exhibited by purely physical systems. Of the three strands of psychological research examined in this essay, this is the one that poses the most serious challenge for Christianity, for it strikes at the very existence of the soul.

As with concerns about human error, the possibility that the human mind might be entirely mechanical was also anticipated by Descartes. In the *Discourse on Method*, Descartes was happy to admit that bodies – whether of humans or other animals – were just machines:

> You won't find that at all strange if you know how many kinds of automata or moving machines the skill of man can construct with the use of very few parts, in comparison with the great multitude of bones, muscles, nerves, arteries, veins and all the other parts that are in the body of any animal, and if this knowledge leads you to regard an animal body as a machine. Having been made by the hands of God, it is incomparably better organised – and capable of movements that are much more wonderful – than any that can be devised by man, but still it is just a machine. (*Discourse on Method*, AT 55)

Descartes was also prepared to concede that the behavior of all nonhuman animals could be controlled by their biological machinery. Aware of the slippery slope that this train of reasoning threatened to open up, Descartes argued that there were aspects of *human* behavior that could *not* be attributed to purely physical or biological mechanisms, such as conversation:

> We can easily conceive of a machine so constructed that it utters words, and even utters words that correspond to bodily actions that will cause a change in its organs (touch it in one spot and it asks "What do you mean?", touch it in another and it cries out "That hurts!", and so on); but not that such a machine should produce different sequences of words so as to give an appropriately meaningful answer to whatever is said in its presence – which is something that the dullest of men can do. (*Discourse on Method*, AT 56)

But this argument is hostage to fortune. If a machine *could* "give an appropriately meaningful answer" to any utterance, Descartes would have to concede that humans are just machines, too. Three hundred years later, the very same test was proposed by the British computer scientist Alan Turing, but by then the presumption had been reversed. Turing assumed that the test would eventually be passed (Turing 1950).

Like Descartes, Turing noted the theological problems that this would pose. The very idea of a humanlike robot suggests that we too might be purely physical entities, devoid of souls. People seem to perceive this instinctively, even without conscious reflection, and this may be the reason why androids so often evoke spooky feelings, as Freud noted in his essay on "The Uncanny" (Freud 1919). A story from Descartes's own life illustrates the visceral reactions aroused by such automata. While sailing to Sweden, some sailors crept into Descartes's cabin and discovered a humanoid robot which the philosopher had constructed himself. When shown the contraption, the ship's captain was horrified, and – convinced that it was some instrument of dark magic – ordered it to be thrown overboard (Wood 2002).

Other historical episodes provide further support for the idea that this horror of robots has theological roots. Four centuries before Descartes, Albert Magnus is said to have made several metal androids, which could move, answer questions, and solve problems. His android butler, 30 years in the making, could answer the door at the sound of a knock. Thomas Aquinas, his pupil, destroyed the android, thinking the devil was in it. In 1727, the French inventor Jacques de Vaucanson built some clockwork androids which could serve dinner and clear the tables for his fellow monks (he was a novice in the order of the Minimes at the time). When the head of the order saw the automata, he declared that Vaucanson had profane tendencies, and ordered that his workshop be destroyed (Wood 2002). Some years later, the French physician Julien Offray de La Mettrie had to flee Holland when the Church forced his publisher to deliver up all the copies of his new book, *L'Homme machine* (Man a Machine), for burning.

The cognitive revolution which swept through psychology in the 1960s, displacing the behaviorist paradigm that had held sway since the 1920s, is based on the assumption that the human mind can be modeled entirely in computational terms. If one day had to be singled out as the birthday of cognitive science, it is surely September 11, 1956. It was on that day that three seminal papers were presented at a historic meeting at the Massachusetts Institute of Technology (MIT). One of these was the paper by Allen Newell and Herbert Simon about a "logic theory machine," which inaugurated the modern discipline of artificial intelligence (Newell and Simon 1956).

The contemporaneous invention of integrated circuits, in which large numbers of components were packed onto a small silicon chip, gave cognitive scientists the means to turn their computational models into real machines. An early example of the new generation of "cognitive robots" was Shakey. Developed at the Artificial Intelligence Center at Stanford Research Institute between 1966 and 1972, Shakey had a complex cognitive architecture in which distinct functions such as perception, planning, and natural language processing were implemented by separate programs, which reflected the emphasis of cognitive psychology on the functional decomposition of mental processes.

It is this strategy of functional decomposition which provides the solid theoretical support for the intuitive notion that cognitive robots pose deep theological problems. By breaking the mind down into successively smaller components, cognitive science avoids the homunculus fallacy – the idea that cognition can be explained by positing the existence of a homunculus (a little man, or soul) inside the head which performs cognitive tasks such as face recognition or logical reasoning. This is, of course, no explanation at all, since it begs the question of how the homunculus is performing the task. Functional decomposition avoids the infinite regress inherent in the homunculus fallacy by stipulating that the components must be simpler at each step, until they become trivial to build (Dennett 1978). At this point there is no place left in the machine for any ghost to hide.

Conclusion

I have argued that the various developments in scientific psychology over the past century pose deep problems for Christianity. These problems are implicit in many areas of psychological research, but for reasons of space I have focused on three strands in particular. The study of human error suggests that many religious beliefs are natural consequences of systematic cognitive biases. Research into the placebo effect provides a biological explanation for many so-called miracles. And the development of cognitive robots demonstrates that psychological properties can be exhibited by purely physical systems. Taken together, these three strands of psychological research are far more corrosive of Christian faith than the earlier scientific revolutions inspired by Copernicus and Darwin.

Note

1   This phrase is translated as "severe blows" by James Strachey in the *Standard Edition*, but I have chosen to follow Joan Riviere's earlier translation in using the word "wound."

References

Atran, Scott 2002. *In Gods We Trust: The Evolutionary Landscape of Religion*. Oxford: Oxford University Press.

Barrett, Justin. 2000. Exploring the Natural Foundations of Religion. *Trends in Cognitive Science*, 4, pp. 29–34.

Bartlett, Frederic. 1932. *Remembering*. Cambridge: Cambridge University Press.

Boyer, Pascal. 2001. *Religion Explained: The Evolutionary Origins of Religious Thought*. New York: Basic Books.

Dennett, Daniel C. 1978. *Brainstorms*. Cambridge, MA: MIT Press.

Dennett, Daniel. 2006. *Breaking the Spell: Religion as a Natural Phenomenon*. London: Allen Lane.

Evans, Dylan. 2003. *Placebo: The Belief Effect*. London: HarperCollins.

Freud, Sigmund. 1917. A Difficulty in the Path of Psycho-Analysis. In J. Strachey, ed. *The Standard Edition of the Complete Psychological Works of Sigmund Freud*, vol. 17. London: Hogarth Press, pp. 135–144.

Freud, Sigmund. 1919. The "Uncanny." In J. Strachey, ed. *The Standard Edition of the Complete Psychological Works of Sigmund Freud*, vol. 17. London: Hogarth Press, pp. 217–256.

Haselton, Martie G. and Nettle, Daniel. 2006. The Paranoid Optimist: An Integrative Evolutionary Model of Cognitive Biases. *Personality and Social Psychology Review*, 10(1), pp. 47–66.

Humphrey, Nicholas. 1996. *Leaps of Faith: Science, Miracles, and the Search for Supernatural Consolation*. New York: Basic Books.

Koriat, A., Lichtenstein, S., and Fischhoff, B. 1980. Reasons for Confidence. *Journal of Experimental Psychology: Human Learning and Memory*, 6, pp. 107–118.

Krummenacher, Peter, Mohr, C., Haker, H., and Brugger, P. 2010. Dopamine, Paranormal Belief, and the Detection of Meaningful Stimuli. *Journal of Cognitive Neuroscience*, 22(8), pp. 1670–1681.

Lewis, C. S. 1952. *Mere Christianity*. London: Macmillan.

Newell, Allen and Simon, Herbert. 1956. The Logic Theory Machine: A Complex Information Processing System. *Information Theory, IRE Transactions on Information Theory*, 2(3), pp. 61–79.

Randi, James. 1989. *The Faith Healers*. Amherst, NY: Prometheus Books.

Skinner, B. F. 1948. "Superstition" in the Pigeon. *Journal of Experimental Psychology*, 38, pp. 168–172.

Turing, Alan. 1950. Computing Machinery and Intelligence. *Mind*, 59(236), pp. 433–460.

Wood, Gaby. 2002. *Living Dolls: A Magical History of the Quest for Mechanical Life*. London: Faber and Faber.

Further Reading

Dennett, Daniel. 2006. *Breaking the Spell: Religion as a Natural Phenomenon*. London: Allen Lane. A highly readable philosophical commentary on contemporary research in the psychology, sociology, and anthropology of religion.

Humphrey, Nicholas. 1996. *Leaps of Faith: Science, Miracles, and the Search for Supernatural Consolation*. New York: Basic Books. An idiosyncratic book, full of surprises and original conjectures, Humphrey's speculations on the psychology of Jesus remain the most plausible account of how a normal human being could have come to think he was the messiah.

James, William. 1997 [1902]. *The Varieties of Religious Experience*. New York: Simon & Schuster. Though opinions are still divided over the merits of this work – the pragmatist philosopher Charles Peirce saying that its great virtue is its "penetration into the hearts of people," while George Santayana retorts that its great weakness is its "tendency to disintegrate the idea of truth, to recommend belief without reason and to encourage superstition" –it is, nevertheless, a pioneering work.

Skinner, B. F. 1948. "Superstition" in the Pigeon. *Journal of Experimental Psychology*, 38, pp. 168–172. While not specifically about Christianity, Skinner's article remains a fundamental reference point for psychological theories about the origins of religious and superstitious beliefs.

30

Sociology and Christianity

JOHN H. EVANS AND MICHAEL S. EVANS

This chapter is concerned with the word "and" in our title, focusing on the relationship between sociology and Christianity. The central questions are: does sociology influence Christianity and does Christianity influence sociology? Sociology has of course had a relationship with Christianity since the formation of modern sociology in the late nineteenth century, in that it could be argued that sociology emerged from a form of Christianity. The nature of this relationship has never been clear or institutionalized, as different sociological practitioners at various historical points engaged in different relationships. What is clear to us is that – compared to most social scientific and humanities fields – the relationship between the area of academic study (sociology) and Christianity has been highly contentious, with a number of fairly explicit attempts to define the proper relationship.

Christianity is of course many things: rituals, practices, beliefs, and institutions, to name just a few components. While we have no doubt that the rituals and institutions of Christianity have influenced sociology – and vice versa – we are unaware of any existing scholarship in these areas. We will focus, like the existing literature, on Christianity as a set of beliefs or ideas. When these ideas are formalized by elites we will call these ideas "theology." We will call the formalization of sociological ideas "theories and methods." So, the first question is whether Christian and sociological ideas have influenced each other. We are also interested in sociological and Christian activities, and examine whether Christian ideas influence sociological activities, and whether sociological ideas influence Christian activities.

The relationship between Christianity and sociology probably looks quite different depending upon the side from which one starts. Therefore, it is important to explicitly state that the authors of this chapter start from academic sociology and look at theology, having both been trained in the mainstream of the former and not the latter. We have no doubt that a different essay would be written by someone looking from the other side.

Relationships between Christianity and Sociology

Christianity shaped Western culture, and continues to do so. Sociology, as part of "science," similarly has shaped and continues to shape our culture. It is clear that these two institutions

The Blackwell Companion to Science and Christianity, First Edition. Edited by J. B. Stump and Alan G. Padgett.
© 2012 Blackwell Publishing Ltd. Published 2012 by Blackwell Publishing Ltd.

Table 30.1   Relationships between Christianity and sociology.

	Maintain idea boundary, but influence activities	Blend ideas
Christianity influences sociology	1	3
Sociology influences Christianity	2	4

must have an influence on each other, despite boundaries that have been constructed. The remainder of this chapter will be organized by two generic relationships, represented in columns in Table 30.1. The discussions of both of these relationships will be subdivided by the direction of influence (the rows in Table 30.1).

Each cell in the table represents a family of claims by sociologists or theologians about what the relationship between sociology and Christianity should be, is, or has been. For example, when we describe the works in cell 1, we are making generalizations about scholars who have advocated that Christian and sociological *ideas* maintain a strong boundary, but that Christian ideas do or should influence sociological *work*. While we sort these claims into these four categories, individual scholars often could fit into multiple categories, believing, for example, that Christian ideas influence sociological work and that sociological ideas influence Christian activities.

We think that the four categories are useful generalizations for understanding how scholars have conceived of the relationship between Christianity and sociology specifically. We recognize that our categories may sometimes align with more general approaches, such as Barbour's (2000) influential fourfold typology of relationships between science and religion. For example, what we describe as Christianity influencing sociology by blending ideas (cell 3) might be considered an example of "integration" in Barbour's terms. But to be clear, our focus here is on the specific relationships between sociology and Christianity rather than on the proposed general relationships between science and religion.

Cell 1: Maintaining the Idea Boundary While Admitting the Influence of Christian Ideas on Sociological Work

The first European sociologists or proto-sociologists were deeply influenced by the Enlightenment notion that we should not be looking to religious traditions for our knowledge. We should not forget that Auguste Comte, often depicted as at least the European father of sociology, thought he was going to replace religion with a new religion of science called sociology. If we turn to what is jokingly referred to by undergraduates as the "holy trinity" of original sociological theorists – Marx, Weber, and Durkheim – we see that each was deeply interested in religion, and each presumed that religious belief was not true. Religion was the result of people not truly understanding the social forces around them.

This impulse took highly pragmatic form with the emergence of sociology in the USA. In its earliest forms, "sociology" referred to social reform and its supporting apparatus, and could be applied equally to "settlement houses" such as Hull House, the Christian Social Gospel movement, or to large-scale data collection efforts such as William Bliss's *Encyclopedia of Social Reform*. Even as sociology moved from the streets into the universities at the turn of the twentieth century, it still had significant overlap with social work and with

Christian projects for social improvement. Given its goals of eliminating social problems and improving social conditions, academic sociology had a sort of natural constituency in religious communities.

Yet as a fledgling academic discipline, American sociology faced specific institutional trials. Evans (2009) calls these trials a "dual challenge of credibility." On one hand, sociology had substantial support from a religious audience and institutional base outside of the university. On the other hand, academic sociologists had to attract participation from university scientists to bolster their institutional legitimacy and establish themselves as credible scientists among the biologists, chemists, and physicists. Yet to do this meant abandoning in some respects the very religious constituency most supportive of the sociological project.

The solution was to turn religious supporters from contributors to consumers, so that sociological theories would be seen as autonomous from religious influence but would still benefit in some ways from religious support. This transformation of the "sociological public" happened in numerous ways. Authors changed the content of textbooks to move religion from a source of theory and purpose to an object of study in its own right (Smith 2003). Articles from proponents of Christian Sociology, a movement linking academic sociology to Social Gospel goals, were slowly phased out of the discipline's primary journal, the *American Journal of Sociology* (Evans 2009). Influential academic sociologists populated their new departments with colleagues who were not seen as religiously influenced. And Christian Sociologists became increasingly marginalized within the primary professional association (Turner and Turner 1990). The result is that the basic structures of sociology as a discipline and as a profession depended, and perhaps continue to depend, on a distinctive and strong boundary between sociological and religious ideas.

The incredibly strong boundary against the influence of Christian ideas on sociology is indicated by sociological definitions of religion itself. The most commonly used definitions of religion include dividing the world into sacred and profane. The sacred, when studying Christianity, is typically something like belief in the supernatural. The profane world operates through rational processes, while the sacred world is beyond rationality, the argument goes. For example, in one popular textbook religion is defined "as a system of beliefs and practices by which a group of people interprets and responds to what they feel is sacred and, usually, supernatural as well" (Johnstone 1997, 13).

Religious belief is thus that which is beyond rationality. With mainstream sociology firmly committed to rational explanations, there is no way that something beyond rationality is supposed to influence sociological ideas. This view was reinforced by the secularization assumption that has historically been a dominant theme in sociology. The assumption, put simply, was that scientific truth will eventually win out over the irrational – read "religious" – side of human experience. According to one social science summary:

> The era of the Enlightenment generated a rational view of the world based on empirical standards of proof, scientific knowledge of natural phenomena, and technological mastery of the universe. Rationalism was thought to have rendered the central claims of the Church implausible in modern societies, blowing away the vestiges of superstitious dogma in Western Europe. (Norris and Inglehart 2004, 7)

To be clear, we are not advocating value neutrality or claiming that sociology is essentially scientific. Rather, we are pointing out that sociologists generally work from this set of assumptions and maintain a boundary between sociology and religious influence accordingly. With this boundary solidly in place, sociology remains utterly "scientific," uninfluenced by any of the "irrational" religious ideas or methods of knowing from Christianity. However, it is acceptable within this paradigm for sociological activity to be influenced by Christianity via the religious beliefs of individual sociologists which influence *topic selection*. This is most famously called Weberian value neutrality in research. As two authors debating this issue recently put it: "we also think that having religious motivations in sociological research is epistemologically and scientifically unobjectionable. In the classic Weberian formulation, social scientists inevitably research intellectual problems generated by specific value commitments" (Smilde and May 2010, 9). For example, if a mainline Protestant sociologist has really been influenced by the beatitudes, he or she may decide that what is most important to understand scientifically is the process by which rich societies produce or tolerate poverty. Christian ideas would then influence the work of sociology, but not the sociological ideas embodied in methods and theories. This works because it keeps sociology itself – defined as its theories and methods – sacrosanct and distinct from religion. It keeps sociology as a science, which allows it to maintain its legitimacy in academia.

Therefore, in this proposed relationship, Christianity influences sociology because Christianity causes certain practitioners to focus on particular topics. For example, Gerardo Marti, while simultaneously studying a congregation as a sociologist and being one of its pastors, clearly embodies this distinction, writing:

> For this study, I operated primarily as a scholar working on behalf of other scholars to generate new knowledge about the processes of ethnic transcendence and congregational diversification. I hoped my analysis would be of use to others examining other multiethnic settings. I also hoped it would provide useful information for church leaders who desire to build integrated congregations effectively. (Marti 2005, 204)

It is difficult to empirically assess how much sociological work is occurring using the ideal relationship represented in cell 1 of Table 30.1. One challenge to counting is that people operating in this tradition rarely if ever say that their topic selection was influenced by their religion. This is probably for a number of reasons. First, they do not want it to be perceived that their sociological *ideas* are influenced by Christian ideas (e.g., cell 3). Second, given that Christianity has shaped American culture, many of the topics one could be motivated to examine from the Christian tradition are already nearly universally considered problems, at least by people with PhDs who work at American universities (e.g., racial injustice, violence against women). Third, in practice sociologists operating in this tradition do not care about the analyst's motivations, since it is not supposed to influence their conclusions anyway. In fact, there is a sociological tradition that *does* encourage the analyst to list all of their personal values at the front of their book, and this is the tradition that rejects value neutrality, advocating for sociological work to occur in cell 3. As we will see, Christians who have advocated for the relationships represented in cell 3 do so by repeating the theoretical arguments against Weberian value neutrality (cell 1).

Cell 2: Maintaining the Idea Boundary While Admitting the Sociological Influence on Christian Activity

This cell retains the high wall where the sociological and Christian ideas do not influence each other, but sociology influences Christian activities. Typically, sociology informs religious leaders about the practices or beliefs of religious people, using sociological methods, and the leaders use this information to change their practices.

Probably the most obvious and explicit example in cell 2 (Table 30.1) is the field of "congregational studies," which is essentially applied sociology. In this area of inquiry, scholars with sociological training go to a Christian congregation and conduct interviews, surveys, and other analyses to try to teach the congregation about itself or its social environment (Ammerman *et al.* 1998). The congregation is then encouraged to change its beliefs or practices on the basis of the findings. More generally, this influence is widespread, as Christian leaders read sociological texts to see what the believers "really" think about various issues. For example, there can be no doubt that denominational leaders are aware of the social science research regarding the political orientation of their members.

The leadership in different Christian traditions has different reactions to using sociology to study the beliefs and practices of their members. Catholic sociologists claim the Catholic Church has been resistant to it (Varacalli 1990, 256). On the other hand, in some Protestant denominations, there is essentially an office of sociological investigation of the views of the laity. For example, the Presbyterian Church (USA) has a social science research office that conducts regular surveys of the clergy and laity on various issues.

Cell 3: The Influence of Christian Ideas on Sociological Ideas

In the relationship summarized in cells 3 and 4 of Table 30.1, the ideas of sociology and Christianity do influence each other. It has been extremely transgressive for mainstream sociologists to claim that sociological theories and methods are influenced by Christianity (cell 3). It has been less transgressive for theologians to admit an influence from sociology (cell 4). Sociology is supposed to be scientific and not influenced by ideas ultimately based upon faith, but almost all Christian theology has assumed that "secular" thought may contribute to Christian thought. From the perspective of the sociological work in cell 3, Christian ideas could influence sociological theories intentionally or unintentionally. As we will summarize below, unintentional influence occurs when the background ideas of the culture are Christian, and sociologists embedded in this culture produce implicitly Christian theories. There is also a long history of scholars trying to explicitly use Christian theology to influence sociological theory.

From its inception sociology has unintentionally incorporated a specific understanding of modernity grounded in Christian ideas. Despite subsequent institutional divergence and ongoing boundary work, Christianity and sociology share what Charles Taylor calls a "modern social imaginary," the constitutive self-understandings that shape our use and deployment of social categories. In this sense, we have never been secular, whether or not Christianity is explicitly invoked.

In sociology this is perhaps most evident in the attempt to identify universal and abstract social laws that govern society. Christianity is built on the idea that salvation is universally accessible, but that there is only one true path to salvation. The meaning of Christ is universal and independent of any other meaning or action. Thus the entire premise of Christianity is that some meaning systems (specifically, the meaning of Christ) can be completely abstracted from their local context and applied universally. In sociology this Christian concept of a universal and abstract meaning system manifests as the positivist approach to finding social laws or rules that, though varying in time, place, and extent of expression, nevertheless lie at the heart of social reality. For much of mainstream sociology, the goal is to identify such laws or rules, for example by using statistical techniques to establish objective analyses that eliminate possible bias from subjective (meaning local and variable) perspectives. Sociology can thus be described as the systematic pursuit of abstract and universal meaning systems in society. This is a pursuit that only makes sense within a particular Western notion of modernity driven by Christian ideas, as it is neither common nor sensible for religion or social organization in non-Western societies (see Asad 1993).

Another key Christian idea in modernity is that what is true determines what is good. That is, once the various distractions of the social world are identified and set aside, the truth that remains will guide the proper selection and implementation of the good in society. For Christianity this is, variously, the truth of the Bible, the truth of Jesus' teachings, the truth of magisterial declaration, the truth of discernment, or the truth of revelation. For sociology this is the truth of scientific method, the truth of value neutrality, and the truth that emerges once the illusions (or delusions) of good are disproven through systematic study of causes and effects. Again, the divergence is based on institutional distinctions, not on commitment to underlying principles. Both Christianity and sociology intend to debunk illusory good, whether that is the immoral lure of sexual deviance or the immoral lure of neoliberal ideology, in favor of the true.

Were it the case that these abstract ideas did not generate meaningful differences in the execution of sociological research, we might dismiss them as so much theoretical hand-waving. However, it is increasingly clear that Christian ideas influence how sociology is done, particularly in how they define the categories with which social scientists work.

Given the paucity of sociological self-reflection on this point, it is helpful to look to the related field of anthropology for examples. Fenella Cannell offers the example of "interiority," an individual's inner consciousness, the part of consciousness that reflects on one's own circumstances and place in the world. Such a concept largely goes unquestioned, though it may encompass many different kinds of experiences analytically. Yet Cannell points out that the concept of "interiority" itself depends on the separation of the world into hierarchies and strata, in particular those that distinguish between life and afterlife, human and divine. Thus the current application of the concept as individual self-reflection originates "in the need of the Christian to consider the fate of his or her own soul" (Cannell 2006, 15). Further, as Webb Keane (2002) notes, such a notion of interiority is intertwined with Protestant notions of sincerity. When someone speaks sincerely, it is because they speak from a place of interiority that is not skewed by outside influences.

An example in sociology proper is the concept of agency. It is hard to imagine sociological theory without a concept of agency. Yet as it is argued among sociologists, agency has primarily been seen as something that is exercised by individuals within and against larger (social) structures. While there are wide variations in how this is interpreted, and many arguments about the relationships that mark structure and agency, Keane helpfully notes that the Protestant origins of the idea of individual agency as separated from divine agency grounds much of what social scientists understand to be (or recognize as) agency. The conceptual apparatus that imagines a world built around motivated willful actors with freedom to make meaningful choices is a Protestant conceptual apparatus wherein such freedom of choice and action is necessary to answer fundamental questions about who should be saved and what they should do to be saved.

Many of the criticisms of Christianity are leveled at sociology by scholars working from postcolonial and subaltern studies perspectives. Talal Asad (1993) famously points out that the version of modernity that tries to render religion as a human universal is grounded in the Christian assumption about abstraction and universality, such that otherwise well-meaning secular social scientists are failing to recognize that their universal project is actually based on the imposition of parochial notions of modernity on other cultures and societies.

If one looks closely at American sociology since its founding, one also sees repeated calls for an intentional integration of Christian and sociological ideas. At their most general, these calls are for, in the words of one scholar, conducting "sociology as if religion is real" (Swatos 1987, viii). What is most striking about these calls is that they emerge in brief episodes and then die out quickly, that they never change how mainstream sociology operates, and do not even lead to an identifiable body of research using their own claims. Theoretical statements abound, but with a few exceptions (e.g., a few chapters in Swatos) empirical sociology research from, say, an evangelical perspective, cannot be found.

The American Catholic Sociological Society, founded in 1938, makes a good case study of how difficult it is to explicitly try to influence sociological ideas with Christian ideas. While there were many reasons for the founding of a separate academic society, one was clearly the anti-modernism of the Catholic hierarchy during this era, which led to a suspicion of main-stream sociology. In the early days there were clearly two main factions. The motivation of this first group was to "facilitate the Americanization or assimilation of this group" into the sociology that had rejected them (Kivisto 1989, 353). More important for us is the second faction, which wanted to "forge a distinctly Catholic sociology" that would "become an agency for developing a theologically grounded sociological position, one that sought to utilize interpretive tools from the social sciences that harmonized with Catholic faith." This was sometimes even called a "supernatural sociology" or a "sacred sociology" (Kivisto 1989, 355, 356). This second group was advocating a relationship that places it squarely in cell 3.

While the exact meaning of sacred sociology has never entirely developed, it is usually stated in terms of a rejection of the logical positivist tradition in mainstream sociology and specifically a rejection of the idea that one's religious ideas can be removed from one's socio-logical analysis and theories (i.e., a rejection of cell 1). Joseph Varacalli, who was one who did not abandon the idea of a Catholic sociology, offers some examples of sociological pre-suppositions that would flow from Catholic theology, such as: there is an objective moral order, a human nature tending toward sin, and that humans have spiritual and material needs (Varacalli 1990, 254–255).

Advocates of a cell 1 perspective were present in the society, even at the beginning, and this group grew with time. In a 1942 address, the president of the society argued for separat-ing the roles of social philosopher, social scientist, and social reformer. Sociologists should conduct sociology "in the interest of a theological inspired social reform" – note the parallel with value neutrality – and "he did not think that the Catholic sociologist qua sociologist inquired into the dynamics of the social world in a manner distinct from other sociologists" (Kivisto 1989, 357). A later Catholic sociologist is described as viewing "Catholic sociologists as producing knowledge that should inform Catholic social thought and programs aimed at implementing Catholic social values" (Kivisto 1989, 359).

By the 1950s, "calls for creating a Catholic sociology had virtually disappeared" (Kivisto 1989, 358). The weakening of the anti-modernist impulse of the hierarchy over time may have had a role, and Peter Kivisto explains this shift as the result of the increasing acceptance and assimilation of Catholics in post-war America. Joseph Varacalli agrees about the declining number of people advocating a cell 3 relationship, writing that the decline was the result of "the desire of young Catholic sociologists trained in secular universities to gain society-wide recognition by conforming to the standards of the mainstream, outer and secular profession of sociology" (Varacalli 1990, 251). Indeed, the society is now called the "Association for the

Sociology of Religion," and the name of its journal has changed from the *Catholic Sociological Review* to *Sociology of Religion*. Varacalli also sees a collapse of cell 2, in that the Catholic Church never accepted the help that sociology could offer for two reasons: it thought that truth could be derived solely through theology and philosophy, and that the hierarchy correctly perceived that value-free scientific sociology was the carrier of "Protestant and secular thought into the Catholic body" (Varacalli 1990, 251, 256).

Similar attempts by Protestants show similar results. In the UK, Protestant sociology had deep roots. However, the British Protestant version of "Christian Sociology, as a self-conscious movement, declined after the war [WWII] because of the increasingly secular context, the complexity of the issues, and competition from empiricist, academic sociology" (Lyon 1983a, 233). Like Catholics, David Lyon concludes that both the US and UK versions of Christian sociology failed to make a link between Christian ideas about humanness and sociological theory, and died around World War Two, lying dormant until the late 1970s (Lyon 1983a, 237).

After 1980 there was a glimmer again, but again nothing came to fruition, possibly because of the lack of an organizational mechanism (Lyon 1983a, 239). The decade produced at least a small shelf of books and a file folder of articles and chapters advocating some version of a Christian sociology. Almost all are in obscure venues, having little to no influence on the field. They are jeremiads, leaving no research tradition in mainstream sociology nor within a distinctly evangelical sociology (of which we are aware). Indeed, the authors of this chapter – trained in mainstream sociology – were unaware of almost all of them until beginning to write this article.

Interestingly, the Christian idea that sociological theory is seen to need a Christian account of a person (in contrast to a secular sociological account) remains constant across time and across the Catholic and Protestant versions. For example, David Lyon, in a book published by InterVarsity Press, attributes the troubles within mainstream sociology to its views of humanness, and argues for a Christian view of humanness as a replacement (Lyon 1983b). Moreover, the way to convince mainstream sociology remains a critique of positivism and a critique of the possibility of value free sociology (cells 1 and 2).

The Christian Sociological Society is still active. Our impression is that it primarily functions in immigration mode analogous to the Catholic Sociological Society in the 1940s, because while Catholics have gained acceptance within academia, evangelicals are still looked down upon. However, the explicit influence of evangelical ideas on mainstream sociological theory still seems as unlikely as the influence of Catholic ideas on mainstream sociology in the 1940s. While books are occasionally published that claim to be sociological studies from an evangelical perspective, the supporting research comes from evangelical research groups (e.g., the Barna Group) that are outside of academic sociology, demonstrating the ongoing resilience of the institutional boundary. In sum, Christian ideas have influenced sociological theory and method, but the influence has largely been unintentional. Intentional projects have largely failed. When we turn to our final cell in our fourfold scheme, we can see that far more openness has existed for the other direction of this relationship.

Cell 4: The Influence of Sociological Ideas on Christian Ideas

Christian theology does not draw such high boundaries against influence from secular sources, and the influence of Christian theology on mainstream sociology has been almost nothing compared to the influence of mainstream sociology on theology. We can draw a distinction between theologians importing sociological ideas, and the more rare case of sociologists trying to influence Christian ideas.

Sociological influences on theology are many (Roberts 2005). A prominent example is narrative theology, which is a general term for an approach to theology characterized by an understanding of Christianity as a way of constructing stories about the world. For narrative theologians, there is no essential or enduring component to Christianity that is located in particular beliefs, doctrines, rituals, or practices. Such things are important, but they are not foundational. Rather, they are constituted in and through communities that share common purpose and understanding of the world and organize their use of language and material accordingly. This approach has many variations, but the underlying commonality is an understanding of the world as constituted by language (following Wittgenstein), and the power of ordering language through narrative (Comstock 1987).

In sociological terms, narrative theology is what happens when you start from the assumption that the world as we understand it is socially constructed. What matters for narrative theologians is not whether there is something "really real," but whether the constructions that we create make sense within a Christian framework as realized by a particular community. Put another way, narrative theology represents a "cultural turn" in theology. Rather than seeing pluralism of practice or doctrine as aberration or heterodox, narrative theologians evaluate whether or not any given second-order structure is consistent with the story that Christianity tells (primarily through the Bible) and with the intentional community in which the second-order structure resides (or exists).

Two different examples of sociology's influence on narrative theology can be found in the work of (respectively) Stanley Hauerwas and John Milbank. Hauerwas's written work focuses on the role of the church in society, and in particular how we should "speak not of the truth of Christians' beliefs but of the truthfulness of their lives" in "demonstrating Christian virtues in our communities of faith" (Comstock 1987, 704). For Hauerwas, the dependence on unyielding foundations (such as magisterial doctrine) interferes with the possibilities for constructing a good Christian life through community, and should therefore be deprecated. In contrast, Milbank (2006) focuses on confronting the "ontology of violence" that marks social science understandings of society with an "ontology of peace" consistent with Christian narratives. For Milbank, such "radical orthodoxy" provides the only way to truly enact social change, as you cannot challenge an ontology when you share its premises and assumptions. On the one hand, Milbank would see sociology as a secular heresy. He sees Christian theology as corrupted by the interaction of sociology and theology, shows the myriad influences of the latter on the former, and calls for a radical divide between the two. In Roberts's summary of Milbank, "secularity and secular discourse are *heresy* in relation to orthodox Christianity, and the archeological investigations will show that all 'scientific' social theories are in fact 'theologies or anti-theologies' in disguise" (Roberts 2005, 379). So, while decrying the existence of cell 4, and calling for its end, Milbank nonetheless uses a "*Nietzschean* postmodernity" that is "offered to theologians for their positive appropriation" (379). This strikes us as requiring the narrative theology that was itself influenced by social theory. Both Hauerwas and Milbank, as narrative theologians, accept social construction as critical to understanding social life. However, each in his own way turns this sociological insight toward theological ends, and in particular how such insight might inform a Christian life.

We can gesture to many other examples of the influence of sociological ideas on theology. For example, it is claimed that H. Richard Niebuhr was strongly influenced by sociologist George Herbert Mead, ultimately creating a "sociological theology" (Garrett 1987, 42). Liberation theology obviously draws heavily on Marx, and the theology of Hans Küng and Gregory Baum extensively use Marx, Hegel, Freud, Durkheim, and Weber (McAllister 1987,

27). Richard H. Roberts writes that Bonhoeffer incorporated both Tönnies's *Gemeinschaft* and *Gesellschaft* distinctions and secularization theory in his work (Roberts 2005, 375–376).

Much more rare are card-carrying sociologists who try to argue that sociological ideas influence Christian theology. Most famous is undoubtedly Peter Berger, the most influential sociological proponent of the human construction of religion, who wrote in 1967 that only after the theologian

> has really grasped what it means to say that religion is a human product or projection can he begin to search, within this array of projections, for what may turn out to be signals of transcendence. . . . An "empirical theology" is, of course, methodologically impossible. But a theology that proceeds in a step-by-step correlation with what can be said about man empirically is well worth a serious try. (Berger 1967, 185)

Berger most explicitly engaged in this project in his 1979 *The Heretical Imperative*, which argued against what he called the "deductive" and "reductive" methods in theology, and in favor of an "inductive" method, simultaneously critiquing theologians such as Barth and Bultmann (Berger 1979).

This impulse does not end with the mainline Protestant Berger. For example, Richard Perkins, in a book published by an evangelical publishing house, writes that:

> Christians need to have their parochial view of the world – *including* Christianity – challenged by the skeptical orientation of modern sociology. We need to be able to critique in a reflexive way (and jettison if necessary) some of the reified cultural baggage accumulated over the centuries. In particular, the commitment of evangelicals to an unbiblical ideology of individualism indicates the degree to which Christian thinking has been influenced by our cultural context. (Perkins 1987, 176–177)

Sociologists trying to influence Christian ideas with sociological ideas remain rare.

Conclusion

Mainstream sociologists have been happy with the dominance of the arguments in cells 1 and 2. While some work in cell 3 exists, it has had little lasting influence on mainstream sociology. Likewise, mainstream sociologists generally do not care about the existence of work in cell 4. While Milbank would say that sociological influence on Christian theology has been a disaster, others may disagree, and we will leave it for others to make that evaluation. It is, however, clear that the two fields cannot be hermetically sealed and that influence will occur. Perhaps what would be best is for this influence to be transparent, because then we can better see the advantages and pitfalls of such influence. We hope that this will ensure that any boundary is not simply a product of institutional boundary work, but also a site for useful and generative engagement of ideas.

References

Ammerman, Nancy T., Carroll, Jackson W., Dudley, Carl S., and McKinney, William. 1998. *Studying Congregations: A New Handbook*. Nashville, TN: Abingdon Press.

Asad, Talal. 1993. *Genealogies of Religion: Discipline and Reasons of Power in Christianity and Islam*. Baltimore, MD: Johns Hopkins University Press.

Barbour, Ian. 2000. *When Science Meets Religion: Enemies, Strangers, or Partners?* San Francisco: HarperSanFrancisco.

Berger, Peter L. 1967. *The Sacred Canopy: Elements of a Sociological Theory of Religion*. New York: Doubleday.

Berger, Peter L. 1979. *The Heretical Imperative: Contemporary Possibilities of Religious Affirmation*. Garden City, NY: Anchor.

Cannell, Fenella. 2006. The Anthropology of Christianity. In Fenella Cannell, ed. *The Anthropology of Christianity*. Durham, NC: Duke University Press, pp. 1–50.

Comstock, Gary L. 1987. Two Types of Narrative Theology. *Journal of the American Academy of Religion*, 55, pp. 687–717.

Evans, Michael S. 2009. Defining the Public, Defining Sociology: Hybrid Science–Public Relations and Boundary-Work in Early American Sociology. *Public Understanding of Science*, 185, pp. 5–22.

Garrett, William R. 1987. The Sociological Theology of H. Richard Niebuhr. In William H. Swatos, ed. *Religious Sociology: Interfaces and Boundaries*. New York: Greenwood Press, pp. 41–55.

Johnstone, Ronald L. 1997. *Religion in Society: A Sociology of Religion*. Upper Saddle River, NJ: Prentice-Hall.

Keane, Webb. 2002. Sincerity, "Modernity," and the Protestants. *Cultural Anthropology*, 17, pp. 65–92.

Kivisto, Peter. 1989. The Brief Career of Catholic Sociology. *Sociological Analysis*, 50, pp. 351–361.

Lyon, David. 1983a. The Idea of a Christian Sociology: Some Historical Precedents and Current Concerns. *Sociological Analysis*, 44, pp. 227–242.

Lyon, David. 1983b. *Sociology and the Human Image*. Downers Grove, IL: InterVarsity Press.

Marti, Gerardo. 2005. *A Mosaic of Believers: Diversity and Innovation in a Multiethnic Church*. Bloomington, IN: Indiana University Press.

McAllister, Ronald J. 1987. Theology Lessons for Sociology. In William H. Swatos, ed. *Religious Sociology: Interfaces and Boundaries*. New York: Greenwood Press, pp. 27–39.

Milbank, John. 2006. *Theology and Social Theory: Beyond Secular Reason*. Oxford: Wiley-Blackwell.

Norris, Pippa and Inglehart, Ronald. 2004. *Sacred and Secular: Religion and Politics Worldwide*. New York: Cambridge University Press.

Perkins, Richard. 1987. *Looking Both Ways: Exploring the Interface between Christianity and Sociology*. Grand Rapids, MI: Baker.

Roberts, Richard H. 2005. Theology and the Social Sciences. In David F. Ford, ed. *The Modern Theologians*. Oxford: Blackwell, pp. 370–380.

Smilde, David and May, Matthew. 2010. *The Emerging Strong Program in the Sociology of Religion*. Social Science Research Council Working Papers. New York: Social Science Research Council.

Smith, Christian. 2003. Secularizing American Higher Education: The Case of Early American Sociology. In Christian Smith, ed. *The Secular Revolution: Power, Interests, and Conflict in the Secularization of American Public Life*. Berkeley, CA: University of California Press, pp. 97–159.

Swatos, William H., Jr. 1987. *Religious Sociology: Interfaces and Boundaries*. New York: Greenwood Press.

Turner, Stephen and Turner, Jonathan. 1990. *The Impossible Science: An Institutional Analysis of American Sociology*. Newbury Park, CA: Sage Publications.

Varacalli, Joseph A. 1990. Catholic Sociology in America: A Comment on the Fiftieth Anniversary Issue of Sociological Analysis. *International Journal of Politics, Culture and Society*, 48, pp. 249–262.

Further Reading

Asad, Talal. 1993. *Genealogies of Religion: Discipline and Reasons of Power in Christianity and Islam*. Baltimore, MD: Johns Hopkins University Press. This book collects several of Asad's essays that detail how religion emerged as a specific historical category underpinning Western ideas about modernity and universality.

Comstock, Gary L. 1987. Two Types of Narrative Theology. *Journal of the American Academy of Religion*, 55, pp. 687–717. In addition to identifying important differences between strains of narrative theology as it emerged, Comstock provides a useful overview of key concepts and arguments that continue to drive its development.

Perkins, Richard. 1987. *Looking Both Ways: Exploring the Interface between Christianity and Sociology*. Grand Rapids, MI: Baker. A good example of an attempt to merge ideas from Christianity and sociology from an evangelical perspective.

Taylor, Charles. 2004. *Modern Social Imaginaries*. Durham, NC: Duke University Press. Taylor contrasts explicit rules of moral order with the less explicit shared self-understandings and expectations that constitute a "social imaginary," and suggests that the historical development of the economy, public sphere, and democratic self-rule as cultural forms have defined Western modernity's distinctive social imaginary.

31

Economics and Christian Faith

ROBIN J. KLAY

For thousands of years, societies have struggled with the tension between commerce and godliness, between being successful and being good. From the biblical authors, to Christian scholars in the Middle Ages, to Reformers, lively debate took place on the morality of charging interest, private property rights, just prices in local markets, and the exploitation of the poor. With the rise of modern economies during the nineteenth century, some secular and Christian scholars began questioning whether it was possible for Christian faith and markets to coexist. Today, it is quite common to hear either: (1) that Christians should decry markets and find a *middle way* between godless capitalism and godless socialism; or (2) that Christianity itself is responsible for having opted for markets and abandoned *social democratic* values, for example, by pursuing material wealth at the expense of environmental degradation.

The objective of this chapter is not to survey and assess the history of this fractious dialogue. Instead I will present evidence that the following two extreme assertions are wrong: (1) that capitalism is fundamentally evil; or (2) that the narrow pursuit of self-interest in free and competitive markets produces everything necessary for a prosperous economy. The first part will examine those aspects of market economies most often misunderstood by critics, demonstrating their economic value and moral integrity. The second part considers what might be the economic benefits of Christian faith and values for societies in which many people are Christians.

Defending Markets and Capitalism

Over the last two centuries many Christian writers have vigorously criticized markets and capitalism for the following reasons, claiming that:

- *Private property* is a platform for selfishness.
- *Exchange/trade* presents opportunities for powerful sellers to exploit uninformed consumers, and for powerful buyers to exploit vulnerable sellers of commodities like coffee and textiles.

The Blackwell Companion to Science and Christianity, First Edition. Edited by J. B. Stump and Alan G. Padgett.
© 2012 Blackwell Publishing Ltd. Published 2012 by Blackwell Publishing Ltd.

- *Specialization* is an abandonment of wholesome self-sufficiency in which households provide for their own food, shelter, clothing, education, and entertainment. It also alienates employees from meaningful work when employees cannot connect their labor directly with the people who buy their output.
- *Middlemen and speculators* are parasites and high rollers, prospering at the expense of real producers.
- *Businesses* have the sole aim of maximizing earnings. Beating out the competition rules all their decisions. Therefore, profitable businesses are those that squeeze workers, consumers, and communities the most.
- *Financial capital* is a tool used to get something for nothing, especially by exploiting the poor.

Related to all criticisms of capitalism is a suspicion of market incentives. Thus, business's pursuit of profit is considered to be an inferior motive for production, playing to human greed at the expense of the godly values needed for true human flourishing. Let us examine these critiques in greater detail.[1]

Private property

It does not require a major in economics to understand the value of certain market features like private property rights and financial capital. *Private property* is a socially useful, morally defensible way of assigning rights and responsibilities for the use of land and other assets. Beginning with the early Church Fathers, an argument has been made that free persons have rights to the fruit of their labor.[2] If a family's labor enables them to acquire land and other assets, they have the right to use and dispose of these as they like. A just society should protect people against theft by jealous neighbors, pillage by intruders, and confiscation by their own governments.

Aristotle was the first to argue for the social usefulness of private property as an alternative to holding everything in common. First, people take better care of property that is their own. The opposite is referred to as the "tragedy of the commons": the economic value of a resource, like the ocean, is depleted because each user wants to harvest as much as possible before others. Resources deteriorate when extractions exceed their ability to replenish themselves. By contrast, a person who owns a field, factory, or forest has an incentive to protect its value, so that it will continue to be a reliable source of income and enjoyment into the future.

In addition to preserving the value of resources, owners typically invest to increase their productivity. Persons who rent or lease the land on which they work tend to make fewer improvements like drainage and erosion prevention. Likewise, those who do not own the buildings they occupy (or are subject to rent controls) tend not to add amenities or invest in their upkeep. Continuous investment to improve and augment resources (land, labor, and capital) happens only in economies based largely on private ownership. As a direct result, their citizens enjoy sustained growth in living standards.

Aristotle mentioned another very important value of private property ownership, namely, that it enables owners to act generously toward others. He writes, "No one, when men have all things in common, will any longer set an example of liberality [i.e., generosity] or do any liberal action" (*Politics*, book II, 1263b; quoted in Combee and

Norton 1991, 9). This virtuous outcome of private property ownership deserves wider appreciation.

People who work and live in poor neighborhoods and countries frequently testify to being warmly welcomed by poor families into their homes for a drink or meal. I have seen no one more proud or generous than the builder-owners of Habitat for Humanity homes in Oaxaca, Mexico. With only 500 square feet of house to their names, these families offer bedrooms to strangers, donate time to making improvements in the shacks of poorer families, and tend to sick neighbors.

We often hear that communities benefit from the generosity of wealthy families. This is certainly true, especially in America. However, it is the generosity of hundreds of millions of working-class and low-income families that speaks volumes about the potential for moral good to be generated in economies based on private property.[3]

Exchange and trade

Adam Smith identified the widespread, inherently human, propensity to "truck and barter" as the motivating force that enables people to raise their living standards. Monkeys do not improve their lives by trading up with each other (bananas for snails) or with other species (bananas for a lion's protection). But humans have always looked for casual and systematic opportunities to trade goods they have in abundance for goods they lack. Historically, trades were conducted by barter, which seriously limited potential mutual benefits. Once money was introduced it became possible to trade across greater distances and for a wider range of goods.

By making themselves useful to others through trade, humans accomplish what no other species can, taking full advantage of differences among themselves. Through trade, a great variety of skills, lands, climates, and interests around the world are made available to meet the needs of all market participants. The human inclination to trade and its increasingly complex organization over time are impressive social innovations. Notably, exchange is morally superior to many alternatives, since it requires free agreement among the parties.

Furthermore, trade opens opportunities for people of very different religions, races, nationalities, values, and tastes to create mutual benefits and to develop mutual understanding. When Americans want to sell to foreigners, like the Chinese, US businesses must take into account their needs, and vice versa. For example, a US company is entering the Chinese market with revolutionary clean-coal technology, because Chinese demand for energy is growing rapidly but threatens to make pollution levels much worse. As a result, ongoing economic relationships create understanding that deepens because people in both societies come to know each other better.

Smith considered progress toward freer exchange and trade over wider areas as *the* key to raising the living standards of the common people. (These were the *masses* who Marx later insisted could improve their lot only through violent revolution, led by those who could *see through* market dependence on exploitation.) With fewer barriers to the free movement of workers, and lower barriers to international trade in goods, a typical craftsman of Smith's day (the late eighteenth century) was better clothed and fed than were kings during previous centuries. Further improvements came with legal reform. Craftsmen were no longer barred from moving to towns for better wages and gained access to a wide assortment of goods brought from far and near to local markets.

Specialization

This brings us naturally to another characteristic of markets. As markets grow wider and richer, living standards rise through regional specialization in producing certain products. When this happens, engineers, for example, do not have to grow their own food. Farmers do not have to make their own clothes or build their own airplanes. Instead, all of them contribute skills to market networks circling the globe. Thus, French and Chilean vintners produce wines sold in Virginia, the Virgin Islands, and Vietnam; while Indian entrepreneurs supply software to banks in Chicago, Cambridge, and Cartagena.

The advantages of specialization are readily apparent in places like Oaxaca, Mexico, where some families have begun to specialize in growing pineapples or papayas for sale to expanding markets. Unlike their largely self-sufficient neighbors, these famers earn enough to build their own houses and keep their children in school. They expect to enjoy their old age, living with extended families, because they can afford better access to health care and education for themselves and their children.

Middlemen

As markets grow, it becomes beneficial for some people to specialize in the tasks of *middlemen*. If farmers in central Washington State had to truck their cherries to Seattle for sale at the local farmers' market, they would not be successful. They are experts at growing cherries, not trucking and marketing. Neither do these dry-climate farmers want to run the risk that Seattle rain might close the market for days, leaving them with truckloads of unsold, wasting fruit. Instead, farmers sell most of their crop to wholesalers, who in turn sell to retailers around the country and world. Cherry farmers do not resent middlemen (e.g., wholesalers and retailers), because their expertise enables farmers to make a good living in agriculture.

It is a sign of real poverty wherever farmers must undertake all the tasks needed to finance, raise, transport, and sell their crops. By contrast, in well-developed markets, firms specialize in tasks that contribute value to consumers. Some firms sell farmers inputs, ranging from fertilizer to financing. Others provide crop storage and make bulk shipments to processors and wholesalers. Retailers then sell the food to consumers.

Specialization and productivity improvements have lowered the cost of food reaching the tables of American consumers – far below what food would cost if all components were supplied by famers themselves. Between 1901 and 2002/3, the share of household budgets spent on food in America dropped from 42.5% to 13.2%.[4] The fraction of retail food prices earned by farmers has also fallen. This is not a sign that middlemen gouge consumers or cheat producers. Instead, each link in the production chain contributes value. Innovations in transportation and product handling are clear examples. Wholesalers add value by ensuring product arrival in the right quantities and at the right times for sale to retailers. In turn, food retailers now offer consumers an increasing array of farm products on a continuous basis. This is an obvious advantage to consumers because they could not possibly buy a year's worth of foods like cherries, corn, and cucumbers.

The popular movement encouraging families to eat only locally grown food is well-meaning but wrongheaded. It is one thing for families to faithfully buy summer fruit from farmer friends. It is quite another to claim that if communities bought only locally grown products, they would be better off. Imagine the scene. Texans stop buying Michigan blueberries in favor of local citrus fruits. Michiganders stop buying Texas grapefruit in favor of Michigan blueberries. Now extend the argument to all states and crops.

Consumers would have to forgo fruits and vegetables out of season or preserve them in great quantities. Many farmers, limited to selling in local markets, would go out of business. In a word, we would all be worse off: farmers, consumers, middlemen, and many businesses associated with the agricultural industry.

Speculators and financial markets

One of the specialized activities upon which many farmers depend is the *futures market*. Let us take the example of the Swart family, which has a corn and soybean operation in Iowa. Farming has always been risky because of unpredicted weather and changing market prices. The Swarts reduced some risks by purchasing insurance to cover their harvesters and other expensive machinery. They can further lower risks by agreeing, six months in advance (or longer), to sell contracts (5,000 bushels each) for their fall corn crop. For example, in mid-July 2010, they could arrange to sell corn six months later at a price of $3.91 per bushel. By committing to this contract, the Swarts can concentrate their attention and skills on farming. They no longer have to worry about the price of corn falling to $2.50 per bushel by mid-January, because someone has agreed to buy their corn at the price of $3.91.

For persons unfamiliar with futures markets, the question naturally arises, "Who would want to buy corn six months before delivery?" Two groups of people have an interest in buying corn futures. Any company for which corn is an input wants to protect itself against the risk that corn will cost much more if they wait to buy in six months. To eliminate this risk they purchase the Swarts's contracts for delivery in January. This arrangement allows companies specializing in neither farming nor *commodity futures* to stick to their primary task of processing corn for sale to the ultimate customers, such as farmers buying corn for cattle feed and families buying corn cereals.

A third group of participants in futures markets are *speculators* who buy and sell *corn futures*. These are financial instruments similar to futures contracts for other commodities and currencies. The buyer of a corn future never actually takes delivery on the corn. Just as in stock markets, successful futures speculators are so well tuned into the markets that they buy low and sell high often enough to earn good incomes.

Commodity futures markets do not work well if the only participants are farmers and processors. The additional presence of speculators is said to thicken markets. Prices in these markets are less volatile than they would otherwise be without speculators, because their purchase and sale of futures contracts has the effect of incorporating information relevant to commodity market trends over the coming months. For example, some specialists in corn futures might believe that China's demand for grains will grow faster over the coming year – thereby putting upward pressure on world corn prices. If so, these specialists may bet on rising corn prices by buying futures contracts today, with the expectation of being able to sell them off at high prices in six months. The greater the number of persons in a futures market – buyers, sellers, and speculators – the less any one future's transaction will affect the market price.

If quite a few speculators start buying more corn futures today, thereby driving their price well above $3.91 per bushel, some farmers will take this as a signal to plant more corn. Of course, as more farmers do this, the price of corn will rise less than speculators had predicted. In this way, the presence of speculators prevents price swings from being as great as they might otherwise be. Farmers are protected from sharp price drops, and corn processors from sharp price increases. Both farmers and processors benefit by shifting the risk of price changes onto speculators, who thankfully specialize in risky futures contracts to earn their living.

Mutually positive market outcomes contrast sharply with what happens when governments try to modify markets in favor of one party. Thus, when the US, the EU, or Japan "protects farmers" by limiting foreign food imports, consumers must pay much higher prices. In some African countries, governments have created export marketing monopolies to "protect farmers from foreign exploitation." In doing so, they typically exploit their own farmers by paying them a pittance. Furthermore, when governments attempt to "protect the urban poor" by imposing ceiling prices on basic necessities (e.g., bread in Egypt, tortillas in Mexico, and rental apartments in New York City), severe shortages appear. What could have been mutually advantageous market exchanges become, instead, devices that favor one party at the expense of another.

Businesses and the profit incentive

Businesses exist because there is a need to coordinate many tasks under a single roof and manage large numbers of workers for different tasks. Imagine an economy without businesses. Each person contracts with the next one in a series of steps needed to produce a car. Joe agrees to make and sell windshields at the price of $500 each to Jill, who agrees to make car bodies and sell them to Jim at a price of $7000 each, who agrees to make and sell them, and so on. There would have to be hundreds of *Joes* making windshields, thousands of *Jills* making car bodies, and hundreds of thousands of workers in total. It is easy to see that making products this way, with each worker being his or her own contractor, would be extremely cumbersome, inefficient, and costly.

The creation of businesses (as a social institution) is an innovation that has greatly improved efficiency.[5] The historical development of better business models rivals all patents ever created for their importance to human society. The genius of business is more than efficient production. What businesses do is to coordinate the production and distribution of goods and services in environments of constantly changing technologies, suppliers, competitors, and consumer tastes. Only when businesses are owned privately (not by governments) do they respond so adroitly to challenging environments that living standards rise over time.

Successful businesses in competitive markets notice and respond to changing opportunities and threats. Sony, for example, after developing the first radio to fit in the hand, did not rest on its profitable laurels. The entry of other electronic companies into the new market pushed Sony to develop newer technologies, like miniature tape recorders and DVDs. Businesses also compete by hiring better workers, inventing new ways to handle inventory, and introducing quality improvements.

The profit motive makes businesses alert to new opportunities, for example a chance to expand into new markets. In March 2009, the Indian car company Tata Motors surprised the global automobile industry by announcing its readiness to market the Nano, at a record low price of $2200, to rising middle-class families in fast-growing Asian markets. The profit incentive has also encouraged fishermen co-ops in South India to buy cell phones, with which they can contact nearby urban markets to determine the varieties of fish to catch for the day's best price. After Hurricane Katrina, the profit incentive first led local outlets to raise the prices of water pumps, which signaled firms around the country to make and ship pumps in large numbers to places where they were badly needed.

Few economists believe that a narrowly conceived profit incentive – for example, letting *maximum quarterly* earnings determine all decisions – explains the behaviour of businesses. In order to hire and keep good employees, businesses must consider their employees' ideas, offer them chances for advancement, train and retrain competent workers, motivate and reward them. In order to keep investors, firms have to think well beyond next quarter's returns.

Far from being myopically focused on short-term profit at the expense of competitors, workers, and consumers, businesses that achieve durable success are masters at continuously listening to consumers; facilitating collaboration between managers and employees; coordinating with suppliers; and being attentive to the wellbeing of the communities in which they operate.

Financial and human capital

Financial capital is what businesses require to fund their activities. Having begun with founders' equity investments, businesses can borrow money from banks and sell bonds. They may also sell stock. For the use of these funds, businesses pay dividends to stockholders and interest to bondholders. Fundamentally these funds derive from saving made earlier and concurrently by households and businesses. In the latter case, saving takes the form of retained earnings out of profits, which are plowed back into expanding production capacity.

One must keep in mind that businesses could not be created and expanded without savers. They forgo current consumption in exchange for interest on bank deposits, bonds, and market fund accounts; or for dividends on stocks. Consider the case of stocks and bonds that a saver purchases directly, or indirectly through a fund, from business X. The saver depends on the business to make profitable use of his/her funds by expanding facilities, researching new products, lowering costs, and serving customers as well or better than its competitors. Only businesses that excel at all these activities are able to continue borrowing and selling stock. If businesses did not increase productivity over time, savers would not receive rewards for sacrificing a portion of their current incomes. In such an environment, saving would take the form of burying money in a safe place. (Recall Jesus' parable in which he chastised the servant who just buried the master's money instead of using the funds to multiply their value; Matt. 25:14–30.)

It is a remarkable fact about market economies that they reward savers precisely because they grow! It is an even more remarkable fact about human beings that families believe in the future enough to save, and that businesses believe in the future enough to invest savings to grow their productive capacity.

Over the last several decades economists have devoted research to the study of *human capital*. Persons are said to "invest" in developing their gifts and skills through education and training. Notice that this, too, requires saving. Hence, families save to pay for their children's education and businesses invest in recruiting, training, and retaining the best possible employees. As is true of all investment, such activities are funded by saving out of current revenue with the hope of greater gains in the future.

An interesting fact about the word "credit" is that its origin is the Latin word *credere*, to believe. We have followed the chain from belief in the future to saving, and belief in the future to investment by firms and families. Investment is made possible by some combination of saving ahead of time and borrowing from the accumulated savings of others. In the latter case, we say that a bank, for example, offers credit (a loan) to a business. Banks offer credit only to those in whom they *believe*. The deal works if both parties believe that the loan will make the borrower more productive, and therefore able to pay interest and repay principle out of increased revenues. It is their shared belief in the future of the borrower, his or her character and project (in addition to any collateral) that makes lending, borrowing, and saving possible.

Hope in the future, trust among people and organizations, sacrifice, creativity, insight, delight in collaboration, the passion to build and share – these are qualities that infuse economies in which markets work their miracle by enabling free people to become more productive and enjoy rising living standards. However, these foundational qualities of human society are typically left unacknowledged by contemporary economists. How do economies benefit from the Christian faith and the lives of Christians? How might economists investigate these issues? This is the topic of the second part of this chapter.

Taking stock

The study of economics uncovers the value of markets, whose prominent features we have just discussed. It does not, however, prove that all operations of private property, exchange and trade, specialization, middlemen, speculators, businesses, and capital are honest and contribute to the common good. The press calls our attention to instances when large companies are accused of shortsighted or illegal behavior motivated by greed. As individuals, too, we rightly question ourselves about the stewardship of our property, our honesty when selling a used car, and the pressure we feel to buy the latest devices.

Markets give people reasons to think carefully about alternative uses of their money, time, and skills. They close some options while opening up new ones. They respond to new ideas. Along with constant change, they also offer insurance against particular risks. They provide consumers with goods and services to meet their needs and desires for housing, clothing, food, and entertainment; as well as the resources required to build families, churches, programs for young and old, and community spirit.

What markets cannot do is tell us the meaning of our work, the purpose of our recreation, or the value of empty space and silence. They cannot tell us which job to take, how much to save, what risks to assume, or whom we should help. Markets do not force people to think only in terms of money and material wealth. They do give everyone many choices in all these matters. It is a supreme and uniquely human responsibility to determine the values that guide these choices, in the light of life's ultimate purposes. Christians believe that God offers every person high goals and moral choices, as well as the example of Christ, to meet life's challenges.

Christian Faith and Economics

Economics and Christian faith seem unlikely partners to many people. One is thought to be about money and the other about ultimate values. Instead, as we saw in the previous section, many characteristics of markets are extremely useful, require specialized skills found only in well-developed economies, and enable the vast majority of families to do better over time. We now consider whether specifically Christian values make a difference in an economy. In the process, we take note of secular economists' failure to recognize that behaviors crucial to economic success, like saving and investment, are deeply rooted in fundamental values, including those of distinctly Christian origin.

Economists are beginning to study social capital – those skills, habits, and values acquired through family and community.[6] In societies like the United States, formal and informal organizations at local, state, and regional levels build valuable social capital. A bare sampling of such organizations would include: neighborhood picnics and recreation programs; beach clean-up days and soup kitchens; cultural centers and fund raisers to return a son for burial in Mexico; chess clubs and sports teams. Most of us cannot imagine our communities without these, in addition to religious and artistic organizations. They build trust, pride, friendship, sensitivity, and a willingness to sacrifice. They also develop organizational skills in leaders and members.

In communities with a strong social fabric, public safety is cheaper and property loss is less than elsewhere, meaning lower taxes and insurance rates. Communities like these attract new residents and businesses. The economic benefits of strong social networks include new and better jobs, higher incomes, and greater tax revenue. These towns get written up nationally for the health and happiness of their residents, often leading to increased tourist revenue. A common bonus for the cities so honored is becoming eligible for private and public grants to further improve residents' lives. Values taught and practiced in communities like these have an impact far beyond the surrounding geographical area. What firm, neighborhood, town, or state would not eagerly recruit and warmly welcome people who contribute positively to their community?

We may assume that many personal and social values formed in Christian communities are broadly shared by people of other faiths. Still, one might ask whether the presence of many Christians in a community adds unique values and economic rewards. Are certain values emphasized and practiced more by Christians than by people of other religious traditions? Perhaps. No simple answers can be given to these questions. It is the case that the practice of values within religious/ethical traditions is the key to positive outcomes for their community, not simply membership and belief.

Among the seven classical virtues, the theological ones – faith, hope, and love – are especially relevant to the question of what economic difference Christians make, if any, in their communities. I suspect that from communities in which the theological virtues are taught and practiced by Christians, powerful economic consequences follow, along with spiritual ones. However, this is likely to be true only when Christians also practice the cardinal virtues: justice, courage, temperance, and prudence. Indeed, exploring this hypothesis is the task undertaken by Deidre N. McCloskey in her book *The Bourgeois Virtues: Ethics for an Age of Commerce* (2007). As a highly regarded senior economist, who publicly revealed her decision to become a Christian, McCloskey sets a high standard for all economists. Her analysis is scholarly, fair, and inspiring.

It is an empirically testable hypothesis that communities with a large proportion of Christians tend to be economically better off than very similar communities with few Christians.[7] A statistical test of this question requires holding constant (taking into account) traits that have important economic consequences, such as education, wealth, age distribution, health, and immigration status, to determine what specific difference a strong Christian presence makes in a community's income level and growth rates (or some other measure of economic success).

Healthy economic life requires sustained hope that encourages saving and investment in one's future. When hope is vitally present, people make sacrifices to save for their children's education; and they accept the inevitable risks entailed in business investment. Not surprisingly, these are the very behaviors that create more abundant futures for which people hope, sacrifice, and plan. If, as it seems, the practice of hope is declining, our society will face threats of economic stagnation.

Noting that low saving rates cause slower income growth, economists have frequently called attention to falling US saving rates, which fell from an average of 9–11% of personal income in 1952–1982 to about 1% in 2007.[8] Indeed, poor countries with high saving rates, like China, are enjoying historically unmatched growth rates in their living standards. Typically, saving rates show a tendency to fall as average incomes rise substantially. As a result, economists in advanced economies are often asked for professional advice about tax reform that might stimulate saving and investment. However, if a society's deepest springs of hope start to dry up, economists will be ill equipped to offer policy solutions.

Christians need pastoral guidance about how to approach economic and other challenges with a combination of reason and faith. This they need much more urgently than pastoral encouragement to support specific social and political causes, like debt relief for Third World countries or an end to gun control.

Many Christian clergy and theologians believe that they have a duty to teach Christians how to care about social issues. By itself, this makes sense. It is wise and potentially useful for Christians to probe Scripture and to recover Church teaching about stewardship over creation and the responsibility to care for the poor. It is, however, treacherous for Christian leaders to assign themselves the job of determining the best economic means to accomplish social/ethical goals. It is beyond their realm of expertise to advocate for approaches identified closely with their own political ideologies.

When clergy take up public policy positions, they abandon their primary responsibility to teach, lead worship, and serve the sacraments to people who reasonably and faithfully differ in their support for political, economic, and social causes. The error is compounded when persons at the highest levels of church administration pick moral winners and losers in the realm of applied politics and economics, claiming to speak for the Church or their denomination. When the Christian faith is identified with particular economic positions – left, right, or center – some people who sincerely want to know Christ may avoid coming near a church. Their discomfort with the political views of church pastors and leaders can become an obstacle to welcoming God's love and call in their lives.

Urging caution by Christian communities lest they raise barriers to the Gospel has a strong scriptural legacy. St Paul (1 Cor. 8: 1–7) advised his readers not to take sides with Jewish Christians who insisted on strict observance of Old Testament dietary laws, because Gentiles might be kept from responding to the Gospel.

Without question, Christian families need guidance from the Church and clergy about how to raise children to be strong in faith, hope, and love and practiced at exercising even the *mundane* virtue of prudence (wisdom). They must be taught spiritual practices like prayer and worship – in order to experience their value to mind, body, spirit, and entire communities.

Families must hear that achieving the highest goals for themselves and others requires budgeting wisely, saving consistently, giving regularly, and applying faith-with-reason in all things. John Wesley's teaching on the subject is often summed up with these words:

> Do all the good you can,
> By all the means you can,
> In all the ways you can,
> In all the places you can,
> At all the times you can,
> To all the people you can,
> As long as ever you can.[9]

Churches should help their members, young and old, to identify and develop their gifts and callings from God.

The Church teaches that God calls laypersons in particular to join reason with faith in every sphere of life. For the glory of God and the benefit of all, each person receives a unique calling(s) from God to exercise faith and reason in his or her areas of expertise.[10] Indeed, the Christian doctrine of *vocation* compares favorably with the value economists attach to specialization. Vocations into many different professions set loose diverse talents and skills for the benefit of the whole society, more so as specialization increases. If each generation of Christians becomes grounded in these truths and tasks, they will bring even greater spiritual and material blessings to humanity.

Conclusion

We have shown how the study of economics illuminates major features of market economies and found them not to be the source of social evil. We have also suggested that one contribution Christianity could make to the study of economics is its emphasis on reasoned hope. Societies marked by the practice of the classical Christian virtues, like hope, produce risk-taking entrepreneurship, creative innovation, and strong saving for the future. These are the very behaviors that raise living standards. Taken together, the practice of virtue and rising living standards may be signs of God's providence in communities.[11] Perhaps Christian economists will push the profession to study the impact of moral values and spiritual practices on economic wellbeing.

Notes

1   For a typical moral critique of markets and profits by theologians, see Loy (1997).
2   For a good summary of Church teaching on the right to property, see "Article 7 – The Seventh Commandment" in the *Catechism of the Catholic Church*, paragraph 2401, on "The Universal Destination and the Private Ownership of Goods."
3   Economist Arthur C. Brooks (2007) offers a stunning, detailed exploration of statistically reliable relationships among Americans between giving (and not giving), income levels, religious engagement, and a person's views about the proper role of government.
4   Figures from the US Bureau of Labor Statistics: http://www.bls.gov/opub/uscs/reflections.pdf.
5   See a masterful treatment of the subject in Baumol (2004).
6   Glenn Loury (2002) was among the first economists to apply the concept of social capital to income differences between races. The nineteenth-century French writer Alexis de Tocqueville was struck by the vitality of social networks in every American hamlet – enabling them to provide for themselves and to solve common problems without resort to government. See his *Democracy in America*, 1835–1840, which is available in many editions, including online.
7   Economist Feler Bose is conducting research on this topic, using village-level studies, in which he compares Christian villages with Hindu villages in the same Tamil region of India, and their respective economic success.
8   Figures from US Department of Commerce, Bureau of Economic Analysis, National Income and Product Accounts: http://www.bea.gov/national/nipaweb/PrintGraph.asp?Freq=Year.
9   The quotation isn't direct, but paraphrases the three rules from Wesley (2007, 124–136): gain all you can; save all you can; give all you can.

10   See the most important papal statement on the topic of the vocation of laypersons in the *Decree on the Apostolate of the Laity*, Pope Paul VI, November 18, 1965.

11   Acknowledgement of God's blessings in and through economic relationships must be distinguished from the wealth gospel. It is noteworthy that from the Psalmist through the Scottish Enlightenment, believers were heard praising God for his work among his chosen people and far beyond. Their praise rose up to God for blessings in the natural world and through certain social institutions in the economy and the state. Contemporary economists and theologians no longer accept Max Weber's thesis that Calvinists created capitalism. Neither do most economists and lay Christians believe that God mechanically rewards those who "claim his promises" without a lot of wisdom and sweat in addition to faith.

References

Baumol, William J. 2004. *The Free Market Innovation Machine: Analyzing the Great Miracle of Capitalism*. Princeton, NJ: Princeton University Press.

Brooks, Arthur C. 2007. *Who Really Cares? The Surprising Truth about Compassionate Conservatism*. New York: Basic Books.

Combee, Jerry and Norton, Edgar, eds. 1991. *Economic Justice in Perspective: A Book of Readings*. Upper Saddle River, NJ: Prentice-Hall.

Loy, David R. 1997. The Religion of the Market. *Journal of the American Academy of Religion*, 65(2), pp. 275–290.

Loury, Glenn. 2002. *The Anatomy of Racial Inequality*. Cambridge, MA: Harvard University Press.

McCloskey, Deidre N. 2007. *The Bourgeois Virtues: Ethics for an Age of Commerce*. Chicago: University of Chicago Press.

Wesley, John. 2007. *The Works of John Wesley*, 3rd edn, vol. 6. Grand Rapids, MI: Baker Books.

Further Reading

Klay, Robin and Lunn, John. 2005. What Bearing, If Any, Does the Christian Doctrine of Providence Have upon the Operation of the Market Economy? *Journal of Markets and Morality*, 6(2), pp. 493–504. An attempt to show compatibility between the market system and a key Christian doctrine (providence), while specifically affirming personal responsibility for economic choices and the Church's role in building and sustaining the moral and cultural fabric of society.

Nelson, Robert H. 1998. Economic Religion versus Christian Values. *Journal of Markets and Morality*, 1(2), pp. 142–157. A critique of the Chicago school of economics' claim to explain virtually all of human behavior as single-minded searches for the best individual "deals" – not just in the market but also in marriage and family.

Novak, Michael. 1990. *The Spirit of Democratic Capitalism*, revised edn. Lanham, MD: Madison Books. One of the most comprehensive attempts to connect major Christian doctrines (e.g., sin, man's creation in the image of God) with free markets, in the context of political democracy and strong moral-cultural institutions.

Woods, Thomas E., Jr. 2005. *The Church and the Market: A Catholic Defense of the Free Market Economy*. Lanham, MA: Lexington Books. A good example of one economist's attempt to show how Catholic social teaching is compatible with sound economic principles, especially those emphasized in Austrian economics.

Part VII
Christian Bioethics

32

Shaping Human Life at the Molecular Level

JAMES C. PETERSON

The Gospel of John says that on at least one occasion Jesus turned water instantly into the best wine at a wedding feast (John 2:1–10). Now that is molecular enhancement. Jesus is also described as a builder in his hometown until about the age of 30, hewing the stone and wood of the natural world for his neighbors (Mark 6:1–3). Such shaping of the natural world to service was one expression of Jesus' teaching to love God and neighbor. The world is God's, and human beings have a special part in it. In the opening of Genesis the first humans live in a garden, not a wilderness. A garden requires tending (more roses or more aphids?) and the first human beings were directed to do so (Gen. 2:15). They were responsible to God to make decisions so that both they and the garden might flourish. Such stewardship gives a context for issues of ecology and the environment addressed in Chapter 35 of this volume. Chapter 33 considers responsibility for human life at the embryonic level. This chapter focuses on God-given stewardship of the human body that naturally includes genetics. The current practice of genetic testing will receive particular attention.

Body Matters

The human body matters in the Christian tradition. It is not a kind of prison for the soul as Plato thought. It is not to be disdained as with the Manicheans. It is part of God's good and gracious provision. When the Apostle Paul writes of subduing the flesh (Rom. 8:1–14), he is not rejecting the materiality of the human body, rather he is referring to the harmful habits that we often build up in how we use our bodies. Our bodies are where we have the most opportunity to decide, and they come to embody our decisions. I can choose what I look at with my eyes, where I go with my feet, what I touch with my hands. Unless there are immediately disastrous results each choice tends to reinforce seeing and acting in that way again as the patterns become embedded in our muscle memory and neural net. Habits become part of our bodies. This has important implications for Christian spirituality and discipleship.

The Blackwell Companion to Science and Christianity, First Edition. Edited by J. B. Stump and Alan G. Padgett.

As the primary locus of my own decisions, the body is where I develop momentum toward God or away from God. It is also where I can learn to love my neighbors as myself by seeing and providing for their needs, or to turn away from them. This eventually constitutive orientation toward God and others is so important for the follower of Christ that Jesus describes a great separation on the last day between those people who are his and those who are not. Those who are his can be recognized by how they are caring for their neighbors, bringing food to the hungry, water to the thirsty, visiting those who are sick or in prison (Matt. 25:31–46). To be clear, these body actions to care for the embodied needs of others are not described as ways of earning one's way into God's family, but are characteristic of those who by grace *are* part of God's family (Eph. 2:1–10).

The human body plays a pivotal role in human life and purpose. As human beings we are deeply physical beings living at multiple levels (Green 2008). Whatever happens at one level has ripple effects for the other levels of human life. When the body is tired the soul finds it hard to pray. Further, the human body is so intricately complex that it is a wonder that it works at all. The stakes are high in a body vulnerable to disruption. A small change at a strategic point can wreak havoc. For example, a change in one base pair out of 3 billion in a person's DNA, from a C to a T, might convert a glutamine codon (CAG) to a STOP codon (TAG). The result is a loss of the intended protein and its function. The implications can be as lethal as cystic fibrosis. A primary task for being human is to do what we can to maintain our bodies, restore them when they lose function, and to develop them when possible. Just to maintain the blood that courses through the veins of one person, each day the spleen destroys about 200 billion worn-out red blood cells, and bone marrow replaces them with 200 billion new red blood cells. If that system starts to break down, say by a disease that causes the kidneys not to make enough erythropoietin to trigger adequate red blood-cell formation, medical care makes every effort to restore the kidneys' function. If we could intervene to keep a person's blood replacement going before the system broke down, say with a vaccine that enhanced the immune system to protect the person from developing the kidney disease in the first place, such would be most welcome. We should sustain, restore, and develop our bodies where we can. Some people are genetically predisposed to lose bone mass as they age, facing the crippling of osteoporosis. We encourage the consumption of calcium and weight-bearing exercise to maintain their present bone mass. If a bone snaps, we realign it in its proper place to encourage it to knit back together. If, as often occurs, the body rejoins the bone at that point so that it is stronger than it was before, we are pleased. We do and should maintain, restore, and improve our bodies.

How we find our bodies at a given point is not a God-given standard that we are prohibited from changing (Albertson 2010). It is appropriate to intervene. We should brush our teeth. If they are ignored they will go away. Further when a tooth develops a cavity, it is right to fill it to save the tooth. It is even better to treat teeth with fluoride to strengthen the enamel beyond its natural ability so that no cavities develop in the first place. Maintain, restore, and improve. When a child is born with a cleft palate, there is no debate whether we should do surgery so that the child can eat and speak. If we could do a kind of genetic micro-surgery so that the roof of the child's mouth grew together from the beginning without later cutting and stitches for the baby and her future children, would that not be better? In yet other words: sustain, repair, and develop.

Now the opening words of Genesis are "In the beginning God created the heavens and the earth." This affirmation is at the start of the Apostles' Creed as well: "We believe in God the Father, maker of heaven and earth." That God created the world is sometimes confused with the idea that creation as we experience it now is God's perfect intent for creation forever. This is deeply mistaken in at least two ways. First, the major Christian traditions agree that God has revealed a plan ultimately to transform his people from what we are now. Paul writes of the perishable transformed to the imperishable, a new form of the body suitable to live with God forever (1 Cor. 15:42–44). The Apostle John writes of the old earth and heaven passing away and a new heaven and earth given by God (Rev. 21:1). Some traditions emphasize continuity in this change between the present creation and the one to come (Volf 2001, 99–102), but it is still held in common that what is now is not what will always be. Change is promised.

Second, human life is characterized by misplaced priorities that the tradition identifies as sin. When human beings prioritize anything over the one true God they end up harming themselves and each other. Augustine wrote in the fourth century of our era that human beings were created right with God and one another, but lost this blessed state by their poor choices. Later, in the seventeenth century, Milton would describe this condition as a paradise lost. In contrast, St Irenaeus wrote before Augustine that human beings did not have initial perfection so much as a chance at developing (Irenaeus, book 4, chapter 11). Tragically, they turned from their potential to grow toward God and in God's service to dissolution and grief, instead. What both Augustine and Irenaeus see is that human beings do not currently live as we could. Paul wrote of the present creation groaning as if in childbirth to be liberated to what God has planned for it (Rom. 8:19–23). We are not yet all we are meant to be. Our natural circumstances now are not the standard for what we can and should be. Human beings are not to remain static. We are called and empowered by God's grace to grow and develop into human beings fulfilled in right relationship with God and each other forever. We are not to remain the same as we are now. We are to grow in the capacity, relationship, and calling first described in the opening chapter of Genesis as the image of God.

As creatures created to be creative, it is God's design to work in, through, and with us. Physical change is part of that process. God instructed Abraham to show his commitment to covenant with God by circumcision (Gen. 17:10). Circumcision is the cutting off of a normal part of the male human body. It is clear that altering the body is not inherently contrary to God's will; in fact here it was given as a sign of following God. Physical change at the molecular level is not the point of human life, but it too can be an instrumental good. This is not to advocate transhumanism. Transhumanism hopes for human fulfillment in merely extending individual capability and life span. Even fulfilled at its most dreamed-of level, it would not produce whole human life. Christian faith calls for life in right mission and community with God and one another. Life is to be shaped at all levels out of love for God and one another, not self-absorption. We best grow to serve, not to displace into ultimately pointless self-aggrandizement. It is not that self-love is inherently wrong. Jesus taught that we should love our neighbors as ourselves, not more than ourselves. Our hardwiring is such that we are naturally much more directly aware of our own desires, such as hunger, than of someone else's. To consider the needs of others as being as important as our own is actually quite a high standard and one that requires significant sacrifice of immediate self-interest. The problem is not in caring for oneself, it is in not caring for God decisively more and our neighbors as much as ourselves.

Could intervening in the human body at the molecular level affect our default tendency to self-centeredness? Sin, placing anything other than God at the center of one's life, is more complex than physical disposition, yet physical disposition pays a role in basic heart orientation and how it is carried out. Most human tendencies can be channeled in positive or harmful ways. Molecular change cannot single-handedly resolve what we do, but there may eventually be ways to contribute positively, such as by building up the usually present human reticence against murdering another. Also, genetic intervention might be able to contribute to rolling back some of the embodied tendencies toward sin. Parents and day-care workers will still be more formative for perception and practice than molecular intervention is likely to be. But where it can contribute its part, as is expected of every other resource, it could be welcome as yet another expression of love for God and neighbor.

Direction

So if human life at the molecular level, as at every other level, is to be shaped to God's service out of love for God and one another, what should it look like? I have argued thus far that intentionally modifying our bodies can be not only permissible, but even part of our calling to responsible stewardship of what God has entrusted to us. However, there is a long history of human beings misdirecting their developed capabilities. One of the worst relatively recent examples was the racist mass murder that the Nazis perpetrated in the name of the health of the people. The worst evils are often perpetrated in the name of recognized goods. The Nazis also commandeered the education system, but we do not now reject schooling. The Nazis co-opted the medical system, but we do not now inherently mistrust all physicians and nurses. In biblical terms, the destruction of the tower of Babel was a warning against putting bricks together to try to be God, but it is not a warning against putting bricks together to build homes. That something can be turned into an idol or turned to abuse means that it requires caution, not that it is necessarily harmful of itself.

So how can we genuinely serve in this area? In postmodern times consensus on the required discernment is often hard to find. Rather than agreeing on *what* we will do, we often agree on *who* will decide what we will do. This would not be a bad course in regard to much of molecular intervention, in that one choice pursued by all risks the most marked danger. Disseminating decisions widely would limit unintentional damage by courses that turn out to be mistaken, make it difficult for one large group to use choices against another, encourage the opportunity of trying a wide variety of directions, and enhance the rich diversity of life. Yet some choices for oneself or others might be so ill-advised that there would be sufficient consensus in a public to limit them. We face similar life-shaping choices, dialogue, and limitations in how we provide education and medical care.

Three guides for individuals and the public have been proposed that draw attention to important considerations, although they can be damaging if treated as final standards. One of these distinctions is between intervention that is somatic and intervention that has germ-line effects. "Somatic" means that the effect of the intervention is felt by only one recipient. This has the marked advantage of honoring the recipient's choice if they are competent to so decide, and limits any unexpected damage to just that one person. However, many somatic treatments end up having effects in descendants (the germ line). If a young patient is somatically treated for heart disease and then lives to have children of his own, the genetic tendency toward that kind of heart disease is now passed on to others who would not have been born if the disease had run its course. Now the genes for that disease are more prevalent. That is a germ-line effect from what was intended to be a somatic treatment. A further question for the distinction is that if a treatment is safe enough for the person who requests it, why not for the recipient's children? If a genetic treatment becomes available to stop Huntingdon's disease (HD), which kills its carriers usually in their thirties or forties, why free only the presenting patient, and not their children? As much as possible people should be consulted about what will affect them, but countless formative decisions are made for us before we can speak for ourselves. My first language and where I grew up shaped me deeply, but were not my choice. That is the human condition. Why rule out help that we are confident will be appreciated? If not, to insist on only acting with competent consent would also stop life-saving surgery for children with appendicitis.

A second distinction that is argued is that between gift and artifact. Children should be born and received as gifts, not something that we choose and make (President's Council on Bioethics, 2003). There is a great truth here that all children should be welcomed and nurtured whatever their abilities (Hall 2008). But such is quite different from saying that all children should be left as they are. When a child is born with a blocked intestine, it does not mean that she should be left to die as if this were simply God's design and will for her. If we know a way to help her thrive, we should provide it. That we have done a tonsillectomy for Johnny does not make him any less a gift or a person. Our motivation may be precisely that we care about him as a beloved person.

A third distinction often invoked is that between correction and enhancement. It is crucial to realize that all intervention can be described as enhancement. If a high temperature is relieved, the body's ability to regulate temperature has been enhanced. If one sets a broken arm bone, one has enhanced the recipient's ability to heal that arm. Granted, some define cure as a subset of enhancement that is limited to normal, but what then is "normal"? Is normal having teeth that do not meet well for maximum use and lifespan, hence braces would be an unacceptable enhancement? Is the typical lifespan of 30 in Uganda the appropriate norm because it is the average there? For that matter, ability is spread over a range in most populations. Some people see better than others. If those above the average remain where they are while those below are brought up to average, the average will go up and more people would be eligible for improvement to average. There would be little long-term difference between cure and enhancement so defined. What is normal or healthy is not as easily described as this demarcation assumes (Tengland 2007). Further, why should normal be normative? I have argued earlier that what is now is not final for the Christian tradition.

In contrast, there are three standards that have gained wide consensus for centuries that can help us better discern helpful intervention. John Rawls (1971) thought that they are recognizable to all free, rational people. They are nonmaleficence, autonomy, and fairness. The most widely used textbook for bioethics (Beauchamp and Childress 2008) uses basically the same set, with nonmaleficence differentiated into nonmaleficence and beneficence. These authors describe these principles as the consensus of a long Western tradition, and indeed it is a long tradition. One can see these three principles 2700 hundred years ago when the prophet Micah (Mic. 6:8) wrote, "What does God require of you? That you seek justice, love kindness, and walk humbly with God." "Seeking justice" in Micah parallels the fairness and justice just referred to. "Love kindness" can be seen in nonmaleficence and beneficence. "To walk humbly with God" would require an attitude of respect and openness, communicated in the later lists as respect for persons or autonomy.

These principles are not always defined precisely the same way and of themselves do not offer an order of priority. When two seem to conflict, which takes precedence? They do, however, raise key questions and concerns for deliberation. I propose here a version of the list as it might apply to shaping life at the molecular level, such as in genetic or neurological intervention. Considering loving kindness and nonmaleficence: (1) is the intervention reasonably safe? This question has a long history, as seen in *primum non nocere*; at least do not make the patient worse (Peters 2004). Avoiding harm has become almost the exclusive norm in some legal jurisdictions (Brunk 2004). It does require for application answers to further questions such as what constitutes a "harm" or what is significant risk. My intent is to be informed by the Christian tradition for a contextualized description that is needed by any actual practice (Walzer 1994).

Taking into account loving kindness and beneficence: (2) is the proposed intervention offering a genuine improvement? Note the standard is improvement, not perfection (Greely *et al.* 2008). It is a false dichotomy to characterize the options as either trying to surpass our species or doing nothing at all. Results can become quite complicated as the outcome of multiple consequences at interactive levels. For example, some transhumanist proposals to relieve negative emotions may incur too high a cost in lost relationship and care for others. The ultimate context of a Christian vision of enhancement is not personal preference, rather God's revealed calling.

Walking humbly and respect for persons lead us to ask: (3) does the intervention increase recipient choice? This question is intended to ensure that no one is or feels predestined by others (Habermas 2003). If choices made on behalf of others increase their choices, the recipients are still the ones who make many of the most formative decisions for themselves. Increasing choice would not lead to accepting the request of a deaf couple for prenatal genetic diagnosis to implant only embryos that would lead to deaf children (Murray 1996). While people can lead fulfilling lives in deaf culture, the range of choices is less for the deaf child than for one who can hear. Choice for a recipient should not be unnecessarily restricted.

Each of the key principles listed above includes some sense of justice or fairness: (4) is this intervention the best available use of always finite resources?

Genetic Testing

How might the above standards apply in practice? Intervention in the human body at the molecular level is likely to include eventually a wide range of potential practices such as turning certain genes on or off, or changing neural pathways with genetically designed or nano-built pharmaceuticals. The type of molecular intervention most widespread at this point is genetic testing. It is easier to read the human genome than it is to change it. The impact of genetic testing and the questions that it raises are already substantial. Working through some of these challenges can begin to unpack how we could deal with related questions to come. I have already argued that sustaining, restoring, and developing the human body is part of human responsibility in the Christian tradition, and that four questions might structure our thinking about what we should do. Addressing specific cases brings to the fore yet more considerations. For example, the respect for persons or autonomy advocated in the last section as a key question to consider can be complicated to pursue in practice.

One might be puzzled when a physician asks many questions about one's parents and siblings. This is your appointment, not theirs. Yet a physician will often start with such questions. They are a primitive genetic test. By learning something of genes in the family, the physician gains some idea of what genes the patient may have inherited. That is helpful information. Genetics makes a difference, sometimes more weighty than environment. Winston Churchill was overweight, had an ever-present cigar, and enjoyed copious alcohol consumption. He died at 90. Sergei Grinkov was a seemingly healthy non-smoker, light drinker, and Olympic athlete but died of heart failure at 28. Genes matter. Of course one receives only half of each parent's genes and the inherited genes may have been hidden in the parent that passed them on. What is needed is some way of reading precisely which genes a particular person has inherited. The cost of doing that is dropping exponentially. Francis Collins projects that the reading of an entire individual's genome will soon be affordable for many.

Yet even if we can read a person's genome, we do not yet know what most of the DNA is doing. There are key steps between the genetic code and how it is expressed as studied in epigenetics. Further, our 23 000 genes live in the context of over a million genes in the bacteria that inhabit our gut and skin in interrelated symbiosis with us. Despite this complexity and our just beginning knowledge of genetics, genetic testing is already in active use for five major applications. It can be used to support a diagnosis, to better target conventional treatment, to plan for disease effects, to help avoid disease effects, and to discern carrier status. Most of the ethical questions that are raised overlap with concerns about other therapies, but some challenges are heightened and some are quite new. I have advocated in this chapter for respect for the presenting person, sometimes called autonomy. This is a demanding standard when genetic testing provides unintended revelations. Finding two copies of the APOE4 allele when testing for a particular problem with cholesterol can indicate greater risk for early onset dementia. The cardiologist looking for one concern has discovered another. An adult interested in bearing a child might want to know if she has HD. As a dominant single-gene disease, a test result that she will experience HD reveals that her parent will too, even if her parent did not want to know that information. The overall uptake for predictive testing is about 18% of the adult at-risk HD population in Canada (Creighton *et al.* 2003, 462–475). In other words, 82% of Canadians with an HD parent do not want to know if they will have the disease. This is why minors should not be tested for conditions that have no current treatment or effect on planning. Most minors decide not to be tested for HD when they become adults and can choose for themselves. There would need to be a compelling reason to take that choice away from them.

Another example is that of misattributed paternity. When a couple has a child whose care is extremely taxing, it is not unusual for them to ask for genetic counseling concerning the chance that the next child they have together will be so afflicted. In these cases a small percentage are found to be at no risk for repetition because it is genetically revealed that the presented father is not the biological father. It may seem simple to lie to the couple about paternity, but such deception undermines that patient–physician relationship as well as future relationships with other care providers. Furthermore, deception misleads the future decisions of the patients. For example, if they separate, the presented father will continue to believe that he is carrying a genetic disease when in fact he is not. Deception in addition denies the patients information that they asked for in the informed consent that is required by respect for persons. That this situation can arise is a reminder that the presenting couple should be told about the possibility of misattributed paternity being discovered before the test is conducted. If such disclosure is listed along with many other potential revelations before the test is done, the couple can decide to withdraw if they so wish. If they proceed, the results are rarely a complete surprise. Care providers should present such findings gently, for example to the woman first in case she may want to be the one to present the finding. If a woman seeks reproductive counseling without her spouse, the provider is not obligated to find and inform the spouse, but if a couple presents as a couple, then they as a couple are the informed patients and should not be deceived.

A further complication of genetic testing is that while genes are formative they do not act unilaterally. Genes are important, but are usually not determinative, so genetic test results will most often be in probabilities. If an identical twin has diabetes 1, the chance of the other twin having diabetes 1 is about 50%. That is a much higher risk than for the general population, but identical genes do not lead to identical disease experiences. Half of the identical twins will never develop the disease. This raises the problem of how to communicate such probabilities. Which would you rather hear, that this will not significantly affect you 9 times out of 10 or that you have a 1 in 10 chance that this will significantly affect you? These two descriptions convey identical probabilities. But as seen in the success of lotteries, most people do not comprehend probabilities very well. If informed consent is actually to occur out of respect for persons, significant resources are required for patients not only to receive genetically based information, but also to understand the import of it. Written or video explanations and personal attention from, for example, a genetic counselor become crucial.

The standard of nonmaleficence is challenged by genetic testing in the status of developing life. Genetic testing in the earliest days of conception can be used in prenatal genetic diagnosis to decide which embryos to implant, or later for fetus selection. Such selection would be nonmaleficent and could indeed be kind and helpful before a fellow human being is present but difficult to justify once one is. This requires, then, careful thought about stages of development unaddressed in earlier eras. While the Christian Church has long exhorted against abortion, this was with reference to stopping pregnancy after the first missed period or after what Church leaders called formation. Thomas Aquinas, for example, recognized the presence of an ensouled body only after there was a body to ensoul. By his understanding of the best science of his day, that was at least 40 days after sperm and egg met. Modern science has not settled the matter in that it describes a continuous process of syngamy that takes the first 24 hours after sperm and egg meet to actually merge genetic endowment, that two-thirds of that which combines egg and sperm never implants, and that whether there is one egg and two individuals beginning (identical twins) or two eggs and one person (a mosaic) is not settled until 14 days after sperm and egg first begin to combine. The Roman Catholic response has been to rule against contravening at any point in the process, including a prohibition on physical contraception. There is clear warrant in the Christian tradition to extend an inclusive love of neighbor, especially for the most vulnerable, but such concern does not directly tell us of itself when in the development of human life there is a neighbor present to love.

The Christian commitment to justice raises concern that genetic testing substantially changes the insurance industry that so many people depend on for access or supplement to medical care, or for life insurance. Insurance depends on an equality of ignorance between the insurance company and the person insured. The insured pays into the insurance company because she may need coverage later. The insurance company accepts the insured in hopes that she will not, in which case it can apply her premiums to someone who does need the payout. Insurance companies do not print money; they just transfer it. Genetic testing undermines the required uncertainty. If the prospective insured knows from genetic tests that she will likely need an insurance company payout, she is more likely to buy insurance, indeed the most generous policy she can, while the person who hits the genetic lottery with little risk of disease is likely to favor other expenses. The insurance company then does not have enough money coming in to pay claims going out. Conversely, if the insurance company knows from genetic testing that the potential insured is likely to require large payouts, the company will not want to insure for that condition or will require premiums that are large enough to meet the expected payout, hence more a savings plan than insurance. The premiums may well be too high for the potential insured to purchase. Insurance is then available for everything except what the purchaser is most likely to need. Legislation to prohibit insurers from requiring genetic test results can be circumvented by companies offering discounts to those who volunteer genetic test results. Those who do not avail themselves of the discount would be assumed to be the ones at higher risk. Coverage is lost if the insurer knows genetic test results. Coverage is lost if the insurer does not know the genetic test results. Genetic testing is increasingly changing the context such that the financing of medical care and life insurance will need to change quite dramatically if all are to receive the care that they need.

Conclusion

Life, and so bioethics, is complicated. It requires working together in Christian community to thoughtfully think through the challenges to serve God and one another as best we can. I have argued that God's people are called in part to sustain, restore, and develop the human body. Developing the human body is not the end purpose of life, but the body does have a role to play as God shapes people into those who can enjoy and glorify God forever. Rightly developing the body will include making widely disseminated choices that are safe, lead to genuine improvement, increase choice rather than predestine recipients, and are fair in using resources. The Christian tradition and community can give context and valuation to help work through these complex decisions that come with new opportunities to serve.

References

Albertson, David and King, Cabell, eds. 2010. *Without Nature? A New Condition for Theology*. New York: Fordham University Press.

Beauchamp, Thomas and Childress, James. 2008. *Principles of Biomedical Ethics*, 6th edn. New York: Oxford University Press.

Brunk, Conrad G. 2004. Religion, Risk, and the Technological Society. In D. J. Hawkins, ed. *The Twenty-First Century Confronts Its Gods: Globalization, Technology, and War*. Albany, NY: State University of New York Press, pp. 45–58.

Creighton, S., Almqvist, E. M., MacGregor, D. *et al.* 2003. Predictive, Pre-natal, and Diagnostic Testing for Huntington's Disease: The Experience in Canada from 1987 to 2000. *Clinical Genetics*, 63, pp. 462–475.

Greely, H., Sahakian, B., Harris, J. *et al.* 2008. Towards Responsible Use of Cognitive-Enhancing Drugs by the Healthy. *Nature*, 456(11), pp. 702–705.

Green, Joel B. 2008. *Body, Soul, and Human Life: The Nature of Humanity in the Bible*. Grand Rapids, MI: Baker Academic.

Habermas, Jürgen. 2003. *The Future of Human Nature*. Cambridge: Polity Press.

Hall, Amy Laura. 2008. *Conceiving Parenthood: American Protestantism and the Spirit of Reproduction*. Grand Rapids, MI: Eerdmans.

Irenaeus, *Against Heresies*, online at http://www.ccel.org/ccel/schaff/anf01.i.html (accessed November 28, 2011).

Murray, Thomas. 1996. *The Worth of the Child*. Berkeley: University of California Press.

Peters, Phillip G., Jr. 2004. *How Safe Is Safe Enough? Obligations to the Children of Reproductive Technology*. Oxford: Oxford University Press.

Peterson, James C. and Mutter, Kelvin F. 2010. Some Pains Are Worth Their Price: Discerning the Cause of Pain to Guide Its Alleviation. *Journal of Spirituality in Mental Health*, 12, pp. 182–194.

President's Council on Bioethics. 2003. *Beyond Therapy*. Washington, DC: The President's Council on Bioethics.

Rawls, John. 1971. *A Theory of Justice*. Cambridge, MA: Harvard University Press.

Tengland, Per-Anders. 2007. A Two-Dimensional Theory of Health. *Theoretical Medicine and Bioethics*, 28, pp. 257–284.

Volf, Miroslav. 2001. *Work in the Spirit: Toward a Theology of Work*. Eugene, OR: Wipf and Stock.

Walzer, Michael. 1994. *Thick and Thin: Moral Argument at Home and Abroad*. Notre Dame, IN: University of Notre Dame Press.

Further Reading

Baily, Mary Ann and Murray, Thomas, eds. 2009. *Ethics and Newborn Genetic Screening: New Technologies, New Challenges*. Baltimore, MD: Johns Hopkins University Press. Thoughtfully tests the criteria for public policy choices in genetic screening.

Cole-Turner, Ron, ed. 2008. *Design and Destiny: Jewish and Christian Perspectives on Human Germline Modification*. Cambridge, MA: MIT Press. An array of fine scholars consider religious views of germline intervention.

Peters, Ted. 1996. *For the Love of Children: Genetic Technology and the Future of the Family*. Louisville, KY: Westminster John Knox Press. Open to new technology while keeping focus on the people most affected by its use.

Peterson, James C. 2010. *Changing Human Nature: Ecology, Ethics, Genes, and God*. Grand Rapids, MI: Eerdmans. A nuanced theological argument to be conscious and conscientious about human change.

Stassen, Glenn and Gushee, David. 2003. *Kingdom Ethics: Following Jesus in Contemporary Contexts*. Downers Grove, IL: InterVarsity Press. With clarity and fairness introduces the broad context of Christian ethics, including chapters on particular issues including genetics.

33

An Inclusive Framework for Stem Cell Research

JOHN F. KILNER

While much controversy surrounds the field of stem cell research, the predicament is far from hopeless.[1] Contrary to common assumptions, the key ethical challenge here is more basic than one's view of human embryos and the public relevance of religious convictions. Such issues need to be located in a broader discussion of inclusiveness.

Most people share a concern to include particularly vulnerable people in efforts to preserve life and health. Christian ethics can help foster a constructive way forward because it aspires to give an account of what authentically *human* flourishing looks like – not merely some more narrow account of *Christian* flourishing. In fact, as argued elsewhere, in some ways Christian ethics is better able to explain concerns about vulnerable people and inclusiveness than other contemporary ethics that affirm similar sensitivities (Hollman and Kilner 2006).

Arthur Dyck, at Harvard University, is a good example of a Christian ethicist who engages the challenges of the twenty-first century by emphasizing the importance of fostering an "inclusive community" (2005, 199). In order for community and humanity to flourish, he argues, certain conditions are necessary. Prominent among them is "that no human being fall outside [that is, not benefit from] the moral responsibilities to protect life" (2005, 308).

Such an inclusive ethics appears to underlie international understandings of human rights that go far beyond the Christian community, such as the United Nations Universal Declaration of Human Rights. Nevertheless, the biblically based recognition that even the weakest member of the human community has been created and is loved by God provides a powerful basis for an inclusive ethics that other outlooks are hard-pressed to match (Mitchell et al. 2007).

Traci West is one of many other Christian ethicists, diverse in many ways, who agree on the central importance of an inclusive ethics. In her book *Disruptive Christian Ethics*, she adds an important insight regarding inclusiveness and vulnerability. A shortcoming of many discussions of controversial issues is that not all the voices of those who have a serious stake in the issue are heard (2006, 107–109). Accordingly, in the following development of an inclusive framework for stem cell research, it will be important to hear from a range of major

The Blackwell Companion to Science and Christianity, First Edition. Edited by J. B. Stump and Alan G. Padgett.
© 2012 Blackwell Publishing Ltd. Published 2012 by Blackwell Publishing Ltd.

stakeholders – paying careful attention to giving voice to the weakest and most vulnerable among them.

Unfortunately, this endeavor is sometimes minimized, or sidelined completely, in the rush to defend or advance some particular activity – perhaps adult stem cell research, or embryonic stem cell research, or new ways to produce "embryonic-like" stem cells. A kind of counterfeit inclusiveness is operative here, in which including all forms of research is considered to be an evident good, regardless of what is at stake for all of the people involved.

It is crucial from the outset to be clear about the object of inclusiveness. It is all of the *people* with a stake in stem cell research who are to be taken into account. There is no *a priori* moral mandate to include all of the forms and activities of stem cell research in what is ultimately pursued. Research is for people; people do not exist to meet the needs of research. To hear some defenses of all possible forms that stem cell research can take, one would think that the activities of research are more important than the people who have a stake in what those activities entail and yield. An inclusive approach will need to reject an idolatry of technology in favor of holding every potential technological innovation accountable to the flourishing of the entire human community, including those who are most vulnerable.

Unless the argument for including a particular group is advanced only by a few self-interested people, or what is at stake for the group at issue is manifestly less significant than what is at stake for others, there should be a strong presumption in favor of inclusion. The argument for inclusion need not, in the end, convince everyone. But if the argument raises reasonable doubt, and the stakes for the group are high, then it will be important to include that group. Practically speaking, such inclusion entails focusing on efforts to meet people's needs in a way that seeks to benefit all, rather than benefiting some groups at the expense of others.

In the case of stem cell research, the needs of various groups are being emphasized by different people today. Some people are quickest to champion the needs of the potential beneficiaries of stem cell research. These are the patients who are ill or injured and are eagerly awaiting lifesaving and life-changing treatments that this research will almost certainly yield. People personally committed to the wellbeing of those suffering in this way play a crucial role in sensitizing everyone to the huge stakes involved in enabling stem cell research to move forward rapidly (e.g., Bellomo 2006).

Other people are more concerned about those who donate the bodily materials that the research requires. Such donors include those who risk harm by providing eggs or somatic cells for the research cloning necessary to produce embryonic stem cells genetically matched to the patients using them. A growing chorus of voices is calling attention to these potentially exploited donors (Hyun 2006).

Still other people are particularly attentive to the subjects of the research. Those subjects include patients on whom any form of new stem cell treatment is tried (National Research Council 2005). More controversial, though, are the human embryos most intimately involved as subjects in one of the forms of stem cell research: embryonic stem cell research. Should we also pay attention to those who are speaking up for them? Only if it is reasonable to include human embryos among the vulnerable members of the human community is there a place for them in an inclusive approach to stem cell research. Thus, it will be important to consider whether arguments for excluding human embryos are valid beyond a reasonable doubt.

Meanwhile, it will be important to remember that "stem cell research" is not a single issue or technology – people are not simply *for* or *against* "stem cell research." This is a cluster of technologies, some forms of which are more conducive to an inclusive approach to human flourishing than others. Human flourishing requires distinguishing the different impacts of various forms of stem cell research on each stakeholder group.

The Beneficiaries of Treatment

In terms of stakeholders, an inclusive approach manifestly requires a deep commitment to the healing and wellbeing of patients and their loved ones. Huge numbers of people are suffering today from illnesses and injuries that most likely can be cured or at least significantly helped by stem cell treatments. Unfortunately, many people are not intimately related to any of these sufferers, or at least do not appreciate what stem cell treatments have the potential to do for them.

This lack of appreciation is why public figures suffering themselves or emotionally close to those in need play such an important role in the current stem cell debate. The way that people identify with them is an opportunity. However, it is also a danger. Because such figures typically have excellent access to health care, it is easy to take for granted that those in need will receive stem cell treatments once they become available. However, far too many people – even in relatively wealthy nations – do not have sufficient access to the more basic health care that they need. While determining what forms of stem cell research should go forward, it is critical to address the ethics of access at the same time (Peters *et al.* 2008, 74, 238; Cohen 2007, chapter 7).

Since the goal here is to benefit suffering patients without harming others in the process, the nearly universal support for so-called "adult" stem cell (ASC) research is not surprising. This imprecisely named category of stem cell research can encompass work on all stem cells that exist in human bodies at any age of development, except for embryonic stem cells (ESCs) derived from human embryos.[2] Typically, none of the sources of the research materials or the subjects of the research to be discussed later is harmed by this research, so the benefits to patients can be celebrated by all. Moreover, the possibility that the stem cells involved can be obtained from a patient's own body enhances the likelihood that treatment will be affordable and accessible.

The health benefits of ASC treatments are already considerable and growing rapidly.[3] In fact, somewhat more controversial reports suggest that very select ASCs may have a flexibility (and thus medical usefulness) much closer to that of ESCs than traditionally thought (e.g., Conrad *et al.* 2008). That could enable them to produce cells that other ASCs cannot produce. Should further research confirm their existence, that would be good news indeed for all those whose illnesses or injuries can be helped by stem cell treatments. And that would be good news for a world seeking an inclusive approach to stem cell research committed to benefiting all, rather than some at the expense of others.

The Sources of Materials

The second set of vulnerable people with a stake in stem cell research includes those who donate the bodily materials necessary for stem cell treatments. In ASC treatment, the primary bodily material is the stem cells themselves. Where possible, the cells will come from the patient being treated. One reason is that such cells will be genetically matched to the patient and therefore less likely to be rejected by the body's immune system. When using the patient's own cells is not possible, donors should be able to provide the needed cells without incurring serious risk. This would be done much the way that blood or tissue donors make donations already, with careful attention to appropriate informed consent procedures.

If ESC treatments are developed in humans, however, ESCs will have the disadvantage of not being genetically matched to the patient unless an ethically controversial cloning process using the patient's genetic material produces the embryo.[4] Experience with organ transplantation suggests that drugs can lessen – but not necessarily eliminate – rejection problems if a genetic match is not present. Moreover, the drugs themselves can introduce new problems. So it is likely that attempts at human cloning, with the need for a supply of eggs and genetic material, will accompany the pursuit of ESC research. Recent investigations suggest that the huge supply of eggs needed will have to be human eggs, because animal eggs appear inadequate for the human genetic reprogramming required. Moreover, not all human eggs can be used, since only high-quality eggs appear sufficient for this demanding process.

Some believe that human egg donation is not a big problem, and that the many eggs needed to generate ESCs genetically matched to each patient would not be difficult to obtain. However, those who call attention to the difficulties here provide a great service. The journal *Science* has reported that up to 10% of egg donors may experience severe ovarian hyperstimulation syndrome, which can cause pain and occasionally leads to hospitalization, renal failure, potential future infertility, and even death (Magnus and Cho 2005). At issue here is not just the immediate risk, but also the longer-term cancer risk that has been inadequately studied (Pearson 2006). Moreover, coercion of donors can also be a problem, in three ways:

- *informational* coercion (risks may not be explained fully);
- *vocational* coercion (research workers may be urged to donate by their boss);
- *financial* coercion (financially strapped women may be offered money to prompt donation that would not have occurred otherwise).

It might seem that women should be able to assess what donating their eggs is worth to them. However, Debora Spar argues in *The Baby Business* (2006) that this is not the case. The normal protections of the market – information, competition, and transparency – are largely absent in this situation. Customers – that is, researchers now, but ultimately very ill patients – are desperate; the norm of rational trade-offs does not apply. Similarly, enough money can induce poorer women, including students, to take risks as "donors" that human beings should not have to take in order to meet their basic needs.

"But we *have* to obtain those eggs," some will say, because developing the cures to help hurting people requires it. Such thinking is detrimental to an inclusive approach if it inclines us toward justifying harming some in order to benefit others. We need to appreciate deeply the suffering of patients who need stem cell treatments *and* the suffering of women who can all too easily be pressured into egg extraction. Our aspiration for inclusiveness should strengthen our resolve to alleviate both – and certainly not to add substantially to the suffering of one group in order to lessen the suffering of another.

The donation of other body ("somatic") cells is not immune from similar issues of coercion. But an even greater danger of exploitation of the vulnerable has to do with the problem of "therapeutic misconception" (Hyun 2006). This problem can occur when donors have no prospect of personally benefiting from the experiment in which they are participating. They may nevertheless think that they will benefit – and they may participate only because of that mistaken idea. The result is a violation of informed consent. The informed consent process must be more proactive than it has traditionally been in order to prevent this misconception – even at the risk of losing donors.

The Subjects of Research

The third group of vulnerable people connected with stem cell research includes the subjects of that research. Regarding ASC research, standard research ethics guidelines apply. In particular, the temptation to harm some in order to benefit many must be fastidiously resisted. For instance, in their zeal to help children with diabetes, researchers prematurely subjected several children to a risky adult stem cell study before experiments on consenting adults had demonstrated sufficient benefit to justify the risk (Manier 2007). An inclusive approach would encourage the aggressive pursuit of treatments for children suffering from diabetes without exposing some children to serious harm in the process.

ESC research presents a unique challenge, in that the human embryos involved in the research typically are taken apart and then die in the process. How serious a matter is that? Many people see embryos as persons, worthy of the same protections that should be given to other persons – or at least have a reasonable doubt about the claim that embryos are not persons in this fullest sense.

Scientific and philosophical considerations

People's concerns about embryos often begin with the science. They may be familiar with the publicly posted definition of the human embryo provided by the US National Institutes of Health: "the developing organism from the time of fertilization until the end of the eighth week of gestation" (National Institutes of Health 2011). Or as international embryology textbooks have put it, the life history of a new individual has begun at conception (e.g., O'Rahilly 2001, 8, 33).

Accordingly, many people recognize that even the early embryo, at the blastocyst stage, is not just "human life" – as blood cells are alive and human. Rather a human embryo is a human organism – a being that is human – who, unless fatally disabled or injured, can typically develop throughout the human lifespan as long as suitable nurture and environment are provided. A child or an adult is also a human being who, unless fatally disabled or injured, can typically develop throughout the human lifespan as long as suitable nurture and environment are provided. Recognizing this parallel gives many people pause.

They are struck by the difference between a bunch of human cells that are gathered together in the same place – such as a group of skin cells – and an integrated human organism, or being, that has already begun developing in an increasingly complex way toward adulthood. They note that living adult bodies could also be described as "some cells," but that adults, like embryos, are not "*just* some cells." They are also biologically integrated (self-organizing) beings.

That human embryos are, biologically, human beings is enough to persuade many that they warrant the protections due to all other human beings. Other people resist making this equation because they see something added to human beings after the embryonic stage that gives them a more protectable status as "persons." In this context, "persons" (or people) are human beings who actually (not just potentially) have all of the characteristics necessary to warrant the same treatment as a typical adult human being (e.g., the right not to be killed). Are all human beings "persons"? Let us consider some views that have been offered:

- *Location*: some suggest that even if embryos implanted in a womb are persons, those in dishes in a lab are not, because they cannot develop there into born human beings. However, people are people regardless of where someone puts them. If someone chooses not to put adults where they can obtain what they need in order to live, that does not invalidate their personhood; nor would that seem, to many, to invalidate an embryo's personhood.
- *Formation*: others suggest that only embryos whose neurological "primitive streak" has formed – generally by about 14 days after fertilization – should be considered persons, because the primitive streak provides biological evidence that these organisms will have human brains and related capacities such as self-awareness and reasoning in the future. However, if it is the biological evidence that such capacities will develop in the future that matters, that is already present genetically after fertilization.
- *Individuation*: still others suggest that because early embryos can divide and become more than one embryo, as in the case of identical twins, they are not in their final form yet and do not qualify as persons. However, embryos are changing form in all sorts of ways throughout their development. So the question really is whether division per se demonstrates that what was thought to be something (a person) was not really that thing. Division is not an unusual phenomenon. For instance, a country may divide into two countries. The division does not mean that there was not a country present before the division. Division simply suggests that multiple entities (countries or persons) were in some unrecognized way present previously – or at least can be in the future. One (or more) was genuinely present prior to division.
- *Intention*: a fourth consideration has primarily to do with embryos produced through cloning for the purpose of ESC research. The idea is that embryos produced through cloning and intended to be implanted and born may be persons; but they are not persons if they are intended only for research and thus death before they are 14 days old. However, as many see it, people are people regardless of what others intend to do to them; and such is the case with people at any stage of their development, whether embryonic or adult.

In other words, many would say that embryos are *persons with potential* rather than *potential persons*. Sperm and eggs – in fact, every body cell in this age of cloning – have the potential to become persons. So it is understandable that some may refer to them as "potential persons." But such language is inappropriate regarding human embryos. They already are beings or organisms that are human. That human embryos have not yet manifested their full potential no more invalidates their personhood than young adults' personhood is invalidated by the fact that they have not yet manifested their full potential.

It is not surprising, then, to find an analysis of the many current debates over ESC research concluding that proponents of ESC research "have a serious intellectual problem." They have not been able to refute the central scientific and philosophical arguments for viewing human embryos as true persons (Shields 2007, 18, 20). Unless all reasonable doubt on these matters can be removed, it makes sense that ESC research be viewed as an example of the objectionable, non-inclusive approach to meeting human need – that is, severely harming some to benefit others.

Explicitly Christian considerations

The discussion to this point illustrates that the basis for being protective of human embryos is scientific and philosophical, not necessarily religious. In other words, this is a *human* concern, which can stand on its own without uniquely Christian or other religious justifications. However, there are additional considerations that carry weight for many who take the Bible seriously.[5]

For instance, Genesis 1 and 9 suggest that the preciousness of the life of human beings is rooted in humanity being created in the image of God – a distinction that is in place when a being is established as human as opposed to plant or animal. Needless to say, it is only in light of the relatively recent understanding of genetics that this distinction is now understood to be in place genetically at the embryonic stage.

Later biblical passages reflect such an outlook regarding early human life. For example, in the Psalms (for example, Pss. 51, 139), King David comments on the earliest days of his existence – which he says took place when he began to grow within his mother. David considers the "me" who is speaking as an adult to be the same "me" (person) who was conceived in his mother's womb. Many who look to New Testament writings such as Luke 1 find a similar mindset there. God becomes a human being and identifies completely with what it means to be human, not by taking the form of an adult, but by becoming a human embryo.

God's coming is a profound signal that the world is far from what God intends it to be and is badly in need of healing. There is no more graphic illustration of this predicament than the huge number of embryos who die before implanting in their mothers' wombs. That is a tragedy to be lamented and rectified, to the extent possible, not a justification for killing even more embryos.

Anti-inclusive thinking

Sometimes people, overwhelmed with the importance of helping suffering patients or protecting endangered egg donors, imply or even assert that it does not matter whether embryos are persons. So much can be done through ESC research that will benefit so many people to so great a degree, they maintain, that this itself is sufficient justification for the research. Such a view embodies the heart of the anti-inclusive outlook at work here – namely, that if enough benefit can be generated for enough people, then whatever must be done to a minority in order to achieve that great end can be justified.

If a minority must be treated badly enough, there is a natural tendency to bring into question the full humanity of those mistreated, in order to better justify the mistreatment. For instance, in debates over ESC research, it may be claimed that if embryos are human beings, surely they are not truly persons as adults or children are: people know a fellow person when they see one.

Why is this line of thinking so upsetting to many people? What concerns them is that this line of thinking has done great harm all over the world. There was a time in many countries when using black slaves as property was so economically beneficial that people advocated doing it. That made some people uncomfortable unless slaves could be defined as less than fully human. That was not hard to do because there were obvious visual differences between these black slaves and their white owners. Even the US Supreme Court conveniently ruled in the Dred Scott case that black slaves were mere property from which to profit, rather than persons sharing in the basic equality of all persons.

What unsettles many today is that it was as clear to the Court then that Dred Scott was not a full human being as it is clear to others today that an embryo is not a human being. It is quite easy to underestimate what we can mentally justify, many worry, if the economic or medical benefits that we aspire to are attractive enough. Sadly, yielding to this temptation has a long history leading up to the advent of ESC research, as chronicled in the book *Useful Bodies* (Goodman *et al.* 2003).

New cell sources

What if embryonic stem cells could be obtained without doing harm to embryos? (For the purposes of discussion, the cells in view here will simply be called "pluripotent" stem cells (PSCs). Whether they actually come from embryos or not, this term emphasizes the ultimate goal for the stem cells in view here: the highly prized capacity of giving rise to all cell types in the body.) If such cells could be obtained without doing harm, then the major ethical obstacle would be removed. Two basic approaches to avoiding this obstacle have been proposed. One involves producing PSCs without harming embryos. The other involves using only "unwanted" embryos that will be dying anyway.

Producing PSCs without doing harm could take numerous forms, as three of the options examined in a US President's Council on Bioethics report (2005) illustrate. One, *embryo biopsy*, typically involves removing a single cell from an eight-cell embryo, developing a PSC line from that cell and allowing the embryo to continue to develop to a successful birth. A second approach, *altered nuclear transfer*, typically involves a process similar to the cloning technique of somatic cell nuclear transfer. In this approach, the genetic material from a body cell is altered before being placed in an egg whose nucleus has been removed. The resulting entity – not a viable embryo but rather a generator of PSCs – could never develop into a born human being. A third approach, *dedifferentiation of body cells*, involves reversing the differentiation process that "turns off" or blocks most of the genetic code in cells as they become more specialized. The goal is to "reactivate" most of the genetic code so that the induced pluripotent stem cells (iPSCs) have the pluripotency of ESCs, without reactivating the entire code and giving the cells totipotency (that is, the ability to develop into an entire born human being).

Since one inclusive goal in view here is to generate maximally beneficial cells without harming human embryos, there are at least four practical and ethical criteria that can be used to evaluate sources of pluripotent stem cells:

(1) *Workability*: can the technique actually produce stem cells?
(2) *Pluripotency*: do any cells produced have the flexibility to give rise to all cell types in the body?
(3) *Compatibility*: do the cells genetically match the patient to be treated, in order to minimize the risks of rejection?
(4) *Safety*: are donors or recipients of the cells harmed by the technique?

At this point in time, the fourth approach, *dedifferentiation of body cells*, is where the great breakthrough has occurred. Although prospects for this technology appeared remote when the President's Council issued its paper, they improved considerably in 2007, when two different sets of researchers demonstrated that easily accessible cells like human skin cells can be reprogrammed to a pluripotent state. What sets this approach apart at the present time is its demonstrated or likely ability to meet all four criteria. Not only does the technique work, but the iPSCs produced are pluripotent, they can genetically match the patient to be treated, and their production does not harm adult cell donors, human embryos, or, likely, the recipients.

As a result, a significant amount of stem cell research has already begun to focus on iPSC rather than ESC research. The work of stem cell pioneer George Daley of Children's Hospital in Boston is a case in point. As he concludes in *Nature Medicine*: despite any limitations of current iPSCs, "there's no reason in my mind to think that we're not going to have iPS cells that function as well as embryonic stem cells" (Dolgin 2010). Two studies published in *Cell Stem Cell* during late 2010 are telling in this regard. A Massachusetts Institute of Technology study found "little difference" between iPSCs and ESCs, and a Harvard University study demonstrated a new "highly efficient" and safe way (using RNA) to produce iPSCs that "very closely recapitulate" ESCs.

It turns out, then, that there is at least one emerging approach to producing PSCs – iPSC research – that is more in line with an inclusive ethics than using human embryos. It is more attractive for other ethically significant reasons as well. Yet, just as the tendency of ESCs to produce cancer in mice has made it very difficult to test them safely in human beings, so iPSCs and all other forms of stem cells must remain accountable to appropriate standards of human safety. An inclusive ethics supportive of all subjects of the research requires no less.

Unwanted embryos?

What about the other proposed way to obtain embryonic stem cells without doing harm – using only "unwanted" embryos that will be dying anyway? Proponents of using leftover embryos for stem cell research typically hold that using such embryos is in line with the ethical treatment of human beings. But many appropriately question that assumption. They look to other settings where decisions have been made to let healthy people die, to see if it is considered ethically acceptable to remove their vital body parts before they have actually died.

That issue has been publicly addressed at length by the US United Network for Organ Sharing with regard to removing vital organs from prisoners on death row. The fact that people will inevitably be dying has been found to be an insufficient justification for killing them even earlier. The ends in view – obtaining vital bodily materials for sick patients – may be admirable. But harming (especially killing) some to benefit others has been deemed unacceptable. It is profoundly at odds with an inclusive outlook committed to the wellbeing of all vulnerable groups in society.

Meanwhile, there is another basic problem with the notion that unwanted embryos could provide an acceptable source of stem cells. It is the false assumption that these embryos are unwanted. Consider the example of the United States. The number of frozen embryos there has often been estimated to be about 400 000, based on a study by the RAND Corporation (Hoffman *et al.* 2003). Many people mistakenly assume from this figure that there is a huge supply of leftover embryos that must be thrown away if they are not used for embryonic stem cell research (e.g., Herold 2006).

The RAND report itself reveals quite a different picture. The vast majority of the 400 000 – 88.2% of them – are not "left over" according to that report. Instead, they are eagerly wanted by the very people who produced them. Those people are planning to implant them in the future in order to have more children.

Because only about two-thirds of the remaining 11.8% are likely to survive thawing, only 30 000 frozen embryos are likely to be viable and unwanted by those who produced them. But even these embryos are not truly unwanted. They are very much wanted – by women yearning to adopt them and carry them to term in their own wombs. There are so many such women, in fact, that there are now well over 200 agencies in the USA facilitating embryo donation for reproductive purposes.

Some women prefer embryo adoption to the adoption of born children because of the opportunity to ensure the healthy development of their child while in the womb. Others are motivated by the opportunity to rescue a young one who otherwise would perish, perhaps inspired by the proverbial call to "rescue those being led away to death" (Prov. 24:11).

Snowflakes alone, just one of the hundreds of agencies,[6] has provided approximately 3000 embryos for adoption already – and those numbers are expected to escalate in the near future. Such figures suggest that giving 30 000 embryos a chance at life through an expanded embryo adoption or donation effort is realistic.

Some respond by claiming that many parents with extra embryos do not now seek out embryo donation, so society should encourage the use of these embryos in stem cell research. However, the echoes of the Dred Scott experience are unsettling. Many claimed then that owners of slaves should be allowed to do what they wanted with them. The fallacy of this outlook is now evident: the liberty of all stakeholders, including the slaves, was not adequately considered. So it is today, many would say, regarding ownership of embryos.

Conclusion

An inclusive framework for stem cell research, then, will listen to all who are speaking up for vulnerable groups with a substantial stake in this research. No such groups will be excluded unless exclusion is warranted beyond a reasonable doubt. There are at least minimally plausible reasons for including patients, embryos, and other donors and research subjects among the relevant vulnerable groups. Accordingly, while an inclusive approach will not welcome ESC research, it presently appears that developing the full range of stem cell treatments that patients need, using ASCs and iPSCs, is both welcome and realistic. How to use precious resources to benefit all, rather than harming some to benefit others, is worthy of society's best efforts.

Notes

1 This chapter abbreviates and updates the framework in Kilner (2009), where more extensive scientific documentation is included.
2 This categorization corresponds with whether the stem cells can be obtained without causing the death of the source of the cells. Accordingly, stem cells from fetuses are commonly considered "adult" rather than "embryonic" if they can be obtained without killing the fetuses in order to obtain them. "Non-embryonic" would be a more precise term than "adult" to describe the alternative to ESCs, but the more familiar term will be employed here.

3   See for example the research reports gathered at www. stemcellresearch.org.
4   Regarding various ethical as well as scientific problems with human cloning, see President's Council on Bioethics (2002).
5   For a fuller discussion of how the central biblical themes of creation, corruption, and redemption shape an understanding of human embryos not dependent on a few specific verses, see Kilner (2011).
6   For Snowflakes, a directory of agencies, and another example, see http://www.nightlight.org/ programs_SnowflakesFrozenEmbryoFaqs.html#General; http://www.miracleswaiting.org/clinics. html, and http://www.embryodonation.org/about.html.

References

Bellomo, Michael. 2006. *The Stem Cell Divide*. New York: Amacom.

Cohen, Cynthia B. 2007. *Renewing the Stuff of Life*. Oxford: Oxford University Press.

Conrad, Sabine, Renninger, Markus, Hennenlotter, Jörg *et al.* 2008. Generation of Pluripotent Stem Cells from Adult Human Testis. *Nature*, 456(November 20), pp. 344–349.

Dolgin, Elie. 2010. Straight Talk with George Daley. *Nature Medicine*, 16(June), p. 624.

Dyck, Arthur J. 2005. *Rethinking Rights and Responsibilities*. Washington, DC: Georgetown University Press.

Goodman, Jordan, McElligott, Anthony, and Marks, Lara, eds. 2003. *Useful Bodies*. Baltimore, MD: Johns Hopkins University Press.

Herold, Eve. 2006. *Stem Cell Wars*. New York: Palgrave Macmillan.

Hoffman, David I., Zellman, Gail L., and Fair, C. Christine. 2003. *How Many Frozen Human Embryos Are Available for Research?* Santa Monica, CA: RAND Corporation.

Hollman, Jay and Kilner, John. 2006. Are Christian Voices Needed in Public Bioethics Debates? Care for Persons with Disabilities as a Test Case. *Ethics and Medicine*, 22(3), pp. 143–150.

Hyun, Insoo. 2006. Magic Eggs and the Frontier of Stem Cell Science. *Hastings Center Report*, 36(2), pp. 16–19.

Kilner, John F. 2009. An Inclusive Ethics for the Twenty-First Century: Implications for Stem Cell Research. *Journal of Religious Ethics*, 37(December), pp. 683–722.

Kilner, John F. 2011. *Why the Church Needs Bioethics*. Grand Rapids, MI: Zondervan.

Magnus, David and Cho, Mildred K. 2005. Issues in Oocyte Donation for Stem Cell Research. *Science*, 308(June 17), pp. 1747–1748.

Manier, Jeremy. 2007. Hope, Risk in Diabetes Trial. *Chicago Tribune*, 11 April, p. 10.

Mitchell, C. Ben, Pellegrino, Edmund D., Elshtain, Jean Bethke *et al.* 2007. *Biotechnology and the Human Good*. Washington, DC: Georgetown University Press.

National Institutes of Health. 2011. Stem Cell Information. Bethesda, MD: National Institutes of Health, US Department of Health and Human Services, online at http://stemcells.nih.gov/info/glossary (accessed November 14, 2011).

National Research Council. 2005. *Guidelines for Human Embryonic Stem Cell Research*. Washington, DC: National Academies Press.

O'Rahilly, Ronan. 2001. *Human Embryology and Teratology*. Wilmington, DE: Wiley-Liss.

Pearson, Helen. 2006. Health Effects of Egg Donation May Take Decades to Emerge. *Nature*, 442(August 10), pp. 607–608.

Peters, Ted, Lebacqz, Karen, and Bennett, Gaymon. 2008. *Sacred Cells?* Lanham, MD: Rowman & Littlefield.

President's Council on Bioethics. 2002. *Human Cloning and Human Dignity*. Washington, DC: The President's Council on Bioethics.

President's Council on Bioethics. 2005. *Alternative Sources of Human Pluripotent Stem Cells*. Washington, DC: The President's Council on Bioethics.

Shields, Jon A. 2007. The Stem Cell Fight. *Society*, 44(4), pp. 18–21.

Spar, Debora L. 2006. *The Baby Business*. Cambridge, MA: Harvard Business School Press.
West, Traci C. 2006. *Disruptive Christian Ethics*. Louisville, KY: Westminster John Knox Press.

Further Reading

Dyck, Arthur J. 2005. *Rethinking Rights and Responsibilities*. Washington, DC: Georgetown University Press. Provides an ethical basis for responsible community life with applications to bioethics, in a way that is conducive to Christian thinking but not dependent on it.

Kilner, John F. 2009. An Inclusive Ethics for the Twenty-First Century: Implications for Stem Cell Research. *Journal of Religious Ethics*, 37(December), pp. 683–722. Contains extensive documentation from scientific, ethics-related, Christian, and other sources as well as a substantially expanded discussion of the issues addressed in the present chapter.

Mitchell, C. Ben, Pellegrino, Edmund D., Elshtain, Jean Bethke *et al.* 2007. *Biotechnology and the Human Good*. Washington, DC: Georgetown University Press. Features a team of leading Christian ethicists evaluating which narratives, worldviews, and concepts are most conducive to human flourishing in current efforts to heal and enhance human beings.

President's Council on Bioethics. 2005. *Alternative Sources of Human Pluripotent Stem Cells*. Washington, DC: The President's Council on Bioethics. Explores the science and ethics of several potential ways to produce stem cells that are as flexible as embryonic stem cells, involving varying degrees of safety for the embryos involved.

Waters, Brent and Cole-Turner, Ronald. 2000. *God and the Embryo: Religious Voices on Stem Cells and Cloning*. Washington, DC: Georgetown University Press. Maps a range of religious views held by religious ethicists as well as position statements from various Christian church denominations and other groups.

Zacharias, David G., *et al.* 2011. The Science and Ethics of Induced Pluripotency: What Will Become of Embryonic Stem Cells? *Mayo Clinic Proceedings*. 86(July), pp. 634–640. Evaluates the relative merits of embryonic vs. induced pluripotent stem cells in light of scientific, resource-related, and ethical concerns.

34

The Problem of Transhumanism in the Light of Philosophy and Theology

PHILIPPE GAGNON

Our purpose in this chapter is to examine from the perspective of philosophy and theology the recent cultural movement calling itself transhumanism. The term was first used in its current sense, it seems, by Julian Huxley (1957, 13–17). The movement gained traction in the 1960s, and has reached the status of a significant cultural and intellectual voice in the present century, with magazines, lectures, internet sites, books, global associations, and even its own "Transhumanist Declaration" (World Transhumanist Association 1998). The transhuman ideal is based upon a reconception of evolution, a perfecting and transcending of the human race through the next step in progress: not through biological mutation but through science and technology. H+ (a common abbreviation) means the enhancement of human beings as a whole, the inevitable advance of our species which combines biology with technology, enhancing our bodies and brains with scientific innovation, seeking to overcome the limitations of our flesh (see Bostrom 2005).

Humanism as Historical Reality

In this chapter we will bring the transhumanist ideal into conversation with Western philosophy and Christian theology. Seeing this current movement in the longer vision of Western philosophy will both help us to understand it and bring out some problems which it recapitulates in its own techno-human way. What Christian theology will say to the transhuman ideal, as a kind of alternative story of salvation, will also bring both greater understanding of this hope in technological advance and critical issues from the stance of faith in God.

To begin with, an assessment of transhumanism requires that one address the "trans-" function in the expression. In the Western philosophical tradition, there has been some ambivalence when it comes to situating human beings within nature, and transhumanism seems to be in a similar place. For some ancient and medieval philosophies, relying on various understandings of the Hermetic tradition, we were considered a symbolic representation of

---

The Blackwell Companion to Science and Christianity, First Edition. Edited by J. B. Stump and Alan G. Padgett.

the whole cosmos, a microcosm within a macrocosm (Peck 1979, 49–52). Another reaction to humanity's place in the natural order came from the project of establishing a foundation of knowledge that would be indubitable, which Descartes sought in the self-affectation of the knower in a direct experience of mental attention. It was soon realized that for Descartes the substance of non-mental things had been reduced to extension, thus ceasing to have any density, and thus emphasizing a connection to God through our mental life exclusive of the body. Spinoza's reaction to this was to turn the problem on its head and declare that the material and the spiritual are two faces of one and the same reality. Along with this came the denial that human beings can be an "empire within an empire" (*Ethics* III, preface). This anti-anthropocentrism has had a long-lasting life. Along with this element of his thought came the development of an ontology of "enjoyment," with an explicit desire to find more in philosophy than a meditation on and a preparation for death. The "sage" rather meditates on life (*Ethics*, IV, prop. 67).

In the Western tradition, the humanistic project is centered on an affirmation of Self, a denial of one's enslavement to fate or the will of the gods. It takes the form, around the Renaissance, of the development of a sense of value in the service of honor. In Shakespeare's play *Julius Caesar*, we find Brutus guilty of regicide in the name of a higher law. This law is not transcendent, it is felt by one within oneself. In the sphere of action, it can lead to the commission of crimes in the name of an unspeakable urge. In the sphere of sentiments, we will see it enacted in the perennial vitality of the medieval legend of Tristan and Isolde, whose love is immanent and requires satisfaction, yet with a tonality of sadness in that it cannot be realized in this world. Whereas Tristan retains a connection to the tragic, the *virtù* of Renaissance neo-paganism knows no limit from outside. It culminates in the affirmation "I am" interpreted as freedom to make values and to choose how and when to apply them.

According to Carroll (2008, 26), reason's greatest authority does not come out in Newton, or in Descartes's or Kant's rationalism, but in Shakespeare. The Bard of Avon captured the downfall of the humanist utopia, because he did not try to salvage some of it like Erasmus, or to deny its having any value like Luther, but preferred to invite us to live without illusions, describing what he saw. He decided to look at things apart from any grand narrative so that, as Santayana had seen, with him we stop looking at the medieval supra-lunar world, the world of Dante, and rest our gaze on the sub-lunar world (1921, 152–154). We cannot describe this vision as tragic; there is no such thing as a humanist tragedy. The implications of man having been made the measure of all things are drawn as they never were: whereas for classical tragedy death is not ultimate, in *Hamlet* it is.

Hence, we see that an exaltation of the free individual imposing his will through might leaves one in front of nothing but emptiness. Learned men, especially, have no answer to death. Secular humanism leaves behind it a failure to invent a grand narrative (Stoeger 2000).

Manifestations of an Overhuman Idea

When one looks around, one finds a dual attitude to this saddening admission made by Nietzsche: we can no longer believe in God. There is something of a tiredness in the way he devoted all his energy to a parody of the Renaissance hero who knows no other law than his own, which he termed the *Übermensch* (the Over-Human), with little left to disprove God. But is it possible to stop trying to be like the gods in an attempt to live a form of *beata vita*? Will we see around us, in line with the "experiments in living" advocated by John Stuart Mill in *On Liberty* (1859, chapter 3), then revived in a different and influential way by Foucault, some new quest to make oneself the center of things? Or is this postmodern mood a search for what may look like anesthesia from deep anguish-driven questioning (Lipovetsky 2005)? This might be what is left from a universe with its "center everywhere and its circumference nowhere." Despite appearances, one still tries to create a node in a complex web and pull the energies in one's own direction. On the darker side, we will see a disenchanted world and the breeding of a human herd, our having to invent new rules to regulate life alongside products of our technology, something to which Sloterdijk – in an important reply to Heidegger's "Letter on Humanism" – had the courage to call attention (2009; see also 1989). Sloterdijk might have enlisted Nietzsche too quickly in the materialism of the engineers of cybernetic control of the masses.

The Spirit of Technology

Transhumanism can mean overcoming our garment of flesh, and it can also mean transcending this humanistic ideal, which keeps something Promethean and invites us to measure up with the gods. Descartes's project of refoundation was aimed at establishing our freedom from the hardships of this world. The reformation of human knowledge through the sciences was built on the idea that one ought to increase the welfare of humankind if it is in one's power. Descartes added in the sixth part of the *Discourse on Method* that with knowledge we could become "as if" masters and possessors of nature (the adverb *"comme"* in the original is usually overlooked). We need to remember the context for these oft-quoted words. This is a time when disease can strike unexpectedly and kill half a city, when crop or grain shipments not making it on time bring famine, where nature has the face of a shrew rather than that of a mother (Broad 1959, 29–31). The Enlightenment project of promoting modern science sometimes masked a fear of this world; it was intended to fight against the Fall of man and the curses inflicted on him (Harrison 2007). The theme of the vengeance of nature is a very real one in the subconscious of the promoters of an age of technological advancement (Daston 2010, 17).

There is an ambiguity in Descartes's ontology of substance, which we may find to some degree in Galileo's understanding of matter as representing "primary" qualities. This can lead to a reduction of phenomena to numerical magnitudes standing for them. It comes out in the fact that some Christian thinkers, such as Gassendi, thought it useful to adopt a reduction of the world outside the soul to matter and motion. Those Christian scientists had it in mind to *conjoin* the heuristic advantage of treating the world *as though* it would only be mechanical forces in motion, and the affirmation that God initially was responsible for setting it in motion. For some of them, like Robert Boyle, it seemed an advantage as it canceled any talk of pantheism or of a nature rivaling its creator (Daston 1995, 52–53). Yet the ironic result of trying to have nature's source of initiative be neither God nor nature itself is an estrangement of human beings from nature.

Some reactions of the Catholic Church indicate that its officials were quite aware of possible implications of the view of nature and matter adopted by Galileo and those he inspired (von Weizsäcker 1964, 111–112). In the case of Descartes, he advocated the causal and mechanical explanation of the achievements of human thinking, but also posited an *"ingenuum,"* an inscrutable center of decision, moving beyond the usual dichotomy associated with his philosophy of the mind and body relationship (see Brown 2006, 58–60). There is a folly of the rationalist project where some philosophers have come to forget that for Descartes, in Husserlian language, the mind had not been reduced. This led them to abuse the intelligibility of mathematics, laying more than Descartes on a foundation about which he himself had occasional doubts and in which we may well find total intelligibility because this is where we have chosen to secure it all in the first place.

Technology as Driving Force

How shall we understand technology as it was generated against such a background? It is the "other" of the intelligible reconstruction in pure relational knowledge of measurements at first carried by the slaves. It got tied to the production of work through heat and its modeling which revolutionized industry through the transforming power of fire. Following this revolution one can safely say that it became increasingly difficult to separate pure science from the technology needed to set up experimental apparatuses (Prigogine and Stengers 1984, 103–107, 136). Technology has something of an unexpected discovery: it is about making things happen by suddenly hitting upon the right functional schema. Nature's technology proceeds as we do, in the sense of using available resources and fitting them into functional trade-offs that make sense for the purposes of the situation. There is a difference, however, in that natural inventions have level upon level of order, or multiply realized orders.

The project of transforming and steering the available energies from nature easily turns into a denial of there being anything else than its own effort. Some students of technology have spoken of its whole project being animated by this spirit of unceasing transformation through a *logos* that will spare nothing on its way. Names such as Ellul (1980, 126–128) or Hottois (1988, 88–89) come to mind. Must we posit such a *logos* of technology? There seems to be one, an immanent energy that drives itself toward a sort of autism, but is it, as Ellul imagined, a purely processual force destined to carry everything in the end? The answer is "yes," but problematically so. The technological force is that of a human creature in denial in front of the presence of an order she has not made. Such judgments can therefore be misleading if they scapegoat something that is devoid of intentionality. No more than a computer can be "alive" is technology animated by a will that makes it a substance.

The Place of Evolution

A common perception of our having evolved is that we are the product of successive meaningless accidents. Von Bertalanffy warned that such a paradigm was not sustainable and that the real question is not to oppose mindless and undirected mutations to a "ghost in the machine" that would betray a misunderstanding of science and an outmoded spiritualism (1974, 84–85). Nature is creative but she does not work like we do. She tends to create patterns and order.

When we look at biology since the nineteenth century, we should be careful to notice the mingling of a mechanistic ideal with the will of Darwin to get close to the Newtonian ideal of enunciating a general law which subsumes its particular instances, with what is otherwise the hidden potency emphasized by the Romantics in the running commentaries on Diderot's and La Mettrie's legacy when they spoke of sensation as in-built in matter.

One way to make sense of technology's conceptual advance is to see our inventions as compressing time, providing us with an advance, technically speaking a negentropy. When it is realized that our universe will not sustain carbon-based life forever, the reactions can be to count on our creativity to wormhole ourselves into a different universe, or to affirm that we have ways to migrate elsewhere within this galaxy so that its run-down could be as it were displaced. Technology induces in us an impression of control over the future. Interestingly, it is cosmologists who have, in their attempt to protest against our downfall, revived the idea that we would be fundamentally minds, or some informational pattern, whereas most biologists still defend the value of Darwin's insights that are in the end mechanistic ones, as if mechanism did not have its own demise (Baker 2002, 183). Popular scientific writers on evolution such as Gould have spoken much about the erroneous belief in the brain as driving force of evolution (1980, 130–133), but it is possible to bypass talks of brain size and ask whether mind and consciousness are not in the end the key factors. Such a perspective has been recently defended by Lanza and Berman (2010), but one could say that from the inception of the theory of evolution through natural selection, this line of thinking has been present with Alfred Russel Wallace (1903).

The point of the cybernetic turn embedded in transhumanism, be it in perception (making it happen as we *understand* how circuits are saturated) or in making things create themselves, from von Neumann to Schöffer, is really about creating a responsive environment: an "enchanted" world. It is also about canceling the effects of time: think of information archiving, where the past is recreated and becomes available through some atemporal present (Munnik 2005, 32–33).

The idea of creating life artificially, when forced on us with present-day technological capabilities, ends up copying that which nature has already done and playing with its tolerable perturbations without going beyond the boundaries of structural stability (responses to Venter *et al.* 2010 illustrate this). Tinkering attempts, like that of using different nucleic acids' "letters" to understand how chromosomal information is passed on between generations, brings us to optimality limits, where we are not well placed to predict what could come out of such manipulations in terms of, for example, the invention of new *Bauplans*, or the re-utilization of the same architect genes. If hox genes mutate as much as they do (Carroll *et al.* 2008, 67), it is not clear that homologies between body plans spanning a range from the earthworm to man through the lobster would be the result of random switching of genes. They could very well establish that nucleic acids are a storehouse of data rather than a program (Atlan and Koppel 1990).

In forms of biological experimentation that deny any order in nature other than a randomly stabilized interplay of mechanical forces, in what Stuart Newman calls "biological postmodernism," our species is either defined as a statistical result or apprehended as an indefinite force capable of self-transforming. Research in genetic engineering is thus split between those who try to achieve a reassembling of parts into novel organisms either through the use of non-naturally occurring molecules, or by shifting parts that are present naturally into some already living organism (Cole-Turner 2010, 137–142).

The Kind of Being That We Are

Attempts to save in the human a non-material element that would not die end up reinforcing dualism. We can understand why if we recall that in transhuman "evolution" our bodies come out looking awfully irrational from the "natural" evolutionary story. They are evolved, which entails that they could have been considerably different. This lack of control implies that we are *connected* with the rest of the cosmos, that there is a unity of all things.

Therefore, to the question that asks why there has been a movement such as transhumanism, the answer would be: because being human means to be inserted in a dramatic becoming that does not seem to obey rational planning with its preemptive annihilation of time's effects. This carries with it the temptation to make the move Descartes made when he split the universe too rapidly in two substantial realms. It is then that we start to hear talk that we could be some software that can be saved from its implementation in "meat" (Hacking 2005, 163–165). Not only could we avoid dying, but we could entertain the possibility of being born with a different hereditary makeup. By choosing when to be born, or what type of constitution to have, some will think: "might we not escape the 'thrownness' sentiment and the estrangement in front of cosmic time?" Inevitably, there comes with it a radicalization of a core idea of Greek philosophy: we *are* an immortal "soul," a "pattern" in today's language.

It is a fallacy, although one only to be detected with subtlety, to say that, since man transforms everything he touches, we cannot assign him any nature. The reasoning goes like this:

(1)   If something is natural, then it is not artificial.
(2)   Man is the maker of all the artifices.
(3)   So, man does not have a nature.

The argument in fact draws on four terms, not three. The problem is the soundness of this reasoning. The minor premise calls on a capacity to draw out. The artifices in question do not concern the human being acting on his nature, as long as we have not created life *in toto*. It is assumed that to be in a nature puts one in a situation where everything would be given and somehow fixed through instincts or natural processes, which would imply the false assertion that there is no invention in nature but endless repetition of the same. What these problems reveal is not that human beings are without nature, but that we do not possess the adequate concepts to form an image of a nature capable of changing while staying the same. This is an old *aporia* in philosophy.

Limits and Motivations of Nature's Manipulation

Let us emphasize that Christianity is concerned with the very long term, its goal is nothing less than the redemption of all creation, including changing the mentalities of crude and barbaric individuals to make them inherit the Kingdom of God. If naturally occurring organisms like our very bodies are to be re-engineered by us, we will have to recognize that time and its effects are not on our side. This is captured by Bergson in *Creative Evolution* with his metaphor of the cube of sugar which has to melt in the glass (1913, 9–10), defining time as an unrestricted stream of self-referring duration (as opposed to Einstein's and Minkowski's view of physical time). Christian hope, past and future, needs to be thought of against this background of an organic whole reinforming all its states. This has a connection with reproduction, not in the sense of surviving *hic et nunc*, but rather through a duty to conquer time as opposed to space. The covenant of God with Abraham is sealed on the male reproductive organ (Gen. 17:11) and equally blessed is the womb of Sarah (Gen. 17:15–19). As Heschel showed, the desire of the Israelite is to embrace the spirit of *Shabbat* personified in the feminine (1975, 50–57).

Evolution has brought time into the center of a consideration of what it means to be human, or indeed to be a living creature. The three humiliations inflicted on human pride of which Freud spoke, referring respectively to Copernicus, Darwin, and himself, are built on space, body, and mind (Weinert 2009). There is no real consideration of time in any of them. It matters that our planet is not conceived as central anymore, that our bodies are not the perfect result of a transcendent form, and that we do not control all that is in our minds, but in the end those successive "dethronings" do nothing to address the question that asks about existence itself. Freud was to later put it correctly (1962, 35): what value is there in stretching the duration of our lives if it is to spend more time awaiting liberation from death? Any serious eschatological hope for meaning and fulfillment is skirted or ignored by transhumanism, which may envision nothing more than mere endless life, time extended without fulfillment.

As for the mind, if we say, like Gelernter (1994, 122–147), that we will program on a computer its allusive character or its metaphorization capacities through simulating emotions, it is hard to see how we could program a theory that would make a theory of its own incompleteness. What in effect would be the converse of such a position? Are we going to program in the mind a *theory* of what *life* is, of all its rhythms and cycles? It is the total sensitive incarnation which is lacking in the computer, to be as much of a summary of the universe as we are.

Artificial intelligence created programs that would not only perform logical operations or calculations faster and more accurately than human beings, but also neural networks that would learn by trial and error like we do. In the perspective of connectionism, what was advocated was a study of the cooperation of a great number of "cells," used here in an electronics sense, in the production of a pattern that would be general enough to give human beings' subjective impression of integration and preemption.

With hindsight, it is possible to see that a displacement from a focus on cognition needed to happen. The lesson could have been drawn around the suggestions of Turing, which amounted to saying that there is no priorly set limit to the algebraic operations that a machine eventually could perform. If a human thinker finds a function that a machine could not compute, Chaitin's Ω number, for instance (2006, 129–141), this is nonetheless unapproachable for the human mind. If a problem is correctly posed, someone will eventually be able to reconstruct the mechanical route to its solution.

So it seems that at the heart of this problem of transhumanism is not a question as to whether we should value the machine or not. Machines are humanly contrived apparatuses serving inferential and deductive rationality. We can use expert systems to assist in a diagnosis. We can even speak of augmented intelligence, from all manner of prostheses to "ubiquitous programming" with sensors disseminated in the environment so as to not interfere with human activity (Weiser 1994, 125–127). All of these are to some degree extensions of the human body. Such tools are "piloted" by a decisional center. They allow us more freedom to divagate and explore, making creativity equivalent to error in terms of this predefined codification.

The real question and enigma is the desire to flee out of humanity, of the risks and limitations of our "being human." It is the dementia of one who constantly swerves in order to be certain that he will not have deficiencies or be handicapped (Sandel 2004, 57–58). The goal is to reinforce that which we need nature to do if she is to perform according to a criterion we have predefined. What if we no longer had this servant that the body is, whose limits we can push back and which allows us to surpass ourselves? What would be an anthropological situation in which there no longer exists some self-overcoming? All that we want we would obtain, never again encountering this hard resistance of reality and the physical order.

As for our human bodies, it has always been justifiable to fight illnesses and grave deformities. "Improving" on our nature would come with all the shortcomings of our shortsightedness in electing a perspective to be valued. The lack of consensus about the "ideal type," its fleeting character, would run the risk of having for itself complete license until a perception started to look different and we "felt" we could *decree* some forms out of "humanness" (Lerderberg 2002, 38). The proximity of this to eugenics does not need to be emphasized. Our moral sense protests against it, yet if we try to define the nature we *possess*, we fall on traits we share with other sentient beings.

The Place of Fiction and the Reclaiming of Eschatology

The human orphan in a cosmic drama that surpasses us is bound to respond in a way that will reflect our dual capacities, limited by space and matter which can also be challenges to overcome, and apparently unlimited when it comes to a projection of our will. To the *rational utopia*, which would protest our having to work so hard to acquire fragments of knowledge only to see them disappear at death and try accordingly to push backwards our downfall, there is often contrasted a response which calls for the rediscovery of our animalness and the connection we bear with an emotive grounding to the "there is" ("*il y a*," a technical term among phenomenologists) that has put us where we are. Adherents of this *poetic utopia* do not always have means of rationally articulating the meaning of their quest.

On the one hand, there is the ideal of ubiquitous presence, used by fascists in the 1930s through radio waves carrying the human voice everywhere and hence usurping a prerogative of the angelic world. This, if used for conditioning, would make of man a blasphemer in the style of the master of the Golem. The same presence everywhere can also, on the other hand, be equivalent to a communication that would affect its own conditions of production, creating a loop where every act of emission would be informed by everything else instantaneously, such as was contemplated by Marshall McLuhan. This would redeem the Golem, since the secret of life would be intimately connected with the act of writing which shapes the future and, as Sloterdijk recalled, connects grammar and magic (2009, 13). If life is written down as a set of hereditary instructions, an algorithm, could one be any more guilty of writing on the already written, than one could be guilty for having to use language?

Sloterdijk's "Rules for the Human Zoo" moves from Heidegger's "angelism" to Nietzsche's "beastianism." Nietzsche wrote that there was no end or goal of humanity, save the production of the highest specimen: "the *goal of humanity* cannot lie in its end but only *in its highest exemplars*" (1983, 111). Many transhumanist proposals are thought experiments, they are to be understood as "world-making," so that behind the question of whether one should advocate "playing God" is the danger of stifling this vocation to creativity if we flip downward at the way the world is any efforts at inventing a better one.

One cannot make sense of the manner in which this reaction is conditioned by and is a response to nihilism if one does not move from metaphysical to fictional nihilism. It serves no purpose to oppose to Nietzsche an ontology of light and peace in reaction to some purported violent promotion of the void. He probed and found that reason and knowledge do not give us reasons stemming directly from reality, or put differently, values. Those imaginative procedures are "secreted" by the absence of a metaphysical viewpoint, and yet to oppose them a full-fledged realist metaphysics is besides the point. Recent apologetics, from writers such as J. Milbank and D. B. Hart, has misconstrued Nietzsche's stance by reading this mask-wearing philosopher like a first-person metaphysical realist (Hyman 2000, 434–436). The highest fruit of earthly becoming should be its offering to eternity, but how could we avoid this specimen being *this* or *that*, inevitably failing to represent all that the earth was capable of as possibilities? It is this that drove Nietzsche mad and led him to affirm eternal recurrence.

From Autonomy to Theonomy

The Christian faith affirms at the core of its hope the promise that God will be all in all (1 Cor. 15:28). What does this promise mean for the problem here considered? How will the kingdom of freely offered grace be allowed to make its appearance in the midst of our chiaroscuro? Let us think about the vocation of lording over creation: does that mean and entail preserving some mind capacities? Does it mean improving on them? Some promoters of artificial life and intelligence, such as H. Moravec, have not failed to offer such an interpretation. Theologians have at times also taken this route (see Foerst 2004).

What place have we left for the animal, that sketch of ourselves? What room is left for a non-anthropocentric universe, that of Psalm 104, or of chapters 38–40 of the Book of Job? Those questions would pose a larger one: does Christianity require a communion with nature? It does in the sense of having been created for a communion supremely instantiated in the face to face of man and woman (*ish* and *isha*). In the sense of Romanticism, of the *Hymnen an die Nacht* of Novalis, the answer is problematic and more likely to be negative. Romanticism rests on an enclosing within the finite sphere of nature from which we have been freed by the cross. Christianity justifies a certain form of dominion of human beings over nature, and hence allows for some exploitation of it. Vitalistic naturalism is not a Christian position. God's Noachic covenant (Gen. 8:15–22) is not primarily a teaching about nature, but a statement to the effect that it is righteousness of the heart that will keep the balances of the earth ('*adamah*, from which '*adam* was modeled) forever standing, since they rest on God's ultimate solidity mediated through the human *vizir* he instituted. This being said, we need not pit the lessons of poetic utopia against Christianity. The Spinozist ontology introduced at the beginning, revived by Nietzsche and Freud, calls us to rediscover our dependence on nature instead of cultivating the illusion that we can dominate it. If poetic utopia is not from Christianity, it is hard to think it could be dispensed with altogether when it comes to prophetically expressing God's ultimate will, just as it would be hard to think of the compiler of the Genesis creation story not having borrowed anything from surrounding Near Eastern mythopoeic narratives.

Our obedience calls more for a conversion of the will than a prescription never to modify nature. If our intention is saved, we will foster those positive traits that are an inverse image of the ones Sandel stigmatized in the wrongful ethics of control. The problem is displaced, not so much toward some unconditional, forbidden modification of nature but towards the fruits of time to be poured into the bosom of eternity, so that they will carry something more than the mirroring of our own flawed passions, greed, and biases. We would not want a world made in our image if this is what it meant. It is to the credit of Dante's insight to have captured this in the *Inferno*.

Jewish rabbinic ethics has left us with this teaching recalled by Lévinas: we disrupt the cosmos not when artificializing it, but when we fail to acknowledge the cucumbers through our act of gratefulness and see instead in them the illusion of more production of cucumbers (Lévinas 1994, 141–142). It is not making things unnatural that bewitches the human creature into defying the Lord. We can make synthetic meat if we want. Our fault lay in eating it on *Shabbat* and not observing the final destination of creation.

The Christian God created through the Word something akin to an intellectual act and he had in front of him not passive atoms to shuffle, but a matter pregnant from an act of the Spirit. He does not create like an artisan, poking his hammer in slate. Reserving a space for that which we have not made comprises a range where even matter would be included. If God has let creation be what it is, if he created (*bara*) in a way that is unrepresentable to us (which in the Old Testament means less "to make" than "to make a *new* thing appear") and through withdrawing, there is room for nature's own intelligence, and further for the misuse of it, for ranges of exploratory "dead ends." Not all we see in nature ought to be preserved.

Transhumanism can be seen as an anticipation of a godlike life, but it will not do to simply speak of putting God at the center in the manner of Spinoza read by Heine. One has to locate the "blind spot" present in this project when, fueled by a desire for immortality, it flashes its gaze on the other "shore" of our experience of a "valley of tears" and imagines cities that are "cybernetic" (Schöffer 1972), or organisms such as cyborgs that have come to be from a finitely intentional act of mind and who do not know suffering, since it thus simulates for us the attainment of divine life *hic et nunc*, against a parousiac realization of justice.

If human beings are in the process of being fully formed, ethical problems themselves will be modified. For a being who has learned to partly control and certainly reduce suffering, the fear of consequences will not be experienced in the same way. When suffering has been eradicated, two possibilities present themselves: to propel ourselves in a painless life, pursuing a garden of pleasure and ecstasy, or to turn our gaze on the agonizing earth, almost as if she took over our suffering. No one, however, can tell us what *physical* sense there would be in a planet such as ours existing forever as we know it. The other strategy, that of a transfer of our lives in an endless absence of obstacles and trials, in an eternal repose, has a fantasy character about it, as if by pulling ourselves out of the universal connectedness of all creatures, we had forgotten the boredom and eternal suffering that would accompany a swelling-up of our deficiencies to the dimensions of endless time and space.

There is a theological response that will be shared by all Christians: the human person is made in the image of God. As *imago Dei*, humankind does not need to build a world in its image, but to steer creation with a heart and mind in God's likeness. A full answer to the problems inherent within the dream of transhumanism would have to include a revaluation of personhood, but the nature of the human creature might not just be in personhood. Even the grounding of personhood in the life of the Trinity needs to be balanced against the recognition that "person" used as a concept to speak of God is more dissimilar from "person" used to speak of us than it is similar (Lateran Council IV, chapter 2). Nature might bear a greater work which exceeds the order she represents, but this might in turn only be visible in a theological axiology: an eternal fountain of energy and life that would make the person possible.

What is incompatible with Christianity in the transhuman ideal is the will to measure oneself against God, to act as if we could value ourselves only through work and autistic "busying" while God would have rested. To reject dependency on other creatures betrays a refusal of feebleness, of the weaving of a web, of the network that surrounds us. It is the refusal to accept that resources which do not belong to us belong to other living beings.

Whereas humanism affirmed human nature to the point of creating in the soul a sense of horror, transhumanism denies it. In both cases, what complements this nature has not been acknowledged. Whether we affirm it or deny it any value, we have all along been incapable of seeing in the need for relationality a parable of who God is. Christianity is the real challenge to transhumanism, not the other way around. It teaches that to realize the fullness of our nature, to have it all, one must lay it down, not by aggrandizing a mentalized and abstract version of it, but by accepting that something be given at the gateway where our independence is destroyed.

This is why we are promised a new name and a new self (Rev. 14:3). Impatience with the self is therefore inscribed in us, but by having invented a world of constant agitation, we have gotten tired of being, of the effort implicit in evolving in a noosphere and having to constantly decide. We seek to dismiss the "I am" and fuse in a pantheistic way like a flame everywhere disseminated and locally nowhere. Never have we seen a more pressing need to understand how the Spirit of God is a flame that can call to life this haze of dust, because it is also the water where life could first appear.

References

Atlan, H. and Koppel, M. 1990. The Cellular Computer DNA: Program or Data. *Bulletin of Mathematical Biology*, 52(3), pp. 335–348.

Baker, A. 2002. Theology and the Crisis in Darwinism. *Modern Theology*, 18(2), pp. 183–215.

Bergson, H. 1913. *Creative Evolution*. Translated by A. Mitchell. New York: H. Holt.

Bostrom, N. 2005. A History of Transhumanist Thought. *Journal of Evolution and Technology*, 14(1), online at http://jtpress.org/volume14/bostrom.html.

Broad, C. D. 1959. *A Short History of Science*. Garden City, NY: Doubleday.

Brown, D. 2006. *Descartes and the Passionate Mind*. Cambridge: Cambridge University Press.

Carroll, J. 2008. *The Wreck of Western Culture: Humanism Revisited*. Wilmington, DE: ISI Books.

Carroll, S., Prud'homme, B., and Gompel, N. 2008. Regulating Evolution. *Scientific American*, 298(5), pp. 60–67.

Chaitin, G. 2006. *Meta Math! The Quest for Omega*. New York: Vintage.

Cole-Turner, Ronald. 2010. Synthetic Biology: Theological Questions about Biological Engineering. In D. Albertson and C. King, eds. *Without Nature? A New Condition for Theology*. New York: Fordham University Press, pp. 136–151.

Daston, Lorraine. 1995. How Nature Became the Other: Anthropomorphism and Anthropocentrism in Early Modern Natural Philosophy. In S. Maasen, E. Mendelsohn, and P. Weingart, eds. *Biology as Society, Society as Biology: Metaphors*. Dordrecht: Kluwer, pp. 37–56.

Daston, Lorraine. 2010. The World in Order. In D. Albertson and C. King, eds. *Without Nature? A New Condition for Theology*. New York: Fordham University Press, pp. 15–34.

Ellul, J. 1980. *The Technological System*. Translated by J. Neugroschel. New York: Continuum.

Foerst, A. 2004. *God in the Machine*. New York: Dutton.

Freud, S. 1962. *Civilization and Its Discontents*. Translated by J. Strachey. New York: Norton.

Gelernter, D. 1994. *The Muse in the Machine*. New York: Free Press.

Gould, S. J. 1980. *The Panda's Thumb*. New York: Norton.

Hacking, I. 2005. The Cartesian Vision Fulfilled: Analogue Bodies and Digital Minds. *Interdisciplinary Science Reviews*, 32(2), pp. 153–166.

Harrison, P. 2007. *The Fall of Man and the Foundations of Science*. Cambridge: Cambridge University Press.

Heschel, A. J. 1975. *The Sabbath*. New York: Farrar, Straus & Giroux.

Hottois, G., ed. 1988. *Évaluer la technique*. Paris: Vrin.

Huxley, J. 1957. Transhumanism. In *New Bottles for New Wine*. London: Chatto & Windus, pp. 13–17.

Hyman, G. 2000. John Milbank and Nihilism: A Metaphysical (Mis)Reading? *Literature and Theology*, 14(4), pp. 430–443.

Lanza, R. and Berman, B. 2010. *Biocentrism*. Dallas, TX: BenBella Books.

Lederberg, Joshua. 2002. Experimental Genetics and Human Evolution. In W. Kristol and E. Cohen, eds. *The Future Is Now*. Lanham, MD: Rowman & Littlefield, pp. 33–40.

Lévinas, E. 1994. *Nine Talmudic Readings*. Translated by A. Aronowicz. Bloomington, IN: Indiana University Press.

Lipovetsky, G. 2005. *Hypermodern Times*. Translated by A. Brown. Cambridge: Polity Press.

Munnik, René. 2005. ICT and the Character of Finitude. In U. Görman, W. Drees, and H. Meisinger, eds. *Creative Creatures*. London: T&T Clark, pp. 15–33.

Nietzsche, F. 1983. *Untimely Meditations*. Translated by R. J. Hollingdale. Cambridge: Cambridge University Press.

Peck, Russell A. 1979. Number as Cosmic Language. In D. Jeffrey, ed. *By Things Seen: Reference and Recognition in Medieval Thought*. Ottawa: University of Ottawa Press, pp. 47–80.

Prigogine, I. and Stengers, I. 1984. *Order Out of Chaos*. New York: Bantam.

Sandel, M. 2004. The Case against Perfection. Atlantic Monthly, April, pp. 51–62.

Santayana, G. 1921. *Interpretations of Poetry and Religion*. New York: Scribner.

Schöffer, N. 1972. *La Ville cybernétique*. Paris: Denoël.

Sloterdijk, P. 1989. *Thinker on Stage: Nietzsche's Materialism*. Translated by J. Owen Daniel. Minneapolis, MN: University of Minnesota Press.

Sloterdijk, P. 2009. Rules for the Human Zoo: A Response to the *Letter on Humanism*. Translated by M. Varney Rorty. *Environment and Planning D: Society and Space*, 27(1), pp. 12–28.

Stroeger, William R. 2000. Cultural Cosmology and the Impact of the Natural Sciences on Philosophy and Culture. In J. Polkinghorne and M. Weiker, eds. *The Ends of God and the End of the World*. Harrisburg, PA: Trinity Press, pp. 65–77.

Venter, C. G., Gibson, D. G., Glass, John I. *et al.* 2010. Creation of a Bacterial Cell Controlled by a Chemically Synthesized Genome. *Science Express*, May 20, pp. 1–7.

von Bertalanffy, L. 1974. *Robots, Men, and Minds*. New York: G. Braziller.

von Weizsäcker, C. F. 1964. *The Relevance of Science*. London: Collins.

Wallace, A. R. 1903. *Man's Place in the Universe*. London: Chapman & Hall.

Weinert, F. 2009. *Copernicus, Darwin, and Freud*. Oxford: Wiley-Blackwell.

Weiser, M. 1994. Commentary. *Human–Computer Interaction*, 9(2), pp. 125–127.

World Transhumanist Association. 1998. Transhumanist Declaration, online at http://humanityplus.org/learn/transhumanist-declaration (accessed July 2011).

Further Reading

Albertson, D. and King, C., eds. 2010. *Without Nature? A New Condition for Theology*. New York: Fordham University Press. A collection of essays addressing the difficult question of nature's fixity and the human quest for improvement, typically with a theological dimension.

Ehrenberg, A. 2010. *The Weariness of the Self*. Translated by D. Homel *et al*. Montreal: McGill. Helps to penetrate the discomfort with one's identities of substitution and shows how much of the transhumanist question is related to the absence of an agreed-upon anthropology.

Hansell, G. R. and Grassie, W., eds. 2011. *H+/−: Transhumanism and Its Critics*. Philadelphia, PA: Metanexus Institute. Recent essays by specialists laying down the reasons why they think transhumanism must be pursued, followed by dissenting viewpoints.

Janicaud, D. 2005. *On the Human Condition*. Translated by E. Brennan. London: Routledge. Furthers several of the points mentioned in an inevitably sketchier way in this chapter.

Kurzweil, R. 2000. *The Age of Spiritual Machines*. New York: Penguin. Provides a synopsis of work done in artificial intelligence and mind reproduction in machines.

Wiener, N. 1966. *God & Golem Inc.: A Comment on Certain Points Where Cybernetics Impinges on Religion*. Cambridge, MA: MIT Press. Essential reading for understanding the vision that the father of cybernetics contemplated, seeking a humanism that would counterbalance machine and intelligence hybridization.

35

Ecology and the Environment

LISA H. SIDERIS

In everyday use, the terms "ecology" and "environment" may connote something normative – a social movement, Earth Day gatherings, a vision of proper relationships between humans and the rest of the natural world. In Christian environmental ethics or "ecological theology" this is frequently the case. Yet ecology, of course, is also – some would say primarily – a branch of science, and research on the environment may not have any obvious connection to environmentalism. A scholarly work that purports to be about Christianity and ecology may or may not have much to do with ecology as a science, except in a very general way, and the chances are good that it will have even less to do with *evolutionary* science, despite the importance of evolution for understanding the workings of nature. At the same time, however, Christian environmentalism is quite engaged with ideas and developments in certain areas of science. In order to understand this state of affairs, it is necessary to get a sense of how Christian environmentalism came into being and what forces have shaped it.

Green Critiques of Religion and Science

The academic field of religious environmentalism emerged somewhat later than the popular environmental movement of the 1960s. Ecotheology was a product of environmental critiques of both religious and scientific worldviews. The Judeo-Christian tradition in particular has often been the target of such critiques. The best known of these is Lynn White's essay "The Historical Roots of our Ecologic Crisis" published in the journal *Science* in 1967. White put forth what now seems an obvious claim that how people regard the natural world depends on how they understand themselves and their relationship to that world. Above all, "human ecology is deeply conditioned by beliefs about our nature and destiny – that is, by religion" (White 1967, 1206). Of course, beliefs about our nature and destiny also have much to do with science, and as ecotheology has evolved, its relationship to science has become complicated and quite interesting.

The Blackwell Companion to Science and Christianity, First Edition. Edited by J. B. Stump and Alan G. Padgett.
© 2012 Blackwell Publishing Ltd. Published 2012 by Blackwell Publishing Ltd.

White's critique encompassed aspects of both science and religion. He took aim at the Genesis doctrine of creation that granted humans, as creatures in God's image, virtually unlimited dominion over the natural world, established a dualism between the physical and the spiritual (privileging the latter), and treated nature as incidental to the quest for human transcendence and other-worldly salvation. White argued that this worldview had driven out ancient pagan views that posited a natural world inhabited and animated by spirits. Though the point is often overlooked, White also believed that science and technology, as outgrowths of Judeo-Christianity (more specifically, of Western Christianity), also encouraged human mastery of and dominion over nature. Asian perspectives were less problematic, White asserted, insofar as they lack the nature–spirit dualism of Christianity. The belief that Buddhist traditions, for example, are inherently "greener" persists in ecotheology, as does a disagreement over whether religious or scientific attitudes toward nature are, on the whole, more culpable for environmental problems.

Because the Christian tradition received much of the blame, early responses to critiques such as White's emerged largely from Christian theologians. Some of these defended Christianity by pointing out that biblical dominion, for example, implies human responsibility and stewardship of nature, not despotism; but a surprising number of theologians more or less conceded many of White's points and set to work to rehabilitate the tradition (or to recover forgotten teachings and practices) in order to produce a more environmentally friendly version. Many Christian theologians focused on expanding Christian ethics – ethics of neighborly love and liberation – to include our nonhuman neighbors. The resulting ethics, however, have not been entirely compatible with scientific perspectives on the natural world. Ambivalence and selective use of science – as well as occasional outbreaks of enthusiasm for it – characterize much of Christian ecotheology.

The environmental movement in America in the 1960s was both inspired by science – at least in popular works and media – and nurtured by a deep distrust of scientific authority. Religious environmentalism within the academy shows a similar tendency to distrust science and its claims to authority. A central text that generated ecological concerns in both popular and academic circles was Rachel Carson's Silent Spring (1962). Writing in an era of unprecedented enthusiasm for chemical wonders such as DDT, Carson criticized indiscriminate use of pesticides and portrayed the chemical control of nature as a scientific and moral issue. Carson condemned inordinate faith in science and reckless disregard for the long-term consequences of chemical pest control. She dismissed the methods of chemical engineering and entomology as primitive, "Stone Age" science, "as crude as the cave man's club" (297). Silent Spring called for greater caution and humility among scientists and chemical engineers, and urged citizens to cast a wary eye on science's promise of a better and safer future. The branch of science that Carson upheld as offering the greatest promise was ecology, because it alone provided solutions through biological pest control (what is now called integrated pest management), and offered holistic, rather than compartmentalized, understanding of the natural world. This big-picture perspective could suggest to humans which interventions in nature were prudent and which might wreak greater havoc on what Carson called the "fabric of nature." Shortly after Silent Spring, ecologist Paul Sears dubbed ecology the "subversive science" because "ecology affords a continuing critique of man's operations within the ecosystem" (Sears 1962, 12). Like Carson he understood ecology as the least "particulate" and "specialized" of the sciences, and thus the least likely to provide shortsighted solutions without regard to larger ecological wholes and future generations. In this portrait of ecology as science of a different sort – inherently holistic, potentially subversive, and refreshingly countercultural – we see the merging of ecology as a normative perspective and ecology as a scientific discipline. For these early environmentalists, and many who read them, ecology was bound up with citizens' right to know what was in their food, air, and water and with the growing conviction that "we should no longer accept the counsel of those who tell us that we must fill our world with poisonous chemicals" (Carson 1962, 278).

Few Christian environmentalists, past or present, take their cues directly from writers like Carson. Though she wrote with reverence and a sense of wonder for the natural world, Carson's arguments made no direct appeal to traditional religion or religious morality.[1] A certain suspicion of science, and a sense of ecology as countercultural, nevertheless pervades much of Christian ecological theology. Carolyn Merchant, whose book *The Death of Nature* (1980) strongly influenced a generation of environmentalists, likewise dubs ecology a "subversive science," a science of interconnectedness that "reawakened interest in the values and concepts associated historically with the premodern organic world" (1980, xx). By *organic* Merchant means the world before nature was effectively "killed" by the mechanical philosophy of the sixteenth and seventeenth centuries. These scientific paradigms are blamed for reducing nature to dead matter in motion and disregarding the interconnected nature of life. The exception is often physics – not the physics of the scientific revolution but the "new physics" of the twentieth and twenty-first centuries. Fondness for recent discoveries in physics is accompanied by a peculiar turning away from modern biology. Christian ecotheologians cast an especially jaundiced eye on modern versions of Darwinism.

The Problem of Suffering and the Turn to Physics

The turn away from evolutionary biology in favor of physics would likely have puzzled Carson, who understood Darwinian dynamics such as predator–prey relationships to be the engine of nature. We tamper with this engine at great risk to ourselves and other life forms. Chemical tampering generates more intractable problems: bioaccumulation of pesticides up the food chain, and pesticide resistance that threatens to transform nature's mixture of "weak" and "strong" insects into a population of "entirely tough resistant strains" (Carson 1962, 272). Among some Christian ecotheologians, however, it is precisely this portrait of Darwinian struggle between weak and strong that makes it an awkward fit with their religion. The common association of evolutionary theory with forms of Social Darwinism may partially account for uneasiness with evolutionary theory. If Darwinism is understood – however erroneously – to entail victory of the strong and fit over the weak or disadvantaged, it flies in the face of Christian ethics that prescribes preferential concern for the poor, sick, hungry, and downtrodden. The theory of natural selection brings the problem of suffering, and more generally, issues of theodicy, to the forefront. For example, some Christians advocate treating all organisms as valuable and attending, as Jesus would, to the bodily needs of organisms that comprise nature's "poorest" and "neediest" (McFague 1997, 149) We ought to care for *nature's* marginalized, despised, and oppressed beings, "healing the wounds of nature and feeding its starving creatures" just as a Christian community would focus on "feeding and healing its needy human beings" (McFague 1997, 149).

For a number of prominent Christian theologians, the idea that humans have obligations to reduce suffering in nature takes seriously a vision of the natural world as fallen from a more perfect condition and in need of restoration. This goal of restoring or redeeming nature finds support in biblical ideals of a past – or future – perfection and assumes nature's suffering to be symptomatic of its corrupted state. Ecofeminist theologian Rosemary Radford Ruether envisions restoration of nature that ushers in "right relations" among all creatures and heals "nature's enmity." Passages of Isaiah suggest to her that "even the carnivorous conflict between animals will be overcome in the Peaceable Kingdom" (Ruether 1994, 213). For fellow ecofeminist Sallie McFague, ethical insights can be gleaned from biblical stories "in which the lion and the lamb, the child and the snake, lie down together; where there is food for all; where neither people nor animals are destroying one another" (McFague 1997, 158). A "peaceable kingdom of shalom and ecological harmony" in which "predatorial behavior will no longer characterize human and non-human relations" informs Michael Northcott's interpretation of God's will for creation (Northcott 1996, 194). Charles Birch anticipates a time when "paradise is regained, and everyone not only goes back to a nonmeat diet, but the friendliest relations subsist between all species" (Birch 1990, 67). Often it seems that the sort of natural community envisioned by many ecotheologians could come about only if evolutionary processes were halted.

Darwin himself, who recoiled from suffering in any form, felt this problem keenly with regard to the natural world. According to his *Autobiography* his refusal to accept that a benevolent Creator would have made a natural world so filled with suffering, sentient beings ultimately turned him away from theism. "A being so powerful and so full of knowledge as a God who could create the universe, is to our finite minds omnipotent and omniscient, and it revolts our understanding to suppose that his benevolence is not unbounded, for what advantage can there be in the sufferings of millions of the lower animals throughout almost endless time?" (Darwin 1958, 90). The amount of suffering in the natural world accords well with the theory of natural selection, Darwin believed, but not with belief in God.

Christian ecotheologians have taken up Darwin's problem of theodicy and run with it – in a variety of directions. As recurring motifs of peaceable kingdoms and restored Eden suggest, one approach sees the task of ecological ethics as eliminating suffering as much as possible, often without much clarity regarding natural as opposed to human or cultural sources of suffering. Another common approach is to portray nature as a place where suffering and conflict is in a minor key, whereas instances of symbiosis, cooperation, and benign forms of interdependence are much the norm. Here again, ecology is seen as more than a science of biotic communities; it provides "guidelines" and exhibits principles of "cooperation and interdependency" (Ruether 1994, 56–57). Ecology, understood as a blueprint for communal harmony and right relationships, is foregrounded, while evolution, evocative of pain, and strife, recedes into the background.

A number of related approaches can loosely be categorized as liberation theologies. Liberation theology emerged in Latin American during the 1960s with Gustavo Gutiérrez's *Theology of Liberation* (1973). The movement put the gospel of Jesus into dialogue with Marxist perspectives on struggle and oppression, in order to address earthly injustices – social, economic, and political. Liberation theology influences the work of Christian ecofeminists such as McFague and Ruether who discern parallels between oppression of women and minorities and the oppression of nonhuman life forms, as well as by process thinkers such as Charles Birch and John Cobb who integrate the philosophy of Alfred North Whitehead with Christian theology. Process theologians understand God as inseparable from, and affected by, natural processes. God is posited as a force or presence that "lures" the natural world forward in noncoercive ways; the direction nature takes is a product both of God's intentionality and the actions of all organisms. This account understands all entities as potential subjects capable of experience, subjecthood, and creative response. All therefore have value and should be shielded from unnecessary suffering. Science and the scientific worldview are themselves major sources of unnecessary suffering, some process thinkers point out. Charles Birch and

John Cobb call for liberation of life from objectifying and mechanistic scientific categories and conceptions. Most scientific investigation regards living entities as mere objects or machines, not subjects, they argue. "If we can liberate the concept of life we might better be able to liberate life itself" Birch and Cobb argue (1981, 68).

What many of these ecotheologians have in common is advocacy of an "ecological model," an alternative paradigm to the objectifying and reductionist approaches they criticize. Despite its name, the ecological model is largely informed by "developments in other sciences, especially the so-called 'new physics'" (Hay 2002, 129). This is particularly true of some process thinkers. The new or "postmodern" physics – quantum theory and special relativity – reveals a universe of complex, interrelated events, not an atomistic array of objects. Radical continuity and relationality of all entities to their environments, as well as the dissolution of absolute distinctions between subject and object or observer and the observed, are the welcome messages of the new physics, according to this account. As claims to objectivity in science are undermined, so are harmful attitudes that objectify life.

The turn to physics in ecotheology is also motivated by rejection of a so-called "neo-Darwinian paradigm." Neo-Darwinism often has no consistent or clear meaning in this context. In the history of science, the term refers to the synthesis of Darwin's theory of natural selection with modern genetics (the rediscovery of Mendel's work on genes, and the later discovery of DNA). In theological contexts, however, the term acts as a kind of "code for views of the evolutionary process that a variety of persons and groups are not comfortable with" (Goodenough 2005, 370). Critics charge that neo-Darwinism entails, for example, commitment to atheistic worldviews, genetic determinism, purposeless variation, and a blind, uncaring, mechanical process of natural selection. In other words, neo-Darwinism is the latest version of mechanical philosophies like those that Merchant faulted for bringing death to what was once a vital, enchanted world; but the mechanical model in its neo-Darwinian incarnation is even more pernicious insofar as it mechanizes humans as well, who are portrayed as robots – "survival machines" – programmed by their genes (Dawkins 2006a). Now even humans "are asked to interpret ourselves as matter in motion" (Cobb 2007, 43). Ecology and the new physics, by contrast, are understood as sister sciences pointing to a more accurate and ethically rich picture of interconnectedness, relationality, and active subjecthood. "Both the new physics, with its stress on self-organising, spontaneous systems, and ecology, with its insistence on the primacy of relationality, are at least potential rivals to the mechanistic paradigm" (Hay 2002, 151). It is worth noting that many of these complaints against neo-Darwinism are also voiced by proponents of intelligent design (ID) who show a similar distaste for the perceived excesses of materialism in modern biology. ID critics charge that modern biology is committed to a conception of matter as reductionistic as those promulgated in the seventeenth century. Michael Behe contends that nature shows "irreducible" complexity, and like process theologians who discern purpose, initiative, and active agency in all entities, he insists on a more "active" and self-organizing view of life than modern gene-centered biology allows (Behe 1996).[2]

"Storied" Nature and the Rapprochement of Science and Religion

In contrast to apparent convergence between some process thinkers and design arguments, ecotheologian John Haught has defended evolutionary theism against incursions from ID. A Roman Catholic theologian who served as an expert witness in the 2005 *Kitzmiller vs. Dover* trial over intelligent design, Haught considers Darwin's theory a gift to theology that enriches rather than diminishes it. In his view, ID bears a striking resemblance to the scientism of neo-Darwinian and neo-atheist writers such as Dawkins and Daniel Dennett. Invoking a metaphor of nature as a book, he argues that both ID and materialist biology display a basic "reading problem," and excessive literalism with regard to Darwin's theory. Haught advocates layered explanation or explanatory pluralism, which entails that virtually any phenomenon in our experience can be explained at different levels. Science appropriately deals with questions at the level of natural causes, not questions about ultimate meaning and purpose. Essentially both ID and materialist biology conflate science with ideology. Both "compress what could be a rich hierarchy of explanations into a one-dimensional Flatland where scientific and ultimate levels either become indistinguishable, or else they are forced to compete for the single explanatory slot available" (Haught 2003, 91).

Though influenced by some of the same philosophers and theologians as process thinkers such as Whitehead as well as Teilhard de Chardin, Haught posits greater independence and autonomy of the natural world from God. He emphasizes nature's contingency and spontaneity – key features of a Darwinian account – as consistent with a theological interpretation of God as differentiated from creation. It might appear that this move simply reasserts the dualism of God and nature that critics such as White see as integral to Christianity's neglect of nature. Haught's account is somewhat more nuanced in that he sees God's relationship to the universe as one of interdependence and "dialogical intimacy," not separation. Citing Teilhard, he stresses that "true union differentiates" (Haught 2007, 54). Interestingly, Haught's account directly takes up Darwin's claim that a God whose benevolence is "not unbounded" would not create a world with so much suffering and waste. Nature's autonomy and spontaneity reflect the noncontrolling, self-giving, "boundless love" of God, Haught argues. It is a sign of God's infinite love of the world that he allows it to *be*, much as a parent enables a child's autonomy. "A more directive, dictatorial deity might bring the universe to completion in one magical moment." Such a world might have greater stability and fewer tragic elements, "But what a bland, lifeless, storyless world that would be" (Haught 2007, 54–55).

What does appreciation of these features of the natural world imply for ecological ethics? Haught is less clear on this point. Like many ecotheologians influenced by Teilhard, he sees humans as part of the "great work," or great story of God's creation. Realizing our embeddedness in this great story revitalizes ethical engagement and discourages environmentally destructive practices. Humans play a significant role in "renewing and extending" creation into the future (Haught 2010, 147). Haught interprets the cosmos as akin to an unfinished, unperfected but compelling narrative and understands God as beckoning us – and the universe as a whole – toward a future of undefined promise. God "arrives from out of the future to give new life to the creation and fresh hope to human history" (Haught 2010, 135). Haught believes that this conception of a universe oriented toward future fulfillment and completion can ground ecological-ethical responsibility, but it could just as well undermine it, since humans may place responsibility for the fate of nature in God's hands. It is also questionable whether Haught's future-oriented universe is scientifically coherent. His claim that nature is most intelligible with reference to a metaphysics of the future implies that current scientific knowledge – based upon present experimentation, as well as the causal efficacy of the past – is unreliable at best.

Science as the source of a rich narrative, a "story of the universe," resonates with many Christian thinkers. Like Haught, environmental philosopher and theologian Holmes Rolston III, considered by many to be the founder of environmental ethics, likens nature to a story whose meaning acquires greater depth with the advent of Darwinian theory: "One reason that evolution is a much richer and more welcome theory than was the former belief in fixity of species is that it makes possible vaster depths of story" (Rolston 2006, 275). Rolston sees "systemic" processes such as speciation, predator–prey interactions, and other ecosystem dynamics as productive of higher values, even though (or precisely because) these processes often entail suffering for individual organisms. In some of his writing, Rolston grafts these ideas onto a central Christian paradigm of "cruciform nature" where suffering is generative of values in the system as a whole. Rolston cites examples of the intelligence, beauty, and speed that is achieved by predator species in the evolutionary process and argues that much of what is valuable in nature could not have occurred in the absence of predation. Predation is an instance of value *capture* rather than value loss: the prey organism's life is lost, but at the species level both predator and prey gain. The predatory process allows species "to rise higher on the trophic pyramid, funded by capturing resources from below for greater achieve-ments in sentience, cognition and mobility" (Rolston 1992a, 254). As for the prey, its species too "may gain as the population is regulated, as selection for better skills at avoiding predation takes place" (Rolston 1992a, 254).

By locating the value of evolution in systems rather than (only) in individual organisms, Rolston argues, we can see nature's narrative not as one of unmitigated or pointless pain but one of "suffering through to something higher" (Rolston 2006, 145). This accords well with the Christian tradition which never eschews suffering as a means of achieving divine pur-poses: "The way of nature," Rolston argues, "is the way of the cross" (2006, 146). Beyond the continuous production of systemic values in nature that are driven by pain and other "disvalues," there is no further redemption for organisms, and no perfected state against which the present natural world is to be judged. Rolston resists any censuring of nature with reference to ideals of its past or future: "A peaceable natural kingdom, where the lion lies down with the lamb . . . is a cultural metaphor and cannot be interpreted in censure of natural history" (Rolston 1992b, 131). Biblical injunctions to feed hungry persons do not require feeding hungry animals in nature. Because Rolston believes that suffering is not neces-sarily contrary to the intentions of the Creator, he endorses a largely noninterventionist environmental ethic. Interventions in "wild" nature are warranted primarily when human past interventions have compromised or disrupted nature's functioning, but we do not inter-vene to protect individual organisms from the forces of natural selection and ecosystem interactions, though they involve pain, hunger, and disease. Seen from a systemic standpoint, pain in natural contexts is instrumental, not pointless, even though it may not benefit the individual organism who suffers. Critics charge Rolston with setting up too rigid a distinction between nature and culture, but his arguments offer guidelines not found in much of eco-theology regarding when we ought and ought not to intervene in the suffering of nonhuman animals.

A movement gaining great momentum within ecotheology, and with the scientifically literate public, is the Universe Story (variously called The Great Story and The New Story). Some offshoots of this movement go by the name Epic of Evolution, and its proponents range from atheists to religious naturalists to more or less traditional Christians. I focus here primarily on figures who have emerged within the Christian tradition, but as some general background will suggest, the movement has a much broader reach. The central figure in this movement is Thomas Berry, a Roman Catholic priest who was strongly influenced by Teil-hard's work, as well as Eastern philosophy and religion, Native American religions, and the science of cosmology. Berry characterized himself as a "geologian" – a historian of the earth and earth processes. The New Story tells the scientific narrative of the universe – the whole, unfolding cosmogenesis – in mythopoeic form. Because the Universe Story is proffered as a common creation myth for all life and all cultures, Berry and his co-author (cosmologist Brian Swimme) avoid the strongly Christian language of Teilhard. We find ourselves in a new "ecozoic age" in which the universe, in the form of humans, has become conscious of itself. This story allows us to know our place in the universe, to experience profound kinship with all life, and to discern our obligations to safeguard the future unfolding of the great story. Each of our lives comprises a personal evolution embedded within the great cosmic unfolding. The Universe Story thus confers meaning to individual lives while reminding us that, from the grand perspective of the cosmos, it makes little sense to think of our species as having dominion over earth. Since Berry's death in 2009 at age 94, his work has been carried forward most notably by Mary Evelyn Tucker, a theologian with expertise in Confucianism and founder of the Forum on Religion and Ecology. Tucker has teamed up with Brian Swimme to create a documentary film called *Journey of the Universe* that "draws together scientific discoveries in astronomy, geology, biology, ecology, and biodiversity with humanistic insights concerning the nature of the universe . . . to inspire a new and closer relationship with Earth in a period of growing environmental and social crisis."[3]

The idea that scientific narratives of nature have mythic potential and ethical import is integral to the work of some ecotheologians. However, the core idea of these movements – captured in the phrase "the epic of evolution" – can be traced to sociobiologist and entomologist E. O. Wilson. The phrase appears in his Pulitzer Prize-winning *On Human Nature* (1978) and in *Consilience* (1999). "The epic of evolution is probably the best myth we will ever have" Wilson argues (1978, 201). Wilson's phrase is featured prominently on a variety of web sites advocating the Epic of Evolution and the Universe Story. Though Wilson has often characterized science and religion as competitors for explanatory power – a struggle he predicts science will eventually win – his phrase has been appropriated by many who want to see reconciliation between science and religion (as opposed to religion *superseded* by science). One of the most prominent advocates of a sacralized epic of evolution – if prominence can be gauged by media attention – is Michael Dowd, a conservative Christian pastor turned evolutionary "evangelist." Along with his wife, science writer Connie Barlow, Dowd tours the country in a van decorated with symbols of a Jesus fish kissing a Darwin fish.[4] Together they spread the gospel of evolution, and host "evolutionary revivals" for audiences that include children and adults, in both secular and religious venues (ranging widely over the more moderate Christian denominations).

Dowd's book *Thank God for Evolution* (2008) encourages people to see the meaning of their lives within the context of the sacred narrative of evolution. Like Berry before him, Dowd is influenced by thinkers such as Teilhard but also by contemporary work in evolutionary biology and psychology. He combines insights from evolutionary theorists who are often engaged in heated disputes with one another over the details of evolutionary processes: Richard Dawkins and Simon Conway Morris, for example, or E. O. Wilson and Stephen Jay Gould. Dowd writes glowing reviews of Dawkins's work – he seems to regard Dawkins's *The Greatest Show on Earth* (2009) as a sort of companion book to *Thank God for Evolution* – and he counts among his favorite evolutionary psychologists Stephen Pinker and David Sloan Wilson, from whom he draws, respectively, his views about our unchosen animal nature and the general trajectory of cooperative social arrangements in evolution. Dowd enthusiastically embraces evolutionary psychology's potential to explain human failings that have traditionally been blamed on sin or Satan – drug, food, and sex addictions, infidelity, impulses to cruelty – as well as gender differences and other inherited tendencies "deeply rooted in our reptilian brain" (Dowd 2008, 171). "From a science-based, evolutionary perspective, there is no place for belief in a literal Satan" he notes; "nevertheless, personalizing or relationalizing the forces of evil – especially those within us – can be helpful, whether or not we choose to use the words Satan or the Devil" (Dowd 2008, 169).

Perhaps the more pressing question is whether there is any place in this account for belief in a literal *God*. Dowd has drawn fire from some Christians for his support of the new atheists. Dowd's internet essay titled "Thank God for the New Atheists" depicts Dawkins and Sam Harris as prophets of God who "call us into right relationship with our time" and with "Reality."[5] Judging by Dawkins's commentary on forms of religious naturalism based in scientific narratives, it seems unlikely that he would return Dowd's compliments. Dawkins has taken scientists to task – notably, biologist and epic of evolution advocate Ursula Goodenough – who resort to religious language to express feelings of wonder and awe, when they do not believe in a supreme being, an afterlife, or any of the trappings of traditional religion. "As far as I can tell," Dawkins writes in *A Devil's Chaplain*, "my 'atheistic' views are identical to Ursula Goodenough's 'religious' ones. One of us is misusing the English language, and I don't think it's me" (Dawkins 2003, 146). What Dawkins dismisses as "neo-deistic pseudo-religion" (Dawkins 2003, 146) would likely encompass Dowd's worldview as well, as Dowd often equates God with a great "wholeness" or the universe itself.

Regarding questions of ecological ethics, Dowd's account, like Thomas Berry's, aims to create a sense of belonging with the universe, to motivate responsible behavior and appropriate moral sensibilities toward all life. An important upshot of the sacred story is the recognition of our true selves as an expanded self, undifferentiated from our environment. Echoing the insights of deep ecology, Dowd argues that "what we imagine as our environment is actually not 'out there' separate from us. Rather, each one of us in inextricably linked to vast, ancient, and potent cosmological, geological, and biological processes. . . . Earth is my larger self" (Dowd 2008, 290). Great Story cosmology tells us that whatever we do to the earth we do to our Self (248).

Conclusion: Science and the Future of Christianity

The rise of Christian environmentalism in the last several decades might be characterized as a story of disenchantment and re-enchantment. That is, the impetus for this movement can be traced to the widespread perception that the natural world has been systematically disenchanted – stripped of value, purged of sacred, awesome, or wondrous dimensions. Since science and religion are both deemed culpable for nature's disenchantment, and since there is little consensus as to which is more culpable and why, options for re-enchantment continue to emerge from both scientific and religious perspectives – and sometimes from combinations of both. Which of these major forces – science or religion – has the potential to recapture awe and wonder, and to instill a sense of connection to other life forms and the universe generally? As I see it, some form of this question drives much of the current discussion about science, religion, and the environment. Writers like Richard Dawkins and E. O. Wilson seek to persuade us that science provides all the wonder, awe, and meaning we shall ever need: "the true evolutionary epic, retold as poetry, is as intrinsically ennobling as any religious epic" (Wilson 1999, 265). Scientific forms are superior to religious forms of wonder, because scientific wonder is grounded in empirical realities or evoked by an increasingly comprehensive understanding of the structure of our universe (Dawkins 1998; Wilson 1999). As more and more religious believers are persuaded that science does indeed have the potential to weave powerful narratives in mythopoeic language with universal appeal and ethical import, what will become of traditional faiths such as Christianity? Is religion even necessary for such forms of enchantment? The answer depends in part on how one defines religion. Dawkins sees all religious belief as delusional and has made clear his hope that reason will prevail (2006b). Some scholars of religion believe that a science-inspired, global form of civic "green religion" that stresses "ecological interdependence, an affective connection to the earth as home and to nonhumans as kin" may gain ascendance over traditional faiths not easily reconciled with science (Taylor 2010, 196–197).

As religious environmentalists turn to science for materials from which to construct a new mythology, it is worth remembering that science is not the same thing as nature. One need not be an opponent of science to appreciate that the forms of wonder it generates, and the knowledge it produces, may or may not be conducive to positive feelings of connection with or ethical behavior toward the natural world. Rachel Carson, who was no enemy of science, would remind us that wonder in science may come at the expense of natural and human wellbeing. Some Christians, moreover, would want to remind us that God is not the same thing as nature, either. Although the trend in Christian environmentalism has, on the whole, been toward nondualism of spirit and matter or reconceptualization of God as inseparable from natural processes, some Christian environmentalists retain very sharp distinctions between the Creator and the Creation. One such example is the Evangelical Environmental Network (EEN), a conservative Christian organization promoting "creation care" modeled on the teachings of Jesus and applied to issues of environmental justice and climate change.[6] EEN affirms belief in a transcendent God who remains wholly other to his Creation and they remain vigilant against idolizing the latter. The natural world deserves our care simply because it is the work of God and belongs ultimately to God. For the many Christians who are not also scholars of religion, such an approach to environmental problems may have far greater common-sense appeal than abstruse theories of academic theologians or scientists. For the present time at least, Christians concerned about environmental issues have a wide range of options from which to choose.

Notes

1   For a discussion of Carson and other nature writers and environmentalists who exemplify green spirituality, see Taylor (2010). Carson's environmental commitments were strongly influenced by her Presbyterian upbringing. See Sideris (2008).
2   The similarity to ID is particularly apparent in some of process theologian David Ray Griffin's work.
3   Film description available at http://www.journeyoftheuniverse.org/synopsis/.
4   A cancer diagnosis in 2009 led to the canceling of many of Dowd's speaking engagements.
5   Available at http://www.everydaychristian.com/blogs/post/7748/.
6   EEN campaigns against sport-utility vehicles with advertisements asking "What Would Jesus Drive?"

References

Behe, Michael. 1996. *Darwin's Black Box*. New York: The Free Press.

Birch, Charles. 1990. Christian Obligation for the Liberation of Nature. In Charles Birch and William Eakin, eds. *Liberating Life: Contemporary Approaches to Ecological Theology*. Maryknoll, NY: Orbis, pp. 57–71.

Birch, Charles and Cobb, John. 1981. *The Liberation of Life*. New York: Cambridge University Press.

Carson, Rachel. 1962. *Silent Spring*. Boston, MA: Houghton Mifflin.

Cobb, John. 2007. The Limitations of Neo-Darwinism and Evidence for a Whiteheadian Theory of Evolution. *Worldviews: Global Religions, Culture, and Ecology*, 11(1), pp. 32–43.

Darwin, Charles. 1958. *The Autobiography of Charles Darwin*. Nora Barlow, ed. New York: Norton.

Dawkins, Richard. 1998. *Unweaving the Rainbow*. Boston, MA: Houghton Mifflin.

Dawkins, Richard. 2003. *A Devil's Chaplain*. Boston, MA: Houghton Mifflin.

Dawkins, Richard. 2006a. *The Selfish Gene*. Oxford: Oxford University Press.

Dawkins, Richard. 2006b. *The God Delusion*. London: Bantam.

Dawkins, Richard. 2009. *The Greatest Show on Earth*. New York: Free Press.

Dowd, Michael. 2008. *Thank God for Evolution*. New York: Viking.

Goodenough, Ursula. 2005. Reductionism and Holism, Chance and Selection, Mechanism and Mind. *Zygon*, 40(2), pp. 369–380.

Gutiérrez, Gustavo. 1973. *A Theology of Liberation*. Translated by Caridad Inda and John Eagleson. Maryknoll, NY: Orbis.

Haught, John. 2003. *Deeper than Darwin*. Boulder, CO: Westview Press.

Haught, John. 2007. Darwin and Contemporary Theology. *Worldviews: Global Religions, Culture, and Ecology*, 11(1), pp. 44–57.

Haught, John. 2010. *Making Sense of Evolution*. Louisville, KY: Westminster John Knox.

Hay, Peter. 2002. *Main Currents in Western Environmental Thought*. Bloomington, IN: Indiana University Press.

McFague, Sallie. 1997. *Super, Natural Christians: How We Should Love Nature*. Minneapolis, MN: Fortress.

Merchant, Carolyn. 1980. *The Death of Nature: Women, Ecology and the Scientific Revolution*. San Francisco, CA: Harper & Row.

Northcott, Michael. 1996. *The Environment and Christian Ethics*. Cambridge: Cambridge University Press.

Rolston, Holmes, III. 1992a. Disvalues in Nature. *The Monist*, 75, pp. 250–278.

Rolston, Holmes, III. 1992b. Wildlife and Wildlands. In Dieter Hessel, ed. *After Nature's Revolt*. Minneapolis, MN: Fortress, pp. 122–143.

Rolston, Holmes, III. 2006. *Science and Religion: A Critical Survey*. West Conshohocken, PA: Templeton Foundation Press.

Ruether, Rosemary Radford. 1994. *Gaia and God: An Ecofeminist Ethic of Earth Healing*. San Francisco, CA: HarperCollins.

Sears, Paul. 1962. Ecology – a Subversive Subject. Bioscience, July, pp. 11–13.

Sideris, Lisa. 2008. "The Secular and Religious Sources of Rachel Carson's Sense of Wonder." In Lisa Sideris and Kathleen Dean Moore, eds. *Rachel Carson: Legacy and Challenge*. Albany, NY: State University of New York Press, pp. 232–250.

Taylor, Bron. 2010. *Dark Green Religion: Nature Spirituality and the Planetary Future*. Berkeley, CA: University of California Press.

White, Lynn, Jr. 1967. The Historical Roots of Our Ecologic Crisis. *Science*, 155(3767), pp. 1203–1207.

Wilson, E. O. 1978. *On Human Nature*. Cambridge, MA: Harvard University Press.

Wilson, E. O. 1999. *Consilience: The Unity of Knowledge*. New York: Vintage.

Further Reading

Dawkins, Richard. 2006. *The God Delusion*. London: Bantam. Dawkins's statement on religious faith as "belief without evidence" and arguments against the existence of God hypothesis.

Sideris, Lisa. 2003. *Environmental Ethics, Ecological Theology, and Natural Selection*. New York: Columbia University Press. Examines the neglect or distortion of evolutionary theory in Christian ecotheology.

Swimme, Brian and Berry, Thomas. 1992. *The Universe Story*. San Francisco, CA: Harper. A mythopoeic account of the complete history of our universe.

Taylor, Bron, ed. 2005. *Encyclopedia of Religion and Nature*. London: Continuum. Definitive, multicultural guide to the religion–nature interface, including new religious movements and green spirituality.

Part VIII
Metaphysical Implications

36

Free Will and Rational Choice

E. J. LOWE

The mutual metaphysical implications of science and Christianity are many, subtle, and highly controversial. This is above all true in the arena of human reason and action. Very arguably, rational choice requires free will, in the robust and "libertarian" rather than "compatibilist" sense of the latter. But some see science as inimical to such a notion of free will and hence as a threat to human reason. In this chapter, I shall contrast two very different conceptions of rational human action. One of these, which is currently dominant amongst scientifically minded analytical philosophers, is hostile to libertarian conceptions of free will and rational agency. The other, whose merits will be advanced here, is libertarian and yet consistent, I believe, with everything that modern science – as opposed to modern scientistic philosophy – tells us with any assurance about the nature of the human mind and brain. The key notion that any account of human rationality must be able to accommodate and explain, in my view, is the notion of *responsiveness to reasons* – that is, the peculiar kind of ability that a rational mind has to respond to a reason *as* a reason and *for the sake* of that reason. I shall argue that causal accounts of this phenomenon are constitutively incapable of capturing it adequately and that only a certain kind of libertarian account can hope to succeed. In the first of the chapter's three sections, I shall briefly set out the currently dominant "standard" causal theory of rational action. (I can afford to be brief, since the view is so well known.) In the second, I shall present, a little more fully, my preferred libertarian alternative. And in the third I shall examine in some detail the notion of responsiveness to reasons and offer a libertarian account of it.

The "Standard" Causal Theory of Rational Action

According to the "standard" causal theory of rational action, ultimately inspired by the ideas of David Hume (1978, book II, part III) and currently best articulated in the work of Donald Davidson (1980), actions are *events that are intentional under some description.* For example, the

The Blackwell Companion to Science and Christianity, First Edition. Edited by J. B. Stump and Alan G. Padgett.
© 2012 Blackwell Publishing Ltd. Published 2012 by Blackwell Publishing Ltd.

event of my arm's moving is an action of mine if, say, under the description "reaching for the salt-cellar" it is intentional of me – that is, if it can truly be said of me that, in moving my arm, I intentionally reached for the salt-cellar. An automatic blink of my eye is not an action of mine on this view, because it is not intentional of me under *any* description. An event which is intentional of me under one description may not be intentional of me under another description. For example, the event of my arm's moving may not be intentional of me under the description "displacing some molecules of air." Intentional and unintentional actions are not two different classes of action, on this view: *any* action will be intentional under some descriptions and not under others.

On this view, moreover, actions are events that are *caused by beliefs and desires* (or, more generally, "pro-attitudes") of the agent, which constitute the agent's *reasons* for performing them. For instance, my action of reaching for the salt-cellar was at least partly caused by, say, my desire that my food taste more salty and my belief that the salt-cellar was not empty. These beliefs and desires (or, more exactly, their "onsets") are mental events which, supposedly, are in principle identifiable with neural events in the agent's brain. In sum, as the famous Davidsonian slogan has it, *reasons are causes*.

We need, on many versions of this view, to distinguish between "normative" and "motivational" reasons for action – it is the *latter* that are supposedly causes of action, not the former. *Normative* reasons are sorts of things that may constitute the *propositional contents* of the beliefs and desires of agents and may in some sense "justify" their actions (hence the "normative" status of such reasons), whereas these beliefs and desires themselves are the sorts of things that may qualify as *motivational* reasons. (Supposedly, following Hume, a motivational reason must always at least *include* a desire, or "pro-attitude": belief *alone* is allegedly never sufficient to motivate action, or move the mind to act.) For example, *that the salt-cellar is not empty* might constitute at least part of a normative reason for me to reach for it (since I wouldn't perhaps be justified in reaching for it if it were empty), but it is only my *belief* that it is not empty that can help (along with some desire of mine) to *cause* my reaching for it and so contribute to my "motivational" reasons for so acting.

The next thing to focus on is what we may call *Davidson's "master argument" for the claim that reasons are causes* (Davidson 1980, 9–19). The argument takes as its starting point the following question. An agent may possess various different reasons for acting in a certain way on a given occasion (various different combinations of belief and desire), but what makes one of these *the* reason *for which* he actually *acts*? For instance, I may desire that my food taste more salty and also desire to show off my expensive new wristwatch, both of which desires could be satisfied by my reaching for the salt-cellar – but for which of these reasons did I *actually* reach for it? Davidson says: the only workable answer is that it was the desire that actually helped to *cause* my reaching that was (part of) my (motivational) reason for so acting. On this view, only in a *causal* sense of "because" does it make sense to say that I reached for the salt-cellar *because* I wanted my food to taste more salty, rather than because I wanted to show off my new watch. The reason that "moved" me so to act was the reason that *caused* me so to act, and this was (at least in part) my desire that my food taste more salty.

However, there is a notorious problem for the standard view: the problem of "deviant causal chains." This is well illustrated by Davidson's own famous example of the nervous climber (Davidson 1980, 79). An agent may, it seems, possess a reason for φing and be *caused* to φ by that reason (belief/desire complex), and yet not φ *intentionally*, and so *a fortiori* not φ *for that reason*. In the example, the climber strongly desires to let go of the rope supporting his colleague, because he fears for his own safety. At the same time, he strongly desires to save his colleague. However, he is "so unnerved" by the enormity of his desire to let go that *this desire causes him to let go*. And yet, contrary to what the "standard" theory seems to imply, we surely want and ought to say he lets go *unintentionally*. Spelling out "the right way" for a belief/desire complex to cause an action so as to render it intentional of the agent under the appropriate description has proved to be very difficult, and indeed I think that the task is an impossible one. This, in my view, is one of the most prominent symptoms of the inadequacy of the standard causal theory of rational action.

In sum, then, the standard view has in its favor its apparent ability to answer *Davidson's challenge* – what makes one of an agent's reasons *the* reason *for which* s/he acted? – but it has against it the problem of deviant causal chains. I would add that it also has against it, in my opinion, our strong intuition that our actions are at least sometimes *genuinely free*, in the sense of being *uncaused by prior events*, including (the onsets of) any of our own beliefs and desires. But I shall say more about that in the next section.

An Alternative "Libertarian" Account of Rational Action

I shall now set out a radically different view of rational human action, which differs from the "standard" causal view in almost every respect. According to this view, which I favor (Lowe 2008), most actions are *not* events; rather, they are *causings* of events by agents. For example, my action of raising my arm is my causing my arm to rise, or my bringing about the event of my arm's rising. On this view, *I* am a cause of what I do in such a case: an *agent*-cause and hence (since agents are "substances') a *substance*-cause. (By a "substance" I just mean a persisting bearer of properties which can survive changes in at least some of those properties – so that "substances" in this sense certainly include human persons.) On this view, moreover, an action is intentional only if it is *voluntary*, that is, only if the agent performs it *by* exercising his or her power of *volition* or *will*. An exercise of the will – an "act of will" – is a *volition* or *willing*. If I raise my arm *by willing to raise it*, then I raise it intentionally. (If, though, I raise my arm – that is, cause my arm to rise – by willing to do *something else* which just happens to cause my arm to rise, not knowing that this effect will ensue, then I do *not* raise my arm intentionally. For instance, if I am intentionally pulling on a rope but am unaware that my other arm is caught up in it, as a result of which my other arm is caused to rise, then although I do thereby *raise my other arm*, I do not do so intentionally.)

Volitions, according to this view, are mental episodes which are (1) *events* – not causings of events – but also *actions*, and (2) have intentional contents of a *non-propositional* kind (a volition is always a volition to φ, for some action-type φ). To say that volitions are not causings of events is not at all to deny that they cause events: it is just to deny that volition *consists in* the causing of some event, in the way that the action of raising an arm does (because it consists in the causing of an arm-rising). That volitions – unlike beliefs and desires – are not propositional attitudes is an important feature of the present view. It is most implausible to contend that an agent wills *that p*, for some proposition *p*, as opposed to saying that an agent *wills to* φ, for some action-type φ. For what, plausibly, could *p* be in any particular case? When I voluntarily raise my arm, can it plausibly be said that I will *that my arm rises*? No, because this makes willing no different from "wishful thinking." On the other hand, can it plausibly be said that I will *that I raise my arm*? Again, no: because this would imply, most implausibly, that human infants and higher primates – inasmuch as they very probably lack any first-person conception of themselves as agents and thinkers – would be incapable of willing. (Clearly, an agent could not will *that he himself* φ, without possessing a conception of *himself* as the prospective agent of the action φ.)

Volitions, on the present view, are completely *uncaused*. That is to say, exercises of the will are completely *spontaneous*. In this respect (only), they are like manifestations of the radioactive powers of decay possessed by some atoms. A radium atom has a power or capacity to undergo spontaneous radioactive decay: when it does decay, nothing whatever *causes* it to decay. (It is wrong even to say that such events have "probabilistic" causes. For, although there is indeed a certain objective probability that any given radium atom will decay within a specified period of time, this probability is fixed and perfectly insensitive to the atom's environmental conditions and even to such factors as the atom's *age*.)

Putative examples of an agent's being *caused* to will (or decide/choose) in such-and-such a way are misdescriptions, in my view. (I take "will," "decide," and "choose" to be synonyms for present purposes.) For instance, in certain so-called "Frankfurt-style cases" (Frankfurt 1988) – in which a neuroscientist is supposed to be able to *cause* an agent *A* to decide/choose to perform a certain action, if *A* doesn't "decide for herself" to do it – all that could really happen, were the neuroscientist to intervene, would be for *A*'s will to be entirely *bypassed*, not *activated*, by this other agent. (This verdict is to some extent borne out empirically by some of Wilder Penfield's famous experiments (Penfield 1958), in which conscious subjects being prepared for brain surgery felt that their limbs were being "made" to move in various ways, when implanted electrodes stimulated corresponding regions of their motor cortex: they resolutely denied, however, that *they themselves* were moving their limbs.) Frankfurt-style cases were invented, of course, in an attempt to show that an agent's moral responsibility for her actions does not require her to have an "ability to do otherwise." What I am saying, though, is that even if the imagined neuroscientist were able to make the agent behave *as if* she were φing, this could never be achieved by *making* the agent *will* to φ – and, hence, never by *making* the agent do the same as she *actually* does in deciding "for herself" to φ. Consequently, these invented cases cannot serve to show that an agent may φ *voluntarily* despite "lacking an ability to do otherwise," that is, despite having *no alternative* other than to φ voluntarily: for, in the intervention scenario, the agent would *not* be doing exactly the same as she was doing in the non-intervention scenario – she would *not* be φing voluntarily. Indeed, she would not really be *doing* anything at all. (This point is connected to the important fact, to be discussed in the section on responsiveness, below, that the will is distinctive in being a *two-way* power.)

There is, on the present view, no distinction to be drawn between "normative" and "motivational" reasons for action. *All* reasons for action are *normative* reasons. (Indeed, the notion of a reason is evidently an *essentially* normative notion, so it is mysterious how anyone could suppose that there could be *non*-normative reasons.) A *reason* (for an agent *A*) to φ is a *consideration* (fact, state of affairs, circumstance) which "speaks in favor of" (*A*'s) φing. (Note that reasons are thus *agent-relative*: what would be a reason for *A* to φ might not be a reason for *B* to φ. As for the expression "speak in favor of," this is just shorthand for the kind of *rational support* – which may, of course, be less than fully *conclusive* in many cases – that a reason supplies for an agent's acting in a certain way, and is best illustrated by means of concrete examples.) For instance, the fact that a falling roof-slate is about to hit my head is a reason for me to jump out of its way. Reasons, then, are "external', *worldly* items, not (in general) "internal" mental states of agents – although sometimes the fact *that* an agent has a certain mental state can be a reason for that agent to act in a certain way. For example, the fact that *A* believes that he is being pursued by Martians is (probably) a reason for *A* to seek psychiatric help. By contrast, the fact (if it is indeed a fact) that *A is* being pursued by Martians is a reason for *A* to take evasive action, by hiding or fleeing (compare Dancy 2000, 125). Of course, *A* cannot act *for* a certain reason unless *A* is at least *aware* of that reason, and this will normally involve *A's believing* that the state of affairs / circumstance which constitutes that reason does in fact obtain. For instance, only if I am *aware* that the slate is about to hit my head can I take evasive action by jumping out of its way *for that reason*. But it is *the fact that the slate is falling*, not my *awareness* of that fact, nor even *the fact that I am aware of it*, that is a reason for me to jump out of the way.

Something needs to be said at this point concerning *misinformed* action. If I merely *thought* that a slate was about hit my head and jumped out of the way on that account, when in reality I was in no such danger, would I be acting *rationally*? What I *took* to be my reason for so acting was, in this case, not any *actual* state of affairs or circumstance. So it might be said that, if reasons for action are indeed such "external" states of affairs or circumstances, then in this case I must have *acted for no reason*, since there *was* no reason for me to jump. Philosophers who maintain that reasons are *not* such "external" states of affairs or circumstances, but instead are "internal" *states of mind of the agent*, such as beliefs and desires, take comfort from such examples. But they are wrong to do so. The examples do not show that reasons are "internal" in this sense. It is *true* that, in the case just described, *there was no reason for me to jump*: that is precisely what I would and should say, on being informed that no slate was in fact falling. So it is *wrong* to say that I still jumped "for a reason," namely, for the reason that I *believed* that a slate was falling. My false belief gave me *no reason at all* to jump. However, although in this case *I jumped for no reason*, this is not to say that I acted *irrationally*, that is to say, in a manner which took no proper account of the sources of information available to me at the time. Taking proper account of such sources cannot require an agent to verify those sources beyond any possibility of error. The degree to which we should trust our sources of evidence when deciding how to act needs to be proportionate to, amongst other things, the timescale of our action. Timely action can often require a lower standard of evidence than action that can be pursued at leisure.

There is, incidentally, *another*, albeit closely related, notion of "internality" connected with the concept of a reason for action, which I would not want to reject altogether. (The "internal"–"external" *terminology* was introduced by Bernard Williams (1981), but its deployment in the literature on action is often confusing (for discussion, see Dancy 2000, 15–17). I do not intend my own usage to defer to that of any other author and hope that it is sufficiently clear in itself.) The fact that an opera is playing at the theater tonight might be a reason for *A* to buy a ticket, but not a reason for *B* to buy a ticket, because *A* but not *B likes opera*. Here, *A's desires* are a relevant factor. The *reason* for *A* to buy a ticket is an "external" state of affairs or circumstance, namely, the fact that an opera is playing. But that fact *constitutes* a reason for *A* to buy a ticket at least partly in virtue of *A's* liking for opera, which is clearly an "internal" mental state of *A's*. This is not to say, however, that *A's* desire to attend the opera tonight is *itself* (part of) a *reason* for *A* to buy a ticket. Furthermore, there are plenty of cases in which the reasons for an agent to φ on a given occasion obtain quite independently of any desires that the agent may have, and may even run quite contrary to the agent's desires. For instance, I have a *reason* to help a stranger in distress, however I might dislike the prospect of doing so. So it certainly isn't the case that all reasons for action are at least partly constituted as such by the desires of the agents for whom they are reasons.

One other important point that needs to be made is this, in connection with my opposition to the "standard" causal theory of rational action. *Sometimes*, to be sure, an agent's behavior is indeed caused by beliefs and desires of that agent – but I maintain that such behavior is never *rational*, at best only (what I would call) *reasonable*, precisely because it isn't initiated by a free (uncaused) *act of will* on the part of the agent, performed "in the light of" reasons for so acting of which the agent was aware. If I "automatically" or "instinctively" jump out of the way of a falling slate, being caused so to act by my beliefs and desires (perhaps only unconscious ones), then I may well be *behaving reasonably* (in my own best interests), but I am not *acting rationally*, since I didn't freely *choose* (will) so to act "in the light of" a reason for so acting of which I was aware, such as the fact that the slate was falling (and could cause me serious harm).

Responsiveness to Reasons

But *what is it* to act freely "in the light of" one or more reasons? And when an agent does so act, in virtue of what can we say that s/he acted *for a specific one of those reasons* rather than another? This, once more, is "Davidson's challenge." My answer to the second question is that the reason *for which* the agent acted is the reason that the agent *chose* to act upon – and hence that it is the agent him/herself who *makes* a certain reason *the* reason for which s/he acted (compare Searle 2001, chapter 3). We choose not only *how* to act (*what to do*), but also *on what/which reason* to act, when more than one reason presents itself. (Indeed, we also choose how to *weight* reasons, that is, how to assign them different degrees of importance or significance – and this is a matter of considered judgment, exercised when we deliberate about how to act.) But – it may be asked – doesn't this just push our question back a stage and so not really answer it? Mustn't we now say that an agent chooses a "first-order" reason to act upon "in the light of" various "second-order" reasons, favoring this or that "first-order" reason – and so on? Well, *sometimes* such further reflection on "higher-order" reasons may take place – and properly so, time permitting – but it obviously cannot do so with respect to *every* reason that an agent chooses, on pain of generating a vicious infinite regress. *Eventually*, in any process of deliberation that comes to an end and issues in action, a (finite) number of choices *must actually be made*. (Part of what constitutes good judgment where deliberation is concerned is *knowing when to stop!*) And these choices, by my account, will all be *entirely uncaused*. However, if the final choice to act in a certain way has in fact been made "in the light of" reasons reflected on by the agent, and the agent has chosen so to act for a chosen one of those reasons, the chosen action will thereby be *rational*, and in that respect quite unlike the spontaneous decay of a radium atom – it won't just be *random*, or a matter of *pure chance*. Or so I claim.

However, in order to be entitled to this answer, I need to be able to explain, *in a non-causal way*, what it is for an agent to be *responsive* to reasons, that is, to choose to act *for the sake of* a reason, and more specifically for the sake of a *particular* reason, R. It evidently isn't enough, for this purpose, just to point out that an agent can often *appreciate* or *acknowledge* that R is a good, or indeed an optimal, reason to φ and then *go on to φ*: for we can envisage an agent appreciating this and yet remaining "passive" – not φing. (It is at this point that the "standard" causal theory insists that we must insert a "motivating" reason to "get the agent to act," in the form of a desire or other "pro-attitude" – a "reason" which will *cause* the agent to φ.) However, that this is a real possibility – that the agent should be able to acknowledge the cogency of R and yet *not act on R* – *is precisely what we should expect* on a genuinely libertarian account of free action. For such an account admits that agents may exhibit genuine "weakness of will" or *akrasia* – something that, it seems clear, the "standard" causal theory cannot really allow for. (It cannot because, according to that theory, whenever the agent *acts*, his or her action is caused by a belief/desire complex which *by definition* includes the agent's "strongest" desire at the time. On this view, the reason that the agent *really* took to be "the best" or "most preferable" is the one that actually *caused* him or her to act, despite any protestations to the contrary that s/he might make *ex post facto*. For instance, if it was *actually* my desire to show off my new watch that caused me to reach for the salt-cellar, then *that* was in fact my strongest desire. So I couldn't, on this view, be described as doing what I didn't *really* most want to do, or acting for a reason that was for me less preferable at the time than some other reason that I had for acting in the same or another way. If I were to protest that I *really* took my desire that my food taste more salty to be the better reason for me to reach for the salt-cellar, but "succumbed" to what I took to be the less good reason, in the shape of my desire to show off my new watch, this would apparently make no sense on the "standard" view.)

So let us look more carefully at this important phenomenon of akrasia, which I shall continue to refer to by that technical term, since the phrase "weakness of will" is not entirely apposite for a theory like mine which emphasizes the autonomy of the will. (In cases of akrasia, I still want to say that agent exercises his or her will freely, not that it is somehow subordinated to an overpowering force, such as a strong desire, since on my view exercises of the will can never be *caused* to occur.) Akrasia in general arises when the agent can truly say, in the words of Ovid, *video meliora, proboque; deteriora sequor* – I see the better path and approve, but follow the worse. However, falling under the general case there are more specific cases to consider. Most interestingly, for our present purposes, in a case of (what I shall henceforth call) *extreme* akrasia, the agent A acknowledges that s/he had better φ, for reason R, and yet simply *declines* to choose to φ, and declines *for no reason*. (In non-extreme cases, A either does choose to φ, but for another reason S which A takes to be less good than R, or else chooses to do something else, ψ, for yet another reason T, again despite judging that the better choice would be to do φ for reason R. In all such non-extreme cases, A may still be described *as acting for a reason*, albeit for what A judges to be a *sub-optimal* reason.) However, *declining* to choose to φ is in fact still a *choice* on the part of A, not the mere *absence* of choice. For the will (as I conceive of it) is a *two-way* power to choose to act *or to refrain* from acting in any specific way available to the agent. In a case of extreme akrasia, the agent freely chooses *not* to φ, but does so *for no reason whatever*. Thus, akratic action of this kind is certainly not *rational* action (just as one would expect). But it is the very *possibility* of extreme akrasia, I suggest, that explains how rational action (as I conceive of it) can properly be described as action that is genuinely *responsive* to reasons, in a *non-causal* sense of "responsiveness." It is this idea that I now need to spell out more fully.

On my account, whenever an agent A *does* choose to φ *for* reason R, A not only freely chooses to φ but also freely chooses R as his/her reason for φing, and thereby φs *for* reason R. (This is our answer to "Davidson's challenge.") A's choice of R as his/her reason to φ reflects A's acknowledgement that R is indeed a (good) reason for A to φ – it reflects A's appreciation that R is indeed a consideration which "speaks in favor of" A's φing. By actually *choosing* to φ *for* reason R, A is "responding" to *that* reason, R. But nothing is *making* (causing) A so to respond, because A exercises this choice while fully retaining the *power* "to do otherwise" – to *refrain* from choosing to φ, and thus to choose *not* to φ, even *for no reason at all*. Because a free agent A always has it *within his/her power* to refrain, even for no reason at all, to act in a given way φ for a particular reason R, when A *does* in fact choose to φ for reason R, A thereby *manifests* his or her responsiveness to R – exhibits the fact that s/he is genuinely responding *to that reason for so acting*. If the only alternative to φing for reason R were to φ for *another* reason, S, or to act in another way, ψ, for yet another reason, T, then we might fairly be asked to explain what "made" the agent respond to one of these reasons *rather than another.* And simply to say that the agent freely *chose* one of them might seem merely to postpone the question. We need to be able to represent the agent as having *another* option *besides* responding to this or that reason, in order to make it clear in what way his or her responding to *any* reason can be something that s/he is genuinely *doing freely*, not being "made" to do. But, I claim, it is the constant availability of extreme akrasia that provides this needed "other option." Precisely because it is always *possible* for the agent simply to "say no" to any available course of action, *for no reason whatever*, when the agent freely *rejects* this option and follows the path of reason (*whichever* reason it might be), s/he thereby *evinces* or *demonstrates* his or her real power to *respond*, but *freely*, to the "call of reason." Reason does not and cannot *compel* the agent to respond, because the agent always retains the power to decline to follow *any* path that reason recommends.

Somewhat surprisingly, then, it is the very possibility of akratic, irrational choice that makes available and reveals a free agent's capacity to manifest a genuine *responsiveness* to reasons which is non-causal in character. The "standard" view's inability to accommodate genuine akrasia is, I believe, a deeply revealing symptom of its inability to confer upon agents a *genuine* responsiveness to reasons – an ability to act for reasons *for reason's sake*, rather than because the mind is *moved* (even by its own mental states) so to act.

To draw these matters to a conclusion, I now want to explain more fully why I think that no *causal* account of rational human choice and action can ever hope to capture the true nature of our genuine responsiveness to reasons – quite apart from the problem of deviant causal chains which afflicts such accounts. At bottom, the problem for all such accounts is that – to invoke a slogan of my own – *causation is "blind to reason."* I should emphasize that, most importantly, this is *not* the same as saying that causation is necessarily *insensitive to informational content.* After all, causally successive machine-states of a computer can exhibit such sensitivity, if the computer has been suitably "programmed." Thus, to take a very simple example, a computer can be programmed in such a way that a machine-state with the informational content p always causes a successor machine-state with the informational content q, where p entails q. However, such a causal sequence of machine-states cannot constitute a genuine *process of reasoning*: at best, it can merely *mimic* such a process. The "blindness to reason" of causation consists, rather, in the fact that a cause (an "*event*-cause," that is, as opposed to an *agent*-cause) never brings about its effect *in recognition of the cogency of reasons for doing so* – which is precisely what a genuinely rational agent must be able to do. For event-causes are tied to their effects purely by universal laws of succession. I have tried, however, to explain how the two-way power of will or choice gives agents precisely this needed capacity to respond to a reason *in recognition of its cogency as a reason.* In making an agent's responses to reasons genuinely free and autonomous, it makes them genuine responses to reasons qua *reasons*, as opposed to mere causally generated reactions to prior mental states of the agent – reactions which may be sensitive to the *informational contents* of those states but not to the *cogency* of the reasons "in the light of" which the agent acts.

The key point in all this is that *cogency* is an irreducibly *normative* notion and as such an *essentially contestable* notion. There is never an incontestably "right answer" to the question of whether or not the fact that p is a good reason for an agent A to φ. It is essentially a matter for rational debate and considered judgment. Consequently, no universal causal law of succession can properly connect *reasons* for action to *actions*. Only a free responsiveness to reasons qua reasons can do this, and can do so only on a case-by-case basis, each case depending on its merits as judged by rational agents. The implication of all this is that a wholly "naturalistic" account of rational human action is simply metaphysically impossible, if by such an account is meant one that appeals only to non-normative causal considerations, of a sort that may be accommodated by the physical sciences. If we insist that nothing other than a wholly naturalistic account is available, then we condemn ourselves to the status of *irrational* beings, incapable of displaying a genuine responsiveness to reasons. Hence, we could never *rationally* believe that we belong *wholly* to the natural, causal order, in the way that machines and lower forms of animal life do. For either we *do* belong wholly to that order, in which case we are not truly rational beings and are consequently incapable of rational belief, or else we do *not*, in which case to believe that we *do* belong wholly to it is radically mistaken and irrational.

References

Dancy, Jonathan. 2000. *Practical Reality*. Oxford: Oxford University Press.

Davidson, Donald. 1980. *Essays on Actions and Events*. Oxford: Clarendon Press.

Frankfurt, H. G. 1988. *The Importance of What We Care About: Philosophical Essays*. Cambridge: Cambridge University Press.

Hume, David. 1978. *A Treatise of Human Nature*. L. A. Selby-Bigge and P. H. Nidditch, eds. Oxford: Clarendon Press.

Lowe, E. J. 2008. *Personal Agency: The Metaphysics of Mind and Action*. Oxford: Oxford University Press.

Penfield, Wilder. 1958. *The Excitable Cortex in Conscious Man*. Liverpool: Liverpool University Press.

Searle, John R. 2001. *Rationality in Action*. Cambridge, MA: MIT Press.

Williams, Bernard. 1981. *Moral Luck: Philosophical Papers 1973–1980*. Cambridge: Cambridge University Press.

Further Reading

Ginet, Carl. 1990. *On Action*. Cambridge: Cambridge University Press. Deals with foundational issues of the theory of action, arguing for a volitional view.

Hornsby, Jennifer. 1980. *Actions*. London: Routledge & Kegan Paul. A seminal work in the field influenced by Davidson's work.

Kane, Robert, ed. 2002. *The Oxford Handbook of Free Will*. Oxford: Oxford University Press. A comprehensive reference to current scholarship on the problem of free will.

McCann, Hugh J. 1998. *The Works of Agency: On Human Action, Will, and Freedom*. Ithaca, NY: Cornell University Press. A collection of essays arguing for a non-causal theory of the relation between intentions and actions.

O'Connor, Timothy. 2000. *Persons and Causes: The Metaphysics of Free Will*. New York: Oxford University Press. Reworks the traditional account of free will as reasons-guided agent causation.

37

Science, Religion, and Infinity

GRAHAM OPPY

Oppy (2006) contains an extensive discussion of the understanding and application of a conception of the infinite that is fundamentally mathematical: questions about the mathematically infinite are questions about the cardinality of collections, or the divisibility of time and space, or about the magnitude of measurable properties, and so forth. But – following the discussion of Anaximander and other early philosophers – we might wonder whether the discussion of the mathematically infinite really does exhaust the discussion of the infinite. Is it the case that the concept of the infinite is, in all essentials, the concept of the mathematically infinite – or is it rather the case that the concept of the infinite is importantly ambiguous in such a way that we can also discern something that might properly be called a non-mathematical conception of the infinite? In order to address this question, I shall largely follow the lead of Sweeney (1992), which surveys the range of attributions of "infinity" to monotheistic gods.

Brief History

Etymologically, "infinite" comes from the Latin *infinitas*: "in" = "not" and "finis" = "end," "boundary," "limit," "termination," "determining factor," and so forth. So, to be "infinite" is to be not possessed of an end, or boundary, or limit, or termination, or determining factor. There are two Greek terms – *apeiria* and *aoristia* – that are at least sometimes translated using the word "infinite." Etymologically, to be "apeiria" is to be in the state of having no end, or limit, or boundary; whereas to be "aoristia" is to be without boundary, measure, decision, determination, and so forth. According to Sweeney's – perhaps controversial – interpretation, "apeiria" can signify either absence of determination and form, or presence of infinite power, whereas "aoristia" only signifies absence of determination because of absence of form.

The Blackwell Companion to Science and Christianity, First Edition. Edited by J. B. Stump and Alan G. Padgett.
© 2012 Blackwell Publishing Ltd. Published 2012 by Blackwell Publishing Ltd.

Anaximander

As just noted, the origins of our words "infinite" and "infinity" can be traced back to the Greek word *peras* (πέραος), which can be translated by "limit," or "bound," or "frontier," or "border," and which has connotations of being "clear" or "definite." The Greek *to apeiron* (ἄπειρον) – the "negation" or "opposite" of *peras* – thus can be understood to refer to that which is unlimited, or boundless, or – in some cases – unclear and indefinite.

When *to apeiron* makes its first significant recorded appearance – in the work of Anaximander of Miletus[1] – it is typically taken to be used to refer to "the boundless, imperishable, ultimate source of everything that is" (Moore 1998, 772). Thus, in this early usage, *to apeiron* has connotations – "imperishable," "ultimate source of everything" – that are quite separate – or, at any rate, separable – from considerations about the absence of "limits," or "bounds," or "frontiers," or "borders," or "clarity," or "definiteness."

As Moore points out, most of the Greeks associated much more negative connotations with *to apeiron* than are evident in the early usage of Anaximander: for the Pythagoreans, and – at least to some extent, for Plato – *to apeiron* "subsumed . . . all that was bad . . . it was the imposition of limits on the unlimited that accounted for all the numerically definite phenomena that surround us" (Moore 1998, 773). Again, on this kind of usage of the term, *to apeiron* has connotations – "chaotic," "irrational," "disorderly" – that are quite separate – or, at any rate, separable – from considerations about the absence of "limits," or "bounds," or "frontiers," or "borders," or "clarity," or "definiteness."

Aristotle

As with so many topics, the first systematic treatment of infinity that we have is found in Aristotle. There is discussion of the infinite in at least the following Aristotelian texts: *Physics* III, 4–8. 10; *Metaphysics* K, 10; *Metaphysics* L, 7; and *Concerning the Heavens* I, 5–7. Of these, the most important discussion is that in the *Physics*, where it seems that Aristotle divides that which can properly be said to be infinite into the following three categories: (i) that which is "intrinsically" "intraversable" – for example a point or a quality; (ii) that which is "intrinsically" "traversable," but in which the process of "traversal" is "extrinsically" or "metaphorically" "endless" – for example the depth of the sea or a journey to Alpha Centauri; and (iii) that which is "intrinsically" "traversable," and in which the process of "traversal" is itself "intrinsically "endless" either with respect to "addition" – for example the natural numbers – or with respect to "division" – for example a finite volume of space – or with respect to both "addition" and "division" – for example time. Of these three categories, it is really only the last that can properly be said to deserve the label "infinite" – and, as many commentators have stressed, in this case we have a mathematical and quantitative concept of the infinite. Indeed, if we eliminate "traversability" in favor of "measurability" – thus dispensing with the metaphor of travel in favor of the more abstract and precise notion of measure – and then eliminate the notion of "measurability" in favor of the notion of "being possessed of finite measure" – thus dispensing with the ambiguous modal notion (measurable by whom?) in favor of an unambiguous non-modal notion – we arrive at what is plausibly the generic modern conception of the infinite: *that which exceeds all finite measure.*

While it might be said that the analysis that Aristotle offers of the infinite is not very far removed from the generic modern conception of the infinite, there are conceptual associations that Aristotle makes in connection with the infinite that have a much more distant ring. As Sweeney notes, Aristotle associates finitude with intelligibility, actuality, and perfection, whereas he associates infinitude with unintelligibility, potentiality, imperfection, privation, and wholeness. According to Aristotle – at least on Sweeney's account – an infinite line is imperfect because it lacks endpoints, and hence can be neither measured nor described. Since Aristotle takes the Prime Mover to be perfect, he does not allow that it is infinite, though he does accept that the results of the exercise of the power of the Prime Mover – the rotations of the heavenly spheres – are infinite. If one says that the Prime Mover's power is infinite then, for Aristotle, one is not really providing an "intrinsic" description of that power, but rather saying something about what is brought about by the exercise of that power.[2]

Plotinus

Against Aristotle – according to Sweeney – Plotinus supposes that "form" and "being" are always "determining" or "terminating." Given that "matter" is "below" "form" and "being," it turns out that "matter" is "infinite" – "imperfect" and not "determined." On the other hand, the "One Itself" "transcends" "form" and "being" – and all other "forms" of "determination" – being both "infinite" and "perfect." While the "One Itself" – the head of the Neoplatonic scale of being – is conceptually distinct from familiar monotheistic gods, it shares with them the feature that there is claimed to be a sense in which it, itself, can properly be said to be "infinite." Of course, one might well be given to think that this conception of "the infinite" is only dubiously related to the key mathematical, quantitative concept that Aristotle analyzed, but, nonetheless, we clearly do have a long historical tradition of use of the label "infinite" to describe "that which exceeds all forms of determination."

Early Christian thinkers

According to Sweeney, Augustine, Pseudo-Dionysius, John Damascene, Gregory of Nyssa, and others from that era agreed that God is "infinite." By this, it seems that they mean that God is "all-powerful," "eternal," "immense," "incomprehensible," and – perhaps – "beyond being." Philo claims that God is "infinite" because "incomprehensible," "omnipotent," and "all-good." Augustine says that that which is incorporeal is both complete and infinite: complete because whole, yet infinite because not confined by spatial location. John Damascene says that Divinity is both infinite and incomprehensible – and that this alone is comprehensible of Divinity. Once again, these uses of the term "infinite" have very little relationship to the key mathematical quantitative concept that Aristotle analyzed.

Medieval scholasticism

According to Sweeney, little attention was paid to the notion of the infinite by Christian authors between the tenth century and the middle of the thirteenth century. Many theologians failed to mention the attribute at all; and those who did seem to have mentioned it only in connection with God's incomprehensibility, or eternity, or deeds, that is the results of the exercise of God's powers. Bonaventure, Aquinas, and other thinkers accepted Aristotle's account of quantitative infinity and agreed that there is one world that is finite in extent.

However, they also held that there is a conception of "infinity" that applies directly to God, but that is not Neoplatonic in its formulation. Thus, for example, while Aquinas accepts the claim that "forms" and "acts" are "determinative," he also holds that "matter" and "potency" are "determinative," and not merely "negations," or "privations," or "mental constructs," or the like. Anything that escapes the "determinations" imposed by "matter" and "potency" is properly said to be both "infinite" and "infinitely perfect." While the connection between "incorporeality" and "infinity" harks back to Augustine – and other early Christian thinkers – the connection between "actuality" – "absence of potency" – and "infinity" seems to be something new. Of course, there is a serious question about the intelligibility of the application of the description "without potency" – but we shall not be able to pursue that question here. On the account given by Aquinas, God is properly said to be "intrinsically" "infinite," because "essentially lacking in any kind of potentiality."[3]

Modernity

There has been a proliferation of conceptions of divine infinity since the beginnings of early modern philosophy. Sweeney notes that some philosophers – for example Spinoza – suppose that God is infinite because the underlying reality of all which otherwise is mere mode or manifestation. Sweeney also notes that other philosophers – for example Mill, James, and Whitehead – respond to Spinoza's contention that nothing other than God is real because nothing other than God is infinite, by insisting that God too is finite, and, in that way, allowing that there are really things other than God. Moving beyond Sweeney's account, it seems to me to be plausible to add that, in more recent times, there has been an increasing willingness, on the part of monotheistic philosophers and theologians, to suppose that at least some of the divine attributes are properly to be understood in terms of a quantitative, mathematical conception of the infinite. Thus, for example, there are philosophers – such as Swinburne (1977) – who suppose that it is quite proper to describe God's knowledge as infinite because God knows infinitely many true propositions; and who suppose that it is quite proper to describe God's power as infinite because there are infinitely many actions that God could perform; and who suppose that it is quite proper to describe God's eternity as infinite because it endures for an infinite amount of time; and so forth. It is well known that Cantor's development of transfinite arithmetic had theological motivations (see Dauben 1990), and that there are many subsequent philosophers and theologians who have supposed that there are respects in which God is actually mathematically infinite.

How We Talk

In current English, we have the adjective "infinite," the noun "infinity," and the substantive "the infinite." The standard use of the substantive form is "as a designation of the Deity or the absolute Being"; and so, of course, there is one standard use of the adjectival and noun forms that rides piggyback upon this standard use of the substantive form. It seems to me that it is plausible to see the current use of the substantive "the Infinite" as a direct descendant of Anaximander's use of *to apeiron* with more or less the same connotations – "imperishable," "ultimate source of everything" – except, of course, that *to apeiron* is personalized, that is, taken to have personal attributes and attitudes, in Christian theology.[4]

However, in current English, we also have uses of the adjective and noun forms that are not obviously related to the standard use of the substantive form. In particular, there are uses of these terms in mathematics, including geometry, and applications of these terms to space and time, in which most of the connotations associated with the substantive form seem to play no role at all. While these uses of the term do have more or less clear connections to the absence of "limits," or "bounds," or "frontiers," or "borders," they have very little to do with considerations about the absence of "clarity" or "distinctness," and nothing at all to do with considerations about "the ultimate, imperishable, source of everything."

It is not clear to me whether this separation of considerations was achieved by the Pythagoreans. Given their metaphysical belief that the positive integers are the ultimate constituents of the world, it is a plausible conjecture that they did not recognize the discussion of "limits," or "bounds," or "frontiers," or "borders" – and the application of these terms to, say, space and time – as a separate topic for investigation in its own right. But, whatever the truth about this matter may be, it seems that some of the contemporaries and immediate successors of the Pythagoreans *did* come to see the discussion of these topics as an independent subject matter. It is, I think, plausible to view Zeno's paradoxes as a contribution to such a discussion; and, even if that is not so, it is surely right – as I suggested above – to see Aristotle's treatment of infinity as an investigation of "limits" and "bounds" – in the context of space, time, and matter – in their own right. (In *Physics*, book III, Aristotle makes mention of Anaximander's views about "the ultimate source of everything." But those views are entirely incidental to the theory of "limits" and "bounds" that Aristotle proceeds to elaborate and defend.)

However, once it is recognized that the investigation of "limits" and "bounds" – in the context of space, time, and matter – is a legitimate subject matter in its own right, then various questions arise about the application of the results of *that* investigation to the subject matter with which Anaximander was primarily concerned: "the ultimate source of everything." Even if it is true – as I think it is – that the historical entanglement of talk about "limits" and "bounds" with talk about "the ultimate source of everything" persists into the present, it is important to ask whether this entanglement has any *essential* significance for either the investigation of "limits" and "bounds" as a subject matter in its own right, or for the investigation of "the ultimate source of everything" (as a subject matter in its own right). As I mentioned initially, we might well suspect that there is one conception of "the infinite" that is appropriate to mathematics and science; and a quite different conception of "the infinite" that is appropriate to theology – and, if that is right, we might also suspect that considerations about "the infinite" will hold little genuine interest for those who are interested in interactions between scientific and theological investigations.

Science and Infinity

Infinity is ubiquitous in classical mathematics. Classical set theory – which many suppose is foundational for classical mathematics – is committed to a mind-boggling infinite hierarchy of sets;[5] classical analysis – which is one of the fundamental tools in most applications of mathematics to science – is committed to an uncountable infinity of real numbers; classical geometries are committed to manifolds of uncountably many points; and so on.

Classical mathematics is ubiquitous in contemporary science. For example, classical analysis is a standard tool in all theoretical branches of physics and chemistry, and in all fields in which there are applications of physical and chemical theories: experimental physics, experimental chemistry, cosmology, astronomy, meteorology, geology, paleontology, engineering, electronics, computing, communications, systems analysis, and so forth.

Should we then conclude that infinity is ubiquitous in contemporary science? Certainly not immediately. First, classical mathematics is not accepted universally: there are finitists, intuitionists, and constructivists who oppose classical mathematics on philosophical grounds, primarily because of its commitments to the infinite. Second, it is not universally accepted that use of classical mathematics incurs ontological and theoretical commitments: for instance, fictionalists insist that we should treat all mathematics as useful fiction, hence not as reality-limning theory that brings with it commitment to infinite domains of entities. Third, it is not universally accepted that there are *ineliminable* uses of classical mathematics in practical applications of theoretical science: perhaps, for example, differential equations are useful only as approximations to difference equations, whose exact solutions would belong to merely finite mathematics. Fourth, even if it is granted that there are ineliminable uses of classical mathematics in practical applications of theoretical science, it is not universally accepted that there are cases in which commitment to real infinities emerge: it is not universally accepted, for example, that just because we model space-time with classical manifolds, it immediately follows that we are committed to the infinite divisibility of space-time.

Setting the foregoing considerations aside, we can ask directly whether there are cases in contemporary science in which there is assignment of infinite values to physical quantities. Perhaps surprisingly, the answer to this question is "Yes!" For example, on the standard Kelvin absolute temperature scale, there are systems in which infinite temperatures are actually attained –for example there are states of nuclear spins of lithium ions in lithium fluoride crystals that have temperature $\pm\infty$ on the standard Kelvin absolute temperature scale (Oppy 2006, 133–136). However, this fact does not reflect a deep feature of the physical world: it is merely a matter of convenience that we continue to use the Kelvin absolute temperature scale when we could operate with an equally acceptable temperature scale on which there are no assignments of infinite temperatures to actual physical systems.

Taking account of this kind of case, we might refine our original question: are there cases in contemporary science in which there is assignment of ineliminable infinite values to physical quantities (i.e., assignments of infinite values to physical quantities that cannot be eliminated by reparamaterization, renormalization, or the like)? I think that the answer to this question is "No!" Of course, there are cases in which very good scientific theories produce models in which there are ineliminable infinities. In the 1960s, Hawking and Penrose established that there are generic essential singularities in general relativistic space-times: there are ineliminable infinite values in standard general relativistic models of the universe (Oppy 2006, 128–131). However, the standard response to this observation amongst working cosmologists is that we know that general relativistic models of the universe are inadequate – and, in particular, that they are inadequate at precisely the places where the ineliminable infinities arise. (Why so? Because the ineliminable infinities arise where quantum considerations should dominate – and yet there is no taking account of quantum considerations in general relativistic models.)

Can we infer from the treatment of singularities in general relativistic space-times that there is no place for ineliminable infinities in contemporary science? I don't think so. While it is true that, for example, cosmologists do take the view that the presence of singularities in their cosmological models points to inadequacies in the models (rather than to the presence of genuine infinities in the world), there are other kinds of infinities about which cosmologists remain undecided and open-minded. Does the universe have an infinite spatial volume? Does the universe contain an infinite amount of mass-energy? Are there infinitely many universes? Does causal reality have an infinite past? Unless we are prepared to accept *a priori* philosophical answers to these kinds of questions, the most that we can say is that we can place lower bounds on some of the quantities that are here under discussion: we know that the universe is at least *so* big; and we know that there is at least *so much* mass-energy in the universe. And, in other cases, the best that we can say is that the questions remain controversial: some cosmologists incline towards infinitely many universes and/or an infinite causal past; some cosmologists do not.

This quick tour of science and infinity may seem disappointingly inconclusive to some. However, there are a couple of definite concluding observations that we can make. First, to the extent that there are genuine open scientific questions about the application of the concept of infinity to the world, those questions concern the finite measurability of features of the world. (How big? How old? How many stars? And so forth.) And, second, the other associations that are sometimes picked up by the word "infinity" and its cognates have nothing at all to do with contemporary science. Science is not in the business of speculating about "the ultimate source of everything," or the "imperishable foundations of the perishable," or the like. Nor is it in the business of speculating about "irrational," or "disorderly," or "chaotic," or "unclear," or "indefinite" elements of reality that lie "beneath" or "beyond" the physical universe that we inhabit.[6]

Religion and Infinity

Our initial examination of the etymology (and current use) of the word "infinity" and its cognates revealed three rather different sets of connotations. First, "infinity" is associated with the denial of ends, limits, boundaries, borders, frontiers, measures, and so on: the infinite is unending, unlimited, unbounded, immeasurable, and so forth. Second, "infinity" is – or, at any rate, has been – associated with the denial of determination, form, clarity, definition, decision, and so on: the infinite is unclear, indefinite, indeterminate, unformed, undecided, and so forth. Third "infinity" is – at least in some places, at some times – associated with permanence, imperishability, and the ultimate source or ground or origin of everything else.

We can see reflections of all of these sets of connotations in religious talk about divine infinity – and, indeed, in Christian talk about God's infinity. First, we may be told that the divine is temporally unending (eternal or sempiternal), unlimited in knowledge and power, unbounded in goodness and compassion, and so forth. Second, we may be told that the divine exceeds human comprehension, can only be described or thought of in terms of what it is not, and so on. Third, we may be told that the divine is permanent, imperishable, and the ultimate source, or ground, or origin of everything else.

Some may object that there is a cheat in the accounting that has just been made. On the one hand, from the standpoint of ontology and metaphysics, it may be deemed acceptable to say that the divine is temporally unending (eternal or sempiternal), unlimited in knowledge and power, unbounded in goodness and compassion, and so forth; it may also seem acceptable to say that the divine is permanent, imperishable, and the ultimate source, or ground, or origin of everything else. But, from this ontological or metaphysical standpoint, it may well be deemed unacceptable to say that the divine is unclear, indefinite, indeterminate, unformed, undecided, and so forth. On the other hand, from the standpoint of epistemology, it may be deemed acceptable to say that the divine is unclear, indefinite, indeterminate, unformed, undecided, and so forth, provided that this is understood to be an expression of the thought that the divine exceeds human comprehension, can only be described or thought of in terms of what it is not, and so on – but, in that case, there is at least *prima facie* reason to be suspicious of the claim that it is acceptable to say that the divine is temporally unending (eternal or sempiternal), unlimited in knowledge and power, unbounded in goodness and compassion, and so forth; and there may also be at least *prima facie* reason to be suspicious of the claim that it is acceptable to say that the divine is permanent, imperishable, and the ultimate source, or ground, or origin of everything else.

There is considerable diversity of opinion concerning the extent to which we can make true assertions about the attributes of divinity. Some say that we can make no true assertions about divinity. Some say that we can make no true *literal* assertions about the attributes of divinity: while we can make true assertions about divinity, those true assertions can only be metaphorical, or figural, or the like. Some say that can make no true *positive* assertions about divinity: we can only truly say what divinity is not, but we cannot truly say what divinity is. Some say that we can make no true literal positive assertions about the attributes of divinity: we can only truly literally say what divinity is not, but we cannot truly literally say what divinity is (though we can make true positive assertions about the attributes of divinity, so long as those assertions are metaphorical, or figurative, or the like).

How we respond to the accusation that our prior accounting of talk about "infinity" involved cheating depends, at least in part, upon the stance that we take on these questions about the possibility of true, positive, literal claims about divinity.

If we suppose that we can make true, literal, positive assertions about the attributes of divinity – and, in particular, if we suppose that we can truly, literally, say that the divine is temporally unending (eternal or sempiternal), unlimited in knowledge and power, unbounded in goodness and compassion, permanent, imperishable, the ultimate source, or ground, or origin of everything else, and so forth – then, I think, we ought simply to deny that the divine is unclear, indefinite, indeterminate, unformed, undecided, and so on. Moreover, if we take this line, we are free to go on to say that, in some respects, the divine is infinite in the standard, mathematical sense: perhaps, for example, the collection of propositions that is known by the divine exceeds all finite measure; and, perhaps, the range of actions that could be carried out by the divine exceeds all finite measure; and so forth.

However, if we suppose that we can *only* truly say what the divine is not, then it seems to me that, while we are then obliged to say that the divine is not clear, and not definite, and not determinate, and not formed, and not decided, and so on, we are also then obliged to say that the divine is not unending, and not unlimited in knowledge and power, and not unbounded in goodness and compassion, not permanent, not imperishable, and not the ultimate source, or ground, or origin of everything else. Moreover, if we take this line, then we can go on only to say that the divine is not finite; but we cannot insist that the divine is infinite in the standard, mathematical sense. For to say that the divine exceeds all finite measure (in some respect or other) surely would be to say something about what the divine is, not merely what it is not.

Of course, there are many intermediate positions here – between the view that says that we can make a wide range of true, literal, positive assertions about the attributes of the divine, and the view that says that we can only truly say what the divine is not – but the important point to which I wish to draw attention is the significance of the distinction between the infinite and the non-finite for all of the positions in the range. It is one thing to say that something is non-finite – that is, to say that something does not have a finite measure; it is quite another thing to say that something is infinite – that is, to say that it exceeds all finite measure. Something can be non-finite because it is a kind of thing to which the concept of measure has no application; however, something can only be infinite – in the standard, mathematical sense – if it is the kind of thing to which the concept of measure has application.

We can make sense of the idea that the universe is infinite in extent because (i) we have a measure concept that applies to finite volumes, and (ii) we can then form the concept of a volume that exceeds all finite measure. Correspondingly, we can make sense of the idea that the divine is infinite – in the standard, mathematical sense – with respect to an attribute F, provided that (i) we have a measure concept that applies to the attribute F, and (ii) we can make sense of the idea that the divine possesses the attribute F in a manner that exceeds all finite measure. So, for example, if we suppose that amount of knowledge can be measured by number of propositions known, then we can make sense of the idea that the divine has infinite knowledge by supposing that there are infinitely many propositions that are known to the divine.

Those who are inclined to look favorably on the view that we can only truly say what the divine is *not* are often also inclined to look favorably on the view that the divine and the mundane have no features in common: there are no properties that are shared by the divine and the mundane. Some who take this kind of view may go so far as to say that God does not have knowledge in the same sense that human beings do; and perhaps those people will then go on to deny that God has infinite knowledge in the sense explained in the previous paragraph. (It may be true that one human being is more knowledgeable than a second if that first knows more propositions than the second; but it is not true that God knows more than human beings because God knows more propositions than human beings do.) Of course, someone who takes this line will deny that God has finite knowledge; but that denial does not amount to an acceptance of the claim that God has infinite knowledge, on the standard mathematical account of the infinite.

I am inclined to think that it is incoherent to suppose that one can only truly say what the divine is not; and I am inclined to think that there is a range of opinion at that end of my scale that is also incoherent.[7] However, for the purposes of the present chapter, it does not matter whether these suspicions of mine are well founded. The significant point that emerges from the preceding discussion is that there is considerable complexity involved in the proper interpretation of *literal* religious talk about divine infinity. Some literal talk about divine "infinity" will clearly be properly interpreted as talk about divine non-finitude: the divine is not limited, not bounded, not terminating, not ending, and so forth. Some literal talk about divine "infinity" is properly interpreted as talk about divine infinitude: the divine possesses knowledge that exceeds all finite measure; the divine possesses power that exceeds all finite measure; the divine possesses goodness that exceeds all finite measure; the divine possesses compassion that exceeds all finite measure; and so on. And some literal talk about divine "infinity" is properly interpreted as talk that really has no direct connection to either finitude or infinitude: the divine is imperishable, unchanging, the ultimate source of everything else, and so forth.[8] Whenever we come across talk about divine "infinity," we need to think carefully about the proper interpretation to put upon that talk.

Concluding Remarks

Given the preceding accounts of the role of the concept of the infinite in contemporary science, and the various ways in which talk about divine infinity can be properly interpreted, we can fairly quickly conclude that the suspicions I aired at the beginning of this chapter are largely borne out. Over time, the standard mathematical concept of the infinite has emerged as one refinement of the notion of the non-finite. As that refinement has taken place, there has been some take-up of the standard mathematical concept of the infinite in talk about the divine; but there has also been continued use of the notion of the non-finite in that talk. To the extent that talk about divine infinity is merely talk about the non-finitude of the divine – or talk about the permanence, and so on of the divine – that talk does not even share sense with scientific conceptions of infinity (and so there is not even the possibility that conflict or cooperation between science and religion might emerge at that point). However, to the extent that talk about divine infinity is talk about the infinity of the divine (in the standard mathematical sense), such talk does at least share sense with scientific conceptions of infinity. But, even if this at least leaves open the possibility that conflict or cooperation between science and religion might emerge at this point, it seems rather implausible to suppose that considerations about infinity could be a significant locus of either conflict or cooperation between science and religion.

Notes

1   Anaximander's account of his first principle is reported in Plato's *Philebus* (16C, 23C), and Aristotle's *Metaphysics* (987a15–19).

2   One might well wonder whether it is really possible to make sense of the distinction between "intrinsic" and "extrinsic" characterizations of powers. However, I shall not attempt to explore this question here.

3   According to Sweeney (1992), no one prior to Richard Fishacre gives any evidence of having supposed that a monotheistic god could be "intrinsically" infinite – that is, roughly, not merely infinite in its relations to other entities, but infinite "in itself." Moreover, according to Sweeney (1992), it is not until Aquinas observes that "matter or potency determines form" – because "matter or potency limits the perfection of form" – no less than "form determines matter or potency" – because "form confers perfection on matter or potency" – that any philosopher or theologian arrives at a clear understanding of how it can be that a monotheistic god is "intrinsically" infinite. For Aquinas, according to Sweeney (1992), it is *because* a monotheistic god has no matter or potency that it can properly be said to be "intrinsically infinite": it is not "limited" or "determined" by "matter or potency." I think that one might well doubt whether the categories to which Sweeney here appeals – "matter," "form," "potency," "act," "determination," "limit" – are suitable to the kind of fundamental inquiry that metaphysicians pursue; however, I won't try to argue for this suspicion here.

4   Of course, most, if not all, Christian theology *repudiates* other connotations that many of Anaximander's contemporaries associated with the term: "chaotic," "irrational," "disorderly," and so forth. I think that there are the raw materials for an interesting investigation in the history of ideas here. The early philosophers were, I think, mostly disposed to view "ultimate" reality as a mixture of "good" and "evil" (or "chaos" and "order," or the like). An advantage of this view is that it seems to comport well with observation: the world is mixed, so it is natural to suppose that "ultimate" reality is also mixed. On the other hand, Christianity teaches that "ultimate" reality is unalloyed "good" (or "order," or the like). An advantage of this view is that it seems to comport well with what we would like: it would be better if "ultimate" reality were not mixed. I think that it would be very interesting to trace out the history of ideas here, to try to establish how and why the Christian view came to be widely accepted.

5   See, for example, Devlin (1990) and Rucker (1982). And, for an introduction to an alternative way of thinking about the foundations of the theory of numbers, see Conway (1976).

6   For further discussion of the role of infinity in science, see, for example, Barrow (2005) and Gamow
    (1946).
7   For some arguments in support of the position that I announce here, see Oppy (2011).
8   Of course, there are similar points to make about non-literal – metaphorical, figurative – talk about
    divine "infinity"; but we don't have time and space to set out the details here.

References

Barrow, J. 2005. *The Infinite Book*. London: Vintage.

Conway, J. 1976. *On Numbers and Games*. London: Academic.

Dauben, J. 1990. *Georg Cantor: His Mathematics and Philosophy of the Infinite*. Princeton: Princeton University Press.

Devlin, K. 1991. *The Joy of Sets*. Berlin: Springer.

Gamow, G. 1946. *1, 2, 3 . . . Infinity*. London: Macmillan.

Moore, A. W. 1998. Infinity. In E. Craig, ed. *The Routledge Encyclopaedia of Philosophy*. London: Routledge.

Oppy, G. 2006. *Philosophical Perspectives on Infinity*. Cambridge: Cambridge University Press.

Oppy, G. 2011. God and Infinity: Directions for Future Research. In M. Heller and H. Woodin, eds. *Infinity: New Research Frontiers*. Cambridge: Cambridge University Press, pp. 233–254.

Rucker, R. 1982. *Infinity and the Mind*. Hassocks, Sussex: Harvester.

Sweeney, L. 1992. *Divine Infinity in Greek and Medieval Thought*. New York: Peter Lang.

Further Reading

Benardete, J. 1964. *Infinity: An Essay in Metaphysics*. Oxford: Clarendon Press. A brilliant, unfairly neglected work: contains seeds for almost all recent philosophical discussion of infinity.

Maor, E. 1991. *To Infinity and Beyond: A Cultural History of the Infinite*. Princeton: Princeton University Press. A lovely account of mathematical fascination with infinity.

Moore, A. W. 1990. *The Infinite*. London: Routledge. An excellent introduction to Western thought about infinity – a great place to start.

Vilenkin, N. 1995. *In Search of Infinity*. Berlin: Springer. A useful introduction to mathematical and scientific thinking about the infinite.

Woodin, H. and Heller, M., eds. 2011. *Infinity: New Research Frontiers*. Cambridge: Cambridge University Press. A more advanced interdisciplinary study of infinity, with contributions from mathematics, physics, cosmology, philosophy, and theology.

38

God and Abstract Objects

WILLIAM LANE CRAIG

To the uninitiated, platonism, science, and Christianity might seem poles apart. Neither the average scientist nor the average Christian, after all, finds abstract objects relevant to his quotidian affairs. Appearances are in this case deceptive, however, for the principal argument for platonism today is that physical science requires the existence of abstract objects. This claim in itself demands careful scrutiny, since the very truth of science is at stake. But the importance of the issue is amplified for Christian theists because platonism is at the same time potentially a dagger in the heart of the Christian doctrines of divine aseity and *creatio ex nihilo*. In this chapter I shall first briefly introduce platonism and the argument for the reality of abstract objects based on their scientific indispensability; then I shall consider a series of responses that can be made to this argument, and close with what I take to be a serious theological objection to platonism.

Platonism

What is platonism? Platonism is the ontological thesis there exist mind-independent, abstract entities. This characterization raises the question of what it means to be abstract. Metaphysicians take the distinction between concrete and abstract to be exclusive and exhaustive and typically provide paradigm examples of each kind of object: if such things exist at all, people, electrons, mermaids, and planets would be concrete objects, whereas mathematical objects (like numbers, sets, and functions), properties, and propositions would be abstract objects. Can we say something more about the definitive characteristics of an abstract object? It is frequently asserted that concrete objects just are spatio-temporal objects and that therefore any existing entity which is not spatio-temporal is an abstract object. But this cannot be right, for God, if he exists, is usually taken to transcend space and time and yet is a paradigm example of a concrete object, being a personal agent who effects things in the world. Perhaps that provides a clue to distinguishing between concrete and abstract entities. It is virtually

The Blackwell Companion to Science and Christianity, First Edition. Edited by J. B. Stump and Alan G. Padgett.
© 2012 Blackwell Publishing Ltd. Published 2012 by Blackwell Publishing Ltd.

universally agreed that abstract objects, if they exist, are causally impotent, that is to say, they do not stand in cause–effect relations. Numbers, for example, do not cause anything. More than that, their causal impotence seems to be an essential feature of abstract objects. The number seven, for example, does not just happen to lack all causal effects; there is no possible world in which seven could effect something. Their essential causal impotence serves to distinguish abstract objects from any entities which just happen to be causally isolated in the world, but which could have had effects, and from God, who could have refrained from creating and so could have stood in no causal relations.

Our characterization of platonism also raises the question of what it means to be mind-independent. Mind-independence serves to distinguish platonism from conceptualism, which ascribes to *abstracta* a sort of ideal existence only. Intuitively, one would like to say that mind-independent objects are those that would still exist even if there were no minds. But in a theistic context, it is metaphysically impossible that no minds exist, since God exists necessarily. Even if we allow counterfactuals with impossible antecedents to have non-trivial truth values, it avails us nothing, for the distinction between mind-dependent and mind-independent objects then collapses, since in the absence of God, nothing would exist. Even objects normally taken to be mind-independent, like physical objects, turn out to be mind-dependent. When the platonist ascribes mind-independence to abstract objects, he means that such objects exist as entities in the external world. They are not just the contents of consciousness, either of human or of divine minds. Even if the products of divine intellectual activity, they nonetheless exist *extra Deum*. They are objects existing in the world, even if not in the spatio-temporal realm.

I think it is fair to say that it is hard to believe that such queer objects really exist. Indeed, even many would-be platonists embrace what has aptly been called a "lightweight platonism" which looks suspiciously very much like conceptualism or even nominalism (see Linnebo 2009; Craig 2011). They admit that abstract objects are not objects in the ordinary sense of the word but just in the sense that they are the referents of certain abstract singular terms. On this view it would seem fair to say that Wednesday, for example, is an object, since it may be referred to in true sentences like "Today is Wednesday." If abstract objects have no more reality than Wednesdays, then the affirmation that they exist may have no significance for ontology.

The Indispensability Argument for Platonism

So why should we go beyond lightweight platonism and affirm the existence of objects so strange as abstract objects? The answer given by contemporary platonists is that the truth of our best scientific theories demands it. Reference to and quantification over abstract objects, particularly mathematical objects, is simply indispensable to natural science, and therefore the truth of those theories requires that the abstract objects referred to and quantified over exist. The truth of mathematical statements, at least those that find application in scientific theories, is guaranteed by the truth of those theories. Customary semantics requires that if singular terms (like names, definite descriptions, and demonstrative expressions) fail to refer to any object and if quantifying expressions like "all" or "some" do not appropriately delimit the range of objects to which the predicate is ascribed, then the sentences containing such expressions cannot be true. Since the mathematical sentences comprised by our best scientific theories are true, it follows that the objects referred to and quantified over must exist. Anyone who regards scientific theories as true must therefore be a platonist.

What might be said in response to the Indispensability Argument? Both of its central claims have been vigorously challenged.

Challenge to the Truth of Mathematical Statements: Fictionalism

Consider first challenges to the truth of sentences referring to or quantifying over abstract objects. Fictionalists accept the customary semantics and so agree that such sentences cannot be true unless abstract objects exist. Since abstract objects do not exist, it follows that the sentences in question cannot be true. Fictionalism treats abstract objects as more or less useful fictions. Sentences referring to or quantifying over abstract objects are akin to statements of fictional discourse. Just as "Hamlet was a Danish prince" is not true because the name "Hamlet" fails to refer to an object, so "2 + 2 = 4" is not true because there are no objects which are the referents of the names "2 + 2" and "4." What can be truly said is that according to Shakespeare's play Hamlet was a Danish prince, so that we may characterize the statement "Hamlet was a Danish prince" as fictionally true. Analogously, mathematical sentences, while not literally true, can be said to be fictionally true, for example, 2 + 2 = 4 according to the standard model for arithmetic based on the Peano Axioms.

In dealing with the Indispensability Argument, there are two routes open to the Fictionalist. One route, taken by Hartry Field, is to challenge the assumption that mathematics is indispensable for science and to provide a nominalized science in its place. Field adopts a paraphrastic strategy for rewriting scientific theories so that no reference to or quantification over mathematical objects occurs. The second route, adopted by Mark Balaguer (1998), is to admit that reference to mathematical entities cannot be paraphrased away but to maintain that however indispensable mathematics may be for scientific practice, it contributes nothing of content to our knowledge of the world. Although Balaguer disagrees with the consensus view that Field's nominalization program is a failure, he nevertheless prefers to concede that mathematics is inextricably woven into empirical science and to maintain that while the nominalistic content of empirical science is for the most part true, its platonistic content is fictional. If, *per impossibile*, all the abstract objects in the mathematical realm were to disappear, there would be, given their causal isolation, no impact whatsoever on the physical world. Therefore, even if all mathematical objects did not exist, the nominalistic content of science would remain true. The platonistic content of science is something that science says incidentally in its effort to say what it really wants to say, namely, what is contained in its nominalistic content. On Fictionalism, then, scientific theories containing mathematical sentences are literally false.

Challenges to the Customary Semantics
for Mathematical Discourse

Fictionalists accept the customary semantics for singular terms and existential quantification. More fundamental challenges to the Indispensability Argument call into question the customary semantics which it presupposes. One form of this challenge is to accept the customary semantics for non-mathematical discourse but to provide a different semantics for mathematical discourse.

Constructibilism

For example, Charles Chihara (1990) has developed a semantics for mathematical statements called Constructibilism which preserves the truth of mathematical statements without committing us ontologically to mathematical objects. This is achieved by rewriting ordinary Zermelo–Fraenkel set theory by replacing the existential quantifier with what Chihara calls a constructibility quantifier, so that existence claims are replaced by claims about what is constructible. The primitive constructibility quantifier Cx is to be understood as asserting, "It is possible to construct an x such that . . ." What is constructible on Chihara's theory are certain open sentence tokens, that is to say, sentence tokens containing unbound variables, and assertions of set membership are rewritten as assertions about some individual's satisfying an open sentence. Chihara does not claim that his semantics represents how mathematicians actually understand their language or that it should replace standard mathematical language but claims merely that it shows how mathematical statements may be regarded as true without any commitment to abstract objects.

Deductivism

A second proposed nominalistic semantics for mathematical sentences is counterfactual If–Then-ism or Deductivism. Traditional Deductivism interpreted mathematical statements to be disguised conditionals to the effect that if certain axioms are true, then certain theorems are true. So "$2 + 2 = 4$" is the assertion that if the Peano Axioms are true, then $2 + 2 = 4$. The problem with this view is that on Nominalism the Peano Axioms are in fact false, given their existence assertions about mathematical objects, and so the statements of arithmetic are vacuously true. It is on this view equally vacuously true that "$2 + 2 = 5$," since that claim is also materially implied by the false antecedent of the conditional. This problem can be solved, however, by interpreting the relevant conditionals not as material implications but as counterfactual conditionals to the effect that if the Peano Axioms were true, then the theorems of standard mathematics would be true. Since counterfactuals are not truth functional, there is no implication that if the Peano Axioms were true, then would it would be the case that $2 + 2 = 5$. Geoffrey Hellman's Modal Structuralism (1989) would appear to be a variation on this approach. Hellman takes arithmetic statements like $2 + 2 = 4$ to be statements about possible structures to the effect that if a certain structure were to exist, then it would be the case, say, that the object in the position named "$2 + 2$" in that structure is the object in the fourth place in that structure. Counterfactual Deductivism need not commit one to the contingency of mathematical objects and their existence in some possible world if one is willing to countenance non-trivial counterfactuals with impossible antecedents, as seems plausible.

Figuralism

Finally, a third proposal for a semantics of abstract object talk is Figuralism. Stephen Yablo (2000) is impressed with the similarities between abstract object talk and figurative talk such as we find in understatement, hyperbole, metonymy, and metaphor. An assertion like "It's raining cats and dogs!" is literally false, but to stop there is to miss the whole point of such language. When a speaker uses figurative language, the literal content is not what the speaker is asserting. There is what Yablo calls a "real content" to figurative statements which may well be true. This is not to say that figurative statements can always be successfully paraphrased into expressions of their real content. Numbers may be indispensable as representational aids for the expression of the real content of mathematical language. The real content of mathematical statements is logical truths, which is why mathematics seems necessary and *a priori*. For example, the real content of "2 + 3 = 5" is the logical truth employing numerical quantifiers:

$$[\exists_2 x(Fx)\ \&\ \exists_3 y(Gy)\ \&\ \exists z(Fz\ \&\ Gz)] \supset \exists_5 u(Fu \lor Gu).$$

Yablo extends his analysis to include other sorts of abstract object talk as well. For example:

The truth value of:	is held to turn on:
Argument A is valid	the existence of *counter-models*
It is possible that B	the existence of *worlds*
There are as many Cs as Ds	the existence of 1 : 1 *functions*
There are over five Es	the *number* of Es
He did it F-ly	the *event* of his doing it being F
There are Gs which —	there being a *set* of Gs which —
She is H	her relation to the *property* H-ness.

The entities on the right are not what the expressions on the left are really about. We simulate belief, perhaps quite unconsciously, that the entities on the right exist, but they are mere figures of speech which are vehicles of the real content. Figurative speech may be true – herein lies the difference between Figuralism and Fictionalism – but the representational aids it employs are not ontologically committing.

Challenges to the Customary Semantics in General

The above strategies all accept the customary semantics in general but seek to develop a special semantics for abstract object talk in particular. Even more fundamental challenges to the Indispensability Argument call into question the customary semantics *tout court*.

Defense of irreferential terms: Free Logic

One such alternative to the customary semantics is provided by Free Logic. Free Logics are logics whose quantifiers remain ontologically committing but whose general and singular terms are devoid of existential import. Karel Lambert (2003) complains that modern logic still retains existence assumptions that ought not to characterize a purely formal discipline. These assumptions surface in standard logic's treatment of statements of identity. According to standard modern logic, identity statements presuppose existence assumptions, that is to say, their truth requires the existence of the objects referred to in the identity statement.[1] This is evident in the fact that from $t = t$, where t is some singular term, it follows that $\exists x(x = t)$.

For if we substitute the predicate "$= t$" for "P" in $Pt \supset \exists x(Px)$, a theorem of modern logic, we have $t = t \supset \exists x(x = t)$. But, then, absurdly, it would follow from "Vulcan = Vulcan" that there is some object identical with Vulcan, that is to say, that Vulcan exists. Standard logic avoids this untoward result by restricting the terms in true identity statements to those designating existing objects. As a result standard logic becomes limited in its application to certain inferences and does not permit us to discriminate between inferences where the referentiality of the terms is crucial and those where it is not.

Proponents of Free Logic therefore propose to rid logic of all existence assumptions with respect to both general and singular terms. Free Logic has thus become almost synonymous with the logic of irreferential (or non-denoting, vacuous, empty) singular terms. It does not presuppose (like Meinongianism) that the referents of such terms are non-existent objects; rather there just are no referents. Because Free Logic retains the existential force of the quantifiers of standard logic, it is consistent with the customary view that one is committed by existential quantification to the objects quantified over in true statements. But Free Logic avoids gratuitous commitments by modifying Existential Generalization (EG) and Universal Instantiation (UI). EG now becomes $\exists x(x = t) \supset [Pt \supset \exists x(Px)]$, and UI is replaced by $\forall y(\forall x(Px) \supset Py)$.

The Free Logician will point out that the Indispensability Argument must rely crucially on EG if it is not to be question-begging. When a scientific statement Pt includes a singular term t, we shall not be ontologically committed to a referent of t unless we can infer "Therefore, there is something that is P," or $\exists x(Px)$. But in Free Logic such existential generalization is not valid. We should also need to know that $\exists x(x = t)$, to assume which is question-begging. If t is an irreferential term like "3," as the nominalist believes, then the truth of "$2 < 3 < 4$" does not commit us to the reality of 3. Should the platonist simply begin with an existential assertion, for example, "3 is a number between 2 and 4," he begs the question. The nominalist Free Logician will, like the Fictionalist, regard this statement as false.

Reference to non-existent objects: neo-Meinongianism

Proponents of Free Logic have challenged the customary semantics for general and singular terms, but they have taken over unchallenged the customary semantics view of the existential quantifier. Other nominalist schools of thought have been more critical. Perhaps the most radical is neo-Meinongianism, which, in contrast to Free Logic, retains the referentiality of singular terms but rejects the existential quantifier of traditional logic. According to neo-Meinongianism, singular terms in true statements do refer to objects, but these objects may not exist. When Meinong affirmed that "There are things that do not exist," no contradiction was involved because for Meinong *es gibt* ("there is/are") is not, as neo-Meinongian Richard Routley puts it, "existentially loaded" (Routley 1979, 76). The expression does not imply that something exists. Routley takes the quantifiers of classical logic to be existentially loaded and therefore proposes a reform of classical logic by replacing it with a neutral quantified logic. Like the Free Logician, Routley faults the traditional scheme of EG: $Fa \supset (\exists x)Fx$. His rejection of traditional EG is the result of the neo-Meinongian repudiation of what Routley calls the Ontological Assumption, to wit, the assumption that a statement has the value *true* and is about something only if the subject of the statement refers to an existent object. The correct scheme of EG will involve the use of an existence predicate E: $Fa \ \& \ Ea \supset (\exists x)Fx$. In neutral quantification logic the existential quantifier will be replaced by a quantifier of particularization P to be interpreted as "for some item." So "Some things do not exist" is symbolized (Px)(¬Ex). EG will be replaced by a Principle of Particularization $Fa \supset (Px)Fx$, that is, for some item, Fx.

Routley, in contrast to Meinong, who thought that abstract objects subsist, takes abstract objects to be items that do not exist and so discourse about them to be properly formalized by a neutral quantification logic (Routley 1979, 45). By replacing the existentially loaded quantifier of classical logic with a neutral logic featuring a quantifier of particularization, we may affirm, in contrast to the Fictionalist, that it is true that "There is a number 4" without committing ourselves to the reality of mathematical objects.

Existentially neutral quantifiers: Neutral Logic

The appeal to Neutral Logic is independent of Meinongianism. Advocates of Neutralism like Jody Azzouni (1998, 2004, 2007, 2010) do not advocate a reform of classical logic to replace the existential quantifier but challenge the assumption that the quantifier of classical logic is ontologically committing. The purpose of the existential quantifier is simply to facilitate logical inferences. It can carry out that function without making ontological commitments to objects, existent or non-existent. Why, Azzouni asks, should we think that this quantifier has any different meaning or carries any more ontological force than "there is/are" in ordinary language, which is clearly non-committing?

Philosophers typically discriminate between two interpretations of the existential quantifier: the objectual (or referential) and the substitutional. The objectual interpretation of the quantifier conceives it as ranging over a domain of objects and picking out some of those objects as the values of the variable bound by it. The substitutional interpretation takes the variable to be a sort of place-holder for particular linguistic expressions which can be substituted for it to form sentences. The substitutional interpretation is generally recognized not to be ontologically committing. But Azzouni maintains that even the objectual interpretation of the quantifier is not ontologically committing until one so stipulates. The claim that it must be ontologically committing overlooks the fact that the quantifiers of the metalanguage used to establish the domain of the object language quantifiers are similarly ambiguous. Whether the items in the domain D of the object language quantifier actually exist will depend on how one construes the "there is" of the metalanguage establishing D. Even referential use of the quantifier in the object language need not be ontologically committing if the quantifiers in the metalanguage are not ontologically committing. If, when we say that there is an element in D, we are using ordinary language, then we are not committed to the reality of the objects in D which we quantify over. There is no reason to think that one cannot set up as one's domain of quantification a wholly imaginary realm of objects. D is then non-empty, but objectual quantification in the object language of the domain will not be ontologically committing. It will be contextual factors that will tip us off to whether locutions are being used in ontologically committing ways.

Reference without ontological commitment: deflationary reference

Neutral Logic will obviate any automatic ontological commitments thought to arise from existential quantification. This takes us back to questions of reference. The neo-Meinongian, like the Free Logician, continues to assume with the customary semantics that singular terms, when used referentially, must designate some mind-independent object. But why should we think that? It is an experiential datum that referring is a speech act carried out by an intentional agent. Absent an agent, ink marks on paper or noises do not refer to anything at all. Referring is an intentional activity of persons, and words are mere instruments. We need to take seriously the fact, given lip service everywhere, that it is *persons* who refer to things *by means of* their words, so that words at best refer only in a derivative sense, if at all.

As obvious as this point is, theorists of reference remain strangely oblivious to the fact. Reference continues to be very widely construed as a relation obtaining between words and objects in the world. By contrast, Arvid Båve's (2009) new deflationary theory of reference features a central schema for reference formulated in terms of the referring activity of agents:

(R)   *a* refers to *b* iff *a* says something (which is) about *b*,

where "*a*" always stands for a speaker. This account is deflationary because it does not attempt to tell us anything about the nature of reference itself. It leaves it entirely open whether reference is a relation (as Frege and Meinong assumed) or whether it is an intentional property of a mind (as held by Brentano and Husserl). Taking reference to be a relation between a speaker and some object makes (R) ontologically committing to either existing or non-existing objects. But Båve's theory is ontologically neutral when it comes to the question of whether there must be objects corresponding to the singular terms we use successfully to refer. On his account, if I assert "1 + 1 = 2," then I have said something about 2; it follows from (R) that I have thus referred to 2. But it does not follow that there is some such object, existent or non-existent, as the number 2. One has the option of avoiding the inference to "There is something to which I have referred" by restricting, with the Free Logicians, EG, or the option of granting the inference but rendering it harmless by denying, with the Neutral Logicians, that the so-called existential quantifier is ontologically committing. Hence, Båve recognizes the neutrality of his theory for the debate between nominalists and realists.

So what does it mean to say that *a* says something "about" *b*, as stipulated on the right-hand side of the biconditional (R)? Båve offers the following schema as implicitly defining "about":

(A)   That S(*t*) is about *t*,

where S( ) is a sentence context with a slot for singular terms. Again, Båve's account of aboutness is extraordinarily deflationary. It does not tell us what aboutness is but simply provides a schema for determining what a that-clause containing a singular term (or, presumably, terms) is about. So, for example, that Ponce de Leon sought the Fountain of Youth is about Ponce de Leon and about the Fountain of Youth because the singular terms "Ponce de Leon" and "the Fountain of Youth" fill the blanks in the sentence context "— sought —."

There is nothing in the deflationary schema (A) that entails that aboutness is a relation between propositions and objects. So if I assert, "Ponce de Leon sought the Fountain of Youth," I have said something which is both true and about the Fountain of Youth (as well as about Ponce de Leon); but we are not entitled to infer with Meinong that there are non-existent objects like the Fountain of Youth which this sentence is about. I can say things about Pegasus, the accident that was prevented, or numbers without committing myself to there being objects of which I am speaking.

Theological Objection to Platonism

So much for responses to the case for platonism. What reasons are there for rejecting platonism? The two objections usually urged against platonism are the epistemological objection and the uniqueness objection (Benacerraf 1965, 1973). Whether platonists can successfully defeat these objections may remain a moot question here. My concern is one that is scarcely ever broached in the philosophical literature: that platonism is theologically untenable. If this contention is correct, then, given the truth of classical theism, it will defeat all forms of platonism, even versions crafted to avoid the epistemological and uniqueness objections. The reason for platonism's theological unacceptability for orthodox theists is that it is incompatible with the doctrine of *creatio ex nihilo* and so fundamentally compromises divine aseity.

In the prologue of the Gospel of John, the evangelist presents a vision of God as the Creator of all things: "In the beginning was the Word, and the Word was with God, and the Word was God. He was in the beginning with God. All things came into being through him, and without him not one thing came into being" (John 1:1–3). God through his Word is responsible for the existence of literally everything other than God himself. Apart from God every existent belongs to the creaturely realm, the class of things which have come into being (*geneta*), and so owe their existence to God's creative Word or Reason (*logos*), who is later identified as Christ (John 1:14–18). John 1:1–3 is thus fraught with metaphysical significance, for taken *prima facie* it tells us that God alone exists eternally and *a se*. It entails that there are no objects of any sort which are co-eternal with God and uncreated via the Logos by God.

God's unique status as the only eternal, uncreated being is typical for Judaism (Copan and Craig 2004, 29–145). John himself identifies the Logos alone as existing with God (and being God) in the beginning. Everything else is then created through the Logos. It is who or what God is that requires the domain of John's quantifier to be unrestricted, whatever beings might be found to lie in the domain. Indeed, given the striking similarities of John's Logos doctrine to that of the Alexandrian Jewish philosopher Philo (20 BC to AD 50), it is not all implausible that John thought that the intelligible realm of what we would today call abstract objects was contained, as Philo held, in the divine Logos (see Leonhardt-Balzer 2004, 309–310, 318–319). Everything else has been created by God.

The evangelist's conviction that God is the Creator of everything that exists aside from God himself eventually attained credal status at the Council of Nicaea. In language redolent of the prologue to the Fourth Gospel (John 1:3) and of Paul (Col. 1:16), the Council affirmed:

> I believe in one God, the Father Almighty, Maker of heaven and earth and of all things visible and invisible;
> And in one Lord, Jesus Christ, the only Son of God, begotten of the Father before all ages, light from light, true God from true God, begotten not made, consubstantial with the Father, through whom all things came into being.

At face value the Council affirms that God alone is uncreated and that all else was created by him.

An examination of ante-Nicene theological reflection on divine aseity confirms the *prima face* reading. Like the Arian heretics, the ante-Nicene and Nicene Church Fathers rejected any suggestion that there might exist *ageneta* apart from God alone.[2] According to patristic scholar

Harry Austryn Wolfson, the Church Fathers all accepted the following three principles (Wolfson 1970, 414):

(1) God alone is uncreated.
(2) Nothing is co-eternal with God.
(3) Eternality implies deity.

Each of these principles implies that there are no *ageneta* other than God.

Lest it be suggested that *abstracta* were somehow exempted from these principles, we should note that the ante-Nicene Church Fathers explicitly rejected the view that entities such as properties and numbers are *ageneta*. The Fathers were familiar with the metaphysical worldviews of Plato and Pythagoras and agreed with them that there is one *agenetos* from which all reality derives; but the Fathers identified this *agenetos*, not with an impersonal form or number, but with the Hebrew God, who has created all things (other than himself) *ex nihilo*.[3] If confronted by a modern-day platonist defending an ontology which included causally effete objects which were *ageneta* and so co-eternal with God, they would have rejected such an account as blasphemous, since such an account would impugn God's aseity by denying its uniqueness and undermine *creatio ex nihilo* by denying that God is the universal ground of being. The Fathers could not therefore exempt such objects from God's creative power, since he is the sole and all-originating *agenetos*.

Can an accommodation between platonism and classical theism be reached? The easiest and most obvious proposal is Absolute Creationism, which maintains that God has created any abstract objects that exist. Unfortunately, Absolute Creationism faces two difficulties, the first troublesome and the second truly serious. First, Absolute Creationism misconstrues either the scope or nature of creation. From a biblical perspective creation is an inherently temporal concept implying a temporal beginning of existence for any created thing (Copan and Craig 2004, chapters 1–4); yet it is plausible that many types of abstract objects, if they exist, exist necessarily and so have no beginning of existence. So if we think of abstract objects as part of the order of dependent beings existing apart from God, then the scope of *creatio ex nihilo* becomes miniscule. The overwhelming bulk of things is merely sustained in being but not, properly speaking, created by God. If, to avoid this difficulty, we expand the meaning of "creation" so as to make any dependent being the object of God's creation, then we have radically subverted God's freedom with respect to creating. The vast majority of being flows from him with an inexorable necessity independent of his will. Thus, the ontology of Absolute Creationism is incompatible with the doctrine of *creatio ex nihilo*, attenuating either God's freedom or the scope of creation.

The second and more serious problem with Absolute Creationism is that it appears to be logically incoherent. Simply stated, the problem is that the creation of certain abstract objects presupposes the existence of those objects, so that a vicious explanatory circle is formed (Bergmann and Brower 2006). For example, God cannot create the property of *being powerful* unless he already has the property of *being powerful*. (If one maintains that God can be powerful without exemplifying the property of *being powerful*, then one has thereby ceded the palm of victory to the nominalist, who denies that the truth of "God is powerful" entails the existence of a property.) The challenge facing Absolute Creationists is to find a way out of this explanatory circle.[4] Indeed, I should say that the chief problem posed by the existence of abstract objects to classical theism stems not from their necessary existence but from, in certain cases, their uncreatability. It is not the existence of abstract objects as such that poses a serious challenge to divine aseity but rather the putative existence of uncreatables.

Conclusion

Given the failure of Absolute Creationism, the Christian theist cannot consistently embrace platonism, because such a doctrine compromises *creatio ex nihilo* and divine aseity by its postulation of uncreatables. Fortunately, there are abundant responses to the Indispensability Argument for platonism. The Indispensability Argument is at root an exercise in meta-ontology, not simply ontology. Behind it lie certain metaontological assumptions about the nature of reference and quantification that must be surfaced and examined. A deflationary theory of reference and neutral logical interpretation of first-order quantification are intuitive, defensible, and effective strategies for undercutting the Indispensability Argument. Nominalism or conceptualism remain open options for the Christian theist.

Notes

1 Standard logic cannot therefore distinguish the truth value of "Zeus = Zeus" and "Zeus = Allah." Nor can we on standard logic affirm the truth of "Aristotle = Aristotle," since Aristotle no longer exists and so there is no thing with which he can be identified.
2 Justin *Dialogue* 5; Methodius *On Free Will* 5; Irenaeus *Against Heresies* 4.38.3; Tertullian *Against Praxeas* 5.13–15; Hippolytus *Against Noetus* 10.1; Hippolytus *Refutation of All Heresies* 10.28; Epiphanius *Panarion* 33.7.6; Athanasius *Defense of the Nicene Definition* 7: "On the Arian symbol 'Agenetos'"; Athanasius *Discourses against the Arians* 1.9.30–34; Athanasius *On the Councils of Ariminum and Seleucia* 46–47; Athanasius *Statement of Faith* 3.
3 Athenagoras *Plea for the Christians* 15, 24; Tatian *Address to the Greeks* 4.10–14; Methodius *Concerning Free Will*; Hippolytus *Refutation* 6.16, 18, 19, 24, 43. Combining the Gospel of John's Logos doctrine with Philo's, the Greek Apologists grounded the intelligible realm in God rather than in some independent realm of self-subsisting entities like numbers or forms. According to Wolfson, every Church Father who addressed the issue rejected the view that the ideas were self-subsisting entities but instead located the intelligible world in the Logos and, hence, in the mind of God. For a discussion of texts taken from pseudo-Justin, Irenaeus, Tertullian, Clement of Alexandria, Origen, and Augustine, see Wolfson (1970, chapter 13).
4 I consider some suggested escape routes in Copan and Craig (2004, 176–180) and find them unavailing.

References

Azzouni, Jody. 1998. On "On What There Is." *Pacific Philosophical Quarterly*, 79, pp. 1–18.
Azzouni, Jody. 2004. *Deflating Existential Consequence: A Case for Nominalism*. Oxford: University Press.
Azzouni, Jody. 2007. Ontological Commitment in the Vernacular. *Noûs*, 41, pp. 204–226.

Azzouni, Jody. 2010. Ontology and the Word "Exist": Uneasy Relations. *Philosophia Mathematica*, 18, pp. 74–101.

Balaguer, Mark. 1998. *Platonism and Anti-Platonism in Mathematics*. New York: Oxford University Press.

Båve, Arvid. 2009. A Deflationary Theory of Reference. *Synthese*, 169, pp. 51–73.

Benacerraf, Paul. 1965. What Numbers Could Not Be. *Philosophical Review*, 74, pp. 47–73.

Benacerraf, Paul. 1973. Mathematical Truth. *Journal of Philosophy*, 70, pp. 661–679.

Bergmann, Michael and Brower, Jeffrey. 2006. A Theistic Argument against Platonism (and in Support of Truthmakers and Divine Simplicity). *Oxford Studies in Metaphysics*, 2, pp. 357–386.

Chihara, Charles. 1990. *Constructibility and Mathematical Existence*. Oxford: Clarendon Press.

Copan, Paul and Craig, William Lane. 2004. *Creation out of Nothing*. Grand Rapids, MI: Baker.

Craig, William Lane. 2011. Why Are (Some) Platonists so Insouciant? *Philosophy*, 86(2), pp. 213–229.

Hellman, Geoffrey. 1989. *Mathematics without Numbers*. Oxford: Oxford University Press.

Lambert, Karel. 2003. *Free Logic*. Cambridge: Cambridge University Press.

Leonhardt-Balzer, Jutta. 2004. Der Logos und die Schöpfung: Streiflichter bei Philo (Op 20–25) und im Johannesprolog (Joh 1, 1–18). In J. Frey and U. Schnelle, eds. *Kontexte des Johannesevangelium*. Tübingen: Mohr-Siebeck, pp. 295–319.

Linnebo, Øystein. 2009. Platonism in the Philosophy of Mathematics. In *Stanford Encyclopedia of Philosophy*, online at http://plato.stanford.edu/entries/platonism-mathematics/ (accessed July 18, 2009).

Routley [Sylvan], Richard. 1979. *Exploring Meinong's Jungle and Beyond*. Canberra: Australian National University Research School of Social Sciences.

Wolfson, Harry Austryn. 1970. *The Philosophy of the Church Fathers*, vol. 1, *Faith, Trinity, and Incarnation*, 3rd revised edn. Cambridge, MA: Harvard University Press.

Yablo, Stephen. 2000. A Paradox of Existence. In A. Everett and T. Hofweber, eds. *Empty Names, Fiction, and the Puzzles of Non-Existence*. Stanford: Center for the Study of Language and Information, pp. 275–312.

Further Reading

Azzouni, Jody. 2004. *Deflating Existential Consequence: A Case for Nominalism*. Oxford: University Press. A penetrating account and defense of how mathematical statements can be true without the existence of mathematical objects.

Balaguer, Mark. 1998. *Platonism and Anti-Platonism in Mathematics*. New York: Oxford University Press. An influential book defending both factionalism and full-blooded platonism and concluding that no good arguments exist either for or against mathematical platonism.

Balaguer, Mark. 2009. Platonism in Metaphysics. In *The Stanford Encyclopedia of Philosophy*, online at http://plato.stanford.edu/entries/platonism/ (accessed April 7, 2009). A helpful survey article which surveys platonism as it pertains to abstract objects.

Båve, Arvid. 2009. A Deflationary Theory of Reference. *Synthese*, 169, pp. 51–73. A rigorous account of an important new deflationary theory of reference.

Linnebo, Øystein. 2009. Platonism in the Philosophy of Mathematics. In *The Stanford Encyclopedia of Philosophy*, online at http://plato.stanford.edu/entries/platonism-mathematics/ (accessed July 18, 2009). An introductory article focused specifically on the uses of platonism in mathematics.

39

Laws of Nature

LYDIA JAEGER

Introduction

Talk about laws of nature is commonplace in current scientific practice. Quite routinely, the central task of the natural sciences, and more precisely of physics,[1] is described as being the formulation of the laws of nature. Despite its familiarity, the concept of law of nature is of rather recent origin. It originated in the seventeenth century, when the leaders of the scientific revolution liked to describe their procedures as a breakaway from Greek science, as transmitted by the medieval scholastics. Laws of nature were introduced as a rival explanation of natural phenomena, which were meant to replace the Aristotelian categories. Many of the founding fathers of modern science explicitly linked the new laws of nature to their belief in the Creator God. This chapter explores the characteristics of the modern concept of natural law, explains its biblical and theological roots, and explores the extent to which this theological background is still relevant for the contemporary use of the concept.

The Early Modern Concept of Laws of Nature

The frequent use of the metaphor of laws of nature during modern times is in stark contrast with earlier periods of history. Only two or three instances have survived of Greek pre-Christian sources which employ the metaphor of law resembling the modern sense (Ruby 1986, 354). Although the metaphor can sometimes be found in Roman (particularly Stoic) and medieval sources, it is not until the scientific revolution that laws of nature become a stock expression in scientific contexts. Of particular influence was Descartes, who in his *Principia philosophiae* called the three fundamental rules at the basis of his mechanistic kinematics "the first laws or principles of nature." The law metaphor would acquire lasting fame when Newton incorporated it into what would become "classical" mechanics. In his *Principia*

The Blackwell Companion to Science and Christianity, First Edition. Edited by J. B. Stump and Alan G. Padgett.
© 2012 Blackwell Publishing Ltd. Published 2012 by Blackwell Publishing Ltd.

(1687), he formulated three laws of motion and the law of universal gravitation and used them to explain the motion of a great variety of physical systems. These laws have been regarded ever since as the paradigm of a successful science of nature.

In the minds of the founders of modern science,[2] laws of nature frequently took the place of the substantial forms which scholastic science had employed in order to explain order in nature. In the preface to the *Principia*, Newton writes: "The moderns – rejecting substantial forms and occult qualities – have undertaken to reduce the phenomena of nature to mathematical laws" (Newton 1999, 381). The transition is particularly clear in Descartes's posthumously published *Le Monde* (*The World*). In the sixth chapter of this work, the philosopher invites the reader to imagine a world filled with matter allowing for a geometric description, but which is without any form in the scholastic sense of the word. The laws of nature ensure the natural order, despite the absence of any Aristotelian ordering principle:

> For God has so marvellously established these laws, that while we had supposed that he creates nothing more than what I said, and even that he put in this neither order nor proportion, but that he composes Chaos, the most confused and the most tangled that the Poets could describe: they are sufficient to cause the parts of this Chaos to untangle themselves, and ready themselves in such good order, that they will have the form of a very perfect World, and in which one sees not only Light, but also all the other things, from the general to the particular, that inhabit this real world. (Descartes 1909, 34f.)

The introduction of laws of nature, in the place of Aristotelian categories, is more than a change in vocabulary. Laws of nature allow for a wider range of governing principles than were known in Aristotelian-inspired natural philosophy. Aristotle explained change in terms of properties of entities considered individually. For substantial forms are individual categories, based on the inherent properties of things. A physical account in this framework must use only local conditions and local interaction. These were defined entirely by the properties of the individual substances, taken separately. But modern science gives a prominent place to forces of interaction that depend on the relative distance between two objects (as in Newton's law of gravitation and in Coulomb's law of electrostatic interaction). The role of global constraints may be less obvious, but is nevertheless crucial. Although many early scientists looked for explanations in terms of local conditions and interactions, in classical mechanics forces of inertia continue to resist a local explanation.

The Universality of Laws of Nature

The modern concept of laws of nature is linked to a significant shift in the way the natural order is perceived. Two expressions coined by Alexandre Koyré can serve to characterize the major difference between the conflicting conceptions: the medievals think in terms of a "Cosmos: closed unity of a hierarchical order," whereas the modern view presupposes a "Universe: open ensemble linked by the unity of its laws" (Koyré 1966, 165). Earlier centuries were influenced by the Greek idea of *analogia entis* ("analogy of being"): everything which exists is ordered on a scale reaching from the lowest existing things to human beings, angels, and up to the divine; each entity behaves in accordance with its own nature defined by its position in this cosmic hierarchy. The new philosophers of nature instead adopt universal laws: the same law would govern the movement of all (material) things. Such universal laws are easily interpreted in the framework of creation: the omnipotence and omnipresence of the Creator guarantee their universal validity. It is thus no accident that seventeenth-century thinkers routinely attribute them to God's action.

Creation offers an asymmetric view of reality: on the one hand stands the all-powerful Creator, on whom everything depends and who does not depend on anything; on the other hand there is the world which is created in all its parts. Such a perspective does not sit well with a hierarchical worldview classifying things on a scale according to their greater or lesser proximity with God – despite medieval attempts (most prominently by Aquinas) to integrate Christian and Greek insights. Creation unites all of reality under Almighty God, it encourages the adoption of universal laws. As Francis Oakley has shown, early modern discussions of laws of nature are continuous with medieval debates on the absolute and ordained power of God (Oakley 1984, 72ff.). The sinologue Joseph Needham (1951) even argued that the absence of the concepts of the divine Creator-Lawgiver and thus of imposed laws is one of the main reasons for the different direction in which science has evolved in China.

Given the huge influence which the Bible has had on Western civilization, it is significant that laws instituted by God and governing all of nature can be found in several passages of the Old Testament. Clearly, they do not take on the precise mathematical form characteristic of modern scientific laws. Nonetheless, these texts show that the idea of universal laws sits comfortably with biblical monotheism – combining wisdom and omnipotence in one Godhead. In the midst of adversity, the psalmist finds courage in the fact that the whole universe serves God's law (Ps. 119:89–91):[3]

> Forever, Lord, your word is established in the heavens.
> Your faithfulness endures from generation to generation;
> You founded the earth and it holds firm.
> Because of your judgments, they remain standing even today;
> For the whole universe is your servant.

Jeremiah 33:25 speaks of the "laws[4] of heaven and earth." Psalm 148 uses the process of enumeration to imply the submission of all creatures to God's law.[5]

The universality of the created order is also indirectly expressed in those passages which emphasize the obedience of the sea and its waves to the law instituted at creation. Thus speaks Wisdom personified:

> The Lord possessed me at the beginning of his activity,
> Before his most ancient works.
> . . .
> When he established his law for the sea,
> That the waters might not disobey his commandment,[6]
> When he arranged the foundations of the earth.
> Then I was before him, like a master workman;
> I was daily his delight, rejoicing before him always.
>
> (Prov. 8:22, 29–30; cf. Jer. 31:35–36; Job 38:8–11)

In the ancient Near East, the sea symbolizes the forces of chaos threatening the natural order. If even the sea has to submit to God's law, the created order extends to all that exists.

An additional indication of the universal validity of the laws established at creation comes from texts which affirm their reign over natural domains in which pre-scientific observation can hardly discover any order. A prominent example is a passage from the Book of Job affirming nomological order concerning the weather:

> He determined the weight of the wind,
> And fixed the measure of the waters.
> When he determined a law for the rain
> And a trajectory for the lightning and thunder.[7]
>
> (Job 28:25–27; cf. 38:25)

The chaotic nature of the weather continues to mock any effort to predict it, even using sophisticated contemporary scientific methods. Even less could the Old Testament believer have derived its lawful structure from observation. His conviction that it does not deviate from the created order rested on his knowledge of God's omnipotence, sovereign over all reality.

Coming back to modern science, two immediate consequences of the universality of the laws should be mentioned. First, Aristotle distinguished between natural and violent movements. In Aristotelian science, the nature of each body determines its "natural" place. If it is moved out of its place, it will naturally try to return there. For example, heavy things have a tendency to move towards the earth; once there, they remain at rest. "Violent" movements go against this natural order. The intervention of an exterior agent, the "motor," is demanded only for the second type of movement, whereas the natural movements simply express the nature of the object and do not stand in need of a causal explanation. Modern physics has given up this Aristotelian distinction between natural and violent movements and applies instead the same laws to all kinematic phenomena.

Second, the scientific revolution built on a shift in the major analogy used to comprehend the world: no longer was it seen in analogy to an animal, with its inherent tendencies and strivings, but as a machine. As Kepler wrote (to Herward von Hohenberg, February 10, 1605), the movement of the celestial bodies is to be conceived "not on the model of a divine, animate being, but on the model of a clock" (Harrison 2008, 20). This shift presupposes the rejection of the Aristotelian exclusion of artifacts from the realm of natural philosophy. A created cosmos is as a whole an artifact, produced by God. It thus becomes possible to transfer the kinds of mathematical reasoning already in use in mechanics (meaning the theory of machines) to the description of nature itself. As Descartes put it, "the rules of mechanics . . . are the same as those of nature" (Descartes, 1992, part V, 73).

The Book of Nature Written in the Language of Mathematics

A very striking aspect of laws of nature, as we know them today, is their mathematical character: modern scientific descriptions are more powerful than older accounts of natural phenomena exactly because they are more precise in virtue of the mathematical devices used. This is particularly true for physics, but other scientific disciplines also often strive to get closer to the ideal set by mathematical physics. The possibility of applying mathematical rules to nature is such a powerful presupposition of current scientific practice that we often take it for granted. But the exact status of mathematics with regard to natural science was under discussion when laws first became a dominant feature of it. Galileo is famous for claiming (for example in a letter to Fortunio Liceti in 1641) that the book of nature is written in mathematical language:

The book of philosophy [that is natural philosophy] stands perpetually open before our eyes, though since it is written in characters different from those of our alphabet it cannot be read by everyone; and the characters of such a book are triangles, squares, circles, spheres, cones, pyramids, and other mathematical figures, most apt for such a reading. (Quoted in Drake 1978, 412)

Aristotle had argued that each science should be built up deductively from its own fundamental principles, thus proscribing the use of mathematics in natural philosophy. Mathematical methods could nevertheless be used in what he called "subalternate sciences," that is scientific disciplines which applied mathematical tools to their subject matter, as for example astronomy, optics, and mechanics. As causal explanations were the prerogative of natural philosophy, mathematics could therefore tell us how something behaved, but not why it did so. From the sixteenth century onwards, these disciplines were known as "mixed mathematical sciences," the whose status did not compare to that of natural philosophy. They used rules framed in mathematical language (like the rules of refraction and reflection in optics); these were, however, more akin to calculation tools than to universal laws of *nature* in modern science (Harrison 2008, 16). In astronomy, such mathematical rules lent themselves to an instrumental reading, as all efforts continuously failed to provide an account of Ptolemaic (and Copernican) astronomy in terms of principles derived from Aristotelian philosophy of nature. As long as one stuck to the Aristotelian framework, it was impossible to consider that they provided a description of how the world was "in reality." The title of Newton's *magnum opus*, *Mathematical Principles of Natural Philosophy*, must thus have been shocking to the ears of more than one scholar trained in the scholastic tradition.

The re-emergence of a Christian Platonism in the Renaissance certainly helped to pave the way for the modern concept of law of nature. Nevertheless, Plato himself had taught that mathematical forms are realized only imperfectly in material objects (*Timaeus* 50b, 53b, 56c). When pressed to justify their use of mathematics in deducing the structures of the material world, early modern scientists referred to God's omnipotence and wisdom in creation. Kepler defended himself along these lines in his *Mysterium Cosmographicum* (*The Secret of the World*) in 1596:

I shall have the physicists [i.e., the natural philosophers] against me in these chapters, because I have deduced the natural properties of the planets from immaterial things and mathematical figures. . . . I wish to respond briefly as follows: that God the Creator, since he is a mind, and does what he wants, is not prohibited, in attributing powers and appointing circles, from having regard to things which are either immaterial or based on imagination. (Quoted in Harrison 2008, 19)

John Henry sees the same dynamics at work in Descartes's reference to created laws:

Descartes, writing . . . as a mathematician in the forefront of efforts to develop the new physico-mathematics proposes precise laws of interaction in physics (inspired, as Ruby might have said, by the use of laws in the subordinate mathematical sciences). Almost immediately, however, Descartes realizes he is now playing a somewhat different game. While putative laws in the abstract system of mathematics needed no justification beyond their definition, the new *physical* laws that he was proposing needed a metaphysical underpinning. In pursuit of this new metaphysics, Descartes had to consider the nature of God's interactions with the world and turned, accordingly, to traditional providentialist theology. (Henry 2004, 97)

What had been devices for calculation, now acquired the status of a universal order. It was God's infinite rationality and his sovereignty over the world which turned mathematical rules into laws of nature.

Exact Science in a Material World

One obstacle to applying mathematics to our world was a certain conception of matter with Greek (and more specifically Platonic) roots. It takes matter to be a source of defect, prohibiting exact mathematical descriptions of material objects. This point of view is illustrated by Simplicio, the representative of scholastic thinking in Galileo's *Dialogue on the Great World Systems*. He considers that "it is the imperfection of matter that makes the matters taken in concrete to disagree with those taken in abstract." To the contrary, Galileo's spokesman Salviati insists that material objects can be described by exact mathematical formula: "What happens in the concrete does in like manner hold true in the abstract." If a round object touches a plane surface in more than one point, this is not because it is material, but because it is not truly a sphere (Galilei 1953, Second Day, 220, 222).[8] The two perspectives profoundly diverge in the way they treat the observed deviation from the spherical form: for Simplicio, the material imperfection is the end of all possible explanation. Salviati, however, seeks an exact mathematical description of how the object deviates from the ideal form. If it is not exactly a sphere, it is exactly something else!

As creation sees everything produced by God, it provides the framework for a renewed understanding of matter. In opposition to the Greek conception of a demiurge imparting form to pre-existing matter, the Creator produced all that exists, matter included. Matter, being created by a wise and all-powerful God, cannot pose any threat to order, nor to an understanding of this order by rational exploration. The contingency of our world is no longer explained by matter, only partially informed by order, but is grounded in the freedom of God "who works out everything according to the purpose of his will" (Eph. 1:11) and who created all things by his will (Rev. 4:11). Wolfhart Pannenberg takes this changed view of contingency to be one of the major contributions that Christian theology has made to the philosophy of science (Pannenberg 1993, 36f., 115f.). The new philosophy of nature which took shape in the seventeenth century was based on the conviction that the perceptible, the material, in itself, is the subject of rational knowledge and thus of mathematical description. On this point it is in perfect agreement with the idea of creation: since all that exists is the work of an infinitely wise God, nothing is fundamentally irrational and unintelligible.

Quantum Mechanics: An Aristotelian Comeback?

Physics went through profound transformations at the beginning of the twentieth century. Classical Newtonian mechanics was replaced first by Einstein's special and general relativity and then by quantum mechanics. Quantum theory in particular revolutionized our understanding of such very basic scientific categories as object, substance, and causality. Nevertheless prominent aspects of early modern laws carry over into this changed framework. These theories continue to build on the conviction that an exact mathematical description is possible for nature and should be searched for. They claim universal validity. The contingency inherent in our world is not seen as an obstacle to scientific endeavor, but is an incentive to careful experimental exploration combined with theory-building. Although it might not amount to logical proof, the typical curriculum of physics speaks in favor of a basic continuity between early modern and contemporary physics. Whereas the student learns near to nothing about Aristotelian or any other pre-modern science (and even dedicated researchers ignore it, unless they have some historical inclinations), every freshman has first to learn classical mechanics before being introduced to Einsteinian and quantum physics.

Notwithstanding much continuity, contemporary physical theories have novel features. Of particular concern to many is the probabilistic nature of quantum mechanics. Some – most famously Einstein – take it to be a sign of incompleteness. In most circumstances, quantum theory allows only for probabilistic predictions. Thus it is tempting to postulate a deeper deterministic reality of which quantum mechanics provides only a partial description. Einstein conceived the famous Einstein-Podolsky-Rosen experiment in 1930 precisely in order to prove the incompleteness of the quantum description. Building on Einstein's genius, J. S. Bell was able to prove about 30 years later the exact opposite. He showed that one reaches contradictory results if one postulates that quantum theory is only a partial description of a hidden reality.

Thus, the strangeness of the microscopic world does not point to a limit that mathematical description might encounter there. As much as Galilean and Newtonian physics, contemporary physics is based on the conviction that mathematical calculations apply to our "lowly" world; there is no question of merely approximate realizations of mathematical forms which would exist only in the world of Ideas. In fact, the probabilistic laws of quantum theory have an exact mathematical form. Recent mathematical results even allow the development of a probability-free version of quantum mechanics. Probability predictions logically follow from the description of individual quantum systems by the state of the system and the assumption that the objective properties of the system can be obtained with certainty by measurements (Mittelstaedt 1998, 47–57, 62–64). It is therefore unwarranted to believe in another level of reality behind the atomic world, which could not be described by mathematics.

Einstein resisted the probabilist character of quantum mechanics because of his deterministic view of nature, inspired by Spinoza. In such a perspective, our ignorance is the only possible source of the appearance of indeterminacy, thus his conclusion that quantum mechanics must be incomplete. Against Spinoza and his necessitarian deduction of the natural order from God's *nature*, Christian doctrines of creation stress the contingency of the world, depending on God's free *will*. Although classical physics works with deterministic theories, a perspective inspired by creation must remain agnostic about the deterministic (or indeterministic) nature of the world. Instead of positing a certain conception of natural order, it inspires open-minded exploration in order to see which kind of world God in his freedom has decided to create. Thus biblical faith sees divine providence as much at work in the regularities of natural laws as in events resulting from chance (cf. Prov. 16:33).

Laws of Nature Grounded in God's Covenant Faithfulness

The Hebrew prophet Jeremiah once compared the laws established at creation to a covenant which God has made with nature's regular rhythms:

> This is what the Lord says: If you can break my covenant with the day and with the night, so that day and night no longer come at their appointed time. (Jer. 33:20)

> This is what the Lord says: If I had not established my covenant with the day and with the night, if I had not established the laws of heaven and earth. (Jer. 33:25)

The explicit comparison is unique in the biblical canon. It most certainly harks back to the Noachic covenant after the Flood. In the Book of Genesis, God makes a covenant not only with Noah's family but with all living creatures. God guarantees the daily and annual cycles, so that their habitat will not be destroyed again (Gen. 8:21f.; 9:9–17).

It might be interesting to consider this quite peculiar understanding of laws in parallel with the interpretation of the causal efficiency of sacraments found in some medieval theologians. Around 1240 in Oxford, the Dominicans Richard Fishacre and Robert Kilwardby taught that the sacraments were efficient not in virtue of their inherent nature, but in virtue of God's promise, who faithfully kept the covenant or pact made with the Church. They meant to safeguard God's sovereign freedom, while at the same time rejecting occasionalism. Fishacre used the image of a coin which a royal minister gives to a pauper in compensation for some work done and which guarantees him free access to a meal. Parisian Franciscan theologians took up the idea, in particular Bonaventure (1221–1274). Of less restricted scope, the coin could now be exchanged against 100 marks everywhere in the kingdom. The image is the first known instance of fiduciary money, where the value of the coin is not based on the inherent price of the metal used, but on the king's promise to redeem it when asked to. Thomas Aquinas takes up this interpretation of the sacraments – often called juridical or volitional causality and which William Courtenay names covenantal – but rejects it as insufficient. The coin is now a lead denarius and in this form is found in debates on sacramental efficiency until now (Courtenay 1972, 185–202).

Covenantal causality offers a fascinating model for understanding laws of nature in a theistic framework.[9] In fact, it allows for the stability of the natural order, without limiting God's freedom, as it is the Creator himself who, by his faithfulness, guarantees nature's regular behavior. Laws of nature are not seen as independent of divine action; there is no space here for a deistic universe evolving according to its own autonomous laws. Understanding constant laws as based on God's covenant faithfulness allows us to harmoniously articulate a fixed order of nature with ongoing divine involvement in the world. The very permanence of the laws expresses God's free commitment to the covenant he has established.

Covenantal causality at the same time resists any attempt to deify nature, as a covenant builds on the difference between the two partners. Describing God's relation to nature in such terms is in tune with the asymmetrical relation at the heart of the notion of creation: God as the omnipotent and independent Creator giving rise to the world. A demythologized view of reality is crucial to modern science: only a non-divine nature can be the subject of human experimental exploration and constructive theorizing. This not only implies the crucial distinction between the covenant partners that nature is not divine; it also validates the world as truly existing. Thus it does not reduce to occasionalism, but recognizes nature's causal nexus as a sound object of human exploration.

Laws without a Lawgiver?

Contemporary philosophers of science do not agree on why laws of nature are valid. Various explications are offered for the necessity intuitively attached to the concept of law: a law does not simply express what is, but what *should* be. Some ground this necessity in relations between universals; the most elaborate version of this account is today defended by David Armstrong (Armstrong 1997, 220–262). Others derive this necessity from the working of dispositions. Nancy Cartwright has combined such an Aristotelian-type account with the contention that laws do not apply universally, but hold only in limited contexts, most typically in carefully orchestrated laboratory conditions (Cartwright 1999, 49–103). Some take the necessity attached to laws as a primitive notion which cannot be derived from any non-nomological categories (Carroll 1994, 1–16). Still others take their inspiration from Hume and try to do without necessity, offering different substitutes in its place. David Lewis worked out a detailed account along these lines. He takes laws of nature to be certain regularities which play a particularly important role in our best scientific theories in that they optimize both simplicity and information content taken together (Lewis 1973, 73).

The question of why laws of nature are valid is not a recent one. Hume and Kant, to name just two giants of modern philosophy, struggled with it, each putting forward his own answer. Faced with conflicting accounts, where the long-standing discussion does not seem to be able to bring philosophers of science closer to an agreement, one cannot help but wonder if the loss of the theological framework in which the concept was originally born explains the difficulty in reaching a satisfactory answer. In fact, it is not at all obvious how to account for laws unfailingly "obeyed" by unconscious, non-personal entities without a divine all-powerful Lawgiver.[10] This fact is recognized even by some atheistic philosophers; Nancy Cartwright finds good reason here to resist the concept altogether (Cartwright 1993, 299):

> I think that in the concept of law there is a little too much of God. We try to finesse the issue with possible worlds, fictive regularities, and *ceteris paribus* clauses. But in the end the concept of a law does not make sense without the supposition of a law-giver.

But science will not easily do away with one of its key concepts since the scientific revolution in the seventeenth century. Therefore it seems as if the theological commitment implicit in the concept of laws of nature is bound to stay with us.[11]

Notes

1   This chapter concentrates on the notion of laws of nature as used in physics. Physics is often seen as the paradigm science. For instance, many nineteenth-century evolutionists, including Charles Darwin himself, drew a parallel between the laws of Newtonian mechanics and the law of biological evolution (Harrison 2008, 28f.). The question of how far the form of physical laws can be transferred to other sciences, like biology or even sociology, gives rise to fascinating problems. Nevertheless, it will not be addressed here.

2   "Science" is an anachronistic term when applied in this sense to the early modern period. Historically, it would be more accurate to speak of natural philosophy. Nevertheless, I consider that there is enough continuity to warrant the retroactive use of "science."

3   The translation of the biblical texts which is offered in this chapter follows as closely as possible the Hebrew original. "Judgments" translates *mišpàṣîm*. Although the word can be used without a legal connotation ("habit, custom"), it is routinely employed in the legal sphere. The legal use conforms well to the context of the psalm celebrating God's law. The implicit subject of the last sentence ("they") is best understood to be the whole visible realm.

4   Hebrew *huqqôt*, plural of *huqqâ*. It means either (spatial or temporal) limit or law. In this passage, it is clearly the second sense which is correct.

5   Hebrew _hòq_ (v. 6), similar semantic range to _huqqâ_.
6   "Law" translates the Hebrew word _hòq_; "commandment" _pè(h)_.
7   "Law" translates the Hebrew word _hòq_; "trajectory" _dèrèk_.
8   Ernan McMullin pointed out to me that Galileo was not entirely consistent on this issue. At one point he writes that "conclusions demonstrated in the abstract are altered in the concrete," but that demonstration in the abstract ought to be sufficient for the purposes of science (Galilei 1974, Fourth Day, 223).
9   The following remarks are no more than promissory notes on further developments. Unfortunately, I do not know of any author who offers a substantial account of laws of nature along the lines of covenantal causality.
10 The other option would be animism, attributing quasi-personal strivings to all natural objects, a vision not hospitable to natural science as we know it.
11 For a thorough critique of the substitute which Cartwright offers for laws – Aristotelian-type capacities of limited scope – see Jaeger 2007, 195–257. I am indebted to John Brooke, Peter Harrison, Ernan McMullin, and Peter Mittelstaedt, who commented on an earlier version of this chapter. I would also like to thank Jonathan and Rachel Vaughan who assisted me with translating some French citations and smoothing my style.

References

Armstrong, David M. 1997. _A World of States of Affairs_. Cambridge: Cambridge University Press.

Carroll, John. 1994. _Laws of Nature_. Cambridge: Cambridge University Press.

Cartwright, Nancy. 1993. Is Natural Science "Natural" Enough: A Reply to Philip Allport. _Synthese_, 94, pp. 291–301.

Cartwright, Nancy. 1999. _The Dappled World: A Study of the Boundaries of Science_. Cambridge: Cambridge University Press.

Courtenay, William J. 1972. The King and the Leaden Coin: The Economic Background of "Sine Qua Non" Causality. _Traditio_, 28, pp. 185–209.

Descartes, René. 1909. _Le Monde ou Traité de lumière_. In Charles Adam and Paul Tannery, eds. _Oeuvres de Descartes_, vol. 6. Paris: Cerf/Vrin, pp. 1–118.

Descartes, René. 1992. _Discours de la méthode_. Geneviève Rodis-Lewis, ed. Paris: Flammarion.

Drake, Stillman. 1978. _Galileo at Work: His Scientific Biography_. Chicago: University of Chicago Press.

Galilei, Galileo. 1953. _Dialogue on the Great World Systems_, revised edn. Translated by T. Salusbury. Chicago: University of Chicago Press.

Galilei, Galileo. 1974. _Two New Sciences_. Translated by Stillman Drake. Madison, WI: University of Wisconsin Press.

Harrison, Peter. 2008. The Development of the Concept of Laws of Nature. In Fraser Watts, ed. _Creation: Law and Probability_. Aldershot: Ashgate, pp. 13–35.

Henry, John. 2004. Metaphysics and the Origins of Modern Science: Descartes and the Importance of Laws of Nature. _Early Science and Medicine_, 9, pp. 73–114.

Jaeger, Lydia. 2007. _Lois de la nature et raisons du coeur: les convictions religieuses dans le débat épistémologique contemporain_ [Laws of Nature and Reasons of the Heart: The Religious Convictions in the Contemporary Debate in Philosophy of Science]. Bern: Peter Lang.

Koyré, Alexandre. 1966. Galilée et la loi d'inertie. In _Études galiléennes_. Paris: Hermann.

Lewis, David K. 1973. _Counterfactuals_. Oxford: Blackwell.

Mittelstaedt, Peter. 1998. _The Interpretation of Quantum Mechanics and the Measurement Process_. Cambridge: Cambridge University Press.

Needham, Joseph. 1951. Human Laws and the Laws of Nature in China and the West. _Journal of the History of Ideas_, 12, pp. 3–30, 194–230.

Newton, Isaac. 1999. *The Principia: Mathematical Principles of Natural Philosophy.* Translated by I. Bernhard Cohen and Anne Whitman. Berkeley, CA: University of California Press.

Oakley, Francis. 1984. *Omnipotence, Covenant, and Order: An Excursion in the History of Ideas from Abelard to Leibniz.* Ithaca, NY: Cornell University Press.

Pannenberg, Wolfhart. 1993. *Toward a Theology of Nature: Essays on Science and Faith.* Ted Peters, ed. Louisville, KY: Westminster John Knox Press.

Ruby, Jane E. 1986. The Origins of Scientific Law. *Journal of the History of Ideas,* 47, pp. 341–359.

Further Reading

Harrison, Peter. 2008. The Development of the Concept of Laws of Nature. In Fraser Watts, ed. *Creation: Law and Probability.* Aldershot: Ashgate, pp. 13–35. A study of the theological considerations which played a role in the emergence of the idea of mathematical laws in science.

Henry, John. 2004. Metaphysics and the Origins of Modern Science: Descartes and the Importance of Laws of Nature. *Early Science and Medicine,* 9, pp. 73–114. Recent synthesis of all major historical explanations of the origin of the modern concept. Henry attributes the major role to Descartes and explains the role of theological considerations for his concept of laws.

Jaeger, Lydia. 2010. *Einstein, Polanyi and the Laws of Nature.* West Conshohocken, PA: Templeton Foundation Press. Of particular interest is the section of the book presenting a thorough exegesis of all biblical texts which use legal metaphors with regard to natural phenomena.

Pannenberg, Wolfhart. 1993. *Toward a Theology of Nature: Essays on Science and Faith.* Ted Peters, ed. Louisville, KY: Westminster John Knox Press. The chapter "Contingency and Natural Law," written in 1970 (pp. 72–122), is particularly relevant to our subject.

van Fraassen, Bas C. 1989. *Laws and Symmetry.* Oxford: Clarendon Press. Critique of major current philosophical accounts of laws of nature. Instead of taking laws of nature as a clue to scientific practice, the author argues for an empiricist view of science.

Part IX
The Mind

40

Christianity, Neuroscience, and Dualism

J. P. MORELAND

Christianity is a dualist, interactionist religion in this sense: God, angels/demons, and the souls of men and beasts are immaterial substances that can causally interact with the world. Specifically, human persons are (or have) souls that are spiritual substances that retain personal identity in a disembodied intermediate state between death and final resurrection. Most scholars agree that this was the Pharisees' view in intertestamental Judaism, and Jesus (Matt. 22:23–33) and Paul (Acts 23:6–10) side with the Pharisees on this issue over against the Sadducees (Wright 2003, 131–134, 190–206, 366–367, 424–426). In my view, Christian physicalism involves a politically correct revision of the biblical text that fails to be convincing (see Green 2008; cf. Cooper 2000, 2007, 2009a, 2009b). Throughout history, most people have been substance and property dualists. Thus, Jaegwon Kim's concession seems right: "We commonly think that we, as persons, have a mental and bodily dimension. . . . Something like this dualism of personhood, I believe, is common lore shared across most cultures and religious traditions" (Kim 2001, 30).

Today, many hold that, while broadly logically possible, dualism is no longer plausible in light of advances in modern science. This attitude is especially prominent outside Christian circles, but it is not limited to non-Christian thinkers. Christian philosopher Nancey Murphy (1998a, 1998b) claims that physicalism is not primarily a philosophical thesis, but the hard core of a scientific research program for which there is ample evidence. This evidence consists in the fact that "biology, neuroscience, and cognitive science have provided accounts of the dependence on physical processes of *specific* faculties once attributed to the soul" (Murphy 1998a, 17; cf. 13, 27; 1998b, 139–143; cf. Murphy and Brown 2009). Dualism cannot be *proven* false – a dualist can always claim that these accounts describe only correlations or functional relations between soul and brain/body – but advances in science make it a view with little justification. According to Murphy, "science has provided a massive amount of evidence suggesting that we need not postulate the existence of an entity such as a soul or mind in order to explain life and consciousness" (Murphy 1998a, 18).

I disagree. My purpose in what follows is not to argue directly for some form of dualism. I have done that elsewhere (e.g., Moreland and Rae 2000; Moreland 2008, 2009). Rather, I shall argue that once we get clear on the central first- and second-order issues in philosophy

The Blackwell Companion to Science and Christianity, First Edition. Edited by J. B. Stump and Alan G. Padgett.
© 2012 Blackwell Publishing Ltd. Published 2012 by Blackwell Publishing Ltd.

of mind, it becomes evident that stating and resolving those issues is basically a (theological and) philosophical matter for which discoveries in the physical sciences are largely irrelevant. These philosophical issues are, with rare exceptions, autonomous from (and authoritative with respect to) the so-called deliverances of the physical sciences.

In what follows, I shall (1) clarify certain preliminary notions; (2) defend my central thesis by focusing on a paradigm case regarding property dualism that is representative of the dialectic in the literature in philosophy of mind; (3) respond to two potential defeaters of my thesis.

Clarification of Important Preliminaries Relevant to the Autonomy Thesis

Two preliminaries need clarification: identification of the central issues in philosophy of mind and the nature of the Autonomy and Authority Theses.

These central topics tend to revolve around three interrelated families of issues (Churchland 1988):

(1) Ontological questions. To what is a mental or physical property or event identical? To what is the owner of mental properties/events identical? What is a human person? How are mental properties related to mental events (e.g., do the latter exemplify or realize the former?)? Are there essences and, if so, what is the essence of a mental event or of a human person?

(2) Epistemological questions. How do we acquire knowledge about other minds and about our own minds? Is there a proper epistemic order to first-person knowledge of one's own mind and third-person knowledge of other minds? How reliable is first-person introspection and what is its nature (e.g., a non-doxastic seeming or a disposition to believe)? If reliable, should first-person introspection be limited to providing knowledge about mental states or should it be extended to include knowledge about one's own ego?

(3) Semantic questions. What is a meaning? What is a linguistic entity and how is it related to a meaning? Is thought reducible to or a necessary condition for language use? How do the terms in our common-sense psychological vocabulary get their meaning?

The main second-order topics in philosophy of mind are these:

(4) Methodological questions. How should one proceed in analyzing and resolving the first-order issues that constitute the philosophy of mind? What is the proper order between philosophy and science? What is the role of thought experiments in philosophy of mind and how does the "first-person point of view" factor into generating the materials for formulating those thought experiments?

In order to clarify the Autonomy and Authority Theses, I can do no better than cite advocate George Bealer's statement of them:

> I wish to recommend two theses. [1] *The autonomy of philosophy*: Among the central questions of philosophy that can be answered by one standard theoretical means or another, most can in

principle be answered by philosophical investigation and argument without relying substantively on the sciences. [2] *The authority of philosophy*: Insofar as science and philosophy purport to answer the same central philosophical questions, in most cases the support that science could in principle provide for those answers is not as strong as that which philosophy could in principle provide for its answers. So, should there be conflicts, the authority of philosophy in most cases can be greater in principle. (Bealer 1996, 1)

Of the two, the Autonomy Thesis is less controversial and, in my view, clearly correct, at least in certain areas outside philosophy of mind. Debates about universals, the status of the identity of indiscernibles, and so forth are carried out with virtually no regard whatever for the latest findings in science. Most of the first- and second-order topics in philosophy of mind are similarly autonomous, or so I shall shortly argue.

The Principle of Authority is more controversial but not for the reason that may first come to mind. At first glance, ambivalence towards the principle may arise from the idea that science is a superior guide to joint areas of exploration. I disagree. The controversial nature of the Authority Principle derives from the fact that, in those cases where philosophical considerations carry more weight than scientific ones, it is usually open to someone to adopt an anti-realist depiction of the relevant scientific view, operationalize the relevant terms that constitute it, and avoid epistemic conflict by resorting to an autonomy depiction of the philosophical and scientific aspects of the disputed area.

Two Paradigm Case Studies on Behalf of the Autonomy Thesis

Once we get before us the four families of questions listed above, it becomes evident that scientific discoveries play virtually no role at all in formulating or resolving those issues. To support this claim further, I have selected, almost at random, the following paradigm case debate about the nature of mental properties/events in philosophy-of-mind literature to serve as an illustration of the Autonomy Thesis: Paul Churchland's treatment of two different approaches to closely related semantic and epistemic issues (Churchland 1988, chapters 3 and 4).

According to Churchland, a popular physicalist approach to these issues is the network theory of meaning for the terms in our psychological vocabulary. Here, one looks not for an ontological analysis of meaning itself, but rather for a theory about how psychological terms get meaning. On this view, the best way to proceed is to start with a third-person perspective and focus on publicly accessible language to see how terms in folk psychology get their usage. These terms primarily function as theoretical terms used to explain/predict other people's behavior. Moreover, says Churchland, as theoretical terms, they get their meaning by their relations to laws, principles, and other terms in the entire theory in which they are embedded.

For Churchland, the epistemic approach most suited to this semantic theory starts with third-person questions about knowledge of other minds and assimilates first-person to third-person knowledge. We are justified in applying a mental term to another creature just in case this provides the best explanation for and prediction of the creature's behavior. Churchland claims that one's justification need owe nothing at all to one's examination of one's own case and, thus, one could justifiably apply a mental term such as "pain" to a creature and, thus, know its meaning, even if one had never had the relevant experience.

Churchland characterizes self-consciousness as the ability to use a linguistic network to judge that one's various mental states satisfy the interlocking network of folk psychology. Thus, self-consciousness is largely something that is learned. Moreover, for Churchland, all perception is theory-laden, including self-"perception," and self-consciousness is essentially linguistic behavior of a certain sort.

Space considerations prevent me from presenting Churchland's largely accurate depiction of a dualist approach to these questions, but it involves a commitment to such things as irreducible self-presenting properties, first-person introspection and ostensive definition, epistemic movement from the first to the third person, non-doxastic mental states as temporally and epistemically prior to concepts and judgments, and meanings that are not essentially linguistic.

Who's right and what factors are relevant to this question? The answer is complicated and the dialogue involves thought experiments that, in my view, derive their force from first-person introspection, debates about private languages, analyses of the relationship between thought and language, and so on. What is less complicated is that factual information in the physical sciences is virtually irrelevant to these issues. Almost no book in philosophy of mind where these issues are discussed contains any detailed scientific information that plays a role in the discussion. Curiously, while Churchland himself is a physicalist and an advocate of naturalism as a second-order methodological thesis, and while he does include scientific information in *Matter and Consciousness*, that scientific information comes in the second half of the book and it plays absolutely no role whatever in presenting the core philosophical issues and arguments in the first half of the book. Thus, his actual practice underscores the Autonomy Thesis.

The Autonomy Thesis is also justified by the actual nature of the debates about the ontological status of the entity that contains consciousness. Space considerations forbid a presentation of the dialectic between substance dualists and their physicalist opponents, but this is not necessary here. I believe that by listing the five main arguments for (some version of) substance dualism, it will become virtually self-evident to an honest reader that the nature of the task of stating, defending, or criticizing these arguments underscores the Autonomy Thesis.

Argument 1

In acts of introspection, one is aware of: (1) one's self as an unextended center of consciousness; (2) various capacities of thought, sensation, belief, desire, and volition which one exercises and which are essential, internal aspects of the kind of thing one is; (3) one's sensations as being such that there is no possible world in which they could exist and not be one's own. The best explanation for this fact is to take mental states to be modes of the self and mental properties to be kind-defining properties.

Argument 1 is actually two arguments that draw their force from what substance dualists claim people know about themselves from attending to themselves and their conscious states. Put more formally and in the first person, these two variants of an argument from introspection look like this:

Variant One:

(1) I am an unextended center of consciousness (justified by introspection).
(2) No physical object is an unextended center of consciousness.

(3) Therefore, I am not a physical object.
(4) Either I am a physical object or an immaterial substance.
(5) Therefore, I am an immaterial substance.

Variant Two:

(1) My sensations (and other states of consciousness) are either externally or internally related to me.
(2) If I am a physical object, then my sensations are externally related to me such that there is a possible world in which those sensations exist and are not so related to me.
(3) There is no possible world in which my sensations exist without being mine (justified by introspection).
(4) Therefore, I am not a physical object and my sensations are internally related to me.
(5) If a sensation is internally related to me, then it is a mode of my self.
(6) If an entity x is a mode of some entity y, then x is an inseparable entity dependent for its existence on y such that (a) x is modally distinct from and internally related to y and (b) x provides information about the nature of the thing y of which it is a mode.
(7) Therefore, I am a thing whose nature is to have sensations (and other states of consciousness).

Stewart Goetz and Geoffrey Madell have advanced versions of argument one (Goetz 2001, 89–104; Madell 1981; cf. Madell 1988, 103–125).

Argument 2

Personal identity at and through time is primitive and absolute. Moreover, counter-examples exist which show that the various bodily or psychological (e.g., memory) conditions proffered for personal identity are neither necessary nor sufficient. Put linguistically, talk about persons is not analyzable into talk about their bodies or connected mental lives. Further, the primitive unity of consciousness cannot be accounted for if the self is a bodily or physical mereological compound. These facts are not innocuous but, rather, have important metaphysical implications. Substance dualism, according to which the soul is taken as a substance with an essence constituted by the potential for thought, belief, desire, sensation, and volition, is the best explanation of these facts. Different versions of this argument have been advanced by Richard Swinburne and William Hasker (Swinburne 1997, 145–173; Hasker 1999, 122–146). Some nonreductive physicalists who advocate a material composition view of human persons have offered responses to some of these points.[1]

Argument 3

The indexicality of thought provides evidence for the truth of substance dualism. A complete, third-person physical description of the world will fail to capture the fact expressed by "I am J. P. Moreland." No amount of information non-indexically expressed captures the content conveyed by this assertion. The first person indexical "I" is irreducible and uneliminable, and this feature of "I" is not innocuous, but rather, is explained by claiming that "I" refers to a non-physical entity – the substantial self with at least the power of self-awareness. Moreover, if mental predicates are added to the third-person descriptive language, this still fails to capture the state of affairs expressed by statements like "I am thinking that P." Finally, the system of indexical reference (e.g., "I," "here," "there," "this," "that") must have a unifying center that underlies it. This unifying center is the same entity referred to by "I" in expressions like "I am thinking that P," namely, the conscious substantial subject taken as a self conscious, self-referring particular (see Madell 1988, 103–125). More formally:

(1) Statements using the first person indexical "I" express facts about persons that cannot be expressed in statements without the first-person indexical.
(2) If I am a physical object, then all the facts about me can be expressed in statements without the first-person indexical.
(3) Therefore, I am not a physical object.
(4) I am either a physical object or an immaterial substance.
(5) Therefore, I am an immaterial substance.

Geoffrey Madell and H. D. Lewis have advocated this type of argument (see Madell 1981; Lewis 1982).

Argument 4

Some have argued for substance dualism on the grounds that libertarian freedom is true, and either a necessary condition for libertarian freedom is substance dualism or the latter is the best explanation for the former. The argument may be put this way (using only the form in which substance dualism is a necessary condition for libertarian freedom):

(1) Human beings exercise libertarian agency.
(2) No material object (one which is such that all of its properties, parts, and capacities are at least and only physical) can exercise libertarian agency.
(3) Therefore, human beings are not material objects.[2]
(4) Human beings are either material objects or immaterial substances.
(5) Therefore, they are immaterial substances.

Substance dualist John Foster has employed this sort of argument (Foster 1991, 266–280; cf. O'Connor 2000; Moreland 2002).

Argument 5

A modal argument for substance dualism has been advanced by Keith Yandell and Charles Taliaferro, and while it comes in many forms, it may be fairly stated as follows (Yandell 1995; Taliaferro 1995):

(1) If x is identical to y, then whatever is true of x is true of y and vice versa.
(2) I can strongly conceive of myself as existing disembodied or, indeed, without any physical particular existing.
(3) If I can strongly conceive of some state of affairs S that S possibly obtains, then I have good grounds for believing of S that S is possible.

(4)   Therefore, I have good grounds for believing of myself that it is possible for me to exist and be disembodied.

(5)   If some entity x is such that it is possible for x to exist without y, then (i) x is not identical to y and (ii) y is not essential to x.

(6)   My physical body is not such that it is possible for it to exist disembodied or without any physical particular existing.

(7)   Therefore, I have good grounds for believing of myself that I am not identical to a physical particular, including my physical body and that no physical particular, including my physical body is essential to me.

A parallel argument can be developed to show that possessing the ultimate capacities for consciousness is essential to one's self. Issues in the physical sciences have virtually nothing at all to do with stating and resolving the issues that constitute the core of the debate about substance dualism.

An Autonomy Thesis advocate takes the thesis to be fairly obvious and invites others to attend to the actual dialogical issues as they pepper the pages of literature in philosophy of mind, believing that one will simply be able to see that those issues are largely philosophical and not scientific. This is precisely what I have tried to do in this section. Rather than elaborate on this further, I shall instead turn to a consideration of two prominent counter-arguments offered by Murphy to the Autonomy Thesis.

Response to Two Counter-Arguments

First, Murphy claims that while substance dualism cannot be proven false, nevertheless, "biology, neuroscience, and cognitive science have provided accounts of the dependence on physical processes of *specific* faculties once attributed to the soul" (Murphy 1998a, 17; cf. 3, 27; 1998b, 139–143).

For Murphy, "science has provided a massive amount of evidence suggesting that we need not postulate the existence of an entity such as a soul or mind in order to explain life and consciousness" (Murphy 1998a, 18). Thus, since advances in science have provided detailed accounts of mental/physical dependencies which make postulation of the soul otiose, the Autonomy Thesis is false, at least in this case.

I offer three responses. First, many substance dualists believe in a substantial ego not primarily because it is a theoretical postulate with superior explanatory power. Rather, they take the ego to be something of which people are directly aware. The point is not that dualists are right about this. Given this dualist approach, the point is that advances in our knowledge of mental/physical dependencies are simply beside the point. And the further debate about which approach is the fundamental one for defending substance dualism is not something for which advances in scientific knowledge are relevant.

Second, in those cases where substance dualism *is* postulated as the best explanation for a range of purported facts, typically, those facts are distinctively philosophical and not the scientific ones Murphy mentions. Arguments from the unity of consciousness, the possibility of disembodied survival or body switches, the best view of an agent to support agent causation, the metaphysical implications from the use of the indexical "I" (see above) are typical of arguments offered by substance dualists, and the facts Murphy mentions are not particularly relevant for assessing these arguments. Those and related scientific facts (e.g., split-brain phenomena) may provide difficulties for certain versions of substance dualism, but they are not decisive – dualists have provided reasonable responses to them – and, in any case, they are less important than the philosophical issues mentioned above.

Finally, the discovery of "the dependence on physical processes of *specific* faculties once attributed to the soul" does not provide sufficient grounds for attributing those faculties to the brain rather than to the soul. (After all, are dualists supposed to think that mental/physical correlations or causal relations are vague and unwieldy and not specific and regular?) To see this it is important to get clear on the use of "faculty" as the term has been historically used in discussions of substances in general and the soul in particular (Tennant 1956, 1–138, especially 33–43). Roughly, a faculty of some particular substance is a natural grouping of resembling capacities or potentialities possessed by that thing. For example, the various capacities to hear sounds would constitute a person's auditory faculty. Moreover, a capacity gets its identity and proper metaphysical categorization from the type of property it actualizes. The nature of a capacity-to-exemplify-F is properly characterized by F itself. Thus, the capacity to reflect light is properly considered a physical, optical capacity. For property dualists, the capacities for various mental states are mental and not physical capacities. Thus, the faculties that are constituted by those capacities are mental and not physical faculties.

Now, arguably, a particular is the kind of thing it is in virtue of the actual and potential properties/faculties essential and intrinsic to it. Thus, a description of the faculties of a thing provides accurate information about the kind of particular that has those faculties. For example, a description of the (irreducible) dispositions of gold provides us with information about the sort of thing gold is.

A description of a particular's capacities/faculties is a more accurate source of information about its nature than is an analysis of the causal/functional conditions relevant for the particular to act in various ways. The latter can either be clues to the intrinsic nature of that particular or else information about some other entity that the particular relates to in exhibiting a particular causal action.

For example, if Smith needs to use a magnet to pick up certain unreachable iron filings, information about the precise nature of the magnet and its role in Smith's action does not tell us much about the nature of Smith (except that he is dependent in his functional abilities on other things, e.g., the magnet). We surely would not conclude that the actual and potential properties of a magnet are clues to Smith's inner nature.

Similarly, functional dependence on/causal relations to the brain are of much less value in telling us what kind of thing a human person is than is a careful description of the kind-defining mental capacities, that is, faculties, human persons as such possess. In this case, various forms of physicalism and substance dualism are empirically equivalent theses and, in fact, there is no non-question-begging theoretical virtue (e.g., simplicity) that can settle the debate if it is limited to being a scientific debate. But it should not be so limited and, indeed, paradigm case substance dualists such as F. R. Tennant approached the subject of the nature of the self and its relationship to faculties from a distinctively first-person introspective point of view. The choice to side with Murphy over against Tennant cannot be made on the basis of detailed scientific correlations. Rather, it must be made on the basis of factors such as one's evaluation of the strength of first-person awareness of the self and its conscious life.

Murphy's second argument is that we should take physicalism not merely as a philosophical thesis, but primarily as the hard core of a scientific research program. If we look at physicalism not as a philosophical thesis but as a scientific theory, then there is ample scientific evidence for it (Murphy 1998b, 127–148).

If one follows Murphy's advice, then the Autonomy Thesis will have to be set aside. But for at least two reasons, I think Murphy's recommendation is ill-advised. For one thing, it is unclear how physicalism in any of its forms is actually used as the "hard core of a scientific research program" in a way relevant to debates in philosophy of mind. To see this, it will be helpful to get before us some important points made by Alvin Plantinga and Bas C. van Fraasen.

Plantinga contrasts Duhemian and Augustinian science derived, respectively, from the ideas of Pierre Duhem and St Augustine (Plantinga 1996, 177–221). According to Duhem, religious and, more importantly, metaphysical doctrines have often entered into physical theory. Many scientists have sought explanations of the phenomena, the appearances, in terms of underlying material causes. A proffered characterization of those causes often employs divisive metaphysical commitments as when Aristotelians, Cartesians, and atomists gave disparate accounts of the phenomenon of magnetism.

If the aim of physical theory is to explain phenomena in terms of the ultimate nature of their causes, says Duhem, then physical science becomes subordinate to metaphysics and is no longer an autonomous science. Thus, estimates of the worth of a physical theory will depend upon the metaphysics one adopts. When practitioners of an area of physical science embrace different metaphysical schemes, progress is impeded because there is a compromise in the cooperation needed for progress. Successful science, if it is to be common to all, should not employ religious or metaphysical commitments only acceptable to some, including theism or physicalist naturalism. For Duhem, it is not the absence of metaphysics as such that serves the prudential interests of science, but of metaphysical views that divide us.

Augustinian science stands in contrast to Duhemian science. An Augustinian approach to science eschews methodological naturalism, and employs religious or metaphysical commitments specific to a group of practitioners not widely shared throughout the scientific community. Augustinian science sanctions the use of scientific data to justify a religious or metaphysical proposition specific to a group of practitioners.

According to Plantinga, Duhemian science will not "employ assumptions like those, for example, that seem to underlie much cognitive science. For example, it could not properly assume that mind-body dualism is false, or that human beings are material objects; these are metaphysical assumptions that divide us" (Plantinga 1996, 209–210). More generally, the fact that there is a distinction between Duhemian and Augustinian science and that the former can be practiced at all seems to justify the Autonomy Thesis by showing that the progress of and data derived in accordance with Duhemian science are usually not of fundamental importance for resolving the deeper metaphysical issues that divide practitioners into different Augustinian camps.

Aspects of van Fraasen's philosophy of science lead to a similar conclusion. Van Fraasen argues that the theoretical postulates of a scientific theory typically go beyond the observational evidence and several different metaphysical characterizations are empirically equivalent (van Fraasen 1980; 1984, 250–259). For van Fraasen, the primary goal of a scientific theory is to be empirically adequate, and acceptance of the unobservable metaphysical postulates of a theory is merely a pragmatic stance taken by advocates of a research program to continue searching for greater empirical adequacy.

This is what is actually going on when scientists employ physicalism as the hard core of a scientific research program. They are simply proffering either physically detectable operational definitions of mental states or are straightforwardly searching for physical correlates/causal relations for those mental states. There is not a single discovery in neuroscience (or cognitive science) that requires or even provides adequate justification for abandoning property or substance dualism, since the main issues in neuroscience and philosophy of mind conform to the Autonomy Thesis. The actual success of, say, neuroscience is strictly due to its Duhemian nature. This is why in the last few decades three Nobel Prize winners in neuro-science or related fields were a substance dualist (John C. Eccles), an emergent property dualist (Roger Sperry), and a strict physicalist (Francis Crick). What divided them were philo-sophical differences, not differences about scientific facts.

In fact, in a recent article, Crick and Christof Koch (1998, 97–107) acknowledge that one of the main attitudes among neuroscientists is that the nature of consciousness is "a philo-sophical problem, and so best left to philosophers." This posture comports perfectly with Duhemian science. Elsewhere, they claim that "scientists should concentrate on questions that can be experimentally resolved and leave metaphysical speculations to 'late-night con-versations over beer'" (Horgan 1994, 91). Methodologically, they set aside philosophical ques-tions about the nature of consciousness and study the neural correlates and causal/functional roles of conscious states. If this is all it means to say that physicalism is "the hard core of a scientific research program," a dualist will heartily agree and, in any case, such a Duhemian appropriation of physicalism underscores and does not provide a counter-argument to the Autonomy Thesis.

The mistaken notion that progress in neuroscience requires an Augustinian commitment to physicalism as an essential component of that progress derives, not from the actual physical facts of neuroscience or the actual way neuroscience is practiced as evidenced by the Duhemian approach of Crick and Koch, but from the sociological fact that many contem-porary neuroscientists just happen to be physicalists, and many people, including some philosophers, seem overly impressed with the cultural authority of science.

Second, when scientists study the causal correlates/functional relations between con-scious states and the brain, they must rely on first-person reports about those states themselves. To see this, consider the binding problem. Scientists are seeking to find a region of the brain that "unifies" all the different stimuli that activate various parts of the brain. But exactly why would anyone think that such unification should be sought? Certainly not from an empirical investigation of the brain itself. Rather, we know from first-person intro-spection of our own substantial selves and our conscious states that all of our experiences are unified into one field of consciousness and, in fact, are possessed by one unified I, and it is on the basis of this knowledge that the scientific research program is justified and moti-vated. Moreover, William Hasker has argued that the phenomena which underlie this research are best explained by (emergent) substance dualism (see Hasker 1999, 122–146, 171–203). Whether Hasker is right or not is itself a philosophical matter that illustrates the Autonomy Thesis.

Given that (1) substance/property dualism are widely acknowledged to be the common-sense position based on first-person introspection, and (2) the task of arguing for or against dualism so grounded is a philosophical one, and (3) neuroscientific research must rely on first-person introspective reports, the Autonomy Thesis seems to capture adequately the role of pre-philosophical intuitions and distinctively philosophical issues in neuroscience. The debate between dualists and physicalists is not about scientific facts. It is about things such as the status of first-person introspection as a source of justification for common-sense beliefs about the self and consciousness, the status of philosophical knowledge, and the proper philosophical interpretation of the role of physicalism in scientific research.

The truth of the Autonomy Thesis is what philosophers should have expected all along, and it constitutes philosophical self-understanding throughout the history of philosophy up to and including the present. In his 1886 lectures on the limitations of scientific materialism,

John Tyndall claimed that "The chasm between the two classes of phenomena" is of such a nature that we might establish empirical association between them, but it

> would still remain intellectually impassable. Let the consciousness of love, for example, be associated with a right-handed spiral motion of the molecules in the brain, and the consciousness of hate with a left-handed spiral motion. We should then know when we love that the motion is in one direction, and when we hate that the motion is in the other; but the "WHY" would remain as unanswerable as before. (Tyndall 1897, 89)

Little has changed since Tyndall made this remark. Specifically, no advance in knowledge of the specificity of detail regarding the correlations between mental and physical states provides any evidence against dualism or, more importantly, against the Autonomy Thesis. When philosophers discuss topics in philosophy of mind, they do not employ specific information in the physical sciences, because it is not relevant to their issues. In evaluating functionalism, it does not matter if one claims that a functional state is realized by brain state alpha or by a more detailed description of the relevant brain state. Scientific data play virtually no role at all in philosophy-of-mind literature. In fact, it is rare for a philosophical text in philosophy of mind to include any scientific information. The same cannot be said, however, of scientific discussions of topics in these areas. For example, after claiming to set aside philosophical issues in order to focus on the more important empirical issues, Crick and Koch's discussion of consciousness and neuroscience is literally teeming with philosophical claims about topics philosophical and with which they qua scientists are inadequately equipped to deal. For example, they claim that "Philosophers, in their carefree way, have invented a creature they call a 'zombie,' who is supposed to act just as normal people do but to be completely *un*conscious. This seems to us to be an untenable scientific idea" (Crick and Koch 1998, 3).

Relatedly, in considering whether two people in a similar brain state would experience the same quale, they say that

> One is therefore tempted to use the philosopher's favorite tool, the thought experiment. Unfortunately, this enterprise is fraught with hazards, since it inevitably makes assumptions about how brains behave, and most of these assumptions have so little experimental support that conclusions based on them are valueless. (Crick and Koch 1998, 15)

Crick and Koch have a poor grasp on the role of thought experiments in philosophical argumentation. (Does the Knowledge Argument advocate make assumptions about how brains work in the actual world?) Moreover, when compared to philosophical treatments of topics in philosophy of mind, the discussion by Crick and Koch illustrates an asymmetry between neuroscience and philosophy of mind and, therefore, the Autonomy Thesis. Scientists cannot adequately discuss the central topics in philosophy of mind without making substantive philosophical claims, but philosophers need not discuss scientific data to treat adequately these same philosophical issues.

If I am right about all this, then if someone is going to be a mind/body physicalist, he or she cannot appeal to science to justify that commitment. It may well be that in first-person introspection one discovers oneself to be constituted by animality, or there may be overriding philosophical and theological arguments for physicalism, though I suspect that even these arguments are not the real reason for physicalism's popularity among many academics. Explaining why I have these suspicions must be left for another occasion. But one thing seems clear. Whenever and wherever that dialogue takes place, it will be a nice illustration of the Autonomy Thesis (see Moreland 2008, 2009).

Notes

1   Cf. van Inwagen 1990 (especially chapters 2 and 9); 1995; Baker 1995; Merricks 1994; 1999.
2   See Foster 1991, 266–280; Gillett 1993, 81–100; Moreland 1997, 351–381. But cf. O'Connor 1995, 178–180.

References

Baker, Lynn Rudder. 1995. Need a Christian Be a Mind/Body Dualist? *Faith and Philosophy*, 12(4), pp. 489–504.

Bealer, George. 1996. On the Possibility of Philosophical Knowledge. *Philosophical Perspectives*, 10, pp. 1–34.

Churchland, Paul M. 1988. *Matter and Consciousness: A Contemporary Introduction to the Philosophy of Mind*, revised edn. Cambridge, MA: MIT Press.

Cooper, John W. 2000. *Body, Soul and Life Everlasting: Biblical Anthropology and the Monism–Dualism Debate*, revised edn. Grand Rapids, MI: Eerdmans.

Cooper, John W. 2007. The Bible and Dualism Once Again: A Reply to Joel B. Green and Nancey Murphy. *Philosophia Christi*, 9(2), pp. 459–469.

Cooper, John W. 2009a. The Current Body–Soul Debate: A Case for Dualistic Holism. *Southern Baptist Journal of Theology*, 13(2), pp. 32–50.

Cooper, John W. 2009b. Exaggerated Rumors of Dualism's Demise: A Review Essay on *Body, Soul, and Human Life*. *Philosophia Christi*, 11(2), pp. 453–464.

Crick, Francis and Koch, Christof. 1998. Consciousness and Neuroscience. *Cerebral Cortex*, 8(2), pp. 97–107.

Foster, John. 1991. *The Immaterial Self: A Defence of the Cartesian Dualist Conception of the Mind*. London: Routledge.

Gillett, Grant. 1993. Actions, Causes, and Mental Ascriptions. In Howard Robinson, ed. *Objections to Physicalism*. Oxford: Clarendon Press, pp. 101–126.

Goetz, Stewart. 2001. Modal Dualism: A Critique. In Kevin Corcoran, ed. *Soul, Body and Survival: Essays on the Metaphysics of Human Persons*. Ithaca, NY: Cornell University Press, pp. 89–104.

Green, Joel B. 2008. *Body, Soul and Human Life: The Nature of Humanity in the Bible*. Grand Rapids, MI: Baker Academic.

Hasker, William. 1999. *The Emergent Self*. Ithaca, NY: Cornell University Press.

Horgan, John. 1994. Can Science Explain Consciousness? *Scientific American* (July), p. 91.

Kim, Jaegwon. 2001. Lonely Souls: Causality and Substance Dualism. In Kevin Corcoran, ed. *Soul, Body, and Survival: Essays on the Metaphysics of Human Persons*. Ithaca, NY: Cornell University Press, pp. 30–44.

Lewis, H. D. 1982. *The Elusive Self*. Philadelphia: The Westminster Press.

Madell, Geoffrey. 1981. *The Identity of the Self*. Edinburgh: Edinburgh University Press.

Madell, Geoffrey. 1988. *Mind and Materialism*. Edinburgh: Edinburgh University Press.

Merricks, Trenton. 1994. A New Objection to *A Priori* Arguments for Dualism. *American Philosophical Quarterly*, 31(1), pp. 81–85.

Merricks, Trenton. 1999. The Resurrection of the Body and the Life Everlasting. In Michael J. Murray, ed. *Reason for the Hope Within*. Grand Rapids, MI: Eerdmans, pp. 261–286.

Moreland, J. P. 1997. Naturalism and Libertarian Agency. *Philosophy and Theology*, 10(2), pp. 351–381.

Moreland, J. P. 2002. Timothy O'Connor and the Harmony Thesis: A Critique. *Metaphysica*, 3(2), pp. 5–40.

Moreland, J. P. 2008. *Consciousness and the Existence of God: A Theistic Argument*. New York: Routledge.

Moreland, J. P. 2009. *The Recalcitrant Imago Dei: Human Persons and the Failure of Naturalism*. London: SCM Press.

Moreland, J. P. and Rae, Scott B. 2000. *Body and Soul: Human Nature and the Crisis in Ethics*. Downers Grove, IL: InterVarsity Press.

Murphy, Nancey. 1998a. Human Nature: Historical, Scientific, and Religious Issues. In Warren S. Brown, Nancey Murphy. and H. Newton Malony, eds. *Whatever Happened to the Soul? Scientific and Theological Portraits of Human Nature*. Minneapolis: Fortress Press, pp. 1–30.

Murphy, Nancey. 1998b. Nonreductive Physicalism: Philosophical issues. In Warren S. Brown, Nancey Murphy, and H. Newton Malony, eds. *Whatever Happened to the Soul? Scientific and Theological Portraits of Human Nature*. Minneapolis: Fortress Press, pp. 127–148.

Murphy, Nancey and Brown, Warren S. 2009. *Did My Neurons Make Me Do It? Philosophical and Neurobiological Perspectives on Moral Responsibility and Free Will*. New York: Oxford University Press.

O'Connor, Timothy. 1995. Agent Causation. In Timothy O'Connor, ed. *Agents, Causes, and Events: Essays on Indeterminism and Free Will*. New York: Oxford University Press, pp. 173–200.

O'Connor, Timothy. 2000. *Persons and Causes: The Metaphysics of Free Will*. New York: Oxford University Press.

Plantinga, Alvin. 1996. Methodological Naturalism. In Jitse M. van der Meer, ed. *Facets of Faith and Science, vol. 1, Historiography and Modes of Interaction*. Lanham, MD: University Press of America, pp. 177–221.

Swinburne, Richard. 1997. *The Evolution of the Soul*, revised edn. Oxford: Clarendon Press.

Taliaferro, Charles. 1995. Animals, Brains, and Spirits. *Faith and Philosophy*, 12(4), pp. 567–581.

Tennant, F. R. 1956. *Philosophical Theology*, vol. I, *The Soul and Its Faculties*. Cambridge: Cambridge University Press.

Tyndall, John. 1897. Scientific Materialism. In *Fragments of Science: A Series of Detached Essays, Addresses, and Reviews*, vol. 2. New York: D. Appleton & Company.

van Fraassen, Bas C. 1980. *The Scientific Image*. Oxford: Oxford University Press.

van Fraassen, Bas C. 1984. To Save the Phenomena. In Jarrett Leplin, ed. *Scientific Realism*. Berkeley: University of California Press, pp. 250–259.

van Inwagen, Peter. 1990. *Material Beings*. Ithaca, NY: Cornell University Press.

van Inwagen, Peter. 1995. Dualism and Materialism: Athens and Jerusalem? *Faith and Philosophy*, 12(4), pp. 475–488.

Wright, N. T. 2003. *Christian Origins and the Question of God, vol. 3, The Resurrection of the Son of God*. Minneapolis: Fortress Press.

Yandell, Keith. 1995. A Defense of Dualism. *Faith and Philosophy*, 12(4), pp. 548–566.

Further Reading

Baker, Mark C. and Goetz, Stewart. 2010. *Soul Hypothesis*. New York: Continuum. A multidisciplinary defense of the soul.

Beauregard, Mario and O'Leary, Denyse. 2007. *The Spiritual Brain*. New York: HarperCollins. A defense of the claim that neuroscience is fully supportive of substance dualism.

Goetz, Stewart and Taliaferro, Charles. 2011. *A Brief History of the Soul*. Oxford: Wiley-Blackwell. A history of the nature of and case for and against the soul that illustrates powerfully that these issues are not scientific.

Moreland, J. P. 2009. *The Recalcitrant Imago Dei*. London: SCM Press. Contains a description of five irreducible, unleiminable features of human persons that cannot be adequately explained by scientific naturalism but which are so explained by Western theism.

41

The Emergence of Persons

WILLIAM HASKER

Alternatives to Emergence

A viable theory of the nature of human persons needs to be an emergentist theory. The case for this claim can't be set out in full here, but a brief sketch will be offered. The main alternatives to emergence are reductive materialist views and traditional dualism. Reductive versions of materialism hold little appeal for those who are interested in developing a view of human persons that is congruent with religious faith; there are just too many points at which the two approaches will clash. But that kind of materialism also faces formidable difficulties of a purely philosophical nature. There is the notorious "hard problem" of consciousness, the unsolved problem of explaining how conscious states are either reducible to or metaphysically necessitated by states of the physical organism. There is the problem of mental causation: given that, as such views assert, the physical domain is causally closed, how can mental states as such make a difference to what goes on in the world?[1] (Even token-identity theories founder on this point; a mental event which is identical with some physical event may have causal consequences, but the consequences will be those that follow from the physical characteristics of the event, not those that result from its phenomenal or intentional character.) On reductive materialist views, neither intentionality nor teleology can be fundamental features of reality. (As Jerry Fodor remarked, "If aboutness is real, it must really be something else."[2]) Such views, I surmise, will not be live alternatives for most philosophers who are interested in the project represented by the present volume.

Traditional dualist views – Cartesian and Thomistic are the main varieties – avoid these difficulties but face others in their place. On both sorts of views, the human soul is a special divine creation, whose origin does not depend on the physical organism. They differ, however, in the kind of relationship posited between the soul and the organism. For Cartesian views, the biological functions of the organism are independent of the soul, which is concerned only with conscious experience, or, as Descartes said, with "thinking." For Thomistic views, the soul is "the form of the body," and is essential for biological functioning, as it is for conscious experience. Cartesian views have difficulty in giving a plausible account of the intimate

The Blackwell Companion to Science and Christianity, First Edition. Edited by J. B. Stump and Alan G. Padgett.

dependence of highly sophisticated mental processes on specific aspects of brain function. Thomistic views are somewhat less troubled by this, but by insisting that the soul is essential for biological functioning they are committed to a vitalist view concerning the nature of life that has been emphatically rejected by the life sciences for about a century. Both sorts of views confront an awkward situation in dealing with biological evolution. More complex and highly evolved organisms presumably require more complex souls, endowed with correspondingly enhanced powers. (Descartes's attempt to limit souls to human beings entails the unacceptable consequence that only humans have conscious experiences, the rest of the animal realm consisting of cleverly constructed automata.) But what is the relationship between the increasing biological complexity and the gradually (or perhaps stepwise) increasing powers of the divinely created souls? Are we to suppose that God waits until natural evolutionary processes have produced a more complex organism, and then supplies the more sophisticated soul? (But then, how would the requisite modifications in the organism be selected for, if they are as yet unable to function because the soul is inadequate to support the functions in question?) Or do the more advanced souls come first and somehow guide the process of evolutionary development? Or, finally, does each major evolutionary advance require a simultaneous "double nudge," which at the same time impels the physical modifications and supplies a more advanced soul? Perhaps each of these alternatives is logically possible, but I doubt that any of them will commend itself as plausible in the light of reflection.

This is, to repeat, a mere sketch of a critique which needs to be much more fully developed – and has been more fully developed elsewhere.[3] But life is short, and editors are jealous of space, so we must proceed to consider the emergentist views with which this chapter is primarily concerned.

Emergence and Its Varieties

The core idea of emergence can be explained as follows:

> When elements of a certain sort are arranged in the right way, something new comes into being, something that was not there before. The new thing is not just a rearrangement of what was there before, but neither is it something dropped into the situation from the outside. It "emerges," comes into being, through the operation of the constituent elements, yet the new thing is something different and surprising; we would not have expected it before it appears. (Hasker 2005, 76)

As applied to the human person, this means that the person emerges as a result of the structure and functioning of the human body; more generally, mind or consciousness arises whenever there is a suitably composed and functioning organism. This very general conception of emergence, however, needs to be further specified. Emergence comes in various degrees; the weaker versions tend to be uncontroversial but metaphysically trivial, while the stronger versions are more consequential but whether they actually occur is in dispute. For our present purposes there are two varieties of emergence that are especially pertinent.

The first variety of emergence to be considered can be labeled as *the emergence of novel causal powers*. What this means is that, given the right configuration and functioning of the underlying elements, new forms of causality arise; there are new causal powers that did not operate until the elements were in the correct configuration. Furthermore, the operation of these powers cannot be inferred from the laws that govern the functioning of the elements apart from the special configuration in question. What this means in the case of the mind is this: once the physical stuff of the brain and nervous system achieves the right state of functional complexity, new phenomena are produced, namely the phenomena of conscious awareness. Furthermore, these new phenomena are themselves causally efficacious, in that because they occur the physical system itself behaves in ways it otherwise would not have done. For a concrete example: when I reach a decision to pay a visit to the grocery store, this results in my body's making the appropriate movements (getting my coat on, going out to the car, turning on the ignition, etc.), movements that would not have occurred had I not reached that particular decision. There is a temptation, to which many philosophers succumb, to insist that the movements of my body are themselves fully explained in terms of the ordinary laws of physics and chemistry, and thus to deny that the mind has any actual control over one's bodily movements. This of course is the doctrine of the "causal closure of the physical domain," noted above as a central cause for the difficulties of reductive materialism. (This leads to the view of the mind known as *epiphenomenalism*, according to which mental properties and consciousness exist but are without causal consequences.) In contrast to this, the theory of emergent causal powers, applied in this instance, insists that what emerges from the function of the brain[4] is mental states that are causally efficacious – that make a difference in the physical goings-on in the world.

By postulating emergent causal powers, an emergentist theory can provide answers to many of the questions that prove themselves recalcitrant for reductive materialism. Emergence theory does give an account of how conscious experience arises from the functioning of the biological organism. This is not, of course, the sort of theory the reductivists are seeking – but whether an adequate theory needs to conform to their strictures is precisely the point in dispute. By making conscious experiences causally effective it banishes the threat of epiphenomenalism; it also solves the problem of mental causation and is able to recognize intentionality and teleology as fundamental factors in the world. Perhaps most surprising, this sort of emergence theory harmonizes better with biological evolution than either traditional dualism or reductive materialism. The difficulties for dualism posed by evolution have already been noted, and evolution is widely appealed to as a reason to discount dualism altogether. But reductive materialism also has a problem with evolution: namely, the problem of *explaining how it is possible for humans to achieve conscious knowledge and awareness of many aspects of the world*. That we do have such knowledge is for materialists undeniable; indeed it is the conspicuous success of the natural sciences in achieving knowledge of the world that provides a great deal of the motivation for materialist theories. But how is our ability to achieve such knowledge to be explained? If materialists are asked to explain the cognitive abilities of human beings, the answer that is invariably given (and probably that must be given) is in terms of Darwinian evolution. Awareness of life-supporting or life-threatening features of the environment (for example, the presence of predators or prey, or the location of food resources) can have a major effect on an organism's ability to survive and reproduce, and in this way genetic variations that enhance such awareness are selected for; they are more likely to be passed on to successor generations. There is of course a question as to how this applies to mental capabilities that have little relation to survival and reproductive success, such as higher mathematics. But reductive materialism faces a more fundamental objection: on this view, with its dogma of the causal closure of the physical domain, *conscious experiences have no physical consequences and cannot be subject to evolutionary selection*. The selection process, after all, is physical in nature, and only features that have physical consequences can be selected for or against. To be sure, a predator might happen to be in a neurological state that enables it to hunt down and overcome its prey in an especially effective way. There is in principle no obstacle to a Darwinian explanation of this fact. The question remains, however, *what is responsible for the fact that a physical state of the organism that is evolutionarily successful is correlated with a conscious state that involves a true apprehension of the world?* If reductive materialism cannot answer this question, it is in deep trouble – but it is hard to see how any credible answer is possible. Emergentism, on the other hand, has no difficulty with such a question: mental states are causally efficacious in virtue of their phenomenal and intentional properties, and because of this they are indeed subject to evolutionary selection.

The other type of emergence to be considered here may be designated as the *emergence of individuals*. Given the proper configuration of the underlying substrate, a completely *new individual* comes into existence, one that does not consist of previously existing "stuff" of any kind. This sort of emergence will also involve emergent causal powers, in two distinct ways. The emergence of the individuals in question is not entailed by the causal laws that operate outside the emergence situation; thus the emergence of such individuals itself represents an emergent causal power of the substrate in such a configuration. Furthermore, the emergent individual will exert causal powers that would not otherwise exist. (Absent this, there would be little reason to postulate the emergent individuals.) So the emergence of individuals is not an alternative to the emergence of powers, but rather a second level of emergence in addition to the emergence of novel causal powers.

Claims about the emergence of individuals in this sense are less common than claims for emergent causal powers, but they do exist. Interestingly, one advocate for the emergence of individuals is Wilfrid Sellars, whose "sensa" are emergent in precisely the sense described (Sellars 1971, 408). More relevant to the present topic, Karl Popper seems to have thought of the human mind as an emergent individual in this sense (Popper and Eccles 1977, part I; cf. Hasker 1999, 185–188). Still more recently, Dean Zimmerman (2006) and Peter Unger (2006) have expressed support for the notion of the mind as an emergent individual. The application of this notion will be further developed in the following section.

Emergent Dualism and Emergentist Materialism

In describing these two varieties of emergence, we have set the stage for presenting the two main types of theories concerning the emergence of persons. Both theories involve both of the varieties of emergence surveyed in the previous section, albeit in somewhat different ways. The first theory to be discussed is *emergent dualism*,[5] a view I have developed over several decades (see Hasker 1974, 1982, 1999, 2005, 2010, and forthcoming). This view embraces the emergent causal powers described above, but maintains that these powers are exercised by a new individual, not composed of the microparticles of physics, which emerges given the right configuration and functioning of the brain. (On my view the emergent self is spatially extended, but this conclusion is not strictly required by other aspects of the theory.) Similar individuals will emerge also in those lower organisms which possess some degree of conscious awareness – thus, "animal souls." (Emergent dualism, unlike Cartesian dualism, faces no embarrassment over the question of the souls of beasts.)

One might wonder at this point why an emergentist theory needs to introduce such a new individual, since the benefits of emergentism, as described above, could apparently be secured merely by postulating emergent causal powers. The answer to this question lies in the *unity-of-consciousness argument* which is derived from Leibniz and Kant. In a familiar passage Leibniz writes:

> In imagining that there is a machine whose construction would enable it to think, to sense, and to have perception, one could conceive it enlarged while retaining the same proportions, so that one could enter into it, just like into a windmill. Supposing this, one should, when visiting within it, find only parts pushing one another, and never anything by which to explain a perception. Thus it is in the simple substance, and not in the composite or in the machine, that one must look for perception. (Leibniz 1991, par. 19)

The problem Leibniz is pointing out here does not lie, as many have supposed, in the limitations of seventeenth-century technology. If instead of his "parts pushing one another" we fill the machine with vacuum tubes, transistors, or for that matter with neurons, exactly the same problem remains. The problem does not lie in the pushes and pulls but rather in the *complexity* of the machine, the fact that it is made up of many distinct parts, coupled with the fact that *a complex state of consciousness cannot exist distributed among the parts of a complex object*. The emergent self of emergent dualism fills the role of the "simple substance" which, as argued by Leibniz, is needed to account for perception and other conscious states (cf. Hasker 1999, chapter 5; 2010).

The other type of view to be discussed here may be termed *emergentist materialism*; it affirms that what is distinctive about persons is the emergence of the distinctive personal powers (reason, moral discernment, free will, and the like), these powers being properties of the physical organism itself. It is "materialist" in the sense that human beings are held to be physical objects with no non-physical parts (such as the "souls" embraced by various forms of dualism), but not in the stronger sense implied by reductive materialism. A view of this sort has been capably developed by Timothy O'Connor (see 1994, 2000a, 2000b, 2003; O'Connor and Jacobs 2003, 2010; O'Connor and Churchill 2010).

Since emergentist materialism denies the existence of a non-physical soul, it might seem that it lacks the resources needed to meet the challenge of the unity-of-consciousness argument.[6] This, however, is not correct; the needed resources make their appearance in the two articles by O'Connor and Jacobs (2003, 2010).[7] In order to understand their response to this argument it becomes necessary to go into some of detail regarding the ontology adopted by these two philosophers.

The ontology in question, which owes much to D. M. Armstrong, is described by them as an "ontology of immanent universals." Each and every substance (for instance, an electron which they dub "eleanore") involves features or universals that exist in that substance but can also exist in many others. But given this:

> There must be something more to eleanore than a mere cluster of universals, since it is a particular thing, and no cluster of universals can yield particularity. This something extra can only be eleanore's *particularity* or *thisness*, a non-qualitative aspect necessarily unique to it. Eleanore, then, is constituted by a cluster of universals, plus such a particularity, bound in some sort of non-mereological structure, which we shall call a "state of affairs." (O'Connor and Jacobs 2003, 546)

Eleanore's particularity or thisness, then, is an ontological constituent of eleanore though not, in the proper sense, a "part" of eleanore. It needs to be noted, however, that these thisnesses are more sparingly distributed in the world than one might be inclined to think. They write:

Anyone who embraces this ontology in a serious way should posit distinctive particularities in only mereological simples and those composites that exhibit some kind of objective, ontological unity. Substances exhibiting ontologically emergent properties are natural candidates. Those lacking such features, however much they may appear to be unified to the uneducated eye, are individual objects only by a courtesy born of practical concerns. (O'Connor and Jacobs 2003, 547)

We arrive, then, at a metaphysic that exhibits some striking similarities to that expounded by Peter van Inwagen in his *Material Beings* (van Inwagen 1990). What exists are physical simples and some organisms; strictly speaking there are no chairs but only "simples arranged chair-wise."

Given all this, we are ready for a more detailed account of what O'Connor and Jacobs term the emergence of a "new substance."[8] At an early stage in the development of an organism, we have a number of atoms that have certain properties and are arranged in a certain way. (Note that at this stage no organism as such exists.) These atoms, together with God[9] and perhaps certain features of the environment, bring about (that is, cause) the existence of something new, an organism, which has both a particularity of its own and new, emergent causal powers. The organism, then, is a complex whole which involves the physical simples, with their own properties and relations, the emergent causal powers, and the particularity or thisness which unifies the simples and makes it the case that they compose a single thing, an organism. Furthermore, the organism's possession of the emergent powers – powers which, as the unity-of-consciousness argument has shown, cannot exist distributed among the parts of the organism – consists precisely in the composition relation between those powers and the particularity. The particularity, then, is the "simple" entity that plays the same role as Leibniz's simple substance or the self of emergent dualism, and in view of this emergentist materialism is not threatened by the unity-of-consciousness argument. Emergentist materialism does after all involve the emergence of new individuals, though in a different sense than is postulated by emergent dualism.

Evaluating the Two Emergentisms

The two views discussed here, emergentist materialism and emergent dualism, arguably represent the best available options for an emergentist philosophy of mind. And if the general case for emergentism is cogent, they may be the most promising possibilities for a general account of the mind. (They are by no means the currently most popular options, but that is another matter!) The task of evaluating these two emergentisms against one another is, however, only beginning. The comments that will be offered here should be taken as tentative first steps towards that project.

It might occur to us that in the context set by the present volume emergent dualism enjoys an immediate advantage over emergentist materialism, one that, unless countered, might by itself be sufficient to guarantee victory. This advantage concerns the belief in survival after death, a belief that is central to Christianity, as to many other religious traditions. To be sure, the typical Christian belief affirms the resurrection of the body rather than a future existence as an unembodied soul, and this may seem to neutralize the advantage of the dualistic alternative. Belief in the resurrection, however, has traditionally been coupled with, rather than opposed to, belief in an incorporeal soul. Furthermore, attempts to conceive of a resurrection

without a soul have encountered serious difficulties over the personal identity of the resurrected (or recreated) person with the individual who previously lived. It is not clear that, in
spite of strenuous efforts, these difficulties have been overcome; if they have not, that confers
an advantage on dualist views for which the continuity of the soul ensures personal identity.
This advantage, if it exists, will not play a major role in the present discussion. O'Connor and
Jacobs (2010), and in another context Dean Zimmerman (2010), have recently argued that a
certain type of materialist resurrection (popularly known as body-splitting) can overcome
difficulties over the identity of a resurrected body with the body that previously lived and
died. Whether these attempts succeed is an important question that demands a full-scale
treatment on its own account (see Hasker 2011).

On the other side of the ledger, O'Connor and his co-authors have a number of complaints
about emergent dualism, complaints that in their opinion should greatly reduce its attractive-
ness. Early on, O'Connor seems to have considered the whole notion of the emergence of a
mental substance to be highly implausible: this sort of emergence, he wrote, "would involve
the generation of fundamentally new substance in the world – amounting to creation *ex
nihilo*. That's a lot to swallow" (O'Connor 2000b, 110). More recently, however, it seems that
O'Connor is not in a strong position to press this objection. The "creation *ex nihilo*" idea
seems to be a way of pointing out that an organism is said to be able to generate a mental
substance that is not made out of any previously existing stuff.[10] But O'Connor and Jacobs's
proposed account of the resurrection also involves creation *ex nihilo*. This account credits
ordinary physical particles – electrons and so on – with the capacity, under certain circumstances, to produce additional particles through "immanent causal fission," where once again
there is no previously existing material to account for the mass-energy of the new particles
(O'Connor and Jacobs 2010, 70ff.). If the latter supposition is such that it is possibly true, why
not the former? Difficulty in swallowing turns out, not surprisingly, to vary depending on
whose theory is on the menu. To those who find their account of the resurrection hard to
accept O'Connor and Jacobs remonstrate, "If you find this wildly implausible, even given
theism, you ought to carefully examine the source of your incredulity" (79). They quote with
satisfaction Alexander's dictum that truths about the powers latent in the constituents of the
universe are to be discovered empirically and then accepted "with the natural piety of
the investigator" (80).

An additional objection is directed at a more specific feature of emergent dualism.
O'Connor and Jacobs complain that on this view:

> One is apparently asked to contemplate a composite physical system's giving rise, all in one go,
> to a whole, self-contained, organized system of properties bound up with a distinct individual.
> Applied to human beings, the view will imply that at an early stage of physical development, a
> self emerges, having all the capacities of an adult human self, most of which, however, lie
> dormant owing to immaturity in the physical system from which it emerges. (O'Connor and
> Jacobs 2003, 549)

The problem presumably is not that the emergent individual comes into existence "all at one
go," for this will be true also of the emergent substance featured in emergentist materialism.
The problem is rather that, at a very early stage of the organism's development, the emergent
self will be possessed of "all the capacities of an adult human self," most of which cannot
yet be utilized (and some which may never be able to be utilized) because of the inadequate
development of the organism. This does indeed sound problematic, but why attribute such
a view to emergent dualism? At an early stage the powers of the emergent self will be limited

in a way that corresponds to the limited capacities of the generating brain and nervous system. Later on, the increasing functional complexity of the neural substrate leads to a corresponding augmentation of the mind's powers. In another article, however, O'Connor seeks to block this move, writing:

> For we cannot say, as we should want to do, that as the underlying physical structure *develops*, the emergent self does likewise, as there doesn't seem to be conceptual space for changing mereological complexity within a nonphysical simple. (O'Connor 2003, 3)

This criticism involves the entirely gratuitous assumption that growth in the powers of the emergent self must come about through "changing mereological complexity" – that is, through the *addition of parts* to the mind/self/soul. This assumption is simply false in relation to emergent dualism. The growth in powers will occur, as stated above, as a consequence of the gradually increasing functional complexity of the brain and nervous system. The outcome of this criticism may be that we come to appreciate the *similarity* of emergentist materialism and emergent dualism in a way we might not otherwise have done.[11]

Frankly, I am doubtful that any knock-down argument will appear that will show conclusively that one of these views is unacceptable or that one is obviously preferable to the other. As so often in philosophy, we may have to fall back on very general considerations of coherence and plausibility, matters concerning which even the best-intentioned of thinkers are likely to disagree. And, of course, I cannot pretend to occupy the role of a disinterested adjudicator in such a dispute! The thoughts that are put forward here, then, should be understood as tentative early steps in a process that needs to be continued by others.

With regard to emergent dualism, it must be acknowledged that this is not, after all, the simplest or most obvious solution to the mind–body problem. It's just that (as Winston Churchill said about democracy) it begins to look better, the more one considers the alternatives! The original objection offered by O'Connor – that the emergence *ex nihilo* of a whole new substance is implausible – will be felt by many, even if (as we saw) O'Connor is not himself in a strong position to press his objection. Again, the assertion that ordinary, everyday matter has within itself the potentiality to generate something with the amazing capacities we find in the human mind may well strain one's credulity. (This is so, even though the assertion is made also by O'Connor's own view and by materialist philosophies of mind in general.) For that matter, the very word "dualism" is enough by itself to ensure that the view will be seen as an unwelcome intruder in many gatherings of philosophers!

Where emergentist materialism is concerned, it may in a sense be problematic that the view is tied so closely to a particular system of ontology. To be sure, any philosopher writing on the mind–body problem will have some views about ontology and will tend to reflect them in his or her writing. In many cases, however, it is possible to consider the views concerning the philosophy of mind without directly engaging issues of ontology.[12] That is not the case with O'Connor and Jacobs's proposal, though. In order for the view to get off the ground, one has to accept the general notion of an ontology in which, in some fairly literal sense, organisms are constituted by a "non-mereological structure" involving a thisness together with immanent universals.[13] Probably we have to accept also the "compositional nihilism" concerning ordinary physical things (those without emergent causal powers); otherwise we wouldn't get the "big bang" when the new thisnesses, together with their corresponding powers, come to be. My intention is not to claim that these views are evidently false; to say that would mean entering another, and very large, debate. My point is merely that it is in some sense a tactical disadvantage for the view that in order to adopt it one must buy into such specific, and highly disputed, theses of general ontology.

While the problem of materialism and the resurrection has not been stressed here, the problem remains on the agenda and it cannot be taken for granted that an acceptable solution is possible. Beyond this, I can only mention some ways in which the metaphysic we are asked to embrace seems problematic. I have little grasp on the "particularities" of composite substances or on the "non-mereological composition relation" that unites them with their component simple substances and with their properties. I understand the role played by these items in the system, but can form no conception of what they might actually be or of why we should suppose that such things actually exist. I suspect this puzzlement will be shared by a good many philosophers whose views about universals tend towards nominalism or conceptualism.

Particularly problematic, it seems to me, is the relation between the material substances that we persons are said to be, our particularities, and our emergent mental properties. Such properties are properties of the person, but what is crucial for their existence is the "non-mereological composition relation" between the properties and the particularity. Indeed, the having of the property *consists entirely* of this composition relation; it *does not in any degree consist* of the properties of, and the relations between, the organism's physical parts. Logically speaking, this property of the physical organism is *completely independent* of any of the physical properties of the organism or its parts. (To be sure, the properties of the organism's parts may, and no doubt do, play a *causal role* in bringing it about that the organism has the emergent property. Causal relations, however, are by common consent logically contingent.) To repeat: the organism's having the property does not consist in any way of the organism or its parts being in any particular physical state; instead it consists entirely of the composition relation between the property and the particularity. But the particularity is not a concrete entity of any kind; it certainly isn't a material entity, and that's the only kind of concrete entity that is available. If the reader's sensibilities resonate with this complaint to any degree, then perhaps he or she will see the point of the contention that there does need to be a concrete entity of some sort, an entity in whose states the having of the emergent property by the substance might consist. Emergent dualism offers a candidate for this role, but it is not a candidate that will be cast for the part by the view now under consideration.

All this, to be sure, reflects my own partial and no doubt biased perspective; in no way does it represents the "view from nowhere" to which philosophers longingly but hopelessly aspire. Others are cordially invited to take their turn in assessing these matters from their own partial and biased perspectives.[14]

Notes

1 This problem applies also to many versions of what is termed "nonreductive physicalism": insofar as they affirm causal closure they cannot avoid being causally reductionist, even if they reject a metaphysical reduction of conscious states to physical states of the organism.
2 Fodor 1987, 9; quoted in Searle 1992, 51. Searle responds: "On the contrary, aboutness (i.e., intentionality) is real, and it is not something else" (51).
3 For my own approach to both reductive materialism and traditional dualism, see Hasker 1999, chapters 1–3 and 6.

4   As a matter of convenience I will often refer to the physical substrate of our conscious life simply as "the brain," while recognizing that it may actually consist of more or of less than the entire brain.

5   Strangely enough, Timothy O'Connor and John Ross Churchill refer to their quite different view as "emergent dualism" (O'Connor and Churchill 2010). This is surprising, because I have been using this label for my own view for over a decade, a fact of which O'Connor, at least, is well aware. I would suggest to O'Connor and Churchill that they should return the intellectual property they have "borrowed," and set about devising an appropriate label for their own position. In the meantime, I will continue to refer to that position as "emergentist materialism."

6   I myself previously supposed this; the following account replaces and corrects what is said on this score in Hasker (forthcoming).

7   Interestingly, O'Connor and Jacobs characterize O'Connor's previously stated view as "mere property emergence" (2003, 549).

8   The description here is adapted from one given by Jonathan Jacobs in private correspondence.

9   God is mentioned here in order to allow for the possibility that God acts in some special way (different from his ordinary conservation of all creatures) in the origins of individual human persons. O'Connor and Jacobs are not committed with regard to whether this actually occurs.

10   We need not, however, exclude the possibility that the generation of a mind consumes energy. For a dualist view that posits exchange of energy between the physical and mental realms, see Hart 1988.

11   The criticism may arise because of a supposition that the emergent self is more similar to a Cartesian ego than in fact it is. A Cartesian ego does seem to be self-contained in a way that suggests that all of its powers must be inherent in it from the very beginning.

12   O'Connor is a philosopher who takes ontology very seriously, but in considering his earlier, property-emergence theory I did not find that his ontological views became anywhere near as prominent as they are in the present context.

13   Or possibly tropes; they do allow for this as a possible, though less favored, alternative.

14   My thanks to Jonathan Jacobs for an extremely helpful discussion based on an earlier version of this material.

References

Fodor, Jerry. 1987. *Psychosemantics*. Cambridge, MA: MIT Press.

Hart, W. D. 1988. *The Engines of the Soul*. Cambridge: Cambridge University Press.

Hasker, William. 1974. The Souls of Beasts and Men. *Religious Studies*, 10, pp. 265–277.

Hasker, William. 1982. Emergentism. *Religious Studies*, 18, pp. 473–488.

Hasker, William. 1999. *The Emergent Self*. Ithaca, NY: Cornell University Press.

Hasker, William. 2005. On Behalf of Emergent Dualism. In Joel B. Green and Stuart L. Palmer, eds. *In Search of the Soul: Four Views of the Mind–Body Problem*. Downers Grove, IL: InterVarsity Press, pp. 75–100.

Hasker, William. 2010. Persons and the Unity of Consciousness. In Robert C. Koons and George Bealer, eds. *The Waning of Materialism: New Essays*. Oxford: Oxford University Press, pp. 175–190.

Hasker, William. 2011. Materialism and the Resurrection: Are the Prospects Improving? *European Journal for Philosophy of Religion*, 3(1), pp. 83–103.

Hasker, William. Forthcoming. Is Materialism Equivalent to Dualism? In Benedikt Paul Göcke, ed. *The Case for Dualism*. Notre Dame: University of Notre Dame Press.

Leibniz, Gottfried Wilhelm. 1991. Monadology. In Nicholas Rescher, ed. *G. W. Leibniz's* Monadology: *An Edition for Students*. Pittsburgh, PA: University of Pittsburgh Press.

O'Connor, Timothy. 1994. Emergent Properties. *American Philosophical Quarterly*, 31, pp. 91–104.

O'Connor, Timothy. 2000a. *Persons and Causes: The Metaphysics of Free Will*. Oxford: Oxford University Press.

O'Connor, Timothy. 2000b. Causality, Mind, and Free Will. In James E. Tomberlin, ed. *Philosophical Perspectives 14: Action and Freedom*. Oxford: Blackwell, pp. 105–117.

O'Connor, Timothy. 2003. Groundwork for an Emergentist Account of the Mental. *Progress in Complexity, Information and Design*, 2.3.1, pp. 1–14.

O'Connor, Timothy and Churchill, John Ross. 2010. Nonreductive Physicalism or Emergent Dualism? The Argument from Mental Causation. In Robert C. Koons and George Bealer, eds. *The Waning of Materialism: New Essays*. Oxford: Oxford University Press, pp. 261–279.

O'Connor, Timothy and Jacobs, Jonathan D. 2003. Emergent Individuals. *Philosophical Quarterly*, 53(213), pp. 540–555.

O'Connor, Timothy and Jacobs, Jonathan D. 2010. Emergent Individuals and the Resurrection. *European Journal for the Philosophy of Religion*, 2(2), pp. 69–88.

Popper, Karl R. and Eccles, John C. 1977. *The Self and Its Brain*. New York: Springer International.

Searle, John. 1992. *The Rediscovery of the Mind*. Cambridge, MA: MIT Press.

Sellars, Wilfrid. 1971. Science, Sense Impressions, and Sensa: A Reply to Cornman. *Review of Metaphysics*, 24(March), pp. 391–447.

Unger, Peter. 2006. *All the Power in the World*. Oxford: Oxford University Press.

van Inwagen, Peter. 1990. *Material Beings*. Ithaca, NY: Cornell University Press.

Zimmerman, Dean. 2006. Dualism in the Philosophy of Mind. In Donald M. Borchert, ed. *The Encyclopedia of Philosophy*, 2nd edn, vol. 3. New York: Macmillan Reference, pp. 113–122.

Zimmerman, Dean. 2010. Bodily Resurrection: The Falling Elevator Model Revisited. In George Gasser, ed. *Personal Identity and Resurrection: How Do We Survive Our Death?* Farnham, UK: Ashgate Publishing, pp. 33–50.

Further Reading

Armstrong, D. M. 1997. *A World of States of Affairs*. Cambridge: Cambridge University Press. A work on ontology that explains some of the concepts that are central to O'Connor and Jacobs's theory.

Beckerman, A., Flohr, H., and Kim, J., eds. 1992. *Emergence or Reduction? Essays on the Prospects of Nonreductive Physicalism*. Berlin: de Gruyter. Essays debating the comparative merits of emergentism versus reductionism.

Clayton, Philip and Davies, Paul, eds. 2006. *The Re-emergence of Emergence: The Emergentist Hypothesis from Science to Religion*. Oxford: Oxford University Press. Essays illustrating the application of emergence in the physical sciences, biology, consciousness studies, and religion.

Koons, Robert C. and Bealer, George, eds. 2010. *The Waning of Materialism: New Essays*. Oxford: Oxford University Press. Contains a number of essays critical of various aspects of reductive materialism, and presenting alternatives.

42

Christianity and the Extended-Mind Thesis

LYNNE RUDDER BAKER

The Extended-Mind Thesis belongs to cognitive science. Although the background assumptions of cognitive science are far removed from those of Christianity, Christians may wonder whether the Extended-Mind Thesis is even compatible with Christianity. Investigation of the compatibility of Christianity and the Extended-Mind Thesis is made more difficult by the fact that there is not just one thesis labeled the "Extended-Mind Thesis," but at least two theses to be disentangled.

The family of theses called the "Extended-Mind Thesis" share, I believe, an assumption. The common assumption is that

> certain forms of human cognizing include inextricable tangles of feedback, feedforward, and feed-around loops: loops that promiscuously criss-cross the boundaries of the brain, body, and the world. The local mechanisms, if this is correct, are not all in the head. Cognition leaks out into body and world. (A. Clark 2008, xxviii)

I'll call the general approach to the mind as having the capacity to extend out into the environment, beyond the brain and body "EM," for "the Extended-Mind Thesis." EM is really a family of theses that has two main branches – claims about cognitive processes and states, and claims about the subjects of those processes. Neither of these claims is straightforwardly confirmable or disconfirmable, inasmuch as both concern how to conceptualize processes and their subjects. What is new about EM are not empirical data, but how to think about the data.

After saying what I find appealing in EM, I shall suggest what a Christian like me might say about several versions of EM theses. Then, I'll make an important distinction that I think has not been given enough attention in cognitive science – a distinction between personal and subpersonal levels of reality. I'll use the personal/subpersonal distinction to show how what I find appealing in EM can be accommodated by Christians.

Now turn to certain features of the Extended-Mind Thesis that some find attractive. First, EM makes it essential to us that we have bodies, but not that we have the all-organic bodies that most of us now have. Second, EM emphasizes our integration into our environments.

The Blackwell Companion to Science and Christianity, First Edition. Edited by J. B. Stump and Alan G. Padgett.
© 2012 Blackwell Publishing Ltd. Published 2012 by Blackwell Publishing Ltd.

As an externalist in philosophy of mind, I believe that our intentional mental states are ontologically dependent on the environment (Baker 2007a, 2007d); this externalism is congenial to the hypothesis that many physical mechanisms of mind are not entirely in the brain. Third, EM leads to a way to understand the amazing innovations of biotechnology. Recent advances in biotechnology – from cochlear implants, to all manner of brain–machine interfaces that allow monkeys to move paralyzed limbs at will – suggest that the physical mechanisms of mind need not all be organic either. The increasing integration of the biological with the nonbiological makes the line between them very faint. Here are a couple of examples:

- Graeme Clark, inventor of the cochlear implant, envisions new field of "medical bionics" which will produce, among other things, bionic nerve and spinal repair for paraplegia and quadripledia, a bionic eye for blindness, bionic bladder neck for control of incontinence, bionic muscles, and implantable bionic sensors (G. Clark 2007, 78).
- Another fertile ground concerns brain–machine interfaces. John Donoghue has developed a neural implant – a "neuromotor prosthesis" – and connects them to a robotic prosthesis that will allow a paralyzed patient to move her limbs. "We're effectively rewiring the nervous system – not biologically but with real wires," says Donoghue (Sender 2004, 74–75).

Like the Copernican hypothesis and numerous other surprising empirical hypotheses, the hypothesis that the mechanisms of cognition may have components that are not neural, and not even biological, should be dealt with by Christianity. I want to show how one version of the Extended-Mind Thesis may be used to accommodate biotechnology in a way that is compatible with Christianity. To do this, I'll canvass the two main streams of EM.

Two Versions of the Extended-Mind Thesis

The EM family all endorse the claim that our minds and the cognitive processes and states that constitute them extend beyond our brains and bodies. The locus classicus of this thesis is "The Extended Mind" by Andy Clark and David Chalmers, published in *Analysis* in 1998. Clark and Chalmers colorfully put forward a Parity Principle, which is a mainstay of the extended-mind thesis:

> If, as we confront some task, a part of the world functions as a process which, *were it done in the head,* we would have no hesitation in recognizing as part of the cognitive process, then that part of the world *is* . . . part of the cognitive process. Cognitive processes ain't (all) in the head! (A. Clark and Chalmers 1998, 8)

Clark and Chalmers extend this claim from cognitive processes to cognitive states, like belief. The paradigmatic example concerns a character called "Otto," who has suffered neural damage and cannot form new memories. So, he writes down what he wants to remember in his notebook, which contains the information that in other people is stored in brain-based memory. Walking down Fifth Avenue in New York one day, he wants to go to MoMA. He automatically looks in his notebook and retrieves the address of MoMA. The information he needs "is reliably there when needed, available to consciousness and available to guide action, in just the way that we expect a belief to be" (A. Clark and Chalmers 1998, 13). Otto's notebook plays the same causal role in his cognitive economy as parts of your brain play in your cognitive economy.

The extended-mind thesis rejects the traditional "brain-bound" view that "locates all our mental machinery firmly in the head and central nervous system" (A. Clark 2008, 82). By contrast to the traditional view, the Extended-Mind Thesis allows "at least some aspects of human cognition to be realized by the ongoing work of the body and/or the extraorganismic environment" (A. Clark 2008, 82). Again, EM is the modal claim that it is possible that a human mind is not bound by brain or skin.

The EM family comprises two kinds of theses: one concerning systems that may have biological and nonbiological components, the other concerning processing and states of these systems. "Extended minds" may be extended – that is, not bound by brain and skin – in either way, either as extended systems or as extended processes and states. So, we can distinguish two kinds of EM theses:

The extended-systems thesis (ES): cognitive systems need not be confined to brains or human bodies, but may spread out into the environment. Cognitive systems have no privileged parts that could be unified subjects of the cognitive processes.

The extended-cognition thesis (EC): cognitive processes and states may be spread out into the environment. What is extended is just the cognitive loop of causally connected elements that may extend into the world.

ES concerns material things (systems), and EC concerns properties of material things (processing, states).

It may be thought that EC entails ES, but that is not the case. EC is compatible with a number of views on the subjects of these processes. EC and ES are conceptually and logically distinct, as a number of cognitive scientists would agree. For example, Robert Wilson appeals to mental states that are "larger than individual organisms"; although, he says, mental states may be locationally wide, extending into the world, the subject of those states remains the individual organism (Wilson 2004, 197–198). And Susan Hurley and Mark Rowlands also distinguish between the Extended-Mind Thesis as a thesis concerning processing and as a thesis concerning the subjects of these processes (Rowlands 2009, 629; Hurley 1998, 36). So, one can hold EC without holding ES. In any case, we can consider ES on its own since, as we shall see, some philosophers do seem to take us to be extended systems in the sense of ES. I shall discuss these first.

Extended Systems and Christianity

Full disclosure: "Persons and the Metaphysics of Resurrection" (Baker 2007c) argues that Christians should not be committed to the view that human beings have immaterial souls: human beings are persons constituted by, but not identical to, bodies (Baker 2007b). However, for present purposes, I do not begin with specific assumptions about what we are.

Clark and Chalmers suggest that the Extended-Mind Thesis does not stop with subpersonal items – processes, states, vehicles of content – but goes all the way to the personal level, to the person, the self, the agent: "Otto *himself* is best regarded as an extended system, a coupling of biological organism and external resources" (Clark and Chalmers 1998, 18). More recently, Clark said, "Otto-and-his-notebook exhibit enough of the central features and dynamics of a normal agent having (amongst others) the dispositional belief that MoMA is on 53rd St. to warrant thinking of him as such" (A. Clark 2005, 7). On ES, biological entities can "couple" with nonbiological entities in the environment, and coupling may result in a cognitive system with biological and nonbiological parts. We are "creatures whose minds are special precisely because they are tailor-made for multiple mergers and coalitions" (A. Clark 2003, 7). Instead of a unified subject of processing, ES recognizes only systems that may not be "brain-bound" or "skin-bound."

Another image that is frequently used by proponents of ES is that we are just "grab bags of tools." As Clark put it: "We have been designed, by Mother Nature, to exploit deep neural plasticity in order to become one with our best and most reliable tools. . . . Tools-R-us, and always have been" (A. Clark 2003, 6–7). Indeed, Clark suggests, we should abandon "the seductive idea that all these various neural and nonneural tools need a kind of privileged user. Instead it is just tools all the way down" (A. Clark 2003, 6–7, 136). According to Daniel Dennett, another proponent of ES, we are (in Clark's words), only "a grab bag of tools and an ongoing narrative: a story we, as the ensemble of tools, spin to make sense of our actions, proclivities, and projects" (A. Clark 2003, 6–7, 138).

ES construes "the extended mind [to] imply an extended self" (Clark and Chalmers 1998, 18). As Chalmers says in his Foreword to *Supersizing the Mind*, "a sort of two-way coupling between organism and environment . . . is at the heart of the extended mind thesis." Although Chalmers goes on to say that he "tentatively conclude[s] that the extension of the mind is compatible with retaining an internal conscious core," he does not elaborate (A. Clark 2008, xv). Moreover, Clark developed the idea that we are "natural-born cyborgs." Natural-born cyborgs are "systems continuously renegotiating their own limits, components, data stores, and interfaces" (A. Clark 2008, 42). So I shall construe ES to be an interpretation of EM that is

> a kind of no-self (or nearly-no-self) theory, according to which (what we ordinarily think of as) the self is a hastily cobbled together coalition of biological and non-biological elements, whose membership shifts and alters over time and between contexts. (A. Clark 2004, 177)

I take ES to be a thesis about how to understand what we are – we readers of this sentence – and I take ES to hold that we are extended systems. When we are born, we do not (yet) have any nonorganic parts; but over time we acquire and lose nonorganic parts. If a system is individuated by its parts, then we are not a single extended system, but rather a (somewhat haphazard) series of extended systems. If I understand correctly, according to ES, we are series of extended systems (often scattered objects) that process information and have cognitive states without there being any privileged element that is the subject of the processing.

Is ES compatible with Christianity? Although I believe that Christianity is compatible with a number of different conceptions of what we are, I also believe that there is a constraint on the conceptions of the human person that are compatible with Christianity. The constraint is fairly broad – indeed, broad enough to be endorsed by secular humanists and atheists. The constraint that Christian (and other humanistic) conceptions of human persons impose is that human persons can act intentionally and reflect on what they do; in short, Christianity takes human beings to be reflective and responsible agents. Although I shall not argue for it here, I believe that Christianity can get along without attributing to us a self (or soul) as an inner part, and that it can (and should!) get along without attributing to us libertarian free will. Nevertheless, Christian doctrine cannot get along without regarding us as reflective and responsible agents.

Here are some well-known features of how Christianity sees human persons. Human persons are sinners, who are called to repentance and are subject to judgment. A sinner is an agent; she does things intentionally. A sinner who repents must sincerely regret what she has done. To sincerely regret what one has done, one must be able to reflect on her experience.

The stories of Christianity continually take human persons to be reflective and responsible agents. The Old and New Testaments are riddled with examples. Cain killed Abel and later was questioned by God; Jacob stole his brother's birthright; Noah built an Ark and saved a pair of each species; Judas betrayed Jesus and later hanged himself – these are all examples of responsible agency. There are also countless examples of being reflective agents: David said, "O Lord my God, I cried to thee for help, and thou hast healed me" (Ps. 30:2). The Virgin Mary thought that God had looked with favor upon her. Paul said, "I am . . . unfit to be called an apostle, because I persecuted the church of God" (1 Cor. 15:9). So, through and through, Christianity takes us to be responsible and reflective agents.

What does it take to be a reflective and responsible agent? Although this is a difficult question, I think that there is a clear necessary condition for one to be a reflective and responsible agent: The same person who is held responsible must realize that she herself does or has done things intentionally. To realize that one does or has done things intentionally, one must have a robust first-person perspective. She must be in a position to affirm: I know that I – I, myself – do things intentionally. One must be able to refer to oneself without the aid of a name, description, or third-person pronoun. A robust first-person perspective is also a necessary condition for being a reflective being. "I know that I saw a light." "I know that I was saying my prayers." On my view, a robust first-person perspective is a defining characteristic of human beings (Baker 2000, 2007b). It is also a necessary condition for being a reflective and responsible agent.

Does ES have room for reflective and responsible agents? Could "a hastily cobbled together coalition of biological and non-biological elements, whose membership shifts and alters over time and between contexts" (A. Clark 2004, 177) be a reflective and responsible agent? I do not see how: suppose that while the notebook was guiding the extended system (Otto-and-his-notebook) to MoMA, the extended system mugged someone. For Otto to be responsible, he – an extended system with organic and inorganic parts – would have to be able to reflect on what he did. But if, as ES would have it, Otto is nothing but an assemblage of organic and inorganic parts, with no part privileged, there is no subject to do the reflecting. The standard move by some cognitive scientists here is to agree that there is no subject, and to try to explain (perhaps by invoking a "user-illusion") how it could *seem* that there are subjects of reflection. I have argued against such cognitive scientists (Baker 2007c, 2009, 2011). Suffice it to say that we have no idea of how an extended system – an assemblage of organic and nonorganic parts with no privileged part – could reflect on itself. And if the extended system cannot reflect on itself, it cannot be a responsible agent.

Someone may object that if an extended system has a part (organic Otto) that should be held responsible, then the whole extended system should be held responsible. Not only does it seem ridiculous to hold Otto-and-his-notebook responsible, but also that suggestion is inconsistent with EM.

In the first place, the objection makes an unextended human being (organic Otto) "a privileged user" – the one whose responsibility is to be attributed to the whole system. And as we have seen, ES denies that any of the components of an extended system is in a privileged position. We are just grab bags of tools with no privileged user.

In the second place, the suggestion is ad hoc and not generalizable. Some extended systems have more than one unextended human being as a component. There is social extension as well as physical extension. For example, "the waiter at my favorite restaurant might act as a repository of my beliefs about my favorite meals" (Clark and Chalmers 1998, 17–18). In this case, the waiter and I are a transitory extended system. Suppose that while the waiter is recalling my favorite meals, I repent of something, and the waiter never repents of anything. If I repent and the waiter does not, then it is false that the extended system – the-waiter-and-I – repented. Hence the suggestion that if a proper part of an extended system repents, then the extended system repents leads to contradiction.

In sum, an extended system with no privileged parts has no robust first-person perspective and thus cannot be a reflective and responsible agent. So, ES seems incompatible with Christian doctrines about human persons.

Let me conclude the discussion of ES by emphasizing that, perhaps surprisingly, ES is also incompatible with secular humanism or any atheistic view that takes us to be reflective and responsible agents. Acknowledgment of agency is not specific to Christianity or to any religious view. Regardless of Christianity, seeing "agents themselves as spread into the world" (Clark and Chalmers 1998, 18) or as "hastily cobbled together coalition of biological and non-biological elements, whose membership shifts and alters over time and between contexts" is a nonstarter.

But ES is not the only way to interpret the Extended-Mind Thesis. Let us turn to the more plausible EC.

Extended Cognition and Christianity

The core idea of EM is that human cognizing concerns "inextricable tangles of feedback, feedforward, and feed-around loops that promiscuously criss-cross the boundaries of brain, body and world" (A. Clark 2008, xxviii). The cognitive processing of Otto's finding the location of MoMA loops from neural processes through visual processes to motor processes that manipulate the notebook and back to neural processes again. The fact that the processing does not take place entirely in the brain is irrelevant to its outcome: Otto now knows how to find MoMA just as if he had remembered it.

Cognitive processing, of the sort that finds MoMA for Otto, is *subpersonal* processing – whether it takes place wholly in the brain or not. Brains are as subpersonal as notebooks. As long as the various mechanisms (the brain alone or in concert with the notebook) play the functional roles that lead to Otto's learning MoMA's location, it does not matter where those mechanisms are located. And it does not matter whether there are artifactual as well as organic links in the causal chain. Although what cognitive science has to tell us is primarily subpersonal, the concern of Christianity for human persons is *not* primarily subpersonal: What Christianity cares about is that persons are sinners, who repent and are forgiven, and, Christians hope, are resurrected after death. What Christianity has to say to people is all at the *personal* level.

Your brain's normal functioning, or your cochlear implant's stimulating your auditory nerve, or your leg's moving while you walk to the bank are subpersonal-level phenomena. Your thought about the political situation is at the personal level. On my view, personal-level phenomena are *constituted* by subpersonal-level phenomena, without being identical to the constituting subpersonal-level phenomena (Baker 2007b, 111–116). Whatever physical phenomena – whether wholly in your brain or not – constitute your thinking are at a subpersonal level. The vehicle that carries your thought – whether in your brain, body, or environment

– is subpersonal. Remembering and believing are personal-level phenomena; the functioning of the mechanisms of memory and belief are at the subpersonal level. Doing what you want to do is at the personal level – indeed, doing what you want to do is at the level of agency; proper neural functioning (motor control) required for doing what you want to do is at a subpersonal level. Finding the location of MoMA is at the personal level; cognitive processing is at a subpersonal level. If we are to understand reality, it is crucial to keep straight which levels we are talking about.

Since the terms "information-processing" and "cognition" are often used for phenomena at both personal (moving the cursor) and the subpersonal (a process in the brain), it is easy to conflate the personal and subpersonal levels, or to see levels only as different ways to describe the same phenomena rather than to see levels as ontologically distinct. In *The Metaphysics of Everyday Life* (Baker 2007b, 234–239), I argued that there are indefinitely many ontologically distinct levels. So, taking the personal and subpersonal levels to be ontologically distinct, and not just levels of description, I want to suggest that EC should be interpreted at a subpersonal level, and thus that this version of EM is compatible with Christianity, the concern of which is at the personal level.

To make EC compatible with Christianity, we should clearly distinguish EC from ES: EC can allow objects in the environment to be part of x's cognitive processing without being part of x. For example, on a construal of EC that is compatible with Christianity, the notebook is a part of Otto's cognitive processing without being a part of Otto.

We can make this plausible by requiring that parts of a person's body be causally integrated with other parts and more or less permanently attached. So, in order to be part of Otto, the notebook would have to be causally integrated into Otto's subpersonal parts more permanently. On this view, the result of implanting a neural device would be to give someone a new body, a hybrid – part organic and part bionic – a replacement of his old biological (animal) body. A bionic eye would have the same effect and be part of a new hybrid body; but putting on eyeglasses would not result in a new body. Wearing glasses is too transitory. So is using a notebook for memory storage.

So, I think that a person's body has parts that are more or less permanently attached and causally integrated with the person's other parts. But the parts of a person's body need not all be organic as long as they are suitably related to each other. This construal of EC seems to fit with our conception of the body of a human being.

I take the success of brain–machine interfaces and neural implants to be conclusive evidence that the (subpersonal) physical mechanisms of cognition can include nonbiological as well as biological items and that some persons today have nonorganic components in their brains and bodies. So, I think we need to make room in our religious views for people just like you and me, except that various of their mental and physical activities require machines. The line between the biological and the nonbiological becomes fainter with increasing integration.

The Upshot

Our conscious mental lives are at the personal level: we say our prayers, we balance our checkbooks, we find the location of MoMA. These mental phenomena are made possible by machinery at the subpersonal level. Instead of referring to Otto's notebook (a material object), we can refer to the processing loop that includes a state of the notebook, and an interaction between Otto's visual system and the relevant state of the notebook. But the notebook is not thereby a part of Otto. (The claim that the notebook is a part of Otto or his body moves to a version of ES, not of EC.) What EC adds to the traditional view is that subpersonal processing may have parts that are not parts of the brain, or even of the person whose processing it is.

The point is this: it does not matter *how* the processing is done and what subpersonal items (brain, notebook) it involves. It does not matter how Otto finds the location of MoMA as long as he finds it. The subpersonal processing is the machinery by which we, for example, say our prayers or balance our checkbooks or find the location of MoMA. That we do such things as these is at the personal level, the level of Christian concern. How we do them is at the subpersonal level.

As mentioned earlier, Christianity takes us to be reflective and responsible agents. If brain-bound people are reflective and responsible agents, so are people with extended cognition (where EC is clearly distinguished from ES). The subpersonal features of our mental lives – the machinery that makes them possible – just seem irrelevant to Christianity. As long as we are reflective and responsible agents, there is no problem for Christianity. Indeed, perhaps our being such agents, or perhaps our having the robust first-person perspectives necessary for being such agents, is evidence of our being made in God's image. So, EC does not seem at odds with Christianity.

It seems to me fine for a Christian to hold that some personal-level mental states and processes have subpersonal vehicles with nonbiological parts – whether these parts are neural implants, brain–machine interfaces, robotic limbs, or wireless transmitters to computers. Such a person is constituted by a body that has both organic and nonorganic parts. Indeed, it seems not much of a stretch to suppose that with enough bionic parts, one's body would not be an animal body at all. But if one's first-person perspective remained intact, one would continue to exist – but constituted by a nonorganic body.

This possibility seems very congenial to Christian doctrine. The doctrine of resurrection is a doctrine of *bodily* resurrection, and unlike organic bodies, the resurrected body is to be incorruptible (1 Cor. 15). God could, of course, transform our corruptible organic (or bionic) bodies into incorruptible bodies; to do so would be to change the corruptible bodies into different bodies – different bodies with different persistence conditions. Although there is a tradition in Christianity that a person's resurrection body will be the same body that she had on earth, such an interpretation of the doctrine of resurrection seems metaphysically mistaken. The same body could not have different persistence conditions at different times. So, if the Christian doctrine of resurrection as bodily is correct, resurrected bodies are not the same bodies as our earthly bodies, but the person with a resurrected body is the same person who on earth had an earthly body. So, it seems to follow from Christian doctrine that we are not identical to our organic bodies, and that is the conclusion that EM supports as well.

Conclusion

The Extended-Mind Thesis, on one version, EC, seems compatible with relevant doctrines of Christianity. Neural implants, brain-controlled robotic limbs, and other causally integrated prostheses may be parts of a person's body; but the person continues to exist as long as her first-person perspective is exemplified. Moreover, if we interpret the Extended-Mind Thesis as applying only to subpersonal processing and states, EC shows a way Christians can accommodate at least some of the innovations in biotechnology that may seem to threaten our very existence.

References

Baker, Lynne Rudder. 2000. *Persons and Bodies: A Constitution View*. Cambridge: Cambridge University Press.

Baker, Lynne Rudder. 2007a. First-Person Externalism. *Modern Schoolman*, 84, pp. 155–170.

Baker, Lynne Rudder. 2007b. *The Metaphysics of Everyday Life*. Cambridge: Cambridge University Press.

Baker, Lynne Rudder. 2007c. Naturalism and the First-Person Perspective. In Georg Gasser, ed. *How Successful Is Naturalism?* Frankfurt: Ontos-Verlag, pp. 203–227.

Baker, Lynne Rudder. 2007d. Social Externalism and the First-Person Perspective. *Erkenntnis*, 67, pp. 287–300.

Baker, Lynne Rudder. 2009. Persons and the Extended-Mind Thesis. *Zygon*, 44(3), pp. 642–658.

Baker, Lynne Rudder. 2011. Does Naturalism Rest on a Mistake? *American Philosophical Quarterly*, 48(2), pp. 161–174.

Clark, Andy. 2003. *Natural-Born Cyborgs: Minds, Technologies, and the Future of Human Intelligence*. Oxford: Oxford University Press.

Clark, Andy. 2004. Author's Reply: Review Symposium on Andy Clark's *Natural-Born Cyborgs*. *Metascience*, 13(2), pp. 169–181.

Clark, Andy. 2005. Intrinsic Content, Active Memory and the Extended Mind. *Analysis*, 65(1), pp. 1–11.

Clark, Andy. 2008. *Supersizing the Mind: Embodiment, Action, and Cognitive Extension*. Oxford: Oxford University Press.

Clark, Andy and Chalmers, David. 1998. The Extended Mind. *Analysis*, 58(1), pp. 7–19.

Clark, Graeme. 2007. *Restoring the Senses*. Sydney: Australian Broadcasting System.

Hurley, Susan L. 1998. *Consciousness in Action*. Cambridge, MA: Harvard University Press.

Rowlands, Mark. 2009. The Extended Mind. *Zygon*, 44(3), pp. 628–641.

Sender, Aaron J. 2004. Neuroscience: John Donoghue. *Discover Magazine*, online at http://discovermagazine.com/2004/nov/neuroscience (accessed June 20, 2011).

Wilson, Robert A. 2004. *Boundaries of the Mind: The Individual in the Fragile Sciences*. Cambridge: Cambridge University Press.

Further Reading

Adams, Fred and Aizawa, Kenneth. 2008. *The Bounds of Cognition*. Oxford: Wiley-Blackwell. A critique of the Extended-Mind Hypothesis.

Clark, Andy. 2004. Author's Reply: Review Symposium on Andy Clark's *Natural-Born Cyborgs*. *Metascience*, 13(2), pp. 169–181. Clark's response to a wide range of criticisms.

Cooper, John W. 1989. *Body, Soul and Life Everlasting*. Grand Rapids, MI: Eerdmans. A biblically based defense of soul/body dualism – at odds with both my view and the ES hypothesis.

Taliaferro, Charles. 1994. *Consciousness and the Mind of God*. Cambridge: Cambridge University Press. Argues that physicalism should not lead to atheism.

43

In Whose Image?
Artificial Intelligence and the Imago Dei

NOREEN HERZFELD

Introduction: In Whose Image?

Despite a legacy of broken expectations, artificial intelligence retains a hold on the human imagination. Scarcely a month goes by without a news article reporting a new advance in the field – a machine that smiles, robotic pets for the elderly, an IBM machine that plays the game show *Jeopardy*. On the more practical side, search engines now recommend books, or recipes, or dates; computer-generated avatars guide us through online shops or attack us in a new generation of video games; robotic arms do delicate surgery; and vacuum cleaners scuttle about picking up crumbs and dog hair, plugging themselves into an outlet when their batteries feel a little low. While it is not yet the age of the Jetsons, so called "intelligent" computers are an increasingly common part of our lives.

While each of these "intelligent" computers accomplishes some task or amuses us in some way, the Holy Grail of artificial intelligence, a computer that truly thinks like a human being, one we can talk to or trust as we might another person, continues to elude us. Yet we still hold out hopes for such a machine. We desire a computer that is created "in our image" just as we see ourselves as created in the image of our God. Understanding ourselves as created in the image of God connects us to God, reassures us that God is not wholly Other, wholly different from or indifferent to the human condition. Computers that are as similar to ourselves as possible could better connect us to them and to the work they do, making them easier to interact with in an increasingly technological world.

We stand in the middle looking out toward God and toward our own creation in the computer. We see an image linking us in both directions. In this chapter we will examine what we perceive the nature of those images to be and how we can best use that imaging to understand ourselves and our relationship to both our Creator and our creation.

The Blackwell Companion to Science and Christianity, First Edition. Edited by J. B. Stump and Alan G. Padgett.
© 2012 Blackwell Publishing Ltd. Published 2012 by Blackwell Publishing Ltd.

"In the Image of God He Created Them"

Then God said, "Let us make humankind in our image, according to our likeness; and let them have dominion over the fish of the sea, and over the birds of the air, and over the cattle, and over all the wild animals of the earth, and over every creeping thing that creeps upon the earth." So God created humankind in his image, in the image of God he created them, male and female he created them. (Gen. 1:26–27)

Genesis 1 culminates in the creation of humanity in the image of God. What constitutes this image, however, goes unsaid. This has left the image as a matter of interpretation, and these interpretations have varied widely through history, encompassing everything from the most prosaic, such as our ability to walk upright, to the more sublime, such as our capacity for self-transcendence.[1] Most interpretations fit into three broad categories: substantive interpretations, which view the image as some individually held property that is a part of our nature, most often associated with reason; functional interpretations, in which the image of God is seen in action, specifically our exercise of dominion over the earth; and relational interpretations, in which God's image is found within the relationships we establish and maintain.

David Cairns (1953, 60) writes: "In all the Christian writers up to Aquinas we find the image of God conceived of as man's power of reason." This follows from Aristotle, who described humans as the *animal rational*, the only creature with reason, which must, therefore, be our most Godlike faculty. Early Christian writers who discuss the image of God in terms of reason or the rational mind include Clement of Alexandria (*Stromateis* 5.14), Origen (*Against Celsus* 4.85), Gregory of Nazianzus (*Orations* 38.11), Gregory of Nyssa (*On the Making of Man* 5), and Augustine (*On the Trinity* 12–14). We find a similar approach throughout the Middle Ages and Reformation. We think, therefore we are like God and unlike the animals.

Among contemporary theologians, Reinhold Niebuhr remains closest to this classical view of what we share with God. He sees the divine image in a reason that encompasses rationality, free will, and an ability to move beyond the self. He (1996, 161–162) writes:

It will suffice to assert by way of summary that the Biblical conception of "image of God" has influenced Christian thought, particularly since Augustine . . . to interpret human nature in terms which include his rational faculties but which suggest something beyond them. The ablest non-theological analysis of human nature in modern times, by Heidegger, defines this Christian emphasis succinctly as "the idea of 'transcendence,' namely that man is something which reaches beyond itself – that he is more than a rational creature."

Niebuhr sees this capacity for self-transcendence as both a consequence of reason and the defining arbiter of human freedom, for it is only this that allows us to view ourselves objectively and therefore to choose how to live. The divine image gives us the ability to see beyond our finite bodily nature, to think in terms of infinity, though we remain finite creatures, a paradox that Niebuhr sees as the root of the primary tensions of the human condition and, thus, the root of sin (1963, 42).

For all its intuitive appeal, this interpretation of the image of God has the drawback of being curiously inward and static. However narrowly or broadly reason or any other characteristic is conceived, all substantive interpretations presuppose that what makes us like God, and therefore most human, is found by looking within; the image of God is found in the human individual, irrespective of his or her actions or surroundings. And the actions that have stemmed from reason are not always Godlike. After all, Hitler and his minions thought the Final Solution to be eminently reasonable.

Even more telling is the argument that the image of God as reason is a bit of a stretch because reason is nowhere mentioned in the Genesis 1 text. This has led biblical scholars to an examination of the text itself in its historical and literary context. In a 1915 article, "Zum Terminus 'Bild Gottes'," Johannes Hehn introduced a new way of looking at the concept of the image of God. Hehn suggested that the image of God be understood as a job description rather than an attribute of human nature (1915, 36–52). Old Testament scholar Gerhard von Rad extended Hehn's work into a dynamic, functional approach that locates the image of God not in an internal quality, but in the external realm of our actions. In his commentary on Genesis, von Rad argues for the translation "as the image of God" rather than "in the image of God." Von Rad (1961, 56) notes:

> Just as powerful earthly kings, to indicate their claim to dominion, erect an image of themselves in the provinces of their empire where they do not personally appear, so man is placed upon earth in God's image, as God's sovereign emblem. He is really only God's representative, summoned to maintain and enforce God's claim to dominion over the earth.

This understanding of the image of God as the human function of exercising dominion, in effect, acting as God's deputy on earth, has been in the ascendancy among Old Testament exegetes throughout the twentieth century. There are several strengths to this interpretation. First, it emphasizes a holistic view of human beings. While substantive interpretations have frequently split the intellectual or spiritual capacities of the human from the physical, it is the whole of man, both physical and intellectual, that exerts dominion over the earth. Second, the phrase "image of God" is considered within its textual context; creation in God's image is immediately followed by the commission to exercise dominion over all the other creatures. A third strength of a functional interpretation, not mentioned by von Rad, but crucial in light of the current ecological debate, is that a functional interpretation supports human responsibility for the environment by positing a universal divine plan in which humans are given not only dominion but responsibility for the wellbeing of the natural world.

However, a functional interpretation does not exhaust all the possibilities in the Genesis text. While the idea of human creation in the image of God appears in the context of human dominion, it is also closely followed by the phrase "in the image of God he created them, male and female he created them." These linked phrases raise the possibility that the image is found primarily in relationship. The most influential proponent of a relational interpretation is Karl Barth. According to Barth (1958, 184–185), the image of God "does not consist in anything that man is or does" but is identified with the fact that the human being is a counterpart to God. Barth begins, not with observation of the qualities or actions of human beings, but with the nature of God. He interprets the plural in "Let us make man" as referring not to a heavenly court but to the nature of God himself, a Trinity that contains both an "I" that can issue a divine call and a "Thou" capable of a divine response. This I–Thou confrontation, existing within the Godhead, forms the ground of human creation, thus rooting our very nature in relationship with an other. This relationship can take two forms, the human–God relationship and the human–human relationship. The image is in the relationship itself, not our capacity for relationship. Thus it is not a quality for Barth, nor is it held by humans as individuals. It exists first in our relationship to God and secondarily in our relationships with each other (1958, 182).

Since sexual differentiation and some form of relationship exist also among animals, in what way does Barth's conception of the image of God distinguish humanity from the rest of creation? Barth admits that we share creation as male and female, at least in a formal sense, with the animals. He notes, however, that among humans, differentiation by gender is the only differentiation; while animals are divided according to their kind, humans are divided only by gender. Barth (1958, 186) writes:

> This is the particular dignity ascribed to the sex relationship. It is wholly creaturely, and common to man and beast. But as the only real principle of differentiation and relationship, as the original form not only of man's confrontation of God but also of all intercourse between man and man, it is the true *humanum* and therefore the true creaturely image of God.

Barth also finds evidence for a relationship as the center of our being and what we share with God in the character of Jesus, in whom he sees human nature as it was intended to be. What is significant about Jesus is his active giving of himself to others.

> If we see Him alone, we do not see Him at all. If we see him, we see with and around Him in ever widening circles His disciples, the people, His enemies, and the countless multitudes who never have heard His name. We see Him as theirs, determined by them and for them, belonging to each and every one of them. (Barth 1958, 216)

Although many theologians have differed sharply with Barth on the details of what constitutes authentic relationship, or whether the male–female differentiation mentioned in Genesis 1 is an adequate model for all human relationships, a relational model of the image of God has become the dominant approach among systematic theologians in the mid- to late twentieth century.[2] The relational approach is not, however, without its critics. Alexander Altmann notes that although he begins with an exegesis of Genesis 1, Barth bases his exegesis on an *a priori* assumption regarding the nature of the Trinity, an assumption based on Christology and thus alien to the text of Genesis, a text which is, in its origin, not Christian, but Hebrew (1968, 235).

Each of the substantive, functional, and relational interpretations of the image of God arises out of a different methodology. For Niebuhr, the question of the image of God in human beings is considered in the context of a study of the human condition. He begins *The Nature and Destiny of Man* with an examination of human experience. Von Rad begins with the text of Genesis, and uses the exegetical methods of literary and historical criticism. Barth begins with the nature of God, considering the text through the lens of Trinitarian theology. These differing approaches result in three different analogies between God and humankind. The substantive interpretation posits an analogy of nature, that God and the human being share some trait or quality that is essential to our being. The functionalist interpretation posits an analogy of function. We need have nothing in common with God's nature; we image God when we perform actions in God's stead. The relational interpretation finds an analogy of relationship, that there is a relationship within God that we mirror when we are in relationship with God or with one another. Each of these approaches locates the core of humanity in a radically different sphere. These three approaches also differ on whether the image of God is expressed individually or corporately. The substantive approach finds the locus of the image in the individual, while the functional and relational interpretations find the image corporately.

These three interpretations are not necessarily mutually exclusive. Niebuhr, though he interprets the image of God in a substantive sense in *The Nature and Destiny of Man*, also highlights the importance of dialogue with self, God, and others. Similarly, Barth presupposes a degree of rationality in noting the importance of speech in establishing relationship. Many authors today see the image of God as a composite made up of aspects of each of these interpretations. Elizabeth Johnson, in making a case for the divine image in women, states that women express the image of God in their exercise of stewardship over the earth, in their kinship with holy mystery, in rationality and intelligence, in their social nature and their communion with others, and in their bodiliness. For Johnson, the image of God is roughly akin to the concept of personhood, the whole of women's being that is created and blessed by God (1992, 71). As Paul Ricoeur has said, the concept of the image of God contains a "wealth of meaning" not exhausted in a single interpretation. "Each century has the task of elaborating its thought ever anew on the basis of that indestructible symbol" (1965, 110).

In the Image of Humans

As we turn now to the field of artificial intelligence, similar questions to those we addressed regarding the image of God arise. In our quest to create artificial intelligence we are creating in our own image. Is this image some inner trait or capacity that we hope to share with the computer, do we simply want machines to do certain tasks for us, or do we hope for machines with whom we can enter into relationships? If, through artificial intelligence, we are looking for a true and viable image of ourselves, is this image the same as what we perceive to be God's image in us?

The first approach to creating in our own image by designing artificially intelligent computers assumed that what mattered was strictly mental. Like rationality as the image of God, the image of the human was seen as intelligence, loosely understood as problem-solving. This assumption fits our intuitive notion of intelligence, based as it is on the model of activities that we consider indicative of highly intelligent people, such as the ability to play chess or solve complicated equations in mathematics or physics. AI researchers, following rationalist philosophers such as Wittgenstein and Whitehead, believed that human thought could be represented by a set of basic facts which could then be combined, according to set rules, into more complex ideas. This approach to AI has been called symbolic AI. It assumes intelligence is basically an internal process of symbol manipulation.

Symbolic AI met with immediate success in areas in which problems are highly rule-based. Game-playing is an obvious example of one such area. The game of chess takes place in a world in which the only objects are the 32 pieces moving on a 64-square board, and these objects are moved according to a limited number of rules. In 1997 the computer Deep Blue beat then reigning world chess champion Gary Kasparov, a victory that was greeted with both amazement and fear as computers seemed poised to take over many of the mental functions of human beings.

Those fears have not been realized, however. While the field of artificial intelligence continues to produce machines that excel in mental calculations and problem-solving, we have come to a much broader understanding of intelligence and its different forms. Just as theologians moved from a disembodied rationality as God's image in us to seeing that image actively, as our functioning as God's hands in the world, so scientists also have come to see intelligence as the ability to act within an environment. This means that, first of all, intelligence must be embodied. Of course any intelligent agent would be embodied in some way. Deep Blue did not have what we would think of as a body; it could not pick up the chess pieces and physically move them. However, the program was embodied in a bank of super-computers. So the question is not whether intelligence requires a physical body, but what kind of body.

One thing it does seem to require is mobility. A recent example is the development of mobile robots used in hospitals to help doctors who may not be on-site give diagnoses or recommend changes in treatment. While these robots might be seen as a simple advance in videoconferencing, their ability to roll right up to a patient's bed seems to give both doctor and patient a new level of trust and wider options in exchanging information. This is one example of how our physical makeup determines how we interact with the world. Philoso-pher John Haugeland (1997, 26) explains how this shapes our intelligence:

> Think how much "knowledge" is contained in the traditional shape and heft of a hammer, as well as in the muscles and reflexes acquired in learning to use it – though, again, no one need ever have thought of it. Multiply that by our food and hygiene practices, our manner of dress, the layout of buildings, cities, and farms. To be sure, some of this was explicitly figured out, at least once upon a time; but a lot of it wasn't – it just evolved that way (because it worked). Yet a great deal, perhaps even the bulk, of the basic expertise that makes human intelligence what it is, is maintained and brought to bear in these "physical" structures. It is neither stored nor used inside the head of anyone – it's in their bodies and, even more, out there in the world.

According to Haugeland, much of what we consider to be human intelligence is not an internal quality of the mind. Our designs and behaviors arise through and out of interaction with the environment.

One might argue that interaction with the environment is needed for the kind of intelli-gence that allows us to do things, but that there are other forms of intelligence – making plans or decisions, ruminating over events and ideas – that are ruled by the conscious mind alone. Recent experiments in neuroscience tell us that the situation is more complex. In 1983 Benjamin Libet conducted a series of experiments in which the subject was asked to make the simple decision to move a finger and to record the moment this decision was made. Sensors recorded the nerve impulse from brain to finger, and found that the impulse was on its way roughly half a second before persons consciously registered their decision. The sub-conscious mind and the body had things underway before the conscious introspective mind knew anything about it (Libet 1999, 46). Even that most abstract of fields, mathematics, has its roots in our interaction with the environment. In the book Where *Mathematics Comes From: How the Embodied Mind Brings Mathematics into Being*, authors Lakoff and Núñez (2000) argue that mathematical ideas are metaphorical in nature, grounded in our everyday expe-riences of the world. The concept of number requires experience of objects that can be numbered.

Computers that move and act much like humans in the world have been a mainstay in science fiction books and movies. In recent years prominent AI researchers, such as Rodney Brooks at MIT, have moved away from a more abstract mental version of AI toward the field of robotics as well. Brooks has noted that to be truly intelligent, computers must learn as we do from the continuity and the surprises of the real world. Brooks, and others at a variety of AI labs, have built a series of robots that act within the world on the basis of data acquired through sensors.[3] Brooks began with a series of insects, later moving on to the humanoid robots Cog and Kismet, which acquired a few of the rudimentary skills of a baby through interaction with human beings. None of these robots come close to human-like intelligence, but some seem to have a niche in their environment. Consider the Roomba, a vacuum cleaner that navigates around a room looking for dirt, avoids furniture and stairs, and plugs itself in when it needs to be recharged. One might argue that Roomba shows as much intelligence as many animals, in its ability to navigate in a local environment, avoid hazards, and forage for sustenance.

We take Roomba's abilities as a minimal form of intelligence. Hardly our image. Even Deep Blue does not express what counts in human intelligence. After all, after their famous match, Kasparov went on to play a major role in Russian politics. Deep Blue did nothing. Roomba interacts primarily within a static material environment. Humans do not. We find ourselves continuously in new environments, interacting with new situations and, especially, with each other. Just as theologians came to realize it might be relationships that ultimately matter, computers cannot be intelligent if they cannot move easily within the realm of relationships.

This has been recognized from the very beginning of the field of artificial intelligence. In his landmark paper "Computing Machinery and Intelligence," first published in 1950, Alan Turing asked how one might determine if a computer were intelligent and proposed a test based on a parlor game called the imitation game in which an interrogator questions a man and a woman and tries to tell from their written responses which is which. In Turing's version, the interrogator's subjects are a human and a machine. If the interrogator fails as often as she succeeds in determining which was the human, and which the machine, the machine could be considered as having intelligence. Turing predicted that by the year 2000, "it will be possible to programme computers . . . to make them play the imitation game so well that an average interrogator will not have more than a 70 percent chance of making the right identification after five minutes of questioning" (Turing 1997, 29–32). This, like most predictions in AI, was overly optimistic. No computer has yet come close to passing the Turing Test.[4]

The ability to converse is not just a test of intelligence. It may also be a precondition. Winograd and Flores assert that cognition is dependent upon both language and relationships. Objects we have no words for do not exist for us in the same way as those we name. Without words to describe difference, distinctions cannot long be held in mind or shared with others. Conversation also binds us to one another: "To be human is to be the kind of being that generates commitments, through speaking and listening. Without our ability to create and accept (or decline) commitments we are acting in a less than fully human way, and we are not fully using language" (Winograd and Flores 1991, 68). Understanding, for Winograd and Flores, arises in listening, not to the meaning of individual words, but to the commitments expressed through dialogue. Thus understanding is both predicated on and produces social ties.[5]

Social ties bring us to a fourth aspect of intelligence – it is also emotional. To navigate the world of relationships, one needs to express and perceive emotions, to manage one's own emotions, and to use emotions to facilitate thought. While we often think that our emotions obscure rational thought, they are actually necessary for cognition. Neuroscientist Antonio Damasio describes patients who have had an injury to the parts of the brain that govern the ability to feel emotions and subsequently lose the ability to make effective decisions, even decisions as simple as what to have for lunch (1999, 133). There is also a tie between emotions and self-consciousness. We can only conceive of ourselves in relation some external object. Similarly, it is the gift of consciousness that allows us to feel emotions at all:

> Consciousness provides us with a self enriched by the record of our own individual experience. When we face each new moment of life as conscious beings, we bring to bear on that moment the circumstances of our anticipated future, those circumstances that are presumed to bring on more joys or more sorrows. (Damasio 2003, 270)

According to Marvin Minsky (1985, 163), "The question is not whether intelligent machines can have any emotions, but whether machines can be intelligent without emotions." This, however, is proving to be a difficult task. Computers can be programmed to recognize emotions in facial expressions or tone of voice, and a robot or a video avatar can be programmed to express a variety of emotions, physically or verbally. However, feeling emotion requires a level of self-consciousness current machines lack. This has led Winograd and Flores to assume that a human-like AI might be an impossible dream (1991, 123–124).

Who Are We?

While computers that act in the environment are here to stay as useful tools, Turing, Damasio, Winograd, and Flores all view the true image of who we are that we wish to pass on to computers as the ability to enter into relationships. Though they approach it in different ways, each suggests that the idea of an individual intelligence is meaningless, that intelligence has meaning only in encounter. Whether a computer could have the capability of entering into true relationship with human beings remains to be seen.

What is interesting is that interpretations of the image of God in humanity and the image of humanity we would like to pass on to computers have passed through similar trajectories. Both begin with mental experience, expressed variously as rationality or problem solving, but move to a more holistic approach, incorporating action within the world. And in contemplating which actions matter the most, both theologians and artificial intelligence researchers have settled on being in relationship.

Why this similarity? Perhaps these two images tell us more about our self-understanding than they do about the nature of either God or computers. They tell us what we value in ourselves – mind, agency, and relationality. In different times and circumstances we have held one of these three above the other, projecting it as what we must share with God and what we would like to share with our own creation. Yet the three stand in a dialectical tension. Without mind there is neither agency nor relationship. Yet without relationships there is no mind.

We think of this bestowing of an image as a one-way process, from God to us, from us to the computer. However, there is a risk. Theologians have long warned against our tendency to reverse the direction of the image between God and humans, to make God in our own image and likeness. This is idolatry, for when we project our own attributes and desires onto God we create a god who is our own fabrication, embodying our values and satisfying our narcissistic whims. There is a similar risk in the image connecting humans to computers. As we give computers more and more human traits we have a tendency to see them not as our tools but as our children. But we are infinitely more adaptable than our machines. Viewing our machines as fellow creatures is unlikely to change them, and more likely to subtly shape our image of ourselves, of what our lives and relationships are about. This, too, is a form of idolatry, for insofar as we allow computers to shape our lives we have made them into gods of silicon.

We stand in the middle, between our Creator and our own creation. We come to know what we value in ourselves through our understanding of these relationships. Ultimately we know more what God is not than what God is. We do not know the mind of God; we cannot ever be sure whether our actions are those God would ordain; we live in a relationship of love with God and each other, yet we all too often find these relationships as broken as they are whole. Similarly, with computers, we will never succeed in creating a machine that thinks exactly as we do; computers will function differently in our world; and we must ever be wary that we do not substitute relationships with machines, or even relationships with each other that are totally mediated by machines, for the real thing.

Notes

1   Some have looked for the *imago Dei* in a quality of the human being, such as our physical form (Gunkel), the ability to stand upright (Koehler), our rationality or intellect (Aquinas), our personality (Procksch), or our capacity for self-transcendence (Niebuhr). Others have thought of God's image as dynamic, rooted in human actions such as our dominion over the animals (Gross, von Rad). A third approach defines the image as emergent in the interrelationship of two beings, human with human, or human with divine (Barth, Brunner). See Westermann 1984, 147–148, for a summary.
2   One finds similar interpretations in Brunner, Berkouwer, Pannenberg, and Küng, among others.
3   For descriptions of a variety of mobile robots developed at MIT, see Brooks 1990.
4   In 1991 Hugh Loebner began funding a yearly competition that offers $100 000 for the first program to pass a Turing Test. The first four years of the competition allowed the area of questioning to be restricted. Since 1995, the areas of questioning have been unrestricted. Judgments on the relative success of various programs differ; however, Loebner has yet to part with his money.
5   Winograd and Flores feel so strongly about the connection between knowing an object and being able to speak of it in terms of language that they baldly state, "Nothing exists except through language" (1991, 73).

References

Altmann, Alexander. 1968. Homo Imago Dei in Jewish and Christian Theology. *Journal of Religion*, 48, pp. 235–259.

Barth, Karl. 1958. *Church Dogmatics*, vol. 3. Edinburgh: T. & T. Clark.

Brooks, Rodney. 1990. Elephants Don't Play Chess. *Robotics and Autonomous Systems*, 6, pp. 3–15.

Cairns, David. 1953. *The Image of God in Man*. London: SCM Press.

Damasio, Antonio. 1999. *The Feeling of What Happens: Body and Emotion in the Making of Consciousness*. New York: Harcourt, Brace, & Company.

Haugeland, John. 1997. What Is Mind Design? In John Haugeland, ed. *Mind Design II: Philosophy, Psychology, Artificial Intelligence*. Cambridge, MA: MIT Press, pp. 1–28.

Hehn, Johannes. 1915. Zum Terminus "Bild Gottes." In *Festschrift Eduard Sachau zum Siebzigsten Geburtstag*. Berlin: G. Reimer, pp. 36–52.

Johnson, Elizabeth. 1992. *She Who Is: The Mystery of God in Feminist Theological Discourse*. New York: Crossroad Press.

Lakoff, George and Núñez, Rafael. 2000. *Where Mathematics Comes From: How the Embodied Mind Brings Mathematics into Being*. New York: Basic Books.

Libet, Benjamin. 1999. Do We Have Free Will? *Journal of Consciousness Studies*, 6 (8–9), pp. 47–57.

Minsky, Marvin. 1985. *The Society of Mind*. New York: Simon & Schuster.

Niebuhr, Reinhold. 1963. *Moral Man and Immoral Society: A Study in Ethics and Politics*. London: SCM Press.

Niebuhr, Reinhold. 1996. *The Nature and Destiny of Man: A Christian Interpretation*, vol. 1, Human Nature. Louisville: Westminster John Knox Press.

Ricoeur, Paul. 1965. *History and Truth*. Evanston, IL: Northwestern University Press.

Turing, Alan. 1997. Computing Machinery and Intelligence. In John Haugeland, ed. *Mind Design II: Philosophy, Psychology, Artificial Intelligence*. Cambridge, MA: MIT Press, pp. 29–56.

von Rad, Gerhard. 1961. *Genesis: A Commentary*. Philadelphia: Westminster Press.

Westermann, Claus. 1984. *Genesis 1–11: A Commentary*. Minneapolis, MN: Augsburg Press.

Winograd, Terry and Flores, Fernando. 1991. *Understanding Computers and Cognition: A New Foundation for Design*. Reading, MA: Addison-Wesley.

Further Reading

Cairns, David. 1953. *The Image of God in Man*. London: SCM Press. Provides a complete summary of how the *imago Dei* has been understood by theologians from the early Church Fathers to the twentieth century.

Damasio, Antonio. 2003. *Looking for Spinoza: Joy, Sorrow, and the Feeling Brain*. New York: Harcourt, Brace, & Company. Presents a very readable summary of current neuroscientific research into the origin of emotions.

Herzfeld, Noreen. 2002. *In Our Image: Artificial Intelligence and the Human Spirit*. Minneapolis, MN: Fortress Press. Compares our understanding of how we are in God's image with our desire to create an artificial intelligence in our own image.

Westermann, Claus. 1984. *Genesis 1–11: A Commentary*. Minneapolis, MN: Augsburg Press. Looks at the concept of the image of God through a historical/literary criticism of the relevant passages.

44

How Science Lost Its Soul, and Religion Handed It Back

JULIAN BAGGINI

Like "Does God exist?" or "Is religion the root of evil?", the question "Are science and religion compatible?" tends to evoke a weary sigh in the serious religious thinker. The issue has been discussed to death, and very little, if anything, new emerges with each iteration. Nevertheless, we have to guard against the fallacy I call *argumentum ad fatigum*: mistaking one's own tired-ness with a debate for the debate's exhaustion. The question of science's relation to religion remains lively, I suspect, because most of the commonly trotted out lines on the subject just don't get to the heart of it. Something meaty always remains, inviting us to get our teeth into it, only for us to get stuck masticating the same old fat.

Not all atheists believe that science and religion are simply incompatible, but I think it is empirically true that most believe science is at the very least more supportive of atheism than it is of faith. But if this is so, how do they account for the scientists who maintain something like a traditional religious belief? Surveys have repeatedly suggested that such scientists are a minority, and that non-belief is much more prevalent among scientists than it is the general population. One recent book put the number of atheist or agnostic scientists at elite academic institutions at 64%, compared to 6% of the general population (Howard Ecklund 2010, 16). Yet enough scientists are able to combine faith and science to make us ask how they can do so.

Some, like Jerry Coyne, dismiss this breezily:

> [The] existence of religious scientists, or religious people who accept science, doesn't prove that the two areas are compatible. It shows only that people can hold two conflicting notions in their heads at the same time. If that meant compatibility, we could make a good case, based on the commonness of marital infidelity, that monogamy and adultery are perfectly compatible. (Coyne 2010)

Coyne may be right, but the principle of charity demands that we at least see if a better explanation than "people are irrational" is at hand to explain this datum.

I'm going to start with a broad-brush overview of the general relation between science, atheism, and belief before taking as a case study the existence or otherwise of souls. First,

The Blackwell Companion to Science and Christianity, First Edition. Edited by J. B. Stump and Alan G. Padgett.
© 2012 Blackwell Publishing Ltd. Published 2012 by Blackwell Publishing Ltd.

I'll look at a fairly standard argument for why atheists believe science leads us to reject the existence of souls. Then I'll try to unpack some of the reasons why, nonetheless, others argue that science either leads to or is as consistent with belief in souls. In my conclusion, I'll try to draw out some of the lessons we might learn about the relationships atheism and religious belief have with science.

No Use for That Hypothesis

It is crucial to the atheist argument that there is no atheist science, just science. On this view, science is, in its premises at least, neutral on religious belief. It is concerned with finding what the scientific evidence would lead us to believe, irrespective of any prior convictions we might have about religion. Its conclusions may support or undermine religious belief, but it is not ideologically or methodologically irreligious. We can call this the *integrity of the scientific domain*: science is based on scientific evidence and methodology, no more and no less. In this respect, the scientific endeavor is simply to be as objective as is humanly possible. That does not mean this view of science is premised on the possibility of being able to leave all personal prejudice or subjective experience completely behind, but that it tries to minimize the role such contingencies play in our understanding (see Nagel 1986, 13–19 and 25–28). If we did not think that such greater objectivity were possible, then higher learning in almost every-thing – science, history, economics, psychology – would be pointless. We may as well just stick with our unreflective prejudices.

So, science aims to be as objective as possible, and as such it does not start with a presup-position of theism or atheism, even though individual scientists will of course have their own views on this. Most atheists believe that, from this starting point, a picture will emerge of the world that has no place for God or the supernatural. Just as Laplace is reputed to have said to Napoleon, they dismiss God with a *"Je n'ai pas eu besoin de cette hypothèse"* ("I had no use for that hypothesis").

The usual rejoinder at this point is to say that there is a difference between an absence of proof and a proof of absence. That God does not play a role in scientific explanations of the world does not disprove God's existence, it simply reveals a lack of scientific proof for it. The atheist is typically unimpressed by this move, arguing that in the absence of any good reason to believe in something, belief in it is irrational. God is just one of an infinite set of things we have no reason to believe in, other members of which are commonly said to include Santa Claus, unicorns, or teapots orbiting the moon. Belief in these things is irrational purely because we have no reason to think they do exist. The same logic should apply to God.

The scientific argument against God really is that simple, as it is, I would argue, with all the big debates about science and religion. The atheist cases rest not in the complex details of biology or quantum physics, but with the big, glaring data of evident truths about the world. Why then, if the argument is so strong and simple, does religious belief persist among some scientists?

There is no single answer to this, but practically all answers, I suggest, share a common form. Religious scientists almost all hold that there is some datum or data which supports whatever divine reality it is they are defending, and which is either more important than the scientific data or is itself a scientific datum that secular enquiry has missed. Both types of claim can be understood as challenges to the way in which the integrity of the scientific domain is understood by atheists. On the one hand, it can be argued that there are data that belong in the domain, but which secular scientists rule out or play down for ideological, non-scientific reasons. Call this the *missing-data* approach. On the other, it can be argued that too much emphasis is placed on the integrity of the scientific domain. To insist, *a priori*, that scientific data are the only data worth taking account of when trying to understand the fundamental nature of the world is not to be scientific but *scientistic*: it is not to value science as a powerful means of understanding the world but to claim that science is the only truthful way of understanding the world. Call this the *additional-data* approach.

The appeal of the additional-data approach is one reason the atheist case is not as compelling as it often appears to its advocates, because the demand that only scientific evidence is admissible is a stipulation that one can rationally disagree with. What atheists see as a scientific argument critics can dismiss as a *scientistic* one, on the grounds that it rules out *a priori* any other evidence, such as that of religious experience, which for others is as indubitable a datum as the result of any scientific experiment. To put it another way, I said above that the purely scientific question concerns "what the scientific evidence would lead us to believe, irrespective of any prior convictions we might have about religion." But a religious believer can ask why we must accept this stipulation, since it rests on an assumption that only scientific data have any value in determining our views about the fundamental nature of reality.

In the case of both the missing- and additional-data approaches, it is argued that the neglected data can explain the holes or mysteries that the secular scientific accounts leave behind. But when a religious person mentions holes or mysteries left by science, they are usually accused of falling into an intellectual hole – or rather gap – of their own. "The God of the gaps" is a deity whose existence is defended solely on the grounds that he is needed to fill the spaces left by empirical enquiry. The term comes from the nineteenth-century evangelist Henry Drummond, who wrote:

> There are reverent minds who ceaselessly scan the fields of Nature and the books of Science in search of gaps – gaps which they will fill up with God. As if God lived in the gaps? What view of Nature or of Truth is theirs whose interest in Science is not in what it can explain but in what it cannot, whose quest is ignorance not knowledge, whose daily dread is that the cloud may lift, and who, as darkness melts from this field or from that, begin to tremble for the place of His abode? (Drummond 1894, 333)

So today, for instance, when physics accounts for everything from the big bang onwards, the God of the gaps is invoked as necessary to explain why the big bang banged in the first place.

This god is disreputable for two reasons. First of all, it is precarious to rest the case for God on current gaps in our knowledge, for there is always a risk that these gaps will in time be closed. Not so long ago, we could not account for the emergence of life on earth, but those who used that as a reason to postulate the existence of God found the whole basis of their case swept away with the development of modern biology.

Second, one has to be careful not to misread Sherlock Holmes's principle that "Once you have excluded the impossible, whatever remains, however improbable, must be the truth" (Doyle 2008, 632). This is strictly true, but of course, the problem is that we often don't know what we don't know, so rather than having considered all the remaining possibilities, others remain which we just haven't thought of yet. Consider, for instance, the hypotheses on the table at around AD 1500 for explaining life. None of them were anywhere near good enough as explanations. The rational thing would not have been to have accepted the one which hadn't yet been shown to be conclusively false, but to admit that we didn't yet know how to explain it. It is not enough that a hypothesis is the best available if it is not well supported by evidence. The problem of the God of the gaps is that it doesn't really explain anything at all. All it does is gesture towards a divine mystery in place of a terrestrial one.

None of this is, I think, controversial. Religious thinkers are as keen to avoid a God of the gaps as atheist critics are to find him lurking in their opponents' arguments. The complications come when trying to distinguish this kind of gap-filling from the more reputable variety. In science, it is common and good practice to identify anomalies and incompleteness in theories as signs that they may need replacing or improving. We owe the emergence of quantum theory, for instance, to the recognition that Newtonian mechanics just doesn't accurately describe what is going on at the very smallest level. Quantum theory is not, however, a "physics of the gaps," because it fills the hole it identifies with a better theory, one which explains and predicts with great accuracy. Identifying the gaps in Newtonian physics did not in itself provide any grounds in favor of rival theories. All it did was open up ground for other theories to step in, if and when they were sufficiently well supported by evidence.

This is why so many theologians accused of postulating a God of the gaps reject the charge. They claim that their God is not just a hand-waving replacement of one mystery for another. They claim that their God actually does a good job of explaining the data that science cannot.

To examine further how these disagreements over data and the integrity of the scientific domain play out, I'm going to look, not at God's existence, but two contemporary defenses of the existence of souls. The question here is, what kind of things are you and I? Are we purely physical or do we have some other non-physical part? Could this part survive our death? If we take a scientific look at this, then we will encounter two very simple, compelling data:

(1) We are human beings, a biological species in the same family as the chimpanzee.
(2) All the sound evidence we have suggests that a properly functioning brain is necessary and sufficient for consciousness.

When basing conclusions on evidence, it is always worth bearing in mind Hume's maxim that "A wise man . . . proportions his belief to the evidence" and that "a weaker evidence can never destroy a stronger" (Hume 2010, 137, 138). There are many other data that could and perhaps should be weighed up when assessing the nature of persons, but none come close to being as firm as these two. I would go so far as to say that they are as close to being certain facts as we can get. Therefore whatever other data about human persons we need to explain, they must be either made compatible with these or left as unsolved mysteries in need of explanation. The only alternative would be to take the other data as true and leave these apparent truths as merely apparent anomalies, which would fail the test of proportioning belief to evidence.

What our scientific understanding has to say about souls is therefore very simple: it seems to me that all the evidence points to us being entirely biological creatures and I find no evidence at all that suggests otherwise. Non-material souls which are the bearers of our identities are therefore like unicorns and orbiting teapots: we have no reason to suppose they exist, so it would therefore be irrational to believe that they do. This does not amount to proof of their non-existence, but that is not needed. One needs *reasons to believe*, and in their absence, defeasible non-belief is the only rational alternative.

How then, if the case is so simple and clear, is it possible for intelligent philosophers and theologians to argue for the existence of souls? First, as an example of the missing-data approach, I'll look at the substance dualism of Richard Swinburne. Second, as an example of the additional-data approach, I'll look at a non-reductive materialism defended by a number of different Christian scientists.

Swinburne on Souls

Since it takes the missing-data approach, if Richard Swinburne's argument for the existence of souls is to work, it must do two things. First, it must show that there is indeed something that rival accounts cannot explain; and second, it must show that it does not just provide an alternative, but one which both fits with and is supported by the evidence.

Take the question of what's missing in rival accounts first of all. Swinburne's target here is physicalism. Swinburne argues that "There are data which are not taken account of by the physicalist," data which physicalism not only "can't explain, but can't describe." (All direct quotations from Swinburne are from an interview with the author.) There are several such data, but I'll focus on two here.

The first is that "We have thoughts and feelings and so on and the occurrence of these does not entail the occurrence of goings-on in the brain or conversely." This is one aspect of the famous "hard problem of consciousness": how it is that a purely physical brain can give rise to subjective experience? The hard problem with the hard problem, however, is pinning down exactly what it is. For Swinburne, the problem is a logical one. Brain events do not entail mental events and vice versa. But is this really the hard problem? It doesn't look like it. Mental events could never logically entail physical ones or vice versa because there is nothing in the concept of the mental that entails the physical or vice versa. But nothing follows at all from this about what the actual empirical relation between the two is. Take a very simple analogy. Imagine when it was first established that surgery was often followed by infections in patients solely because doctors did not wash their hands. That solves the "easy problem" of frequent post-surgical infection: we now know what gives rise to it. But the hard problem still remained: by what mechanism do unclean hands lead to infection? For a while, they had no idea. Now imagine that an Oxford don pipes up and says, "But unclean hands do not entail infection or vice versa." In one sense this is true, but beside the point. If all causal relations were discoverable by the analysis of logical entailment between concepts, we wouldn't need empirical science.

In many, but not all ways, the mind–body problem is like the dirt–infection problem. That the two are causally related is not in doubt. The gap is (or, some claim, was) in explaining why and how there is such a relation. But in Swinburne's argument, the gap is interpreted quite differently. The fact that mind does not entail matter and vice versa is taken as a reason for thinking that there is something other than matter responsible for consciousness. Again, there is a sense in which this is right. In the dirt–infection case, for instance, we only properly understand why there is a link when we know what it is in the dirt which is causing the infection. In that sense, *dirt* isn't the cause of infection, rather *something in the dirt* is. You could describe this in terms of *something other than the dirt* being responsible, but this is misleading, because the causal agent is part of the dirt, not something additional to it. In the mind–body case, we know that the mere existence of matter is not sufficient to give rise to consciousness, but it does not follow that postulating *something other than matter* is needed to do the job. Rather, we could look at, not parts of the matter, but the way in which the matter is organized, if we are to explain how it gives rise to consciousness.

Of course, it could be argued that we cannot specify in advance whether the better explanation is that the way brains work gives rise to consciousness or whether something other than a functioning brain – but somehow always accompanying it – is what does the trick. But, first, the way Swinburne describes the problem suggests that the former is not a possibility, when clearly it is.

Let us assume, however, that both possibilities are allowed. In that case, a gap has been correctly identified. Could it still not be argued that a non-material soul better explains the data than the physical explanation? Very few philosophers would agree with Swinburne, on the basis that the leap over the gap to souls seems to be possible only on the misuse of the Sherlock Holmes principle.

This is where Swinburne's argument really becomes interesting, however. Whenever he is called to defend his position, he is always at pains to point out that his conclusions are supported by a whole network of arguments. If the only reason to postulate non-material souls were the failure of material minds to explain consciousness, the argument would indeed be weak. But Swinburne's philosophy is a mutually supporting system of arguments. So, when, for example, God is called upon to do some explanatory work, it is noted that there are independent arguments as to why God is thought to exist. Swinburne's argument for souls does not stand up without his arguments for God's existence, but these he thinks are robust. Atheists who refuse to engage with this whole system are therefore dismissed as not engaging with the argument in its entirety. So, for instance, when I put it to him that his soul hypothesis required "a personal God who is keeping an eye on every corner of the world" he replied, "That's why you don't like souls. There's a serious point as to why some modern philosophers who don't like the idea of God are so hostile to what seem to me compelling arguments for the soul."

This kind of move is resisted by atheists, but their problem is that their arguments also depend on an interlocking network of claims, none of which is absolutely proven. It may be an exaggeration to say we're all coherentists these days, but certainly almost everyone does accept that our picture of the world does not rest on a single foundation but stands or falls on the basis of a whole network of interlocking and interdependent claims. The structure of Swinburne's argument is therefore impeccable: he describes a gap in the physicalist theory and claims that the dualist alternative explains the data better, both fitting with and supporting the evidence. The disagreement concerns the merits of this alternative explanation. But Swinburne is able to say that the reason that most people do not accept this is because the set of interlocking and interdependent beliefs they use to assess the credibility of claims is itself a physicalist one. As he put it to me, "The only reason people deny what stares them in the face is because they're captured by the physicalist dogma current in our time." In other words, what is claimed as the integrity of the scientific domain is actually a more restrictive *a priori* ruling which says that the non-physical has no role in scientific explanation. Swinburne, in contrast, argues that it is properly scientific to accept the existence of anything that is required to account for the phenomenon, whether it already has a place in the scientific picture or not. To use an analogy, just as it is scientific to postulate the existence of hitherto unknown dark matter if that's what the equations of physics demand, so it is scientific to postulate the existence of hitherto unacknowledged non-physical substance if that is what the fact of consciousness demands.

I can't hope to settle the dispute between Swinburne and his critics here. What is of interest for our purposes is simply *how* one could possibly resolve it. The naive scientific hope is that the facts settle disputes. But the issue here is about which facts count, and how much. The data can't answer the problem if the problem is which data to appeal to. What's worse, judgments about what data count and how much are not autonomous and discrete. They are made within the context of a whole set of overlapping beliefs and commitments about scientific method, epistemology, and ontology.

Material Souls

The additional-data approach appears in some ways to be more accepting of secular science because it accepts in its entirety its data and the central conclusions drawn from it. In the case of souls, there are those who, far from arguing for substance dualism, actually argue that that is not an authentically Christian doctrine at all. Scripture and the early Church Fathers never talked of souls separate from bodies. Rather, they believed in the resurrection of the body. Christ is the model here. It is not incidental that he rose from the dead as a fully embodied person, not just a spirit. This was the only kind of life after death that made sense.

The idea of soul these happily materialist theologians embrace is more of an Aristotelian than a Cartesian one. Soul is not a non-physical entity, but refers to the unique way in which a physical person is constructed, to make an individual, conscious entity. The idea is similar to one put forward by the contemporary neuroscientist Susan Greenfield, that the self is the "personalization of the brain," which, in broad terms at least, is an orthodox view among her colleagues (Greenfield 2000, 185–186). Similarly, the soul is what makes your body and brain you, rather than someone else.

To put it more technically, this view (endorsed by most of the contributors to Brown *et al.* 1998) embraces non-reductive materialism. On this view, the soul is constituted by, but not reducible to, its physical parts. Many atheists would agree, even though they would resist using the word "soul." They would agree that the self emerges from the incredibly complicated workings of the brain and the body, and that a purely physical account of these workings, no matter how comprehensive, would not give you an account of the self that they give rise to.

If that were the end of it, there would be no difference between these Christian believers in materialist souls and their atheist counterparts. But that is not the end of it. There are additional data which make them believe that these souls can enjoy a life after death. It is not that the soul is naturally immortal, just as long as God doesn't destroy it. Rather, eternal life is a gift of God. The theologians are embracing the physicalist picture that, in their naiveté, the atheists thought put an end to all talk of the soul, but for the additional claim that an all-powerful God would do what many philosophers agree is possible in thought experiments: recreate a self, perhaps using some of the original matter, but perhaps using new stuff.

On what grounds do they maintain this? On the grounds of additional data the atheist does not accept. These are the "data" that Christ has risen from the dead, and that the Bible is the word of God. At this point, the atheist will protest that this is not reasonable or rational. Consider, for example, the likely atheist response to what the theologian Justin Thacker says (this and all other direct quotations are from an interview with Thacker by the author):

> If there is a conflict between contemporary science and God, then God wins every time, and God has revealed himself to us through the Bible. . . . There are some things which I think the Bible is unbelievably clear about and that have scientific consequences. Let's take the resurrection of Jesus Christ. If science somehow, and I can't even imagine how, but if it told me that the resurrection of Jesus Christ was just categorically impossible, could not happen, I would disbe-

lieve that and continue to believe what the Bible teaches about the resurrection of Jesus Christ, because if you take away the resurrection there is no Christian faith, it just doesn't exist.

The problem for the atheist is, what's the knock-down argument against this? At the moment, what Thacker believes is apparently consistent with the science. It's just that it adds to the science something that is outside its scope: a benevolent, all-powerful God. But Thacker believes in this God on the basis of experiences he finds utterly compelling. Such beliefs are considered "properly basic," to use Plantinga's phrase, and not in need of epistemic justification.

Whatever Works for You

It's hard to avoid the depressing conclusion that the differing judgments made by Swinburne, Thacker, and their critics are all being driven by substantive worldviews, which, once adopted, are like those arcade games where you have to bash down bumps with a hammer, only for a new one to appear elsewhere. The complex, interrelated nature of comprehensive ontological and metaphysical theories means that you can never decisively nail them. Judgments about which beliefs are properly basic, and how evidence should be made are just that – judgments – and there is no way for reason to adjudicate between them.

It would be too pessimistic, however, to conclude that we just have to shrug our shoulders and accept "whatever works for you." There are two ways in which such web-like sets of beliefs can be subjected to scrutiny.

The first is that, when comparing competing explanations, not every element of the case is of equal importance. Some "nodes" in a web are more critical than others. In the Swinburne case, I would argue (but for lack of space here will simply assert) that the two most important nodes in the physicalist argument are, first, that we are a biological species, human beings; and second, that all the sound evidence we have suggests that a properly functioning brain is necessary and sufficient for consciousness. These are rock solid, and, if true, incompatible with the dualist view. In contrast, the most critical node in the case for souls is that there is an explanatory gap between the existence of matter and the existence of minds. But this is compatible with the physicalist case. That is what makes the atheist case stronger.

In the case of Thacker *et al.*, the greatest vulnerability is clearly a belief in the infallibility of the Bible. Christians who hold this (and not all do, of course) and use it as a key datum are vulnerable. But even here, it is amazing how ingenuity can lead otherwise intelligent people to maintain a belief in the divinity of the Bible in the face of what appears to be clear counter-evidence.

The second means of scrutiny is that one can assess, one by one, how well-argued particular elements of the case are. The fact that they form an interconnected net does not mean that there is no way of making any discrete criticisms. In the Swinburne case, I will again just have to assert that most philosophers would agree that most of his individual arguments are weak. If this is correct, then any web that links them together is also going to be weak. No number of bad arguments add up to a good one.

In Thacker's case, the most obvious weakness is that the apparent consistency between the method of life after death and non-reductive materialism is arguably superficial, because the kind of physicality that such accounts require is actually importantly different from that of the physical sciences. As Thacker explains it:

If Jesus' resurrection body is the paradigm for our resurrection bodies – which the New Testament sets out for us and the history of the Christian tradition has accepted since – then the form of physicality that Jesus had is also a different kind of physicality. In many ways it was normal – he ate fish, he invited Thomas to touch him, he said "see that I am flesh and blood, I'm not a ghost, I'm not a spirit" – but at the same time he did just appear through walls; at first he was unrecognizable, for instance, by the two on the road to Emmaus. Tom Wright, the bishop of Durham, calls it a trans-physicality, which means it's physical, but it's a different kind of physicality to the physicality we have.

But "a different kind of physicality" is as mysterious and beyond science as a different kind of substance, such as that of the immaterial soul. This is not decisive if, like Thacker, the data of Christ and the Bible are compelling. There is nothing logically contradictory about saying that our understanding of matter is extremely limited, and we just don't know how God might be able to modify and change it in a new heaven and a new earth. But it is possible to question the data of Christ and the Bible for different reasons.

This brief discussion of the defense of souls has obviously only scratched the surface of the issues that would have to be resolved to settle the debates. But that is not my aim here. Rather, it is simply to make clearer how it is that religious believers can persist in holding beliefs that purely secular scientists see no grounds for holding. Sometimes, it is just because, as Jerry Coyne suggested, people can hold contradictory beliefs. Sometimes it is because people cling on to an unstable and unsecure God of the gaps. But neither explanation is enough to explain why many people who think the issue through very thoroughly, some of them scientists, hold such beliefs.

To explain this, we have to appreciate the truth of the old adage that an argument is only as sound as its premises. In science, the premises are the empirical data. The problem is that believers and non-believers alike can accept the data which are unarguable, but that leaves plenty of scope to argue about what the data mean and how important each datum is. And it also leaves room to argue that scientists are missing some data, because they are blinded by their secular prejudices, or that there is relevant additional data of experience that are not strictly scientific.

As I have suggested, the pessimistic conclusion one could draw from this is that there is so much room for people to choose their fundamental premises that there is simply no way to conclusively show which view is more rationally grounded. I think that's too pessimistic. The point is rather that there is no shortcut. Very few nodes in a net of belief are so critical that destroying them brings the whole thing down. And very few nodes can be critiqued wholly independently of everything else in the net. Rather, the net has to be unstitched piece by piece.

In practice, this is probably little different from the pessimistic conclusion. When people have strong desires to believe something, it is always possible to convince oneself that a decisive argument against one node wasn't decisive after all, or that you have found a reply to it. Mending and making-do can enable one to think a web of belief still holds together, even after a good critic has ripped it to shreds.

These considerations together show why it is naive for the atheist to think that the theist is disproved on the basis of fairly obvious empirical data. While I agree that the case against souls is much more robust than the case for them, it is not surprising that a minority of those who subject these issues to rigorous philosophical scrutiny, who may have any number of reasons to be well disposed towards religious belief, don't side with the naturalists. This is because there is no algorithm for determining which data are most important, or for what makes for an overall more complete and satisfying understanding of a given phenomenon. The jibe that they are simply taking advantage of "wriggle room" grossly underestimates the size of the cell they're in. The reality is that there is room not just to wriggle, but to dance a little jig.

References

Brown, Warren S., Murphy, Nancey, and Malony, H. Newton, eds. 1998. *Whatever Happened to the Soul? Scientific and Theological Portraits of Human Nature*. Minneapolis: Fortress.

Coyne, Jerry. 2010. Science and Religion Aren't Friends. USA Today, October 11.

Doyle, Arthur Conan. 2008. *The Complete Stories of Sherlock Holmes*. London: Wordsworth.

Drummond, Henry. 1894. *The Ascent of Man*. New York: James Pott & Co. Publishers.

Greenfield, Susan. 2000. *The Private Life of the Brain*. New York: John Wiley & Sons, Inc.

Howard Ecklund, Elaine. 2010. *Science vs. Religion: What Scientists Really Think*. New York: Oxford University Press.

Hume, David. 2010. Of Miracles. In Julian Baggini, ed. *Hume on Religion*. London: Philosophy Press, pp. 137–152.

Nagel, Thomas. 1986. *The View from Nowhere*. Oxford: Oxford University Press.

Further Reading

Baggini, Julian. 2011. *The Ego Trick*. London: Granta. An interdisciplinary examination of self and identity, including interviews as well as argument.

Brown, Warren S., Murphy, Nancey, and Malony, H. Newton, eds. 1998. *Whatever Happened to the Soul? Scientific and Theological Portraits of Human Nature*. Minneapolis: Fortress. A collection that represents the Christian non-reductive physicalist understanding of the soul.

Feinberg, Todd E. 2001. *Altered Egos: How the Brain Creates the Self*. New York: Oxford University Press. One of the best accounts of the neurological basis of sense of identity.

Martin, Raymond and Barresi, John. 2006. *The Rise and Fall of Soul and Self: An Intellectual History of Personal Identity*. New York: Columbia University Press. An astonishingly comprehensive and clear journey through the entire history of the soul and identity debate.

Swinburne, Richard. 1997. *The Evolution of the Soul*, revised edn. Oxford: Oxford University Press. The fullest contemporary argument for the dualistic soul.

Part X
Theology

45

The Trinity and Scientific Reality

JOHN POLKINGHORNE

If God is indeed the Creator of the universe, then it would be reasonable to expect that, to a discerning eye, the dimension of reality that is explored by science might be found to display some pale reflection of the nature of its Creator. However, the intimations of divinity thus conveyed may be expected to be veiled and indirect, and that is why there is need for discernment if they are to be detected. Just as God does not write messages on the clouds for all to read, so the universe will not be found to be full of items stamped "Made by God." Divine revelation is more subtle than that. What might be expected is that there are certain aspects to the history and nature of the universe as known to science, but not explained by it, which seem too remarkable to be treated simply as inexplicable brute facts and which can become satisfyingly intelligible when viewed in the light of theological insight.

Scientists are motivated in their research by a deep desire to gain understanding, but the restricted character of science's enquiry means that this thirst for comprehensive understanding cannot be quenched by science alone. The first five sections of this chapter draw attention to a number of aspects of the scientific account of reality which it would be intellectually lazy simply to treat as happy accidents. It is claimed that they can be delivered from that unsatisfactory status by being set in the wider and more profound context of understanding that theistic belief can afford. As the cumulative discussion of these cosmic properties unfolds, it will be argued that the accessible range of explanatory plausibility narrows down from a very general kind of theism into something very like Christian Trinitarian theology. A final section then follows which seeks to argue that the Christian search for truth that led to Trinitarian belief, bears an analogous relationship to science's search for truth in its own domain of enquiry.

Science has discovered that the universe is endowed with certain remarkable properties. I discuss these in the following five sections.

Deep Intelligibility

It is hardly remarkable that human beings can understand the world of everyday experience, since the evolutionary pressure for survival can be expected to have so shaped the brains of

The Blackwell Companion to Science and Christianity, First Edition. Edited by J. B. Stump and Alan G. Padgett.
© 2012 Blackwell Publishing Ltd. Published 2012 by Blackwell Publishing Ltd.

our ancestors that they were capable of making sense of what was going on around them. Yet the human power of scientific understanding far exceeds the requirements of mundane necessity, or anything that could plausibly be considered as a spin-off from such a necessity. There is the subatomic world of quantum physics, remote from direct impact upon our daily lives and requiring for its understanding modes of thought that are completely contrary to those of common sense (see, for example, Polkinghorne 2002). In the quantum world entities can be in states which are an unpicturable mixture of "being here" and "being there." Light can sometimes display wave-like properties and sometimes behave as if it were a collection of tiny particles, an ambidexterity that lies far beyond the comprehension of mundane understanding. There are the vast domains of cosmic curved space-time, whose geometrical properties are quite different from everyday Euclidean expectation. Yet these counterintuitive regimes have proved to be open to scientific exploration and understanding. The universe is astonishingly rationally transparent to us, exhibiting a remarkable degree of profound intelligibility. Moreover, it has turned out that the key to unlocking the deep secrets of the physical world is provided by that seemingly most abstract of disciplines, mathematics. It is an actual technique of discovery in fundamental physics to seek theories that are expressed in terms of equations that possess the unmistakable character of mathematical beauty. Like all forms of beauty, mathematical beauty is easier to discern than describe, but it is something that the mathematicians can recognize and agree about. This search for beautiful equations is no act of aesthetic indulgence on the part of the physicists. Rather, it has been found to be a heuristic strategy of proven effectiveness, supported by much accumulated scientific experience. It has turned out time and again that it is just such theories that are the ones which will yield the long-term fruitfulness of explanation that persuades us that they truly describe aspects of physical reality. Paul Dirac, one of the founding figures of modern quantum theory, once said that he had made his discoveries by an unrelenting (and, one must say, highly successful) quest for beautiful equations. He said it was a "very profitable religion" to have followed.

Thus science has discovered that the universe is both rationally transparent and rationally beautiful. Cosmic transparency has been the basis of the very possibility of success in fundamental physics, and the beautiful order disclosed has given fundamental physicists the gift of wonder as the reward for their labors. Scientists are happy to exploit the remarkable opportunities that they have been given, but science itself can offer no explanation of their great good fortune. Yet these aspects of physical reality are surely too significant just to be treated as if they were merely incredibly happy accidents. Theological insight can make cosmic intelligibility itself intelligible. The rational transparency and beauty of the universe speaks of a world shot through with signs of mind, and it is an attractive and coherent possibility to believe that this is so because the divine Mind of the Creator lies behind its marvellous order.

Here is a first step in making a connection between physics and theology. In itself it is only a small step, since cosmic intelligibility would seem to be as well explained by the spectator god of deism as by the Trinitarian God of Christianity, but there is more still to be explored.

Intrinsic Fertility

The universe that we observe today sprang forth from the singularity of the big bang 13.7 billion years ago. The very early universe was extremely simple, being just an almost uniform expanding ball of energy. That world has now become very rich and complex, with the human brain the most complicated product of its long history that is known to us. Although it seems that there was no life in the universe until it was about 10 billion years old, and hominid life appeared only yesterday in cosmic terms, there is a real sense in which the universe was pregnant with the possibility of carbon-based life from the beginning. As physicists have come to understand the many processes which turned that initial ball of energy into the present home of saints and scientists, they have come to realize that this fertile history was possible only because the laws of nature – the given physical fabric of the world – took a very specific, "finely tuned" form. A universe capable of evolving carbon-based life has to be a very specific universe indeed, an insight that has come to be called "the anthropic principle" (see Holder 2004 for further discussion). Here, just one example drawn from many will have to serve to illustrate the point. The chemistry of life is the chemistry of carbon, since that element plays a vital role in the structure of the long-chain molecules that are the biochemical foundation of all forms of life. The only place in the entire universe where carbon is made is in the interior nuclear furnaces of the stars. We are all people of stardust, made of the ashes of dead stars. The chain of stellar nuclear processes that make carbon and the other heavy elements which are necessary for life is wonderfully and delicately balanced. If the laws of nuclear physics in our world had been only a little bit different from what they actually are, the chain would have been broken and there would be no carbon and no possibility of carbon-based life.

Science itself does not explain the laws of nature, since it simply accepts them as the given foundation on which to build its explanation of particular phenomena. Yet the fine-tuned specificity of these laws is a fact about the universe so significant that it surely should not be treated as if it too were just a happy accident. If possible, it demands some further explanation. Belief that the universe is a divine creation offers an obvious explanation of why the world is endowed with anthropic potentiality, for that fact can then be understood as an expression of the Creator's fruitful intention. Those wishing to avoid such a conclusion have been driven to the rather desperate expedient of conjecturing that our universe is part of a vast multiverse, an enormous portfolio of different worlds, all separate from each other and unobservable by us and possessing a great variety of different laws of nature, of which our world is simply one among a trillion. The "explanation" of anthropic fertility is then supposed to be that, simply by chance, our universe happens to be the winning ticket in this vast multiversial lottery. Belief in a Creator seems both more economical and better motivated (for example, it also explains cosmic intelligibility). Yet one must acknowledge that this is again an insight that would be as consistent with deism as it is with Christian theism. However, further consideration of other properties of physical reality will begin to narrow the range of theological plausibility.

An Evolving World

The processes that turned the initial ball of energy into the world we see today have been evolutionary in character. That is to say, they have involved an interplay between the effects of regularity and contingency, necessity and chance. It is a fundamental scientific insight that situations in which true novelty can emerge are always "at the edge of chaos," regimes where the orderly and the disorderly interlace each other. Too far on the orderly side of that frontier and things are too rigid for anything truly new to be possible. Too far on the disorderly side and things are too haphazard for anything new that emerged to be able to persist. The familiar story of biological evolution illustrates the point. If there were no genetic mutations (only order) there would be no new forms of life. If there were unceasing genetic mutations (only disorder), no species could become established on which the sifting effect of natural selection could be at work. Biological fruitfulness has depended on there being some genetic mutation, but not too much.

It is important to recognize that the operation of evolutionary process is not limited to the history of terrestrial life. The first stars were formed by an evolutionary interaction in which the small fluctuations of density initially present in the primordial ball of energy (a contingent pattern) came, through the operation of gravity (lawful regularity), to be seed sites for the condensation of stars, by a kind of snowballing process resulting from locally enhanced gravitational attraction.

When the *Origin of Species* was published there were some Christian theologians who from the start welcomed Darwin's ideas. Charles Kingsley coined a phrase that neatly encapsulates the theological way to think about an evolving world. He said that the Creator, instead of bringing into being a ready-made world, had done something cleverer than that in producing a world so endowed with potentiality that creatures could be allowed "to make themselves" through the processes of evolutionary exploration. It came to be recognized that this picture of creation was fittingly consonant with the Christian understanding that the divine nature is one of love. The Christian God could neither be the indifferent Spectator of deism nor the Cosmic Tyrant who held the whole of creation under tight divine control alone. The gift of love must always include a due degree of independence granted to the objects of love, which are allowed to be themselves and to make themselves. Such an evolving creation is a great good, but it has an inevitable shadow side. Its fertile process lies at the edge of chaos and so there will be ragged edges and blind alleys in its history, as well as great fruitfulness. Genetic mutations will sometimes result in new forms of life; sometimes they will result in malignancy. This insight offers theology some modest assistance as it tries to wrestle with the perplexing problems of theodicy.

The history of an evolving creation is not to be thought of as the performance of a fixed score, decreed from all eternity. It is more like an unfolding improvisation in which both Creator and creatures have roles to play. Seeing creation as an unfolding process leads to a concept of continuous creation, complementing the concept of the Creator holding the world in being through an act of creation out of nothing. Creation is not simply a single timeless act, but it is also a temporal process. The God who is the Ordainer of nature is to be thought of as acting as much through unfolding natural processes as in any other way. It is not the case that if something happened in a way that science is fully capable of describing, then God had no hand in it. The quest for a "God of the gaps" was not only a bad apologetic strategy (always open to defeat by the next advance in knowledge), but was also a bad theological mistake.

The recognition of the fact of continuous creation is the point at which the purely spectatorial god of deism – a once-for-all initiator who then simply watches it all happen – drops out of theological plausibility. There remains, however, the question of whether we can take all that science can tell us with appropriate seriousness and still believe in a God who is providentially active in history, interacting with creation in particular ways that go beyond the general sustaining of natural process. Can we think of God as being involved in the contingent aspects of evolution as well as in the lawful regularity that constrains it? Christian theology uses personal language about God (however stretched that language necessarily is), calling God "Father" rather than "Force," precisely because it believes that in particular circumstances divine providence acts to bring about particular consequences. The coherence of holding this belief, while taking modern science seriously, is the issue to be explored in the following section.

Causal Structure

In the eighteenth and nineteenth centuries, it seemed to many as if the deterministic equations of Newtonian physics implied that the universe is a world of clockwork mechanism, with its Creator simply the great cosmic Clockmaker. There was always something suspicious about this idea, since human experience of choice and responsibility surely indicates that persons are not just automata. However, in the twentieth century the discovery of intrinsic unpredictabilities present in nature, both at the microscopic level of quantum physics and, later, at the macroscopic level of the exquisitely sensitive systems of chaos theory, showed that the universe is something more subtle than a merely mechanical world. The word "intrinsic" is important here, for the unpredictabilities involved are of a kind that cannot be removed by more careful measurement or by more precise calculation. They are properties of physical reality.

Unpredictability might be epistemological or ontological in character. In the former case, it would just be the consequence of an unavoidable ignorance of all the factors involved, which if actually known would be sufficient fully to predict a particular outcome. The fall of a die would be a homely example of epistemic unpredictability. Ontological unpredictability is much more radical in its character, for it corresponds to the presence of real indeterminacy. The Copenhagen interpretation of quantum physics, stemming from the thought of Niels Bohr, has this character. It considers the Heisenberg uncertainty principle to be a principle of radical indeterminism and not simply a principle of necessary ignorance. Yet physics itself does not enforce this conclusion. There is an alternative interpretation of quantum theory, due to David Bohm (see Bohm and Hiley 1993), which is fully deterministic, in which uncertainty does indeed arise from unavoidable ignorance of all the causal factors involved. The theories of Bohr and Bohm both lead to identical empirical consequences, so that the choice between them cannot be made on the ground of physics alone, but is a matter requiring also metaphysical decision. Almost all physicists side with Bohr, one of the reasons being that Bohm's theory, though very ingenious and instructive, has about it an air of unnatural contrivance which fails to make it metaphysically persuasive. The lesson to derive from this quantum controversy is the recognition that while physics constrains our ideas about causality, it is not sufficient on its own to determine them. I have suggested that we should take a similar metaphysical approach to interpreting the unpredictabilities of chaos theory, seeing them as indications of further causal openness in physical process, now present at the macroscopic level (Polkinghorne 1991 34–48). The issue cannot be settled by appealing to the deterministic equations from which chaos theory took its mathematical origin, since we know that classical physics can offer only an approximate account of reality.

The strategy of interpreting intrinsic unpredictability ontologically is a natural one to take for those of a realist disposition in the philosophy of science, for whom what we know, or cannot know, is taken to be a reliable guide to what is the case. To do so does not imply that the future is some sort of random lottery, but simply that there are more causal factors active in bringing it about than those which science can describe in its reductionist terms of the exchange of energy between constituents. It would be natural to suppose that these additional causal factors include the exercise of human agency and divine providential interaction, both taking place within the open grain of created nature. What this discussion certainly shows is that physics has not established the causal closure of the world on its terms alone. This judgment is reinforced by the recognition that the account of causal structure offered by physics is not only metaphysically ambiguous, but it is also distinctly patchy in its character. Often the connections between different regimes are not well understood. For example there is no fully adequate account of how the apparently clear and reliable world of everyday experience emerges from its cloudy and fitful quantum substrate. Microscopic quantum theory and macroscopic chaos theory, as presently formulated, are incompatible with each other. Quantum physics has a scale (giving a meaning to "large" and "small" and set by Planck's constant), while chaos theory is notoriously fractal in character, looking the same on any scale on which it is sampled. The two theories just do not fit consistently together.

The conclusion is that one can take absolutely seriously all that physics can actually tell us about the causal structure of the universe, without being driven to deny human agency or exclude that providential activity of God within its history to which many religious traditions, including Christianity, bear witness.

Relationality

In the eighteenth century, physical thinking had a strongly atomistic character, but the succeeding two centuries have seen an increasing recovery of the importance of relationality. Among the greatest triumphs of nineteenth-century physics was James Clerk Maxwell's theory of electromagnetism. It relational significance does not derive from its being a field theory, since fields, while spread out in space and varying in time, have a local character in the sense that changes occurring at two separated locations are independent and have no immediate effect upon each other. What was relationally significant in Maxwell's theory was the intimate linkage it revealed between electricity and magnetism, two sets of phenomena which superficially had seemed completely unrelated to each other.

A unifying trend of this kind has proved to be a continuing feature of physical thinking. Albert Einstein's discovery of general relativity showed how space, time, and matter form an integrated system in which matter curves space-time and this curvature in turn influences the motion of particles of matter. The Newtonian picture of isolated atoms colliding in the container of absolute space, and in the course of the unfolding of absolute time, has had to be replaced by an altogether more relational account, in which space, time, and matter are joined together in a kind of physical package deal.

The quest for further unification has continued. In the 1960s, Steven Weinberg and Abdus Salam were independently able to integrate electromagnetism and the weak nuclear force, responsible for such phenomena as radioactive nuclear decay, in a single electroweak theory. Today, most physicists entertain the belief that there is a Grand Unified Theory, capable of combining in a single account all the forces of nature, including gravity, though so far no fully satisfactory theory of this kind has been successfully formulated.

The extreme sensitivity of chaotic systems to the slightest influence coming from their environment means that they can never adequately be considered in separation from that environment. However, the most striking discovery of intrinsic relationality in physics has been quantum entanglement. In the 1930s, Einstein and two young colleagues noticed that quantum theory implied that two quantum entities which had once interacted with each other could, in consequence, be in a state in which they retained a power of instantaneous influence on each other, however far they became separated. This mutual connection is a true ontological effect, producing real change in both entities, and not simply epistemological, revealing something that had always been the case. The entangled particles effectively constitute a single, non-local, system. Einstein thought that this togetherness-in-separation was so "spooky" that it must imply that there was something wrong with modern quantum theory, which he had always disliked. However, in the 1980s, clever experiments demonstrated that quantum entanglement is indeed a property of nature. The instantaneous action-at-a-distance that this implies is not a violation of special relativity, since careful analysis shows that it cannot be used to send information that would permit the synchronization of separated clocks, something that is forbidden by special relativity. Quantum entanglement shows us that even the subatomic quantum world cannot be treated atomistically.

Today a further scientific development of considerable potential significance is taking place through the study of complex systems, treated holistically as integrated entities and not decomposed into their constituent parts in science's traditionally reductionist manner. Current complexity theory is at the natural history stage of the study of many particular examples and it has not yet reached the mature scientific status of attaining a properly formulated general theory, explaining the underlying source of its diverse phenomena. The systems so far studied are far less complicated than even a single living cell, but nevertheless astonishing holistic properties have been discovered which were wholly unforeseeable from the point of view of a constituent-based analysis. These complex systems display very remarkable self-organizing powers to generate patterns of dynamically ordered holistic behavior (see Prigogine and Stengers 1984; Kauffman 1995). A simple example is provided by Bénard convection. Fluid is confined between two horizontal plates and the lower is maintained at a higher temperature than the upper. In certain well-defined circumstances, the transfer of heat between the two plates is carried by the convective motion of hot fluid, in a process which takes place within an orderly pattern of hexagonal convection cells. This spontaneously structured behavior involves the correlated motions of literally trillions upon trillions of fluid molecules.

The discovery of phenomena of this kind strongly suggests that the traditional reductionist physics based on the exchange of energy between constituents will need complementing by a holistic theory of the behavior of systems considered as totalities, reflecting the fact expressed in the slogan, "More is different" – the whole is more than the sum of its parts. A key concept in this holistic theory, when it is finally formulated, will surely be "information," meaning the specification of the dynamical pattern of total energy flow in the system. It is a plausible expectation that, as complexity theory comes of age, information will take its place alongside energy as a key category in physical thinking.

The developments briefly outlined above, when taken together, imply the need for scientific recognition that, far from being simply atomistic, "Reality is Relational." This will come as no surprise to Trinitarian theologians, whose discourse invokes the concept of "Being as Communion" (Zizioulas 1985). Of course, quantum entanglement and the like does not logically necessitate belief in a Creator whose inner nature is the unity of three Persons in one God, but it is strikingly consonant with that belief. In a similar way, information is not identical with spirit, but there is a glimmer of consonant connection between them. A universe for whose understanding information is a vital concept, is one to which the theological concept of the Spirit at work on the inside of creation does not seem wholly alien.

Our exploration of contemporary knowledge of the character of physical reality has been a process which has cumulatively suggested that Trinitarian theology offers a metaphysical setting in which to attain a deep understanding of remarkable cosmic properties that have been discovered by science but not explained by it (Polkinghorne 2004). Intelligibility and intrinsic fertility suggest that a divine Mind and Purpose lies behind the universe. Evolutionary process encourages a concept of continuously unfolding creation. An analysis of causal structure shows that science has not established a degree of causal closure that would deny belief in the reality of human agency and providential action. The widespread importance of relationality is highly consonant with belief in a Trinitarian Creator. The arguments presented have been an exercise in a theology of nature. That is to say, the claim is not that the universe *must* be thought of as a Trinitarian creation, but that, given this belief, one is in possession of a deeply coherent and persuasive way of understanding the way the world is. The next task is to see how theology can offer from within its own resources a well-formulated defense of its Trinitarian belief.

Trinitarian Belief

Scientists have often found that the world is surprising, manifesting properties that are strange beyond any human power to anticipate. In 1899 any competent student of philosophy could have "proved" the impossibility of anything behaving sometimes like a wave and sometimes like a particle. After all a wave is spread out and oscillating, while a particle is concentrated and point-like. Nevertheless this is exactly how light has been found to behave, and it is a striking example of the deep intelligibility of the universe that quantum theory has enabled us to make sense of this seemingly paradoxical fact. Nature's power to correct and transcend our prior expectations should lead scientists to have a natural inclination to humility in their encounter with reality, allowing it to speak for itself, whether they are acting as investigators of the physical universe or as persons seeking to discern what further reality might lie beyond it. Therefore, the natural question for a scientist to ask about any proposal is not, "Is it reasonable?", for that would rashly presume prior knowledge of the shape that rationality had to take. Instead the natural question for the scientist to ask is one that is at once more open and more demanding, "What makes you think that might be the case?" No proposal is to be ruled out of court from the start, however seemingly counterintuitive, but it will be entertained only if some adequately motivating evidence can be presented in its support. The natural style of thinking for the scientist is what I have called "bottom-up thinking" (Polkinghorne 1994), seeking to be guided by experience in the quest for truthful understanding and not presuming already to be in possession of a sufficient set of clear and certain ideas that could form an *a priori* basis for the argument. I believe that it is possible to pursue theological enquiry in this bottom-up fashion, and this section seeks to give a brief sketch how this strategy might be used to approach Trinitarian thinking about nature of God, in a manner that should be congenial to a scientist.

The New Testament provides the record of the foundational experiences that led to the Christian movement, but its pages do not contain a carefully articulated statement of Trinitarian doctrine, although there are two isolated verses which have a remarkably Trinitarian ring to them (Matt. 28:19 and 2 Cor. 13:13). What is to be found in the New Testament are records of those experiences and insights of first-century Christians which were to inspire later generations to develop an understanding of the nature of God of a more subtle and complex kind than could be expressed simply by an unnuanced assertion of monotheism. Most of the New Testament writers were Jews, for whom the great affirmation "Hear, O Israel, The Lord is our God, The Lord alone" (Deut. 6:4) was central to their religious belief. They knew that the One whom Jesus called Father is indeed the Creator of the world. Yet, when these writers came to speak of their experiences of the transforming power of the risen Christ, time and again, despite their Jewish monotheism, they were driven to use divine-sounding language about him. The earliest Christian confession seems to have been "Jesus is Lord" (see, for example, Rom. 10:9; 1 Cor. 12:3). Paul calls Jesus "Lord" more than 200 times in his letters, and he can even use language about him which echoes what the Hebrew Scriptures say about The Lord, the God of Israel (for example, compare Phil. 2:10–11 and Isa. 45:23) . While in everyday speech the Greek *kyrios* could amount to no more than a common courtesy (rather like the English "sir"), in the theologically centered writings of the New Testament, readers would inevitably be reminded that "Lord" was the word that pious Jews used as a circumlocution for the unutterably sacred divine name of God, so that its use as a title was fraught with significance. This impression was surely reinforced by the way in which Paul, in opening his letters, habitually bracketed together God and Christ in the greeting, "Grace to you and peace from God our Father and the Lord Jesus Christ" (Rom. 1:7, etc.). Of course, both writer and readers knew that Jesus of Nazareth was a human being who had been alive in Palestine within living memory, but purely human terms did not seem to suffice to describe their experience of him. At the same time, these early Christians felt a divine power at work within them, which they variously called "the Spirit of God," "the Spirit of Christ," or simply "the Spirit" (for example, see Rom. 8:9, where all three terms are used in the same verse). Here there seemed to be a third, and distinguishable, form of encounter with divine reality. One might say that these early Christians knew God in three ways, the Father (Creator of heaven and earth), the Son (God made manifest in a human life), and the Holy Spirit (God at work in their hearts). Yet they also believed that there was a single divine Will and Purpose at work in the world.

The New Testament does not discuss explicitly how these diverse insights into the reality of God can be combined and understood in a coherent fashion. Its concern is to witness to its experience, not to construct a fundamental theological theory. However, later generations of Christians could not leave these matters unaddressed and this led eventually to the formulation of Trinitarian doctrine at the Councils of Nicea (325) and Constantinople (381), and to much further discussion which has continued up to the present day. That is a complex and fascinating story which I shall not attempt to tell here in what could only be an inadequate summary fashion. The important point for the present discussion is that the Trinitarian doctrine of the three divine Persons, united by love in a single divine Nature, did not arise from unbridled metaphysical speculation, but from wrestling with making sense of actual religious experience. The bottom-up thinker should be prepared to give serious consideration to the counterintuitive concept of the triune God, and he or she can do so without incurring the risk of committing intellectual suicide by having to submit to a demand for belief unsupported by motivating evidence.

Theory-making in theology is much more difficult than theorizing in science, essentially because God transcends us while we transcend the physical world. Often theology has to be content with circumscribing the domain in which truth must lie, without being able to offer a detailed map of the terrain. In the case of Trinitarian theology, the Church concluded that it could identify two extreme positions which would not be true to the scriptural witness and to its own worshipful encounter with God. One came to be called modalism, the idea that Father, Son, and Holy Spirit simply label different aspects of human encounter with an undifferentiated divine Reality. This view does not seem to do justice to the distinctive and differentiated character of actual Christian experience. A paradigm counterexample drawn from Scripture was provided by the story of the baptism of Jesus, with the heavenly voice of the Father proclaiming the beloved nature of the Son, and the Spirit descending upon Christ in the form of a dove. At the other extreme, the Church rejected a tritheistic understanding that would treat the Trinity as if it were a mini-pantheon of three wholly distinct gods, for the Church's experience testified to the unity of the divine Will and Purpose at work in creation.

A good scientific theory often reinforces its persuasiveness by offering deeper understanding of phenomena not explicitly taken into account in its initial formulation. Something similar to this can be claimed for Trinitarian theology. If the inner nature of God is constituted by the eternal exchange of love between the three divine Persons, this gives a much more profound understanding of the central Christian assertion that "God is love" (1 John 4:16) than could be afforded by something like the Aristotelian notion of an isolated deity absorbed in the narcissistic contemplation of his own perfection.

It is along the lines sketched in this section that Christian believers can defend their Trinitarian belief as truly arising from a motivated appeal to actual evidence, and this provides for them the resource from which they can offer their response to the question, "What makes you think that might be the case?"

References

Bohm, David and Hiley, Basil J. 1993. *The Undivided Universe*. London: Routledge.

Holder, Rodney D. 2004. *God, the Multiverse and Everything*. Aldershot: Ashgate.

Kauffman, Stuart. 1995. *At Home in the Universe*. New York: Oxford University Press.

Polkinghorne, John. 1991. *Reason and Reality*. London: SPCK.

Polkinghorne, John. 1994. *Science and Christian Belief: Theological Reflections of a Bottom-Up Thinker*. London: SPCK.

Prigogine, Ilya and Stengers, Isabelle. 1984. *Order Out of Chaos*. London: Heinemann.

Further Reading

Polkinghorne, John. 2002. *Quantum Theory: A Very Short Introduction*. Oxford: Oxford University Press. A slim volume that explores in more detail many of the points made in this chapter concerning quantum theory.

Polkinghorne, John. 2004. *Science and the Trinity*. London: SPCK. Explores more fully several of the key points made in this chapter concerning Trinity, science, and reality.

Zizioulas, John D. 1985. *Being as Communion: Studies in Personhood and the Church*. Crestwood, NY: St Vladimir's Seminary Press. An influential interpretation and exploration of the doctrine of the Trinity; develops for our time the ancient Eastern Orthodox viewpoint.

46

God and Miracle in
an Age of Science

ALAN G. PADGETT

One of the important issues which the Enlightenment has bequeathed to us is the question of miracles in the light of modern science. This topic is one of the areas where Christianity and science overlap, and some would say conflict. Is it rational or otherwise intellectually legitimate to accept the occurrence of genuine miracles and at the same time embrace the teachings of modern science and a robust conception of the laws of nature? In this chapter I will argue for the positive case. The topic of miracles is quite extensive, and we cannot cover everything. We are not going to discuss issues of knowing or testimony concerning miracles, for example, nor go into details concerning special divine action. Instead we will start with the question of just what a miracle is, at least for Christian thought. I will argue that for many miracles it is wrong to believe they "violate" the laws of nature, a confused term which I shall conclude should be replaced with several more nuanced terms, including "physical impossibility" (see also Walker 1982; Corner 2005, 1–7). Now Christian theology is grounded in Scripture, and so we will first work out a biblically informed conception of miracles before considering the metaphysical issue of their relationship to the acceptance of science and the laws of nature.

Miracles: A Theological Definition

It is often remarked by biblical theologians that the concept of "miracle" in the Hebrew Bible and New Testament does not imply something beyond the capacity of nature to bring about.[1] The Hebrew biblical terms sometimes translated as "miracle" are better translated as "sign" (*ôt*) or "wonder" (*môpet*) and are often seen together as "signs and wonders." Similarly, the NT uses the Greek terms "sign" (*semeion*) and "wonder" (*teras*) along with "power" in the sense of mighty deed (*dynamis*). In Scripture, these signs and wonders performed by God or God's human agent may or may not be beyond the capacity of nature. For example, Isaiah walked three years naked through Jerusalem as a "sign and wonder" (Isa. 20:4). On the other

The Blackwell Companion to Science and Christianity, First Edition. Edited by J. B. Stump and Alan G. Padgett.
© 2012 Blackwell Publishing Ltd. Published 2012 by Blackwell Publishing Ltd.

hand, some biblical miracles do seem to be beyond the capacities of nature to bring about. The standard Christian example is the bodily resurrection of Jesus from the dead (Acts 2:22–24). Another example is one of the seven "signs" performed by Jesus in the first part of John's Gospel, for instance turning water into wine (John 2:11).

What is of central importance for the biblical authors is not the question of natural law, but a very different issue. There is indeed an important difference between genuine or true miracles and false ones. True miracles are done by God or God's human agent: they are a special divine action. They point to God's work of salvation and redemption (e.g., Exod. 7:1–7; John 2:11), or put differently, they are wondrous deeds that act as *signs* of the reign and realm ("kingdom") of God in the world.[2] There are, however, *false* miracles which are done by false prophets (e.g., Deut. 13:2; Matt. 24:24). The difference here has nothing to do with the capacities of the natural world. Rather, the difference is spiritual: false miracles are used by evil beings to lead people away from God, just as true miracles act as signs of God's reign and realm. Again, the miracles in question do not have to be beyond the capacities of nature to bring about, but they may sometimes be physically impossible or strictly extra-ordinary (as I will define it). In his monograph on miracles, *Signs of God*, Mark Corner (2005, 2–7) rightly defines miracles (*true* miracles, I would insist) as special divine actions that need not violate the laws of nature; but he fails to distinguish between true and false miracles. Thus not *all* miracles are special divine actions – false miracles are not.

Christian theology should recover in our time this biblical, spiritual understanding of what counts as a *true miracle*. It is far more helpful in our scientific age than Hume's definition. This means rejecting what has become a standard meaning for "miracle" among theologians and philosophers, that is, a miracle must be a "violation" of a law of nature (e.g., Swinburne 1970, 6). To insist on keeping Hume's definition of miracle as a violation of natural law would mean that some of the key miracles in biblical salvation history (for example, the return of Israel from exile) would not be miracles at all on this definition – which is absurd. As we have seen, what the Bible calls "signs and wonders" may or may not be beyond the powers of nature. We should on biblical and theological grounds resist the claim of Aquinas that "a thing is called a miracle by comparison with the power of nature which it surpasses. So the more the power of nature is surpassed, the greater the miracle" (*Summa Theologiae* I, q.105, a.8). The greatness of a miracle, in theological terms, has to do with its importance for salvation and special revelation, *not* how far it exceeds the capacity of natural things to bring it about. In order to address the concerns of modern thinkers like Hume, therefore, we will need to use another term to speak of events which, in the words of Aquinas, are "beyond the order commonly observed in natural things" (*praeter ordinem communiter observatum in rebus*) (*Summa contra gentiles*, iii.100). For this purpose I suggest we use two terms instead of "violation": (a) physically impossible or (b) strictly extra-ordinary event.

Violation and Intervention: A Critique of Metaphors

The first problem with the commonly asserted notion of a violation of natural law is theological and rhetorical. Because our language gives shape to our social reality, these are important considerations. I find the very term "violation" to be unacceptable and confusing. To speak of God "violating" or "breaking" the laws of nature is, at best, rather loose. It is better to speak of God doing something that is physically impossible for two reasons. The first is greater precision. If we could replace "violate" and "break" with doing the physically impossible we would go a long way toward clarity and precision in our discussion of miracles and the laws of nature.

The second reason is more philosophical, having to do with our understanding of nature. The metaphor or picture which this kind of language evokes I find objectionable on natural philosophical grounds. They suggest that the laws of nature are independent of the world, or hold some universal determinative power. Later in the chapter I will give reasons to reject this kind of natural philosophy for laws of nature. I will also argue that what is meant by the terms "violation of the laws of nature" is best expressed as a physical impossibility rather than something that is very highly improbable (strictly extra-ordinary).

While on the subject of language and rhetoric, I also object (with other scholars) to the terms "intervention" or "interference" when speaking of true miracles (as seen, for example, in Lewis 1960, 12). In his recent book on miracles, Mark Corner makes an argument very much in line with this point (2005, 7):

> [T]here is a danger implicit in this notion of "intervention." It implies that human beings ordinarily inhabit a self-sufficient universe which they interpret and manage of their own accord . . . If God "intervenes" in the world, that implies that the Deity ordinarily stands apart from it.

In other words, the picture of God and the world which "intervention" evokes, rhetorically, is already theological deficient. It assumes a deistic notion of God and the world. Much to be preferred, at least in academic circles, is the more neutral "special divine action" (on God's part) or "physically impossible" (on nature's part).

To take up an important example: in one of the better recent books on miracles René Latourelle provides a careful biblical, philosophical, and theological analysis of miracles, resulting in a careful definition. His definition is marred, however, by the term "intervention" for which I will substitute "wondrous action." We can then adopt it as a definition of *true* miracle:

> A [true] miracle is a religious wonder that expresses, in the cosmic order (human beings and the universe), a special and utterly free [wondrous action] of the God of power and love, who thereby gives human beings a sign of the uninterrupted presence of his word of salvation in the world. (Latourelle 1988, 276)

True miracles will always be wonders in some sense, and therefore extra-ordinary in some way. But they need not be strictly extraordinary nor physically impossible.

Physically Impossible and SEE: Definition

I have argued that among the genuine miracles which are part of the biblical witness, some are within the order commonly observed in natural things, while other events are beyond it. As part of our consideration of miracles, we have mentioned that some events brought about by God are physically impossible. For the purpose of analysis, we must now make a distinction among the meanings of the terms "laws of nature". Sometimes by laws of nature philosophers have meant sentences of a certain type, in human natural and artificial languages. Let us agree to call these "laws of natural science," or just laws of science. These will change as science and/or natural philosophy change over time. Yet sometimes by laws of nature philosophers have meant something outside of human knowing: the existing, actual principles of nature which structure and order the natural world. Let us agree to call these *principia*, from the Latin *principia naturae* used by late medieval and early modern natural scientists.

We are now ready for a preliminary definition of the physically impossible. A physically impossible event is an event which is not possible for nature itself to bring about, that is, an event which is impossible from the point of view of the principles of nature (*principia*) as they really are. There are different kinds of possibility, necessity, and impossibility: this kind has to do with the structures of nature, and what they can and cannot bring about. It is physically possible for a human to fly when aided; however it is physically *impossible* for me to fly without the aid of a glider or similar help. To fill out the physically impossible, we should note that the past is relevant here, along with the nature of the physical thing we are speaking of, and the context in which the event takes place.

When speaking of miracles, however, we sometimes need to refer to events that are more than merely wonderful or extraordinary, but neither are they physically impossible. This is because our concept of the *principia* has changed over time. Perhaps at one time a mechanistic world picture made plausible the idea that every physical event is fully determined by the *principia* and prior physical events. But the advent of more recent theories in natural science has made much more complex our understanding of nature. Quantum theory, chaos theory, quantum cosmology, evolutionary biology, ecology, and neurobiology have worked to bring us a more complex, dynamic, and holistic understanding of the natural world. In this context, the thesis of global physical determinism seems unlikely.[3] We had better allow for the fact that some of the *principia* in the actual world have to do with *probabilities* rather than fixed outcomes. They tell us what a proportion of events will be like, rather than what all events will be like of a certain type. What is more, taken as a whole the *principia* are probabilistic. They do not, strictly speaking, make certain kinds of events *physically impossible* so much as make them *highly improbable*.

So we need another definition of an event that is somehow "beyond" nature, but based on probability: I will call this a strictly extra-ordinary event (SEE), that is, an event in the natural history of the world which is *very highly improbable*, but not quite physically impossible. A fair coin flipped one time which lands on its edge is not physically impossible – but it is very, very unlikely and so an SEE.

Both the physically impossible and the strictly extra-ordinary are concepts based upon the orders of nature. It is true that some of the laws of physics can lead to deterministic results, as long as the system is a simple one and the circumstances are right. A good example of this is our ability to predict and retrodict, with striking accuracy, a solar eclipse. But let us say that the present conditions and the laws of astronomy predict a total solar eclipse for Buenos Aires on July 1, 2111. But between now and then a massive asteroid strikes the moon and changes its orbit, so that the predicted event does not take place. Examples like this can be multiplied many times, since physics is based upon simplified, abstract models in which the conditions are assumed to be just right. Taken out of these models, and understood as simple empirical generalizations, which apply with universal and non-probabilistic force, many of the laws of physics may prove false.[4]

In her important work *How the Laws of Physics Lie*, Nancy Cartwright comes to two significant and convincing conclusions (1983, 128–129):

(1)   We need to "distinguish between the tidy and simple mathematical equations of abstract theory, and the intricate and messy descriptions in either words or formulae, which

express our knowledge of what happens in real systems made of real materials, like helium-neon lasers or turbo-jet engines."

(2) "Nature is not governed by simple quantitative equations of the kind we write in our fundamental theories."

Of course this does not mean that these laws of science are in fact false (*pace* Cartwright), but only that their nature and justification is more complicated than has sometimes been assumed. This is why we need to refer to the actual *principia* of nature, as well as to what is highly probable or improbable given them.

In very broad terms, the physically impossible cannot be brought about by natural things operating under their own power, given the *principia* and prior physical events. SEEs may well occur from time to time, but would not be normal, frequent, or regular events. Excluding what is logically impossible, this analysis leaves us with four categories of events in the world of nature:

(1) physically impossible
(2) strictly extra-ordinary (and not (1))
(3) extraordinary (and neither (1) nor (2))
(4) ordinary.

Just because it is a wonder, no miracle will be (4) except in some romantic or figurative sense, but we have seen that for Christian Scripture a miracle may be (1), (2), or (3). Having come up with a workable definition of SEE, we are now ready to explore more fully the relationship between miracle, the strictly extra-ordinary, and the physically impossible.

So far I have argued that not all miracles are SEEs or physically impossible. Equally true is the fact that not all physically impossible events or SEEs are miracles! This is because of the implicit spiritual meanings associated with the term "miracle" in Christian thought. We now turn to the relationship between miracles, natural order, and natural science.

Miracles, Science, and the Order of Nature

In this section I will argue that, first, SEEs are bound to occur from time to time, and thus the rare SEE in no way undermines the reliability of scientific knowledge. I will argue, second, that a very rare occurrence of a physically impossible event would not undermine the reliability of scientific knowledge, as long as it did not happen on a regular basis.

If we are right to understand the *principia* as not only including some probabilistic principles, but also of being (as a whole) probabilistic, then certain interesting facts about SEEs result. Because the *principia* in the actual world are probabilistic, some chance events must have occurred in the long history of the space-time continuum for our very large universe. In other words, given a large and old universe, some weird things are bound to happen! SEEs are entailed by the probabilistic character of the *principia* plus the long history of a large cosmos. If the *principia* are based on probabilities, then given billions upon billions of events, some will be strictly extra-ordinary.

It turns out, then, that some SEEs are not "violations" of the *principia*; on the contrary, they are entailed by their probabilistic character. Yet to be compatible with the *principia*, such events must not be repeating or repeatable. A repeating (or repeatable) SEE would not be compatible with the actual *principia* even when they are understood to be probabilistic. Mary Hesse was not quite right to claim that "statistical laws in science are in fact violated if events occur which according to them are excessively improbable" (1965, 38). As we have seen, a one-off or non-repeating SEE may well be required by the *principia*. But she is right if the event in question (and events like it in the relevant way) happens regularly, or can be repeated for scientific study (see also Smart 1964; Swinburne 1970, 26–32; Kellenberg 1979). Smart argues that non-repeating counter-instances do not make laws of science false: Swinburne concludes, "If, as seems natural, we understand by physically impossible what is ruled out by the laws of nature, then our account of laws of nature suggests that it makes sense to suppose that on occasion the physically impossible occurs" (1970, 28). J. L. Mackie, no friend to theism or miracles, makes the same point in his study of causation: "an occasional violation does not itself necessarily overthrow the independently established conclusion that this *is* a law of working" (1974, 20).[5] So a one-off SEE does not undermine science. Some SEEs will occur from time to time in any case, and a non-repeating SEE does not "overthrow" the laws of science.

But what about the physically impossible? Are not some miracles affirmed by a Christian and biblical faith not merely extraordinary but simply impossible given the nature of the world? First of all, to repeat points already made, some miracles are in accordance with the laws of science and/or the *principia*. Others may not be physically impossible but SEE. But some miracles, like the bodily resurrection of Jesus, are physically impossible. In nature, dead bodies that have been dead for three days stay that way. The resurrection of Jesus is beyond nature. What about miracles like this? *As long as they are not repeating and not repeatable*, they do not "violate" the laws of nature. Because the laws of nature are descriptive of the normal and ordinary ways in which natural things work, one-off events, even physically impossible ones, do not undermine these laws. A one-off event, even a physically impossible one, neither *makes* nor *breaks* any of the laws of nature. If it is a true miracle, it is another example of God at work in the world – but not an "interference" or an "intervention" into the causal nexus of the *principia* as if somehow God were not always active there!

So the bodily resurrection of Jesus violates nothing. It breaks nothing. It is not and cannot be a principle of nature, and these principles are rules or structures of how natural things do operate – not how they *must* do so. Certainly, some kind of necessity attaches to the principles and laws of nature – but it is causal and natural rather than absolute. Perhaps another biblical example of miracle can clarify this point, this time an SEE. Take the miraculous catch of fish (Luke 5:1–11) which Luke places just before Jesus calls the disciples, giving them the famous promise that "from now on you will fish for people" (v. 10). The power of the miracle is such that it helped to stimulate their trust in Jesus, and "they left all and followed him" (v. 11). But the miracle itself is not physically impossible. After fishing all night, Simon, James, John, and their partners caught nothing – and suddenly their nets were simply loaded with fish after Jesus told them to try again. Even though not physically impossible, this true miracle and its exact timing are very highly improbable. It is not really a *natural* event, and it counts as an SEE. The very highly improbable character of this event strongly suggests it will not be repeatable by investigators today, either. It does not undermine our faith in natural science. It does not "violate" or "break" the very structures of nature (*principia*) any more than the bodily resurrection of Jesus. Both are brought about by the God of nature, who is always at work in the cosmos. God upholds everything moment by moment, including all matter-energy and the *principia*. Thus God can act in a way that is in continuity with the nature world, even when the event is an SEE or physically impossible. In the miraculous catch of fish God may have worked with creatures like fish and water to perform this true miracle, but it is not a violation of anything. Nothing was "broken" here, as if the universe were a fragile clock in which any "interference" would destroy the mechanism. The created causes of fish, boats, nets, and waves retained their integrity as creatures while cooperating with the divine will. We should conclude that true miracles are *not* "interventions" by God into an otherwise self-sustaining causal nexus.

SEE as violation of the laws of science

Perhaps an SEE might turn out to be physically impossible on another analysis. Analytic philosophers have sometimes voiced their objections to miracles not in terms of the *principia* but in terms of the laws of science. According to this line of reasoning, a true law of science is falsified by a single counter-instance, just because they are universal empirical generalizations which tell us what can and cannot happen physically.[6] The problem here is twofold: (1) the use of the term "miracle" to mean nothing more than a physically impossible event, and (2) the utilization of an earlier and now dubious conception of the "laws of nature" (i.e., laws of science).[7] As we have seen, the laws of physics (for example) are true in their models, but they may not be universally true when understood to be simple empirical generalizations taken out of their models. Indeed, one of the goals of a complicated experiment in physics is to create an environment where reality is as close as possible to the mathematical model(s) being tested; in this way scientists attempt to exclude extraneous forces and chance outcomes resulting from the incursion of outside forces.

Thus a one-off SEE need not falsify the laws of science.

Physically impossible miracles: can they happen?

I have argued so far that a miracle need not be physically impossible. Many miracles may be extraordinary, others may be non-repeating SEEs. But some true miracles may well be physically impossible. Could they still happen within the world of nature? For a true miracle, God or God's agent brings about the event in question. Yes, a true miracle which is also physically impossible is incompatible with the *principia* and prior physical events. But this does not mean the event in question simply cannot occur in the natural world. Nature cannot bring about a physically impossible miracle: but God can. God creates and upholds the *principia* (and all creation) throughout time. They are not independent creatures, and they do not operate on their own. They pose no limit upon the absolute power of God, except as God elects to self-limit the divine will so as to empower creatures and allow them to be what they are in freedom.[8] A physically impossible miracle is possible by divine omnipotence – not by the powers of the natural world. A true miracle may be physically impossible but still *possible* because it is *God* that brings it about.[9] But would not such a miraculous event undermine modern science? Not at all.

One might put the point in these terms: earlier philosophers focused on the qualities of the laws of science as *laws*. This led them to assert that they are universal non-probabilistic empirical generalizations. I have concluded (following other philosophers of science) that we should focus on the fact that these are laws of *science*; their truth must be affirmed in a modest and modified manner more in keeping with their typical status as true approximations. The fact is that a unique and non-repeating counter-instance to a law of science (even if it is physically impossible in my sense) does not undermine science, nor does it falsify the laws of science. Since the laws of science are true approximations of the natural world, a single non-repeating counter-instance, even one that is physically impossible, need not falsify or otherwise undermine them. True, some theologians, philosophers, and scientists continue to assume that natural science entails a kind of "no miracles" rule, but usually without much argument (e.g., Griffin 2000) and often assuming too rigid an understanding of the laws of science and/or the *principia*.

Conclusions

In this chapter we have reviewed and responded to many of the Enlightenment worries about belief in true miracles. We have found reasons to alter our loose language and thinking about miracles and the laws of nature. We should reject the idea that miracles are a "violation" of the laws of nature, along with the language of "intervention" and "interference": these do not helpfully or accurately describe God's action in a true miracle. Instead, we found reasons to recover a biblical understanding of true miracle as an event brought about by God or God's agent which serves as a sign of God's reign and realm, independent of any question of the laws of nature. I defined another technical term, strictly extra-ordinary event, as an event that is very highly improbable but need not be physically impossible. One-off strictly extra-ordinary miracles do not "violate" the laws of nature, and the rare physically impossible event does not undermine science.

   None of this suggests that religion should be irrational. I am not advocating superstition, or abandoning a scientific outlook on reality. Science has its place: but so does faith in God. Hard thinking about any miracle claim is called for: thinking which is both theological and scientific. True miracles may be extraordinary, strictly extra-ordinary, or physically impossible. Even a one-off physically impossible miracle (while incompatible with the *principia*) need not falsify the laws of science, nor undermine natural science. A firm belief that true miracles occur, understood in the right way, is perfectly consistent with a robust and realist notion of the laws of nature, and a full acceptance of natural science.

Notes

My thanks to the Director and members of the Center for Philosophy of Religion, University of Notre Dame for warm conversation and questions around early versions of this chapter, during a wonderful year as Crosson Fellow there. I also thank Jim Stump, once again, for helpful suggestions.

1   See among others McCasland (1957); DeGroot (1966); Brown (1986); Sant and Collins (2006).

2   Other philosophers have made similar points, including Blondel (1907), a hundred years ago, and in recent times Swinburne (1970, 2) and Mawson (2001). On the other hand, Basinger and Basinger object to the criterion of "religious significance" for miracles because they feel there is no "set of objective and *independent* criteria" (their italics) by which a theist can "always determine whether an event contributes to some holy, just purpose" (1986, 22). This objection is misplaced. It assumes we cannot know some event is a genuine miracle without knowing its full effect – which places our capacity to know how God is at work far above reasonable expectations for everyday humans!

3   So already in 1939 (Eddington, 63–64): "In the current indeterministic system of physics . . . [t]he present system of fundamental laws does not furnish a complete set of rules for the calculation of

the future. It is not even part of such a set, for it is concerned only with the calculation of probabilities." For more current arguments against determinism, see Popper (1982) and Earman (1986).

4   Philosophers of religion have not always taken this fact on board when defining laws of nature, e.g., Johnson (1999, 9). Likewise Saunders (2002) misinterprets of the laws of mathematical physics as too universal and deterministic in relationship to the real world.

5   A "basic law of working" is Mackie's term for a true law of concrete operation, similar to what we are here calling *principia*.6   For a recent discussion of this issue see Mavrodes (1985) and Hoffman (1985).

7   Mumford (2001) argues that miracles are logically possible. He uses "miracle" to mean nothing more than a physically impossible event brought about by a supernatural cause, wrongly dismissing the essential spiritual and moral force of a genuine miracle. But Mumford (2004) does have an attractive and sophisticated theory of the laws of nature.

8   On this theme of self-limitation to empower creatures see Polkinghorne (2001).

9   Numerous philosophers, theologians, and scientists have come to similar conclusions, from Mozely's Bampton lectures (Mozley 1865) to Blondel (1907), and now to Polkinghorne (2000). For a review of the history and the debates, see Brown (1984).

References

Basinger, David and Basinger, Randall. 1986. *Philosophy and Miracle*. Lewiston: Edwin Mellen.

Blondel, Maurice. 1907. La notion et la rôle du miracle. *Annales de philosophie chrétienne*, 105, pp. 337–361.

Brown, Colin. 1984. *Miracles and the Critical Mind*. Grand Rapids, MI: Eerdmans.

Brown, Colin. 1986. Miracle. In G. W. Bromiley, ed. *International Standard Bible Encyclopedia*, revised edn, vol. 3. Grand Rapids, MI: Eerdmans, pp. 371–381.

Cartwright, Nancy. 1983. *How the Laws of Physics Lie*. Oxford: Oxford University Press.

Corner, Mark. 2005. *Signs of God: Miracles and Their Interpretation*. Aldershot: Ashgate.

DeGroot, A. 1966. *The Bible on Miracles*. De Pere, WI: St Norbert Abbey Press.

Earman, John. 1986. *A Primer on Determinism*. Dordrecht: Reidel.

Eddington, Arthur. 1939. *The Philosophy of Physical Science*. Cambridge: Cambridge University Press.

Griffin, David R. 2000. *Religion and Scientific Naturalism*. Albany, NY: State University of New York Press.

Hesse, Mary. 1965. Miracles and the Laws of Nature. In C. F. D. Moule, ed. *Miracles*. London: Mowbray, pp. 35–42.

Hoffman, Joshua. 1985. Comments on "Miracles and the Laws of Nature." *Faith and Philosophy*, 2, pp. 347–352.

Johnson, David. 1999. *Hume, Holism and Miracles*. Ithaca, NY: Cornell University Press.

Kellenberger, J. 1979. Miracles. *International Journal for Philosophy of Religion*, 10, pp. 145–162.

Latourelle, René. 1988. *The Miracles of Jesus and the Theology of Miracles*. New York: Paulist Press.

Lewis, C. S. 1960. *Miracles*. New York: Macmillan.

Mackie, J. L. 1974. *The Cement of the Universe*. Oxford: Oxford University Press.

Mavrodes, George. 1985. Miracles and the Laws of Nature. *Faith and Philosophy*, 2, pp. 333–346.

Mawson, T. J. 2001. Miracles and Laws of Nature. *Religious Studies*, 37, pp. 33–58.

McCasland, S. V. 1957. Signs and *Wonders*. *Journal of Biblical Literature*, 76, pp. 149–152.

Mozely, J. B. 1865. *Eight Lectures on Miracles*. London: n.p.

Mumford, Stephen. 2001. Miracles: Metaphysics and Modality. *Religious Studies*, 37, pp. 191–202.

Mumford, Stephen. 2004. *Laws in Nature*. London: Routledge.

Polkinghorne, John. 2000. *The End of the World and the Ends of God*. Harrisburg, PA: Trinity Press International.

Polkinghorne, John, ed. 2001. *The Work of Love: Creation as Kenosis*. Grand Rapids, MI: Eerdmans.

Popper, Karl. 1982. *The Open Universe*. Totowa: Rowman & Littlefield.

Sant, C. and Collins, R. F. 2006. Miracles (in the Bible). In T. Carson, J. Cerrito *et al.*, eds. *New Catholic Encyclopedia*, 2nd edn, vol. 9. Detroit: Thompson/Gale, pp. 661–664.

Saunders, Nicholas. 2002. *Divine Action and Modern Science*. Cambridge: Cambridge University Press.

Smart, Ninian. 1964. Miracles and David Hume. In Ninian Smart, ed. *Philosophers and Religious Truth*. London: SCM, pp. 25–67.

Swinburne, Richard. 1970. *The Concept of Miracle*. London: Macmillan.

Walker, Ian. 1982. Miracles and Violations. *International Journal for Philosophy of Religion*, 13, pp. 103–108.

Further Reading

Brown, Colin. 1984. *Miracles and the Critical Mind*. Grand Rapids, MI: Eerdmans. A good historical survey of the issues and main thinkers.

Corner, Mark. 2005. *Signs of God: Miracles and Their Interpretation*. Aldershot: Ashgate. A helpful and critical overview of the topic, with a sustained argument from the author in light of recent debates.

Gwynne, Paul. 1996. *Special Divine Action*. Rome: Gregorian University Press. A good recent monograph on the specific topic of special divine action, with a critical overview of various authors and issues.

Latourelle, René. 1988. *The Miracles of Jesus and the Theology of Miracles*. New York: Paulist Press. A learned combination of biblical studies, philosophy, and theology, with a focus on the Gospel accounts.

Swinburne, Richard, ed. 1990. *Miracles*. New York: Macmillan. A fine anthology of significant essays from philosophers.

47

Eschatology in Science and Theology

ROBERT JOHN RUSSELL

Introduction

Among the variety of scholarly surveys of historical and contemporary approaches to Christian eschatology, few treat the challenge of scientific cosmology to eschatology.[1] It is the purpose of this chapter to do so. We begin with the place of eschatology in Christian theology. Next we summarize the predictions for the far future of the universe according to scientific cosmology. These predictions – 'freeze or fry' – severely challenge those versions of eschatology which are based on the bodily Resurrection of Jesus and the transformation of the universe into the new creation. Several recent approaches to this challenge are outlined and some suggestions made for future research.

The Place of Eschatology in Christian Theology

The meaning of eschatology in the classic Christian theological texts is as an apocalyptic event in the distant future. It refers to the topic of "last things" (general resurrection, last judgment, heaven and hell, the end of the world, etc.) and it is routinely consigned to the end of dogmatics. Following the eighteenth-century Enlightenment, however, eschatology was usually reinterpreted in terms of philosophical, ethical, social, political, economic, and historical categories, and little attention was given to traditional issues and the universe as such. In the twentieth century we find C. H. Dodd arguing that the eschaton was "realized" in the ministry of Jesus and the history of the Church. Because of the conflict with modern science, Rudolf Bultmann viewed eschatology as mythology and reinterpreted it in lived, existentialist categories. Feminist, Black, Latin American, and other contemporary liberation theologies use eschatological texts to challenge patriarchy, racism, sexism, political and economic oppression, and the abuse of the natural world. Followers of the Jesus Seminar typically construct a non-eschatological Jesus preaching a Gospel of social transformation.

The Blackwell Companion to Science and Christianity, First Edition. Edited by J. B. Stump and Alan G. Padgett.
© 2012 Blackwell Publishing Ltd. Published 2012 by Blackwell Publishing Ltd.

This raises two questions for us: can an eschatology be constructed which combines both future hope for a universal transformation of the world and the present realization of that hope in the world? And can it do so in the full light of contemporary scientific cosmology? It is these questions which will be taken up here.

Karl Barth (1933, 314) took a decisive stand in the direction of the first question with his claim that "Christianity that is not entirely and altogether eschatology has entirely and altogether nothing to do with Christ." Paul Tillich (1967, 3:394–396) saw the eschaton in terms of our present experience of the eternal *as well as* the aim and end of history in its "elevation" into the eternal. The Vatican II document *Lumen Gentium* points to the immediacy *and* the futurity of the Kingdom of God in proclaiming that "the human race as well as the entire world . . . will be perfectly established in Christ. . . . The final age of the world has already come upon us" (Abbott 1966, 78–79).

Others have responded to both of these questions. For Wolfhart Pannenberg, eschatology determines the entire content of systematic theology. Here God as Trinity acts from the eschatological future in the historical life, ministry, death, and Resurrection of Jesus. Pannenberg sees Easter as a "proleptic" event which transforms world history into eschatological reign of God (Pannenberg 1998, chapter 5). And while he is primarily interested in the present-day implications of eschatology for political, social, and economic liberation, Jürgen Moltmann (1996) is also committed to the coming of the universal new creation in and through the person of Jesus Christ.

What is notable is that, in these eschatologies, the new creation is neither a 'replacement' of the present creation – that is, not as a second *ex nihilo* – nor the mere working out of the natural, evolutionary processes of the world. Instead eschatology involves the complete transformation of the world by a radically new act of God beginning at Easter and continuing into the future. For biblical scholars and theologians such as Raymond Brown, Gerald O'Collins, William Lane Craig, Phem Perkins, Ted Peters, Janet Martin Soskice, Sandra Schneiders, Richard Swinburne, and N. T. Wright, eschatology as transformation is derived in large measure from a view of the Resurrection which emphasizes elements of continuity and discontinuity between the historical Jesus of Nazareth and the Risen Jesus. In this view, the empty tomb plays a key role in pointing to an irreducible element of *physical/material continuity* within an overarching discontinuity between the historical Jesus and the Risen Lord. Some of these scholars view the transformation of the world into the New Creation as happening not only synchronically at the end of time but also diachronically throughout the entire course of world history.

Clearly it is *these* eschatologies which face the severest challenge from contemporary science, particularly from cosmology. When we expand the domain of eschatology from the anthropological and even eco-terrestrial context of 'world history' to the cosmos itself, we encounter science's grim prediction that all life must inevitably be extinguished as stars go supernova and following this that the *far* future of the universe is either endless cold or unimaginable heat. What response can we give to this challenge?

The Challenge of Scientific Cosmology

The standard scientific model of the universe that dominated most of the last century is the "Big Bang cosmology." Based on Albert Einstein's special and general theories of relativity and massive amounts of astronomical evidence, the Big Bang portrays the universe as expanding in time from an origin or "singularity" labeled "$t = 0$" some 13.75 billion years ago.[2] The standard Big Bang model includes three varieties: In the first two the universe is "open": infinite in size and destined to expand endlessly as its temperature falls exponentially towards absolute zero. In the third model the universe is "closed": finite in size, and it will eventually recontract while its temperature and density soar to infinity. The far future in the open models is aptly termed "freeze" and in the closed model "fry."

It turns out that these models were beset by a number of important technical problems, not the least of which was the singularity, $t = 0$. In the 1980s Alan Guth and others developed so-called "inflationary" models to address these problems. Inflation depicts the very early universe (c. the "Planck time," 10^{-43} seconds) as undergoing an exponentially rapid expansion before settling down to normal expansion rates. As a result of this rapid expansion, the universe is thought to be much larger than what the Big Bang models describe as the "visible universe." In inflationary cosmology the actual universe consists of countless domains or regions, one of which is our visible universe. Recent developments in "quantum cosmology" depict our universe as emerging from a prior "superspace" of universes that are multiply connected. Other developments involve superstring theory, the "multiverse" and "brane cosmology." These are highly speculative theories that offer very different accounts of the origin of our universe. Nevertheless they all result in a standard Big Bang expanding universe after the Planck time.

What about the scientific prognoses for the future of the universe – is it 'freeze' (open and destined to expand and cool forever) or 'fry' (closed and destined to recollapse to a singularity and an infinite temperature)? There is now growing evidence supporting the 'freeze' prognosis: an open universe expanding and cooling forever with the rate of expansion as increasing in time. But whether the future is 'freeze' or 'fry' the prospects for life are grim (Barrow and Tipler 1986):

- near future: in 5 billion years, the sun will become a red giant, engulfing the orbits of earth and Mars. In 40–50 billion years, star formation in our galaxy will have ended. This leaves our two scenarios:
- far future: (1) *fry*. If the universe is *closed*, then in 10^{12} years the universe will reach its maximum size and then recollapse back to a singularity; (2) *freeze*. If the universe is *open*, then in 10^{31} years, protons and neutrons will decay into positrons, electrons, neutrinos, and photons. The universe will continue to cool and expand forever, and all of its early structure, from galaxies to living organisms, will vanish forever leaving no trace that they ever existed.

In both cases, life as we know it is doomed to extinction in the relatively near, cosmic future. Clearly none of this provides a scientific background on which a credible Christian eschatology based on the bodily Resurrection of Jesus can be deployed. Crisis indeed!

Eschatology and Cosmology: A Variety of Minimalist Responses

We first turn to a variety of minimalist responses to the challenge of eschatology and cosmology.

Conflict

A number of distinguished scientists have given pessimistic, 'dysteleological' readings of scientific cosmology. In 1903, long before Big Bang cosmology was on the horizon, Bertrand Russell (1963, 41) wrote darkly: "All the labors of the ages, all the devotion, all the inspiration, all the noon-day brightness of human genius . . . must inevitably be buried beneath the debris of the universe in ruins." Over 70 years later his detailed knowledge of modern cosmology brought Steven Weinberg (1977, 154–155) to a strikingly similar conclusion: "It is very hard to realize that this all is just a tiny part of an overwhelmingly hostile universe . . . [which] faces a future extinction of endless cold or intolerable heat. The more the universe seems comprehensible, the more it also seems pointless."

Similar positions can be found among those few theologians who have seriously considered the meaning of eschatology in light of cosmology. In 1966 John Macquarrie (1977, 356) wrote: "[I]f it were shown that the universe is indeed headed for an all-enveloping death, then this might . . . falsify Christian faith and abolish Christian hope." Three decades later, Kathryn Tanner (2000, 222) echoed this view: "If the scientists are right . . . hope for an everlasting and consummate fulfillment of this world is futile." Ted Peters (1993, 175–176) also wrote unequivocally about the threat posed by science:

> Should the final future as forecasted by the combination of big bang cosmology and the second law of thermodynamics come to pass . . . we would have proof that our faith has been in vain. It would turn out to be that there is no God, at least not the God in whom followers of Jesus have put their faith.

Pannenberg (1981, 12–15) has listed the conflict between eschatology and cosmology as one of five key questions in the theology–science dialogue.

Faced with this conflict one option might be to capitulate and reduce eschatology to scientific cosmology. In 1979 physicist Freeman Dyson published a ground-breaking paper on what he called "physical eschatology." Working with an open universe that expands and cools forever, Dyson argued that if life can be reduced to information processing and thus freed from its biological basis, then life can continue into the *infinite* future. It will be conscious of its history, capable of processing new experiences, storing them through new forms of non-biologically based memory, and ultimately remolding the universe to its own purposes. "An open universe need not evolve into a state of permanent quiescence. . . . In the open cosmology, history has no end" (Dyson 2002, 103, 121). A decade later, physicists John Barrow and Frank Tipler (1986) reframed Dyson's arguments for the closed universe. Their crucial insight was that if the rate of processing could continually increase, an infinite amount of information could be processed (thus, they claimed, constituting 'eternal life') even in the finite time remaining before the closed universe 'fries'.

The scientific details of these scenarios are fascinating, and to his immense credit, Dyson did undermine Weinberg's dysteleology. Moreover Dyson, Tipler, and Barrow all suggested various connections between physical cosmology and Christian eschatology somewhat in the spirit of Teilhard de Cardin. These moves should not go unacknowledged. But what are the theological consequences of attempting to reduce Christian eschatology to physical cosmology? Willem B. Drees (1990) and Fred W. Hallberg (1988) pointed to theological strengths and weaknesses, while John Polkinghorne (1989, 96), Ian Barbour (1990, 151–152),

Arthur Peacocke (1993, 345), Philip Clayton (1997, 132–136), and Mark Worthing (1996, chapter 5) have criticized these ideas on both theological and philosophical grounds. Tipler (1989) and Pannenberg (1989) have engaged in an extensive interaction to which Drees (1997), R. Russell (1997; 1989; 1994), and others have replied,[3] but Tipler's scientific claims have been attacked aggressively by Hyung Sup Choi (1995) and William R. Stoeger and George Ellis (1995).

On balance I believe that "physical eschatology" does *not* hold out genuine promise for an eschatology of "new creation." Nevertheless if we set aside the reductionist assumptions, theological oversimplifications, and scientific controversies that habitually accompany both Weinberg's conclusions and the Dyson-Barrow-Tipler response to it, we may yet discover some vital clues from scientific cosmology for our constructive attempt to relate it to Christian eschatology.

Two worlds

Perhaps those supporting a "two-worlds" model of theology and science are right. Then cosmology is simply irrelevant to eschatology; if so, the conflict would be over. The cost, however, is that we're stuck in the 'dead end to progress' that the new approaches to theology and science are trying to avoid.

Interestingly one can draft a "two-worlds" model simply by exaggerating the fact that all scientific theories are provisional. There is wisdom to this view. Scientific theories are eventually replaced by, or incorporated into, new and broader theories. In light of this perhaps we need not be too concerned about the present conflict between eschatology and cosmology; instead we should 'wait and see." But there is reason to be cautious about relying too heavily on the provisionality of science. It is one thing to acknowledge the current situation of conflict, as Pannenberg, Tanner, and Peters do, and to soften the conflict by remembering the provisionality of scientific theories. It is quite another thing to overcome the conflict categorically by adopting a "two-worlds" cul-de-sac per se.

Can we 'split the difference' and claim that cosmology is irrelevant to Christian eschatology while maintaining that other scientific theories, such as evolution, may be highly relevant to theology? This form of irrelevancy is doctrine-specific and avoids a full-scale "two-worlds" model. Arthur Peacocke is an example of this view. Although he disagrees with scholars who reduce the Resurrection of Jesus to the subjective experience of his disciples, he does not seem to connect the Resurrection with the eschatological transformation of the universe. Instead, eschatology refers to "our movement towards and into God beginning *in the present* . . . it transcends any literal sense of 'the future.' Our ultimate destiny is Dante's 'beatific vision'" (Peacocke 1993, 344–345). In taking this position Peacocke avoids a conflict with cosmology, but the cost seems to be that the universe has no eschatological destiny.[4]

In process theology the consequent nature of God is continually enriched through God's experience and enjoyment of the world. Moreover, through God's memory of us we obtain what Whitehead called "objective immortality" and this is the basis for process eschatology (Cobb and Griffin 1976, 118–124). In attempting to bring Whitehead's views closer to Christian eschatology and its insistence on the importance of personal eternal life, some process theologians, such as Ian Barbour (1990, 241) and Marjorie Suchocki (1982), add to this "subjective immortality." Here a person continues after death to be "a center of experience" within God.

Dialogue and Interaction: Eschatology and the Transformation of the Universe

The idea of a hope after death and an end that fulfills history as a whole is as intrinsic to the Christian tradition as it is foreign to the project of science. (Clayton 2005, 134)

We now briefly survey some of the most promising directions for dealing with an eschatology of God's transformation of the universe into the new creation in light of science.[5]

Jürgen Moltmann (1985, 208) offers a threefold concept of creation: "*creatio originalis – creatio continua – creatio nova*" where the latter leads to eschatology. In the process Moltmann provides some crucial reasons for requiring that eschatology be cosmic in scope. One is to avoid a gnostic reading of redemption that would be a redemption from, and not of, both body and world. A second reason is given in his doctrine of the Trinity in which the Redeemer is the Creator. Thus without redeeming all that God creates, God would contradict Godself. Finally cosmic eschatology is essential because of Moltmann's theological anthropology:

> Because there is no such thing as a soul separate from the body, and no humanity detached from nature . . . there is no redemption for human beings either without the redemption of nature. . . . Consequently it is impossible to conceive of any salvation for men and women without "a new heaven and a new earth." There can be no eternal life for human beings without the change in the cosmic conditions of life. (Moltmann 1996, 259–261)

Moltmann's constructive approach then is to "work out the tangents, or points of access" for the dialogue

Denis Edwards (1995, 145–152) draws on the writings of Pierre Teilhard de Chardin, Karl Rahner, and Moltmann to view salvation as God's transforming the universe as a whole and all that is within it, from clusters of galaxies to subatomic particles. Edwards then raises a crucial question: will "every sparrow that falls" be redeemed (Matt. 10:29; Luke 12:6)? While Moltmann claims that every creature (i.e., "victim" of evolution) will find *individual* fulfillment in God, Edwards leaves this question open.

According to *Ted Peters* (1993, 168–173), Pannenberg's theme of prolepsis can be interpreted in terms of what he calls "temporal holism." For Peters the cosmos is both created and redeemed proleptically from the future by the Trinitarian God (Peters 1992, 134–139; 2006). Prolepsis ties together *futurum*, the ordinary sense of future resulting from present causes, and *adventus*, the appearance of something absolutely new, namely the kingdom of God and the renewal of creation. The creation, from alpha to omega, will be consummated and transformed into the eschatological future which lies beyond, but which will include, this creation as a whole. Having said this, Peters, as we saw above, is ruthlessly honest about the challenge from science.

Wolfhart Pannenberg enters into an explicit conversation with Barrow and Tipler in his extended discussion of the doctrine of creation in *Systematic Theology*, vol. 2. Here he suggests that some of their underlying ideas might be used theologically without in any way "adopting" the Barrow–Tipler model (Pannenberg 1994, 158–161). These ideas include the permanent role of intelligent life in the universe; the divine reality as both emerging at the final "omega point" and as present throughout the history of the universe; and the "constitutive function" eschatology has for the whole universe. In vol. 3, however, where the doctrine of eschatology is discussed in detail, little more is added (Pannenberg 1998, 586–590).

John Polkinghorne (1994, chapter 9; 2000; 2002) has offered very promising insights for responding to the challenge of cosmology. He bases his eschatology of the transformation of the universe into the new creation by analogy with the bodily Resurrection of Jesus Christ for which he proposes the term creation *ex vetere*: "The new is not a second creation *ex nihilo*, but it is a resurrected world created *ex vetere*. Involved in its coming to be must be both continuity and discontinuity, just as the Lord's risen body bears the scars of the passion but is also transmuted and glorified" (Polkinghorne 2000, 29–30).

A crucial question is then, if the nature of the new creation cannot be based on current science, why is science relevant to our discussion of it? In response, Polkinghorne focuses on the element of continuity in the transformation of the universe because science can offer helpful insights here. He starts with special relativity, quantum mechanics, chaos theory, and thermodynamics and 'distills' out of them general features of the universe which might be a clue to the new creation: relationality and holism, energy and pattern (form), mathematics. There must also be a degree of continuity to preserve the individual identities of persons through the transformation.

What then are the next steps in the dialogue? In recent writings I have proposed a method in which we can expand the usual approach to theology and science to allow for their genuine interaction (R. Russell 2008, Introduction and chapter 10). According to this method, not only should theology critically incorporate the discoveries of science in theological reconstruction. In addition such reconstructed theology might offer either insights for future research programs in science or criteria by which to select between competing research programs. Of course all such scientific research programs would have to be tested strictly by the scientific community and would presuppose methodological naturalism.

Still we must first deal explicitly with the impasse between a cosmic future of "freeze or fry" and an eschatological future of new creation. My response to the impasse is to recognize that the challenge is not from *science* but from a combination of *philosophical and theological assumptions* we routinely bring to science. The first assumption is philosophical: namely that the events science predicts must come to pass. Instead we can suppose that the laws of nature are descriptive, not prescriptive. In this case predicted events do not necessarily occur. The next step is theological: namely that the efficacy described by the laws of nature does not reside in the processes of nature which science describes, but instead it is the result of God's ongoing and faithful action as Creator. Finally, we can believe theologically that God is free to act in radically new ways, not only in human history but also in the ongoing history of the universe. Because of this, we can claim that the scientific predictions are *right but inapplicable* since God did act in a radically new way at Easter and will continue to act to bring about the new creation. In doing so, we are not in a conflict with science but with a philosophical interpretation brought to science. In short, the future of the universe *would have been* what science predicts (i.e., 'freeze' or 'fry') had God *not* acted at Easter and *did God not continue* to act in the future.

With this in place we can move ahead to reconstruct eschatology in light of science and, hopefully, to suggest promising insights from such an eschatology for research programs in science. The first step is to recognize that eschatology must work critically with science's description of the *past and present* history of the universe. This description, in turn, might shed light on elements of continuity in the transformation of the universe. In particular, since our starting point is God's act to transform the universe into the new creation, it follows that God must have created the universe *such that it is transformable* by God's action. Specifically, God must have created it with precisely those conditions and characteristics which it needs as preconditions in order to be transformable by God's new act. As Polkinghorne argues, science can be of immense help to the theological task of understanding something about that transformation if we can find a way to identify, with at least some probability, these needed *"elements of continuity"* in that transformation. Next, I would add to this that science might also shed light on which conditions and characteristics of the present creation we do *not* expect to be continued into the new creation, or what I call *"elements of discontinuity"* between creation and new creation. This would include those physical and biological processes which underlie disease, suffering and death; temporality marred by the loss of the past and the unavailability of the future; and ontological determinism, which undercuts genuine personhood and relationality.

Our project also involves the possibility that eschatology might stimulate creative insights in research science by focusing on the elements of continuity and discontinuity. This includes revising our view of nature as creation and, in turn, the philosophy of space, time, matter, and causality underlying contemporary physics, selecting which theoretical programs to pursue among those already "on the table," and inspiring the construction of new scientific research programs. For example could an eschatological interpretation of temporality and relationality lead to implications about nature as it is now and, in turn, aspects of nature as it is now that physics has so far overlooked? Could the assumption of their existence generate concrete suggestions for research programs in physics? Pannenberg (1990; 1998, chapter 15) can be taken to argue that with Augustine durational time was limited to human subjectivity, leaving time in nature as merely point-like, and this view of time was then built into Newtonian science. What might physics look like if time as durational was used instead of time as point-like in contemporary physics? Finally, could we start with the discontinuous aspects of creation that we expect not to be a part of the new creation (e.g., 'natural evil'), and glean some sense of what must even now be merely epiphenomenal and ultimately transitory characteristics of creation compared to those characteristics which must be crucial to the possibility of the new creation? Questions like these are central to my current research (R. Russell 2008, chapters 7, 8, and especially 10; forthcoming).

Conclusions and Future Research

Systematic theology requires critical attention to eschatology, including the bodily Resurrection of Jesus and its implications for the new creation as the transformation of the universe, in light of the challenges raised by scientific cosmology. In my opinion we are now ready to engage that challenge extensively. The engagement will involve both the theological reconstruction of eschatology in light of science and the indication of directions for potential research in science from this new eschatological perspective on the universe at present. This engagement represents an instance of the methodology of creative mutual interaction between theology and science. The value of this interaction can only be assessed when, over time, its results have been carefully articulated by a variety of scholars with a diversity of theological and scientific interests and views.

Notes

1   The few exceptions include Schwarz (2000); Körtner (1995); Bauckham and Hart (1999); and Peters (2003).

2 For non-technical introductions, see Trefil and Hazen (2000, chapter 15).

3 See *Zygon*, March, 1999.

4 Peacocke (1993, 126–128, esp. n. 72). For a critique see R. Russell (2002, 13–14).

5 Strict limits on length mean that I have not included many others deserving discussion in a longer treatment, notably Pierre Teilhard de Chardin and Karl Heim.

References

Abbott, Walter M., SJ, ed. 1966. *The Documents of Vatican II*. New York: America Press, 48.

Barbour, Ian G. 1990. *Religion in an Age of Science: The Gifford Lectures 1989–1991*, vol. 1. San Francisco, CA: Harper & Row.

Barrow, John D. and Tipler, Frank J. 1986. *The Anthropic Cosmological Principle*. Oxford: Clarendon Press.

Barth, Karl. 1933. *The Epistle to the Romans*, 6th edn. Translated by Edwyn C. Hoskyns. London: Oxford University Press.

Bauckham, Richard and Hart, Trevor. 1999. *Hope against Hope: Christian Eschatology at the Turn of the Millennium*. Grand Rapids, MI: Eerdmans.

Choi, Hyung Sup. 1995. A Physicist Comments on Tipler's "The Physics of Immortality." *CTNS Bulletin*, 15(2), pp. 21–22.

Clayton, Philip. 1997. *God and Contemporary Science*. Grand Rapids, MI: Eerdmans.

Clayton, Philip. 2005. Eschatology as Metaphysics under the Guise of Hope. In Joseph Bracken, ed. *World without End: Essays in Honor of Marjorie Suchocki*. Grand Rapids, MI: Eerdmans, pp. 128–149.

Cobb, John B., Jr., and Griffin, David Ray. 1976. *Process Theology: An Introductory Exposition*. Philadelphia, PA: Westminster Press.

Drees, Willem B. 1990. *Beyond the Big Bang: Quantum Cosmologies and God*. La Salle, IL: Open Court.

Drees, Willem B. 1997. Contingency, Time, and the Theological Ambiguity of Science. In Carol Rausch Albright and Joel Haugen, eds. *Beginning with the End: God, Science, and Wolfhart Pannenberg*. Chicago: Open Court, pp. 217–248.

Dyson, Freeman. 2002. Time without End: Physics and Biology in an Open Universe. In George F. R. Ellis, ed. *The Far Future Universe: Eschatology from a Cosmic Perspective*. Randor, PA: Templeton Foundation Press, pp. 103–139.

Edwards, Denis. 1995. *Jesus the Wisdom of God: An Ecological Theology*. Homebush: St Pauls.

Hallberg, Fred W. 1988. Barrow and Tipler's Anthropic Cosmological Principle. *Zygon*, 23(2), pp. 139–157.

Körtner, Ulrich H. 1995. *The End of the World: A Theological Interpretation*. Translated by Douglas W. Stott. Louisville, KY: Westminster John Knox Press.

Macquarrie, John. 1977. *Principles of Christian Theology*, 2nd edn. New York: Charles Scribner's Sons.

Moltmann, Jürgen. 1985. *God in Creation: A New Theology of Creation and the Spirit of God*. San Francisco, CA: Harper & Row.

Moltmann, Jürgen. 1996. *The Coming of God: Christian Eschatology*. Translated by Margaret Kohl. Minneapolis, MN: Fortress Press.

Pannenberg, Wolfhart. 1981. Theological Questions to Scientists. In A. R. Peacocke, ed. *The Sciences and Theology in the Twentieth Century*. Notre Dame, IN: University of Notre Dame Press, pp. 3–16.

Pannenberg, Wolfhart. 1989. Theological Appropriation of Scientific Understandings: Response to Hefner, Wicken, Eaves, and Tipler. *Zygon*, 24(2), pp. 255–271.

Pannenberg, Wolfhart. 1990. *Metaphysics and the Idea of God*. Grand Rapids, MI: Eerdmans.

Pannenberg, Wolfhart. 1994. *Systematic Theology*, vol. 2. Translated by G. W. Bromiley. Grand Rapids, MI: Eerdmans.

Pannenberg, Wolfhart. 1998. *Systematic Theology*, vol. 3. Translated by G. W. Bromiley. Grand Rapids, MI: Eerdmans.

Peacocke, Arthur. 1993. *Theology for a Scientific Age: Being and Becoming – Natural, Divine and Human*, enlarged edn. Minneapolis MN: Fortress Press.

Peters, Ted. 1992. *God – The World's Future: Systematic Theology for a Postmodern Era*. Minneapolis, MN: Fortress Press.

Peters, Ted. 1993. *God as Trinity: Relationality and Temporality in the Divine Life*. Louisville, KY: Westminster John Knox Press.

Peters, Ted. 2003. Where Are We Going? Eschatology. In William C. Placher, ed. *Essentials of Christian Theology*. Louisville, KY: Westminster John Knox Press, pp. 347–365.

Peters, Ted. 2006. *Anticipating Omega: Science, Faith, and Our Ultimate Future*. Göttingen: Vandenhoeck & Ruprecht.

Polkinghorne, John. 1989. *Science and Providence: God's Interaction with the World*. Boston, MA: Shambhala Publications.

Polkinghorne, John. 1994. *The Faith of a Physicist: Reflections of a Bottom-Up Thinker*. Princeton, NJ: Princeton University Press.

Polkinghorne, John. 2000. Eschatology: Some Questions and Some Insights from Science. In John Polkinghorne and Michael Welker, eds. *The End of the World and the Ends of God: Science and Theology on Eschatology*. Harrisburg, PA: Trinity Press International, pp. 29–41.

Polkinghorne, John. 2002. *The God of Hope and the End of the World*. New Haven, CT: Yale University Press.

Russell, Bertrand. 1963. A Free Man's Worship. In *Mysticism and Logic, and Other Essays*. London: Allen & Unwin, pp. 40–47.

Russell, Robert John. 1989. Cosmology, Creation, and Contingency. In Ted Peters, ed. *Cosmos as Creation: Theology and Science in Consonance*. Nashville, TN: Abingdon Press, pp. 201–204.

Russell, Robert John. 1994. Cosmology from Alpha to Omega. *Zygon*, 29(4), pp. 570–572.

Russell, Robert John. 1997. Cosmology and Eschatology: The Implications of Tipler's "Omega Point" Theory to Pannenberg's Theological Program. In Carol Rausch Albright and Joel Haugen, eds. *Beginning with the End: God, Science, and Wolfhart Pannenberg*. Chicago: Open Court, pp. 195–216.

Russell, Robert John. 2002. Bodily Resurrection, Eschatology and Scientific Cosmology: The Mutual Interaction of Christian Theology and Science. In Ted Peters, Robert John Russell, and Michael Welker. *Resurrection: Theological and Scientific Assessments*. Grand Rapids, MI: Eerdmans, pp. 3–30.

Russell, Robert John. 2008. *Cosmology from Alpha to Omega: The Creative Mutual Interaction of Theology and Science*. Minneapolis, MN: Fortress Press.

Russell, Robert John. Forthcoming. *Time in Eternity: Pannenberg, Physics, and Eschatology*. Notre Dame, IN: University of Notre Dame Press.

Schwarz, Hans. 2000. *Eschatology*. Grand Rapids, MI: Eerdmans.

Stoeger, William, S.J. and Ellis, George. 1995. A Response to Tipler's Omega-Point Theory. *Science and Christian Belief*, 7(2), pp. 163–172.

Suchocki, Marjorie Hewitt. 1982. *God, Christ, Church: A Practical Guide to Process Theology*. New York: Crossroad.

Tanner, Kathryn. 2000. Eschatology without a Future? In John Polkinghorne and Michael Welker. *The End of the World and the Ends of God*. Harrisburg, PA: Trinity Press International, pp. 222–237.

Tillich, Paul. 1967. *Systematic Theology: Three Volumes in One*. Chicago: University of Chicago Press.

Tipler, Frank J. 1989. The Omega Point as Eschaton: Answers to Pannenberg's Questions for Scientists. *Zygon*, 24(2), pp. 217–253.

Trefil, James and Hazen, Robert M. 2000. *The Sciences: An Integrated Approach*, 2nd edn. New York: John Wiley & Sons, Inc.

Weinberg, Steven. 1977. *The First Three Minutes: A Modern View of the Origin of the Universe*. New York: Basic Books.

Worthing, Mark W. 1996. *God, Creation, and Contemporary Physics*. Minneapolis, MN: Fortress Press.

Further Reading

Dyson, Freeman. 2002. Time without End: Physics and Biology in an Open Universe. In George F. R. Ellis, ed. *The Far Future Universe: Eschatology from a Cosmic Perspective*. Randor, PA: Templeton Foundation Press, pp. 103–139. An attempt to place Christian eschatology strictly within the confines of scientific cosmology.

Peters, Ted. 2006. *Anticipating Omega: Science, Faith, and Our Ultimate Future*. Göttingen: Vandenhoeck & Ruprecht. Required reading in theology and science with a thorough and pioneering treatment of Christian eschatology in light of science.

Polkinghorne, John. 2002. *The God of Hope and the End of the World*. New Haven, CT: Yale University Press. Perhaps the most important and extensive treatment of Christian eschatology in relation to the natural sciences.

Russell, Robert John. Forthcoming. *Time in Eternity: Pannenberg, Physics, and Eschatology*. Notre Dame, IN: University of Notre Dame Press. A book-length rendition of Russell's method of "creative mutual interaction" which first reformulates Christian theology in light of science and then shows its value in pointing to new directions for scientific research, with a special focus on Christian eschatology.

48

The Quest for Transcendence in Theology and Cosmology

ALEXEI V. NESTERUK

Because theology refers to the Divine, contemporary discussions of science and Christian theology at least implicitly address the issue of transcendence. But most of these discussions do not clarify the sense of their references to the Divine or see any problem for science relating to the transcendent. They presume that one can relate the things of *this* world to the *signs* of the Divine *presence* in the universe without any serious attempt either to disclose the sense of this presence or to relate this presence specifically to the God of Christian faith – the transcendent Creator of the world.

At first the difficulty seems to lie almost wholly on the side of science. Seen in a banal sense, the objective of science is to study the natural world by using empirical or theoretical means in order to reveal its immanent rational structure, which does not need any reference beyond either the material or its intelligible representations. In all scientific cases the reality of the "external world" is affirmed in the rubrics of the constituting subjectivity and thus made immanent to it. While studying scientific phenomena, the enquiring thinker does not even venture to guess about the "true other" of the phenomena (including "the other" of theoretical constructs) simply because in this context the intellect does not reflect upon its own facticity. Science functions in conditions where transcendence is fundamentally inconceivable and impossible. In this sense any scientific enterprise manifests a radical fight against transcendence.

But transcendence means more than just the old-fashioned "passing beyond" the world (what is sometimes called a vertical transcendence). It also includes, after the fashion of Heidegger, a horizontal transcendence beyond the limits which constitute human knowledge and experience by understanding that we are incomplete and open to reconstitution by our incomplete future. Certainly these heuristic distinctions between the vertical and horizontal in transcendence are intertwined, inflecting each other. So, transcendence can describe either an epistemic invocation or existential participation in the *truly other*, the other which is not in being (which would make no sense for the distinction between science and theology), but neither is beyond being (which would make it impossible for human beings to reach it). Understood in this way, transcendence is no less a problem for theology taken in its philosophical mode than it is for science. If theology were involved in the dialogue with science

The Blackwell Companion to Science and Christianity, First Edition. Edited by J. B. Stump and Alan G. Padgett.
© 2012 Blackwell Publishing Ltd. Published 2012 by Blackwell Publishing Ltd.

only in its philosophical mode, the question of transcendence would be framed in a theoretical dimension and therefore subject to the limitations imposed by our present horizons. But Christian theology offers new ways of thinking about the problem of transcendence in the dialogue with science.

In a Christian perspective, any abstract philosophical speculation on transcendence contains elements of religious faith, for there is no pure reason, and all understanding originates in the life world whose horizons are structured by existential faith in the reality of life as gift of God. All philosophical insights in the science–theology dialogue seek elucidation in the same way that faith seeks understanding, an elucidation implying transcendence in a practical sense when Christian life itself relates to the truly other intrinsically present in discursive and linguistic formulae of this dialogue. So we begin with the transcendent in this practical dimension of faith.

Transcendence in Eucharistic Experience

Christian theology understands that the *fullness* of truth it asserts in words and deeds is sustained by the constant *presence* of the Divine in its Word (Scripture), in its institution (Church), and in the works of creation (the Universe). But such a presence does not once and for all exhaust the meaning of that which is intended and signified by theological proclamations. Theology, understood experientially, relies on faith in God who is *present* in the world in his empirical *absence*. This faith is endorsed through individual worship and liturgical cycles, activating such human qualities as love, receptiveness of grace, gratitude for creation and life, and the transfer of goodness. All of these manifest transcendence through change that is a constant overcoming and transfiguration of humanity, its ongoing incarnation in the world.

Patristic writers insisted that a faculty for perceiving transcendence is inherent in what they called human nature and is granted to man at the moment of creation. According to St Maximus the Confessor, "the faculties which search out divine realities were implanted by the Creator in the essence of human nature at its very entrance into being" (Maximus the Confessor 1981, 239). In a different place he says, "when God the Logos created human nature He . . . implanted in it a certain noetic capacity through which men could enjoy Him in an inexpressible way. By this capacity I mean the intellect's natural longing for God" (Maximus the Confessor 1981, 243). However, Maximus is eager to comment that this capacity is only a potential possibility, for "the divine realities themselves are revealed to man through grace by the power of the Holy Spirit descending upon him" (Maximus the Confessor 1981, 239). The actual performance of the faculty for transcendence comes from the *intentional* search for communion with God which is activated by the Holy Spirit. He clarifies this point:

> Our intellect . . . possesses the capacity for a union that transcends its *nature* and that unites it with what is beyond its natural scope. It is through this union that divine realities are apprehended, not by means of our own natural capacities, but by virtue of the fact that we entirely transcend ourselves and belong entirely to God. (Maximus the Confessor 1981, 276)

However, the actual possibility of achieving the goal is realized in liturgical invocations of Eucharistic communities. It is through individual worship and liturgical participation that Christians are predisposed to ecclesial transformation in order to surpass a hypostasis of biological existence (Zizioulas 1997, 63). Since the Eucharist affirms the true presence of

Christ through his body and blood – that is his true presence in our midst in spite of his being with God the Father – communion brings transcendence and transfigures communicants under the pressure of its donation (Gal. 2:20; 2 Cor. 5:17). There is a mutual movement in transcendence: God descends to us (that is, transcends) in liturgical acts in order for us being able to ascend (that is, transcend) to him (Athanasius of Alexandria 1996, 93). Thus experiencing the transcendent is not solely an effort on the side of man. Without the grace of God the ascent to God would involve climbing an impossible ladder between man and transcendent God.

Eucharistic Experience in Science?

The Eucharistic dialectic of transcendence and immanence is particularly relevant to the theology of the Incarnation when applied to rubrics of spatial structure of the universe. The universe in its immanent form, which sustains God's presence in humanity, has, as the foundation of its facticity, the transcendent Divinity of Christ (the Logos-Word of God). Christ remains at the right hand of the Father, sustaining the immanent universe through his creative Word.

In the same way as the Eucharistic acts actualize transcendence for the Eucharistic community, the scientific exploration and articulation of the universe appear to suspend the spatial and temporal extensions of the universe when they symbolically return the cultivated and cared universe back to its Creator. This para-eucharistic dimension, if effectuated, could give to scientific research the status of transcending.

Scientific activity per se is devoid of the thanksgiving dimension. However, in some limiting cases, science has to exercise a sort of "transcendence" when it refers to the non-objectifiable hypotheses invoking intelligible realities (for example, the multiverse) which are still immanent to the structures of human subjectivity. Certainly one can build a hermeneutic of transcendence while remaining in what we take to be scientific discourse: cosmology, for example, produces theories of creation out of "nothing" or it posits the multiverse. These are examples of the belief that this universe can be explained by an appeal to an extended sense of physical reality. However, in no way – either hermeneutically or in terms of scientific practices – is the whole edifice of science capable of having any insight into the other-worldly, because every premise and possibility of scientific discourse presupposes the conditions of the given facticity of being. Science cannot inquire into the underlying sense of this facticity (and thus its own facticity): it can explicate the sense of this facticity by referring to other orders of reality in this world, but to get insight beyond this reality or to enter into physical communication with the other would contradict not only the spirit and objectives of science but would represent an existential impossibility (Marcel 1965, 24).

Let us note that theology in this respect is clear: in *theosis* the body will be transfigured (as well as the whole nature) but the ontological difference between man and God (the transcendent) will remain. Even if some parts of scientific discourse contain the rhetoric of transcendence, the hermeneutical circle cannot be broken "ontologically." The ontological breakthrough could come only if science occurred at the level of communion. Correspondingly, only in this case would the dialogue between theology and science exceed the hermeneutic of transcendence and have existential implications.

The difference between theology and science in their stance on the possibility of transcendence becomes clear: ecclesial, experiential theology claims that it is possible to retain signs of the presence of the Divine – unconditioned by thought or speech – in the *events of communion*, that is to retain God's transcendence in immanence. However, this claim becomes problematic not only in science, but even in theology taken in its philosophical mode. Indeed, since the events of communion are pre-theoretical, it represents a difficulty for philosophical theology to express theoretically pre-theoretical experience (that is, the experience of faith).

The Apophatic Approach in Philosophical Theology

The problem is how to employ thought and speech in order to express that which cannot be thought and spoken of. This difficulty, however, is not novel for theology, for it reflects a classical problem of incongruence in knowledge of God by man, which since the Church Fathers has been reflected in the term "apophaticism." The apophatic approach in theology adopts the view that knowledge of God cannot be exhausted by reason, its linguistic means, or, in general terms, by any of its signifiers. In this sense theology operates with metaphors and allegories which reflect existential, pre-categorical, and pre-theoretical truth.

As an example one can quote the seventh-century writer St Isaac the Syrian, who outlined the essence of the apophatic approach by distinguishing between knowing things of this world and the Divine: "Knowledge adheres to the domain of nature. . . . Knowledge does not venture to step over into the domain which lies outside nature" (Isaac the Syrian 1923, 243). So accurate designations can be established only concerning earthly things. This is not the case, however, if reason trespasses the boundaries of its legitimate sphere and attempts to discuss things which are not of this world. In this case "faith makes its course above nature" (243), such that knowledge aspires towards the things of the age to come which do not possess a true name but can only be apprehended by simple cognition which is exalted above all perceptibility, all signs, forms, all colors, and composite denominations. When knowledge elevates itself above earthly things, therefore, the *Fathers use any designations they like to describe it, for no one knows their real names* (250).

In the twentieth-century theologian Thomas Torrance one finds a similar thought:

> If there is to be real knowledge of God, there cannot but be an incongruence between God as the known and man as the knower, but if that knowledge is to take place it must rest upon the reality and grace of the Object known – just as in all true knowledge, where we are unable to reduce the relation between our thought and speech and the reality of things to relations of thought and speech, we nevertheless allow their reality to shine through to us and act upon us. (Torrance, 1997, 54)

In both theologians one finds a characteristic response to the problem of philosophical theology in appropriating existential truth about God within the limits of the ego. To overcome the phenomenalization of the transcendent, and thus to preserve transcendence in immanence, one needs to allow the Divine to shine through us by adjusting our subjectivity and thus constituting it or giving "new birth" to it.

Characteristically in apophatic knowledge, the Divine cannot be fully phenomenalized and thus deprived of transcendence. One can talk of the providential withdrawal of God to preserve the authenticity of transcendence. Or, in the experience of saints, the bliss of God's grace is a short-term experience which never allows a recipient to contemplate its fullness and thus acquire complete knowledge of God. It is through this unavailability of the fullness of grace that God shows himself through manifestations which cannot be phenom-enalized. God has to withdraw to preserve his hypostasis as he is in himself, for otherwise his face would be affected by the subjectivity of one who attempts to see God. While the basic ontological difference between God and created beings is preserved and God's undisclosed-ness (concealment or darkness) makes his experience authentic and ever advancing, at the same time God is not absent completely, and he appears as presence in response to our call or invocation. By retaining his transcendence (that is, being distinct and *different* from the world and us) God avoids phenomenality, that is, he does not show himself as an *object*. God, who shows himself, acts as the *self* by giving the *self*, and under the pressure of that donation must show himself not as an object but as sheer manifestation, or Personal communion. In this case the phenomenalization of God as manifestation is an *event* of meeting between a human subject and the Person of God who gives himself. As an event, such a meeting cannot be a product of any procession or production, or to have transitive and relational features; it happens on God's volition in hypostatic events in which God's presence-in-absence is contem-plated in an inexpressible way. All spatial and temporal connotations of "presence" and "absence" pertaining to ordinary things disappear in God's manifestations. This means that no demonstrated knowledge of these events can be developed.

So the Fathers of the Church and theologians, in order to speak at all, have felt free to use symbolism and allegory. Their language conveys the reality of the presence and absence of God as they are given to man. Even if the accounts of their experience reflect a mystical union between man and God (as the ultimate goal of Christian life), they do not eliminate an ontological element in the dichotomy of presence-in-absence of God: the presence-in-presence is achieved (through the gift of grace) on the moral level and is strictly hypostatic, whereas the whole creation still experiences God's presence-in-absence as a basic ontological difference. Deification as a potential possibility is thus a never-ending transcendence.

The Possibility of Dialogue in Science and Theology

In summary, we can rearticulate the main problem for relating theology and science: theology is imbued with transcendence in practical and theoretical modalities, but the methodology of science, with its adherence to the immanent hermeneutical circle, precludes transcend-ence. And since even the discursive part of theology is in need of justification of its own ability to retain Divine transcendence within the sphere of phenomenal consciousness, science, if it engages theology and refers to God, needs a similar sort of justification.

Thus the problem of mediation between theology and science requires one to deal with the generic issue of the *possibility of transcendence* in science given the conditions of its straightforward impossibility. Any possible discourse of transcendence in science ceases to be a scientific enterprise: it transforms into a philosophical or theological reflection upon science. Such a discourse is carried out not by working scientists but by philosophically oriented thinkers who interrogate science in a way similar to philosophical theology. They pose the question of whether the intrinsic immanence of scientific assertions about reality can contain pointers to the transcendent. If they do, how might theoretical speech in scientific discourse retain the signs of that allegedly other-worldly (or trans-historical) ground of the overall facticity (including the facticity of scientific research), which is fundamentally pre- and trans-theoretical? It is important to realize that such discussion must have a *personal* dimension to be truly relevant for the science–religion dialogue. While this was always considered the norm in theology (see, e.g., Zizioulas 1997), the personal aspect of transcendence in the scientific context is far from evident and clear.

Indeed, in theology transcendence is referred to the Divine, and the subject of transcendence is a faithful Christian, a person who is a subject of experience of God. This feature is implanted in the definition of *theologia* as spiritual knowledge, which is attained through personal communion. Theology thus is not only *the* way, but also *the* reality of God conferred to the *person* in an ecstatic rapture, in the form of the blessings of the age to come (Peter of Damaskos 1984, 277). Through its function in the Church's tradition, theology creates reality in the same way as God reveals himself to us. However theology is ontological, that is, its mode of existence is hypostatic, so that it is just an illusion and fallacy to assert an anonymous experience of God. If one remains "outside" the subject, one is not able to understand even the meaning of what it is. In short, theology is a *personal* achievement, a gift bestowed by God. Therefore any feasible transcendence is personal, and the ways of achieving it are related to a particular subject of transcendence.

There is a sharp contrast to what we have just said, when one asserts transcendence in philosophical theology. Its subject is an anonymous transcendental consciousness, and the "object" of transcendence is the intended ideal remaining within a hermeneutical circle of philosophical definitions. In this sense the methods of transcendence are purely discursive, without any practical references on how to break the circle and leading to no existential change. The situation becomes even more acute in science because it is not a personal enterprise. Scientific consciousness is impersonal, so there does not seem to be a particular subject to which transcendence can be referred. Also, in contrast to theology, where the object of transcendence is the Divine Person, it is not clear what the physical or metaphysical limit is to which transcendence in science could potentially refer. Transcendence in science implies that its subject transcends science as such through philosophical enlightenment and transfiguring communion, and transcendence if effectuated must affect its subject (as happens in theology). The subject of transcendence is constituted under the pressure of that which, by definition, exceeds the categories of thought, which attempts to circumscribe this transcendence. It is clear that this type of transcendence "in" science, if effected, would position it on the edge of the impossible, that it would lead to the transcendence of science in the sense that, instead of a collective and objective way of affirming the world, it becomes subjected to a personal experience of communion with the transcendent, which is not subject to a scientific demonstration at all. This new, philosophically enlightened activity would have to deal with such phenomena – open-ended and unlimited in their manifestation – which would exceed capacities of any *a priori* structures of subjectivity.

Here one notes that when using words about "science" one mostly refers to the natural sciences, which are the major counterpart of the dialogue with theology. Correspondingly there are indeed some significant difficulties in dealing with the phenomena leading to transcendence in the natural sciences. However, there are many interesting examples of cases in the human sciences, art, philosophy, and certainly theology where the excess of intuition blocks discursive description and simple logical interpretation while retaining the phenomenon's donation and thus entailing transcendence. The French philosopher Jean-Luc Marion called these situations with an excess of intuition over logic "saturated phenomena" (Marion 2001). The challenge of investigating transcendence in the science–religion dialogue is to attempt to identify whether such saturated phenomena can be detected by the natural sciences. Are there philosophically enlightened minds capable of making investigations in the natural sciences while being subjected to transfiguring communion with the transcendent?

Transcendence-in-Immanence in Cosmology

If we want to engage theology with those branches of scientific activity which deal with the phenomena where the excess of intuition over logic prevails, we must ask whether those fragments of knowledge qualify as truly scientific. Indeed, to assert that "saturated phenomena" are present in science is equivalent to recognizing that these phenomena cannot be exhaustively described by scientific methods. Our knowledge of them (represented by the logic of signifiers) cannot be complete because there always remains (behind their manifestations in observations and mental reflections) a context which is an inevitable constituting counterpart of their knowledge. To claim that such an apophatic methodology is valid for some cases in science would admit the possibility of transcendence in a very sophisticated sense. Apophaticism would imply here not simply the inexhaustibility of the content of some phenomena, but the acceptance that these phenomena appear in certain series of *contexts* which cannot be articulated in a first-order reflection. However, in spite of the fact that these contexts escape all intentionality related to the first-order enquiry, their complete disregard would distort the phenomenon as constituted. It is the presence of these contexts that saturates intuition over logic in studying the phenomenon. The silent context of that which is *visible* (and open to articulation) in science provides the coherent and conceptual completion of the most operative definition of "phenomenon": this context appears as itself, of itself, and starting from itself (Heidegger 1962, 54). Thus the "saturated phenomena" within scientific discourse reveal themselves as that unobjectifiable presence of contexts which are at the very foundation of the discourse; it is these contexts which constitute scientific thinking and drive it to its discursive self-manifestation.

Reiterating the above, one can say that the very contingent facticity of science, that is, its being given in the entirety of its distinct stages (not in a sociological, but in a philosophical sense), represents a saturated phenomenon since it is itself a historical *event* (which, like all events, exceeds any quantification). The facticity of scientific facts and theoretically determined statements about the universe are path-dependent and non-repeatable. We have no access to the formation or underlying conditions of the appearance of these events. They are phenomenologically detached from our present state of subjectivity. Being given in our historically contingent image, they escape the totality of objectification in a transcendental sense. Thus science itself must employ certain hermeneutics. When contemporary cosmology attempts to predicate the foundations of the present display of the universe in terms of its initial conditions in the remote past (Big Bang), this exercise of reasoning represents a hermeneutics, approximation, and aberration of that origin of all from whose mystery we are phenomenologically detached. Thus we are left with only varieties of cosmic narratives (Nesteruk 2008, 239–246). The intuition of the creation and beginning of the universe thus forms the narrative-like context of our perception of the universe as a whole, in spite of the fact that, according to physical cosmology, we can observe only a tiny bit of it. The universe then manifests itself as a "saturated phenomenon," because the intuitive saturation of its wholeness surpasses all possible horizons of its representation in the cosmological discourse. The contingent facticity of the universe is being given to humanity's gaze as its witness (humanity as a transcendental subject cannot constitute the fact of this givenness). But in return it is this unconditional donation of the universe which comprehends humanity (as constituted transcendental subjectivity).

In such a vision of the universe one sees a certain breakdown of scientific methodology. The universe as a whole cannot be understood like ordinary objects, because it is present in the foundation and possibility of every contingent intention in the scientific exploration of the world seen as a collection of objects. The donating intuition of the universe as the background of all existence saturates any attempt to discover it within one of the objects. It is not limited; its excess can neither be divided nor put together because of a homogeneous magnitude of its parts. The excess of the donating intuition could not be measured on the basis of its parts since this intuition surpasses the sum of these parts. The "phenomenon of the universe," which is always exceeded by the intuition that saturates it, should probably be called immeasurable. This lack of measure does not operate here through the enormity of an unlimited quantity which stands behind the universe. It is rather marked by the impossibility of applying a successive synthesis to it, as if one could foresee a complex whole on the basis of its parts. Since the universe as a whole, as a saturated phenomenon, exceeds any summation of its parts, which are in many ways inaccessible to the subjectivity undertaking such a summation, the idea of a successive synthesis has to be replaced by what one could call an instantaneous synthesis (a synthesis of communion), the representation of which "precedes" and goes beyond possible (unobservable and imagined) components, rather than resulting from them.

There is another clarification of the excess of intuition over logic which happens in our encounter with the universe. We can perceive only the particular side of the universe which is turned to us by the surface of the past null cone. One cannot acquire a more particular knowledge of the universe because what we see through the light cone of the past imposes itself on us with a certain force and overwhelms and fascinates us. At this stage the successive synthesis, attempted later in physical cosmology, is suspended exactly at the moment when the first impression from the universe occurred, because another synthesis has been achieved that is instantaneous and irreducible to the sum of all possible parts of the universe. This type of communion accompanied by amazement, and the sense of awe arises without any common measure of the phenomena which precede, announce, or explain it. The "I" is unable to constitute the phenomenon of the universe as a whole, and experiences itself as being constituted by this phenomenon through communion and participation. The sought and intended identity of the universe as unfulfilled intentionality returns to the "I" who is constituted by the universe as if the "I" is being gazed at by it. The "I" experiences itself as the subject of a dialogue which is initiated through donation of the universe to humanity.

The response of humanity to the invitation to participate in this dialogue has certain aspects of gratitude for the gift of being-in-the-universe. In the case of the universe, the "I" does not have any dominant point of view over the intuition that overwhelms it. The universe as a saturated phenomenon engulfs subjectivity by removing its parts and spatial extension. In a temporal sense, the universe is always already there, so that all events of subjectivity's life unfold from the never-ending donating event of the universe as constant coming-into-being in which the unforeseeable nature of every moment entails the unending historicity and unpredictability of existence. It is the inability to comprehend the pre-theoretical and pre-conceptual in the givenness of the universe to the "I" (as well as the givenness of the "I" to itself), that indicates that we deal here with the problem of transcendence-in-immanence: the universe shows itself to the "I" in the categories of its immanent consciousness remaining incomprehensible, and hence retaining its inexhaustibility – or transcendence – with respect to conceptual thinking. The diversity and plurality in knowledge of the universe in any immanent-like cosmology, including a physical one, brings to a characteristic expression an apophatic conviction that all signifiers in our experience of the universe do not exhaust that which is signified. As was conjectured by Bohm and Peat, each scientific theory bears the inscription "this is not a universe," meaning that "every kind of thought, mathematics included, is an abstraction which does not and cannot cover the whole of reality." This is why "perhaps every theory of the universe should have in it the fundamental statement 'this is not a universe'" (Bohm and Peat 1987, 8–9). Such an understanding of what is implied in the notion of the universe definitely extends beyond its physical definition in cosmology, where the universe, in one way or another, is treated as "an" or "the" object. However, even on physical grounds one must admit that the universe is unique, it is not subject to experimentation, and it cannot be rerun from the beginning. Seen in this perspective, cosmological discourse acquires a transcendental meaning in which the universe is not considered as *the manifest*, but as *the manifestation* related to humanity. Correspondingly, the universe as the world cannot be treated as an astronomical concept. It is rather a transcendental notion related to our immediate experience of life in the universe and with the universe (see Nesteruk 2010, 186–189).

Conclusion

If one now extends the philosophical insight above towards a theological sensibility, the situation with "knowledge" of the universe as a saturated phenomenon becomes characteristically similar to knowledge of God in theology. Recall that what is called "knowledge" in theology is related to a sort of mystical awareness based on personal participation and communion with the Divine, so that any discursive theologizing of an academic kind is deeply rooted in this communion. One cannot be detached from the subject of theology's enquiry; one needs faith and participation in that which is studied. Knowledge of God cannot be objective (in the sense of scientific rationality), because it depends on a mode of personal experience and involvement. This suggests that theology implies a special understanding of "objectivity," different from a natural attitude where reason attempts to separate itself from attachments (contexts) in order to be detached from the finite object (which is constituted as freed from attachments). Thus in theology, no prior assessment of the attachments to its "object" is possible, for the definitiveness of the perceptive intellect is revealed to itself only through its relationship with the divine as God-given capacity. This is the moment where the intuition saturates the intellect in its attempt to grasp its own facticity. It is this saturation which indicates the inseparable union of consciousness and its source in the Divine. Any imagined deprivation of this donating intuition of its source (that is the objectifying of the Divine) would mean the immediate cessation of subjectivity in general. Thus we face an interesting reversal with respect to scientific knowledge: the "objective" knowledge of God presupposes saturation over all discursive images of the Divine, which paradoxically means the impossibility of detachment from communion with God.

The commonly accepted objectivity in scientific cosmology based on the presupposition of detachment from all personal, subjective commitments also becomes impossible. Paraphrasing the words of Torrance, formulated in a theological context, it is sheer attachment to the universe that detaches us from our preconceptions about it; while detaching ourselves from our preconceptions we become free for the universe, and therefore free for true "knowledge" of it (Torrance 1996, 36). Then a philosophically enlightened insight into cosmology is constituted in conversation and communion with the universe which *communicates itself* to us in acts of donation; while gazing at us it *requires of us an answering relation* in receiving, acknowledging, understanding, and in active personal participation in the relationship it establishes between us (Torrance 1996, 39). It is this answering relation in receiving, acknowledging, understanding, and active personal participation in the relationship with the universe that constitutes the "I" of a cosmologist who is manifested through cosmic narratives created in response to the universe. Certainly within a Christian theological sensibility one must not assign any para-hypostatic features to the universe, such as actively invoking in us a conscious response. The response is provoked by the fact of our inseparability from the universe, but as an action and event it is rooted in the ability of people to articulate their own existence and the existence of the universe.

The universe is a saturated phenomenon because of the sheer attachment to it through embodiment: thus it is not an object. Correspondingly knowledge of the universe unfolds in series of never-ending contexts which effectively form the cosmological narrative and its author. In its immanence, to the subject looking at the universe, it retains its hidden transcendent identity. Thus transcending the universe means a never-ending change in the narrative about the universe and in humanity – its author.

References

Athanasius of Alexandria. 1996. *On the Incarnation*. Crestwood, NY: St Vladimir's Seminary Press.

Bohm, David and Peat, David. 1987. *Science, Order, and Creativity*. New York: Bantam.

Heidegger, Martin. 1962. *Being and Time*. Oxford: Blackwell.

Isaac the Syrian. 1923. Homily 51. In A. J. Wensinck, trans. *Mystical Treatises by Isaac of Nineveh*. Amsterdam: Koninklijke Akademie van Wetenschappen.

Marcel, Gabriel. 1965. *Being and Having*. London: Collins.

Marion, Jean-Luc. 2001. The Saturated Phenomenon. In D. Janicaud, J.-F. Courtine, J.-L. Marion, M. Henry, and P. Ricoeur *Phenomenology and "The Theological Turn": The French Debate*. New York: Fordham University Press, pp. 176–216.

Maximus the Confessor. 1981. Various Texts on Theology, the Divine Economy, and Virtue and Vice. In G. E. H. Palmer, P. Sherrard, and K. Ware, eds. *St. Nikodimos of the Holy Mountain and St. Makarios of Corinth, The Philokalia*, vol. 2. London: Faber and Faber, pp. 164–284.

Nesteruk, Alexei V. 2008. *The Universe as Communion: Towards a Neo-Patristic Synthesis of Theology and Science*. London: T&T Clark.

Nesteruk, Alexei. 2010. Transcendence-in-Immanence in Theology and Cosmology: A New Phenomenological Turn in the Debate. *Studies in Science and Theology*, 12, pp. 179–198.

Peter of Damaskos. 1984. Twenty-Four Discourses. In G. E. H. Palmer, P. Sherrard, and K. Ware, eds. *St. Nikodimos of the Holy Mountain and St. Makarios of Corinth, The Philokalia*, vol. 3. London: Faber and Faber, pp. 211–281.

Torrance, Thomas. 1996. *Theological Science*. Edinburgh: T&T Clark.

Torrance, Thomas. 1997. *Space, Time and Incarnation*. Edinburgh: T&T Clark.

Zizioulas, John D. 1997. *Being as Communion: Studies in Personhood and the Church*. Crestwood, NY: St Vladimir's Seminary Press.

Further Reading

Caputo, J. D. and Scanlon, Michael J., eds. 2007. *Transcendence and Beyond: A Postmodern Inquiry*. Bloomington, IN: Indiana University Press. A modern discussion on the possibility of transcendence in philosophical theology.

Clayton, Philip and Peacock, Arthur, eds. 2004. *In Whom We Live and Move and Have Our Being: Reflections on Panentheism in a Scientific Age*. Grand Rapids, MI: Eerdmans. A remarkable collection of essays on God's presence in the world, covering subjects from patristics to contemporary dialogue between theology and science.

Ellis, George. 2007. Issues in the Philosophy of Cosmology. In J. Butterfield and J. Earman, eds. *Philosophy of Physics*. Netherlands: Elsevier, pp. 1183–1283. A comprehensive assessment of the present state of affairs in modern cosmology, including a philosophical outline of its limits and claims for realism of its theoretical models.

Nesteruk, Alexei V. 2008. *The Universe as Communion: Towards a Neo-Patristic Synthesis of Theology and Science*. London: T&T Clark. A contemporary book on the Eastern Orthodox perspective of the science–theology dialogue related in particular to a possibility of transcendence in cosmology if the latter is reinstated through the change of attitude and ontological repentance to the status of communion.

Schwartz, Regina M., ed. 2004. *Transcendence: Philosophy, Literature, and Theology Approach the Beyond*. London: Routledge. An outstanding collection of essays by leading contemporary thinkers along the lines "transcending" not only modernity's reductionisms, but also postmodernity's overconfidence in tackling the issue of transcendence.

Zizioulas, John D. 2006. *Communion and Otherness*. London: T&T Clark. An important theological book with links to contemporary philosophy asserting the central role of the person in establishing true identity through communion with the Divine.

Part XI

Significant Figures of the Twentieth Century in Science and Christianity

49

Pierre Teilhard de Chardin

JAMES F. SALMON, SJ IN COLLABORATION WITH NICOLE SCHMITZ-MOORMANN

Introduction

Born in 1881 in the French Auvergne, Teilhard died in New York City on Easter Sunday in 1955. Throughout his life, in his private journal and non-scientific writings, Teilhard's objective was to reconcile his religious faith with personal experience as a geologist and paleontologist. Because of his unique vision and popularity at the time as a public speaker, he was often asked to speak about his personal background. Writing about his early life, Teilhard relates as a "starting point" an early "psychological disposition" and "for want of a better name I shall call it a *Sense of Plenitude.*" He inherited both his father's interest in natural philosophy (called natural science today) and his mother's Christian piety, especially her devotion to the person of Jesus Christ. He writes in 1950, five years before his death, "to show how starting from the point at which a spark was first struck, as a point that was built into me congenitally, the World gradually caught fire for me, burst into flames; how this happened all *during* my life, and *as a result of* my whole life, until it formed a great luminous mass, lit from within, that surrounded me" (HM 15).[1] Teilhard continues:

> But what was more, there was a gradual variation of intensity and colour that was related to the complex interplay of three universal components, the Cosmic, the Human, and the Christic – these (at least the first and the last) asserted themselves explicitly in me from the very first moments of my existence, but it has taken me more than sixty years of ardent effort to discover that they were no more than the successive heralding of, or approximate outlines of one and the same fundamental reality . . . a universe that is Person.

We shall return to that theme in Teilhard's idea of "universe that is Person."

Very early in his Jesuit life Teilhard writes that he confided to his spiritual director that he decided to forgo a primary interest in rocks and natural philosophy in order to dedicate himself to the spiritual life. The director responded that he would be forgoing his Jesuit vocation if he did that because the Jesuit vocation is to find God present in all things no matter

The Blackwell Companion to Science and Christianity, First Edition. Edited by J. B. Stump and Alan G. Padgett.
© 2012 Blackwell Publishing Ltd. Published 2012 by Blackwell Publishing Ltd.

what one is doing, as taught by the order's founder, Ignatius Loyola. From then on Teilhard relates that he always felt he was fulfilling his vocation as a Jesuit priest through his scientific activities.

Teilhard found a proper role for the risen Christ lacking in seminary studies of Scripture and theology. The universal Christ of St Paul seemed to have neither meaning nor value in the teaching except as an expansion of Christ who was born of Mary and died on a cross. How does this impression of Teilhard relate to the letters attributed to St Paul, to John's Gospel in the New Testament, and to the writings of early Eastern Fathers of the Church? Teilhard felt that these writings had not been brought out and interpreted sufficiently by theologians and Church authorities. He felt it to be a major weakness in the rather traditional Western scholastic theological training of Jesuits at the time.

Because of his natural interest in science he was sent by his Jesuit superiors to study in Paris and prepare for a career in science. Of course he became aware in his studies of the general acceptance and significance of evolution by those with whom he worked and studied. In 1914 at the age of 33 he was drafted into the French Army before completing his doctoral studies. He served as a stretcher-carrier four years in a North African infantry regiment in the bloody trench warfare of World War One. He was honored for battlefield heroism, receiving the prestigious Medal of Honor. It was during this period that he began to write down in private copy books, his "journals," reflections not of "some bygone period of my life, but rather to the most advanced stage of my inner exploration in search of the Heart of things" (HM 35).

Cosmic Life

The origin of Teilhard's viewpoint about human existence in the cosmos and the role of Christ came long before World War One. He wrote in one of his wartime essays, "My Universe": "However far back I go into my memories (even before the age of ten) I can distinguish in myself the presence of a strictly dominating passion: the passion for the Absolute. . . . At one time it would be a piece of metal; at another, I would take a leap to the other extreme and find satisfaction in the thought of God-the-Spirit" (HM 197). When the metal rusted he turned his interest to rocks, an attraction that endured for the rest of his life. This double attraction and his final solution are implied even in the four headings in his 1916 essay "Cosmic Life": Awakening to the Cosmos; Communion with Earth; Communion with God; Communion with God through Earth.

During that World War One period he sent essays that he composed to Marguerite Teillard-Chambon, his cousin and confidante throughout his life. He composed all 13 of the short essays during breaks while in the trenches or during brief stays away from the "Front." Marguerite would comment on them and then he would further develop his viewpoints to share with her. Writing about his final essay during the war period, he told her:

> I've already begun, and got well into, "The Universal Element," for which, as you know, my ideas were already completely in order. It won't be long, but clear and full of substance. It will, I think, be the most central exposition of my ideas I've produced, and I'll be able to make good use of it to let people know and assess my position, in a private way. I find it interesting to look back on the road I've travelled since three years ago (exactly) when I was writing "Cosmic Life" (W 289).

"Cosmic Life" was the first essay he wrote while in the Army, and "The Universal Element" was written after the armistice, before he went back to Paris to continue research with the world-famous geologist and paleontologist Marcellin Boule at the Paris Museum of Natural History to obtain a doctorate in geology.

Two Attractions in Human Lives

Significant themes within Teilhard's focus during the war and the remainder of his life may be cited. One is his experience of two points of view, "which establishes at all times and in all things, a relationship between themselves and the Absolute – both in them and around them" (W 290). He called them two rival stars. In his essay "The Universal Element," the headings are: (I) Existence; (II) The Nature of the Universal Element, which includes (A) The Pantheist Solution, (B) The Christian Solution; (III) The Properties of Christ, the Universal Element. The two points of view of pantheism and Christianity exert contrary attractions: the religion of earth, which has "led us astray in the worship of a great Whole in which individuals were supposed to become lost like a drop of water, dissolved like a grain of salt in the sea" (P 186), and the religion of heaven, based on communion with the earth and communion with God (W 28–57). In his spiritual treatise *The Divine Milieu* he emphasizes this mutual exclusion and his proposed solution to show "how easily the two stars, whose divergent attractions were disorganizing your faith, are brought into conjunction" (D 9).

Teilhard also returns to this theme of two attractors in 1923. He introduces the essay "Pantheism and Christianity" thus : "In this note I write to try to bring face to face two great religious powers: the only two powers, truth to say, that today share between them the world of human thought. They are Christianity and pantheism." He writes of a principal concern of Christians, generally speaking, to oppose the two doctrines, whereas his approach is the exact reverse:

> I would like to make it clear that pantheism (in the current restricted meaning of the word) is only the defective form in which is expressed a well-justified (and, moreover, ineradicable) tendency in the human soul, a tendency which can be fully satisfied only in Christianity. The tendency is to recognize the *importance, in one's religious calculations of the Whole*. (C 56–57)

This "tendency" recalls his own early "psychological disposition" towards, or need for, a "Sense of Plenitude" that somehow fulfills the attractions of the two stars, the earth and God. Within this theme of two stars, among Teilhard's principal interests were philosophical and theological concerns about Christian evolutionism. The combination of Jesuit seminary training and life as a professional scientist stimulated obvious questions about how evolution could be understood, first by himself, and then by communication to others. In relation to Hebrew and Christian interpretations of revelation, the question was regularly asked by colleagues and friends. His answers came at a time when many people, including influential Christian churchmen, thought differently. He wrote:

> Using the word "evolution" in its most generally accepted meaning, and in a purely experiential context, I would say that man's origin by way of *evolution* is now an *indubitable* fact for science. There can be no two ways about it; the question is settled – so finally that to continue to debate it in the schools is as much a waste of time as it would be to go on arguing whether or not the revolution of the earth is an impossibility. (C 139)

The remainder of his essay discusses first what he called a proposal for "hyperphysics" and his theological conclusions. He added an appendix titled "Original Sin and Evolution." His description has become a generally accepted solution by many Christian scholars to the issue of sin and redemption, based on biblical teaching for an evolutionary universe.

A second significant theme in Teilhard's writings can be found in the introduction to an essay he wrote in 1945. He suggests in "Christianity and Evolution: Suggestions for a New Theology," dated "Peking, 11 November, 1945": "In the course of the last twenty years I have put forward in a long series of essays the views which gradually took shape in my mind on the emergence in the thought of modern man of a Christian evolutionism. Unfortunately, or fortunately, many of these pieces have never been published" (C 173). This fact was the result of a decision in 1925 by authorities in the Roman Catholic Church and the Jesuit order to prohibit publication of any of Teilhard's writings in philosophy and theology during his lifetime. His disappointment, and remarkable obedience in accepting that decision, is a special topic that is not covered in this survey. However, the authorities did permit publication of his scientific writings, which were collected and published in 11 volumes after his death (SW). These technical publications made him well known as a significant geologist and paleontologist in the small community of interested scientists, especially in China. When he returned from internment by the Japanese in Peking from 1939 to 1945, he was elected a member of the French Academy of Sciences for his contributions to the scientific profession.

Law of Complexity-Consciousness

In a preliminary note to *The Human Phenomenon*, Teilhard describes his "hyperphysics":

> Take any major book written about the world by one of the great modern scientists such as Poincaré, Einstein, Jeans, and the others. It is impossible to attempt a general scientific interpretation of the universe without *seeming* to intend to explain it right to the end. But only take a closer look at it, and you will see that this "hyperphysics" still is not metaphysics. (P 2)

By thus describing his purpose, Teilhard had hoped to satisfy Church authorities that he was not writing about philosophy or theology in the book, but only describing phenomena revealed by evolutionary science. Some scientists, not aware of Teilhard's real reason for proposing the essay as science, were critical of the book, especially the Nobel laureate Peter Medawar (Medawar 1961).

Since he was familiar with the hypothesis of the origin of the universe by explosion of a "primeval atom" first proposed by abbé Georges Lemaître in the 1930s, and later generally accepted within the science community, Teilhard assumed the origin of both matter and energy to be explained by Big Bang cosmology. However, he observed that neither Aristotelian nor Newtonian concepts of matter could fully explain growing awareness of the increasing complexity of matter and the general complementary increase over time of some form of consciousness. These conclusions had been established by paleontologists and others through their investigations of fossils.

In his writings Teilhard refers to the tendency for matter, under favorable conditions, to construct naturally organized and elaborate arrangements, so-called self-organization of matter. The gradual formations seemed to manifest over long durations gradual increases of growing psychic power and interiorization in their arrangements, as the complexity increased; for example, from molecules to cells, to animals, to humans. Teilhard proposed the phenomenon to be a law of nature, the law of complexity-consciousness, which has continued to be verified by research projects (P 216).[2]

The phenomenon of self-organization of matter appeared to be a scientific mystery. It also contradicted a basic law of physics. The roots of the scientific paradox can be understood by referring back to one decade, 1850–1860. In that period Darwin and Wallace developed the theory of biological evolution, and Clausius and Kelvin independently stated the second law of thermodynamics, sometimes called the law of entropy. A law of physics seemed to deny biological evolution. The law of entropy said the world is becoming more and more disorganized while paleontology and biology were finding that earth became more and more complex and organized as time passed. Many scientists were unaware of the entropy–evolution dilemma, or disregarded possible theoretical resolutions, and left it as one of the scientific mysteries. Teilhard wondered about the issue throughout his life as a scientist. His correspondence indicates that he was also curious whether there is any philosophical or theological significance to this process of seemingly complementary increases of complexity and consciousness as evolution has occurred. His now well-known explanations, given at the time in unpublished essays and private letters to friends, have caused Ian Barbour (1968) and some commentators to call him a process thinker. Long after Teilhard died, a theoretical discovery by physical chemist Ilya Prigogine and colleagues solved an important aspect of this dilemma of self-organization of matter.

In an important essay written in 1944 before leaving internment in China, he wrote an essay, "Centrology." In it he stressed that understanding our world would require interpreting the process of gradual increasing complexity accompanied by increasing consciousness. Specifically, could the process be related to a concept of what he called increasing "centricity" or interiorization of matter?[3] He wrote that perhaps in this world of becoming and increasing interiorization, what he called consciousness, the traditional description of being itself could be improved by relating it to the concept of union. He wrote:

> Underlying this experimental and undeniable interdependence of the two variables (centricity and complexity) we can distinguish a fundamental ontological relation between *being* and *union*; it may be expressed in two converse and indubitably complementary forms: 1. The one passive: "*Plus esse = plus a pluribus uniri*" (passive evolution). 2. The other active: "*Plus esse = plus plura unire*" (active evolution). (A 113)

The first description may be translated: "to be = to be more united out of many, and realizes the passive aspect of being." His description of the active aspect of evolution may be translated: "to be = to unite more the many." Thus for Teilhard, being is realized in its unity as maintained union.

The importance of grasping union for Teilhard as fundamental to understanding experience came early. He wrote on October 8, 1917 to Marguerite:

> When I get back down the line, if God grants me the time, I have almost made up my mind to make a start on an essay in philosophical synthesis (you'll smile to hear this ambitious plan) called *L'Union Créatrice*. I think this essential if I am to make myself understood by those before whom I shall sooner or later have to defend my ideas or forward them. (W 151)

Thus the concept of union for Teilhard does not rely merely on materialistic functions, like the synthesis of water from the union of hydrogen and oxygen. The concept goes beyond, as a metaphysical concept to explain stability and change. It is based on classical Platonic and Aristotelian metaphysical principles of matter and form to explain the modern cultural human experience of transition from a world of being to one of becoming.

From 1917 onwards Teilhard worked on the concept of union under its different variations. It is the most frequently mentioned word in his private journals. What seems significant is that the approach may offer an opportunity to expand and explore a metaphysics and analogy of being to a metaphysics and analogy of becoming, which includes the dynamic element that some consider absent in the classical philosophies identified with Aristotle and Thomas Aquinas.

The proposal of the role of union to explain ongoing complexity in creation permits investigation of differences that occur in nature like that between fusion and union. In fusion the individual components lose their identity, whereas in union the parts continue to maintain their individual identity. Teilhard recognized the individual parts become something more than their individuality, as part of a new whole. In evolution the individual identity of the parts in making the whole is important, especially among humans, in which respect for the other becomes important. In that case he saw that union differentiates and, in the case of humans, union personalizes. He wrote in his private journal on June 25, 1952: "L'Union différencie (personnalise), Péking, 1937." For Christians, this ongoing arrangement through-out creation has been cited as of striking theological interest because of the doctrines of marriage as covenant of two people, and of faith in the reality of three divine Persons in one God. This insight into interpretation of union in a triune God has been compared to the ancient Hebrew testimony in biblical writings to the mystery of natural manifestations of Jahweh, as described in Psalm 104. To date, the metaphysical implications of this doctrine for theological reflection have not been thoroughly investigated.

Matter-Spirit

Early in his career Teilhard noticed matter's complementary increases of psychic emergence with complexity of matter. Essays in 1925, 1926, and 1930 concerned with the gradual emer-gence of humans forced him to clarify his thoughts so that by 1938 he was ready to summarize his understanding of the issue. The proposal in his book *The Human Phenomenon* offered a possibility that has intrigued some philosophers and scientists:

> No concept is more familiar to us than spiritual energy. And yet nothing remains more obscure to us scientifically. . . . To think we must eat. But on the other hand, so many thoughts come out of the same piece of bread. . . . The two energies – physical and psychical – spread respec-tively through the internal and external layers of the world behave on the whole in the same way. . . . On the one hand, the objectivity of the effort and work of the psyche is so certain that the whole of ethics resides in it. And on the other, the nature of this interior power is so impal-pable that the whole of mechanics could be built up without it. (P 29)

Teilhard's solution to this issue of understanding the nature of matter proposed that matter must have properties and require concepts that go beyond what Newton and modern science assumed to be *Weltstoff*. In "Centrology," his solution to the issue of complementary increases of complexity and psychic energy is outlined. He proposes that matter must have "two aspects, spiritual and material" and "the real necessarily and complementarily call for one another like two sides of one and the same object – or, rather like the two terms 'a quo' and 'ad quem' of one and the same movement." He continues:

> Even in pre-living particles, we saw, we must conceive some sort of curvature which prefigures and initiates the appearance of freedom and a "within." *In fact, physical determinisms ("laws") are simply the effects of large numbers, in other words, of materialized freedom.* . . . From this point of view there is nothing in the universe except spirit, in different states or degrees of organization or plurality. (A 124–125)

In a footnote he supports his concept that there must be some form of spirituality in matter itself:

> By *atomic complexity* I mean here the number of atoms contained in the particle in question. That particles of low atomic complexity should appear "inanimate" to us is completely in line with the analogies we find in science. A number of fundamental properties of matter (variation of mass with velocity, the curvature of space, etc.) become perceptible to us only in the infinitely large or the infinitely small. From this point of view, we might say that biology is simply the "physics of very large complexes" – the physics of this third infinite (that of complexity, in which life appears. (A 102)

Teilhard's concept that pure matter, *Weltstoff*, is in reality matter-spirit has not been considered seriously. There seem to be two principal reasons for this lack of popularity among members of both the philosophical and scientific communities. The first is that it changes the clear description of matter, *Weltstoff*, proposed by Isaac Newton, who is considered the father of modern science. In his *Mathematical Principles of Natural Philosophy*, Newton described matter as mass, which can be simply weighed and measured. He eliminated the important role of Aristotle's abstract metaphysical principles like matter and form to describe nature. Aristotle's metaphysical principles had been accepted by philosophers and scientists for over a thousand years. Thus Newton's brilliant concept of how to deal with matter became a new philosophical foundation for the successful scientific revolution that followed.

A second objection to Teilhard's general approach to the interpretation of the concept of matter was his use of the word "energy." Because he was not sure that Newton's description of matter could explain the self-organization and psychic emergence that has been found in evolution, Teilhard proposed that the material or "a quo" aspect in matter could be described by what he called "tangential energy," and the spiritual or "ad quem" aspect could be explained by what he called "radial energy." Thus, in order to explain evolution Teilhard proposed:

> We shall assume that all energy is essentially psychic. But we shall add that in each individual element this fundamental energy is divided into two distinct components: a tangential energy making the element interdependent with all elements of the same order in the universe as itself (that is, of the same complexity and same "centricity"), and a radial energy attracting the element in the direction of an ever more complex and centered state, toward what is ahead. (P 30)

Teilhard adds a supportive footnote to his description of the two energies:

> Note by the way, that the less centered an element is (that is, the weaker its radial energy), the more its tangential energy is shown through powerful mechanical effects. Between strongly centered particles (that is, particles with a high radial energy), the tangential seems to become "interiorized" and to disappear, in the eyes of physics.

Of course these descriptions of matter and energy were based on Teilhard's observations of phenomena. Aristotle's metaphysics has been inadequate to fully explain the dynamism of our dynamic biological world. Moreover, Newton's concepts so far have been shown inadequate to fully explain the irreversibility of an expanding universe, the so-called arrow of time. Teilhard's proposal of *Weltstoff* as matter-spirit remains neither verified nor falsified.

Teilhard's Omega Point and Christogenesis

On September 23, 1919, referring to the universal Christ, Teilhard wrote in his journal: "The purpose of this note is to bring to the notice of my friends, more skilled than I am in sacred science and better placed to exert intellectual influence, how necessary, how vitally necessary, it is that we should make plain the eminently Catholic notion of Christ A and Ω [alpha and omega]." The application of alpha and omega had been attributed to Christ in the Book of Revelation: "I am the alpha and the omega, the first and the last, the beginning and the end" (22:13). "The concepts had been used before by authors who "borrowed the symbolism not from Hellenistic, but rather from Jewish sources" (Hartman 1954, 56).

After his wartime experience, his familiarity with the growing culture of evolution in his environment, and his devotion to the resurrected Christ, Teilhard probably adopted omega as a concept. He was concerned that the modern mind did not take seriously enough the significance of the passages about Christ, the Word of God, that are portrayed in John's Gospel in such verses as "All things came to be through him, and without him nothing came to be" (1:3) and in some of the passages in Paul's letters about the resurrected Christ.

The two aspects of Teilhard's omega have often been misunderstood. In *The Human Phenomenon* only one aspect of omega is described. The book is written in the language of observation of natural phenomena. It includes conclusions and speculations commonly used by scientists in writings about what has been observed about their areas of specialization, what he called "hyperphysics." That description, for his part, eliminated directly the language of professional metaphysics and theology. Thus he fulfilled the directives of the Church authorities.

The second aspect of Teilhard's omega is described in many of his shorter essays and correspondence with friends. Most of this material was, like his books, not published until after his death. In these essays one finds the scriptural and theological basis for his vision. There the concepts in his evolutionary vision are found in his essay, "The Christic." He relates Christogenesis, the evolution of the universe groping to reach a final point, the Omega Point, of becoming fully *in Christ*. There the resurrected Christ-the-Evolver will be seen to be what St Paul wrote of the risen Christ: "all in all." Throughout this process of Christogenesis, Christ is transcendent to and immanent in the process of evolution as Christ-Omega lures creation towards the Omega Point. The term *"in Christ"* appears 155 times in the Pauline writings (Murphy-O'Connor 1982, 183). Teilhard wrote in "The Christic" a month before he died: "When all is said and done, what constitutes the impregnable superiority of Christianity over all other types of Faith, is that it is ever more consciously identified with a *Christogenesis*, in other words with an awareness of the rise of a *certain universal Presence* which is at once *immortalizing and unifying*" (HM 90).

Building the Earth: The United Nations

In 1948, after recovering from a heart attack in Paris, Teilhard was offered the opportunity to accept the chair in geology at the College of France. However, his Jesuit superiors advised that it would probably be best to leave France permanently. Reports of his public talks in Paris, addressing controversial issues and attracting many people, worried certain Church officials in Rome. He was invited by the Viking Fund to come to New York City and prepare a future major symposium on human origins under the Fund's sponsorship at the University of California, Berkeley.

Teilhard outlined his perspectives in an important supper-talk to anthropologists in New York City, "On the Trend and Significance of Human Socialization" (SW 4243–4253, from which other quotations from Teilhard in this section also come). It encapsulates his point of view about topics that appeared in his non-technical essays after World War Two. The talk began:

> Under our very eyes a most extraordinary biological phenomenon is going on. In the course of the last ten or twelve thousand years of active socialization, human life has succeeded in expanding all over the continental earth. Now, however, and because the limits of the earth have been reached by the rising tide of civilization, it seems that this expansional process is in some way reflecting (reversing) on itself. First Life had to fill the surface of the earth. Now, in turn, it seems that Earth is *closing back* on itself, compressing more and more tightly, on its curved and limited area the continuously growing human mass. And in order to counteract this growing pressure, human mass, is *forced to super organize itself.*

Teilhard compares this process to natural crystallization that minimizes a volume of matter in new and more organized ways. The increased complex and conscious arrangement of matter is helpful to understand human unitary socialization:

> Life is nothing else but the cosmic process under which a fraction of the *Weltstoff*, instead of disintegrating into energy, is continuously shifting toward evermore complex types of arrangements, the degree of arrangement being somewhat measured by the degree of what we call consciousness (consciousness is probably a universal propriety of Matter, but which does not become apparent except when complexity reaches very high values).

He speaks to skeptics about the implications of natural theology: "Let me insist on the fact that I am not introducing here any undue metaphysics. I do not venture here to speak of 'finalité,' *purpose* (entelecheia), – no more so than when I am recognizing the flowing of a river or the spiraled movement of a galaxy."

Can socialization proceed further? Teilhard answers that, according to a common biological interpretation, the social phenomenon is a by-product of evolution. Evolution leads to individuation that includes numbers of individuals at the same time. Although there is some compensation, "this process of association always remains a dangerous antagonistic force." His own more scientific choice regards socialization as a direct and genuine prolongation of evolution to higher arrangements with growing consciousness. "Man is *not yet achieved*, zoologically; – and this evolutive achievement is to come to him *through unitary socialization.*" A positive psychological atmosphere about a Future could replace post-war experience of the "cosmic sea around us in which we have lost our bearings . . . modern Mankind has no clear idea where the Universe is driving. Anxiety – Bore." In the hope of continuing evolution to a Future, "the positive psychological atmosphere could be developed on Earth in which many social, political, religious unitary transformations . . . would become possible and easy." In this environment, the main role of anthropologists should change from a descriptive science of the human past and present to an operative science for the future, a science of the development of man, anthropogenesis. Through inventive power and collaboration humans can be in charge of controlling their own evolution. His thinking intrigued leaders at the United Nations.

When representatives of the American Teilhard Association requested a small room for a meeting at United Nations headquarters in 2005 to mark the fiftieth anniversary of Teilhard's death, the invitation reached the office of the Secretary-General, Kofi Annan. His is said to have replied: "They may not have a small room – they will have the main chamber." Eventually 750 people gathered in the General Council Chamber to discuss Teilhard's perspectives for a better world. In a message from Kofi Annan to the Association at the time, the then Secretary-General wrote about the significance of Teilhard's thought for his predecessors, Dag Hammarskjöld, U Thant, and Javier Pérez de Cuéllar, adding "Finally, I am convinced that Pere Teilhard de Chardin is a thinker for the twenty-first century."[4]

Robert Muller, Assistant Secretary-General of the United Nations during those years, relates two conversations between Teilhard and Emmanuel de Breuvery, his close Jesuit friend, who was in charge of the Natural Resources Division at the UN:

> Father de Breuvery often discussed with Teilhard his work at the UN. Father de Breuvery once quoted to me Teilhard as saying: *"Mon Père* someday people will understand that the sun, and only the sun, from which most other forms of energy are derived, is our great clean source of energy. Among the civilizations in the universe the earth is a very primitive one, since it uses the energy of its planet. Others utilize the energy of their sun, and still others harness the energy of the cosmos. You must take a very long-term view, a view of hundreds of thousands of years, and prepare the minds of the political leaders to think in terms of solar energy." (Muller 2005, 120)

Muller continues:

> On another occasion Father de Breuvery told me: Last night I exploded in front of Teilhard against UN bureaucracy. He looked at me with his kind eyes and said: *"Mon Père,* you must be patient. Mankind is still very young. Give it another five hundred thousand years and the problem of bureaucracy will also be solved."

Notes

1   Teilhard is best known for two books, *The Human Phenomenon* and *The Divine Milieu.* Other material covered in this chapter comes from relatively short unpublished essays, correspondence, and his private journals. The essays were collected after his death by an international committee of scholars familiar with Teilhard's thought, translated, and published in many languages. The titles of the essays were Teilhard's, but the committee placed them in specific books and titled the books. Citations are given by abbreviated book title, with the page where the citation is found. A list of these abbreviated book titles appears at the end of this chapter.

2   Based on Teilhard's original concept of matter, a development of the concept which permits reasonable emergence of consciousness, freedom, and information in cosmic evolution was developed by the late K. Schmitz-Moormann in collaboration with J. Salmon, SJ (1997, 38–48) and later expanded by Salmon (forthcoming).

3   By centricity Teilhard means level of interiorization or the psychic level of the entity.
4   Secretary-General Kofi Annan, April 7, 2005, "Message du Secrétaire général à l'occasion du colloque des amis du Père Teilhard de Chardin," online at http://www.un.org/apps/sg/sgstats.asp?nid=1389 (accessed November 11, 2011).

List of Abbreviations of Cited Works of Teilhard

A   1970. *Activation of Energy*. Translated by René Hague. New York: Harcourt Brace Jovanovich.
C   1971. *Christianity and Evolution*. Translated by René Hague. New York: Harcourt Brace Jovanovich.
D   1960. *The Divine Milieu*. Translator unknown. New York: Harper & Row.
HM   1976. *The Heart of Matter*. Translated by René Hague. New York: Harcourt Brace Jovanovich.
P   1999. *The Human Phenomenon*. Translated by Sarah Appleton-Weber. Portland: Sussex Academic Press.
SW   1971. *Pierre Teilhard de Chardin L'Oeuvre scientifique*, vol. 10, *1945–1955*. Olten and Freiburg im Breisgau: Walter-Verlag.
W   1968. *Writings in Time of War*. Translated by René Hague. New York: Harper & Row.

References

Barbour, I. 1968. Five Ways of Reading Teilhard. *Soundings*, 2(2), pp. 115–145.
Hartman, L. 1954. *Encyclopedic Dictionary of the Bible*. New York: McGraw-Hill.
Medawar, P. 1961. Critical Notice: Review of *"The Phenomenon of Man."* *Mind*, 70(277), pp. 99–106.
Muller, R. 2005. *Most of All They Taught Me Happiness*. Los Angeles: Amare Media LLC.
Murphy-O'Connor, J. 1982. *Becoming Human Together*. Wilmington, DE: Michael Glazier, Inc.
Salmon, James F., SJ. Forthcoming. *Creation and Evolution*.
Schmitz-Moormann, K. and Salmon, James F., SJ. 1997. *Theology of Creation in an Evolutionary World*. Cleveland, OH: Pilgrim Press.

Further Reading

Mooney, C. 1964. *Teilhard de Chardin and the Mystery of Christ*. New York: Harper & Row. An attempt to organize the theological thought of Teilhard into a synthesis, which he himself never did.
Salmon, J. and Farina, J., eds. 2011. *The Legacy of Pierre Teilhard de Chardin*. New York: Paulist Press. A collection of essays, five by theologians and five by scientists, who are well-known scholars in their respective disciplines.
Schmitz-Moormann, K. and Salmon, James F. 1997. *Theology of Creation in an Evolutionary World*. Cleveland, OH: Pilgrim Press. A Teilhardian interpretation of the scientific understanding of the world.

50

Thomas F. Torrance

TAPIO LUOMA

The question of how to relate theology and science has often been thought of as an effort to build a bridge between the two disciplines. The crucial point here is not only the manner in which the two sides meet each other but also what kinds of materials are used as arguments. At least as important is the foundation on both sides of the divide upon which the construction work will get started. In this respect, the theology–science dialogue of past decades is full of variations ranging from physics to neurobiology on the scientific side, and from the doctrine of creation to ecclesiology on the theological side. Each of them offers insightful ideas and, at best, provides us with fruitful concepts and interesting prospects for future dialogue.

Considered from the standpoint of theology, the doctrine of creation quite naturally touches scientific questions of the origin and structure of the universe, the more philosophical ideas of determinism and contingency, as well as the idea of God. It is no surprise, therefore, that a lot of theology–science dialogue has proceeded along this route. One of the problems of this approach, however, can be detected in the observation that this discussion, as necessary and fruitful as it is, can go on without any significant reference to specifically Christian doctrines and remains on quite a general religious and philosophical level.

The theological work of Thomas Forsyth Torrance (1913–2007) is of the utmost importance precisely in this respect. His treatises do contain important aspects of, for example, the doctrine of creation and its implications for theology–science dialogue, but one cannot find the core of his ideas there. Instead, the doctrine of Christ or Christology is his starting point for constructing links to natural sciences. He draws his insights especially from patristic theology of the first Christian centuries as well as from the work of John Calvin and, most important of all, Karl Barth. In his mature years, he increasingly applied insights from another unique doctrine of Christianity, the doctrine of the Trinity, to his discussion of the relationship between theology and science.

In an unparalleled way Torrance binds together his deep knowledge of the theology of the Church Fathers, the Swiss Reformer and the outstanding Swiss theological figure of the twentieth century, and the ideas of modern physics and philosophy of science. All this he

The Blackwell Companion to Science and Christianity, First Edition. Edited by J. B. Stump and Alan G. Padgett.
© 2012 Blackwell Publishing Ltd. Published 2012 by Blackwell Publishing Ltd.

does as a Reformed theologian from a specific Barthian point of departure. Contrary to what has usually been assumed, Torrance gives evidence of the ability of the Barthian theological paradigm to enter into serious dialogue with the natural sciences and philosophy of science. It is precisely this feature in Torrance's work which makes it interesting, challenging, and insightful not only from the viewpoint of theology or science or philosophy but also from that of the Christian Church and its everyday life.

Torrance's Life

Thomas Forsyth Torrance was born in 1913 in Chengdu, China, the second of six children. His parents were working as missionaries, and Thomas's personal experience in a missionary field left a lasting influence in his theology and thought. Even as an academic he wanted to contribute to the proclamation of Church in a way that reflected his central theological ideas. His deep concern for church life resulted also in the many important positions he held in his own church, the Church of Scotland, as well as in the ecumenical movement. His interest in ecumenism had undoubtedly deep roots in the Reformed tradition of his father and the Anglican faith of his mother. His efforts to bring the Reformed and the Orthodox traditions into dialogue are among the most remarkable achievements of his ecumenical activity.

Thomas Torrance studied in the Faculty of Divinity at the University of Edinburgh. Of utmost importance for his theological development was his contact with Karl Barth, who was his teacher during his studies in Basel, Switzerland. In the University of Edinburgh Torrance was appointed Professor of Church History in 1950 but in 1952 accepted the professorship of Christian Dogmatics, an office he held until his retirement in 1979. He wrote a large body of works, ranging from church history to Reformation theology and from ecumenism to philosophy of science. He was also a vigorous participant in discussions not only of theology but also of the praxis of the Church. Within Torrance's own context, in Scotland and in the Church of Scotland, he had a controversial position: from the standpoint of Calvinist orthodoxy, Torrance was too liberal, and from the standpoint of the modernist branch of Scottish Reformed tradition he was too conservative. As a result, his views were more warmly welcomed abroad than in his own country (McGrath 1999, 3–107; Luoma 2002, 18–9).

Space and Time as the Stage of God's Revelation

One of the basic arguments Torrance makes with regard to the relationship between theology and natural sciences is that both disciplines share in the same single rationality and that there is only one basic way of knowing. This means that in their efforts to understand more deeply the structures of the universe the natural sciences apply the same kind of reasoning as a theologian who tries to understand more fully God and God's relation to the world. At the same time, it belongs to the nature of single rationality that the true reality of each object of investigation is respected. Therefore it would be a violation against the other discipline to try to carry out scientific investigation in the field of theology or to interpret the objects of the natural sciences with the methods and questions of theology. Although both disciplines share in the same rationality, each has its own distinct fields of investigation (Torrance 1980, 9).

Torrance holds that the common rationality of human questioning and the common way of knowing as the basis of all honest thinking and inquiry have their roots in creation. Because God has created the universe and given the human being a unique position as its "spokesman" in every field of knowing, there cannot be several ways of being in relation to reality. Any scholar, even a natural scientist, is a "priest of creation" whose calling is to give articulate expression to the inherent rationality of the universe. In this way scientific endeavor is always a religious task, a task without which nature would remain dumb and unable to become articulate (Torrance 1980, 5–6; 1982a, 24–27).

This one single rationality uniting human beings and the rest of creation cannot operate without its bearers, space and time. Torrance says:

> In creating man, endowed with mind as well as with soul and body, out of nothing, God created within the universe an intelligent counterpart to the rational order immanent in the creation through the functioning of space and time. (Torrance 1980, 55)

Space and time as the two basic elements of all existence and a point of interest of scientific thinking from ancient times thus form the actual scene in which the human being carries out her duty to interpret reality. Space and time set the limits of human existence and knowing. If there ever is any kind of knowing or being in this universe, it must comply with the conditions of space and time. This is more or less self-evident for the natural sciences, but so it is also for theology. Human knowledge of God would be totally impossible without space and time, because together they form the setting in which God actually makes himself known and open to human understanding. We can know God only to the extent God wants to be known, within the conditions of God's sovereign choice (Luoma 2002, 53–60).

Torrance wants to develop his idea of the interaction of theology and natural science from a definite Christian viewpoint. He does not favor discussions about God in general, about God's existence or omnipotence or other central issues of philosophical theology. Instead, Torrance starts from what Christian theology sees as the sole point of human ability to know anything of God, namely God's revelation. Space and time as bearers of intelligibility and rationality should be taken with utmost seriousness. Therefore God's revelation in space and time must precede any proposition or idea of God. Space and time themselves reveal important features of their Creator, but Christian theology must never be satisfied with this approach only.

According to Torrance, the final meeting point of God and man in space and time is Jesus Christ, the second Person of the triune God. In him God has entered as a human the conditions of space and time and complied within the limits of finite created being. The Christian doctrine of incarnation is the traditional explication of the conviction that the infinite has become finite, the eternal has become temporal, or using the language of the New Testament, "the Word was made flesh." As true God and true human being, Jesus is the only point of entrance into knowledge of and communion with God.

The doctrine of Christology offers Torrance the structure for how he sees the relationship between theology and natural sciences. Their common ground in space and time and, within them, their mutual sharing in the same single rationality and intelligibility present a challenge to both disciplines to appreciate reality as it truly is, without efforts to clamp human ideas or preconceptions upon reality. There should be no *a priori* knowledge of nature or God but only knowledge based on the real subject matter of the field of investigation (Torrance 1980, 90; 1985, 24).

The Theological Character of Space and Time

For Torrance, space and time are not only the setting in which God's revelation of the incarnation of Christ takes place. The innermost being of space and time itself is deeply infected by the conviction that they are created and, first of all, that God himself has entered them in the Incarnation. They are not neutral categories in which something happens, but rather they are profoundly involved in every event, even in God's becoming human being.

In his argumentation, Torrance makes use of his vast knowledge of the patristic theology of the early Church. Again, the doctrine of Christ is of utmost importance here. If Jesus Christ is God incarnate in space and time, then it is important to reflect on the actual relationship between Christ's divinity and humanity. The Council of Nicaea in 325 CE settled a long dispute concerning the issue. There had been a strenuous conflict in which one party, led by Archdeacon Arius, insisted that Christ as a figure in space and time is a created being whose nature is not ultimately divine. Arius held that it would be gross blasphemy against the sovereignty and unity of God to claim that Christ is somehow ontologically participating in the Divinity. For him, Christ is a divine being, he is the Son of God, but there is no possibility of calling him God. He is only God-like.

The leader of the other party, Bishop Athanasius, struggled long after the Nicene Council against Arius's theology, claiming that it is actually Arius who was blaspheming against God and his majesty by insisting that God has not become incarnate himself. Athanasius determinedly defended the Nicene solution that the Son of God is of one being, *homoousios* in Greek, with God the Father. This means that Christ must not be seen as a mere creature or superficial appearance of the divine but someone who is ontologically identical with God. Therefore the Christian Church throughout the world explicates its faith in the Nicene Creed:

> We believe in one Lord, Jesus Christ, the only Son of God, eternally begotten of the Father, God from God, Light from Light, true God from true God, begotten, not made, of one Being with the Father.

Torrance underlines the implications of this conviction pointing out that what we see in Christ we see in the Father, and what God the Father is in himself can be seen in God the Son, Jesus Christ. God does not hide himself from us but lays himself open for us in his Son. This further implies that the relationship between God in his being and God in his incarnate substance emphasizes the ontological unity of the two Persons of the Godhead. Although the Person of the Father remains outside the sphere of creation, the incarnate Person of the Son is ontologically involved in it.

Torrance holds that the theological idea of *homoousion*, the belief that the Son is of one being with the Father, in a significant way anticipated the feature of physics that later became known as the relational notion of space. Its counterpart, the absolute (or receptacle or container) notion of space, has traditionally claimed that space has strict boundaries, thus making it a closed container in which events occur and things exist. This is the usual common-sense idea of the nature of space, and in the field of physics it provided Isaac Newton, for instance, with the insights upon which he constructed his pioneering scientific work.

The relational notion, however, does not concentrate on the boundaries of space but understands it rather as a field of relations between objects. Space as an independent category vanishes and becomes integrated into objects and events and their more or less complicated relations. In philosophy of physics the debate between adherents of the two notions has been occasionally quite vigorous, and remains unsettled so far.

As noted, Torrance is in favor of the relational notion. Behind this there are two reasons. First of all, Torrance makes the claim that the Nicene theologians had to think of the relationship between God the Father and God the Son and their identical being (*homoousion*) strictly in relational terms, so that the idea of space and time was itself affected. This further anticipated the rise of relational notion of space and time in later physics, especially in the theories of relativity of Albert Einstein. This feature is an example of Torrance's idea of how theology has made a substantial contribution to science, or, as Torrance says, "far from theology being based on natural science, the opposite, if anything, is nearer the truth" (Torrance 1980, 44).

The second reason for Torrance's sympathy for the relational notion of space and time is that it is more helpful for understanding the idea of incarnation than the container notion. If space and time can be conceived, not as containers with strict boundaries, but, rather, as consisting of relations, then there are fewer rational obstacles to conceiving the idea of God's becoming a human being. In the final analysis, Torrance's idea of relational space and time refers not only to the horizontal relations between objects but also to the vertical relations between the objects and the Creator of all. The ultimate nature of everything in space and time is contingent, dependent on God.

Realism Based on Theology

Space and time as the stage of God's revelation, his unique self-disclosure in the incarnation of Jesus Christ, were seen to bear a deep theological character: the Christological concept of *homoousion* makes it clear, according to Torrance, that the relation between the historical figure of Jesus Christ as the Son of God and God the Father can be conceived only in terms of relationality. Torrance prefers talking about *onto-relations*, referring thus to such connections that belong to the innermost essence of things and persons. This means that what created beings ultimately are is basically determined by their mutual relations. They are not a superficial attachment to their being but deeply integrated into it.

In the thinking of Torrance, the idea of onto-relations, as entertained in theology in the Christian doctrine of the *homoousion* relation between God the Son and God the Father, is a strong indication of outspoken realism in whatever science or field of inquiry. This explicates the conviction that whatever we observe in space and time can be trusted to bear a direct relation to the innermost being of the objects of our observation. If we had to rely on mere appearances and leave the actual being aside, as is the case in the Kantian scientific paradigm, then we could not have proper access to the things we observe. For Torrance, then, the originally theological concept of *homoousion* can be seen as applicable to other disciplines as well because it coins a realist attitude toward human observations: what we observe is of the same being, *homoousion*, with the object of our observation.

With these insights Torrance is contributing to the theology–science dialogue with special reference to the relation of epistemology and ontology. His viewpoint is strongly theological, and precisely this feature makes his approach interesting. Torrance holds that every scientific endeavor must respect reality as such and not force it into the straitjacket of human thought. He reminds us: "We must submit ourselves modestly, with our questions, to the object in order that it and not we ourselves may be the pivotal point in the inquiry" (Torrance 1969, 120).

The roots of Torrance's view of realism are not solely in the patristic theology of the early Church but especially in the theology of Karl Barth. This feature is most significant because it proves that the Barthian theological paradigm is not so incapable of entering into serious dialogue with the natural sciences as has usually been thought. There is a vast literature on realism and its different aspects in the philosophy of science. There have also been efforts to see Torrance as an adherent to one or more strands of realism. One cannot, however, understand his view of realism without taking into account his thoroughly theological way of argumentation as well as his commitment to the basic structure of Karl Barth's thinking.

When Torrance underscores that there is only one way of gaining knowledge of reality he is actually referring to an idea of compulsion: the power of reality has to be taken seriously, and any scientific effort should submit itself to the demands of reality if it wants to be science in the first place. Even the nature of questions put to the object of inquiry should be determined by the reality under study (Torrance 1969, 120; Polkinghorne 2004, 77). Torrance makes extensive use of modern quantum physics to show that reality must be left to speak for itself, although this speech goes far beyond the understanding and preconceived ideas of a scientist. Torrance favors Albert Einstein's realist view of quantum phenomena and, conversely, feels critical towards the so-called Copenhagen interpretation. The problem with the latter lies in its claim that we do not have direct access to quantum phenomena themselves but only to their appearances as expressed in their statistical explication. This leads to the conclusion that atoms are not real in the same sense as observable phenomena (Heisenberg 1959, 160).

From Torrance's point of view, this cannot but cut off our observations from their ontological nucleus: the idea of *homoousion* is thereby denied because what we discern in reality cannot be seen to participate in the same being of reality itself. This defect further implies that reality cannot exercise its compelling power over our observations and our explications of it because we leave ourselves satisfied with a phenomenal or superficial level only.

It would be too much to say, however, that Torrance is adhering to the correspondence theory of truth, the idea in epistemology wherein a sentence or proposition is true just in case it correctly describes the facts, and false when it fails to do so. Instead Torrance held something like a *realist* theory of truth (see Armstrong 2004). Torrance holds that truly scientific propositions have a *referential* relation to reality, indicating that what we say of an object of inquiry on the basis of what we have gotten to know of it refers to the object in a way that remains open to further possible refinement. Although realist scientific propositions must be seen as reaching reality as it is in itself, not only superficial phenomena but its innermost being, these propositions as human intellectual constructions always fall short of reality itself (Torrance 1982b, 171).

As stated above, the motivation behind Torrance's thinking in this respect does not lie in general considerations in the field of philosophy of science but, rather, in the total structure of his theology. It is not difficult to discern the traditional Calvinist emphasis on the majesty of God compelling us to consent humbly to the divine reality as it is. The roots of Torrance's view of realism can be found still deeper in the heart of Reformed theology and in one of its most characteristic doctrines, the doctrine of election.

Torrance is not fond of the idea of election entertained within Reformed orthodoxy in which it is held that God's eternal degree has decided in a sovereign manner the fate of every single human person. The problem with this view is, according to Torrance, that there is no crucial place for Christ, his Incarnation, and his atoning work. Instead, salvation is considered as lacking any direct link to how God has decided to act. This is negligent of how things really are and therefore this approach reveals only human constructions of thought which do not obey God's own way of acting in the process of salvation. There is no evangelical consolation in this line of thought, leaving a Christian in a deterministic trap in which she cannot but continually ask whether she belongs to the company of the elect or not.

While traditional Calvinistic orthodoxy claims that God's sovereign election affects single human beings, Karl Barth's interpretation insists that God's election chooses only one individual amongst the vast numbers of humankind, namely Jesus Christ (Barth 1956, 50–51, 516). In and through him salvation belongs to the whole of humankind because Christ has taken our humanity upon himself. It is precisely this Barthian approach that Torrance makes use of in his efforts to relate science and theology. And, consequently, it is here where his thought elaborates further Barth's original position and where this theologically based realism finds its application in wider spheres of philosophy of science.

The crucial point in Torrance's argument is the idea of the rationality or intelligibility of all creation. Because there is, basically, only one rationality pervading the whole universe, we have no option but to obey its compelling power. This objective rationality must determine what we think of reality (Torrance 1981, 29). Because this universe is given, created by God, its rationality and intelligibility are also something created and integrated into the universe by God. God has elected precisely this universe as his creation to bear rationality that exercises its compelling power upon human minds.

According to traditional Calvinist orthodoxy God's election applies to all rational creatures, referring to angels and human beings (Heppe 1984, 152). Now Torrance remarkably enlarges the horizon of God's election: not only angels and humans bear rationality but the whole of creation is seen as a rational entity. Torrance's view of the rationality of the whole of creation is based on the Christological doctrine of the Word or *Logos*, insisting that because God has created the universe through his Word, thereby he gave it its rationality and intelligibility. He makes use of St Athanasius's idea according to which all rational order in the universe is "to be traced back to its creative source in the Word of God" (Torrance 1988, 103). This Word has become incarnate in Jesus Christ, who is *homoousios*, of same being with God the Father.

The discussion above indicates clearly that it is difficult to categorize Torrance's view of realism along the lines stemming from philosophy of science only. His contribution to theology–science dialogue in this respect lies in his conviction that what we discern in our investigations is ontologically linked to the innermost essence of the object of our investigation. The concept of *homoousion*, then, binds together theological and epistemological dimensions in a unique patristic, Reformed, and Barthian way, revealing another possibility of constructing a bridge between theology and natural sciences. The usefulness of such an approach, however, undoubtedly remains under debate.

The Threat of Dualism

Torrance's program in the theology–science dialogue is based, as we have seen, on the idea of realism, the actual characteristic of which is to be detected in the concept of *homoousion*, to be of the same being. Torrance holds that realism has not affected science and theology to the extent that it should have. The constant threat to realism lies in the human tendency to focus only on a phenomenal level of reality so that the ontological connection between our perceptions and the essence of the objects of our investigations is damaged or even destroyed. Torrance calls this threat dualism.

Related to dualism is Torrance's effort to draw a picture of Western thinking through his unique periodization. Torrance holds that the history of ideas and science can be seen as consisting of three distinct eras, each of which has struggled with dualistic modes of thinking. The era of Ptolemaic cosmology introduced a deep divide between "the intelligible realm of celestial realities and the sensible realm of terrestrial phenomena" (Torrance 1971, 29; 1975, 267). During this period in history the Christian Church tried to find its way into a coherent understanding of the relation between God and Jesus, the Father and the Son. The split between the two realms was overcome, according to Torrance, only through the realistic approach indicated in the concept of *homoousion*.

The second phase in Western history is the time of Newtonian cosmology. Dualism now found another application in Isaac Newton's view of absolute or the container notion of space and time as the counter-pole of a relative, apparent notion of space and time. Torrance claims that this led to the introduction of hard causalism and determinism into the fabric of Western thinking and posed a severe threat to any realistic understanding of the universe. Accordingly, God's role was reduced to that of an explanation for those phenomena that were not conceivable according to the strict mechanistic laws of nature (Torrance 1975, 268–269; 1980, 70).

While Torrance sees the first two eras as contaminated by dualistic modes of thinking, the third is full of hope. The present period of Einsteinian cosmology has been able to move forward from dualistic thinking, for example with its discoveries of the deep integration of space and time. Torrance holds that Albert Einstein put the development of modern thinking on a new path with his theories of relativity, thus creating a novel understanding of the deep connection between epistemology with ontology, between knowing with being. In other words, the compelling force of realism can once again be seen as exercising its power on our knowing so that we are not held captives of a phenomenal level only but have an access to the innermost being of reality and its events (Torrance 1980, 70.) The realism coined in the concept of *homoousion* is relevant again.

Torrance's view of the intellectual background presumptions of Western science and thinking in general is another indication of his theological position. The three periods are valued according to their ability to nurture a realist standpoint, realist in the sense of an obedient consent to the demands and compelling power of reality. For Torrance dualism is

> a paradigmatic, most often unconsciously applied but deeply internalized way of perceiving reality which is seen as consisting of two principles. In the final analysis the poles are God and the world, or the Creator and the creation, between which there is no real interaction of dynamic relation as indications of the ontological and epistemological openness of God and the universe toward each other, thus offering a negation of the *homoousion*. (Luoma 2002, 92)

Torrance is quite explicit in his claims that Isaac Newton's dualism has a lot to do with the scientist's religious views, the details of which are well known to be rather unorthodox. Torrance maintains that the mechanistic and deterministic currents in Newton's idea of absolute versus relative space and time bear an analogy to Arius and his struggle against the Nicene theology. Torrance notes that Newton favored Arius and was personally opposed to the doctrines of Christ's divinity and the Trinity, which could not but reveal its connection to his overall view of the structure of the universe. Because both Arius and Newton operated with the notion of container space, there was no possibility for them to conceive the Incarnation in the orthodox way, underlining the true entering of eternal and omnipresent God into temporality and locality. In the final analysis, both Arius and Newton operated with the Greek dualistic thinking that makes a sharp distinction between the intelligible world, approachable only through reason, and the sensible world, conceivable only through the senses (Torrance 1975, 269–269).

A Scientific Lesson to Learn

Torrance's grand program for theology and natural sciences includes the thought that realism, as Torrance defines it, is something that was originally introduced into the fabric of Western thinking by the patristic theology of the early Church. Torrance agrees with scholars who claim that the biblical idea of God creating the universe, explicating the vast categorical difference between God and creation, contributed significantly to the Western intellectual world. The point is that investigation of nature without fear of entering into the domain of God became possible in the first place. Such a fear was common among ancient civilizations for religious reasons because they were not able to draw such a sharp distinction between God and God's creation as the Judaeo-Christian view could (Jaki 1986, viii; Hooykaas 1984, 13–16).

Torrance takes this argument further. He makes the claim that not only the doctrine of creation but also that of Incarnation helped to reflect fruitfully the structure of nature. The core of Torrance's claim is that God's relation to the created universe came into new light through the Incarnation. Thinking through the relation of God the Father and God the Son incarnate made theologians respect the actual way in which God chose to reveal himself within the structures of space and time. The doctrine of Incarnation, with the idea of God becoming a human being, also implicitly fostered a novel understanding of the universe. Torrance holds that ontologically the doctrine of Incarnation confirmed what the doctrine of creation had earlier laid a basis for. These are the "three masterful ideas," as Torrance calls them: rationality, freedom, and contingency of the universe. Without taking them into account any realist approach in investigations would be deficient (Torrance 1980, 52–60).

Torrance describes the interaction between theology and natural sciences first as a movement from the former to the latter. The core issue is realism and how a realist epistemology can guarantee that human knowledge reaches the ontology of reality. According to Torrance, now theology has a lesson to learn. Following Karl Barth, Torrance is quite critical towards modern theology, which, in his opinion, has largely forgotten its realist basis but is satisfied with a superficial and phenomenal level only. This is most evident in studies of the historical Jesus and, related to that, of historical biblical texts. This has led to the situation where modern theology can cope only with the phenomenal Jesus or the phenomenal Bible, without asking the question what is behind them on an ontological level. Both Jesus and the Bible have been detached from their ontological context (Torrance 1982a, 52–83).

The lesson of realism, sadly forgotten in theology, is now taught to it by the natural sciences. Torrance appreciates James Clerk Maxwell and Albert Einstein as pioneers of a realist attitude towards scientific enterprise. Torrance holds that for both scientists the idea of ontology was of the utmost importance. Maxwell used the idea of a field, thus introducing a dynamic and relational view of reality as opposed to the strictly mechanical, causal, and therefore deterministic understanding so strongly prevailing after Isaac Newton. Einstein developed further this un-mechanistic approach with his theories of relativity. Both Maxwell and Einstein saw, according to Torrance, the immense relevance of ontology and the need to take it seriously even if it contradicted common sense. The point is not to see particles or events of the universe only but, first of all, the relations between them (Torrance 1984, 232–236). In the debate over whether Maxwell and Einstein truly saw processes of nature as indeterministic, Torrance makes his own point quite clear. He argues at length in favor of indeterminism in the thinking of the two scientists, although in this respect views differ significantly (Torrance 1980, 112–132; 1985, 72–76; Luoma 2002, 106–112, 148).

Torrance claims that just as physics has been able to throw away the burden of determinism and mechanistic ideas, theology should now do the same and return to the realist basis of its own enterprise to get proper knowledge of God. Theology should take seriously the ontological context to which the central issues of Christianity are attached, the Bible and especially Jesus Christ. The patristic understanding of the *homoousion* relation between God the Father and God the Son must be seen as characteristic of the whole Godhead, the Trinity, in which the relations of love prevail between the three divine Persons, Persons who are *homoousioi*, of the same being with each other.

Conclusion

Thomas F. Torrance is widely regarded as one of the most significant Anglo-Saxon theologians in the Reformed tradition. The impact of his thinking is seen in that an international research organization bearing Torrance's name has been established (T. F. Torrance Theological Fellowship) to promote his theological legacy. At the same time, Torrance's thought has also met with criticism not only in scientific circles but also within his own Reformed tradition. This makes any evaluation of the reception of his views quite a complex task. Comments from the sphere of the natural sciences are actually quite rare; those existing come often from scholars with both a theological and scientific background.

However, the dialogue of science and theology can benefit from Torrance's work in many ways. Despite the obvious problems in Torrance's reading of history of science and theology, and despite his personal preferences with regard to certain scientific figures, his call for deeper interdisciplinary interaction should be taken seriously. We can detect many points in his thought that challenge further reflection. Here I name only three.

First, Torrance's approach invites not only academic theology but also Christian worshipping communities to conversation. This is of utmost importance in our times, when we increasingly see fragmented religion as an obstacle to dialogue and understanding. Second, Torrance's conviction that there is only one reality common to all people emphasizes the obligation of all scientists in every field to respect reality, no matter how differently we interpret it. Consequently, and third, Torrance makes a wise argument when he holds that basically there is only one rationality and only one basic way of knowing. This unites all scientific disciplines to seek answers to the questions put to us by the universe and its diverse existence in a common enterprise. In the final analysis, theology and natural sciences are *homoousioi*, of the same being.

References

Armstrong, D. M. 2004. *Truth and Truth-Makers*. Cambridge: Cambridge University Press.

Barth, Karl. 1956. *Church Dogmatics*, vol. 4.1. G. W. Bromiley and T. F. Torrance, eds. Edinburgh: T. & T. Clark.

Heisenberg, Werner. 1959. *Physics and Philosophy: The Revolution in Modern Science*. London: George Allen & Unwin.

Heppe, Heinrich. 1984. *Reformed Dogmatics: Set Out and Illustrated from the Sources*. Grand Rapids, MI: Baker Book House.

Hooykaas, R. 1984. *Religion and the Rise of Modern Science*. Edinburgh: Scottish Academic Press.

Jaki, Stanley L. 1986. *Science and Creation: From Eternal Cycles to an Oscillating Universe*. Edinburgh: Scottish Academic Press.

Luoma, Tapio. 2002. *Incarnation and Physics: Natural Science in the Theology of Thomas F. Torrance*. New York: Oxford University Press.

McGrath, Alister E. 1999. *Thomas F. Torrance: An Intellectual Biography*. Edinburgh: T&T Clark.

Polkinghorne, John. 2004. *Science and the Trinity: The Christian Encounter with Reality*. New Haven, CT: Yale University Press.

Torrance, Thomas F. 1969. *Theological Science*. Oxford: Oxford University Press.

Torrance, Thomas F. 1971. *God and Rationality*. London: Oxford University Press.

Torrance, Thomas F. 1975. *Theology in Reconciliation: Essays towards Evangelical and Catholic Unity in East and West*. London: Geoffrey Chapman.

Torrance, Thomas F. 1980. *The Ground and Grammar of Theology*. Charlottesville: University Press of Virginia.

Torrance, Thomas F. 1981. *Divine and Contingent Order*. Oxford: Oxford University Press.

Torrance, Thomas F. 1982a. *Reality and Evangelical Theology*. Philadelphia: The Westminster Press.

Torrance, Thomas F. 1982b. Theological Realism. In Brian Hebblethwaite and Stewart Sutherland, eds. *The Philosophical Frontiers of Christian Theology: Essays Presented to D. M. McKinnon*. Cambridge: Cambridge University Press, pp. 169–196.

Torrance, Thomas F. 1984. *Transformation and Convergence in the Frame of Knowledge: Explorations in the Interrelations of Scientific and Theological Enterprise*. Belfast: Christian Journals Limited.

Torrance, Thomas F. 1985. *Reality and Scientific Theology*. Edinburgh: Scottish Academic Press.

Torrance, Thomas F. 1988. *The Trinitarian Faith: The Evangelical Theology of the Ancient Catholic Church*. Edinburgh: T&T Clark.

Further Reading

Colyer, Elmer M. 2007. *How to Read T. F. Torrance: Understanding His Trinitarian and Scientific Theology*. Downers Grove, IL: InterVarsity Press. A highly useful introduction to the totality of Torrance's thinking.

Holder, Rodney D. 2009. Thomas Torrance: "Retreat to Commitment" or a New Place for Natural Theology? *Theology and Science*, 7(3), pp. 275–296. A critical look at Torrance's evaluation of natural theology.

Pannenberg, Wolfhart. 2006. Contributions from Systematic Theology. In Philip Clayton and Zachary Simpson, eds. *The Oxford Handbook of Religion and Science*. Oxford: Oxford University Press, pp. 359–371. An article by another significant theologian with a special interest in natural sciences.

Smart, J. J. C., ed. 1979. *Problems of Space and Time*. New York: Macmillan. An informative compilation of classic texts on space and time.

Torrance, Thomas F. 1989. *The Christian Frame of Mind: Reason, Order and Openness in Theology and Natural Science*. Colorado Springs, CO: Helmers & Howard. Usefully collects the central themes of Torrance's views on theology and natural science.

51

Arthur Peacocke

TAEDE A. SMEDES

Biography

With physicists John Polkinghorne and Ian Barbour, Arthur Robert Peacocke (born on November 29, 1948) was known as one of the three "scientist-theologians" (a term coined by Polkinghorne). For many people, Peacocke has become a personification of the synthesis of science and Christian theology. Peacocke was trained as a biochemist, and taught at the University of Birmingham from 1948 until his appointment as university lecturer in biochemistry in the University of Oxford in 1959. Peacocke wrote two textbooks in biochemistry, but is best known for his work in the field of science and theology that started when he took up a second career as a theologian in the Anglican Church: Peacocke was ordained a deacon and a priest in the Church of England in 1971. From 1973 until 1984 he was Dean and Fellow of Clare College, Cambridge. From 1985 to 1988 and from 1995 to 1999 he was the director of the Ian Ramsey Centre. He founded the Society of Ordained Scientists in 1986 to further advance the development of the field of science and religion. He delivered the Bampton Lectures in 1978 (published in 1979 as *Creation and the World of Science*) and the Gifford Lectures at St Andrews in 1993 (incorporated in the second edition of his book *Theology for a Scientific Age: Being and Becoming – Natural, Divine and Human*, published in 1993). In 2001 Peacocke received the Templeton Prize. He published more than 200 papers and a dozen books, such as *Science and the Christian Experiment* (1971, winner of the prestigious Lecomte du Noüy Prize in 1973), *God and the New Biology* (1986), and an extensive summary of his theological ideas in *Paths from Science towards God: The End of All Our Exploring* (2001). Peacocke died on October 21, 2006, at the age of 81.

This chapter is intended to give an introduction to Peacocke's thought by way of a topical overview of those ideas that have proven most influential in the field of science and religion and that Peacocke himself has elaborated most fully in his works: the importance of theological consonance with the sciences; methodological considerations concerning metaphors and models; Peacocke's critical realism, inference to the best explanation, and natural theology; the panentheistic and kenotic image of God; the scientific, emergent ontology of the world

The Blackwell Companion to Science and Christianity, First Edition. Edited by J. B. Stump and Alan G. Padgett.
© 2012 Blackwell Publishing Ltd. Published 2012 by Blackwell Publishing Ltd.

as a result of the interplay of chance and necessity; divine action and downward causation; and, finally, the meaning of Christ for humanity.

The Relevance of the Sciences for Theology

Many scholars who attempt to bring science and theology together are motivated by the attempt to debunk the view that science and religion are generally in a state of conflict. Although Peacocke refers occasionally to the conflict view, his motivation for engaging in the interaction between science and religion lies elsewhere. In almost all of his works, Peacocke emphasizes that if theology today does not engage with the natural sciences in a serious and constructive manner, it will ultimately lose touch with culture and will be relegated to obscurity in a cultural ghetto. Peacocke thus is concerned with the cultural place of religion and theology. He acknowledges that the encounter between scientific knowledge and traditional theology at first is not easy: "Today it is the scientific worldview that constitutes the challenge to received understandings of nature, humanity and God – in a way that can be initially devastating yet is potentially creative" (Peacocke 2001, 15). The sciences initially may have a corrosive effect on theology, but in the end also invite new articulations and justifications of religious assertions about God and about God's relation to nature and humanity.

Thus Peacocke argues "for re-examining the claimed cognitive content of Christian theology in the light of the new knowledge derivable from the sciences, since both enterprises purport to be dealing with what they regard as realities" (Peacocke 1993, 6). In other words, Peacocke regards it as his task to bring together science and theology in order to critically examine and assess traditional theological ideas and doctrines in the light of the natural sciences. Theology should strive towards consonance with the sciences. Any exploration of the Divine should be based on methods, instruments, and knowledge that have proven their value to us. Theology should thus adopt the methodological principles inherent in the natural sciences. One major principle is "inference to the best explanation." Peacocke holds that theology should aim at God as the best explanation, not only for religious experiences, but ultimately for the universe as a whole, "by application of the criteria of reasonableness that are used generally to assess ideas and, in particular, in appraising scientific models and theories – namely, fit with the data, internal coherence, comprehensiveness, fruitfulness and general cogency" (Peacocke 1993, 15, cf. also 17).

Philosophically, Peacocke commits himself to a metaphysical position he calls "emergentist monism," and which "affirms that natural realities, although basically physical, evidence various levels of complexity with distinctive internal inter-relationships between their components, such that new properties, and also new realities, emerge in those complexes" (Peacocke 2007, 14). This is a monistic and even materialistic view,

> in the sense that everything can be broken down into whatever physicists deem ultimately to constitute matter/energy (e.g., quarks, superstrings?). No extra entities or forces, other than the basic four forces of physics, are to be inserted at higher levels of complexity in order to account for their properties. (Peacocke 2007, 12)

However, as we will see later, although physicalist or materialist in nature, it is also non-reductionist, in that Peacocke takes the scientific concept of emergence seriously and allows for the possibility that "properties, concepts, and explanations used to describe the higher-level wholes are not logically reducible to those used to describe their constituent parts" (Peacocke 2007, 13).

Monism is often contrasted with dualism. Peacocke, however, allows for one dualist element in his theology, and that is

> the distinction between the Being of God and that of everything else (the "world" = all-that-is, all-that-is-created). Talk of the "supernatural" as a level of being in the world, other than God, therefore becomes superfluous and misleading, and a genuine naturalism is thus entirely compatible with theism – for God is the only super-natural entity or being. (Peacocke 2001, 51)

Peacocke calls his own view *theistic naturalism*, which unifies his emergentist monism with a specific view of divine action according to which "natural processes, characterized by the laws and regularities discovered by the natural sciences, are themselves actions of God, who continuously gives them existence" (Peacocke 2007, 17).

Metaphors, Models, and the Doctrine of God

Critical realism, models, and metaphors

For Peacocke the doctrine of God is central, but he distances himself from "the God of the philosophers," that is, the concept of God that is derived from philosophical analysis. For Peacocke (1993, 98), the Christian doctrine of God "is not a philosophical and metaphysical theory; it is, rather, an attempt to understand and to come to terms with a profound religious experience centred on the life, death, resurrection and teaching of Jesus." To communicate this experience, religious discourse uses concepts, models, and images. Peacocke acknowledges that, therefore, theological language is profoundly metaphorical. For example, in the Christian tradition, God is described as Father, Creator, King, Sovereign, Shepherd, and Judge. The relationship of God to the world is depicted sometimes in terms of monarchical models (e.g., King, Sovereign), sometimes in terms of organic models (e.g., creation as an emanation of God's life-giving energy, or as a manifestation of God's Wisdom or Word). Peacocke acknowledges that theological models

> are so deeply embedded in Christian language that it is extremely difficult to frame theories and concepts entirely devoid of metaphor, for even abstract words like "transcendent," "immanent," and "pan-en-theism" partake of spatial metaphors. (Peacocke 1984, 41)

Models and metaphors are also omnipresent in the natural sciences, and Peacocke acknowledges that there are similarities in the use of models and metaphors in both science and theology. For example, both scientific and theological models are analogical and metaphorical and not explicitly descriptive; they are candidates for reality, but not literal pictures, though more than merely useful fictions; they are concerned less with picturing things in themselves than with depicting processes, relations, and structures; and models are formulated and propounded in the context of a community (Peacocke 1984, 41–43). Yet, there are also differences between the roles that models play in the sciences and in theology. In theology, models and associated metaphors are indispensable, especially when it comes to so-called "root-metaphors," like the model of God as the personal source of all being, the transcendent

Creator who is also immanently active in creation. The centrality of root-metaphors in theology, according to Peacocke, is totally unlike the role of models in the natural sciences. Another difference is that "theological models do have a component of evaluation and an evocative ability that is lacking in scientific models" (Peacocke 1984, 44).

But however affective and personal theological models may be, they still purport to be explanatory. Peacocke refers to the work of Janet Martin Soskice, who argues that theological models (like scientific models) are *reality depicting*, which for Peacocke entails that

> Christian believers take their models to depict reality, otherwise they would be affectively and
> personally ineffectual and inoperative. Yet the reality such believers seek to depict is one that the
> creature cannot claim to describe as it is in itself – *ex hypothesi* God as transcendent is beyond all
> explicit depiction whether by language or visual image. (Peacocke 1984, 44)

Accordingly, Peacocke adopts the position of *theological critical realism*, which he regards as "the most appropriate and adequate philosophy concerning religious language and theological propositions" (Peacocke 1993, 14), and wherein

> negative theology and positive theology meet: the former recognizes that, having referred to
> God, whatever we say will be fallible and revisable and *ex hypothesi* inadequate; the latter that to
> say nothing is more misleading than to say something, and that then we have to speak metaphori-
> cally. So we have good grounds for affirming that metaphorical language, the language expound-
> ing the theological models that explicate religious experience, can be referential and can depict
> reality without at the same time being naively and unrevisably descriptive. And this character
> theological models share with scientific models of the natural world. (Peacocke 1984, 45–46)

In other words, when theologians speak about God, they do so hoping "to speak realistically of God through revisable metaphor and model" (Peacocke 1984, 46).

Peacocke (1993, 21) also argues that critical realism is the "bridge" between theology and the sciences:

> [S]ince the aim of a critical-realist theology is to articulate intellectually and to formulate, by
> means of metaphor and model, experiences of God, then it behooves such a theology to take
> seriously the critical-realist perspective of the sciences on the natural, including the human,
> world. For on that theology's own presuppositions, God himself has given the world the kind
> of being it has and it must be in some respects, to be ascertained, revelatory of God's nature and
> purposes. So theology should seek to be at least consonant with scientific perspectives on the
> natural world. Correspondingly, the sciences should not be surprised if their perspectives are
> seen to be partial and incomplete and to raise questions not answerable from within their own
> purview and by their own methods, since there are other realities – there is a Reality – to be
> taken into account which is not discernible by the sciences as such. A critical-realist science and
> theology cannot but regard themselves as mutually interacting approaches to reality.

Natural theology and God

Peacocke's adherence to inference to the best explanation leads him on the path towards a natural theology. He writes (2001, 30):

> I urge that IBE [inference to the best explanation] is the procedure that best leads to public truth
> about the relation of nature, humanity and God which is both communicable and convincing

by its reasonableness through reflection on our most reliable and generally available knowledge of nature and humanity. To most in Western culture such knowledge is preeminently forthcoming from the sciences. Such an approach might even open a path towards God for the many wistful agnostics and the "cultured despisers" of any form of theism.

In other words, the path that Peacocke proposes as one which will lead to a "revised theology" (i.e., "a very radical revision of past notions concerning what Christians can in the future hold as credible, defensible and reasonable" (Peacocke 2001, 33)), is a path from science towards God, and thus of natural theology, though Peacocke is hesitant about using the term "natural theology" for the approach that he is defending. Traditionally, natural theology intended to provide deductive arguments as proofs for the existence and attributes of God from natural phenomena. Peacocke argues that such a natural theology is no longer a valid option. There is no hard proof, but Peacocke holds that one could make a case for God, based on the principle of inference to the best explanation. Because God is the Creator of the universe, nature provides clues, pointers, or analogies as to the nature of God. Science studies the nature and structure of the universe, and theology interprets these as pointers to an Ultimate Reality. Such an approach conforms to Peacocke's methodological aim, that theology should strive for maximum consonance with science, though this obviously resonates with traditional forms of natural theology.

First, there is the claim that the existence of the universe as a whole is not self-explanatory. The question "Why is there anything at all?" is raised but not answered by science. Peacocke argues we have reason to regard the world as contingent, that is, not-necessary. There are reasons to believe the organization of the world could have been different from what it actually is, and for all we know the world might not have come into existence at all. If the world is contingent, then it is dependent on something else, and hence the explanation of its actual existence must be given by something distinct from the universe. According to Peacocke, there must be an "Ultimate Reality" (where the initial capitals denote its uniqueness) that is the ground and source of the world's existence. This Ultimate Reality must be self-existent, that is, "the only reality with the source of its being in itself" (Peacocke 2001, 39). Unlike our universe, this Reality exists necessarily: it is not dependent upon anything outside itself and there is nothing that can explain its coming into existence except itself.

Concerning the internal structure of the universe, Peacocke believes one can make tentative inferences as to the existence and especially the nature of this Ultimate Reality. Our universe is a conglomerate of various entities, structures, and processes. It is a collection of these various elements, and yet we talk about the universe as a unity. The Ultimate Reality, according to Peacocke, is a single Reality, a unity or "Oneness" that is of such a nature that it has the capacity to give rise to all these diversified and complex features. In Peacocke's words (2001, 40), the Ultimate Reality is a "*diversity-in-unity, one Being of unfathomable richness, capable of multiple expression and variegated outreach.*" Furthermore, through science, humans rationally investigate the universe and its features. Through mathematics and the equations of fundamental physics, science unveils an inherent rationality underlying the cosmos, and as the source of this rational cosmos, the Ultimate Reality must therefore possess rationality supremely and unsurpassedly (Peacocke 2001, 41). This maximal rationality, in Peacocke's view, also entails that the Ultimate Reality is omniscient and omnipotent: it knows all that is logically possible to know and is able to do whatever it is logically possible to do. Finally, because of the "anthropic" features of our world (i.e., the precarious conditions of our universe that led to our contingently being here), together with the idea that "the personal is the highest level of unification of the physical, mental and spiritual of which we are aware"

(Peacocke 2001, 42), this Reality can also be said to be personal or supra-personal. Summarizing, Peacocke argues from features of our world to the existence of a transcendent, omnipotent, omniscient, and personal Ultimate Reality. He claims that this Reality is worshipped in the Christian religion under the name of God, who is then furthermore considered the Creator of all-that-is.

A kenotic view of God's power and knowledge

One of the original features in Peacocke's thought that has proven influential in the field of science and religion is his concept of a *kenotic* (i.e., self-limited) God. According to Peacocke, God's power and knowledge can be limited either by self-limitation or for logical reasons. First, God is bound to the laws of logic, which (because God is supremely rational) are internal to God's nature. Violating the laws of logic would entail that God becomes inconsistent with his own nature. God's omniscience and omnipotence thus entail that God is able to do and know what is logically possible to do and know. Logic poses a limit to God's knowledge and power, but because the laws of logic are internal to God's nature, logical limitations are internal limitations.

Peacocke also argues that God's omnipotence and omniscience are also limited with regard to the autonomy of many structures and processes of the world which God has chosen to respect. As the Ultimately Reality and Creator, God cannot be limited involuntarily by anything external to God, thus any limitation of God's powers (other than those of a logical nature) entails self-limitation of God's knowledge and power, so that these limitations are internal to God's own nature.

God's self-limited omnipotence implies "that God has so made the world that there are certain areas over which he has chosen not to have power" (Peacocke 1993, 121f.). Peacocke argues that God chose to let creation be other over-against God-self as a consequence of divine love. Creation has an autonomy which God chose voluntarily not to influence. First, there is human free will. According to Peacocke, humans have free will and thus are free to respond to God's call to co-create the universe in accordance with God's intentions. A second area that God has chosen as a limit on God's power consists of certain physical processes, such as quantum indeterminacy and the unpredictability of nonlinear macroscopic systems (i.e., chaos, self-organizing and emergent processes). The unpredictability in quantum mechanics and nonlinear systems arises because the Heisenberg Uncertainty Principle "sets a limit to the accuracy with which the determining initial conditions *can* be known" (Peacocke 1993, 122). According to Peacocke, it was God's free choice that this limit should pertain to God's power and knowledge; the unpredictability of those systems is thus irreducible even to God and limits the range of God's power in the world.

God's self-limited omniscience entails "that God may also have so made the world that, at any given time, there are certain systems whose future states cannot be known even to him since they are in principle not knowable" (Peacocke 1993, 122). Such systems are again human free choice, quantum indeterminacy, and the unpredictability of nonlinear systems. God can only know what is logically possible to know. Since the future does not yet exist, Peacocke argues that it has no content to be known, so that God logically cannot know the future. Yet, this does not preclude God from knowing the possibilities of the future and the probabilities of each possibility to become actual (Peacocke 1993, 122f.; 2001, 45). If God knows the possibilities of the future evolution of some systems and their probabilities, God might also be able to influence those systems to lure them to evolving in accordance with God's intentions. However, this influencing should not be seen as interventions in the causal nexus of the universe, for Peacocke regards intervention as scientifically and theologically unacceptable. Not only would intervention reduce God to "a kind of semi-magical arbitrary Great Fixer or occasional Meddler in the divinely created, natural and historical networks of causes and effects" (Peacocke 2001, 57), but a view of divine intervention, interpreted as God breaking or suspending the natural order, would make our conception of God logically inconsistent. Since for Peacocke the causal nexus is a "rational" feature of the world that mirrors God's superior rationality, breaking or suspending the created rational order would entail an act against God's own rationality, thus becoming inconsistent with God's own nature.

The Nature of the Cosmos and Panentheism

Chance, necessity, and the emergence of novelty

Because of God's self-limited power and knowledge, God has bestowed autonomy upon creation that results in an ongoing, open-ended process, an interplay of randomness (chance) and natural lawfulness (necessity) that allows for the emergence of novelty that even God cannot foresee. According to Peacocke, chance is a genuine (ontological) feature of the world, for example at the quantum level, but also in the (macroscopic) case of, for example, random mutations in DNA. However, the effects of randomness are constrained by a lawlike framework. The result is a dynamic view of nature as a process involving both chance and necessity. If rigid laws alone governed the universe, all patterns would repeat themselves indefinitely and no genuine novelty would emerge. So, the laws are not rigid, but can be compared to "rules" of a game: they limit the outcome, but not too tightly, for they still leave room for countless possible outcomes. If chance had absolute freedom, there would be no stability for form, pattern, or organization to occur, and no life would be possible. So, because of the limiting capacity of the lawlike framework, the universe is a dynamic stability of form and structure. And the natural sciences show that it is the dynamic interplay between necessity and chance that constitutes our richly patterned, creative, dynamic, and self-organizing cosmos.

Peacocke was one of the first scholars in science and religion to incorporate the results of the sciences of emergent and self-organizing systems in his thinking. These sciences increasingly lead to

> a picture of the world as consisting of complex hierarchies – a series of levels of organization of matter in which each successive member of the whole series is a whole constituted of parts preceding it in the series. The wholes are organized systems of parts that are dynamically and spatially interrelated. (Peacocke 2001, 48)

In other words, Peacocke regards the basic structure of the universe as a hierarchy of complex, emergent systems, that is, systems which are built from the same fundamental building blocks, yet which as a whole exhibit features that emerge from the causal interactions between constituents but that are not explanatorily reducible to the properties of those building blocks themselves. For example, the "wetness" of water is an emergent feature, which does not pertain to the individual H_2O molecules that are the building blocks of water.

Because of the emergent nature of the different levels, the concepts employed to describe systems on each level in the ontological hierarchy of complexity are applicable to those levels only. The concept of "wetness" is such a higher-level concept, which does not pertain to the lower level of the atomic building blocks. According to Peacocke, this ontological distinction between higher-level and lower-level concepts warrants a non-reductionism about theories: on higher levels concepts are introduced that are inapplicable to lower-level systems and pertain to features that are only present at those higher levels. In other words, Peacocke adheres explicitly to conceptual and explanatory non-reductionism (though in his writing he has expressed his acceptance of methodological reductionism that has proven its worth in science). Peacocke concludes that with increasing complexity emerges novelty in the sense that higher levels of complexity display new features not present at lower levels.

Perhaps the most controversial feature of Peacocke's thought is connected to this idea of higher levels having a causal influence on lower levels, or, as Peacocke calls it, "downward" or "top-down" causation. In his view the lower levels give rise to emergent features at higher levels of complexity. But higher-level systems also exert causal and/or constraining influence upon the sub-systems and building blocks from which they emerge. In complex systems there is thus a "whole–part influence" (Peacocke 2001, 52; in Peacocke 1993, Peacocke prefers the term "top-down causation," while in other works he used the term "whole–part constraint"). An example of how this works is the operation of human DNA, which has the potential to create an entire human body, that is, all the organs and tissues that make up the complex structure of human bodies. Yet, during the process of growth, DNA is merely a building block with many possibilities. Given an arbitrary DNA molecule, it is not predetermined what organ or tissue it will help develop. It is the larger "system" in which the molecule is embedded that co-determines what will eventually come out of it. So the context together with the DNA molecule "collapses" all the possibilities into one actual organ, and as such the DNA gives form to (thus "in-forms") the human body. There is thus, in the case of the growth of a human organism, a whole–part influence, where building blocks and the larger context together determine the outcome.

The world-as-a-whole: a "System-of-systems"

Peacocke brings the different ideas about chance, necessity, and complexity together in a metaphysical proposal to see the world not as a conglomerate of individual systems, but as an interconnected and interdependent System-of-systems (cf. Peacocke 2001, 55). Peacocke thus proposes to see the universe-as-a-whole as an object with an autonomy and integrity in its own right. Such a world, as an interlocking system of complex systems, is, according to Peacocke, a lawlike and causally closed world in which God does not intervene.

The universe as a System-of-systems is also described by Peacocke as a cosmic hierarchy of systems or levels, where systems on each level are more complex than those on the previous level, such as: atom, molecule, macromolecule, sub-cellular organelle, cell, multi-cellular functioning organ, whole living organism, populations of organisms, and ecosystems (Peacocke 1979, 113). This hierarchy of complexity is a series of systems that become more and more encompassing, from the lowest level (the atom) to the most encompassing system (the universe-as-a-whole). Each level is a whole that needs to be dealt with theoretically on its own particular level, and corresponds, in Peacocke's view, to the different sciences. In other words, the cosmic hierarchy of systems corresponds with a hierarchy of sciences. Each science, dealing with a specific system or level, uses its own irreducible concepts and theories to describe and explain the characteristics of systems at that specific level. Peacocke distinguishes roughly between four levels of sciences: (1) the level of the physical world (the physical sciences); (2) living organisms (the biological sciences); (3) the behavior of living organisms (the behavioral sciences); and (4) human culture (the humanities, including theology) (Peacocke 1993, 214–244). It is, however, important to stress that Peacocke's ideas of a cosmic hierarchy are not to be interpreted as a hierarchy of priority, as if higher, more complex levels are more important than the lower levels. For Peacocke, each level is a whole that needs to be dealt with conceptually and theoretically on its own particular level. There is not a single branch of science to be prioritized over others.

God's relation to the System-of-systems: panentheism and divine action

Although Peacocke is not too enthusiastic about process thought, he accepts panentheism as the view that is the most adequate to philosophically articulate what is the essence of the Christian doctrine of God. Peacocke summarizes his panentheistic view as follows:

> Panentheism is the belief that the *Being of God includes and penetrates all-that-is*, so that every part of it exists in God and (as against pantheism) that *God's being is more than it and is not exhausted by it*. In contrast to classical philosophical theism, with its reliance on the concept of necessary substance, panentheism takes embodied personhood for its model of God and so places much greater stress on the immanence of God in, with and under the events of the world. . . . The total network of regular, natural events, in this perspective, is viewed as in itself the creative and sustaining *action* of God. . . . *God is the immanent creator creating in and through the processes of the natural order*. This points us in the direction of postulating that the ontological gap(s) between the world and God is/are located simply everywhere – or, more precisely, because the world is "in God," God can influence the world in its totality, as a System-of-systems. (Peacocke 2001, 57f.)

In Peacocke's panentheist model, God is both transcendent to creation (as the ontological "Other") as well as immanently present in it. Because of God's immanent omnipresence, God is able to know and do all that is logically possible to do and know, within the limits that Godself has set. Peacocke is eager to point to the fact that his panentheism does not require the idea that the world is "God's body." There is an ontological difference between the world as created and God as Creator, and Peacocke argues that this distinction becomes blurred in the notion of the world as God's body. Instead, Peacocke argues that the infinite God made space for the world to come into existence "in" God, be it also as ontologically distinct from God. Peacocke (2001, 142) also uses the image of the world being inside the "womb of God." All-that-is is in God, but God is also "more than" the universe.

Peacocke's panentheist view of God's relationship to the world is developed through the analogy of human personhood, where he takes the human person as a psychosomatic unity of which the mental and the physical are two modalities. Human persons can have intentions, which they can realize by performing particular bodily actions. Peacocke sees human action as a paradigm case of whole–part influence: persons exert causal influence on their bodies and their surroundings, but at the same time these influence persons as well. There is thus a kind of feedback loop between persons, their bodies, and their surroundings. Analogously, God transcends the universe, but is at the same time "internally present to all of the world's entities, structures and processes in a way analogous to the way we as persons are present and act in our bodies" (Peacocke 2001, 140).

According to Peacocke's panentheist view, the workings of the natural world can all be regarded as divine actions. This does not mean that the network of natural events is identical with God; Peacocke is no pantheist. It does mean that, because God is immanently present in creation, God is creating in and through the processes of the natural order. God "unfolds the created potentialities of the universe through a process in which its possibilities and propensities become actualized" (Peacocke 2001, 136). It is through chance that God explores the many possibilities inherent in creation; chance thus functions for God as a "search radar" (Peacocke 1979, 95). Peacocke often refers to the analogy of a (jazz) musician who improvises within the constraints of a certain chord schema to describe God's use of chance within the constraints set by natural law.

But within this framework of general providence, God also implements his particular intentions which are responses to free decisions and actions performed by creation itself. This is done, according to Peacocke, through downward causation or whole–part influence. God acts on the world-as-a-whole, while the effects of God's actions are both general and particular: they affect the universe-as-a-whole and also instantiate particular patterns of events which express God's intentions. Peacocke often describes God's influence on the universe in terms of action through "information flow."

But God does not govern everything. The world has a certain autonomy, which God respects. This entails for Peacocke that God has taken a risk in creating the universe. In giving up total control in the act of creation, this act itself involves an element of risk "whereby God renders Godself vulnerable in a way that only now we are able to perceive" (Peacocke 2001, 89). And because of God's personhood, Peacocke holds that God suffers in and with the suffering of creation.

Humanity and Christ

Because God can influence patterns of events in the world through top-down information flow, Peacocke believes God can communicate with humans, for "it must be possible for God to influence those patterns of events in human brains which constitute human thoughts, including thoughts of God and a sense of personal interaction with God" (Peacocke 2001, 123f.). Religious experiences and divine revelations are always mediated, according to Peacocke. As for the future of humanity, this is where Christ comes into the picture. For Peacocke (2007, 36f.), "the capacities of human nature are transformed by the causal efficacy of the divine presence upon it, such that the risen Jesus becomes the paradigm or paragon of what God intends human beings to be and to become." Christ is encountered as "a new emergent, a new reality" within created humanity (37). In Christ there is continuity with the rest of humanity and so with the rest of nature within which *homo sapiens* evolved, but there is also a discontinuity "constituted by what is distinctive in this relation to God and in what, through him (his teaching, life, death, and resurrection), the early witnesses experienced of God" (2007, 37). This continuity and discontinuity is characteristic of emergent phenomena, so that Peacocke (2007, 37) concludes: "In Jesus the Christ a new reality has emerged and a new *ontology* is inaugurated." Consequently:

> Jesus the Christ may therefore be seen as a specific, indeed for Christians a unique, focal point at which the diverse meanings written into the many levels of creation coalesce, like rays of light, with an intensity that so illuminates the purposes of God for us that we are better able to inter-

pret God's meanings communicated in his creative activity over a wider range of human experience of nature and history. (Peacocke 2007, 40)

References

Peacocke, Arthur. 1979. *Creation and the World of Science: The Bampton Lectures 1978.* Oxford: Clarendon Press.

Peacocke, Arthur. 1984. *Intimations of Reality: Critical Realism in Science and Religion.* Notre Dame, IN: University of Notre Dame Press.

Peacocke, Arthur. 1993. *Theology for a Scientific Age: Being and Becoming – Natural, Divine and Human,* enlarged edn. London: SCM Press.

Peacocke, Arthur. 2001. *Paths from Science towards God: The End of All Our Exploring.* Oxford: Oneworld.

Peacocke, Arthur. 2007. *All That Is: A Naturalistic Faith for the Twenty-First Century.* Philip Clayton, ed. Minneapolis, MN: Fortress Press.

Further Reading

Clayton, Philip and Peacocke, Arthur, eds. 2004. *In Whom We Live and Move and Have Our Being: Panentheistic Reflections on God's Presence in a Scientific World.* Grand Rapids, MI: Eerdmans. An influential volume with many different perspectives on panentheism, showing how deeply this view of God has influenced work in science and religion.

Peacocke, Arthur. 1993. *Theology for a Scientific Age: Being and Becoming – Natural, Divine and Human,* enlarged edn. London: SCM Press. The seminal text for understanding Peacocke's important contribution to the discipline of science and religion.

Peacocke, Arthur. 2007. *All That Is: A Naturalistic Faith for the Twenty-First Century.* Philip Clayton, ed. Minneapolis, MN: Fortress Press. Contains the last essay by Peacocke as well as his "Nunc Dimittis," and a host of responses to Peacocke's work by science and religion scholars showing the impact of Peacocke's work on the field.

Polkinghorne, John. 1996. *Scientists as Theologians: A Comparison of the Writings of Ian Barbour, Arthur Peacocke and John Polkinghorne.* London: SPCK. Polkinghorne summarizes the similarities and differences between his view and the ideas of his fellow scientist-theologians Peacocke and Barbour.

Saunders, Nicholas. 2002. *Divine Action and Modern Science.* Cambridge: Cambridge University Press. A critical philosophical and scientific analysis of models of divine action, describing Peacocke's view on downward causation, which Saunders thinks is "the most promising current theory of SDA [special divine action]" (213).

Smedes, Taede. 2004. *Chaos, Complexity, and God: Divine Action and Scientism.* Leuven: Peeters. A comparison and critical assessment of Polkinghorne's and Peacocke's thought, focused on their ideas concerning divine action, chaos theory, and complexity.

52

Ian G. Barbour

NATHAN J. HALLANGER

Ian Graeme Barbour is widely regarded as catalyzing a resurgence in scholarly work focused on the constructive engagement between science and religion. Beginning with his contributions in the 1960s, Barbour has been a key conversation partner in developing a framework for analyzing, understanding, and critiquing interactions of various types between science and religion, in both academic and cultural contexts. His description of critical realism has been influential in providing a means of bringing science and religion into dialogue. His fourfold typology is used in courses in colleges, universities, and seminaries the world over. His embrace of process theology serves as a model for a theology of nature. For these reasons and his myriad other contributions to the field, Barbour is considered by many to be the father of the contemporary dialogue between science and religion. Given his role as a key figure in the dialogue, this chapter will outline briefly his life and academic background before examining some of Barbour's key contributions and approaches to specific issues in science and religion, and conclude with some reflections on Barbour's legacy.

Life

Ian Graeme Barbour was born in China in 1923, his parents having both taken teaching posts at Yenching University, his mother in religious education, his father in geology. Barbour has described his family's relationship with Pierre Teilhard de Chardin, who was in China on paleontological expeditions during Barbour's youth (Barbour 2004, 17). After several family moves to the United States and the United Kingdom during his youth, he enrolled at Swarthmore College and majored in physics. He was influenced by working with Quakers one summer to register as a conscientious objector during World War Two, and he spent three years on civil service projects during the war. He then pursued a graduate degree in physics, receiving his master's degree from Duke University. He subsequently earned his PhD from the University of Chicago, where he studied cosmic-ray physics and worked with Enrico

The Blackwell Companion to Science and Christianity, First Edition. Edited by J. B. Stump and Alan G. Padgett.
© 2012 Blackwell Publishing Ltd. Published 2012 by Blackwell Publishing Ltd.

Fermi and Edward Teller. As Barbour notes, Teller was recruiting students in the post-war years to work on the hydrogen bomb, but Barbour "wanted to teach in a liberal arts college" (Barbour 2004, 18). Given his preference for college teaching, Barbour was hired to teach physics at Kalamazoo College in Michigan beginning in 1949.

A Ford Foundation fellowship to study theology and ethics in 1953 served as a turning point for Barbour. He took courses at Yale Divinity School, ultimately extending his fellowship for a second year, which allowed him to complete a degree in divinity. The fascination he felt in studying at Yale meant that Barbour, sensitive to his own vocational journey,

> then faced a difficult decision. I believed that vocational choice should reflect a person's abilities, interests and (in a religious context) response to God and human needs. I enjoyed physics and was familiar enough with it that I could teach and still have time for other activities. Moreover I knew that scientists are respected in the academic world, and their voices carry some weight on educational, ethical and religious issues. In addition, I shared the Reformation's conviction that any useful vocation can serve God and human need. But I increasingly felt that it would be more interesting and more significant to spend at least part of my time learning and teaching in religious studies. (Barbour 2004, 19)

The opportunity to combine physics and religious studies presented itself at Carleton College, where Barbour was offered a teaching position in both physics and philosophy. A religion department was formed at Carleton in 1960, and Barbour served as its chair. In 1963 he spent a study year at Harvard University, where a seminar with Gordon Kaufman introduced him to the process philosophy of Alfred North Whitehead and some of Whitehead's interpreters, including Charles Hartshorne, John Cobb, and David Ray Griffin.

Barbour published *Issues in Science and Religion* in 1966, which marked the beginning of a new chapter in the history of religion and science. Barbour's carefully researched and reasoned approach influenced a generation of scholars to take up questions related to science and religion as their primary vocation, and in fact created the very possibility that such a choice could be made (not without difficulty, to be sure). Along with Arthur Peacocke and John Polkinghorne, Barbour was now at the leading edge of a new academic field focused on interdisciplinary engagement between the natural sciences and religion.

Barbour's work in science and religion continued into the 1970s, with the publication of *Myths, Models, and Paradigms* in 1974. Earlier work with colleagues on questions related to developing environmental concerns led to *Earth Might Be Fair: Reflections on Ethics, Religion, and Ecology* (1973). Ongoing concerns "about ethical issues in the application of science" led Barbour to work on an NSF- and NEH-funded project focused on science, technology, and public policy (Barbour 2004, 20). The volume *Technology, Environment, and Human Values* (1980) emerged from this work.

Barbour was named the first Winifred and Atherton Bean Professor of Science, Technology, and Society at Carleton College in 1981, a post he held until his retirement in 1986. Barbour was invited to deliver the prestigious Gifford lectures in 1989/1990, the content of which was published in two books, *Religion in an Age of Science* (1990) and *Ethics in an Age of Technology* (1993).

Barbour's work in the field was recognized in 1999 when he received the Templeton Prize for Progress in Religion. He donated a signification portion of the monetary award that comes with the Templeton Prize to the Center for Theology and the Natural Sciences (CTNS) in Berkeley, California, to support its work fostering constructive engagement between science and religion.

In 2000, Barbour published a brief, accessible volume titled *When Science Meets Religion: Enemies, Strangers, or Partners?* which he structured using the fourfold typology he had developed in his earlier *Religion in an Age of Science*. He continued his research and writing, publishing a volume that explored evolution, human nature, and the environment, *Nature, Human Nature, and God* (2002). On the occasion of his eightieth birthday Barbour was honored with a volume dedicated to engaging his thought, *Fifty Years in Science and Religion: Ian G. Barbour and His Legacy* (Russell 2004).

Barbour has continued to write and publish, engaging in dialogue and debate about aspects of his own work, methodology in science and religion, and specific topics in the science and religion dialogue.

Key Contributions

With a career spanning more than six decades, Barbour has witnessed, participated in, and contributed to the intellectual development of science and religion. Barbour is considered by many the founder of the contemporary dialogue between science and religion. Much of Barbour's work focuses on methodology, or how it is that one goes about relating science and religion, and that will be the primary focus in what follows. But Barbour also has been concerned with specific aspects of engagement, from physics to neuroscience to evolutionary biology. Barbour is unique in that his contributions have been influential among different groups working in distinct contexts, with research scholars, teachers, students, religious leaders, scientists, theologians, and the wider public. In assessing the various contributions Barbour has made, one can see the levels of engagement he has fostered across these various publics or audiences of his work.

What follows are brief explorations of three of Barbour's distinctive contributions, two in methodology and one in theological reflection. First, I will review his critical insight about methodology in the 1960s, focused on critical realism. Then, I look at Barbour's fourfold typology, the most developed version of which appears in the 1990s. Finally, I explore his model for a theology of nature as a method for theology itself.

Beyond Instrumentalism and Classical Realism: Critical Realism

Already in *Issues in Science and Religion*, Barbour had begun developing a model for understanding method in the sciences. Barbour faced a challenge related to the sources and methods for obtaining knowledge, a challenge that one could argue continues to the present. Fundamentally, Barbour believed that the challenge to religion was one of epistemology: "For many people today the challenge to religious belief arises not from any conflict of content between science and religion but from the assumption that the scientific method is the only road to knowledge" (Barbour 1966, 137). What was needed, then, was an understanding of knowledge that accurately captured and accounted for the success of the scientific method yet accounted for its limits. Against the backdrop of developments in early twentieth-century philosophy of science, which was evolving from empiricist, positivist understandings of science – which emphasized observation and data – to an understanding of science that included cultural, societal, and other factors as having an effect on the way the sciences operate, Barbour set out to identify a middle course that could both accurately capture how scientists operated and provide for a nuanced understanding of the limits of scientific knowledge.

Barbour analyzes four options for how theories are understood in science: (1) as "summaries of data"; (2) as "useful tools"; (3) as "mental structures"; and (4) as "representations of the world" (Barbour 1966, 162–171). In terms of philosophy of science these options are associated with positivism, instrumentalism, idealism, and realism respectively. Barbour describes realism's key differences from the other three as follows:

> Against the positivist, the realist asserts that the real is not the observable. Against the instrumentalist, he affirms that valid concepts are true as well as useful. Against the idealist, he maintains that concepts represent the structure of events in the world. The patterns in the data are not imposed by us, but originate at least in part in *objective relationships in nature*. (Barbour 1966, 168)

Realist interpretations of scientific theories are how scientists normally view their work, Barbour argues, yet one cannot overlook "the role of man's mind in the creation of theories" (Barbour 1966, 172). In other words, "naïve realism" that asserts that scientific concepts can be "thought of as exact and complete replicas of nature as it is in itself," is not an accurate description of the scientific process (Barbour 1966, 172).

Navigating primarily between classical or naive realism on the one hand and instrumentalism on the other, Barbour develops a middle path he labels "critical realism." Instead of viewing theories as literal, photographic representations of reality or as useful constructs used to control and predict, critical realism "sees theories as limited accounts of aspects of the world as it interacts with us" (Barbour 2004, 23). On this account, scientific theories are expressed in models and metaphors, requiring human imagination and cognition, that describe aspects of the natural world. These models "are to be taken seriously but not literally," for they "make tentative ontological claims that there are entities in the world something like those postulated in the models" (Barbour 1990, 43). Through critical realism Barbour is attempting to hold together the scientist's commitment to a correspondence between theory and an objective reality with a recognition that science also requires interpretation. "There is no simple access to the world as it exists in itself independently of being known, and mental constructs influence the interpretation of all experience," Barbour writes (Barbour 1966, 172). Critical realism serves to bridge the gap between a purely interpretive and purely objective understanding of reality.

If theories are limited accounts of a single reality, then a question arises as to the criteria by which one adjudicates competing theories. If all theories capture "partial, revisable, abstract but referential knowledge of the world," then how might one go about assessing a particular theory? (Russell 2004, 46).

Barbour provides four criteria for assessing theories in science. First, and most importantly, a theory can be judged on its agreement with data. Barbour believes in a correspondence theory of truth, where what is true is what most closely describes an objective reality separate from the thinking subject. Thus, that which is true must correspond with that reality. Yet agreement with data does not provide unassailable proof that a theory is true. Rather, this criterion is a strong indicator of a theory's explanatory potential. Interestingly, Barbour notes that the converse is also the case, that *lack* of agreement with the data does not prove a theory definitively false, for "*ad hoc* modifications or unexplained anomalies can be tolerated for an indefinite period" (Barbour 1990, 34–35).

Second, one can assess a theory based on the criterion of coherence. There are two levels of coherence one can explore in this context. One level explores the degree to which a theory is consistent with other theories. If reality is a single reality, then those theories that purport to provide referential knowledge of the world should cohere with one another. Another level involves the internal coherence of a theory, having to do with how well the component parts of a theory fit together. Here one might speak of a theory's simplicity, elegance, and so forth (Barbour 1990, 34).

Third, a theory can be judged according to its scope. Better theories are more adept at incorporating a wide range of knowledge in a comprehensive fashion. A theory would be valued if its scope "unifies previously disparate domains, if it is supported by a variety of kinds of evidence, or if it is applicable to wide ranges of the relevant variables" (Barbour 1990, 34).

Finally, fertility can serve as a criterion in assessing a theory. For Barbour the key question to ask in this context is, "Is the theory fruitful in encouraging further theoretical elaboration, in generating new hypotheses, and in suggesting new experiments?" Those theories that exhibit fertility have both explanatory power for past observation but also predictive power in generating future research programs.

Behind the criteria lies Barbour's attempt to incorporate various theories of truth. It was noted above that Barbour espouses a correspondence theory of truth, which aligns with his inclusion of the first criterion focused on agreement with data. By combining this emphasis on correspondence with additional criteria, Barbour ties together three theories of truth: correspondence, coherence, and pragmatic. By supplementing the primary criterion of agreement with data with additional criteria, Barbour accounts for additional theories of truth in assessing a theory's applicability.

Given a critical realist understanding of scientific theories, including criteria by which such theories should be assessed, Barbour provides a means by which to engage in work that "bridges" science and religion (Russell 2004). Barbour carefully describes the manner in which theory construction in religion is analogous to theory construction in science. By so doing, he is making an argument about the cognitive status of religious claims, just as his description of critical realism in science argues for a particular way of viewing the nature of scientific theories. Religious claims are not simply descriptions of a reality to which one has little access; such claims have cognitive content and are based on a set of data, such as revelation, religious experience, and tradition.[1]

Yet he is careful to point out where there are differences between method in science and in religion. "Science," writes Barbour, "is clearly more objective than religion. . . . The kinds of data from which religion draws are radically different from those in science, and the possibility of testing religious beliefs is much more limited" (Barbour 2000, 26–27). Moreover, religion strives to function as a "way of life" rather than simply a thought pattern or system (27).

Barbour's Typology: Four Ways of Relating Science and Religion

If critical realism is a critical contribution to methodology, Barbour's framework for understanding various approaches to relating science and religion serves as a key insight for education and understanding various thinkers and options. Developed over his decades of research and writing, Barbour describes his fourfold typology in full form in *Religion in an Age of Science*: conflict, independence, dialogue, and integration (Barbour 1990, chapter 1).

Barbour begins by describing conflict as a way of relating science and religion. Either science or religion can be victorious and true, but not both. Further, conflict assumes that victory for one spells defeat for the other. And so it goes with conflict between science and religion. A contemporary example of conflict could include the so-called "new atheists," who argue that religion is not merely a harmless fantasy but a destructive delusion that should be abandoned for the good of society. Richard Dawkins, Christopher Hitchens, and Sam Harris would be included in Barbour's description of scientific materialism as an example of conflict between religion and science. Scientific materialism makes two assertions, one about epistemology and one about metaphysics. First, science and the scientific method provide the only reliable way to knowledge, to the exclusion of other ways of knowing, and second, "matter is the fundamental reality in the universe" (Barbour 1990, 4). Scientific materialism is often accompanied by reductionism, either by reducing all scientific explanations to the most fundamental theories in chemistry and physics (epistemological), or by asserting that explanation of a system's component parts is the most fundamental reality (metaphysical) (Barbour 1990, 4).

Within the category of conflict, Barbour also includes biblical literalism. Barbour's rationale is that biblical literalism shares with scientific materialism the belief that one must choose between science and religion, and that both "seek knowledge with a sure foundation." Both biblical literalism and scientific materialism make the mistake of "[failing] to observe the proper boundaries of science" (Barbour 1990, 4).

Conflict between science and religion is not an ideal situation for scientific, theological, and philosophical reasons. Moving beyond conflict, Barbour identifies three possible ways of relating science and religion.

If one wants to minimize conflict between science and religion, then independence is one option. Religion and science can be viewed as separate ways of knowing and explaining the world, and what matters is a discipline's ability to defend its theories according to the norms and context of that discipline. In other words, there are different methods employed by science and by religion. Moreover, religion and science speak different languages – science speaks of fact, religion speaks of value; science describes how, religion describes why; and so on. The late biologist Stephen Jay Gould labeled this independence "non-overlapping magisteria" to denote this separation of powers between science and religion (Gould 1999, 5). With different methods, domains of exploration, and language, science and religion cannot be in conflict, for they operate in separate spheres. Moving beyond conflict to independence has positive and negative impacts: "If science and religion were totally independent, the possibility of conflict would be avoided, but the possibility of constructive dialogue and mutual enrichment would also be ruled out" (Barbour 1990, 16).

Clearly, Barbour aims to move beyond conflict and independence to greater interaction. Dialogue provides one model for making that move. Why the necessity for moving beyond conflict and independence? For Barbour, there are a number of arguments. First, human experience does not divide itself into discrete experiences that align with disciplinary boundaries; instead, humanity experiences reality as a whole. Second, for Christians, God is the creator of all that is, and if God is the source of the whole of the cosmos, then Christians should seek explanations that do not separate religious faith from the natural world. Finally, the need for a response to the environmental crisis demands a strong theology of nature, grounded in biblical faith commitments and engaged with scientific knowledge of the world.

Given those demands, dialogue between science and religion is a much-needed contribution to scholarly discourse. The potential for dialogue lies in limit or boundary questions and in the recognition of parallels between method in science and religion. Limit questions are those raised by science but that cannot be answered by science alone. The early origins of the universe are one context where limit questions arise, particularly as one gets closer to $t = 0$, the origin of time at the big bang, and to speculations about what might have preceded $t = 0$. The orderliness and intelligibility of the universe lead to questions about the nature of nature, and the source of order and intelligibility. Science cannot answer these questions on the basis of science alone, so dialogue with religion is necessary. Additionally, a greater understanding of cultural, societal, and individual factors in the scientific method, combined with a recognition that religion has content that goes beyond the merely subjective, has led to recognition of parallels between scientific and theological method. Though religion does have an added aspect of personal commitment and involvement, religion and science both assess theories in their domains using similar criteria, including scope, coherence, and fruitfulness. Finally, scientific concepts can serve as models for theological reflection, leading to new insights within theology (Barbour 2000, 2–3). Dialogue in any case requires a respectful approach to disciplines – and individuals – in religion and in science.

Integration is one additional option for thinking about relating science and religion. Unlike dialogue, which "starts from general characteristics of science or of nature" (Barbour 1997, 90), integration focuses on "the relationships between theological doctrines and particular scientific theories" (98). Natural theology and a theology of nature are examples of the integration between science and religion. Whereas natural theology looks to design in nature as supportive of God's existence, a theology of nature develops theories and doctrines that are heavily informed by theories in science. A systematic synthesis of science and religion such as process theology is one version of a natural theology. More will be said about a theology of nature and process thought in the next section below.

Barbour's fourfold typology has been critiqued and expanded upon by a wide range of authors. Ted Peters expands upon Barbour's typology in describing eight ways in which science and religion interact. One of Peters's concerns is that by including scientific creationists within "conflict," one fails to see the complexity of creationists' relationship to science. Rather than viewing science as conflicting with religion, Peters (1996) argues, young-earth creationists reject "scientism" rather than science itself. To such individuals, science and religion do not conflict; only scientism and religion do.

Christian Berg has questioned the usefulness of Barbour's fourfold typology, and proposed as an alternative three dimensions to describe aspects of the relationship between science and religion: epistemology, metaphysics, and ethics (Berg 2004, 69). Among other arguments in favor of dimensions, Berg believes that these three are "more observer-independent than relational categories" such as those Barbour employs (Berg 2004, 71).

Barbour has noted, too, that his typology has been criticized as "too simple and too static to illuminate the complex and changing historical interactions of science and religion" (Barbour 2004, 24–25). He has responded that the typology is useful in identifying common patterns and themes, recognizing that attention needs to be paid to distinguishing features of each position or individual's thought by "continual return to empirical data" (Barbour 2004, 25).

A Theology of Nature and Process Thought

Since his early writings, Barbour has described his project as a "theology of nature" to capture the set of methodological and theological commitments he is making in bridging science and religion. By way of comparison and in contrast to Barbour, one approach included in integration between science and religion is "natural theology." Natural theology has a long history in Christian theology as a means of discerning evidence or proof of God's existence or presence in the world by examining the natural world. Among the better-known examples of natural theology is William Paley, the nineteenth-century theologian. Paley described God's relationship to nature using the analogy of the watch and a watchmaker. Just as the intricate construction of a watch's mechanism leads one to postulate the work of a skilled watchmaker, the intricate and complex structures of the natural world lead one to postulate a skillful creator God. Evidence of complexity or apparent design lends proof to the existence of the creator.

Unlike Paley, Barbour argues for a theology of nature. His approach begins with a commitment to the theology of a worshipping community, based on the historical revelation of God. But it incorporates the natural order, emphasizing "the continuity between nature and grace, between impersonal and personal realms, and between language about nature and language about God" (Barbour 1966, 454). The Bible affirms God as the source of all creation, and the world described by science is the same world of God's active presence. Therefore, theological and doctrinal assertions should be informed by scientific descriptions of the natural world as God's creation.

Such an approach may result in revisions to classical religious commitments. In a theology of nature, "some traditional doctrines," according to Barbour, "need to be reformulated in the light of current science" (Barbour 1997, 100). The doctrines of creation, providence, and human nature are prime candidates for such reformulation, for science has provided significant insights into all three areas.

For Barbour a theology of nature has implications for how one engages science and religion, for if there is in fact one world whose origin lies in God, then one should not be content to keep science and religion separate. Additionally, if religion is to affirm God's active presence in the world, then an understanding of the processes and mechanisms of the natural world is essential for understanding divine action. Barbour summarizes his commitment to a theology of nature informed by process philosophy as follows:

> I am in basic agreement with the "Theology of Nature" position, coupled with a cautious use of process philosophy. Too much reliance on science in natural theology can lead to the neglect of the areas of experience that I consider most important religiously. As I see it, the center of the Christian life is an experience of reorientation, the healing of our brokenness in the new wholeness, and the expression of a new relationship to God and to the neighbor . . . the centrality of redemption need not lead us to belittle creation, for our personal and social lives are intimately bound to the rest of the created order. We are redeemed in and with the world, not from the world. Part of our task, then, is to articulate a theology of nature, for which we will have to draw from both religious and scientific sources. (Barbour 1997, 195)

From early in his career, the process philosophy of Alfred North Whitehead and theologians influenced by him have influenced Barbour's theology, a fact he identifies as the most controversial aspect of his work (Barbour 2004, 25). Process thought provides a philosophical bridge for thinking about wholeness and dynamism in creation, while opening up the possibilities for freedom and novelty to arise from natural, regularized processes. Two examples of Barbour's engagement with process philosophy will serve as models for how he integrates science and religion.

Among its advantages, Barbour sees process philosophy as supporting an ecological view of the natural world, in that it holds that entities are relational and experiential. In the process view, "All creatures have value to God and to each other, and all have intrinsic value as centers of experience" (Barbour 2002, 131). Here Barbour points to panexperientialism in process philosophy, the notion that one can attribute experience even to lower-level entities. Distinctions need to be made between the kinds of experience possible among lower-level entities, as opposed to higher-level experience such as consciousness, yet Barbour argues that every entity has an interior experience. What this means for environmental ethics is that one should exhibit concern for all forms of life, but that one should prioritize life that is capable of higher-order experience (Barbour 2002, 131). In addition to its attribution of experience, process theology emphasizes God's immanence. God is present in the evolution of each new event yet transcends nature itself. This suggests an attitude toward nature that is neither worship nor exploitation, Barbour argues, but instead focuses on respect and appreciation of nature as "the scene of God's continuing activity" (Barbour 2002, 132).

In addition to its support of care for creation, process theology for Barbour provides insights into understanding God's power in relation to creation. Classical Christian commitments to omnipotence typically view God's power as a combination of (potential) coercive power with love. Rather than coercive power, Barbour interprets process theology as placing an emphasis on empowerment. Moreover, while one approach to understanding God's power in relationship to freedom is to argue that God self-limits God's power to allow for human freedom and novelty, Barbour endorses process arguments that there are metaphysical limitations to God's power. The future is open and unknowable even to God, given human freedom and God's experience of the temporal aspect of reality. To Barbour this is preferable to seeing God's power as a self-limitation, which suggests that God could choose to overcome that self-limitation if God so chose (which would simply raise the theodicy question once again).

In assessing the feasibility of applying these and other process concepts to theology, Barbour returns to the four criteria identified for evaluating scientific theories: agreement with data, coherence, scope, and fertility. Barbour recognizes that agreement with data for religion includes engaging the biblical record and the experience of a religious community, and believes that process theology does fit with these religious data. Process theology is coherent with the core of Christian faith, God's love revealed in Christ, as well as an internally coherent system that integrates many facets of experience. In terms of scope, process attempts to bring together "diverse types of experience – scientific, religious, moral, and aesthetic" (Barbour 1990, 266). Finally, Barbour believes that process theology has the potential to foster new thinking, ethical action, and personal transformation. After a review of these criteria, Barbour concludes, "I believe that by these four criteria the reformulations of classical tradition proposed in process theology are indeed justified" (Barbour 1990, 267).

Barbour describes integration as a way of relating science and religion, focuses on a theology of nature as one way of integrating the two disciplines, and evaluates the viability of process theology to accomplish such integration, weighing the strengths and weaknesses of process thought at each stage. Barbour thus demonstrates the manner in which one might go about engaging science and religion constructively, even if one ultimately rejects process theology as the proper means of integration. He also shows how to apply the criteria for assessing theories in a theological context, recognizing the distinctive features and aspects of theological method.

Conclusion

Ian G. Barbour has contributed much to those interested in exploring the intersections between science and religion. Those reflecting on the intellectual history of the era encompassing the last half of the twentieth century would be wise to pay attention to Barbour's contributions, for he provides a set of philosophical tools and frameworks that catalyzed further work in bringing disciplines into creative interaction. Critical realism serves as a bridge between science and religion by ensuring clear understandings of epistemology in science and in religion. Barbour's fourfold typology for ways of relating science and religion provides an accessible framework for learning about various positions, and his efforts at developing a theology of nature informed by process philosophy suggest one logical path for faith in an age of science. These aspects of Barbour's work have had wide-ranging impact.

Constructive engagement between science and religion is more widespread in Christian theology now than it was in the 1960s. Barbour and those whom he has influenced have provided ways of engaging science and religion in dialogue and perhaps integration. Yet there are areas still unexplored. Barbour himself points to one future direction for development: "The future dialogue must be interreligious as well as interdisciplinary" (Barbour 2004, 21). Barbour and those who have built on his work naturally focused at first on Christian religion and science, though a number of efforts have been undertaken to broaden the scope to include wider representation from the world's religions in dialogue. Engagement with science may serve as a common ground for inter-religious engagement.[2]

Whatever the future direction of engagement between science and religion, Barbour has left a significant legacy. The work in the field to date has accomplished much, and ongoing work must engage in the body of work that has originated with Barbour's insights. As Barbour himself would expect, such work should not be done uncritically, but by evaluating any proposal according to agreement with data, coherence, scope, and fertility. The enduring test will be whether or not the bridge between science and religion built by Barbour and those he has influenced can bear the weight of future traffic.

Notes

1   Robert John Russell has extended this thinking in describing "creative mutual interaction" between science and theology. See Russell (2008).
2   Barbour here cites the Science and the Spiritual Quest (SSQ) project and the fact that, in his opinion, "The participants were more open to each other's religious views because they respected each other as scientists, and they brought to their discussion some of the spirit of inquiry they had known in science, even as they acknowledged the differences between fields" (Barbour 2004, 21).

References

Barbour, Ian G. 1966. *Issues in Science and Religion*. Englewood Cliffs, NJ: Prentice-Hall.

Barbour, Ian G., ed. 1973. *Earth Might Be Fair: Reflections on Ethics, Religion and Ecology*. Englewood Cliffs, NJ: Prentice Hall.

Barbour, Ian G. 1974. *Myths, Models, and Paradigms: A Comparative Study in Science and Religion*. London: SCM Press.

Barbour, Ian G. 1980. *Technology, Environment, and Human Values*. Westport, CT: Praeger.

Barbour, Ian G. 1990. *Religion in an Age of Science: The Gifford Lectures 1989–1991*, vol. 1. San Francisco: Harper & Row.

Barbour, Ian G. 1993. *Ethics in an Age of Technology: The Gifford Lectures 1989–1991*, vol. 2. San Francisco: HarperCollins.

Barbour, Ian G. 1997. *Religion and Science: Historical and Contemporary Issues*, revised edn. San Francisco: HarperSanFrancisco.

Barbour, Ian G. 2000. *When Science Meets Religion: Enemies, Strangers, or Partners?* San Francisco: HarperSanFrancisco.

Barbour, Ian G. 2002. *Nature, Human Nature, and God*. Minneapolis: Fortress Press.

Barbour, Ian G. 2004. A Personal Odyssey. In Robert John Russell, ed. *Fifty Years in Science and Religion: Ian G. Barbour and His Legacy*. Aldershot: Ashgate, pp. 17–28.

Berg, Christian. 2004. Barbour's Way(s) of Relating Science and Theology. In Robert John Russell, ed. *Fifty Years in Science and Religion: Ian G. Barbour and His Legacy*. Aldershot: Ashgate, pp. 61–75.

Gould, Stephen Jay. 1999. *Rocks of Ages: Science and Religion in the Fullness of Life*. New York: Ballantine Books.

Peters, Ted. 1996. Theology and Science: Where Are We? *Zygon*, 31, pp. 323–343.

Russell, Robert John, ed. 2004. *Fifty Years in Science and Religion: Ian G. Barbour and His Legacy*. Aldershot: Ashgate.

Russell, Robert John. 2008. *Cosmology from Alpha to Omega: The Creative Mutual Interaction of Theology and Science*. Minneapolis: Fortress Press.

Further Reading

Barbour, Ian G. 1997. *Religion and Science: Historical and Contemporary Issues*, revised edn. San Francisco: HarperSanFrancisco. The revised edition of the first volume of Barbour's Gifford lectures provides the most encompassing and in-depth overview of the historical, philosophical, and theological challenges with which Barbour is most concerned in religion and science.

Barbour, Ian G. 2000. *When Science Meets Religion: Enemies, Strangers, or Partners?* San Francisco: HarperSanFrancisco. This short, accessible volume is structured around Barbour's fourfold typology, and provides examples of how the typology is operative in specific areas of science and religion.

Barbour, Ian G. 2002. *Nature, Human Nature, and God*. Minneapolis: Fortress Press. Barbour's most recent book, covering topics in evolution, genetics, human nature, neuroscience, artificial intelligence, and environmental ethics. Additionally, the volume includes Barbour's fullest exploration of his own constructive process theology.

Russell, Robert John, ed. 2004. *Fifty Years in Science and Religion: Ian G. Barbour and His Legacy*. Aldershot: Ashgate. A *Festschrift* honoring Barbour's eightieth birthday, this volume brings together 20 authors who provide critical insights into Barbour's contributions to methodology, ethics, and theology. The opening chapter is a brief autobiography by Barbour.

53

Wolfhart Pannenberg

HANS SCHWARZ

Born in 1928, Wolfhart Pannenberg is one of the two most prominent theologians of Germany in the latter part of the twentieth century, the other being Jürgen Moltmann (b. 1926). While Pannenberg claimed that he "never became a Hegelian," he "decided that theology has to be developed on at least the same level of sophistication as Hegel's philosophy" (Pannenberg 1988, 16). Indeed, the breadth of his undertakings certainly has a resemblance to Hegel, as does the unashamed wedding together of reason and revelation. At times he can be carried away in his determination to make the Christian faith credible, for instance in comparing the working of the Holy Spirit with field theory in physics. Yet he remains one of the most thought-provoking theologians of the latter part of the twentieth century, and in his astounding command of the history of thought also one of the most erudite.

As with Hegel, history became Pannenberg's most important reference point, as evidenced in his provocative "Dogmatic Theses on the Doctrine of Revelation" in *Revelation as History* (1961). In thesis 3 Pannenberg claimed: "In contradistinction to the special appearances of the Godhead, revelation in history is open to everyone. It has universal character" (Pannenberg 1961, 135). With this claim Pannenberg wanted to redirect our attention from the "ghetto" of a special salvation history toward God's self-disclosure in the open court of universal history. This was an outright rejection of the then prevailing existential history favored by Rudolf Bultmann (1884–1976) and of Barth's abandoning the natural world in favor of God's total otherness. Pannenberg's claim that revelation can be maintained in the court of reason opened the possibility of engaging in a dialogue with the secular sciences, of correlating their truth claims with those of theology, and of achieving a coherent picture of the world which is both reasonable and open to the notion of revelation. But how can this be executed?

Theology as the Science of God

Like Thomas F. Torrance (1913–2007), Pannenberg asserts that theology is not inferior in status to the sciences. Pannenberg's assertion was intensified by the challenge to theology in

The Blackwell Companion to Science and Christianity, First Edition. Edited by J. B. Stump and Alan G. Padgett.
© 2012 Blackwell Publishing Ltd. Published 2012 by Blackwell Publishing Ltd.

Germany in the 1970s as to whether it was indeed a science and belonged in a modern university or whether it should be excluded from the academic discourse. In direct contradiction
to Karl Barth, Pannenberg picked up on the demand of Heinrich Scholz (1884–1956), who
was a student of Adolf von Harnack and first became a philosopher of religion and later
made a name for himself as a logician. When Scholz taught with Barth at the University of
Münster he challenged Barth with the presupposition that theology, just like any other intellectual discipline which aspired to be considered a science, must undisputedly have formal
consistency, internal coherence, and be subject to external control and verification (Scholz
1931, 231ff.). But Barth claimed that theology can "flatly declare" that this concept of modern
science is unacceptable. Theology cannot "take over the obligation to submit to measurement
by the canons valid for other sciences" (Barth 1936, 8–9.). Theology is a science *sui generis* on
account of God's self-disclosure. Yet Pannenberg had made it clear that this self-disclosure
does not occur in a separate realm apart from all other reality and picked up the challenge
posed by Scholz.

Pannenberg contends that if theology does not subject its claims to rational examination
it inadvertently nourishes the suspicion that theological claims have nothing to do with
empirical reality but are only language events, that is, they only show what one believes. But
there is more to these claims. For instance, when one asserts in the words of the Apostles'
Creed "I believe in God the Father almighty, creator of heaven and earth," one does not only
claim a certain belief, but this belief includes a claim which can be empirically examined
(Pannenberg 1974, 13f.). The logical consistency of an assertion results from the fact that
every claim implies truth and excludes untruth. Similarly, internal coherence implies that the
assertions concerning a certain object can be distinguished from the object itself. Therefore
different assertions can be made concerning the same object. It is there that Pannenberg
notices a difficulty for contemporary theology. If the object investigated by theology is the
Word of God, "it appears that the object cannot be clearly distinguished from statements
about it" (Pannenberg 1974, 15). Is it really the Word of God or is it just a human word?
When we consider God and not just God's word as the object of theology, then the difficulty
still exists as to how God is accessible as a reality distinct from the assertions of theologians.
Pannenberg questions whether God appears only in assertions of theologians, especially
when these assertions are not taken seriously today as true assertions but appear to be fig-
ments of the faithful and of theologians. According to Pannenberg this is the point at which
the question of theology's object, or even the question whether theology has an object at all,
leads directly to Scholz's third requirement: that of external control and verifiability of theological statements. This means that the issue of whether theology has an actual object cannot
be determined apart from answering the question whether that object can be verified.

But how can one examine the truth claim of theological assertions? Claims concerning
God's activities cannot be examined against their object, since the reality of God itself is in
dispute. Such an examination would contradict the notion of God as the all-determining
reality. Such a reality is not at our disposal so that human claims could be verified. Claims
concerning God, God's activity, and God's self-disclosure cannot be directly verified with
regard to its object. This does not mean for Pannenberg that the criterion of verifiability
cannot be met, since one can "test propositions in terms of their implications. Propositions
about divine reality or divine activity can be tested according to their implications for our
understanding of finite reality, insofar, that is, as God is asserted to be *the all-determining
reality*" (Pannenberg 1974, 16). Pannenberg concedes that the notion of God as the all-
determining reality does not sufficiently settle the issue of divine reality, but at least in monotheism this is the fundamental presupposition for all talk about God. Therefore, claims

concerning God can be examined as to whether their content is indeed determined for all finite experience, at least as it is accessible to us. If such claims are verified then the implication is that "nothing real can be understood fully in its uniqueness without reference to the God thus proposed, and, in turn, one must expect that a deeper understanding of all reality is only possible in reference to the supposed divine reality" (Pannenberg 1974, 16). To the extent that this is true, Pannenberg concludes that theological claims have proven truthful. With this approach Pannenberg led theology out of its ghetto and gave it the tremendous task of adding a depth dimension to all (scientific) pursuits. By bringing theological claims alongside (secular) scientific ones, he also challenged its apodictic character.

Provisionality of All Knowledge

While for Barth it is only in obedience to the word of God that this word becomes recognizable as God's word, for Pannenberg it is clear that "all thought rests ultimately on unprovable assumptions" (Pannenberg 1974, 13). Whether we are Christians or not, we always live to some extent by faith. Pannenberg illustrates his point: thinking in modern science is thinking in hypotheses and assumptions and this also characterizes its peculiar rationality. Each claim is logically hypothetical, since such a claim can be true or false. Only by admitting its hypothetical character can we examine its status as a claim to truth, because otherwise it would be an apodictic statement but not a claim to truth. In every science, theology included, we encounter provisional statements.

The provisionality of all knowledge does not mean that this knowledge does not contain any truth but that the result of its verification has not come to a final conclusion. "A final judgment is impossible for someone who stands within this still open process, and not at its end" (Pannenberg 1976, 343). Only in the end, when the whole historical process has come to its conclusion, do we know which claim is true and which is false. At present, however, we must judge a truth claim by how well a hypothesis can interpret convincingly our total experience of reality. Neither mere existential certainty ("I am sure this is true") nor the force of logic ("this is the most elegant way of reasoning") makes a hypothesis true, but the substantiation of a hypothesis in all the dimensions of our experience accessible at any particular time. A reformulation of a hypothesis with regard to its truth content, then, must show that it can explain the experience of all reality to which it pertains in a more differentiated and convincing way than the older formulation. We can see this in an exemplary way with the theory of evolution, which as a hypothesis has seen continuous reformulation as new evidences have surfaced. Pannenberg cautions that:

> A strict verification in the sense of logical positivism, by tracing theological assertions to sense observations, is certainly impossible. But such strict verification is not possible even for the posited laws of physics because no general rule can be exhaustively tested by a finite number of cases to which it applies. (Pannenberg 1974, 21)

Conversely, however, a single exception can already falsify a general law. Without circumventing the necessity for provisional and ultimate verification, Pannenberg does not want to narrow down verification to a sense experience, especially since we must consider the whole of reality and the whole of experience. While he does not want to leave everything open until the end of history when there is the final verification (or falsification) of theological claims, he notes that theological hypotheses can already illuminate present experience and thereby witness to their truth content. Yet why do we even need a theological dimension? Should we not just stay with the natural sciences and the insights into reality offered by them?

Necessity for the Theological Dimension

In his youthful work *What Is Man? Anthropology in the Theological Perspective*, originally a series of radio addresses in the winter of 1961/62, Pannenberg already claimed that humans are not tied to their environment but are open for the world:

> 1. Man's openness to the world presupposes a relation to God. . . . 2. Man's openness is not yet grasped with sufficient depth if one speaks only of man's destiny for culture. . . . 3. The animal's bondage to its environment corresponds, not to man's relation to the world of nature or to his familiarity with his cultural world, but to his infinite dependence on God. What the environment is for animals, God is for man. God is the goal in which alone his striving can find rest and his destiny be fulfilled. (Pannenberg 1970b, 12f.)

This conclusion sounds very much like what Augustine wrote in the opening sentence of his *Confessions*: "Thou hast made us for thyself and restless is our heart until it comes to rest in thee" (Augustine 1955, 31).

More than a decade later in his *Anthropology in Theological Perspective* Pannenberg elaborates on this claim:

> Even when we move beyond all experience or idea of perceptible objects they continue to be exocentric, related to something other than themselves, but now to an Other beyond all the objects of their world, an Other that at the same time embraces this entire world and thus ensures the possible unification of the life of human beings in the world, despite the multiplicity and heterogeneity of the world's actions on them. A mere very general horizon containing all objects would have no inherent existence. In fact, when human beings reach out to a very general horizon embracing all the individual objects of actual or possible perception, they are relating themselves exocentrically to a *reality* prior to them; in this reaching out they are therefore implicitly affirming at the same time the divine reality, even though they have not yet grasped this thematically as such, much less in this or that particular structure. (Pannenberg 1983, 69)

There is a certain relatedness of humans to God even if this relationship attests itself in a very diffuse way. It is not only Christians but also modern atheists who look for an anthropological basis for the universal validity of their claims. We may think here of Ludwig Feuerbach, Karl Marx, Friedrich Nietzsche, Sigmund Freud, and their followers.

Pannenberg then poses the issue which he wants to address:

> If it can be shown that religion is simply a product of the human imagination and an expression of a human self-alienation, the roots of which are analyzed in a critical approach to religion, then religious faith and especially Christianity with its tradition and message will lose any claim to universal credibility in the life of the modern age. The Christian faith must then accept being lumped together with any and every form of superstition. (Pannenberg 1983, 15)

Since anthropology is the terrain on which the battle is fought over whether the Christian faith rests on truth or on fiction, Christian theology must have a foundation in general anthropological studies. There is the danger, however, that theology then focuses only on the human being instead of on God and lets the true subject matter of theology fall by the wayside. But this does not mean that theology should evade anthropology, because in so doing the impression is given that theological assertions are purely subjective assurances. Pannenberg contends against Barth: "Theologians will be able to defend the truth, precisely of their talk about God, only if they first respond to the atheistic critique of religion as being on the terrain of anthropology" (Pannenberg 1983, 16). Then he continues his argument for an anthropological base, saying: "In the modern age anthropology has become, not only in fact but also with objective necessity, the terrain on which theologians must base their claim of universal validity for what they say" (Pannenberg 1983, 16). He pleads for a "critical appropriation" of secular anthropology, because there the relation between anthropological findings and the subject matter of theology has in large measure been lost from sight. Since the God of the Bible is indeed the creator of all reality, such critical appropriation for theological use must be possible.

Pannenberg does not argue for a point of contact in (secular) anthropology, since that would mean that anthropology would be the avenue through which the eternal subject matter of theology is conveyed to humanity. Critical appropriation means something quite different:

> The aim is to lay theological claim to the human phenomena described in the anthropological disciplines. To this end, the secular description is accepted as simply a provisional version of the objective reality, a version that needs to be expanded and deepened by showing that the anthropological datum itself contains a further and theologically relevant dimension. (Pannenberg 1983, 19f.)

But how can such a theological anthropology be attained? Pannenberg shows that traditional dogmatic anthropology has two central themes: the image of God in human beings and human sin. These themes still surface when one connects anthropological phenomena with the reality of God. The tension between closeness to God and distance from God may shed a special light on the empirically derived anthropological phenomena.

Pannenberg now turns his attention "directly to the phenomena of human existence as investigated in human biology, psychology, cultural anthropology, or sociology and examines the findings of these disciplines with an eye to implications that may be relevant to religion and theology" (Pannenberg 1983, 21). For instance with regard to societal institutions Pannenberg concludes:

> The legitimacy crisis of the secular state is not a question solely of public morality and of appropriate political reforms. It has deeper roots in the loss of the religious foundation for moral obligation and the authority of law. The crisis is repeated every time the discovery is made that the state is justifying its power by manipulating public awareness. (Pannenberg 1983, 472)

The theological perspective, as Pannenberg convincingly shows, is not just an option for secular anthropology but an integral dimension without which anthropology loses sight of the whole human being and its relatedness with other human beings and the world.

Posing Theological Questions to Scientists

Pannenberg does not just focus on anthropology. In *The Apostles' Creed in the Light of Today's Questions* he writes: "If the Christian God cannot be understood as the creator of the world, my personal experience of being indebted to him for everything can well be pious self-deception. Even the devout man knows very well that this material world is the foundation of his existence" (Pannenberg 1972, 36). Anthropology by necessity leads to cosmology. In 1970, with the physicist A. M. Klaus Müller (1931–1995), Pannenberg had already treated the concept of contingency extensively (Pannenberg 1970a). As Pannenberg explained, for the biblical understanding of God the creator it is essential that God acts freely and unrestrictedly not only in laying the foundations of the universe but also in the subsequent course of events: "This 'continuous creation' is basically characterized by contingency because future acts of God cannot be deduced from the past course of events. And yet there emerge regularities and persistent forms of created reality giving expression to the faithfulness and identity of God in affirming the world that he created" (Pannenberg 1981, 44).

Contingency is not only theologically relevant for the beginning of creation, where God could, so to speak, push the button after which the creation unfolded. Unless we opt for a non-biblical deistic God, contingency is also relevant for the subsequent upholding of creation and each creative activity of God in the unfolding process of the universe and of life within it. Moreover Pannenberg is convinced that the affirmation of divine reality "can be justified only on the condition that the affirmed reality can be understood as the origin of all that is real" (Pannenberg 1970a, 75). The scope of history in which the reality of God needs to be asserted and rationally justified extends both to human history and the history of the universe.

Though nature is the field of modern natural science, a God who is not the origin and perfecter of this nature which science investigates could not be the power that determines all reality of being, and therefore could not truly be God. As a result Pannenberg sees the necessity of looking for common ground on which scientific and theological concerns can be discussed without losing sight of the specific differences of their respective ways of thinking. The Judeo-Christian understanding of the world was characterized by the experience of contingency. "New and unforeseen events take place constantly that are experienced as the work of almighty God" (Pannenberg 1970a, 76). An understanding of nature characterized by such contingency stood in fundamental contrast to the unbreakable order in the natural events as seen in the Greek view of the eternal recurrence of the same, or in the understanding of classical modern science regarding the thoroughgoing regularity of nature. This strict determinism of all natural occurrences by laws, known and still unknown, that are always alike has been shown to be an illusion.

Contemporary physics has produced a more realistic consciousness of the limits of physical and scientific laws as such. Pannenberg writes: "The micro structure of natural events can be described only by statements of probability, and this obviously not because of the limitedness of present physical knowledge but because of the nature of the matter itself" (Pannenberg 1970a, 77). Furthermore new observations make it necessary for formulas, previously considered as constantly valid, to be regarded as mere approximations of more general regularities. "Thus the possibility exists that the laws of nature that are today familiar to humanity are limited in time and space in their field of application, so that they do not have to be applicable in every former or future time and not everywhere in the same way" (Pannenberg 1970a, 78). Pannenberg is aware that such insights into the limited scope of scientific explanations cannot be founded by exploiting still-existing gaps in the pursuit of scientific discoveries, since such gaps could quickly be bridged. A more fundamental issue emerged in modern science: in every new stage of research, the total process of natural events presents itself again as a mesh of contingency and regularities. Or differently stated: every formula in science contains a certain degree of provisionality, and scientific discoveries thrive on surprises.

The provisionality of our knowledge of nature implies that at no point in time can we grasp the whole of nature. Theologically speaking, only in the eschatological future will we be able to look at creation as a whole and understand it. In the present we can obtain some insight into the nature of creation, since at least in partial aspects in each case there is regularity, while in the world process as a whole, as well as in individual events, there is a contingency of occurrences. If contingency rules supreme, what happens then to the so-called laws of nature? Pannenberg responds: "If the world process as a whole represents a unique process that as a whole is unrepeatable, then it also cannot be understood in its entirety as the application of a law" (Pannenberg 1970a, 106). Since each individual occurrence participates in the uniqueness of the total process, not a single event is exhaustively expressed by the applicable laws. This means that the formulation of natural laws is possible only if one abstracts from the peculiarities that characterize the individuality of each event and focuses just on that which is typical and common to various occurrences. On this basis statements concerning the unique world process are made in such a way that one thinks of the unique total process as a chain of individual events. The regularities of nature, however, which can be described by natural laws, have then a certain but limited stability. This means they are not strictly unchangeable.

The belief in the inviolable regularities of natural processes made possible a methodological atheism which is an intrinsic feature of modern science. As Pannenberg claims, however, these regularities are based on the unfailing faithfulness of the creator God to God's creation and do not ensue from themselves. They then form the basis for individual and more precarious transitory natural systems from stars, mountains, and oceans, to plant and animal life, and finally to the rise of the human species. Therefore the abstract investigation of the regularities underlying the emergence of the natural forms, as it occurs in modern science, need not separate these regularities from their natural context in God's creation, and thus from God's own self. Yet Pannenberg discerns a strong tendency in modern science toward such separation "by putting the knowledge of the abstract regularities of nature to the use of man to whatever purpose he thinks fit" (Pannenberg 1981, 39). This opens the floodgates to the abuse of science and of nature, its object of investigation. Therefore one must ask what has been abstracted and what has been methodically disregarded. It soon becomes clear that God the creator and the nature of things as creatures are abstracted from the mathematical language of science. Theologians then must pose questions to scientists concerning the compatibility of modern science with faith in the biblical God as creator and redeemer of humanity and the whole of creation. While Pannenberg is more concerned with dogmatic issues and only implicitly with ethical ones regarding the mutual interaction of science and theology, such interaction would also militate against the abuse of nature and its resources.

In view of the importance of contingency in the natural processes, the first and foremost issue with which scientists are confronted is the principle of inertia. Pannenberg contends that "the introduction of this principle in modern science played a major role in depriving God of his function in the conservation of nature and in finally rendering him an unnecessary hypothesis in the understanding of natural processes" (Pannenberg 1981, 39). If things or events continue by themselves there is at most a need for an initial impetus by an uncreated creator but not for a continuously active presence of God. God is relegated to inactivity. But this principle of inertia is not as self-evident as one often assumes. If the stuff of the universe consists of events rather than of solid bodies, and if these are already the products of the regularities of events, then their inertia or self-persistence is no more self-evident than any other natural regularity. Pannenberg suggests that "the phenomenon of inertia may tacitly imply the framework of a field of force to provide the conditions for such a phenomenon to exist" (Pannenberg 1981, 42). With this notion of a field of force, which Pannenberg then equates with God's enlivening Spirit, Pannenberg aroused the attention of many scientists and also stirred up much controversy, as we will see later. Yet there are two important facets to his line of argument: (1) do things go on in the world as they always have? and (2) is there an active God to uphold the whole world process? To clarify the issue, he asks whether the reality of nature must be understood as contingent and whether the natural processes must be understood as irreversible.

As we have noted, contingency is essential for the theological notion of a continuous creation because the future activity of God as the all-determining reality cannot be deduced from the past course of events. Yet through this activity emerge regularities and persistent forms of reality which show the faithfulness of God who affirms the world God has created. God stays with it and sustains it. In referring to God's activity in and with creation, Pannenberg introduces a historical dimension which also adds continuity of the natural processes. The natural laws formulated by science to describe these regularities, however, are abstract from the contingent conditions of their occurrence. In other words science proceeds as if these regularities were self-explanatory as regularities. But the category of history provides a more comprehensive description of the continuous process of nature by comprising the contingency of events together with the emergence of regularities. If the God of history who provides continuity were thought to be outside the created process, God is separate from nature and would act in a supernatural way. Such extra-categorical activity would be rejected by any serious scientist. Therefore it is crucial to see whether this continuity manifests itself also inside the process of nature. To elucidate his point Pannenberg refers to the biblical notion of the divine Spirit as the origin of life.

Scientific Metaphors in Theology

In the biblical tradition life is not considered as a function of the organism, rather the life-giving power is seen as an agent that influences the organism from the outside. Now Pannenberg comes to the decisive point:

> This view of life as originating from a transcendent source is an indispensable presupposition for the hope in a resurrection to a new life beyond death. Only if the source of life transcends the organism is it conceivable that the individual be given a new life that is no longer separate from the divine spirit, the source of life. (Pannenberg 1981, 45)

Though this view is from an ancient context which is quite different from ours today, Pannenberg notes that even in modern biology a living organism is not a closed system. Pannenberg now describes the evolution of life through the power of the divine Spirit in terms of a generalized field theory. With this theory he wants to express "the biblical idea of the divine spirit as the power of life that transcends the living organism and at the same time is intimately present in the individual" (Pannenberg 1981, 45f.). Pannenberg contends:

> Since the field concept as such corresponds to the old concept of *pneuma* and was derived from it in the history of thought, theologians should consider it obvious to relate also the field concept of modern physics to the Christian doctrine of the dynamic presence of the divine Spirit in all of creation. (Pannenberg 1989, 40)

In proposing the concept of a field only as a model Pannenberg does not intend to equate the activity of the Spirit with the field theories in physics. The fundamental differences between views in physics and theology in describing the reality of the world does not allow for Pannenberg to interpret field theories in physics and use them directly for theological issues. For theology one can use them only as approximations to the reality which is also the object matter in theological discourse about creation. Since the Holy Spirit is regarded as one person of the Trinity, Pannenberg also sees theological restraints in equating the Spirit with a field. "The person of the Holy Spirit is not himself to be understood as the field, but as a unique manifestation (singularity) of the field of the divine essentiality" (Pannenberg 1994, 83). The activity of the Spirit in creation is not exhausted in the field character of the divine essence. But this said, one must also consider that God's transcendence cannot be conceived of without considering a spatial dimension. While it is inappropriate to think of God as localized in space and to be distinguished from other parts of space, one must note that by creating, God gives the creatures space next to God's self and this 'next to' or 'in opposition to' remains enveloped by God's presence. God's essence and activity cannot be divorced from space.

Microcosmic events can be understood as manifestations of the future, since they are the foundation for macrocosmic events which seem to proceed according to the laws of nature as traditionally understood. Pannenberg sees here considerable theological consequences: "The force field of future possibility is thus responsible for the fact that the process of nature, which as a whole tends towards the dissolution of creatures through increase of entropy also offers space for the rise of new structures of increasing differentiation and complexity" (Pannenberg 1991, 100f.). This would allow for increasing differentiation and complexity as it has occurred in the evolution of life. Pannenberg cautions that "even though field concepts may speak of a force field as the origin of what is possible in the future, we have here an extension of such usage" (Pannenberg 1991, 101). We note here again a deepening of scientific insights, similar to what we noticed with his interpretation of anthropology.

Pannenberg even includes angels into his field concept. He suggests: "From the point of view of the field structure of spiritual dynamics one could consider identifying the subject matter intended in the conception of angels with the emergence of relatively independent parts of the cosmic field" (Pannenberg 1989, 41). If one keeps in mind the idea that angels are personal spirits that can be explained by "the fact that the concept of person in the phenomenology of religion is related to the impact of more or less incomprehensible 'powers,'" then the problem of personhood in the doctrine of angels can be overcome. Considering the "background of the biblical language about angels as personal realities, they may very well be related to fields of forces or dynamic spheres, the activity of which may be experienced as good or bad" (Pannenberg 1989, 41).

As noted above, Pannenberg's use of the field concept has created considerable discussion.[1] While he insists that the theological understanding and application of the concept will be different from those in the natural sciences, his use is more than a metaphorical one. He makes great effort to show how his own theological use connects to the use of field theory in physics to the point that he sometimes seems to (con)fuse both concepts. This reminds us of the physico-theology of bygone days. Since Pannenberg is deeply convinced that God as the creator is the all-encompassing entity, he endeavors to show that when the events of nature and history are properly understood, knowledge of their being rooted in God and God's will is conveyed. Therefore he sees no need for an alternative creationistic science, but simply states: "Our task as theologians is to relate to the natural sciences as they actually exist. We cannot create our own sciences. Yet we must go beyond what the sciences provide and include our understanding of God if we are properly to understand nature" (Pannenberg 1989, 48).

There is a new consonance between theology and science, if science admits to its own partial knowledge which needs deepening to tell the whole story. Pannenberg has led theology out of its self-imposed ghetto and made it into a dialogue partner of equal standing with the natural sciences.

Note

1   See especially Worthing (1998, 120–124). Worthing (1996, 377–385) has also carefully and extensively dealt with Pannenberg's use of the field-theory concept. Pannenberg was somewhat concerned about this and cautioned him to tone down his criticism, otherwise "he would make a fool of himself." Yet Pannenberg's use of the field concept has met a similar fate to Bultmann's use of demythologization. Both Pannenberg and Bultmann always claimed to be misunderstood.

References

Augustine of Hippo. 1955. *The Confessions.* Trans. and ed. Albert C. Outler. Philadelphia: Westminster.

Barth, Karl. 1936. *The Doctrine of the Word of God (Prolegomena to Church Dogmatics, being Vol. 1, Part 1).* Translated by G. T. Thomson. Edinburgh: T. & T. Clark.

Pannenberg, Wolfhart. 1961. Dogmatic Theses on the Doctrine of Revelation. In Wolfhart Pannenberg, ed. *Revelation as History.* Translated by D. Granskou. New York: Macmillan, pp. 123–158.

Pannenberg, Wolfhart. 1970a. Contingency and Natural Law. Translated by Wilhelm C. Linss. In *Toward a Theology of Nature: Essays on Science and Faith.* Ted Peters, ed. Louisville: Westminster John Knox, 1993, pp. 72–122.

Pannenberg, Wolfhart. 1970b. *What Is Man? Anthropology in the Theological Perspective.* Minneapolis: Fortress.

Pannenberg, Wolfhart. 1972. *The Apostles' Creed in the Light of Today's Questions.* Translated by Margaret Kohl. Philadelphia: Westminster.

Pannenberg, Wolfhart. 1974. Is There Any Truth in God-Talk? The Problem of Theological Statements from the Perspective of Philosophy of Science. Translated by Linda Maloney. In *The Historicity of Nature: Essays on Science and Theology.* Niels Henrik Gregersen, ed. West Conshohocken, PA: Templeton Foundation Press, 2008, pp. 11–22.

Pannenberg, Wolfhart. 1976. *Theology and the Philosophy of Science.* Translated by Francis McDonagh. Philadelphia: Westminster.

Pannenberg, Wolfhart. 1981. Theological Questions to Scientists. In Carol Rausch Albright and Joel Haugen, eds. *Beginning with the End: God, Science, and Wolfhart Pannenberg.* Chicago: Open Court, 1997, pp. 37–50.

Pannenberg, Wolfhart. 1983. *Anthropology in Theological Perspective.* Translated by Matthew J. O'Connell. Philadelphia: Westminster.

Pannenberg, Wolfhart. 1988. An Autobiographical Sketch. In Carl E. Braaten and Philip Clayton, eds. *The Theology of Wolfhart Pannenberg.* Minneapolis: Augsburg, pp. 11–18.

Pannenberg, Wolfhart. 1989. The Doctrine of Creation and Modern Science. In *Toward a Theology of Nature: Essays on Science and Faith.* Ted Peters, ed. Louisville: Westminster John Knox Press, 1993 pp. 29–49.

Pannenberg, Wolfhart. 1994. *Systematic Theology,* vol. 2. Translated by Geoffrey W. Bromiley. Grand Rapids, MI: Eerdmans.

Scholz, Heinrich. 1931. Wie ist eine evangelische Theologie als Wissenschaft möglich? In Gerhard
    Sauter, ed. *Theologie als Wissenschaft*. Munich: Chr. Kaiser, 1971, pp. 221–264.

Further Reading

Albright, Carol Rausch and Haugen, Joel, eds. 1997. *Beginning with the End: God, Science, and Wolfhart
    Pannenberg*. Chicago: Open Court. Contains five contributions by Pannenberg and responses by
    his critics.
Pannenberg, Wolfhart. 1993. *Toward a Theology of Nature: Essays on Science and Faith*. Ted Peters, ed.
    Louisville: Westminster John Knox Press. Contains seven essays by Pannenberg and a helpful
    introduction by the editor.
Pannenberg, Wolfhart. 2008. *The Historicity of Nature: Essays on Science and Theology*. Niels Henrik
    Gregersen, ed. West Conshohocken, PA: Templeton Foundation Press. Contains 16 essays by Pannen-
    berg and an introduction by the editor.
Worthing, Mark William. 1996. *Foundations and Functions of Theology as Universal Science: Theological
    Method and Apologetic Praxis in Wolfhart Pannenberg and Karl Rahner*. Frankfurt am Main: Peter Lang.
    An extensive review of Pannenberg's position as it relates to his engagement with the natural
    sciences.
Worthing, Mark William. 1998. *God, Creation, and Contemporary Physics*. Minneapolis: Fortress. Contin-
    ues the review of Pannenberg's engagement with the natural sciences.

54

John Polkinghorne

CHRISTOPHER C. KNIGHT

Biography

John Charlton Polkinghorne, one of the most significant figures in the dialogue between science and theology in the last two decades of the twentieth century and the first decade of the twenty-first, was born in 1930. Much of his working life has been spent in the University of Cambridge, where as an undergraduate he read mathematics at Trinity College, remaining to work for his doctorate in mathematical physics in the group led by Paul Dirac. After a Harkness fellowship at the California Institute of Technology (where he collaborated with Murray Gell-Mann), he worked for two years as a lecturer at the University of Edinburgh before returning, in 1958, to a lectureship in Cambridge. He was promoted to reader in 1965 and to a professorship in mathematical physics in 1968, a position which he held until 1979. During this period he was elected a Fellow of the Royal Society.

In his undergraduate years, the distinctive evangelical approach of the (non-denominational) Christian Union played a significant role in Polkinghorne's religious development, and throughout his career in physics his Christian commitment remained strong. By the late 1970s, it seemed to him that his best mathematical work probably lay behind him, and that an appropriate step would be to offer himself for the ordained ministry of the Anglican Church. Having been accepted for training for that ministry, he resigned his university chair and studied for two years at Westcott House, Cambridge, in the accelerated scheme for ordination preparation available to older candidates. Ordained deacon in 1981 and priest in 1982, he worked first as an assistant curate in Bristol and subsequently as vicar of Blean, in Kent. During this period of parish ministry, Polkinghorne's first book of thoughts about the relationship between science and theology was published.

While perhaps rather simplistic by the standard of his later theological work, this book – The Way the World Is (Polkinghorne 1983) – made clear that Polkinghorne might have a significant part to play in the new phase of the dialogue between science and theology that had recently been inaugurated by books like Ian Barbour's Issues in Science and Religion (1966) and Arthur Peacock's Science and the Christian Experiment (1971). This possibility was no doubt

The Blackwell Companion to Science and Christianity, First Edition. Edited by J. B. Stump and Alan G. Padgett.
© 2012 Blackwell Publishing Ltd. Published 2012 by Blackwell Publishing Ltd.

a factor in Polkinghorne's return to Cambridge in 1986 – first as Dean and Chaplain of Trinity Hall and subsequently as President of Queens' College.

This return to Cambridge allowed Polkinghorne not only the time to pursue the theological agenda outlined in his first book on the science–theology dialogue, but also to carry forward the teaching on that dialogue that Arthur Peacocke had fostered within the university until his recent move to Oxford. In the year of Polkinghorne's return, his book *One World* (1986) appeared, soon to be followed by two more volumes, *Science and Creation* (1988) and *Science and Providence* (1989). In this trilogy – still perhaps the best introduction to Polkinghorne's thinking – he not only manifested the extraordinarily effective style of communication that was to characterize all his later work on the science–theology dialogue, but also set out the main outlines of the theology that he was to defend and expand in the more than 20 books that followed.

The Scientist-Theologians

One of these later books – *Scientists as Theologians* (1996) – had a significant subtitle: *A Comparison of the Writings of Ian Barbour, Arthur Peacocke and John Polkinghorne*. The appropriateness of such a book lay in the fact that these three writers were not only (as Polkinghorne called them) "scientist-theologians" – people who had started as scientists and had brought their scientific knowledge and commitment to bear on theological issues. In addition, they had become, and were to remain for some years, the three leading figures in the science–theology dialogue. Thus a comparison of their views (albeit inevitably written from Polkinghorne's own perspective) was of major interest to everyone involved in that dialogue. (Ian Barbour was, in fact, to write a much shorter comparison (Barbour 2010) from his own point of view some years later.) Indeed, in many ways, the work of Polkinghorne is still perhaps best understood in terms of this kind of comparison, since the three manifest many similarities – attributable perhaps to their scientific backgrounds – but also some significant differences.

One of the things that unites the work of all three of these scientist-theologians is a determination to show that our current scientific understanding – including aspects of it that some Christians have found problematical, such as evolutionary theory – is consonant with a commitment to religious faith in general and to the Christian faith in particular. In this sense, there is clearly an apologetic motivation to at least some of their work. Central to this apologetic, for all three, is a rejection of the sort of reductionism in which religious experience and faith are seen as being explicable in purely psychological or biological terms. Each, in his own way, defends the concept of *emergence* as a way of countering the notion that ultimately the only valid description of any complex system is that which deals with the components of that system at the lowest level of complexity. Each regards the reductionistic methodology of the sciences as valid, but argues that a recognition of the appropriateness of this methodology does not imply that high levels of complexity in the world may be understood fully in terms of the properties of the components of which they are made up. New emergent properties, they argue, arise with growing complexity in the cosmos, and any full appreciation of the created order must recognize that these new emergent levels of complexity have an autonomous aspect.

It may be, as some have suggested, that a fully coherent view of emergence requires a more sophisticated philosophical analysis (of the kind begun by people like Philip Clayton) than these three scientist-theologians provide. Nevertheless, their own perspectives have clearly inspired much of this later and more thorough work, and in apologetic terms their antireductionist stance has been highly effective. Largely as a result of their work, ontological reductionism is now widely seen in Christian circles as no more than a questionable assumption, often adopted through philosophical laziness in much contemporary criticism of religious belief.

Does the lack of a fully convincing analysis of emergence in the scientist-theologians' work perhaps point to a general weakness in their work, arising from their being underequipped to grapple adequately with philosophical issues? Some have thought this to be the case, and have asked in particular whether Polkinghorne – perhaps more than the other two scientist-theologians – sometimes deals with complex philosophical issues in too cavalier a manner, regarding them as issues that can be answered simply in terms of his experience as a physicist. However, others have argued that this impression is mistaken and arises only because Polkinghorne has in general been writing for a broad audience, for which too much emphasis on such issues would have been counterproductive. (Certainly he makes regular references to these issues in a way that makes clear that he is aware of them.) Some have, nevertheless, still posed awkward questions of this kind in the light of Polkinghorne's approach to another position broadly shared by all three scientist-theologians: their view of the "critical realism" that is to be attributed to the languages of science and theology.

All three scientist-theologians argue that scientific and religious languages point to the reality of the world. They share a scientific background in which it is generally assumed that scientific language provides descriptions of reality that relate directly to ontology, and they attribute a comparable sort of "realism" to the language of their faith community. Their view that theological language can be seen as puzzle-solving on the basis of experience, in a way that is comparable to how scientific language is developed, is held by many to be not unreasonable, so that their view of theological language has seemed justifiable. The fact that they are clearly aware of the historical development of scientific language, which makes the adoption of a "naive" realism impossible, has also reassured many that their views are philosophically sound, with the result that their conclusions have been widely accepted. It is inadequate, they all say, to see either scientific or theological language simply as a social construction without genuine reference, and they opt for a sort of realism that is "critical" in the sense of allowing for future development of the sort that Karl Popper spoke of (in the scientific context) in terms of "increasing verisimilitude."

This kind of argument is, however, a problematical one for many philosophers and theologians, some of whom prefer a purely instrumentalist view of one or both languages, and some of whom (e.g., Knight 2001, 91–106) adopt a critical realism of a rather more subtle kind. In relation to these arguments, some suggest, none of the three scientist-theologians has grappled fully with the philosophical problems of the position that they defend, and of the three, it is perhaps Polkinghorne who manifests the least subtle understanding. While both Peacocke (1984) and Barbour (1976) have clearly grappled with the issues that arise from various philosophical analyses of both scientific and religious language, Polkinghorne's slogan that "epistemology models ontology" – despite being argued for at length (e.g., Polkinghorne 1991) – arises, in their view, as much from a sort of "gut instinct" as from a comparable grappling with the philosophical issues.

Bottom-Up Thinking and Consonance

In this context, Polkinghorne's categorization of himself as a "bottom-up thinker" (e.g., Polkinghorne 1994) is clearly a significant factor in his justification of his view. Valid thinking, in both science and theology, does not, for him, start with broad theory but with experience of various kinds. He recognizes that in each case the community that attempts to interpret this experience has an effect on the data that arise from it. So his approach is by no means a simplistic one that fails to acknowledge the theory-laden nature of data and the way in which theoretical concepts in both science and theology are culturally influenced and paradigm-dependent. He insists that it is the surprising nature of the results of such thinking that leads to his belief that these results relate to the ontology of the real world. Scientific findings are sometimes surprising, he says, and therefore so too might theological ones be. We must, he suggests, be open to these surprises when the evidence – approached in a "bottom-up" way – leads us towards them.

Polkinghorne's attempts at this kind of thinking in theology suggest to some, however, that he may be more open to "surprises" that are congenial to the conservative Christian than to the atheist. (The biblical historians he tends to cite, for example, do not really reflect the breadth of the community of such historians.) In an age in which there has been widespread criticism, from within the Christian community, of the basic understanding which that community has inherited – or at least of the categories through which that understanding has been articulated – it has been surprising to some that while Polkinghorne's knowledge of theological thinking has increased, his understanding of the Christian faith has remained fundamentally unchanged. While by no means a fundamentalist, he exhibits a trust in the biblical record and in the sort of Protestant version of Nicene orthodoxy with which his adult faith began that many find difficult to understand. Is it only his "bottom-up thinking," they ask, that has led him to this position? Or has the apologetic component of his work – perhaps in an unconscious way – led him to give greater weight to those aspects of experience that are congenial to an essentially conservative theological outlook?

However we may judge this question, there is undoubtedly a positive aspect to the effect of Polkinghorne's relatively conservative position, for despite all his talk about bottom-up thinking, he in fact exhibits – especially in his later work – a subtle awareness of the tension between inference from experience and something more subtle and complex. He is, among the scientist-theologians, undoubtedly the one who most clearly perceives the need for a carefully nuanced theological appraisal of competing positions that arise within the science–theology dialogue. While Barbour famously spoke of those approaches that assume real interaction between science and theology as falling into the categories of *dialogue* and *integration*, Polkinghorne has spoken in terms of a different categorization: of *consonance* – something to pursue in his view – and of a more questionable *assimilation* (into which he sees both Barbour and Peacocke as sometimes falling). His own position, Polkinghorne stresses, is one that argues for *consonance* between science and theology. Science "does not determine theological thought but constrains it" in the sense that the "scientific and theological accounts of the world must fit together in a mutually consistent way." More radical approaches than his own, he goes on to say, involve "assimilation" in the sense that they allow "a degree of accommodation of the one to the other that could seem to threaten [theology's] justified autonomy" (Polkinghorne 1996, 6–7).

Traditional Theological Concerns

In this wariness of allowing too much modification to traditional Christian beliefs on the supposed basis of scientific or other secular insights, there seems, especially in Polkinghorne's earlier work, to have been an influence on him from the work of Thomas Torrance. However, in his later work Polkinghorne seems in some respects to have moved away from Torrance's perspectives (with their Barthian overtones) and towards something more subtle and in accordance with the sacramental emphasis of his own Anglican tradition. This is brought out in particular in his book *Science and the Trinity* (Polkinghorne 2004), which sets his whole way of thinking in its Christian context. Here he speaks, in particular, of the way in which the totality of his Christian ecclesial experience influences his thought. While still defending his earlier notion of the appropriateness of being a bottom-up thinker who "seeks to move from experience to understanding," in this later work he clearly recognizes the complexity of this experience for the Christian. A substantial part of this experience is, he says, "vicarious, deriving from the acceptance of the accounts of the foundational events and insights recorded in scripture. A further part also comes to us externally, from the testimony of outstanding religious figures." However, he goes on, "for a living encounter between faith and understanding, there must be an internal resource." For him, he explains, this "centres on a certain degree of faithfulness in prayer, worship and service. A particularly important part of this experience is located in my regular participation, week by week, in the Eucharistic celebration of the Church. . . . For me, theological thinking proceeds by a kind of 'liturgy-assisted logic'" (Polkinghorne 2004, 118–120).

In expanding on this, Polkinghorne cites a figure who has clearly been important to him in the latter part of his career, the German protestant theologian Michael Welker, with whom he has collaborated on a number of occasions, not least in work focused on the Christian eschatological hope (Polkinghorne and Welker 2000; Polkinghorne 2002b). While his perspectives do not always coincide with Welker's, this collaboration does seem to have had a positive effect on Polkinghorne's later work, making it theologically more nuanced and rich. In certain respects, however, it may also have reinforced an aspect of Polkinghorne's approach that was present from the beginning, and which perhaps has its roots in his experience of evangelical Protestantism in early adulthood. This is his focus on Scripture, which he reads in a way that is far from fundamentalist but is still relatively conservative.

It is sometimes said, in this context, that Polkinghorne – with his attempt to hold Scripture, tradition, and reason in a creative tension – is a typically Anglican theologian. However, both his early background and his later collaborative work have possibly meant that, consciously or unconsciously, he interprets this balance in a way that makes the solid, learned Protestantism of people like Welker – reflected in one strand of Anglican theological thinking – more congenial than other strands of that thinking (such as that which has been influenced by neo-Thomism). Informally, at least, Polkinghorne has sometimes claimed as a virtue that his perspectives may not always be in accordance with the tradition of Christian philosophical thinking, but that they are, in his view, "biblical." In this respect his "Anglican" approach differs in emphasis from the approach of Arthur Peacocke, whose combination of a strong sacramental understanding of the cosmos and openness to new insights in biblical scholarship is perhaps more characteristic of the Anglicanism of their generation.

An example of this leaning towards supposedly biblical perspectives at the expense of the traditional thinking of the post-biblical era may be found in Polkinghorne's insistence on the wrongness of the classical notion of divine eternity, in which God is seen (as Aquinas put it) as wholly outside the order of time, so that the whole course of time is subject to eternity in one simple glance. As with the other scientist-theologians, this essentially philosophical perspective is discarded by Polkinghorne in favor of the notion of a God who does not know the future. In his rejection of the classical Christian understanding of divine eternity, there are clearly many factors at play, but one of the most significant seems to be his notion of a "personal" God who acts by responding – much as any temporal, created agent must – to events in the world.

Here again, an essentially "biblical" notion – that of a "personal" God who acts in response to events – is upheld at the expense of a traditional but more complex philosophical understanding of the way in which God may be seen as more than personal. What Wesley Wildman has said of Robert J. Russell's personalistic theism seems here applicable to that of Polkinghorne (to whom Russell is close in his basic views). This kind of theism is, says Wildman, "of the distinctively modern kind, which sprang up when the seeds of the Hebrew Bible's anthropomorphism germinated in the fertile soil of an increasingly literate culture. . . . It is a distinctively Protestant deviation from the mainstream Christian view, preferring the Jerusalem to the Athens side of the famous tension that has dominated Christian theology from the beginning." What happened, Wildman asks, "to the classical doctrines of aseity and immutability, the affirmations that God is self-contained and does not change through acting and feeling? What happened to God as the ground of being or being itself, as pure act and first cause?" How is the holder of this kind of view "to deflect the classical intuition that God as a being can be no God at all but merely an idol of the human imagination?" (Wildman 2006, 166).

Polkinghorne's answer to such questions has been, essentially, that the classical Christian notion of God is based too much on a flawed philosophy and too little on the revelation of God in Christ. In this, moreover, his position is not significantly different from that of the other scientist-theologians, even though their view of the content of that Christian revelation is less conservative than his. All three are, in fact, willing to set aside aspects of classical Christian philosophical theism, not because of a mistrust of systematic theology, but because of a perception of the need to develop such a theology anew. In the outlines of a systematic theology that each has offered, the differences between them relate primarily to historical and Christological understanding, with Polkinghorne's "biblical" outlook leading him to be more conservative than the other two scientist-theologians on these issues.

In particular, while Barbour's theism is strongly influenced by process philosophy (of which Polkinghorne is suspicious), and Peacocke's involves a rather modified Trinitarianism (affected by Geoffrey Lampe's thinking about the Holy Spirit), Polkinghorne remains a staunch defender of Nicene Trinitarianism (albeit with a sense of modesty about what can be said about the Trinity, which not all defenders of a Trinitarian theology share). On the subject of Christ himself, Polkinghorne is a defender of a traditional position. For Barbour, the intent of classical Christological doctrines is now best preserved through the categories of relationship and history, so that Jesus is understood by him primarily as a man responsive to God's call. He finds helpful Peacocke's use of evolutionary categories to develop a contemporary Christology, so that just as Christ is, for Peacocke, a new emergent in history, so for Barbour he may be seen as a continuation and intensification of what had occurred previously. For Polkinghorne, however, these approaches by the other scientist-theologians are fundamentally flawed, just as is their rejection of the notion of Jesus' virginal conception and their questioning of his bodily Resurrection. Polkinghorne defends the notion of a preexistent second person of the Trinity becoming incarnate with two natures, and – though by no means a biblical fundamentalist – he accepts, far more readily than the other two, the basic integrity of the biblical texts that he sees as fundamental to this defense.

Polkinghorne's defense of traditional theological perspectives is not, however, based solely on theological arguments of the sort that would be common in any conservative Christian milieu. The scientific and philosophical perspectives that he brings to his arguments are often both ingenious and engaging. In relation to the Christian eschatological hope, for example, his use of the notion of the soul as an information-bearing pattern that can be re-embodied in a new kind of matter and time has proved, for many, an extremely helpful notion. Similarly, in his reflection on the Resurrection, his notion of laws of nature as both "reflections of the faithfulness of the Creator who ordains them" and, at the same time, "not as immutable necessities, but as holding simply for as long as the Creator determines that they should do so" (Polkinghorne 2002a, 46), ties in intriguingly with his notion of Christ's Resurrection as a foretaste of an eschatological future with a new set of such laws.

Divine Action

Polkinghorne's acute intelligence is also brought to bear in the particular model of divine action that he proposes, which is of the kind that – in order to avoid a "God of the gaps" approach – seeks to identify some sort of "causal joint" between God and the world, through which God can act without setting aside the laws of nature. While his theological motivation for attempting this kind of model is similar, as we have noted, to that of Robert John Russell, Polkinghorne's scientific insight into quantum mechanics leads him to reject the specific model that Russell and others have developed from the earlier work of William Pollard, which focuses on quantum indeterminacy. Polkinghorne's focus is, rather, on the way in which both quantum mechanics and chaotic phenomena point, in his view, to a more "subtle and supple" universe than these phenomena in themselves indicate – one in which the "cloudy unpredict-abilities of physical process" can be interpreted as "the sites of ontological openness" (Polk-inghorne 1996, 40).

What is interesting here is that Polkinghorne does not base himself on scientific insights as such. By using deterministic chaos theory to posit a non-deterministic aspect of the universe – as yet unknown to science – he is in fact extrapolating from scientific insights in a way that is motivated by theological considerations. His understanding of "the way the world is" is clearly, here, a scientifically informed account of "the way the world ought to be" if his fundamental theological instincts are correct. However, as we have seen from the perceptive comments of Wesley Wildman, these theological instincts are of a very particular kind, and are by no means shared by all Christians. The nature of God and of his relationship to the creation are understood in a number of ways within the Christian world, and Polkinghorne's type of theism – while at present the predominant one within the science–theology dialogue – is not the only one.

Indeed, even within this broad and currently dominant stream of thinking, there are interesting variations, not only in relation to aspects of Trinitarian and Christological formula-tion (of the sort already noted) but also in relation to the broader relationship between God and the world. The most important of these variations, as they impinge on the science–religion dialogue, are brought out by Polkinghorne's criticisms of two aspects of the under-standing of Arthur Peacocke, one of which Polkinghorne thinks distances God too much from the world, and one of which brings God too close. The first of these criticisms is leveled at Peacocke's sense that God's "personal" involvement with the world is restricted to what Peacocke calls God's "providential" action, as distinct from his action as Creator (which latter he interprets entirely naturalistically). For Polkinghorne, this kind of understanding leans towards a kind of deism. Over and above what he calls divine action in its "impersonal, rela-tively deistic mode" he says, it is necessary to recognize examples of "Creatorly action in a more personal mode"; otherwise, he thinks, one will be guilty of an "implicit deism . . . whose nakedness is only thinly covered by a garment of personalized metaphor" (Polkinghorne 1994, 78–79). The second type of criticism focuses on Peacocke's panentheism – his sense that the world is in some sense "in God." This too, for Polkinghorne poses a threat to a proper understanding of the relationship between God and the world (and here too the difference between the two men has major implications, not least on understandings of divine action (see Peacocke and Clayton 2004)).

Natural Theology

How, then, is Polkinghorne's theological work ultimately to be understood and evaluated? One approach might be to see him as someone who fits much more clearly than he himself might recognize as a proponent of *natural theology*. He himself tends to use this term in the rather narrow sense in which it is defined in terms of attempts to "prove" the existence of God, either through purely philosophical arguments (as in the scholastic period) or through design arguments (of the kind associated with early modern science). He himself has seen such attempts as deeply flawed, but has nevertheless defended a more modest "revived and revised" natural theology, in which, for example, considerations related to the anthropic cosmological principle are seen as giving rise to "a meta-question . . . to which theism provides a persuasive (but not logically coercive) answer" (Polkinghorne 1991, 80). However, in the wider historical sense of the term *natural theology* – which Polkinghorne actually points towards in speaking of such a revision – he may arguably be seen as a remarkable example of a natural theologian.

What I mean by this is that Polkinghorne's characteristic approach exhibits significant parallels with the practice of natural theology that Jaroslav Pelikan has spoken of as characteristic of the pre-scholastic period, and especially of the three Cappadocian Fathers, Basil the Great, Gregory of Nazianzus, and Gregory of Nyssa. This natural theology was, for Pelikan, essentially an encounter between Christian conviction and the philosophy and science of a particular epoch and culture. It involved what he calls "natural theology as apologetic" and "natural theology as presupposition" (Pelikan 1993). The first of these categories relates to making the Christian faith seem reasonable in relation to the philosophical and scientific understanding of a particular period. The second relates to the way in which the semi-instinctive philosophical and scientific presuppositions of a particular epoch and culture inevitably affect the articulation of religious faith, even though this faith ultimately has roots less in apologetic argument than in the experience of the individual and of the historical faith community with which that individual identifies. These two categories of natural theology did not, for the Cappadocians, exist in isolation from one another, but there was, inevitably, a complex interplay between them.

The same interplay of apologetic and presupposition, it might be argued, has been characteristic of the development of Polkinghorne's work, for the scientific and philosophical understandings our own era have, in a way that exhibits significant parallels with the work of those Fathers of the Church, clearly both influenced him and been used by him in his defense and articulation of the Christian faith. The same might also be said of the other scientist-theologians, and indeed Arthur Peacocke once spoke of his hope that, through the modern science–theology dialogue, "a new coherent theology might emerge . . . and so continue in our own day what, for example, the Cappadocian Fathers . . . did in their time in relation to contemporary philosophy and science" (Peacocke 1986, 128).

Might one, in the light of this comment, perhaps push the comparison with the Cappadocians further? Just as there were three Cappadocian Fathers, who worked largely on the basis of a common understanding – but with significant differences of stress and of willingness to speculate beyond the bounds of accepted views – so there have been three principal scientist-theologians, and their work has had something of the same character as theirs, at least in its basic interplay of natural theology as apologetic and natural theology as presupposition. Might one, perhaps, see in Peacocke's work something of the speculative adventurousness of Gregory of Nyssa, with Polkinghorne as the more cautious and conservative Basil, and Barbour as the Nazianzen in-between? Certainly the parallels should not be pushed too far, but the comparison is an interesting one.

Of course, the importance of Polkinghorne and the other two scientist-theologians may ultimately not match that of the Cappadocians in Christian history, since the sort of synthesis which these modern scientist-theologians have sought has not yet been fully developed. Moreover, if such a synthesis does eventually emerge, it may, some think, be based on different foundations from those they have laid. Even if their work is judged simply as an inspiration to attempt a Cappadocian-type synthesis, however, their work has an importance that can hardly be overestimated. And in this endeavor, Polkinghorne's contribution has been an immense one, especially in relation to the need to demonstrate that contemporary scientific understanding may be seen as consonant not only with theism but with the fundamental categories of Christian belief. In the history of Christian theology, his place is an assured one.

References

Barbour, Ian. 1966. *Issues in Science and Religion*. Englewood Cliffs, NJ: Prentice-Hall.

Barbour, Ian. 1976. *Myths, Models, and Paradigms: A Comparative Study in Science and Religion*. New York: Harper & Row.

Barbour, Ian. 2010. John Polkinghorne on Three Scientist-Theologians. *Theology and Science*, 8, pp. 247–264.

Knight, Christopher C. 2001. *Wrestling with the Divine: Religion, Science, and Revelation*. Minneapolis, MN: Fortress.

Peacocke, Arthur. 1971. *Science and the Christian Experiment*. Oxford: Oxford University Press.

Peacocke, Arthur. 1984. *Intimations of Realty: Critical Realism in Science and Theology*. Notre Dame, IN: University of Notre Dame Press.

Peacocke, Arthur. 1986. *God and the New Biology*. London: J. Dent & Sons.

Peacocke, Arthur and Clayton, Philip, eds. 2004. *In Whom We Live and Move and Have Our Being: Panentheistic Reflections on God's Presence in a Scientific World*. Grand Rapids, MI: Eerdmans.

Pelikan, Jaroslav. 1993. *Christianity and Classical Culture: The Metamorphosis of Natural Theology in the Christian Encounter with Hellenism*. New Haven, CT: Yale University Press.

Polkinghorne, John. 1983. *The Way the World Is: The Christian Perspective of a Scientist*. London: Triangle.

Polkinghorne, John. 1986. *One World: The Interaction of Science and Theology*. London: SPCK.

Polkinghorne, John. 1988. *Science and Creation: The Search for Understanding*. London: SPCK.

Polkinghorne, John. 1989. *Science and Providence: God's Interaction with the World*. London: SPCK.

Polkinghorne, John. 1991. *Reason and Reality: The Relationship between Science and Theology*. London: SPCK.

Polkinghorne, John. 1994. *Science and Christian Belief: Theological Reflections of a Bottom-Up Thinker*. London: SPCK.

Polkinghorne, John. 1996. *Scientists as Theologians: A Comparison of the Writings of Ian Barbour, Arthur Peacocke and John Polkinghorne*. London: SPCK.

Polkinghorne, John. 2002a. Eschatological Credibility: Emergent and Teleological Processes. In Ted Peters, Robert John Russell, and Michael Welker, eds. *Resurrection: Theological and Scientific Assessments*. Grand Rapids, MI: Eerdmans, pp. 43–55.

Polkinghorne, John. 2002b. *The God of Hope and the End of the World*. London: SPCK.

Polkinghorne, John. 2004. *Science and the Trinity: The Christian Encounter with Reality*. London: SPCK.

Polkinghorne, John and Welker, Michael, eds. 2000. *The Ends of the World and the Ends of God: Science and Theology on Eschatology*. Harrisburg, PA: Trinity International Press.

Wildman, Wesley. 2006. Robert John Russell's Theology of God's Action. In Ted Peters and Nathan Hallanger, eds. *God's Action in the World: Essays in Honour of Robert John Russell*. Aldershot: Ashgate, pp. 147–170.

Further Reading

Nelson, Dean and Giberson, Karl. 2011. *Quantum Leap: How John Polkinghorne Found God in Science and Religion*. Oxford: Lion. A brief and simple biographical introduction to Polkinghorne's beliefs, especially useful for those who are unfamiliar with those beliefs.

Polkinghorne, John. 1996. *Scientists as Theologians: A Comparison of the Writings of Ian Barbour, Arthur Peacocke and John Polkinghorne*. London: SPCK. Polkinghorne's reflections on his own theological work in comparison with that of the two other leading scientist-theologians of his time.

Polkinghorne, John. 2005. *Exploring Reality: The Intertwining of Science and Religion*. New Haven, CT: Yale University Press. Polkinghorne's mature reflections on a number of topics covered in his earlier books.

Steinke, Johannes Maria. 2006. *John Polkinghorne – Konsonanz von Naturwissenschaft und Theologie*. Göttingen: Vandenhoek & Ruprecht. A philosophical appraisal and critique of Polkinghorne's notion of the consonance of scientific understanding and religious faith.

Watts, Fraser and Knight, Christopher C., eds. 2012. *God and Physics: An Exploration of the Work of John Polkinghorne*. Aldershot: Ashgate. Essays by Polkinghorne on his life's theological work and by numerous other authors on aspects of that work.

Index
